Rand H. Morimoto, Ph.D., MCITP
Michael Noel, MVP, MCITP
Chris Amaris, MCSE
Andrew Abbate, MCITP
Mark Weinhardt, MCSE

Technical Edit by Guy Yardeni

Microsoft®
Exchange
Server 2010

UNLEASHED

SAMS | 800 East 96th Street, Indianapolis, Indiana 46240 USA

Microsoft® Exchange Server 2010 Unleashed

ISBN-13: 978-0-672-33046-9

ISBN-10: 0-672-33046-6

Library of Congress Cataloging-in-Publication Data

Microsoft Exchange server 2010 unleashed / Rand H. Morimoto ... [et al.].
    p. cm.
  Includes bibliographical references and index.
  ISBN 978-0-672-33046-9 (alk. paper)
  1. Microsoft Exchange server. 2. Client/server computing. 3. Electronic mail systems. I. Morimoto, Rand.
  QA76.9.C55M52988 2009
  004.692—dc22

2009034389

Printed in the United States of America

Third Printing: August 2010

Trademarks

All terms mentioned in this book that are known to be trademarks or service marks have been appropriately capitalized. Sams Publishing cannot attest to the accuracy of this information. Use of a term in this book should not be regarded as affecting the validity of any trademark or service mark.

Warning and Disclaimer

Every effort has been made to make this book as complete and as accurate as possible, but no warranty or fitness is implied. The information provided is on an "as is" basis. The authors and the publisher shall have neither liability nor responsibility to any person or entity with respect to any loss or damages arising from the information contained in this book.

Bulk Sales

Sams Publishing offers excellent discounts on this book when ordered in quantity for bulk purchases or special sales. For more information, please contact

U.S. Corporate and Government Sales
1-800-382-3419
corpsales@pearsontechgroup.com

For sales outside of the U.S., please contact

International Sales
international@pearsoned.com

Editor-in-Chief
Karen Gettman

Executive Editor
Neil Rowe

Development Editor
Mark Renfrow

Managing Editor
Kristy Hart

Project Editor
Betsy Harris

Copy Editor
Apostrophe Editing Services

Indexer
Erika Millen

Proofreaders
Water Crest Publishing
Williams Woods Publishing

Technical Editor
Guy Yardeni, CISSP, MCITP, MCSE: Security

Publishing Coordinator
Cindy Teeters

Book Designer
Gary Adair

Compositor
Jake McFarland

Contributing Writers
Alex Lewis, CISSP, MVP
Jeff Guillet, MVP, MCITP, CISSP
Kim Amaris, PMP
Ross Mistry, MVP, MCTS
Scott Chimner, CISSP, MCITP, MCTS
Tyson Kopczynski, CISSP, GSEC, GCIH, MCTS

Contents at a Glance

Table of Contents

Part VII: Unified Communications in an Exchange Server 2010 Environment

Part IX: Data Protection and Disaster Recovery of Exchange Server 2010

31   Database Availability Group Replication in Exchange Server 2010   1027

About the Authors

Rand H. Morimoto, Ph.D., MVP, MCITP, CISSP, has been in the computer industry for more than 30 years and has authored, coauthored, or been a contributing writer for dozens of books on Windows, Security, Exchange, BizTalk, and Remote and Mobile Computing. Rand is the president of Convergent Computing, an IT-consulting firm in the San Francisco Bay area that has been one of the key early adopter program partners with Microsoft, implementing beta versions of Microsoft Exchange Server 2010, SharePoint 2010, and Windows 2008 R2 in production environments more than 18 months before the initial product releases.

Michael Noel, MCITP, CISSP, MVP, is an internationally recognized technology expert, bestselling author, and well-known public speaker on a broad range of IT topics. He authored multiple major industry books that have been translated into more than a dozen languages worldwide. Significant titles include *SharePoint 2010 Unleashed, Exchange 2007 Unleashed, SharePoint 2007 Unleashed, Windows Server 2008 R2 Unleashed, ISA Server 2006 Unleashed,* and many more. Currently a partner at Convergent Computing (www.cco.com) in the San Francisco Bay area, Michael's writings and extensive public-speaking experience across six continents leverage his real-world expertise helping organizations realize business value from Information Technology infrastructure.

Chris Amaris, MCSE, CISSP/ISSAP, CHS III, is the chief technology officer and cofounder of Convergent Computing. He has more than 20 years experience consulting for Fortune 500 companies, leading companies in the technology selection, design, planning, and implementation of complex Information Technology projects. Chris has worked with Microsoft Exchange since the early beta days of version 4.0. He specializes in messaging, security, performance tuning, systems management, and migration. A Certified Information Systems Security Professional (CISSP) with an Information System Security Architecture Professional (ISSAP) concentration, Certified Homeland Security (CHS III), Windows 2003 MCSE, Novell CNE, Banyan CBE, and a Certified Project Manager, Chris is also an author, writer, and technical editor for a number of IT books, including *Network Security for Government and Corporate Executives, Windows Server 2008 Unleashed,* and *Microsoft Operations Manager 2005 Unleashed.* Chris presents on Messaging, Operations Management, Security, and Information Technology topics worldwide.

Andrew Abbate, MCITP, is a 16-year veteran of consulting and IT with a wealth of practical knowledge on Exchange and Active Directory. Starting with his first migration of MS Mail to Exchange 4.0 through early adopter migrations to Exchange 2007, Andrew worked with some of the largest and most complex Exchange environments in North America. In addition to his Exchange background, Andrew has written several other books covering topics such as Windows 2003, Active Directory, and Information Security. Andrew currently enjoys the position of principal consultant and partner at Convergent Computing where he continues to consult with both large and small clients to help improve their IT practices.

Mark Weinhardt, MCSE, has worked in various aspects of the computing industry for more than 20 years. With a background in military communications, Mark understands the importance of maintaining a reliable and secure infrastructure and has preserved that mentality with his transition to the private sector. Mark worked as a consultant with Convergent Computing for more than 11 years and is currently a senior exchange engineer at Yahoo! Inc., working with a fantastic team. With an infectious enthusiasm for technology, Mark has performed Windows and Exchange designs and implementations for companies throughout Northern California.

Dedication

*I dedicate this book to Trecia; I will never forget
how you make me laugh and smile...*

—Rand H. Morimoto, Ph.D., MVP, MCITP, CISSP

*This book is dedicated to my sister Elizabeth. You brighten the world
with your intelligence, dynamism, and passion for life.*

—Michael Noel, MCITP, CISSP, MVP

*I dedicate this book to my wife, Sophia, who is also my best friend.
I also dedicate the book to my children, Michelle, Megan,
Zoe, Zachary, and Ian. They inspire me to strive.*

—Chris Amaris, MCSE, MVP, CISSP/ISSAP, CHS III

*I dedicate this book to my good friend and mentor, Vic Chapman,
who helped me make some of my biggest strides in IT and consulting early in my career. Without his support and his taking a chance
on a young consultant, I wouldn't be where I am today. If only he
could fix my chipping....*

—Andrew Abbate, MCSE, MCSA

*I dedicate this book to my parents, John and Pat Weinhardt,
who taught me to stand proud, and to my brother James and
his wife Wendy, who are teaching my nephews Colin James
and Logan Andrew the same thing.*

*And to my girlfriend Shirley, who put up with the late nights
and weekends of solitude as I disappeared in the lab.
Thank you for your support Baby Girl.... I love you.*

—Mark Weinhardt, MCSE

*I dedicate this book to my wife Allison, who puts up with me
and with the demands of the profession while still managing
to make me smile every day and to my daughters Maya and
Zoe for the power of their smiles.*

—Guy Yardeni (Tech Editor), CISSP, MCITP, MCSE: Security

Acknowledgments

Rand H. Morimoto, Ph.D., MVP, MCITP, CISSP. I want to thank Microsoft (including Melissa Travers and Robin Martin-Emerson) for allowing us the opportunity to work with the technologies months before general release so that we could put together content like this book in time for the product launch! A big thanks out to the Sams Publishing team (Neil, Mark, Betsy, and all the folks behind the scenes) in working with our tight time schedule as we write, edit, and produce a book of this size literally in weeks!

I also wanted to thank the consultants at Convergent Computing and our early adopter clients who fiddle with these new technologies really early on and then take the leap of faith in putting the products into production to experience (and at times feel the pain) as we work through best practices. The early adopter experiences give us the knowledge and experience we need to share with all who use this book as their guide in their production environments based on the lessons learned.

To Chip and Kelly, now that this book is done, okay well actually after I finish the *Windows 2008 R2 Unleashed* book that I'm jumping into right now, you actually might find Daddy in bed when you wake up in the middle of the night instead of down on the couch writing at all hours of the night. And thank you, Mom, for your constant love and support! For all those afternoons and evenings that you struggled to help me get my homework done because I couldn't string together words into a sentence to write a book report; I guess after all these years and several books later, I can finally say I figured it out.

Michael Noel, MCITP, CISSP, MVP. Another set of late nights, another book written, but much of the credit should go to the people behind the scenes that make the final product a reality. Thanks to the team at Sams Publishing that works hard to edit technical language, create diagrams, manage timelines, and deal with difficult and perpetually tardy authors. Special thanks to Neil Rowe at Sams, who has worked with me on countless volumes to date.

An excellent team of writers also makes for a quality product, and this group is the best in the business. Thanks to lead author Rand Morimoto, my coauthors Andrew, Chris, and Mark, and the excellent supporting contributing writers for the massive effort it takes to cram the sum of hundreds of combined years of IT experience into one volume.

And, of course, I would never be able to do this without the loving support of my family; my wife Marina, my beautiful daughter Julia, Val, Liza, and everyone else. I love you all and thanks once again for putting up with the late nights and occasional grumpiness!

Chris Amaris, MCSE, MVP, CISSP. Writing these books is a lot like eating really spicy food. You think it sounds like fun when the idea comes up, you wonder what you were thinking in the middle of it, and you think "Yeah, I did it!" when it is all over. I want to thank Rand Morimoto for once again letting me back in the game at a Scoville rating of 100,000.

I would also like to thank Sophia for handling all the myriad of family tasks like driving to math classes, games and practices, and cooking dinners while I scrambled to meet deadlines. I could not do it without you.

And thanks to Stanley Wong for letting me cool off in Phoenix after finishing the book!

Andrew Abbate, MCITP. Sometimes I think writing this front matter is harder than writing the book itself. A book feels like a living thing sometimes, and there are so many people involved in bringing it to life that it's hard to make sure everyone gets the credit they deserve. I'll start off with thanking Sams for giving us another opportunity to reach such a large audience. They seem to get better and better each year at making this an easy process, and please pass along my thanks to whomever worked up the new templates; huge time saver. Once again I'd like to thank the rest of the author team–you guys are great when it comes to bouncing ideas off of and gathering up tips and tricks from working with this product. You always make the process easier.

Last and certainly not least, I'd like to thank my friends for being supportive and accepting of the fact that I disappear for months on end when I start one of these projects. You should see more of me soon.

Mark Weinhardt, MCSE. I would like to thank Rand once again for the opportunity to get my hands dirty with a new product, to work with my former coworkers (and current friends), and to share what we've learned with the public. I'd also like to thank my coauthors, who are among the best in the business, for their tireless commitment to excellence.

And thank you to my girlfriend Shirley, for understanding as I put much of my personal life on hold during this endeavor.

Lastly, thank you to my friends and coworkers (on both the East and West coast) for your support. I am thankful for you all each and every day. "Be excellent to each other...."

We Want to Hear from You!

As the reader of this book, *you* are our most important critic and commentator. We value your opinion and want to know what we're doing right, what we could do better, what areas you'd like to see us publish in, and any other words of wisdom you're willing to pass our way.

As an executive editor for Sams Publishing, I welcome your comments. You can email or write me directly to let me know what you did or didn't like about this book—and what we can do to make our books better.

Please note that I cannot help you with technical problems related to the topic of this book. We do have a User Services group, however, where I will forward specific technical questions related to the book.

When you write, please be sure to include this book's title and author and your name, email address, and phone number. I will carefully review your comments and share them with the authors and editors who worked on the book.

Email: feedback@samspublishing.com

Mail: Neil Rowe
            Executive Editor
            Sams Publishing
            800 East 96th Street
            Indianapolis, IN 46240 USA

Reader Services

Visit our website and register this book at informit.com/register for convenient access to any updates, downloads, or errata that might be available for this book.

Introduction

In the past 15 years, we have written a book on every version of Exchange Server since its inception built on at least two years of early adopter beta experience. This book, *Microsoft Exchange Server 2010 Unleashed*, is the latest of our efforts. However, because Exchange Server 2010 is effectively based on Exchange Server 2007 and could potentially be considered a major service pack update to the product, there are enough differences in the new release that it required complete rethinking of the way we wrote this book.

Rather than being just an email and calendaring product, Microsoft added a handful of new server roles to Exchange Server 2007 to improve security and reliability that Microsoft further enhanced in Exchange Server 2010. In addition, Exchange Server 2010 greatly expands on Microsoft's offering in the areas of unified messaging that it entered into the marketplace with Exchange Server 2007. Exchange Server 2010 has not enhanced the Unified Messaging server role, but Exchange Server is now clearly the backbone of an entire unified communications strategy that Microsoft has built over the past several years. Beyond just email and calendaring, Exchange Server 2010 is now the foundation for voice and mobile communications.

Just a decade and a half ago, email was just one of a number of different ways people communicated. Early implementations of Exchange Server (v4.0, v5.0) had organizations tolerant if a server was down for a day or two. Today, email has become an extremely important, if not primary, method of communication for organizations. Downtime on an Exchange server can bring an entire organization to its knees. With Exchange Server 2010 adding voice mail and mobile communications into the messaging environment, an Exchange Server 2010 server and environment can no longer tolerate failures caused by viruses and spam, nor system downtime caused by server crashes or database corruption.

You will find that the improvements Microsoft has made to Exchange Server 2010 are not only evolutionary improvements, but highly critical if not absolutely essential to Microsoft's responsibility to help organizations maintain a safe, secure, and reliable communications infrastructure. This book covers all the aspects of Exchange Server 2010 from introducing the technologies, to properly planning and designing Exchange Server, to the implementation, management, and support of an Exchange Server 2010 environment built on tips, tricks, and best practices from more than two years of early adopter implementations in the field.

This book is organized into 10 parts, each part focusing on core Exchange Server 2010 areas, with several chapters making up each part:

> ▶ **Part I: Microsoft Exchange Server 2010 Overview**—This part provides an intro-
> duction to Exchange Server 2010, not only from the perspective of a general tech-
> nology overview, but also to note what is truly new in Exchange Server 2010 that
> made it compelling enough for organizations to implement the technology in beta

in a production environment. This part also covers best practices of planning, proto-type testing, and migration techniques.

▶ **Part II: Planning and Designing an Exchange Server 2010 Environment—** This part covers the design of an underlying Windows Server 2003/2008 and Active Directory environment in addition to the Exchange Server 2010 unified communications environment. Because organizations of varying sizes have different needs and requirements, as appropriate, this part addresses core Exchange Server 2010 design plans and concepts appropriate for most organizations, and specific attention is given to enterprise-level design and planning considerations for some of the largest Exchange Server implementations in the world. This part also covers the integration of Exchange 2010 in a non-Windows environment as well as tips, tricks, and best practices for getting a Windows Server 2003/2008 Active Directory, DNS, and domain structure properly planned and architected.

▶ **Part III: Implementing Exchange Server 2010 Services—**This part covers the core implementation of Exchange Server 2010 as well as the new Edge Services role that has been added to the Exchange Server organizational structure to provide protection against viruses and spam. In addition, this section has a chapter on the Exchange Management Script based on PowerShell, the Microsoft scripting solution that is the basis of the configuration, administration, and operations of Exchange Server 2010.

▶ **Part IV: Securing an Exchange Server 2010 Environment—**Security is on everyone's mind these days, and it was absolutely critical to have several chapters that covered security. The chapters in this part of the book include client-level, server-level, and transport-level security that is at the backbone of security for a network environment. A dedicated chapter on email encryption was necessary to cover the use of certificate-based encryption technologies to enable an organization the ability to provide person-to-person encrypted message communications. In addition, chapters on Microsoft ISA Server 2006 enhancing security at the edge and a chapter on enterprise policy environment addressing regulatory compliance security enhancements added to Exchange Server 2010 round out this extensive part on security.

▶ **Part V: Migrations and Coexistence with Exchange Server 2010—**This part is dedicated to migrations, client access servers (CASs), and Hub Transport servers. This part provides a chapter specifically on migrating from Windows 2003 Server to Windows Server 2008 for organizations that want to migrate to a base Windows 2008 environment during their migration to Exchange Server 2010. And, of course, this part includes a chapter on migrating from Exchange Server 2003 and Exchange Server 2007 to the new Exchange Server 2010 unified communications environment. Because Microsoft does not provide migrations from Exchange Server 5.5 or Exchange Server 2000 to Exchange Server 2010, nor does it provide in-place upgrades to Exchange Server 2010, there are fewer options to choose from, which means that the method you are left with needs to be planned, tested, and executed with the utmost care to minimize, if not eliminate, any interruption to users. This part of the book includes a chapter that covers the planning and implementation of the CAS role and the Hub Transport role, two updated roles to Exchange Server 2010 that are critical to the Exchange Server 2010 organizational environment.

▶ **Part VI: Exchange Server 2010 Administration and Management**—In this part, five chapters focus on the administration and management of an Exchange Server 2010 environment. The administration and management of mailboxes, distribution lists, sites, and administration have been greatly enhanced in Exchange Server 2010. Although you can continue to perform many of the tasks the way you did in the past, because of significant changes in replication, background transaction processing, secured communications, integrated mobile communications, and changes in Windows Server 2003 Active Directory, there are better ways to work with Exchange Server 2010. These chapters drill down into specialty areas helpful to administrators of varying levels of responsibility.

▶ **Part VII: Unified Communications in an Exchange Server 2010 Environment**—This section has been completely updated for Exchange Server 2010 with the revised Unified Messaging role, new mobility functionality, and tight integration with SharePoint 2007/2010. As previously mentioned in this introduction, Exchange Server 2010 not only improves voice mail to Exchange Server, but also the addition of voice integration takes Exchange Server 2010 far beyond just an email and calendaring solution. This addition takes Exchange Server into an area where communication is conducted on personal computers, mobile handheld devices, and from remote kiosks and terminal systems. The chapters in this part of the book highlight all the enhanced technologies and integration capabilities that make Exchange Server 2010 the core foundation to the future of an organization's communications infrastructure.

▶ **Part VIII: Client Access to Exchange Server 2010**—This part of the book focuses on the enhancements to the Outlook Web App client, various Outlook client capabilities, and Outlook for non-Windows systems. Outlook Web App is no longer just a simple browser client, but one that can effectively be a full primary user client to Exchange Server, including access to network file shares, an entry point to SharePoint shares, and a remote voice mail collection point. In addition, Outlook Web App now has full functionality for non-Windows users, such as users who access Exchange Outlook Web App from an Apple Mac computer. Being that Exchange Server 2010 now includes voice and mobile communications as a major component of the Exchange Server environment, client access as well as the distribution, management, and support of the client becomes even more important.

▶ **Part IX: Data Protection and Disaster Recovery of Exchange Server 2010**— As organizations implement Exchange Server 2010 and make it their central store for email, calendars, contacts, voice and fax communications, and mobile communications, it is no longer an option to set up and support an environment where downtime is even a possibility. This part of the book covers the new continuous backup technologies built in to Exchange Server 2010 intended to keep Exchange Server 2010 operating in a nonstop environment. Additional chapters in this part address backing up and restoring Exchange Server data, along with the recovery of an Exchange Server 2010 environment in the event of a disaster.

▶ **Part X: Optimizing Exchange Server 2010 Environments**—This last part of the book addresses optimization in terms of server and Exchange Server 2010 organizational environment optimization, optimization of the new Database Availability Group (DAG) storage and replication system, and system optimization that goes far beyond the basics. Rather than simply tuning an Exchange server with the appropriate amount of RAM and disk space, Exchange Server 2010 takes on a whole new area of load balancing data storage across distributed storage subsystems in which information is managed and replicated as an integral part of Exchange Server 2010.

The real-world experience we have had in working with Exchange Server 2010 and our commitment to writing this book based on years of field experience in early adopter Exchange Server 2010 environments enable us to relay to you information that we hope will be valuable in your successful planning, implementation, and migration to an Exchange Server 2010 environment.

Exchange Server 2010 Technology Primer

Microsoft Exchange Server 2010 is the latest release of the messaging and communications system from Microsoft built on the Windows operating system. This chapter introduces you to "What is Exchange Server 2010?" not just from the perspective of what's new in Exchange Server 2010 compared to previous versions, but also from the perspective of those who are new to Exchange Server. This chapter discusses the background of Exchange Server, the previous versions, and the general concepts of the Exchange Server messaging system, so that regardless of whether you are an Exchange Server 2003 or 2007 expert, or you are new to working with Exchange Server, you are prepared to dive into the remainder of this book on planning, testing, implementing, administering, managing, and supporting an Exchange Server 2010 environment.

What Is Exchange Server 2010?

At its core, Microsoft Exchange Server 2010 is an email, calendaring, and address book system that runs on a centralized Windows Server 2008 server system. However, with the release of Exchange Server 2010, now the seventh major release of Exchange Server in the 15-year history of the product, Microsoft has made significant improvements in the areas of security, reliability, scalability, mobility, and unified communications. For those Exchange Server experts who are already very familiar with the product, you might choose to skip this section, jump to the "Exchange Server 2010 Versions and Licensing" section (because Microsoft has a slightly different way of licensing Exchange Server

2010), and then jump to the "What's New in Exchange Server 2010" section to discover the latest and greatest in Exchange Server 2010.

So, back to the basics of Exchange Server, with a centralized Exchange server holding mail messages, calendar appointments, contacts, and other user information, the Exchange Server environment provides a server-based storage of information. Users throughout the organization connect to the Exchange server from Microsoft Outlook, from a web browser, or from a variety of other client systems to get access to their email and other information.

For larger organizations, multiple Exchange servers can be added to the environment hosting mailbox information of the users. Microsoft has split the roles of servers in an Exchange Server environment, where some servers are dedicated for antivirus and anti-spam filtering, and other servers are dedicated to routing messages throughout the organization. The "Understanding Exchange Server 2010 Server Roles and Mail Flow" section discusses these roles in more detail.

Understanding the Evolution of Exchange Server

For those new to Microsoft Exchange Server, this section covers the history of the Exchange Server product line. Sometimes as a newcomer to a technology, it's hard to jump right into the technology because everyone working with the technology refers to previous versions without taking into consideration that some people might not remember what was in the last revision, or in the product a couple of revisions back. So, this section is intended to give you a little history of Exchange Server so that the version numbers and major notable features and functions make sense.

Exchange Server 4.0

The first version of Microsoft Exchange Server, despite the 4.0 designation, was Exchange Server 4.0. Some people ask, "What happened to Exchange Server 1.0, 2.0, and 3.0?" For a bit of trivia, prior to Exchange Server 4.0, Microsoft had MS-Mail 3.0 (and MS-Mail 2.0); prior to that, it was a product called Network Courier Mail that Microsoft bought in the early 1990s.

Microsoft Exchange Server 4.0 had nothing in common with MS-Mail 3.0; they were completely different products and different technologies. The first rollouts of Exchange Server 4.0 back in 1996 were on Windows NT Server 3.51, which anyone with old NT 3.x experience knows that it was a challenging operating system to keep fully operational. "Blue screens" in which the operating system would just lock up were common. Anything that caused a system error usually resulted in a blue screen, which meant that every patch, update, service pack addition, installation of antivirus software, and so on frequently caused complete server failures.

However, Exchange Server 4.0 was a major breakthrough, and organizations started to migrate from MS-Mail (or at that time, cc:Mail was another popular mail system) to Exchange Server 4.0. One of the biggest reasons organizations were migrating to Exchange Server 4.0 was that in 1996, the Internet was just opening up to the public. The specifications for the World Wide Web had just been released. Organizations were connecting systems to the Internet, and one of the first real applications that took advantage of the

Internet was Microsoft Exchange Server 4.0. Organizations were able to connect their Exchange 4.0 server to the Internet and easily and simply send and receive emails to anyone else with an Internet-connected email system. MS-Mail 3.0 at the time had a Simple Mail Transfer Protocol (SMTP) gateway; however, it worked more on a scheduled dial-up basis, whereas Exchange Server 4.0 had a persistent connection to, typically, Integrated Services Digital Network (ISDN) or 56-KB frame connections to the Internet. And with Windows NT 4.0 shipping and being a much more solid infrastructure to work from, Exchange Server 4.0 was much more reliable than MS-Mail was for centralized organization-wide email communications.

Exchange Server 5.0

Exchange Server 5.0 came out in 1997 and was built to run on Windows NT 4.0, which proved to add more reliability to the Exchange Server product. In addition, Exchange Server 5.0 supported the first version of Outlook that to this day has a similar mailbox folder concept with the Inbox, Sent Items, Calendar, Contacts, and other common folders duplicated by mail systems throughout the industry. With the support for the Microsoft Outlook (97) client, Exchange Server also included calendaring directly within the Exchange Server product. In Exchange Server 5.0, the calendaring product was Schedule+, which was an add-on to Exchange Server 4.0, meaning that a user's email and calendaring weren't tied together, so Exchange Server 5.0 tied email, calendaring, and address books all together. With a service pack to Exchange Server 5.0, Microsoft also released the first version of Outlook Web Access (OWA) so that those who accessed the new World Wide Web could get remote access to their email on Exchange Server. Back in 1997, this was a big thing as web mail was a new concept, and Exchange Server 5.0 had web mail built into the messaging product.

Exchange Server 5.0 also had better third-party support for things such as fax gateways, unified voice mail add-in products, and document-sharing tools, leveraging shared public folders in Exchange Server. With better reliability, third-party product support, and a growing base of customers now migrating from MS-Mail and cc:Mail to Exchange Server, the Microsoft Exchange Server marketshare started to skyrocket.

Exchange Server 5.5

In 1998, Microsoft released Exchange Server 5.5, which until just a year or two ago, some organizations were still running in their networking environment. With Exchange Server 5.5, Microsoft worked out the bugs and quirks of their first two revisions of the Exchange Server product, and significantly better integration occurred between email, calendar, contacts, and tasks than in previous releases of Exchange Server. Microsoft also expanded the support for a larger Exchange Server database used to store messages. So, instead of being limited to 16GB of mail with earlier releases of Exchange Server, organizations could upgrade to the Enterprise Edition of Exchange Server 5.5 that provided more than 16GB of data storage. With larger storage capabilities, Exchange Server 5.5 greatly supported large corporate, government, and organizational messaging environments.

Along with Exchange Server 5.5, OWA was improved to provide a faster and easier-to-use web client. The concept of site connectors was expanded with Exchange Server 5.5 to provide a larger enterprise Exchange Server environment with distribution of administration, message routing, and multilanguage support. Most organizations that hadn't migrated off of Exchange Server 5.5 earlier had made their migration to Exchange Server 2000 and 2003. Exchange Server 5.5 for the most part is now out of environments or will soon be migrated to Exchange Server 2003 in anticipation of the organization ultimately migrating to Exchange Server 2010.

NOTE

The last supported direct migration path from Microsoft from Exchange Server 5.5 was with the Exchange Server 2003 product in which a connector and migration tools enabled integration of Exchange Server 5.5 and 2003 environments to coexist. Exchange Server 2007 and Exchange Server 2010 do not support Exchange Server 5.5 at all, and if an organization still has Exchange 5.5 servers, it must either migrate first to Exchange Server 2003 or export its mail out of Exchange Server 5.5 before beginning the process of implementing Exchange Server 2007 or Exchange Server 2010.

Exchange 2000 Server

Exchange 2000 Server came out in 2000 right after the release of Windows 2000 Server and the first version of Microsoft Active Directory. The biggest change in Exchange 2000 is that it used Active Directory for the Global Address List (GAL), instead of Windows NT having its list of network logon users and Exchange Server 5.5 having its own directory of email users. Active Directory combined a network and email user account into one single account, making the administration and management of Exchange Server much simpler. Exchange 2000 also went to an ActiveX version of the OWA client instead of a straight Hypertext Markup Language (HTML) version of the web access, thus providing users with drag-and-drop capabilities, pull-down bars, and other functionality that made the web access function much easier for remote users.

Exchange 2000, which is required to run on top of Windows 2000, became much more reliable than Exchange Server 5.5, which ran on top of Windows NT 4.0. However, because Exchange Server 5.5 can run on top of Windows 2000, many organizations made the shift to Exchange Server 5.5 on top of Windows 2000. These organizations also gained better performance and reliability, which is why many organizations did not migrate from Exchange Server 5.5. However, Windows 2000 provided Exchange 2000 a stable operating system platform from the beginning. Also by 2000, Novell's popularity was dramatically decreasing and organizations were migrating from Novell GroupWise to Exchange 2000, so the Microsoft marketshare continued to grow.

Exchange Server 2003

Exchange Server 2003 was a major update to the Exchange Server messaging system that supported Active Directory. Although Exchange 2000 had Active Directory support, organizations found that Exchange Server 2003 on top of Active Directory 2003 provided a more reliable experience, better performance, and integration support between Exchange Server and AD. Exchange Server 2003 added mobility for users to synchronize their Pocket PC mobile devices to Exchange Server. In addition, OWA got yet another major face-lift, mirroring the OWA interface with the normal Microsoft Office Outlook desktop client. With better remote support, Exchange Server 2003 became more than an office-based messaging system—it also greatly enhanced an organization's ability to provide remote and mobile users with email anytime and anywhere.

Exchange Server 2003, running on top of Windows Server 2003, took advantage of additional operating system enhancements, making Exchange Server 2003 an even more reliable and manageable messaging system. Windows 2003 clustering finally worked so that organizations that put Exchange Server 2003 on top of Windows 2003 were able to do active-active and active-passive clustering. In addition, clustering went from two-node clusters to four-node clusters, providing even more redundancy and recoverability.

Exchange Server 2003 also introduced the concept of a recovery storage group (RSG) that allowed an organization to mount an Exchange Server database for test and recovery purposes. Prior to Exchange Server 2003, an Exchange Server database could only be mounted on an Exchange server, typically with the exact same server name and for the sole purpose of making the database accessible to users. The recovery storage group in Exchange Server 2003 allowed an Exchange Server database from another Exchange server to be mounted in an offline manner so that the Exchange Server administrator can extract corrupt or lost messages, or possibly even have the database in a "ready mode" to allow for faster recovery of a failed Exchange server.

Exchange Server 2003 Service Pack 2

Although not a major release of Exchange Server, it is significant to note a major service pack for Exchange Server 2003, which is Exchange Server 2003 Service Pack 2. Exchange Server Service Pack 1 introduced cyclic redundancy check (CRC) error checking of the Exchange Server database. For 10 years, information written to Exchange Server was done without error checking, so prior to 2005, Microsoft Exchange Server had a bad reputation for having corruption in its databases any time the databases got too large. Early Exchange Server administrators are likely familiar with the utilities EDBUtil and ISInteg, which were used regularly to fix database corruption. Those utilities are, for the most part, not used anymore because error correction repairs are performed in realtime to the Exchange Server databases. With the release of Exchange Server 2003 SP1, error checking brought Exchange Server to a whole new world in better reliability.

Exchange Server 2003 SP2 added to the reliability and security of Exchange Server by introducing support for SenderID message integrity checks, as well as enhanced journaling of messages that captured a copy of messages in Exchange Server and locked the original copies of the messages in a tamperproof database that allowed for better support for regulatory compliance auditing and message integrity.

Exchange Server 2003 SP2 also added in direct push for mobile devices. Instead of having a Windows Mobile or Pocket PC device constantly "pull" messages down from Exchange Server, Exchange Server 2003 SP2 pushes messages to mobile devices, thus preventing constant polling by the mobile device. This increases battery life and enables Exchange Server and mobile devices to remain synchronized in real time.

Exchange Server 2007

Exchange Server 2007 was the most recent, major product release prior to the current Exchange Server 2010 product line. Exchange Server 2007 was released in 2007 and changed the direction of Exchange Server in several ways. Exchange Server 2007 completely eliminated the concept of routing groups being separate from Active Directory sites. Prior to Exchange Server 2007, organizations would have both Active Directory sites and Exchange Server routing groups, and in most organizations they were identical and effectively required separate parallel configuration. Exchange Server 2007 eliminated the separate routing group and instead looked to Active Directory's sites and services to identify the subnets of various sites, and used the routing topology specified in Active Directory to move email along the same path and route as Active Directory replication.

Exchange Server 2007 also eliminated the Exchange bridgehead server as a role that simply routed mail from bridgehead server to bridgehead server, to a server (called a Hub Transport server) where every piece of email goes through. The Hub Transport server could be seen as a major central point of failure because every inbound, outbound, or even user-to-user email must pass through a Hub Transport server. However, because every piece of mail goes through the Hub Transport server, policies and rules can be set so that every email message can be filtered so a single policy can be applied to not only Hub Transport to Hub Transport messages, but also even to messages between users with mailboxes on the same Exchange server. Read more about Hub Transport servers in Chapter 17, "Implementing Client Access and Hub Transport Servers."

Outlook Web Access in Exchange Server 2007 was also dramatically improved, being more than 95 percent feature complete with the full 32-bit version of Outlook. Web users have full control over mailbox rules, out-of-office rules, access digitally rights managed content, and both provision and deprovision of their Windows Mobile devices within the OWA interface.

And finally, one of the major improvements in Exchange Server 2007 is the introduction of Continuous Replication (CR), a major enhancement in mail system redundancy. Prior to Exchange Server 2007, a user's mailbox was on only one server. If that server failed or if the database was corrupt, a third-party solution needed to be leveraged to minimize Exchange Server system outage. The most common method for fast database recovery was the use of Storage Area Network (SAN) snapshots. Exchange Server Cluster Continuous Replication (CCR) provided organizations with a primary and secondary copy of the Exchange Server database. If the primary database failed, the secondary copy of the database automatically came online within 20–30 seconds, the user's Outlook 2007 reconnected to the new server automatically, and the user never knew that the primary Exchange server had failed. And unlike many third-party solutions in the past that didn't gracefully fail back to the primary server, Exchange Server 2007's CCR failed back to the primary server just as it failed forward, providing organizations with a clean high-availability solution.

Exchange Server 2007 Service Pack 1

Exchange Server 2007 Service Pack 1 was released late in 2007 and was seen by many as the first real version of Exchange Server 2007 with the addition of key components for the product version. Exchange Server 2007 SP1 enabled the access of Public Folders in OWA, something that many organizations could not upgrade to the initial Exchange Server 2007 release because OWA users needed access to their Public Folders. Exchange Server 2007 SP1 also included Standby Continuous Replication (SCR) that provided a second tier replication of Exchange Server databases. Where Exchange Server CCR provided a primary and secondary copy of the Exchange Server databases using instant failover clustering technology, SCR allowed for a replica of the Exchange Server databases to be created to a remote site with replication occurring in a 20-minute delayed manner. SCR provided organizations with the capability to replicate information across a wide area network to potentially an offsite data center.

Along the lines of high availability and disaster recovery came the concept of a stretched or geo-cluster in Exchange Server, where Exchange Server 2007 SP1 could be installed on top of Windows Server 2008 that provided a geographically distributed cluster to split the Exchange Server CCR replicated data. With the Exchange Server CCR cluster split across a WAN link, if a primary server (and now site) failed, the secondary CCR cluster server would immediately become available for users to automatically reconnect to their mail. Stretch clusters for CCR provided not only high availability for mail, but also disaster recovery in a single solution.

Exchange Server 2010 Versions and Licensing

One major change to Exchange Server 2010 (as it was with Exchange Server 2007) is that it only comes in an x64-bit version that requires Windows 2008 x64-bit to run as the core operating system. Although Exchange Server 2010 requires Windows x64-bit to run the Exchange server software, an organization can still run 32-bit Windows 2003 domain controllers, global catalog servers, and even Windows NT 4.0 and Windows 2000 member servers throughout the environment. Just the Exchange Server 2010 servers need to run x64-bit.

This means that organizations need to make sure their server hardware is x64-bit. Prior to the release of Exchange Server 2007 and Exchange Server 2010, most organizations were buying x64-bit hardware anyway because many hardware vendors stopped shipping 32-bit hardware as much as 2 to 3 years prior to the release of Exchange Server 2010. The benefit of x64-bit hardware is that you can still run 32-bit Windows and 32-bit software on the hardware until such time that you want to just reinstall 64-bit Windows and 64-bit software on the systems.

> **NOTE**
>
> Organizations with volume licensing agreements with Microsoft do not need to purchase or upgrade their Windows licenses from 32-bit to 64-bit. A Windows 2003 (or 2008) server license is a Windows 2003 (or 2008) server license, so regardless of whether the system is 32-bit or 64-bit, the organization's server licenses remain the same.

Choosing the Standard Edition of Exchange Server 2010

As with previous versions of Exchange Server, Microsoft has two different versions: a Standard Edition and an Enterprise Edition of the software. The Exchange Server 2010, Standard Edition is the basic message server version of the software. The Standard Edition supports five data stores. The Standard Edition has full support for web access, mobile access, and general Outlook email functionality.

The Standard Edition is a good version of Exchange Server to support a messaging system for a small organization, or as a dedicated Edge Transport, Hub Transport, or client access server for a larger environment. Many small and medium-sized organizations find the capabilities of the Standard Edition sufficient for most messaging server services, and even large organizations use the Standard Edition for message routing servers or as the primary server in a remote office. The Standard Edition meets the needs of effectively any environment wherein a server with a limited database storage capacity is sufficient.

Expanding into the Exchange Server 2010 Enterprise Edition

The Exchange Server 2010, Enterprise Edition is focused at server systems that require more Exchange Server messaging databases and support for continuous replication for higher availability. With support for up to 150 databases per server, the Enterprise Edition of Exchange Server 2010 is the appropriate version of messaging system for organizations that have a lot of mailboxes or a lot of mail storage. The Enterprise Edition is also appropriate for an organization that wants to set up continuous replication for higher reliability and redundancy of the Exchange Server environment.

Table 1.1 summarizes the differences between the Standard and Enterprise Editions.

TABLE 1.1   Exchange Server 2010 Standard Versus Enterprise Editions

Exchange Server 2010 Function	Standard Edition	Enterprise Edition
Number of data stores supported	5	50+
OS support	Windows 2008 and 2008R2 x64-bit	Windows 2008 and 2008R2 x64-bit

Exchange Enterprise CAL Versus Standard CAL

The basic differences of the Exchange Enterprise versus Standard server editions is the differing number of databases supported and higher-availability clustering support. Beyond these basic differences on the server side, there is also a separate concept of an Enterprise client access license (CAL) and a Standard CAL. Either CAL can be used against either server edition and has no association between the server versions. Rather, the Enterprise CAL adds user functionality, such as providing the user with a license for unified messaging (voice mail in Exchange Server 2010), per-user journaling for archiving and compliance support, and the ability to use Exchange Server hosted services for message filtering, or providing enhanced antispam and antivirus functionality using ForeFront Security for Exchange Server.

Organizations that had software assurance for Exchange Server will get upgraded to the Standard Exchange Server CAL, and those that want to add on unified messaging and the enhanced archiving, retention policies, and litigation hold technologies can purchase the upgrade for their licenses to the Enterprise CAL license.

> **NOTE**
>
> The feature differences between what an organization can run if it owned the Enterprise CAL versus the Standard CAL is merely a legal function. All Exchange Server 2010 servers support the Enterprise CAL features (unified messaging, per mailbox journaling, and so on), so the reason an organization would purchase the Enterprise CAL would be to legally have the right to use these enhanced features.

What's New in Exchange Server 2010?

Exchange Server 2010, being the seventh major release of the Exchange Server product, adds to the existing technology base of more recent versions of Exchange Server, such as Exchange Server 2003 and Exchange Server 2007. Exchange Server administrators familiar with Exchange Server 2003 and 2007 will find that Exchange Server 2010 is about 70% to 80% the same; however, the 20% to 30% that is different is drastically different and requires some relearning of the changes.

What's the Same Between Exchange Server 2003/2007 and Exchange Server 2010?

The core infrastructure of Exchange Server 2003 and 2007 versus Exchange Server 2010 is basically the same. Microsoft continues to use the Jet EDB database as the main database store. Some time ago, it was rumored that Microsoft would migrate Exchange Server to run off SQL Server; however, neither Exchange Server 2010 nor versions coming out from Microsoft in the foreseeable future will change the basic EDB database structure.

Exchange Server 2010 still has the concept of a Mailbox server where EDBs are stored and where user mailbox data resides. Storage groups remain the same where databases are created, and then databases are grouped together in storage groups to combine the management tasks of databases into common groupings.

Users can use the Microsoft Outlook client and can access Exchange Server using OWA, as shown in Figure 1.1, for browser-based access, as well as synchronize with Exchange Server from their Windows Mobile and Pocket PC mobile devices.

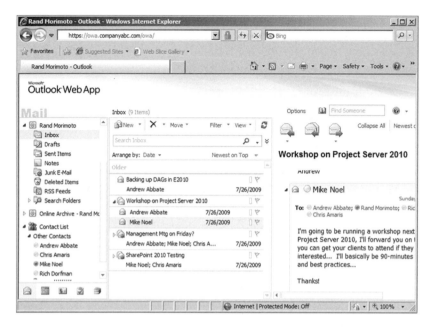

FIGURE 1.1   The new Outlook Web App in Exchange Server 2010.

Exchange Server 2010 still uses the VSSBackup application programming interface (API) to freeze the state of the Exchange Server database to perform a backup of the Exchange Server database.

One of the most important things that the users of an Exchange Server 2010 environment who get migrated from Exchange Server 2003 or 2007 to Exchange Server 2010 will notice is that nothing is new or different from the end-user standpoint, assuming you keep the same Outlook client that the user has been using. A migration from Exchange Server 2003 and 2007 to Exchange Server 2010 does not require an upgrade to the Outlook 2010 client. Effectively, the user's mailbox is moved from an old server to a new server, and the user still has the exact same look, feel, and functionality as they had with Exchange Server 2003 and 2007. This relatively seamless cutover of user mailboxes, covered in Chapter 16, "Transitioning from Exchange Server 2003/2007 to Exchange Server 2010," minimizes user interruption as part of the migration process. Users will notice enhanced features with the new OWA, and even more enhancements if/when their systems are upgraded to Outlook 2010.

What's Missing in Exchange Server 2010 That Was in Previous Versions?

A common question that is asked is "What is missing in Exchange Server 2010 that was in previous versions of Exchange Server?" Although the balance of this section of the chapter covers the new features—which could arguably be said to be missing because they have drastically changed—this portion of the chapter focuses on things that are completely gone or do not exist in Exchange Server 2010.

In Exchange Server 2010, the concept of the recovery storage group has been removed. Exchange Server 2003 introduced the recovery storage group as a way to restore an Exchange Server database to an Exchange server that wasn't the original server on which the database was created or was running. With Exchange Server 2007 and Exchange Server 2010, Microsoft has added a whole new series of technologies that are addressed in the "Making Exchange Server 2010 Extremely Reliable and Recoverable" section later in this chapter. The new technologies do a better job of replicating Exchange Server databases and making Exchange Server recoverable both from a local database crash and from a server or entire site failure.

Relative to Exchange Server databases, the STM database has been removed, so Exchange Server is now back to just the EDB database as it was in Exchange Server 2000 and prior versions. Rather than completely removing the STM database, Microsoft incorporated the streaming data technology into the new EDB database, so instead of having two databases for each mailbox and trying to reconcile the storage of information within those two databases, the combined mailbox database is now the standard.

Also gone in Exchange Server 2010 is the concept of a storage group. With Exchange Server 2007, when an organization implemented Continuous Replication, each database had to be in its own storage group. With database recoverability as an important topic in Exchange Server 2010 in which all databases should have a replica, the need for storage groups has been removed, and Exchange Server Mailbox servers simply have databases on them.

From an administration standpoint, the concept of administrative groups and routing groups has been completely removed. Administrative groups were introduced with Exchange Server 2000 as a method of grouping together users to identify who would manage and administer groups of mailboxes. Administrative groups were brought forward from Exchange Server 5.5 where administration was done based on sites connected by site connectors. In Exchange Server 2010 (as in Exchange Server 2007), administration is now completely consolidated into an enterprise view of users and mailboxes. The administration of the users and mailboxes is handled as delegated rights of administrators, not by a group of users and servers. So, rather than grouping together servers and users into special containers, an administrator is merely assigned rights to manage specific users, mailboxes, servers, or preexisting containers.

As noted in the preceding paragraph, routing groups have also been removed. Rather than having to group servers by routing groups, Exchange Server 2010 has done away with separate routing groups within Exchange Server. Instead, the Active Directory Sites and Services now uses its configuration to determine organizational sites and the routing of message communications to those sites.

An administrator might likely also notice that ExOLEDB, WebDAV, CDOEX, and Store Events are gone in Exchange Server 2010. Exchange Server 2010 now uses Exchange Web Services (EWS) as the primary method to provide Web services to client systems.

With the release of Exchange Server 2007, Microsoft had noted that public folders were going to be deemphasized, which basically means they would be going away in a future version of Exchange Server. What you will find is when you install Exchange Server 2010 from scratch, public folders are not created at all. You need to manually add public folders to a Mailbox server and extend public folder access from the server system. During a migration, if the organization has public folders, they will continue to operate in Exchange Server 2010. So as much as Microsoft has stated that public folders are being deemphasized, they are still completely and fully supported in Exchange Server 2010, and because of the prevalent use of public folders in enterprises, it would seem that public folders will continue to be in Exchange Server for the foreseeable future. Microsoft has created excellent hooks between Exchange Server 2010 and SharePoint 2007/2010 that enable a user to click on what used to be a folder for public folders, but instead a SharePoint share is rendered in the user's Outlook or OWA screen. You can do pretty much everything you were able to do with public folders with SharePoint 2007/2010—and then some. More on SharePoint integration with Exchange Server 2010 is covered in Chapter 25, "Collaborating Within an Exchange Server Environment Using Microsoft Office SharePoint Server 2007."

Several things have drastically changed in Exchange Server 2010, such as a completely new Exchange Server administration tool, a new Exchange Server scripting language, and the removal of front-end and bridgehead servers with new server roles that will be covered in the next handful of sections.

Exploring the New Exchange Management Console

One of the first things an administrator will notice and have to relearn is the new Microsoft Exchange Management Console, or EMC tool, shown in Figure 1.2, which is used for administering and managing the Exchange Server 2010 environment. The Exchange Management Console looks nothing like the old Exchange Systems Manager. Microsoft made a drastic departure from the administrative tree structure used with Exchange Server for the past decade and, instead, revamped the entire structure to be focused to the way Exchange Server is managed and administered in the real world.

Rather than organizing users and servers by administrative groups and routing groups that broke up an organization and made it difficult for the enterprise Exchange Server administrators to see all users and all servers in the organization, Exchange Server 2010 now organizes objects as a whole. The administrator sees all users, all servers, and all resources in the Exchange Server organization in a single view. The Exchange Server administrator(s) can regroup users, computers, and resources into smaller delegation groups; however, this is done by filtering views, not by creating fixed containers and groupings. This filtering method of organization objects allows an organization the flexibility to simply change the groupings for administration, management, or operations without having to completely reorganize the entire Exchange Server architecture.

More on the Exchange Management Console is covered in Chapter 18, "Administering an Exchange Server 2010 Environment."

Providing Exchange Server 2010 on an x64-Bit Platform Only

Another major change to Exchange Server 2010 (as was Exchange Server 2007) is that they only run on an x64-bit platform. Up until Exchange Server 2007, Exchange Server ran primarily on a 32-bit platform, and although 64-bit had been supported, the way the core

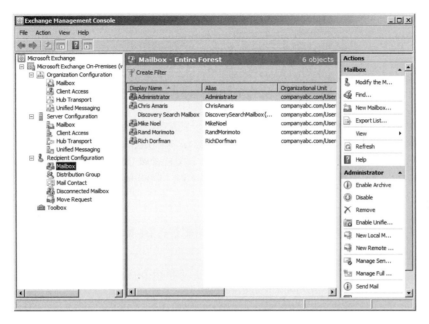

FIGURE 1.2   The new Exchange Management Console.

Exchange Server environment was designed, 64-bit didn't provide significant improvements until Exchange Server 2007 and Exchange Server 2010 became available.

The Microsoft Exchange Server development team made the decision to go solely to a 64-bit environment because of the significant benefits that 64-bit Windows and 64-bit technologies provide in server scalability and management. One of the biggest problems with earlier versions of Exchange Server on a 32-bit platform is the support for only 4GB of memory on an Exchange server. Just a few years ago, no one thought 4GB of RAM was a limitation. However, with Exchange Server and the amount of messaging transactions an organization can send and receive, what is required for an Exchange server to process far exceeded the memory space available in just 4GB of RAM. Because the processing of messages, write transactions to disk, logging for rollback recoverability, and the addition of spam and virus protection takes away from available memory in the system, 4GB would be used up quite quickly.

To compensate for the lack of available memory in 32-bit Exchange Server, Microsoft Exchange Server 2003 and prior depended heavily on caching transactions to disk. As an example, for an organization with 5,000 users on an Exchange Server 2003 server in a large enterprise, the Exchange Server 2003 server would have 4GB of RAM and need about 100GB of disk storage to have as available spool memory. In very large enterprises with tens of thousands of users, the Exchange servers could easily take up 500GB or even terabytes of disk space for spooling.

With 64-bit Windows and its support for 8TB of RAM memory, an Exchange Server 2010 server with 5,000 users now needs 32GB of RAM, but can do with just 5GB or less of spool disk space. Not only does the additional RAM memory eliminate the need for hundreds of gigabytes of spool disk space, but the additional memory allows an Exchange Server 2010 server to support three to six times as many users per server, and provides a 50% to 80% increase in system efficiency of transactions.

Likewise, the 64-bit operating system also has proven to provide better support for significantly larger Exchange Server EDB databases. Most organizations wouldn't think of having an Exchange Server 2000 or 2003 database greater than 80GB to 100GB in size; however, with a 64-bit operating system, Exchange Server 2010 supports databases that easily run in the hundreds of gigabyte size.

Server configuration and server optimization are covered in Chapter 3, "Understanding Core Exchange Server 2010 Design Plans," and in Chapter 34, "Optimizing an Exchange Server 2010 Environment."

Improvements in Exchange Server 2010 Relative to Security and Compliance

One of the improvement goals Microsoft has had with all of their products over the past few years has been to constantly improve the security in the products. More recently with all the regulatory compliance laws and policies being implemented, Microsoft has focused a lot of security enhancements to address privacy, information archiving, and compliance support. The release of Exchange Server 2007 and Exchange Server 2010 was no different—Microsoft added in several new enhancements in the areas of security and compliance support.

One of the additions to Exchange Server 2007 and Exchange Server 2010 is the creation of an Edge Transport server role that supplements the traditional Exchange Server database server as a system in the Exchange Server organization environment. Whereas the Exchange Server database server holds user data, the Edge Transport server is dedicated to provide the first line of defense relative to virus and spam blocking. Organizations with Exchange Server have had servers in their demilitarized zone (DMZ) typically as SMTP relay servers that collect messages, perform antivirus and antispam filtering, and route the messages internal to the organization. However, most of the message relay servers in the DMZ have typically had no tie back to Exchange Server, so when messages come in for email addresses for individuals who don't even exist in the organization, the DMZ mail relays didn't really have a way to know, so they blindly processed antispam and antivirus checks, and then forwarded messages on to the Exchange server. The Exchange server would realize when individuals did not exist and would bounce or delete the message. This meant that the Exchange server would still have to process hundreds if not thousands or tens of thousands of invalid messages.

The Edge Transport server role, covered in detail in Chapter 8, "Implementing Edge Services for an Exchange Server 2010 Environment," brings forward in a tightly encrypted format specific details out of Active Directory into the Edge Transport server (such as a valid list of email addresses), so that before a message is even processed for spam or virus filtering, the message determines if the recipient even exists in the organization. Only messages destined to valid recipients are processed for antispam and antivirus filtering. In many cases, this means that 50%, 60%, or even 70% of all messages are immediately deleted because a valid recipient does not exist in the organization. A simple rule of this type greatly improves the efficiency of Exchange Server for routing good messages, not spam.

Another major enhancement in Exchange Server 2007 and Exchange Server 2010 is the addition of the Hub Transport server. For many, the Hub Transport server merely replaces the bridgehead server that handled routing in earlier versions of Exchange Server. However, the Hub Transport server in Exchange Server 2010 does more than just bridgehead routing; it also acts as the policy compliance management server. Policies can be configured in Exchange Server 2010 so that after a message is filtered for spam and viruses, the message goes to the policy server to be assessed whether the message meets or fits into any regulated message policy, and appropriate actions are taken. The same is true for outbound messages: The messages go to the policy server, the content of the message is analyzed, and if the message is determined to meet specific message policy criteria, the message can be routed unchanged, or the message might be held or modified based on the policy. As an example, an organization might want any communications referencing a specific product code name or a message that has content that looks like private health information, such as Social Security number, date of birth, or health records of an individual, to be held so that encryption can be enforced on the message before it continues its route. More details on the role of policy compliance are in Chapter 14, "Understanding Exchange Policy Enforcement Security," and information on the Hub Transport server role is covered in Chapter 17.

Other security enhancements in Exchange Server 2007 and Exchange Server 2010 include default server-to-server Transport Layer Security (TLS) for server-to-server traffic so that message communications no longer transmits between Exchange servers unsecured. Even the Edge Transport and Hub Transport servers have the ability to check to see if a destination server supports TLS, and if it does support TLS communications, the transport out of Exchange Server 2010 is encrypted. More details on server encryption and transport communication encryption are discussed in Chapter 11, "Server and Transport-Level Security," and Chapter 13, "Securing Exchange Server 2010 with ISA Server."

Not new to Exchange Server 2010, but key in an organization's effort to maintain security and privacy of information, is the ability to encrypt email messages and content at the client level. Exchange Server 2010 encrypts content between the Exchange Server 2010 server and an Outlook 2010 client by default, and provides full support for certificate-based Public Key Infrastructure (PKI) encryption of mail messages. More details on client-level security and encrypted email are covered in Chapter 10, "Client-Level Secured Messaging," and in Chapter 12, "Integrating Certificate-Based Public Key Infrastructure (PKI) in Exchange Server 2010."

Exchange Server 2010 as the Focal Point for Remote and Mobile Communications

Starting with Exchange Server 2003, Microsoft has added significant focus on support for remote and mobile access to Exchange Server. Remote and mobile access takes on two forms for Exchange Server: One is in the support of remote access users to Exchange Server with the improvement of the OWA client and mobile laptop user, and mobility is enhanced in the areas of access and synchronization with Windows Mobile and Pocket PC devices.

Remote access to Exchange Server has become extremely important as users want to access Exchange Server outside of the business office, potentially from a home computer, an Internet café kiosk system, or from a laptop they are carrying with them. OWA 2010 is now nearly feature complete compared to the full Outlook client with full support for filters, spell checking, drag and drop of messages, out of office rules management, calendar and contact access, and the like. Many early adopters to Exchange Server 2010 have found the new OWA to be so feature complete that when they are remote, they only use OWA as their method to check and manage their messages. More on OWA in Exchange Server 2010 is covered in Chapter 28, "Leveraging the Capabilities of the Outlook Web App (OWA) Client."

A new feature of OWA in Exchange Server 2007 and Exchange Server 2010 is the direct file access feature. Direct file access is a new function that allows the administrator of a network to share internal network shares through OWA. Normally, for a user to access an internal Universal Naming Convention (UNC) such as \\server\share\, the user needs to be on the local area network (LAN) or they need to have a virtual private network (VPN) connection to securely connect to the network from a remote location. With direct file access, after a user is logged on to OWA, any network shares that the network administrators specifically allow to be accessed using direct file access can be accessed from the remote user, as shown in Figure 1.3. For organizations that have implemented direct file access in Exchange Server 2010, most have gotten rid of their need for VPNs because between OWA and direct file access, a user can access email, calendar, contacts, and internal file shares. From a security perspective, whatever file-level security has been enabled on the network shares relative to user access are activated as part of the remote access security for the user to the direct file access share privileges.

Additional remote access improvements in Exchange Server 2007 and Exchange Server 2010 include just a name change of what used to be called RPC over HTTPS to what is now called Outlook Anywhere. RPC over HTTPS, or Outlook Anywhere, is the ability for a user running Outlook 2003, 2007, or 2010 to connect to an Exchange server using HTTPS and synchronize with the server using 128-bit encryption without using VPN access. The remote connection between the Outlook client and Exchange Server is encrypted so that the synchronization is protected. Although a VPN connection is no longer needed, Outlook Anywhere also does not require special ports or configurations to be opened up on firewalls or special settings to be configured. Outlook Anywhere uses the same connection address that the organization uses for OWA. So, if users normally type in https://owa.companyabc.com to get access to OWA, the Outlook Anywhere connection point for the Outlook user is also owa.companyabc.com. Between direct file access and Outlook Anywhere, an organization can seriously evaluate whether it needs to continue providing remote VPN access to the network, or possibly provide VPN access to a limited number of users whose remote access needs go beyond the requirements provided by OWA, direct file access, and Outlook Anywhere.

A major improvement in Exchange Server 2010 is its capability to provide the "premium client" for Outlook Web App to more than just Windows Internet Explorer users. The

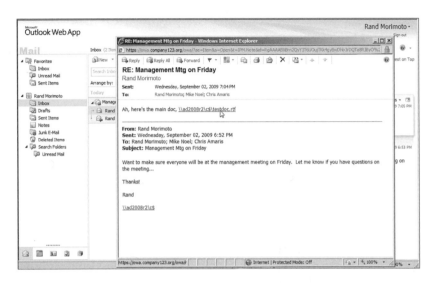

FIGURE 1.3   Direct file access in Exchange Server 2010.

premium client in Outlook Web App provides drag-and-drop capabilities and full access to OWA features. For users running browsers such as FireFox for Windows or Safari for the Apple Mac, the user experience has been in "light client mode." The light client required a user to first select messages through a check-box process and then choose from a menu to move, delete, or modify the messages as a separate step. Effectively light client users were provided a far inferior experience to Outlook Web App. With Exchange Server 2010, Microsoft expanded the premium client support in Outlook Web App to include variations of FireFox for Windows and Safari for the Apple Mac. Additional browser and platform support will be added to Exchange Server 2010 through updates and service packs over time.

On mobility, Microsoft has greatly enhanced the capabilities of remote access of users who have Windows Mobile and Pocket PC devices. Exchange Server 2010 had a significant improvement to ActiveSync that extends the direct push function that was included in Exchange Server 2003 SP2 and Exchange Server 2007 that has the Exchange server push or send messages to Windows Mobile devices instead of having the Windows Mobile devices constantly poll the Exchange server for new messages. New to Exchange Server 2007 and Exchange Server 2010 mobility is the ability for Windows Mobile systems to remotely search for old messages. In the past, a mobile device only had access to the messages that were synchronized by ActiveSync to the device, which usually meant 2–3 days of historical calendar appointments, and only the Inbox for messages. With Exchange Server 2010, a Windows Mobile device can query all folders to which the user has access to find messages and download them to the mobile device at any time. In addition, just as OWA has the direct file access feature that brings down files from network shares without setting up a VPN connection, Exchange Server 2010 provides direct file access to Windows

Mobile users. You can find more discussion on mobility in Exchange Server 2010 in Chapter 23, "Designing and Implementing Mobility in Exchange Server 2010."

Improving Unified Messaging in Exchange Server 2010

One of the major improvements to Exchange Server 2010 is the updates to unified messaging. Unified messaging is the capability for Exchange Server 2010 to be the voice mail server for an organization. Rather than having a separate voice mail system connected to the organization's phone system, Exchange Server 2010 can be integrated into the phone system to be able to take messages on incoming calls, and the messages are stored in the user's Exchange Server mailbox for playback from the phone or by accessing the message from within Outlook, OWA, or Windows Mobile, as shown in Figure 1.4.

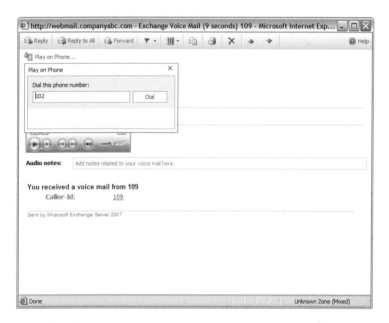

FIGURE 1.4   Voice mail client to Exchange Server 2010 unified messaging.

Unified messaging is not new to Exchange Server; in fact, many organizations, including Cisco, Avaya, Nortel, and so on, have had voice mail to Exchange Server add-ons for years. Microsoft claims to not be directly competing against organizations with unified messaging solutions for Exchange Server already, but rather wants to provide a better infrastructure to support a tightly integrated unified messaging system into Exchange Server 2010.

One of the benefits of unified messaging in Exchange Server from any vendor is the concept of a single data store for inbound email messages and voice mail messages. Rather than checking Outlook for emails, and calling into a phone voice mail system for voice messages, having all messages go in to Exchange Server provides a single point of message control. A single point for message access allows Exchange Server 2010 to provide anywhere access to all messages, whether it is from an Outlook client, from OWA, or from a Windows Mobile device.

Unified messaging is significant in Exchange Server 2010 because it is the foundation that Microsoft has built upon that provides unified communications across their entire product line. Microsoft has been tightly integrating instant messaging (IM), voice over IP (VoIP) telephone integration, videoconferencing, data conferencing, and so forth into a complete, centralized communications system. Today, Microsoft has several new products they have introduced to the marketplace, including Office Communications Server 2007, Office Roundtable, and SharePoint 2007 and 2010, that integrate technologies together in a unified communications backbone. Exchange Server 2010 is the core to the unified communications strategy that Microsoft is setting forth because Exchange Server is the point of connection for email, contacts, remote access, mobile access, and, now, voice communications.

More information on unified messaging and the capabilities provided out of the box from Microsoft on unified messaging is in Chapter 24, "Designing and Configuring Unified Messaging in Exchange Server 2010."

Making Exchange Server 2010 Extremely Reliable and Recoverable

In addition to security and mobility as core areas in which Microsoft has invested heavily for all of their products, Microsoft has added significant improvements in making Exchange Server 2010 more reliable and more recoverable. As messaging has become critical to business communications, Exchange Server 2010 becomes an important component in making sure an organization can effectively communicate between employees as well as from employees to customers, to vendors, to business partners, and to the public. Add voice communications into the new Exchange Server unified communications strategy, and it becomes even more important that Exchange Server 2010 is extremely reliable.

With Exchange Server 2010, Microsoft included a new continuous backup and replication technology that effectively allows Exchange Server to now hold up to 16 copies of a user's mailbox information. In the past, Exchange Server only had one copy of a user's mailbox sitting in an Exchange Server database. In the event that the database holding the user's information became corrupt or the server holding the user's information failed, the way to get the user's mailbox back up and running was to typically restore the data to another server. Several hardware and software utility vendors have created snapshot technologies that replicate a user's mailbox information to another server; however, as much as the user's data can be available on another system in another site, the user's Outlook client was still pointing to the old Exchange server where the mailbox used to reside. So, as much as the data was available, business continuity couldn't continue until the user's Outlook profile was changed to redirect the user to the new location of the data.

Exchange Server 2007 introduced Continuous Replication in three forms: Local Continuous Replication (LCR), Cluster Continuous Replication (CCR), and Standby Continuous Replication (SCR) that effectively duplicates the Exchange Server databases on another server on the network. In the case of Local Continuous Replication, the user's data is replicated on a separate drive within a single server, so effectively a server has two databases with a copy of the data stored in each of the databases. CCR provided the replication of the user's mailbox across servers and sites so that if a user's mailbox is lost either because of a hard drive or database failure, a server failure, or the complete loss of a site, a replicated copy of the user's mailbox information resides on another server potentially in another site. SCR provided for the delayed replication of an Exchange Server database to a server in a remote location providing a solution for disaster recovery in case the primary site fails. In addition, for the past decade, Microsoft Exchange Server supported single copy clusters that provided for two or more servers to host a single copy of the mail for the purpose of Exchange Server scalability and server redundancy.

However, with Exchange Server 2010, Microsoft eliminated single copy clusters, Local Continuous Replication, Clustered Continuous Replication, and Standby Continuous Replication in place of an updated Database Availability Group (DAG) replication technology. The DAG is effectively CCR, but instead of a single active and single passive copy of the database, DAG provides up to 16 copies of the mail and provides a staging failover of data from primary to replica copies of the mail.

DAGs still use log shipping as the method of replication of information between servers. Log shipping means that the 1-MB log files that note the information written to an Exchange server are transferred to other servers, and the logs are replayed on that server to build up the content of the replica system from data known to be accurate. If during a replication cycle a log file does not completely transfer to the remote system, individual log transactions are backed out of the replicated system and the information is re-sent. Unlike bit-level transfers of data between source and destination used in Storage Area Networks (SANs) or most other Exchange Server database replication solutions, if a system fails, bits don't transfer, and Exchange Server has no idea what the bits were, what to request for a resend of data, or how to notify an administrator what file or content the bits referenced. Microsoft's implementation of log shipping provides organizations with a clean method of knowing what was replicated and what was not.

In addition, because log shipping is done with small 1-MB log files, Exchange Server 2010 replication can be conducted over relatively low-bandwidth connections. Dependent on the amount of data written to an Exchange server, a T1 line can potentially be used to successfully keep a source and destination replica server up to date. Other uses of the DAG include staging the replication of data so that a third or fourth copy of the replica resides "offline" in a remote data center; instead of having the data center actively be a failover destination, the remote location can be used to simply be the point where data is backed up to tape, or a location where data can be recovered if a catastrophic enterprise environment failure occurs. More details on continuous backup are covered in Chapter 31, "Database Availability Group Replication in Exchange Server 2010," and in Chapter 33, "Recovering from a Disaster in an Exchange Server 2010 Environment."

Another major point about having data come live on a remote system is to redirect a user's Outlook clients to the location of their data. With Outlook 2007 and Outlook 2010, shown in Figure 1.5, Microsoft no longer hard-codes the Mailbox server name to the user's Outlook profile, but rather has the user connect to the client access server (CAS) with merely the user's logon name and password; the CAS parses Active Directory and Exchange Server and directs the user's Outlook client to the appropriate server that is currently hosting the user's mailbox. This automatic swap over at the client level provides the business continuity functionality that is needed in a server failover scenario.

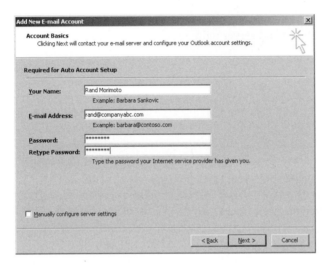

FIGURE 1.5   Automatic client configuration in Outlook 2007/2010.

Improving Configuration, Administration, and Management Through the Exchange Management Shell

Improved in Exchange Server 2010 is a command-line shell known as Exchange Management Shell, or EMS. The command-line shell, shown in Figure 1.6, provides an administrator with the ability to configure, administer, and manage an Exchange Server 2010 server environment using text commands instead of solely a graphical user interface (GUI). In fact with Exchange Server 2010, the GUI administration tool, Exchange Management Console, is nothing more than a front end to the Exchange Management Shell. Every GUI check box or pull-down function executes an EMS script in the back end. Experience with Exchange Server 2010 has shown that 80% to 90% of an administrator's tasks can be done through the graphic Exchange Management Console; however, on a regular basis, the Exchange Server administrator has to do things through the scripted interface because a GUI option does not exist. Throughout this book, the various chapters relating to administrative tasks note the EMS text command that needs to be run to perform certain tasks. Chapter 9, "Using the Windows PowerShell in an Exchange Server 2010 Environment," is dedicated to providing details on the Exchange Management Shell.

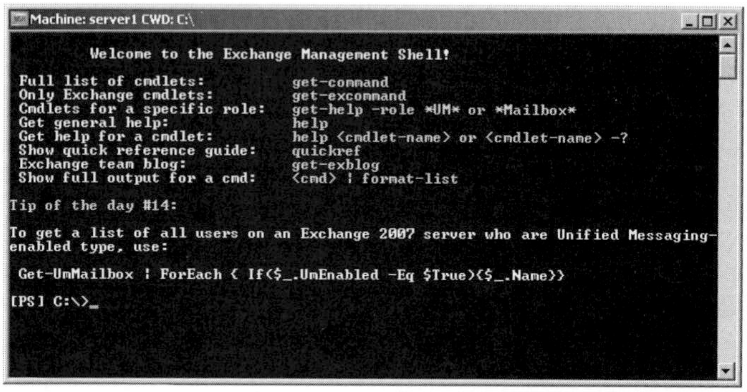

FIGURE 1.6   Sample Exchange Management Shell interface.

Exchange Server administrators have found that the EMS is very easy to use for day-to-day tasks. For example, tasks such as adding mailboxes or moving mailboxes used to require dozens of key clicks, but can now be scripted and simply cut/pasted into the EMS tool to be executed. As an example, a common task is moving a mailbox to a different database. Through the graphical management console, the task would take dozens of key clicks to move the mailboxes of a group of users. With EMS, it just takes a simple command such as the following:

```
Get-mailbox –server SERVER1 ¦ move-mailbox -targetdatabase
➥"SERVER2\Mailbox Database 1"
```

By creating a library of commands, an administrator can just search and replace words such as server names, usernames, or other object data, replace it in the command-line script, and then paste the script into EMS to have it execute. EMS is not only a necessity to do many tasks that are not available from the GUI, but it also makes administering and managing Exchange Server 2010 much easier for redundant tasks or for complex tasks that can be cut and pasted from a script library.

Although EMS was included in Exchange Server 2007, the execution of commands in EMS typically had to be initiated from the server in which the command was executed. With Exchange Server 2010 and the use of PowerShell v2 remoting technologies, an EMS command can be executed on one server with the effect taking place on another remote server.

Understanding Exchange Server 2010 Server Roles and Mail Flow

As briefly introduced previously in this chapter, Exchange Server 2010, like Exchange Server 2007, now has several new server roles, where different servers have different specializations. Instead of just having a Mailbox server and a front-end server to host data and provide a connecting point for client systems, these server roles provide improvements in security with servers dedicated to antivirus and antispam functions, message routing and policy compliance functions, and voice mail communications.

Identifying Exchange Server 2010 Server Roles

Each server role in Exchange Server 2010 provides several functions. The five server roles in Exchange Server 2010, shown in Figure 1.7, are as follows:

- ▶ Edge Transport server role

- ▶ Hub Transport server role

- ▶ Client Access server role

- ▶ Mailbox server role

- ▶ Unified Messaging server role

The various server roles can be combined onto a single server with the exception of the Edge Transport server role. For security reasons, the Edge Transport server role must be installed on a server that provides no other Exchange server role functions, and is recommended to be a system that provides no other Windows functions to limit the attack surface on the Edge Transport server.

Edge Transport Server Role

The Edge Transport server role is a dedicated server function that performs spam and virus filtering as the first point of entry of messages into an Exchange Server environment. Rather than having unwanted messages go directly to an Exchange Server back-end server taxing the database server with filtering of messages, the Edge Transport server offloads this task. Rather than spam and virus filtering thousands of messages for recipients who do not exist in the environment, the Edge Transport server accesses and stores a copy of certain Active Directory data, such as all valid Exchange Server 2010 email recipient mail

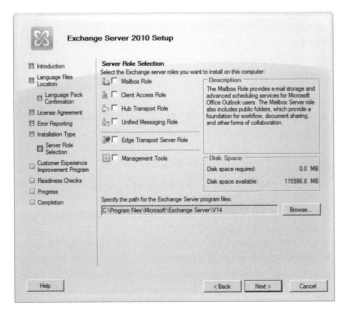

FIGURE 1.7   Server Role Selection option on Exchange Server 2010 installation.

addresses. This is so incoming messages can be checked against this Active Directory Application Mode (ADAM) directory, and messages for recipients who do not exist in the organization are immediately deleted.

In addition, the Edge Transport server role performs a safelist aggregation function as well, where it gathers safelist information from Outlook clients and brings the safelists out to the edge. By bringing individual users' safelists to the edge, the Edge Transport server can now take into consideration individual user preferences to receive certain types of messages so that the messages are forwarded on to the recipient even if the Edge Server's antispam software would normally quarantine or delete the message.

After a first pass at deleting messages for nonexistent recipients, a spam and virus scan can then be run on the remaining messages. After being determined to be clean, the messages can be forwarded on to either a Hub Transport server or to an Exchange Server 2010 back-end server. More details on the Edge Transport server role are covered in Chapter 8.

Hub Transport Server Role

For those familiar with earlier versions of Exchange Server, the Hub Transport server role replaces what was formerly known as the bridgehead server. The function of the Hub Transport server is to intelligently route messages within an Exchange Server 2010 environment. By default, SMTP transport is very inefficient at routing messages to multiple recipients because it takes a message and sends multiple copies throughout an organization. As an example, if a message with a 5-MB attachment is sent to 10 recipients in an SMTP network, typically at the sendmail routing server, the 10 recipients are identified from the directory, and 10 individual 5-MB messages are transmitted from the sendmail server to the mail recipients, even if all of the recipients' mailboxes reside on a single server.

The Hub Transport server takes a message destined to multiple recipients, identifies the most efficient route to send the message, and keeps the message intact for multiple recipients to the most appropriate endpoint. So, if all of the recipients are on a single server in a remote location, only one copy of the 5-MB message is transmitted to the remote server. At that server, the message is then broken apart with a copy of the message dropped into each of the recipient's mailboxes at the endpoint.

The Hub Transport server in Exchange Server 2010 does more than just intelligent bridgehead routing, though; it also acts as the policy compliance management server. Policies can be configured in Exchange Server 2010 so that after a message is filtered for spam and viruses, the message goes to the policy server to be assessed whether the message meets or fits into any regulated message policy, and appropriate actions are taken. The same is true for outbound messages; the messages go to the policy server, the content of the message is analyzed, and if the message is determined to meet specific message policy criteria, the message can be routed unchanged, or the message can be held or modified based on the policy. As an example, an organization might want any communications referencing a specific product code name, or a message that has content that looks like private health information, such as Social Security number, date of birth, or health records of an individual, to be held or encryption to be enforced on the message before it continues its route. More information on the role of policy compliance is found in Chapter 14, and information on the Hub Transport server role is found in Chapter 17.

Client Access Server Role

The Client Access server role in Exchange Server 2010 performs many of the tasks that were formerly performed by the Exchange Server front-end server, such as providing a connecting point for client systems. A client system can be an Office Outlook client, a Windows Mobile handheld device, a connecting point for OWA, or a remote laptop user using Outlook Anywhere to perform an encrypted synchronization of their mailbox content.

Unlike a front-end server in previous versions of Exchange Server that effectively just passed user communications on to the back-end Mailbox server, the CAS does intelligent assessment of where a user's mailbox resides, and then provides the appropriate access and connectivity. This is because Exchange Server 2010 now has replicated mailbox technology (covered in the "Making Exchange Server 2010 Extremely Reliable and Recoverable" section earlier in this chapter), where a user's mailbox can be active on a different server in the event of a primary mailbox server failure. By allowing the CAS server to redirect the user to the appropriate destination, there is more flexibility in providing redundancy and recoverability of mailbox access in the event of a system failure. More on the role of the Client Access server role is found in Chapter 17.

Mailbox Server Role

The Mailbox server role is merely a server that holds users' mailbox information. It is the server that has the Exchange Server EDB databases. However, rather than just being a database server, the Exchange Server 2010 Mailbox server role can be configured to perform several functions that keep the mailbox data online and replicated. For organizations that want to create high availability for Exchange Server data, the Mailbox server role systems would likely be clustered, and not just a local cluster with a shared drive (and, thus, a single point of failure on the data), but rather one that uses the new Exchange Server 2010 cluster continuous replication (CCR) technology.

Database Availablility Group replication allows the Exchange Server to replicate data transactions between Mailbox servers across a wide area network, or WAN. In the event of a primary Mailbox server failure, the secondary data source can be activated on a redundant server with a second copy of the data intact. Downtime and loss of data can be drastically minimized, if not completely eliminated, with the ability to replicate mailbox data on a real-time basis. You can find more details on Exchange Server 2010 Mailbox server recovery in Chapter 31.

NOTE

A major architecture change with Exchange Server 2010 is how Outlook clients connect to Exchange Server. In previous versions of Exchange Server, even Exchange Server 2007, the Outlook client initially connected to the Exchange Server front end or client access server, but thereafter, MAPI communications would communicate directly to the mailbox server. With Exchange Server 2010, all communications (initial connection and ongoing MAPI communications) goes through the client access server. Therefore, architecturally, the client access server in Exchange Server 2010 needs to be close to the Mailbox server, and a high-speed connection should exist between the servers for optimum performance. More on server placement and architecture in Chapter 3.

Unified Messaging Server Role

The Unified Messaging server role has been updated in Exchange Server 2010. Unified messaging is the capability for Exchange Server 2010 to be the voice mail server for an organization. Rather than having a separate voice mail system connected to the organization's phone system, an Exchange Server 2010 unified messaging server can be integrated into the phone system to be able to take messages on incoming calls, and the messages are stored in the users' Exchange Server mailboxes for playback from the phone or by accessing the message from within Outlook, OWA, or Windows Mobile.

Typically, the Unified Messaging server role will be set up on a dedicated server to isolate the tasks of mailbox management from unified voice communications and routing. However, the Unified Messaging server role can be combined as part of a limited server environment when the performance and separation of tasks is not required in the organization. You can find more information on unified messaging in Chapter 24.

How Messages Get to Exchange Server from the Internet

To follow the flow of messages in an Exchange Server 2010 environment with all the various server roles, the following flow occurs:

1. An incoming message from the Internet first goes to the Edge Transport server.
2. The Edge Transport server performs first-level recipient validation, as well as spam and virus filtering. The message is then passed on to the Hub Transport server.
3. The Hub Transport server performs compliance content assessment and then looks at the internal routing for messages and forwards the message to another Hub Transport server or directly to a Mailbox server.
4. The Mailbox server places the incoming message into the user's mailbox and notifies the user that a message has arrived.
5. The user launches Outlook, OWA, their Windows Mobile device, or another client system and connects to the client access server. The client access server confirms the destination point of the user's mailbox and provides the user access to their mailbox data.
6. In parallel, if a voice mail message comes in for a user, the Unified Messaging server processes the incoming voice message, and then takes the message and places the voice message into the user's mailbox residing on the Mailbox server for the recipient.

How Messages Route Within an Internal Exchange Server Environment

Internal messages are routed through Exchange Server in a similar manner. The process for a mail user to send a message to another mail user in the organization or to the Internet is as follows:

1. A message is created by a user in Outlook, on their Windows Mobile device, or on OWA where the user is connected to the client access server.
2. The message is stored on the user's Mailbox server as an Outbox message and, likely, a copy is stored in the user's Sent Items folder on the Mailbox server.

3. The Mailbox server then typically sends the message to a Hub Transport server that performs compliance content assessment and then looks at the internal routing for messages and forwards the message to another Hub Transport server, directly to a Mailbox server, or out to the Internet.

4. For internal messages, the Mailbox server places the incoming message into the user's mailbox and notifies the user that a message has arrived.

5. The message recipient launches Outlook, OWA, their Windows Mobile device, or another client system and connects to the client access server. The client access server confirms the destination point of the user's mailbox and provides the user access to their mailbox data.

Understanding the Importance of Active Directory for an Exchange Server 2010 Environment

Unlike previous versions of Exchange Server that leveraged Active Directory but still had separate components specific to routing of messages or separate administration roles, Exchange Server 2010 has done away with many of the Exchange Server-specific functions and now relies heavily on Active Directory. With Exchange Server 2010, as with Exchange Server 2007, the directory now provides the sole source for users, administrative roles, sites, server locations, and security functions. With this reliance on Active Directory, an Exchange Server 2010 environment needs to have a very reliable and properly configured Active Directory.

The Role of the Directory in an Exchange Server 2010 Environment

The directory in Active Directory is leveraged by Exchange Server 2010 to not only act as the lookup point for users' email addresses and contact information, but is now used as an authoritative directory to validate users within the organization. When messages come in from the Internet, rather than being processed for spam and virus filtering, a message is first checked to see if the recipient even exists in the environment. If the recipient is not in Active Directory, the message is quarantined or deleted completely, eliminating the task of processing messages for nonexistent recipients that takes up to 60%, 70%, and even 80% of a server's processing time.

Active Directory works in conjunction with Active Directory Application Mode, or ADAM, using a tool called EdgeSync on an Exchange Server 2010 Edge Transport server to move a portion of Active Directory to the edge in an encrypted, secure manner. In addition, Active Directory is leveraged on the Hub Transport server to process rules for compliance and regulatory content assessment. Using Active Directory user, group, organizational unit, site, domain, and forest level rules, content can be assessed and filtered at the Hub Transport server level.

The Role of Domain Name System (DNS) for Internal and External Message Routing

Exchange Server 2010 no longer maintains a separate message routing table nor does it provide a lookup table for servers within an Exchange Server environment. Rather, Exchange Server 2010 now uses DNS exclusively to determine name resolution and to identify servers and destination points from which to communicate. Unlike previous versions of Exchange Server that could still communicate using NetBIOS naming and Windows Internet Naming Service (WINS), Exchange Server 2010 solely depends on DNS. With the dependence on DNS in Exchange Server message transport and communications, it is extremely important that DNS is configured properly. More information on DNS is presented in Chapter 6, "Understanding Network Services and Active Directory Domain Controller Placement for Exchange Server 2010."

The Role of Sites in Exchange Server 2010

Exchange Server 2010 no longer has separate routing rules like routing groups for information on proper routing of messages within an Exchange Server environment. Rather, Exchange Server 2010 now uses Active Directory Sites and Services to determine how to route messages and to determine the most efficient route to transport messages within an organization. With the dependence on Active Directory Sites and Services in Exchange Server message transport and routing, it is extremely important that Active Directory Sites and Services be configured properly. You can find more details on Active Directory Sites and Services in Chapter 6.

Installing and Migrating to Exchange Server 2010

With an overview on what Exchange Server is and what is new in Exchange Server 2010, organizations usually turn to understanding how to plan, implement, or migrate to Exchange Server 2010, and how to administer, manage, and support the environment on an ongoing basis.

Installing Exchange Server 2010 from Scratch

Some organizations choose to install Exchange Server 2010 from scratch. This might occur for an organization that is new to email, or at least new to Exchange Server. This is common for an organization that had a different email platform, such as Lotus Notes, Novell GroupWise, or a sendmail/POP3/IMAP messaging system. Other times organizations implement Exchange Server from scratch is when an organization undergoes a major merger and consolidation and is better off creating the new environment from scratch rather than trying to consolidate or modify an existing environment.

Whatever the case might be, this book begins with design planning and implementation preparation tasks in Chapter 3. This is a good chapter for any size organization to plan and prepare for Exchange Server. For a larger organization, Chapter 4, "Architecting an

Enterprise-Level Exchange Server Environment," covers the planning and implementation of Exchange Server 2010 with tips, tricks, and best practices specific to large enterprise environments.

After a design plan has been identified, Chapter 7, "Installing Exchange Server 2010," will help the implementer of Exchange Server walk through the steps of installing Windows Active Directory and Exchange Server 2010, and configure the basic server roles as necessary.

Migrating to Exchange Server 2010

For an organization that has an existing Exchange Server environment, the organization would likely migrate to Exchange Server 2010. The Exchange Server migration path is pretty limited. You cannot migrate directly from Exchange Server 2000 or earlier directly into Exchange Server 2010. The only supported migrations from Microsoft are migrations from Exchange Server 2003 and Exchange Server 2007 to Exchange Server 2010. Furthermore, there is no support to perform an in-place upgrade of any Exchange server to Exchange Server 2010 primarily because Exchange Server 2010 runs on an x64-bit platform with a completely new set of binary files.

So because of this limited support, the process of migrating to Exchange Server 2010 is drastically simplified. There are specific tips, tricks, and best practices created in migrating from Exchange Server 2003 and Exchange Server 2007 to Exchange Server 2010 that help an organization more reliably and more effectively perform their migration. The steps for migration are outlined in Chapter 16.

Managing and Administering Exchange Server 2010

After an Exchange Server 2010 environment has been properly designed and implemented, the administrators of the organization need to be able to jump in and begin managing and administering the messaging environment. Because Exchange Server 2010 is more than just email message boxes and calendars, there is more to manage and administer. Chapter 18 goes through the top administrative tasks performed by Exchange Server administrators, such as adding users, deleting users, moving mailboxes, adding users to distribution lists, and so on. These tasks can now be performed both from the Exchange Management Console GUI and from the Exchange Management Shell command-line interface.

With Exchange Server 2010, a handful of ongoing management and maintenance tasks have proven to be important in keeping the Exchange Server environment operational. These management and maintenance tasks are covered in Chapter 19, "Exchange Server 2010 Management and Maintenance Practices." The tasks include daily, weekly, and monthly maintenance routines intended to keep Exchange Server operational on an ongoing basis.

Monitoring Exchange Server Using Microsoft System Center Operations Manager (SCOM)

Part of any best practice in network systems management is to monitor servers and services to ensure that the system is operating properly, and to provide proactive alerts if something is no longer operating. Chapter 20, "Using Operations Manager to Monitor Exchange Server 2010," covers the SCOM product used to monitor and alert on Exchange Server 2010 activities. There is a dedicated Exchange Server 2010 management pack that provides specific monitoring functions for Exchange Server 2010.

Summary

This chapter highlighted the new features, functions, migration tools, and management utilities in Exchange Server 2010 that will help administrators take advantage of the capabilities of the new messaging system. An upgrade to Exchange Server 2010 is more than just a simple upgrade from one messaging system to another, but should take into account the new ways Exchange Server 2010 will be leveraged as the depository for more than just email messages, but also voice and mobile communications.

Planning and implementing a new implementation or an upgrade to Exchange Server 2010 is an opportunity for the organization to make Exchange Server 2010 a highly reliable and fully recoverable communications infrastructure environment. The new capabilities of Exchange Server 2010 allow an organization to change the way users access the system remotely, improve security both in the background and at the client, and have the tools available to maintain, manage, and recover from a disaster.

The steps to proper planning and successful implementation are highlighted throughout this book, with tips, tricks, and best practices noted throughout the chapters.

Best Practices

The following are best practices from this chapter:

▶ Spend a moment to understand what is new in Exchange Server 2010 and how the focal point of Exchange Server 2010 as the infrastructure foundation for unified communications requires a rethinking of the current architecture and ultimate redesign of an organization's Exchange Server environment.

▶ Plan for the implementation of Exchange Server 2010 by reviewing the architecture recommendations for a basic Exchange Server configuration environment covered in Chapter 3, with more specific recommendations for larger enterprises covered in Chapter 4.

▶ Use the step-by-step installation procedures for implementing Exchange Server 2010 covered in Chapter 7.

▶ Use the step-by-step migration process covered in Chapter 16 to properly plan a migration from Exchange Server 2003 and Exchange Server 2007.

▶ Consider using the new Outlook Web App 2010 not only as a web browser client, but possibly as the primary mail client for many users and as a replacement of the need for VPNs in an organization through the use of the direct file access technology in OWA.

▶ Leverage the Outlook Anywhere functionality to enable remote, full-client Outlook users connectivity to Exchange Server 2010 without the need to implement VPNs or other secured connection systems.

▶ Implement the Database Availability Group (DAG) technology covered in Chapter 31 to create a more redundant Exchange Server environment for fast and fully supported recovery of Exchange Server mailboxes.

▶ Test the mailbox recovery process highlighted in Chapter 33 to ensure that if you need to recover from mailbox deletion or corruption, you have successfully tested the functionality.

▶ For better Exchange server management, administration, and reporting, review Chapters 18 and 19 on tips and techniques for managing and administering Exchange Server 2010.

▶ Leverage Microsoft System Center Operations Manager to better proactively monitor and respond to Exchange Server 2010 operational problems before the problem impacts users.

▶ To minimize spam and unwanted messaging, enable Exchange Server 2010 Edge Transport servers to perform front-line filtering.

▶ Consider using the Exchange Server 2010 built-in remote and mobile capabilities for Windows Mobile phones and devices for the communication of messages, calendars, and contacts.

▶ Review exiting enterprise configurations for network settings that can be modified or reconfigured with an upgrade to Exchange Server 2010.

CHAPTER 2

Planning, Prototyping, Migrating, and Deploying Exchange Server 2010

Implementing a new messaging environment or upgrading an existing one can be both an exciting time and a stressful time for an administrator. Messaging has changed drastically over the years, steadily growing from an occasionally used way to send short messages to a highly critical collaboration tool that sends hundreds of times more messages each day than the U.S. Post Office. Users depend on Exchange Server to track their tasks, keep their appointments, store important pieces of information, and communicate quickly and easily with co-workers and vendors. As users become more and more dependent on these types of tools, their requirements increase in terms of accessibility and reliability. The ultimate goal of the end users is for email to be much like the telephone. They never want to have to think twice about whether they'll have access to it and whether or not they'll get a dial tone. Proper planning is the key to being able to deliver this level of functionality and reliability. This chapter helps Exchange Server administrators to properly plan out their build or upgrade through standardized processes of planning, prototyping, and migrating or deploying Microsoft Exchange Server 2010.

Email has become a business-critical tool and, as such, the upgrade process should never be taken lightly. Although an upgrade from Exchange Server 2003 or Exchange Server 2007 might at first appear to be a simple process, its success relies on your understanding of current issues with the messaging environment, defining both the objectives of the upgrade and its potential effects on the user community. Adding more features and complexity to the messaging "ecosystem" might not result in ecstatic users, but reducing spam and the resulting impact on Inboxes might more than justify the cost of the upgrade.

Reducing the number of milliseconds it takes to send an email probably won't get noticed, but being able to guarantee access to email anywhere and anytime should. Be aware of who your audience is for the upgrade and make sure you understand their existing pain points and how they use Exchange Server and Outlook. An enthusiastic user community tends to generate support and momentum for projects, which allows you to extend the functionality of the messaging system and increase the productivity of your users. Productive users result in happy management. Happy management results in project approval. It's a very positive circle to create. As such, it's important for an administrator to understand the potential benefits that come with Exchange Server 2010 and to ensure that the correct functions are mapped to the appropriate user need.

Important decisions include whether the entire network operating system (NOS) needs to be upgraded (if Active Directory [AD] is not yet in place) or only a subset of it, and what other infrastructure components need to be changed or replaced. It is also very important to realize that Exchange Server 2010 is a 64-bit application and, therefore, needs a 64-bit operating system and 64-bit capable hardware to run. This means that some of your existing tools or integrated applications might or might not work. Testing cannot be underestimated in this process. Pay special attention to the fact that unlike Exchange Server 2007, there will be no 32-bit code available for Exchange Server 2010. This means that if an administrator is going to run the Exchange Server 2010 management tools from his or her own workstation, that workstation must be running a 64-bit version of Windows.

The examples used in this chapter assume that the environments being migrated are primarily based on Exchange Server 2003 or Exchange Server 2007 and, except where noted, that Active Directory is already in place. Please note that an Exchange Server environment must be in Exchange Server 2000 Native mode or higher. Exchange Server 2010 cannot be introduced into an organization that still has Exchange Server 5.5 servers. This would require migrating into a new forest and is discussed later in this chapter. The same process can be applied to other messaging migration projects, such as GroupWise or Notes. The migration process is covered in detail in Chapters 15, "Migrating from Active Directory 2000/2003 to Active Directory 2008," and 16, "Transitioning from Exchange Server 2003/2007 to Exchange Server 2010."

Initiation, Planning, Testing, and Pilot: The Four Phases to the Upgrade

This chapter presents a structured process for upgrading to Exchange Server 2010 and highlights some best practice recommendations to enhance the success of the project. The standard project management phases of initiation, planning, testing, and implementation can be used for organizations of any size and can be applied to most any information technology (IT) project. Transitioning each phase is a "go/no-go" decision, in which the results of the phase are reviewed, and the decision makers determine whether or not the project should move forward. Any problems that were encountered are assessed to determine whether they require attention before moving forward. This ensures that issues identified are addressed, rather than being overlooked, to inevitably crop up at the worst possible moment. You can also use this go/no-go point to feedback results of the testing back into your plans. If you determine that something will be an issue when rolled out, take the fix for the issue and work it back into your process. Now retest with the altered procedure to make sure it works as expected. In this way, you will eventually reach a production rollout with no surprises.

Documentation Required During the Phases

A number of documents are produced during each phase to ensure that the phase is well defined and ultimately successful. In the initiation phase, the goals and requirements of the project can be identified and documented in a Statement of Work document. In the planning phase, more time and energy can be applied to detailing the end state of the migration into a Design document, including the majority of the technical decisions. Although this document paints the picture of what the end state will look like, the road map of how to get there is detailed in the Project Schedule and Migration documents. These documents are only drafts during this phase, because they need to be validated in the prototype phase before they can be considered "final."

Consider tracking the options that were discussed during the design process and document the reasons why a particular choice was made. This allows for future members of your team to understand why particular decisions were made.

The prototype phase validates that the new technologies will effectively meet the organization's needs, and determines whether modifications to the project are needed. Any additional documents that would help with the implementation process, such as Server Build documents, Business Continuity or Disaster Recovery documents, and checklists for workstation configurations, are also created during the testing phase. Finally, the appropriate Maintenance documents are created during the prototype phase so that they can be properly tested without impacting production users. The prototype phase is also when the majority of team cross training should occur, as it's an excellent opportunity to demonstrate the creation and modification of Exchange Server-related objects without impacting a production environment.

These phases and the documents to be created are discussed in more detail later in this chapter.

The following list summarizes the standard phases of an Exchange Server 2010 upgrade and the standard documents created in each phase:

▶ **Initiation phase**—Statement of Work document that reflects the goals and objectives of the key stakeholders of the project.

▶ **Planning phase**—Design document draft, Migration document draft, and Migration schedule draft (Gantt chart).

▶ **Prototype phase**—Design document final, Migration document final, Migration schedule final (Gantt chart), Server Build documents, Migration checklists, Maintenance documents, and Training documents for end users and administrators.

▶ **Implementation phase**—As-built documents for all servers.

For smaller environments, not all of these items are required, but it's important to have each document created before it is needed, to avoid delays during the migration process. For example, having a Statement of Work document that is well constructed and agreed upon in the initiation phase clears the way for the creation of the Design document and Migration document. A detailed Migration Schedule Gantt chart facilitates scheduling of resources for the actual work and clarifies the roles and responsibilities. Remember to have the appropriate groups review the documentation and get their approval to consider the document "done." This avoids potential issues in which a group might change their minds and claim that they never agreed to a design decision or migration process.

Initiation Phase: Defining the Scope and Goals

Upgrading to Exchange Server 2010 can be a simple process for basic messaging environments, or as challenging as a complete network operating system upgrade for more complex organizations. In most environments, Exchange Server is implemented on multiple servers, and an upgrade affects a number of other software applications. In fact, changes to the Exchange Server environment might affect the daily lives of the employees to a much greater extent than moving from Windows NT to Windows Server 2003 (or even more than an upgrade from a non-Microsoft environment) because they will most likely receive a new Outlook client and change the way they access email remotely. With an operating system upgrade, the end users often don't even know that anything has changed.

The upgrade process is also a great opportunity to help the business achieve its business objectives by leveraging the messaging components of the technology infrastructure and to help justify the never-ending IT expenses. Messaging, in essence, enables the sharing of information and access to data and other resources within the company to help the company deliver its products or services. With this critical purpose in mind, it makes sense to engage in a structured and organized process to determine the goals of the project, control the variables and risks involved, and make sure that a clear definition of the end state has been crafted. The Statement of Work is the key deliverable from this phase that paints the overall picture of the upgrade project and gains support from the key decision makers (and allocates an initial budget).

Be sure to take into account any regulatory compliances that you need to maintain. This includes things such as HIPAA, Sarbanes-Oxley, or the Gramm-Leach-Bliley Act. These types of regulatory compliances will likely influence your decisions about how your systems will be deployed and managed. It is much easier to account for these requirements during the planning phase than it is after you've deployed Exchange Server 2010.

The Scope of the Project

Before the entire Statement of Work can be written, time should be allocated to define the scope of the project. The scope of the project simply defines what is included in the project and what is not. For a simpler environment, this might be very easy to define—for example, an environment in which there is only one server used for email and scheduling, with a dedicated backup device and virus-protection software. If this organization has not migrated to Active Directory yet, the scope might expand to include the upgrade of additional servers or simply upgrade the single server. Depending on the version of Active Directory in place, there would likely be a schema updated in the scope as well. A desktop upgrade might be included in the scope of the project if the features and benefits of Outlook 2007 are desired. In any case, it's important to clarify this level of detail at the beginning of the planning process. "Scope creep" is a lot more manageable if it can be predicted in advance! If the scope starts to grow to be out of hand, consider breaking it up into multiple projects. For example, if you have a large upgrade to Exchange Server 2010, you can split off the upgrading of desktops to Outlook 2007 to be a separate project. This can also help prevent a project from stalling out because of too many dependencies on other groups or projects.

> **NOTE**
>
> An example of a scope of work for a small organization is as follows:
>
> ▶ Upgrade the Exchange Server 2003 Windows 2003 server to Exchange Server 2010 with Windows Server 2008 64-bit.
>
> ▶ Upgrade the tape backup and virus-protection software to Exchange Server 2010–compatible versions.
>
> ▶ Upgrade the Outlook client to Outlook 2007 on all workstations.
>
> ▶ Provide secure Outlook Web App (OWA) access to all remote users.

In a larger company, "what's in" and "what's out" can be significantly more complicated. A company with multiple servers dedicated to Exchange Server functions—such as load-balanced client access servers and clustered mailbox servers, multiple Hub Transport servers, or servers dedicated to faxing or conferencing—requires the scope definition to get that much more detailed. Multiple sites and even different messaging systems complicate the scope, especially if the company has grown via mergers over the last few years. Odds are that larger environments will have a mix of hardware ranging in age from 0 to 3 years old. Changes in the architecture of Exchange Server 2010 mean that companies will likely be looking at changes in their standard hardware specs, as well as their storage requirements for Exchange Server. Always be sure to look at the big picture and account for as much as you can in the scope.

> **NOTE**
>
> An example of a scope of work for a larger organization is as follows:
>
> ▶ Upgrade the four Exchange Server 2007 Windows 2003 mailbox clusters to two Exchange Server 2010 mailbox servers in DAG on Windows Server 2008 64-bit.
>
> ▶ Replace the two Exchange Server 2007 on Windows 2003 client access servers with two Exchange Server 2010 on Windows 2008 client access servers.
>
> ▶ Migrate the mailbox data from the SAN storage to local disks on the new Exchange Server 2010 mailbox servers.
>
> ▶ Provide Outlook Web App (OWA) access to all remote users.

▶ Upgrade the enterprise tape backup and virus-protection software on all servers to the latest versions that are Windows Server 2008–compatible and Exchange Server 2010–compatible.

▶ Implement unified messaging on Exchange Server 2010.

▶ Upgrade the Outlook client to Outlook 2007. Provide OWA access to all remote users.

The scope of work might change as the initiation phase continues and, in the more detailed planning phase, as the Design and Migration documents are created and reviewed. This is especially true for more complex migration projects after the detailed planning phase is completed and the all-important budget is created. At this point, the scope might need to be reduced, so that the budget requested can be reduced.

It is in your best interest to circulate your plans among other groups not only to get their buy-in on the migration, but also to give them a chance to see how it might impact their projects. Often, the group managing the phone systems will look at a project like an Exchange Server 2010 upgrade and take the opportunity to make changes to their systems to further integrate with Exchange Server. Knowing about these integration plans early in your process makes it easier to accept them. Altering a deployed environment after the fact is almost always more expensive and more complicated. Do everything you can to keep your project stable and uneventful.

Identifying the Goals

As a next step in the initiation phase, it helps to spend time clearly identifying the goals of the project before getting too caught up in the technical details. All too often, everyone runs up the whiteboard and starts scribbling and debating technology before agreeing on the goals. Although this conversation is healthy and necessary, it should be part of the planning phase, after the high-level goals for the project and initial scope have been defined. Even if there is a very short timeline for the project, the goals—from high-level business objectives, to departmental goals, to the specific technology goals—should be specified.

It is important to have the correct audience in the goal-setting phase of the initiation phase. This will likely be the meeting with the largest attendance. Try to gather goals and objectives from groups such as the following:

▶ Information technology

▶ Help desk

▶ Upper management

▶ Business unit representatives

▶ Telecom

▶ Enterprise backup

By talking to this diverse group of people, you can capture existing pain points of the users and maintainers of the messaging environment and try to alleviate those issues. You can also get a much more accurate feel for how your end users actually utilize Exchange Server and ensure that you account for those items.

One of the biggest values you get out of clearly identifying your goals is that it simplifies the technical decisions that will be made later. Anytime there is contention around a given decision, you can always ask yourself "Does this decision support my originally stated goals?" and if not, it is probably not the right decision.

High-Level Business Goals

The vision statement of an organization is an excellent place to start because it tells the world where the company excels and what differentiates that company from its competitors. There will typically be several key objectives behind this vision, which are not so publicly stated, that can be related to the Exchange Server 2010 upgrade. These should be uncovered and clarified, or it will be difficult, if not impossible, to judge whether the project succeeds or fails from a business standpoint.

> **NOTE**
>
> High-level business goals that pertain to an Exchange Server 2010 upgrade can include better leveraging of company knowledge and resources through efficient communications and collaboration, controlling IT costs to lower overhead and enabling products to be more competitively priced, or improving security to meet governmental requirements. An IT group that understands these larger goals and can serve as an enabler for business practices through technology is an amazing asset to any company.

Although this process sounds basic, it might be more difficult if the company hasn't documented or updated its business objectives in some time (or ever). Different divisions of larger companies might even have conflicting business goals, which can make matters more complicated. High-level business goals of a company can also change rapidly, whether in response to changing economic conditions or as affected by a new key stakeholder or leader in the company. So even if a company has a standard vision statement in place, it is worth taking the time to review and ensure that it still accurately reflects the opinions of the key stakeholders.

This process helps clarify how the messaging upgrade fits into the overall company strategy and should help ensure that support will be there to approve the project and keep its momentum going. In this time of economic uncertainty, a project must be strategic and directly influence the delivery of the company's services and products; otherwise, the danger exists of a key stakeholder "pulling the plug" at the first sign of trouble or shifting attention to a more urgent project.

For example, a consulting organization might have a stated vision of providing the latest and greatest processes and information to its clients, and the internal goal could be to make its internal assets (data) available to all employees at all times to best leverage the knowledge gained in other engagements. The Exchange Server environment plays a key role in meeting this goal because employees have become so dependent on Outlook for communicating and organizing information, and many of the employees rely on portable devices such as BlackBerries or Windows Mobile devices.

A different company, one which specializes in providing low-cost products to the marketplace, might have an internal goal of cost control, which can be met by Exchange Server 2010 through reduction in the total server count, storage technologies, and more cost-effective management to help reduce downtime. For this company, user productivity is measured carefully, and the enhancements in the Outlook 2007 client would contribute positively.

High-Level Messaging Goals

At this point, the business goals that will guide and justify the Exchange Server upgrade should be clearly defined, and the manner in which Exchange Server 2010's enhanced features will be valuable to the company are starting to become clear. The discussion can now turn to learning from key stakeholders what goals they have that are specific to the messaging environment that will be put in place and how Exchange Server 2010 might improve their day-to-day business processes.

The high-level goals tend to come up immediately, and be fairly vague in nature; but they can be clarified to determine the specific requirements. A CEO of the company might simply state "I need access to all of my email and calendar data from anywhere." The CTO of the same company might request "zero downtime of the Exchange servers and easy integration with other automated business systems." The CFO might want to "reduce the costs of the email system and associated technologies." If the managers in different departments are involved in the conversation, a second level of goals might well be expressed. The IT manager might want geographic redundancy, the ability to restore a single user's mailbox, and reduced user complaints about spam and performance. The marketing manager might want better tools to organize the ever-increasing amount of "stuff" in his employees' Inboxes and mail folders.

Time spent gathering this information helps ensure that the project is successful and the technology goals match up with the business goals. It also matters who is spearheading the process and asking the questions because the answers might be very different if asked by the president of the company rather than an outside consultant who has no direct influence over the career of the interviewee. By involving the people whose employees will be most affected by the upgrade and listening to their needs, you can create very powerful allies in getting approval for the technology and hardware necessary to support their goals and objectives.

NOTE

An example of some common high-level messaging goals include a desire to have no downtime of the Exchange servers, access to email and calendars from anywhere, better functionality of the OWA client, and increased virus and spam protection.

A specific trend or theme to look for in the expression of these goals is whether they are focused on fixing and stabilizing or on adding new functionality. When a company is fixated on simply "making things work properly," it might make sense to hold off on implementing a variety of new functionality (such as videoconferencing or providing Windows-powered mobile devices using the Windows Mobile operating system) at the same time. Make sure you listen to your audience and design an environment that supports their needs and addresses their concerns. Avoid the pitfalls of enabling new functions simply because they seem "cool."

Business Unit or Departmental Messaging Goals

After these higher-level goals have been identified, the conversations can be expanded to include departmental managers and team leads. The results will start to reveal the complexity of the project and the details needed to complete the Statement of Work for the migration project. For an Exchange Server upgrade project to be completely successful, these individuals, as well as the end users, need to benefit in measurable ways.

Based on the business and technology goals identified thus far, the relative importance of different departments will start to become clear. Some organizations are IT-driven, especially if they are dependent on the network infrastructure to deliver the company's products and services. Others can survive quite well if technology isn't available for a day or even longer.

> **NOTE**
>
> Examples of some departmental goals include a desire to ensure encrypted transmission of human resource and personnel emails, an OWA client that has the same functionality as the Outlook client, and support for Smartphone and Windows Mobile devices. The IT department might also like better mailbox recovery tools and Exchange Server-specific management tools that can be used to centralize and simplify the management of Exchange Server.

All departments use email, but the Sales department might also receive voice mails through the Outlook client and updates on product pricing, and, therefore, need the best possible reliability and performance. This includes ensuring that viruses don't make it into employee Inboxes and that spam be reduced as much as possible.

Certain key executives are rarely in the office and might not be happy with the existing OWA client. They might also carry BlackBerry wireless devices or Windows Mobile phones and need to make sure that they remain fully functional during and after the upgrade.

The Marketing department might use the email system for sharing graphics files via public folders, which have grown to an almost unmanageable size, but this enables them to share the data with strategic partners outside of the company. This practice won't change, and the amount of data to be managed will continue to grow over time.

The Finance and Human Resources departments might be concerned about security and want to make sure that all email information and attached files are as safe as possible when traveling within the organization, or being sent to clients over the Internet.

The IT department could have a very aggressive service level agreement (SLA) to meet and be interested in clustering, reducing the number of servers that need to be managed, and improving the management tools in place. In addition, Exchange Server 2010's integration with Active Directory will facilitate the management of users and groups and additions and changes to existing user information.

In the process of clarifying these goals, the features of the Exchange Server messaging system that are most important to the different departments and executives should become apparent.

A user focus group might also be helpful, which can be composed of employee volunteers and select managers, to engage in detailed discussions and brainstorming sessions. In this way, the end users can participate in the initial planning process and help influence the decisions that will affect their day-to-day work experience.

Other outcomes of these discussions should include an understanding of which stakeholders will be involved in the project and the goals that are primary for each person and each department. A sense of excitement should start to build over the possibilities presented by the new technologies that will be introduced to make managers' lives easier and workers' days more productive.

This process also serves an additional benefit of giving people a sense of how big the project really is and where they'll see the benefits that affect them the most. A major change like an Exchange Server upgrade should always be well communicated to the end-user community so that they will know what changes to expect, when to expect them, and how to prepare for them.

Initiation Phase: Creating the Statement of Work

Executives generally require a documented Statement of Work that reflects strategic thinking, an understanding of the goals and objectives of the organization, and a sense of confidence that the project will be successful and beneficial to the company. The document needs to be clear and specific and keep its audience in mind. This generally means not going into too much technical detail in the Statement of Work. This document also needs to give an estimate of the duration of the project, the costs involved, and the resources required. The document should be written such that it can be understood by someone who knows nothing about the technology that is being proposed. This is a classic example of where one needs to understand the point of view of their audience and to tailor the information to what that target audience will want to see.

The initial scope of work might have changed and evolved as discussions with the executives, managers, and stakeholders reveal problems that weren't obvious and requirements that hadn't been foreseen. Although the scope started out as a "simple Exchange Server upgrade," it might have expanded to include an upgrade to Active Directory, the addition of new features for remote access to the messaging environment, the rollout of new 64-bit capable servers or management, and business continuity features.

The following is a standard outline for the Statement of Work document:

1. Scope of Work
2. Goals and Objectives
3. Timeline and Milestones
4. Resources
5. Risks and Assumptions
6. Dependencies
7. Initial Budget

The following sections cover the different components of the Statement of Work. This document is arguably the most important in the entire process because it can convince the executives who hold the purse strings to move forward with the project—or, of course, to stop the project in its tracks.

Summarizing the Scope of Work

At this point in the initiation phase, a number of conversations have occurred that have clarified the basic scope of the project, the high-level business goals as they pertain to the messaging upgrade, and the more specific goals for each department and of key stakeholders. Armed with this wealth of information, the lead consultant on the project should now organize the data to include in the Statement of Work and get sign-off to complete the phase and move to the more detailed planning phase.

The Scope section of the Statement of Work document should answer these essential questions:

▶ How many Exchange Server and Windows servers need to be upgraded?

▶ Where do these servers reside?

▶ What additional applications need to be upgraded (especially backup, virus protection, disaster recovery, and remote access) as part of the project?

▶ What additional hardware needs to be upgraded or modified to support the new servers and applications (especially tape backup devices, SANs, routers)?

▶ Will laptop configurations be changed? If so, will you need physical access to them?

▶ Will the desktop configurations be changed?

The answers to these questions might still be unclear at this point, and require additional attention during the planning phase.

Summarizing the Goals

As discussed earlier, a number of conversations have been held previously on the topic of goals, so there might be a fairly long list of objectives at this point. A structure to organize these goals is suggested in the following list:

▶ Business continuity/disaster recovery (clustering, storage, backup, and restore)

▶ Performance (memory allocation improvements, public folders, email)

▶ Security (server, email)

▶ Mobility (Outlook Web App, Windows Mobile, and Outlook Anywhere support)

▶ Collaboration (Public Folders, SharePoint Portal, Office Communications Server integrations)

▶ Serviceability (administration, management, deployment)

▶ Development (Collaboration Data Objects, managed application programming interface [API])

By using a framework such as this, any "holes" in the goals and objectives of the project will be more obvious. Some of the less-glamorous objectives, such as a stable network, data-recovery abilities, or protection from the hostile outside world, might not have been identified in the discussions. This is the time to bring up topics that might have been missed, before moving into the more detailed planning phase.

It might also be valuable to categorize portions of the upgrade as "fixes" for existing pain points, as opposed to "new" capabilities that will be added to the environment.

Summarizing the Timeline and Milestones

A bulleted list of tasks is typically all that is needed to help define the time frame for the upgrade, although more complex projects will benefit from a high-level Gantt chart. The time frame should be broken down by phase to clarify how much time is to be allocated for the planning phase and testing phases. The actual implementation of the upgrade also should be estimated. A good rule of thumb at this point is that no task represented on the project plan should have a duration of less then 1 day. If it logically has a shorter duration, it's probably too detailed to call out at this point.

Depending on the complexity of the project, a time frame of 1 to 2 months could be considered a "short" time frame, with 2 to 4 months offering a more comfortable window for projects involving more servers, users, and messaging-related applications. Additional time should be included if an outside consulting firm will assist with part or the entire project. Be sure to account for things such as acquiring hardware, application testing, and shipping of hardware to remote locations. These types of items can often be overlooked, yet they can easily add weeks to the timeline of a project like this.

Because every project is different, it's impossible to provide rules for how much time to allocate to which phase. Experience has shown that allocating additional time for the planning and testing phase helps the upgrade go more smoothly, resulting in a happier user base. If little or no planning is done, the testing phase will most likely miss key requirements for the success of the project. Remember also to allocate time during the process for training of the administrative staff and end users.

Be aware of your own internal processes and try to account for them. If your environment requires, for example, that the security group perform a security audit on any server before it is released into production, be sure to account for this in the timeline. Also be sure to let that other group know that you will be submitting a potentially large number of servers for them to audit so that they can also prepare their own resources to be ready for you. Careful teamwork and communication around these types of activities can save a lot of time overall.

The key to successfully meeting a short timeline is to understand the added risks involved and define the scope of the project so that the risks are controlled. This might include putting off some of the functionality that is not essential, or contracting outside assistance to speed up the process and leverage the experience of a firm that has performed similar upgrades many times. Hardware and software procurement can also pose delays, so for shorter time frames, they should be procured as soon as possible after the ideal configuration has been defined. Don't be afraid to make certain portions of the original project "out of scope" and spin them into separate projects. Keeping your project realistic makes it easier to complete successfully.

Summarizing the Resources Required

Typical roles that need to be filled for an Exchange Server 2003 upgrade project include the following:

- ▶ Project sponsor or champion
- ▶ Exchange Server 2010 design consultant
- ▶ Exchange Server 2010 technical lead
- ▶ Exchange Server 2010 consulting engineer
- ▶ Project manager
- ▶ Systems engineer(s)
- ▶ Technical writer
- ▶ Administrative trainer
- ▶ End-user trainer

The organization should objectively consider the experience and skills, as well as available time of internal resources, before deciding whether outside help is needed. For the most part, few companies completely outsource the whole project, choosing instead to leverage internal resources for the tasks that make sense and hiring external experts for the planning phase and testing phases. Often, internal resources simply can't devote 100% of their energy to planning and testing the messaging technologies because their daily duties get in the way. Contracted resources, on the other hand, are able to focus just on the messaging project. Most successful projects include a mix of internal and external resources. This allows the internal resources to gain valuable knowledge from the external resources and end up with a strong knowledge of their own environment from their direct involvement with the design and deployment.

The resulting messaging environment needs to be supported after the dust settles, so it makes sense for the administrative staff to receive training in the early phases of the upgrade (such as planning and testing) rather than after the implementation. Many consultants provide hands-on training during the testing and implementation phases. It is easier to perform most of the training in the prototype phase because you will have a working environment that doesn't have any users on it. This allows the administrative staff to practice moving mailboxes, recovering data and entire servers, and rebuilding servers from scratch without impacting any production users.

For larger projects, a team might be created for the planning phase, a separate team allocated for the testing phase, and a third team for the implementation. Ideally, the individuals who perform the testing participate in the implementation for reasons of continuity. Implementation teams can benefit from less-experienced resources for basic server builds and workstation upgrades. By properly assigning the project tasks to the right resources, you can maximize the chances for overall success. By providing for a bit of overlap between tasks and resources, you can also cross-train your staff so that they can more easily support each other.

Summarizing the Risks and Assumptions

More time is spent discussing the details of the risks that could affect the successful outcome of the project during the planning phase; however, if there are immediately obvious risks, they should be included in the Statement of Work.

Basic risks could include the following:

▶ Existing Exchange Server problems, such as a corrupt database or lack of maintenance

▶ Lack of in-house expertise and bandwidth for the project

▶ Using existing hardware that might not have enough random access memory (RAM), storage capacity, processor speed, or the ability to support a 64-bit operating system

▶ Wide area network (WAN) or local area network (LAN) connectivity issues, making downtime a possibility

▶ A production environment that cannot experience any downtime or financial losses will occur

▶ Customized applications that interface with Exchange Server and that need to be tested and possibly rewritten for Exchange Server 2010

▶ Short timeline that will require cutting corners in the testing process

Summarizing the Initial Budget

The decision makers will want to start getting a sense for the cost of the project, at least for the planning phase of the project. Some information might already be quite clear, such as how many servers need to be purchased. If the existing servers are more than a few years old and don't support a 64-bit operating system, chances are they need to be replaced, and price quotes can easily be gathered for new machines. Software upgrades and licenses can also easily be gathered, and costs for peripheral devices such as tape drives or SANs or host bus adapters should be included.

If external help is needed for the planning, testing, and implementation, some educated guesses should be made about the order of magnitude of these costs. Some organizations set aside a percentage of the overall budget for the planning phase, assuming outside assistance, and then determine whether they can do the testing and implementation on their own.

As mentioned previously, training should also not be forgotten for both the administrative staff and the end users.

Getting Approval on the Statement of Work

After the initial information has been presented in the Statement of Work format, formally present it and discuss it with the stakeholders. If the process has gone smoothly this far, the Statement of Work should be approved, or, if not, items that are still unclear can be clarified. After this document has been agreed upon, a great foundation is in place to move forward with the planning phase.

Planning Phase: Discovery

The planning phase enables the Exchange Server 2010 design consultant time to paint the detailed picture of what the end state of the upgrade will look like, and also to detail exactly how the network will evolve to this new state. The goals of the project are clear, what's in and what's out are documented, the resources required are defined, the timeline for the planning phase and an initial sketch of the risks are anticipated, and the budget is estimated.

Understanding the Existing Environment

If an organization has multiple Exchange servers in place, third-party add-on applications, multiple sites, complex remote access, or regulatory security requirements, it makes sense to perform a full network audit. If an outside company is spearheading the planning phase, this is its first real look at the configuration of the existing hardware and network, and it is essential to help create an appropriate end state and migration process. Standard questionnaires are helpful to collect data on the different servers that will be affected by the upgrade. Typically, these questionnaires are sent to the groups that manage the Exchange Server-related systems in various locations as they generally have the best information on those systems, including any issues or "quirks" they might have.

The discovery process typically starts with onsite interviews with the IT resources responsible for the different areas of the network and proceeds with a hands-on review of the network configuration. Focus groups or white boarding sessions can also help dredge up concerns or issues that might not have been shared previously. External consultants often generate better results because they have extensive experience with network reviews and analysis and with predicting the problems that can emerge midway through a project. Consider holding at least some of the interview sessions with only specific groups present. Sometimes, some groups don't want to bring up specific issues with other groups present.

Network performance can be assessed at the same time to predict the level of performance the end users will see and whether they are accessing email, public folders, or calendars from within the company, from home, or from an Internet kiosk in an airport. This is also a great time to get a baseline of system performance and bandwidth consumption. Having this baseline is very important and allows you to accurately rate the new environment. It can be very hard to deal with comments of "the new environment seems slower" if you have no previous performance data to compare it with.

Existing network security policies might be affected by the upgrade, and should be reviewed. If AD is being implemented, group policies—which define user and computer configurations and provide the ability to centralize logon scripts and printer access—can be leveraged.

Anyone using Exchange Server is familiar with the challenges of effectively managing the data that builds up, and in grooming and maintaining these databases. The existing database structure should be reviewed at least briefly so the Exchange Server 2010 design consultant understands where the databases reside, how many there are and their respective sizes, and whether regular maintenance has been performed. Serious issues with the database(s) crashing in the past should be covered. Methods of backing up this data should also be reviewed.

Desktop configurations should be reviewed if the upgrade involves an upgrade to the Outlook client. If there are a variety of different desktop configurations, operating systems, and models, the testing phase might need to expand to include these.

Disaster recovery plans or SLAs can be vital to the IT department's ability to meet the needs of the user community, and should be available for review at this time.

Remote and mobile connections to the messaging system should be reviewed in this phase as OWA is used by most organizations, as well as Terminal Services, or virtual private networks (VPNs). The features in Exchange Server 2010 might enable the organization to simplify this process; VPNs might not be needed if the design allows Outlook to be accessed via Hypertext Transfer Protocol Secure (HTTPS).

Although the amount of time required for this discovery process varies greatly, the goals are to fully understand the messaging infrastructure in place as the foundation on which the upgrade will be built. New information might come to light in this process that will require modifications to the Statement of Work document. Always review the initial documentation at the end of a phase so that any changes can be fed back into the processes, and you can determine if any tests need to be repeated as a result of the changes.

Understanding the Geographic Distribution of Resources

If network diagrams exist, they should be reviewed to make sure they are up to date and contain enough information (such as server names, roles, applications managed, switches, routers, firewalls, IP address information, gateways, and so forth) to fully define the location and function of each device that plays a role in the upgrade. These diagrams can then be modified to show the end state of the project. Also critical to these network diagrams is an understanding of not only the bandwidth rating of the connection, but also the average utilization. Connection latency is also a useful piece of information because improvements in Outlook 2007 and Exchange Server 2010 might allow you to use configurations that were previously unavailable to you because of high latency on a WAN connection. On the flip side of this, many of the new technologies in Exchange Server 2010 will encourage administrators to replicate more mailbox data than ever before. This can create a noticeable increase in bandwidth requirements for Exchange Server.

Existing utility servers—such as bridgehead servers, front-end servers, domain name system (DNS) naming servers, and Dynamic Host Configuration Protocol (DHCP) or Windows Internet Naming Service (WINS) servers—should be listed in these diagrams as well.

Has connectivity failure been planned for a partial or fully meshed environment? Connections to the outside world and other organizations need to be reviewed and fully understood at the same level, especially with an eye toward the existing security features. If this is an area that can be improved in the new Exchange Server 2010 design, be sure to track this as a goal of the project.

Companies with multiple sites bring added challenges to the table. As much as possible, the same level of information should be gathered on all the sites that will be involved in and affected by the messaging upgrade. Also, a centralized IT environment has different requirements from a distributed management model. It's important to fully understand these aspects of the environment to successfully plan for your upgrade.

If time permits, the number of support personnel in each location should be taken into account, as well as their ability to support the new environment. Some smaller sites might not have dedicated support staff and network monitoring, and management tools, such as System Center Operations Manager or System Center Configuration Manager might be required.

How is directory information replicated between sites, and what domain design is in place? If the company already has Active Directory in place, is a single domain with a simple organizational unit (OU) structure in place, or are there multiple domains with a complex OU structure? Global catalog placement should also be clarified. Did the existing Exchange Server environment span multiple administrative groups? Who managed what functions in each administrative group? Is this administrative model going to change in the new Exchange Server 2010 environment?

The answers to these questions directly shape the design of the solution, the testing phase, and the implementation process. Keep in mind that each decision made in the planning phase needs to support the original goals and objectives of the project. When in doubt, always return to these goals and ask yourself if a particular decision is in line with those goals.

Planning Phase: Creating the Design Document

When the initial discovery work is complete, you can turn your attention to the Design document itself, which paints a detailed picture of the end state of the messaging system upgrade. In essence, this document expands on the Statement of Work document and summarizes the process that was followed and the decisions that were made along the way. When possible, include a little information on what the options were and why a particular decision was made. This helps other people to understand why decisions were made if they were not directly involved in the design process.

The second key deliverable in the planning phase is the Migration document, which tells the story of how the end state will be reached. Typically, these documents are separate, because the Design document gives the "what" and "why" information, and the Migration document gives the "how" and "when" information. This is a good example of writing documents slightly differently based on who the audience will be.

Collaboration Sessions: Making the Design Decisions

Just as the planning phase kicked off with discovery efforts and review of the networking environment, the design phase will start with more meetings with the stakeholders and the project team for collaborative design discussions. This process covers the new features that Exchange Server 2010 offers and how these could be beneficial to the organization as a whole and to specific departments or key users in support of the already defined goals. Typically, several half-day sessions are required to discuss the new features and whether implementing them makes sense. Try to leave a bit of time between sessions to give participants a chance to let the information sink in and make sure there won't be any unintended side effects of a given decision.

By this point in the process, quite a bit of thought has already gone into what the end state will look like, and that is reflected in the Statement of Work document. This means that everyone attending these sessions should be on the same page in terms of goals and expectations for the project. If they aren't, this is the time to resolve differing opinions, because the Design document is the plan of record for the results of the messaging upgrade.

The collaborative sessions should be led by someone with hands-on experience in designing and implementing Exchange Server 2010 solutions. This might be an in-house expert or it might be an external consultant. Agendas should be provided in advance to keep the sessions on track and enable attendees to prepare for specific questions. A technical writer should be invited to take notes and start to become familiar with the project as a whole because that individual will most likely be active in creating the Design document and additional documents required.

The specifics of the upgrade should be discussed in depth, especially the role that each server will play in the upgrade. A diagram is typically created during this process (or an existing Visio diagram updated) that defines the locations and roles of all Exchange Server 2010 servers and any legacy Exchange servers that need to be kept in place. This includes plans for the number of mailbox servers, the number of client access servers needed to support the remote users, the placement of Edge Transport servers to allow for redundancy, and the placement of Hub Transport servers to ensure that mail can be routed efficiently.

The migration process should be discussed as well because it is likely to have the largest impact on the end users. This is the time to account for overlapping projects that might impact your Exchange Server 2010 rollout. Also pay careful attention to the availability of the resources you defined previously. You don't want any surprises, such as having your Exchange Server 2010 expert on vacation during the critical phases of your migration.

Disaster Recovery Options

Although a full disaster recovery assessment is most likely out of the scope of the messaging upgrade project, the topic should be covered at this phase in the project. Take this opportunity to review your existing disaster recovery plans for your existing environment and think about how it will need to change with the new design.

Most people would agree that the average organization would be severely affected if the messaging environment were to go offline for an extended period of time. Communications between employees would have to be in person or over the phone, document sharing would be more complex, communication with clients would be affected, and productivity of the remote workforce would suffer. Employees in the field rarely carry pagers any more, and some have even discarded their cell phones, so many employees would be hard to reach. This dependence on messaging makes it critical to adequately cover the topic of disaster recovery as it pertains to the Exchange Server messaging environment.

Existing SLAs should be reviewed and input gathered on the "real" level of disaster recovery planning and testing that has been completed. Few companies have spent the necessary time and energy to create plans of action for the different failures that could take place, such as power failures in one or more locations, Exchange Server database corruptions, or server failures. A complete disaster recovery plan should include offsite data and application access as well. For more details on items that should be considered, see Chapter 33, "Recovering from a Disaster in an Exchange Server 2010 Environment."

Design Document Structure

The Design document expands on the content created for the Statement of Work document defined previously, but goes into greater detail and provides historical information on the decisions that were made. This is helpful if questions come up later in the testing or implementation process, such as "Whose idea was that?" or "Why did we make that decision?"

The following is a sample table of contents for the Exchange Server 2010 Design document:

1. Executive Summary
2. Goals and Objectives
    - Business Objectives
    - Departmental Goals
3. Background
    - Overview of Process
    - Summary of Discovery Process
4. Exchange Server Design
    - Exchange Server 2010 Design Diagram
    - Exchange Mailbox Server Placement

- ► Exchange Mailbox Replication

- ► Exchange Client Access Server Placement

- ► Exchange Edge Transport Server Placement

- ► Exchange Hub Transport Server Placement

- ► Exchange Unified Messaging Server Placement

- ► Organization (definition of and number of Exchange Server organizations)

- ► Mailbox Databases (definition of and number of)

- ► Mixed Mode Versus Native Mode (choice and decision)

- ► Global Catalog Placement (definition and placement)

- ► Recipient Policies (definition and usage)

- ► Server Specifications (recommendations and decisions, role for each server defined, redundancy, disaster recovery options discussed)

- ► Virus Protection (selected product with configuration)

- ► Administrative Model (options defined, and decisions made for level of administration permitted by administrative group)

- ► System Policies (definition and decisions on which policies will be used)

- ► Exchange Monitoring (product selection and features described)

- ► Exchange Backup/Recovery (product selection and features described)

5. Budget Estimate

- ► Hardware and Software Estimate

Executive Summary

The Executive Summary should summarize the high-level solution for the reader in under one page by expanding upon the scope created previously. The importance of the testing phase can be explained and the budget summarized. The goal with this document is to really understand your audience. The executives probably don't care that you are implementing Database Availability Groups, but they might be interested to hear that you are designing for "four 9s" of uptime.

Design Goals and Objectives

Goals and objectives have been discussed earlier in this chapter and should be distilled down to the most important and universal goals. They can be broken down by department if needed. The goals and objectives listed can be used as a checklist of sign-off criteria for the project. The project is complete and successful when the goals are all met.

Background

In the background section, the material gathered in the discovery portion of the planning phase should be included in summary form (details can always be attached as appendixes);

also helpful is a brief narrative of the process the project team followed to assemble this document and make the decisions summarized in the design portion of the document.

Agreeing on the Design

When the document is complete, it should be presented to the project stakeholders and reviewed to make sure that it fully meets their requirements and to see whether any additional concerns come up. If there were significant changes since the initiation phase's Statement of Work document, they should be highlighted and reviewed at this point. Again, it is valuable in terms of time and effort to identify any issues at this stage in the project, especially when the Migration document still needs to be created.

Some organizations choose to use the Design document to get competitive proposals from service providers, and having this information levels the playing field and results in proposals that promise the same end results.

Creating the Migration Document

With the Design document completed and agreed to by the decision makers, the Migration document can now be created. There are always different ways to reach the desired Exchange Server 2010 configuration, and the Migration document presents the method best suited to the needs of the organization in terms of timeline, division of labor, and costs. Just like the Design document, the migration plan is based on the goals and objectives defined in the initiation and planning processes. The Migration document makes the project real; it presents specific information on "who does what" in the actual testing and migration process, assigns costs to the resources as applicable, and creates a specific timeline with milestones and due dates. Having accurate information in the migration timeline will make it much easier to ensure that resources, both people and hardware/software, are available in time.

The Migration document should present enough detail about the testing and upgrade process that the resources performing the work have guidance and understand the purpose and goals of each step. The Migration document is not a step-by-step handbook of how to configure the servers, implement the security features, and move mailboxes. The Migration document is still fairly high level, and the resources performing the work need real-world experience and troubleshooting skills.

Additional collaborative meetings might be needed at this point to brainstorm and decide both on the exact steps that will be followed and when the testing and upgrade will be. It is critical to plan the migration as carefully as possible and to always make the decisions that support the goals of the migration process. Remember, the primary goal of the migration isn't just to put a new system into place; your users won't appreciate the new functionality of Exchange Server 2010 if it was a painful process for them to get there.

Part V of this book, "Migrations and Coexistence with Exchange Server 2010," provides additional information about the various strategies and processes for moving from previous versions of Exchange Server to Exchange Server 2010.

The Project Schedule

A project schedule or Gantt chart is a standard component of the Migration document, and it presents tasks organized by the order in which they need to be completed, in essence creating a detailed road map of how the organization will get from the current state, test the solution, and then implement it.

Other important information is included in the project schedule, such as resources assigned to each task, start dates and durations, key checkpoints, and milestones. Milestones by definition have no duration and represent events such as the arrival of hardware items, sign-off approval on a series of tasks, and similar events. Some additional time should be allocated (contingency time) if possible during the testing phase or between phases, in case stumbling blocks are encountered. This reduces the chances of having to shift the entire project back and potentially throw off the availability of resources.

A good rule of thumb is to have each task line represent at least four hours of activities; otherwise, the schedule can become too long and cumbersome. Another good rule is that a task should not be less than 1% of the total project, thus limiting the project to 100 lines. The project schedule is not intended to provide detailed information to the individuals performing the tasks, but to help schedule, budget, and manage the project. Tracking the completion of the project plan items versus time is a great way to quickly spot when you are at risk of falling behind and compromising the timeline.

To create a project schedule, a product such as Microsoft Project is recommended, which facilitates the process of starting with the high-level steps and then filling in the individual tasks. The high-level tasks should be established first and can include testing the server configurations and desktop designs and performing one or more pilot implementations, the upgrade or migration process, and the support phase.

Dependencies can also be created between tasks to clarify that Task 40 needs to be completed before Task 50 can start. A variety of additional tools and reports are built in to see whether resources are overburdened (for example, being expected to work 20 hours in one day), which can be used for resource leveling. A baseline can also be set, which represents the initial schedule, and then the actual events can be tracked and compared to the baseline to see whether the project is ahead or behind schedule.

Microsoft Project is also extremely useful in creating budgetary information and creating what-if scenarios to see how best to allocate the organization's budget for outside assistance, support, or training.

If the timeline is very short, the Gantt chart can be used to see if multiple tasks take place simultaneously or if this will cause conflicts.

Create the Migration Document

With the project schedule completed, the Migration document will come together quite easily because it essentially fills out the "story" told by the Gantt chart. Typically, the Migration document is similar to the structure of the Design document (another reason why many organizations want to combine the two), but the Design document relates the design decisions made and details the end state of the upgrade, and the Migration document details the process and steps to be taken.

The following is a sample table of contents for the Migration document:

1. Executive Summary
2. Goals and Objectives of the Migration Process
3. Background
4. Summary of Migration-Specific Decisions
5. Risks and Assumptions
6. Roles and Responsibilities
7. Timeline and Milestones
8. Training Plan
9. Migration Process

    ▶ Hardware and Software Procurement Process

    ▶ Prototype Proof of Concept Process

    ▶ Server Configuration and Testing

    ▶ Desktop Configuration and Testing

    ▶ Documentation Required from Prototype

    ▶ Pilot Phase(s) Detailed

    ▶ Migration/Upgrade Detailed

    ▶ Support Phase Detailed

    ▶ Support Documentation Detailed

10. Budget Estimate

    ▶ Labor Costs for Prototype Phase

    ▶ Labor Costs for Pilot Phase

    ▶ Labor Costs for Migration/Upgrade Phase

    ▶ Labor Costs for Support Phase

    ▶ Costs for Training

11. Project Schedule (Gantt Chart)

The following sections delve into the information that should be covered in each section. Part V of this book provides in-depth information on the steps involved in migrating to Exchange Server 2010 from Exchange Server 2003 or Exchange Server 2007.

Executive Summary

As with the Design document, the executive summary section summarizes what the Migration document covers, the scope of the project, and the budget requested. Again, keep in mind your audience for this summary and what they would be interested in. Avoid being too technical is this summary, focus on the high level of what they are getting from this project and when then can expect to get it.

Goals and Objectives of the Migration Process

The goals and objectives of the migration overlap with those of the overall project, but should focus also on what the goals are for use and development of internal resources and the experience of the user community. A goal of the overall project could be "no interruption of messaging services," and this would certainly be a goal to include in the Migration document. This is one of the reasons that many project management methodologies recommend always having an "end-user advocate" for this type of project.

Sub-phases of the Migration document have their own specific goals that might not have been included in the Design document. For example, a primary goal of the prototype phase, which takes place in a lab environment so it won't interfere with the production network, is to validate the design and to test compatibility with messaging-related applications. Other goals of the prototype phase can include hands-on training for the migration team, creating documents for configuration of the production servers, and creating and validating the functionality of the desktop configurations.

Background

A summary of the migration-specific decisions should be provided to answer questions such as: "Why are we doing it that way?" There is always a variety of ways to implement new messaging technologies, such as using built-in tools as opposed to using third-party tools. Because a number of conversations will have taken place during the planning phase to compare the merits of one method versus another, it is worth summarizing them early in the document for anyone who wasn't involved in those conversations.

Risks and Assumptions

Risks pertaining to the phases of the migration should be detailed, and, typically, are more specific than in the Design document. For example, a risk of the prototype phase might be that the hardware available won't perform adequately and needs to be upgraded. Faxing, virus protection, or backup software might not meet the requirements of the Design document and, therefore, need upgrading. Custom-designed messaging applications or Exchange Server add-ons might turn out not to be Exchange Server 2010 compatible.

Roles and Responsibilities

The Design document focuses on the high-level "who does what"; the Migration document should be much more specific because the budget for labor services is part of this deliverable. Rather than just defining the roles (such as project sponsor, Exchange Server 2010 design specialist, Exchange Server 2010 technical lead, and project manager), the Migration document specifically indicates the level of involvement of each resource throughout the prototype, pilot, and migration phases. The project sponsor should stay involved throughout the process, and regular project status meetings keep the team on the same page. At this point, everyone involved in the project should know exactly what they are and are not responsible for doing.

The project manager is expected to keep the project on time, on budget, and within scope, but generally needs support from the project sponsor and key stakeholders involved in the project. Depending on how the project manager role is defined, this individual might be either a full-time resource, overseeing the activities on a daily basis, or a part-time resource, measuring the progress, ensuring effective communications, and raising flags when needed. A cautionary note: Expecting the project manager to be a technical resource such as the Exchange Server 2010 technical lead can lead to a conflict of interest and generally does not yield the best results. Projects tend to be more successful if even 10% of an experienced project manager's time can be allocated to assist.

Timeline and Milestones

Specific target dates can be listed, and should be available directly from the project schedule already created. This summary can be very helpful to executives and managers, whereas the Gantt chart contains too much information. Constraints that were identified in the discovery process need to be kept in mind here because there might be important dates (such as the end of the fiscal year), seasonal demands on the company that black out certain date ranges, and key company events or holidays. Again, be aware of other large projects going on in your environment that might impact your timeline. There's no point trying to deploy new servers on the same weekend that the data center will be powered off for facility upgrades.

Training Plan

It is useful during the planning of any upgrade to examine the skill sets of the people who will be performing the upgrade and managing the new environment to see if there are any gaps that need to be filled with training. Often, training happens during the prototype testing process in a hands-on fashion for the project team, with the alternate choice being classroom-style training, often provided by an outside company. Ask yourself if the end users require training to use new client-side tools. Also pay attention to how the new environment will integrate into existing systems such as backup or monitoring. Determine if those groups need any training specific to interact with Exchange Server 2010 components.

Migration Process

The project schedule Gantt chart line items should be included and expanded upon so that it is clear to the resources doing the work what is expected of them. The information does not need to be on the level of step-by-step instructions, but it should clarify the process and results expected from each task. For example, the Gantt chart might indicate that an Exchange server needs to be configured, and in the Migration document, information would be added about which service pack is to be used for the NOS and for Exchange Server, how the hard drives are to be configured, and which additional applications (virus protection, tape backup, faxing, network management) need to be installed.

If the Gantt chart lists a task of, for example, "Configure and test Outlook 2007 on sales workstation," the Migration document gives a similar level of detail: Which image should be used to configure the base workstation configuration, which additional applications and version of Office should be loaded, how the workstation is to be locked down, and what testing process should be followed (is it scripted, or will an end user from the department do the testing?).

Documentation also should be described in more detail. The Gantt chart might simply list "Create as-Built documents," with as-built defined as "document containing key server configuration information and screenshots so that a knowledgeable resource can rebuild the system from scratch."

Sign-off conditions for the prototype phase are important and should be included. Who needs to sign off on the results of the prototype phase to indicate that the goals were all met and that the design agreed upon is ready to be created in the production environment?

Similar levels of information are included for the pilot phase and the all-important migration itself. Typically during the pilot phase, all the upgraded functionality needs to be tested, including remote access to email, voice mail access, BlackBerry and personal information managers, and public folders. Be aware that pilot testing might require external coordination. For example, if you are testing access through OWA in Exchange Server 2010, you might need to acquire an additional external IP address and arrange to have an address record created in DNS to allow your external testers to reach it without having to disturb your existing OWA systems.

The migration plan should also account for support tasks that need to occur after the Exchange Server 2010 infrastructure is fully in place. If you are using an outside consulting firm for assistance in the design and implementation, you should make sure that they will leave staff onsite for a period of time immediately after the upgrade to be available to support user issues or to troubleshoot any technical issues that crop up.

If documentation is specified as part of the support phase, such as Exchange Server maintenance documents, disaster recovery plans, or procedural guides, expectations for these documents should be included to help the technical writers make sure the documents are satisfactory.

Budget Estimate

At this point in the process, the budgetary numbers should be within 10%–20% of the final costs, bearing in mind any risks already identified that could affect the budget. Breaking the budget into prototype, pilot, migration, support, and training sections helps the decision makers understand how the budget will be allocated and make adjustments if needed. No matter how much thought has gone into estimating the resources required and risks that could affect the budget, the later phases of the project might change based on the outcome of the prototype phase or the pilot phase.

The Prototype Phase

Depending on the design that was decided on by the organization, the prototype phase varies greatly in complexity and duration. It is still critical to perform a prototype, even for the simplest environments, to validate the design, test the mailbox migration process, and ensure that there won't be any surprises during the actual upgrade. The prototype lab should be isolated from the production network via a virtual LAN (VLAN) or physical separation to avoid interfering with the lives of users.

The prototype phase also gives the project team a chance to get acquainted with the new features of Exchange Server 2010 and any new add-on applications that will be used and to configure the hardware in a low-stress environment. If an external company is assisting in this phase, informal or formal knowledge transfer should take place. Ideally, the prototype lab exactly mirrors the final messaging configuration so that training in this environment will be fully applicable to the administration and support skills needed after the upgrade.

Always take advantage of the unique opportunities granted to you in the prototype phase. Because the prototype is built as a replica of the planned production design, you can practice disaster recovery, server deployment, mailbox moves, and application integrations with no concerns about impacting users the way they would be in production.

What Is Needed for the Lab?

At a bare minimum, the lab should include a new Exchange Server 2010 server, one each of the standard desktop and laptop configurations, the tape drive that will be used to back up the public and private Information Stores, and application software as defined in the Design document. Connectivity to the Internet should be available for testing OWA and Windows Mobile access. You will also need at least one domain controller that is configured as a global catalog. The preferred method to deploy this domain controller is to promote a spare domain controller in production and after it has fully replicated, remove it from the network and move it to the lab network. After being isolated, seize the Flexible Single Master Operations (FSMO) roles on the lab domain controller. In production, use NTDSUTIL to perform a metadata cleanup to remove the references to the temporary domain controller. In this way, you have an accurate view of Active Directory for the prototype phase. This can be especially helpful because directory problems that would show up in a production migration will appear in the lab.

Existing data stores should be checked for integrity and then imported to Exchange Server 2010 to ensure that the process goes smoothly. Exchange Server 2010 comes with improved mailbox migration tools, which are more resistant to failure when corrupt mailboxes are encountered and are multithreaded for better performance.

> **NOTE**
>
> The recommended route for customers with Exchange Server 2007 or 2003 servers to get to Exchange Server 2010 is to install an Exchange Server 2010 server into the environment and move mailboxes. If hardware availability is limited, consider upgrading one location at a time and use the "replaced" server as the new Exchange Server 2010 server in the next site. This assumes the hardware is capable of running Exchange Server 2010 and is appropriately sized. This method is often referred to as a "leap frog" upgrade.

If site consolidation or server consolidation are goals of the project, the prototype lab can be used for these purposes. Multiforest connectivity can now be tested, but this requires a

Microsoft Identity Integration Services server in one or more of the forests to enable directory synchronization.

Exchange Server 2010 also comes with a number of new tools to aid in the testing and migration process, which are covered in detail in Chapters 15 and 16. These include a prescriptive guide that walks through the deployment process, preparation tools that scan the topology and provide recommendations, and validation tools.

For more complex environments and larger companies, the lab should be kept in place even after the upgrade is completed. Although this requires the purchase of at least one additional Exchange server and related software, it provides a handy environment for testing patches and upgrades to the production environment, performing offline database maintenance, and in worst-case scenarios, a server to scavenge from in times of dire need.

Depending on the complexity of the Exchange Server environment, this long-term lab might potentially be run in a virtual environment. Deploying the lab via VMware or Microsoft's Hyper-V allows you to mimic the interactions of multiple servers and server roles on a single box. Both VMware and Microsoft's Hyper-V solutions support 64-bit guest operating systems and, therefore, are viable options for an Exchange Server 2010 lab environment.

After the lab is configured to match the end state documented in the Design document, representative users from different departments with different levels of experience and feature requirements should be brought in and given a chance to play with the desktop configurations and test new features and remote access. Input should be solicited to see whether any changes need to be made to the client configurations or features offered, and to help get a sense for the training and support requirements.

Disaster Recovery Testing

Another important testing process that can be performed prior to implementation of the new solution on the live network is business continuity or disaster recovery testing. Ideally, this was covered in the design process, and disaster recovery requirements were included in the design itself. Definitely take advantage of practicing your disaster recovery process in the prototype phase. This is likely your only opportunity to create and destroy servers without regard for impacting end users.

Documentation from the Prototype

During the prototype phase, a number of useful documents can be created that will be useful to the deployment team during the pilot and production upgrade phases, and to the administrators when the upgrade is complete.

As-built documents capture the key configuration information on the Exchange Server 2010 systems so that they can easily be replicated during the upgrade or rebuilt from scratch in case of catastrophic failure. Generally, the as-built documents include actual screenshots of key configuration screens to facilitate data entry. Having carefully prepared as-built documents allows you to go into production with a well-tested build process. Not unlike a disaster recovery situation, you want to simply follow your own instructions during the deployment; you don't want to have to learn as you go.

Assuming that disaster recovery requirements for the project were defined as suggested previously, this is a perfect time to summarize the testing that was performed in the lab and record the steps a knowledgeable administrator should take in the failure scenarios tested.

One last item of value to take out of the prototype phase is a well-documented list of any surprises that came up during the testing. If you tested the move mailbox process from an Exchange Server 2007 server that was restored from production and you had errors moving mailboxes, you can expect to have these exact same errors in the production move. If you were able to solve the issues in the lab, you should have well-documented notes on how to deal with the same error in production. Being prepared in this manner is the key to a smooth migration.

Final Validation of the Migration Document

When the testing is complete, the migration plan should be reviewed a final time to make sure that the testing process didn't reveal any showstoppers that will require a change in the way the upgrade will take place or in the components of the final messaging solution.

The end users who have had a chance to get their feet wet and play with the new Outlook 2007 client and learn about the new capabilities and enhanced performance of Exchange Server 2010 should be spreading the word by now, and the whole company should be excited about the upgrade!

The Pilot Phase: Deploying Services to a Limited Number of Users

With the testing completed, the Exchange Server 2010 upgrade team has all the tools needed for a successful upgrade, assuming the steps outlined so far in this chapter have been followed. The Design document is updated based on the prototype testing results so that the end state that the executives and decision makers are expecting has been conceptually proven. Unpleasant surprises or frantic midnight emails requesting more budget are nonexistent. The road map of how to get to the end state is created in detail, with the project schedule outlining the sequential steps to be taken and the Migration document providing the details of each step. Documentation on the exact server configurations and desktop configuration are created to assist the systems engineers who will be building and configuring the production hardware.

The project team has gained valuable experience in the safe lab environment, processes have been tested, and the team is brimming with confidence. End users representing the different departments, who tested and approved the proposed desktop configurations, are excited about the new features that will soon be available.

To be on the safe side, a rollback strategy should be clarified, in case unforeseen difficulties are encountered when the new servers are introduced to the network. Disaster recovery testing can also be done as part of the first pilot, so that the processes are tested with a small amount of data and a limited number of users.

The First Server in the Pilot

The pilot phase officially starts when the schema is extended and the first Exchange Server 2010 server is implemented in the production environment. The same testing and sign-off criteria that were used in the lab environment can be used to verify that the server is functioning properly and coexisting with the present Exchange servers. Surprises might be waiting that will require some troubleshooting because the production environment will add variables that weren't present in the lab, such as large quantities of data-consuming bandwidth, non-Windows servers, network management applications, and applications that have nothing to do with messaging but might interfere with Exchange Server 2010.

The migration of the first group of mailboxes is the next test of the thoroughness of the preparation process. Depending on the complexity of the complete design, it might make sense to limit the functionality offered by the first pilot phase to basic Exchange Server 2010 functionality, and make sure that the foundation is stable before adding on the higher-end features, such as voice mail integration, mobile messaging, and faxing. The first server should have virus-protection software and backup software installed. Remote access via OWA is an important item to test as soon as possible because there can be complexities involved with demilitarized zone (DMZ) configurations and firewalls.

Choosing the Pilot Group

The first group of users, preferably more than 10, represents a sampling of different types of users. If all members of the first pilot group are in the same department, the feedback won't be as thorough and revealing as it could be if different users from different departments with varied needs and expectations are chosen. It's generally a good idea to avoid managers and executives in the first round, no matter how eager they are, because they will be more likely to be the most demanding, be the least tolerant of interruptions to network functionality, and have the most complex needs.

Although a great deal of testing has taken place already, these initial pilot users should understand that there will most likely be some fine-tuning that needs to take place after their workstations are upgraded; they should allocate time from their workdays to test the upgrades carefully with the systems engineer performing the upgrade. This will correctly set the expectation for the pilot users, as well as allow the upgrade team to get the feedback they need before moving into the full migration.

After the initial pilot group is successfully upgraded and functional, the number of users can be increased because the upgrade team will be more efficient and the processes fine-tuned to where they are 99% error free.

For a multisite messaging environment, the pilot process should be carefully constructed to include the additional offices. It might make sense to fully implement Exchange Server 2010 and the related messaging applications in the headquarters before any of the other locations, but issues related to WAN connectivity might crop up later, and then the impact is greater than if a small pilot group is rolled out at HQ and several of the other offices. It is important to plan where the project team and help desk resources will be, and they ideally should travel to the other offices during those pilots, especially if no one from the other office participated in the lab testing phase. Be sure to have sufficient coverage for issues that might arise if the pilot groups span multiple time zones.

The help desk should be ready to support standard user issues, and the impact can be judged for the first few sub-phases of the pilot. Issues encountered can be collected and tracked in a knowledge base, and the most common issues or questions can be posted on the company intranet or in public folders, or used to create general training for the user community.

Gauging the Success of the Pilot Phase

When the pilot phase is complete, a sampling of the participants should be asked for input on the process and the results. Few companies do this on a formal basis, but the results can be very surprising and educational. Employees should be informed of when the upgrade will take place, that no data will be lost, and that someone will be there to answer questions immediately after the upgrade. Little changes to the workstation environment, such as the loss of favorites or shortcuts, or a change in the network resources they have access to, can be very distressing and result in disgruntled pilot testers. Your goal is for your employees to be happy about the upgrade experience after it's been done. Their opinions will reach the rest of your users and they'll be a lot more cooperative if they aren't expecting to have problems.

A project team meeting should be organized to share learning points and review the final outcome of the project. The company executives must now make the go-no-go decision for the full migration, so they must be updated on the results of the pilot process.

The Production Migration/Upgrade

When the pilot phase is officially completed and any lingering problems have been resolved with the upgrade process, there will typically be 10%–20% of the total user community upgraded. The project team will have all the tools it needs to complete the remainder of the upgrade without serious issues. Small problems with individual workstations or laptops will probably still occur, but the help desk should be familiar with how to handle these issues by this point.

A key event at this point is the migration of large amounts of Exchange Server data. The public and private Information Stores should be analyzed with eseutil and isinteg, and complete backup copies should be made in case of serious problems. The project team should make sure that the entire user community is prepared for the migration and that training has been completed by the time a user's workstation is upgraded.

It is helpful to have a checklist for the tasks that need to be completed on the different types of workstations and laptops so that the same steps are taken for each unit, and any issues encountered can be recorded for follow-up if they aren't critical. Laptops will most likely be the most problematic because of the variation in models, features, and user requirements, and because the mobile employees often have unique needs when compared to workers who remain in the office. If home computers need to be upgraded with the Outlook 2007 client and if, for instance, the company VPN is being retired, these visits need to be coordinated.

As with the pilot phase, the satisfaction of the user community should be verified. New public folders or SharePoint discussions can be started, and supplemental training can be offered for users who might need some extra or repeat training.

> **TIP**
>
> If at all possible, get your users to clean up their mailboxes and clear their deleted items prior to the migration, as this can result in a very large time savings. Experience has shown that typically 50% of the data moved in an Exchange Server migration is Sent Items and Deleted Items. The time it takes to move a mailbox is more affected by the item count than the overall size of the mailbox in gigabytes.

Decommissioning the Old Exchange Server Environment

As mentioned previously, some upgrades require legacy Exchange servers to be kept online, if they are running applications that aren't ready or can't be upgraded right away to Exchange Server 2010. Even in environments where the Exchange Server 2003 or 2007 servers should be completely removed, this should not necessarily be done right away.

Supporting the New Exchange Server 2010 Environment

After the dust has settled and any lingering issues with users or functionality have been resolved, the project team can be officially disbanded and returned to their normal jobs. If they haven't been created already, Exchange Server Maintenance documents should be created to detail the daily, weekly, monthly, and quarterly steps to ensure that the environment is performing normally and the databases are healthy.

If the prototype lab is still in place, this is an ideal testing ground for these processes and for testing patches and new applications. By following the Exchange Server Maintenance documents and keeping up with regular maintenance tasks, you will be much less likely to have issues with your Exchange Server 2010 environment in the future.

Summary

Someone famous once said, "It's not the destination, it's the journey." In the case of an Exchange Server 2010 upgrade, or any project for that matter, it's both. This chapter has shown that the key to success in a major undertaking such as an Exchange Server 2010 upgrade is to follow a strong methodology that accounts for both the journey and the destination.

The use of a discovery phase allows the people who will be involved in the project to gather as much information as they can about the existing state of the environment, as well as the needs of the environment. This prepares them to make design decisions that will allow them to support the needs of the business without putting the existing environment at risk.

A design phase allows the group to work interactively to design a new end state that best provides for the needs of the company. A key concept to keep in mind during a design phase is that there is no "one perfect design"—there is only a design that is most appropriate for you and your needs and limitations.

A prototype phase allows you to validate your design and your migration methodologies by testing them in a safe replica environment. This allows you to discover potential problems before they come up in a production migration. Always take advantage of the prototype phase to try out the "what-if" questions that will result in you and your team having a stronger knowledge of how the new environment will work.

The pilot phase allows you to try your migration steps in the real world with reduced exposure to problems through a controlled membership of pilot users. Take this opportunity to get feedback from the pilot users to update or modify your steps to reduce impact on users or administrators. Remember, if you need to make major changes after the pilot, run a second pilot and keep running pilots until you feel your process is sufficient. This shouldn't take too much feedback if you took full advantage of the prototype phase.

The implementation phase allows you to push through the migration full force and get all the users migrated to the new environment.

Utilize a support and retirement phase to make sure you have time to retire old servers and to make sure you have a bit of extra time with the enhanced support and help desk to make sure everyone is happy after the migration (or at least happy about Exchange Server 2010).

By following this standard methodology, you will greatly increase the chances of having a smooth and uneventful migration. This will help build credibility for the IT organization and make it that much easier to get projects approved in the future.

Best Practices

The following are best practices from this chapter:

- ▶ An upgrade to Exchange Server 2010 should follow a process that keeps the project on schedule. Set up such a process with a four-phase approach, including initiation, planning, testing, and implementation.

- ▶ Documentation is important to keep track of plans, procedures, and schedules. Create some of the documentation that could be expected for an upgrade project, including a Statement of Work document, a Design document, a project schedule, and a Migration document.

- ▶ Key to the initiation phase is the definition of the scope of work. Create such a definition, identifying the key goals of the project.

▶ Make sure that the goals of the project are not just IT goals, but also include goals and objectives of the organization and business units of the organization. This ensures that business needs are tied to the migration initiative, which can later be quantified to determine cost savings or tangible business process improvements.

▶ Set milestones in a project that can ensure that key steps are being achieved and the project is progressing at an acceptable rate. Review any drastic variation in attaining milestone tasks and timelines to determine whether the project should be modified or changed, or the plans reviewed.

▶ Allocate skilled or qualified resources that can help the organization to better achieve technical success and keep it on schedule. Failure to include qualified personnel can have a drastic impact on the overall success of the project.

▶ Identify risks and assumptions in a project to provide the project manager with the ability to assess situations and proactive work and avoid actions that might cause project failures.

▶ Plan the design around what is best for the organization, and then create the migration process to take into account the existing configuration of the systems within the organization. Although understanding the existing environment is important to the success of the project, an implementation or migration project should not predetermine the actions of the organization based on the existing enterprise configuration.

▶ Ensure that key stakeholders are involved in the ultimate design of the Exchange Server 2010 implementation. Without stakeholder agreement on the design, the project might not be completed and approved.

▶ Document decisions made in the collaborative design sessions, as well as in the migration planning process, ensure that key decisions are agreed upon and accepted by the participants of the process. Anyone with questions on the decisions can ask for clarification before the project begins rather than stopping the project midstream.

▶ Test assumptions and validate procedures in the prototype phase. Rather than learning for the first time in a production environment that a migration will fail because an Exchange Server database is corrupt or has inconsistencies, the entire process can be tested in a lab environment without impacting users.

▶ Test the process in a live production environment with a limited number of users in the prototype phase. Although key executives (such as the CIO or IT director) may want to be part of the initial pilot phase, it is usually not recommended to take such high-visibility users in the first phase. The pilot phase should be with users who will accept an incident of lost email or inability to send or receive messages for a couple of days while problems are worked out. In many cases, a prepilot phase could include the more tolerant users, with a formal pilot phase including insistent executives of the organization.

▶ Migrate, implement, or upgrade after all testing has been validated. The production process should be exactly that: a process that methodically follows procedures to implement or migrate mailboxes into the Exchange Server 2010 environment.

CHAPTER 3

Understanding Core Exchange Server 2010 Design Plans

The fundamental capabilities of Microsoft Exchange Server 2010 are impressive. Improvements to security, reliability, and scalability enhance an already road-tested and stable Exchange Server platform. Along with these impressive credentials comes an equally impressive design task. Proper design of an Exchange Server 2010 platform will do more than practically anything to reduce headaches and support calls in the future. Many complexities of Exchange Server might seem daunting, but with a full understanding of the fundamental components and improvements, the task of designing the Exchange Server 2010 environment becomes manageable.

This chapter focuses specifically on the Exchange Server 2010 components required for design. Key decision-making factors influencing design are presented and tied into overall strategy. All critical pieces of information required to design Exchange Server 2010 implementations are outlined and explained. Enterprise Exchange Server design and planning concepts are expanded in Chapter 4, "Architecting an Enterprise-Level Exchange Server Environment."

Planning for Exchange Server 2010

Designing Exchange Server used to be a fairly simple task. When an organization needed email and the decision was made to go with Exchange Server, the only real decision to make was how many Exchange servers were needed. Primarily, organizations really needed only email and eschewed any "bells and whistles."

Exchange Server 2010, on the other hand, takes messaging to a whole new level. No longer do organizations require only an email system, but high level of system availability and resilience and other messaging and unified communications functionality. After the productivity capabilities of an enterprise email platform have been demonstrated, the need for more productivity improvements arises. Consequently, it is wise to understand the integral design components of Exchange Server before beginning a design project.

Outlining Significant Changes in Exchange Server 2010

Exchange Server 2010 is the evolution of a product that has consistently been improving over the years from its roots. Since the Exchange 5.x days, Microsoft has released dramatic improvements with Exchange 2000 Server and later Exchange Server 2003. Microsoft then followed upon the success of Exchange Server 2003 with some major architectural changes with Exchange Server 2007. This latest version, Exchange Server 2010, uses a similar architecture to Exchange Server 2007 but adds, extends, and perfects elements of Exchange Server design.

The major areas of improvement in Exchange Server 2010 include many of the concepts and technologies introduced in Exchange Server 2007 but expand upon them and include additional improvements. Key areas improved upon in Exchange Server 2010 architecture include the following:

▶ **Database Availability Groups (DAGs)**—The Exchange Server 2007 concept of Clustered Continuous Replication (CCR) has been greatly improved and replaced with a concept called Database Availability Groups (DAGs), which allow a copy of an Exchange Server mailbox database to exist in up to 16 locations within an Exchange Server organization. Because Continuous Replication is no longer limited to two servers, there is no longer any need for concepts such as Standby Continuous Replication (SCR) or Local Continuous Replication (LCR) because they are all superseded by DAG technology.

▶ **Transport and access improvements**—All client access is now funneled through the Client Access server (CAS) role in an organization, which allows for improvements in client access and limited end-user disruption during mailbox moves and maintenance. In addition, Exchange Server 2010 guards against lost emails due to hardware failures by keeping "shadow copies" of mail data on Hub and Edge Transport servers that can be re-sent in the event of loss.

▶ **Integrated archiving capabilities**—Exchange Server 2010 provides users and administrators the ability to archive messages for the purpose of cleaning up a mailbox of old messages, as well as for legal reasons for applying a retention policy on key messages. In addition, a second archive mailbox can be associated with a user's primary mailbox, allowing seamless access to the archived messages from OWA or full Outlook. Users can simply drag and drop messages into their archive folder, or a policy or rule can be set to have messages automatically moved to the archive folder.

▶ **"Access anywhere" improvements**—Microsoft has focused a great deal of Exchange Server 2010 development time on new access methods for Exchange Server, including an enhanced Outlook Web App (OWA) that works with a variety of Microsoft and third-party browsers, Microsoft ActiveSync improvements, improved

Outlook Voice Access (OVA), unified messaging support, and Outlook Anywhere enhancements. Having these multiple access methods greatly increases the design flexibility of Exchange Server because end users can access email via multiple methods.

▶ **Protection and compliance enhancements**—Exchange Server 2010 now includes a variety of antispam, antivirus, and compliance mechanisms to protect the integrity of messaging data. Exchange Server 2010 also includes the capability to establish a second, integrated archive mailbox for users that is made available through all traditional access mechanisms, including OWA. This allows for older archived items to be available to users without the mail actually being stored in the individual's mailbox, enabling an organization to do better storage management and content management of mail messages throughout the enterprise.

▶ **Admin tools improvements and Exchange PowerShell scripting**—Introduced as the primary management tool for Exchange Server 2007, Exchange Server 2010 improves upon PowerShell capabilities and adds additional PowerShell applets and functions. Indeed, the graphical user interface (GUI) itself sits on top of the scripting engine and simply fires scripts based on the task that an administrator chooses in the GUI. This allows for an unprecedented level of control.

It is important to incorporate the concepts of these improvements into any Exchange Server design project because their principles often drive the design process.

Reviewing Exchange Server and Operating System Requirements

Exchange Server 2010 has some specific requirements, both hardware and software, that must be taken into account when designing. These requirements fall into several categories:

▶ Hardware

▶ Operating system

▶ Active Directory

▶ Exchange Server version

Each requirement must be addressed before Exchange Server 2010 can be deployed.

Reviewing Hardware Requirements

It is important to design Exchange Server hardware to scale out to the user load, which is expected for up to 3 years from the date of implementation. This helps retain the value of the investment put into Exchange Server. Specific hardware configuration advice is offered in later sections of this book.

Reviewing Operating System (OS) Requirements

Exchange Server 2010 is optimized for installation on Windows Server 2008 (Service Pack 2 or later) or Windows Server 2008 R2. The increases in security and the fundamental changes to Internet Information Services (IIS) in Windows Server 2008 provide the basis for many of the improvements in Exchange Server 2010. The specific compatibility matrix, which indicates compatibility between Exchange Server versions and operating systems, is illustrated in Table 3.1.

TABLE 3.1   Exchange Server Version Compatibility

Version	Win NT 4.0	Windows 2000	Windows 2003	Windows 2003 R2	Windows 2008	Windows 2008 R2
Exchange Server 5.5	Yes	Yes	No	No	No	No
Exchange 2000 Server	No	Yes	No	No	No	No
Exchange Server 2003	No	Yes	Yes	Yes	No	No
Exchange Server 2007	No	No	Yes*	Yes*	Yes*	Yes*
Exchange Server 2010	No	No	No	No	Yes*	Yes*

64-bit editions only supported

Understanding Active Directory (AD) Requirements

Exchange Server originally maintained its own directory. With the advent of Exchange 2000 Server, however, the directory for Exchange Server was moved to the Microsoft Active Directory, the enterprise directory system for Windows. This gave greater flexibility and consolidated directories but at the same time increased the complexity and dependencies for Exchange Server. Exchange Server 2010 uses the same model but requires specific AD functional levels and domain controller specifics to run properly.

Exchange Server 2010, while requiring an AD forest in all deployment scenarios, has certain flexibility when it comes to the type of AD it uses. It is possible to deploy Exchange Server in the following scenarios:

▶ **Single forest**—The simplest and most traditional design for Exchange Server is one where Exchange Server is installed within the same forest used for user accounts. This design also has the least amount of complexity and synchronization concerns to worry about.

▶ **Resource forest**—The Resource forest model in Exchange Server 2010 involves the deployment of a dedicated forest exclusively used for Exchange Server itself, and the only user accounts within it are those that serve as a placeholder for a mailbox. These user accounts are not logged onto by the end users, but rather the end users are given access to them across cross-forest trusts from their particular user forest to the Exchange Server forest. More information on this deployment model can be found in Chapter 4.

▶ **Multiple forests**—Different multiple forest models for Exchange Server are presently available, but they do require a greater degree of administration and synchronization. In these models, different Exchange Server organizations live in different forests across an organization. These different Exchange Server organizations are periodically synchronized to maintain a common Global Address List (GAL). More information on this deployment model can also be found in Chapter 4.

It is important to determine which design model will be chosen before proceeding with an Exchange Server deployment because it is complex and expensive to change the AD structure of Exchange Server after it has been deployed.

Outlining Exchange Server Version Requirements

As with previous versions of Exchange Server, there are separate Enterprise and Standard versions of the Exchange Server 2010 product. The Standard Edition supports all Exchange Server 2010 functionality with the exception of the fact that it is limited to no more than five databases on a single server.

NOTE

Unlike previous versions of the software, Microsoft provides only a single set of media for Exchange Server 2010. When installed, server version can be set by simply inputting a licensed key. A server can be upgraded from the Trial version to Standard/Enterprise or from Standard to Enterprise. It cannot, however, be downgraded.

Scaling Exchange Server 2010

Exchange 2000 originally provided the basis for servers that could easily scale out to thousands of users in a single site, if necessary. Exchange Server 2003 further improved the situation by introducing Messaging Application Programming Interface (MAPI) compression and RPC over HTTP. Exchange Server 2007 and its 64-bit architecture allowed for even further scalability and reduced IO levels. Finally, Exchange Server 2010 and the separation of client traffic to load-balanced Client Access Servers enable the client tier to be much more scalable than with previous versions.

Site consolidation concepts enable organizations that might have previously deployed Exchange servers in remote locations to have those clients access their mailboxes across wide area network (WAN) links or dial-up connections by using the enhanced Outlook 2007/2010 or OWA clients. This solves the problem that previously existed of having to deploy Exchange servers and global catalog (GC) servers in remote locations, with only a handful of users, and greatly reduces the infrastructure costs of setting up Exchange Server.

Having Exchange Server 2010 Coexist with an Existing Network Infrastructure

In a design scenario, it is necessary to identify any systems that require access to email data or services. For example, it might be necessary to enable a third-party monitoring application to relay mail off the Simple Mail Transfer Protocol (SMTP) engine of Exchange Server so that alerts can be sent. Identifying these needs during the design portion of a project is subsequently important.

Identifying Third-Party Product Functionality

Microsoft built specific hooks into Exchange Server 2010 to enable third-party applications to improve upon the built-in functionality provided by the system. For example, built-in support for antivirus scanning, backups, and unified messaging exist right out of the box, although functionality is limited without the addition of third-party software. The most common additions to Exchange Server implementation are the following:

▶ Antivirus

▶ Backup

▶ Phone/PBX integration

▶ Fax software

Understanding AD Design Concepts for Exchange Server 2010

After all objectives, dependencies, and requirements have been mapped out, the process of designing the Exchange Server 2010 environment can begin. Decisions should be made in the following key areas:

▶ AD design

▶ Exchange server placement

▶ Global catalog placement

▶ Client access methods

Understanding the AD Forest

Because Exchange Server 2010 relies on the Windows Server 2008 AD for its directory, it is therefore important to include AD in the design plans. In many situations, an AD implementation, whether based on Windows 2000 Server, Windows Server 2003, or Windows Server 2008, AD already exists in the organization. In these cases, it is necessary only to plan for the inclusion of Exchange Server into the forest.

> **NOTE**
>
> Exchange Server 2010 has several key requirements for AD. First, all domains and the forest must be at Windows Server 2003 functional levels or higher. Second, it requires that at least one domain controller in each site that includes Exchange Server be at least Windows Server 2003 SP2 or Windows Server 2008.

If an AD structure is not already in place, a new AD forest must be established. Designing the AD forest infrastructure can be complex, and can require nearly as much thought into design as the actual Exchange Server configuration itself. Therefore, it is important to fully understand the concepts behind AD before beginning an Exchange Server 2010 design.

In short, a single "instance" of AD consists of a single AD forest. A forest is composed of AD trees, which are contiguous domain namespaces in the forest. Each tree is composed of one or more domains, as illustrated in Figure 3.1.

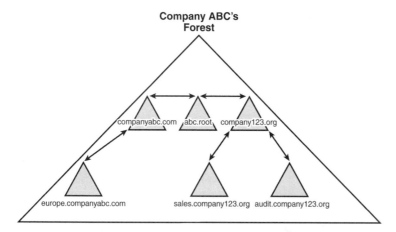

FIGURE 3.1　Multitree forest design.

Certain cases exist for using more than one AD forest in an organization:

▶ **Political limitations**—Some organizations have specific political reasons that force the creation of multiple AD forests. For example, if a merged corporate entity requires separate divisions to maintain completely separate information technology (IT) infrastructures, more than one forest is necessary.

▶ **Security concerns**—Although the AD domain serves as a de facto security boundary, the "ultimate" security boundary is effectively the forest. In other words, it is possible for user accounts in a domain in a forest to hack into domains within the same forest. Although these types of vulnerabilities are not common and are difficult to do, highly security-conscious organizations should implement separate AD forests.

▶ **Application functionality**—A single AD forest shares a common directory schema, which is the underlying structure of the directory and must be unique across the entire forest. In some cases, separate branches of an organization require that certain applications, which need extensions to the schema, be installed. This might not be possible or might conflict with the schema requirements of other branches. These cases might require the creation of a separate forest.

▶ **Exchange-specific functionality (resource forest)**—In certain circumstances, it might be necessary to install Exchange Server 2010 into a separate forest, to enable Exchange Server to reside in a separate schema and forest instance. An example of this type of setup is an organization with two existing AD forests that creates a third forest specifically for Exchange Server and uses cross-forest trusts to assign mailbox permissions.

The simplest designs often work the best. The same principle applies to AD design. The designer should start with the assumption that a simple forest and domain structure will work for the environment. However, when factors such as those previously described create constraints, multiple forests can be established to satisfy the requirements of the constraints.

Understanding the AD Domain Structure

After the AD forest structure has been chosen, the domain structure can be laid out. As with the forest structure, it is often wise to consider a single domain model for the Exchange Server 2010 directory. In fact, if deploying Exchange Server is the only consideration, this is often the best choice.

There is one major exception to the single domain model: the placeholder domain model. The placeholder domain model has an isolated domain serving as the root domain in the forest. The user domain, which contains all production user accounts, would be located in a separate domain in the forest, as illustrated in Figure 3.2.

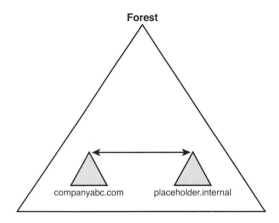

FIGURE 3.2   The placeholder domain model.

The placeholder domain structure increases security in the forest by segregating high-level schema-access accounts into a completely separate domain from the regular user domain. Access to the placeholder domain can be audited and restricted to maintain tighter control on the critical schema. The downside to this model, however, is the fact that the additional domain requires a separate set of domain controllers, which increases the infrastructure costs of the environment. In general, this makes this domain model less desirable for smaller organizations because the trade-off between increased cost and less security is too great. Larger organizations can consider the increased security provided by this model, however.

Reviewing AD Infrastructure Components

Several key components of AD must be installed within an organization to ensure proper Exchange Server 2010 and AD functionality. In smaller environments, many of these components can be installed on a single machine, but all need to be located within an environment to ensure server functionality.

Outlining the Domain Name System (DNS) Impact on Exchange Server 2010 Design

In addition to being tightly integrated with AD, Exchange Server 2010 is joined with the Domain Name System (DNS). DNS serves as the lookup agent for Exchange Server 2010, AD, and most new Microsoft applications and services. DNS translates common names into computer-recognizable IP addresses. For example, the name www.cco.com translates into the IP address of 12.155.166.151. AD and Exchange Server 2010 require that at least one DNS server be made available so that name resolution properly occurs.

Given the dependency that both Exchange Server 2010 and AD have on DNS, it is an extremely important design element. For an in-depth look at DNS and its role in Exchange Server 2010, see Chapter 6, "Understanding Network Services and Active Directory Domain Controller Placement for Exchange Server 2010."

Reviewing DNS Namespace Considerations for Exchange Server

Given Exchange Server 2010's dependency on DNS, a common DNS namespace must be chosen for the AD structure to reside in. In multiple tree domain models, this could be composed of several DNS trees, but in small organization environments, this normally means choosing a single DNS namespace for the AD domain.

There is a great deal of confusion between the DNS namespace in which AD resides and the email DNS namespace in which mail is delivered. Although they are often the same, in many cases there are differences between the two namespaces. For example, CompanyABC's AD structure is composed of a single domain named abc.internal, and the email domain to which mail is delivered is companyabc.com. The separate namespace, in this case, was created to reduce the security vulnerability of maintaining the same DNS namespace both internally and externally (published to the Internet).

For simplicity, CompanyABC could have chosen companyabc.com as its AD namespace. This choice increases the simplicity of the environment by making the AD logon user principal name (UPN) and the email address the same. For example, the user Pete Handley is pete@companyabc.com for logon, and pete@companyabc.com for email. This option is the choice for many organizations because the need for user simplicity often trumps the higher security.

Optimally Locating Global Catalog Servers

Because all Exchange Server directory lookups use AD, it is vital that the essential AD global catalog information is made available to each Exchange server in the organization. For many small offices with a single site, this simply means that it is important to have a full global catalog server available in the main site.

The global catalog is an index of the AD database that contains a partial copy of its contents. All objects within the AD tree are referenced within the global catalog, which enables users to search for objects located in other domains. Every attribute of each object is not replicated to the global catalogs, only those attributes that are commonly used in search operations, such as first name and last name. Exchange Server 2010 uses the global catalog for the email-based lookups of names, email addresses, and other mail-related attributes.

> **NOTE**
>
> Exchange Server 2010 cannot make use of Windows Server 2008 Read Only Domain Controllers (RODCs) or Read Only Global Catalog (ROGC) servers, so be sure to plan for full GCs and DCs for Exchange Server.

Because full global catalog replication can consume more bandwidth than standard domain controller replication, it is important to design a site structure to reflect the available WAN link capacity. If a sufficient amount of capacity is available, a full global catalog server can be deployed. If, however, capacity is limited, universal group membership caching can be enabled to reduce the bandwidth load.

Understanding Multiple Forests Design Concepts Using Microsoft Forefront Identity Manager (FIM)

Forefront Identity Manager (FIM) enables out-of-the-box replication of objects between two separate AD forests. This concept becomes important for organizations with multiple Exchange Server implementations that want a common Global Address List for the company. Previous iterations of FIM required an in-depth knowledge of scripting to be able to synchronize objects between two forests. FIM, on the other hand, includes built-in scripts that can establish replication between two Exchange Server 2010 AD forests, making integration between forests easier.

Determining Exchange Server 2010 Placement

Previous versions of Exchange Server essentially forced many organizations into deploying servers in sites with greater than a dozen or so users. With the concept of site consolidation in Exchange Server 2010, however, smaller numbers of Exchange servers can service clients in multiple locations, even if they are separated by slow WAN links. For small and medium-sized organizations, this essentially means that a small handful of servers is required, depending on availability needs. Larger organizations require a larger number of Exchange servers, depending on the number of sites and users. In addition, Exchange Server 2010 introduces new server role concepts, which should be understood so that the right server can be deployed in the right location.

Understanding Exchange Server 2010 Server Roles

Exchange Server 2010 firmed up the server role concept outlined with Exchange Server 2007. Before Exchange Server 2007/2010, server functionality was loosely termed, such as referring to an Exchange server as an OWA or front-end server, bridgehead server, or a mailbox or back-end server. In reality, there was no set terminology that was used for Exchange server roles. Exchange Server 2010, on the other hand, distinctly defines specific roles that a server can hold. Multiple roles can reside on a single server, or multiple servers can have the same role. By standardizing on these roles, it becomes easier to design an Exchange Server environment by designating specific roles for servers in specific locations.

The server roles included in Exchange Server 2010 include the following:

- **Client access server (CAS)**—The CAS role allows for client connections via nonstandard methods such as Outlook Web App (OWA), Exchange ActiveSync, Post Office Protocol 3 (POP3), and Internet Message Access Protocol (IMAP). Exchange Server 2010 also forces MAPI traffic and effectively all client traffic through the CAS layer. CAS servers are the replacement for Exchange 2000/2003 front-end servers and can be load balanced for redundancy purposes. As with the other server roles, the CAS role can coexist with other roles for smaller organizations with a single server, for example.

- **Edge Transport server**—The Edge Transport server role was introduced with Exchange Server 2007, and consists of a standalone server that typically resides in the demilitarized zone (DMZ) of a firewall. This server filters inbound SMTP mail traffic from the Internet for viruses and spam, and then forwards it to internal Hub Transport servers. Edge Transport servers keep a local AD Application Mode (ADAM) instance that is synchronized with the internal AD structure via a mechanism called EdgeSync. This helps to reduce the surface attack area of Exchange Server. The Edge Transport role can only exist by itself on a server, it cannot be combined with other roles.

- **Hub Transport server**—The Hub Transport server role acts as a mail bridgehead for mail sent between servers in one AD site and mail sent to other AD sites. There needs to be at least one Hub Transport server within an AD site that contains a server with the mailbox role, but there can also be multiple Hub Transport servers to provide for redundancy and load balancing. HT roles are also responsible for message compliance and rules. The HT role can be combined with other roles on a server, and is often combined with the CAS role.

- **Mailbox server**—The mailbox server role is intuitive; it acts as the storehouse for mail data in users' mailboxes and down-level public folders if required. All connections to the mailbox servers are proxied through the CAS servers.

- **Unified Messaging server**—The Unified Messaging server role allows a user's Inbox to be used for voice messaging and fax capabilities.

Any or all of these roles can be installed on a single server or on multiple servers. For smaller organizations, a single server holding all Exchange Server roles is sufficient. For larger organizations, a more complex configuration might be required. For more information on designing large and complex Exchange Server implementations, see Chapter 4.

Understanding Environment Sizing Considerations

In some cases with very small organizations, the number of users is small enough to warrant the installation of all AD and Exchange Server 2010 components on a single server. This scenario is possible, as long as all necessary components—DNS, a global catalog domain controller, and Exchange Server 2010—are installed on the same hardware. In general, however, it is best to separate AD and Exchange Server onto separate hardware wherever possible.

Identifying Client Access Points

At its core, Exchange Server 2010 essentially acts as a storehouse for mailbox data. Access to the mail within the mailboxes can take place through multiple means, some of which might be required by specific services or applications in the environment. A good understanding of what these services are and if and how your design should support them is warranted.

Outlining MAPI Client Access with Outlook 2007

The "heavy" client of Outlook, Outlook 2007, has gone through a significant number of changes, both to the look and feel of the application, and to the back-end mail functionality. The look and feel has been streamlined based on Microsoft research and customer feedback. The latest Outlook client, Outlook 2010, uses the Office ribbon introduced with Office 2007 to improve the client experience. Outlook connects with Exchange servers via CAS servers, improving the scalability of the environment.

In addition to MAPI compression, Outlook 2010/2007 expands upon the Outlook 2003 ability to run in cached mode, which automatically detects slow connections between client and server and adjusts Outlook functionality to match the speed of the link. When a slow link is detected, Outlook can be configured to download only email header information. When emails are opened, the entire email is downloaded, including attachments if necessary. This drastically reduces the amount of bits across the wire that is sent because only those emails that are required are sent across the connection.

The Outlook 2010/2007 client is the most effective and full-functioning client for users who are physically located close to an Exchange server. With the enhancements in cached mode functionality, however, Outlook 2010/2007 can also be effectively used in remote locations. When making the decision about which client to deploy as part of a design, you should keep these concepts in mind.

Accessing Exchange Server with Outlook Web App (OWA)

The Outlook Web App (OWA) client in Exchange Server 2010 has been enhanced and optimized for performance and usability. There is now very little difference between the full function client and OWA. With this in mind, OWA is now an even more efficient client for remote access to the Exchange server. The one major piece of functionality that OWA does not have, but the full Outlook 2007 client does, is offline mail access support. If this is required, the full client should be deployed.

Using Exchange ActiveSync (EAS)

Exchange ActiveSync (EAS) support in Exchange Server 2010 allows a mobile client, such as a Pocket PC device or mobile phone, to synchronize with the Exchange server, allowing for access to email from a handheld device. EAS also supports Direct Push technology, which allows for instantaneous email delivery to supported handheld devices such as Windows Mobile 5.0/6.x or other third-party ActiveSync enabled devices.

Understanding the Simple Mail Transport Protocol (SMTP)

The Simple Mail Transfer Protocol (SMTP) is an industry-standard protocol that is widely used across the Internet for mail delivery. SMTP is built in to Exchange servers and is used by Exchange Server systems for relaying mail messages from one system to another, which is similar to the way that mail is relayed across SMTP servers on the Internet. Exchange Server is dependent on SMTP for mail delivery and uses it for internal and external mail access.

By default, Exchange Server 2010 uses DNS to route messages destined for the Internet out of the Exchange Server topology. If, however, a user wants to forward messages to a smarthost before they are transmitted to the Internet, an SMTP connector can be manually set up to enable mail relay out of the Exchange Server system. SMTP connectors also reduce the risk and load on an Exchange server by off-loading the DNS lookup tasks to the SMTP smarthost. SMTP connectors can be specifically designed in an environment for this type of functionality.

Using Outlook Anywhere (Previously Known as RPC over HTTP)

One very effective and improved client access method to Exchange Server 2010 is known as Outlook Anywhere. This technology was previously referred to as RPC over HTTP(s) or Outlook over HTTP(s). This technology enables standard Outlook 2010/2007/2003 access across firewalls. The Outlook client encapsulates Outlook RPC packets into HTTP or HTTPS packets and sends them across standard web ports (80 and 443), where they are then extracted by the Exchange Server 2010 system. This technology enables Outlook to communicate using its standard RPC protocol, but across firewalls and routers that normally do not allow RPC traffic. The potential uses of this protocol are significant because many situations do not require the use of cumbersome VPN clients.

Configuring Exchange Server 2010 for Maximum Performance and Reliability

After decisions have been made about AD design, Exchange server placement, and client access, optimization of the Exchange server itself helps ensure efficiency, reliability, and security for the messaging platform.

Designing an Optimal Operating System Configuration for Exchange Server

As previously mentioned, Exchange Server 2010 only operates on the Windows Server 2008 (Service Pack 2 or later) or Windows Server 2008 R2 operating systems. The enhancements to the operating system, especially in regard to security, make Windows Server 2008 the optimal choice for Exchange Server. The Standard Edition of Windows Server 2008 is sufficient for any Exchange Server installation.

> **NOTE**
>
> Contrary to popular misconception, the Enterprise Edition of Exchange Server can be installed on the Standard Edition of the operating system, and vice versa. Although there has been a lot of confusion on this concept, both versions of Exchange Server were designed to interoperate with either version of Windows.

Configuring Disk Options for Performance

The single most important design element that improves the efficiency and speed of Exchange Server is the separation of the Exchange Server database and the Exchange Server logs onto a separate hard drive volume. Because of the inherent differences in the type of hard drive operations performed (logs perform primarily write operations, databases primarily read), separating these elements onto separate volumes dramatically increases server performance. Figure 3.3 illustrates some examples of how the database and log volumes can be configured.

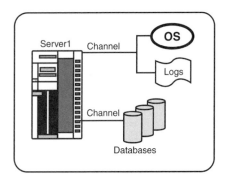
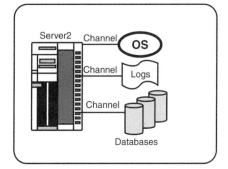

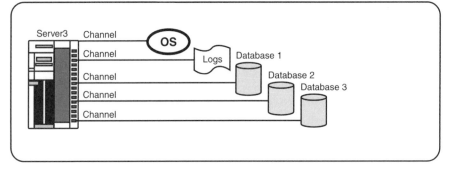

FIGURE 3.3   Database and log volume configuration.

On Server1, the OS and logs are located on the same mirrored C:\ volume and the database is located on a separate RAID-5 drive set. With Server2, the configuration is taken up a notch, with the OS only on C:\, the logs on D:\, and the database on the RAID-5 E:\ volume. Finally, Server3 is configured in the optimal configuration, with separate volumes for each database and a volume for the log files. The more advanced a configuration, the more detailed and complex the drive configuration can get. However, the most important factor that must be remembered is to separate the Exchange Server database from the logs wherever possible.

> **NOTE**
>
> With the use of Database Availability Groups (DAGs) in Exchange Server 2010, the performance of the disk infrastructure has become less of a concern. DAGs enable an organization's mailboxes to be spread across multiple servers and to exist in multiple locations (up to 16), which reduces the need for expensive SAN disks and enables Exchange Server to be installed on DAS or SATA disk.

Working with Multiple Exchange Server Databases

Exchange Server 2010 Database Availability Groups (DAGs) allow for multiple databases to be installed across multiple servers and to have multiple versions of those databases in more than one location. This allows for the creation of multiple large databases that reside on cheaper disks, which in turn allows for larger mailbox sizes. It also has the following advantages:

- ▶ **Reduce database restore time**—Multiple databases (rather than a smaller number of larger databases) take less time to restore from tape. This concept can be helpful if there is a group of users who require quicker recovery time (such as management). All mailboxes for this group could then be placed in a separate database to provide quicker recovery time in the event of a server or database failure.

- ▶ **Provide for separate mailbox limit policies**—Each database can be configured with different mailbox storage limits. For example, the standard user database could have a 200-MB limit on mailboxes, and the management database could have a 500-MB limit.

- ▶ **Mitigate risk by distributing user load**—By distributing user load across multiple databases, the risk of losing all user mail connectivity is reduced. For example, if a single database failed that contained all users, no one would be able to mail. If those users were divided across three databases, however, only one third of those users would be unable to mail in the event of a database failure.

Monitoring Design Concepts with System Center Operations Manager 2007 R2

The enhancements to Exchange Server 2010 do not stop with the improvements to the product itself. New functionality has been added to the Exchange Management Pack for System Center Operations Manager that enables OpsMgr to monitor Exchange servers for critical events and performance data. The OpsMgr Management Pack is preconfigured to monitor for Exchange Server-specific information and to enable administrators to proactively monitor Exchange servers. For more information on using OpsMgr to monitor Exchange Server 2010, see Chapter 20, "Using Operations Manager to Monitor Exchange Server 2010."

Securing and Maintaining an Exchange Server 2010 Implementation

One of the greatest advantages of Exchange Server 2010 is its emphasis on security. Along with Windows Server 2008, Exchange Server 2010 was developed during and after the Microsoft Trustworthy Computing initiative, which effectively put a greater emphasis on security over new features in the products. In Exchange Server 2010, this means that the OS and the application were designed with services "Secure by Default."

With Secure by Default, all nonessential functionality in Exchange Server must be turned on if needed. This is a complete change from the previous Microsoft model, which had all services, add-ons, and options turned on and running at all times, presenting much larger security vulnerabilities than was necessary. Designing security effectively becomes much easier in Exchange Server 2010 because it now becomes necessary only to identify components to turn on, as opposed to identifying everything that needs to be turned off.

In addition to being secure by default, Exchange Server 2010 server roles are built in to templates used by the Security Configuration Wizard (SCW), which was introduced in Service Pack 1 for Windows Server 2003. Using the SCW against Exchange Server helps to reduce the surface attack area of a server.

Patching the Operating System Using Windows Server Update Services

Although Windows Server 2008 presents a much smaller target for hackers, viruses, and exploits by virtue of the Secure by Default concept, it is still important to keep the OS up to date against critical security patches and updates. Currently, two approaches can be used to automate the installation of server patches. The first method involves configuring the Windows Server 2008 Automatic Updates client to download patches from Microsoft and install them on a schedule. The second option is to set up an internal server to coordinate patch distribution and management. The solution that Microsoft supplies for this functionality is known as Windows Server Update Services (WSUS).

WSUS enables a centralized server to hold copies of OS patches for distribution to clients on a preset schedule. WSUS can be used to automate the distribution of patches to Exchange Server 2010 servers, so that the OS components will remain secure between service packs. WSUS might not be necessary in smaller environments, but can be considered in medium-sized to large organizations that want greater control over their patch management strategy.

Summary

Exchange Server 2010 offers a broad range of functionality and improvements to messaging and is well suited for organizations of any size. With proper thought for the major design topics, a robust and reliable Exchange Server email solution can be put into place that will perfectly complement the needs of any organization.

When Exchange Server design concepts have been fully understood, the task of designing the Exchange Server 2010 infrastructure can take place.

Best Practices

The following are best practices from this chapter:

- ▶ Use Database Availability Groups (DAGs) to distribute multiple copies of all mailboxes to multiple locations, taking advantage of HA and DR capabilities that are built into Exchange Server 2010.

- ▶ Separate the Exchange Server log and database files onto separate physical volumes whenever possible, but also be cognizant of the fact that Exchange Server can be installed on slower, cheaper disks when using DAGs.

- ▶ Plan for a Windows Server 2003 functional forest and at least one Windows Server 2003 SP2 or Windows Server 2008 domain controller in each site that will run Exchange Server.

- ▶ Integrate an antivirus and backup strategy into Exchange Server design.

- ▶ Keep a local copy of a full global catalog close to any Exchange servers.

- ▶ Keep the OS and Exchange Server up to date through service packs and software patches, either manually or via Windows Server Update Services.

- ▶ Keep the AD design simple, with a single forest and single domain, unless a specific need exists to create more complexity.

- ▶ Identify the client access methods that will be supported and match them with the appropriate Exchange Server 2010 technology.

- ▶ Monitor DNS functionality closely in the environment on the AD domain controllers.

CHAPTER 4

Architecting an Enterprise-Level Exchange Server Environment

Microsoft Exchange Server 2010 was designed to accommodate the needs of multiple organizations, from the small businesses to large, multinational corporations. In addition to the scalability features present in previous versions of Exchange Server, Exchange Server 2010 offers more opportunities to scale the back-end server environment to the specific needs of any group.

This chapter addresses specific design guidelines for midsize to large enterprise organizations. Throughout the chapter, specific examples of enterprise organizations are presented and general recommendations are made. This chapter assumes a base knowledge of design components that can be obtained by reading Chapter 3, "Understanding Core Exchange Server 2010 Design Plans."

Designing Active Directory for Exchange Server 2010

Active Directory Domain Services (AD DS), often referred to simply as Active Directory (AD), is a necessary and fundamental component of any Exchange Server 2010 implementation. That said, organizations do not necessarily need to panic about setting up Active Directory in addition to Exchange Server, as long as a few straightforward design steps are followed. The following areas of Active Directory must be addressed to properly design and deploy Exchange Server 2010:

▶ Forest and domain design

▶ AD site and replication topology layout

▶ Domain controller and global catalog placement

▶ Domain name system (DNS) configuration

Understanding Forest and Domain Design

Because Exchange Server 2007 uses Active Directory for its underlying directory structure, it is necessary to link Exchange Server with a unique Active Directory forest.

In many cases, an existing Active Directory forest and domain structure is already in place in organizations considering Exchange Server 2010 deployment. In these cases, Exchange Server can be installed on top of the existing AD environment, and no additional AD design decisions need to be made. It is important to note that Exchange Server 2010 requires that the AD forest be at least at Windows Server 2003 functional level and also requires that at least one Windows Server 2003 SP2 or Windows Server 2008 RTM/R2 Global Catalog is installed in each AD site in which Exchange servers reside. Finally, the schema master for the forest must be either a Windows Server 2003 SP2 or Windows Server 2008 (RTM or R2) domain controller.

In some cases, there might not be an existing AD infrastructure in place, and one needs to be deployed to support Exchange Server. In these scenarios, design decisions need to be made for the AD structure in which Exchange Server will be installed. In some specific cases, Exchange Server might be deployed as part of a separate forest by itself, as illustrated in Figure 4.1. This model is known as the Exchange Resource Forest model. This is often the case in an organization with multiple existing AD forests.

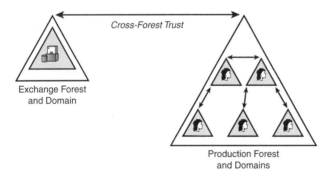

FIGURE 4.1   Understanding the Exchange Resource Forest model.

In any case, AD should be designed with simplicity in mind. A single-forest, single-domain model, for example, solves the needs of many organizations. If Exchange Server itself is all that is required of AD, this type of deployment is the best practice to consider.

> **NOTE**
>
> The addition of Exchange Server 2010 into an Active Directory forest requires an extension of the AD forest's Active Directory schema.
>
> Considerations for this factor must be taken into account when deploying Exchange Server onto an existing AD forest.

Microsoft has gotten serious recently about support for Exchange Server across multiple forests. This was previously an onerous task to set up, but the ability to synchronize between separate Exchange Server organizations has been simplified through the use of Identity Lifecycle Manager (ILM) 2007. ILM now comes with a series of preconfigured scripts to replicate between Exchange Server forests, enabling organizations that, for one reason or another, cannot use a common forest to unite the email structure through object replication.

Outlining AD Site and Replication Topology Layout

Active Directory sites should mirror existing network topology. Where there are pools of highly connected AD domain controllers, for example, Active Directory sites should be created to optimize replication. Smaller organizations have the luxury of a simplified AD site design. In general, the number of sites is small—or, in most cases, composed of a single physical location. Midsize and larger organizations might require the creation of multiple Active Directory sites to mirror the wide area network (WAN) connectivity of the organization.

Exchange Server 2010 no longer uses a separate replication mechanism (routing groups) from Active Directory, and Exchange Server replication takes place within the context of Active Directory sites. This makes proper AD site topology creation a critical component of an Exchange Server deployment.

Reviewing Domain Controller and Global Catalog Placement Concepts

In small or midsize organizations, you have effectively two options regarding domain controller placement. The first option involves using the same physical server for domain controller and Exchange Server duties. This option is feasible, though not recommended, for smaller organizations if budget constraints preclude the addition of more than one server. This type of deployment strategy is not feasible for mid-sized and enterprise organizations, however, and the domain controller functions should be separated onto dedicated systems.

Configuring DNS

Because AD and Exchange Server are completely dependent on DNS for lookups and overall functionality, configuring DNS is an important factor to consider. As a common AD best practice, DNS is installed on the domain controller(s), which enables the creation of Active Directory–integrated DNS zones. AD–integrated zones enable DNS data to be stored in AD with multiple read/write copies of the zone available for redundancy purposes. Although using other non-Microsoft DNS for AD is supported, it is not recommended.

The main decision regarding DNS layout is the decision about the namespace to be used within the organization. The DNS namespace is the same as the AD domain information, and it is difficult to change later. The two options in this case are to configure DNS to use either a published, external namespace that is easy to understand, such as cco.com, or an internal, secure namespace that is difficult to hack into, such as cconet.internal. In general, the more security-conscious an organization, the more often the internal namespace will be chosen.

Determining Hardware and Software Components

Justifying hardware and software purchases is often a difficult task for organizations of any size. It is, therefore, important to balance the need for performance and redundancy with the available funds in the budget, and, thus, deploy the optimal Exchange Server hardware and software configuration.

Unlike versions of Exchange Server prior to Exchange Server 2007, Exchange Server 2010 requires the use of 64-bit capable systems, so it is critical to order the appropriate equipment when deploying Exchange Server 2010 systems.

Designing Server Number and Placement

Exchange Server scales very well to a large number of mailboxes on a single machine, depending on the hardware chosen for the Exchange server. Subsequently, Exchange Server 2010 is optimal for organizations that want to limit the amount of servers that are deployed and supported in an environment.

Exchange 2000 Server previously had one major exception to this concept, however. If multiple sites required high-speed access to an Exchange server, multiple servers were necessary for deployment. Exchange Server 2010, on the other hand, expands upon the concept of site consolidation, introduced in Exchange Server 2003. This concept enables smaller sites to use the Exchange servers in the larger sites through the more efficient bandwidth usage present in Outlook 2007 and Outlook 2003 and other mobile technologies.

Providing for Server Redundancy and Optimization

The ability of the Exchange server to recover from hardware failures is more than just a "nice-to-have" feature. Many server models come with an array of redundancy features, such as multiple fans and power supplies and mirrored disk capabilities. These features incur additional costs, however, so it is wise to perform a cost-benefit analysis to determine what redundancy features are required. Midsize and larger organizations should seriously consider robust redundancy options, however, because the increased reliability and uptime is often well worth the up-front costs.

Exchange Server 2010 further expands the redundancy options with the concept of Database Availability Groups (DAGs), which enable for a mailbox database to reside in up to 16 different locations at one time. This enables for unprecedented levels of redundancy and frees the architect from the requirement to focus heavily on server level redundancy because the loss of a single server is no longer a catastrophic event.

One of the most critical but overlooked performance strategies for Exchange Server is the concept of separating the Exchange Server logs and database onto separate physical drive sets. Because Exchange Server logs are very write-intensive, and the database is read-intensive, having these components on the same disk set would degrade performance. Separating these components onto different disk sets, however, is the best way to get the most out of Exchange Server.

Reviewing Server Memory and Processor Recommendations

Exchange Server is a resource-hungry application that, left to its own devices, will consume a good portion of any amount of processor or memory that is given to it. The amount of processors and random access memory (RAM) required should reflect the budgetary needs of the organization. In general, midsize and larger organizations should consider multiprocessor servers and greater amounts of RAM—8GB or 16GB or more. This helps increase the amount of mailboxes that can be homed to any particular server.

> **NOTE**
>
> The rule of thumb when sizing an Exchange Server 2010 mailbox server is to start with 2GB of RAM for a server; then add 5MB of RAM for each mailbox that will be homed on it. For example, on a server with 3,000 mailboxes, at least 17GB of RAM would be required (2GB + (3000*.005GB)).

Outlining Server Operating System Considerations

The base operating system (OS) for Exchange Server, Windows Server, comes in two versions, Enterprise and Standard. Some midsize and larger organizations could deploy the Enterprise Edition of the Windows Server product, namely for clustering support. If this functionality is not required, the Standard Edition of the OS is sufficient.

Designing Exchange Server Roles in an Exchange Server Environment

Exchange Server 2010 was designed to be resilient and be able to adapt to a wide variety of deployment scenarios. Part of this design revolves around the concept that individual servers can play one or more roles for an organization. Each of these roles provides for specific functionality that is commonly performed by Exchange servers, such as mailbox server or Client Access server (formerly referred to as an OWA server).

Central to the understanding of Exchange Server 2010 and how to design and architect it is the understanding of these individual roles. During the design process, understanding server roles is central to proper server placement.

The individual server roles in Exchange Server 2010 are as follows:

- ▶ Mailbox server role
- ▶ Client Access server role
- ▶ Edge Transport role
- ▶ Hub Transport role
- ▶ Unified Messaging role

Each of these roles is described in more detail in the subsequent sections.

Planning for the Mailbox Server Role

The Mailbox server role is the central role in an Exchange Server topology as it is the server that stores the actual mailboxes of the user. Therefore, mailbox servers are often the most critical for an organization, and are given the most attention.

With the Enterprise Edition of Exchange Server, a mailbox server can hold anywhere from 1 to 50 databases on it. Each of the databases are theoretically unlimited in size, although it is wise to keep an individual database limited to 100GB or less for performance and recovery scenarios.

> **NOTE**
>
> In large organizations, a single server or a cluster of servers is often dedicated to individual server roles. That said, a single server can also be assigned other roles, such as the Client Access server role, in the interest of consolidating the number of servers deployed. The only limitation to this is the Edge server role, which must exist by itself and cannot be installed on a server that holds other roles.

Planning for the Client Access Server Role

The Client Access server role in Exchange Server is the role that controls access to mailboxes from all clients, including the full version of Outlook. It is the component that controls access to mailboxes via the following mechanisms:

- MAPI on the Middle Tier (MoMT)—Standard Outlook method of access
- Outlook Web App (OWA)
- Exchange ActiveSync
- Outlook Anywhere (formerly RPC over HTTP)
- Post Office Protocol 3 (POP3)
- Internet Message Access Protocol (IMAP4)

In addition, CAS systems also handle the following two special services in an Exchange Server topology:

- **Autodiscover service**—The Autodiscover service allows clients to determine their synchronization settings (such as mailbox server and so on) by entering in their SMTP address and their credentials. It is supported across standard OWA connections.

- **Availability service**—The Availability service is the replacement for Free/Busy functionality in Exchange Server 2000/2003. It is responsible for making a user's calendar availability visible to other users making meeting requests.

Client access servers in Exchange Server 2010 are the only way that clients can access their mailbox in Exchange Server 2010, which differs from previous versions of Exchange Server that required direct access to mailbox servers. By separating client traffic to a load-balanced array of CAS servers, Exchange Server architects have more flexibility in design and failover; using concepts such as DAG becomes easier and more efficient.

Planning for the Edge Transport Role

The Edge Transport role was introduced with Exchange Server 2007 and is enhanced in Exchange Server 2007. Edge Transport servers are standalone, workgroup members that are meant to reside in the demilitarized zone (DMZ) of a firewall. They do not require access to any internal resources, except for a one-way synchronization of specific configuration information from Active Directory via a process called EdgeSync.

Edge Transport servers hold a small instance of Active Directory Lightweight Domain Services (AD LDS), which is used to store specific configuration information, such as the location of Hub Transport servers within the topology. AD LDS can be thought of as a scaled-down version of a separate Active Directory forest that runs as a service on a machine.

The Edge Transport role is the role that provides for spam and virus filtering, as Microsoft has moved the emphasis on this type of protection to incoming and outgoing messages. Essentially, this role is a method in which Microsoft intends to capture some of the market taken by SMTP relay systems and virus scanners, which have traditionally been taken by third-party products provided by virus-scanning companies and UNIX SendMail hosts.

In large organizations, redundancy can be built in to Edge Transport services through simple DNS round-robin, Windows Network Load Balancing, or with the use of a third-party hardware load balancer.

Planning for the Hub Transport Role

The Hub Transport role is a server role that is responsible for the distribution of mail messages within an Exchange Server organization. There must be at least one Hub Transport role defined for each Active Directory site that contains a mailbox server.

> **NOTE**
>
> The Hub Transport role can be added to a server running any other role, with only one exception. It cannot be added to a server that is an Edge Transport server.

Several special considerations exist for Hub Transport servers as follows:

- Multiple Hub Transport servers can be established in a site to provide for redundancy and load balancing.

- Exchange Server 2010 built-in protection features (antivirus and antispam) are not enabled by default on Hub Transport servers. Instead, they are enabled on Edge Transport servers. If needed, they can be enabled on a Hub Transport server by running a Management Shell script.

- Messaging policy and compliance features are enabled on Hub Transport servers and can be used to add disclaimers, control attachment sizes, encrypt messages, and block specific content.

Planning for the Unified Messaging Role

The Unified Messaging role in Exchange Server 2010 was originally introduced with Exchange Server 2007 but has come of age in this latest version. This role enables voice mail to be fully integrated into a user's mailbox.

The Unified Messaging role can be installed on multiple servers, although it is recommended that it only be installed when the infrastructure to support it exists in the organization. As Exchange Server 2010 progresses, this role will become more important.

Understanding a Sample Deployment Scenario

A better understanding of Exchange Server roles can be achieved by looking at sample deployment scenarios that utilize these roles. For example, Figure 4.2 illustrates a large enterprise deployment of Exchange Server that takes advantage of all the unique server roles.

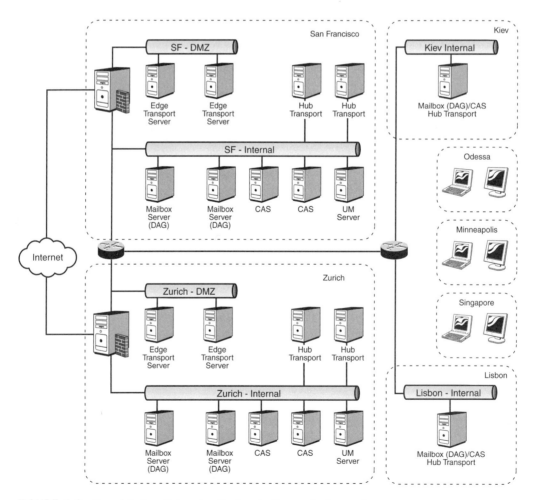

FIGURE 4.2   Examining an Enterprise Exchange Server deployment.

In this design, the following key deployment features are illustrated:

▶ DAGs distributed across multiple mailbox servers, with at least three copies of each mailbox database across the organization.

▶ Dedicated Hub Transport servers distribute mail between the two major sites in San Francisco and Zurich.

▶ Medium-sized sites such as Kiev and Lisbon make use of combined CAS/Mailbox/Hub Transport server systems.

▶ Client access servers are set up in the two main sites, to provide for client access mechanisms in those sites.

▶ Edge Transport servers process inbound and outbound mail in the DMZ locations in San Francisco and Zurich.

▶ Unified Messaging servers exist in the main hub sites and are provided as a service for users in those locations. The servers are directly connected to PBX systems in those locations.

▶ Smaller sites such as Minneapolis, Odessa, and Singapore have their mailboxes hosted in the two hub locations and use the client access servers with Outlook Anywhere to access their mailboxes remotely.

Designing Exchange Server Infrastructure

After Active Directory and the physical OS has been chosen and deployed, the Exchange Server infrastructure can be set up and optimized for the specific needs of the organization. With these needs in mind, you can do several things to optimize an Exchange Server 2010 setup, as detailed in the following sections.

Determining the Exchange Server Version

When installing Exchange Server, the choice of Exchange Server version needs to be made. As with Windows Server 2008, there are two versions of Exchange Server, Standard and Enterprise. The Standard Edition enables all Exchange Server 2010 functionality except it does not enable for more than five mailbox databases on a server.

Determining Exchange Server Database Layout

As previously mentioned, the Enterprise Edition of Exchange Server enables the concept of multiple databases, up to a maximum of 150. This enables a greater amount of design freedom and gives administrators more flexibility. This type of flexibility is even more important when designing infrastructures that include multiple copies of a single database.

Outlining Exchange Server Recovery Options

Deploying Exchange Server requires considerable thought about backup and recovery solutions. Because Exchange Server is a live, active database, special considerations need to be taken into account when designing the backup strategy for email.

Microsoft designed Exchange Server 2010 to use the backup application programming interfaces (APIs) from Windows Server 2008. These APIs support the Volume Shadow Copy Service, which enables Exchange Server databases to be backed up through creation of a "shadow copy" of the entire disk at the beginning of the backup. The shadow copy is then used for the backup, so that the production disk is not affected.

> **NOTE**
>
> The Windows Server 2003/2008 backup utility can be used to back up Exchange Server using the traditional online backup approach. Volume Shadow Copy requires a third-party solution that has been written to support the Windows Server 2003/2008 backup and restore APIs. Microsoft also offers enterprise Exchange Server backup using the System Center Data Protection Manager (DPM) product.

For more information on backup and recovery options, see Chapter 32, "Backing Up the Exchange Server 2010 Environment."

Considering Exchange Server Antivirus and Antispam Design

Viruses are a major problem for all organizations today. Email is especially vulnerable because it is typically unauthenticated and insecure. Consequently, design of an Exchange Server implementation should include consideration for antivirus options.

Exchange Server 2010 enhances the Virus Scanning Application Programming Interface (VSAPI) that was introduced in Exchange 2000 Server and improved in Exchange Server 2003 and 2007. The enhanced VSAPI engine enables quarantine of email messages, as opposed to simply attachments, and enables virus scanning on gateway servers. Third-party virus products can be written to tie directly into the new VSAPI and use its functionality.

Spam, unsolicited email, has become another major headache for most organizations. In response to this, Exchange Server 2010 has some built-in antispam functionality that enables email messages to contain a spam rating. This helps determine which emails are legitimate, and can be used by third-party antispam products as well.

Monitoring Exchange Server

Email services are required in many organizations. The expectations of uptime and reliability are increasing, and end users are beginning to expect email to be as available as phone service. Therefore, the ability to monitor Exchange Server events, alerts, and performance data is optimal.

Exchange Server 2010 is an organism with multiple components, each busy processing tasks, writing to event logs, and running optimization routines. You can monitor Exchange Server using one of several methods, the most optimal being System Center Operations Manager 2007 (previously named Microsoft Operations Manager or MOM). SCOM 2007 is essentially a monitoring, alerting, and reporting product that gathers event information and performance data, and generates reports about Microsoft servers. An

Exchange Server-specific management pack for SCOM contains hundreds of prepackaged counters and events for Exchange Server 2010. Use of the management pack is ideal in midsize and larger environments to proactively monitor Exchange Server.

Although close monitoring of multiple Exchange servers is best supported through the use of SCOM, this might not be the most ideal approach for smaller organizations because SCOM is geared toward medium and large organizations. Exchange Server monitoring for small organizations can be accomplished through old-fashioned approaches, such as manual reviews of event log information, performance counters using perfmon, and simple Simple Network Management Protocol (SNMP) utilities to monitor uptime.

Integrating Client Access into Exchange Server 2010 Design

Although the Exchange server is a powerful systems component, it is only half the equation for an email platform. The client systems comprise the other half, and are a necessary ingredient that should be carefully determined in advance.

Outlining Client Access Methods

Great effort has been put into optimizing and streamlining the client access approaches available in Exchange Server 2010. Not only have traditional approaches such as the Outlook client been enhanced, but support for nontraditional access with POP3 and IMAP clients is also available. The following options exist for client access with Exchange Server 2010:

- **Outlook MAPI**—Traditional MAPI access has been replaced with MAPI on the Middle Tier (MoMT), which enables Outlook clients to communicate through the CAS servers. Outlook versions that support access to Exchange Server 2010 servers are limited to the 2003, 2007, and 2010 versions of Outlook.

- **Outlook Web App (OWA)**—The Outlook Web App (OWA) client is now nearly indistinguishable from the full Outlook client. The one major component missing is offline capability, but nearly every other Outlook functionality is part of OWA.

- **ActiveSync**—ActiveSync provides for synchronized access to email from a handheld device, such as a Pocket PC, Windows Mobile, iPhone, or other ActiveSync-enabled device. It allows for real-time send and receive functionality to and from the handheld, through the use of push technology.

- **Outlook Anywhere**—Outlook Anywhere (previously known as RPC over HTTP) is a method by which a full Outlook client can dynamically send and receive messages directly from an Exchange server over an HTTP or Hypertext Transfer Protocol Secure (HTTPS) web connection. This allows for virtual private network (VPN)–free access to Exchange Server data, over a secured HTTPS connection.

- **Post Office Protocol 3 (POP3)**—The Post Office Protocol 3 (POP3) is a legacy protocol that is supported in Exchange Server 2010. POP3 enables simple retrieval of mail data via applications that use the POP3 protocol. Mail messages, however, cannot be sent with POP3 and must use the SMTP engine in Exchange Server. By default, POP3 is not turned on and must be explicitly activated.

▶ **Internet Message Access Protocol (IMAP)**—Legacy Interactive Mail Access Protocol (IMAP) access to Exchange Server is also available, which can enable an Exchange server to be accessed via IMAP applications, such as some UNIX mail clients. As with the POP3 protocol, IMAP support must be explicitly turned on.

NOTE

Exchange Server 2010 supports the option of disallowing MAPI access or allowing only specific Outlook clients MAPI access. This can be configured if an organization desires only OWA access to an Exchange server. It can also, for security reasons, stipulate that only Outlook 2007 and Outlook 2003 can access the Exchange server. The Registry key required for this functionality is the following:

```
Location:HKLM\System\CurrentControlSet\Services\MSExchangeIS\ParametersSystem

Value Name: Disable MAPI Clients

Data Type: REG_SZ

String: Version # (i.e. v4, v5, etc)
```

See Microsoft TechNet Article 288894 for more information:

http://support.microsoft.com/default.aspx?scid=KB;EN-US;288894

Each organization will have individual needs that determine which client or set of clients will be supported. In general, the full Outlook client offers the richest messaging experience with Exchange Server 2010, but many of the other access mechanisms, such as Outlook Web App, are also valid. The important design consideration is identifying what will be supported, and then enabling support for that client or protocol. Any methods that will not be supported should be disabled or left turned off for security reasons.

Summary

Exchange Server 2010 offers a broad range of functionality and improvements to messaging and is well suited for organizations of any size. With proper thought into the major design topics, a robust and reliable Exchange Server email solution can be put into place that will perfectly complement the needs of organizations of any size.

In short, Exchange Server easily scales up to support thousands of users on multiple servers, and it also scales down very well. Single Exchange server implementations can easily support hundreds of users, even those that are scattered in various locations. This flexibility helps establish Exchange Server as the premier messaging solution for organizations of any size.

Best Practices

The following are best practices from this chapter:

▶ Try to create an Active Directory design that is as simple as possible. Expand the directory tree with multiple subdomains and forests at a later date only if absolutely necessary.

▶ Even if the organization has high bandwidth between sites, create a site to better control replication and traffic between sites.

▶ Highly consider the use of Database Availability Groups (DAGs) that enable a mailbox to exist in up to 16 locations at one time. Consider a design approach that focuses on a DAG as a primary redundancy mechanism.

▶ Minimize the number of servers needed by consolidating services into as few systems as possible; however, after systems have been consolidated, take the leftover spare systems and create redundancy between systems.

CHAPTER 5

Integrating Exchange Server 2010 in a Non-Windows Environment

In many organizations, multiple technologies work side by side with Exchange Server. Certain organizations even have multiple messaging platforms in use. For some of these organizations, consolidation of these platforms into a single platform takes place, but for other organizations, consolidation is not an option, and coexistence in one form or another must be established.

Previous versions of Microsoft Exchange Server supported embedded connectors to competing messaging platforms, such as Novell GroupWise and Lotus Notes. Exchange Server 2010 servers, however, no longer support these connectors, and organizations are faced with the choice of leaving an Exchange 2003 server in place to support these connectors, or finding other methods of synchronizing address lists and other information between the various platforms.

Fortunately, Microsoft provides multiple tools to allow for synchronization between the directory component of Exchange Server, Active Directory (AD), and the various other products. This chapter focuses on the integration of AD with non-Windows environments, such as UNIX and Lightweight Directory Access Protocol (LDAP) directories. Various tools, such as Forefront Identity Manager and Services for UNIX, that can be used to accomplish this are presented, and the pros and cons of each are analyzed.

Synchronizing Directory Information with Forefront Identity Manager (FIM)

In most enterprises today, each individual application or system has its own user database or directory to track who is permitted to use that resource. Identity and access control data reside in different directories as well as applications such as specialized network resource directories, mail servers, human resource, voice mail, payroll, and many other applications.

Each has its own definition of the user's "identity" (for example, name, title, ID numbers, roles, membership in groups). Many have their own password and process for authenticating users. Each has its own tool for managing user accounts and, sometimes, its own dedicated administrator responsible for this task. In addition, most enterprises have multiple processes for requesting resources and for granting and changing access rights. Some of these are automated, but many are paper-based. Many differ from business unit to business unit, even when performing the same function.

Administration of these multiple repositories often leads to time-consuming and redundant efforts in administration and provisioning. It also causes frustration for users, requiring them to remember multiple IDs and passwords for different applications and systems. The larger the organization, the greater the potential variety of these repositories and the effort required to keep them updated.

In response to this problem, Microsoft developed Microsoft Metadirectory Services (MMS) to provide for identity synchronization between different directories. As the product improved, it was rereleased under the new name Microsoft Identity Integration Server (MIIS). For a third time, the tool was renamed, this time as Identity Lifecycle Manager (ILM) 2007. The latest and fourth rename of this tool took place shortly before the release of Exchange Server 2010; Microsoft has now incorporated this tool into its Forefront security line and named it Forefront Identity Manager (FIM).

The use of FIM for Exchange Server 2010 is particularly useful because it can synchronize information between the AD forest that contains Exchange Server and the other messaging systems in use within the organization.

Understanding FIM

FIM is a system that manages and coordinates identity information from multiple data sources in an organization, enabling you to combine that information into a single logical view that represents all of the identity information for a given user or resource.

FIM enables a company to synchronize identity information across a wide variety of heterogeneous directory and nondirectory identity stores. This enables customers to automate the process of updating identity information across heterogeneous platforms while maintaining the integrity and ownership of that data across the enterprise.

Password management capabilities enable end users or help desk staff to easily reset passwords across multiple systems from one easy-to-use web interface. End users and help desk staff no longer have to use multiple tools to change their passwords across multiple systems.

> **NOTE**
>
> At the time of the writing of this chapter, the released production version of FIM was the previously named Identity Lifecycle Manager (ILM) 2007 product. The long awaited 2.0 version of ILM was only recently renamed to FIM and is anticipated for release soon.

Understanding FIM Concepts

It is important to understand some key terms used with FIM before comprehending how it can be used to integrate various directories. Keep in mind that the following terms are used to describe FIM concepts but might also help give you a broader understanding of how metadirectories function in general:

- **Management agent (MA)**—A FIM MA is a tool used to communicate with a specific type of directory. For example, an Active Directory MA enables FIM to import or export data and perform tasks within Active Directory.

- **Connected directory (CD)**—A connected directory is a directory that FIM communicates with using a configured MA. An example of a connected directory is an Active Directory forest.

- **Connector namespace (CS)**—The connector namespace is the replicated information and container hierarchy extracted from or destined to the respective connected directory.

- **Metaverse namespace (MV)**—The metaverse namespace is the authoritative directory data created from the information gathered from each of the respective connector namespaces.

- **Metadirectory**—Within FIM, the metadirectory is made up of all the connector namespaces plus the authoritative metaverse namespace.

- **Attributes**—Attributes are the fields of information that are exported from or imported to directory entries. Common directory entry attributes are name, alias, email address, phone number, employee ID, or other information.

FIM can be used for many tasks, but is most commonly used for managing directory entry identity information. The intention here is to manage user accounts by synchronizing attributes, such as logon ID, first name, last name, telephone number, title, and department. For example, if a user named Jane Doe is promoted and her title is changed from manager to vice president, the title change could first be entered in the HR or Payroll databases; then through FIM MAs, the change could be replicated to other directories within the organization. This ensures that when someone looks up the title attribute for Jane Doe, it is the same in all the directories synchronized with FIM. This is a common and basic use of FIM referred to as identity management. Other common uses of FIM include account provisioning and group management.

> **NOTE**
>
> FIM is a versatile and powerful directory synchronization tool that can be used to simplify and automate some directory management tasks. Because of the nature of FIM, it can also be a very dangerous tool as MAs can have full access to the connected directories. Misconfiguration of FIM MAs could result in data loss, so careful planning and extensive lab testing should be performed before FIM is released to the production directories of any organization. In many cases, it might be prudent to contact Microsoft consulting services and certified Microsoft solution provider/partners to help an organization decide whether FIM is right for its environment, or even to design and facilitate the implementation.

Exploring FIM Account Provisioning

FIM enables administrators to easily provision and deprovision users' accounts and identity information, such as distribution, email and security groups across systems, and platforms. Administrators will be able to quickly create new accounts for employees based on events or changes in authoritative stores such as the human resources system. In addition, as employees leave a company, they can be immediately deprovisioned from those same systems.

Account provisioning in FIM enables advanced configurations of directory MAs, along with special provisioning agents, to be used to automate account creation and deletion in several directories. For example, if a new user account is created in Active Directory, the Active Directory MA could tag this account. Then, when the respective MAs are run for other connected directories, a new user account could be automatically generated.

One enhancement of FIM over previous versions is that password synchronization is now supported for specific directories that manage passwords within the directory. FIM provides an application programming interface (API) accessed through the Windows Management Instrumentation (WMI). For connected directories that manage passwords in the directory's store, password management is activated when an MA is configured in MA Designer. In addition to enabling password management for each MA, Management Agent Designer returns a system name attribute using the WMI interface for each connector space object.

Outlining the Role of Management Agents (MAs) in FIM

An MA links a specific connected data source to the metadirectory. The MA is responsible for moving data from the connected data source and the metadirectory. When data in the metadirectory is modified, the MA can also export the data to the connected data source to keep the connected data source synchronized with the metadirectory. Generally, there is at least one MA for each connected directory. FIM includes MAs for multiple directory sources, as shown in Figure 5.1.

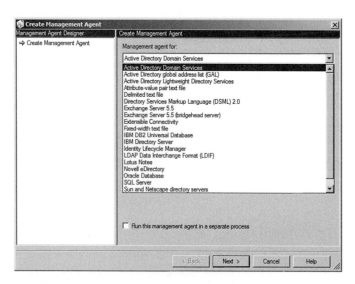

FIGURE 5.1   Potential management agents for FIM.

NOTE

FIM includes integrated support for synchronization with additional directories such as Oracle, SAP, Lotus Notes, and more. In addition, it also introduced the ability for end users to reset their own passwords via a web management interface.

MAs contain rules that govern how an object's attributes are mapped, how connected directory objects are found in the metaverse, and when connected directory objects should be created or deleted.

These agents are used to configure how FIM will communicate and interact with the connected directories when the agent is run. When an MA is first created, all the configuration of that agent can be performed during that instance. The elements that can be configured include which type of directory objects will be replicated to the connector namespace, which attributes will be replicated, directory entry join and projection rules, attribute flow rules between the connector namespace and the metaverse namespace, plus more. If a necessary configuration is unknown during the MA creation, it can be revisited and modified later.

Defining FIM and Group Management

Just as FIM can perform identity management for user accounts, it also can perform management tasks for groups. When a group is projected into the metaverse namespace, the group membership attribute can be replicated to other connected directories through their MAs. This enables a group membership change to occur in one directory and be replicated to other directories automatically.

Installing FIM with SQL Server

Both versions of FIM require a licensed version of SQL Server 2005 or 2008 to run, and an install of the product will prompt for the location of a SQL server.

It is not necessarily required to install a new instance of SQL because an existing SQL instance can be used as well. If an existing SQL 2005/2008 server is not available, SQL can be installed on the same system as FIM.

Deploying FIM for Identity Management with Novell eDirectory

FIM can be an effective tool for managing identities between Novell eDirectory environments and Active Directory. Identity information could include names, email and physical addresses, titles, department affiliations, and much more. Generally speaking, identity information is the type of data commonly found in corporate phone books or intranets. To use FIM for identity management between Active Directory and Novell eDirectory, follow these high-level steps:

1. Install FIM and the latest service packs and patches.

2. Create an MA for each of the directories, including an Active Directory MA and a Novell eDirectory MA.

3. Configure the MAs to import directory object types into their respective connector namespaces.

4. Configure one of the MAs—for example, the Active Directory MA—to project the connector space directory objects and directory hierarchy into the metaverse namespace.

5. Within each of the MAs, a function can be configured called attribute flow, which defines which directory object attributes from each directory will be projected into the respective metaverse directory objects. Configure the attribute flow rules for each MA.

6. Configure the account-joining properties for directory objects. This is the most crucial step because it determines how the objects in each directory are related to one another within the metaverse namespace. To configure the account join, certain criteria can be used, such as employee ID or first name and last name combination. The key is to find the most unique combination to avoid problems when two objects with similar names are located—for example, if two users named Tom Jones exist in Active Directory.

7. After completely configuring the MAs and account joins, configure MA run profiles to tell the MA what to perform with the connected directory and connector namespace. For example, perform a full import or export of data. The first time the MA is run, the connected directory information is imported to create the initial connector namespace.

8. After running the MAs once, you can run them a second time to propagate the authoritative metaverse data to the respective connector namespaces and out to the connected directories.

These steps outline the most common use of FIM; these steps can be used to simplify account maintenance tasks when several directories need to be managed simultaneously. When more sophisticated functionality using FIM is needed, such as the automatic creation and deletion of directory entries, extensive scripting and customization of FIM can be done to create a more complete enterprise account provisioning system.

Managing Identity Information Between LDAP Directories and Exchange Server 2010

LDAP directories are commonplace today and can be found in many business environments. UNIX applications in particular make wide use of the LDAP standard for directories. Along with this proliferation of LDAP directory structures comes a need to synchronize the information contained within them to an Exchange Server 2010 environment. The Enterprise version of FIM contains MAs that support synchronization to LDAP directories. Consequently, a good understanding of LDAP concepts is required before syncing between the environments.

Understanding LDAP from a Historical Perspective

To understand LDAP better, it is useful to consider the X.500 and Directory Access Protocol (DAP) from which it is derived. In X.500, the Directory System Agent (DSA) is the database in which directory information is stored. This database is hierarchical in form, designed to provide fast and efficient search and retrieval. The Directory User Agent (DUA) provides functionality that can be implemented in all sorts of user interfaces through dedicated DUA clients, web server gateways, or email applications. The DAP is a protocol used in X.500 directory services for controlling communications between the DUA and DSA agents. The agents represent the user or program and the directory, respectively.

The X.500 directory services are application-layer processes. Directory services can be used to provide global, unified naming services for all elements in a network, translate between network names and addresses, provide descriptions of objects in a directory, and provide unique names for all objects in the directory. These X.500 objects are hierarchical with different levels for each category of information, such as country, state, city, and organization. These objects can be files (as in a file system directory listing), network entities (as in a network naming service such as NDS), or other types of entities.

Lightweight protocols combine routing and transport services in a more streamlined fashion than do traditional network and transport-layer protocols. This makes it possible to transmit more efficiently over high-speed networks—such as Asynchronous Transfer Mode (ATM) or Fiber Distributed Data Interface (FDDI)—and media—such as fiber-optic cable.

Lightweight protocols also use various measures and refinements to streamline and speed up transmissions, such as using a fixed header and trailer size to save the overhead of transmitting a destination address with each packet.

LDAP is a subset of the X.500 protocol. LDAP clients are, therefore, smaller, faster, and easier to implement than X.500 clients. LDAP is vendor-independent and works with, but does not require, X.500. Contrary to X.500, LDAP supports TCP/IP, which is necessary for any type of Internet access. LDAP is an open protocol, and applications are independent of the server platform hosting the directory.

Active Directory is not a pure X.500 directory. Instead, it uses LDAP as the access protocol and supports the X.500 information model without requiring systems to host the entire X.500 overhead. The result is the high level of interoperability required for administering real-world, heterogeneous networks.

Active Directory supports access via LDAP from any LDAP-enabled client. LDAP names are less intuitive than Internet names, but the complexity of LDAP naming is usually hidden within an application. LDAP names use the X.500 naming convention called attributed naming.

An LDAP uniform resource locator (URL) names the server holding Active Directory services and the attributed name of the object—for example:

```
LDAP://Server1.companyabc.com/CN=JDoe,OU=Users,DC=companyabc,DC=com
```

By combining the best of the DNS and X.500 naming standards, LDAP, other key protocols, and a rich set of APIs, Active Directory enables a single point of administration for all resources, including files, peripheral devices, host connections, databases, web access, users, other arbitrary objects, services, and network resources.

Understanding How LDAP Works

LDAP directory service is based on a client/server model. One or more LDAP servers contain the data making up the LDAP directory tree. An LDAP client connects to an LDAP server and asks it a question. The server responds with the answer or with a pointer to where the client can get more information (typically, another LDAP server). No matter which LDAP server a client connects to, it sees the same view of the directory; a name presented to one LDAP server references the same entry it would at another LDAP server. This is an important feature of a global directory service such as LDAP.

Outlining the Differences Between LDAP2 and LDAP3 Implementations

LDAP3 defines a number of improvements that enable a more efficient implementation of the Internet directory user agent access model. These changes include the following:

- ▶ Use of UTF-8 for all text string attributes to support extended character sets

- ▶ Operational attributes that the directory maintains for its own use—for example, to log the date and time when another attribute has been modified

- ▶ Referrals enabling a server to direct a client to another server that might have the data that the client requested

▶ Schema publishing with the directory, enabling a client to discover the object classes and attributes that a server supports

▶ Extended searching operations to enable paging and sorting of results, and client-defined searching and sorting controls

▶ Stronger security through a Simple Authentication and Security Layer (SASL) based authentication mechanism

▶ Extended operations, providing additional features without changing the protocol version

LDAP3 is compatible with LDAP2. An LDAP2 client can connect to an LDAP3 server (this is a requirement of an LDAP3 server). However, an LDAP3 server can choose not to talk to an LDAP2 client if LDAP3 features are critical to its application.

NOTE

LDAP was built on Internet-defined standards and is composed of the following Request for Comments (RFCs):

▶**RFC 2251**—Lightweight Directory Access Protocol (v3)

▶**RFC 2255**—The LDAP URL format

▶**RFC 2256**—A summary of the X.500(96) user schema for use with LDAP3

▶**RFC 2253**—Lightweight Directory Access Protocol (v3): UTF-8 string representation of distinguished names

▶**RFC 2254**—The string representation of LDAP search filters

---

Using Services for UNIX to Integrate UNIX Systems with an Active Directory/Exchange Server 2010 Environment

In many cases, it might be necessary to integrate many of the components of an existing UNIX implementation with the Exchange Server 2010 forest. In these cases, Windows Server 2008 Services for UNIX (SFU) can provide needed interoperability between the UNIX and Windows/Exchange Server environments.

Understanding and Using Windows Server 2008 UNIX Integration Components

Microsoft has a long history of not "playing well" with other technologies. With Windows 2008, Microsoft introduces native support for Windows Server 2008 UNIX Integration, a series of technologies that was previously included in a product line called Windows Services for UNIX (SFU). With Windows Server 2008, each of the components of the old SFU product is included as an integrated service in the Windows Server 2008 OS.

For many years, UNIX and Windows systems were viewed as separate, incompatible environments that were physically, technically, and ideologically different. Over the years, however, organizations found that supporting two completely separate topologies within their environments was inefficient and expensive; a great deal of redundant work was also required to maintain multiple sets of user accounts, passwords, environments, and so on.

Slowly, the means to interoperate between these environments was developed. At first, most of the interoperability tools were written to join UNIX with Windows, as evidenced by Samba, a method for Linux/UNIX platforms to access Windows file shares. Microsoft's tools always seemed a step behind what was available elsewhere. With the release of the new Windows Server 2008 UNIX Integration tools, Microsoft leapfrogs traditional solutions, such as Samba, and becomes a leader for cross-platform integration. Password synchronization, the capability to run UNIX scripts on Windows, joint security credentials, and the like were presented as viable options and can now be considered as part of a migration to or interoperability scenario with Windows Server 2008.

The Development of Windows Server 2008 UNIX Integration Components

Windows Server 2008 UNIX Integration has made large strides in its development since the original attempts Microsoft made into the area. Originally released as a package of products called Services for UNIX (SFU), it received initial skepticism. Since then, the line of technologies has developed into a formidable integration and migration utility that enables for a great deal of inter-environment flexibility. The first versions of the software, 1.x and 2.x, were limited in many ways; however, subsequent updates to the software vastly improved its capabilities and further integrated it with the core operating system.

A watershed development in the development of Services for UNIX was the introduction of the 3.0 version of the software. This version enhanced support for UNIX through the addition or enhancement of nearly all components. Included was the Interix product as well as an extension to the POSIX infrastructure of Windows to support UNIX scripting and applications natively on a Windows Server.

Then, version 3.5 of Services for UNIX was released, which included several functionality improvements over Windows Server for UNIX 3.0. The following components and improvements were made in the 3.5 release:

▶ Greater support for Windows Server Active Directory authentication

▶ Improved utilities for international language support

▶ Threaded application support in Interix (separated into a separate application in Windows Server 2008 named the Subsystem for UNIX Applications)

▶ Support for the Volume Shadow Copy Service of Windows Server 2008

Finally, we come to the Windows Server 2008 version of Services for UNIX, which was broken into several components that became embedded into the operating system. No longer are the components part of a separate "package." Instead, the components have been built into the various server roles on the operating system.

Here is the structure of major improvements for the Windows Server 2008 UNIX Integration:

▶ x64 bit Windows Server OS Support

▶ AD Lookup capabilities through the inclusion of GID and UID fields in the AD Schema

▶ Enhanced UNIX support with multiple versions supported, including the following: Solaris v9, Red Hat Linux v9, IBM AIX version 5L 5.2, and Hewlett Packard HP-UX version 11i

▶ Capability for the Telnet Server component to accept both Windows and UNIX clients

▶ Extended NIS interoperability including allowing a Windows Server 2008 system to act as an NIS master in a mixed environment

▶ Removal of the User Mapping Component and transfer of the functionality directly into the AD Schema

▶ NFS server functionality expanded to Mac OSX and higher clients

▶ Subsystem for UNIX-based Applications (SUA) enables POSIX-compliant UNIX application to be run on Windows Server 2008, including many common UNIX tools and scripts

▶ Easier porting of native UNIX and Linux scripts to the SUA environment

Understanding the UNIX Interoperability Components in Windows Server 2008

Windows Server 2008 UNIX Integration is composed of several key components, each of which provides a specific integration task with different UNIX environments. Any or all of these components can be used as part of Windows Server 2008 UNIX Integration as the installation of the suite and can be customized, depending on an organization's needs. The major components of Windows Server 2008 UNIX Integration are as follows:

▶ Services for NFS (includes Server for NFS and Client for NFS)

▶ Telnet Server (supports Windows and UNIX Clients)

▶ Identity Management for UNIX (includes the server for Network Information Services and Password Synch components)

▶ Subsystem for UNIX-based Applications (SUA)

Each component can be installed as part of a server role. For example, the Services for NFS components are installed as part of the File Services role in Windows Server 2008. Each component is described in more detail in the following sections.

Prerequisites for Windows Server 2008 UNIX Integration

Windows Server 2008 UNIX Services interoperate with various flavors of UNIX but were tested and specifically written for use with the following UNIX versions:

- ▶ Sun Solaris 7.x, 8.x, 9.x or 10
- ▶ Red Hat Linux 8.0 and later
- ▶ Hewlett-Packard HP-UX 11i
- ▶ IBM AIX 5L 5.2
- ▶ Apple Macintosh OS X

> **NOTE**
>
> The Windows Server 2008 UNIX Integration is not limited to these versions of Sun Solaris, Red Hat Linux, HP-UX, IBM AIX and Apple OS X. It actually performs quite well in various other similar versions and implementations of UNIX, Linux, and Mac OS X.

Installing Services for Network File Server (NFS)

The installation of Windows Server 2008 UNIX Integration for Windows Server 2008 is as simple as adding specific server roles to a server using the Add Roles Wizard. The individual components can be installed as part of different roles added to the server. For example, to add the Services for NFS role, simply add the File Services role to a server via the following process:

1. Open Server Manager (Start, All Programs, Administrative Tools, Server Manager).
2. Click on the Roles node in the task pane and then click the Add Roles link.
3. From the Add Roles Wizard welcome screen, click Next to continue.
4. From the list of roles to install, check the box for File Services and click Next to continue.
5. From the Introduction to File Services dialog box, click Next to continue.
6. From the Select Role Services dialog box, as shown in Figure 5.2, keep the File Server box checked and check the box for Services for Network File System. Click Next to continue.
7. From the confirmation dialog box, review the settings and click the Install button.
8. Click Close when the wizard completes.

Services for NFS streamlines the sharing of information between UNIX and Windows Server 2008, enabling users from both environments to seamlessly access data from each separate environment, without the need for specialized client software. Utilizing the Services for NFS and NFS Client enables for this level of functionality and provides for a more integrated environment.

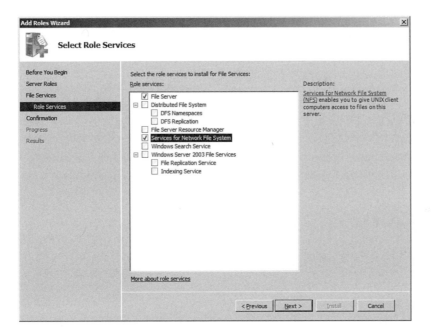

FIGURE 5.2   Installing Services for NFS.

Using and Administering Services for NFS

The Services for NFS component acts as a UNIX-standard NFS server by providing disk space from any Windows-based computer on a network to NFS clients, translating its NFS requests to Windows SMB-based requests. No additional client software is necessary, and the Windows Server 2008 server acts and functions like a normal NFS-based UNIX server for these clients. This is a great way to bring a standardized share format to a heterogeneous network as UNIX and Apple clients might have difficulties using standard Windows file protocols such as CIFS.

After installing Services for UNIX, several tasks need to be performed before accepting UNIX clients to the Windows file shares. These tasks include the following, covered in more detail in the next section of this book:

▶ Configure AD DS Lookup for UNIX GID and UID

▶ Configure the Server for NFS and Client for NFS Components

▶ Create NFS Shared Network Resources

Configure Active Directory Lookup for UNIX GID and UID Information

So that NTFS permissions can be properly mapped to UNIX user accounts, Integration with Active Directory Domain Services (AD DS) must be set up between AD DS and UNIX. This requires the proper schema extensions to be enabled in the Domain. By default,

Windows Server 2008 AD DS includes these schema extensions. If installing Services for NFS into a downlevel schema version of AD, such as with Windows Server 2003, the schema must be extended first to Windows Server 2008 levels.

To enable AD DS Lookup for Services for NFS, do the following:

1. Open the Services for Network File System MMC Console (Start, All Programs, Administrative Tools, Services for Network File System).

2. Right-click the Services for NFS node in the node pane and choose Properties.

3. Check the box to enable Active Directory Identity mapping, and enter the name of the domain where Identity mapping will be enabled in, as shown in Figure 5.3.

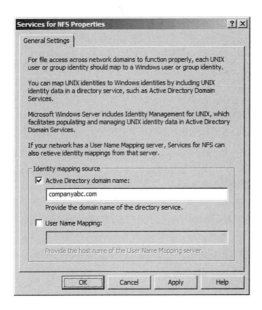

FIGURE 5.3   Enabling AD DS mapping for Services for NFS.

4. Click OK to save the changes.

NOTE

Windows Server 2008 Services for NFS still supports legacy User Name Mapping Service, although installation of the User Name Mapping Service itself cannot be done on a Windows 2008 server. It is preferable to use the AD DS integration, however, rather than the User Name Mapping Service.

Configuring Client for NFS and Server for NFS Settings

After enabling the lookup method used for Services for NFS, you can configure the individual Server for NFS and Client for NFS settings by right-clicking the individual nodes and choosing properties. This enables you to change default file permissions levels, TCP and UDP settings, mount types, and filename support levels. For example, in Figure 5.4, the screen for customizing Client for NFS permissions displays.

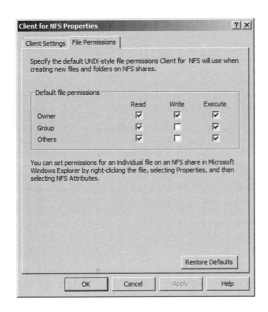

FIGURE 5.4   Customizing Client for NFS settings.

Creating NFS Shared Network Resources

Configuring a Shared Resource with Server for NFS requires opening the command prompt window with elevated privileges (Start, All Programs, Accessories, right-click command prompt, Run as Administrator) and then creating the share using the nfsshare command-line utility. Type nfsshare /? for exact syntax.

To create an NFS Shared Network resource using the GUI interface, perform the following tasks:

1. From Windows Explorer on the server, navigate to the folder that will be shared; right-click it and choose Properties.

2. Select the NFS Sharing tab.

3. Click the button for Manage NFS Sharing.

4. Check the box to Share the folder, as shown in Figure 5.5. Configure if anonymous access will be allowed (not normally recommended) or configure any special permissions by clicking the Permissions button.

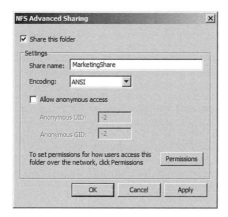

FIGURE 5.5   Creating a shared resource for NFS.

5. Click OK and then Close to save the changes.

Understanding the Identity Management for UNIX Components

The goal of single sign-on, in which users on a network log in once and then have access to multiple resources and environments, is still a long way off. It is common for a regular user to maintain and use three or more separate usernames and associated sets of passwords. Windows Server 2008 UNIX Integration goes a long way toward making SSO a reality, however, with the Identity Management for UNIX Role Service.

Identity Management for UNIX is an additional role service on a Windows Server 2008 machine that includes three major components as follows:

▶ **Server for Network Information Services (SNIS)**—Server for NIS enables a Windows AD DS environment to integrate directly with a UNIX NIS environment by exporting NIS domain maps to AD entries. This enables an AD Domain Controller to act as the master NIS server.

▶ **Password Synchronization**—Installing the Password Synchronization role on a server enables for passwords to be changed once and to have that change propagated to both UNIX and AD DS environments.

▶ **Administrative Tools**—Installing this role service gives administrators to tools necessary to administer the SNIS and Password Synch components.

The Identity Management for UNIX components have some other important prerequisites and limitations that must be taken into account before considering them for use in an environment. These factors include the following:

▶ Server for Network Information Services (SNIS) must be installed on an Active Directory domain controller. In addition, all domain controllers in the domain must be running Server for NIS.

▶ SNIS must not be subservient to a UNIX NIS Server—it can be subservient only to another Windows-based server running Server for NIS. This requirement can be a politically sensitive one and should be broached carefully because some UNIX administrators will be hesitant to make the Windows-based NIS the primary NIS server.

▶ The SNIS Authentication component must be installed on all domain controllers in the domain in which security credentials will be utilized.

Installing Identity Management for UNIX Components

To install one or all of the Identity Management for UNIX components on a Windows Server 2008 domain controller, perform the following steps:

1. Open Server Manager (Start, All Programs, Administrative Tools, Server Manager).

2. Click on the Roles node in the task pane and then click the Add Role Services link in the Active Directory Domain Services section.

3. Check the box next to Identity Management for UNIX, which should automatically check the remaining boxes as well, as shown in Figure 5.6. Click Next to continue.

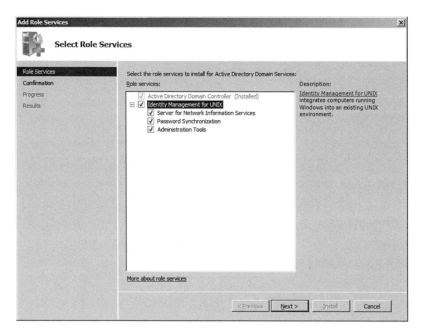

FIGURE 5.6   Installing the Identity Management for UNIX components.

4. Review the installation options and click Install to begin the process.

5. Click Close when complete and choose Yes to restart the server.

6. After restart, the server should continue with the configuration of the server. Let it finish and click Close when the process is complete.

Configuring Password Change Capabilities

To enable password change functionality, a connection to a UNIX server must be enabled. To set up this connection, perform the following steps:

1. Open the MMC Admin Console (Start, All Programs, Microsoft Identity Management for UNIX).

2. From the Node pane, navigate to Password Synchronization, UNIX-Based Computers.

3. Right-click UNIX-Based Computers and choose Add Computer from the drop-down box.

4. Enter a Computer name of the UNIX box, and specify whether to synch passwords to/from UNIX. Enter the port required for password synch and an encryption key that is mutually agreed upon by the UNIX server, similar to what is shown in Figure 5.7. Click OK.

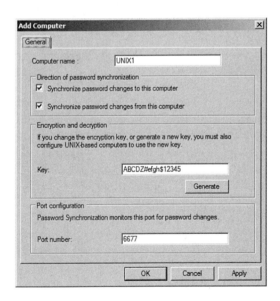

FIGURE 5.7   Configuring password synch to UNIX systems.

5. Click OK to confirm the addition of the UNIX system.

Adding NIS Users to Active Directory

For users who want their existing NIS servers to continue to provide authentication for UNIX and Linux servers, the SNIS component might not be the best choice. Instead, there is a package of Korn shell scripts downloadable from Microsoft.com that simplifies adding existing NIS users to AD. The getusers.ksh script gets a list of all users in an NIS database including the comment field. This script must be run with an account with the permission to run ypcat passwd. The makeusers.ksh script imports these users to Active Directory. The makeusers.ksh script must be run by a user with domain admin privileges. The –e flag enables accounts because by default the accounts are created in a disabled state. This is a perfect solution for migrations that require the existing NIS servers to remain intact indefinitely.

Administrative Improvements with Windows Server 2008

One of the main focuses of Windows Server 2008 UNIX Integration was the ability to gain a better measure of centralized control over multiple environments. Tools such as an enhanced Telnet server and client, ActivePerl 5.6 for scripting, and a centralized MMC Admin console make the administration of the Windows Server 2008 UNIX Integration components easier than ever. Combined with the improved MMC interface in Windows Server 2008, it is easier than ever to manage mixed environments from the Windows platform.

Performing Remote Administration with Telnet Server and Client

Windows Server 2008 UNIX Integration uses a single Telnet service to provide for Telnet functionality to both Windows and UNIX clients. This was a change over the way that it previously was, as two separate components were installed. This version of Windows Server 2008 Telnet server supports NT LAN Manager (NTLM) authentication in addition to basic login that supports UNIX users.

To install the Telnet Server component, perform the following steps:

1. Open Server Manager (Start, All Programs, Administrative Tools, Server Manager).
2. Click the Features node in the task pane and then click the Add Features link.
3. Check the box next to the Telnet server role, as shown in Figure 5.8. Click Next to continue.
4. Review the settings and click Install.
5. When the wizard finishes, click Close.

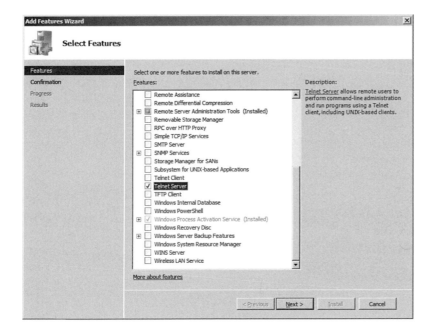

FIGURE 5.8   Installing the Telnet server role for UNIX clients.

Scripting with ActivePerl

With Windows Server 2008 UNIX Integration tools, you can write scripts using the ActivePerl tool, which was fully ported from UNIX Perl. Perl scripts can be used in a Windows environment, and ActivePerl directly supports use of the Windows Scripting Host (WSH), which enables Perl scripts to be executed on WSH server systems.

Summary

Exchange Server 2010 running on Active Directory already goes far toward the goal of maintaining a single directory system for managing enterprise user accounts. The addition of advanced tools such as FIM, Services for NetWare, and Services for UNIX further extends the capabilities of an organization to achieve this goal by providing for single metadirectory functionality. Proper use of these tools can significantly reduce the overhead associated with maintaining separate Exchange Server, UNIX, Novell eDirectory, LDAP, and other directory implementations.

Best Practices

The following are best practices from this chapter:

► Keep an Exchange Server 2003 system in the organization only if the functionality in the legacy GroupWise Connector or Lotus Notes Connector for Exchange is required. These connectors are not supported on an Exchange Server 2010 system.

► Use Forefront Identity Manager (FIM) for synchronization between the Exchange Server 2010 directory service, Active Directory, and non-AD directories, such as Novell eDirectory, LDAP, and UNIX directories.

► Deploy Windows Server 2008 UNIX Integration components to integrate UNIX directories and functionality into an Exchange Server 2010 environment.

► Use account provisioning in FIM to reduce the overhead associated with creating and deleting user accounts.

5

Understanding Network Services and Active Directory Domain Controller Placement for Exchange Server 2010

W ith Microsoft Exchange Server relying on Active Directory and domain name system (DNS) to function, it is important for an organization to make sure that critical networking services are configured and operating properly and that domain controllers have been deployed and configured to adequately support the environment. Exchange Server 2010 has removed its reliance on NetBios and WINS for its networking services and is now very dependent upon the successful operation of Active Directory and DNS. This chapter covers best practices for the design, implementation, and validation that Windows networking services and Active Directory are working properly in an Exchange Server 2010 environment.

Domain Name System and Its Role in Exchange Server 2010

For computer systems to communicate with each other, whether you are talking about a local area network (LAN), a wide area network (WAN), or the Internet, they must have the ability to identify one another using some type of name resolution. Several strategies have been developed over the years, but the most reliable one to date (and the current industry standard) is the use of a DNS.

Accurate name resolution is critical in a mail environment as well. For a message to reach its destination, it might pass through several systems that need to know where it came from and where it is going.

In the past, Microsoft has continued to support the Windows Internet Naming Service, commonly known as WINS, as an alternative way of performing name resolution within an environment. WINS provided a distributed database for registering and querying dynamic mappings of NetBIOS names for computers and groups. WINS mapped these NetBIOS names to IP addresses, and was originally designed to resolve problems that surrounded NetBIOS name resolution in routed networks.

However, in Microsoft Exchange Server 2010, support for WINS/NetBIOS broadcasts has been done away with. This makes the importance of DNS in Exchange Server 2010 greater than ever because if DNS is not configured and working properly, Exchange Server 2010 will not work at all.

Even Lightweight Directory Access Protocol (LDAP) queries for local mailbox users require the DNS client to be properly configured and functioning on your Exchange Server 2010 servers.

This first half of this chapter details how DNS interacts with Exchange Server 2010 and offers troubleshooting techniques and best practices to ensure the system functions properly. The second half of this chapter covers the proper placement and optimized configuration of Active Directory services for the successful operation of Exchange Server 2010.

Domain Name System Defined

The Internet, as well as most home and business networks, relies on Internet Protocol (IP) addresses to allow computers to connect to one another. If we had to remember the IP addresses of every website, server, workstation, and printer that we connect to on a daily basis, it would be very difficult to accomplish anything!

The domain name system, commonly abbreviated as DNS, is a hierarchical, distributed database used to resolve, or translate, domain and host names to IP addresses. Using DNS, users, computers, and applications that query DNS can specify remote systems by fully qualified domain names (FQDNs).

DNS is the primary method for name resolution for the Microsoft Windows Server platforms. DNS is also a requirement for deploying Active Directory (AD), though Active Directory is not a requirement for deploying DNS. That being said, in a Microsoft Windows environment, integrating DNS and Active Directory enables DNS servers to take advantage of the security, performance, and fault-tolerance capabilities designed into Active Directory.

Using DNS

DNS is composed of two components: clients and servers. Servers store information about specific components.

When a DNS client needs to contact a host system, it first attempts to do so by using local resources. The client first checks its local cache, which is created by saving the results of previous queries. Items in the local cache remain until one of three things occurs:

1. The Time-to-Live (TTL) period, which is set on each item, expires.
2. The client runs the `ipconfig /flushdns` command.
3. The DNS client is shut down.

Next, the client attempts to resolve the query using the local HOSTS file, which, on Windows systems, is located in the `%systemroot%\system32\drivers\etc` directory. This file is used to manually map host names to IP addresses, and remains in place even if the system is rebooted.

Finally, if the client is unable to resolve the query locally, it forwards the request to a DNS server for resolution. The DNS server attempts to resolve the client's query as detailed next:

▶ If the query result is found in any of the zones for which the DNS server is authoritative, the server responds to the host with an authoritative answer.

▶ If the result is in the zone entries of the DNS server, the server checks its own local cache for the information.

If the DNS server is unable to resolve the query, it forwards the request to other DNS servers, sending what is known as a recursive query. The server forwards to other servers that are listed as "forwarders," or to a set of servers configured in the DNS server's "Root Hints" file.

The DNS query is forwarded through communications channels on the Internet until it reaches a DNS server that is listed as being authoritative for the zone listed in the query. That DNS server then sends back a reply—either an "affirmative," with the IP address requested, or a "negative" stating that the host in question could not be resolved.

Understanding Who Needs DNS

Not all situations require the use of DNS. There are other name resolution mechanisms that exist besides DNS, some of which come standard with the operating system (OS) that companies deploy. Although not all scenarios have the requirement of a complex name resolution structure, DNS makes life easier by managing name servers in a domain, sometimes with little overhead.

In the past, an organization with a standalone, non-interconnected network could get away with using only host files or WINS to provide NetBIOS-to-IP address name translation. Some very small environments could also use broadcast protocols such as NetBEUI to provide name resolution. In modern networks, however, DNS becomes a necessity, especially in Active Directory environments.

As stated before, WINS is no longer used by Exchange Server with the release of Exchange Server 2010. The proper installation and configuration of DNS is critical to the successful deployment of Exchange Server 2010.

Outlining the Types of DNS Servers

DNS is an integral and necessary part of any Windows Active Directory implementation. In addition, it has evolved to be the primary naming service for UNIX operating systems and the Internet. Because of Microsoft's decision to make Windows 2000 Server, Windows Server 2003, and Windows Server 2008 Internet-compatible, DNS has replaced WINS as the default name resolution technology. Microsoft followed Internet Engineering Task Force (IETF) standards and made its DNS server compatible with other DNS implementations.

Examining UNIX BIND DNS

Many organizations have significant investment in UNIX DNS implementations. Microsoft Exchange Server heavily relies on Active Directory, and Active Directory heavily relies on DNS. Microsoft Active Directory can coexist and use third-party DNS implementations as long as they support active updates and SRV records. In some cases, organizations choose not to migrate away from the already implemented UNIX DNS environment; instead, they coexist with Microsoft DNS. Companies using UNIX DNS for Microsoft AD clients should consider the following:

▶ The UNIX DNS installation should be at least 8.1.2.

▶ For incremental zone transfers, the UNIX DNS implementation should be at least 8.2.1.

Exploring Third-Party (Checkpoint-Meta IP or Lucent Vital QIP) DNS

Third-party DNS implementations can provide significant enhancements in enterprise class IP management. They either provide integrated management of UNIX, Linux, and Microsoft DNS and Dynamic Host Configuration Protocol (DHCP) servers from a central location or can be used in place of the previously mentioned implementations. The most recent versions fully support Dynamic DNS updates, SRV records, and incremental zone transfer, which should be considered a necessity if Active Directory uses the third-party DNS servers.

Examining DNS Compatibility Between DNS Platforms

In theory, DNS clients should be able to query any DNS server. Active Directory, however, has some unique requirements. Clients that authenticate to Active Directory look specifically for server resources, which means that the DNS server has to support SRV records. In Active Directory, DNS clients can dynamically update the DNS server with their IP address using Dynamic DNS. It is important to note that Dynamic DNS is not supported by all DNS implementations.

Examining DNS Components

As previously mentioned, name servers, or DNS servers, are systems that store information about the domain namespace. Name servers can have either the entire domain namespace or just a portion of the namespace. When a name server only has a part of the domain namespace, the portion of the namespace is called a zone.

DNS Zones

There is a subtle difference between zones and domains. All top-level domains, and many domains at the second and lower levels, are broken into zones—smaller, more manageable units by delegation. A zone is the primary delegation mechanism in DNS over which a particular server can resolve requests. Any server that hosts a zone is said to be authoritative for that zone, with the exception of stub zones, defined later in the chapter.

A name server can have authority over more than one zone. Different portions of the DNS namespace can be divided into zones, each of which can be hosted on a DNS server or group of servers.

Forward Lookup Zones

A forward lookup zone is created to do forward lookups on the DNS database, resolving names to IP addresses and resource information.

Reverse Lookup Zones

A reverse lookup zone performs the opposite operation as the forward lookup zone. IP addresses are matched up with a common name in a reverse lookup zone. This is similar to knowing the phone number but not knowing the name associated with it. Reverse lookup zones must be manually created, and do not exist in every implementation. Reverse lookup zones are primarily populated with PTR records, which serve to point the reverse lookup query to the appropriate name.

TIP

It is good practice for the Simple Mail Transfer Protocol (SMTP) mail server to have a record in the reverse lookup zone. Spam control sites check for the existence of this record. It is possible to be placed on a spammer list if the site does not have a PTR record for the MX entry in the DNS reverse lookup zone.

Active Directory–Integrated Zones

A Windows 2003 or Windows 2008 DNS server can store zone information in two distinct formats: Active Directory–integrated or standard text file. An Active Directory–integrated zone is an available option when the DNS server is installed on an Active Directory domain controller. When a DNS zone is installed as an Active Directory zone, the DNS information is automatically updated on other server AD domain controllers with DNS by using Active Directory's multimaster update techniques. Zone information stored in the Active Directory allows DNS zone transfers to be part of the Active Directory replication process secured by Kerberos authentication.

Primary Zones

In traditional (non-Active Directory–integrated) DNS, a single server serves as the master DNS server for a zone, and all changes made to that particular zone are done on that particular server. A single DNS server can host multiple zones, and can be primary for one and secondary for another. If a zone is primary, however, all requested changes for that particular zone must be done on the server that holds the master copy of the zone. As illustrated in Figure 6.1, companyabc.com is set up on DC1 as an Active Directory–integrated primary zone. However, DC1 also holds a secondary zone copy of the amaris.org zone.

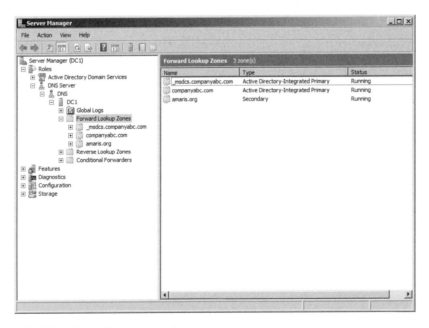

FIGURE 6.1   DNS primary and secondary zones.

Creating a new primary zone manually is a fairly straightforward process. The following procedure outlines the creation of a standard zone for the companyabc.com DNS namespace:

1. Open the Server Manager.
2. Navigate to Roles\DNS Server\DNS\<Servername>\Forward Lookup Zones.

3. Right-click Forward Lookup Zones, and choose New Zone.

4. Click Next on the welcome screen.

5. Select Primary Zone from the list of zone types available. Also, determine if the zone will be stored in Active Directory. If not, uncheck the Store the Zone in Active Directory check box. Click Next to continue.

6. If the zone is Active Directory–integrated, the replication scope needs to be selected. The replication can be to all DNS servers in the forest, all DNS servers in the domain, or just to the domain controllers in the domain for Windows 2000 compatibility.

7. Type the name of the primary zone to be created, and click Next.

8. Determine whether dynamic updates will be allowed in this zone. By default, Allow Only Secure Dynamic Updates is selected. Click Next to continue.

9. Click Finish on the Summary page to create the zone.

Secondary Zones

A secondary zone is established to provide redundancy and load balancing for the primary zone. Secondary zones are not necessary if the zone has been set up as the Active Directory–integrated zone because the zone will be replicated to all domain controllers in the domain. With secondary zones, each copy of the DNS zone database is read-only, however, because all recordkeeping is done on the primary zone copy. A single DNS server can contain several zones that are primary and several that are secondary. The zone creation process is similar to the one outlined in the preceding section on primary zones, but with the difference being that the zone is transferred from an existing primary server.

Stub Zones (Delegated Zones)

A stub zone is a zone that contains no information about the members in a domain but simply serves to forward queries to a list of designated name servers for different domains. A stub zone contains only NS, SOA, and glue records. Glue records are A records that work in conjunction with a particular NS record to resolve the IP address of a particular name server. A server that hosts a stub zone for a namespace is not authoritative for that zone.

A stub zone effectively serves as a placeholder for a zone that is authoritative on another server. It allows a server to forward queries that are made to a specific zone to the list of name servers in that zone.

DNS Queries

The primary function of DNS is to provide name resolution for requesting clients, so the query mechanism is one of the most important elements in the system. Two types of queries are commonly made to a DNS database: recursive and iterative.

Recursive Queries

Recursive queries are most often performed by resolvers, or clients that need to have a specific name resolved by a DNS server. Recursive queries are also accomplished by a DNS server if forwarders are configured to be used on a particular name server. A recursive query asks whether a particular record can be resolved by a particular name server. The response to a recursive query is either negative or positive.

Iterative Queries

Iterative queries ask a DNS server to either resolve the query or make a best-guess referral to a DNS server that might contain more accurate information about where the query can be resolved. Another iterative query is then performed to the referred server and so on until a result, positive or negative, is obtained.

DNS Replication or Zone Transfer

Copying the DNS database from one server to another is accomplished through a process known as a zone transfer. Zone transfers are required for any zone that has more than one name server responsible for the contents of that zone. The mechanism for zone transfer varies, however, depending on the version of DNS and whether the zone is Active Directory–integrated.

Primary-Secondary (Master-Slave) (RW-RO)

The primary name server holds the authoritative copy of the zone. For redundancy and load sharing, a secondary or slave name server should be set up. The DNS name resolution does not care if it is dealing with a primary or secondary server.

The main difference between the primary and secondary server is where the data comes from. Primary servers read it from a text file, and the secondary server loads it from another name server over the network via the zone transfer process. A slave name server is not limited to loading its data from a primary master name server; a slave server can load a zone from another slave server.

A big advantage of using a secondary name server is that only one set of DNS databases needs to be maintained because all secondary name servers are read-only (RO) databases. All updates to the zone file have to be done at the server holding the primary zone file.

AD-Integrated Replication

One of the most significant changes from Windows Server 2000 to Windows Server 2008 is the location where the zone file is stored in Active Directory. Windows Server 2008 Active Directory–integrated zones are stored in the application partition, whereas in Windows 2000 Server, the zones were part of the global catalog (GC). This change in the location of the zone file reduces cross-forest replication traffic because the application partition is unique to each domain.

DNS Resource Records

In the DNS hierarchy, objects are identified through the use of resource records (RRs). These records are used for basic lookups of users and resources within the specified domain and are unique for the domain in which they are located. Because DNS is not a flat namespace, multiple identical RRs can exist at different levels in a DNS hierarchy.

Start of Authority Record

The Start of Authority (SOA) record indicates that this name server is the best source for information within the zone. An SOA record is required for each zone. The server referenced by the SOA record maintains and updates the zone file.

The SOA record also contains other useful information, such as the latest serial number for the zone file, the email address of the responsible person for the zone, and Time to Live (TTL).

Host Records

A host (A) record is the most common form of DNS records; its data is an Internet address in a dotted decimal form (for example, `10.32.1.132`). There should be only one A record for each address of a host.

Name Server Records

Name server (NS) records indicate which servers are available for name resolution for that zone. All DNS servers are listed as NS records within a particular zone. When slave servers are configured for the zone, they will have an NS record as well.

Mail Exchange Record

A mail exchange (MX) specifies a mail forwarder or delivery server for SMTP servers. MX records are the cornerstone of a successful Internet mail routing strategy.

One of the advantages of a DNS over HOSTS files is its support for advanced mail routing. LMHOST files allowed only attempts to deliver mail to the host's IP address. If that failed, they could either defer the delivery of the message and try again later or bounce the message back to the sender. DNS offers a solution to this problem, by allowing the setup of backup mail server records.

Mail server records are also MX records, but with a higher-priority number as the primary MX record for the domain. In Figure 6.2, `microsoft.com` has a single mail server, with the priority of `10`.

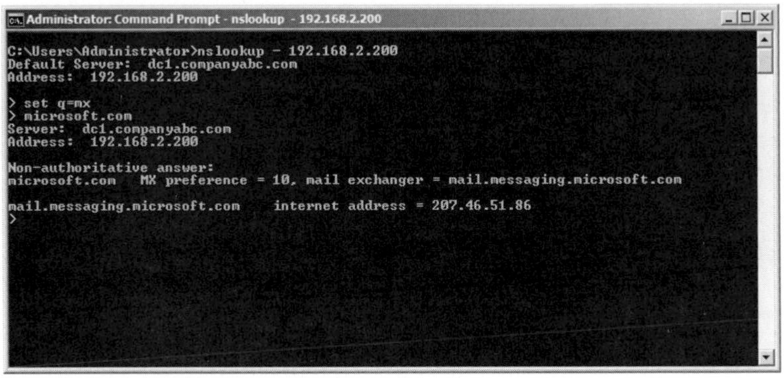

FIGURE 6.2   `Microsoft.com` mail server entry.

The preference value associated with an MX record determines the order in which a mailer uses a record. The preference value of an MX record is important only in relation to the other servers for the same domain. Mail servers attempt to use the MX record with the lower number first; if that server is not available, they try to contact the server with a higher number, and so on.

MX record preferences can also be used for load sharing. When several mail hosts have the same preference number associated with them, a sender can choose which mail server to contact first.

Mail routing based on preference numbers sounds simple enough, but there are major caveats that mail administrators have to understand. When troubleshooting mail routing problems, administrators use the following concepts to pinpoint the problem.

Mail routing algorithms based on preference numbers can create routing loops in some situations. The logic in mail servers helps circumvent this problem:

```
Companyabc.com  IN    MX    10    m1.companyabc.com
Companyabc.com  IN    MX    20    m2.companyabc.com
Companyabc.com  IN    MX    30    m3.companyabc.com
```

Using this example, if a message is sent from a client to Bob@companyabc.com from an email address outside of companyabc.com, the sending mail server looks up the receiving mail server for companyabc.com based on the MX records set up for that domain. If the first mail server with the lowest priority is down (m1.companyabc.com), the mail server attempts to contact the second server (m2.companyabc.com). m2 tries to forward the message to m1.companyabc.com because that server is on the top of the list based on preferences. When m2 notices that m1 is down, it tries to contact the second server on the list, (itself), creating a routing loop. If m2 tries to send the message to m3, m3 tries to contact m1, then m2, and then itself, creating a routing loop. To prevent these loops from happening, mail servers discard certain addresses from the list before they decide where to send a message. A mailer sorts the available mail host based on preference number first, and then checks the canonical name of the domain name on which it's running. If the local host appears as a mail exchange, the mailer discards that MX record and all MX records with the same or higher preference value. In this example, m2 does not try to send mail to m1 and m3 for final delivery.

The second common mistake administrators have to look out for with an MX record is the alias name. Most mailers do not check for alias names; they check for canonical names. Unless an administrator uses canonical names for MX records, there is no guarantee that the mailer will find itself, which could result in a mail loop.

Hosts listed as mail exchangers must have A records listed in the zone so that mailers can find address records for each MX record and attempt mail delivery.

Another common mistake when configuring mail hosts is the configuration of the hosted domain local to the server. Internet service providers (ISPs) and organizations commonly host mail for several domains on the same mail server. As mergers and acquisitions happen, this situation becomes more common. The following MX record illustrates that the mail server for companyabc.com is really the server mail.companyisp.com:

```
companyabc.com IN MX 10 mail.companyisp.com
```

Unless `mail.companyisp.com` is set up to recognize `companyabc.com` as a local domain, it tries to relay the message to itself, creating a routing loop and resulting in the following error message:

```
554 MX list for companyabc.com points back to mail.companyisp.com
```

In this situation, if `mail.companyisp.com` was configured not to relay messages to unknown domains, it would refuse delivery of the mail.

Service (SRV) Record

Service (SRV) records are RRs that indicate which resources perform a particular service. Domain controllers in Active Directory are referenced by SRV records that define specific services, such as the global catalog, LDAP, and Kerberos. SRV records are relatively new additions to DNS and did not exist in the original implementation of the standard. Each SRV record contains information about a particular functionality that a resource provides. For example, an LDAP server can add an SRV record indicating that it can handle LDAP requests for a particular zone. SRV records can be very useful for Active Directory because domain controllers can advertise that they can handle GC requests.

> **NOTE**
>
> Because SRV records are a relatively new addition to DNS, they are not supported by several down-level DNS implementations, such as UNIX BIND 4.1 and NT 4.0 DNS. It is, therefore, critical that the DNS environment that is used for Windows Server 2008 Active Directory has the capability to create SRV records. For UNIX BIND servers, version 8.1.2 or higher is required.

Canonical Name Record

A canonical name (CNAME) record represents a server alias or allows any one of the member servers to be referred to by multiple names in DNS. The record redirects queries made to the A record for the particular host. CNAME records are useful when migrating servers, and for situations in which friendly names, such as mail.companyabc.com, are required to point to more complex, server-naming conventions, such as `sfoexch01.companyabc.com`.

> **CAUTION**
>
> Though DNS entries for MX records can be pointed to canonical (CNAME) host records, doing so is not advised, and is not a Microsoft recommended best practice. Increased administrative overhead and the possibility of misrouted messages can result. Microsoft recommends that mail/DNS administrators always link MX records to fully qualified principal names or domain literals. For further details, see Microsoft Knowledge Base Article #153001 at http://support.microsoft.com/kb/153001/.

Other Records

Other, less common forms of records that might exist in DNS have specific purposes, and there might be cause to create them. The following is a sample list, but it is by no means exhaustive:

▶ **AAAA**—Maps a standard IP address into a 128-bit IPv6 address. This type of record becomes more prevalent as IPv6 is adopted.

▶ **ISDN**—Maps a specific DNS name to an ISDN telephone number.

▶ **KEY**—Stores a public key used for encryption for a particular domain.

▶ **RP**—Specifies the responsible person for a domain.

▶ **WKS**—Designates a particular well-known service.

▶ **MB**—Indicates which host contains a specific mailbox.

Multihomed DNS Servers

For multihomed DNS servers, an administrator can configure the DNS service to selectively enable and bind only to IP addresses that are specified using the DNS console. By default, however, the DNS service binds to all IP interfaces configured for the computer.

This can include the following:

▶ Any additional IP addresses configured for a single network connection.

▶ Individual IP addresses configured for each separate connection where more than one network connection is installed on the server computer.

▶ For multihomed DNS servers, an administrator can restrict DNS service for selected IP addresses. When this feature is used, the DNS service listens for and answers only DNS requests that are sent to the IP addresses specified on the Interface tab in the Server properties.

By default, the DNS service listens on all IP addresses and accepts all client requests sent to its default service port (UDP 53 or TCP 53 for zone transfer requests). Some DNS resolvers require that the source address of a DNS response be the same as the destination address that was used in the query. If these addresses differ, clients could reject the response. To accommodate these resolvers, you can specify the list of allowed interfaces for the DNS server. When a list is set, the DNS service binds sockets only to allowed IP addresses used on the computer.

In addition to providing support for clients that require explicit bindings to be used, specifying interfaces can be useful for other reasons:

▶ If an administrator does not want to use some of the IP addresses or interfaces on a multihomed server computer.

▶ If the server computer is configured to use a large number of IP addresses and the administrator does not want the added expense of binding to all of them.

When configuring additional IP addresses and enabling them for use with the Windows Server 2008 DNS server, consider the following additional system resources that are consumed at the server computer:

▶ DNS server performance overhead increases slightly, which can affect DNS query reception for the server.

▶ Although Windows Server 2008 provides the means to configure multiple IP addresses for use with any of the installed network adapters, there is no performance benefit for doing so.

▶ Even if the DNS server is handling multiple zones registered for Internet use, it is not necessary or required by the Internet registration process to have different IP addresses registered for each zone.

▶ Each additional address might only slightly increase server performance. In instances when a large overall number of IP addresses are enabled for use, server performance can be degraded noticeably.

▶ In general, when adding network adapter hardware to the server computer, assign only a single primary IP address for each network connection.

▶ Whenever possible, remove nonessential IP addresses from existing server TCP/IP configurations.

Using DNS to Route SMTP Mail in Exchange Server 2010

The primary protocol for sending email on the Internet today is known as Simple Mail Transfer Protocol, or SMTP. SMTP has been used for quite some time in UNIX and Linux environments, and has been incorporated into Active Directory as an alternative transport mechanism for site traffic.

Domains that want to participate in electronic mail exchange need to set up MX record(s) for their published zone. This advertises the system that will handle mail for the particular domain, so that SMTP mail will find the way to its destination.

Understanding SMTP Mail Routing

Email is arguably the most widely used TCP/IP and Internet application today. SMTP defines a set of rules for addressing, sending, and receiving mail between systems. As a result of a user mail request, the SMTP sender establishes a two-way connection with the SMTP receiver. The SMTP receiver can be either the ultimate destination or an intermediate (mail gateway). The SMTP sender generates commands that are replied to by the receiver. All this communication takes place over TCP port 25. When the connection is established, a series of commands and replies are exchanged between the client and server. This connection is similar to a phone conversation, and the commands and responses are equivalent to verbal communication.

NOTE

In various implementations, there is a possibility of exchanging mail between the TCP/IP SMTP mailing system and the locally used mailing systems. These applications are called mail gateways or mail bridges. Sending mail through a mail gateway may alter the end-to-end delivery specification because SMTP guarantees delivery only to the mail gateway host, not to the real destination host, which is located beyond the TCP/IP network. When a mail gateway is used, the SMTP end-to-end transmission is host-to-gateway, gateway-to-host, or gateway-to-gateway; the behavior beyond the gateway is not defined by SMTP.

Examining Client DNS Use for Exchange Server

Before users can access their mailboxes on an Exchange server, they must be authenticated. Authentication requires a DNS lookup to locate a domain controller on which the users' accounts can be authenticated.

Clients normally cannot deliver messages directly to destination mail hosts. They typically use a mail server to relay messages to destinations. Using SMTP, clients connect to a mail server, which first verifies that the client is allowed to relay through this server, and then accepts the message destined for other domains.

A client uses DNS to resolve the name of a mail server. For example, when configuring an Outlook mail client to connect to an Exchange server, only the short name and not the FQDN is used to connect to the server. The short name is resolved by DNS to the FQDN of the Exchange server to which the client is connected.

Understanding DNS Requirements for Exchange Server 2010

In Active Directory, all client logons and lookups are directed to local domain controllers and GC servers through references to the SRV records in DNS. Each configuration has its DNS and resource requirements. Exchange Server relies on other servers for client authentication and uses DNS to find those servers. In an Active Directory domain controller configuration, on the other hand, the Exchange server also participates in the authentication process for Active Directory.

Using DNS in Exchange Server 2010

As has been stated, Active Directory and DNS access are vital to an Exchange Server implementation. It is critical that the host records for all Exchange Server 2010 servers be properly registered and configured in the domain name system (DNS) server for the Active Directory forest. Clients, as well as other servers, will use DNS to locate and communicate with Exchange Server 2010 servers.

Any computer acting in one of the Exchange Server 2010 organizational server roles must be domain members and registered in DNS. The five server roles are as follows:

- ▶ Edge Transport
- ▶ Hub Transport
- ▶ Mailbox
- ▶ Client Access
- ▶ Unified Messaging

All server roles, with the exception of the Edge Transport, can be deployed on a single server. Although there are five roles listed, only the Hub Transport, Client Access, and Mailbox server roles are required for a minimal Exchange Server 2010 installation.

Configuring Edge Transport Server DNS Settings

For the Edge Transport server(s), which reside in the perimeter network, to communicate with the Hub Transport servers in your Exchange Server environment, they must be able to locate each other using host name resolution. This is accomplished by creating host records in a forward lookup zone on the internal DNS server that each server is configured to query, or by editing the local Hosts file for each server.

Before installing the Edge Transport server role, you have to configure a DNS suffix for the server name. After you have installed the Edge Transport server role, the server name cannot be changed.

To complete this task, you must log on to the Edge Transport server as a user who is a member of the local Administrators group.

To use Windows Control Panel to configure the DNS suffix, complete the following steps:

1. Open Windows Control Panel.
2. Double-click on System to open the System Properties dialog box.
3. Click the Computer Name tab.
4. Click Change.
5. On the Computer Name Changes page, click More.
6. In the Primary DNS Suffix of This Computer field, type a DNS domain name and suffix for the Edge Transport server.

DNS and SMTP RFC Standards

In 1984, the first DNS architecture was designed. The result was released as RFC 882 and 883. These were superseded by RFC 1034 (Domain Names—concepts and facilities) and 1035 (Domain Names—implementation and specification), the current specifications of the DNS. RFCs 1034 and 1035 have been improved by many other RFCs, which describe fixes for potential DNS security problems, implementation problems, best practices, and performance improvements to the current standard.

RFC 2821 defines the SMTP, which replaced the earlier versions of RFC 821 and 822.

Interoperability with Older Versions of Exchange Server

Exchange Server 2010 can be deployed in an existing Exchange Server 2003 or Exchange
Server 2007 organization, as long as the organization is operating in Native mode. This
interoperability is supported; however, there are many differences between the older
systems and the newer, especially in how the servers are administered and how server-to-
server communication occurs.

Understanding Mixed Exchange Server Environments

For Exchange Server 2010 to communicate properly with Exchange Server 2003, the
routing group connectors between the Exchange Server 2010 Hub Transport servers and
the older bridgehead servers must be configured correctly. When you install an Exchange
Server 2010 server into an existing organization, the server is recognized by the Exchange
Server 2003 organization. However, because server-to-server communications differ greatly,
you must configure routing group connectors to let the different versions communicate
and transfer messages. This is because of the fact that Exchange Server 2003 used SMTP as
the primary communication protocol between Exchange servers, but in Exchange Server
2010, the server roles use remote procedure calls (RPCs) for server-to-server communication and allow the Hub Transport server to manage the transport of SMTP traffic.

Exchange Server 2010 communicates directly from the Exchange Server 2010 Hub
Transport role to the Exchange Server 2007 Hub Transport role. However, the Exchange
2007 servers must be at Exchange 2007 Service Pack 2. Similarly, the Exchange Server 2010
Hub Transport role can interoperate with the Exchange Server 2007 Edge Transport role.

Routing in Exchange Server 2010

Although Exchange Server 2003 uses routing groups to define the Exchange Server routing
topology, Exchange Server 2010 uses Active Directory sites to do so, so an Exchange-
specific routing configuration is no longer needed in a pure Exchange Server 2010 organization or in a mixed Exchange Server 2007/2010 organization.

For the two routing topologies to coexist, all Exchange Server 2010 servers are automatically added to a routing group when the server is installed. This Exchange Server 2010
routing group is recognized in the Exchange System Manager for Exchange Server 2003 as
an Exchange Routing Group within Exchange Administrative Group.

For Exchange Server 2010 to coexist with Exchange 2000 Server or Exchange Server 2003,
you need to perform the following task:

> ▶ A two-way routing group connector must be created from the Exchange Server
> routing group to each Exchange Server 2003 routing group that Exchange Server
> 2010 will communicate with directly.

NOTE

The first routing group connector is created during installation of the first Hub Transport
server when installed in an existing Exchange Server organization.

These connectors allow mail to be routed from Exchange Server 2003 to Exchange Server 2010.

SMTP Mail Security, Virus Checking, and Proxies

Spamming and security issues are daily concerns for email administrators. As the Internet grows, so too does the amount of spam that mail servers have to confront. Unwanted messages not only can take up a lot of space on mail servers, but can also carry dangerous payloads or viruses. Administrators have to maintain a multilayered defense against spam and viruses.

There are several security areas that have to be addressed:

▶ Gateway security to control access to the mail server delivering messages to/from the Internet.

▶ Mail database security where messages are stored.

▶ Client mail security where messages are opened and processed.

Gateway security is a primary concern for administrators because a misconfigured gateway can become a gateway used by spammers to relay messages. Unauthenticated message relay is the mechanism spammers rely on to deliver their messages. When a server is used for unauthenticated message relay, it not only puts a huge load on server resources, but also might get the server placed on a spam list. Companies relying on spam lists to control their incoming mail traffic refuse mail delivered from servers listed in the database; therefore, controlling who can relay messages through the mail relay gateway is a major concern.

Application-level firewalls such as Microsoft Internet Security and Acceleration (ISA) Server 2006 allow mail proxying on behalf of the internal mail server. Essentially, mail hosts trying to connect to the local mail server have to talk to the proxy gateway, which is responsible for relaying those messages to the internal server. Going one step further, these proxy gateways can also perform additional functions to check the message they are relaying to the internal host or to control the payload passed along to the internal server.

This configuration is also helpful in stopping dangerous viruses from being spread through email. For example, dangerous scripts could potentially be attached to email, which could execute as soon as the user opens the mail. A safe configuration allows only permitted attachment types to pass through. Even those attachments have to pass virus checking before they are passed to an internal mail server.

The following process describes how one server contacts another server to send email messages that include virus checking:

1. The sender contacts its SMTP gateway for message delivery.

2. The SMTP gateway looks up the MX record for the recipient domain and establishes communication with it. The application proxy acting as the SMTP server for the recipient's domain receives the message. Before the recipient gateway establishes communication with the sender gateway, it can check whether the sender SMTP gateway is

listed on any known spam lists. If the server is not located on any spam lists, communication can resume and the message can be accepted by the proxy server.

3. The application proxy forwards the message for virus checking.

4. After virus checking, the mail is routed back to the application proxy.

5. Mail is delivered to the internal SMTP gateway.

6. The recipient picks up the mail message.

> **NOTE**
>
> Application proxy and virus or spam checking might be done within the same host. In that case, steps 2–5 are done in one step without having to transfer a message to a separate host.

Third-party products can be used for virus checking not only at the gateway level, but also directly on an Exchange Server email database. Database-level scans can be scheduled to run at night when the load is lower on the server; real-time scans can perform virus checking in real time before any message is written to the database.

The final checkpoint for any multilayered virus protection is on the workstation. The file system and the email system can be protected by the same antivirus product. Messages can be scanned before a user is able to open the message or before a message is sent.

Protecting email communications and message integrity puts a large load on administrators. Threats are best dealt with using a multilayered approach from the client to the server to the gateway. When each step along the way is protected against malicious attacks, the global result is a secure, well-balanced email system.

The Edge Transport Servers Role in Antivirus and Antispam Protection

In Exchange Server 2010, the introduction of the Edge Transport server role was brought about by the increased need to protect organizations from unwanted message traffic. The Edge Transport server is designed to provide improved antivirus and antispam protection for the Exchange Server environment. This server role also applies policies to messages in transport between organizations. The Edge Transport server role is deployed outside the Active Directory forest in the perimeter network and can be deployed as a smarthost and SMTP relay server for an existing Exchange Server 2010 organization.

Actually, you can add an Edge Transport server to any existing Exchange Server environment without making any other organizational changes or upgrading the internal Exchange servers. There are no preparation steps needed in Active Directory to install the Edge Transport server. If you are currently using the antispam capabilities of the Intelligent Message Filter in Exchange Server 2010, you can still use the Edge Transport server as an additional layer of antispam protection.

SMTP Server Scalability and Load Balancing

In a larger environment, administrators might set up more than one SMTP server for inbound and/or outbound mail processing. Windows Server 2008 and Exchange Server 2010 provide a very flexible platform to scale and balance the load of SMTP mail services. DNS and Network Load Balancing (NLB) are key components for these tasks.

Administrators should not forget about hardware failover and scalability. Multinetwork interface cards are highly recommended. Two network cards can be teamed together for higher throughput, can be used in failover configuration, or can be load-balanced by using one network card for front-end communication and another for back-end services, such as backup.

Network design can also incorporate fault tolerance by creating redundant network routes and by using technologies that can group devices together for the purpose of load balancing and delivery failover. Load balancing is the process where requests can be spread across multiple devices to keep individual service load at an acceptable level.

Using NLB, Exchange Server SMTP processes can be handed off to a group of servers for processing, or incoming traffic can be handled by a group of servers before it gets routed to an Exchange server. The following example outlines a possible configuration for using NLB in conjunction with Exchange Server.

DNS, in this example, has been set up to point to the name of the NLB cluster IP address. Externally, the DNS MX record points to a single mail relay gateway for companyabc.com. Exchange server uses smarthost configuration to send all SMTP messages to the NLB cluster. The NLB cluster is configured in balanced mode where the servers share equal load. Only port 25 traffic is allowed on the cluster servers. This configuration would off-load SMTP mail processing from the Exchange servers because all they have to do is to pass the message along to the cluster for delivery. They do not need to contact any outside SMTP gateway to transfer the message. This configuration allows scalability because when the load increases, administrators can add more SMTP gateways to the cluster. This setup also addresses load balancing because the NLB cluster is smart enough to notice whether one of the cluster nodes has failed or is down for maintenance. An additional ramification of this configuration is that message tracking will not work beyond the Exchange servers.

> **NOTE**
>
> Administrators should not forget about the ramifications of antivirus and spam checking software with NLB. These packages in Gateway mode can also be used as the SMTP gateway for an organization. In an NLB clustered mode, an organization would need to purchase three sets of licenses to cover each NLB node.

A less used but possible configuration for SMTP mail load balancing uses DNS to distribute the load between multiple SMTP servers. This configuration, known as DNS round-robin, does not provide as robust a message-routing environment as the NLB solution.

Configuring DNS to Support Exchange Servers

Because DNS is already required and integrated with Active Directory before Exchange
Server is installed, most companies already have a robust DNS environment in place.
Exchange Server by itself accesses DNS servers to find resources on the local network, such
as global catalog servers and domain controllers. It also uses DNS to search for MX records
of other domains.

External DNS Servers for the Internet

The external DNS server for Exchange Server (or any other mail system) is responsible for
giving out the correct MX and A records for the domain for which it is authoritative.
Administrators should take security precautions regarding who can change these
records—and how. Intentionally or accidentally changing these records can result in
undelivered mail.

Most companies let their ISP host the external DNS entries for their domain. ISPs provide
internal administrators with methods of managing DNS entries for their domain. In some
cases, it has to be done over the phone, but normally a secure web interface is provided
for management. Although this setup is convenient and ISPs usually take care of load
balancing and redundancy, some companies opt to host their own zone records for the
Internet. In this case, companies have to host their own DNS server in-house with the ISP
responsible only for forwarding all requests to their DNS server. When hosting an external
DNS server, in-house administrators have to think about security issues and DNS configuration issues.

Internal DNS Servers for Outbound Mail Routing

Exchange SMTP gateways are responsible for delivering mail to external hosts. As with any
name process involving resolving names to IP addresses, DNS plays a major part in
successful mail delivery.

Exchange Server can route mail to outbound destinations two ways. One is by using
smarthosts to offload all processing of messages destined to other domains. As seen in the
previous section, an NLB cluster can be used to route Internet mail to its final destination.

The second way is the default, with Exchange Server 2010 taking care of delivering
messages to other domains. In this scenario, Exchange Server queries DNS servers for other
domains' MX records and A records for address resolution.

Troubleshooting DNS Problems

Troubleshooting is part of everyday life for administrators. DNS is no exception to this
rule. Therefore, understanding how to use the following tools to troubleshoot DNS not
only helps avoid mistakes when configuring DNS-related services, but also provides
administrators with a useful toolbox to resolve issues.

Using Event Viewer to Troubleshoot

The first place to look for help when something is not working, or appears to not be working, is the system logs. With Windows Server 2008, the DNS logs are conveniently located directly in the DNS MMC console. Parsing this set of logs can help the administrator troubleshoot DNS replication issues, query problems, and other issues.

For more advanced event log diagnosis, administrators can turn on Debug Logging on a per-server basis. Debugging should be turned on only for troubleshooting because log files can fill up fast. To enable Debug Logging, follow these steps:

1. Open the Server Manager. Expand the Roles, DNS Server, and then DNS.
2. Right-click on the server name, and choose Properties.
3. Select the Debug Logging tab.
4. Check the Log Packets for Debugging check box.
5. Configure any additional settings as required, and click OK.

Turn off these settings after the troubleshooting is complete.

Troubleshooting Using the `ipconfig` Utility

The `ipconfig` utility is used not only for basic TCP/IP troubleshooting, but can also be used to directly resolve DNS issues. These functions can be invoked from the command prompt with the correct flag, detailed as follows:

▶ **ipconfig /displaydns**—This command displays all locally cached DNS entries. This is also known as the DNS resolver cache.

▶ **ipconfig /flushdns**—This switch can be used to save administrators from a lot of headaches when troubleshooting DNS problems. This command flushes the local DNS cache. The default cache time for positive replies is 1 day; for negative replies, it is 15 minutes.

▶ **ipconfig /registerdns**—This flag informs the client to automatically reregister itself in DNS, if the particular zone supports dynamic zone updates.

> **NOTE**
>
> Client-side DNS caching is configurable in the Registry via the following key:
>
>   \\HKLM\System\CurrentControlSet\Services\Dnscache\Parameters
>
>   MaxCacheEntryTtlLimit = 1 (default = 86400)
>
>   NegativeCacheTime = 0 (default = 300)
>
> These DWORD values need to be created. The first entry overwrites the TTL number in the cached address to 1 second, essentially disabling the local cache. The second entry changes the negative cache from 15 minutes to 0, essentially disabling the negative cache facility.

Monitoring Exchange Server Using Performance Monitor

Performance Monitor is a built-in, often-overlooked utility that enables a great deal of insight into issues in a network. Many critical DNS counters can be monitored relating to queries, zone transfers, memory use, and other important factors.

Using `nslookup` for DNS Exchange Server Lookup

In both Windows and UNIX environments, `nslookup` is a command-line administrative tool for testing and troubleshooting DNS servers. Simple query structure can provide powerful results for troubleshooting. A simple query contacts the default DNS server for the system and looks up the inputted name.

To test a lookup for www.companyabc.com, type

```
nslookup www.companyabc.com
```

at the command prompt. `nslookup` can also be used to look up other DNS resource types—for example, an MX or SOA record for a company. To look up an MX record for a company type, use the following steps, as illustrated in Figure 6.3:

1. Open a command prompt instance.
2. Type `nslookup` and press Enter.
3. Type `set query=mx` (or simply `set q=mx`), and press Enter.
4. Type `microsoft.com` and press Enter.

An MX record output not only shows all the MX records that are used for that domain, their preference number, and the IP address they are associated with, but it also shows the name server for the domain.

By default, `nslookup` queries the local DNS server the system is set up to query. Another powerful feature of `nslookup` is that it can switch between servers to query. This feature enables administrators to verify that all servers answer with the same record as expected. For example, if an organization is moving from one ISP to another, it might use this technique because the IP addresses for its servers might change during the move. The DNS

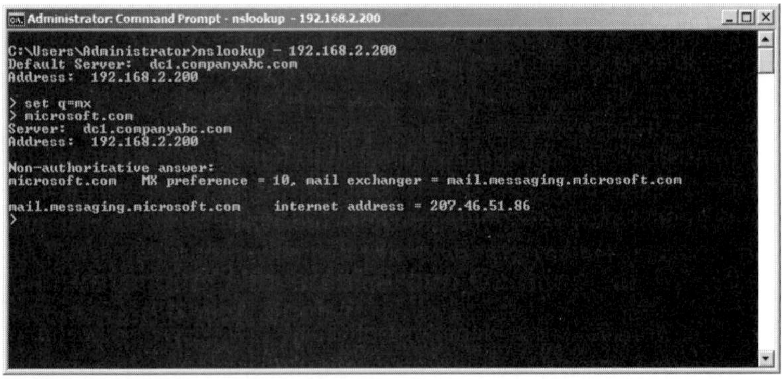

FIGURE 6.3   `nslookup` MX query.

change takes an administrator only a few minutes to do, but replication of the changes through the Internet might take 24 to 72 hours. During this time, some servers might still use the old IP address for the mail server. To verify that the DNS records are replicated to other DNS servers, an administrator can query several DNS servers for the answer through the following technique:

1. Open a command prompt instance.

2. Type `nslookup` and press Enter.

3. Type `server <server IP address>` for the DNS server you want to query.

4. Type `set query=mx` (or simply `set q=mx`), and press Enter.

5. Type `microsoft.com` and press Enter.

Repeat from step 3 for other DNS servers.

`nslookup` can also help find out the version of BIND used on a remote UNIX DNS server. An administrator might find it useful to determine which version of BIND each server is running for troubleshooting purposes. To determine this, the following steps must be performed:

1. From the command line, type `nslookup`, and then press Enter.

2. Type `server <server IP address>` for the IP address of the DNS server queried.

3. Type `set class=chaos` and then press Enter.

4. Type `set type=txt` and then press Enter.

5. Type `version.bind` and then press Enter.

If the administrator of the BIND DNS server has configured the server to accept this query, the BIND version that the server is running is returned. As previously mentioned, the BIND version must be 8.1.2 or later to support SRV records.

Troubleshooting with DNSLINT

`DNSLINT` is a Microsoft Windows utility that helps administrators diagnose common DNS name resolution issues. The utility is not installed by default on Windows servers and has to be downloaded from Microsoft. Microsoft Knowledge Base Article #321046 found at http://support.microsoft.com/kb/321046 contains the link to download this utility.

When this command-line utility runs, it generates a Hypertext Markup Language (HTML) file in the directory it runs from. It can help administrators with Active Directory troubleshooting and also with mail-related name resolution and verification. Running `DNSLINT /d <domain_name> /c` tests DNS information as known on authoritative DNS servers for the domain being tested; it also checks SMTP, Post Office Protocol version 3 (POP3), and Internet Message Access Protocol (IMAP) connectivity on the server. For the complete options for this utility, run `DNSLINT /?`.

Using `dnscmd` for Advanced DNS Troubleshooting

The `dnscmd` utility is essentially a command-line version of the MMC DNS console. Installed as part of the Windows Server 2003 support tools or installed natively with Windows Server 2008, this utility enables administrators to create zones, modify zone records, and perform other vital administrative functions. To install the support tools, run the support tools setup from the Windows Server 2003 CD (located in the `\support\tools` directory). You can view the full functionality of this utility by typing `DNSCMD /?` at the command line.

Global Catalog and Domain Controller Placement

When deploying Exchange Server 2010 in your environment, Active Directory is a critical component. Exchange Server 2010 uses the Active Directory directory service to store and share directory information with Microsoft Windows.

If you have already deployed Active Directory into your environment, it is important that you have a solid understanding of your existing implementation and how Exchange Server will fit into your structure. If you have not deployed AD, you need to design the environment with your Exchange Server environment in mind.

In addition, you need to evaluate your organization's administrative model, as the marriage of Exchange Server 2010 and AD allows you to administer Exchange Server along with the operating system.

When integrating Exchange Server 2010 and Active Directory, the placement domain controllers and global catalog servers is paramount; without proper placement of these key items, your Exchange Server environment will not be able to perform optimally.

The remainder of this chapter discusses these items and offers troubleshooting techniques for directory access problems. In addition, best-practice recommendations are offered for the placement of domain controllers and global catalog servers.

Understanding Active Directory Structure

Active Directory (AD) is a standards-based LDAP directory service developed by Microsoft that stores information about network resources and makes it accessible to users and applications, such as Exchange Server 2010. Directory services are vital in any network infrastructure because they provide a way to name, locate, manage, and secure information about the resources contained.

The Active Directory directory service provides single-logon capability and a central repository for the information for your entire organization. User and computer management are greatly simplified and network resources are easier than ever to access.

In addition, Active Directory is heavily utilized by Exchange Server, and stores all of your Exchange Server attributes: email addresses, mailbox locations, home servers, and a variety of other information.

Exploring AD Domains

An Active Directory domain is the main logical boundary of Active Directory. In a stand-alone sense, an AD domain looks very much like a Windows NT domain. Users and computers are all stored and managed from within the boundaries of the domain.

However, several major changes have been made to the structure of the domain and how it relates to other domains within the Active Directory structure.

Domains in Active Directory serve as a security boundary for objects and contain their own security policies. For example, different domains can contain different password policies for users. Keep in mind that domains are a logical organization of objects and can easily span multiple physical locations. Consequently, it is no longer necessary to set up multiple domains for different remote offices or sites because replication concerns can be addressed with the proper use of Active Directory sites, which are described in greater detail later in this chapter.

Exploring AD Trees

An Active Directory tree is composed of multiple domains connected by two-way transitive trusts. Each domain in an Active Directory tree shares a common schema and global catalog. The transitive trust relationship between domains is automatic, which is a change from the domain structure of NT 4.0, wherein all trusts had to be manually set up. The transitive trust relationship means that because the asia domain trusts the root companyabc domain, and the europe domain trusts the companyabc domain, the asia domain also trusts the europe domain. The trusts flow through the domain structure.

Exploring AD Forests

Forests are a group of interconnected domain trees. Implicit trusts connect the roots of each tree into a common forest.

The overlying characteristics that tie together all domains and domain trees into a common forest are the existence of a common schema and a common global catalog. However, domains and domain trees in a forest do not need to share a common namespace. For example, the domains microsoft.com and msnbc.com could theoretically be part of the same forest, but maintain their own separate namespaces (for obvious reasons).

> **NOTE**
>
> Each separate instance of Exchange Server 2010 requires a completely separate AD forest. In other words, AD cannot support more than one Exchange Server organization in a single forest. This is an important factor to bear in mind when examining AD integration concepts.

Understanding AD Replication with Exchange Server 2010

An understanding of the relationship between Exchange Server and Active Directory is not complete without an understanding of the replication engine within AD itself. This is especially true because any changes made to the structure of Exchange Server must be replicated across the AD infrastructure.

Active Directory replaced the concept of Primary Domain Controllers (PDCs) and Backup Domain Controllers (BDCs) with the concept of multiple domain controllers that each contains a master read/write copy of domain information. Changes that are made on any

domain controller within the environment are replicated to all other domain controllers
in what is known as multimaster replication.

Active Directory differs from most directory service implementations in that the replication of directory information is accomplished independently from the actual logical directory design. The concept of Active Directory sites is completely independent from the
logical structure of Active Directory forests, trees, and domains. In fact, a single site in
Active Directory can actually host domain controllers from different domains or different
trees within the same forest. This enables the creation of a replication topology based on
your WAN structure, and your directory topology can mirror your organizational structure.

From an Exchange Server point of view, the most important concept to keep in mind is
the delay that replication causes between when a change is made in Exchange Server and
when that change is replicated throughout the entire AD structure. The reason for these
types of discrepancies lies in the fact that not all AD changes are replicated immediately.
This concept is known as replication latency. Because the overhead required in immediately replicating change information to all domain controllers is large, the default schedule for replication is not as often as you might want. To immediately replicate changes
made to Exchange Server or any AD changes, use the following procedure:

1. Open Server Manager and expand Roles, Active Directory Domain Services, and then
   Active Directory Sites and Services.

2. Drill down to Sites, sitename, Servers, servername, NTDS Settings. The server name
   chosen should be the server you are connected to, and from which the desired
   change should be replicated.

3. Right-click each connection object and choose Replicate Now, as illustrated in
   Figure 6.4.

Examining the Role of Domain Controllers in AD

Even before the existence of Active Directory, Exchange Server has relied on domain
controllers to authenticate user accounts. With the advent of Active Directory, this has not
changed. Exchange Server still relies on domain controllers to provide all authentication
services. To provide optimal logon authentication response times, the proper placement of
domain controllers is crucial.

Examining Domain Controller Authentication in Active Directory

To understand how Exchange Server manages security, an analysis of Active Directory
authentication is required. This information aids in troubleshooting the environment, as
well as in gaining a better understanding of Exchange Server 2010 as a whole.

Each object in Exchange Server, including all mailboxes, can have security directly applied
for the purposes of limiting and controlling access to those resources. For example, a
particular administrator might be granted access to control a certain set of Exchange
servers, and users can be granted access to mailboxes. What makes Exchange Server particularly useful is that security rights can be assigned not only at the object level, but also at

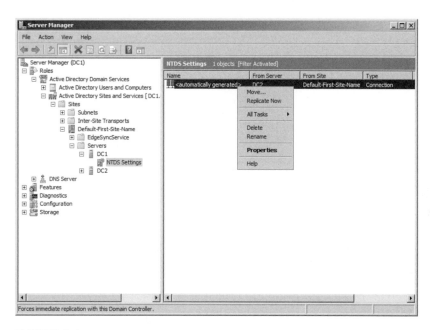

FIGURE 6.4   Forcing AD replication.

the attribute level. This enables granular administration, by allowing tasks such as a Telecom group being able to modify only the phone number field of a user, for example.

When a user logs on to a domain, the domain controller performs a lookup to ensure a match between the username and password. If a match is made, the client is then authenticated and given the rights to gain access to resources.

Because the domain controllers provide users with the permission to access the resources, it is important to provide local access to domain controllers for all Exchange servers. If a local domain controller became unavailable, for example, users would be unable to authenticate to their mailboxes in Exchange Server, effectively locking them out.

Determining Domain Controller Placement with Exchange Server 2010

Because Exchange Server relies on the security authentication performed by Active Directory domain controllers, the placement of these domain controllers becomes critical to the overall performance of your messaging environment. If a domain controller cannot be reached in a reasonable amount of time, access to messages and network resources is delayed.

At a minimum, at least one Active Directory domain controller must be within close proximity to any Exchange server to ensure speedy authentication for local users and mailboxes. Additional Active Directory domain controllers can be implemented to provide increased performance in heavily utilized sites or to provide redundancy in the event of a domain controller failure.

For organizations with a high concentration of Exchange server and clients, a significant demand for directory services can negatively impact all aspects of network performance. The presence of other applications and services that require authentication, directory services, or directory replication can cause your Exchange Server performance to suffer. A current best practice to avoid these pitfalls is to create a dedicated Active Directory site, with dedicated domain controllers and global catalog servers. By segmenting a Service Delivery Location (SDL) into multiple Active Directory sites, you can separate the directory traffic generated by Exchange servers and Microsoft Outlook clients from other directory service traffic.

> **NOTE**
>
> When reading the preceding information, you might be tempted to place the domain controller role directly on the Exchange Server 2010 server to ensure fast authentication. However, this configuration rarely has the desired effect because both roles are resource intensive and can slow down the performance of both the Active Directory and Exchange Server services. Placement of the Active Directory and Exchange Server roles on different servers in close proximity and with a fast network connection will give the greatest performance.

In addition, you can deploy more than one Active Directory domain controller in close proximity to users for user authentication. This enables the distribution of domain controller tasks and builds redundancy into the design. Because each Microsoft Windows Server 2008 domain controller is a multimaster, in the event of a failure of one domain controller, others are able to continue to function and allow uninterrupted authentication.

Defining the Global Catalog

The global catalog is an index of the Active Directory database that stores a full replica of all objects in the directory for its host domain, and a partial replica of all objects contained in the directory of every domain in the forest. In other words, a global catalog contains a replica of every object in Active Directory, but with a limited number of each object's attributes.

Global catalog servers, often referred to as GCs, are Active Directory domain controllers that house a copy of the global catalog. A global catalog server performs two key roles:

▶ Provides universal group membership information to a domain controller when a logon process is initiated.

▶ Enables finding directory information regardless of which domain in the forest contains the data.

Access to a global catalog server is necessary for a user to authenticate to the domain. If a global catalog is not available when a user initiates a network logon process, the user is only able to log on to the local computer, and cannot access network resources.

With such an important role to play, it is a common practice to locate at least one global catalog server in each physical location, as it is referenced often by clients and by applications such as Exchange Server.

Understanding the Relationship Between Exchange Server 2010 and the AD Global Catalog

In the past, an Exchange server could continue to operate by itself with few dependencies on other system components. Because all components of the mail system were locally confined to the same server, downtime was an all-or-nothing prospect. The segregation of the directory into Active Directory has changed the playing field somewhat. In many cases, down-level clients no longer operate independently in the event of a global catalog server failure. Keep this in mind, especially when designing and deploying a domain controller and global catalog infrastructure.

> **NOTE**
>
> Because Outlook clients and Exchange Server can behave erratically if the global catalog they have been using goes down, it is important to scrutinize which systems receive a copy of the global catalog. In other words, it is not wise to set up a GC/DC on a workstation or substandard hardware, simply to offload some work from the production domain controllers. If that server fails, the effect on the clients is the same as if their Exchange server failed.

Understanding Global Catalog Structure

The global catalog is an oft-misunderstood concept with Active Directory. In addition, design mistakes with global catalog placement can potentially cripple a network, so a full understanding of what the global catalog is and how it works is warranted.

As mentioned earlier, Active Directory was developed as a standards-based LDAP implementation, and the AD structure acts as an X.500 tree. Queries against the Active Directory must, therefore, have some method of traversing the directory tree to find objects. This means that queries that are sent to a domain controller in a subdomain need to be referred to other domain controllers in other domains in the forest. In large forests, this can significantly increase the time it takes to perform queries.

In Active Directory, the global catalog serves as a mechanism for improving query response time. The global catalog contains a partial set of all objects (users, computers, and other AD objects) in the entire AD forest. The most commonly searched attributes are stored and replicated in the global catalog (that is, first name, username, and email address). By storing a read-only copy of objects from other domains locally, full tree searches across the entire forest are accomplished significantly faster. So, in a large forest, a server that holds a copy of the global catalog contains information replicated from all domains in the forest.

Using Best Practices for Global Catalog Placement

All users accessing Exchange Server resources should have fast access to a global catalog server. At least one global catalog server must be installed on each domain that contains an Exchange server; however, to achieve the best performance in larger organizations, additional global catalog servers should definitely be considered.

As a starting point, per site, there should be a 4:1 ratio of Exchange Server processor cores to global catalog server 32-bit processor cores. So, if you have four Exchange servers, each with four processors, you should have four processors running your global catalog servers. For global catalog servers with 64-bit processor cores, the ratio is 8:1 ratio of Exchange Server processor cores to global catalog server 64-bit processor cores. Of course, Exchange Server 2010 processor cores are always 64-bit.

Bear in mind, however, that increased global catalog server usage, very large Active Directory implementations, or the use of extremely large distribution lists might necessitate more global catalog servers.

NOTE

With respect to the global catalog processor ratio rule, the 4:1 processor ratio rule from prior versions of Exchange Server, which assumes a result of one global catalog server being deployed for every two mailbox servers, applies to any environment where the database file (the .dit file) for Active Directory is larger than 1GB, and, therefore, cannot fit into memory. Exchange Server 2010 is undergoing a variety of performance tests, and more prescriptive guidance is expected in the RTM version of Exchange Server 2010.

Promoting a Domain Controller to a Global Catalog

Although any domain controller can easily be promoted to a global catalog server, the promotion can have a significant impact on network operations and performance while the topology is updated and the copy of the catalog is passed to the server.

During the promotion, the server immediately notifies DNS if it's new status. In the early days of Active Directory, this often caused problems, as the Exchange servers would immediately begin utilizing the global catalog server before it had finished building the catalog. This problem was rectified in Exchange 2000, Service Pack 2, with the addition of a mechanism that detects the readiness of a global catalog server and prevents Exchange Server from querying new servers until a full copy of the catalog has been received.

The procedure to promote a domain controller to a global catalog server is as follows:

1. On the domain controller, open Server Manager and expand Roles, Active Directory Domain Services, and then click Active Directory Sites and Service.

2. In the console tree, double-click Sites, double-click the name of the site, and then double-click Servers.

3. Double-click the target domain controller.

4. In the details pane, right-click NTDS Settings, and then click Properties.

5. On the General tab, click to select the Global Catalog check box, as shown in Figure 6.5.

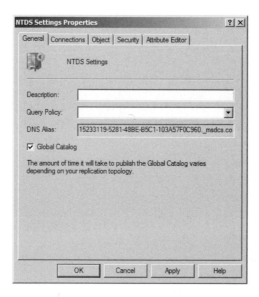

FIGURE 6.5   Making a domain controller a Global Catalog server.

6. Click OK to finalize the operation.

In older versions of the Windows Server operating system, it was necessary to restart the domain controller after a promotion to a global catalog; however, as of Windows Server 2003, this step is no longer necessary.

Verifying Global Catalog Creation

When a domain controller receives the orders to become a global catalog server, there is a period of time when the GC information replicates to that domain controller. Depending on the size of the global catalog, this could take a significant period of time. To determine when a domain controller has received the full subset of information, use the replmon (replication monitor) utility from the Windows Server 2003 support tools. The replmon utility indicates which portions of the AD database are replicated to different domain controllers in a forest and how recently they have been updated.

NOTE

Unfortunately, the replmon tool did not survive the transition from Windows Server 2003 to Windows Server 2008. It is not included in the tools shipped with Windows Server 2008. However, the Windows Server 2003 Support Tools can be installed on a Windows Server 2008 domain controller to gain access to the tool. The compatibility warning can be safely ignored.

Replmon enables an administrator to determine the replication status of each domain-naming context in the forest. Because a global catalog server should have a copy of each domain-naming context in the forest, determine the replication status of the new GC with replmon. For example, the fully replicated global catalog server in Figure 6.6 contains the default naming contexts, such as Schema, Configuration, and DnsZones, in addition to domain-naming contexts for all domains. In this example, the companyabc.com domain has been replicated successfully to the DC2 domain controller.

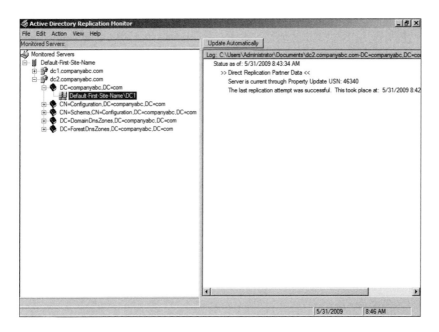

FIGURE 6.6   Replmon GC creation verification.

Global Catalog and Outlook in Exchange Server 2010

In Exchange Server 2003 and Exchange Server 2007, Outlook clients would make direct calls to global catalog servers. This made them susceptible to failure or demotion of domain controllers with global catalogs. In many cases, the failure of a global catalog server would require the restart of all Outlook clients that were using it for lookups.

In Exchange Server 2010, the Outlook client access to the directory has been changed. Outlook clients communicate with the RPC Client Access Service on a CAS. This service proxies the global catalog lookups for the Outlook clients rather than having them query the global catalog directly. This reduces the direct dependency of Outlook clients on the global catalog, allowing for better scalability and faster recovery if a global catalog failure occurs.

Deploying Domain Controllers Using the Install from Media Option

When deploying a remote site infrastructure to support Exchange Server 2010, take care to examine best-practice deployment techniques for domain controllers to optimize the procedure. In the past, deploying domain controller and/or global catalog servers to remote sites was a rather strenuous affair. Because each new domain controller would need to replicate a local copy of the Active Directory for itself, careful consideration into replication bandwidth was taken into account. In many cases, this required one of these options:

▶ The domain controller was set up remotely at the start of a weekend or other period of low bandwidth.

▶ The domain controller hardware was physically set up in the home office of an organization and then shipped to the remote location.

This procedure was unwieldy and time-consuming with Windows 2000 Active Directory. Fortunately, Windows Server 2003 and Windows Server 2008 addressed this issue through use of the Install from Media option for Active Directory domain controllers.

The concept behind the media-based GC/DC replication is straightforward. A current, running domain controller backs up the directory through a normal backup process. The backup files are then copied to a backup media, such as a CD or tape, and shipped to the remote GC destination. Upon arrival, the dcpromo command can be run with the /adv switch (dcpromo /adv), which activates the advanced options including to install from media, as illustrated in Figure 6.7.

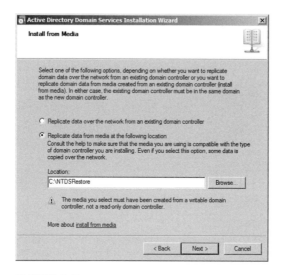

FIGURE 6.7   Install from media option.

After the dcpromo command restores the directory information from the backup, an incremental update of the changes made since the media was created is performed. Because of
this, you still need network connectivity throughout the dcpromo process, although the
amount of replication required is significantly less. Because some dcpromo operations in
very large organizations have been known to take days and even weeks, this concept can
dramatically help deploy remote domain controllers.

> **NOTE**
>
> If the copy of the global catalog that has been backed up is older than the tombstone
> date for objects in the Active Directory (which by default is 60 days), this type of
> dcpromo will fail. This built-in safety mechanism prevents the introduction of lingering
> objects and also assures that the information is relatively up to date and no significant
> incremental replication is required.

Understanding Universal Group Caching for AD Sites

Windows Server 2008 Active Directory enables the creation of AD sites that cache universal group membership. Any time a user uses a universal group, the membership of that
group is cached on the local domain controller and is used when the next request comes
for that group's membership. This also lessens the replication traffic that would occur if a
global catalog was placed in remote sites.

One of the main sources of replication traffic is group membership queries. In Windows
2000 Server Active Directory, every time clients logged on, their universal group membership was queried, requiring a global catalog to be contacted. This significantly increased
logon and query time for clients who did not have local global catalog servers.
Consequently, many organizations had stipulated that every site, no matter the size, have
a local global catalog server to ensure quick authentication and directory lookups. The
downside of this was that replication across the directory was increased because every site
would receive a copy of every item in the entire AD, even though only a small portion of
those items would be referenced by an average site.

Universal group caching solved this problem because only those groups that are commonly
referenced by a site are stored locally, and requests for group replication are limited to the
items in the cache. This helps limit replication and keep domain logons speedy.

Universal group caching capability is established on a per-site basis, through the following technique:

1. On the domain controller, open Server Manager and expand Roles, Active Directory
   Domain Services, and then click Active Directory Sites and Service.
2. Navigate to Sites, sitename.
3. Right-click NTDS Site Settings, and choose Properties.
4. Check the Enable Universal Group Membership Caching check box, as shown in
   Figure 6.8.
5. Click OK to save the changes.

FIGURE 6.8   Universal group caching.

NOTE

Universal group (UG) caching is useful for minimizing remote-site replication traffic and optimizing user logons. Universal group caching does not replace the need for local global catalog servers in sites with Exchange servers, however, because it does not replace the use of the GC port (3268), which is required by Exchange Server. UG caching can still be used in remote sites without Exchange servers that use the site consolidation strategies of Exchange Server previously mentioned.

Exploring DSAccess, DSProxy, and the Categorizer

The relationship that Exchange Server 2010 has with Active Directory is complex and often misunderstood. Because the directory is no longer local, special services were written for Exchange Server to access and process information in AD. Understanding how these systems work is critical for understanding how Exchange Server interacts with AD.

Understanding DSAccess

DSAccess is one of the most critical services for Exchange Server 2010. DSAccess, via the `dsacccess.dll` file, is used to discover current Active Directory topology and direct Exchange Server to various AD components. DSAccess dynamically produces a list of published AD domain controllers and global catalog servers and directs Exchange Server resources to the appropriate AD resources.

In addition to simple referrals from Exchange Server to AD, DSAccess intelligently detects global catalog and domain controller failures, and directs Exchange Server to failover

systems dynamically, reducing the potential for downtime caused by a failed global
catalog server. DSAccess also caches LDAP queries made from Exchange Server to AD,
speeding up query response time in the process.

On start of the Exchange Server 2010 services, the DSAccess queries Active Directory and
determines which domain controllers and global catalogs are available. It also chooses one
as the Configuration Domain Controller. A 2081 event in the Application event log is
generated. DSAccess then polls the Active Directory every 15 minutes to identify changes
to site structure, domain controller placement, or other structural changes to Active
Directory. A 2080 event in the Application event log is generated each time. By making
effective use of LDAP searches and global catalog port queries, domain controller and
global catalog server suitability is determined. Through this mechanism, a single point of
contact for the Active Directory is chosen and maintained, which is known as the configuration domain controller.

Determining the DSAccess Roles

DSAccess lists identified domain controllers on the Exchange server properties page and
identifies servers belonging to either of two groups, as shown in Figure 6.9:

▶ **Domain Controller Servers Being Used by Exchange**—Domain controllers that
have been identified by DSAccess to be fully operational are shown here.

▶ **Global Catalog Servers Being Used by Exchange**—Global catalog servers are
shown here.

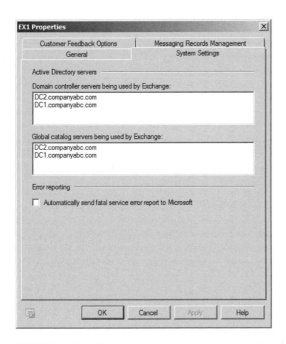

FIGURE 6.9 Viewing domain controllers and global catalog servers used by Exchange Server.

A third role, known as the configuration domain controller, was visible on the properties page in Exchange Server 2003; however, it is not in the same location in
Exchange Server 2010:

▶ **Configuration domain controller**—A single AD domain controller is chosen as
the configuration domain controller to reduce the problems associated with replication latency among AD domain controllers. In other words, if multiple domain controllers were chosen to act as the configuration domain controller, changes Exchange
Server makes to the directory could conflict with each other. The configuration
domain controller role is transferred to other local domain controllers in a site every
eight hours.

To determine the default configuration domain controller, view the Event Viewer application log and search for Event ID 2081. The results of the dsaccess query are listed here as
well, as shown in Figure 6.10.

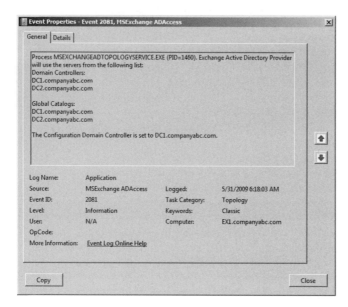

FIGURE 6.10   Identifying the default configuration domain controller.

In addition, the default configuration domain controller can be changed to one of your
choice by performing the following steps:

1. In the Exchange Management Console, select Server Configuration.

2. In the action pane on the right side, click Modify Configuration Domain Controller.

3. Select the Specify a Domain Controller radio button. You can then click Browse in
the Domain section to select the appropriate domain. Then, you can then click

Browse in the Configuration domain controller section, shown in Figure 6.11, to manually select the configuration domain controller.

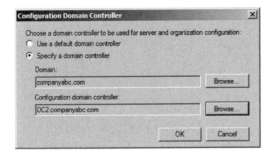

FIGURE 6.11   Manually setting the configuration domain controller.

Understanding DSProxy

DSProxy is a component of Exchange Server that parses Active Directory and creates an address book for down-level Outlook (pre–Outlook 2000 SR2) clients. These clients assume that Exchange Server uses its own directory, as opposed to directly using the Active Directory by itself, as Outlook 2000 SR2 and greater clients do. The DSProxy service provides these higher-level clients with a referral to CAS server for directory lookups. This enables Exchange Server 2010 clients to obtain all their directory information from the Exchange Server 2010 CAS server role and eliminates the need for them to contact an Active Directory global catalog server directly.

NOTE

DSProxy uses Name Service Provider Interface (NSPI) instead of LDAP for address list lookups, because NSPI is a more efficient interface for that type of lookup. Only global catalog servers support NSPI, so they are necessary for all client address list lookups.

Outlining the Role of the Categorizer

The SMTP Categorizer is a component of Exchange Server that is used to submit mail messages to their proper destination. When a mail message is sent, the Categorizer queries the DSAccess component to locate an Active Directory server list, which is then directly queried for information that can be used to deliver the message.

Although the Categorizer in Exchange Server gets a list of all global catalog servers from DSAccess, it normally opens only a single LDAP connection to a GC server to send mail, unless a large number of messages are queued for delivery.

> **TIP**
>
> Problems with the Categorizer are often the cause of DNS or AD lookup issues. When troubleshooting mail-flow problems, use message tracking in Exchange Server 2010 to follow the course of a message. If the message stops at the Categorizer, it is often wise to start troubleshooting the issue from a directory access perspective.

Understanding AD Functionality Modes and Their Relationship to Exchange Server Groups

The most recent versions of Exchange Server, as well as Active Directory, were designed to break through the constraints that had limited previous Exchange Server implementations. However, realistically, it was understood that the products would have to maintain a certain level of compatibility with previous NT domains and Exchange Server 5.5 organizations. After all, not all companies have the resources to completely replace their entire network and messaging infrastructure at once. This requirement stipulated the creation of several functional modes for AD and Exchange Server that allow backward compatibility, while necessarily limiting some of the enhanced functionality—at least for the duration of the migration/upgrade process. Several of the limitations of the AD functional modes in particular impact Exchange Server 2010, specifically Active Directory group functionality. Consequently, a firm grasp of these concepts is warranted.

Understanding Windows Group Types

Groups in Windows Server 2008 come in two flavors: security and distribution. In addition, groups can be organized into different scopes: machine local, domain local, global, and universal. It might seem complex, but the concept, once defined, is simple.

Defining Security Groups

The type of group that most administrators are most familiar with is the security group. A security group is primarily used to apply permissions to resources, enabling multiple users to be administered more easily. For example, users in the Sales department can be added as members to the Sales Department security group, which would then be given permission to specific resources in the environment. When a new member is added to the Sales department, instead of modifying every resource that the department relies on, you can simply add the new member to the security group and the appropriate permissions would be inherited by the new user. This concept should be familiar to anyone who has administered down-level Windows networks, such as NT or Windows 2000.

Defining Distribution Groups

The concept of distribution groups as it exists in Windows Server 2008 was first introduced in Windows 2000 with the deployment of Active Directory. Essentially, a distribution group is a group whose members are able to receive mail messages that are sent to the group. Any application that has the capability of using Active Directory for address book lookups can use this functionality in Windows Server 2008.

> **NOTE**
>
> Distribution groups can be used to create email distribution lists that cannot be used to apply security. However, if separation of security and email functionality is not required, you can make security groups mail-enabled instead of using distribution groups.

Outlining Mail-Enabled Security Groups in Exchange Server 2010

With the introduction of Exchange Server into an Active Directory environment came a new concept: mail-enabled groups. These groups are essentially security groups that are referenced by an email address, and can be used to send SMTP messages to the members of the group. This type of functionality becomes possible only with the inclusion of Exchange 2000 or greater, and Exchange Server actually extends the forest schema to enable Exchange Server-related information, such as SMTP addresses, to be associated with each group.

Most organizations will find that the use of mail-enabled security groups will satisfy the majority of their group requirements. For example, a single group called Marketing, which contains all users in that department, could also be mail-enabled to allow users in Exchange Server to send emails to everyone in the department.

Explaining Group Scope

Groups in Active Directory work the way that previous group structures, particularly in Windows NT, have worked, but with a few modifications to their design. As mentioned earlier, group scope in Active Directory is divided into several groups:

▶ **Machine local groups**—Machine local groups, also known as local groups, previously existed in Windows NT 4.0 and can theoretically contain members from any trusted location. Users and groups in the local domain, as well as in other trusted domains and forests, can be included in this type of group. However, local groups allow resources only on the machine they are located on to be accessed, which greatly reduces their usability.

▶ **Domain local groups**—Domain local groups are essentially the same as local groups in Windows NT, and are used to administer resources located only on their own domain. They can contain users and groups from any other trusted domain and are typically used to grant access to resources for groups in different domains.

▶ **Global groups**—Global groups are on the opposite side of domain local groups. They can contain only users in the domain in which they exist, but are used to grant access to resources in other trusted domains. These types of groups are best used to supply security membership to user accounts who share a similar function, such as the sales global group.

▶ **Universal groups**—Universal groups can contain users and groups from any domain in the forest, and can grant access to any resource in the forest. With this added power comes a few caveats: First, universal groups are available only in Windows 2000, 2003, or 2008 AD Native mode domains. Second, all members of each universal group are stored in the global catalog, increasing the replication load. Universal group membership replication has been noticeably streamlined and optimized in Windows Server 2008, however, because the membership of each group is incrementally replicated.

Universal groups are particularly important for Exchange Server environments. For example, when migrating from Exchange Server 5.5 to later versions of Exchange Server, the Exchange Server 5.5 distribution lists were converted into universal groups for the proper application of public folder and calendaring permissions. An AD domain that contains accounts that have security access to Exchange Server 5.5 mailboxes must be in AD Native mode before performing the migration. This is because the universal groups are made as Universal Security groups, which are only available in AD Native mode.

Functional Levels in Windows Server 2008 Active Directory

Active Directory was designed to be backward-compatible. This helps to maintain backward compatibility with Windows NT domain controllers. Four separate functional levels exist at the domain level in Windows Server 2003 and Windows Server 2008, and three separate functional levels exist at the forest level:

▶ **Windows 2000 Native**—Installed into a Windows 2000 Active Directory that is running in Windows 2000 Native mode, Windows Server 2003 runs itself at a Windows 2000/2003 functional level. Only Windows 2000 and Windows Server 2003 domain controllers can exist in this environment.

▶ **Windows Server 2003**—Functionality on this level opens the environment to features such as schema deactivation, domain rename, domain controller rename, and cross-forest trusts. To get to this level, first all domain controllers must be updated to Windows Server 2003 or Windows Server 2008. Only after this can the domains, and then the forest, be updated to Windows Server 2003 functionality.

▶ **Windows Server 2008**—The most functional of all the various levels, Windows Server 2008 functionality is the eventual goal of all Windows Server 2008 Active Directory implementations. Functionality on this level opens the environment to features such as DFS replication of SYSVOL, Advanced Encryption Standard (AES) support for Kerberos, last interactive logon information, and finer-grained password policies. To get to this level, first all domain controllers must be updated to Windows Server 2008. Only after this can the domains, and then the forest, be updated to Windows Server 2008 functionality.

NOTE

Beginning with Exchange Server 2003 Service Pack 1, Microsoft extended the ability to perform domain rename on an Active Directory forest that was previously extended for Exchange Server. Before SP1, it was not possible to rename an AD domain within a forest that contained Exchange Server.

As previously mentioned, it is preferable to convert AD domains into at least Windows
2000 Native mode, or Windows Server 2003 Functional mode before migrating Exchange
5.5 servers that use those domains. The universal group capabilities that these modes
provide for make this necessary. And if possible, upgrade all domain controllers to Windows
Server 2008 and raise the functional level to Windows Server 2008 Functional mode.

To change domain and forest functional levels in Active Directory to the highest level for
Windows Server 2008, follow these steps:

1. Open Active Directory Domains and Trusts from Administrative Tools.

2. In the left scope pane, right-click your domain name, and select Raise Domain
   Functional Level.

3. Click on the Available Domain Functional Level option, select Windows Server 2008,
   and then choose Raise.

4. At the warning screen, click OK, and then click OK again to complete the task.

5. Repeat the steps for all domains in the forest.

6. Perform the same steps on the forest root, except this time click Raise Forest
   Functional Level, and follow the prompts.

After the domains and the forest have been upgraded, the Functional mode will indicate
Windows Server 2008, as shown in Figure 6.12.

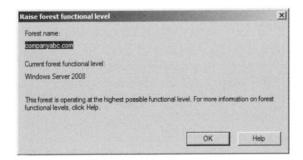

FIGURE 6.12 Windows Server 2008 forest functional level.

Summary

Exchange Server 2010 is a complicated, but extremely powerful, messaging tool. With the
scalability and performance enhancements comes an increased degree of interdependence
with other system components, most notably the DNS and the global catalog. Access to
the global catalog and AD domain controllers is critical and cannot be overlooked. A good
Exchange Server deployment plan takes these factors into account.

Best Practices

The following are best practices from this chapter:

- ▶ Use Microsoft Windows 2003/2008 DNS for client AD name resolution whenever possible. If not possible, ensure that the UNIX BIND version is 8.1.2 or higher to support SRV records.

- ▶ Administrators should set up redundant name resolution servers in the event that one server fails.

- ▶ Use caching-only DNS servers to help leverage load and minimize zone transfer traffic across WAN links.

- ▶ Make any DNS implementations compliant with the standard DNS character set so that zone transfers are supported to and from non-Unicode-compliant DNS implementations, such as UNIX BIND servers. This includes a–z, A–Z, 0–9, and the hyphen (-) character.

- ▶ Set up multiple MX records for all mail servers for redundancy. ISPs usually function as a secondary mail relay gateway for the hosted domain.

- ▶ It is wise to segregate inbound and outbound SMTP traffic from direct exposure to the Internet by deploying an SMTP smarthost in the demilitarized zone (DMZ) of the firewall.

- ▶ Deploy at least one domain controller in each physical location with more than 10 users.

- ▶ When possible, create a dedicated Active Directory site for Exchange Server, with dedicated domain controllers and global catalog servers.

- ▶ Promote or demote global catalog servers and domain controllers during off-hours.

- ▶ Use Exchange Server 2010 site consolidation concepts to reduce the total number of deployed Exchange servers and global catalog servers.

- ▶ Place at least one GC in close network proximity to any major service (such as Exchange Server 2010) that requires use of the global catalog (3268) port.

- ▶ Deploy enough global catalog processor cores to support the deployed Exchange Server 2010 processor cores. Consider deploying 64-bit global catalog processor cores to increase the ratio.

- ▶ Ensure that the AD domain is in Windows Server 2008 Functional mode before migrating to Exchange Server 2010.

- ▶ Do not use substandard hardware for global catalog servers, as a simple hardware failure can affect Outlook clients.

- ▶ Consider the use of universal group caching for domain controllers in sites without local Exchange servers.

CHAPTER 7

Installing Exchange Server 2010

Installing an Exchange Server is like taking a hike through the woods. If you have a map and can accurately follow the directions, you can quickly and safely arrive at your destination. If you get lost in the process (or try to "wing it") you may or may NOT reach your destination, but even if you do, it is likely that you will take a lot longer and travel over more challenging roads.

To those who have worked with Exchange Server 2007 in the past, the Exchange Server 2010 Installation Wizard will seem very familiar. The Wizard walks the administrator through the installation of several of the prerequisites and allows for the selection of specific server roles for deployment. However, the installation wizard does *not* cover all twists and turns. There are steps that must be taken to prepare the Active Directory environment and steps that must be taken to prepare the underlying operating system on the server you are installing on.

This chapter will focus on the installation process for a new Microsoft Exchange Server 2010 server in a typical configuration. In addition, this chapter assumes that the supporting infrastructure and server operating system do not exist and includes step-by-step instructions on how to install Windows Server 2008, Active Directory, supporting configuration settings, and the Exchange Server 2010 prerequisites from scratch.

Understanding the Exchange Server 2010 Server Roles

As with Exchange Server 2007, Exchange Server 2010 has various roles that can be installed on the server to perform specific functions. There are five major server roles, most of which are modular and can reside on a single server (for small environments) or be distributed to multiple servers throughout an organization.

The roles are as follows:

▶ Edge Transport server role

▶ Client Access server role

▶ Hub Transport server role

▶ Mailbox server role

▶ Unified Messaging server role

Edge Transport Server Role—Establishing Perimeter Security

The Edge Transport server role provides antivirus and antispam message protection for the Exchange Server infrastructure. Edge Transport servers act as message hygiene gateways and are designed to reside in a perimeter network or demilitarized zone (DMZ). This allows them to block harmful traffic *before* it reaches the corporate network.

Edge Transport servers are often utilized as the SMTP gateway for sending and receiving mail to and from the Internet.

For more information on the Edge Transport server role and details on how to install and configure the role, review Chapter 8, "Implementing Edge Services for an Exchange Server 2010 Environment."

Client Access Server Role—Providing User Connectivity

As its name suggests, a client access server is responsible for providing connectivity between the user community and their data. Like the front-end servers found in Exchange Server 2003, client access servers manage connectivity via Outlook Web Access and ActiveSync, and like the client access servers in Exchange Server 2007, they also manage connectivity from POP and IMAP users.

In Exchange Server 2010, however, the client access servers also manage MAPI (such as Outlook) client connectivity. In a pure Exchange Server 2010 environment, clients never have to connect directly to their mailbox servers—all connectivity is to the client access server.

By taking responsibility for managing these additional connections, client access servers allow Mailbox servers to focus on their primary role—processing messaging requests.

For more information on the Client Access server role and details on how to install and configure the role, review Chapter 17, "Implementing Client Access and Hub Transport Servers."

Hub Transport Servers—Routing the Mail

The Hub Transport server role is responsible for moving mail between Exchange Mailbox servers, similar to how bridgehead servers worked in the past. This role can be configured on a dedicated server or it can be deployed on an existing mailbox server.

A Hub Transport server must be deployed in each Active Directory site that contains an Exchange Server 2010 Mailbox server, as all message routing in other sites goes through one or more Hub Transport servers.

Even if the sender and recipient are on the same Mailbox server, the message will route through a local Hub Transport server. This ensures that all messages are subject to any transport rules that may be configured for the environment.

For more information on the Hub Transport server role and details on how to install and configure the role, review Chapter 17.

Unified Messaging Servers—Combining All the Data

The Unified Messaging server role was introduced with Exchange Server 2007. It acts as a gateway for combining email, voice, and fax data into a single mailbox. All this data can be accessed via the mailbox or a telephone.

For more information on the Unified Messaging server and detailed steps on installing and configuring the role, refer to Chapter 24, "Designing and Configuring Unified Messaging in Exchange Server 2010."

Mailbox Servers—What It's All About

The Mailbox server role is the core role within Exchange Server 2010. Without mailbox servers to store the user data, all of the other server roles would be without purpose.

The Mailbox servers host mailboxes and mail enabled objects such as contacts and distribution lists.

Understanding the Prerequisites for Exchange Server 2010

Before installing Exchange Server 2010, the administrator should become familiar with the prerequisites for each of the server roles. This section covers the prerequisites for the implementation of Exchange Server 2010 in a Windows networking environment.

Active Directory Infrastructure

Exchange Server 2010 relies on an Active Directory infrastructure to do its job. AD Sites and Services, DNS, Global Catalog Servers, Domain Controllers—all must be in place and configured properly for Exchange Server to function well.

The importance of each of these services, and the steps to deploy them, will be explained in greater detail later in the chapter.

Windows Server 2008—64-Bit All the Way

From inception through Exchange Server 2003, Exchange Server was always a 32-bit application. While this technology was able to handle the needs of organizations in the past, organizations today have more demanding messaging requirements.

In a world with ever-increasing message traffic, the need for highly available systems that allow access from multiple client technologies, through the Internet, and through continuous synchronization with wireless devices resulted in the desire for increased productivity through increased performance.

To address these growing needs, Microsoft released a 64-bit version of their Exchange Server 2007 server for production environments. While they still produced a 32-bit version of the product, it was intended primarily for non-production environments.

With Exchange Server 2010, 32-bit support has gone away, and the product is only being released in a 64-bit version.

By utilizing 64-bit architecture, Exchange Server has significantly enhanced processor and memory utilization. This ensures higher performance gains, the ability to handle an ever-increasing volume of messages, the capability of supporting more users per server, and more simultaneously connected mail clients. This last item is critical as more and more organizations take advantage of the capabilities of Outlook Web App (OWA) and ActiveSync.

The Exchange Server 2010 application can only be installed on a 64-bit edition of the Windows Server 2008 Service Pack 2 (or later) operating system. Either the standard or enterprise edition of Windows Server can be utilized; however, if you plan on taking advantage of some of the more advanced features of Exchange Server 2010 (such as database availability groups and mailbox database copies) you must use the Enterprise edition.

NOTE

The Exchange Server 2010 management tools can be installed on a 64-bit edition of the Windows Server 2008 Service Pack 2 (or later) operating system, or on the Windows Vista Service Pack 2 (or later) operating system.

Microsoft .NET Framework 3.5

The Microsoft .NET Framework is a Microsoft Windows component that allows the ability to build, deploy, and run Web Services and other applications. The .NET framework is a key offering from Microsoft, and most new applications created for the Windows platform rely on it in one way or another.

.Net Framework 3.5 builds on the features added in previous releases and includes service packs for both .NET Framework 2.0 and .NET Framework 3.0. Additionally, there are a number of new features which have been added.

Windows Server 2008 ships with .NET Framework 3.0 already installed. However, Exchange Server 2010 requires .NET Framework 3.5 or above. When applying updates to the Windows Server 2008 server, if you elect to apply all updates the latest version of .NET Framework will be installed. If you elect to selectively install updates, make *sure* you install this update.

Windows Remote Management 2.0

The Exchange Management Shell is a command line interface that enables you to manage your Microsoft Exchange organization without having to rely on a GUI interface.

The Windows Remote Management (WinRM) 2.0 is the transport mechanism that enables your local version of Windows PowerShell to connect to remote Exchange servers, whether that server is in the next rack or across the country. Utilizing WinRM 2.0, administrators can manage servers, devices, and applications throughout their organization from a single management server.

Windows Remote Management 2.0 can be downloaded and installed from the Internet, and instructions on how to do so are included later in this chapter.

Windows PowerShell V2

Administrators who are familiar with Exchange Server 2007 have most likely had some experience with Windows PowerShell. For many, the implementation of PowerShell addressed one of the most glaring shortcomings of older Windows installations—the lack of a usable command line interface for performing administrative tasks.

PowerShell is an extensible command-line shell and scripting language from Microsoft that integrates with the .NET Framework to allow administrators to perform just about any task in an Exchange environment from a command line. From simple to complex, scripts can be written using the PowerShell scripting language to save administrators from time consuming and repetitive tasks.

While some have found the PowerShell scripting language to be difficult to learn and challenging to implement, few who have seen the results of this product being put into action can complain about the results.

Windows PowerShell V2 introduces several new features to PowerShell 1.0 that extend its capabilities including:

▶ **PowerShell Remoting**—Allows scripts and cmdlets to be executed on a remote machine, or several remote machines

▶ **Windows PowerShell Integrated Scripting Environment (ISE)**—GUI-based PowerShell host that provides an integrated debugger, syntax highlighting, tab completion, and up to eight PowerShell consoles.

▶ **Script Debugging**—Allows breakpoints to be set in a PowerShell script or function.

▶ **Eventing**—Allows listening, forwarding, and acting on management and system events.

Windows PowerShell V2 can be downloaded and installed from the Internet, and instructions on how to do so are included later in this chapter.

Microsoft Management Console 3.0

The Microsoft Management Console (MMC) was originally released back in 1996 with the Windows NT 4.0 Option Pack. This was the first time Microsoft released a consistent and integrated management tool that aimed at standardizing the way administrators conducted administrative and operational tasks on Microsoft software. Since 1996, Microsoft has been updating and improving its management console and releasing new versions.

The Exchange Server 2010 Management Console utilizes MMC 3.0, but as Windows Server 2008 ships with the product already installed, it is not listed as a prerequisite and you do not have to install it separately.

Internet Information Services (IIS) 7.0

Internet Information Services (IIS) remains a critical component that allows users to connect to Exchange services over the Internet using Outlook Web App (OWA), Outlook Mobile Access (OMA) and ActiveSync.

As with the MMC above, IIS 7.0 is installed by default with Windows Server 2008.

Understanding High Availability and Site Resilience in Exchange Server 2010

In Exchange Server 2007, Microsoft introduced new technologies that allowed organizations to deploy their Exchange environments with improved availability. Known as "Continuous Replication," this technology was offered in three flavors—Local Continuous Replication (LCR), Cluster Continuous Replication (CCR), and Standby Continuous Replication (SCR).

Although these options were a significant improvement over previous technologies, organizations found that the technologies were challenging to implement, as they required a significant amount of time and experience to deploy. This was largely due to the fact that some parts of the technology were owned by the Windows operating system, and some parts were owned by Exchange Server.

Exchange Server 2010 has built on these technologies and combined the on-site data replication features of CCR with the off-site data replication features of SCR. This combination of technologies is known as a database availability group (DAG). This architecture is designed to provide recovery from disk-level, server-level and site-level failures.

A few characteristics of Mailbox Database copies follow:

▶ Designed for mailbox databases only. Public folder replication is still the preferred method of redundancy and high availability for public folders.

▶ Up to 16 copies of a mailbox database can be created on multiple servers.

▶ Mailbox servers in a DAG can host other Exchange Server roles (Client Access, Hub Transport, and Unified Messaging).

▶ Exchange Server 2010 mailbox databases can only be replicated to other Exchange Server 2010 servers within a DAG. You cannot replicate a database outside of the DAG, or to an Exchange Server 2007 server.

Exchange Server 2010 Hardware Requirements

Microsoft maintains a list of minimum hardware requirements to install Exchange Server 2010. For the latest list of requirements, go to http://technet.microsoft.com and search for "Exchange 2010 System Requirements."

Table 7.1 shows the minimum and recommended hardware requirements for Exchange Server 2010, as stated by Microsoft.

TABLE 7.1   Minimum Hardware Requirements

Hardware	Minimum Requirements
Processor	X64 architecture-based computer with Intel Processor that supports Intel 64 Intel Extended Memory 64 Technology (formerly known as Intel EM64T)
	AMD processor that supports AMD64 platform
	Note—Intel Itanium IA64 processors are NOT supported.

TABLE 7.1   Minimum Hardware Requirements

Hardware	Minimum Requirements
Memory	Edge Transport Server—Minimum: 2GB. Maximum: 16GB. **Recommended:** 1GB per core (2GB Minimum, 8GB Maximum) Hub Transport Server—Minimum: 2GB. Maximum: 16GB. **Recommended:** 1GB per core (2GB Minimum, 8GB Maximum) Client Access Server—Minimum: 2GB. Maximum: 16GB. **Recommended:** 2GB per core (8GB Minimum, 16GB Maximum) Unified Messaging Server—Minimum: 4GB. Maximum: 8GB. **Recommended:** 1GB per core (4GB Minimum, 8GB Maximum) Mailbox Server—Minimum: 2GB. Maximum: 64GB. **Recommended:** 2GB plus 2-4MB per mailbox Multiple Roles (combinations of Hub Transport, Client Access, and Mailbox Server Roles)—Minimum: 4GB Maximum: 64GB. Recommended: 8GB plus 2-4MB per mailbox.
Disk space	At least 1.2GB on the hard disk where Exchange Server 2010 will be installed. An additional 500MB for each Unified Messaging language pack that will be installed. 200MB on the system drive. A hard disk drive that stores the message queue databases on an Edge Transport server or Hub Transport server with at least 500MB.

NOTE

These hardware requirements from Microsoft are the bare minimum and should not be used in best-practice scenarios. In addition, hardware requirements can change because of features and functionality required by the company, for example, the implementation of Unified Messaging voice mail services or clustering on an Exchange Server 2010 server can require more memory. See Chapter 34, "Optimizing an Exchange Server 2010 Environment," for more tips and best practices on sizing the server for your environment.

Understanding the Active Directory Requirements for Exchange Server 2010

An Active Directory (AD) infrastructure running on Windows Server 2003 or Windows Server 2008 must be in place before an organization can deploy Exchange Server 2010. Exchange Server depends on the services provided by AD to successfully function and the design and implementation of the AD environment can have an enormous impact on the success of the Exchange Server deployment. Mistakes made in the planning or implementation of AD can be costly and difficult to correct later.

If AD is already deployed, it is important that the team designing the Exchange Server infrastructure have a solid understanding of the existing AD environment. Organizations with an AD infrastructure already in place need to evaluate how Exchange Server can fit into their environment. If AD has not been deployed, the organization or team designing Exchange Server needs to plan their implementation with a thought as to what their messaging infrastructure will look like.

This section is designed to give a basic understanding of the AD infrastructure required to support an Exchange Server 2010 implementation. Many facets are involved when planning a production AD infrastructure—forest model, domain model, group policies, and delegation of administration to name a few, and the information needed to design an AD infrastructure from end to end is beyond the scope of this book.

Some of the AD factors that should be considered when deploying Exchange Server 2010 include the following:

- Global Catalog Server Placement

- AD Sites and Services

- Forest and Domain Functional Levels

- Flexible Single Master Operations Role Placement

- Permissions Needed to Install Exchange

- Bandwidth and Latency in the Network

NOTE

For in-depth guidance on designing, implementing, and maintaining an AD infrastructure, refer to *Windows Server 2003 Unleashed, R2 Edition*, by Sams Publishing (ISBN: 0-672-32898-4), or *Windows Server 2008 Unleashed*, by Sams Publishing (ISBN: 0-672-32930-1).

Global Catalog Server Placement

As was the case in Exchange 2000 Server through Exchange Server 2007, Exchange Server 2010 requires a global catalog infrastructure to function. The global catalog maintains an index of the Active Directory database for objects within its domain. Additionally, it stores partial copies of data for all other domains within a forest.

Just as important, Exchange Server relies on global catalog servers to resolve email addresses for users within the organization. Failure to contact a global catalog server causes emails to bounce, as the recipient's name cannot be resolved.

Sizing a global catalog infrastructure and server placement is discussed in depth later in this chapter in the section entitled "Establishing a Proper Global Catalog Placement Strategy."

Active Directory Sites and Services

In Exchange Server 2003 and earlier, Exchange Server utilized dedicated routing topology for transporting messages throughout the organization. Beginning with Exchange Server 2007, Microsoft redesigned the product to be a "site-aware" application. This continues in Exchange Server 2010.

Site-aware applications are able to determine what site they (and other servers) belong to by querying Active Directory. The site attribute of all Exchange server objects is maintained by the Microsoft Exchange Active Directory Topology Service. Additionally, Exchange Server 2010 servers utilize site membership to identify which Domain Controllers and Global Catalog servers should be utilized to process Active Directory queries.

The Exchange Server 2010 servers utilize Active Directory site membership as follows:

Hub Transport Servers—Gather information from Active Directory to determine mail routing inside the organization. When a message hits the Microsoft Exchange Transport service, the Hub Transport server resolves the recipient's information and queries Active Directory to match an email address to the recipient's account. The result of this query includes the fully qualified domain name (FQDN) of the user's mailbox server.

From the FQDN, the AD site of the recipient's Mailbox server is determined and, if the Mailbox server is in the same site as the Hub Transport server, the message is delivered. If the Mailbox server is in another site, the message is relayed to a Hub Transport server in that site, and the message is then delivered to the user's mailbox server.

Client Access Servers—When a client access server receives a connection request from a user, it contacts AD to determine which mailbox server houses the user's mailbox and which site that server belongs to. If the mailbox server is in a different site, the connection is redirected to a client access server in the same site as the mailbox server.

Mailbox Servers—Query Active Directory to determine which Hub Transport servers are located in their site. Messages are submitted to local Hub Transport servers for routing and transport.

Unified Messaging Servers—Utilize Active Directory site membership information to determine what Hub Transport servers are located in the same site as the UM server. Messages for routing and transport are delivered to a Hub Transport server in the same site as the UM server.

Forest and Domain Functional Levels

With each new edition of the Windows Server and Exchange Server operating systems, new functionalities are introduced. Some of these enhancements require that the Active Directory infrastructure be upgraded before you can take advantage of the new capabilities. At times, these capabilities cannot be implemented until all domain controllers in an environment have been upgraded to the same level.

To support this, Active Directory has Forest and Domain functional levels that determine what enhancements are enabled or disabled. By raising the functional level of an environment, new functionalities are enabled. By maintaining an older functional level, interoperability with older domain controllers is supported.

Forest Functional Levels

Windows Server 2003 supports three forest functional levels:

- ▶ **Windows 2000 Native**—Required while any Windows Server 2000 domain controllers remain in your forest. Supports domain controllers running Windows NT 4.0, Windows 2000 server, and Windows Server 2003.

- ▶ **Windows Server 2003 Interim**—A special functional level only implemented during NT 4.0 to Windows 2003 upgrades.

- ▶ **Windows Server 2003**—All DCs in the forest must be running Windows Server 2003, and all domains in the forest must be at the Windows 2003 Domain functional level before you can raise your forest functional level to Windows Server 2003.

Windows Server 2008 supports three forest functional levels:

- ▶ **Windows 2000 Native**—Supports Windows 2000, Windows Server 2003, and Windows Server 2008 domain controllers.

- ▶ **Windows Server 2003**—Allows for a mix of Windows Server 2003 and Windows Server 2008 functional level domains.

- ▶ **Windows Server 2008**—Ensures all domain controllers in the forest are running Windows Server 2008 and all domains have been raised to the Windows Server 2008 domain functional level.

NOTE

To install Exchange Server 2010, the Active Directory forest functional level MUST be Windows Server 2003 or higher.

Windows 2000 Native and Windows Server 2003 Interim modes are NOT supported.

Domain Functional Levels

Windows Server 2003 supports four domain functional levels:

- ▶ **Windows 2000 Mixed**—Allows Windows Server 2003 domain controllers to interoperate with other domain controllers running Windows Server 2003, Windows 2000 Server, and Windows NT 4.0.

- ▶ **Windows 2000 Native**—Allows domain controllers running Windows Server 2003 to interact with domain controllers running either Windows Server 2003 or Windows 2000 Server.

- ▶ **Windows Server 2003 Interim**—Supports only domain controllers running Windows Server 2003 and Windows NT 4.0.

- ▶ **Windows Server 2003**—Supports only Windows Server 2003 domain controllers.

Windows Server 2008 supports three domain functional levels:

▶ **Windows 2000 Native**—Allows domain controllers running Windows Server 2008 to interact with domain controllers running either Windows Server 2008, Windows Server 2003, or Windows 2000 Server.

▶ **Windows Server 2003**—Supports an environment comprised of a mixture of Windows Server 2003 and Windows Server 2008 domain controllers.

▶ **Windows Server 2008**—Only available after all domain controllers in a domain are running Windows Server 2008.

> **NOTE**
>
> To install Exchange Server 2010, the Active Directory domain functional level MUST be Windows Server 2003 or higher for each domain in the Active Directory forest that will house an Exchange Server 2010 server.
>
> Windows 2000 Mixed, Windows 2000 Native, and Windows Server 2003 Interim modes are NOT supported.

Understanding Flexible Single Master Operations Roles

Active Directory uses a multimaster replication scheme for replicating directory information between domain controllers; however, certain domain and enterprise wide operations are not well suited for a multimaster model. Some services are better suited to a single master operation to prevent the introduction of conflicts while an Operations Master is offline. These services are referred to as Operations Master or Flexible Single Master Operations (FSMO) roles.

FSMO roles can be either "forestwide" or "domainwide." The forestwide roles consist of the Schema Master and the Domain Naming Master. The domainwide roles consist of the Relative ID (RID) Master, the Primary Domain Controller (PDC) Emulator, and the Infrastructure Master. A brief description of each is as follows:

▶ **Schema Master**—Maintains all modifications to the schema throughout the Active Directory forest, as no other domain controller is allowed to write to the schema. The schema determines what types of objects are permitted in the forest and the attributes of those objects.

▶ **Domain Naming Master**—Maintains a list of the names of all domains in the forest and is required to add any new domains (or to remove existing ones).

▶ **RID Master**—Allocates security RIDs to domain controllers to assign to new AD security users, groups, or computer objects. RIDs are the part of the Security Identifier (SID) that identifies an account or group within a domain. The RID master also manages objects moving between domains.

▶ **PDC Emulator**—Processes all password changes in the domain. If a user logon attempt fails due to a bad password, the request is forwarded to the PDC emulator to check the password against the most recent one. This allows a user to log in immediately after a password change instead of having to wait for that change to replicate throughout the active directory.

▶ **Infrastructure Master**—Maintains security identifiers, GUIDs, and DNS for objects referenced across domains. This role is also responsible for ensuring that cross-domain group-to-user references are correctly maintained.

When designing the FSMO role placement of an Active Directory environment, the following best practices should be considered:

▶ If a domain has only one domain controller, that domain controller holds all the domain roles. However, this configuration is not recommended (even for smaller organizations), as it creates a single point of failure.

▶ The Schema Master and Domain Naming Master should be placed on the same domain controller in the root or placeholder domain. This server can (and should) also be configured as a global catalog server.

▶ Place the RID and PDC emulator roles on the same domain controller. If the load on this server justifies separating the roles, place them on domain controllers in the same domain and AD site and ensure the two domain controllers are direct replication partners of each other.

▶ As a general rule, the infrastructure master should be deployed on a domain controller that is NOT also a global catalog server. This domain controller should have a direct connection to a GC server, preferably in the same Active Directory site. Global catalog servers hold a partial replica of every object in the forest and the infrastructure master, when placed on a global catalog server, will never update anything as it does not contain any references to objects that it does not hold. There are two exceptions to this rule:

   1. Single domain forest: In a forest with a single AD domain, there are no phantoms and the infrastructure master has no work to do. In this case, the infrastructure master can be placed on any domain, including those that are also global catalog servers.

   2. Multidomain forests where *every* domain controller is a global catalog server. When *every* domain controller in a domain that is part of a multidomain forest is configured as a global catalog server, there are no phantoms or work for the infrastructure master to do. The infrastructure master can be placed on any domain controller in the domain.

NOTE

As stated by Microsoft, to install Exchange Server 2010, the Schema master should have "the latest 32-bit or 64-bit edition of the Windows Server 2003 Standard or Enterprise operating system or the latest 32-bit or 64-bit edition of the Windows Server 2008 Standard or Enterprise operating system."

Additionally, in each Active Directory site where you plan to install Exchange Server 2010, you must have at least one Global Catalog server that meets the same criteria.

Understanding How DNS and AD Namespace Are Used in Exchange Server 2010

The first step in the actual design of the AD structure is the decision on a common domain name system (DNS) namespace that AD will occupy. AD revolves around (and is inseparable from) DNS and this decision is one of the most important ones to make. The namespace chosen can be as straightforward as companyabc.com, for example, or it can be more complex. Multiple factors must be considered, however, before this decision can be made. Is it better to register an AD namespace on the Internet and potentially expose it to intruders, or is it better to choose an unregistered, internal namespace? Is it necessary to tie in multiple namespaces into the same forest? These and other questions must be answered before the design process can proceed.

Impact Forests Have on an Exchange Server 2010 Design

An AD forest and an Exchange Server organization are tightly integrated. Exchange Server relies on AD as its directory repository for mailboxes, mail-enabled objects, Exchange servers, and much more. An AD forest can only host a single Exchange organization and an Exchange organization can only span one AD forest.

It is recommended that a single AD forest should be utilized to minimize complexity and administration when designing and implementing a company's Exchange Server implementation. However, there will be times when a single AD forest will not meet the company's business, security, or political requirements.

If multiple AD forests are necessary to satisfy the company's requirements, it must be decided on which forest the Exchange organization will be hosted. It is possible to have an Exchange Server reside in a single forest, a dedicated resource forest, or to implement multiple Exchange organizations in multiple forests.

The Role of a Domain in Exchange Server 2010

After the AD forest structure has been laid out, the domain structure can be contemplated. Unlike the forest structure, an Exchange Server 2010 organization can span multiple domains within the forest if needed. Therefore, a user mailbox, Exchange server, or other Exchange object can reside in any domain within the forest where Exchange Server 2010 has been deployed. A company can plan its domain model structure (single domain model or multiple domain model) based on their business and security requirements without a direct negative impact to the Exchange Server 2010 design.

While a single domain model is often considered due to its simplicity, most organizations prefer the placeholder domain model. The placeholder domain model has an isolated domain serving as the root domain in the forest. The user domain, which contains all production user accounts, would be located in a separate domain in the forest, as illustrated in Figure 7.1.

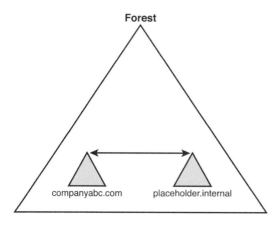

FIGURE 7.1   The placeholder domain model.

The placeholder domain structure increases security in the forest by segregating high-level schema-access accounts into a completely separate domain from the regular user domain. Access to the placeholder domain can be audited and restricted to maintain tighter control on the critical schema. The downside to this model, however, is the fact that the additional domain requires a separate set of domain controllers, which increases the infra- structure costs of the environment. Smaller organizations may have a difficult time justify- ing the extra infrastructure costs to provide the increased security, but whenever the budget allows, this model should definitely be considered.

Planning a Proper Sites and Services Architecture

As stated earlier, one of the major features of Exchange Server 2007 and Exchange Server 2010 is the ability to natively utilize Active Directory Sites and Services for routing mail, rather than having to implement and maintain an independent routing topology using connectors. To take advantage of this capability, you must first remove all pre-Exchange Server 2007 servers from your environment.

If Exchange Server 2010 will be installed into an existing Exchange Server 2003 organiza- tion, the administrators must configure routing group connectors to ensure that the Exchange Server 2010 servers are communicating to legacy servers.

For more information on coexistence of Exchange Server 2010 with legacy versions, review Chapter 15, "Migrating from Active Directory 2000/2003 to Active Directory 2008."

Administrators should be aware of the best practices for designing a proper Sites and Services architecture to support Exchange Server 2010. From a high-level perspective, within AD it is necessary for administrators to create sites, allocate subnets to sites, and then create site links between sites for communication to occur. Similar to Exchange 2000 and 2003, it is possible to set up redundant links between sites and allocate costs to control communication priorities.

Active Directory Sites

The basic unit of AD replication is known as the site. Not to be confused with physical sites or Exchange Server 5.5 sites, the AD site is simply a group of domain controllers connected by high-speed network connections. Each site is established to more effectively replicate directory information across the network. In a nutshell, domain controllers within a single site will, by default, replicate more often than those that exist in other sites. The concept of the site constitutes the centerpiece of replication design in AD.

Associating Subnets with Sites

In most cases, a separate instance of a site in AD physically resides on a separate subnet from other sites. This idea stems from the concept that the site topology most often mimics, or should mimic, the physical network infrastructure of an environment.

In AD, sites are associated with their respective subnets to allow for the intelligent assignment of users to their respective domain controllers. For example, consider the design shown in Figure 7.2.

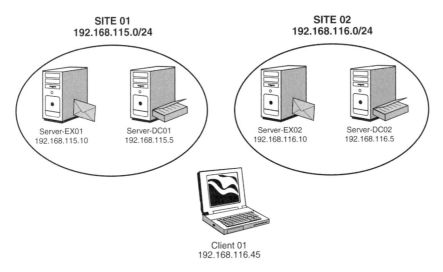

FIGURE 7.2   Sample Exchange Server and Client site assignment.

In this example, Server-EX01 is a physical member of the 192.168.115.0/24 subnet. Server-EX02 and Client01 are both members of the 192.168.116.0/24 subnet. Based on the subnets, Server-EX01 will automatically be assigned to the domain controller Server-DC01 in SITE01 and Server-EX02 and Client01 will be assigned to the domain controller Server-DC02 in SITE02.

Using Site Links

By default, the creation of two sites in AD does not automatically create a connection linking the two sites. This type of functionality must be manually implemented by the creation of a "site link."

A site link is essentially a connection that joins together two sites and allows for replication traffic to flow from one site to another. Multiple site links can be set up and should normally follow the wide area network (WAN) lines of your organization. Multiple site links also assure redundancy so that if one link goes down, replication traffic has an alternate path.

Site link replication schedules can be modified to fit the requirements of your organization. If, for example, the WAN link is saturated during the day, a schedule can be established to replicate information at night. This functionality allows you to easily adjust site links to the needs of any WAN design.

Exchange Server 2010 and Site Membership

After the AD site topology has been created, including adding the appropriate subnets to sites and creating site links between sites, an administrator can now take Exchange Server placement into consideration.

Similar to AD domain controllers, Exchange Server 2010 servers will be associated with sites in AD based on their IP address and subnet mask. As stated earlier, there should be at least one domain controller/global catalog server residing in each site that an Exchange Server 2010 server will be in.

For more information on creating an Exchange Server routing topology, refer to Chapter 4, "Architecting an Enterprise-Level Exchange Server Environment."

> **NOTE**
>
> If an AD infrastructure already exists prior to the design of the Exchange Server 2010 environment, there might be a need to make changes to the AD routing topology to support the Exchange routing requirements.

Establishing a Proper Global Catalog Placement Strategy

Another area of importance is the design and placement of global catalog servers within the environment. The importance of the global catalog server cannot be overstated. The global catalog is used for the address list that users see when they are addressing a message and by Exchange servers every time a message is delivered. If a global catalog server is not available, the recipient's address will not resolve when users address a message, and the message cannot be delivered.

There should be at least one global catalog server in every AD site that contains an Exchange Server 2010 server. The recommendation from Microsoft is as follows:

If Active Directory is running on a 32-bit system, the recommendation is 4:1—for every four processor cores in your mailbox servers, you should have one processor core in a global catalog server. For example, if you have 2 mailbox servers, each with dual quad-core processors, that is 16 processor cores. You should have at least 4 processor cores worth of global catalog computing, so 1 quad core server, or 2 dual core servers should do the trick.

If Active Directory is running on a 64-bit system, the recommended ratio is 1:8. However, you must have enough memory installed on the server to cache the entire Active

Directory database in memory. To confirm the size of your Active Directory database, look at the size of the %WINDIR%\NTDS\NTDS.DIT file.

For optimization, plan on having a global catalog server close to the clients to provide efficient address list access. Making all domain controller servers global catalog servers is recommended for an organization that has a single AD domain model and a single site. Otherwise, for multidomain models, all domain controllers can be configured as global catalog servers *except* for the domain controller hosting the Infrastructure Master FSMO role.

> **NOTE**
>
> It is a best practice to have a minimum of at least two global catalog servers within an AD infrastructure.

Understanding Role Based Access Control

Exchange Server 2010 uses the new *Role Based Access Control* (RBAC) permissions model on the Mailbox, Hub Transport, Unified Messaging, and Client Access server roles. At first glance, this RBAC may seem very similar to the Exchange Server 2007 server permissions model, but it actually allows for much greater flexibility.

Using RBAC allows you to easily control what your administrators and users can (and cannot) access. Rather than applying permissions directly to user accounts, the permissions are applied directly to the role. Members are added to a particular role when they need a particular level of permissions.

In addition, role assignments can be "scoped" to include only specific resources within the organization. The role (and the permissions associated with it) allows certain tasks to be accomplished, while the role scope determines what resources can be administered.

The RBAC model consists of:

▶ **Management Role**—A container for grouping management role entries.

▶ **Management Role Entries**—A cmdlet (including parameters) that is added to a management role. This process grants rights to manage or view the objects associated with that cmdlet.

▶ **Management Role Assignment**—The assignment of a management role to a particular user or a universal security group. This grants the user (or the members of the security group) the ability to perform the management role entries in the management role that they are assigned to.

▶ **Management Role Scope**—Used to target the specific object or objects that the management role assignment is allowed to control. A management role scope can include servers, organizational units, filters on server or recipient objects, and more.

As described by Microsoft, this process allows complete control of the *who* (management role assignment), the *what* (management role and management role entries), and the *where* (management role scope) in the security model.

Role Based Access Control is *not* used on Edge Transport servers, as these servers are designed to sit outside the domain.

Exchange Server 2010 provides several built-in management roles that cannot be modified, nor can the management role entries configured on them. However, the *scope* of the built-in management roles can be modified.

The following built-in management roles are included by default in Exchange Server 2010:

▶ **Organization Management**—Administrators assigned to this role have administrative access to the entire Exchange Server 2010 organization, and can perform almost any task against any Exchange Server 2010 object. Even if a task can only be completed by another role, members of the Organization Management role have the ability to add themselves to any other role.

As this role is very powerful, it is recommended that it only be assigned to users who are responsible for organizational level administration. Changes made by this role can potentially impact the entire Exchange organization.

▶ **View Only Organization Management**—This role is the equivalent to the Exchange View-Only Administrator role in Exchange Server 2007. Members of this role can view the properties of any object in the Exchange organization, but cannot modify the properties of any object.

Useful for personnel who need to be able to view the configuration of objects within the environment, but who do not need the ability to add new or modify existing objects.

▶ **Recipient Management**—Administrators assigned to this role have the ability to create, modify, or delete Exchange Server 2010 recipients within the organization.

▶ **Records Management**—Administrators assigned to this role have the ability to configure compliance features, including transport rules, message classifications, retention policy tags, and others.

Often assigned to administrators or members of an organization's legal department who need the ability to view and modify compliance features in an organization.

▶ **GAL Synchronization Management**—Administrators assigned to this role have the ability to configure global address list (GAL) synchronization between organizations.

Other built-in management roles include the Unified Messaging Management, Unified Messaging Recipient Management, Unified Messaging Prompt Management, and Discovery Management.

NOTE

Membership in the Organization Management Role should be limited to personnel who have advanced knowledge of the Exchange Server operating system and your particular network environment.

Planning Your Exchange Server 2010 Installation

Before installing Exchange Server, you should review the following chapters earlier in this book:

Chapter 1, "Exchange Server 2010 Technology Primer" covers what is new in Exchange Server 2010 and differences between the available versions.

Chapter 2, "Planning, Prototyping, Migrating, and Deploying Exchange Server 2010."

Chapter 3, "Understanding Core Exchange Server 2010 Design Plans."

Chapter 4, "Architecting an Enterprise-Level Exchange Server Environment" addresses the planning and design of an Exchange Server 2010 implementation for a small, medium, or large enterprise organization.

From these chapters, you will learn the industry best practices and recommendations for planning and deploying Exchange Server 2010.

Installing Exchange Server 2010 in a Test Environment

To reduce risks, prevent end-user downtime, and minimize the exposure of the production environment, it is typically recommended that the first implementation of Exchange Server 2010 be conducted in an isolated test lab rather than being installed into a production environment.

Having a test environment isolates functional errors so that if there are any problems they will not be injected into the existing production environment. In addition, the test environment acts as a "Proof of Concept" for the new Exchange Server 2010 design.

Occasionally, organizations attempt to repurpose their test environments into their production environment. Administrators should be cautious, as "shortcuts" are sometimes taken in the lab—the use of evaluation copies of software and/or underpowered hardware may work flawlessly in the lab, but transitioning the equipment to production results in inadequate performance and unnecessary downtime.

Production equipment should be rebuilt and deployed from scratch, not "moved" from a test environment.

Prototyping an Exchange Server 2010 Installation

Some of the steps an organization should go through when planning to build a test Exchange Server environment include the following:

▶ Building Exchange Server 2010 in a lab

▶ Testing email features and functionality

▶ Reviewing Exchange Server 2010 server roles

▶ Verifying design configuration

▶ Testing failover and recovery

▶ Selecting to install on physical hardware or virtual machines

Much of the validation and testing should occur during the testing process. It is much easier, for example, to test a disaster recovery rebuild of Exchange Server in an exclusive test environment than it is to do so in a production environment, where production servers or users could accidentally be impacted.

Additionally, testing application compatibility in a lab environment can be much more effective than attempting to do so in a production environment, where you might suddenly find business critical third-party fax, voice mail, or paging software non functional.

Other items to test and confirm in your lab environment include:

▶ **Sites and Services Configuration**—Ensure replication is completed as expected

▶ **Role Based Access Control**—Ensure the proposed security settings allow proper user and administrative access

Building an Exchange Server 2007 prototype test lab can be a costly affair for companies that want to simulate a large, global implementation. For companies with a global presence where it is necessary to provide messaging services for thousands of employees, in multiple sites throughout the world, mirroring their production site can prove a daunting task. However, without successfully prototyping the installation, upgrade strategy, and application compatibility before they move forward in production, they cannot be assured that the deployment will go smoothly.

The cost of building a lab of this magnitude using physical servers can be prohibitive; there can be AD domain controllers, Exchange 2003 and 2007 servers, and application servers. The cost of building the lab could eat up a large part of the overall budget allocated to the project.

However, with the improvements in server virtualization, companies can significantly lower the costs associated with the prototype phase. Server virtualization enables multiple virtual operating systems to run on a single physical machine, while remaining logically distinct with consistent hardware profiles. For further cost savings, the hardware utilized for the virtual lab can be purchased with an eye toward re-utilization in the production environment once the prototype phase is complete.

Upgrading from Previous Versions of Microsoft Windows

Many organizations already have an existing directory structure in place. It is great if a company has the opportunity to implement a new Windows Server 2003 or Windows Server 2008 AD environment from scratch; however, this is not usually possible for environments with previous versions of Exchange Server deployed.

When upgrading an existing Active Directory infrastructure, the deployment plan should be carefully thought out and tested before implementation in the production environment.

Deploying Active Directory from Scratch

Before installing Exchange Server 2010, there must be an existing Active Directory environment to support it. The environment can be running on either a Windows Server 2003 or Windows Server 2008 platform. The following sections will focus on the steps needed to install an Active Directory environment on a Windows Server 2008 platform from scratch. This example can be followed in a lab environment to prepare it for the deployment of Exchange Server 2010.

This sample deployment will consist of a single site and single domain controller, as might be found in a small organization. The steps we will deploy include:

▶ Installing the Windows Server 2008 operating system

▶ Promoting a Windows Server 2008 Server to a domain controller

▶ Configuring Active Directory Sites and Services

▶ Configuring a global catalog server

Installing the Windows Server 2008 Operating System

Microsoft Exchange Servers rely heavily on the Active Directory environment they are installed in.

For those experienced with installing previous versions of the Windows Server operating system, most of the concepts covered in this section will feel very familiar. The installation of Windows Server 2008 is straightforward, and takes approximately 30 minutes to an hour to complete. The following procedure is based on installing Windows Server from the standard media provided by Microsoft. Many hardware manufacturers include special installation instructions and procedures specific to their hardware platform, but the concepts should be roughly the same.

For our test lab, we will install Windows Server 2008 Enterprise Edition on two machines. One will be promoted later in the chapter to a domain controller. The other will have the Exchange Server 2010 software installed on it.

To install Windows Server 2008 (Standard or Enterprise Edition) perform the following steps:

1. Insert the Windows Server 2008 CD into the CD drive.

2. Power up the server and let it boot to the CD-ROM drive. If there is currently no operating system on the hard drive, it automatically boots into the CD-ROM-based setup.

3. Select the language you wish to install, the Time and Currency Format, and the Keyboard or input method. When ready, click Next to continue.

4. Click Install Now.

5. Select which version of the Windows Server 2008 Operating system you wish to install. For this example, we will be installing Windows Server 2008 Enterprise (Full Installation) on a 64-bit platform. When ready, click Next to continue.

6. Review the Microsoft Software License Terms, click the "I accept the license terms" check box, and click Next to continue.

7. Select Custom (advanced) to install a clean copy of Windows.

8. Select the physical disk on which Windows will be installed and click Next to continue.

The server will begin the installation process, rebooting several times during the process.

1. A default account called Administrator will be created, but you will have to set the password for this account. When prompted The User's Password Must Be Changed Before Logging on the First Time, click OK to continue.

2. Enter the new password for the Administrator account in both the New password and Confirm password fields, and then press Enter. When prompted Your password has been changed, click OK.

Once the installation process has completed and the server reboots, there will be an Initial Configuration Tasks screen. Perform the steps in the Provide Computer Information section as follows:

Set Time Zone

1. Click Set Time Zone. On the Date and Time tab, review the current Date, Time, and Time zone settings and configure them as needed.

2. If desired, up to two additional clocks can be configured for additional time zones with customized display names. If you wish to display more than one clock, select the Additional Clocks tab and configure them.

3. By default, Windows Server 2008 servers are configured to automatically synchronize with time.windows.com. The server is configured to synchronize once a week. If you need to change the source of your time updates, you can click the Internet Time tab.

4. Click OK to return to the Install Configuration Tasks screen.

Configure Networking

Windows Server 2008 has a completely redesigned implementation of the TCP/IP protocol stack which is known as the "Next Generation TCP/IP stack." This updated functionality applies to both Internet Protocol version 4 (IPv4) and Internet Protocol version 6 (IPv6).

1. Click Configure networking, double-click the Local Area Network Connection icon, and then click the Properties tab.

2. Double-click the Internet Protocol Version 4 (TCP/IPv4) option and configure an appropriate IP address, Subnet mask, Default gateway, and preferred DNS server for your environment.

3. Click OK to save your changes.

4. Perform the same steps to configure the Internet Protocol Version 6 (TCP/IPv6).

5. Save all settings and exit the Network Connections utility.

6. Launch Internet Explorer and confirm internet connectivity. Adjust your network settings if necessary to allow the computer access to the Internet.

Provide Computer Name and Domain

Each computer on a Windows network and in Active Directory must have a unique computer name. This name, known as the NetBIOS name, allows users, resources, and other computers to contact this computer on the network.

A standard NetBIOS name is limited to 15 characters and should only consist of letters (A-Z, a-z), digits (0-9), and hyphens (-). For example, weinhardt-dc is a standard computer name, but weinhardt_dc is nonstandard. Although the implementation of a DNS server will allow you to use nonstandard computer names and still find the resources in your environment, servers as critical as domain controllers and Exchange servers should only use standard computer names.

1. Click Provide Computer Name and Domain. If you have already closed your Initial Configuration Tasks screen, you can click Start, right-click Computer, select Properties; then, beside Computer Name, Domain, and Workgroup Settings, click Change Settings.

2. On the Computer Name tab, click Change.

3. Under Computer name, enter the computer name for this machine; then click OK to continue.

4. Acknowledge that you must restart your computer to apply these changes by clicking OK, and then click Close.

5. When prompted You Must Restart Your Computer, click Restart Now.

Enable Automatic Updating and Feedback

Windows Server allows you the option of automatically applying updates as they are released from Microsoft. While this option may be a good idea for some applications, most organizations require change control procedures before updating servers as business critical as domain controllers and Exchange servers.

1. Click on Enable Automatic Updating and Feedback. Although the first option, Enable Windows Automatic Updating and Feedback, states that it is "recommended," in this author's opinion, that setting is NOT recommended for domain controllers or Exchange servers. Instead, click on Manually Configure Settings.

2. Under Windows Automatic Updating, click Change Setting. Set the automatic updates according to your organization's policies. The author recommends selecting either Download Updates but Let Me Choose Whether to Install Them or Check for Updates but Let Me Choose Whether to Download and Install Them. Additionally, the author recommends Include Recommended Updates When Downloading, Installing, or Notifying Me about Updates, as shown in Figure 7.3.

3. When ready, click OK to continue.

4. Review the Windows Error Reporting and Customer Experience Improvement Program settings. The author recommends the default settings, as shown in Figure 7.4. When finished, click Close to continue.

5. Click Download and Install Updates; if prompted to Install new Windows Update Software, click Install Now. As part of the installation process, the Windows Updates application will automatically close and reopen and begin checking for updates.

FIGURE 7.3   Configuring automatic updates.

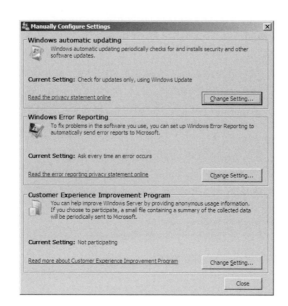

FIGURE 7.4   Configuring Windows Error Reporting and Customer Experience Improvement Program.

6. At this point, you can either click View Available Updates and select which ones to install or simply click Install Updates to automatically download and install all available updates.

7. Accept any license agreements and click Finish to begin installing available updates. Monitor the installation, as you may have additional prompts from the installation process. When finished, if a restart is required, click Restart Now.

8. When the server has rebooted, log on again and return to the Download and Install Updates section.

9. Click the option to Get Updates for More Products.

10. From the Microsoft Update site, place a check mark in the I Accept the Terms of Use box and click Next.

11. Select Use Current Settings and click Install; then on the User Account Control window, click Continue.

12. When complete, your server now checks for updates for all Microsoft products on the server (such as Exchange Server), and not just for the standard Windows updates. Close all windows to finish.

This concludes the installation of the Base operating system for both the Domain Controller and the Exchange Server 2010 server.

Promoting a Windows Server 2008 Server to a Domain Controller

As previously stated, in this example we are creating a new Active Directory environment, creating a new forest and domain, and installing a new domain controller in that domain. This is accomplished by using the Active Directory Domain Services Installation Wizard.

1. The installation wizard can be started from the Add Roles option on the Initial Configuration Tasks window, but the easiest way is simply to kick off the wizard from a command prompt. To do so, from the Start menu select Run, type DCPROMO in the text box, and then click OK. This installs the Active Directory Domain Services binaries and starts the Installation Wizard.

2. When the wizard starts, select Use Advanced Mode Installation and click Next.

> **NOTE**
>
> There are many improvements in the Active Directory Domain Services Installation Wizard in Windows Server 2008. While all of these improvements are available by default, some of the wizard pages will appear only if the administrator selects Use Advanced Mode Installation.
>
> Advanced mode installation can also be selected by running the DCPROMO command with the /ADV switch (dcpromo /adv).

3. On the Operating System Compatibility screen, read the information and then click Next.

4. At the Choose a Deployment Configuration screen, for our purposes, we select Create a New Domain in a New Forest and click Next. Other available options enable you to modify an existing forest by adding a new domain controller in a new or existing domain.

5. Enter the fully qualified domain name (FQDN) of the Forest Root Domain and click Next. For our example, we use `companyabc.lab`.

6. Enter the Domain NetBIOS name. A default name is suggested for you, derived from the Forest Root Domain name in the previous step. In our example, the suggested domain name is COMPANYABC. When you have the domain name entered, click Next.

7. Set the Forest Functional Level. For our purposes, we cannot set the level to Windows 2000, as Exchange Server 2010 requires at least Windows Server 2003 or higher. If you are certain your environment will not contain any Windows Server 2003 domain controllers in the future, you can set it to Windows Server 2008. For our test installation, we select Windows Server 2003 and click Next to continue.

8. Set the Domain Functional Level. As above, we will select Windows Server 2003 and click Next.

9. Microsoft recommends that you install DNS server on the first domain controller, and requires that this server be a Global Catalog. Leave the default settings and click Next to continue. Electing to install Microsoft DNS on the new domain controller will also modify the server's TCP/IP properties to use the new DNS installation for name resolution.

10. If your computer has any IP addresses (either IPv4 or IPv6) that are assigned by a DHCP server, you will receive a notice that static IP addresses should be assigned to all network adapters. Check your IP settings and continue when ready.

11. If no authoritative parent DNS zone exists, you receive the warning shown in Figure 7.5.

FIGURE 7.5   DNS installation error message.

In our example, we are not integrating with an existing DNS infrastructure, so we will simply click Yes to continue.

12. Depending on your server configuration design, select the location where the AD databases will be located. Using the Browse buttons, select the locations for your Database, Log files, and SYSVOL folders. When ready, click Next.

NOTE

When configuring AD database locations, make sure that your server hardware configuration plan takes recoverability and performance into account.

For best performance, install the AD databases on a separate hard disk than the server operating system and server page file.

For best recoverability, use disk fault tolerance such as RAID or disk mirroring for the AD databases.

---

13. Assign a password to the Directory Services Restore Mode Administrator account. This account is used in the event that you have to start the domain controller in Directory Services Restore Mode. This password should be a strong password, containing a combination of upper and lower-case letters, numbers, and special characters. The password should be documented and stored in a secure location. Enter the Directory Services Restore Mode Administrator password and click Next.

14. Review the selections you have made. In the future, when creating additional domain controllers that will be similar to one another, you can export the settings to an "answer file" that you can use for future unattended installations. If you need to make any changes, use the Back button to go to the section you want to change, then use the Next button to return to the review screen. When ready, click Next to continue.

15. The installation wizard now installs DNS and the Active Directory Domain Services. When the installation has completed, click Finish to close the wizard, and then click Restart Now to restart the server.

When the server has rebooted, log on to the new domain. Your default administrator account will now be a domain administrator, and the password is the same. Take the time to review the server's Event Viewer application and system logs to identify any errors or potential problems with your installation before continuing.

Configuring Active Directory Sites and Services

As previously stated, in order for Exchange Server 2010 to successfully deliver mail, it relies heavily on Active Directory Sites and Services to determine what site particular servers belong to.

After the AD domain controller has been installed, it is necessary to configure Sites and Services to support the future Exchange Server deployment. In our example, we are going to configure two sites for a future installation of Exchange servers in two locations. We will cover how to rename the default first site, and how to create the second site from scratch.

Changing Site Properties

To change the AD Default-First-Site-Name, follow these steps:

1. On the domain controller, select Start\Administrative Tools\Active Directory Sites and Services.

2. Click the plus sign (+) to expand the Sites tree.

3. Right-click Default-First-Site-Name in the left pane of the console, and then click Rename.

4. Enter a name, and then press Enter, which changes the default site name to your custom site name. In our sample lab, we will choose FredericksburgVA.

Creating a New Active Directory Site

To create a new site in AD, follow these steps:

1. On the domain controller, open AD Sites and Services.

2. Click the plus sign (+) to expand the Sites tree.

3. Right-click Sites in the left pane of the console, and then click New and Site.

4. Enter the new site name in the New Object-Site dialog box. In this example, SunnyvaleCA was used for the new site name.

5. Click to highlight DEFAULTIPSITELINK, and then click OK.

6. Review the Active Directory Domain Services message box (shown in Figure 7.6) and ensure the configuration was successful, and then click OK.

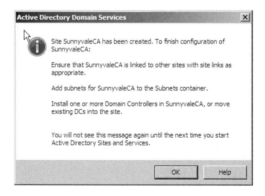

FIGURE 7.6   Active Directory Domain Services message box.

In AD, sites are associated with their respective subnets to allow for the intelligent assignment of users to their respective domain controllers.

To create a new subnet and associate it with a site, follow these steps:

1. Open AD Sites and Services.

2. Click the plus sign (+) to expand the Sites tree.

3. Right-click Subnets and choose New and Subnet.

4. Enter the address prefix using network prefix notation. This requires the address and the prefix length, where the prefix length shows the number of fixed bits in the subnet. The example shown in Figure 7.7 uses the 192.168.80.0/24 subnet, providing us with a Class C (255.255.255.0) subnet. Next, select a site to associate with the subnet and click OK.

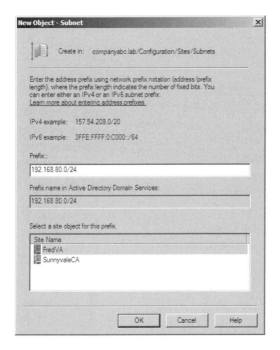

FIGURE 7.7   Associate a subnet to a site.

Perform the same steps to create a second subnet and associate it with the second site.

Configuring a Global Catalog Server

By default, the first domain controller in a domain is automatically configured as a global catalog server. Any additional domain controllers need to be configured manually.

To configure or verify that a domain controller is a global catalog server, follow these steps:

1. Open AD Sites and Services.

2. Click the plus sign (+) to expand the Sites tree.

3. Expand the desired site name, the Servers folder, and then the server object.

4. Right-click the NTDS Settings object, and then click Properties.

5. On the General Tab, ensure the Global Catalog check box is marked if you want the server to be a global catalog server (as illustrated in Figure 7.8). When ready, click OK.

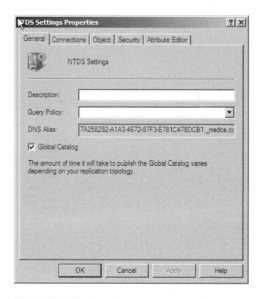

FIGURE 7.8   Configuring a global catalog server.

Preparing Your Environment for Exchange Server 2010

Before deploying Exchange Server 2010, there are several steps that must be done, and several more that *should* be done.

Performing an Active Directory Health Check

This is a step that *should* be done, especially if AD is not being set up from scratch (as it is in our scenario). The existing AD environment should be validated to ensure it is functioning correctly. Since Exchange Server relies so heavily on Active Directory, an extensive health check utilizing tools such as DCDIAG, NETDIAG, and Replication Monitor can help identify any underlying problems that will impact the installation or performance of Exchange Server. A combination of Windows Server 2003 and Windows Server 2008 Support tools can be utilized for these tasks.

For detailed instructions on performing an AD health check, see the Digital ShortCut titled *Performing an AD Health Check* (Sams Publishing, ISBN: 0-7686-6842-5), which can be purchased and downloaded from www.samspublishing.com/bookstore/ product.asp?isbn=0768668425.

Granting the Appropriate Permissions

To install Exchange Server 2010, you must make sure the domain account you will be using is a member of the following groups: Domain Admins, Enterprise Admins, and Schema Admins.

To do so, perform the following steps:

1. On the domain controller, from the Start menu, select Administrative Tools, then Active Directory Users and Computers.

2. Expand your domain name and select the Users organizational unit (OU).

3. Right-click Users and click Find. Enter the name of the account that you will be using to install Exchange Server 2010 and click Find Now.

4. Double-click the user account and select the Member Of tab.

5. Click Add. In the Enter the Object Names to Select field, type `Enterprise Admins`; `Domain Admins`; `Schema Admins` (separated by semicolons as shown). Click Check Names to ensure all group names are resolved, and then click OK. Ensure all three groups show in the Member Of section and click Apply. Click OK to exit the screen.

Installing the Base Operating System on Your Exchange Server

Exchange Server 2010 can be installed only on a 64-bit version of the Windows Server 2008 Operating System. Although either Standard or Enterprise can be used, the Enterprise version is required for some of the more advanced Exchange Server features.

After you complete the setup of the base operating system, perform the following steps to join the server to the domain:

1. Install Windows Server 2008 on your Exchange server by following the installation procedures earlier in this chapter in the section titled Installing Windows Server 2008. Do NOT continue with the installation of Active Directory on this server.

2. Configure your Domain Controller/DNS server as the Preferred DNS Server in the Internet Protocol Version 4 (TCP/IPv4) settings of your new Exchange Server.

3. From the Initial Configuration Tasks screen, click Provide Computer Name and Domain.

4. On the Computer Name tab, click Change.

5. In the Member Of section, select the Domain radio button and type the name of the domain you created. In our example, this is companyabc. Click OK to continue.

6. Enter the administrator name and password for your domain and click OK.

7. When prompted Welcome to the companyabc Domain, click OK; then click OK again to acknowledge that the computer must be restarted. Close all open windows and, when prompted, click Restart now.

8. After the computer restarts, from the log on screen, click Switch User; then click Other User and enter the domain administrator credentials in the following format:

-*domain\administrator,* where domain is the name of your domain, and administrator is the administrative account for that domain.

Prepare Internet Explorer to Accept ActiveX Downloads

The default security settings of Windows Server 2008, combined with the default security settings of Internet Explorer 8.0, can result in some real challenges when attempting to download the prerequisite applications for Exchange Server. To ease the process, perform the following steps.

1. On the new Exchange server, log on with your domain administrative account.

2. Right-click the Internet Explorer icon and click Run as administrator. Ensure you have Internet connectivity by bringing up an Internet website. If you do not, troubleshoot your network settings and resolve any issues before continuing.

3. In Internet Explorer, select Tools, and then Internet Options. Select the Security tab and then the Trusted Sites icon, and click Sites.

4. In the Add This Website to the Zone field, type `https://connect.microsoft.com` and click Add. Then type `http://download.microsoft.com` and click Add. When finished, click Close.

5. Click the Internet icon and click Custom Level. Under the ActiveX Controls and Plug-Ins section, change Download Signed ActiveX Controls to Prompt (recommended).

6. Click OK and click Yes in response to the warning; then click OK again and exit Internet Explorer.

Installing the Prerequisites

There are some software applications that must be installed on the server before you can run the Exchange Setup Wizard. These applications must be installed regardless of which server role you are going to install. Follow the steps below to install these applications.

Installing Windows Remote Management 2.0

1. Log on to the workstation with your domain administrative account.

2. Insert the Exchange Server 2010 CD and allow Autorun to start the Microsoft Exchange Server 2010 Setup Wizard. You can also start the Wizard from a command prompt by typing `d:\setup` (assuming d:\ contains your E2010 installation media).

3. If you have installed all updates for the server, Step 1: Install .NET Framework 3.5 should already be completed.

4. Select Step 2: Install Windows Remote Management 2.0.

5. Select the WinRM on Vista and WS08 (x64) option, and click Download beneath the file. When prompted This Website Wants to Install the Following Add-On, right-click the Internet Explorer Information Bar and select Install This Add-on for All Users on This Computer.

6. Click Install to Install the Microsoft File Transfer Manager.

7. If the Language Update box appears, click OK and install the selected file.

8. When the Confirm Transfer Request box appears, browse to the location where you would like to store your prerequisite installation files. (Note: The browse feature does not allow you to create new folders, so if you are going to want to create a new folder for the storage of these files, do so in Explorer before trying to browse.) When you have selected the location, click Transfer.

9. Once the file has finished downloading, click Close. You can then go to the directory where you stored the download. Double-click the WinRM on Vista and WS08 (x64) Directory; then double-click the installation file. When prompted to Click OK to Install do so.

10. Accept the license terms by clicking I Accept.

11. Once completed, click Restart Now.

Installing Windows PowerShell v2

1. Log on to the workstation with your domain administrative account.

2. Insert the Exchange Server 2010 CD and allow Autorun to start the Microsoft Exchange Server 2010 Setup Wizard. You can also start the Wizard from a command prompt by typing d:\setup (assuming d:\ contains your E2010 installation media).

3. Select Step 3: Install Windows PowerShell v2.

4. From the download page for Windows PowerShell V2, locate the download files and click Download next to the "PowerShell_Setup_amd64.msi" file.

5. Click Run to run the file directly from the download page. If you receive a security warning, click Run again.

6. From the Windows PowerShell Setup Wizard, click Next.

7. On the License Agreement page, click I Accept the Terms in the License Agreement, then click Next, and then click Install.

8. Click Finish when complete and close the Internet Explorer window.

Installing the 2007 Office System Converter: Microsoft Filter Pack

This section is required only for Exchange Server 2010 servers that have the Mailbox role installed on them.

1. Log on to the workstation with your domain administrative account.

2. Open Internet Explorer and go to www.microsoft.com/downloads. Search for 2007 Office Converter Microsoft Filter Pack. Select the Microsoft Filter Pack from the available options.

3. Make sure you are on the 2007 Office System Converter: Microsoft Filter Pack page. Scroll down and click Download for the FilterPackx64.exe file. When prompted, click Run.

4. From the Welcome screen, click Next.

5. From the End-User License Agreement screen, click I Accept the Terms in the Licensing Agreement and click Next.

6. When complete, click OK to exit the installation.

Installing the Active Directory Services Remote Management Tools

These steps will allow an administrator to perform the Schema and Domain prep commands from your Windows Server 2008 server.

1. Open an administrator-enabled command prompt. Right-click Command Prompt and select Run as Administrator.

2. Run the following command:

   ```
   ServerManagerCmd -i RSAT-ADDS
   ```

   The progress of this command will sit at the <10/100> prompt for awhile—be patient and let it finish.

   Upon completion, you see two Warnings in yellow stating You Must Restart This Server to Finish the Installation.

3. After you have successfully installed the Role Administration Tools and the Active Directory Domain Services Tools, reboot the server as instructed.

NOTE

Simply running the `ServerManagerCmd` command above from a normal command prompt will result in a frustrating and poorly documented error:

WriteError: Failed to write the log file: Access to the path 'C:\Windows\logs\ServerManager.log' is denied.

The need to do this is the result of a newly added security component found in both Windows Server 2008 and Windows Vista that is known as "User Access Control" or "UAC." UAC allows administrators to enter their credentials while in a non-administrators user session to accomplish administrative tasks without having to switch users, log off, or utilize the "run as" command. UAC also utilized the Admin Approval Mode (AAM) for all accounts except the built-in Administrator account in Windows Server 2008. AAM is designed to prevent malicious applications from installing without the knowledge of the logged on user.

AAM allows administrators to log on and receive a split user access token—the administrator receives both a full access token and a filtered access token. The filtered access token is used to start Explorer.exe (the process that creates the user's desktop). All applications started by the Explorer.exe process inherit this filtered access token.

In short—with UAC enabled, administrators may have to confirm the installation of some applications or system changes, even when logged in with elevated privileges.

Preparing the Active Directory Forest, Domain, and Exchange Organization

Before you can install Exchange Server, the Active Directory Schema and Domain must be prepared.

Preparing the Schema

1. From the Exchange server, log on with your administrative account. This account must be a member of the Schema Administrators and Enterprise Administrators groups.

2. Copy the contents of your Exchange Server 2010 installation media to a directory on a local drive, such as c:\E2k10Install.

3. From an administrator-enabled command prompt, change to the drive and directory that holds your Exchange Server 2010 installation media and run the following command:

   ```
   Setup /PrepareSchema or Setup /ps
   ```

> **NOTE**
>
> Depending on how you obtain the media for Exchange Server 2010, you may need to copy the installation media to a local drive and run the setup from that local drive. If you do not, your installation may result in the following error:
>
> *An error occurred while copying the file d:\\en\Setup\ServerRoles\Common \en\Details Templates Editor.msc. The error code was 5.*
>
> If you did not copy the installation media locally and you receive this error, delete the contents of the c:\%windir%\temp file, copy the media locally, and run the command again.

4. When completed, the screen should look like the one in Figure 7.9.

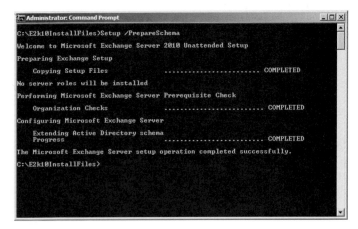

FIGURE 7.9   Preparing the Active Directory Schema.

5. When finished, leave your Command Prompt window open and continue with the next section.

Preparing the Domain and Organization

1. To prepare the Domain and Organization, log on to the Exchange server with your administrative account. This account must be a member of Enterprise Administrators and Domain Administrators groups.

2. From an administrator-enabled command prompt, change to the drive and directory that holds your Exchange Server 2010 installation media and run the following command:

```
Setup /PrepareAD /OrganizationName:SG or Setup /p /on:SG
```

where SG is the Organization Name for your environment. In our lab, we are using TestLab as the Organization Name, so the command will look like this:

```
Setup /PrepareAD /OrganizationName:TestLab
```

3. When completed, the screen should look like the one in Figure 7.10.

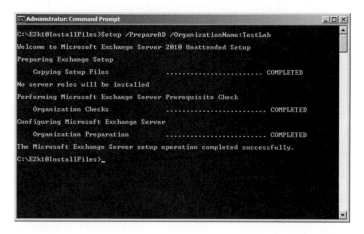

FIGURE 7.10   Preparing the Domain and Creating the Organization.

4. When finished, leave your Command Prompt window open and continue with the next section.

Installing Additional Required Operating System Components

There are several additional operating system components that are prerequisites for all Exchange Server 2010 roles. Additionally, there are specific prerequisites that are required for each of the individual roles.

To determine what prerequisites are needed for each role, review the Exchange Server 2010 Prerequisites document on Microsoft Technet. You can find this by going to http://technet.microsoft.com and searching for "Exchange 2010 Prerequisites."

The following components are required for a server that will contain the Hub Transport, Client Access, and Mailbox roles:

```
ServerManagerCmd -i Web-Server
ServerManagerCmd -i Web-ISAPI-Ext
ServerManagerCmd -i Web-Metabase
ServerManagerCmd -i Web-Lgcy-Mgmt-Console
ServerManagerCmd -i Web-Basic-Auth
```

```
ServerManagerCmd -i Web-Digest-Auth
ServerManagerCmd -i Web-Windows-Auth
ServerManagerCmd -i Web-Dyn-Compression
ServerManagerCmd -i NET-HTTP-Activation
ServerManagerCmd -I RPC-over-HTTP-proxy
```

To install these roles, perform the following steps:

1. Log on with your domain administrator account. From an administrator-enabled Command Prompt, run each of the commands above or, alternately, run the combined command as shown here:

   ```
   ServerManagerCmd -I Web-Server Web-ISAPI-Ext Web-Metabase Web-Lgcy-

   Mgmt-Console Web-Basic-Auth Web-Digest-Auth Web-Windows-Auth Web-Dyn

   -Compression NET-HTTP-Activation RPC-over-HTTP-proxy -Restart
   ```

   Note the addition of the -Restart at the end of the command to ensure the server does not try to restart between component installations.

   When complete, you should see Success: Installation Successful.

2. Reboot the server upon completion.

Installing Exchange Server 2010

Although the installation of all the Active Directory components, prerequisites, operating system components, updates, and hotfixes might seem to have taken forever, we are now finally ready to kick off the Exchange Server 2010 Installation.

Installing Exchange Server 2010 from the GUI Interface

Utilizing the Exchange Server 2010 Installation Wizard is the simplest way of deploying an Exchange server. The GUI interface is extremely intuitive and makes the installation a snap. To install Exchange Server using the Installation Wizard, perform the following tasks:

1. Log on with your domain administrator account. From your Exchange Server 2010 installation media, run the Exchange Installation Wizard (d:\setup.exe, for example).

2. Select Step 4: Choose Exchange Language Option. Select either Install All Languages from the Language Bundle or Install Only Languages from the DVD.

   If you select Install All Languages from the Language Bundle, another screen will appear giving you the option to either download the latest language pack bundle from the Internet or connect to a specific network path for the language files. When the language files have been installed, click Finish to return to the Exchange Server 2010 installation wizard.

3. Select Step 5: Install Microsoft Exchange.

4. From the Introduction screen, click Next to continue.

5. From the License Agreement screen, select I Accept the Terms in the License Agreement and click Next to continue.

6. On the Error Reporting screen, select whether you want to report installation errors to Microsoft. The default is No. Click Next to continue.

7. On the Installation Type screen, if you are installing specific roles, select Custom Exchange Server Installation. In our test environment, we are installing the Hub Transport, Client Access, and Mailbox server roles (as well as the Exchange Management Tools), so we select Typical Exchange Server Installation. Additionally, if you are not installing the Exchange Server application to the default location, click Browse to select the installation directory. When ready, click Next to continue.

8. On the Client Settings screen, if you have clients running either Outlook 2003 (or earlier) or Entourage, select Yes. Otherwise, select No. Selecting Yes creates a public folder database during the installation to support these clients. If No is selected, a public folder database can be created manually any time after the installation completes. When ready, click Next to continue.

9. The Configure Client Access Server External Domain screen is a new addition to the Exchange Installation Wizard (see Figure 7.11). If your client access server will be Internet facing, you can place a check in the box and enter the domain name that you will use (for example, mailservices.domain.com). If your client access server is NOT going to be Internet facing, leave this box unchecked. Click Next to continue.

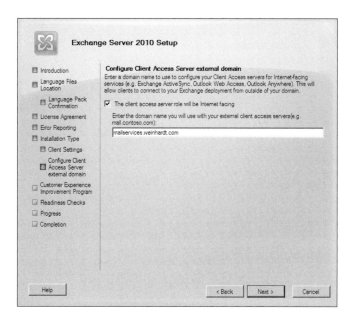

FIGURE 7.11 The New Configure Client Access Server External Domain screen.

10. On the Customer Experience Improvement Program screen, elect whether you want to join the Exchange Customer Experience Improvement Program. Make your selection and click Next to continue.

11. On the Readiness Checks screen, wait while the Install Wizard goes through the prerequisites for each of the selected roles. There may be hotfixes required for the roles being installed—if so, they will be identified as errors in the Readiness Check. Take the recommended actions to resolve them. When all readiness checks show as Completed, click Install to continue.

12. On the Completion screen, review the results of the installation. Ideally, you should see Successfully Installed. No Errors, as shown in Figure 7.12. When ready, uncheck the option to Finalize This Installation Using the Exchange Management Console and click Finish.

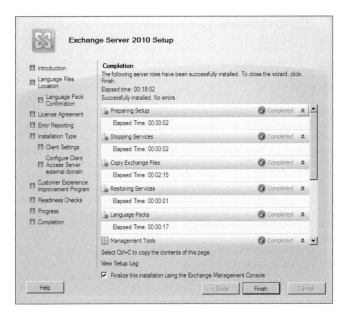

FIGURE 7.12   Completion screen reporting Successfully Installed. No Errors.

13. When you return to the Exchange Sever 2010 Installation Wizard, click Step 5: Get Critical Updates for Microsoft Exchange.

14. Install any available updates for Exchange Server and reboot the server if necessary.

Installing Exchange Server 2010 from the Command Prompt

In several situations (such as the deployment of an Exchange server in a remote location), administrators would prefer to install Exchange Server 2010 from the command prompt.

To do so, perform the following steps:

1. From an administrator-enabled command prompt, change to the drive and directory that contains your installation media.

  2. Run the following command:

```
Setup.com /mode:<setup mode> /roles:<roles to install>
➥[/OptionalParameters]
```

  For our purposes, we will simply run the following command:

```
Setup.com /mode:install /roles:H,C,M
```

The optional parameters cover all of the various configuration possibilities, including the organization name, target directory, source directory, default database name, and others.

All optional parameters can be viewed from the command line by typing:

```
Setup.com /help:install
```

Finalizing the Deployment

After completing the installation of the Exchange server software, there are several post-installation tasks that should be completed to ensure the installation completed successfully. These include the following:

- ▸ Exchange Server 2010 Post-Installation Tasks

- ▸ Review Exchange Installation Logs

- ▸ Review the Event Viewer for Errors and Warnings

- ▸ Verify Server Roles Were Successfully Installed

- ▸ Run the Microsoft Exchange Best Practice Analyzer

Exchange Server 2010 Post-Installation Tasks

After the Exchange installation has completed, open the Exchange Management Console and perform the Exchange Server 2010 Post-Installation Tasks. There are three sections:

- ▸ **Finalize Deployment Tasks**—Tasks required to complete the deployment of your Exchange organization. Apply to features that are enabled, but require additional configuration.

- ▸ **End-to-End Scenario Tasks**—Check list of the recommended tasks to perform after deploying Exchange Server.

- ▸ **Additional Post-Installation Tasks**—Optional steps for configuring Exchange Server features.

Reviewing Exchange Server Installation Logs

After the first Exchange Server 2010 server installation is complete, administrators should review the installation logs located on the root drive of the installation path selected. The typical location of the installation log file is C:\ExchangeSetupLogs.

The log files contain all the details pertaining to the installation of the Exchange server throughout the process.

Review the Event Viewer for Errors and Warnings

After an administrator has verified the installation logs for any anomalies and determined the implementation is a success, it is beneficial to review the Windows Event Viewer logs.

The Application Event Log can contain both positive and negative Exchange Server information about the installation. The Exchange Server events can consist of information, warning, and critical errors. The Application Event Log can be found by launching the Event Viewer included with Windows Server 2008.

Verify Server Roles Were Successfully Installed

Another recommended post-installation task is to verify that the appropriate server roles were installed. This can be conducted by running the get-ExchangeServer ¦fl command from within the Exchange Management Shell. Look at the ServerRole header to determine what roles are installed on the server.

Run the Microsoft Exchange Best Practice Analyzer

The final recommended post-installation task is to run the Exchange Best Practice Analyzer tool included with Exchange Server 2010. The Microsoft Exchange Best Practice Analyzer tool is designed for administrators to determine the overall health of the Exchange topology. The tool analyzes Exchange servers and verifies items that do not adhere to Microsoft best practices against a local repository.

The Exchange Best Practice Analyzer tool can be found by expanding the Toolbox node in the Exchange Management Console.

Summary

The installation of Exchange Server 2010 is a relatively simple process, thanks to the Exchange Server Installation Wizard. However, the key to a successful deployment is proper planning—administrators should know exactly what they are deploying before they begin, and the plan should be confirmed in a test environment before deployment.

A solid understanding of the prerequisites, testing the installation process, and carefully following the installation steps confirmed during the testing phase are critical to a smooth and error-free deployment.

Best Practices

The following are best practices from this chapter:

- ▶ Carefully review and complete all prerequisites before attempting to install Exchange Server 2010. The "trial and error" method is time consuming and frustrating. Proper planning before execution will greatly increase the chance of an error-free installation.

- ▶ For email messages to flow, you MUST install both the Mailbox server role and the Hub Transport server role in each Active Directory site that will house a mailbox server.

- ▶ You must install a client access server in each AD site that has a mailbox server.

- ▶ Use virtual servers when creating a test lab to simulate large production implementations and to minimize hardware costs.

- ▶ For small organizations, it is possible to install the Mailbox, Client Access, and Hub Transport roles all on the same server.

- ▶ Before installing Exchange Server 2007 into a production environment, it is beneficial to prototype the design in a test environment.

- ▶ To install Exchange Server 2010, the Active Directory forest functional level MUST be Windows Server 2003 or higher.

CHAPTER 8

Implementing Edge Services for an Exchange 2010 Environment

The Edge Transport server role provides an important layer of security between the Internet and an organization's messaging environment. Rather than having messages go straight from the Internet directly into an Exchange server, messages first go to an Edge server and are assessed and filtered based on certain policies or rules. The Edge server analyzes messages and can identify spam, content, connection trends, and take the appropriate action to prevent delivery of potentially harmful content, spam, and other undesired messages. The Edge server plays an important role in the messaging infrastructure, protecting the organization from attack, data leakage, and the delivery of unnecessary email, which ultimately can save an organization's reputation, reduce administrative overhead, and increase productivity. Ensuring the delivery of legitimate messages is just as, if not more, important than filtering out unwanted messages. The Edge server addresses this need by providing advanced controls and configuration options to ensure the delivery of legitimate email and assist administrators in troubleshooting.

By default, Edge Services are not installed on an Exchange server in the organization, and an organization can choose to not have an Edge server and still have a fully operational Exchange Server messaging environment. However, by placing an Edge server in the network, the organization substantially improves its ability to eliminate unwanted messages. Edge servers are typically deployed in a workgroup and are not members of Active Directory. Active Directory does, however, play an important role in the effectiveness of the Edge server's functionality.

This chapter focuses on the planning and implementation of Edge Services in an organiza-tion, along with critical configuration and tuning of Edge Services rules to further enhance the effectiveness of the Edge server in filtering messaging content.

Installing and Configuring the Edge Transport Server Components

The first thing that needs to be done is to determine how the Edge Transport server role will be implemented and configured in the Exchange Server environment. This involves planning and designing the placement of the Exchange Edge Transport server location, considering configuration options, and then actually installing the Edge Transport Services onto a server in the network. This section defines the configurable items for the compo-nents available on an Exchange 2010 server when the Edge Transport server role is selected during installation. Several items are identified in this section specific to the appropriate configuration options to properly achieve a secure, effective, and stable Edge Transport server environment.

Planning the Implementation of the Edge Transport Servers in Exchange Server

The first item to consider when installing and configuring the Edge Transport Services is the desired end result of the email message or connection being processed by the Edge Transport server. Determining what type of email should always be rejected, quarantined, or tagged for end-user review or which connections should be blocked and for how long will help reduce the amount of false positives and allow for a moderately aggressive spam filter-ing policy the first time Edge Transport servers begin monitoring email for an organization.

Planning for the Message Processing Order of Edge Services

To assist with the planning for your Edge Transport server deployment, take a moment to become familiar with the order in which filtering agents analyze messages. Understanding the order in which messages are processed will help you determine where you should place filters and assign settings for messages you do or don't want to receive. The Edge Transport Antispam filtering order is as follows:

1. An email message is received from the Internet.
2. The IP Block and Allow Lists are checked for a match to the sending IP address.
3. The IP Block List Providers and IP Allow List Providers are checked for a match to the sending IP address.
4. The Sender Filtering Agent checks the Blocked Senders list for a match.
5. The SenderID Agent performs a Sender Policy Framework (SPF) record lookup against the sending IP address.
6. The Recipient Filtering Agent checks the Blocked Recipients list for a match. This is also where messages addressed to nonexistent recipients get identified.

7. The Content Filtering Agent analyzes the content contained inside the message. Using Safelist Aggregation, the Content Filtering Agent also recognizes block and allow entries obtained from users' Outlook clients.

8. Attachments are analyzed by the Attachment Filter Agent. Edge transport rules run against the message.

9. The message is either delivered to the Hub Transport server, rejected, deleted, sent to the spam quarantine mailbox, or placed in the user's Junk E-Mail folder in the Outlook client.

NOTE

Messages can be identified for delivery or one of the blocking actions at any point in this process, depending on how the Edge Transport server agents have been configured.

TIP

Because the majority of unwanted email delivered today is spam, it is recommended to scan for spam messages before performing virus scanning. This reduces the load placed on the server when it performs virus scanning because virus scanning requires more processing power. This best practice assumes other antimalware mechanisms are in place throughout the network.

TIP

The Microsoft Exchange Server TechCenter, located at http://technet.microsoft.com/en-us/exchange/default.aspx, contains a wealth of information, tools, tips, and virtual labs for Exchange Server administrators.

TIP

The Microsoft Exchange Team Blog, located at www.msexchangeteam.com/, is a great place to stay current on Exchange Server news and communicate with other Exchange Server experts in the industry.

Installing Edge Transport Services on an Exchange Server

With a general concept of what the Edge Transport Services does, the next step is to install Edge Services on a system and begin configuring filters to test the results in your environment.

Unlike some server functions where you can test functionality in a lab environment, such as performance, features, and functions, testing Edge Services filtering is a little harder to do in an isolated setting. You need to have incoming messages, including spam and good messages, to filter to determine the effective results of the filters you create. The only way to truly measure the impact of Edge Services on an organization's email is on a production environment's mail flow.

Many organizations insert an Edge Services system into their network and set the filter settings low enough that no good messages are accidentally filtered. Then, the organization trends the effectiveness of the filters and tunes up the settings over time to be more and more restrictive, effectively increasing the filter catch rate. While the filtering is expanded, quarantine areas are monitored to look for false positive messages ensuring that good messages are not being blocked unintentionally or unnecessarily filtered. This process can take an organization several weeks to work through; however, it provides tight control and oversight on the processing of filtered messages.

Another option that is frequently adopted is where an organization sets up a test network with a live connection to the Internet and creates a "honeypot." A honeypot is an Internet-connected system that purposely attracts messages, including spam and other content, but is not connected to the production network. The process involves establishing a domain on the Internet, setting up an email server to the domain, and then signing up to be on mailing lists with an email account from this test domain. This might include going to the websites of established businesses such as retail stores, mail-order houses, and so on and signing up to receive emails about their promotions and regular newsletters. To get less desirable content, you could sign up to receive notification of events on sites with questionable reputations, such as triple-X sites. Do note that it could take several weeks before your honeypot attracts enough messages to make the filtering effective.

> **TIP**
>
> Prior to deploying any email filtering controls, organizations should first clearly define all domains, subdomains, and email addresses it wants to ensure isn't inadvertently blocked because it could have a direct impact on business. The domains, subdomains, and email addresses identified should first be placed in the Safe Sender's list on the Edge Transport server, with other filters put in place after.
>
> Realize that if you sign up on sites for the purpose of attracting spam, the incoming content might be inappropriate for professional organizations, and you risk exposing the external IP address and incoming ports to questionable systems or sources.

Preparing an Exchange Server 2010 System

As covered in Chapter 7, "Installing Exchange Server 2010," for installing core Exchange Server 2010 systems, the Exchange Edge Transport server role also needs to be installed on a computer running the Windows Server 2008 operating system. The minimum prerequisite required to install Exchange Server 2010 is Windows Server 2008 with at least Service Pack 2, Standard or Enterprise 64-bit Editions. Because this server will be connected to the Internet, hardening the server for security is extremely important; therefore, it is even more important that the server system is properly configured, and has the latest service pack and security updates installed. For more details on installing Windows Server 2008, see Chapter 7.

Installing the Exchange Server 2010 Application on the Server

After the system has Windows Server 2008 installed and is properly configured and updated, you can begin the installation of Exchange Server 2010. To install Exchange Server using the interactive installation process of Exchange Server, use the following steps:

1. Insert the Exchange Server 2010 CD or DVD (Standard or Enterprise).

2. AutoRun should launch a splash screen with options for installing the prerequisites and application. (If AutoRun does not execute, select Start, Run. Then type [Drive]:\setup.exe and click OK.)

3. Ensure all prerequisites for an Edge Transport Server have been met before attempting to install Exchange Server 2010:

    Windows 2008 Standard or Enterprise 64-Bit Edition with Service Pack 2

    Microsoft .NET Framework 3.5

    Windows Remote Management 2.0

    Windows PowerShell V2

    Active Directory Lightweight Directory Services (AD LDS)

4. On the splash screen, click Step 4: Choose Exchange Language Option and select to install all languages from the language bundle or only those on the DVD.

5. Click Step 5: Install Microsoft Exchange.

TIP

To quickly and easily install Active Directory Lightweight Directory Services (AD LDS), simply enter `ServerManagerCmd -i ADLDS` in the PowerShell command prompt.

NOTE

Before Microsoft Exchange Server 2010 can be installed, the Setup Installation Wizard will verify if the necessary prerequisites have been fulfilled. If the prerequisites have not been met, configure the prerequisites as recommended by the Configuration Wizard and run setup again. Prerequisites differ depending on the Exchange 2010 server role you are installing. For more details, see Chapter 7.

---

6. `Setup.exe` copies the setup files locally to the server on which Exchange Server 2010 is being installed.

7. In the Microsoft Exchange Server Installation Wizard dialog box, on the Introduction page, click Next.

8. At the License Agreement page, click I Accept the Terms in the License Agreement, and click Next.

9. At the Error Reporting page, select whether to participate in the Exchange Error Reporting program by sending feedback automatically to Microsoft, and then click Next.

10. At the Installation Type page, select the Custom Exchange Server Installation option and click Next.

11. On the Server Role selection page, select Edge Transport Server Role and click Next (see Figure 8.1).

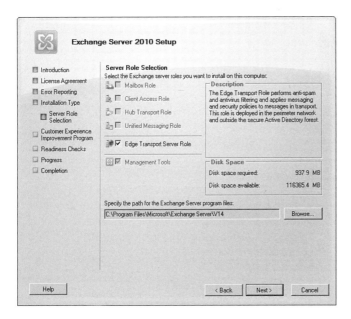

FIGURE 8.1   Adding the Exchange Transport Server role.

NOTE

If there is a need to change the installation folder, click Browse before proceeding and specify a path for the Exchange Server installation.

12. On the Customer Experience Improvement Program (CEIP) page, select one of the following two options: 1) Join the Customer Experience Improvement Program (CEIP) or 2) I Don't Wish to Join the Program at This Time. Click Next.

13. On the Readiness Checks page, the Installation Wizard is verifying that the appropriate Exchange Server prerequisites have been installed. View the status to determine if the organization and server role prerequisite checks completed successfully, and then click Install.

NOTE

If there are any errors returned or prerequisites not met on the Readiness Checks page, it is necessary to address these issues and retry the setup.

14. To complete the Exchange Server 2010 installation, on the Completion page, click Finish. The Exchange Management Console launches displaying the Exchange 2010 Post-Installation tasks.

NOTE

The Verify Deployment and Secure the Edge Transport Server by Using the Security Configuration Wizard tasks should be completed after you have finished configuring the Edge Transport server filters and services. The Security Configuration Wizard can be found under Start, All Programs, Administrative Tools.

NOTE

The Exchange Best Practices Analyzer should be run after you finish configuring the Edge Transport server filters and services. This tool scans the Exchange Server configuration and provides recommendations based on the configuration of the server. The Exchange Best Practices Analyzer can be found in the Toolbox located in the Exchange Management Console.

The Finalize Deployment Tasks, End-to-End Scenario tasks, and Post-Installation Tasks sections in the Exchange Management Console outline the recommended tasks for end-to-end email routing scenarios along with other help topics. For example, the Configure the Spam Confidence Level (SCL) Junk E-Mail Folder Threshold link provides steps for setting the SCL thresholds for delivery to the end user's Junk E-Mail folder in Outlook. Details for configuring these options are covered throughout the balance of this chapter.

Understanding the Edge Transport Components in the Exchange Management Console

8

After the Exchange Server software has been installed on the server system that will become the Edge Transport server, launch the Exchange Management Console to begin the process of configuring filters and parameters. The Exchange Management Console can be launched by doing the following:

1. Click Start, All Programs, Microsoft Exchange Server 2010.
2. Choose the Exchange Management Console program.

If the Edge Transport server role was selected during the Exchange Server 2010 setup process, the Edge Transport object and Toolbox are the only items that will be available in the console tree of the Exchange Management Console. Selecting the Edge Transport object in the console tree of the Exchange Management Console populates the work pane similar to what is shown in Figure 8.2 with the configurable options for the Edge Transport server.

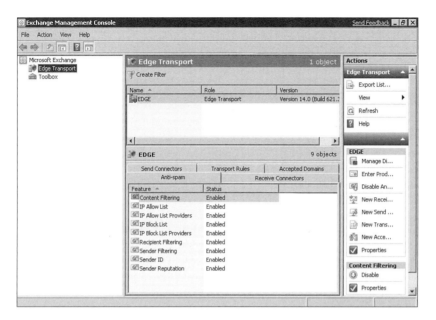

FIGURE 8.2   View of the Exchange Management Console configuration options for the Edge Transport server.

NOTE

All filters, lists, and connector settings are enabled by default. As changes are made and applied, they will be in effect on the Edge Transport server. Careful attention to changes is necessary, especially in a live environment. It is recommended to design and configure the first Edge Transport server offline with the minimal configuration needed for email routing and moderate antispam filtering. In the future, the aggressiveness of the antispam filters can be increased and additional filters can be added or modified. This makes troubleshooting easier and helps ensure delivery of legitimate email, while retaining the benefit of blocking known spam or messages carrying a malicious payload.

Several tabs are displayed within the action pane, including the following:

- ▶ Anti-Spam
- ▶ Receive Connectors
- ▶ Send Connectors
- ▶ Transport Rules
- ▶ Accepted Domains

NOTE

New to an Exchange 2010 Edge Transport Server is the Accepted Domains tab that enables Administrators to specify domains that they use for sending and receiving e-mail. Accepted Domains can be authoritative, internal, or external mail relays.

The Anti-Spam tab is selected by default and includes all the configurable filters, lists, and agents for effective spam filtering. Listed alphabetically, the following nine items are available under the Anti-Spam tab in the work pane:

- Content Filtering
- IP Allow List
- IP Allow List Providers
- IP Block List
- IP Block List Providers
- Recipient Filtering
- Sender Filtering
- Sender ID
- Sender Reputation

To the right of the Anti-Spam tab is the Receive Connectors tab. The Receive Connectors tab is used to configure email routing for messages received into the organization. From here, you can either create a new Receive Connector or modify the default Receive Connector labeled "Default internal receive connector <SERVERNAME>." This connector is enabled by default.

The tab to the right of the Receive Connectors tab is the Send Connectors tab. The Send Connectors tab is used to configure email routing for outgoing messages. From here, you can either create a new Send Connector or modify the default Send Connector labeled "Default internal send connector <SERVERNAME>."

NOTE

The Send Connector does not need to be configured if the Edge Transport server is subscribed to the Exchange Server 2010 organization and is receiving data from Active Directory through EdgeSync. See the "Using EdgeSync to Synchronize Active Directory Information to the Edge Transport Server" section later in this chapter for details on how to set up and configure EdgeSync.

The second to last tab in the action pane of the Exchange Management Console for Edge Transport servers is the Transport Rules tab. The Transport Rules tab allows for the creation of rules that should be applied to email messages passing through the Edge Transport server. Different conditions to check in email messages can be set for a rule.

The last tab in the action pane of the Exchange Management Console for Edge Transport servers is the Accepted Domains tab. The Accepted Domains tab enables for the creation of rules that specify which domains will be sending email to the Edge Transport server. For example, an organization would add any of their domains that are used for sending and receiving e-mail in the Accepted Domains tab.

Take a few minutes to navigate through the different items in the Exchange Management Console to become familiar with the location and options for each Edge Transport server component and service.

Utilizing the Basic Sender and Recipient Connection Filters

Connection filtering combats spam by blocking and/or allowing email messages from specific networks, IP addresses, and IP ranges. Email that is routed through Receive Connectors is processed by the Connection Filtering Agent. These messages are received from the Internet and travel inbound to the Edge Transport server for delivery to the recipient. The connection filtering agents (IP Block List, IP Allow List, IP Block List Providers, and IP Allow List Providers) are all enabled by default and can be configured using the Exchange Management Console or Exchange Management Shell.

An IP Allow List is a manual list of servers you trust to send email to your organization, more specifically those for which email communication cannot be disrupted. An IP Block List works in reverse, blocking email from specific email servers without further processing or retaining copies of the message. IP Block and Allow List Providers make it easier to stop email from known malicious entities or ensure that communication continues for others. This is usually a free service and allows administrators to easily subscribe to these lists and benefit from them.

One example of a real-time block list provider is The Spamhaus Project at www.spamhaus. org. Spamhaus maintains the Spamhaus Block List (SBL) and provides it as a free service for anyone to use. Spamhaus records their block entries in the SBL domain name system (DNS) zone, and that list is updated at regular intervals and then mirrored to servers around the world with direct hourly feeds to major Internet service providers (ISPs).

NOTE

If the message matches an entry from the IP Allow List, the message is assigned a Spam Confidence Level (SCL) rating of 0 regardless of any matches from the IP Block List. SCLs are covered in more detail later in this chapter in the section, "Using Content Filtering to Isolate Inappropriate Content."

NOTE

Changes described in this section are applied only to the local system. This is important to know if you have more than one Edge Transport server in your environment because the change will need to be made locally on all other Edge Transport servers.

To disable the IP Block List, IP Allow List, IP Block List Providers, and IP Allow List Providers agents using the Exchange Management Console, right-click the appropriate agent icon in the action pane and select Disable.

To disable these same agents using the Exchange Management Shell, run the set-< IPAllowListConfig, IPAllowListProvider, IPAllowListProvidersConfig, IPBlockListConfig, IPBlockListProvider, or IPBlockListProvidersConfig> command with the -Enabled $false parameter. For example:

"set-IPBlockListConfig -Enabled $false".

When configuring an IP Block List or IP Allow List, entities to block must be entered manually by the administrator because these lists are created and maintained locally on the server. Unless specified otherwise by the organization, reject email messages received from addresses on IP Block Lists to avoid further processing, increased system overhead, and consumed disk space.

TIP

The IP Block List is administered by and applies only to the organization the Edge server is routing mail for. The IP Block List can be used to define IP addresses that consistently send messages carrying a malicious payload or unacceptable content to the organization, whereas an IP Block List Provider might not identify these messages, which can occur for several reasons.

Configuring an IP Allow List Using the Exchange Management Console

Email administrators can configure Allow Lists on an Edge Transport server to ensure messages from desired source mail senders or organizations are not filtered and blocked at the Edge server. Administrators can define single IP addresses, IP addresses and subnet masks, and/or IP ranges from which to allow email messages.

TIP

In addition to IP v4, Exchange Server 2010's Edge Transport role supports filtering using IP v6 addresses and ranges.

> **NOTE**
>
> In some organizations, the Edge Transport server might sit behind another Simple Mail Transfer Protocol (SMTP) server that receives email from the Internet. In scenarios like this, the SMTP address of each upstream email server must be added to the Transport Configuration object in an Active Directory forest before connection filtering can be used. The SMTP addresses listed in the Transport Configuration object in Active Directory are replicated to the Edge Transport servers via EdgeSync. See the "Using EdgeSync to Synchronize Active Directory Information to the Edge Transport Server" section on how to configure EdgeSync.

To configure an IP Allow List using the Exchange Management Console, do the following:

1. Launch the Exchange Management Console.
2. Select Edge Transport in the console tree.
3. Double-click the IP Allow List item in the action pane.
4. In the IP Allow List Properties window, select the Allowed Addresses tab.
5. Click the Add button or the down arrow and choose the IP address option to add a Classless Internet Domain Routing (CIDR) IP v4 or v6 address or range (for example, 192.168.1.10, 192.168.1.10/24, or 2001:DB8:0:C000::/54).
6. Click OK to add the IP address or address range.
7. The IP addresses or address ranges are shown in the IP Address(es) section of the Allowed Addresses tab in the IP Allow List Properties window.

> **NOTE**
>
> You must first obtain the IP address or address ranges of the email server or servers for those you want included in the IP Allow List.

8. Click Apply to save changes or click OK to save changes and close the window.

> **NOTE**
>
> Entries in an IP Allow List cannot be scheduled to expire.

Alternatively, an IP address and subnet mask, or IP address range can be defined for filtering. To define an allowed IP address and subnet mask, do the following:

1. In the IP Allow List Properties window, select the Allowed Addresses tab.
2. Click the down arrow and select IP and Mask.
3. In the Add Allowed IP Address – IP and Mask window, enter the IP address in the IP Address field (for example, 192.168.1.10).

4. Enter the subnet mask of the IP address in the IP Mask field (for example, 255.255.255.0).

5. Click OK to add the IP address and IP mask.

To define an allowed IP address range, do the following:

1. In the IP Allow List Properties window, select the Allowed Addresses tab.

2. Click the down arrow and select IP Range.

3. In the Add Allowed IP Address – IP Range window, enter the first IP address in the Start Address field (for example, 192.168.1.1).

4. Enter the last IP address in the address range in the End Address field (for example, 192.168.255.255).

5. Click OK to add the IP address range.

Any defined IP addresses, IP addresses and subnet masks, and/or IP address ranges are shown in the IP Address(es) section of the Allowed Addresses tab of the IP Allow List Properties window.

Several list providers are available; the criteria for being added to or removed from their databases along with how often those databases are updated is different. For example, Microsoft provides updates twice per week for their Intelligent Message Filter, which is used with content filtering and the heuristics rules specific to phishing attempts. To configure an IP Allow List Providers using the Exchange Management Console, complete the following steps:

1. Launch the Exchange Management Console.

2. Select Edge Transport in the console tree.

3. Double-click the IP Allow List Providers item in the action pane.

4. In the IP Allow List Providers Properties window, select the Providers tab.

5. Click the Add button to define an IP Allow List Provider.

6. Enter the name of the provider in the Provider Name field.

7. Enter the IP address or fully qualified domain name (FQDN) in the Lookup Domain field.

8. Select Match Any Return Code to identify all delivery status notifications (DSN) and respond to them accordingly.

9. Select Match Specific Mask and Reponses to specify an IP address or subnet mask and respond accordingly or to list multiple IP addresses or subnet masks and respond accordingly.

10. Click OK when you are finished; the newly created provider entry will be displayed in the IP Allow List Providers Properties window.

Configuring an IP Block List Using the Exchange Management Console

The IP Block List is configured using the same procedures as the IP Allow List; however, an entry made in the IP Block List can be scheduled to expire, whereas an entry in the IP Allow List cannot. By default, new entries are set to never expire.

> **NOTE**
>
> You must first obtain the IP address or address ranges of the email server or servers that you want included in the IP Block List.

To configure an IP Block List using the Exchange Management Console, do the following:

1. Launch the Exchange Management Console.
2. Select Edge Transport in the console tree.
3. Double-click the IP Block List item in the action pane.
4. In the IP Block List Properties window, select the Blocked Addresses tab.
5. Click Add to make a new entry.
6. In the Add Blocked IP Address window, enter the CIDR information for the blocked addresses and select Block Until Date and Time.
7. Specify a date and time to expire the entry, and click OK.

Known spam servers and IP addresses sending malicious email should be double-checked for compliance before the expiration date comes due. Consider keeping maintenance logs or check entries frequently to avoid letting unwanted and previously blocked email messages (back) into your organization.

Configuring an IP Block List Provider Using the Exchange Management Console

The IP Block List Providers filter is configured in the same manner as the IP Allow List Providers filter; however, two different options are available in the IP Block List Providers properties that are not available when configuring an IP Allow List Provider.

The first difference can be found in the Add IP Block List Providers window when adding an IP Block List Providers on the Providers tab. A custom message can be specified or the default can be used for the Determine Error Message Returned when a Sender Is Blocked by a Provider option in the Return Status Codes section. To configure a custom error message, click the Error Messages button at the bottom of the window and select Custom Error Message in the IP Block List Providers Error Message window.

> **NOTE**
>
> A maximum of 240 characters can be entered into the Custom Error Message field.

The second difference between the IP Allow List Providers and IP Block List Providers filters is the ability to add exceptions. Exceptions to the IP Block List Provider's database can be configured on the Exceptions tab of the IP Block List Providers Properties window. On the Exceptions tab, you can add email addresses of recipients that should not be blocked in the Do Not Block Messages Sent to the Following E-Mail Addresses, Regardless of Provider Feedback field. Messages sent to addresses in this list will not be blocked if they trigger a match in the IP Block List Providers' database.

> **NOTE**
>
> You must first obtain the necessary DNS zone(s) or IP address(es) to query from the provider hosting the IP Block List being added.

Configuring IP Block and Allow Lists Using the Exchange Management Shell

Connection filtering can also be configured through the Exchange Management Shell. Each shell command has its own parameters you can set based on the action(s) performed by the command. There are four commands: Get, Add, Remove, and Set. Each command works with one or more IP Block and Allow List components.

The Get- command is used to retrieve the configuration of a component. For example, entering Get-IPBlockListConfig displays the IP Block List Configuration on the local system.

The Add- command can be used to add an IP Block or Allow List entry or list provider and to assign an expiration time to the entry. The following example adds an IP range to the block list with an expiration date and time (24-hour format):

```
Add-IPBlockListEntry -IPRange 192.168.1.1/16 -ExpirationTime "12/15/2007 11:30:00"
```

The Remove- command can be used to remove an IP Block or Allow List entry, list provider, or list entry. The following example removes a list provider using the name:

```
Remove-IPAllowListProvider -Identity Spamhaus
```

> **NOTE**
>
> Only static list entries can be removed using this command.

The Set- command allows an administrator to enable or disable the agent or modify the configuration of an IP Block or Allow List or list provider's configuration. The following example enables the Connection Filtering Agent on email distributed internally:

```
Set-IPBlockListConfig -InternalMailEnabled $true
Test-IPBlockListProvider -Identity Spamhaus -Server EDGE2
```

> **NOTE**
>
> The status of an IP Allow or Block List Provider can be tested using the Test-IPAllowListProvider or Test-IPBlockListProvider commands, respectively.

You can test the configuration of a Block or Allow List Provider using the `Test-BlockListProvider` and `Test-AllowListProvider` Exchange Server shell commands, respectively.

The Exchange Management Shell is covered in more detail in Chapter 9, "Using Windows PowerShell in an Exchange Server 2010 Environment."

Configuring Sender Filtering

Sender filtering allows an administrator to block email messages received from specific email addresses, domains, subdomains, and email messages that do not specify a sender. Email that is routed through Receive Connectors is processed by the Sender Filtering Agent. These messages are received from the Internet and travel inbound to the Edge Transport server for delivery to the recipient. Sender filtering, for example, can be a very useful tool when someone in an organization is being harassed by an external person or ex-employee, receiving consistent nondeliverable receipts (NDRs) or strange messages from the same source because of a virus or spam.

> **NOTE**
>
> Changes described in this section are applied only to the local system. This is important if you have more than one Edge Transport server in your environment.

The Sender Filtering Agent is enabled by default and can be configured using the Exchange Management Console or Exchange Management Shell.

To disable the Sender Filtering Agent using the Exchange Management Console, right-click the agent icon in the action pane and select Disable. To disable the Sender Filtering Agent using the Exchange Management Shell, run the `set-SenderFilterConfig` command with the `-Enabled $false` parameter—for example, `set-SenderFilterConfig -Enabled $false`.

The General tab of the Agent Properties window displays a brief description of the agent and its capabilities, its current status, and the last time the agent's settings were modified.

To add email addresses to the Sender Filtering list, double-click the Sender Filtering Agent in the action pane and select the Blocked Senders tab. From here, you can add, edit, or delete entries in the list. Checking the box at the bottom of the window enables the Block Messages that don't have sender information option. If an email address isn't specified in the message received, it will be blocked. This is a fairly common trick used in spammed messages.

Click Add in the Add Blocked Senders window to do the following:

1. Add an individual email address to block.
2. Add a domain and subdomains (if applicable) to block.

The Action tab allows you to specify whether to reject or stamp messages with Block Sender and continue processing them if the address matches an entry in the list. If messages are rejected because of a match in the Sender Filtering Agent, they can be responded to with a "554 5.1.0 Sender Denied" SMTP session error message and the session will also be closed. Stamping the message updates the metadata to indicate the sender was on the block list. This is taken into account by the content filter when it tabulates an SCL. The Sender Reputation filter agent uses the SCL rating when developing a sender reputation level.

Using the Exchange Management Shell to Add Blocked Senders

Sender filtering can also be configured through the Exchange Management Shell. Each shell command has its own parameters you can set based on the action(s) performed by the command. There are two commands: Get and Set.

The Get- command is used to retrieve the configuration of the Sender Filtering Agent. For example, entering Get-SenderFilterConfig displays the Sender Filtering configuration on the local system.

The Set- command allows an administrator to enable or disable the agent and modify the configuration of the agent. The following example enables the Sender Filtering Agent and rejects messages from blank senders on external SMTP connections:

```
Set-SenderFilterConfig -Enabled $true -Action Reject
-BlankSenderBlockingEnabled $true -ExternalMailEnabled $true -Enabled $true
```

Configuring Recipient Filtering

Recipient filtering allows an administrator to block email delivery from the Internet to a specific email address. Email that is routed through Receive Connectors is processed by the Recipient Filtering Agent. In addition, recipient filtering can prevent delivery of email messages to nonexistent accounts in Active Directory. This is extremely effective in stopping spam and virus-laden email to abused or commonly named email accounts (for example, support@companyabc.com or domain@domain.com).

The Recipient Filtering Agent is enabled by default and can be configured using the Exchange Management Console or Exchange Management Shell.

> ### NOTE
>
> Changes described in this section are applied only to the local system. This is important if you have more than one Edge Transport server in your environment.

To disable the Recipient Filtering Agent using the Exchange Management Console, right-click the agent icon in the action pane and select Disable. To disable the Recipient Filtering Agent using the Exchange Management Shell, run the set-RecipientFilterConfig command with the -Enabled $false parameter.

```
Example: set-RecipientFilterConfig -Enabled $false
```

The General tab of the Agent Properties window displays a brief description of the agent and its capabilities, its current status, and the last time the agent's settings were modified.

To add email addresses to the Recipient Filtering list, double-click the recipient Filtering Agent in the action pane and select the Blocked Recipients tab, as shown in Figure 8.3. From here, you can add, edit, or delete entries in the list. You can also enable the Block Messages Sent to Recipients That Do Not Exist in the Directory field. Enabling this feature prevents delivery of email messages to nonexistent accounts in Active Directory.

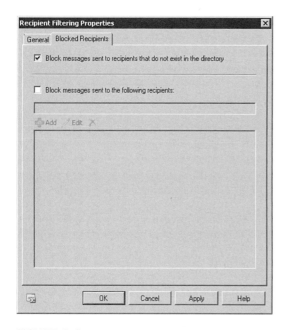

FIGURE 8.3   Blocked Recipients tab in the Exchange Management Console.

NOTE

For the Block Messages Sent to Recipients That Do Not Exist in the Directory feature to work, you must first configure the EdgeSync process and Active Directory Lightweight Directory Services (AD LDS) for recipient lookup. See the "Using EdgeSync to Synchronize Active Directory Information to the Edge Transport Server" section of this chapter for more information.

TIP

Using the Block Messages Sent to Recipients That Do Not Exist in the Directory option can significantly help reduce the amount of email sent to commonly targeted addresses like webmaster@companyabc.com, support@companyabc.com, and john@companyabc.com.

This also reduces the spammer's ability to identify which email addresses are valid when no response or a response other than "nonexistent user" is returned in a nondelivery report (NDR).

Using the Exchange Management Shell to Add Blocked Recipients

Recipient filtering can also be configured through the Exchange Management Shell. Each shell command has its own parameters you can set based on the action(s) performed by the command. There are two commands: `Get` and `Set`.

The `Get-` command is used to retrieve the configuration of the Sender Filtering Agent. For example, entering `Get-RecipientFilterConfig` displays the Recipient Filtering configuration on the local system.

The `Set-` command allows an administrator to enable or disable the agent or modify the configuration of the agent. The following example enables the Recipient Filtering Agent and rejects messages to nonexistent recipients on external SMTP connections:

```
Set-RecipientFilterConfig -Enabled $true -ExternalMailEnabled $true -
RecipientValidationEnabled $true
```

Utilizing SenderID on an Edge Transport Server

SenderID is a very effective defense mechanism against spam, phishing schemes, and mass-mailing computer viruses when an organization has their SenderID information properly registered. One, if not the most common, trick used by malicious email authors is the forging of fields in an email message's header information—specifically, the From address. This is often referred to as spoofing a sender's email address. SenderID processes inbound email from the Internet. These are the messages that are routed through the Receive Connector on the Edge Transport server.

Configuring SenderID

The SenderID Agent is installed and enabled by default when the Exchange Edge Transport server is installed on a Windows Server system. Because it is installed and enabled, the focus of this section is to identify the specific configuration tasks needed in configuring SenderID using the Exchange Management Console or Exchange Management Shell.

> **NOTE**
>
> Changes described in this section are applied only to the local system. This is important if you have more than one Edge Transport server in your environment.

To disable the SenderID Agent using the Exchange Management Console, right-click the agent icon in the action pane and select Disable. To disable the SenderID Agent using the Exchange Management Shell, run the `set-SenderIDConfig` command with the `-Enabled $false` parameter, for example:

```
"set-SenderIDConfig -Enabled $false"
```

The General tab of the Agent Properties window displays a brief description of the agent and its capabilities, its current status, and the last time the agent's settings were modified.

Malicious email crafters forge this field to hide their identity to avoid being discovered or direct any reply traffic to a specific or random domain, purposefully or not. Another reason this field is commonly forged is to trick the recipient into believing the message is from someone they know, thus increasing the likelihood it will be read and actions such as opening an attachment or web page will be carried out.

SenderID's primary purpose is validating that the server sending the message to your email server was authorized to do so for the domain specified in the From field of the message headers. When configured and maintained correctly, SenderID can accurately eliminate malicious email without extensive analysis of the content contained inside. In this section, you learn how to create and look up SPF records, how to configure SenderID, and how SenderID Framework (SIDF) has merged these technologies together.

When configuring SenderID, take into consideration which sending entities should always be allowed to deliver email messages to your organization, regardless of having a published SPF record. For example, in medium to large organizations, a coordinated outreach to the other companies the organization does business with might be necessary to inform them of the impact SenderID could have on email they send to your organization and how to mitigate that impact. Administrators should avoid automatically rejecting or deleting messages initially to help identify any senders that should be "white listed." Following this recommendation drastically reduces the impact the loss of legitimate email can have on an organization.

SenderID is an invaluable tool that can combat more sophisticated spam attacks such as the Reverse NDR attack that delivers spam email to recipients using a forged FROM field and targeting accounts that obviously don't exist. The spam message is sent to bogus e-mail addresses in an organization; however, the NDR is relayed to the address in the FROM field—the target of the spammers campaign. This attack makes it appear to other systems that the organization sending the NDRs could be spamming and places the organization at risk of being placed on a block list. These types of NDRs are also referred to as backscatter.

There are two components to getting SenderID functional on an Edge Transport server: the SenderID Agent and SPF records. SPF records aren't something that is configured on the Edge Transport server, but rather a piece of information SenderID requires to determine how to handle the message.

> **NOTE**
>
> SenderID also works with the Sender Reputation Agent to help the Sender Reputation Agent compute a Sender Reputation Level (SRL) for the sending entity. The Sender Reputation Agent is covered in the section "Configuring the Sender Reputation Agent Using the Exchange Management Console" later in this chapter.

SenderID validates the sending email server by querying the DNS server providing name resolution for the Internet for the sending server's Sender Policy Framework (SPF) record, provided the administrator of the sending system created and published one correctly. SPF is the "part" that makes SenderID work. SPF is an open standard added to the SMTP protocol and was designed by Meng Weng Wong and Mark Lentczner to help combat unwanted email without the use of antispam engines or extensive content filtering. Extensive SPF record creation, supporting different SPF configurations and/or multiple domains, and advanced syntax use is beyond the scope of this text. This section outlines what SPF is, how it works, how it integrates with SenderID, and how to create and activate a basic SPF record.

An SPF record, put simply, is a listing in DNS of what systems are authorized to send email for a specific domain or set of domains. Publishing an SPF record allows others to cross-reference the IP addresses of the mail servers in an organization against that organization's DNS entry for their domain, specifically a mail exchange (MX) record. This is also sometimes referred to as a reverse MX lookup.

The following is a sample SPF record for `CompanyABC.com`:

```
v=spf1 mx ip4:192.168.1.150 -all
```

The following is a sample SPF record for CompanyABC.com using multiple identifiers to include MX and A record lookup in DNS, and to allow email from another domain, Company123.org:

```
v=spf1 mx a:mail.companyabc.com include:company123.org -all
```

An SPF record can contain multiple domain mechanisms and domain modifiers to provide the correct identification and email handling or policy information when queried by other email systems running a SenderID or SPF filtering configuration.

> **NOTE**
>
> More information regarding Sender ID and Sender Policy Framework (SPF) can be found at http://www.ietf.org under Request for Comments (RFC) 4405, 4406, 4407, and 4408.

SPF only needs three pieces of information to work:

▶ The domain of the From address in the message headers

▶ The purported IP address of the email server that sent the message

▶ The HELO or EHLO parameter of the server that sent the message

Using this information, SenderID can determine if the IP address was authorized to send email for the domain listed in the sender's email address.

SenderID Framework (SIDF) is a combination of two similar technologies: Sender Policy Framework (SPF) and Microsoft's CallerID for email.

Creating a Sender Policy Framework Record

This section walks you through setting up an SPF record using the Microsoft Sender ID Framework SPF Record Wizard located at www.microsoft.com/mscorp/safety/content/technologies/senderid/wizard/.

On the Microsoft Sender ID Framework SPF Record Wizard web page, first enter the domain for which you want to create a record (for example, `companyabc.com`) in Step 1 of 4: Identify Your Domain field on the website, and click Next. The website checks DNS information about the domain to see what records, including SPF, exist. If no records exist, you are taken to the next step, Step 2 of 4: Display Published DNS Records. Review the information provided to ensure its accuracy, and click Next when you are ready to proceed to Step 3: Create SPF Record.

In Step 3 of 4: Create SPF Record of the Microsoft Sender ID Framework SPF Record Wizard, seven sections can be configured to support the organization's email structure. On this page, you can create an SPF record to reflect the following:

▶ That the domain does not send email.

▶ That inbound email servers also send email for the domain.

▶ That outbound email servers are different from the domain's inbound email servers.

▶ That all reverse DNS records (PTR) resolve to the domain's outbound email servers.

▶ That a domain's outbound email is routed through another domain (outsourced).

▶ That the domain will send email from an IP address not listed in the SPF record being created.

▶ That the SPF record can be used to validate either the Purported Responsible Address (PRA) derived from the message headers, or from the MAIL FROM (or reverse-path) address derived from the SMTP protocol's MAIL command, or both. The PRA is the [nonforged] IP address of the system responsible for sending the email message and the MAIL FROM tag (often forged) designates the email address the message is being delivered as.

NOTE

Some fields in the form might already contain data when the wizard queried DNS for information about the domain entered in Step 1.

For this example, you will create an SPF record in which companyabc.com's SMTP server is running the Edge Transport server role and handles both incoming and outgoing email. No other domains or IP addresses should be allowed to route email for companyabc.com.

In the form, specify that the domain's inbound email servers can send email by selecting the check box of the same name in the Inbound Mail Servers Send Outbound Mail section of the form. Next, specify that the IP address of the outbound email server for companyabc.com is 192.168.2.150 by adding that IP address to the Outbound Mail Server Addresses field in the form. Accept the default of Discouraged to the question regarding whether legitimate email can or will originate from an IP address not included in this record, and allow the record to be used to validate both the Purported Responsible IP address (PRA) and MAIL FROM address in the message headers. Now that the information has been entered, you can proceed to Step 4 of 4: Generate SPF Record, where the record can be created so it can be reviewed and saved for later use.

The record example for companyabc.com looks like this:

```
v=spf1 mx ip4:192.168.1.150 –all <or> ~all
```

The v=spf1 designates that this is an SPF record and it is version 1. The portion mx IP4:192.168.2.150 signifies the email server at 192.168.2.150 is authorized to send and receive email for company abc.com. The -all closes the record by stating that no one besides the IP addresses in companyabc.com's MX records are authorized to send email using a companyabc.com and can be rejected. From here, you can copy the syntax, paste it into a Notepad or WordPad document, save the file in standard ASCII text (TXT) format, and add it to DNS so other organizations using Edge Transport servers or an implementation of SPF can look up companyabc.com's SPF record.

NOTE

The SPF record must be published in DNS as a text file to be properly recognized. Beyond formatting of input on the form, the Sender ID Framework SPF Record Wizard does not test or validate the settings entered. After the wizard has finished creating your SPF record, take a moment to view it for accuracy before exporting it for use on the DNS servers.

More information about SPF—extensive SPF record creation, supporting different SPF configurations, multiple domains, and advanced syntax use—is beyond the scope of this text. More information can be obtained at the Microsoft website (www.microsoft.com/ mscorp/safety/technologies/senderid/resources.mspx) or Sender Policy Framework (www. openspf.org).

So far, we've covered how SenderID works, how to create and manage simple SPF records, and considered the impact SenderID can have on legitimate email. At this point, the SenderID Agent on the Edge Transport server(s) can be configured.

Configuring the SenderID Agent on the Exchange Edge Transport Server

The SenderID Agent is enabled by default on Exchange Server 2010 Edge Transport servers. Configuration is quick and straightforward because SenderID only relies on a couple of items to function properly. SenderID like other spam-filtering technologies can impact legitimate email but, as discussed earlier, there are ways to mitigate this impact while still identifying messages that don't have an SPF record.

To begin configuring SenderID, do the following:

1. Launch the Exchange Management Console by doing the following on the Exchange server. Click Start, All Programs, Microsoft Exchange Server 2010.

2. Choose Exchange Management Console.

3. Double-click the SenderID Agent in the action pane.

4. Select the Action tab.

From here, you can change the action taken on messages if the SenderID check fails. There are different actions to choose from. One action is to Stamp Message with Sender ID Result and Continue Processing. This is the default action and appends certain information to the message headers for further processing by the Content Filtering Agent. The Content Filtering Agent then takes this information into account when tabulating the overall spam score assigned to the message, also known as the Spam Confidence Level (SCL).

TIP

When you first implement SenderID filtering, it is recommended to "stamp" messages to assist in filtering out false positives and generate a white list of legitimate senders and domains. After the organization is comfortable with the established white list, messages can be rejected.

Another option is to use the "exp" modifier in your SPF record and include a uniform resource locator (URL) to an Internet web page where others can retrieve information about your email policy, SPF records, and contact information. This helps offset false positives when rejecting email messages that fail to comply with SPF.

The actions available if a SenderID check fails include the following:

- ▶ Reject the message.

- ▶ Delete the message.

- ▶ Stamp message with SenderID result and continue processing.

Choosing to reject the message sends an error response to the sending server. The text contained in this error message corresponds to the Sender ID status derived from processing the SPF record of the message.

Choosing to delete the message sends a fake OK SMTP command to the sending server. The message is deleted and the sender is not notified.

Accepting the default action of Stamp Message with Sender ID Result and Continue Processing appends the Sender ID status derived from the SPF record lookup into the message headers for further processing by the Content/IMF filter. This information, often called metadata, is used by the Content/IMF filter to create the SCL.

Using the Exchange Management Shell to Configure SenderID

One limitation of SenderID is the inability to exclude recipients and domains from SenderID filtering through the Exchange Management Console. Exclusion of recipients and domains from SenderID filtering can only be accomplished using the Exchange Management Shell's Set-SenderIdConfig command. The following example enables the SenderID Agent on external SMTP connections, bypasses checking one external domain, and sets the action on spoofed messages:

```
Set-SenderIdConfig -BypassedSenderDomains Microsoft.com -Enabled $true
➥-ExternalMailEnabled $true -SpoofedDomainAction Delete
```

The Get- command is used to retrieve the configuration of the Sender Filtering Agent. For example, entering Get-SenderIDConfig displays the Sender Filtering configuration on the local system.

You can test the configuration of SenderID using the Test-SenderID Exchange shell command. The following example tests to see if the SPF record resolves correctly:

```
Test-SenderId -IPAddress 192.168.1.150 -PurportedResponsibleDomain
➥mail.companyabc.com
```

The Exchange Management Shell is covered in more detail in Chapter 9, "Using Windows PowerShell in an Exchange 2010 Environment."

Using Content Filtering to Isolate Inappropriate Content

Content filtering is not only effective for eliminating spam, but it can also be beneficial for identifying messages containing content deemed unacceptable to the organization, such as sexually derogatory remarks or racial slurs. The content filter processes messages that are routed through the Receive Connector on the Edge Transport server. The Content Filtering Agent is enabled by default and can be configured using the Exchange Management Console or Exchange Management Shell.

NOTE

Changes described in this section are applied only to the local system. This is important if you have more than one Edge Transport server in your environment.

To disable the Content Filtering Agent using the Exchange Management Console, right-click the agent icon in the action pane and select Disable. To disable the Content Filtering Agent using the Exchange Management Shell, run the set-ContentFilterConfig command with the -Enabled $false parameter:

For example "set-ContentFilterConfig -Enabled $false"

The General tab of the Agent Properties window displays a brief description of the agent and its capabilities, its current status, and the last time the agent's settings were modified.

The content filter in Exchange Server 2010 builds on the Intelligent Message Filter technology that Microsoft developed and included in Exchange Server 2003. The Intelligent Message filtering technology, a proprietary message–analyzing filter developed by Microsoft, "learns" which messages are spam and legitimate by analyzing the characteristics contained in both. This filter is updated periodically through Microsoft Software Update Services.

After message analysis has occurred, the content filter assigns an overall score to the message that corresponds with an action you choose based on the needs of the organization. For example, all messages scoring an 8 or higher might be deleted, whereas any message scoring a 3 or lower might be delivered. This message score is often referred to as the SCL. Messages are assigned a score ranging from 0–9, with 9 being the "most confident" score that the message is spam.

The content filter can leverage the end user's Safe Recipients List, Safe Senders List, or trusted contacts list in Outlook (2003 or later) by enabling Safelist Aggregation. Safelist Aggregation uses the entries inside of Outlook to help populate the list of legitimate senders so they can be safely bypassed by the Content Filtering Agent. Configuring Safelist Aggregation is covered in the section "Implementing Safelist Aggregation for Outlook 2003 and Outlook 2007," later in this chapter.

To begin configuring content filtering, launch the Exchange Management Console, and double-click the Content Filtering Agent in the action pane. From here, you can customize the Custom Words list to block and allow certain words or phrases, add recipients to the exclusions list to exempt them from content filtering, and configure the actions to take on messages based on the messages' SCL. Some of these items are not available through the Exchange Management Console and can only be configured through the Exchange Management Shell.

The basic function of configuring the content filter on an Edge Transport server is performed as follows:

1. Enable the Content Filtering Agent (default is enabled).
2. Designate and specify a quarantine mailbox for captured messages.
3. Enable and configure SCL thresholds and actions.
4. Enable or disable puzzle validation.
5. Specify recipient and sender exceptions.
6. Configure Allow phrases and Block phrases.
7. Set the rejection response.

These functions are covered in the balance of this section.

Configuring the Quarantine Mailbox for Captured Messages

Before configuring other content-filtering components, it is advised that you first configure the mailbox that will store messages on which an action of "quarantine" was taken. This action is based on the corresponding SCL for the Quarantine Messages That Have an SCL Rating Larger or Equal To setting in the Exchange Management Console, or the SCLQuarantineEnabled and SCLQuarantineThreshold parameters of the Set-ContentFilterConfig Exchange Management Shell command.

To configure a mailbox for content filtering, complete the following steps:

1. Create a user account with a mailbox in Active Directory if the quarantine mailbox will reside on your internal Exchange servers. Creating mailboxes is covered in Chapter 18, "Administering an Exchange Server 2010 Environment."
2. To configure the mailbox using the Exchange Management Console, select the Action tab of the Content Filter and enter the email address of the mailbox.
3. To configure the mailbox using the Exchange Management Shell, run the `Set-ContentFilterConfig` with the `–QuarantineMailbox` parameter.

   Then run the Exchange Management Console.
4. In the Content Filtering Properties window, select the Custom Words tab.
5. Enter the word or phrase you want to allow in the Messages Containing These Words or Phrases Will Not Be Blocked field. Email messages containing these entries will always be allowed to bypass content filtering.
6. Click Add to include the new entry.
7. To remove an entry, highlight it, and click the Delete button.
8. Click Apply to save your changes or OK to save changes and close the Content Filter dialog box.

Configuring Spam Quarantine

The spam quarantine holds messages that meet or exceed the SCL threshold set in the Content Filtering Agent on the Edge Transport server. Messages marked for quarantine are sent to a quarantine mailbox where they can be reviewed and delivered, if necessary. Administrators who need to resend a quarantined message can use the Send Again feature of Outlook. For more information regarding Microsoft Outlook, refer to Part VIII, "Client Access to Exchange Server 2010."

For messages to be quarantined, an Active Directory user and corresponding mailbox must exist, solely for this purpose. If you are running multiple Edge Transport servers, you might consider having one spam quarantine mailbox per server. Although this might increase the amount of effort needed to find captured messages, it decreases the load expected of one mailbox server. This can also help with troubleshooting configuration differences between Edge Transport servers. Depending on the size of the organization and the amount of Internet email received, the spam quarantine can grow substantially. For more information on creating mailboxes, refer to Part VI, "Exchange Server 2010 Administration and Management."

> **TIP**
>
> It is recommended to dedicate an Exchange Server database to the spam quarantine mailbox, configure an email retention policy or recipient policy to restrict the mailbox size, and set the duration for how long quarantined messages should be retained.

After a mailbox has been created for the use of quarantining spam messages, the spam quarantine mailbox must be specified on the Edge Transport server. The spam quarantine mailbox can only be specified on an Edge Transport server using the Set-ContentFilterConfig command with the QuarantineMailbox parameter.

```
Set-ContentFilterConfig -QuarantineMailbox anti-spam@companyabc.com
```

The Set-ContentFilterConfig command is covered in more detail in the section "Using the Exchange Management Shell to Configure Content Filtering" later in this chapter.

Configuring the Allowed Keyword or Phrases List

Content filtering varies from organization to organization, so Exchange Server 2010 Edge Services has exceptions to allow for keywords or phrases to not cause a message to be filtered or blocked. This is commonly used in the medical profession where the reference to certain drugs, body parts, or human activities is part of the field of business, whereas in other organizations, those references are commonly used in unwanted or unsolicited email messages.

To configure the Exchange Server 2010 Edge Transport server to allow keywords or key phrases, do the following from within the Exchange Management Console:

1. Select the Custom Words tab.

2. Enter the word or phrase you want to allow in the Messages Containing These Words or Phrases Will Not Be Blocked field. Email messages containing these entries will always be allowed to bypass content filtering.

3. Click Add to include the new entry.

4. To remove an entry, highlight it, and click the Delete button.

5. Click Apply to save your changes or OK to save changes and close the Content Filter dialog box.

> **NOTE**
>
> Messages containing an allowed word or phrase are given an SCL score of 0.

Configuring Keyword or Phrases List to Block Messages

The second section of the Custom Words tab allows you to define words or phrases in messages that should be blocked. There are two exceptions to this: use of the allowed word or phrase list and the exclusions list. Entries in this section result in the message being blocked, unless the word or phrase appears in the Messages Containing These Words or Phrases Will Not Be Blocked section or the recipient's email address is listed in the exclusions list.

For example, your organization might have an email policy that states any message containing racial slurs or derogatory terms should be blocked unless the message is sent to or from the organization's attorneys and senior management. To accomplish this, you would use the Block Messages Containing These Words or Phrases section to include the racially discriminatory language, the Messages Containing These Words or Phrases Will Not Be Blocked section could contain the lawyers' names, office names, addresses, and so forth of the law firm the attorneys work for, and the Exceptions tab would hold the email addresses of the company's executive staff. This would ensure any message not deemed appropriate would be blocked unless it contained information about the company's lawyers or were sent or copied to one of the organization's executives.

To configure blocked keywords or phrases, from within the Exchange Management Console, do the following:

1. Select the Custom Words tab.

2. Enter the word or phrase you want to block in the Block Messages Containing These Words or Phrases field. Email messages containing these entries will always be blocked unless they contain a word or phrase that is included in the allow list or are sent to recipients included in the Exceptions tab.

3. Click Add button to include the new entry.

4. To remove an entry, highlight it, and click the Delete button.

5. Click Apply to save your changes or OK to save changes and close the Content Filter dialog box.

> **NOTE**
>
> Messages containing a blocked word or phrase are given an SCL score of 9.

As a recommendation from experience, get creative but, be precise! In the previous example scenario, you could request the law firm to insert a particular code or phrase in messages sent to your company. This makes the message easier for your company to identify and entries in your content filter lists easier to manage, and increases the reliability of content filtering overall. Avoid entering words and phrases that are arbitrary. Instead choose keywords and phrases specific to why you are blocking the message and that won't be mistakenly identified in legitimate messages. This reduces the amount of false positives and processing power needed by the content filter.

Configuring the Exceptions List

The next item in the Content Filter Properties window is the Exceptions tab. The Exceptions tab is used to define email addresses for those you do not want to filter their messages by content. For example, a company might include the human resources', attorneys', or system administrator's mailbox because they might need to view these messages to fulfill the duties of their jobs, whereas the same is not true for the rest of the organization's employees. To configure exceptions, within the Exchange Management Console, do the following:

1. In the Content Filter Properties window, select the Exceptions tab.
2. In the Don't Filter Messages Sent to the Following Recipients field, enter the full email address of the account.
3. Click Add to include the entry in the list.
4. To remove an entry, highlight it, and click the Delete button.
5. To edit the email address of an entry, highlight it, and click the Edit button.
6. Click Apply to save your changes or OK to save changes and close the Content Filter.

> **NOTE**
>
> The exception list is restricted to a maximum of 100 entries.

Setting the Action Tab of the Content Filtering Agent

The last tab of the Content Filtering Agent is the Action tab. The Action tab stores the configuration for what actions should be taken on a message based on the calculated SCL. The SCL can range from 0 to 9; 9 designates a high confidence level that the message is spam or contains a match to a block list, and 0 designates a high confidence level the message is valid or contains a match to an allowed list.

In the Content Filtering Agent, an action of Delete takes priority over the action of Reject, which takes priority over the action of Quarantine. For example, when all three actions are enabled with a threshold of Delete if SCL is 8 or higher, Reject if SCL is 6 or higher, and Quarantine if 4 or higher, a message with an SCL of 9 would get deleted even though it technically is higher than the other thresholds, and a message with an SCL of 5 would get quarantined. This hierarchy is by design. At least one but not all actions need to be enabled to use content filtering.

> **TIP**
>
> To avoid an impact on legitimate email (false positives), start with a more conservative approach, leveraging either high SCL numbers as the threshold or quarantining most spam first. In addition, IP and sender blocking previously defined in this chapter also reduces the amount of false positives. The aggressiveness of the content filter can always be increased and messages that are quarantined can easily be delivered or retrieved.

Fine-Tuning Content Filtering

Content filtering can be used for more than just identifying the content of messages in reviewing whether content is considered spam or whether the content is appropriate for the users of an organization. The content filtering function can be used to delete, reject, or quarantine messages based on an SCL rating where the fine-tuning of the SCL helps keep unwanted messages out of the organization's email system, yet minimizes the potential of false positives where messages are deleted or quarantined even when they are being sent by legitimate senders. This section covers the fine-tuning of content filtering on an Edge Transport server.

Configuring Content Filtering Actions

Several options are available in the Content Filter properties that can be configured. The following goes through the configuration options and notes what the various settings do. To configure content filtering, do the following:

1. In the Content Filter Properties window, select the Action tab.

2. Check the Delete Messages That Have an SCL Rating Larger or Equal To option, and set the threshold appropriately. All messages with the respective SCL are deleted.

3. Check the Reject Messages That Have an SCL Rating Larger or Equal To option, and set the threshold appropriately. All messages with the respective SCL are rejected.

4. Check the Quarantine Messages That Have an SCL Rating Larger or Equal To option, and set the threshold appropriately. All messages with the respective SCL are quarantined.

> **NOTE**
>
> A quarantine mailbox must first be defined. A prompt appears if it is not and the action cannot be enabled. See the section "Configuring the Quarantine Mailbox for Captured Messages" of this chapter for more information.

5. To disable an action, uncheck the box next to it.

6. To change the corresponding SCL threshold of an action, either enter a new number in the box or use the up/down arrows to change the value.

7. Click Apply to save your changes or OK to save changes and close the Content Filter.

Using the Exchange Management Shell to Configure Content Filtering

Content filtering can also be configured through the Exchange Management Shell. Each shell command has its own parameters you can set based on the action(s) performed by the command. There are four commands: Get, Add, Remove, and Set. Each command works with one or more content-filtering components.

The Get- command is used to retrieve the configuration of a component. For example, entering Get-ContentFilterConfig displays the Content Filter configuration on the local system.

The Add-ContentFilterPhrase command can be used to add an acceptable or unacceptable word or phrase to the filter. The following example adds an unacceptable phrase:

```
Add-ContentFilterPhrase -Phrase "this is unacceptable" -Influence BadWord
```

The Remove-ContentFilterPhrase command can be used to remove a blocked or allowed keyword or phrase. The following example removes an unacceptable phrase:

```
Remove-ContentFilterPhrase -Identity "this is unacceptable"
```

> **NOTE**
>
> When replacing the <String> option with a phrase, the phrase must be enclosed with quotation marks and the phrase must be "influenced" so it gets added to the correct list.

The Set command allows an administrator to enable or disable the agent and modify the configuration of the content filter components. The following example enables the Content Filtering Agent on email received on External SMTP connections, bypasses scanning of one domain, enables Outlook 2007 postmark validation, sets the spam quarantine mailbox, and assigns the thresholds for the different actions.

```
Set-ContentFilterConfig -BypassedSenderDomains Microsoft.com -Enabled $true
➥-ExternalMailEnabled $true -OutlookEmailPostmarkValidationEnabled $true
```

```
➥ -QuarantineMailbox anti-spam@companyabc.com -SCLDeleteEnabled $true
➥ -SCLDeleteThreshold 7 -SCLQuarantineEnabled $true -SCLQuarantineThreshold 4]
➥ -SCLRejectEnabled $false
```

Configuring Puzzle Validation for Content Filtering

Puzzle validation in Exchange Server 2010 works in conjunction with the Outlook 2007
Email Postmark validation feature to lower the SCL of a message that was sent using the
Outlook 2007 client. This helps reduce false positives in email messages exchanged
between organizations running exclusively in Exchange Server 2010 and Outlook 2007
messaging environments. Postmark validation is disabled by default.

NOTE

Puzzle validation can only be configured using the `Set-ContentFilterConfig`
Exchange Management Shell command.

When Email Postmark validation is configured for Outlook 2007 clients, and those clients
send an email message, a presolved computational puzzle is inserted into the message that
an Exchange 2010 server running the Content Filtering Agent with Puzzle Validation
enabled will be able to "solve." If the message was marked as spam, but contains an
Outlook 2007 Postmark Validation stamp and the Content Filtering Agent was able to
successfully resolve the inserted "puzzle," then the SCL of the message will be lowered
because the sender's software has technically been validated, making the message unlikely
to be spam. If the message contains an invalid Email Postmark validation header or no
Email Postmark validation at all, the SCL will remain unchanged.

To enable or disable Puzzle Validation and Outlook 2007 Email Postmark validation, run
the following command in the Exchange Management Shell:

```
Set-ContentFilterConfig -OutlookEmailPostmarkValidationEnabled <$true ¦ $false>
```

where `$true` enables puzzle validation and `$false` disables puzzle validation.

Using Content Filtering to Allow and Reject Domain-Level Content

At times, you might want to identify a specific email address or an entire domain on the
Internet that is sending you messages that you either want to completely allow or specifically deny the receipt of messages from that source location. The content filtering function of Edge Transport Services enables you to create a white list that always allows
content to be received from a user or domain, or specifically allows for the denial of
messages from a user or domain.

Do note that each user can also allow and deny message communications, so the choice
to allow or deny content at the server level should take into consideration that the

communication is organization-wide and that making a setting at the Edge Transport server level will have a positive impact on the appropriate receipt of content to all users in the organization.

An example of a deny filter on a user address or entire domain would include a situation where a user or domain is sending inappropriate content to several users in the organization. Rather than having each user make a configuration to block content from a user or domain, it can be set at the server level.

Conversely, if users in an organization want to receive all messages from a user or domain, those names can be added to a white list that will always allow messages to be received by users or the entire domain in the organization.

Configuring the Content Filter Agent to Allow (White List) Specific Senders, and Sending Domains

The Exchange Management Console allows you to exclude specific keywords, phrases, and recipients within your organization from content filtering checks; however, you can only exclude specific senders and sending domains from content filtering through the use of the Exchange Management Shell's Set-ContentFilterConfig command, using the BypassedSenders and BypassedSenderDomains parameters, respectively.

The BypassedSenders parameter allows you to specify up to 100 external email addresses to exclude from content filtering, with each entry separated by a comma:

```
Set-ContentFilterConfig –BypassedSenders fred@companyabc.com,
➥heather@company123.org
```

> **NOTE**
>
> The entry must be the full SMTP address; wildcard (*) use is not supported. For example, you cannot exclude john*@companyabc.com, or john@companyabc.*.

When excluding a specific email address (for example, user@companyabc.com), consider whether it is safe to exclude the domain using the BypassSenderDomains parameter instead (for example, companyabc.com). Not only does this save you time and message retrieval because of false positives, it also consumes fewer entries in your list, leveraging both lists and the allowed maximum of 100 more efficiently.

The BypassedSenderDomains parameter works similarly to the BypassedSenders parameter, allowing you to specify up to 100 external domains to exclude from content filtering, with each entry separated by a comma:

```
Set-ContentFilterConfig –BypassedSenderDomains *.companyabc.com, company123.org
```

> **NOTE**
>
> Wildcard use is supported to designate the exclusion of subdomains under the excluded domain—for example, *.companyabc.com.

Configuring the Content Filter's SMTP Rejection Response

The SMTP Rejection Response is inserted into a SMTP nondelivery report (NDR) that is sent in reply to a rejected message. The default message is Message Rejected Due to Content Restriction. This message can be changed using the `Set-ContentFilterConfig` command with the `-RejectionResponse` parameter. The SMTP Rejection Response cannot exceed 240 characters and must be enclosed in quotation marks.

> **NOTE**
>
> The SMTP Rejection Response cannot exceed 240 characters and must be enclosed in quotation marks:
>
> ```
> Set-ContentFilterConfig -RejectionResponse "Message rejected, an error
> ➥has occurred. Contact your HelpDesk"
> ```

Filtering Content in a Message Attachment

The Microsoft Exchange Edge Transport server can also filter content within attachments of a message. There are times when an organization wants to prevent offensive or malicious content being stored in a Word document, Hypertext Markup Language (HTML) attachment, and so on from being transmitted to users in a network, so a filter can be configured to identify and handle incoming attachment messages.

Understanding Attachment Filtering Processing

A powerful tool in the fight against computer viruses and other malicious email attachments is the use of attachment filtering. Attachment filtering allows you to identify a specific filename or all files of a particular type using Multipurpose Internet Mail Extensions (MIME) recognition. Attachment filtering can be applied to both incoming and outgoing email. This allows you the flexibility of implementing attachment distribution that complies with business requirements or policy. For example, you can choose to block all executable file types (for example, .bat, .exe, .scr) on inbound email to help prevent the spread of new computer viruses or distribution of unacceptable content. On outbound connections, you could elect to block distribution of particular files by name (for example, tradesecrets.doc, salaryinfo.xls), which can help prevent proprietary information from being accidentally or purposefully distributed. SMTP Send and Receive Connectors can be included or excluded from attachment filtering.

8

NOTE

Changes described in this section are applied only to the local system. This is important if you have more than one Edge Transport server in your environment.

Planning Attachment Filtering Processing

One limitation to attachment filtering is that it can only be configured using the Exchange Management Shell. No attachment filtering options are available in the Exchange Management Console.

Exchange Server 2010, Outlook 2007, and Active Directory's Group Policy can work together to orchestrate implementation of an organization's policy on email attachments. Outlook 2007 includes an enabled default list of Level 1 attachments—attachments that will not be allowed. The Level 1 attachment list was derived from their known or potential ability to carry malicious code. Level 2 attachments are attachments that will initiate a prompt requiring that the user first download the attachment prior to running it. This allows any locally installed antimalware product the opportunity to scan the attachment for viral code that might have bypassed email virus scanning, albeit a rare circumstance, but not impossible. By default, there are no Level 2 file types defined in Outlook 2007.

There are over 70 Level 1 files included in Outlook 2007. Some examples of Level 1 file types are shown in the following list. For a complete list, refer to the Microsoft Outlook 2007 documentation:

▶ asp—Active Server Page

▶ crt—Certificate file

▶ .hta—Hypertext application

▶ .msc—Microsoft Management Console snap-in

▶ .msh—Microsoft Shell

Using Group Policy, an administrator can "open up" Level 1 attachments to users so they can choose whether to accept the attachment and/or make modifications to the Level 1 and Level 2 attachment lists. Alternatively, administrators can take full control of this functionality. This flexibility, unfortunately, can pose a security risk. To offset this risk, administrators can use the attachment-filtering component on an Edge Transport server to block specific attachments, regardless of the configuration in place on internal email systems.

First, you need to determine what attachments and/or types of attachments you want blocked and in what direction(s) attachment filtering should take place: inbound, outbound, or both. If you will be blocking a specific attachment, implement the block using the filename. If you want to block all email attachments of a specific type, add the file extension so it can be identified by its MIME type, regardless of the filename.

After you have decided on which attached files or file types you want to identify in email messages, you also need to determine what you want to do with messages containing those attachments. The default action is to block the attachment and the message (Reject). The available actions you can take on messages and attachments defined in the attachment filter include the following:

▸ **Reject**—Stops delivery of the message and planning attachments to the recipient and sends an undeliverable response to the sender.

▸ **Strip**—Delivers the message to the recipient, replacing the attachment in the message with a notification it has been removed. Any attachment not listed in the attachment filter will still be available to the recipient.

▸ **SilentDelete**—Similar to the Reject action in that the message and attachment aren't delivered; however, the SilentDelete action does not send an undeliverable notification to the sender.

Using the Exchange Management Shell to Configure Attachment Filtering

Attachment filtering, as previously mentioned, can only be configured through the Exchange Management Shell. Each shell command has its own parameters you can set based on the action(s) performed by the command. There are four commands: `Get`, `Add`, `Remove`, and `Set`. Each command works with one or more IP Block and Allow List components.

The `Get-` command is used to retrieve the configuration of a component. For example, entering `Get-AttachmentFilterEntry filename` displays the result of whether that file is being identified in messages.

The `Add-` command can be used to add an entry to the Attachment Filter Agent. The following example adds a filename to be blocked:

```
add-AttachmentFilterEntry -name virus.exe -type FileName
```

The Remove- command can be used to remove an attachment filter entry. The following example removes an entry by filename:

```
remove-AttachmentFilterEntry -Identity filename:virus.exe
```

The `Set-` command allows an administrator to modify the configuration of the attachment filter. In attachment filtering, it is primarily used to set the action. The following example configures the action and response options:

```
Set-AttachmentFilterListConfig -Action Reject -RejectResponse "Attachment type not
➥allowed."
```

8

Using Sender/IP Reputation to Filter Content

Sender Reputation when combined with the other antispam technologies in Edge Services can help reduce unwanted email very efficiently and effectively. Sender Reputation, simply put, allows administrators to answer the question, "Can I trust who sends us email, and if I can't, why should I process it?" The Sender Reputation Agent answers this question for you by learning from values obtained in email messages to determine whether the source of the messages is legitimate or if it is sending junk.

Configuring Sender/IP Reputation

Email that is routed through Receive Connectors is processed by the Sender Reputation Agent. These messages are received from the Internet and travel inbound to the Edge Transport server for delivery to the recipient. The Sender Reputation Agent is enabled by default and can be configured using the Exchange Management Console or Exchange Management Shell.

> **NOTE**
>
> Changes described in this section are applied only to the local system. This is important if you have more than one Edge Transport server in your environment.

To disable the Sender Reputation Agent using the Exchange Management Console, right-click the agent icon in the action pane, and select Disable. To disable the Sender Reputation Agent using the Exchange Management Shell, run the set-SenderReputationConfig command with the -Enabled $false parameter:

```
"set-SenderReputationConfig -Enabled $false"
```

The General tab of the Agent Properties window displays a brief description of the agent and its capabilities, its current status, and the last time the agent's settings were modified.

The Sender Reputation Agent works by evaluating several items in an email message(s) and then assigns a score, known as the Sender Reputation Level (SRL). The SRL works very similarly to the SCL assigned to messages themselves. The SRL gets assigned to the IP address from which the email message(s) are originating. The Sender Reputation Agent adds the IP address to the IP Block List when the SRL corresponds with the tolerance threshold you have set for this action. The SRL can be adjusted from 0 to 9. You can also configure the amount of time (in hours, 0 to 48) the flagged IP address should remain on your IP Block List.

The SRL for an IP address is derived from the following four items: an open proxy test, HELO/EHLO validation check, reverse DNS lookup, and SCL ratings derived from messages received from the sending IP address. The Sender Reputation Agent takes the cumulative results of these items into account when composing the SRL.

An open proxy test determines whether the receiving Edge Transport server can communicate back to itself through the network on which the sending IP address resides. Open proxies are easy to establish and are commonly used by spammers to conceal the true identity of the server sending email. When email messages are routed through an open proxy, the information contained in the message changes to reflect that of the local host—that is, the network on the "other side" of the proxy server.

> **NOTE**
>
> Performing an open proxy test is enabled by default. This setting can be changed on the Sender Confidence tab of the Sender Reputation Properties window.

The HELO/EHLO SMTP commands are another item often forged by spammers. Their purpose is to provide the domain name or IP address from which the message originated. Spoofing the From address, using the same domain in the To and From fields, and forging the sending IP address are very common spam tricks.

A reverse DNS lookup is performed to determine if the domain name registered with the sending IP address is the same as that provided with the HELO/EHLO commands.

> **NOTE**
>
> Although there are a couple of similarities, this is not the same as SenderID and the use of SPF records.

The SCL of a message is the last item taken into account by the Sender Reputation Agent when calculating a SRL for a particular IP address. The Sender Reputation Agent tabulates SCL scores obtained from messages previously received from the same IP address.

Configuring the Sender Reputation Agent Using the Exchange Management Console

The Sender Reputation Agent can be configured using the Exchange Management Console interface. To configure the sender reputation from EMC, do the following:

1. Launch the Exchange Management Console.
2. Select Edge Transport in the console tree.
3. Double-click the Sender Reputation agent.
4. The General tab provides a quick overview of the Sender Reputation Agent, along with the last time the agent's settings were modified.

   5. The Sender Confidence tab allows you to enable (default) or disable the open proxy test. This typically remains enabled.
6. The Action tab allows you to set the block threshold for SRL on a scale of 0 to 9. (The default setting is 7, the maximum.)

7. The Action tab also allows you to configure how long (0 to 48 hours) the IP address should remain on the Edge Transport server's IP Block List. (The default setting is 24 hours.)

8. Click Apply to save changes or click OK to save changes and close the window.

Configuring Sender Reputation Using the Exchange Management Shell

Sender Reputation can also be configured through the Exchange Management Shell. Each shell command has its own parameters you can set based on the action(s) performed by the command. There are two commands: Get- and Set-.

The Get- command is used to retrieve the configuration of Sender Reputation. For example, entering Get-SenderReputationConfig displays the Sender Reputation configuration on the local system.

The Set- command allows an administrator to enable or disable the agent and modify the configuration of the agent. The following example enables sender reputation on email received on external SMTP connections, activates the open proxy detection test, and configures the blocking options.

```
Set-SenderReputationConfig -Enabled $true -ExternalMailEnabled $true
➥-OpenProxyDetectionEnabled $true  -ProxyServerName proxy1.companyabc.com
➥-ProxyServerPort  8080 -SenderBlockingEnabled $true -SenderBlockingPeriod 48
➥-SRLBlockThreshold 8
```

Using Address Rewriting to Standardize on Domain Address Naming for an Organization

Address rewriting was created by Microsoft to allow an organization to have all outbound or inbound email appear to be delivered from one domain when several mail-enabled domains could be sending messages through the same systems. This allows a company to provide a consistent appearance when communicating via email. Address rewriting is commonly used on outbound email when companies merge with or acquire other organizations. Address rewriting is also used on outbound email when an organization's network contains several other domains. Using address rewriting in these scenarios results in external recipients seeing email as originating from one domain name even if it is coming from a domain with a completely different name.

> **NOTE**
>
> If you enable address rewriting on external messages, ensure you have enabled address rewriting on inbound messages as well, so that inbound messages will be delivered to the appropriate recipients.

Configuring Address Rewriting

As with many of the components for the Edge Transport server, address rewriting is enabled on inbound email messages so messages that were rewritten when sent externally can be routed back to the appropriate person. Address rewriting can also be beneficial when sending email between internal systems. For example, if an IT department has multiple domains and the organization wants all email communication from the IT department to internal departments (other than IT) to come from *@it.companyabc.com, then address rewriting would be used to accomplish this.

> **NOTE**
>
> Using address rewriting on your outbound email messages eases white-listing of your organization's email for external recipients and business partners by simplifying the answer to their question: "What domain and systems can we expect to receive email from?"

> **NOTE**
>
> Changes described in this section are applied only to the local system. This is important if you have more than one Edge Transport server in your environment.

Some considerations to take into account when using address rewriting are items that will not be rewritten, end result of email addresses being combined, messages that have been secured, and rewriting in both directions.

Address rewriting will not modify messages that are attached to the message being rewritten and also will not modify the SMTP Return-Path, Received, Message-ID, X-MS-TNEF-Correlator, Content-Type Boundary=string headers, and headers located inside of MIME body parts. Message-ID, X-MS-TNEF-Correlator, Content-Type Boundary=string headers, and headers located inside of MIME body parts are used when securing email messages such as with encryption or Microsoft Rights Management and are, therefore, not rewritten purposely to ensure the message isn't modified to ensure delivery and integrity of the content.

To ensure that messages (mainly responses to rewritten messages) get routed to the appropriate person, a few items need to be addressed. First, the end result of the email address must be unique between users so conflicts and incorrect delivery of messages does not occur; second, a proxy address must be configured on the mailbox that matches the rewritten address; and third, address rewriting must be configured on both the Send and Receive Connectors of the Edge Transport server.

To ensure the rewritten email address between domains will remain unique to the user, take into account how each domain creates their usernames. For example, domains that allow simple usernames like Alexa@, Reese@, or support@ will have more conflicts when using address rewriting than organizations that use more unique or defined usernames like

Alexa_Chimner@, RMChimner@, or online-sales-support@. If two domains used simple user-names in their email addresses and the organization wanted to use address rewriting, the end result could contain too many conflicts, presenting the need to change email addresses at least in one domain. This could end up being quite an involved task depending on the number of users in each domain. For example, CompanyABC.com wants to have all email from domains like infosec.companyabc.com, it.companyabc.com, and development.companyabc.com leave the organization as companyabc.com. If two different users named Mike have the same email prefix (mike) in it.companyabc.com and infosec.companyabc.com, there will be a conflict as they would both be rewritten to mike@companyabc.com. This has more of an impact on replies to rewritten messages than it does to new outbound messages.

For information on configuring a proxy address for a mailbox or multiple mailboxes, see Chapter 18.

> **NOTE**
>
> The use of wildcards is supported in limited usage when rewriting addresses. For example, wildcards can only be used on internal domains. Partial wildcard use such as john*@finance.companyabc.com or username@sales*.companyabc.com is not supported, whereas username @*.companyabc.com is. One example of wildcard usage is rewriting *@development.companyabc.com and *@software.companyabc.com to *@support.companyabc.com.

Address rewriting can only be configured through the Exchange Management Shell. No address rewriting options are available in the Exchange Management Console. Each shell command has its own parameters you can set based on the action(s) performed by the command. There are four commands: Get-AddressRewriteEntry, New-AddressRewriteEntry, Set-AddressRewriteEntry, and Remove-AddressRewriteEntry. An example of each is shown later in this chapter.

The Get- command is used to retrieve the configuration of address rewriting. For example, entering Get-AddressRewriteEntry displays the configuration settings on the local system.

The New-AddressRewriteEntry command can be used to add a new rewriting entry. Use of this command requires three parameters: ExternalAddress, InternalAddress, and Name. The following example rewrites all email addresses in both directions for companyabc.com:

```
New-AddressRewriteEntry -Name "Two-way Rewrite entry for companyabc.com"
➥-InternalAddress companyabc.com -ExternalAddress companydef.com
```

The Set- command allows an administrator to activate address rewriting or modify the existing configuration. The following example switches the internal and external domains given in our previous example and updates the description to reflect the change:

```
Set-AddressRewriteEntry -Identity "Two-way Rewrite entry for companyabc.com"
➥-ExternalAddress companydef.com -InternalAddress companyabc.com
➥-Name "Two-way Rewrite entry for companydef.com"
```

The Remove- command can be used to delete an address rewriting entry. The following example removes the entry created in the previous examples:

```
Remove-AddressRewriteEntry -Identity ""Two-way Rewrite entry for companydef.com"
```

Using EdgeSync to Synchronize Active Directory Information to the Edge Transport Server

EdgeSync is a component of the Edge Transport server that allows replication of certain data from Active Directory to the Edge Transport server to support specific antispam and email filtering components. As an example, an organization might want a copy of their recipient email address list at the Edge Transport layer of their security system so that if an email comes in for a user who does not exist in the organization, the message can be purged immediately instead of taking up disk space to queue, route, or even manage unnecessary content.

Understanding the EdgeSync Process

The EdgeSync process runs on the Hub Transport server in an Active Directory forest and replicates data to the Edge Transport server(s). The EdgeSync communication between the Hub and Edge Transport server is secure. For example, EdgeSync is required if you plan on recognizing and taking action on email messages that are sent to nonexistent recipients. See the Recipient Filtering section of this chapter for more information on stopping email to nonexistent recipients. EdgeSync is also required if you intend to recognize entries in Outlook 2003 and 2007 clients, also known as Safelist Aggregation, which is covered later in this section.

> **NOTE**
>
> Active Directory Lightweight Directory Services (AD LDS) must be installed on the Edge Transport server before Exchange Server 2010 is installed because it is required to use EdgeSync. AD LDS works in conjunction with EdgeSync as a directory in which EdgeSync collects directory information. AD LDS can be used in conjunction with an organization's Active Directory in an extranet scenario where employees (in Active Directory) need mail routed through the Edge Transport server, but also nonemployees such as contractors or vendors would be populated in AD LDS and EdgeSync'd into the Edge Transport server system filter tables.

Using EdgeSync to Subscribe the Server to the Exchange Server 2010 Organization

EdgeSync is also used to subscribe the Edge Transport server to the internal Exchange Server 2010 organization. Subscribing the Edge Transport server in this manner automatically defines the Send Connectors on the Edge Transport server after they have been replicated to AD LDS on the Edge Transport server from a Hub Transport server. The Hub Transport server the Edge Transport server has subscribed with will now route all email from its domain addressed to Internet recipients through the subscribed Edge Transport server(s). Send Connectors must be configured manually if the Edge Transport server is not subscribed internally and utilizing EdgeSync. Send and Receive Connectors are covered in more detail in Chapter 17, "Implementing Client Access and Hub Transport Servers."

> **NOTE**
>
> Using EdgeSync overwrites previously defined Send Connector configurations and disables the Send Connector configuration on the Edge Transport server after replication to the Edge Transport server has occurred, unless you deselect having Send Connectors automatically defined when you import the Edge subscription file on the Hub Transport server.

Maintaining the EdgeSync Schedule of Replication

EdgeSync runs on a regularly scheduled basis with configuration data replicated every hour and recipient information replicated every four hours. In Exchange Server 2007's EdgeSync instance, a full replication took place at every interval, whereas with Exchange Server 2010's EdgeSync instance, only changes are now replicated (deltas), significantly reducing bandwidth and time needed for replication. Also new to Exchange Server 2010's EdgeSync process is the support of a customizable EdgeSync schedule, whereas Exchange Server 2007's EdgeSync process was static and not configurable. This ensures the information needed by the Edge Transport server is up to date. EdgeSync replicates the following items from Active Directory to the AD LDS instance on the Edge Transport server:

▶ Outlook 2003 and 2007 Safe Senders and Safe Recipients Lists (Blocked Senders are not replicated)

▶ Valid email recipients listed in AD (used by the Block E-Mail Sent to Non-Existent Recipients feature of the Recipient Filtering Agent)

▶ Message classifications

▶ Accepted and remote domains

▶ Send Connector configuration

▶ List of Hub Transport servers subscribed in Active Directory

▶ Transport Layer Security (TLS) Send and Receive Domain Secure lists

▶ Internal SMTP relay servers lists

Configuring EdgeSync on an Edge Transport Server

Configuring EdgeSync begins with exporting the Edge Transport subscription file for importing on a Hub Transport server that communicates with Active Directory. The Edge Transport subscription file is in Extensible Markup Language (XML) format. This procedure must be repeated for each Edge Transport server:

1. Ensure communication through ports 50389 and 50636 is available from the Hub Transport to the Edge Transport servers.

> **NOTE**
>
> Ports 50389 (LDAP) and 50636 (Secure LDAP) were assigned at installation and cannot be changed on the Edge Transport server.

2. Use the Exchange Management Shell to export the Edge Transport subscription file.
3. Open the Exchange Management Shell.
4. Enter the following:

```
New-EdgeSubscription -FileName "C:\temp\EdgeSubscriptionInfo.xml"
```

> **NOTE**
>
> You must include the full path to the file.

5. Copy the Edge subscription file to the Hub Transport server. (For security reasons, it is recommended to delete the Edge subscription file after it has been copied to the Hub Transport server and replication has been verified.)
6. Use the Exchange Management Console or Shell to import the Edge Transport subscription file on the Hub Transport server.
7. Place a copy of the EdgeSubscriptionInfo.xml file you created in the previous step onto the Hub Transport server (for example, C:\temp\EdgeSubscriptionInfo.xml) to import the Edge subscription file using the Exchange Management Console.
8. Open the Exchange Management Console and select the Hub Transport section under Organization Configuration.
9. In the action pane, click New Edge Subscription to launch the New Edge Subscription Wizard.
10. Click Browse to select an Active Directory site.
11. Click Browse to browse to the location of the Edge subscription file you copied from the Edge Transport server (for example, C:\temp\EdgeSubscriptionInfo.xml), and click Next.
12. Click New.
13. Click Finish when the completion page appears.
14. Alternatively, you can use the Microsoft Exchange Management Shell to import the Edge Transport subscription file:

```
New-EdgeSubscription -filename "C:\temp\EdgeSubscriptionInfo.xml"
➥-CreateInternetSendConnector $true -site "Default-First-Site-Name"
```

15. Verify synchronization to the Edge Transport server's AD LDS instance.
16. Review the application log in Event Viewer for MsExchange EdgeSync events on the Hub and Edge Transport servers.

Configuring EdgeSync Using the Exchange Management Shell

As noted earlier, EdgeSync is not configured through the Exchange Management Console. Five EdgeSync commands exist for use with the Exchange Management Shell:

- ▶ Get-EdgeSubscription

- ▶ New-EdgeSubscription

- ▶ Remove-EdgeSubscription

- ▶ Start-EdgeSynchronization

- ▶ Test-EdgeSynchronization

Each shell command has its own parameters you can set based on the action(s) performed by the command. Each command performs a specific task or set of tasks.

The Get- command is used to retrieve the current configuration for EdgeSync. For example, entering Get- EdgeSubscription -Identity EDGE1 displays EdgeSync configuration on a server named EDGE1. This command can be run on any Exchange 2010 server on the network.

Running the Get-EdgeSubscription command on an Edge Transport server displays that server's EdgeSync subscription, whereas running the Get-EdgeSubscription on a Hub Transport server can also display EdgeSync subscriptions on Edge Transport servers. Use the –Identity parameter to specify the name of the Edge Transport server.

Creating a New EdgeSync Subscription File

The New-EdgeSubscription command is used to add a new Edge subscription to a Hub Transport server and configure the options for adding a new subscription, such as whether to automatically create the Send Connector or specify the Active Directory site. The following example imports a new Edge Transport subscription file, thus subscribing the Edge Transport server to the network. This command is run on the Hub Transport server:

```
New-EdgeSubscription -FileName "C:\temp\EdgeServerSubscription.xml"
```

Removing an EdgeSync Subscription

The Remove-EdgeSubscription command is used to unsubscribe an Edge Transport server from participating in EdgeSync. The following example removes an Edge subscription from Active Directory. This command is run on the Hub Transport server:

```
Remove-EdgeSubscription -Identity EDGE3 -DomainController dc1.companyabc.com
```

> **NOTE**
>
> This unsubscribes the Edge Transport server from the synchronization process on the Hub Transport server.

Starting EdgeSync Synchronization

Edge synchronization can be started by running the `Start-EdgeSynchronization` command on any Exchange 2010 server joined to the Active Directory domain. Starting Edge synchronization comes in handy when you have added a new Edge server, want to test synchronization, or replicate changes immediately. The `Start-EdgeSynchronization` command initializes EdgeSync to all Edge Transport servers:

```
Start-EdgeSynchronization
```

Testing EdgeSync Synchronization

After configuring EdgeSync, it is important to test it for success. Edge synchronization can be tested by running the `Test-EdgeSynchronization` command on any Exchange 2010 server joined to the Active Directory domain. Testing Edge synchronization comes in handy when you have added a new Edge server and want to validate the EdgeSync configuration and replication settings. The `Test-EdgeSynchronization` command produces a detailed report that can be used for troubleshooting. The `Test-EdgeSynchronization` command can be coupled with several different parameters; for example, the `VerifyRecipient` parameter validates that a single recipient was properly replicated to the Edge Transport server from Active Directory:

```
Test-EdgeSynchronization
```

Implementing Safelist Aggregation for Outlook 2003 and Outlook 2007

The Safelist Aggregation component of an Edge Transport server allows an administrator to obtain copies of end users' Safe Senders lists from Outlook 2003 and 2007 clients. Safelist Aggregation essentially provides a mechanism to respect the entries users have made in their Safe Senders lists, which reduces false positives when filtering for spam. By moving the user's safelist to the Edge Transport server, a rule or spam filtering process set up at the Edge won't delete email that a user has deemed desired.

Configuring Safelist Aggregation for Outlook 2003/2007

As with all of the other Edge Transport rule processes, the Edge Transport server must be subscribed to the Exchange Server 2010 organization from which you want to retrieve Safe Senders list entries on Outlook 2003 and 2007 clients. Safe Senders are replicated to the Edge Transport server using EdgeSync. Safelist entries created by users and imported using Safelist Aggregation are recognized when the Content Filtering Agent examines the message.

> **NOTE**
>
> You can only use Safelist Aggregation with the Content Filtering Agent enabled and on an Edge Transport server that has a subscription with the organization's Hub Transport server. Also, entries in the local Contacts list in Outlook and any external account the user sends email to is added to their safelist. These entries are replicated to the Edge Transport server and used with Safelist Aggregation. Outlook's safelist collection is composed of the Safe Senders, Recipients, Domains, and External Contacts. Each user can have a maximum of 1,024 entries in their safelist collection.

Safelist Aggregation can only be enabled with the Exchange Management Shell by running the `Update-SafeList` command against a user's mailbox on a server running under the Mailbox server role. That information must then be replicated to the Edge Transport server using EdgeSync. For more information about the Mailbox server role, see Part II, "Planning and Designing an Exchange Server 2010 Environment."

To configure Safelist Aggregation, complete the following steps:

1. Use the `Update-Safelist` Exchange shell command on a server running under the Mailbox server role to aggregate and copy the safelist collection data from the user's mailbox to the user object in Active Directory:

   ```
   Update-Safelist -Identity HeatherL -DomainController dc2.companyabc.com
   ➥-Type Both
   ```

> **NOTE**
>
> To run the `Update-SafeList` command against multiple mailboxes residing in a particular organizational unit, you must prepend its use with the `Get-Mailbox` command. This could also be useful when included inside of a script. At the end of the `Get-Mailbox` command statement, add the `update-safelist` command:
>
> ```
> Get-Mailbox -OrganizationalUnit CompanyABC.com\Sales\Users ¦ update-safelist
> ```

2. Schedule the `Update-Safelist` command to run frequently:

   ```
   AT 19:00 /every:M,T,W,Th,F,S,Su  cmd /c "C:\Temp\Update-SafeList"
   ```

> **NOTE**
>
> You must use the AT command to schedule Safelist Aggregation. The AT command can call to a batch file or script that includes the commands to run Safelist Aggregation.

3. Verify that EdgeSync is properly replicating from the Hub Transport server to the Edge Transport server. See the section "Using EdgeSync to Synchronize Active

Directory Information to the Edge Transport Server" on configuring EdgeSync in this chapter for more information regarding EdgeSync.

4. Ensure the Content Filtering Agent is enabled on the Edge Transport server on which you want to perform Safelist Aggregation.

Managing and Maintaining an Edge Transport Server

Managing and maintaining an Edge Transport server requires the same server hardware maintenance, Windows patching and updating, and ongoing system monitoring that is covered in Chapter 19, "Exchange Server 2010 Management and Maintenance Practices." However, there are a handful of things specific to the Edge Transport server, such as exporting the Edge Transport server configuration settings so that if the server needs to be recovered, you can more easily import in the settings after performing a server rebuild. In addition, you can view reports on messages and transport communications managed by the Edge Transport server. The details on how to perform these specific Edge Transport tasks are covered in this section.

Exporting and Importing Edge Transport Server Settings

Exporting the Edge Transport configuration from one server for use on another has two apparent benefits:

▶ Disaster recovery preparedness

▶ Cloning the configuration when multiple Edge Transport servers exist in an organization

This section focuses on exporting the Edge Transport configuration for use in these scenarios. For more information on disaster recovery for Exchange Server 2010, see Part IX, "Data Protection and Disaster Recovery of Exchange Server 2010."

Utilizing the process described in this section of the chapter can help ease deployment of Edge Transport servers when a network will have more than one Edge Transport server or changes are frequently made.

> **NOTE**
>
> Exporting and importing the Edge Transport server configuration does not include the Edge subscription file used by a Hub Transport server for EdgeSync replication. When importing the Edge configuration data to a new or restored server, ensure the Edge Transport server has a subscription on the Hub Transport server and that EdgeSync is properly replicating. More information regarding EdgeSync can be found in the "Configuring EdgeSync on an Edge Transport Server" section of this chapter.

Exporting the Edge Transport server configuration requires the use of a script included with Exchange Server 2010 when the Edge Transport server role is selected during installation.

The script exports the configuration to an XML file, which can later be used to restore the configuration to the same system or another. The name of this script is `ExportEdgeConfig.ps1` and is located in the `C:\Program Files\Microsoft\Exchange Server\Scripts\` folder on the Edge Transport server. The `ExportEdgeConfig.ps1` script is executed through the Exchange Management Shell using the `ExportEdgeConfig` command.

Importing the Edge configuration data works in a similar manner, using the `ImportEdgeConfig` command. The name of this script is `ImportEdgeConfig.ps1` and is located in the `C:\Program Files\Microsoft\Exchange Server\Scripts\` folder on the Edge Transport server. The `ImportEdgeConfig.ps1` script is executed through the Exchange Management Shell using the `ImportEdgeConfig` command.

Exporting Edge Transport Server Configuration

Exporting the Edge Transport server configuration is a four-step process. The steps to export and import Edge Transport server configuration settings are shown next:

1. Copy the `ExportEdgeConfig.ps` file from the `C:\Program Files\Microsoft\Exchange Server\Scripts\` folder to the root of your user profile on the Edge Transport server (for example, `C:\Documents and Settings\Administrator\ExportEdgeConfig.ps`).

2. Open the Exchange Management Shell and run the following command:

   ```
   ./ExportEdgeConfig -cloneConfigData:"C:\temp\CloneConfigData.xml"
   ```

3. If the export is successful, a confirmation message appears, showing the location of the exported file.

4. Copy the file to a location where it can be imported by an Edge Transport server.

> **NOTE**
>
> The `CloneConfigData.xml` is intended for use on a server with a clean installation of Exchange Server 2010 under the Edge Transport role—with the same name as the server from which the file was exported.

The following items are exported to file:

- ▶ Log paths for receive and send protocols, pickup directory, and routing table
- ▶ Message tracking log path
- ▶ Status and priority of each transport agent
- ▶ Send and Receive Connector information
- ▶ Accepted and remote domain configurations
- ▶ IP Allow and IP Block List information (Provider Lists are not included)
- ▶ Content filtering configuration

▶ Recipient filtering configuration

▶ Address rewrite entries

▶ Attachment filtering entries

Importing Edge Transport Server Configuration

After you've exported the Edge Transport server configuration information, you can store the information should you ever need to rebuild the Edge server again, or you might need to configure a secondary Edge server with the exact same configuration settings. The import process brings in the saved configuration settings to a freely installed Edge Server configuration.

To import the Edge Transport server configuration to a system, do the following:

1. Copy the `ExportEdgeConfig.ps` file from the `C:\Program Files\Microsoft\Exchange Server\Scripts\` folder to the root of your user profile on the Edge Transport server to which you are importing the `CloneConfigData.xml` file (for example, `C:\Documents and Settings\Administrator\ ExportEdgeConfig.ps`).

2. Copy the `CloneConfigData.xml` file you created during the export process to a location on the server (for example, `C:\temp\CloneConfigData.xml`).

3. Launch the Exchange Management Shell.

4. Run the `ImportEdgeConfig` command to validate the configuration file and create an answer file (`CloneConfigAnswer.xml`).

   ```
   ./importedgeconfig -CloneConfigData:"C:\temp\CloneConfigData.xml" -IsImport
   ➡$false -CloneConfigAnswer:"C:\temp\CloneConfigAnswer.xml"
   ```

5. A confirmation message is displayed if the answer file was properly exported.

6. Open the `CloneConfigAnswer.xml` file that was created in the previous step. If the file is blank, the configuration is correct and no modification is necessary. If any configuration items cause a discrepancy, they will be included in the answer file and must be modified for the correct configuration (for example, server name, invalid SMTP Connector IP address, log file path, and so on). Save your changes.

7. After you have reviewed and made any necessary modifications to the answer file, you must import both the `CloneConfigData.xml` file and the modified `CloneConfigAnswer.xml` file. The following syntax is for the `ImportEdgeConfig` command to accomplish this:

NOTE

If the answer file is blank, the configuration is correct and can be used and there is no need to import the answer file.

```
./importedgeconfig -CloneConfigData:"C:\temp\CloneConfigData.xml" -IsImport
➡$true -CloneConfigAnswer:"C:\temp\CloneConfigAnswer.xml"
```

8. After the XML file(s) have been imported, a message stating "Importing Edge Configuration Information Succeeded" appears.

9. Configure and run EdgeSync and ensure replication is occurring successfully.

Export the Edge Transport server configuration file and test importing it on a regular basis, especially when multiple changes have been made to the Edge Transport server and to ensure the configuration will work in the event of a disaster or outage. Network Load Balancing and other mechanisms can also help offset the impact of a disaster or system outage. For more information on disaster recovery in an Exchange Server 2010 environment, see Part IX.

Viewing Antispam Reports Using Included PowerShell Scripts

The Edge Transport server includes several antispam reports that contain information about the top blocked items, such as IP addresses, domains, and senders, how frequently those items are blocked, how many times those items have been blocked, and who in the organization receives the most spam. The information contained in these reports can assist administrators in fine-tuning the spam-filtering agents to achieve a higher level of spam detection while simultaneously reducing the number of false positives.

Antispam reports can only be generated using an Exchange Management Shell command. Each shell command will parse the logs files to create a report. The logs for each Antispam agent are stored in `C:\Program Files\Microsoft\Exchange Server\TransportRoles\Logs\`.

To run any of the following scripts to generate the respective Antispam report, perform the following steps:

1. Launch the Exchange Management Shell on the Edge Transport server.

2. Change to the `C:\Program Files\Microsoft\Exchange Server\v14\Scripts\` folder using the command `cd $exscripts`.

3. Enter a `./` and the name of the script for the Antispam report you want to review:

    `./Get-AntispamTopBlockedSenderDomains`

A handful of PowerShell scripts are included with Exchange Server 2010 to generate Antispam reports from the log files. Some of the default scripts are as follows:

▶ `Get-AntispamFilteringReport`—Generates a report displaying a summary of messages that have been rejected by connection, command, or filtering agent.

▶ `Get-AntispamSCLHistogram`—Generates a report summarizing the amount of email identified with each SCL threshold (1 to 9 total).

▶ `Get-AntispamTopBlockedSenderDomains`—Generates a report summarizing how many times and how frequently a domain has been blocked.

▶ `Get-AntispamTopBlockedSenderIPs`—Generates a report summarizing how many times and how frequently an IP address of a sending mail server has been blocked.

▶ `Get-AntispamTopBlockedSenders`—Generates a report summarizing how many times and how frequently a sender's email address has been blocked.

▶ `Get-AntispamTopRecipients`—Generates a report summarizing spam volume for recipients and the amount of spam messages received.

Forefront Online Security for Exchange Server 2010

Managing and maintaining an Edge Transport server takes time and is vital to an organization's email security framework. Organizations can offset this responsibility (at a cost) to Microsoft using Forefront Online Security for Exchange Hosted Services, an email hygiene solution that exists in the cloud and is administered by Microsoft. Organizations can also choose to implement a hybrid approach, in which part of the messaging hygiene solutions are provided by Microsoft and some reside on-site. Both have distinct advantages and disadvantages. Offloading spam and virus filtering to Forefront Online Security for Exchange Hosted Services can significantly reduce the amount of processing power and administrative overhead for the organization.

For regulatory compliance, corporate policy, technical limitations, or other reasons, not all organizations might take advantage of Forefront Online Security for Exchange Hosted Services; however, some of the same technologies used with Forefront Online Security for Exchange Hosted Services are built in to the Edge Transport server and Forefront Security for Exchange, so either way Microsoft customers get strong technologies for combating spam and malicious email.

The Forefront Online Security for Exchange Hosted Services utilizes the following antispam technologies to maintain a high level of spam detection and low level of false-positives:

▶ Sender Reputation analysis

▶ Recipient validation

▶ Fingerprinting

▶ Content filtering

▶ Rules-based message scoring

▶ Custom filtering management

Using a Hybrid Solution for Messaging Hygiene

Implementing a hybrid solution where both a hosted and on-site solution is used to filter email provides the most flexibility and protection for the messaging infrastructure and is highly recommended if hosted services are going to be used at all. The most common implementation offloads spam and malware filtering to the Forefront Online Security service while on-site malware scanning and other filtering rules are still used.

It is not uncommon for newer spam campaigns and malware messages to be identified by a cloud-based hosted service before the on-site solution because on-site solutions require periodic updates to be downloaded and installed before the malicious message reaches the network. This is because hosted solutions are updated first and typically on a much more frequent basis. In addition, hosted services handle mail for organizations around the globe, making it possible for a new spammed piece of malware to go undetected in one country or region, and then get detected for all other parts of the world due to the nature of how the hosted service monitors mail and updates the database used to identified unwanted messages.

It is necessary, however, for an onsite solution to add another layer of scanning should a message go undetected by the hosted service, and also to prevent against inside attacks that would not be monitored by the hosted service. This applies more to malware and virus attacks than spam runs. Because both Forefront Online Security for Exchange Hosted Services and Forefront Security for Exchange utilize multiple scan engines, the attack surface is very low; however, no solution is 100% immune to attack.

TIP

Microsoft has more on its Online Services at www.microsoft.com/online/exchange-hosted-services/filtering.mspx with resources available for pricing, more information, or to sign-up for online services.

Summary

The Edge Transport server provides an important layer of security between the general Internet and an organization's messaging environment. If set up properly, an Edge server can successfully filter unwanted content such as spam, viruses, or inappropriate content. If not set up properly, an Edge server can filter desired content and accidentally eliminate critical messages of communications. The focus of this chapter was to provide guidance on implementing, configuring, and fine-tuning an Edge server to improve its impact on the filtering and management of information into a network.

Best Practices

The following are best practices from this chapter:

▶ Filter for spam before processing messages because spam accounts for the majority of mail messages transported on the Internet.

▶ When configuring an Edge server, configure it with minimal configuration rules and then add rules, while testing a successful hit rate on filtration, and then fine-tune the filtering to be more restrictive.

▶ When first implementing filtration, consider stamping questionable messages with the word "Suspect" or something similar rather than deleting the message so you can track which messages might possibly be filtered when they otherwise shouldn't be.

▶ Configure allow lists to ensure messages from desired message senders or organizations are not filtered and that they are successfully received by the intended recipient.

▶ Configure custom block lists to ensure that messages from email senders or specific domains are not transmitted to users, but instead are blocked at the Edge server.

▶ Enable Safelist Aggregation that will collect users' safelists and add safelist users to the Edge server filters to allow content to be allowed instead of blocked by rule.

▶ Use message attachment filtering to assess the content of attachments as part of an appropriate content filtering process.

▶ Enable address rewriting to standardize on domain address names used by the organization.

▶ When an Edge-based application utilizes directory content such as username and email address lists, use EdgeSync to propagate the directory information to the Edge server.

▶ Export Edge Transport server configuration information and store the information along with other server build documentation. The exported Edge Transport configuration information can be imported to a new system in the event of a server replacement or server failure scenario.

CHAPTER 9

Using Windows PowerShell in an Exchange Server 2010 Environment

Microsoft PowerShell is the powerful command-line interface that Microsoft Exchange Server 2010 is based upon. This chapter introduces you to the Exchange Management Shell (EMS), which is the Exchange Server 2010 command-line administration tool based on Windows PowerShell. This chapter discusses the background of PowerShell, what the Exchange Management Shell is, and the general concepts about scripting and command-line administration so that you can use this powerful tool to manage your Exchange Server 2010 environment effectively.

What Is Windows PowerShell?

Microsoft Windows PowerShell is a command-line shell and scripting language that enables Information Technology (IT) professionals to achieve greater levels of productivity, automation, and control in their IT environments.

Windows PowerShell is easy to learn and use because it works in your existing IT environment, and you can leverage your existing scripting investments. It is as powerful (or more powerful) than some programming languages. It plugs into the .NET runtime, also called the common language runtime. An administrator can sit at a PowerShell prompt and access, control, and automate almost everything in Windows.

Windows PowerShell is extremely powerful, in which virtually anything can be written and scripted from the shell. PowerShell is a fully featured command-line shell, similar to a Bash prompt. It is also an extremely powerful administrative scripting tool—think Perl or Ruby with AWK, SED, and

Grep thrown in. And all this is based on .NET—so administrators have direct access to the entire .NET common language runtime, plus the ability to script existing COM (ActiveX) and Windows Management Instrumentation (WMI) objects, similar to what can be done with VBScript but with much more power and ease.

Windows PowerShell includes many system administration utilities, a consistent syntax and naming convention, and improved navigation of common management data such as the Windows Registry, certificate stores, or Windows Management Instrumentation (WMI) repositories. The PowerShell command-line interface uses a common verb-noun structure that makes it easy to read, as well as write. All the items you work with are objects, and you act upon these objects with a specific set of verbs, discussed later in this chapter.

Versions 1.0 and 2.0 of Windows PowerShell are available for free download from the Microsoft Download Center (www.microsoft.com/downloads/en/results.aspx?pocId= &freetext=powershell). The differences between these versions will be discussed in the next section. PowerShell runs on Windows XP, Windows Vista, and Windows Server 2003. Windows PowerShell is included as part of Windows Server 2008 as an optional feature that can be added to the operating system. It is installed by default in Windows 7 and Windows Server 2008 R2.

Understanding the Evolution of PowerShell

This section provides a brief history of Windows PowerShell, so you have an understanding of how and why it was developed. We discuss how Windows PowerShell relates to Exchange Server 2010 and why it is so important for you to master this important and powerful technology.

Monad

The first version of Windows PowerShell was called Monad (also known as Microsoft Shell or MSH). A team at Microsoft, led by the brilliant architect of PowerShell, Jeffrey Snover, realized that Windows needed a new command-line interface that would allow administrators to do everything from the command line. GUIs can do only as much as they are written to do. Changes are sometimes made in the Registry, some in Active Directory (AD) through Active Directory Services Interface (ADSI), and others in less often used or difficult to manage components such as the Exchange Server metabase or Internet Information Services (IIS).

The team developed a fresh, new shell whereby everything in the Windows environment is accessed as an object, and a common set of verbs are used to act upon these objects. These verb-object commands are sometimes combined into useful combinations call cmdlets (pronounced "commandlets") that are specialized .NET classes designed expressly to expose a functionality via PowerShell. The Monad team compiled some of these cmdlets into PowerShell, making them native commands available to all end users.

Various betas of Monad were made available on Microsoft's Download Center between June 2005 and April 2006 when Monad was renamed to Windows PowerShell.

Windows PowerShell v.1.0

The idea that was Monad started to become a full-fledged command-line shell in Windows PowerShell 1.0. Because it is based on .NET classes, PowerShell requires the .NET Framework version 2.0. It is available on both the Microsoft Download Center as a redistributable package and through the Windows Update and Microsoft Update services. The final Release to Web (RTW) version of PowerShell 1.0 was released in November 2006.

The user interface offers tab-completion, in which PowerShell commands and parameters can be viewed or completed by entering the beginning portion of a command and pressing the Tab key. For example, entering "get-" and pressing tab repeatedly steps though all the objects that PowerShell can act upon.

PowerShell also introduced the concept of a pipeline to the shell. PowerShell pipelines are used to compose or combine complex commands, enabling the output of one command to be passed as input to another. A pipeline is created by piping the output of one command to another command, using the ¦ operator. You can even pipeline the output of one pipeline into another.

Scripts written using PowerShell can be saved in a .ps1 file. However, as a security precaution, script execution is disabled by default and must be enabled explicitly within PowerShell. PowerShell scripts can be signed to verify their integrity and use .NET Code Access Security.

Windows PowerShell 1.0 is the underlying platform used by Microsoft Exchange Server 2007. The Exchange Server team built upon that platform to develop and operate Exchange Server 2007, and they developed the Exchange Management Shell (EMS) for administration. EMS is an extension of PowerShell 1.0 with custom cmdlets that were written specifically for Exchange Server administration. When the administrator launches the Exchange Management Shell, PowerShell 1.0 is invoked and special Exchange Server 2007–only cmdlets are loaded, such as the move-mailbox cmdlet. There are 402 cmdlets unique to Exchange Server 2007, and each cmdlet has its own set of help.

One major missing feature in PowerShell 1.0 is the lack of remoting, or the ability to run a PowerShell command on a remote computer. This shortcoming hampered PowerShell 1.0 from being adopted and utilized in large enterprise-class IT centers with thousands of computers. It also prevents administrators from loading the Exchange Management Console or Exchange Management Shell on a workstation for remote administration of Exchange 2007 servers. Plans began for a remotable version of PowerShell.

Windows PowerShell v.2.0

PowerShell V2 includes changes to the scripting language and hosting API, and includes more than 240 new cmdlets.

Major changes in PowerShell V2 include the following:

▶ Background Jobs enables a command sequence, script, or pipeline to be invoked asynchronously.

▶ Transactions enable cmdlets to perform transacted operations. PowerShell V2 includes transaction cmdlets for starting, committing, and rolling back a transaction.

▶ Modules enable script developers and administrators to organize and partition PowerShell scripts in self-contained, reusable units.

▶ Script Debugging enables breakpoints to be set in a PowerShell script or function.

▶ Windows PowerShell Integrated Scripting Environment. PowerShell V2 includes a new GUI-based PowerShell environment that provides an integrated debugger, syntax highlighting, tab completion, and up to eight tabbed PowerShell runspaces.

Most important of the changes in PowerShell V2 is the ability to perform remoting using Windows Remote Management (WinRM) 2.0. This enables administrators to invoke scripts on a remote machine or a large collection of remote machines. It is this capability that lends itself to Exchange Server 2010 and remote management using the Exchange Management Shell (EMS).

Now with Exchange Server 2010, administrators can invoke EMS commands from a remote server or workstation. Because EMS uses WinRM for remote connectivity, it lends itself very well to firewall and cross-forest scenarios. WinRM uses the standard ports 80 and 443 for all communications to and from the target computer, making it easier than ever to perform remote management, even in complex environments.

> **NOTE**
>
> PowerShell V2 is available in x86, x64, and IA64 versions. Even though Exchange Server 2010 is a 64-bit only application, any version of PowerShell V2 is capable of running the Exchange Management Shell remotely.

Introducing the Exchange Management Shell

The Exchange Management Shell in Exchange Server 2010 is the command-line interface that enables Exchange Server administrators to manage, check, and report on any Exchange Server objects. These objects include mailboxes, mailbox stores, DAGs, servers, connectors, and the Exchange Server organization itself—anything that can be managed in Exchange Server 2010 can be managed from the Exchange Management Shell.

The Exchange Management Console (EMC) is actually a graphical user interface (GUI) for the Exchange Management Shell, or EMS. Each task or operation that an administrator does using the Exchange System Console is actually calling an underlying EMS command or series of commands. There is nothing that can be done from the EMC that cannot be done from EMS. However, there are a lot of commands and operations that can only be done from EMS. This is simply because Microsoft has not written a GUI front end for these tasks.

Because EMS is based on PowerShell V2, administrators have access to the full set of features built in to PowerShell, plus custom extensions written by the Exchange Server 2010 team. These Exchange Server 2010-specific commands, or cmdlets, leverage the simplicity and power of PowerShell to perform common and some not-so-common

Exchange Server tasks. Also, because EMS is now based on PowerShell V2, administrators can now perform Exchange Server administration from a remote computer.

> **NOTE**
>
> All connections made to any Exchange server using Exchange Management Shell are remote connections, even when using EMS from a local Exchange server. See the "Starting the Exchange Management Shell" section in this chapter for more information.

Administrators can now do almost every single administrative task with an interactive command line. EMS can be used to quickly check settings, create reports, check the health of the Exchange servers, or, best of all, automate all the administrator's frequent operations.

Scripting and automation are key to lowering total cost of ownership for Exchange Server administrators. By providing a simple platform that enables administrators to create, save, and distribute their own cmdlets, EMS enables administrators to easily extend Exchange Server functionality and administrative tasks that are appropriate for their support structure and line of business. This, combined with Rights-Based Access Control (RBAC), provides a significant benefit to the IT organization.

Since Exchange Server's early beginnings, Exchange Server administrators have requested ways to manage all the buttons and knobs that are built in to Exchange Server. The GUI allows only the administrator to do as much as the GUI was programmed to do. Now that all these objects and settings are available through EMS, administrators are free to develop, customize, save, and distribute their own cmdlets to Exchange Server support staff for maximum effectiveness.

The power of EMS can be used to automate many different types of tasks. Imagine creating 10,000 test user accounts for a test lab with one line of code or setting a 200MB mailbox quota on all Sales Team mailboxes in the organization with one line. That's the power of the Exchange Management Shell.

The Exchange Management Shell and PowerShell replace VBScript, WMI, ADSI, LDP, and more—all within a single command-line interface. Tasks that used to require specialized scripting knowledge can now be easily learned using extensive help within the shell.

Cmdlets that administrators create can be modified to do other tasks. Administrators will quickly build a set of cmdlets that they will use and recycle into new and more complex sets of functions.

A common question asked by administrators is whether complex scripting is required in EMS to do simple tasks. Do administrators have to learn complex syntax and command switches to manage Exchange Server? Exchange Management Shell is extremely powerful, yet very easy to learn, and helps to simplify many tasks that previously had to be done by developers or programmers.

When the Exchange Server 2010 team started designing the Exchange Server command-line and scripting interface, they made sure that 80 percent of Microsoft customers, who normally have little or no scripting experience, can still use the PowerShell/Exchange Server command line to automate or perform their tasks.

EMS makes it easier to administer Exchange Server 2010 by making administration more safe, easy, and fun. It improves the developer experience by making it easier to add command-line management capabilities using Microsoft .NET. It improves the administrative experience by enabling information technology (IT) professionals to write secure automation scripts that can run locally or remotely.

An abundance of resources are available to the administrator who uses EMS and PowerShell. Microsoft is committed to publishing dozens of example scripts and cmdlets highlighting some of the more common administrative tasks. Numerous other websites and utilities are also devoted to PowerShell. Some of these are covered in this chapter.

Understanding the EMS Is the Back End to the Exchange Management Console

The Exchange Management Console is simply a GUI to Exchange Management Shell. Whenever an operation is performed in EMC, it calls a set of cmdlets in EMS and presents the results back to the GUI.

Everything an administrator can do in EMC can be done in EMS but not always vice versa. If the Exchange Server 2010 team were to add every configuration setting to the EMC, it would be too complicated and cumbersome to navigate. Their goal was to put the most-common administrative tasks in EMC.

When administrators perform most operations in EMC, the EMS command used to execute the task is presented in the GUI, similar to the screen shown in Figure 9.1.

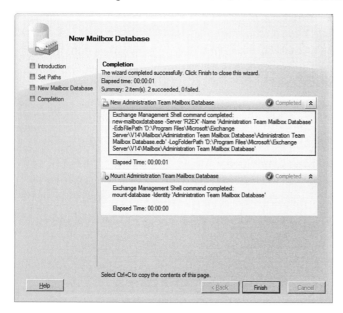

FIGURE 9.1   Sample EMC Wizard showing EMS commands.

Additionally, all the wizards in the Exchange Server 2010 EMC include the command that is created when you use an EMC Wizard to create or modify an Exchange Server object. By clicking the Show Exchange Management Shell Command button in the lower-left corner of the wizard, the wizard completion window shows the command that would be run. It can also be copied to the Clipboard for use in the EMS directly.

Understanding the Exchange Server Task Model

Four major groups of tasks are performed in Exchange Server 2010 administration. Each of these groups and tasks can be fully managed using the Exchange Management Shell. The rich command-line interface in EMS provides more granularity than the Exchange Management Console:

- **Organization management tasks**—Include managing federation or organizational trusts, database management, global rules, email life cycle policies, OWA and ActiveSync policies, email address policies, and unified messaging dial plans.

- **Server management tasks**—Include certificate management as well as managing and configuring all Exchange 2010 server roles, including mailbox servers, client access servers, Hub Transport servers, and Unified Messaging servers.

- **Recipient management tasks**—Include all facets of mailbox, contact, and distribution group management, including creation, moves, deletions, and modifications.

- **Diagnostic tasks**—Include queue management, reporting, and analysis. Performance monitoring and alerts also fall into this group.

Tasks are further broken down into categories based on server role or features:

- **Edge Transport server**—Managing EdgeSync, Active Directory Lightweight Directory Services (ADLDS), receive connectors, and send connectors.

- **Hub Transport, Client Access, Mailbox, and Unified Messaging roles**—Managing transport rules, Outlook Web App configuration, database and DAG configuration, mailbox configuration, and unified messaging configuration.

- **Antispam**—Managing content filtering, recipient filtering, IP Allow and Block filters, SenderID, and Sender Reputation settings.

- **Email life cycle**—Message archiving and journaling, and creating, managing, and deleting Exchange Server 2010 Email Life Cycle folders.

- **Transport**—Managing hub transport rules and policies.

- **Rules**—Creating, managing, and deleting global rules, internal rules, external rules, and journal rules.

Understanding How RBAC Is Used in EMS

As explained in Chapter 18, "Administering an Exchange Server 2010 Environment," Roles-Based Access Control (RBAC) is the new security model used in Exchange Server 2010. RBAC uses management roles to determine what an administrator can do and manage in the Exchange Management Shell (EMS), the Exchange Management Console (EMC), and the Exchange Control Panel (ECP).

For example, an administrator who is assigned the RecipientManagement role can manage mailboxes, distribution groups, contacts, and other recipient objects. Also, the management roles assigned to administrators can be scoped, so they can manage only specific recipients or servers in the Exchange Server 2010 organization. For example, if am RBAC role assignment is scoped to only recipients in San Francisco, the administrator with that role can manage only San Francisco recipients and no others.

RBAC and Its Affect in EMS

An important concept to understand is that RBAC dictates which cmdlets are exposed and available to the administrator, depending on the RBAC management role(s) assigned to that administrator. This might be only a small subset of the many commands and cmdlets that ship with Exchange Server 2010.

Likewise, some RBAC roles use a particular cmdlet but might not have access to all its parameters. For example, if a modified RecipientManagement role does not enable the administrator to change the recipient's office, the -Office parameter will not be used in that administrator's Set-Mailbox cmdlet.

> **NOTE**
>
> The help commands in Exchange Management Shell always show all the parameters available for the cmdlet, regardless of the RBAC roles assigned to the user.

Starting the Exchange Management Shell

Quite a bit happens behind the scenes when the Exchange Management Shell is launched.

When the administrator clicks the Exchange Management Console shortcut to open EMS, Windows PowerShell V2 is launched, and some Exchange Server-specific scripts are run. These scripts find the most suitable Exchange Server 2010 server and attempt to connect to its PowerShell virtual directory in IIS using WinRM. Assuming the administrator has rights to connect, Exchange Server then determines which RBAC management roles have been assigned to the administrator. Finally, it creates an ESM environment that contains all the Exchange Server management cmdlets that the administrator is allowed to use.

As noted earlier, all EMS instances are actually made as remote connections, even if EMS is opened on a local Exchange server. The previous steps occur every time EMS is opened.

> **NOTE**
>
> Simply opening PowerShell V2 is not the same as the Exchange Management Shell. PowerShell does not automatically make a remote connection to the Exchange server and does not include any of the Exchange Server–specific cmdlets, such as Get-Mailbox.

When the administrator opens EMS the first time, all the Exchange Server cmdlets available for that RBAC role will be downloaded to the local computer. Figure 9.2 shows EMS connecting to an Exchange Server 2010 server for the first time and importing the cmdlets to which the administrator has access.

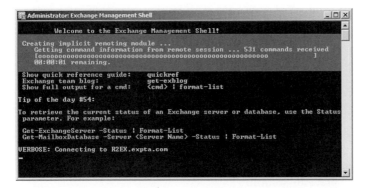

FIGURE 9.2   Connecting to an Exchange Server 2010 server with EMS.

After connecting, the administrator can run EMS and PowerShell cmdlets, as usual.

NOTE

The PowerShell Get-Command cmdlet is useful to see a list of cmdlets to which the administrator has access.

It is important to understand that the Exchange Server–specific cmdlets that are downloaded to the local computer actually run on the Exchange Server 2010 server. For example, when an administrator with the RecipientAdministrator role launches EMS from a remote computer, the cmdlets associated with that role are imported into the remote computer's EMS environment. When the administrator runs an Exchange Server 2010 cmdlet, EMS proxies the command to the Exchange server, on which the command is carried out. The output from the command is then proxied back to the remote computer for display or further processing.

When EMS opens a remote connection to an Exchange Server 2010 server, the connection remains open until EMS is closed. This is made possible by a managed hosting API built into PowerShell and is also utilized by the Exchange Management Console. By keeping the connection open, better performance is achieved in both EMS and EMC.

Starting EMS from a Non-Exchange Server

To use EMS on a remote computer, PowerShell V2 and its prerequisites must be installed on the computer and the Active Directory account must be given remote administration rights.

EMS relies on remoting, which is possible using PowerShell V2, WinRM 2.0, and the .NET Framework 2.0, or greater. All these components are available for free download from the

Microsoft Download Center. PowerShell V2 is installed with the operating system by default in Windows 7 and Windows Server 2008 R2. It must be downloaded and installed on Windows XP SP2 or greater, Windows Vista, and Windows Server 2008.

> **NOTE**
>
> Windows Server 2008 includes Windows PowerShell as an optional feature that can be installed after the operating system is installed. This feature is PowerShell V1, not PowerShell V2 as required by Exchange Server 2010 EMS. You must uninstall the PowerShell feature if it is installed before installing PowerShell V2 from the Microsoft Download Center.

It doesn't matter whether the x86 or x64 version of PowerShell V2 is installed on the local computer because the EMS commands are actually run on the remote Exchange Server 2010 server, as described in the previous section.

After PowerShell V2 is installed, you must also configure the PowerShell script execution policy. By default, Windows PowerShell is set to a secure configuration that prevents any scripts from running. To allow EMS to run its connection scripts, you must set the execution policy to run digitally signed scripts with the following command:

```
Set-ExecutionPolicy RemoteSigned
```

> **NOTE**
>
> Setting the execution policy writes to the Registry. You might need to run PowerShell as an Administrator to configure the execution policy.

The Active Directory account used to install Exchange Server 2010 will be granted remote management rights in PowerShell by default. To grant this right to another Active Directory user, the administrator must use the Set-User cmdlet with the RemotePowerShellEnabled parameter. For example, to grant this right to a user named Keith Johnson, the administrator enters the following at the PowerShell prompt:

```
Set-User 'Keith Johnson' –RemotePowerShellEnabled $True
```

After these one-time prerequisites are met, it's time to run EMS remotely. The Active Directory user (Keith Johnson, in this example) enters the following commands at the PowerShell prompt:

```
$session = New-PSSession -ConfigurationName Microsoft.Exchange -ConnectionUri
➥http://<Exchange2010fqdn>/PowerShell -Authentication Kerberos
Import-PSSession $session
```

The first line defines the variable $session to be the remote PowerShell session object on the Exchange Server 2010 server. The second line tells PowerShell to import the remote session object to this computer. When this second line is executed, PowerShell makes a remote connection to the specified Exchange server over the standard HTTP port 80, authenticates using Kerberos, and imports all the cmdlets that the user has rights to use, based on the RBAC role(s) assigned to the user in Exchange Server.

It's important to understand that EMS will only download the appropriate cmdlets for the RBAC administration role of the user running EMS. For example, a user running EMS who is a member of the Records Management security group gets a small subset of Exchange Server cmdlets to work with. If that same user runs PowerShell using the Windows RunAs command as a user who is a member of the Organization Management group, almost all the Exchange Server cmdlets will be available to work with.

The EMS environment is dynamic. When the remote Exchange Management Shell is closed, the local cmdlets are cleared from the environment. That means that another user running EMS from the same computer will not have access to cmdlets that he doesn't have rights to run.

Connecting to Another Exchange Server Organization

Connecting to an Exchange Server 2010 server in a different Active Directory forest is achieved basically the same way as previously described. The main difference is that we cannot use Kerberos for authentication. For this, we must use explicit credentials. Open a PowerShell prompt and enter the following command:

```
$UserCredential = Get-Credential
```

This causes PowerShell to invoke the Windows GUI to prompt for a username and password, as shown in Figure 9.3.

FIGURE 9.3   Creating the $UserCredential variable.

Now we run the following two PowerShell commands to connect to the remote Exchange Server 2010 server, authenticate, and create the EMS environment:

```
$session = New-PSSession -ConfigurationName Microsoft.Exchange -ConnectionUri
```

```
➥http://<Exchange2010fqdn>/PowerShell -Authentication $UserCredential
Import-PSSession $session
```

Notice that the commands are identical to the previous command, except that we are now passing the $UserCredential variable for authentication instead of using Kerberos.

Creating a Shortcut for Remote EMS

Typing the preceding commands every time you want to run EMS remotely is tedious. The following procedures explain how to create a PowerShell script that runs these commands by clicking a shortcut.

First, open a text editor, such as Notepad, or use the Windows PowerShell Integrated Scripting Environment (ISE), which is new to PowerShell V2. Then enter the same commands, as previously entered:

```
$session = New-PSSession -ConfigurationName Microsoft.Exchange -ConnectionUri
➥http://<Exchange2010fqdn>/PowerShell -Authentication Kerberos
Import-PSSession $session
```

Save the new file as EMS.PS1 somewhere on your local computer or a network share, making note of the path where you saved it. Now create a new shortcut to PowerShell on the Windows desktop. Rename the new shortcut to **Exchange Management Shell**. Right-click the shortcut and select Properties. Add the following text to the end of the Target text:

```
-noexit <path>\EMS.PS1
```

Click OK to save the shortcut. When you double-click the Exchange Management Console icon on the desktop, PowerShell opens, launches the EMS.PS1 script, and remains open after the script executes.

More on How PowerShell and EMS Work Together

The Exchange Management Shell is based on Microsoft PowerShell V2, which provides access to all the objects and classes and .NET classes available in .NET Framework 3.5.1. When the administrator installs Exchange Server 2010, the Exchange Server setup program installs all the cmdlets necessary to manage the Exchange Server 2010 organization. Over time, as Exchange Server 2010 is updated through service rollups, service packs' new functionality will be created and new cmdlets will be included as part of the update.

The cmdlets were written by the Exchange Server team to perform all Exchange Server-specific tasks. There are more than 600 cmdlets unique to Exchange Server 2010, and each cmdlet has its own set of help.

Common PowerShell Functions in EMS

Because the Exchange Management Shell is based on PowerShell, it shares many functions with it.

EMS shares the same verb-noun syntax for all operations and cmdlets as PowerShell does. This gives a consistent logical experience for the administrator while working in the EMS environment.

Comprehensive tab completion is also present in EMS and PowerShell. When the administrator presses the Tab key after typing some text, the TabExpansion PowerShell function is called to generate the list of possible completion matches. Tab completion works on variables and parameters on cmdlets in addition to filename completion. Administrators can also define custom tab completions.

Both EMS and PowerShell offer a comprehensive help system with examples. Administrators can get both general and cmdlet-specific help within the command environment. The help systems support wildcards. Knowing the strong naming conventions used in the environment, administrators can leverage wildcards to guess at what they are looking for.

EMS and PowerShell cmdlets both offer an interactive completion process. The administrator can enter as many cmdlet parameters as he is comfortable with, and the command environment will prompt for the missing required parameters. This is helpful for seldom-used cmdlets.

Unique EMS Functions Specific to Exchange Server

The Exchange Management Shell offers more than 600 unique cmdlets that were written by the Exchange Server team specifically for Exchange Server 2010. Each of these cmdlets has been optimized for performance, and they are the building blocks for all Exchange Server management functions.

Some Exchange Server operations and tasks take time to complete. Moving large mailboxes across a wide area network (WAN), for example, can take several minutes to complete. When long operations like these take place, a textual status bar is presented at the top of the display, indicating the progress of the task.

Understanding the EMS Syntax

The Exchange Management Shell shares the same verb-noun syntax as PowerShell. This provides a consistent set of commands to learn and understand within the command environment.

Understanding the Verb-Noun Construct

EMS uses a strict verb-noun naming construct for all of its cmdlets. The verb is separated from the noun with a hyphen. For example, the cmdlet `get-mailbox` returns all of the mailbox objects in the organization.

The verbs used in both EMS and PowerShell are listed in Table 9.1. There is a high level of verb reuse to provide a consistent, predictable user experience. As in the English language, there are many more nouns than verbs. Examples of nouns used in EMS are mailbox, Mailboxserver, ExchangeServer, TransportSettings, DatabaseAvailabilityGroup, object, service, and so on.

TABLE 9.1   PowerShell and EMS Verbs

Add	Backup	Invoke
Clear	Checkpoint	Register
Close	Compare	Request
Copy	Compress	Restart
Enter	Convert	Resume
Exit	ConvertFrom	Start
Find	ConvertTo	Stop
Format	Dismount	Submit
Get	Edit	Suspend
Hide	Expand	Uninstall
Join	Export	Unregister
Lock	Group	Wait
Move	Import	Debug
New	Initialize	Measure
Open	Limit	Ping
Pop	Merge	Repair
Push	Mount	Resolve
Redo	Out	Test
Remove	Publish	Trace
Rename	Restore	Connect
Reset	Save	Disconnect
Search	Sync	Read

TABLE 9.1   PowerShell and EMS Verbs

Select	Unpublish	Receive
Set	Update	Send
Show	Approve	Write
Skip	Assert	Block
Split	Complete	Grant
Step	Confirm	Protect
Switch	Deny	Revoke
Undo	Disable	Unblock
Unlock	Enable	Unprotect
Watch	Install	Use

Walking Through Cmdlets in EMS

Some cmdlets offer many different switches and parameters. If administrators are not comfortable entering all the parameters for a cmdlet in one line, they can enter as much as they want, press Enter, and EMS prompts for the rest. This provides an easy way to run cmdlets that are not often used and that don't necessarily need to be saved for reuse.

For example, enter `Dismount-Database` and EMS prompts for the missing required parameters:

```
cmdlet Dismount-Database at command pipeline position 1
Supply values for the following parameters:
Identity: MBDB14


Confirm
Are you sure you want to perform this action?
Dismounting database "MBDB14". This may result in reduced availability for mail-
boxes in the database.
[Y] Yes  [A] Yes to All  [N] No  [L] No to All  [?] Help (default is "Y"): y
```

This is the same as entering the following single line at the EMS command line:

```
Dismount-Database MBDB14
```

Getting Help with EMS

The Exchange Management Shell features a QuickRef guide that gives a quick tutorial on common commands and syntax. It provides common tasks and options, tips and tricks, recipient management examples, storage management examples, transport configuration examples, policy configuration, and server management examples. This is presented in a Hypertext Markup Language (HTML) page by simply typing `QuickRef` at the EMS console on the Exchange server.

The Exchange Management Shell includes two basic types of help—command help and conceptual help. Both types can be accessed from the console using the `Get-Help` cmdlet, which also uses the alias `help`.

To retrieve a list of all available help topics, simply type `help *`. To get help with a specific cmdlet, type `help cmdlet-name`. For example, `help move-databasepath` displays the purpose of the cmdlet, all the required and optional parameters, return variables, and examples of its use.

By default, some information appears in the console window as one long, scrolling topic. To view the information a single page at a time, pipe the results to `more`. For example, `Get-ExCommand | More` displays all the Exchange Server–specific cmdlets available in EMS, one page at a time.

Using Pipelining in EMS

Pipelining is the key to the power of EMS. It uses the output of one cmdlet to run through another cmdlet using the ¦ (pipeline) operator. Pipelining provides bulk management changes. To understand this concept, examine this example:

```
Get-mailbox –server MBX1 ¦ set-mailbox -MaxSendSize 5mb
```

The first part of the line, the part before the ¦ pipeline operator, tells EMS to get all the mailbox objects on mailbox server MBX1. It then sends, or pipelines, the resulting set of objects to the next command, which instructs it to set the maximum send size of an email for these users to 5MB.

Another way of saying it is that one process output is consumed by another and another. Consider another example:

```
get-mailbox ¦ where-object { $_.name -like "amy*" } ¦ set-Mailbox -MaxSendSize 10mb
```

In this example, the `get-mailbox` cmdlet returns all the mailbox objects on all servers in the organization. This collection of objects is piped through the `where-object` filter cmdlet that filters the mailbox objects to include only mailboxes with names beginning with amy. The `$_` variable equates to "this object." The resulting set of objects, in turn, is piped through the `set-Mailbox` cmdlet to pass the parameter `–MaxSendSize` and set the value to `10MB`.

Note that EMS is not case-sensitive and that it understands that 10MB equates to 10,240,000 bytes. In this example, the `get-mailbox` cmdlet produces a result, the `where-object` consumes it and produces another result, and this result is consumed by the `set-mailbox` cmdlet to set the new value.

Using the WhatIf Switch and Confirm Parameter

There are times when the administrator writes a simple or complicated script in EMS and wonders what results it will produce. Some cmdlets support the -WhatIf switch and -Confirm parameter. The -WhatIf switch informs the administrator what action the script would take if executed without the -WhatIf switch, and the -Confirm parameter prompts for confirmation before taking action.

For example, suppose the administrator wants to set the Archive Warning Quota for all mailboxes in the Mailbox Store 5 database on server SERVER1. The administrator could use the following command:

```
Get-mailbox -database "SERVER1\Mailbox Store 5" ¦ set-mailbox
-ArchiveWarningQuota 2GB
```

By adding the -WhatIf switch, the following sample result is output to the console for each mailbox:

```
What if: Setting mailbox "companyabc.com/Admins/Keith Johnson"
What if: Setting mailbox "companyabc.com/Users/Jason Guillet"
```

This enables the administrator to easily see all the mailboxes that the set operation would be performed on by the script. If the results are as expected, the administrator presses the up arrow to recall the last typed line, and removes the -WhatIf switch to execute the script.

If the administrator adds the -Confirm parameter, the following is output to the console:

```
Confirm
Are you sure you want to perform this action?
Setting mailbox "companyabc.com/Admins/Keith Johnson".
[Y] Yes  [A] Yes to All  [N] No  [L] No to All  [?] Help
(default is "Y"):
```

Entering Y processes this operation, A processes all operations, N skips this operation, and L cancels further processing.

Creating Your Own Scripts

The Exchange Management Console contains many built-in cmdlets. Administrators can create their own scripts using the PowerShell ISE or a common text editor by using one or more cmdlets, which typically execute in order. The script is stored in a text file with a .PS1 extension.

The PowerShell common language runtime is an interpretive environment, meaning that cmdlets, functions, and scripts are loaded into random access memory (RAM), where they are validated and executed. In EMS, this is performed on the Exchange server.

The Exchange Management Shell and PowerShell define several types of commands that administrators can use in development. These commands include functions, filters, scripts, aliases, and executables (applications). The main command type discussed in this chapter is a simple, small command called a cmdlet. Both EMS and PowerShell supply sets of cmdlets and fully support cmdlet customization to suit the organization's environment. The PowerShell/EMS runtime processes all cmdlets.

An EMS cmdlet is a simple set of Exchange Server-specific commands bundled together to interact with a managed application (Exchange Server) and the operating system. It is similar to a built-in command in any other shell, such as `Cmd.exe`, `Bash`, or `ksh`. A conventional shell processes most commands as separate executable programs. Each program must parse the input and parameters, bind values to the correct parameters, format the output, and display the output.

EMS, in contrast, processes commands as instances of .NET classes and objects. The administrator must provide the necessary parameters and values, and then supply details of object types and formatting. EMS does the rest of the work: parsing the parameters and binding them to their values, formatting the output, and then displaying the output.

Demonstrating Cmdlet Examples

The administrator can run a cmdlet singly or as one of several cmdlets piped together on the command line. For example, the single cmdlet

```
Get-AddressList
```

returns all attributes of an address list or set of address lists. The pipelined command

```
Get-AddressList ¦ export-csv "C:\AddressList.csv"
```

produces a collection of address lists and pipelines it to the export-csv cmdlet, which requires the file path and name parameter to create a CSV file.

The following example is a custom script line that displays all public folders, their message counts, and total message sizes in a table format:

```
get-PublicFolder -recurse ¦ get-PublicFolderStatistics ¦ select-object
➥name,itemCount,totalItemSize
```

Although this is only a single-line command, it can be tedious to type every time it is needed. It can be typed into a text editor and saved as a `.ps1` file, `PFSize.ps1` for example, in the system path so that it can easily be run again and again.

A working knowledge of .NET is required to write more complex functions that access objects and classes that are not exposed using the built-in cmdlets. The following cmdlet example uses the `system.net.mail.smtpClient` class in .NET to send a Simple Mail Transfer Protocol (SMTP) email to a nonauthenticating SMTP server using the EMS or PowerShell command line:

```
$SmtpServer = "server1.companyabc.com"
```

```
$From = "EMStest@companyabc.com"
if ($args.Length -lt 1) {
    $To = "administrator@companyabc.com"
}
else {
    $To = $args[0]
}
$Subject = "Greetings from EMS!"
$Body = "Hello, this is a test from the Exchange Management Shell."
$SmtpClient = new-object system.net.mail.smtpClient
$SmtpClient.host = $SmtpServer
$SmtpClient.Send($From, $To, $Subject, $Body)
```

This cmdlet takes an argument, or parameter. If the cmdlet is saved as TestMail.ps1, the administrator can issue the following command to send a test SMTP email:

```
TestMail testuser@companyabc.com
```

The book *Script the World Using PowerShell* is a good resource for more detail on writing scripts using cmdlets.

Combining Functions to Create a Cmdlet Library

As the administrators become more familiar with EMS and using and writing cmdlets, they will begin to build a library of commonly used cmdlets and scripts. It is common to "recycle" similar cmdlets to use for different tasks. Over time, administrators will find useful scripts and concepts from many resources: colleagues, search engines, scripting blogs, newsgroups, and so on.

It is sometimes useful to put all the cmdlets in a common area where other administrators, users, and developers can peruse them and add to the knowledge base. Often, a fellow administrator needs to perform the same task that another administrator has already written. There is no reason to "reinvent the wheel."

A common practice is to create a network or DFS share where administrators and cmdlet developers have modify permissions and other users have read and execute access permissions. Arrange the folder structure based on business needs and technical requirements.

Modifying and Applying Server Cmdlets to Other Systems

After a cmdlet has been written and tested, it is often useful to run the same cmdlet against many or all servers in the organization. For example, consider the following cmdlet that configures the external URL for OWA on SERVER1:

```
Set-OwaVirtualDirectory -Identity 'SERVER1\owa (Default Web Site)' -ExternalUrl
➥'https://mail.companyabc.com/owa'
```

It is easy to convert this cmdlet so it will run against all client access servers in the Exchange Server organization using pipelining:

```
Get-OwaVirtualDirectory | Set-OwaVirtualDirectory -ExternalUrl
➥'https://mail.companyabc.com/owa'
```

In this example, `Get-OwaVirtualDirectory` returns a collection of all the OWA Virtual Directories in the Exchange Server organization and pipes them to the `Set-OwaVirtualDirectory` cmdlet, where it assigns the value.

Managing Cmdlets

It is a best practice to add the folder(s) that contain the custom cmdlets and scripts to the system path. This enables the administrator to run any one of the cmdlets from anywhere in the EMS console.

Cmdlets with the `.ps1` extension cannot be run directly from the `Cmd.exe` console; they must be run within the PowerShell or Exchange Management Shell.

The cmdlets that ship with Exchange Server 2010 and EMS cannot be modified. They have been optimized and compiled for maximum performance. These native cmdlets are contained in the DLL files in the `%SystemDrive%\Program Files\Microsoft\Exchange Server\bin` folder.

It is a best practice to create a folder to contain the custom `.ps1` files and add that folder to the system path. This facilitates the use of the `.ps1` files within the EMS command line.

Developing a Common Naming Scheme

When developing custom scripts, it is important to use functional names that denote the use of the script. It is a best practice to use the same verb-noun naming that is common in PowerShell and EMS. This provides consistency in the management environment.

A script to send SMTP email from the EMS command line might be called `send-email.ps1`, for example.

Distributing Cmdlets

Cmdlets can be distributed in a number of ways, similar to VBScripts or batch files.

The Microsoft distributed file system (DFS) offers another way to distribute cmdlets. By creating replicas in remote sites, the organization's cmdlet library can be fault tolerant and available locally to all administrators.

Another option for distributing cmdlets is via SharePoint. SharePoint's document management features enable administrators to check in and check out cmdlets as `.ps1` files. This makes managing `.ps1` files simple and provides full-text search capabilities. It also provides security so that only the appropriate administrators have access to certain cmdlets.

> **NOTE**
>
> Because .ps1 files are executable code, they cannot be sent using Outlook due to the Outlook security restrictions. Cmdlets can be zipped into compressed folders and emailed as attachments, or their contents can be pasted into the body of a message.

Introducing the Windows PowerShell Command Log

As mentioned earlier, every time a command executes from the Exchange Management Console, it runs a shell command. Even when you click on an item in the console navigation pane, EMS runs a refresh command to display the contents.

The EMC in Exchange Server 2010 has a new feature that logs how Shell commands are used to complete the actions the administrator performs. The Windows PowerShell Command Log, shown in Figure 9.4, has the ability to log every Shell command that runs whenever an action is performed in the EMC.

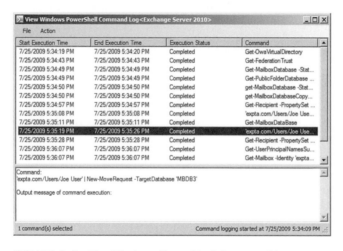

FIGURE 9.4   The Windows PowerShell Command Log.

The administrator can start the log any time after the EMC is opened by selecting View Windows PowerShell Command Log from the View menu in EMC. Click Start Command Logging from the Action menu to begin PowerShell logging. The PowerShell Command Log stays resident and continues to log commands until either logging is stopped or the EMC is closed. It will begin logging again when the EMC is re-opened.

The log contains the following information for each command that's recorded:

Start Execution Time	This field records the time the Shell command started running.
End Execution Time	This field records the time the Shell command ended.

Execution Status   This field records whether the command completed successfully.

Command   This field records the command that was run, the cmdlet, the parameters, and their values.

When the administrator selects a line in the upper pane of the Windows PowerShell Command Log, the details of the highlighted command are displayed in the bottom pane. The details include the complete EMS command that was run and any output from that command.

The administrator can save the output of the log to a log file, or copy the commands to the Clipboard to use the command in EMC directly. This can be done by right-clicking any line in the Windows PowerShell Command Log and selecting Copy Command(s).

Using EMS to Do Administrative Mailbox Tasks

The Exchange Management Shell makes common mailbox management tasks such as adding, modifying, moving, and deleting mailboxes simple. The flexibility of EMS enables the administrator to easily perform bulk tasks that would require much more time and labor if done from the Exchange Management Console.

Creating Mailboxes with EMS

Mailboxes can be created with EMS singly or in bulk. They can be created using the interactive command prompt or by specifying the required parameters from the command line. To enable a mailbox for an existing AD user or InterOrgPerson using the interactive shell, simply enter:

```
Enable-mailbox
```

and answer the prompts for the missing parameters:

```
Supply values for the following parameters:
Identity: companyabc\claire
```

The following example creates a mailbox for the existing user Jason in the DB14 mailbox database:

```
Enable-Mailbox "companyabc\jason" -database "DB14"
```

> **NOTE**
>
> The -Database is an optional parameter. If none is specified, the mailbox will be moved to a random database.

The next example demonstrates using EMS to create 1,000 users in AD and create mailboxes for each user in the Test Mailbox database. This single-line cmdlet is useful in lab scenarios.

```
1..1000 ¦ ForEach {net user "user$_" MyPassword=01 /ADD /Domain; enable-mailbox
"user$_" -database "test mailbox"}
```

Doing this same operation using VBScript would take many more lines of code and require much more development time.

Modifying Mailboxes with EMS

Mailbox attributes can easily be modified using EMS, as well. The following example modifies the mailbox for user Jason in the default domain to accept only emails from amy@companyabc.com:

```
set-Mailbox jason -AcceptMessagesOnlyFrom amy@companyabc.com
```

It is just as easy to make changes on many mailboxes at the same time using pipelining. Consider the following example that sets the mailbox prohibit send quota for all user mailboxes at 2GB:

```
get-Mailbox ¦ set-Mailbox -ProhibitSendQuota 2gb
```

In the following example, we use the –OrganizationalUnit parameter of the Get-Mailbox cmdlet to set the maximum message size that users in the Accounting OU can send to 5MB:

```
get-Mailbox -OrganizationalUnit "Test Users" ¦ set-Mailbox -MaxSendSize 5mb
```

Moving Mailboxes Using EMS

Moving mailboxes with the Exchange Management Shell in Exchange Server 2010 is a bit different than it was in previous versions. The move-mailbox cmdlet has been replaced with four new cmdlets: New-MoveRequest, Get-MoveRequest, Set-MoveRequest, and Remove-MoveRequest.

New-MoveRequest	Begins the process of a mailbox move.
Get-MoveRequest	Gets the status of an in-process mailbox move.
Set-MoveRequest	Changes move request options after the move has begun.
Remove-MoveRequest	Cancels an ongoing mailbox move.

When the Move-Mailbox cmdlet is used to move a mailbox, the cmdlet logs into both the source database and the target database and moves the content from one mailbox to the other mailbox. The move process can take several hours to complete, depending on the mailbox size.

The new MoveRequest cmdlets perform an asynchronous mailbox move because they do not perform the actual move. A new Exchange Server 2010 service running on an Exchange Server 2010 Client Access called the Mailbox Replication Service (MRS) actually performs the move. The New-MoveRequest cmdlet simply sends the request to the Mailbox Replication Service. The benefit of using the service is that it enables the administrator to manage mailbox moves from EMS after the move request has been made.

The `Set-MoveRequest` cmdlet provides the capability to change the options of an in-progress mailbox move. The `Get-MoveRequest` cmdlet reports the current status of a mailbox move.

The `Remove-MoveRequest` cmdlet enables the administrator to cancel a move that is in progress. A move can be canceled at any time before the move completes. If a move is canceled, the mailbox remains on the source server and database.

A simple move of a mailbox from one database to another on the same server is accomplished like this:

```
New-MoveRequest claire –TargetDatabase "accounting database"
```

> **NOTE**
>
> The TargetDatabase is an optional parameter. If none is specified, the mailbox will be moved to a random database.

EMS knows the names of all the databases in the organization. If there is more than one database with the same name, EMS moves the database to the first alphabetic server with that database name. To target a specific server, explicitly name the server in the TargetDatabase parameter. For example:

```
New-MoveRequest claire –TargetDatabase "SERVER2\accounting database"
```

> **NOTE**
>
> EMS will accept only the server name in the TargetDatabase parameter if there is more than one database with the same name in the same organization.

More complex moves are achieved just as easily from the Exchange Management Shell command line. In the following example, the mailbox is moved from the companyabc.com forest to the expta.com forest:

```
New-MoveRequest companyabc\claire -Remote –RemoteHostName mbx1.expta.com
```

Disabling or Removing Mailboxes with EMS

Disabling a mailbox in Exchange Server 2010 removes the Exchange Server attributes from a user in AD, making the AD user non-mail enabled. The AD user account is otherwise untouched. The mailbox is truly deleted by Exchange Server during the online maintenance cycle after exceeding the retention time.

Removing a mailbox in Exchange Server 2010 actually deletes the AD user account and mailbox. Because most Exchange Server administrators might not have rights to delete user accounts in AD, the most common Exchange Server task is to disable the mailbox.

The following example disables a mailbox of a user in the companyabc.com domain:

```
Disable-Mailbox companyabc\claire
```

The next example shows how to delete all the mailboxes in the "Test Database" mail store so that it can be decommissioned:

```
get-Mailbox -database "test database" ¦ disable-Mailbox –whatif
```

The –WhatIf switch in the preceding example runs the task in read-only mode, allowing the administrator to see what would happen by running this command.

The Remove-Mailbox cmdlet is used to remove the AD user account associated with a mailbox, as shown in the following example:

```
Remove-Mailbox claire
```

> **NOTE**
>
> The administrator requires user management rights in Active Directory to perform a Remove-Mailbox task because this task deletes the Active Directory user.

Using EMS for Server Tasks

Thus far, most of the examples have been for managing mailbox resources. EMS can also manage the Exchange servers in your environment. The following example demonstrates how to disable a Unified Messaging server. This enables the administrator to start or stop call processing on a Unified Messaging server so that the Unified Messaging server can be brought online or taken offline in a controlled way:

```
Disable-UMServer UMserver3
```

The next example uses the Set-AttachmentFilterListConfig command to modify the configuration of the Attachment Filter agent on the computer running the Edge server role:

```
Set-AttachmentFilterListConfig -action reject
```

And in this example, the Set-EventLogLevel cmdlet is used to set diagnostic logging for the mailbox replication to high:

```
Set-EventLogLevel 'MSExchange Mailbox Replication\Service' -Level High
```

These are just a few examples of what can be done with the Exchange Management Shell to manage Exchange servers. Many, many more commands are available to the administrator.

Provisioning Databases with EMS

Exchange Server 2010 databases can easily be provisioned and configured using the Exchange Management Shell. This first example creates a new database called "Marketing Storage Group":

```
New-MailboxDatabase -name "Marketing Storage Group" -EdbFilePath "D:\Database
➥Files\Marketing Storage Group.edb"
```

The next example configures circular logging on the "Test Database 2" database:

```
Set-MailboxDatabase -CircularLoggingEnabled $true -Identity "Test Database 2"
```

Managing Databases with EMS

All facets of Exchange Server database administration can be handled with the Exchange Management Shell. Using the following examples, mailbox stores can be created, dismounted, and moved. The first example creates a new Sales Database:

```
New-MailboxDatabase -name "Sales Database" -EdbFilePath "D:\Program Files\
➥Microsoft\Exchange Server\V14\Mailbox\Sales Database.edb"
```

The second example shows how to mount the same mailbox database after it has been created:

```
Mount-database "Sales Database"
```

Use the Move-DatabasePath command to set a new path in Active Directory for the database object and then move the related files to the new location. For example:

```
move-DatabasePath -Identity 'MBDB1' -EdbFilePath 'D:\Program Files\
➥Microsoft\Exchange Server\V14\Mailbox\MBDB1\MBDB1.edb' -LogFolderPath
➥'D:\Program Files\Microsoft\Exchange Server\V14\Mailbox\MBDB1'
```

When the preceding command is run, EMS automatically takes the database offline, moves the database, and mounts it again.

The next example shows how to delete a mailbox database:

```
Remove-MailboxDatabase "sales database"
```

When this command is run, Exchange Management Shell deletes the database and provides a warning, letting the administrator know that the database has been removed from Active Directory but the physical files remain. The following warning is displayed:

```
WARNING: The specified database has been removed. You must remove the database file
located in DatabaseFilePath from your computer manually if it exists. Specified
database: Sales Database
```

Managing Connectors with EMS

All types of connectors can be managed with the Exchange Management Shell. Receive and Send connectors can be created, deleted, and configured. This example gets the existing credential object and creates a new secured Send connector on an Edge or Hub Transport server role and configures it to use that credential:

```
$CredentialObject = Get-Credential
New-SendConnector -Name "Secure E-Mail to Companyabc.org" -Type ToInternet
 -AddressSpaces companyabc.com -AuthenticationCredential $CredentialObject
```

This example modifies an existing Receive connector. The Identity parameter is required when you are running the Set-ReceiveConnector command. This example sets the maximum number of hops, sets the SMTP banner message, and configures the connection timeout value:

```
Set-ReceiveConnector -Identity "Internet Receive Connector" -MaxHopCount 1
➥-Banner "220 Authorized access only" -ConnectionTimeout 00:15:00
```

This command deletes the object and the configuration information for a Receive connector. After this task completes, the object and the configuration information for the Receive connector are deleted:

```
Remove-ReceiveConnector "Companyabc.com Receive Connector"
```

Using EMS to Do Reporting

EMS has built-in reporting features that use a variety of outputs. For example, the following cmdlet verifies server functionality by logging on to the specified user's mailbox and reporting the latency (see Figure 9.5):

```
Test-MapiConnectivity amy@companyabc.com
```

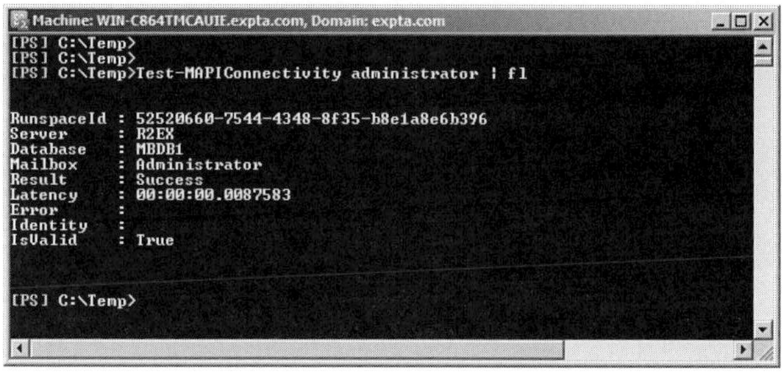

FIGURE 9.5   Output generated by EMS MapiConnectivity Test.

Output is normally sent to the display, but it can also be sent to files using redirection. EMS has special cmdlets that also produce comma-separated values (CSV), Extensible Markup Language (XML), and HTML output. These types of output provide the flexibility that administrators need to manipulate the data using familiar tools, such as Microsoft Excel.

Generating User Distribution Reports

Reports that list user mailbox distribution across all mailbox stores can be helpful to know if the user load is balanced in the organization. The following .ps1 example shows how to produce a report listing the total number of mailbox stores, the number of mailboxes in each store, and the total number of mailboxes.

This .ps1 script contains comments, variables, and error trapping. Comments begin with the "#" symbol and are useful for administrators to understand what the script or cmdlet is doing and are ignored by EMS/PowerShell. Variables always start with the $ symbol and are used to assign values or collections. Error trapping handles exceptions or errors that can occur in the script so that the script continues to run:

```
#Get all mailbox stores in the organization and assign them to the $MailboxDatabases
➥array variable
$MailboxDatabases = get-mailboxdatabase
write-host "There are" $MailboxDatabases.Count "Mailbox Stores in the organization."
write-host ("-"*70)


#Get each database and assign it to the $Database array variable
ForEach ($Database in $MailboxDatabases) {
        #Derive the Mailbox server name from the database
         $MailboxServer = $Database.server.name
        #Derive the database name from the database
         $DatabaseName = $Database.name
        #Assign the full database name to the $FullDatabaseName variable
         $FullDatabaseName = "$MailboxServer" + "\" + "$DatabaseName"
        #Count the number of databases on the server
         $count=0
        get-mailboxdatabase –server $MailboxServer | ForEach-Object {$count++}
        #Get the mailboxes for this database
        If ($count -gt 1) {
                $mailbox = get-mailbox -database $FullDatabaseName
                }
                Else {
                $mailbox = get-mailbox -database $DatabaseName
                }
        write-host "There are" $mailbox.Count.toString("#,#") "mailboxes in"
➥$FullDatabaseName


#The trap statement traps the NullException error which occurs when a database
➥has no mailboxes
```

```
trap{
        write-host "There are no mailboxes in" $FullDatabaseName;
        continue
}
}

write-host ("-"*70)
#Get all mailboxes in the organization
$mailboxes = get-Mailbox
write-host "The total number of mailboxes in the organization is"
➥$mailboxes.count.tostring("#,#")
```

Working with Event Logs

Exchange Server administrators often work with Windows event logs to troubleshoot issues. Because EMS runs in the PowerShell environment, the administrator can take advantage of PowerShell's Get-Eventlog cmdlet to work with event logs.

This example displays all events in the Application Event Log in which the source begins with the word "Exchange." The output is exported to a CSV file for easy manipulation in Microsoft Excel:

```
get-eventlog Application ¦ where {$_.Source -ilike "Exchange*"} ¦ export-csv
➥c:\events.csv
```

Finding Other Resources

Numerous resources are available for both PowerShell and the Exchange Management Shell. Microsoft has generated a lot of excitement about these technologies and is focused on delivering meaningful content and examples in a variety of ways.

Resources on the Web

The following are various PowerShell and Exchange Management Shell resources available on the Internet:

- ▶ **Microsoft Exchange Server 2010 Tech Center**—Exchange Management Shell product documentation (http://technet.microsoft.com/en-us/exchange/default.aspx).

- ▶ **Scripting with Windows PowerShell**—Brings together resources for system administrators who are interested in learning about the Windows PowerShell command-line and scripting environment (http://technet.microsoft.com/en-us/scriptcenter/dd742419.aspx).

- ▶ **TechNet Virtual Lab: Exchange**—Hosted by Microsoft, these virtual labs enable you to connect to an Exchange Server 2010 virtual environment to run various exercises and demos (http://tinyurl.com/nlvj43).

6

▶ **Vivek Sharma's blog**—Vivek is a program manager for the Exchange Management Shell team. His blog includes many samples and explanations for working with EMS (http://www.viveksharma.com/techlog/).

▶ **Scripting newsgroups**—These newsgroups provide a place for scripters of all types and abilities to ask questions and share information (http://www.microsoft.com/communities/newsgroups/list/en-us/default.aspx?dg=microsoft.public.windows.server.scripting).

Utilities and Tools

Several tools have been released or are in current development for working with Exchange Management Shell and PowerShell scripts. Most of these are editors that provide automatic formatting, cmdlet method and property exploration, and debugging:

▶ PowerShell ISE, Microsoft (http://technet.microsoft.com/en-us/library/dd315244.aspx)

▶ Idera PowerShell Plus, Idera (http://www.idera.com/Products/PowerShell/PowerShell-Plus)

▶ PrimalScript, SAPIEN Technologies (http://www.primalscript.com)

Summary

PowerShell is required learning when it comes to Exchange Server 2010. Mastery of PowerShell and Exchange Management Shell sets the distinction between an Exchange Server administrator and an Exchange Server guru. Although having a deep understanding of both technologies can benefit both the administrator and the organization, the simple interface and easily understood syntax makes the administrator more productive from day one.

Both PowerShell and the Exchange Management Shell are continually being developed. Each Exchange Server update rollup and service pack is expected to include additional optimized cmdlets to extend the use and functionality of EMS. The administrator is encouraged to check the Exchange Server 2010 website often for updates.

Best Practices

The following are best practices from this chapter:

▶ Leverage scripting to automate repetitive tasks.

▶ Use the Exchange Management Shell for tasks involving recipient management, organization management, server management, and diagnostics.

▶ Understand cmdlets because they are core to the Exchange Management Shell.

▶ Use cmdlets to enforce strict rules and to validate configurations.

▶ Take advantage of the Exchange Management Shell by automating tasks relative to mailbox management, setting user limits, moving mailboxes between servers, and configuring Exchange parameters.

▶ Use the Exchange Management Shell Quickref guide to get a quick tutorial on common commands and shell syntax.

▶ Create a cmdlet library to reuse cmdlets and scripts in similar scripted functions.

▶ Develop a common naming scheme for cmdlets to make it easier to find and understand the function of cmdlets in your library.

▶ Use the Exchange Management Shell to perform basic administrative tasks, such as creating mailboxes, modifying mailbox settings, moving mailboxes, and disabling mailboxes.

▶ Create EMS scripts to perform server administration tasks, such as provisioning storage groups, managing mailboxes stores, and managing connectors.

▶ Take advantage of EMS for reporting by creating large mail user and user distribution reports.

6

CHAPTER 10

Client-Level Secured Messaging

When discussing the broad topic of securing a messaging environment, it is best to break the subject down to three basic components: client-level, server-level, and transport-level security. You have likely heard the adage "A chain is only as strong as its weakest link;" this saying can easily be applied to an organization's security measures. If you have exceptionally good client-level security, and exceptionally strong server-level security, but your transport-level security is lacking—you are vulnerable to attack. Hackers thrive on researching environments, finding "the weakest link," and exploiting it.

This chapter focuses on client-level security, leaving "Server and Transport-Level Security" for Chapter 11. This book also addresses an additional component of messaging security, client-level encryption, in Chapter 12, "Integrating Certificate-Based Public Key Infrastructure (PKI) in Exchange Server 2010."

Microsoft's Trustworthy Computing Initiative

In 2002, Microsoft Founder and Chairman Bill Gates sent a memo to all employees at Microsoft emphasizing the importance of making the company's software more "trustworthy." He labeled this new effort "Trustworthy Computing" and stated that the company focus needed to shift toward making software that was more secure and helping users become more comfortable with their electronic privacy.

This memo began a shift of focus for the entire organization that continues today. And it is working. Microsoft has recorded a significant reduction of publicly reported vulnerabilities in their products across the board.

However, no matter what security features are built in to a product, you still have to ensure that they are implemented and configured properly to be effective.

Microsoft Exchange Server 2010 was designed, built, and implemented with this new security effort in place. Microsoft has gone to great lengths to provide a rich array of security features at the client, server, and transport layers in Exchange Server 2010 to protect an organization's messaging environment investment.

By actively and aggressively securing each of these three layers, you can ensure your chain has no "weak links."

Securing Your Windows Environment

At its basic components, a Microsoft Exchange Server environment can be reduced to four main components:

- ▶ **Server operating system**—Microsoft's latest server operating system (OS), and the one that Exchange Server 2010 is designed to run on, is Microsoft Windows Server 2008 R2.

- ▶ **Server messaging system**—Exchange Server 2010 is the current messaging system from Microsoft. Exchange Server 2010 provides messaging, calendaring, mobile access, and unified communications for the enterprise.

- ▶ **Client operating system**—Microsoft's latest client operating systems are Microsoft Windows 7 or Windows Vista. Although Exchange Server 2010 can work with older versions of client software, this chapter focuses primarily on the security features available in the latest version of the client OS.

- ▶ **Client messaging application**—Microsoft's latest client messaging application is Microsoft Office Outlook 2007, though Outlook 2010 is scheduled for completion shortly after publication of this book. Again, although Exchange Server can work with older versions of Outlook, this chapter focuses on the latest technologies.

Both the server messaging system and the client messaging application are only as secure as their underlying operating systems. Fortunately, Microsoft Windows Server 2008, Windows 7, and Windows Vista are very secure by default, and with a little knowledge and experience can be made exceptionally secure.

NOTE

Implementing security measures in a computer network is an extremely complex process, and entire books have been devoted to the subject. This chapter endeavors to share best practices and tips and tricks for securing your mail client and the underlying OS, but it is recommended that additional resources focusing solely on security be referenced as well.

The concept of securing Windows 7 and Windows Vista can best be grasped if it is broken down into smaller components. This chapter addresses the following primary areas:

- ▶ Authentication

- ▶ Access control

- ▶ Patch management

- ▶ Communications

This chapter addresses other areas as well, of course, but the recommendations in these key sections will get you off to a good start.

Windows Server 2008 Security Improvements

Although this chapter focuses on client-level security, we must discuss some server features as well because the two work hand in hand to create a secure network. Securing Windows Server 2008 is discussed in greater depth in Chapter 11.

Even from the default installation, Windows Server 2008 and the latest version Windows Server 2008 R2 are significantly more secure than their predecessors. Previous versions installed with most features defaulting to an enabled state, counting on the administrator to disable them if they were not going to be used. This left a lot of openings for malicious intruders, especially in an environment where the administration staff was not well versed in hardening an underlying operating system.

In Windows Server 2008, all features and roles are disabled by default and must be manually turned on, making it more difficult for unauthorized users to exploit vulnerabilities. This is one way of improving server security, known as "reducing the attack surface."

Some of the changes in Windows Server 2008 include the following:

- ▶ After a default installation, many services are disabled, rather than enabled.

- ▶ Internet Information Services (IIS), the built-in web server, has been completely overhauled and is no longer installed by default. In addition, group policies can be implemented that prevent the unauthorized installation of IIS in your environment.

- ▶ Access control lists (ACLs) have been redefined and are stronger by default.

- ▶ Security can be defined by server and user roles.

- ▶ Public Key Infrastructure (PKI) Active Directory Certificate Services (AD CS) has been enhanced and includes advanced support for automatic smart card enrollment, certificate revocation list (CRL) deltas, and more.

- ▶ Wireless security features, such as IEEE 802.1X, are supported.

- ▶ The Security Configuration Wizard included with Windows Server 2008 can further lock down security based on server role and function.

10

Windows 7 Security Improvements

Windows 7 complements Windows Server 2008 R2 from the client perspective by supporting the security features embedded in Windows Server 2008 R2. The following are among the more notable security features in Windows 7:

▶ Core system files and kernel data structures are protected against corruption and deletion.

▶ Software policies can be used to identify and restrict which applications can run.

▶ Wireless security features, such as IEEE 802.1X, are supported.

▶ Sensitive or confidential files can be encrypted using Bitlocker encryption as well as Encrypting File System (EFS).

▶ Communications can be encrypted using IP Security (IPSec).

▶ Kerberos-based authentication is integrated in the core logon process.

▶ Enhanced security devices such as smart cards and biometric devices are supported.

All of the security improvements are supported with Group Policy enhancements to the Windows 7 operating system, providing centralized policy setting and management.

Windows Firewall Protection

In today's messaging environments, users often have to be able to access their emails from noncorporate locations. Gone are the days of accessing email only from the office computer; many users now access their mail from hotels, client sites, or wireless network "hot spots" such as the local coffee house.

Supporting this "anytime, anywhere" availability is important, but organizations must work to minimize potential security risks that can come with enhanced functionality.

Because remote users are often utilizing equipment that is not configured by their organization's security administrators, this equipment can be more susceptible to viruses and intrusions. To minimize security risks, client computers should have the Windows Firewall installed and operating.

Windows Firewall provides a protective boundary that monitors information traveling between a computer and a network (including the Internet). Windows Firewall blocks "unsolicited requests," which are often the result of external users located on a network trying to access your computer. Windows Firewall also helps protect you by blocking computer viruses and worms that try to reach your computer through a network connection.

The Windows Firewall uses stateful packet inspection to monitor all communications to and from the computer and records the outbound connections made from the protected system. Windows Firewall can also be customized to allow exceptions based on an application or port as well as to log security events.

Utilizing Security Templates

Security templates are a practical and effective means to apply standardized security policies and configurations to multiple systems in an environment. These security templates can be customized to meet the minimum security requirements of a particular organization, and can be applied to client computers as well as to servers using the Security Configuration and Analysis Microsoft Management Console (MMC) snap-in.

By utilizing the automatic deployment of security templates to client PCs, administrators can ensure that computers are identically configured and utilize available security measures, even if the system is not able to be managed by Group Policy Objects (GPOs).

> **TIP**
>
> Microsoft provides several security templates based on functional roles within a network environment. These can easily be applied to client computers and servers alike. However, organizations often have unique needs that are not met completely by these default templates so, as a best practice, administrators should always customize the security template to address particular application and access needs.

Using the Security Configuration and Analysis Tool

The Security Configuration and Analysis tool is a utility that can apply security templates to computers. It compares a computer's security configurations against an administrator-defined security template, and reports any differences found between the two. Furthermore, when the security configuration on the computer does not match the settings specified in the template, you can use the tool to update the system accordingly.

This utility has two modes of operation: analysis and configuration. An often-overlooked best practice is to analyze the system prior to making any changes so that you have a baseline frame of reference.

To run the Security Configuration and Analysis tool and analyze a computer, perform the following steps:

1. Start the Microsoft Management Console by selecting Start, Run, typing MMC in the Open text box, and then clicking OK.
2. Select File, click Add/Remove Snap-in.
3. In the Add or Remove Snap-in window, select Security Configuration and Analysis, click Add, and then click OK.
4. In the MMC, right-click the Security Configuration and Analysis snap-in, and select Open Database.
5. Type a database name, select a location to store the database, and then click Open.
6. Select a security template from those listed, or navigate to C:\Windows\inf and select one of the files starting with deflt, as shown in Figure 10.1. After you have selected the appropriate .inf file, click Open.

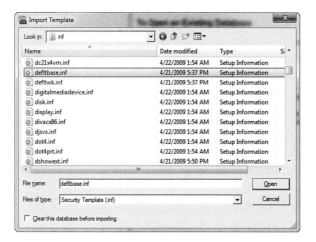

FIGURE 10.1   Using the Security and Configuration Wizard.

7. Back in the MMC, right-click the Security Configuration and Analysis snap-in, and choose Analyze Computer Now.

8. Enter a path to store the generated log file, and click OK to continue.

After the System Security Analysis has completed, the utility displays the security settings that are configured in the template you selected, and what is currently configured on the computer. Items for which the computer is not in compliance with the policy appear with a red "x" beside them.

If you want to configure the system with the security settings in the template, you can do so by performing a few extra steps:

1. In the MMC, right-click the Security Configuration and Analysis snap-in.

2. Select Configure Computer Now.

3. Enter a path for the error log to be written to, and then click OK.

Customizing Security Templates

An administrator might want to use custom security templates for several reasons. The organization might want a simple method of ensuring that attached computer systems meet with defined minimum security criteria. They might desire to ensure configured security settings that work for a particular application can be replicated to other servers of the same nature.

Larger organizations often have the need for customized security templates. For example, a member of the Internal Auditing department might need to regularly connect to employee hard drives, whereas the receptionist is only allowed basic Internet access. By applying different security settings to each of these machines, you can help the company ensure people have access to the data they need, and not to the resources they don't.

TIP

You can download and implement security templates provided by Microsoft, the National Security Agency (NSA), or the National Institute of Standards and Technology (NIST). These templates can be used as baselines, and can be customized to meet the needs of your particular environment. After being customized, you can distribute them to appropriate systems in your organization with minimal effort.

Windows Server 2008/2003, Windows 7/Vista, and Windows XP Professional are equipped with the Security Templates MMC snap-in that enables administrators to quickly and easily customize settings on individual systems. Loading this tool is similar to the Security Configuration and Analysis tool discussed previously. To add the snap-in, follow these steps:

1. Start the Microsoft Management Console by selecting Start, Run, typing MMC in the Open text box, and then clicking OK.

2. Select File, click Add/Remove Snap-in.

3. In the Add or Remove Snap-in window, select Security Templates, click Add, and then click OK.

When the Security Templates snap-in is expanded, it displays the default search path to the security templates folder in the current user's profile. Other paths can be opened to display other security templates that might reside on the system. Expand the default template storage directory (C:\windows\inf\deflt*.inf) to see the available default templates. Rather than editing these default templates, it is recommended that you select the one you are going to use as a baseline, right-click it, and save it as a new template.

After you have created the new template, expand it to display all of the modifiable security settings. From here, you can configure the template to apply the security settings you want, as shown in Figure 10.2.

After you have completed customizing the template, it is an easy process to save the file to an accessible network share, and then use the Security Configuration and Analysis tool to apply it to the appropriate systems.

Keeping Up with Security Patches and Updates

Applying service packs, updates, and hotfixes in a timely manner is critical to maintaining the security of an environment. Whether you are talking about a server operating system, an application such as Exchange Server 2010, a client operating system, or even client applications, keeping your systems up to date with the latest releases ensures that you are protected against known vulnerabilities.

Organizations often underestimate the importance of these updates, so let's look at them in a different light. These updates are released to protect against known vulnerabilities. That means that there is a good possibility that malicious users in the hacker community already know how to exploit them. So, there the system sits, not only does it have an unlocked door, but the criminals know it is unlocked.

10

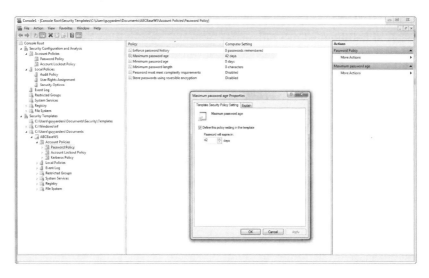

FIGURE 10.2   Editing Security Templates.

In the past, updates often had to be manually implemented on a system-by-system basis and, for companies with hundreds (or thousands) of workstations, it proved to be a monumental task. These manual processes still exist, but rarely need to be used today.

With Windows Server 2008/2003, Windows 7/Vista, and Windows XP, utilities exist that allow you to automate this process and simplify the distribution of updates. Microsoft has provided several options: Windows Update, Microsoft Update, Microsoft Windows Server Update Services (WSUS), and Microsoft System Center Configuration Manager (SCCM). In addition, there are a variety of third-party applications that can assist you with this endeavor.

> **NOTE**
>
> In today's environments, distribution of updates is often considered the "easy" part. Automated methods of deployment have made the process fairly simple. However, one of the most important steps, and one of the most often overlooked, is the thorough and complete testing of updates in a lab environment before the release to a production environment. Strongly consider implementing a patch management system that includes adequate time and resources for testing.

Windows Update

Windows Update, located at http://www.microsoft.com/windowsupdate, is a website that scans a local system and determines whether it has the latest updates applicable to the operating system. Windows Update is a very useful tool when dealing with a small number of systems. One shortcoming of Windows Update is that it only addresses updates to the operating system—not to any applications installed on the computer. Windows Update was designed for Microsoft Windows 2000 SP2 and earlier. Those using later versions of the operating system (including Windows 2000 SP3 and higher, Windows

Server 2008/2003, Windows 7/Vista, and Windows XP) can instead use the Microsoft Update discussed in the following section.

Microsoft Update

For other Microsoft applications on your system, including Microsoft Outlook, use Microsoft Update, located at http://update.microsoft.com. This website offers the same downloads available on the Windows Update site, plus the latest updates for Microsoft Office and other Microsoft applications.

When you visit the website, it scans your computer and allows you to review a list of available updates and select the ones you want to implement.

The site breaks down the available updates into categories, identifying those that are critical to the security and reliability of your computer as high-priority updates.

One other feature of the Microsoft Update website is the ability to review your update history. By selecting this link, you can see the update, the product it applied to, the status of the implementation, the date it was applied, and the method used to apply the patch—for example, Windows Update or Automatic Updates, which is discussed in the next section.

Like Windows Update, Microsoft Update is intended for managing one system at a time. As useful as it is for individual users and small environments, other alternatives should still be considered for larger organizations.

NOTE

You can remove an update by using the Programs and Features (previously known as Add/Remove Programs) applet in Control Panel. When this feature first appeared, it had the reputation of being somewhat unreliable. Sometimes, updates were removed and the system experienced problems afterward. However, this process has been greatly improved over the past several years and is significantly more stable and reliable now.

Automatic Updates

One of the most reliable, and least time consuming, methods of implementing updates from Microsoft is built in to Windows Server 2008/2003, Windows 7/Vista, and Windows XP. Known as Automatic Updates, this feature allows your system to automatically download and install high-priority updates, without manual intervention. Optional updates, however, still need to be implemented using other methods.

With Automatic Updates, you can configure the utility to automatically download and install updates on a daily or weekly basis, at the time of day of your choice (for example, every Saturday at 2:00 a.m.).

Alternatively, you can select one of the following options:

▶ Download Updates for Me, But Let Me Choose When to Install Them.

▶ Notify Me But Don't Automatically Download or Install Them.

▶ Turn Off Automatic Updates.

10

When connecting to Microsoft Update or Windows Update, this method has a few draw-backs that must be mentioned. First, by automatically downloading and applying hotfixes, you are not afforded the opportunity to download and implement them in a test lab prior to deployment. Second, some high-priority updates require a reboot and might automatically restart your system without your prior approval.

To mitigate these shortcomings, you can configure Automatic Updates to not download and install updates directly from Microsoft, but can instead receive updates from a Microsoft Windows Server Update Services (WSUS) server, discussed next.

Windows Server Update Services (WSUS)

Realizing the increased administration and management efforts that challenge administra-tors of larger environments, Microsoft created the Microsoft Software Update Services (SUS), and the newer version called Windows Server Update Services (WSUS). This no-charge add-in component is designed to simplify the process of keeping computers in your organization up to date with the latest updates and service packs. WSUS communi-cates directly and securely with Microsoft to gather the latest security updates for a variety of Microsoft products, including Exchange Server, and enables administrators to manage the distribution of these updates to clients and servers in their environment. By utilizing WSUS, administrators can download updates, test them, and schedule the deployment to additional systems.

Utilizing Background Intelligent Transfer Service (BITS), the application allows administra-tors to download updates in the background, using available network bandwidth, to mini-mize the impact on their user community.

WSUS version 3.0 includes a new MMC-based user interface and has the following features:

▶ Advanced filtering and reporting

▶ Improved performance and reliability

▶ Branch office optimizations and reporting rollup

▶ System Center Operations Manager Management Pack

> **NOTE**
>
> You can find more information on WSUS and download the product from http://technet. microsoft.com/en-us/wsus/default.aspx.

Client-Based Virus Protection

One of the primary reasons why the installation of service packs and software updates in a timely manner is so important is the prevalence of computer viruses. Many viruses are written to exploit specific vulnerabilities that are found in computer operating systems and applications—both on clients and servers. Because Microsoft products are used so widely throughout the world, those who create viruses generally write them specifically to attack Microsoft products. This has resulted in the creation of an entire industry focused solely on protecting businesses and individuals from attack.

Companies truly concerned with protecting their environment from attack should use a multilayer approach to virus protection. By including antivirus applications on gateways, Exchange servers, and on the desktop, outbreaks can be prevented, or quickly detected and dealt with.

Gateway and Exchange server-level antivirus strategies are discussed in more depth in Chapter 11.

There are many ways to distribute viruses, and one of the most effective is by installing unauthorized software on a workstation and turning it into a distribution point. This method might (or might not) utilize an existing messaging system. If it does not, gateway and Exchange server-level antivirus methods might not be able to help at all. By implementing a separate antivirus solution on the desktop itself, you can minimize your exposure to attack.

An aggressive plan should be in place to keep antivirus signature files and engines up to date. Virus outbreaks that once took days (or weeks) to become widespread can now travel around the globe in a matter of hours. Antivirus updates (often referred to as "signature files") should be updated daily at a minimum and more often if your product supports it.

Windows Lockdown Guidelines and Standards

Microsoft has gone to great lengths to provide secure and reliable products. This endeavor was not accomplished in a vacuum—Microsoft has worked closely with companies, government agencies, security consultants, and others to identify and address security issues in the computer industry. Through this concerted effort and teamwork, security standards and guidelines have been developed that are applicable to not only Microsoft products, but also to the computing industry as a whole.

In addition to researching and implementing Microsoft recommended security standards and guidelines, responsible administrators can also use recommended best practices that have been compiled by the National Institute of Standards and Technologies (NIST) and the National Security Agency (NSA).

Both NIST and NSA provide security lockdown configuration standards and guidelines that can be downloaded from their websites (www.nist.gov and www.nsa.gov, respectively).

Exchange Server 2010 Client-Level Security Enhancements

As mentioned earlier, Exchange Server 2010 has several improved security features—especially when combined with Outlook 2007. Some of these features include the following:

> ▶ **Minimizing junk email**—The junk email folder, first introduced in Outlook 2003, helps protect users from junk email. Utilizing the Outlook 2007/2010 junk email filter, Outlook 2007 can disable threatening links and warn you about possibly malicious content within an email message.

▶ **Antiphishing methods**—Exchange Server 2010 acts as the first scan on incoming email and works to determine the legitimacy of the message. If applicable, Exchange Server 2010 can disable links or uniform resource locators (URLs) present in the message to help protect users.

▶ **Information Rights Management (IRM)**—Exchange Server 2010 can help control the distribution of corporate data by preventing recipients from forwarding, copying, or printing confidential email messages. In addition, expiration dates can be applied to messages, after which they cannot be viewed or acted upon. IRM functionality is based on Active Directory Rights Management Services (AD RMS) in Windows Server 2008.

▶ **Managed email folders**—Exchange Server 2010 helps organizations maintain compliance by applying a new approach to document retention. Utilizing managed email folders, users can see and interact with their messages in Outlook 2007/2010 just as they would using regular mail folders, but the managed email folder applies retention, archive, and expiration policies defined by the administrator. Utilizing managed email folders, users and administrators can comply with regulations set by corporate policy or by external agencies.

In addition, Exchange Server 2010 continues to support several security technologies that were present in Exchange Server 2003, including the following:

▶ Support for MAPI (RPC) over HTTP or HTTPS, known as Outlook Anywhere, can be configured to use either Secure Sockets Layer (SSL) or NT LAN Manager (NTLM)–based authentication

▶ Support for authentication methods, such as Kerberos and NTLM

▶ Antispam features such as safe and block lists, as well as advanced filtering mechanisms to help minimize the number of unwanted emails that reach the end user

▶ Protection against web beaconing, which is used by advertisers and spammers to verify email addresses and determine whether emails have been read

▶ Attachment blocking by Exchange Server 2010 before it reaches the intended recipient

▶ Rights management support, which prevents unauthorized users from intercepting emails

Securing Outlook 2007

Exchange Server 2010 and Microsoft Outlook 2007 were designed to work together and, therefore, are tightly integrated. Utilizing these two products together can provide a formidable security front.

Outlook Anywhere

Prior to Exchange Server 2003, Outlook users who needed to connect to Exchange Server over the Internet had to establish a virtual private network (VPN) connection prior to using Outlook. The only alternatives were to open a myriad of remote procedure calls

(RPC) ports to the Internet or make Registry modifications to statically map RPC ports. However, most companies felt that the benefits provided by these two "workarounds" were outweighed by the risks.

With Exchange Server 2003 and Outlook 2003, Microsoft provided an alternate (and very much improved) method for Outlook users to connect over the Internet. Known as RPC over HTTPS, this feature allowed Outlook 2003 users to access their mailboxes securely from remote locations utilizing the Internet and an HTTPS proxy connection. This feature reduced the need for VPN solutions, while still keeping the messaging environment secure.

In Exchange Server 2010, this functionality is known as Outlook Anywhere, and Microsoft has improved the functionality and greatly reduced the difficulty of deployment and management of the feature.

Outlook Anywhere can be used with both Outlook 2003 through 2010 clients and provides the following benefits:

▶ Users can access Exchange servers remotely from the Internet.

▶ Organizations can use the same URL and namespace that is used for Exchange ActiveSync and Outlook Web App.

▶ Organizations can use the same SSL server certificate that is used for Outlook Web App and Exchange ActiveSync.

▶ Unauthenticated requests from Outlook are blocked and cannot access Exchange servers.

▶ Clients must trust server certificates, and certificates must be valid.

▶ No VPN is needed to access Exchange servers across the Internet.

NOTE

For a Windows client to use this feature, the system must be running Windows XP SP1 or higher.

Preparing Your Environment for Outlook Anywhere

Enabling Outlook Anywhere in an Exchange Server 2010 environment is a very straightforward process, and can be done using either the Exchange Management Console or the Exchange Management Shell. However, prior to enabling the product, you must install a valid SSL certificate from a trusted certificate authority (CA).

NOTE

When you install Exchange Server 2010, you have the option of installing a default SSL certificate that is created during the Exchange Server setup process. However, this certificate is not a trusted SSL certificate. It is recommended that you either install your own trusted self-signed SSL certificate, or trust the default SSL certificate that is created during the Exchange Server setup process.

Enabling Outlook Anywhere from the Exchange Management Console

After installing a valid SSL certificate, Outlook Anywhere can be easily enabled from the Exchange Management Console by following these steps:

1. Start the Exchange Management Console. In the console tree, expand the Server Configuration node, and then select the Client Access node.

2. Select the CAS server that will host Outlook Anywhere and in the action pane, click Enable Outlook Anywhere. This starts the Enable Outlook Anywhere Wizard.

3. In the External Host Name field, shown in Figure 10.3, type the appropriate external host name for your organization.

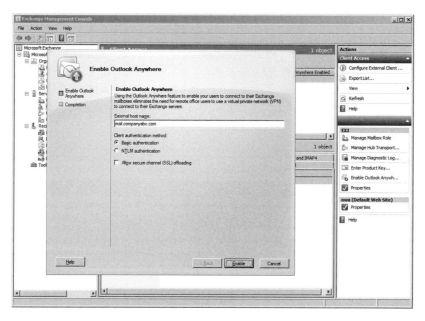

FIGURE 10.3   Enabling Outlook Anywhere.

4. Select the appropriate External Authentication Method, either Basic Authentication or NTLM Authentication.

5. If you are using an SSL accelerator and want to allow SSL offloading, select the Allow Secure Channel (SSL) Offloading check box.

CAUTION

Do not use the Allow Secure Channel (SSL) Offloading option unless you are sure you have an SSL accelerator that can handle SSL offloading. Selecting the option when you do not have this functionality prevents Outlook Anywhere from functioning properly.

6. Click Enable to apply the settings and enable Outlook Anywhere.

7. Review the completion summary to ensure there were no errors, and then click Finish to close the wizard.

8. These steps should be repeated for each CAS server that will host Outlook Anywhere.

Enabling Outlook Anywhere from the Exchange Management Shell

Alternatively, you can enable Outlook Anywhere from the Exchange Management Shell. To do so, run the following command from the shell:

```
enable-OutlookAnywhere -Server:'ServerName' -ExternalHostname:'ExternalHostName'
➥-DefaultAuthenticationMethod:'Basic' -SSLOffloading:$false
```

You can substitute "NTLM" for the DefaultAuthenticationMethod, and replace $false with $true if you are using SSL offloading.

Outlook Anywhere Best Practices

Consider the following best practices when deploying Outlook Anywhere:

▶ **Use at least one client access server per site**—In Exchange Server 2010, a site is considered to be a network location with excellent connectivity between all computers. You should have at least one client access server solely dedicated to providing client access to the Exchange Server 2010 server running the Mailbox server role. For increased performance and reliability, you can have multiple client access servers in each site.

▶ **Enable Outlook Anywhere on at least one client access server**—For each site, there should be at least one client access server with Outlook Anywhere enabled. This allows Outlook clients to connect to the client access server that resides closest to that user's mailbox server. By configuring your environment in this manner, users connect to the client access server in the site with their mailbox server utilizing HTTPS. This minimizes the risk of using RPC across the Internet, which can negatively impact overall performance.

Finally, you must configure your organization's firewall to allow traffic on port 443 because Outlook requests use HTTP over SSL. However, if you are already using either Outlook Web App with SSL, or Exchange ActiveSync with SSL, you do not have to open any additional ports from the Internet.

TIP

Outlook users who will be using Outlook Anywhere as described in this section should be using Cached Exchange mode. Cached Exchange mode optimizes the communications between your Exchange servers and Outlook.

10

Authenticating Users

By default, both Outlook 2003 and Outlook 2007/2010 use the credentials of the user who is currently logged on to the local computer to access the Outlook profile and mailbox. Both applications are also configured to first utilize Kerberos for the authentication process and, if this fails, utilize NT LAN Manager (NTLM). Administrators have the option of setting Outlook to only use Kerberos if they want to implement stronger security methods. The Kerberos/NTLM or NTLM Only options exist for backward compatibility with older systems. When using Kerberos, the user's credentials are encrypted when communicating with Active Directory for authentication.

To view or change the current authentication options in Outlook 2007, perform the following procedure:

1. In Outlook 2007, select Tools, Account Settings.

2. On the Account Settings page, select the email account, and click the Change icon.

3. On the Change E-Mail Account page, click More Settings.

4. Select the Security tab. Under Logon Network Security, select Kerberos Password Authentication from the drop-down box, and then click OK.

5. On the Change E-Mail Account page, click Next to complete the process, click Finish, and then click Close.

User Identification

An additional level of security can be applied to users accessing email through the Outlook client. In the event of a user closing Outlook, but not locking their computer or logging off the network, it is possible for an unauthorized user to access the system, start Outlook, and access the user's email.

It is possible to configure Outlook 2007 to require the user to input their username and password before accessing Outlook. To do so, follow the same steps detailed previously in the "Authenticating Users" section, and place a check mark in the Always Prompt for User Name and Password check box.

It should be noted that few organizations implement this security option, as most find that logging on and off the system properly provides adequate protection.

Blocking Attachments

A common and often effective way for viruses and malicious scripts to spread from user to user is through email. When a user receives a message with an attachment, simply opening the attachment can allow the virus to activate and, if proper security measures are not in place, the virus can do damage to the system or spread to other users.

To mitigate this threat, Microsoft has incorporated attachment blocking in Outlook and Outlook Web App (OWA). By default, Outlook is configured to block attachments that contain file types that can run programs. Known as "executable" files, these blocked file types include those with .exe, .bat, .com, .vbs, and .js on the end of the filename.

It is important to note that this does not automatically protect you from being infected with a virus, as other file formats, including Microsoft Office files such as Word or Excel documents, can potentially contain viruses. However, implementing an antivirus solution on the client PC greatly reduces the possibility of such a file causing harm.

Users who are utilizing Outlook to send an attachment are notified when attaching an executable file that it is likely to be blocked by the recipient.

If the user elects to send the message anyway, it might still be blocked on the receiving end.

Outlook does not provide any way for the end user to unblock these attachments. However, savvy users have found that, in many instances, they can rename the file to a nonexecutable extension (such as .txt) and send the file with instructions on how to rename the file back.

> **NOTE**
>
> File types can be categorized as Level 1 (the user cannot view the file) or Level 2 (the user can open the file only after saving it to disk). By default, Outlook classifies most executable file types as Level 1 and blocks the receipt of the file by users. There are no Level 2 file types by default. However, administrators can use Group Policy to manage how a file type is categorized. For example, if members of your organization regularly receive Visual Basic scripts (.vbs), you can change the categorization from Level 1 to Level 2 for that extension. Extreme caution should be used before changing this setting, as executable attachments are one of the most commonly used methods of distributing viruses.

Protecting Against Spam

Unsolicited email messages are often referred to as spam. These usually unwanted and often offensive messages are utilized as cheap advertising for unscrupulous organizations. In the past several years, the increase in spam traffic has surpassed even the most liberal estimates, and many studies have found that spam traffic accounts for up to 85%–90% of the messaging traffic on the Internet today.

Spam does not just affect your patience and productivity; it affects companies, Internet service providers, and anyone else who is hosting messaging services. The battle against spam is just beginning, and legal battles are well under way against both known spammers and companies that host the messaging services. In some cases, employees are suing employers on grounds that the employer has not taken adequate steps to protect them from offensive materials.

Exchange Server 2010 Antispam Features

Spammers are becoming increasingly more creative and cunning, frequently changing their email addresses, domain names, content, and more to get past a company's protective measures.

Microsoft has provided at least some basic form of antispam technologies in Exchange Server since version 5.5 and Outlook 98. For example, junk mail filters were provided to help identify messages that had either offensive material or other keywords indicating the message was spam. This form of spam prevention placed most, if not all, of the responsibility on the end user to block unwanted email messages.

Exchange Server 2010, when combined with Outlook 2007 or Outlook 2010, provides several methods of reducing unwanted spam messages:

▶ Increased protection through integrated security technologies

▶ Improved email legitimacy assurance

▶ Distribution lists restricted to authenticated users

▶ Connection filtering

▶ Reputation service

▶ Outlook junk email filter lists aggregation

Protecting Against Web Beaconing

A common and very popular format for email messages is Hypertext Markup Language, or HTML. This format is so popular because of the rich content that can be presented, including graphics, images, font formatting, and more. However, HTML-based messages can also present security problems and annoyances because of the ability to hide various codes and images within the message.

One such security problem is called web beaconing. Web beaconing is a term used to describe the method of retrieving valid email addresses and information on whether a recipient has opened a message. Advertisers, spammers, and the like utilize web beaconing to help them become more profitable and improve audience targeting. For instance, when an unsuspecting user opens an email message that contains a web beacon, the user's email address and possibly other information is sent to the solicitor, notifying them that they a) have reached a valid recipient and b) have reached a recipient who is willing to open their message before deleting it. The user is oblivious that their personal information has been given.

Outlook 2003 and 2007 can be used to block web beacons and, consequently, prevent the user's email address from ending up in the wrong hands. By default, if Outlook suspects that the content of a message could be used as a web beacon, it presents a pop-up window warning users that links to images, multimedia, or other external content have been blocked to help protect their privacy. The text content of the email message is viewable by the user, and the user is then presented with an option to unblock the content. This enables the user to make a conscious decision of whether to display all the contents of the message.

This default setting is recommended because it is an excellent way to protect end users from unsolicited emails; however, it is possible to disable this option. To change the default settings in Outlook 2003, do the following:

1. Select Tools, Options.

2. Click the Security tab and then click Change Automatic Download Settings.

3. In the Automatic Picture Download Settings window, choose whether to download pictures or other content automatically. Outlook 2003 can also be customized to

automatically download content from safe lists or from websites listed in the trusted Microsoft Internet Explorer security zones.

To change the default settings for automatic downloading of content in Outlook 2007, do the following:

1. Select Tools, Trust Center.

2. Click the Automatic Download tab. Select the desired settings from the available options. By default, all options are selected.

> **NOTE**
>
> If Automatic Picture Download is turned off, messages from or to email addresses or domain names on the Safe Senders and Safe Recipients lists are treated as exceptions and the blocked content is downloaded. Safe Senders and Safe Recipients lists are discussed in more depth later in this chapter.

Filtering Junk Mail

As mentioned earlier, junk mail filtering has been available in earlier versions of Exchange Server and Outlook. This feature has been improved with each new revision and is useful in minimizing the need for end users to configure junk mail filtering options. In fact, junk mail filtering is primarily controlled by Exchange Server administrators. However, some options can be configured by the users. With junk mail filtering, many unwanted messages can be segregated and set aside before they reach the user's Inbox.

Both Outlook 2003 and Outlook 2007 give you the ability to change the level of protection provided by your junk email filter. To do so, perform the following procedure:

1. Select Tools, Options.

2. On the Preferences tab, in the E-Mail section, click Junk E-Mail.

In addition, both Outlook 2003 and Outlook 2007 provide the following options:

▸ **No Protection (2003) or No Automatic Filtering (2007)**—Although the junk email filter does not perform any filtering on incoming mail, messages sent from the blocked senders list are still moved to the junk email folder.

▸ **Low (the default setting)**—Safe and block lists are consulted with this level of protection, but Outlook also searches for keywords and phrases in the message's subject and body.

▸ **High**—On this setting, the most aggressive filtering is performed. Although you can increase the amount of junk email captured by using this setting, there is the possibility of "false positives," which can result in valid messages being mistakenly filtered out.

▸ **Safe Lists Only**—This setting is the most restrictive because it allows only messages from preapproved senders to be delivered to the Inbox.

Both Outlook 2003 and Outlook 2007 offer you the additional option to Permanently Delete Suspected Junk E-Mail Instead of Moving It to the Junk E-Mail Folder. You should

10

hesitate before using this option because you lose the ability to review the junk email folder to look for missing messages.

Outlook 2007 gives you the following options to battle email phishing attacks:

▶ **Disable Links and Other Functionality in Phishing Messages (Recommended)**—Using this option disables links, the "reply to" feature, and the "reply to all" feature on suspected phishing email messages.

▶ **Warn Me About Suspicious Domain Names in E-Mail Addresses (Recommended)**—Using this option warns you when a message comes from a domain name (for example, @mlcrosoft.com) that uses certain characters to make it appear to be a well-known domain.

Filtering with Safe and Blocked Senders

Both Outlook 2003 and Outlook 2007 allow users to create and manage their own Safe Senders and Blocked Senders. As the name implies, the Safe Senders list is made up of user-defined addresses or domains, and messages from these addresses or domains will never be treated as junk email. Conversely, the Blocked Senders list is made up of user-defined email addresses or domain names, and all messages from them will automatically be treated as junk email.

In addition, both Outlook 2003 and 2007 provide the option to configure a Safe Recipients list. This option is useful when you are a member of an emailing list or group. By adding the list or group to your Safe Recipients list, any messages sent to the email addresses or domain names on that list will not be treated as junk email messages, regardless of the sender.

Both Outlook 2003 and Outlook 2007 allow you the option to automatically treat anyone in your Outlook Contacts list as a Safe Sender. This option is enabled on the Safe Senders tab by selecting the Also Trust E-Mail from My Contacts check box. By default, this feature is enabled.

With Outlook 2003 SP1 and later, there is an additional option. If there are people who are not in your Contacts list, but with whom you regularly correspond, you can select to Automatically Add People I E-Mail to the Safe Senders List. This option is also found on the Safe Senders tab.

To quickly add a sender, domain name, or mailing list to one of these lists, you can right-click the message, select Junk E-Mail, and choose the desired option.

Outlook Email Postmark

In Outlook 2007, the concept of the Outlook Email Postmark is introduced. This feature helps ensure that email placed in the client's Inbox is valid, and that email sent by Outlook 2007 will be trusted by the recipient's email client.

Microsoft has developed this new technology as part of their ongoing effort to minimize junk email. When using the Email Postmark, the sending computer performs a computation, and assigns the resulting work as a token that the email is valid. By making the computation and sending of the message time consuming and resource intensive, mass emailers will find the process detrimental to their productivity; however, the process does not change the user experience for normal email senders.

Exchange Server 2010, upon receiving a message with an Email Postmark, uses it as one method of verification of the reliability of the incoming message.

Blocking Read Receipts

Both Outlook 2003 and Outlook 2007 enable users to request read receipts for the messages that they send. Read receipts tell the sender that the intended recipient has at least opened the email. Automatically sending these read receipts can offer spammers (or others) more insight into your mail reading habits than you might want to share.

By default, both Outlook 2003 and Outlook 2007 block the automatic sending of read receipts. Instead, the recipient is prompted with a message that asks them if they want to send a response.

If you want, you can change this setting to Always Send a Response, or Never Send a Response. To change this behavior, do the following:

1. In Outlook, select Tools, Options.
2. On the Preferences tab, in the E-Mail section, click E-Mail Options.
3. Click the Tracking Options button.
4. Select your desired setting, and then click OK three times to exit the configuration.

Information Rights Management

Introduced in Microsoft Office 2003 products, Information Rights Management (IRM) helps organizations protect digital information from unauthorized use. By integrating with a Windows Server 2008 technology called Active Directory Rights Management Services (AD RMS), IRM enables workers to define how a recipient can use the information contained in a Microsoft Office document.

Users can define exactly who can open, modify, print, forward, or take other actions with protected documents. In addition, users can specify an expiration date, after which the document cannot be viewed or acted upon.

NOTE

To create IRM-protected documents and email messages, the sending user must be using the Professional or Enterprise version of Office 2007/2010. Users of Office Standard can still read and use IRM-protected documents, but cannot create them or apply policies to email messages.

10

IRM granularizes security for supported Microsoft Office applications such as Word, Excel, PowerPoint, and Outlook, as well as any other IRM-aware application. IRM is intended to complement other security technologies, such as Secure/Multipurpose Internet Mail

Extensions (S/MIME) and Pretty Good Privacy (PGP) by securing the contents of information (contained in a document, for example), but it does not provide authentication to the information.

Securing Outlook Web App

Outlook Web App (OWA) provides the interface for users to access their mail across the Internet utilizing a web browser. Over the years, Microsoft improved the OWA client until it was almost as powerful as the actual Microsoft Outlook client.

With OWA 2010, Microsoft has continued this trend, providing an improved user experience and enhanced security over previous versions.

Some of the security-related features in OWA include the following:

▶ Stripping of web beacons, referrals, and other potentially harmful content from messages

▶ Attachment blocking

▶ OWA forms-based (cookie) authentication

▶ Session inactivity timeout

▶ OWA infrastructure using IPSec and Kerberos

▶ Safe and block lists

▶ **Improved logon screen**—In OWA 2010, when you connect from a trusted machine, your previous "private" selection (and your username) is remembered on subsequent connections.

▶ **Junk email management**—OWA 2010 has improved the capabilities of the junk email filter by allowing users to manage their junk email settings from within OWA.

▶ **Protection from harmful content**—If an OWA 2010 user clicks a link that is embedded in an email message, and the link uses a protocol that is not recognized by OWA, the link is blocked, and the user receives a warning stating "Outlook Web App has disabled this link for your protection."

Supported Authentication Methods

Client access servers in Exchange Server 2010 support more authentication methods than Exchange Server 2003 front-end (OWA) servers did.

The following types of authentication are allowed:

▶ **Standard**—Standard authentication methods include Integrated Windows authentication, Digest authentication, and Basic authentication.

▶ **Forms-based authentication**—Using forms-based authentication creates a logon page for OWA. Forms-based authentication uses cookies to store user logon credentials and password information in an encrypted state.

> ▶ **Microsoft Internet Security and Acceleration (ISA) Server forms-based authentication**—By using ISA Server, administrators can securely publish OWA servers by using Mail server publishing rules. ISA Server also allows administrators to configure forms-based authentication and control email attachment availability.

> ▶ **Smart card and certificate authentication**—Certificates can reside on either a client computer or on a smart card. By utilizing certificate authentication, Extensible Authentication Protocol (EAP) and Transport Layer Security (TLS) protocols are used, providing a two-way authentication method where both the client and server prove their identities to each other.

Table 10.1 shows a comparison of authentication methods along with the security level provided relative to password transmission and client requirements.

TABLE 10.1 Authentication Methods for OWA Logon Options

Authentication Method	Security Level Provided	How Passwords Are Sent	Client Requirements
Basic authentication	Low (unless Secure Sockets Layer [SSL] is enabled)	Base 64-encoded clear text.	All browsers support Basic authentication.
Digest authentication	Medium	Hashed by using MD5.	Microsoft Internet Explorer 5 or later versions.
Integrated Windows authentication	Low (unless SSL is enabled)	Hashed when Integrated Windows authentication is used; Kerberos ticket Integrated Windows authentication includes the Kerberos and NTLM authentication methods.	Internet Explorer 2.0 or later versions for Integrated Windows authentication. Microsoft Windows 2000 Server or later versions with Internet Explorer 5 or later versions for Kerberos.
Forms-based authentication	High	Encrypts user authentication information and stores it in a cookie. Requires SSL to keep the cookie secure.	Forms-based authentication is now supported in Internet Explorer, Mozilla Firefox, Apple's Safari, and other browsers.

10

NOTE

When multiple methods of authentication are configured, Internet Information Services (IIS) uses the most restrictive method first. IIS then searches the list of available authentication protocols (starting with the most restrictive), until an authentication method that is supported by both the client and the server is found.

Disabling Web Beacons for Outlook Web App

As previously mentioned in this chapter, web beaconing is a method used to retrieve valid email addresses and recipient information. Web beaconing is often used by unscrupulous advertisers and spammers to improve the accuracy and effectiveness of their spamming campaigns.

Exchange Server 2010 allows the disabling of web beacons for OWA. Administrators can use the Exchange Management Shell to define the type of filtering that is used for web beacon content and enforce it for all users.

To use the Exchange Management Shell to configure web beacon filtering settings, perform the following command from the shell:

```
Set-OwaVirtualDirectory -identity "Owa (Default Web Site)"
➥ -FilterWebBeaconsAndHtmlForms ForceFilter
```

This command configures the filtration of web beacon content in the Outlook virtual directory named OWA in the default IIS website. Possible values for the FilterWebBeaconsandHtmlforms setting are as follows:

- **UserFilterChoice**—Prompts the user to allow or block web beacons
- **ForceFilter**—Blocks all web beacons
- **DisableFilter**—Allows web beacons

Using Safe and Block Lists

OWA 2010 users can now manage their junk email settings from within OWA. Users can enable or disable junk email filtering, create and maintain Safe Senders, Blocked Senders, and Safe Recipient lists, enter email domains or Simple Mail Transfer Protocol (SMTP) addresses, and elect to trust email from their contacts.

> **NOTE**
>
> The option to "always trust contacts" does not function if the user has more than 1,024 contacts. Although this limitation will not be reached for most users, those with an exceptionally large number of contacts should be aware of the limitation.

To access the Junk E-Mail settings in OWA, select Options from the upper-right corner of the screen, and then select Junk E-Mail on the left side of the page.

Summary

As more and more organizations rely heavily on email as a primary communications tool, email security has become increasingly important. Some countries have even gone so far as to implement laws preventing the sending of unsecured email. The risk of an unauthorized or unintended third-party recipient capturing and reviewing corporate email messages is too great to be ignored, especially when there are preventative measures that can so easily and seamlessly be implemented.

Although client-level security is only one piece of the security puzzle, it is a very important one. Each of the three layers—client-level, server-level, and transport-level—must be addressed if you want to ensure your organization's messages are as safe as possible.

Fully implementing client-level security measures requires design and configuration of your operating systems (both client and server), your Exchange Server 2010 server, and your messaging client. In addition, strong antivirus and antispam measures must be implemented to protect your organization and users from malicious attacks.

Only by carefully addressing all of these areas can you ensure a secure messaging environment.

Best Practices

The following are best practices from this chapter:

- ▶ Use security templates provided by Microsoft, the National Security Agency (NSA), or the National Institute of Standards and Technology (NIST) as baselines for customizing the organization's security templates.

- ▶ Customize baseline security templates to reduce the attack surface of workstations and servers. However, implement adequate testing to ensure that required applications function as intended.

- ▶ Keep servers and client computers up to date with the latest service pack and security updates. Use automated processes whenever possible to ensure the timely application of updates.

- ▶ Consult Microsoft, NIST, and NSA security guidelines for securing the operating system.

- ▶ Implement antivirus software in a layered configuration, implementing gateway, server, and client-level antivirus solutions.

- ▶ Authenticate clients to the Exchange Server messaging infrastructure, using Kerberos whenever possible.

- ▶ Outlook Anywhere clients should use Cached Exchange mode to increase performance and minimize network impact whenever possible.

- ▶ Combat spam by utilizing the protective features included in both Exchange Server and Outlook. Fortify these features with additional or third-party measures when necessary.

- ▶ Configure Outlook to always prompt you before sending a read receipt.

- ▶ Review and implement Active Directory Rights Management Services (AD RMS) Information Rights Management technologies for rights-protection of mail content.

10

Server and Transport-Level Security

Securing your Microsoft Exchange Server 2010 organization is a complex process. Two primary components that must be addressed are server-level and transport-level security. In brief, server-level security refers to protecting data that is physically stored on an Exchange server. Transport-level security, on the other hand, refers to protecting data as it is passed into or out of the Exchange server along your network.

When server administrators think of "security," server-level security measures are often the first that come to mind. Because people share information and collaborate by sending messages and attachments that often contain proprietary data, a company's Exchange server can house information that could be potentially damaging if it were to fall into the wrong hands. Server-level security focuses on protecting the data that resides on the Exchange servers from being accessed by nonauthorized users.

As this chapter shows, transport-level security is just as important. Not only does the server need to be secured, the content of information being sent and received by a server also needs to remain protected.

Considering the Importance of Security in an Exchange Server 2010 Environment

Security in a networking environment first starts with considering the importance of a security model within the networking environment. Part of the security model involves internal security practices, and a portion of the security model depends on the level of security built in to the technology products being implemented.

This is a numerical measure of how difficult it is to move along that edge. It could be a measure of time, distance, cost, or any other quantity that can be enumerated. These values are used when deciding on the best route from one vertex to another. When implementing Exchange Server 2010 with security in mind, a lot of the security infrastructure is dependent on the security built in to the Windows 2003 network operating system as well as the Exchange Server 2010 messaging system. Microsoft plays an important role in establishing a secured messaging environment from which an organization can build its security infrastructure.

An organization must then assess its risks and develop a security strategy that is customized to address the risks identified by the organization. Within Exchange Server 2010, the administration function of the Exchange Server messaging system is based on administrative roles in which an administrator allocates roles and levels of security access to other administrators and support personnel in the organization.

Microsoft's Trustworthy Computing Initiative

As the largest software company in the world, Microsoft has always been a target for people who thrive on hacking computer systems, whether they are doing so simply for the challenge, or with malicious intent.

On January 15, 2002, Bill Gates announced the "Trustworthy Computing Initiative" that focused the company in a new direction. The goal of this initiative was to create reliable, secure, and private technologies and committed the company to making products that protect user privacy.

Now, Trustworthy Computing is no longer an initiative; it is a corporate wide tenet that guides the development and maintenance of their products from the moment they are imagined until they are no longer supported. This new way of doing business has resulted in a significant reduction of publicly reported vulnerabilities in Microsoft products across the board.

Secure by Design

Under the Trustworthy Computing Initiative, a process has been implemented known as the Security Development Lifecycle, otherwise known as the SDL, which requires Microsoft developers to create formal threat models when they begin the design of a product. No longer are products envisioned and developed with potential security risks addressed as an afterthought; now all products, including Exchange Server 2010, are developed with an eye toward secure computing from the drawing board.

As an added measure, before a product ships, it is submitted to a final security review, or FSR, where a team of security experts review it to answer just one question—From a security perspective, is this product ready to ship?

Secure by Default

With the original versions of Exchange Server (prior to Exchange Server 2003), the products were shipped with an "implement first, secure later" philosophy. Many services and functions were enabled by default, regardless of whether they would eventually be utilized in an environment.

With later versions of Exchange Server, including Exchange Server 2010, the opposite approach has been taken—by default, many services and functions are *disabled* at the time of installation, only to be enabled by an organization if the determination is made that the function is needed. Thanks to this mentality, organizations are less likely to have features unknowingly enabled that might present a security risk.

Secure by Deployment

Microsoft provides applications and documentation that enable information technology (IT) personnel to implement Exchange Server 2010 securely and successfully. These tools enable an administrator to ensure that all network prerequisites are met, and that the environment is properly configured and ready to accept the implementation of Exchange Server 2010.

Microsoft also provides training resources to ensure that administrators are adequately prepared to deploy Exchange Server 2010. These training resources should be reviewed by any organization implementing Exchange Server 2010, and should be made available to administrators prior to implementation of the product to ensure a successful deployment.

Assessing Your Risks

It has been said that "The only completely secure computer is one that is turned off—and even then, only if no one can find it."

As with most jokes, there is some underlying truth to the statement or it wouldn't be funny. Any computer that is accessible to authorized users is potentially accessible to malicious intruders. When designing security around particular subsets of data, you must strike a balance between security and usability—if you make the environment TOO secure, it is too difficult or time-consuming for valid employees to access the data.

In addition, an organization must consider the value of the data that they are trying to protect. For an email environment, this can be a particularly challenging task, as the actual value of the data contained can be difficult to assess. However, asking yourself "How much would it cost the organization if our email was destroyed, altered, or stolen?" and assigning an accurate monetary value to the data will help you determine how much you can feasibly spend to protect it.

The next step in assessing your risks is to analyze possible security vulnerabilities for the service or functionality with which you are working. The following is a list of some areas of security that you should take into consideration:

▶ **Viruses or Trojan horse messages**—Viruses have existed in the computer world long before the first email message was sent. However, just as email provides users with an easy method of communication, it also is an extremely efficient method of spreading malicious or troublesome code. Once considered the largest problem that email administrators had to face, viruses have been combated by an entire industry devoted to their prevention.

▶ **Spam**—The proliferation of unsolicited messages, often referred to as "spam" mail, has truly become the bane of the messaging world with recent estimates stating that spam accounts for 85%–90% of the messaging traffic on the Internet today. These unsolicited, usually unwanted, and often offensive advertisements cost companies and users billions of dollars annually in lost time and productivity. Unfortunately, because sending bulk messages to thousands (or millions) of recipients can be accomplished with very little expense, offending companies do not need a large response to maintain profitability. It is sad to note that as long as this method of advertising is profitable and effective, spam will be with us to stay. Fortunately, Exchange Server 2010 has several features to help alleviate the problem.

▶ **Address spoofing**—One tool that is commonly used by the distributors of both viruses and spam is known as *address spoofing*. By changing the From line in a Simple Mail Transfer Protocol (SMTP) message, users can often be fooled into opening a message that they think is from a friend or co-worker, only to find that the message originated somewhere else entirely. This method has been especially effective in the distribution of email worms. Because the message appears to come from a known associate, and often has an intriguing Subject line, the unwitting recipient opens the message and, if not properly protected, becomes a distributor of the virus to others.

▶ **Phishing**—Over the past several years, a relatively new type of fraudulent email has emerged. Known as *phishing*, this attack comes in the form of an official looking email message, often appearing to be from a reputable organization, such as a credit card company or a large electronics retailer. The message usually contains a link that, once clicked, brings up an official looking website—often an exact replica of the official site that is being mimicked. However, the fraudulent site has one purpose, to fool you into giving away personal information, such as passwords, credit card numbers, or Social Security numbers. With this information in hand, the offending party can steal your identity, make charges to your credit card, or otherwise profit from your loss.

Exchange Server 2010 Administrative Roles

In Exchange 2000 Server and Exchange Server 2003, there was not a clear separation between administrators of users in Active Directory (AD) and the administration of Exchange Server recipients. Utilizing the previous model, based on predefined security roles, administrators had to be granted high-level permissions to the Active Directory environment to perform even relatively simple Exchange Server recipient–related tasks. In addition, the majority of Exchange Server recipient management had to be accomplished utilizing the Active Directory Users and Computers utility.

Exchange Server 2010 has implemented much greater logical distinction between these two environments. Utilizing newly designed administrator roles, organizations can assign administrators permission to perform Exchange Server-related tasks, while minimizing their ability to directly modify the Active Directory itself. Furthermore, the majority of mail-related configuration items can be administered directly from the Exchange Management Console and Exchange Management Shell.

This is important to Exchange Server security because you no longer have to grant administrative privileges over your Exchange Server environment to domain administrators (who might not have worked with Exchange Server at all). On the other side of the same coin, Exchange Server administrators can be granted permissions over the Exchange Server environment, yet remain restricted in Active Directory. This enables organizations to limit areas of responsibility based on proper administrator aptitude and abilities.

The Exchange Server administrator roles and the permissions associated with each are covered in greater detail in Chapter 18, "Administering an Exchange Server 2010 Environment."

Components of a Secure Messaging Environment

Although network administrators generally focus on server-level security, which protects data stored on the server itself, the administrators must keep in mind that the server they are attempting to protect is connected to a local area network (LAN), and usually the Internet, to allow it to function to its full potential.

To properly protect a server from attack, administrators should implement multiple layers of defense, each reinforcing the other, and each specializing in repelling certain types of attacks. Firewalls, network perimeters, accessibility options for users, security policies, and more are integral components that must be well designed and properly implemented to be effective.

A phrase coined by the military, "defense in depth," is used to describe this strategy. Defense in depth increases a server's security by creating multiple layers of protection between the server and potential attackers. An attacker who successfully maneuvers through the first line of defense finds himself faced with a second challenge, one requiring different skills and tools to bypass, and then a third, and so on.

Hardening Windows Server 2008

Exchange Server 2010 is designed to run on Windows Server 2008 or Windows Server 2008 R2. No matter what steps you take to secure your Exchange Server 2010 servers, if the underlying operating system (OS) is not secure, the Exchange Server installation is vulnerable to attack. Therefore, it is critical that you secure Windows Server 2008 by utilizing a combination of your organization's security standards and industry best practices.

Layered Approach to Server Security

When discussing security measures, whether server-level or transport-level, protective measures work best when they are applied in layers. For example, if a thief were to attempt to steal your car, it might not be very challenging if all they had to do was break the window and hot-wire the vehicle. However, if you were to add a car alarm, or install an ignition block that requires a coded key, the level of difficulty is increased. Each of these obstacles takes additional time, as well as additional skill sets, to overcome.

This same principle applies to both server- and transport-level security methods. By applying multiple layers of security, you can effectively decrease the likelihood of a malicious user successfully tampering with your systems.

Many security features are already built in to Windows Server 2008. Among these are the following:

▶ **Kerberos authentication**—Windows Server 2008 uses the Kerberos authentication protocol to provide a mechanism for authentication between a client and a server, or between two servers.

▶ **NTFS file security**—Utilizing the NTFS file system provides improved performance and reliability over traditional file allocation table (FAT) file systems. NTFS has built-in security features, such as file and folder permissions and the Encrypting File System (EFS).

Windows Server 2008 also includes built-in security tools and features to help secure your environment. Among these are object-based access control, automated security policies, auditing, Public Key Infrastructure (PKI), and trusts between domains.

Physical Security Considerations

The first layer of security for any server, and one that is often overlooked, is preventing physical access to the computer. It takes very little skill or knowledge to simply unplug a computer or to remove it from the network; however, this could have a serious impact on your environment even if the intruder was not able to access your data. In addition, just as security professionals have tools and utilities to assist with the defense of computer systems, hackers have tools and utilities to assist them with their attacks. If a hacker can get physical access to a server, he can use a variety of methods to circumvent basic password security.

At a minimum, servers should be physically secured behind locked doors, preferably in an environmentally controlled area.

Some common physical security methods are the following:

▶ Configure the server BIOS so that it will not boot from a floppy disk drive or CD-ROM.

▶ Password protect the BIOS so that it cannot be reconfigured.

▶ Lock the server case to prevent access to the BIOS jumpers on the motherboard.

▶ Enclose the server in a locked cage or locked room that has limited access.

Restricting Logon Access

All servers should be configured so that only administrators can log on physically to the console. By default, Exchange Server 2010 does not allow any members of the domain users group local logon privileges. This prevents non administrators from logging on to the server even if they can gain physical access to the server.

11

Auditing Security Events

Auditing is a way to gather and keep track of activity on the network, devices, and entire systems. By default, Windows Server 2008 enables some auditing, but there are many additional auditing functions that must be manually turned on to be used. This control allows your system to easily be customized to monitor those features that you desire.

Although the primary use of auditing methods is to identify security breaches, this feature can also be used to monitor suspicious activity and to gain insight into who is accessing the servers and what they are doing. Windows Server 2008's auditing policies must first be enabled before activity can be monitored.

Auditing Policies

Audit policies are the basis for auditing events on a Windows Server 2008 system. Bear in mind that auditing can require a significant amount of server resources and can potentially slow server performance, especially if the server does not have adequate memory or CPU bandwidth available. Also, as more and more data is collected by auditing policies, it can require a significant amount of effort to evaluate. Administrators should be cautious, as gathering too much data can sometimes be overwhelming, effectively diminishing the desired benefits. As such, it is important to take the time to properly plan how your systems will be audited.

Audit policies can track successful or unsuccessful event activity in a Windows Server 2008 environment. These policies can audit the success and failure of events. The types of events that can be monitored include the following:

▶ **Account logon events**—Each time a user attempts to log on, the successful or unsuccessful event can be recorded. Failed logon attempts can include logon failures for unknown user accounts, time restriction violations, expired user accounts, insufficient rights for the user to log on locally, expired account passwords, and locked-out accounts.

▶ **Account management**—When an account is changed, an event can be logged and later examined. Although this pertains more to Windows Server 2008 than Exchange Server 2010, it is still very relevant because permissions granted in Active Directory can have an effect on what data or services an individual has access to in Exchange Server.

▶ **Directory service access**—Whenever a user attempts to access an Active Directory object that has its own system access control list (SACL), the event is logged.

▶ **Logon events**—Logons over the network or by services are logged.

▶ **Object access**—The object access policy logs an event when a user attempts to access a resource such as a printer or shared folder.

▶ **Policy change**—Each time an attempt to change a policy is made, the event is recorded. This can apply to changes made to user rights, account audit policies, and trust policies.

▶ **Privileged use**—Privileged use is a security setting and can include a user employing a user right, changing the system time, and more. Successful or unsuccessful attempts can be logged.

▶ **Process tracking**—An event can be logged for each program or process that a user launches while accessing a system. This information can be very detailed and take a significant amount of resources.

▶ **System events**—The system events policy logs specific system events, such as a computer restart or shutdown.

The audit policies can be enabled or disabled through either the local system policy or Group Policy Objects (GPOs), which can be accessed using the Group Policy Management Console (GPMC).

Keeping Services to a Minimum

Depending on the role that an Exchange Server 2010 server will fulfill, not all services that are installed by default are necessary for the server to function. It is considered a best practice to limit the number of entry points (services) into a server to only those required. Any services that are not necessary for the system to operate properly should be disabled. Although this can be done manually on a server-by-server basis, it can also be performed using a customized security template to ensure all servers in your environment are configured properly.

Locking Down the File System

Files stored on a Windows Server 2008, including mail databases, are only as secure as the permissions that are assigned to protect them. As such, it is good to know that Windows Server 2008 does not grant the *Everyone* group full control over share-level and NTFS-level permissions by default. In addition, critical operating system files and directories are secured to disallow their unauthorized use.

Despite the overall improvements made, a complete understanding of file-level security is recommended to ensure that your files are properly protected.

NOTE

For increased file-level security, the Exchange Server 2010 installation process requires that partitions on the underlying operating system are formatted as NTFS.

Using the Microsoft Baseline Security Analyzer

The Microsoft Baseline Security Analyzer (MBSA) is a tool that identifies common security misconfigurations and missing hotfixes. This information is gathered via local or remote scans of Windows systems. MBSA allows administrators to have the ability to scan a single Windows system and obtain a security assessment, as well as a list of recommended corrective actions. In addition, administrators can use the MBSA tool to scan multiple functional roles of a Windows-based server on the network for vulnerabilities. This allows administrators to ensure systems are up to date with the latest security-related patches.

The MBSA can be downloaded from the Microsoft website at www.microsoft.com/mbsa.

Implementing Industry Standards and Guidelines

As discussed previously, Microsoft has gone to great lengths to provide secure and reliable products. Moreover, it has worked closely with companies, government agencies, security consultants, and others to address security issues in the computer industry.

In addition to Microsoft security standards and guidelines, it is advisable that organizations use recommended best practices compiled by the National Institute of Standards and Technologies (NIST) and the National Security Agency (NSA). Both NIST and NSA provide security lockdown configuration standards and guidelines that can be downloaded from their websites (http://www.nist.gov and http://www.nsa.gov, respectively).

Using the Security Configuration Wizard

The Security Configuration Wizard (SCW) is an attack-surface reduction tool for Windows Server 2008 RTM/R2. The SCW guides administrators in creating security policies based on the minimum functionality required for a server's role or roles.

SCW reviews the computer configuration, including but not limited to, the following:

▶ **Services**—SCW limits the number of services in use.

▶ **Packet filtering**—SCW can configure certain ports and protocols.

▶ **Auditing**—Auditing can be configured based on the computer's role and the organization's security requirements.

▶ **Internet Information Services (IIS)**—SCW can secure IIS, including web extensions and legacy virtual directories.

▶ **Server roles and tasks**—The role (file, database, messaging, web server, and so on), specific tasks (backup, content indexing, and so on), and placement in an environment of a computer is a critical component in any lockdown process or procedure. Application services are also evaluated from products such as Exchange Server, SQL Server, ISA Server, SharePoint Portal Server, and Operations Manager.

CAUTION

The SCW is a very flexible and powerful security analysis and configuration tool. As a result, it is important to keep control over when and how the tool is used because system performance can be greatly degraded while the wizard is running. Equally important is testing possible configurations in a segmented lab environment prior to implementation. Without proper testing, environment functionality can be stricken or completely locked.

The SCW is used to assist in building specific security-related policies and to analyze computers against those policies to ensure compliance. SCW actually combines many of the security-related tasks performed by several other Microsoft security tools. For instance, SCW can take existing security templates created from the Security Configuration and Analysis tool and expand upon the restrictions to meet an organization's security policy requirements. In addition, SCW can analyze computers for any security updates that are needed, integrate with Group Policy, and provide a knowledge base repository.

Running SCW

The SCW is installed by default on all Windows Server 2008 installations and is located in the Administrative Tools section of the Start menu. When you run the SCW, you will have an opportunity to select what roles the server plays. Note that the SCW has already selected the roles that it is aware of, as shown in Figure 11.1.

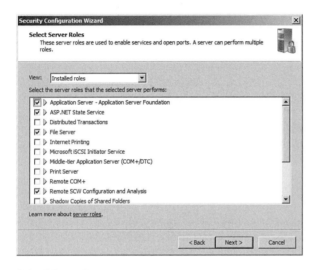

FIGURE 11.1   Reviewing SCW roles.

The SCW continues, giving you the opportunity to select client features (such as domain name system [DNS], Dynamic Host Configuration Protocol [DHCP], or the Automatic Update Client), and installed options (such as a global catalog, Windows Firewall, or time synchronization). Finally, there might be an additional screen for additional services. After you have selected all of the appropriate features, you must confirm service changes.

The SCW continues through network security changes (locking down unused ports), Registry settings, and configuring policy auditing. After finishing, you have the option to apply the security policy to the computer immediately, or save it to apply to this server (or other servers) later.

Securing Servers with Security Templates

Security templates are a practical and effective means to apply security policies and configurations to Exchange servers. Although security templates are provided with Windows Server 2008, it is recommended to customize them prior to applying them using the Security Configuration and Analysis Microsoft Management Console (MMC) snap-in.

This not only ensures that computers are identically configured with the same security configurations, but it also is an easy way to configure appropriate security measures for those computers that are not managed using GPOs.

> **NOTE**
>
> Microsoft creates Exchange Server-specific security templates and distributes them through their website. However, at the time of this writing, the security templates for Exchange Server 2010 have not yet been released.

Keeping Up with Security Patches and Updates

One of the least glamorous, but most important, security measures an organization can take is to ensure all of their products have the latest security patches implemented in a timely fashion. Applying service packs, security updates, and hotfixes for the operating system, as well as applications such as Exchange Server 2010, are crucial to maintaining a secure environment. As security shortcomings are identified, these service packs and hotfixes close the holes, often before they become publicly known, effectively protecting your environment from malicious users.

> **NOTE**
>
> Thoroughly test and evaluate service packs and hotfixes in a lab environment before installing them on production servers. Also, install the appropriate service packs and hotfixes on each production server to keep all systems consistent.

Windows Update

Windows Update is a web service, accessed in Microsoft Internet Explorer (Tools, Windows Update) that scans a local system and determines if the system has all current updates installed. This tool is extremely useful on individual systems, but can be time consuming when used to update multiple systems within an organization.

Windows Server Update Services

Windows Server Update Services (WSUS), an upgrade from its predecessor Software Update Services (SUS), minimizes administration, management, and maintenance of small- to midsized organizations by allowing them to communicate directly and securely with Microsoft to gather the latest security updates and service packs. WSUS is available for Windows Server 2008 and for Exchange servers.

The primary differences between WSUS and its predecessor are as follows:

- ► Support for a greater number of products, including service pack updates
- ► The ability to target computers using Group Policy or scripts
- ► Reports on update installation status
- ► Performs basic hardware inventory

With WSUS, the updates are downloaded from Microsoft to a local WSUS server. They can then be distributed to a lab environment for testing, or to targeted production servers. After being tested and approved, WSUS can be used to automatically distribute the updates throughout your environment. By utilizing this service, updates can be down-loaded from Microsoft once, and distributed locally, saving a significant amount of band-width when compared to hundreds (or thousands) of systems each downloading the updates themselves.

Establishing a Corporate Email Policy

Not all misuse of organizational email systems comes from external sources. Employees improperly utilizing a messaging system can put a company at risk as well, either by over-loading the system, passing confidential data to nonauthorized personnel, or passing material that is offensive in nature, potentially exposing the organization to lawsuits from other personnel.

Established and documented corporate email policies are used to govern and enforce the appropriate use of the messaging environment. However, like most security policies, they cannot be effective if they are not created, approved, implemented, and communicated to the user community.

> **NOTE**
>
> Corporate email policies not only define how the system can and should be used; they also limit an organization's liability in the event of misuse.

The following are possible considerations and guidelines to include in the corporate email policy:

▶ **Personal usage**—The policy should state whether emails of a personal nature are accepted and, if so, to what extent. Some companies place a limit on the number of personal emails that can be sent each day. Others require personal emails to be stored in a separate folder within the email system. Most companies allow the sending and receiving of personal emails because this is often less time consuming than requiring employees to access external mail sources for personal communications.

▶ **Expectation of privacy**—A corporate email policy should plainly state that the messages contained within the system are the property of the organization, and that no expectation of privacy is implied. Email records can be subpoenaed, mailboxes can be reviewed for appropriate use, or data can be retrieved in the event of the termination of someone's employment. By setting the expectation up front, you can make it clear to your users that the email system is a tool for their use, but the messages contained do not belong to them. Note that this type of policy might not be applicable or legal in certain European countries, as privacy laws vary from loca-tion to location.

▶ **Email monitoring**—If the organization monitors the content of its employees' emails, this should be stated in the email policy. Most countries and states allow the monitoring of corporate email by authorized individuals, as long as the employee has been made aware of the policy.

▶ **Prohibited content**—The policy should state that the email system is not to be used for the distribution of offensive or disruptive messages. This includes messages containing inappropriate content such as comments about race, religion, gender, or sexual orientation. The policy should also clearly state that pornographic pictures or emails with sexual content will not be tolerated, as these items are commonly the cause of offense between employees. The policy should mandate that employees receiving any such materials should report them to their supervisor or another appropriate entity for review immediately.

▶ **Confidential data**—Employees should not use the messaging system to discuss sensitive matter, such as potential acquisitions or mergers. Corporate secrets or other proprietary data should not be sent either, as an inadvertent forward could allow the sensitive data to pass to inappropriate personnel.

▶ **Email retention policies**—Many organizations, especially government, health-care, and financial institutions, are required by law to meet or exceed certain email retention policies. These policies should be clearly stated and meticulously enforced. Allowances should be made for employees to save messages of a critical nature—often companies allow them to be saved in separate folders to avoid automatic deletion.

▶ **Point of contact**—The email policy should clearly state where employees can go to have any questions about the corporate email policy answered.

Bear in mind, a corporate email policy that is unknown to the user community is not an effective one. The policy should be distributed to the users in a variety of ways, such as posting on an intranet site, in employee handbooks, on break room bulletin boards, or in company newsletters.

Securing Exchange Server 2010 through Administrative Policies

Whereas a corporate email policy specifically governs the use of the messaging system for users, administrative policies govern the operation and usage of the messaging system in general. Many best practices have been worked out over the years, some of which are as follows:

▶ **Administrative and operator accounts should not have mailboxes**—Many viruses and email worms rely on the permissions of the authenticated user to perform. If the user opening the message has administrative access to the computer, there is a much greater potential for danger.

▶ **Grant permissions to groups rather than users**—By granting permissions to groups, rather than users, you can quickly grant or deny access to a wide range of resources with one change. For example, if your Human Resources department has hundreds of files, in dozens of directories throughout your network, you would have to add (or remove) an individual from the permissions from *each* of these folders when they join or depart the team. However, by granting the permissions instead to an HR group, and then giving the *group* permissions, you can now modify access simply by adding the user to, or removing them from, the group.

▶ **Require complex (strong) passwords for all users**—If left to their own devices, many users select passwords that are easy for them to remember. However, this behavior results in passwords that are also very easy for malicious users to crack. By requiring complex passwords, consisting of upper- and lowercase letters, numbers, and special characters, the likelihood of a breach of security is greatly reduced.

▶ **Require Secure Sockets Layer (SSL) for HTTP, POP3, IMAP4, and Outlook Anywhere clients**—The SSL encryption protects confidential or personal information sent between a client and a server. The SSL protocol uses a combination of public-key and symmetric-key encryption. Symmetric-key encryption is much faster than public-key encryption; however, public-key encryption provides better authentication techniques. An Internal Certificate Authority can be used for these certificates, or they can be purchased from a third-party CA.

▶ **Set policies globally when possible**—Rather than setting policies for individual users or groups, companywide policies should be set, whenever possible, at a global level to ensure compliance.

Securing Groups

An important step in securing your messaging environment is to secure distribution and mail-enabled security groups. For instance, CompanyABC is a medium-sized company with 1,000 users. To facilitate companywide notifications, the HR department created a distribution group called "All Employees," which contains all 1,000 employees. By default, there are no message restrictions for new groups, meaning that anyone can send to this list. If CompanyABC has an Internet Mail SMTP Connector, this group will also have an SMTP address.

Consider what would happen if a new user sent an email to "All Employees" advertising a car for sale. Let's take it one step further and imagine that the user sent it with a read receipt and delivery notification requested. Thousands of messages can now be generated from this one mistake and could negatively impact server performance.

Often, intentions are not as innocent as the new user simply making a mistake. Sending repeated email messages to mail-enabled groups with large memberships is sometimes used in an attempted denial of service (DoS) attack. The attacker sends an SMTP message to the "All Employees" group with a delivery notification receipt requested and spoofs the "Return to" address with the same SMTP address used for the distribution group. So, 1,000 messages are sent, and 1,000 delivery notifications are returned—each of which is then sent to all 1,000 users in the group! From this one spoofed message, the net effect is (1 + 1000) + (1000 * 1000)=1,001,001 messages! By spoofing the distribution list and including a delivery notification receipt, this single email results in more than 1 million messages processed by the system.

Fortunately, for this easy problem, there is an even easier solution. Exchange Server 2010 allows you to configure message restrictions on your distribution groups.

To secure a distribution group so that only authenticated users can use it, do the following:

1. Open the Exchange Management Console.
2. In the console tree, under Recipient Configuration, click Distribution Group.
3. In the results pane, select the distribution group you want to modify, and then click Properties.
4. On the Mail Flow Settings tab, highlight Message Delivery Restrictions, and click Properties.

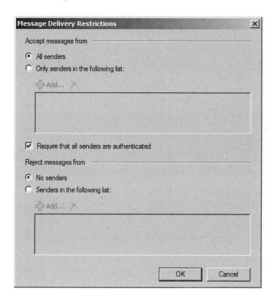

FIGURE 11.2   Restricting the ability to deliver to a distribution group.

5. Ensure there is a check in the Require That All Senders Are Authenticated check box, as shown in Figure 11.2.
6. Click OK when finished, and then click OK again to exit the configuration screen.

In addition, an administrator can further restrict the usage of this distribution group by allowing only a specific individual or security group to use it.

To restrict access to the distribution group to a specific user or group, do the following:

1. Open the Exchange Management Console.
2. In the console tree, under Recipient Configuration, click Distribution Group.
3. In the results pane, select the distribution group you want to modify, and then click Properties.
4. On the Mail Flow Settings tab, highlight Message Delivery Restrictions, and click Properties.
5. Under Accept Messages From, select the Only Senders in the Following List option button.

6. Click Add, and select the users or groups that are to have permission to send to the distribution group.

7. Click OK when finished, and then click OK again to exit the configuration screen.

An additional option allows you to configure the distribution list to reject messages from an individual or from members of a group. This setting is also configured using the Message Delivery Restrictions page.

Using Email Disclaimers

Email disclaimers are notices that are automatically appended to outgoing messages. These disclaimers are primarily intended to reduce liability, and to caution recipients not to misuse the information contained within. The following is a sample email disclaimer:

"The information contained in this message is intended solely for the individual to whom it is specifically and originally addressed. This message and its contents may contain confidential or privileged information. If you are not the intended recipient, you are hereby notified that any disclosure or distribution, or taking any action in reliance on the contents of this information, is strictly prohibited."

When implementing an email disclaimer, you should seek the review and approval of the disclaimer by the organization's legal department, if any.

Creating an Email Disclaimer in Exchange Server 2010

Email disclaimers are easily configured in the Exchange Management Console by performing the following actions:

1. Open the Exchange Management Console.

2. In the console tree, click Organization Configuration, and then click Hub Transport.

3. In the action pane, click New Transport Rule.

4. In the Name field, enter the name of the disclaimer. If you have notes for this disclaimer, enter them in the Comments field.

5. If you want the disclaimer to be created in a disabled state, clear the Enabled check box. Otherwise, leave the Enabled check box selected. Click Next to continue.

6. In the Step 1. Select the Condition(s) dialog box, select all the conditions that you want to be applied to this disclaimer. If you want this disclaimer to be applied to all email messages, do not select any conditions in this step. However, if you want the disclaimer to only be applied to outgoing messages, select Sent to Users Inside or Outside the Corporation, or Partners.

7. If you selected conditions in the previous step, in the Step 2. Edit the rule description by clicking underlined value option, click each blue underlined word.

8. When you click a blue underlined word, a new window opens to prompt you for the values to apply to the condition. Select the values that you want to apply, or type the values manually. If the window requires that you manually add values to a list, type a value. Then click Add. Repeat this process until you have entered all the values, and then click OK to close the window.

9. Repeat the previous step for each condition that you selected. After you configure all the conditions, click Next.

10. In the Step 1. Select the Action(s) dialog box, click Append Disclaimer Text and Fallback to Action if Unable to Apply.

11. In the Step 2. Edit the rule description by clicking an underlined value option, click each blue underlined word. Each word, except Disclaimer Text, is the default value for each field. The fields are Append (or Prepend), Disclaimer Text, and Fallback Action. Click Disclaimer Text and enter the text of your disclaimer.

12. When you click a blue underlined word, a new window opens to prompt you to select the items that you want to add or type values manually. When you are finished, click OK to close the window.

13. Repeat the previous step for each action that you selected. After you configure all the actions, as shown in Figure 11.3, click Next.

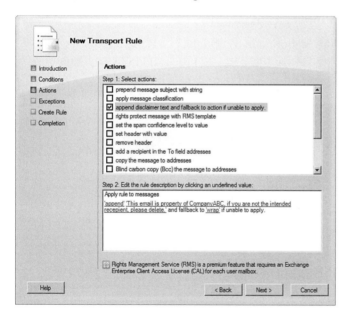

FIGURE 11.3 Reviewing SCW rules.

14. In the Step 1. Select the Exception(s) dialog box, select all the exceptions that you want to be applied to this rule. You are not required to select any exceptions.

15. If you selected exceptions in the previous step, in the Step 2. Edit the rule description by clicking an underlined value option, click each blue underlined word.

16. After you configure any exceptions, click Next.

17. Review the Configuration Summary. If you are happy with the configuration of the new rule, click New. The rule is tested and, if there are no errors, the Completion screen shows 1 item, 1 succeeded, 0 failed. Click Finish.

Standardizing Server Builds

One other easily overlooked component of a secure messaging environment is ensuring that all components are maintained regularly and consistently. Maintaining server builds that are as identical as possible allows an organization to save on administration, maintenance, and troubleshooting.

With standardized systems, all servers can be maintained, patched, and upgraded in similar or identical manners.

Understandably, most organizations cannot afford to standardize on a single hardware platform and replace all of their systems with each and every upgrade. Often, as servers are added to and removed from an environment, different hardware platforms require different server builds to function properly. However, keeping these systems as close as possible in configuration by using automated and/or scripted installations, automated update utilities, and regular monitoring can increase the likelihood that each server added to the environment meets the organization's security requirements.

The Microsoft System Center Configuration Manager product contains a tool called Desired Configuration Management (DCM) that can assist in keeping the configuration standardized across multiple servers. It enables configuration management and standardization and can be enabled simply by deploying SCCM agents to the Exchange servers.

Exchange Server-Level Security Features

As Exchange Server has adapted over the years, Microsoft has recognized the pitfalls encountered by companies overwhelmed by spam and email viruses. To combat this, they have consistently improved the features of their bundled tools to provide organizations with protection that would have had to be addressed with third-party applications in the past.

Exchange Server 2010 Antispam Measures

As previously mentioned, spam is a global problem that affects everyone with an Internet-accessible email address. The spam problem has grown beyond bothersome; it has become an issue that negatively impacts end-user productivity and places a significant burden on messaging systems.

Exchange Server 2010 has many antispam measures built in to the application. These methods are especially effective when coupled with Outlook 2007. A few of these features are as follows:

▶ **Increased protection through integrated security technologies**—Exchange Server 2010 acts as the first line of defense on incoming email messages. The Exchange server determines the legitimacy of the message, and is able to disable links or uniform resource locators (URLs) to help protect the user community. In addition, Exchange Server 2010 offers new antiphishing capabilities to help prevent emails of this nature from reaching your users in the first place.

▶ **Improved email legitimacy assurance**—Email legitimacy is managed through Email Postmark technology when you combine Office Outlook 2007/2010 and Exchange Server autoencryption. Outlook Email Postmark applies a token (actually a computational puzzle that acts as a spam deterrent) to email messages it sends. This token can be read by a receiving Exchange Server 2010 server to confirm the reliability of the incoming message.

▶ **Distribution lists restricted to authenticated users**—Using message delivery restrictions, you can configure a distribution list to accept mail from all senders, or specific senders or groups. In addition, you can require that all senders be authenticated before their message is accepted.

▶ **Connection filtering**—Improvements have been made in the configuration and management of IP Block lists, IP Allow lists, IP Block List providers, and IP Allow List providers. Each of these elements can now be reviewed and configured directly from the Exchange Management Console.

▶ **Content filtering**—Exchange Server 2010 includes the Exchange Intelligent Message Filter, or IMF, which uses the Microsoft SmartScreen patented "machine-learning" technology. This content filter evaluates inbound messages and determines the probability of whether the messages are legitimate, fraudulent, or spam.

In addition, the IMF consolidates information that is collected from connection filtering, sender filtering, recipient filtering, sender reputation, SenderID verification, and Microsoft Office Outlook 2007/2010 Email Postmark validation. The IMF then applies a Spam Confidence Level (SCL) rating to a given message. Based on this rating, an administrator can configure actions on the message based on this SCL rating. These actions might include the following:

 ▶ Delivery to a user Inbox or Junk E-Mail folder.

 ▶ Delivery to the spam quarantine mailbox.

 ▶ Rejection of the message and no delivery.

 ▶ Acceptance and deletion of the message. The server accepts the message and deletes it instead of forwarding it to the recipient mailbox.

▶ **Antispam updates**—Exchange Server 2010 now offers update services for their antispam components. The standard Exchange Server 2010 antispam filter updates every 2 weeks. The Forefront Security for Exchange Server antispam filter updates every 24 hours.

▶ **Spam quarantine**—The spam quarantine provides a temporary storage location for messages that have been identified as spam and that should not be delivered to a user mailbox. Messages that have been labeled as spam are enclosed in a nondelivery report (NDR) and are delivered to a spam quarantine mailbox. Exchange Server administrators can manage these messages and can perform several actions, such as rejecting the message, deleting it, or flagging it as a false positive and releasing it to the originally intended recipient. In addition, messages with an SCL rating that the administrator has defined as "borderline" can be released to the user's Junk E-Mail folder in Outlook. These borderline messages are converted to plain text to provide additional protection for the user.

▶ **Recipient filtering**—In the past, an email that was addressed to a specific domain would enter that domain's messaging service, regardless of whether it was addressed to a valid recipient. This not only utilized bandwidth, but also required Exchange servers to process the messages, create a nondelivery report (NDR), and send that message back out. Now, by using the EdgeSync process on your Hub Transport server, you can replicate recipient data from the enterprise Active Directory into the Exchange Active Directory Application Mode (ADAM) instance on the Edge Transport server. This enables the Recipient Filter agent to perform recipient lookups for inbound messages. Now, you can block messages that are sent to nonexistent users (or to internal use only distribution lists).

▶ **SenderID**—First implemented in Exchange Server 2003 SP2, Sender ID filtering technology primarily targets forgery of email addresses by verifying that each email message actually originates from the Internet domain that it claims to. Sender ID examines the sender's IP address, and compares it to the sending ID record in the originator's public DNS server. This is one way of eliminating spoofed email before it enters your organization and uses your company resources.

▶ **Sender reputation**—The Sender Reputation agent uses patented Microsoft technology to calculate the trustworthiness of unknown senders. This agent collects analytical data from Simple Mail Transfer Protocol (SMTP) sessions, message content, Sender ID verification, and general sender behavior and creates a history of sender characteristics. The agent then uses this knowledge to determine whether a sender should be temporarily added to the Blocked Senders list.

▶ **IP Reputation Service**—Provided by Microsoft exclusively for Exchange Server 2010 customers, this service is an IP Block list that allows administrators to implement and use IP Reputation Service in addition to other real-time Block list services.

▶ **Outlook junk email filter lists aggregation**—This feature helps reduce false positives in antispam filtering by propagating Outlook 2003/2007/2010 Junk Email Filter lists to Mailbox servers and to Edge Transport servers.

Additional Antispam Measures

In the battle against spam, passive measures protect your organization, but more aggressive measures can help lessen the problem overall. The following sections cover some suggestions of ways that your organization can help fight back.

Utilizing Blacklists

Many companies are unknowingly serving as open relays. Many spammers take advantage of this lack of security and utilize the organization's messaging system to send their unsolicited email. When a company or domain is reported as an open relay, the domain can be placed on a blacklist. This blacklist, in turn, can be used by other companies to prevent incoming mail from a known open relay source.

You can find some organizations that maintain blacklists at the following addresses:

▶ **Distributed Sender Blackhold List**—http://www.dsbl.org

▶ **SpamCop Website**—http://www.spamcop.net

▶ **Open Relay Database**—http://ordb.org

Report Spammers

Organizations and laws are getting tougher on spammers, but spam prevention requires users and organizations to report the abuse. Although this often is a difficult task because many times the source is undecipherable, it is nonetheless important to take a proactive stance and report abuses.

Users should contact the system administrator or help desk if they receive or continue to receive spam, virus hoaxes, and other such fraudulent offers. System administrators should report spammers and contact mail abuse organizations, such as those listed earlier in the "Utilizing Blacklists" section.

System administrators should use discretion before reporting or blocking an organization. For example, if your company were to receive spam messages that appeared to originate from Yahoo! or Hotmail, it wouldn't necessarily be in your best interest simply to block those domains. In that example, the cure might be worse than the disease, so to speak.

Third-Party Antispam Products

Although Microsoft has equipped users, system administrators, and third-party organizations with many tools necessary to combat spam, the additional use of a third-party product, or products, can provide additional protection. These third-party products can also provide a multitude of features that help with reporting, customization, and filtering mechanisms to maximize spam blocking, while minimizing false positives.

Do Not Use Open SMTP Relays

By default, Exchange Server 2010 is not configured to allow open relays. If an SMTP relay is necessary in the messaging environment, take the necessary precautions to ensure that only authorized users or systems have access to these SMTP relays.

> **NOTE**
>
> You can use the Exchange Best Practice Analyzer, or other tools such as Sam Spade (www.samspade.org/), to check your environment for open mail relays.

Protecting Exchange Server 2010 from Viruses

Exchange Server 2010 includes many improvements to assist organizations with their antivirus strategies. The product continues to support the Virus Scanning Application Programming Interface (VSAPI). In addition, Microsoft has made a significant investment in the creation of more effective, efficient, and programmable virus scanning at the transport level.

A few of the antivirus measures included in Exchange Server 2010 are listed as follows:

▶ **Transport agents**—Exchange Server 2010 improves upon the concept of transport agents that was introduced with Exchange Server 2007. *Agents* are managed software components that perform a task in response to an application event. These agents act on transport events, much like event sinks in earlier versions of Exchange Server. Third-party developers can write customized agents that are capable of utilizing the Exchange Multipurpose Internet Mail Extensions (MIME) parsing engine allowing extremely robust antivirus scanning. The Exchange Server 2010 MIME parsing engine has evolved over many years of Exchange Server development and is likely the most trusted and capable MIME engine in the industry.

▶ **Antivirus stamping**—Exchange Server 2010 provides antivirus stamping, a method of stamping messages that were scanned for viruses with the version of the antivirus software that performed the scan and the result of the scan. This feature helps reduce the volume of antivirus scanning across an organization because, as the message travels through the messaging system with the antivirus stamp attached, other systems can immediately determine whether additional scanning must be performed on the message.

▶ **Attachment filtering**—In Exchange Server 2010, Microsoft has implemented attachment filtering by a transport agent. By enabling attachment filtering on your organization's Edge Transport server, you can reduce the spread of malicious attachments before they enter the organization.

NOTE

Although Exchange Server 2010 provides features to help minimize an organization's exposure to viruses, it does not have true, built-in antivirus protection, as Exchange Server does not actually scan messages or attachments to look for infection. However, continued support for the built-in Virus Scanning Application Program Interface (VSAPI) allows specialized antivirus programs to connect their applications to your Exchange Server environment to scan messages as they are handled by Exchange Server.

Forefront Security for Exchange Server

Designed by Microsoft specifically for Exchange Server 2010, Forefront Security for Exchange Server is the next generation of Microsoft Antigen for Exchange Server. Because these products were designed specifically to work together, Forefront integrates with Exchange Server 2010 to provide improved protection, performance, and centralized management.

Forefront Security for Exchange Server delivers the following:

▶ Advanced protection against viruses, worms, phishing, and other threats by utilizing up to five antivirus engines simultaneously at each layer of the messaging infrastructure

- ▶ Optimized performance through coordinated scanning across Edge, Hub, and Mail servers and features such as in-memory scanning, multithreaded scanning processes, and performance bias settings

- ▶ Centralized management of remote installation, engine and signature updating, reporting, and alerts through the Forefront Server Security Management Console

Although the client antivirus protection that is provided by Forefront Security for Exchange Server is language independent, the setup, administration of the product, and end-user notifications are currently available in 11 server languages. When Forefront Security for Exchange Server detects a message that appears to be infected with a virus, the system generates a notification message and sends it to the recipient's mailbox. This message is written in the language of the server running Forefront because the server is not able to detect the language of the destination mailbox.

Third-Party Antivirus Products for Exchange Server

In addition, there are many third-party antivirus vendors in the marketplace. At the time of this writing, there was little to no documentation on their websites about future integration with Exchange Server 2010; however, there is no doubt that most of these companies will have compatible products ready by the time the product is released.

Many mechanisms can be used to protect the messaging environment from viruses and other malicious code. Most third-party virus-scanning products scan for known virus signatures and provide some form of heuristics to scan for unknown viruses. Other antivirus products block suspicious or specific types of message attachments at the point of entry before a possible virus reaches the Information Store.

Antivirus products keep viruses from reaching the end user in two fundamental ways:

- ▶ **Gateway scanning**—Gateway scanning works by scanning all messages as they go through the SMTP gateway (typically connected to the Internet). If the message contains a virus or is suspected of carrying a virus, the antivirus product can clean, quarantine, or delete it before it enters your Exchange Server organization.

- ▶ **Mailbox scanning**—Mailbox scanning is useful to remove viruses that have entered the Information Store. For example, a new virus might make it into the Exchange Server environment before a signature file that can detect it is in place. These messages on the Information Store cannot be scanned by a gateway application; however, with an antivirus product that is capable of scanning the Information Store, these messages can be found and deleted.

Antivirus Outsourcing

Although an organization can put in place many gateway antivirus products to address antispam and antivirus issues, outsourcing these tasks has gained popularity in recent years. Companies specializing in antivirus and antispam are able to host your organiza-tion's MX records, scanning all messages bound for your company, and forwarding the clean messages to your organization. Although this removes a level of control from your administrators, many organizations are finding this outsourcing cost-effective, as they no longer have to maintain staff devoted strictly to these measures.

Transport-Level Security Defined

Whereas server-level security focuses on protecting the data stored on the server from internal or external attacks, transport-level security focuses on protecting the data while it is *in transit* from the sender to the recipient. When most people think of transport-level security, they think of protecting data that is leaving their company network, but protect-ing internal communications is equally important.

As mentioned earlier in the chapter, the concept of defense in depth is also critical to transport-level security. This concept is also sometimes called "The Onion Approach" because, like an onion, after you get past a single layer, you find another layer and, beneath that, another. By using a combination of authentication, encryption, and autho-rization, you can add extra layers to protect your more sensitive data.

Encrypting Email Communications

One of the most widespread and effective methods of transport-level security is the use of encrypting message traffic as it travels across the network. Encryption is important for both external and internal email communications. Securing external communications is important to ensure your messages are not intercepted and viewed by random entities on the Internet, and securing internal communications prevents the use of data capture utili-ties by personnel within your organization who are not authorized to view the messages.

Table 11.1 shows measures that are built in to Exchange Server 2010 to assist with the encryption of message traffic that is destined for both internal and external recipients.

TABLE 11.1   Confidential Messaging Improvements in Exchange Server 2010

Feature	Description
Intra-Org Encryption	Introduced with Exchange Server 2007 and improved with Exchange Server 2010, all mail traveling within an Exchange Server organiza-tion is now encrypted by default. Transport Layer Security (TLS) is used for server-to-server traffic, remote procedure calls (RPC) is used for Outlook connections, and Secure Sockets Layer (SSL) is used for client access traffic (Outlook Web App, Exchange ActiveSync, and Web Services). This prevents spoofing and provides confidentiality to messages in transit.
SSL Certificates Automatically Installed	SSL certificates are installed by default in Exchange Server 2010, enabling broad use of SSL and TLS encryption from clients such as Outlook Web App and other SMTP servers.

TABLE 11.1   Confidential Messaging Improvements in Exchange Server 2010

Feature	Description
Opportunistic TLS Encryption	If the destination SMTP server supports TLS (via the STARTTLS SMTP command) when sending outbound email from Exchange Server 2010, Exchange Server will automatically encrypt the outbound content using TLS. In addition, inbound email sent to Exchange Server 2010 from the Internet will be encrypted if the sending server supports TLS (Exchange Server 2010 automatically installs SSL certificates). This is the first step in ensuring the default encryption of Internet-bound messaging traffic, and as more and more sites implement SMTP servers supporting this feature, the ability to encrypt Internet-bound messages by default will increase.
Information Rights Management (IRM)	Administrators can use transport rules on the Hub Transport server role to enforce IRM protection on messages based on subject, content, or sender/recipient. In addition, Exchange Server 2010 prelicenses IRM-protected messages to enable fast client retrieval for users. IRM can be enabled with the addition of Windows Server 2008 Active Directory Rights Management Services (AD RMS) to an environment.

Utilizing Public Key Infrastructure (PKI)

Because Microsoft Exchange Server 2010 is installed on Microsoft Windows Server, it can take advantage of communications security features provided by the underlying operating system.

One of the most widely used security methods is the use of Public Key Infrastructure (PKI), which allows an administrator in an organization to secure traffic across both internal and external networks. Utilizing PKI provides certificate-based services by using a combination of digital certificates, registration authorities, and certificate authorities (CAs) that can be used to provide authentication, authorization, nonrepudiation, confidentiality, and verification. A CA is a digital signature of the certificate issuer.

Chapter 12, "Integrating Certificate-Based Public Key Infrastructure (PKI) in Exchange Server 2010," goes into this technology in greater depth with instructions on how to install certificate services, information on the use of public and private keys, and the use of smart cards in a PKI environment.

Utilizing S/MIME

Another method of providing security to messages while in transit is the use of Secure/Multipurpose Internet Mail Extensions (S/MIME).

S/MIME allows the message traffic to be digitally signed and encrypted, and utilizes digital signatures to ensure message confidentiality. Chapter 12 goes into this technology in depth.

Utilizing TLS and SSL

Transport Layer Security (TLS) is an Internet standard protocol that is included in Microsoft Exchange Server 2010 that allows secure communications by utilizing encryption of traffic sent across a network. In a messaging environment, TLS is specifically utilized when securing server/server and/or client/server communications. Utilizing TLS can help ensure that messages sent across your network are not sent "in the clear," or in a format that is easily intercepted and deciphered.

Configuring your mail servers to utilize TLS and SSL to secure client access is addressed in depth in Chapter 10, "Client-Level Secured Messaging."

Exchange Server 2010 SMTP Connectors

SMTP is a protocol that is used for sending email messages between servers. Because most email systems that are connected to the Internet today utilize SMTP as their messaging standard, it is important to understand how it works with Exchange Server 2010.

Previous versions of Exchange Server supported SMTP, but they relied on a service provided by the underlying Windows operating system. Exchange Server 2010, on the other hand, has its own built-in SMTP server. As a matter of fact, the installation of Exchange Server 2010 requires that you do not have the SMTP service already installed on your underlying Windows platform.

In Exchange Server, for SMTP traffic to travel between computers, SMTP connectors are used. SMTP connectors are logical representations of connections between a source and destination server. These connectors dictate how Edge Transport servers and Hub Transport servers communicate with each other, with the Internet, and with previous versions of Exchange Server.

There are two types of SMTP connector in Exchange Server 2010, Send Connectors and Receive Connectors. Each of these types of connector represents a one-way connection, and the configuration of the connector mandates how messages will be transported.

To secure your Microsoft Exchange Server 2010 environment, you must have an understanding of these connectors and how to configure them properly.

Connector Topology

For messages to flow between servers in an Exchange Server organization, or between the organization and the Internet, several SMTP connectors must be in place and properly configured. These connectors are the minimum that are required for proper end-to-end mail flow. Table 11.2 lists these connectors.

TABLE 11.2   Exchange Server 2010 SMTP Connectors

Purpose	Type	How Created
Send messages between Hub Transport servers in the organization	Send	Implicit connector that is automatically computed based on the system topology.
Send messages from a Hub Transport server to an Edge Transport server	Send	Implicit connector that is automatically computed based on the system topology.
Send messages from an Edge Transport server to a Hub Transport server	Send	Implicit connector that is automatically created by the EdgeSync subscription process.
Send messages from a Hub Transport server to the Internet	Send	Explicit connector that is created by the administrator and is stored in Active Directory.
Send messages from an Edge Transport server to the Internet	Send	Explicit connector that is either created by the administrator on an Edge Transport server or automatically created using the EdgeSync subscription process.
Receive messages on a Hub Transport server from another Hub Transport server or from an Edge Transport server	Receive	Explicit Active Directory connector that is automatically created when the Hub Transport server role is installed. The connector is stored in Active Directory as a child object of the server.
Receive messages on the Edge Transport server from a Hub Transport server or from the Internet	Receive	Explicit connector that is created automatically when the Edge Transport server role is installed. The connector is stored in ADAM. When the Edge Transport server is subscribed to an Active Directory site using EdgeSync, permissions to use this connector are granted to each Hub Transport server in the site.

> **NOTE**
>
> Send and Receive Connectors can be created implicitly, explicitly, or automatically. To say that a connector is created implicitly means that it is computed from the system topology and is not displayed in either the Exchange Management Console or the Exchange Management Shell. A connector that is created explicitly is one that is created when an administrator actively performs a task. Lastly, a connector can be created automatically during the Edge Subscription process.

Understanding Receive Connectors

SMTP Receive Connectors serve the purpose of acting as incoming connection points for SMTP traffic and dictate how incoming SMTP communications are managed on an Exchange Server 2010 transport server. The Receive Connector actively listens for incoming connections that match all settings configured on the connector, such as connections utilizing a particular port or from a particular IP address range.

Receive Connectors have many configurable limits that can be set, such as the following:

▶ Number of active connections allowed

▶ Maximum incoming message size

▶ Maximum recipients per message

Receive Connectors are configured on a single server and determine what particular message traffic that server will listen for. If the Receive Connector is created on a Hub Transport server, it is stored in Active Directory as a child object of that server. However, when it is created on an Edge Transport server, the connector is stored in Active Directory Lightweight Directory Services (AD LDS), previously known as ADAM.

Understanding Send Connectors

SMTP Send Connectors are used for relaying outgoing SMTP communications. Unlike Receive Connectors, Send Connectors are not scoped to a single server. When an Exchange Server 2010 server receives an SMTP message that is addressed to a remote destination, the message is relayed to an appropriate Send Connector that is configured to handle messages intended for that destination.

In Active Directory or in AD LDS, a Send Connector is created as an object in a connectors container. A connector can have more than one source server, which is defined as a Hub Transport server that is associated with that connector.

For example, if a Send Connector is configured to handle message routing to a domain that is external to the organization, whenever a Hub Transport server receives a message destined for that remote domain, the message is routed to the Send Connector to be relayed appropriately.

As with Receive Connectors, a variety of configuration settings can be defined by the administrator. Send Connectors can be created and viewed in either the Exchange Management Console or the Exchange Management Shell, but the majority of the configuration must be accomplished using the Exchange Management Shell. Send Connectors are stored in Active Directory as a configuration object, and can be viewed from the Exchange Management Console by going to the console tree, selecting Organization Configuration, and then selecting Hub Transport. Next, in the results pane, select the Send Connectors tab.

How Connectors Are Created

As previously mentioned, connectors must exist between all messaging servers for SMTP traffic to be passed. However, inside the Active Directory forest, you do not have to create and configure the connectors between Hub Transport servers. These connections are created implicitly. This means that the connections are created by computing a path between AD sites that is based on Active Directory site link costs.

After you install an Edge Transport server and a Hub Transport server, the Edge Transport server must be subscribed to an Active Directory site by using the Edge Transport subscription process. This process enables the EdgeSync service to establish one-way replication of recipients and configuration details from the AD directory service to the AD LDS instance. This subscription process can be accomplished quickly and easily by following the steps listed on the Finalize Deployment tab on the Exchange Management Console. To get to the Finalize Deployment tab, open the Exchange Management Console and click on Microsoft Exchange in the console tree.

When you subscribe the Edge Transport server, data that is stored in Active Directory gets replicated to the AD LDS instance located on the Edge Transport server. Some examples of the data that gets replicated are as follows:

- ► Configuration of Send and Receive Connectors

- ► Domains to accept SMTP traffic from

- ► Remote domains

Connectors can be created using one of the following methods:

- ► **Explicit Active Directory Connector**—When an administrator creates a connector in the Exchange Server organization, an explicit connector is created. This object can be modified by the administrator and changes are replicated throughout the organization.

- ► **Explicit AD LDS Connector**—When an administrator creates a connector on an Edge Transport server, it is stored in AD LDS. Connectors that are created on Edge Transport servers are scoped to a single server. An administrator can modify this object; however, the configuration applies only to that particular connector on that Edge Transport server only.

- ► **Implicit**—Implicit connectors are automatically computed using Active Directory site link information and existing explicit Active Directory connectors. This connector cannot be modified, and cannot be viewed either in Active Directory or AD LDS. The only way to change an implicit connector is to make a change to the system topology. When a change to the topology is made, the connector is recomputed.

- ► **Automatic Explicit AD LDS Connector**—When you subscribe an Edge Transport server, the EdgeSync subscription process creates an Automatic Explicit AD LDS connector inside the Exchange Server organization. This connector is then replicated to the AD LDS instance on the Edge Transport server. This connector cannot be modified on the Edge Transport server, but can be modified in Active Directory. Any changes made in Active Directory are replicated to the Edge Transport server during routine synchronization.

▶ **Automatic Implicit AD LDS Connector**—All implicit connectors are computed from the system topology as described previously. This applies to Automatic Implicit AD LDS connectors as well. One or more Edge Transport servers must have access to the information contained in this connector. This connector cannot be modified in Active Directory; however, if a change is made to the system topology, the connector changes resulting from the topology change will be replicated to the Edge Transport server during routine synchronization.

NOTE

For the Edge Transport servers and the Hub Transport servers to communicate with each other, they must be able to find each other using host resolution in the domain name system (DNS).

Hub Transport Server Connectors

After the Hub Transport server role has been installed on an Exchange Server 2010 server in your environment, you must configure the appropriate Send and Receive Connectors. Until this has been accomplished, the server will be unable to send SMTP messages to, or receive them from, the Internet.

Send Connectors are configured in the Exchange Management Console in the Organization Configuration node, and are stored in AD as a configuration object. The Send Connectors must be configured so that the Hub Transport server knows what source server to forward the message to. Bear in mind, there can be multiple source servers configured on the connector.

Receive Connectors, on the other hand, are configured in the Exchange Management Console in the Server Configuration node, and are stored in AD as a child object of the server. By default, when a Hub Transport server is brought online, it has two default Receive Connectors already configured.

Both Send and Receive Connectors can be viewed and modified using the Exchange Management Shell. As a matter of fact, many configuration settings can *only* be accomplished using the Exchange Management Shell.

So, SMTP Send Connectors handle outgoing messages; SMTP Receive Connectors handle incoming messages. For proper message flow, the Hub Transport server must have the appropriate connectors to allow mail flow to and from the Internet (by relaying through an Edge Transport server), as well as to and from other Hub Transport servers.

A Hub Transport server must have at least three required connectors to function properly. The first two, both of which are Receive Connectors, are created automatically during the installation of the Hub Transport server:

- ▶ A Receive Connector that is configured to accept SMTP messages on port 25 from all remote IP addresses. The usage type for this connector should be "Internal" as well. This connector is automatically generated during the installation of the Hub Transport server.

- ▶ A second Receive Connector that is configured to accept messages on port 587 from all remote IP addresses. This connector is needed to accept SMTP connections from non-MAPI clients who are connecting through a client access server. The usage type for this connector should be set to "Internal." This connector is automatically created during the installation of the Hub Transport server.

The third required connector is a Send Connector:

- ▶ By default, no explicit Send Connector exists on the Hub Transport server, so you must perform one of two actions to create it—either the connector is automatically generated when you create an Edge subscription, or you must manually configure it. After this process has been completed, your environment will be ready to route Internet-bound messages from the Hub Transport server to the Edge Transport server, and then out to the Internet.

Automatic Creation of Send Connectors

To automatically create the Send Connector, you must have a server with the Edge Transport server role and utilize an Edge subscription and the EdgeSync service. To do so, perform the following steps:

1. Install the Hub Transport server role.

2. On the Edge Transport server, export the Edge subscription file. If you have more than one Edge Transport server, each server requires a separate subscription file. The Edge subscription file can be exported in the Microsoft Exchange Shell utilizing the following command:

   ```
   new-edgesubscription - filename "c:\server1info.xml"
   ```

3. Next, you must import the Edge subscription. This file can be accomplished using either the Exchange Management Console or the Exchange Management Shell. To do so using the Exchange Management Shell, run the following command on the Hub Transport server:

   ```
   new-edgesubscription –filename "c:\server1info.xml" –site
      ➥"default-first-site-name"
   ```

4. Verify that synchronization was successful by viewing the Event Viewer application log and inspecting MsExchange EdgeSync events.

Data replicated to AD LDS includes the Internet Send Connector. This connector is stored in AD and the settings for it are written on the Edge Transport server in the local AD LDS instance. The connector has the Edge Transport server as the source server, and is configured to use DNS MX records to automatically route messages.

Manual Creation of Send Connectors

If you decide not to use an Edge subscription, you must manually create and configure the Send Connector. To do so, follow these steps:

1. Start the Exchange Management Console.

2. In the console tree, expand the Organization Configuration node, and then select the Hub Transport node.

3. In the action pane, click New Send Connector. The New SMTP Send Connector Wizard starts.

4. On the Introduction page, type a name for the connector, and then select the intended usage from a drop-down box—the intended usage should be set to Internal for this scenario because it will be sent to the Edge Transport servers. Click Next to continue.

5. On the Address Space page, click Add, and enter * (all domains) as the address space. Leave the Include All Subdomains check box checked, and click OK, as shown in Figure 11.4. Click Next to continue.

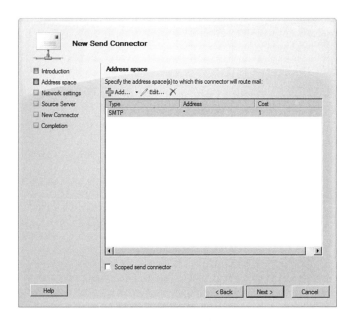

FIGURE 11.4   Configuring a Send Connector.

6. On the Network Settings page, ensure the Route All Mail Through the Following Smart Hosts option button is selected, and then click Add.

7. Enter the IP address or FQDN for the Edge Transport server, click OK, and then click Next to continue.

8. On the Smart Host Security Settings page, select the Exchange Server Authentication option button, and then click Next to continue.

9. Select one or more Hub Transport servers as the source for the connector, and then click Next.

10. Review the Configuration Summary, and then click New to create the connector.

11. From the Completion page, click Finish.

12. Now, you must perform manual configuration of the required connectors on the Edge Transport server. This information is covered in the next section.

Edge Transport Server Connectors

After the installation of the Microsoft Exchange Server 2010 Edge Transport server role, you must configure the appropriate Send and Receive Connectors. Until this has been accomplished, the server will be unable to send SMTP messages to, or receive them from, the Internet and your internal Hub Transport servers.

As discussed in the previous section, to complete the configuration of the Send Connector on an Edge Transport server, you subscribe the server to the organization using EdgeSync, which then replicates the appropriate connectors to the Edge Transport server. If you do not use EdgeSync, you must manually create and configure the connector.

This section covers additional information about Edge Transport server connectors that was not touched on in the previous section.

An Edge Transport server must have at least four required connectors to function properly. The first two, both Send Connectors, are created and configured for you automatically during the EdgeSync process:

▶ A Send Connector must exist that is configured to send messages to the Internet. Typically, the address space for this connector is set to * (all Internet domains). DNS routing is used to resolve destinations. The usage type for this connection is set to "Internet." This connector is created automatically when you use EdgeSync to subscribe the server to an Active Directory site.

▶ A Send Connector must exist that is configured to send messages to the Hub Transport servers in the Exchange Server organization. The address space for this connector can either be *, or you can manually list each of the domains for which you are processing mail. The smart hosts for the connector should be configured as your Hub Transport servers, and the usage type set to "Internal." This connector is also created automatically during the subscription process.

The next two required connectors are Receive Connectors:

▶ A Receive Connector must exist that is configured to accept messages from the Internet. Usually, this connector is configured to accept connections from any IP address range. Furthermore, it is normally configured to allow anonymous access. When configuring the local network bindings for this connection, they should be set to the external-facing IP address of the Edge Transport server, and the usage type should be set to "Internet."

▶ A second Receive Connector must exist that is configured to accept messages from Hub Transport servers in your organization. For security purposes, you can configure this connector to accept connections only from your Hub Transport servers by listing their IP address ranges. The local network bindings for this connector should be configured as the internal-facing IP address of the Edge Transport server, and the usage type should be set to "Internal."

Configuring Receive Connectors on the Edge Transport Server

When you install the Edge Transport server, one Receive Connector is automatically created. This connector is configured by default to accept SMTP traffic from all IP address ranges, and it is bound to all IP addresses associated with the local server. The usage type is set to "Internet," and the connection will accept anonymous connections. It is recommended that you modify the settings of this Receive Connector and create a second one for internal usage. To perform this procedure, follow these steps:

1. Start the Exchange Management Console on the Edge Transport server.

2. In the console tree, select Edge Transport.

3. In the results pane, select the appropriate Edge Transport server and then, on the bottom half of the pane, click the Receive Connectors tab.

4. Select the default connector and, in the action pane, click Properties.

5. Click the Network tab, and edit the existing Local IP Addresses (by default, set to All Available). Configure this address to be the IP address of the Internet-facing network adapter of the Edge Transport server. Save your changes and exit, as no other changes are needed on this connector.

6. Next, in the action pane, click New Receive Connector. On the Introduction page, enter a name for this connector, and select a usage type as Internal. Click Next to continue.

7. On the Remote Network Settings page, modify the Remote IP Addresses and configure them to accept mail from the IP addresses assigned to your Hub Transport servers. Save the settings and click New to create the connector.

8. After the connector has been created, you must make one more modification. Select the connector in the results pane and select Properties in the action pane. Click the Network tab, and double-click the Local IP Address(es) entry, currently set to (All Available). Click the Specify an IP Address option button, and enter the IP address of

the internal-facing network adapter of the Edge Transport server. Save all settings and exit, as no other changes are needed on this connector.

Configuring Send Connectors on the Edge Transport Server

As discussed in the section on Hub Transport servers, the Send Connectors needed on your Edge Transport server are automatically generated by the EdgeSync service. If you elect to not create an Edge subscription, you must manually configure the Send Connectors.

Automatic Creation of Send Connectors

To automatically create the Send Connector on the Edge Transport server, follow the instructions in the previous section titled "Automatic Creation of Send Connectors" in the "Hub Transport Server Connectors" section.

Manual Completion of Send Connectors

To manually complete the configuration of the first Send Connector, do the following:

1. Start the Exchange Management Console on the Edge Transport server.
2. In the console tree, select Edge Transport.
3. In the results pane, select the appropriate Edge Transport server and then, on the bottom half of the pane, click the Send Connectors tab.
4. In the action pane, click New Send Connector.
5. On the Introduction page, type a name for the connector, and set the usage to Internet. Click Next to continue.
6. On the Address Space page, click Add. Set the Domain to * and ensure the Include All Subdomains option is selected. Click Next to continue.
7. On the Network Settings page, select Use Domain Name System (DNS) "MX" Records to Route Mail Automatically. Click Next to continue. Save all settings and exit, as no further configuration is needed on this connector.

To manually complete the configuration of the second Send Connector, do the following:

1. Start the Exchange Management Console on the Edge Transport server.
2. In the console tree, select Edge Transport.
3. In the results pane, select the appropriate Edge Transport server and then, on the bottom half of the pane, click the Send Connectors tab.
4. In the action pane, click New Send Connector.
5. On the Introduction page, type a name for the connector, and set the usage to Internal. Click Next to continue.
6. On the Address Space page, click Add. Set the domain to the domain(s) for which you accept mail. If you have more than one accepted domain, configure additional entries. Ensure the Include All Subdomains option is selected. Click Next to continue.

7. On the Network Settings page, select Route All Mail Through the Following Smart Hosts, and click Add.

8. Enter the IP address or FQDN of one of your Hub Transport servers as the smart host. Click OK to continue. To add additional Hub Transport servers, click Add again. When you are ready, click Next to continue.

9. On the Smart Host Security Settings page, ensure the None option button is selected, and click Next.

10. Review all entries and, after all entries are correct, click New to create the connector.

Setting Message Delivery Limits

One of the most important security measures you can implement on your SMTP connectors is setting message delivery limits. Message delivery limits prevent users from sending large messages through Exchange Server that can tie up Exchange Server resources (processing time, queue availability, disk storage, and more). When this occurs, the results can be just as bad as experiencing a DoS attack. Implementing these limits also encourages users to use alternative delivery methods, such as file shares, compression of attachments, and even document management portals.

In Exchange Server 2010, message delivery limits are set on specific Send and Receive Connectors using the Exchange Management Shell.

To determine the current maximum message size on a particular connector, perform the following procedure. For this example, you will work with a Receive Connector. To perform the same tasks on a Send Connector, replace the `receiveconnector` command with `sendconnector`.

1. Start the Exchange Management Shell.

2. Get a list of the existing connectors by using the following command:

   ```
   get-receiveconnector
   ```

   A list of existing Receive Connectors is returned. For this example, use a connector named "Default VMW-EXCHANGE1."

3. To view the configuration of a specific connector, use the following command:

   ```
   get-receiveconnector "default vmw-exchange1" |format-list
   ```

A detailed configuration of the connector is returned.

By default, the maximum message size is set to 10MB. To change this maximum message size, perform the following procedure:

1. In the Exchange Management Shell, type the following command:

   ```
   set-receiveconnector "default vmw-exchange1" -MaxMessageSize 20MB
   ```

2. If you now view the configuration of the specific connector (as shown previously), you will see that the new `maxmessagesize` limit has been implemented.

> **NOTE**
>
> Configuring a different sending and receiving message size limit can cause potential problems. For example, if you configured a 5MB limit on sent messages, but a 10MB limit on received messages, a user might receive an email from an external source with a 9MB attachment. They would be able to receive the message, but any attempts to forward it to a co-worker would fail because of the sending restriction. A good best practice is to set these limits to the same size.

Another important message delivery limit that can be used to secure Exchange Server 2010 involves the number of recipients that a message can be sent to at any one time. Limiting the maximum number of recipients limits internal users' ability to essentially spam the enterprise with large numbers of emails.

Configuring the maximum number of recipients per message is done similarly to setting the maximum message size previously. The default setting is 200, but you can configure it to whatever number you desire. For this example, you will change this setting to 500 recipients. To do so, type the following command in the Exchange Management Shell:

```
set-receiveconnector "default vmw-exchange1" –MaxRecipientsPerMessage 500
```

The majority of the configuration settings for the Send and Receive Connectors must be configured through the Exchange Management Shell.

Configuring Authoritative Domains

When an Exchange Server organization is responsible for handling message delivery to recipients in a particular domain, the organization is called *authoritative* for that domain. Configuring an authoritative domain in Exchange Server 2010 is a two-step process: First, you create an accepted domain, and second, you set the domain type as authoritative.

An accepted domain is any SMTP namespace that the Edge Transport server(s) in your organization sends messages to or receives messages from. Your organization might have one or more domains, so you might have more than one authoritative domain.

> **NOTE**
>
> If you have subscribed your Edge Transport server to the Exchange Server organization using the EdgeSync process, do not perform these procedures directly on the Edge Transport server. Instead, perform the steps on a Hub Transport server and allow it to replicate to the Edge Transport server during the next synchronization.

To create an authoritative domain, perform the following command in the Exchange Management Shell on your Hub Transport server:

```
New-AcceptedDomain –Name "CompanyABC" –DomainName companyabc.com –DomainType
➥Authoritative
```

> **NOTE**
>
> You must be logged on as an account that is a member of the Organization Management group and that is a member of the local Administrators group on the server. Also, replace this name with your own domain name in place of companyabc.com in the example.

Securing Windows for the Edge Transport Server Role

In Exchange Server 2010, your Edge Transport server roles are installed as standalone servers in your perimeter network (also referred to as the boundary network or screened subnet).

Because these servers exist in your perimeter network, they are more vulnerable to potential attacks than servers located on your internal network. To prepare a server for the Edge Transport server role, you should first utilize the Security Configuration Wizard (SCW) to minimize the attack service of the server by disabling functions that are not needed to perform the functions of an Edge Transport server.

Although it is possible to manually secure the server, the SCW automates the process and applies Microsoft recommended best practices to lock the server down by utilizing a role-based metaphor to determine what services are needed on a particular server. By utilizing the SCW, you can minimize your exposure to exploitation of security vulnerabilities.

One of the challenges to locking down ports and services on a particular server is ensuring you do not remove functionality that is necessary for the server to perform its functions. Often, mistakes can be made that are not immediately visible and that can cause problems in your environment that will require troubleshooting at a later date. However, within Exchange Server 2010, there is an SCW template that can be applied to a computer that has the Edge Transport server role installed that can automatically lock down services and ports that are not needed to perform Edge Transport functionality.

When you run the SCW, you can create a custom policy based on this template that can be applied to all Edge Transport servers in your environment.

Implementing Network Security

Edge Transport servers in a perimeter network are generally configured with two network adapters—one to communicate strictly with the Internet, and the other strictly for internal communications.

Each adapter must have a different level of security applied to it. It is recommended that the Internet-facing (or external) adapter be configured to only allow SMTP traffic on port 25.

The internal adapter, on the other hand, needs the following ports open to properly communicate with the server within your organization:

▶ Port 25/SMTP for SMTP traffic

▶ Ports 50389/TCP and 50636/UDP for Lightweight Directory Access Protocol (LDAP) communication

▶ Port 3389/TCP Remote Desktop Protocol

The LDAP ports are used during the EdgeSync process, and the RDP port is used to allow remote administration of the server.

Administrator Permissions on an Edge Transport Server

By default, when you install an Edge Transport server role, the server is administered using local user accounts. This is because the server is configured as a standalone server in the perimeter network and has no domain membership.

The local Administrators group is granted full control over the Edge Transport server, including administration permissions over the instance of AD LDS on the server. Logging on as an account with membership in the local Administrators group gives you permission to modify the server configuration, security configurations, AD LDS data, and the status of queues and messages currently in transit on the server.

Generally, you would utilize Microsoft Windows Terminal server to administer an Edge Transport server, and the local Administrators group is granted remote logon permissions by default. Rather than allowing all of your administrators to use the default Administrator account, it is recommended that you create a separate local account for each administrator who will be administering your Edge servers, and adding these accounts to the local Administrators group on the server.

Table 11.3 identifies administrative tasks that are commonly performed on an Edge Transport server, and the required group membership needed for each task.

TABLE 11.3   Edge Transport Server Administrative Tasks

Administrative Task	Membership Needed
Backup and restore	Backup Operators
Enable and disable agents	Administrators
Configure connectors	Administrators
Configure antispam policies	Administrators
Configure IP Block lists and IP Allow lists	Administrators
View queues and messages	Users
Manage queues and messages	Administrators

TABLE 11.3   Edge Transport Server Administrative Tasks

Administrative Task	Membership Needed
Create an EdgeSync subscription file	Administrators

Summary

Securing Exchange Server 2010 requires a focus on both server-level and transport-level security measures. Utilizing a combination of techniques including proper planning and design, hardening the underlying operating system, and creating and implementing policies, as well as implementing other built-in security features, goes a long way toward assisting you with a more secure messaging environment.

Furthermore, the proper implementation and configuration of Send and Receive SMTP Connectors in your environment is necessary to allow mail flow in and out of your Exchange Server organization, while minimizing the risk of improper use by malicious users. Securing unneeded services and ports on the Internet-facing Edge Transport servers in your perimeter network is critical to this endeavor.

Best Practices

The following are best practices from this chapter:

- ▶ Accurately assess your messaging environment's risks before attempting to design your security infrastructure.

- ▶ Establish and implement a comprehensive corporate email policy.

- ▶ Establish and implement administrative policies.

- ▶ Create companywide email disclaimers and have them approved prior to implementation by your legal representative.

- ▶ Implement strong antispam and antivirus measures in your environment and devote resources to the maintenance and upkeep of these measures.

- ▶ Plan and implement Exchange Server 2010 security roles.

- ▶ Use a layered approach when hardening Windows Server 2008 and when applying transport-layer security methods.

- ▶ Perform periodic security assessments and include a review of your physical security methods with each.

- ▶ Keep updated with the latest service packs and hotfixes.

- ▶ Standardize Exchange Server 2010 security.

- ▶ Limit the size of incoming and outgoing emails in your environment. Not only does this helps save disk space on your Exchange Server 2010 servers, it also minimizes denial of service (DoS) vulnerabilities. By default, this feature is enabled with a maximum message size of 10MB.

▶ Only allow authenticated users to send email in your environment. This concept can be especially important when applied to sending messages to mail-enabled distribution lists.

▶ Properly configure your SMTP Send and Receive Connectors to control which IP addresses or domains can access them.

▶ Utilize the Security Configuration Wizard on all of your servers, especially any Internet-facing Edge Transport servers located in your perimeter network. Use the SCW template provided by Microsoft to configure a security policy for these servers.

CHAPTER 12

Integrating Certificate-Based Public Key Infrastructure (PKI) in Exchange Server 2010

Exchange Server 2010 uses certificates to secure much of the internal and external traffic. This provides out-of-the-box secured communications for all Exchange Server 2010 transmissions, which prevents both snooping on and tampering with messages sent and received by the systems. Clients can also use certificates to sign and encrypt messages so that they are protected even in storage. Proper issuance of all these certificates and integration with a Public Key Infrastructure (PKI) is important to the security and administration of the Exchange Server 2010 environment.

This chapter compares the various certificate types that you can use with Exchange Server 2010, which server components use certificates, and how to choose the certificates to use with the components. In addition, the chapter covers how to request, install, and maintain these certificates.

As much as Chapter 11, "Server and Transport-Level Security," covered securing a server and encrypting the transport of communications in an Exchange Server environment, hub transport security does not address the privacy of email communications of actual messages between email senders and recipients. This chapter covers email encryption in which the actual email message from a sender is encrypted so that someone trying to intercept the message will not have the ability to read the message because of the encryption on the message itself.

This chapter focuses on certificate-based encryption of messages, including the creation of a certificate server and the installation of certificates within the Microsoft Outlook client software.

Understanding Public Key Infrastructure

Because Microsoft Exchange Server 2010 resides on Microsoft Windows Server 2003 or Windows Server 2008, administrators can rely heavily on the technology of the underlying operating system in their effort to implement a secure messaging environment.

Microsoft Windows Server 2003 and Windows Server 2008 allow for the use of PKI, which enables an administrator to exchange information with strong security and easy administration across both internal and external networks. PKI is an extensible infrastructure used to provide certificate-based services by combining digital certificates, registration authorities, and certificate authorities that can be used to provide authentication, authorization, nonrepudiation, confidentiality, and verification. A certificate authority (CA) is a digital signature of the certificate issuer.

PKI implementations are widespread and are becoming a critical component of modern networks. Windows Server 2003 and Windows Server 2008 fully support the deployment of various PKI configurations, ranging from very simplistic to extremely complex. Entire books have been written on the subject of implementing PKI, but this chapter endeavors to give administrators a basic understanding of the subject and show how PKI can be used to help secure your Exchange Server environment.

Certificate Services in Windows Server 2003 or 2008

Windows Server 2003 and Windows Server 2008 include a built-in CA known as Certificate Services. Certificate Services can be used to create certificates and subsequently manage them and is responsible for ensuring their validity. Certificate Services can also be used to trust external PKIs, such as a third-party PKI, to expand services and secure communication with other organizations.

The type of CA that you install and configure depends on the purpose or purposes of the Windows Server PKI. Certificate Services for Windows Server 2003 or the Active Directory Certificate Services (AD CS) role in Windows Server 2008 can be installed as one of the following CA types:

▶ **Enterprise root CA**—The enterprise root CA is the most trusted CA in an organization and, if utilized, should be installed before any other CA. All other CAs are subordinate to an enterprise root CA. Enterprise root CAs store certificates in Active Directory (AD) by default.

▶ **Enterprise subordinate CA**—An enterprise subordinate CA must get a CA certificate from an enterprise root CA and can then issue certificates to all users and computers in the enterprise. These types of CAs are often used for load balancing of an enterprise root CA. More important, using subordinates provides stronger security for the PKI.

▶ **Stand-alone root CA**—A stand-alone root CA is the root of a hierarchy that is not related to the enterprise domain information, and, therefore, certificates are not stored in AD. Multiple stand-alone CAs can be established for particular purposes.

> ▶ **Stand-alone subordinate** CA—A stand-alone subordinate CA receives its certificate from a stand-alone root CA and can then be used to distribute certificates to users and computers associated with that stand-alone CA.

A Windows Server PKI can also be either online or offline based on the level of security that is required in the organization.

TIP

An enterprise root CA is the most versatile CA in Windows Server 2003 and Windows Server 2008 because it integrates tightly with AD and offers more certificate services. All domain members trust the enterprise CA, and the enterprise CA can be used for autoenrollment of certificates to domain member. If you're unsure as to what CA to use, choose an enterprise root or subordinate CA for use with messaging. Most important, however, is that with any PKI there must be careful planning and design.

PKI Planning Considerations

Any PKI implementation requires thorough planning and design, as noted earlier. Possible planning and design considerations include the following:

- ▶ Multinational legal considerations, including creation and standardization of a formal Certificate Practice Statement (CPS)

- ▶ Policies and procedures for issuing, revoking, and suspending certificates

- ▶ PKI hardware identification and standardization, including employee badge integration

- ▶ Determination of CA hierarchy administration model

- ▶ Creation of a redundant CA infrastructure based on geographical location

- ▶ Policies and procedures for creation of CAs as subordinates and policy enforcers within a greater hierarchy, including qualified subordination and cross-certification

- ▶ Policies and procedures for creation of registration authorities (RAs) and their placement within the CA hierarchy

- ▶ CA trust strategies

- ▶ Policies and procedures for maintaining the CA as a 24x7x365 operation (24 hours a day, 7 days a week, 365 days a year)

- ▶ Policies and procedures for key and certificate management, including, but not limited to, key length, cryptographic algorithms, certificate lifetime, certificate renewal, storage requirements, and more

- ▶ Policies and procedures for securing the PKI

- ▶ Published plans for providing high availability and recoverability

- ▶ Policies and procedures for integrating the CA with Lightweight Directory Access Protocol (LDAP) and/or Active Directory

- ▶ Policies and procedures for integrating with existing applications

- ▶ Policies and procedures for security-related incidents (for example, bulk revocation of certificates)

- ▶ Policies and procedures for delegation of administrative tasks

- ▶ Standards for PKI auditing and reporting

- ▶ Policies and procedures for change control

- ▶ Standards for key length and expiration of certificates

- ▶ Policies and procedures for handling lost certificates (that is, smart card)

- ▶ Policies and procedures for safe distribution of the CA public key to end users

- ▶ Policies and procedures for enrollment (for example, autoenrollment, stations, and so forth)

- ▶ Policies and procedures for incorporating external users and companies

- ▶ Procedures for using certificate templates

As you can see from this list, implementing PKI is not to be taken lightly. Even if the organization is implementing PKI just for enhanced Exchange Server 2010 messaging functionality, the considerations should be planned and designed.

Fundamentals of Private and Public Keys

Encryption techniques can primarily be classified as either symmetrical or asymmetrical. Symmetrical encryption requires that each party in an encryption scheme hold a copy of a private key that is used to encrypt and decrypt information sent between the two parties. One shortcoming of the private key encryption method is that the private key must somehow be transmitted from one party to the other, without it being intercepted and used to decrypt the information.

Asymmetrical encryption uses a combination of two keys that are mathematically related to each other. The first key, known as the private key, is kept closely guarded and is used to encrypt the information. The second key, known as the public key, can be used to decrypt the information. The integrity of the public key is ensured through certificates. The asymmetric approach to encryption ensures that the private key does not fall into the wrong hands and only the intended recipient is able to decrypt the data.

Understanding Certificates

A certificate is essentially a digital document issued by a trusted central authority that is used by the authority to validate a user's identity. Central, trusted authorities such as VeriSign are widely used on the Internet to ensure that software that is being downloaded from Microsoft, for example, is actually originating from Microsoft, and is not in fact a virus in disguise.

Certificates can be used for multiple functions including, but not limited to, the following:

- ▶ Secure email

- ▶ Web-based authentication

- ▶ IP Security (IPSec)

- ▶ Secure web-based communications

- ▶ Code signing

- ▶ Certification hierarchies

Certificates are signed using information from the subject's public key and the CA. Items such as the originator's name, email address, and others can be used.

Certificate Templates

Certificates have multiple functions, and, therefore, multiple types of certificates are available to meet the need. One certificate might be used to sign code, whereas another is used to provide support for secure email. In this one-to-one relationship, a certificate is used for a single purpose. Certificates can also have a one-to-many relationship in which one certificate is used for multiple purposes.

TIP

One of the best examples of a certificate that uses a one-to-many relationship is the user certificate. By default, a user certificate provides support for user authentication, secure email, and the Encrypting File System (EFS).

Windows Server 2003 and Windows Server 2008 contain a large number of certificates, each with an assigned set of settings and purposes. In essence, certificates can be categorized into six different functional areas:

- ▶ **Server authentication**—These certificates are used to authenticate servers to clients and servers to other servers. These are the type used by Exchange Server 2010 servers.

- ▶ **Client authentication**—These certificates are used to provide client authentication to servers or server-side services.

- ▶ **Secure email**—Utilizing these certificates, users can digitally sign and encrypt email messages. These are the type used by Outlook clients.

- ▶ **Encrypting File System**—These certificates are used to encrypt and decrypt files using EFS.

- ▶ **File recovery**—These certificates are used for recovering encrypted EFS files.

- ▶ **Code signing**—These certificates can sign content and applications. Code signing certificates help users and services verify the validity of code.

Manual Encrypted Communications Using Outlook

Specific to this chapter, encryption is used for email communications to allow users to send and receive secured communications. An encryption system is built in to Exchange Server that allows users within an Exchange Server environment to send email messages to other users within their Exchange Server environment in an encrypted manner. The problem with the default encryption in Exchange Server is that it does not provide encryption outside of the company's Exchange Server environment. So, most organizations do not use the built-in email encryption in Exchange Server, but rather use a more standard method of encrypted communications built on the PKI standard.

You have several methods of providing encrypted communications between users within and external to a Microsoft Exchange Server and Outlook email system. Users can each get a certificate from an organization such as VeriSign and perform encrypted communications. Or, an organization can purchase an enterprise license of Pretty Good Privacy (PGP) that provides encryption between users and organizations also using PGP email security. In this example, the use of individual VeriSign certificates is noted.

In this case, a user who wants to encrypt messages between himself and someone else needs to get an individual email certificate and install that certificate in his Microsoft Outlook email client software. In this example using VeriSign, the user would go to www. verisign.com/authentication/individual-authentication/digital-id/index.html and for approximately $20 per year, both individuals wanting to conduct secured communications can purchase a certificate. The individuals share the public portion of their certificates with the other individuals and they can now send encrypted messages back and forth.

To acquire a certificate, do the following:

1. Go to a certificate provider such as VeriSign, and sign up and purchase a digital ID: www.verisign.com/authentication/individual-authentication/digital-id/index.html.

2. Follow the instructions to download and install the certificate in your Outlook client.

3. Have the individual you want to communicate with do the same.

This process of purchasing, downloading, and installing a certificate needs to be done only once per year.

> **NOTE**
>
> If you use multiple computers, you need to install the certificate on each machine on which you run the Outlook client to be able to send and receive encrypted email messages.

After you have downloaded and installed the certificate on your computer, you need to configure Outlook to support the certificate. To do so, do the following:

1. Launch Outlook.

2. For Outlook 2003 and earlier, choose Tools, Options, and then click the Security tab. For Outlook 2007, choose Tools, Trust Center, and then click Email Security.

3. Click the Settings button.

4. In the Security Settings Name text box, type `Email Encryption`. Using the Cryptographic Format list arrow, choose S/MIME. Check the Default Security Setting for This Cryptographic Message Format and the Default Security Settings for all Cryptographic Messages check boxes.

5. Next to the Signing Certificate box, click Choose.

6. From the Select Certificate page, select the certificate that was previously installed and click OK.

7. Using the Hash Algorithm list arrow, choose SHA1. Using the Encryption Algorithm list arrow, choose 3DES.

8. Check the Send These Certificates with Signed Messages check box.

9. The settings should look similar to the ones shown in Figure 12.1. Click OK to apply these settings, and then click OK again.

FIGURE 12.1   Configuring Microsoft Outlook to support encryption certificates.

The Outlook client is now ready to send signed and encrypted emails. Individual users, depending on how computer savvy they are, might have difficulties signing up, downloading, and installing the certificate, and then configuring Outlook to send emails. In addition, because the certificates are individual based, *each* individual user has to do this process themselves every year and for every system on which they conduct email communications.

This process can be completely automated and transparent to the user with a little administrative work. As you will see in the section "Implementing Secured Email Communications with Exchange Server 2010," the issuance of certificates and the configuration of the user's Outlook client can be completed automatically using autoenrollment of certificates as well as using Group Policy Objects in Windows Server 2003 Active Directory.

Installing a Windows Certification Authority Server

The manual processes noted in the previous section showed what is involved in manually enabling security in a Windows and Exchange Server environment. Beyond the complexity for users having to perform critical system tasks to enable and access secured information, the security provided by these manual methods is not even that good. A simple compromise of a shared key can invalidate the security of files, access systems, and secured communications. The better method is to use a certificate-based security system using encryption to provide a significantly higher level of security. In addition, by automating the process, users do not have to be involved in the encryption, transport, or communications between their laptop or desktop, and the network.

This section covers the creation of a certification authority (CA) server system that issues certificates and the process known as autoenrollment of certificates that automatically issues certificates to users and computers in a Windows Server 2003 or Windows Server 2008 Active Directory environment.

> **NOTE**
>
> This section assumes that you have a Windows Server 2008 system that has been fully patched with the latest Windows Server 2008 service pack and updates, and that the server is connected to a Windows Server 2008 Active Directory network. If you are creating this system in a limited lab environment, the certificate server can be added on the same server system as the global catalog server so that a single domain controller and certificate server can be used.

Adding Certificate Services to a Server

Certificate Services is the Windows service that issues, maintains, validates, and revokes certificates to users and computers. It is installed as a Windows Server 2008 role or a Windows 2003 service. In Windows Server 2008, the role is named Active Directory Certificate Services (AD CS).

To install the AD CS role on a Windows Server 2008 system, do the following:

1. On the Windows Server 2008 server that will become your certificate server, launch Server Manager.
2. Right-click on the Roles node and select Add Roles.
3. Click Next.
4. At the Select Server Roles screen, check the Active Directory Certificate Service role and click Next.
5. At the splash screen explaining the AD CS role, click Next.
6. At the Select Role Service screen, check the Certification Authority Web Enrollment service. This allows the CA to issue certificates via the web interface.
7. When you check the box, the wizard automatically checks for the required Roles and Features needed to support web enrollment. If prompted, click the Add Required Role Services button to add the missing roles and features.

8. Click Next to leave the Select Role Services screen.

9. At the Specify Setup Type, choose Enterprise and click Next. This integrates the CA with Active Directory and allows certificates to be issued automatically to domain members.

10. Because this is the first CA in the PKI, at the Specify CA Type screen, select Root CA and click Next.

11. Leave the Create a New Private Key selected and click Next.

12. At the Configure Cryptography for CA screen, leave the defaults and click Next.

13. At the Configure CA Name screen, the name of the CA has been prepopulated, as shown in Figure 12.2. This is composed of the domain and the server name. Adjust if needed and click Next.

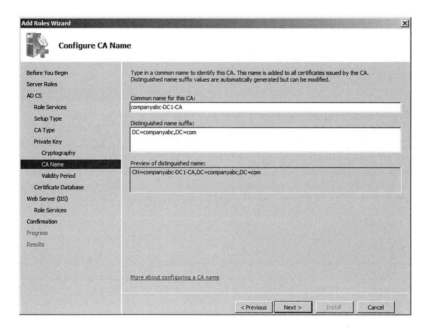

FIGURE 12.2   CA Identifying Information settings.

14. At the Set Validity Period, the default period is 5 years. This is the expiration of the CA and hence the limit on the certificates that the CA can issue. Adjust if needed and click Next.

15. At the Configure Certificate Database, click Next.

16. If any additional roles or features are needed, the wizard steps you through configuring the options for those.

17. At the Confirm Installation Selections screen, review the selections and click Install. The installation proceeds.

18. At the Installation Results screen, confirm that the installation succeeded and click
    Close.

The server is now installed and integrated with Active Directory; all domain members
trust it, and it's ready to issue X.509 certificates.

Server Certificates in Exchange Server 2010

Exchange Server 2010 uses certificates extensively to protect the confidentiality and
integrity of communications. Certificates facilitate the use of industry-standard SSL and
TLS protocols to secure communications by Exchange Server in a flexible manner using
Open Standards. These protocols are native to the Internet as well, allowing easy transition and transport of services over the Internet and intranet.

Components Using Certificates

Key Exchange Server 2010 server components use certificates to authenticate and to
encrypt communications. Components that use certificates include the following:

► **SMTP**—The SMTP component in Exchange Server 2010 uses certificates to encrypt
  and authenticate SMTP traffic between Hub Transport servers and Edge Transport
  servers, between partner organizations, and for opportunistic TLS.

► **EdgeSync Synchronization**—Certificates encrypt the LDAP communications
  between the Hub Transport and Edge Transport servers.

► **Unified Messaging**—Certificates encrypt the SMTP traffic from the UM server to
  the Hub Transport servers, IP gateways, and Office Communications servers (OCS).

► **Autodiscover**—The HTTPS traffic between the CAS and the client are encrypted
  with certificates.

► **POP3/IMAP4**—The Post Office Protocol Version 3 (POP3) and the Internet Message
  Access Protocol Version 4 (IMAP4) protocols are encrypted and authenticated with
  certificates via SSL and TLS to improve the security.

► **Outlook Anywhere**—Certificates are used to secure the Outlook Anywhere HTTP
  communications from the CAS to the client.

► **Outlook Web App**—Certificates secure the Outlook Web App HTTP communications from the CAS to the client.

► **ActiveSync**—Certificates secure the Exchange ActiveSync HTTP communications
  from the CAS to the client.

Many of these services are client-facing, and all the services can be externally facing as
well, creating potential risks to the confidentiality of the services. Certificates enable the
services to be protected with advanced encryption to ensure their privacy.

Self-Signed Versus Public Versus Private Certificates

The difference between self-signed, public, and private certificates is simply where they are issued from. If issued and signed by the owner of the certificate, they are self-signed certificates. If issued by a public CA, they are public certificates. If issued by a private CA, they are private certificates. The difference is all in the level of trust that third parties can place in the certificates.

Public certificates are the gold standard of certificates. The public CAs that issue these certificates are trusted by most operating systems and browsers, which means they trust the certificates issued by the CAs. Examples of public CAs include VeriSign, Thawte, and Digicert. Using a public certificate is easy, but a cost is charged by the public CA for the certificate. Because certificates have expiration dates, this is a recurring cost that the public CAs charge every time the certificate is renewed.

Private certificates are issued by private CAs. A private CA can be created on a number of platforms, including Windows Server 2003 and Windows Server 2008. Certificates issued by these private CAs have no cost. However, these private CAs are not trusted by default by the operating systems and browsers, so the certificates issued by these private CAs are not trusted either. This can lead to annoying pop-up warnings or even failed applications. These can be circumvented by adding the private CA to the list of trusted CAs on the specific computers and deploying a Public Key Infrastructure (PKI). There is typically significant administrative overhead associated with maintaining a private CA.

Self-signed certificates are issued by the computer using the certificate. This is useful because it does not require any additional PKI infrastructure, and the computer can maintain its own certificate. This enables an application such as Exchange Server 2010 to reap the benefits of certificates on installation without having to go through the additional configuration steps to acquire a certificate from a CA. And there is no cost or infrastructure requirement. However, this is the least trusted and least secure of certificates because there is no third-party, public or private, vouching for the certificate.

The server components covered in the previous section all install by default in a protected mode (that is, using SSL/TLS) using self-signed certificates. These default self-signed certificates can be replaced as needed.

Choosing Certificates in Exchange Server 2010

Exchange Server 2010 can use any of the three types of X.509 certificates to encrypt a communication channel. However, how the other end of the communications channel views the certificate that is presented by Exchange Server 2010 is a major factor in which type to use. When the two end points, for example, the Exchange Server 2010 server and a client, negotiate the security of the communications channel, the Exchange Server 2010 certificate is presented to the client. If the client does not trust the CA that issued the Exchange Server 2010 certificate, the communications might fail or the user is prompted with a warning.

By default, Exchange Server 2010 issues self-signed certificates on installation. Self-signed certificates can be used for external communications but are not recommended on a long-term basis. Self-signed certificates are the best option for internal communications, such as for Unified Messaging or EdgeSync services.

It is recommended to use self-signed certificates for internal communications, which are the following:

▶ Between Hub Transport servers

▶ Between Hub Transport and Edge Transport servers

▶ EdgeSync communications

▶ For Unified Messaging communications

▶ Internal-only client access servers

NOTE

Self-signed certificates that are created by Exchange Server expire in one year. The internal components that rely on the default self-signed certificates continue to operate even if the self-signed certificates have expired. However, when the self-signed certificates have expired, events are logged in Event Viewer. It is a best practice to renew the self-signed certificates before they expire.

Public certificates typically have a cost associated with their use but are trusted by all the communication channel endpoints like the clients. This ensures that when the Exchange Server 2010 presents a public certificate during the negotiation of the communications channel, the client accepts it without question.

It is recommended to use public certificates for external client access communications, which are the following:

▶ POP3 and IMAP4

▶ Outlook Web App

▶ Outlook Anywhere

▶ Exchange ActiveSync

▶ Autodiscover

Using public certificates enables users to access services from a wide array of locations such as home systems, Internet kiosks, and other companies' systems without any certificate issues due to the ubiquitous trust of public CAs, such as VeriSign.

Private certificates fall into an interesting area for Exchange Server 2010. Public certificates are identical to private certificates, except that the clients must be configured to trust the issuing CA. This means inserting the private CA certificate into the client's Trusted

Certificate Authority container. When this is done, the client trusts all certificates issues by the private CA just as if it were a public CA.

Using private certificates enables administrators to forego the cost of public certificates with some administrative effort. This is most effective if users access the Exchange Server 2010 services from relatively few locations in which there is a measure of administrative control, such as mobile domain members or home systems. Domain members automatically trust an Enterprise CA via Active Directory, so no configuration is needed. The home users can be given instructions or scripts that configure the home systems to trust the private CA. This is not effective with locations such as Internet kiosks in which the users have no local control.

Names in Certificates

Certificates certify the identity of something, also known as the subject. For users, this is their name and their email address. For Exchange Server 2010 servers, the subject is the server name. In an X.509 certificate, the Subject field contains the identity in the format CN = <subject name>. For example, the Exchange Server 2010 EX1 server self-issued certificate will have CN = EX1 in the Subject field. A user named Chris Amaris from Company ABC might have an autoenrolled certificate with CN = Chris Amaris and E = chrisa@companyabc.com to designate the email address of the subject. Note that the Subject field can contain only one CN reference.

However, multiple DNS names for a single server can be quite common; owa.companyabc.com, autodiscover.companyabc.com, smtp.companyabc.com, and imap.companyabc.com might all reference different services on an Exchange 2010 server supporting Hub Transport and Client Access Server roles. Or even that a server might be referenced by its NetBIOS name (for example, EX1) or by its fully qualified domain name (for example, EX1.companyabc.com). When a receiving application examines the certificate to verify the identity of the server, it might not find the name for the server in the certificate Subject field and fails authentication. These naming dichotomies cannot be represented with only the Subject name.

To address this, there are three name types of X.509 certificates:

▶ Single name certificates

▶ Subject alternative name certificates

▶ Wildcard certificates

These certificates are the same X.509 certificates but have different fields within the certificate populated in different ways. Public CAs charge different amounts depending on how the fields are populated. And some Private CAs and some Public CAs won't issue certain types of certificates. Operating systems and applications might or might not support all usages of these certificates, so care must be taken in how they are deployed.

Single name certificates contain only one subject name in the Subject field and are the default certificate name type. All certificates must contain at least one name. These certificates are supported by all platforms and applications.

Subject Alternative Name certificates (SAN certificates) have one or more names in the
Subject Alternative Name field of the X.509 certificate, typically in the format DNS
Name=<subject name>. When examining the certificate, the receiving application matches
names in both the Subject field and in the Subject Alternative Name field. Exchange
Server 2010 issues self-signed SAN certificates by default. For example, the Exchange Server
2010 EX1 server self-issued certificate is a SAN certificate and will have CN = EX1 in the
Subject field, and DNS Name=EX1 and DNS Name=EX1.companyabc.com in the Subject
Alternative Name field. SAN certificates are supported by most modern public CAs, operating systems, and applications.

Rather than adding each subject name into the SAN field of the certificate, it is convenient to have the certificate represent all potential subject names. This simplifies configuration and avoids the need to reissue certificates if additional names are added later.
Wildcard certificates use the asterisk character (*) to designate all possible subject names
rather than list the names specifically. For example, rather than specifying EX1 and
EX1.companyabc.com, the certificate is issued to the wildcard subject name *.compa-
nyabc.com and matches to both names (and any other host in companyabc.com!).
Wildcard certificate support is being adopted slowly by operating systems, clients, and
applications. There is no common agreement on how to match wildcard certificates to
names, which is hindering the progress on adoption.

Wildcard certificates are supported by Exchange Server 2010, Outlook, Outlook Anywhere,
and Outlook Web App. Windows Mobile 5.0 (Exchange ActiveSync) does not support wildcard certificates.

However, special configuration is sometimes needed on the Exchange Server 2010 server
to support wildcard certificates. For example, if wildcard certificates are used on an
Exchange Server 2010 CAS server, the set-OutlookProvider cmdlet must be run to enable
the Autodiscover service to function properly. The command for Company ABC using a
wildcard certificate would be set-OutlookProvider –Identity EXPR –CertPrincipalName
msstd:*companyabc.com.

To illustrate the emerging support for wildcard certificates, Outlook 2007 does not support
wildcard certificates out of the box and receives a certificate error when accessing an
Exchange Server 2010 CAS server that's configured with a wildcard certificate. Special
configuration is required to make it work. To configure Outlook 2007 to support a wildcard
certificate issue to companyabc.com, execute the following on the Outlook 2007 client:

1. In Outlook 2007, on the Tools menu, click Account Settings.

2. Select the Microsoft Exchange Account Name and then click Change.

3. Click the More Settings button.

4. Select the Connection tab and click the Exchange Proxy Settings button.

5. Select the Connect Using SSL Only check box.

6. Select the Only Connect to Proxy Servers That Have This Principal Name in Their
   Certificate check box, and then in the box that follows, enter
   msstd:*.companyabc.com.

7. Click OK twice.

8. Click Next.

9. Click Finish.

10. Click Close.

Close Outlook and open it again to have the setting take effect. The certificate error will no longer be present.

In general, choosing SAN certificates is the safest and most widely supported certificate name type. Wildcard certificates are a good option if the public CA supports them and additional configuration and testing time is allocated.

Implementing Secured Email Communications with Exchange Server 2010

Encrypted email communications can be sent by manually configuring certificates, or by enabling the autoenrollment of certificates for emails that are issued to users via Group Policy. Email encryption can be automated to the point where users are effectively issued certificates, the certificates are automatically installed, and the user can immediately begin to send and receive messages using encrypted communications.

If you have completed the following steps for the autoenrollment of certificates for a user, the certificate will automatically work for Exchange Outlook encryption.

Note that Exchange Server 2010 provides opportunistic TLS encryption, which essentially means that the Exchange Server 2010 servers encrypt mail with outside organizations if possible. The requirement is that the outside organization supports the STARTTLS command. This is described in RFC 3207, "SMTP Service Extension for Secure SMTP over TLS," and is supported by a number of mail systems in addition to Exchange Server 2010. This encrypts only email between the servers, leaving the messages in the users' inboxes unencrypted. This protects the confidentiality of the email while traveling over the Internet.

> **NOTE**
>
> Opportunistic TLS encryption and the support for the STARTTLS command have been a huge leap forward in the security of intercompany email communications. In the past, most communications between companies were sent in clear-text and completely unprotected, unless the companies spent considerable time and effort to coordinate to secure their email communications. Now, it just happens automatically using the STARTTLS command.

Opportunistic TLS does not protect the confidentiality of the email while it is traveling from the user's desktop to the server, while stored on the server, or when traveling from the receiving user's server to their desktop. Also, there is no guarantee that the email will be encrypted if the opportunistic TLS fails because the email is then transmitted unencrypted. To ensure that the email is truly secure end-to-end during the transmissions and storage, the following procedures must be followed.

Configuring Exchange Server User Certificates Using Autoenrollment

After Certificate Services has been installed on the system, the administrator of the network can issue certificates to users and computers. However, rather than manually generating and issuing certificates, the best practice is to have the certificate server automatically issue certificates to users and computers in Active Directory. This is known as autoenrollment of certificates.

Autoenrollment of certificates requires the following processes to be followed:

1. A certificate template needs to be created.
2. The template needs to be added to the certificate of authority server.
3. A group policy needs to be created to automatically deploy the certificate to the user or computer.

With autoenrollment of certificates, rules are created that define which certificates should be issued to a user or computer. As an example, a rule can be created to create the autoenrollment of a certificate that allows a user to have his certificates automatically created for the encryption of data files. With autoenrollment of encrypted files, the user can simply save files to a shared location, and the files stored in the location will be encrypted.

To have certificates automatically installed for the Exchange Server users in Active Directory, do the following:

1. On the certificate server you just created, launch the Certificate Template Microsoft Management Console (MMC) by clicking Start, Run, typing `mmc.exe` in the Open text box, and then clicking OK.
2. Click File and click Add/Remove Snap-in.
3. Select Certificate Templates and then click Add.
4. Click OK.
5. Click the Certificate Templates folder.
6. Right-click the Exchange User template, select Duplicate Template and click OK.
7. Select the desired certificate and authority version for the template.
8. In the Template Display Name text box, type `AutoEnroll Exchange User`.
9. Make sure the Publish Certificate in Active Directory and the Do Not Automatically Reenroll if a Duplicate Certificate Exists in Active Directory check boxes are both checked. The screen should look similar to Figure 12.3.
10. Select the Subject Name tab.
11. Select the Build from this Active Directory Information and select Subject Name format as the Common name. Check the Include E-Mail Name in the Subject name and E-mail name boxes.
12. Click the Request Handling tab.

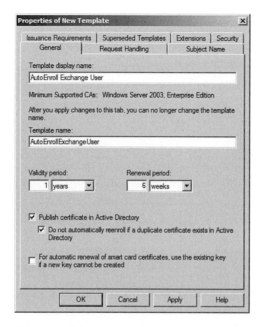

FIGURE 12.3   Creating an AutoEnroll Exchange User template.

13. In the Purpose pull-down, select Signature and encryption.
14. Click the Security tab.
15. Highlight the Authenticated Users name and select the check boxes in the Allow column for the Read, Enroll, and Autoenroll permissions for the Authenticated Users.
16. Click OK.

Adding the Template to the Certificate Server

After an autoenroll Exchange Server user template has been created, the template needs to be added to the certificate server and distributed to users. You can do this by completing the following steps:

1. Launch the Certification Authority Microsoft Management Console (MMC) by clicking Start, Administrative Tools, and then Certification Authority.
2. Expand the Certification Authority folder.
3. Expand the folder for your certificate server.
4. Right-click the Certificate Templates folder, and select New, Certificate Template to Issue.
5. Highlight the AutoEnroll Exchange User template, and then click OK.

NOTE

This step of adding the AutoEnroll Exchange User template you created earlier adds this new template to the certificate server. The AutoEnroll User template allows user certificates to be issued automatically through Group Policy.

Creating a Group Policy to Distribute User Certificates

The next step for autoenrollment is to create a group policy that can then distribute certificates to the users' laptops and desktops automatically. This is done by creating a group policy and having the group policy distribute the certificates created in the previous step. To create this group policy, do the following:

1. Launch the Server Manager and expand the Features, Group Policy Management, Forest, and then Domains.

2. Right-click the domain name of the network (such as companyabc.com), and choose Create a GPO in This Domain, and Link It Here.

3. Enter the name Exchange AutoEnrollment Group Policy Object and click OK.

4. Select the domain and in the right pane, right-click the new GPO and select Edit.

5. Under the User Configuration container, expand the Policies, Windows Settings folder.

6. Expand the Security Settings folder and then click to select the Public Key Policies folder. You see an Object Type named Certificate Services Client - Auto-Enrollment Settings, as shown in Figure 12.4.

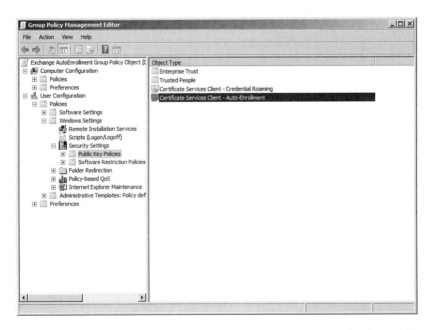

FIGURE 12.4   Expanding folders to access the Autoenrollment Settings object.

7. Right-click the Certificate Services Client - Auto-Enrollment object, and select Properties on the shortcut menu.

8. If needed, set the Configuration Model to Enabled.

9. Check the Renew Expired Certificates, Update Pending Certificates, and Remove Revoked Certificates check boxes and check the Update Certificates That Use Certificate Templates check box. Then click OK.

Validating That Certificates Are Working Properly

The autoenrollment of user certificates has now been configured for all users who log on to the domain. To validate that certificates are working properly, do the following:

1. From a Windows workstation, log on to the domain.

2. Launch the Certificates Microsoft Management Console (MMC) by clicking Start, Run, typing mmc.exe in the Open text box, and then clicking OK.

3. Click File, Add/Remove Snap-in, select the Certificates snap-in, and then click Add.

4. Assuming you logged on as the user for whom you want to verify that certificates are working, choose My User Account, and then click Finish.

5. Click OK.

6. Expand the Certificates – Current User folder.

7. Expand the Personal folder and click to highlight the Certificates folder.

8. You should have a Secure Email certificate created by the Autoenroll Exchange User certificate template, as shown in Figure 12.5.

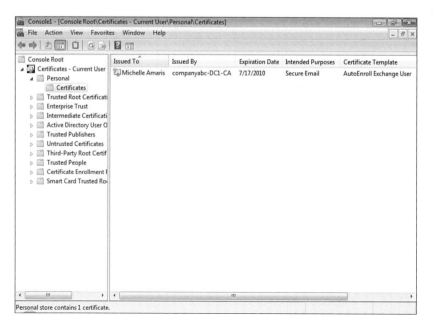

FIGURE 12.5   Exchange Server user certificate added to the user's Certificates folder.

If the Exchange Server user certificate has not pushed to the user's Certificates container, you can easily add the certificate by doing the following:

1. From a Windows workstation, log on to the domain.
2. Launch the Certificates Microsoft Management Console (MMC) by clicking Start, Run, typing `mmc.exe` in the Open text box, and then clicking OK.
3. Click File, Add/Remove Snap-in, select the Certificates snap-in, and then click Add.
4. Assuming you logged on as the user for whom you want to verify that certificates are working, choose My User Account, and then click Finish.
5. Click OK.
6. Right click the Certificates – Current User folder, choose All Tasks, Automatically Enroll and Retrieve Certificates, and then click Next to begin the wizard.
7. Click Next at the Before You Begin screen.
8. Highlight AutoEnroll Exchange User, and then click Next.
9. Click Next to accept the defaults on the Friendly Name and Description page.
10. Click Finish.

Using Outlook to Send and Receive Digitally Signed and Encrypted Emails

After the Windows Server 2008 and Exchange Server 2010 environments have been set up to support a certificate-based infrastructure, the next step is to launch the Outlook client to confirm that certificates are working in the environment, and to then send and receive digitally signed and encrypted messages.

When discussing email security, you need to consider two primary questions:

▶ How do you know the message truly came from the suspected source?

▶ How do you know the message has not been intercepted or tampered with?

Both of these questions can be answered by the use of digital signatures and encryption. Digital signatures provide authentication, nonrepudiation, and data integrity, whereas encryption keeps message contents confidential.

In an Exchange Server environment, both of these solutions can be provided by using Secure/Multipurpose Internet Mail Extensions (S/MIME).

Utilizing S/MIME with Outlook 2003 or Outlook 2007 allows you to do the following:

▶ Digitally sign a message to prove the identity of the sender—S/MIME is the only option supported in Outlook 2007 to digitally sign a message. Although a message protected with Information Rights Management (IRM) can prevent a message from being tampered with, IRM protection is more limited because there is no authority to verify the identity of the sender. Furthermore, with IRM, the Outlook user interface does not show information about the identity of the sender like it does when using S/MIME.

▶ Protect messages from unauthorized users—By utilizing encryption, messages are not sent in "clear text." It is possible for attackers to monitor network traffic and intercept network traffic, but by encrypting the message, you can prevent them from gathering usable data. This protection is especially important for email sent over the Internet, as that is where point-to-point encryption is most valuable and where interoperability standards are most important.

Protecting your messages with S/MIME signatures and encryption is primarily used when users send or receive messages outside of your organization's boundaries, as they are no longer protected by the corporate firewall.

Fundamentals of Digital Signatures and Encryption

The primary purpose of S/MIME is to provide digital signatures and encryption. S/MIME is a small subset of PKI, which addresses a much wider array of security-related capabilities. For instance, PKI supports smart cards, Secure Sockets Layer (SSL), user certificates, and much more.

The International Telecommunication Union (ITU), based in Geneva, Switzerland, has a Telecommunication Standardization Sector (ITU-T) that coordinates standards for telecommunications. X.509 is an ITU-T standard for PKI that specifies (among other things) standard formats for public key certificates and a certification path validation algorithm. Originally issued in 1988, this standard has been revised twice over the years, and Version 3 (the current version) defines the format for certificate extensions used to store information regarding the certificate holder and to define certificate usage.

In short, X.509 is a digital certificate standard that defines the format of the actual certificate used by S/MIME.

The certificate identifies information about the certificate's owner and includes the owner's public key information. X.509 is the industry standard digital certificate and is, by far, the most widely used. PKI products such as Microsoft's Certificate Services (included in Windows Server 2008) adhere to this standard and generate X.509 digital certificates to be used with S/MIME-capable clients.

The Signing Process

When a message sender elects to sign a message, a process is completed where a numerical value is calculated based on the number of set bits in the message. Enclosing the numerical value, known as a checksum, with the original message allows the recipient to apply the same formula to the message.

The random checksum acts as the digital signature, sometimes called a digital ID. This signature is then encrypted using the user's private signing key. The user then sends the message to the recipient, and the message has three components: the message in plain text, the sender's X.509 digital certificate, and the digital certificate.

Upon receipt of the message, the recipient checks its certificate revocation list (CRL) to determine if the sender's certificate has been revoked. If it is found on the CRL, the recipient is warned that the sender's certificate has been revoked.

If the certificate is not on the revocation list, the digital signature is decrypted with the sender's public signing key (which is included in the digital certificate). The recipient's client then generates the checksum based on the plain text message and compares it to the digital signature.

If the checksum generated by the recipient does not match the one generated by the sender, the recipient knows that the message has been garbled or tampered with.

The Encryption Process

When a user elects to encrypt a message, the client generates a random bulk encryption key that is used to encrypt the contents of the message. The bulk encryption key is then encrypted using the recipient's public key. This is known as a lockbox. If the message has multiple recipients, individual lockboxes are created, one for each recipient, using his or her own public encryption key. However, the content of each is still the same bulk signing key. This process prevents the client from having to encrypt the message separately for each recipient, while ensuring the contents remain secure.

For this process to work, the sender must have a copy of the recipient's digital certificate. The certificate can be retrieved from either the Global Address List (GAL) or the sender's Contact list. The digital certificate contains the recipient's public encryption key, which is used to create the lockbox for the bulk encryption key.

When the message is received, the recipient uses his or her private encryption key to decrypt the lockbox, exposing the bulk encryption key that was used to encrypt the original message. The bulk encryption key is then used to decrypt the message.

This process sounds complicated, but it is actually very straightforward—the message is encrypted and needs a key to be decrypted. The key is sent with the message, but it is encrypted itself with the recipient's public key—so, only the intended recipient is able to unlock the key and, in turn, unlock the message.

NOTE

For Exchange Server 2003 SP1 and higher, antivirus software using the Virus Scanning API (VSAPI) 2.5 can scan digitally signed or encrypted messages. This includes Exchange Server 2007 and Exchange Server 2010.

Making Sure Outlook Acknowledges the Certificate

After autoenrollment has issued a certificate to the user and the user has confirmed the certificate has been successfully received, you can confirm that Microsoft Outlook recognizes the certificate for encrypted communications. To do so, do the following:

1. Launch Outlook.
2. For Outlook 2003, choose Tools, Options, and then click the Security tab. For Outlook 2007, choose Tools, Trust Center, and then click Email Security.
3. Click the Settings button.

Under Security Settings Name is the email certificate that enables you to send and receive signed and encrypted communications.

4. Click OK and then click OK again to continue.

Outlook automatically detects the correct autoenrolled certificate and configures Outlook to use the certificate for signing and encrypting email.

Sending a Digitally Signed Email

With the email certificate installed, you can now begin the process of sending and receiving encrypted emails. However, to complete the process, you need to communicate with someone who also has a certificate to send and receive encrypted emails. Email encryption requires both the sender and the receiver to have valid certificates.

The easiest process for setting up encrypted email communications is to send a user a digitally signed email with a copy of your public key certificate attached. With a digitally signed email and a copy of your public key, the recipient can then add your certificate to their address book, and then they can reply to the message sending you their public key. After you have exchanged public keys, you can send and receive encrypted emails.

The process for sending a person a digitally signed email with your public key is as follows:

1. Launch Outlook 2007.
2. Create a new email by selecting Actions, New Mail Message.
3. Enter the recipient's email address that you want to communicate with in the To field, and enter a subject such as "Initial Email for Secured Communications."
4. For the body of the message, you might want to enter text such as "Here is an email message that will help us initiate secured communications. I am attaching a copy of my certificate for you to install; please reply to the message with a copy of your certificate."

> **NOTE**
>
> Writing a message in the body of the email might not be necessary; however, in this day and age of spam filters, if you just send a message with your digital signature and an attachment of your public key, the message will frequently be quarantined in the recipient's spam filter. So, it is best to write a few words describing what you are doing as part of the message.

5. On the Options tab at the top of the page, select Sign and ensure that it is highlighted. To see what settings this affects, you can click the arrow at the bottom of the Options box, and then click the Security Settings button.
6. The Add Digital Signature to This Message and Send This Message as Clear Text Signed check boxes should already be selected, as shown in Figure 12.6.

FIGURE 12.6   Security properties for sending an initial secured message.

7. After selecting the Change Settings button, you should see that the Send These Certificates with Signed Messages check box is already selected. If it is not, select the box so that your certificate is sent with the message, and then click OK.

8. Click OK and then click Close.

9. Click Send to send the message.

Your message will now be sent to the recipient with a copy of your key in a digitally signed email message. When the recipient opens the message, an error will likely appear that says "There are problems with the signature. Click the signature button for details," as shown in Figure 12.7. This message is because the certificate being received is from a domain with which they have not communicated in a secured or encrypted manner in the past.

After confirming that you indeed sent the message and deciding to trust your certificate, the recipient should do the following:

1. Click on the yellow warning icon on the right side of the email message; a warning dialog box opens, as shown in Figure 12.8.

2. Because you (the recipient) have confirmed the validity of the sender, click Trust.

3. A message box opens that warns and prompts that the recipient is trusting the sender. Click Yes to accept the trust.

4. Close and reopen the email. The error no longer appears, and the digital signature is confirmed.

Your certificate has now been installed on the recipient's system; they now need to send you their certificate so you can follow the exact same procedures to install their certificate on your system. They should follow the procedure described in "Sending a Digitally Signed Email" with you accepting their message and trusting their certificate.

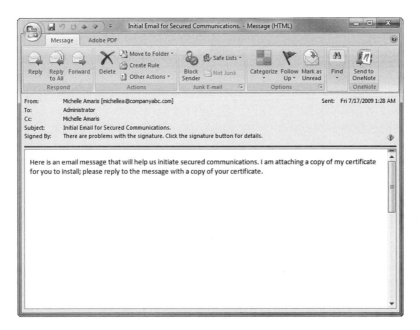

FIGURE 12.7   Initial receipt of a digitally signed but not trusted message.

FIGURE 12.8   Certificate Authority Information warning dialog box.

Sending Encrypted Email Messages

After you have exchanged certificates, you can now send and receive fully encrypted email messages with another individual. To do so, complete the following steps:

1. Launch Outlook 2007.

2. Create a new email by selecting Actions, New Mail Message.

3. Enter the recipient's email address in the To field, and enter a subject such as "Encrypted Email Message."

4. For the body of the message, you might want to enter text such as "Here is an email message that should now be encrypted. Please let me know if you successfully receive this message."

5. On the Options tab at the top of the page, select Encrypt and ensure that it is highlighted. To see what settings this affects, you can click the arrow at the bottom of the Options box, and then click the Security Settings button.

6. The Encrypt Message Contents and Attachments check box should be selected. Click OK, and then click Close.

7. Click Send to send the message.

The recipient will receive an encrypted copy of your message. This process not only works within Microsoft Outlook within an organization, but also works the same way when you want to send and receive encrypted messages to individuals outside of your organization. If the recipient is also running Outlook 2007 or Outlook 2003, the process to install your certificate into their address book is the same as described previously. If the recipient is using a different email system, they might need to detach the certificate, save it, and manually save the certificate into their address book.

Summary

The goal of this chapter was to provide step-by-step procedures that can be followed for the creation of a certificate server, creating the appropriate templates and certificates for users, and having certificates automatically issued to users and computers so that a certificate-based encryption system can be easily implemented in an environment.

When implementing security features in a network environment, it is important to look beyond the security of the computers alone. The data that travels between these computers is often more vulnerable than the data stored on the computers themselves. By implementing security methods such as certificate-based encryption to protect the information contained in the emails, administrators are taking one more step toward a well-rounded security solution.

Best Practices

The following are best practices from this chapter:

▶ Implement a Public Key Infrastructure solution within your environment that meets your organization's security needs.

▶ For environments requiring additional security measures, consider implementing smart cards to use in addition to ordinary network passwords.

▶ Set up autoenrollment of certificates on Windows Server 2003 and Windows Server 2008 to automatically generate certificates for users who have an Active Directory user account.

▶ Use group policies to push certificates to users to minimize the administrative overhead of having users manually download certificates and install the certificates in their Outlook application themselves.

▶ Utilize digital signatures and encryption in your messaging environment by implementing S/MIME for your Outlook 2003 and Outlook 2007 clients.

▶ Use public certificates for client-facing components.

▶ Use self-signed certificates for internally facing components.

CHAPTER 13

Securing Exchange Server 2010 with ISA Server

In today's risk-fraught computing environment, any exposed service is subject to frequent attack from the Internet. This is particularly true for web services, including those offered by Outlook Web App (OWA), Exchange ActiveSync, and Outlook Anywhere. Exploits using the Hypertext Transfer Protocol (HTTP) that these services use are becoming very commonplace, and it is not considered best practice to make an Exchange Client Access server (CAS) directly accessible via the Internet.

Fortunately, the productivity gains of OWA/ActiveSync can still be utilized and made more accessible by securing them behind a reverse-proxy server, such as Microsoft Internet Security and Acceleration (ISA) Server 2006. ISA Server allows for advanced application-layer filtering of network traffic, greatly securing the overall SharePoint environment. In addition, ISA Server supports deployment models in the demilitarized zone (DMZ) of existing firewalls, giving organizations the ability to deploy advanced application-layer filtering for OWA without reconfiguring existing security infrastructure.

This chapter details the ways that Exchange Server services can be secured using the ISA Server 2006 product. Deployment scenarios for securing Exchange Server-related services with ISA are outlined, and specific step-by-step guides are illustrated.

Understanding the Internet Security and Acceleration (ISA) Server 2006

The rise in the prevalence of computer viruses, threats, and exploits on the Internet has made it necessary for organizations of all shapes and sizes to reevaluate their protection strategies for Edge Services such as SharePoint Portal Server. No longer is it possible to ignore or minimize these threats as the damage they can cause can cripple a company's business functions. A solution to the increased sophistication and pervasiveness of these viruses and exploits is becoming increasingly necessary.

Corresponding with the growth of these threats has been the development and maturation of the Internet Security and Acceleration (ISA) Server product from Microsoft. The latest release of the product, ISA Server 2006, is fast becoming a business-critical component of many organizations, which are finding that many of the traditional packet-filtering firewalls and technologies don't necessarily stand up to the modern threats of today. The ISA Server 2006 product provides for that higher level of application security required, particularly for common tools such as Exchange OWA and related services.

> **NOTE**
>
> The next version of ISA Server that will be made available was not yet released at the time of this printing. This next version will be known as Threat Management Gateway (TMG). TMG has many of the fundamental application layer inspection capabilities as ISA Server 2006 but also includes Windows 2008 support, 64-bit capabilities, and improved publishing wizards, among other things. When released, it will be the preferred application layer inspection software for Exchange Server 2010.

Outlining the Need for ISA Server 2006 in Exchange Server Environments

A great deal of confusion exists about the role that ISA Server can play in an Exchange Server environment. Much of that confusion stems from the misconception that ISA Server is only a proxy server. ISA Server 2006 is, on the contrary, a fully functional firewall, virtual private network (VPN), web caching proxy, and application reverse-proxy solution. In addition, ISA Server 2006 addresses specific business needs to provide a secured infrastructure and improve productivity through the proper application of its built-in functionality. Determining how these features can help to improve the security and productivity of an Exchange Server environment is, therefore, of key importance.

In addition to the built-in functionality available within ISA Server 2006, a whole host of third-party integration solutions provide additional levels of security and functionality. Enhanced intrusion detection support, content filtering, web surfing restriction tools, and customized application filters all extend the capabilities of ISA Server and position it as a solution to a wide variety of security needs within organizations of many sizes.

Outlining the High Cost of Security Breaches

It is rare when a week goes by without a high-profile security breach, denial of service (DoS) attack, exploit, virus, or worm appearing in the news. The risks inherent in modern computing have been increasing exponentially, and effective countermeasures are required in any organization that expects to do business across the Internet.

It has become impossible to turn a blind eye toward these security threats. On the contrary, even organizations that would normally not be obvious candidates for attack from the Internet must secure their services as the vast majority of modern attacks do not focus on any one particular target, but sweep the Internet for any destination host, looking for vulnerabilities to exploit. Infection or exploitation of critical business infra-structure can be extremely costly for an organization. Many of the productivity gains in business recently have been attributed to advances in information technology (IT) func-tionality, including Exchange Server-related gains, and the loss of this functionality can severely impact the bottom line.

In addition to productivity losses, the legal environment for businesses has changed significantly in recent years. Regulations such as Sarbanes Oxley (SOX), HIPAA, and Gramm-Leach-Bliley have changed the playing field by requiring a certain level of security and validation of private customer data. Organizations can now be sued or fined for substantial sums if proper security precautions are not taken to protect client data. The atmosphere surrounding these concerns provides the backdrop for the evolution and acceptance of the ISA Server 2006 product.

Outlining the Critical Role of Firewall Technology in a Modern Connected Infrastructure

It is widely understood today that valuable corporate assets such as Exchange OWA cannot be exposed to direct access to the world's users on the Internet. In the beginning, however, the Internet was built on the concept that all connected networks could be trusted. It was not originally designed to provide robust security between networks, so security concepts needed to be developed to secure access between entities on the Internet. Special devices known as firewalls were created to block access to internal network resources for specific companies.

Originally, many organizations were not directly connected to the Internet. Often, even when a connection was created, there was no type of firewall put into place as the percep-tion was that only government or high-security organizations required protection.

With the explosion of viruses, hacking attempts, and worms that began to proliferate, organizations soon began to understand that some type of firewall solution was required to block access to specific, dangerous Transmission Control Protocol (TCP) or User Datagram Protocol (UDP) ports that were used by the Internet's TCP/IP protocol. This type of firewall technology would inspect each arriving packet and accept or reject it based on the TCP or UDP port specified in the packet of information received.

Some of these firewalls were ASIC-based firewalls, which employed the use of solid-state microchips, with built-in packet-filtering technology. These firewalls, many of which are still used and deployed today, provided organizations with a quick-and-dirty way to filter Internet traffic, but did not allow for a high degree of customization because of their static nature.

The development of software-based firewalls coincided with the need for simpler management interfaces and the ability to make software changes to firewalls quickly and easily. The most popular firewall in organizations today, CheckPoint, falls into this category, as do other popular firewalls such as SonicWall and Cisco PIX. ISA Server 2006 was built and developed as a software-based firewall, and provides the same degree of packet-filtering technology that has become a virtual necessity on the Internet today.

More recently, holes in the capabilities of simple packet-based filtering technology has made a more sophisticated approach to filtering traffic for malicious or spurious content a necessity. ISA Server 2006 responds to these needs with the capabilities to perform application-layer filtering on Internet traffic.

Understanding the Growing Need for Application-Layer Filtering

Nearly all organizations with a presence on the Internet have put some type of packet-filtering firewall technology into place to protect the internal network resources from attack. These types of packet-filtering firewall technologies were useful in blocking specific types of network traffic, such as vulnerabilities that utilize the remote procedure calls (RPC) protocol, by simply blocking TCP and UDP ports that the RPC protocol would use. Other ports, on the other hand, were often left wide open to support certain functionality, such as the TCP 80 port, utilized for HTTP web browsing and for access to OWA/ActiveSync. As previously mentioned, a packet-filtering firewall is only able to inspect the header of a packet, simply understanding which port the data is meant to utilize, but is unable to actually read the content. A good analogy to this is if a border guard was instructed to only allow citizens with specific passports to enter the country, but had no way to inspect their luggage for contraband or illegal substances.

The problem that is becoming more evident, however, is that the viruses, exploits, and attacks have adjusted to conform to this new landscape, and have started to realize that they can conceal the true malicious nature of their payload within the identity of an allowed port. For example, they can "piggyback" their destructive payload over a known "good" port that is open on a packet-filtering firewall. Many modern exploits, viruses, and "scumware," such as illegal file-sharing applications, piggyback off the TCP 80 HTTP port, for example. Using the border guard analogy to illustrate, the smugglers realized that if they put their contraband in the luggage of a citizen from a country on the border guards' allowed list, they could smuggle it into the country without worrying that the guard would inspect the package. These types of exploits and attacks are not uncommon, and the list of known application-layer attacks continues to grow.

In the past, when an organization realized that they had been compromised through their traditional packet-filtering firewall, the knee-jerk reaction was to lock down access from the Internet in response to threats. For example, an exploit that arrives over HTTP port 80 might prompt an organization to completely close access to that port on a temporary or semipermanent basis. This approach can greatly impact productivity because OWA access can be affected. This is especially true in a modern connected infrastructure that relies heavily on communications and collaboration with outside vendors and customers. Traditional security techniques involve a trade-off between security and productivity. The tighter a firewall is locked down, for example, the less functional and productive an end user can be.

In direct response to the need to maintain and increase levels of productivity without compromising security, application-layer stateful inspection capabilities were built into ISA Server that can intelligently determine if particular web traffic is legitimate. To illustrate, ISA Server inspects a packet using TCP port 80 to determine if it is a properly formatted HTTP request. Looking back to the border guard analogy, ISA Server is like a border guard who not only checks the passports, but is also given an X-ray machine to check the luggage of each person crossing the border.

The more sophisticated application-layer attacks become, the greater the need becomes for a security solution that can allow for a greater degree of productivity while reducing the type of risks that can exist in an environment that relies on simple packet-based filtering techniques.

Outlining the Inherent Threat in Exchange Server HTTP Traffic

The Internet provides somewhat of a catch-22 when it comes to its goal and purpose. On one hand, the Internet is designed to allow anywhere, anytime access to information, linking systems around the world together and providing for that information to be freely exchanged. On the other hand, this type of transparency comes with a great deal of risk because it effectively means that any one system can be exposed to every connected computer, either friendly or malicious, in the world.

Often, this inherent risk of compromising systems or information through their exposure to the Internet has led to locking down access to that information with firewalls. Of course, this limits the capabilities and usefulness of a free-information exchange system such as what web traffic provides. Many of the web servers need to be made available to anonymous access by the general public, which causes the dilemma, as organizations need to place that information online without putting the servers it is placed on at undue risk.

Fortunately, ISA Server 2006 provides for robust and capable tools to secure web traffic, making it available for remote access but also securing it against attack and exploit. To understand how it does this, it is first necessary to examine how web traffic can be exploited.

Understanding Web (HTTP) Exploits

It is an understatement to say that the computing world was not adequately prepared for the release of the Code Red worm. The Microsoft Internet Information Services (IIS) exploit that Code Red took advantage of was already known, and a patch was made available from Microsoft for several weeks before the release of the worm. In those days, however, less emphasis was placed on patching and updating systems on a regular basis because it was generally believed that it was best to wait for the bugs to get worked out of the patches first.

So, what happened is that a large number of websites were completely unprepared for the huge onslaught of exploits that occurred with the Code Red worm, which sent specially formatted HTTP requests to a web server to attempt to take control of a system. For example, the following URL lists the type of exploits that were performed:

```
http://webmail.companyabc.com/scripts/..%5c../winnt/system32/cmd.exe?/c+dir+c:\
```

This one in particular attempts to launch the command prompt on a web or OWA server. Through the proper manipulation, worms such as Code Red found the method for taking over web servers and using them as drones to attack other web servers.

These types of HTTP attacks were a wake-up call to the broader security community as it became apparent that packet-layer filtering firewalls that could simply open or close a port were worthless against the threat of an exploit that packages its traffic over a legitimately allowed port such as HTTP.

HTTP filtering and securing, fortunately, is something that ISA Server does extremely well, and offers a large number of customization options that allow administrators to have control over the traffic and security of the web server.

Securing Encrypted (Secure Sockets Layer) Web Traffic

As the World Wide Web was maturing, organizations realized that if they encrypted the HTTP packets that were transmitted between a website and a client, it would make it virtually unreadable to anyone who would potentially intercept those packets. This led to the adoption of Secure Sockets Layer (SSL) encryption for HTTP traffic.

Of course, encrypted packets also create somewhat of a dilemma from an intrusion detection and analysis perspective because it is impossible to read the content of the packet to determine what it is trying to do. Indeed, many HTTP exploits in the wild today can be transmitted over secure SSL-encrypted channels. This poses a dangerous situation for organizations that must secure the traffic against interception, but must also proactively monitor and secure their web servers against attack.

ISA Server 2006 is uniquely positioned to solve this problem, fortunately, because it includes the ability to perform end-to-end SSL bridging. By installing the SSL certificate from the OWA server on the ISA server itself, along with a copy of the private key, ISA is able to decrypt the traffic, scan it for exploits, and then reencrypt it before sending it to the Exchange server. Very few products on the marketplace do this type of end-to-end encryption of the packets, and, fortunately, ISA allows for this level of security.

Outlining ISA Server 2006 Messaging Security Mechanisms

As a backdrop to these developments, ISA Server 2006 was designed with messaging security in mind. A great degree of functionality was developed to address email access and communications, with particularly tight integration with Microsoft Exchange Server built in. To illustrate, ISA Server 2006 supports securing the following messaging protocols and access methods:

- ▶ Simple Mail Transfer Protocol (SMTP)

- ▶ Messaging Application Programming Interface (MAPI)

- ▶ Post Office Protocol version 3 (POP3)

- ▶ Internet Message Access Protocol version 4 (IMAP4)

- ▶ Microsoft Exchange Outlook Web App (OWA) with or without forms-based authentication (FBA)

- ▶ Exchange ActiveSync (EAS)

- ▶ Exchange Autodiscover service

- ▶ Exchange Server 2010 EWS

- ▶ Outlook Anywhere (formerly RPC over HTTP)

Securing each of these types of messaging access methods and protocols is detailed in subsequent sections of this chapter. For an understanding of how to initially set up web-related mail access with OWA/ActiveSync, and Outlook Anywhere, it might be wise to review Chapter 23, "Designing and Implementing Mobility in Exchange Server 2010," as this chapter only deals with securing existing OWA/ActiveSync deployments.

Securing Exchange Outlook Web App with ISA Server 2006

As previously mentioned, OWA is one of the most commonly secured services that ISA servers protect. This stems from the critical need to provide remote email services while at the same time securing that access. The success of ISA deployments in this fashion gives tribute to the tight integration Microsoft built between its ISA product and Exchange Server product.

An ISA server used to secure an OWA implementation can be deployed in multiple scenarios, such as an edge firewall, an inline firewall, or a dedicated reverse-proxy server. In all these scenarios, ISA secures OWA traffic by "pretending" to be the CAS server itself, scanning the traffic that is destined for the CAS for exploits, and then repackaging that traffic and sending it on, such as that illustrated in Figure 13.1.

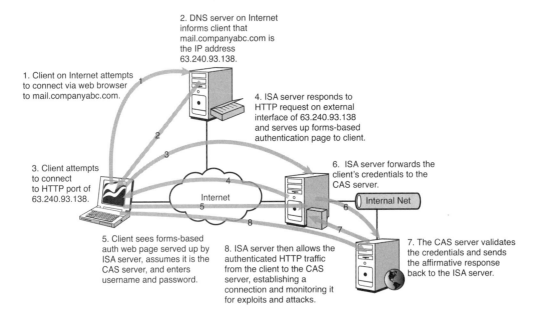

FIGURE 13.1 Explaining OWA publishing with ISA Server 2006.

ISA performs this type of OWA securing through an Exchange Web Client Access rule, which automatically sets up and configures a listener on the ISA server. A listener is an ISA component that listens to specifically defined IP traffic, and processes that traffic for the requesting client as if it were the actual server itself. For example, an OWA listener on an ISA server would respond to OWA requests made to it by scanning them for exploits and then repackaging them and forwarding them on to the OWA server itself. Using listeners, the client cannot tell the difference between the ISA server and the OWA server.

ISA Server is also one of the few products that has the capability to secure web traffic with SSL encryption from end to end. It does this by using the OWA server's own certificate to reencrypt the traffic before sending it on its way. This also allows for the "black box" of SSL traffic to be examined for exploits and viruses at the application layer, and then be reencypted to reduce the chance of unauthorized viewing of OWA traffic. Without the capability to scan this SSL traffic, exploits bound for an OWA server could simply hide themselves in the encrypted traffic and pass right through traditional firewalls.

Exporting and Importing the OWA Certificate to the ISA Server

For ISA to be able to decrypt the SSL traffic bound for the Exchange CAS server, ISA needs to have a copy of the SSL certificate used on the CAS server. This certificate is used by ISA to decode the SSL packets, inspect them, and then reencrypt them and send them on to the CAS server. For this certificate to be installed on the ISA server, it must first be exported from the CAS Server from IIS Manager. By opening up the certificate and then right-clicking and choosing to Export the certificate, it can be exported to a .pfx file. Be sure to select to export the private key, as shown in Figure 13.2.

FIGURE 13.2   Exporting the SSL private key.

CAUTION

It is important to securely transmit this `.pfx` file to the ISA server and to maintain high security over its location. The certificate's security could be compromised if it were to fall into the wrong hands.

After the `.pfx` file has been exported from the CAS server, it can then be imported to the ISA server via the following procedure:

1. From the ISA server, open the MMC console (Start, Run, `mmc.exe`, OK).

2. Click File, Add/Remove Snap-in.

3. Click Add.

4. From the list shown in Figure 13.3, choose the Certificates snap-in and then click Add.

FIGURE 13.3   Customizing an MMC Certificates snap-in console for import of the OWA certificate.

5. Choose Computer Account from the list when asked what certificates the snap-in will manage, and click Next to continue.

6. From the subsequent list in the Select Computer dialog box, choose Local Computer: (the computer this console is running on), and click Finish.

7. Click Close and then click OK.

After the custom MMC console has been created, the certificate that was exported from the CAS server can be imported directly from the console via the following procedure:

1. From the MMC Console root, navigate to Certificates (Local Computer), Personal.

2. Right-click the Personal folder, and choose All Tasks, Import.

3. When the wizard begins, click Next past the Welcome Screen to continue.

4. Browse for and locate the .pfx file that was exported from the CAS server. The location can also be typed into the File Name field. Click Next.

5. Enter the password that was created when the certificate was exported, as illustrated in Figure 13.4. Do not check to mark the key as exportable. Click Next to continue.

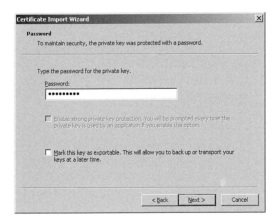

FIGURE 13.4   Installing the OWA certificate on the ISA server.

6. Choose Automatically Select the Certificate Store Based on the Type of Certificate, and click Next to continue.

7. Click Finish to complete the import.

After it is in the certificate store of the ISA server, the OWA SSL certificate can be used as part of publishing rules. Note that any Exchange Server 2010 SSL certificate that uses Subject Alternative Names (SAN) as part of the certificate requires at least ISA Server 2006 Service Pack 1 to use the SAN names in Web Publishing rules.

> **NOTE**
>
> If a rule that makes use of a specific SSL certificate is exported from an ISA server, either for backup purposes or to transfer it to another ISA server, the certificate must also be saved and imported to the destination server, or that particular rule will be broken.

Creating an Outlook Web App Publishing Rule

After the OWA SSL has been installed onto the ISA server, the actual ISA mail publishing rule can be generated to secure OWA via the following procedure:

> **NOTE**
>
> The procedure outlined here illustrates an ISA OWA publishing rule that uses forms-based authentication (FBA) for the site, which allows for a landing page to be generated on the ISA server to preauthenticate user connections to Exchange Server. This FBA page can only be set on ISA, and must be turned off on the Exchange server to work properly. Also note that ISA Server 2006 does not currently have a web publishing definition for Exchange Server 2010; you must use the Exchange Server 2007 definition, which works for Exchange Server 2010. Depending on the timing of the newer version of ISA, TMG, it might be wise to upgrade if securing Exchange Server 2010.

1. From the ISA Management Console, click once on the Firewall Policy node from the console tree.
2. On the Tasks tab of the tasks pane, click the Publish Exchange Web Client Access link.
3. Enter a descriptive name for the publishing rule, such as Outlook Web App, and click Next to continue.
4. From the dialog box shown in Figure 13.5, choose the version of Exchange Server that will be secured. Because Exchange Server 2010 is not an option with the current release of ISA Server, you must select Exchange Server 2007 and then click the Outlook Web App check box. The other check boxes automatically dim. Click Next to continue.
5. The subsequent dialog box allows an administrator to choose whether a single CAS server will be published, or whether a farm of load-balanced CAS servers will be published. In this scenario, a single CAS server will be used. Click Next to continue.
6. In the next dialog box, shown in Figure 13.6, the Use SSL to Connect to the Published Web Server or Server Farm option is illustrated. It is highly recommended to use SSL, and this scenario illustrates that concept. Click Next to continue.
7. On the Internal Publishing Details dialog box, enter the site name that internal users use to access the CAS server. It is recommended that the fully qualified domain name (FQDN), such as mail.companyabc.com, be entered, and that it is different from the physical name of the server itself. Examine the options to connect to an IP address or computer name; this gives additional flexibility to the rule. Click Next to continue.

FIGURE 13.5   Creating an Exchange Server 2010 OWA publishing rule.

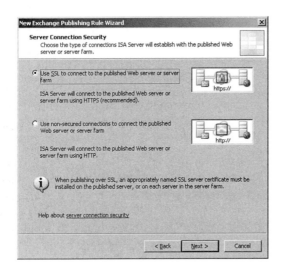

FIGURE 13.6   Choosing SSL publishing options.

8. In the subsequent dialog box, enter to accept requests for "This domain name (type below):" and enter the FQDN of the server, such as mail.companyabc.com. Click Next to continue.

9. Under Web Listener, click New.

10. At the start of the Web Listener Wizard, enter a descriptive name for the listener, such as Exchange HTTP/HTTPS Listener, and click Next to continue.

11. A prompt appears for you to choose between SSL and non-SSL. This prompt refers to the traffic between the client and ISA, which should always be SSL whenever possible. Click Next to continue.

12. Under Web Listener IP Addresses, select the External Network and leave it at All IP Addresses. Click Next to continue.

13. Under Listener SSL Certificates, click Select Certificate.

14. Select the previously installed certificate, as shown in Figure 13.7, and click the Select button.

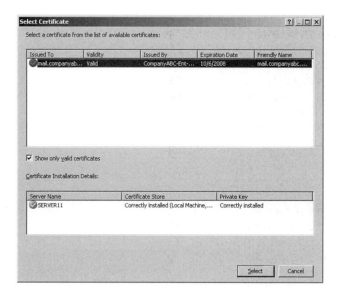

FIGURE 13.7   Choosing a certificate for the listener.

15. Click Next to continue.

16. For the type of authentication, choose HTML Form Authentication, as shown in Figure 13.8. Leave the Windows (Active Directory) option selected, and click Next.

17. The Single Sign On Settings dialog box is powerful; it allows all authentication traffic through a single listener to be processed only once. After the user has authenticated, he can access any other service, be it a SharePoint site, web server, or other web-based service that uses the same domain name for credentials. In this example, enter .companyabc.com into the SSO domain name, as shown in Figure 13.9. Click Next to continue.

18. Click Finish to end the Listener Wizard.

19. Click Next after the new listener is displayed in the Web Listener dialog box.

20. Under Authentication Delegation, choose Basic from the drop-down menu. Basic is used because SSL is the transport mechanism chosen. Click Next to continue.

21. Under User Sets, leave All Authenticated Users selected. In stricter scenarios, only specific Active Directory (AD) groups can be granted rights to OWA using this setting. In this case, the default is fine. Click Next to continue.

22. Click Finish to end the wizard.

FIGURE 13.8   Choosing an authentication type.

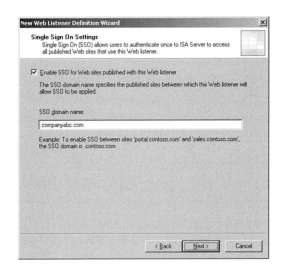

FIGURE 13.9   Enabling the Single Sign On settings.

23. Click Apply in the details pane, and then click OK when finished to commit the changes.

The rule will now appear in the details pane of the ISA server. Double-clicking on the rule brings up the settings, as shown in Figure 13.10. Tabs can be used to navigate around the different rule settings. The rule itself can be configured with additional settings based on the configuration desired. For example, the following rule information is used to configure our basic forms-based authentication web publishing rule for OWA:

▶ **General tab**—For Name, choose Outlook Web App. Also make sure the Enabled option is checked.

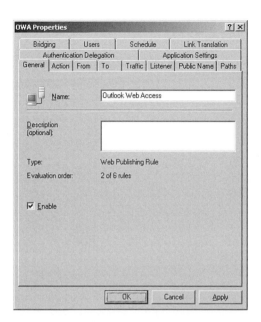

FIGURE 13.10   Viewing the OWA rule.

▶ **Action tab**—For Action to take, choose Allow. Also make sure that the option Log Requests Matching This Rule is checked.

▶ **From tab**—Choose the option This Rule Applies to Traffic from These Sources and select Anywhere as the setting.

▶ **To tab**—For the option This Rule Applies to This Published Site, enter (for this example) mail.companyabc.com. Make sure the option Forward the Original Host Header Instead of the Actual One (which is specified in the Internal site name field) is checked. For the option Specify How the Firewall Proxies Requests to the Published Server, choose Requests Appear to Come from the ISA server.

▶ **Traffic tab**—For the option This Rule Applies to Traffic of the Following Protocols, choose HTTP and HTTPS. Also make sure the option Require 128-bit Encryption for HTTPS Traffic is checked.

▶ **Listener tab**—For Listener properties-Networks, choose External,Port(HTTP)=80, Port(HTTPS)=443, Certificate=mail.companyabc.com, Authentication methods=FBA with AD, and Always Authenticate-No,Domain for Authentication should be COMPANYABC.

▶ **Listener tab, Properties button**—For the Networks tab, select External, All IP addresses. For the Connections tab–Enabled HTTP Connections on Port 80, set to Enable SSL Connections on Port 443. For HTTP to HTTPS Redirection select Redirect Authenticated Traffic from HTTP to HTTPS. For the Forms tab choose Allow Users to Change Their Passwords. Set the Remind Users That Their Password Will Expire in

This Number of Days to 15. For the SSO tab, choose Enable Single Sign On. And for the SSO Domains, enter companyabc.com in this example.

▶ **Public Name tab**—For This Rule Applies to: Requests for the Following Web Sites, enter mail.companyabc.com in this example.

▶ **Paths tab**—For external paths, choose All Are Set to <same as internal>. For internal paths, enter /public/*, /OWA/*, /Exchweb/*, /Exchange/*, /, /autodiscover/*.

▶ **Authentication Delegation tab**—For Method Used by ISA Server to Authenticate to the Published Web Server, choose Basic Authentication.

▶ **Application Settings tab**—For Use Customized HTML Forms Instead of the Default, make sure it is checked. For Type the Custom HTML Form Set Directory, choose Exchange. For Logon type, select As Selected by User. And for Exchange Publishing Attachment Blocking, make sure Public Computers is checked.

▶ **Bridging tab**—For Redirect Requests to SSL Port, enter 443.

▶ **Users tab**—For This Rule Applies to Requests from the Following User Sets, choose All Authenticated Users.

▶ **Schedule tab**—For Schedule, select Always.

▶ **Link Translation tab**—For Apply Link Translation to This Rule, make sure the option is checked.

Different rules require different settings, but the settings outlined in this example are some of the more common and secure ones used to set up this scenario.

NOTE

Exchange ActiveSync, Outlook Anywhere, and Exchange Web Services require their own rules to be set up. The process is very similar, with the only major difference being that a different option is chosen.

Securing POP and IMAP Exchange Server Traffic

The ancillary mail services of the Post Office Protocol version 3 (POP3) and Internet Message Access Protocol version 4 (IMAP4) can be secured through an ISA server. This is particularly important for organizations that require support of these legacy protocols; they are less secure than the newer forms of mail access available.

Creating and Configuring a POP Mail Publishing Rule

POP3 servers are secured in ISA through the creation of a special rule that enables ISA to examine all traffic sent to the POP3 server and perform intrusion detection heuristics on it with an advanced POP intrusion detection filter. The POP server does not necessarily need to be a Microsoft server, such as Exchange Server, but can be run on any POP3-compliant messaging system.

CAUTION

Enable POP support in a messaging environment only if there is no other viable option. POP3 support is less secure than other access methods, and can cause mail delivery and security issues. For example, many POP clients are configured to pull all the mail off the POP server, making it difficult to do disaster recovery of mail data.

After a POP server has been enabled or established on the internal network, it can be secured via modification of an existing rule or creation of a new rule to secure POP traffic as follows:

1. From the ISA console, select the Firewall Policy node from the console tree.

2. In the tasks pane, click the Publish Mail Servers link.

3. Enter a descriptive name for the rule (for example, POP Access), and click Next.

4. Select the Client Access: RPC, IMAP, POP3, SMTP option, and click Next.

5. In the Select Services dialog box, select POP3 (Standard port), and click Next.

6. Enter the internal IP address of the POP server, and click Next.

7. Select to which networks the ISA server will listen by checking the boxes next to them, and click Next.

8. Click Finish, click Apply, and then click OK.

NOTE

By default, enabling a POP publishing rule turns on the POP intrusion detection filter, which can help protect a POP system from potential exploits. That said, POP3 is still an insecure protocol, and it is preferable not to deploy it on a server.

Creating and Configuring an IMAP Mail Publishing Rule

The Internet Message Access Protocol (IMAP) is often used as a mail access method for UNIX systems and even for clients such as Outlook Express. It also can be secured through an ISA server, using the same rule as a POP rule, or through the configuration of a unique IMAP publishing rule.

After the internal IMAP presence has been established, an ISA rule can be created to allow IMAP traffic to the IMAP server. The following procedure outlines this process:

1. From the ISA console, select the Firewall Policy node from the console tree.

2. In the tasks pane, click the Publish Mail Servers link.

3. Enter a descriptive name for the rule (for example, IMAP Access), and click Next.

4. Click the Client Access: RPC, IMAP, POP3, SMTP option button, as shown in Figure 13.11, and click Next.

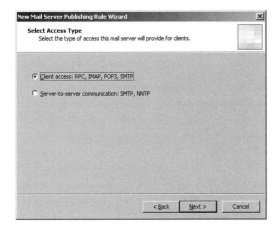

FIGURE 13.11   Setting up an ISA IMAP publishing rule.

5. In the Select Services dialog box, select Secure Ports for IMAP4, and click Next.

6. Enter the internal IP address of the POP server, and click Next.

7. Select to which networks the ISA server will listen by checking the boxes next to them, and click Next.

8. Click Finish.

Managing and Controlling Simple Mail Transfer Protocol (SMTP) Traffic

The Simple Mail Transfer Protocol (SMTP) is the second most commonly used protocol on the Internet, after the web HTTP protocol. It is ubiquitously used as an email transport mechanism on the Internet, and has become a critical tool for online collaboration.

Unfortunately, SMTP is also one of the most abused protocols on the Internet. Unsolicited email (spam), phishing attacks, and email-borne viruses all take advantage of the open, unauthenticated nature of SMTP, and it has become a necessity for organizations to control and monitor SMTP traffic entering and leaving the network.

ISA Server 2006's application-layer inspection capabilities allow for a high degree of SMTP filtering and attack detection. By default, ISA supports the protocol as part of standard rules and policies.

ISA Server 2006 is an ideal candidate for deployment in an environment with an Exchange Server 2010 Edge Transport server, as it can scan the traffic bound for that server for irregularities and potential exploits before delivering messages to the Exchange Server environment.

NOTE

The next version of ISA Server, Threat Management Gateway (TMG) will support installing an Exchange Edge Transport Server directly on the TMG server, improving the overall security and removing any unnecessary hop.

Publishing the SMTP Server for Inbound Mail Access

The first step toward securing SMTP traffic is to create a server publishing rule that protects the internal SMTP server from direct external access. This can be done through an SMTP server publishing rule. In this scenario, an Exchange Server 2010 Edge Transport server in the DMZ of the ISA firewall is published:

1. From the ISA console, select the Firewall Policy node from the console tree.

2. In the tasks pane, click the Publish Mail Servers link.

3. Enter a descriptive name for the rule (for example, SMTP Inbound to Edge Transport Server), and click Next.

4. Select Server-to-Server Communication: SMTP, NTTP, and click Next.

5. In the dialog box shown in Figure 13.12, choose SMTP, and click Next.

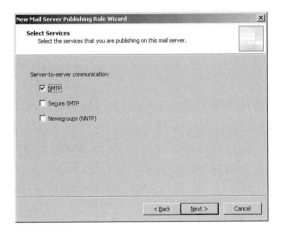

FIGURE 13.12   Setting up an inbound SMTP publishing rule.

6. Enter the internal IP address of the Edge Transport server, and click Next.

7. Select to which networks the ISA server will listen by checking the boxes next to them, and click Next. This is usually the external network. ISA then listens to this network for SMTP requests sent to it and relays them to the Edge Transport server.

8. Click Finish, click Apply, and then click OK.

Creating an SMTP Access Rule in ISA Server 2006

ISA can be easily configured to allow SMTP traffic and to scan that traffic as it passes through the ISA firewall. This can be configured with a simple access rule, set up as follows:

1. On the ISA server, open the ISA console, and choose the Firewall Policy node from the console tree.

2. In the tasks pane, click the Create Access Rule link.

3. Enter a descriptive name, such as Allow SMTP Outbound from Edge Transport Server, and click Next.

4. Select Allow from the rule action list, and click Next.

5. Under This Rule Applies To, select Specified Protocols.

6. Click Add under Protocols, then drill down and choose Common Protocols, SMTP. Click Add.

7. Click Close and then click Next.

8. Under Access Rule Sources, click Add.

9. Drill down to Networks, and select Perimeter (or the network where the Edge Transport server is), click Add, and then click Close. Note that it is often better practice to restrict this to the specific IP address of the Edge Transport server, rather than to a whole network.

10. Under Access Rule Destinations, click Add.

11. Under Networks, select External, click Add, and then click Close.

12. Click Next, click Next, and then click Finish.

13. Click Apply at the top of the details pane, and then click OK to confirm.

Customizing the SMTP Filter

After SMTP rules have been set up to allow the traffic to flow through the SMTP Screener, the ISA SMTP filter can be customized to block specific types of SMTP commands and content. To access the SMTP filter settings on the ISA server, do the following:

1. From the ISA console, click the Add-ins node in the console tree.

2. Under Application Filters in the details pane, double-click on SMTP Filter.

3. Examine and configure the settings in the SMTP Filter Properties dialog box, some of which are shown in Figure 13.13.

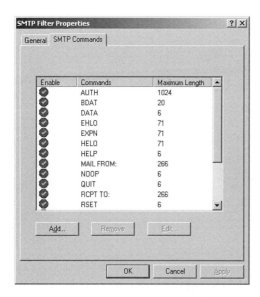

FIGURE 13.13   Configuring SMTP filter settings.

The SMTP Screener filter allows for the following default filtering functionality:

▶ Keyword filtering

▶ Email address/domain name filtering

▶ Attachment filtering

▶ SMTP command filtering

Logging ISA Traffic

One of the most powerful troubleshooting tools at the disposal of SharePoint and ISA administrators is the logging mechanism, which gives live or archived views of the logs on an ISA server, and allows for quick and easy searching and indexing of ISA Server log information, including every packet of data that hits the ISA server.

> **NOTE**
>
> Many of the advanced features of ISA logging are only available when using MSDE or SQL databases for the storage of the logs.

Examining ISA Logs

The ISA logs are accessible via the Logging tab in the details pane of the Monitoring node, as shown in Figure 13.14. They offer administrators the ability to watch, in real time, what is happening to the ISA server, whether it is denying connections, and what rule is being applied for each Allow or Deny statement.

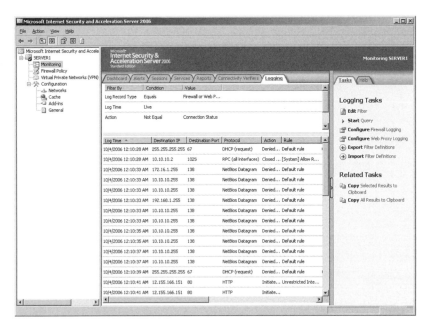

FIGURE 13.14   Examining ISA logging.

The logs include pertinent information on each packet of data, including the following key characteristics:

▶ **Log Time**—The exact time the packet was processed.

▶ **Destination IP**—The destination IP address of the packet.

▶ **Destination Port**—The destination TCP/IP port, such as port 80 for HTTP traffic.

▶ **Protocol**—The specific protocol that the packet utilized, such as HTTP, LDAP, RPC, or others.

▶ **Action**—The type of action the ISA server took on the traffic, such as initiating the connection or denying it.

▶ **Rule**—The particular firewall policy rule applied to the traffic.

▶ **Client IP**—The IP address of the client that sent the packet.

▶ **Client Username**—The username of the requesting client. Note that this is only populated if using the Firewall Client.

▶ **Source Network**—The source network from which the packet came.

▶ **Destination Network**—The network where the destination of the packet is located.

▶ **HTTP Method**—If HTTP traffic, the type of HTTP method utilized, such as GET or POST.

▶ **URL**—If HTTP is used, the exact URL that was requested.

By searching through the logs for specific criteria in these columns, such as all packets sent by a specific IP address, or all URLs that match http://sharepoint.companyabc.com, advanced troubleshooting and monitoring is simplified.

Customizing Logging Filters

What is displayed in the details pane of the Logging tab is a reflection of only those logs that match certain criteria in the log filter. It is highly useful to use the filter to weed out the extraneous log entries, which just distract from the specific monitoring task. For example, on many networks, an abundance of NetBIOS broadcast traffic makes it difficult to read the logs. For this reason, a specific filter can be created to only show traffic that is not NetBIOS traffic. To set up this particular type of rule, do the following:

1. From the ISA Admin console, click the Monitoring node from the console tree, and select the Logging tab in the details pane.

2. On the Tasks tab in the tasks pane, click the Edit Filter link.

3. In the Edit Filter dialog box, change the Filter by, Condition, and Value fields to display Protocol, Not Equal, NetBios Datagram, and then click Add to List.

4. Repeat for the NetBios Name Service and the NetBios Session values, so that the dialog box looks like the one displayed in Figure 13.15.

5. Click Start Query.

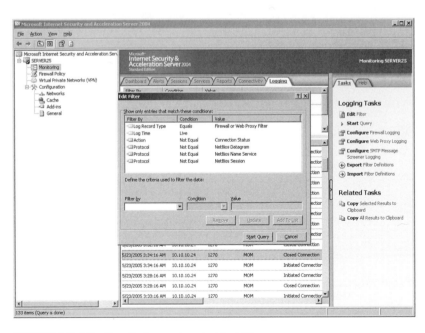

FIGURE 13.15   Creating a custom logging filter.

> **NOTE**
>
> It cannot be stressed enough that this logging mechanism is quite literally the best tool for troubleshooting ISA access. For example, it can be used to tell if traffic from clients is even hitting the ISA server, and if it is, what is happening to it (denied, accepted, and so on).

Monitoring ISA from the ISA Console

In addition to the robust logging mechanism, the ISA Monitoring node also contains various tabs that link to other extended troubleshooting and monitoring tools. Each of these tools performs unique functions, such as generating reports, alerting administrators, or verifying connectivity to critical services. It is, therefore, important to understand how each of these tools work.

Customizing the ISA Dashboard

The ISA Dashboard, shown in Figure 13.16, provides for quick and comprehensive monitoring of a multitude of ISA components from a single screen. The view is customizable, and individual components can be collapsed and/or expanded by clicking the arrow buttons in the upper-right corner of each of the components. All the individual ISA Monitoring elements are summarized here.

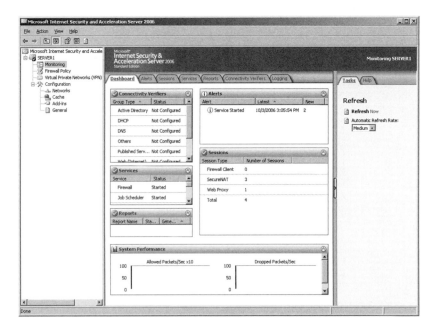

FIGURE 13.16   Viewing the ISA Dashboard.

TIP

The ISA Dashboard is the logical "parking" page for ISA administrators, who can leave the screen set at the Dashboard to allow for quick-glance views of ISA health.

Monitoring and Customizing Alerts

The Alerts tab, shown in Figure 13.17, lists all the status alerts that ISA has generated while it is in operation. It is beneficial to look through these alerts on a regular basis, and acknowledge them when you no longer need to display them on the Dashboard. If alerts need to be permanently removed, they can be reset instead. Resetting or acknowledging alerts is as simple as right-clicking on them and choosing Reset or Acknowledge.

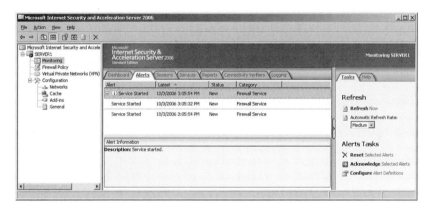

FIGURE 13.17   Viewing the ISA Alerts tab.

Alerts that show up in this list are listed because their default alert definition specified an action to display them in the console. This type of alert behavior is completely customizable, and alerts can be made to do the following actions:

- ▶ Send email

- ▶ Run a program

- ▶ Report to Windows event log

- ▶ Stop selected services

- ▶ Start selected services

For example, it might be necessary to force a stop of the firewall service if a specific type of attack is detected. Configuring alert definitions is relatively straightforward. For example, the following process illustrates how to create an alert that sends an email to an administrator when a SYN attack is detected:

1. From the Alerts tab of the ISA Monitoring node, select the Tasks tab in the tasks pane.

2. Click the Configure Alert Definitions link.

3. On the Alert Definitions tab of the Alert Properties dialog box, shown in Figure 13.18, choose SYN Attack, and click Edit.

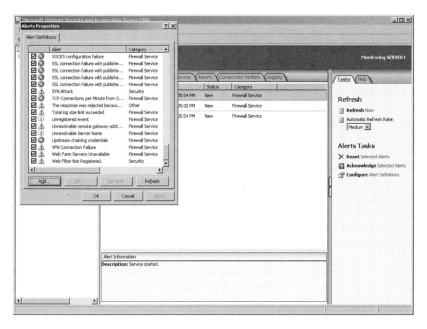

FIGURE 13.18   Creating a custom alert definition.

4. Choose the Actions tab in the SYN Attack Properties dialog box.

5. Check the Send E-mail check box.

6. Enter the SMTP server in the organization, and then complete the From, To, and CC fields, similar to what is shown in Figure 13.19.

7. Click the Test button to try the settings, and then click OK to acknowledge a successful test.

8. Click OK, click OK, click Apply, and then click OK to save the settings.

As is evident from the list, a vast number of existing alert definitions can be configured, and a large number of thresholds can be set. In addition, more potential alerts can be configured by clicking Add on the Alerts Properties dialog box and following the wizard. This allows for an even greater degree of customization.

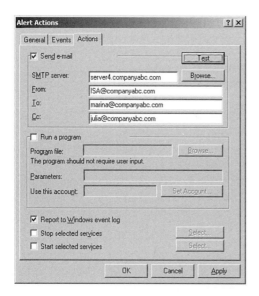

FIGURE 13.19   Setting an alert action for an event.

Monitoring Session and Services Activity

The Services tab, shown in Figure 13.20, allows for a quick-glance view of the ISA services, if they are running, and how long they have been up since last being restarted. The services can also be stopped and started from this tab.

FIGURE 13.20   Monitoring ISA services.

The Sessions tab allows for more interaction, as individual unique sessions to the ISA server can be viewed and disconnected as necessary. For example, it might be necessary to disconnect any users who are on a VPN connection, if a change to the VPN policy has just been issued. This is because VPN clients that have already established a session with the

ISA server are only subject to the laws of the VPN policy that was in effect when they originally logged on. To disconnect a session, right-click on the session, and choose
Disconnect Session, as shown in Figure 13.21.

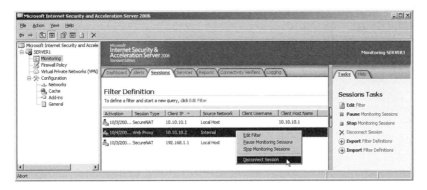

FIGURE 13.21   Disconnecting a session.

Creating Connectivity Verifiers

Connectivity verifiers can be a useful way of extending ISA's capabilities to include moni-
toring of critical services within an environment, such as domain name system (DNS),
Dynamic Host Configuration Protocol (DHCP), HTTP, or other custom services.
Connectivity verifiers are essentially a quick-and-dirty approach to monitoring an envi-
ronment with very little cost, as they take advantage of ISA's alerting capabilities and the
Dashboard to display the verifiers.

For example, the following step-by-step process illustrates setting up a connectivity verifier
that checks the status of an internal SharePoint server:

1. On the Monitoring tab of the ISA console, click the Connectivity tab of the details
   pane.

2. On the Tasks tab of the tasks pane, click the Create New Connectivity Verifier link.

3. Enter a name for the connectivity verifier, such as Web Server Verifier, and click Next.

4. In the Connectivity Verification Details dialog box, enter the server FQDN, the
   group type (which simply determines how it is grouped on the Dashboard), and the
   type of verification method to use—in this case, an HTTP GET request, as shown in
   Figure 13.22.

5. Click Finish.

6. Click Yes when prompted to turn on the rule that allows ISA Server to connect via
   HTTP to selected servers.

7. Click Apply and then click OK.

After being created, connectivity verifiers that fit into the major group types are reflected
on the Dashboard. Creating multiple connectivity verifiers in each of the common group
types can make the Dashboard a more effective monitoring tool.

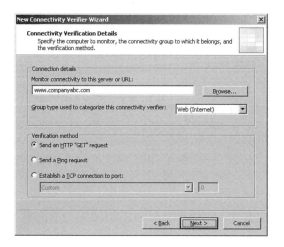

FIGURE 13.22   Configuring a SharePoint HTTP connectivity verifier.

Summary

ISA Server 2006 has often been called the Exchange Server firewall, and for good reason. The capabilities of ISA Server 2006 to secure and protect Exchange Server services, whether through reverse-proxying HTTP traffic, filtering MAPI traffic, or screening SMTP messages, gives it capabilities not present in other firewall solutions. In addition, ISA's ability to be easily deployed in the DMZ of existing firewalls as a dedicated security appliance further extends its capabilities and allows it to be deployed in environments of all shapes and sizes.

Best Practices

The following are best practices from this chapter:

▶ Filter MAPI traffic destined for Exchange servers using ISA Server 2006's RPC filtering technology.

▶ Monitor ISA Server using the MSDE or SQL logging approaches to allow for the greatest level of monitoring functionality.

▶ Secure any edge-facing service such as OWA and Exchange ActiveSync with a reverse-proxy system such as ISA Server 2006.

▶ Deploy ISA reverse-proxy capability in the existing DMZ of a firewall if it is not feasible to replace existing firewall technologies.

CHAPTER 14

Understanding Exchange Policy Enforcement Security

Microsoft Exchange Server 2010 evolved during a time when organizations became more and more aware of the need to gain greater control over the content that traversed through the system. In the past, these types of considerations were not given much thought, and email was pretty much open for all users to send whatever they needed, both internally and externally.

Over time, as specific high-profile lawsuits over email content took place and governmental regulations such as HIPAA and Sarbanes Oxley went into effect, organizations began to take note that they would have to establish policies to control their messaging environments.

Exchange Server 2010 provides for robust integrated support of enterprise policy enforcement, allowing organizations to apply restrictions to mail messages, limiting content that can be sent and creating a framework in which specific retention policies can be created.

This chapter focuses on the Exchange Server 2010 capabilities in this space. The role that governmental policies such as HIPAA and Sarbanes Oxley play in forming these policies is described. Specific information on policy enforcement using transport rules agents and Messaging Records Management are outlined and explained. In addition, best practices for organizations looking to use Exchange Server 2010 for policy management are defined.

What Is Exchange Policy Management in Exchange Server 2010?

Exchange Server 2010 introduces the concept of Exchange Enterprise Policy Management as a built-in component of the application. Microsoft built this structure into Exchange Server as a direct result of the changes in the marketplace that required that certain types of communications such as email be controlled, managed, secured, and audited to levels previously unattainable without third-party products.

Enterprise Policy Management in Exchange Server 2010 is effectively composed of several components, each providing a different layer in the management space. These components are defined as follows:

- **Messaging Records Management (MRM)**—Messaging Records Management in Exchange Server 2010 defines retention settings for individual mail folders within mailboxes.

- **Journaling**—Exchange Server 2010 journaling allows for mailbox-specific archiving of all communications sent to or from specific users, allowing organizations to comply with strict retention policies stipulated by governmental regulations.

- **Edge Transport rules**—Exchange Server 2010 has the ability to apply policies and rules at the edge layer, protecting an organization from spam, spyware, undesired corporate information leakage, and other undesirable emails.

- **Hub Transport rules**—Exchange Server 2010 also allows for Hub Transport-specific rules, which are run against all traffic sent through Hub Transport role servers.

- **Address rewriting**—Edge Transport servers in Exchange Server 2010 can implement a policy to rewrite all of the outgoing Simple Mail Transfer Protocol (SMTP) domain names within a company to a single domain name, thus ensuring consistency with corporate policies.

- **Disclaimers**—Disclaimer policies also run on Edge servers and are created to allow a corporate disclaimer to be appended to the end of every outgoing mail message.

- **Rights Management Services**—Exchange Server 2007 integrates directly with Active Directory Rights Management Services (AD RMS), allowing rights-protected emails to be sent across forest boundaries encrypted.

Each of these components is described in more detail in later sections of this chapter. In addition, step-by-step guides for deploying best practice policies are defined.

Understanding Relevant Governmental Regulations for Policy Enforcement

Multiple governmental and industry regulations have direct consequences for messaging platforms within organizations. Security systems within an organization can be based on proprietary standards; however, as organizations have the need to securely exchange information with other entities, the need to have information systems built on standards becomes crucial. Security standards enable organizations to not only store and transmit information within the enterprise in a secure manner, but also securely exchange information with other entities.

A universal security standard requires the creation of common criteria for a secured environment, the adoption of the standard by an accepted standards organization, the acceptance of the standard by organizations, and the implementation of the standard in enterprise transactions.

There are many initiatives to create security standards. Some of these standards include ISO/IEC 17799, HIPAA, and provisions of the Gramm-Leach-Bliley Act. These initiatives, and how they relate to Exchange Server 2010 Policy Management, are detailed in the subsequent sections of this chapter.

Understanding the ISO/IEC 17799 Security Standard

ISO/IEC 17799 is "a comprehensive set of controls comprising best practices in information security." It is an internationally recognized generic information security standard. Its predecessor, titled BS7799-1, has existed in various forms for a number of years, although the standard only really gained widespread recognition following publication by ISO (the International Organization for Standardization) in December of 2000. Formal certification and accreditation were also introduced around the same time.

ISO/IEC 17799 is organized into 10 major sections, each covering a different topic or area:

- ▶ **Business Continuity Planning**—The objective of this section is to counteract interruptions to business activities and to critical business processes from the effects of major failures or disasters.

- ▶ **System Access Control**—The objectives of this section are a) to control access to information, b) to prevent unauthorized access to information systems, c) to ensure the protection of networked services, d) to prevent unauthorized computer access, e) to detect unauthorized activities, and f) to ensure information security when using mobile computing and telenetworking facilities.

- ▶ **System Development and Maintenance**—The objectives of this section are a) to ensure security is built in to operational systems; b) to prevent loss, modification, or misuse of user data in application systems; c) to protect the confidentiality, authenticity, and integrity of information; d) to ensure information technology (IT) projects and support activities are conducted in a secure manner; and e) to maintain the security of application system software and data.

- ▶ **Physical and Environmental Security**—The objectives of this section are a) to prevent unauthorized access, damage, and interference to business premises and information; b) to prevent loss, damage, or compromise of assets and interruption to business activities; and c) to prevent compromise or theft of information and information-processing facilities.

▶ **Compliance**—The objectives of this section are a) to avoid breaches of any criminal or civil law, statutory, regulatory, or contractual obligations, and of any security requirements; b) to ensure compliance of systems with organizational security policies and standards; and c) to maximize the effectiveness of and to minimize interference to/from the system audit process.

▶ **Personnel Security**—The objectives of this section are a) to reduce risks of human error, theft, fraud, or misuse of facilities; b) to ensure that users are aware of information security threats and concerns, and are equipped to support the corporate security policy in the course of their normal work; and c) to minimize the damage from security incidents and malfunctions and learn from such incidents.

▶ **Security Organization**—The objectives of this section are a) to manage information security within the company; b) to maintain the security of organizational information-processing facilities and information assets accessed by third parties; and c) to maintain the security of information when the responsibility for information processing has been outsourced to another organization.

▶ **Computer and Operations Management**—The objectives of this section are a) to ensure the correct and secure operation of information-processing facilities; b) to minimize the risk of systems failures; c) to protect the integrity of software and information; d) to maintain the integrity and availability of information processing and communication; e) to ensure the safeguarding of information in networks and the protection of the supporting infrastructure; f) to prevent damage to assets and interruptions to business activities; and g) to prevent loss, modification, or misuse of information exchanged between organizations.

▶ **Asset Classification and Control**—The objectives of this section are a) to maintain appropriate protection of corporate assets and b) to ensure that information assets receive an appropriate level of protection.

▶ **Security Policy**—The objectives of this section are a) to provide management direction and b) to provide support for information security.

The first step toward ISO/IEC 17799 certification is to comply with the standard itself. This is a good security practice in its own right, but it is also the longer-term status adopted by a number of organizations that require the assurance of an external measure, yet do not want to proceed with an external or formal process immediately.

In either case, the method and rigor enforced by the standard can be put to good use in terms of better management of risk. It is also being used in some sectors as a market differentiator, as organizations begin to quote their ISO/IEC 17799 status within their individual markets and to potential customers.

Understanding the Health Insurance Portability and Accountability Act of 1996 (HIPAA)

HIPAA is the acronym for the Health Insurance Portability and Accountability Act of 1996. When HIPAA was enacted in 1996, it had two major purposes. One was to allow employees to change jobs while maintaining health-care coverage. The second was to ensure that health-care providers maintain the confidentiality of patient information.

With respect to the portability of insurance, a few decades ago, people stayed in one or two jobs throughout a whole career. In those days, people had no need for HIPAA because their jobs were stable and their employee benefits were retained by a single or limited number of providers. However, today in a time when jobs and even careers are constantly changing, HIPAA provides the continuity of health insurance even through job changes and unemployment.

The original Act was unclear and led to much confusion in the health-care industry specifically how to comply with HIPAA, so several revisions to HIPAA were enacted along with clarification documents.

Early Provisions of HIPAA

The initial actions of HIPAA were clarified and implemented related to consumer rights to health-care coverage. HIPAA increased an individual's ability to get health coverage for themselves and their dependents. It also lowered an employee's chance of losing existing health-care coverage, through a job change or unemployment. HIPAA also helped employees buy health insurance coverage on their own if they lost coverage under an employer's group health plan and have no other health coverage available.

Among its specific protections, HIPAA limited the use of preexisting condition exclusions and prohibited group health plans from discriminating by denying coverage or charging employees extra for coverage based on their individual or family member's past or present poor health. HIPAA provided guarantees to employers or individuals who purchased health insurance so they could renew the coverage regardless of any health conditions of individuals covered under the insurance policy.

HIPAA, however, does not require employers to offer or pay for health coverage to their employees nor does it guarantee health coverage for all workers. HIPAA also does not control the amount that an insurer can charge for coverage nor require group health plans to offer specific benefits. Other provisions do not require an employer or insurer to offer the same level of health-care coverage as a previous provider nor eliminate all use of preexisting condition exclusions.

Later Provisions of HIPAA

After the early provisions for HIPAA relative to consumer rights to health care were defined and implemented, the focus of HIPAA turned to the accountability aspects of the Act. The focus areas were standards for transactions and code sets, privacy of patient information, and security of information.

HIPAA Transaction and Code Sets

The rules for Transactions and Code Sets (TCS) were published on August 17, 2000, and with modifications published in May 2002. The compliance date was October 16, 2002. On December 27, 2001, President Bush signed HR3323, which provided for a delay in the implementation of the TCS rules of HIPAA. This extended the compliance due date to October 16, 2003, if a compliance extension was requested.

Further modifications to the final rule were published in February 2003. This rule finalized provisions applicable to electronic data transaction standards from two related proposed rules published in the May 31, 2002, Federal Register. It adopted modifications to implement specifications for health-care entities and for several electronic transaction standards that were omitted from the May 31, 2002, proposed rules.

The purpose of those regulations was to standardize the electronic exchange of information (transactions) between trading partners. These transactions were mandated to be in the ANSI ASC X12 version 4010 format. The covered transactions include the following:

- ▶ 270 = Eligibility Inquiry
- ▶ 271 = Inquiry and Response
- ▶ 276 = Claim Status Inquiry
- ▶ 277 = Claim Status Inquiry and Response
- ▶ 278 = Authorization Request and Authorization Response
- ▶ 820 = Health Insurance Premium Payment
- ▶ 834 = Beneficiary Enrollment
- ▶ 835 = Remittance/Payment
- ▶ 837 = Claim or Encounter

The HIPAA Code Set Regulations establish a uniform standard of data elements used to document reasons why patients are seen and the procedures performed during health-care encounters. HIPAA specified code sets to be used as follows:

- ▶ Diagnoses—ICD 9
- ▶ Procedures—CPT 4, CDT
- ▶ Supplies/Devices—HCPCS
- ▶ Additional Clinical Data—Health Level Seven (HL7)

HIPAA specified administrative codes set for use in conjunction with certain transactions and HIPAA eliminated local codes.

HIPAA Privacy

As of April 14, 2003, health-care providers and health plans were required to be in compliance with the HIPAA Privacy Regulation. Both the 1996 Congress and the two subsequent administrations agreed that a privacy law was needed to ensure that sensitive personal health information can be shared for core health activities, with safeguards in place to limit the inappropriate use and sharing of patient data. The HIPAA privacy rule took critical steps in that direction to require that privacy and security be built in to the policies and practices of health-care providers, plans, and others involved in health care.

The U.S. Department of Health and Human Services (DHHS) had addressed the concerns with new privacy standards that set a national minimum of basic protections. Congress recognized that advances in electronic technology could erode the privacy of health information. Consequently, Congress incorporated into HIPAA provisions that mandate an adoption of federal privacy protections for certain individually identifiable health information.

The HIPAA Privacy Rule (Standards for Privacy of Individually Identifiable Health Information) provided the first national standards for protecting the privacy of health information. The Privacy Rule regulates how certain entities, called covered entities, use and disclose certain individually identifiable health information, called protected health information (PHI). PHI is individually identifiable health information that is transmitted or maintained in any form or medium (for example, electronic, paper, oral), but excludes certain educational records and employment records. Among other provisions, the Privacy Rule provides for the following:

- ▶ Gives patients more control over their health information.

- ▶ Sets boundaries on the use and release of health records.

- ▶ Establishes appropriate safeguards that the majority of health-care providers and others must achieve to protect the privacy of health information.

- ▶ Holds violators accountable with civil and criminal penalties that can be imposed if they violate patients' privacy rights.

- ▶ Strikes a balance when public health responsibilities support disclosure of certain forms of data.

- ▶ Enables patients to make informed choices based on how individual health information can be used.

- ▶ Enables patients to find out how their information can be used and what disclosures of their information have been made.

- ▶ Generally limits release of information to the minimum reasonably needed for the purpose of the disclosure.

- ▶ Generally gives patients the right to obtain a copy of their own health records and request corrections.

- ▶ Empowers individuals to control certain uses and disclosures of their health information.

The deadline to comply with the Privacy Rule was April 14, 2003, for the majority of the three types of covered entities specified by the rule [45 CFR § 160.102]. The covered entities are the following:

- ▸ Health plans

- ▸ Health-care clearinghouses

- ▸ Health-care providers who transmit health information in electronic form in connection with certain transactions

At DHHS, the Office for Civil Rights (OCR) has oversight and enforcement responsibilities for the Privacy Rule. Comprehensive guidance and OCR answers to hundreds of questions are available at http://www.hhs.gov/ocr/hipaa.

DHHS recognized the importance of sharing PHI to accomplish essential public health objectives and to meet certain other societal needs (for example, administration of justice and law enforcement). Therefore, the Privacy Rule expressly permits PHI to be shared for specified public health purposes. For example, covered entities can disclose PHI, without individual authorization, to a public health authority legally authorized to collect or receive the information for the purpose of preventing or controlling disease, injury, or disability [45 CFR § 164.512(b)]. Further, the Privacy Rule permits covered entities to make disclosures that are required by other laws, including laws that require disclosures for public health purposes. Thus, the Privacy Rule provides for the continued functioning of the U.S public health system.

HIPAA Security

The American public began to register serious concerns about the privacy and security of health records in the early 1990s. Breaches of health privacy, such as press disclosures of individuals' HIV status, network hacking incidents, and misdirected patient emails fueled this concern. At the same time, health-care industry and federal agencies working toward HIPAA "administrative simplification" and increased automation of health information realized that their initiatives would be unsuccessful without incorporating more effective information-security measures. When HIPAA was passed in 1996, it included a mandate for standards that would ensure the security and integrity of health information that is maintained or transmitted electronically. A Notice of Proposed Rulemaking (NPRM) on security was published by DHHS on August 12, 1998.

The Security Rule focuses on both external and internal security threats and vulnerabilities. Threats from "outsiders" include breaking through network firewalls, email attacks through interception or viruses, compromise of passwords, posing as organization "insiders," computer viruses, and modem number prefix scanning. These activities can result in denial of service, such as the disruption of information flow by "crashing" or overloading critical computer servers. The outsider might steal and misuse proprietary information, including individual health information. Attacks can also affect the integrity of information, by corrupting data that is being transmitted.

Internal threats are of equal concern, and are far more likely to occur according to many security experts. Organizations must protect against careless staff or others who are unaware of security issues, and curious or malicious insiders who deliberately take advantage of system vulnerabilities to access and misuse personal health information.

The rule is intended to set a minimum level or "floor" of security. Organizations can choose to implement safeguards that exceed the HIPAA standards—and, in fact, might find that their business strategies require stronger protections. Covered entities are required to

▶ Assess potential risks and vulnerabilities.

▶ Protect against threats to information security or integrity, and against unauthorized use or disclosure.

▶ Implement and maintain security measures that are appropriate to their needs, capabilities, and circumstances.

▶ Ensure compliance with these safeguards by all staff.

Central to HIPAA security is the tenet that information security must be comprehensive. No single policy, practice, or tool can ensure effective overall security. Cultural and organizational issues must be addressed, as well as technological and physical concerns. The safeguards that comprise HIPAA-mandated security focus on protecting "data integrity, confidentiality, and availability" of individually identifiable health information through the following:

▶ **Administrative procedures**—Documented, formal practices to manage the selection and execution of security measures.

▶ **Physical safeguards**—Protection of computer systems and related buildings and equipment from hazards and intrusion.

▶ **Technical security services**—Processes that protect and monitor information access.

▶ **Technical security mechanisms**—Processes that prevent unauthorized access to data that is transmitted over a network.

These regulations established standards for all health plans, clearinghouses, and storage of health-care information to ensure the integrity, confidentiality, and availability of electronic protected health information. Proposed rules were published on August 12, 1998. Final rules were published on February 20, 2003, and compliance had to occur by April 20, 2005.

HIPAA Implications for Exchange Server 2010 Environments

The most important implication that HIPAA requirements have on an Exchange Server 2010 environment is regarding data security. Organizations subject to HIPAA regulations must demonstrate that they are taking significant precautions against confidential patient data being compromised, lost, or stolen. This includes the transmission of this type of data across a medium such as email.

Exchange Server 2010 can help organizations become HIPAA compliant through the use of enterprise policies that define when email data is encrypted, thus securing the transmission of protected data. Information on how to set up these policies is presented in upcoming sections of this chapter.

Understanding the Gramm-Leach-Bliley Act

Information that many would consider private—including bank balances and account numbers—is regularly bought and sold by banks, credit card companies, and other financial institutions. The Gramm-Leach-Bliley Act (GLBA), which is also known as the Financial Services Modernization Act of 1999, provides limited privacy protections against the sale of the private financial information of consumers. In addition, the GLBA codifies protections against pretexting, the practice of obtaining personal information through false pretenses.

The GLBA primarily sought to "modernize" financial services—that is, end regulations that prevented the merger of banks, stock brokerage companies, and insurance companies. The removal of these regulations, however, raised significant risks that these new financial institutions would have access to an incredible amount of personal information, with no restrictions upon its use. Prior to GLBA, the insurance company that maintained health records was distinct from the bank that held the mortgage on a consumer's house or the stockbroker who traded a person's stock. After these companies merged, however, they had the ability to consolidate, analyze, and sell the personal details of their customers' lives. Because of these risks, the GLBA included three simple requirements to protect the personal data of individuals: First, banks, brokerage companies, and insurance companies must securely store personal financial information. Second, they must advise consumers of their policies on sharing of personal financial information. Third, they must give consumers the option to opt out of some sharing of personal financial information.

Privacy Protections Under the GLBA

The GLBA's privacy protections only regulate financial institutions—businesses that are engaged in banking, insuring, stocks and bonds, financial advice, and investing.

First, these financial institutions, regardless of whether they want to disclose the personal information of individuals, must develop precautions to ensure the security and confidentiality of customer records and information, to protect against any anticipated threats or hazards to the security or integrity of such records, and to protect against unauthorized access to or use of such records or information that could result in substantial harm or inconvenience to any customer.

Second, financial institutions are required to provide consumers with a notice of their information-sharing policies when the individual first becomes a customer, and annually thereafter. That notice must inform the consumer of the financial institutions' policies on disclosing nonpublic personal information (NPI) to affiliates and nonaffiliated third parties, disclosing NPI after the customer relationship is terminated, and protecting NPI. "Nonpublic personal information" means all information on applications to obtain financial services (credit card or loan applications), account histories (bank or credit card), and the fact that an individual is or was a customer. This interpretation of NPI makes names, addresses, telephone numbers, Social Security numbers, and other data subject to the GLBA's data-sharing restrictions.

Third, the GLBA gives consumers the right to opt out from a limited amount of NPI sharing. Specifically, a consumer can direct the financial institution to not share information with unaffiliated companies.

Consumers have no right under the GLBA to stop sharing of NPI among affiliates. An affiliate is any company that controls, is controlled by, or is under common control with another company. The individual consumer has absolutely no control over this kind of "corporate family" trading of personal information.

Several exemptions under the GLBA can permit information sharing over the consumer's objection. For instance, if a financial institution wants to engage the services of a separate company, they can transfer personal information to that company by arguing that the information is necessary to the services that the company will perform. A financial institution can transfer information to a marketing or sales company to sell new products (different stocks) or jointly offered products (co-sponsored credit cards). After this unaffiliated third party has an individual's personal information, they can share it with their own "corporate family." However, they themselves cannot likewise transfer the information to further companies through this exemption.

In addition, financial institutions can disclose information to credit reporting agencies and to financial regulatory agencies, as part of the sale of a business, to comply with any other laws or regulations, or as necessary for a transaction requested by the consumer.

Fourth, financial institutions are prohibited from disclosing, other than to a consumer reporting agency, access codes or account numbers to any nonaffiliated third party for use in telemarketing, direct mail marketing, or other marketing through electronic mail. Thus, even if a consumer fails to "opt out" of a financial institution's transfers, the credit card numbers, PINs, or other access codes cannot be sold, as they had been in some previous cases.

Fifth, certain types of "pretexting" were prohibited by the GLBA. Pretexting is the practice of collecting personal information under false pretenses. Pretexters pose as authority figures (law enforcement agents, social workers, potential employers, and so on) and manufacture seductive stories (that the victim is about to receive a sweepstakes award or insurance payment) to elicit personal information about the victim. The GLBA prohibits the use of false, fictitious, or fraudulent statements or documents to get customer information from a financial institution or directly from a customer of a financial institution; the use of forged, counterfeit, lost, or stolen documents to get customer information from a financial institution or directly from a customer of a financial institution; and asking another person to get someone else's customer information using false, fictitious, or fraudulent documents or forged, counterfeit, lost, or stolen documents.

GLBA's Implications for Exchange Server 2010 Environments

GLBA strictly limits the disclosure of personal information outside of a company or its immediate corporate affiliates. Exchange Server policies in regard to email can be set up to monitor communications for specific types of personal data or key phrases, restricting where it can be sent.

Understanding Sarbanes-Oxley

Sarbanes-Oxley (often nicknamed SOX), named for the two congressmen who sponsored it, on the surface doesn't have much to do with IT security. The law was passed to restore the public's confidence in corporate governance by making chief executives of publicly traded companies personally validate financial statements and other information.

President Bush signed the law on July 30, 2002. Initially, companies had to be in compliance by the fall of 2003, but extensions were granted. Large corporations were given until June 15, 2004, to meet the requirements of Sarbanes-Oxley. Smaller companies had to comply by April 15, 2005.

Congress passed the law in quick response to accounting scandals surrounding Enron, Worldcom, and other companies. Sarbanes-Oxley deals with many corporate governance issues, including executive compensation and the use of independent directors. Section 404 mandates that each annual report contain an internal control report, which must state the responsibility of management for establishing and maintaining an adequate internal control structure and procedures for financial reporting. It must also contain an assessment, at the end of the issuer's most recent fiscal year, of the effectiveness of the internal control structure and procedures for financial reporting. The auditor must attest to, and report on, the assessment made by the management of the issuer. It's hard to sign off on the validity of data if the systems maintaining it aren't secure. It is the internal IT systems that keep the records of the organizations. If the IT systems aren't secure, internal controls can also be questioned.

Sarbanes-Oxley doesn't mandate specific internal controls such as strong authentication or the use of encryption. However, if someone can easily get into an organization's IT system, the security hole can establish a condition of noncompliance. Sarbanes-Oxley creates a link between upper management and the security operation staff on what is needed to ensure that proper and auditable security measures are in place. The executives who have to sign off on the internal controls have to ensure the security in their organizations is well established; otherwise, the executive could face criminal penalties if a breach is detected.

Sarbanes-Oxley's Implications for Exchange Server 2010 Environments

SOX controls stipulate that data must be secured and audited to make sure that a third party cannot manipulate financial data. Exchange Server 2010 includes administrative controls that protect an organization from security breaches. In addition, SOX controls look to an organization to establish specific guidelines in regard to data retention and data transfer controls. These factors can be controlled using specific Exchange Server enterprise policies, such as mail retention policies, privacy policies, and confidentiality policies, as outlined in subsequent sections of this chapter.

Using Transport Agents in Exchange Server 2010

Transport agents are part of the core Exchange Server functionality provided to organizations that allow for policies to be enforced within the messaging platform. Microsoft designed these policies with built-in support for third-party add-ons. This allows other companies to build products that directly integrate with Exchange Server 2010 to scan mail and to run specific tasks on the mail that flows through the system.

At their core, Transport agents are just a programmatic method of performing tasks on mail based on a specified criterion. They can range in complexity from a simple "Forward a copy of all emails sent to this person to this particular email address" to "Apply this equation to this email message to determine whether or not it is spam."

Understanding the Role of Transport Agents in Policy Management

Transport agents are especially important for companies looking to bring their messaging platform into compliance with specific governmental regulations, as some of the default transport agents, such as journaling or mail retention policies, offer out-of-the-box functionality that is required by many of these regulations. For situations where built-in functionality might not suffice, the field of third-party add-ons to Exchange Server 2010 transport agents is increasing every day, so organizations can deploy a custom agent to perform a specific task.

Prioritizing Transport Agents

Exchange Server 2010 allows administrators to prioritize the order in which transport agents act on a message. As an SMTP message passes through the transport pipeline, different SMTP events are acted out. These events, with names such as `OnHeloCommand` and `OnConnectEvent`, happen in a specific order every time, and transport agents set to act upon a specific event will only fire when that event has occurred. After it occurs, however, the priority level can be set, determining which transport agent acts first at that particular juncture.

Changing priority on a specific transport rule is as simple as right-clicking on the rule in the details pane and choosing Change Priority.

Using Pipeline Tracing to Troubleshoot Transport Agents

Pipeline tracing with Exchange Server 2010 transport agents is a diagnostic tool that can be used to send a copy of the mail message as it existed before and after a transport rule went into effect. This copy is sent to a specific mailbox.

To enable Pipeline tracing on an Exchange server, run the following command from the Exchange Management Shell:

```
Set-TransportServer Server5 –PipelineTracingEnabled $True
```

where Server5 is the name of the server. To set a specific mailbox to be the pipeline tracing mailbox, run the following command from the shell:

```
Set-TransportServer Server5 -PipelineTracingSenderAddress zack@companyabc.com
```

where `Server5` is the name of the server and only mail from zack@companyabc.com is traced through the pipeline.

Pipeline tracing must be enabled on all Hub Transport and/or Edge Transport servers in the topology for it to be useful as a troubleshooting mechanism.

Outlining the Built-in Transport Agents in Exchange Server 2010

Exchange Server 2010 contains built-in support for a wide variety of transport agents. Some of these agents run off of Hub Transport servers, and others run off of Edge Transport servers.

The Hub Transport server role transport agents are as follows:

- ▶ Journaling agent
- ▶ AD RMS Prelicensing agent
- ▶ Transport Rule agent

The Edge Transport server role transport agents are as follows:

- ▶ Content Filter agent
- ▶ Sender ID agent
- ▶ Recipient Filter agent
- ▶ Connection Filtering agent
- ▶ Attachment Filtering agent
- ▶ Address Rewriting Outbound agent
- ▶ Address Rewriting Inbound agent
- ▶ Edge Rule agent
- ▶ Sender Filter agent
- ▶ Protocol Analysis agent

Understanding the Hub Role Transport Agents in Exchange Server 2010

As previously mentioned, a handful of the default transport agents in Exchange Server 2010 are designed to run on servers running the Hub Transport role in an Exchange Server organization. These agents are designed to run against internal traffic as well as the external traffic that is being routed inside the organization. These agents are the Transport Rule agent, the AD RMS Prelicensing agent, and the Journaling agent, each of which is described further in the following sections.

Working with Transport Rule Agents

Transport Rule agents is the generic term used to describe any server-side rule that is run on the Hub Transport servers. These rules are very similar in design to Outlook rules, but they are run against the entire organization.

To create a simple transport rule to test these chapter concepts, perform the following tasks in Exchange Management Console:

1. From Exchange Management Console, expand Organization Configuration and then click on Hub Transport in the console pane.
2. In the actions pane, click New Transport Rule.
3. From the New Transport Rule Wizard, enter a descriptive name for the rule and ensure that the Enable Rule check box is checked. Click Next to continue.
4. In the Conditions box, shown in Figure 14.1, select which conditions the rule will operate under. In this example, it will fire on messages received from all users inside the company. Click Next to continue.

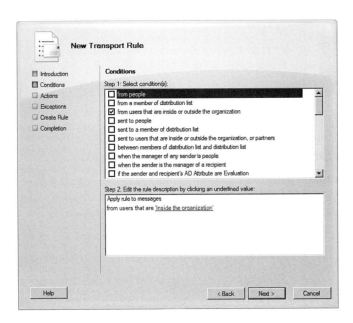

FIGURE 14.1   Creating a transport rule.

5. In the Actions box, select which action to take. Click Next to continue.
6. In the Exceptions box, enter any potential exceptions to the rule, and click Next to continue.

7. Click New to finalize the transport rule creation.

8. Click Finish.

CAUTION

Transport rules are very powerful, and improperly configuring a transport rule can result in the loss of mail data or other issues. Use caution when creating transport rules and always test them in a lab environment first.

Transport rules use Active Directory (AD) replication to replicate any changes made to specific rules. Each Hub Transport server queries AD once every four hours for changes made to transport agents, and then processes all new messages based on the changes made to the rules.

Transport agents are highly customizable, and it is wise to go through the wizards several times to determine what type of rule functionality is available, and if your specific organization can take advantage of them.

NOTE

When a change is made to a transport rule, it can take multiple hours for that change to be enforced. This has to do with the fact that the change must be replicated over AD, which can be set to replicate slowly. In addition, the Hub Transport servers use a cache to avoid constantly asking AD for changes. This cache expires in four hours, so it is important to note how long it can take before a change is properly replicated.

Configuring Rights Management Services Prelicensing Agent

The Rights Management Services (RMS) Prelicensing agent is a transport agent that runs on a Hub Transport server to allow for Rights Management processing of emails. It verifies the authenticity of an email message without prompting the user for authentication.

The RMS transport agent requires Windows Rights Management Services Service Pack 2 or higher to function properly.

Working with Journaling and Mail Retention Policies in Exchange Server 2010

Journaling in Exchange Server 2010 is a method by which all copies of emails sent to or from specific users is backed up and logged. Even if the original email is deleted, the journaling system has access to the original content in the email. Journaling is especially relevant to many organizations looking to comply with governmental regulations such as SEC Rule 17A-4, SOX, GLBA, HIPAA, the Patriot Act, and NASD 3110.

Exploring the Journaling Licensing Differences

Journaling in Exchange Server 2010 goes beyond the capabilities present in the older versions of Exchange Server. Exchange Server now allows for two types of journaling:

▶ **Standard journaling**—Standard journaling is essentially the same journaling mechanism used in pre-Exchange Server 2007 versions of Exchange Server. This form of journaling requires that journaling be turned on to all users in a specific database.

▶ **Premium journaling**—Premium journaling offers new capabilities, such as per-recipient journaling, journal rule replication, and the ability to change the scope of the journaling rule.

Premium journaling allows for the scope of the journaling to be performed to be specified. Options are to limit the scope to Internal, External, or Global. If the scope is not changed from Internal to External, journaling is not performed if the user sending the message is not remote.

14

> **NOTE**
>
> Premium journaling requires an Exchange Server 2010 Enterprise Edition client access license (CAL) to be purchased for each user of the system. This should not be confused with Enterprise server licenses for Exchange, which are per-server licenses as opposed to per-client licenses.

Enabling per Mailbox Journaling

Standard journaling is turned on on a per-database basis. After being turned on, it is on for all mailboxes within that database. To configure a database for mailbox journaling, perform the following steps:

> **CAUTION**
>
> Per-database journaling is very intensive, and can increase the processing and memory needed by 25%. It is, therefore, important to understand the implications of turning on journaling, and to limit the functionality when possible.

1. Within the Exchange Management Console, navigate to Organization Configuration and choose the Mailbox node in the console pane.

2. Right-click on the database in the center pane and choose Properties.

3. On the Maintenance tab, check the Journal Recipient check box, as shown in Figure 14.2. Click Browse to select the mailbox that will be used for journaling.

4. Click OK.

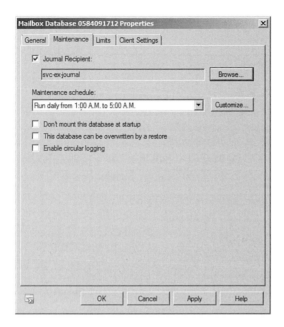

FIGURE 14.2   Enabling journaling on a database.

CAUTION

The mailbox that is used for journaling should be closely guarded and protected, as all the journaled messages from the databases will be stored there.

Creating Journal Rules

Journal rules can be created to activate the premium journaling options available in Exchange Server 2010 to those clients with Enterprise Edition Licensing CALs. To set up a journal rule, do the following:

1. From Exchange Management Console, click Organization Configuration, and then click the Hub Transport node.

2. In the actions pane, click New Journaling Rule.

3. Enter a descriptive name in the Rule Name field.

4. Click Browse to locate a journal email address where journal reports will be sent.

5. Change the scope to the desired level; this determines on which emails the rule will fire.

6. If you need to limit the journaling to a specific user or group of users, you can check the Journal E-mail for Recipient check box and click Browse to locate the group or user, as shown in Figure 14.3. When you are finished, click New.

7. Click Finish.

FIGURE 14.3   Enabling a journaling rule on all email messages.

Setting Up Email Disclaimers

Email disclaimers have long been a desired feature in Exchange Server. In the past, complex SMTP event sinks or third-party products have provided this functionality, but Exchange Server 2010 now includes the built-in ability to apply a legal disclaimer to the end of all email messages. The transport rule topology is used for this mechanism.

To add a disclaimer to the Hub Transport role, do the following:

1. From Exchange Management Console, click on the Hub Transport node under the Organization Configuration.

2. Click New Transport Rule from the actions pane.

3. Under Name, enter a descriptive name for the disclaimer and click Next.

4. Leave the Conditions check boxes blank (so the rule will apply to all messages). Click Next.

5. Click Yes when prompted with the warning about the rule applying to all messages.

6. In the Actions box, check the "Append Disclaimer Text..." check box, as shown in Figure 14.4.

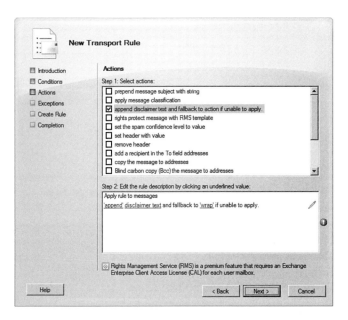

FIGURE 14.4   Creating a disclaimer.

7. Click the blue text shown in the diagram; this opens dialog boxes allowing for the disclaimer to be written. Click Next when you are finished.

8. Leave the Exceptions check boxes blank and click Next.

9. Click New.

10. Click Finish.

Implementing Transport Agent Policies on the Edge

The Edge Transport server role is vital in today's risk-fraught messaging environment as it is responsible for intercepting the onslaught of viruses and spam before they reach the internal network. Special transport rules have been created specifically for Edge servers in Exchange Server 2010. These transport rules include address rewriting policies, content filtering policies, SenderID, and Sender Filtering.

Understanding the Role of EdgeSync in Exchange Policy Management

The EdgeSync service runs as a special synchronization component that keeps specific information from the internal AD forest in sync with an external AD in Application Mode (ADAM) forest. It uses this information to determine if policies have changed. For more information on EdgeSync, see Chapter 8, "Implementing Edge Services for an Exchange Server 2010 Environment."

Implementing Edge Rule Agents

Many of the transport rules in Exchange Server 2010 were designed to work on the Edge Transport role systems. This is especially true for services such as antivirus and antispam. Several other key pieces of functionality are run as policies on Edge Rule agents, as described in this section.

Setting Up Address Rewriting Policies

One of the edge transport rules available by default is the address rewriting policy. This policy allows internal email domains to be rewritten to a common external domain, or any other combination of domain rewriting as necessary.

Address rewriting cannot currently be performed from the graphical user interface (GUI)—it must be scripted. The following illustrates a sample script to set up a rewriting policy:

```
New-AddressRewriteEntry -name "marina@abc.internal to marina@companyabc.com"
-InternalAddress marina@abc.internal -ExternalAddress marina@companyabc.com
```

This sample policy rewrites any instance of marina@abc.internal to marina@companyabc.com.

Configuring Content Filtering Policies

Edge Server role systems have a built-in Content filter running to provide for antispam and antivirus functionality. This agent serves as a direct replacement for the Exchange 2003 Intelligent Message Filter (IMF). The agent works by assigning a Spam Confidence Level of 1-9 for an email. The higher the number, the more likely it is to be spam. Removing the junk messages at the edge is the best way to reduce the load that this type of environment has on the current messaging environment.

Working with Sender Filtering Policies

Sender filtering on an Edge Transport role server allows for antispam functionality on the edge. It can be easily enabled or disabled for a server by following the command outlined as follows:

1. On the Edge server in Exchange Management Console, click Edge Transport.
2. In the work pane, click the Antispam tab.

3. Click Sender Filtering.

4. Click either the Disable or Enable action, depending on how you want to set it up.

Understanding and Configuring SenderID

SenderID is an antispam framework that defines how organizations can create special domain name system (DNS) records, known as Sender Policy Framework (SPF) records, to easily verify that they really are who they purport to be.

SenderID can be disabled or enabled on an Edge Transport server via the following process:

1. On the Edge server in Exchange Management Console, click Edge Transport.

2. In the work pane, click the Antispam tab.

3. Click Sender ID.

4. Click either the Disable or Enable action, depending on the action desired.

Creating Messaging Records Management Policies

Messaging Records Management (MRM) in Exchange Server 2010 allows organizations to create and enforce mailbox retention policies for their messaging environment. It has a very granular administration model, so administrators can turn off the process for individual users.

Understanding the Scope of MRM

MRM is flexible in its approach, as it allows for different policies to be set up for different managed folders. MRM deployment takes place in several steps, as follows:

1. Create any custom managed folders, as necessary.

2. Create Managed Content Settings on specific managed folders.

3. Create any managed folder mailbox policies as necessary to group together specific Managed Content Settings.

4. Apply the managed folder mailbox policy to a mailbox or set of mailboxes.

5. Schedule the Managed Folder Assistant.

For example, an administrator might want to set up a data retention policy that allowed items stored in the Inbox to be stored for one year. That administrator could then create a new custom managed folder named "Data Retention Folder" that had a policy of not deleting items before 10 years. These two managed folders could have the specific Managed Content Settings set on them, and then they would be grouped together into a single managed folder mailbox policy. This policy would then be applied to all mailboxes in the organization. Finally, the administrator could schedule the Managed Folder Assistant to run on a regular basis to enforce these policies.

The step-by-step procedures for setting up this type of scenario are outlined in the following sections.

Creating Custom Managed Folders

The first step is to create a custom folder definition for the 10-year retention folder. This folder will be added as a subfolder in all mailboxes that are added to the policy. To create this custom managed folder, do the following:

1. From Exchange Management Console, expand Organization Configuration and choose the Mailbox node.

2. In the actions pane, click New Managed Custom Folder.

3. Type a descriptive name for the custom folder in the Name field. In addition, list a display name that will be shown when it is viewed in Outlook. As optional settings, you can configure a storage limit, comments, and force users to not be able to minimize the folder, as shown in Figure 14.5.

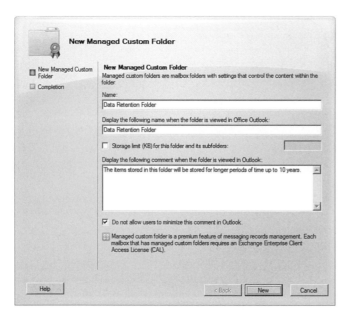

FIGURE 14.5   Creating a managed custom folder.

4. Click New and then click Finish.

Creating Managed Content Settings

The second step is to define the content settings that will be applied to the Inbox and to the custom folder that was created. The content settings define how long the data will be kept before it is deleted. To perform this task, complete the following steps:

1. From the Mailbox node under Organization Configuration, right-click on the newly created custom folder, and choose New Managed Content Settings.

2. Type a descriptive name for the content settings, and then enter in the type of retention policy, as shown in Figure 14.6. In this case, we are setting the policy at 10
   years, or 3,650 days. Click Next when you are finished.

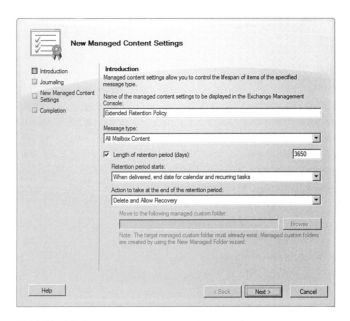

FIGURE 14.6   Creating Managed Content Settings.

3. On the Journaling tab, you have the option to forward a copy of the item to another
   location. Click Next to continue.

4. Click New and then click Finish.

5. Repeat the process for any other custom folders or the default folders. In this example, you would repeat the process for the default Inbox folder, and set the policy
   retention to one year for that folder.

Creating Managed Folder Mailbox Policies

Next, these folders must be added into a single overarching policy. To do so, perform the
following tasks:

1. From Exchange Management Console, in the Mailbox node under Organization
   Configuration, choose the Managed Folder Mailbox Policies tab.

2. Click New Managed Folder Mailbox Policy from the actions pane.

3. Enter a descriptive name for the policy, and then click the Add button.

4. Select a managed folder from the list—in this case, the Inbox and the Data Retention Folder (the custom one created; hold down the Ctrl key while selecting more than one option). Click OK and review the additions to the wizard, as shown in Figure 14.7.

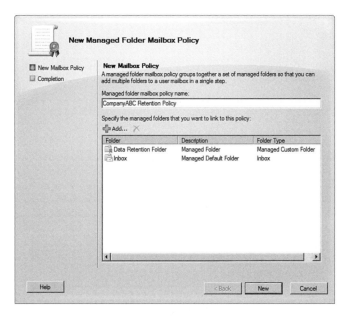

FIGURE 14.7   Creating a managed folder mailbox policy.

5. Click New and then click Finish.

Applying Managed Folder Mailbox Policies to Mailboxes

Finally, the mailboxes themselves must be added into this policy. To do so, follow these steps:

1. In Exchange Management Console, select the Mailbox node under the Recipient Configuration node.

2. Right-click the user who will be added to the policy, and select Properties.

3. Select the Mailbox Settings tab.

4. Click Messaging Records Management, and then click the Properties button.

5. Check the Managed Folder Mailbox Policy check box, and click the Browse button and choose the Managed Folder Mailbox Policy you just created. Click OK. Review the settings, as shown in Figure 14.8.

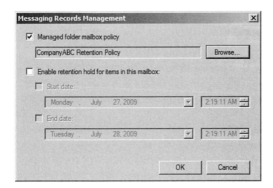

FIGURE 14.8   Applying a managed folder mailbox policy to a mailbox.

6. Click OK and then click OK again to save the changes.

An alternative method to using the GUI is to use the command-line shell. The syntax would be similar to the following example:

```
Set-Mailbox –Identity Carrie –ManagedFolderMailboxPolicy "CompanyABC
Retention Policy"
```

Scheduling the Managed Folder Assistant

You might want to change the default cleanup schedule for policy enforcement from the default, which is set to run from 1:00 a.m. to 5:00 a.m. in the morning. To do so, perform the following steps:

1. From Exchange Management Console, click the Mailbox node under the Server Configuration node.

2. Select the server name from the list, right-click it, and choose Properties on the shortcut menu.

3. Select the Messaging Records Management tab, and change the drop-down box to say Use Custom Schedule.

4. Click the Customize button.

5. Select a time window for the management to occur, similar to what is shown in Figure 14.9.

6. Click OK and then click OK again to save the settings.

The same process outlined in these step-by-step guides can be used to create any number of granular mailbox retention policies, as needed for governmental regulation and/or compliance.

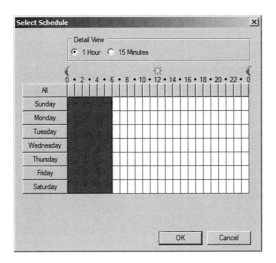

FIGURE 14.9   Scheduling the Managed Folder Assistant.

Summary

Organizations today are subject to any number of strict governmental and industry regulations in regard to messaging retention, email security, and policy enforcement. Fortunately, Exchange Server 2010 has unprecedented levels of policy enforcement built in to the application, helping organizations to become compliant with these regulations and positioning them to better control their messaging environment going forward.

Best Practices

The following are best practices from this chapter:

▶ Establish Messaging Records Management policies to control mailbox retention in Exchange Server 2010.

▶ Fully understand the implications of the various governmental regulations, such as HIPAA, SOX, GLBA, and others.

▶ Use transport agents to control email traffic with well-defined policies. This includes Edge Transport server role transport agents and Hub Transport server role transport agents.

▶ Use Premium journaling when you have Enterprise client access licenses (CALs) and if the need for journaling on individual mailboxes is required.

CHAPTER 15

Migrating from Active Directory 2000/2003 to Active Directory 2008

As organizations plan their migration to Microsoft Exchange Server 2010, many organizations are considering their migration to Active Directory 2008 during their Exchange Server migration project. Although the server that Exchange Server 2010 runs on must be Windows Server 2008 or higher, the entire organization does not need to be on Windows 2008 or Active Directory 2008. Exchange Server 2010 does require that the Forest and Domain functional levels are Windows 2003 or higher; therefore, an organizational update to at least Active Directory 2003 native mode is required. However, as many organizations take the opportunity to migrate Active Directory to 2008 at the same time they migrate to Exchange Server 2010, this chapter focuses on the steps necessary to help those organizations plan, prepare, and implement their migration from Active Directory 2000 or 2003 to Active Directory 2008.

Understanding What Needs to Be Migrated to Windows Server 2008

As you plan your migration to Exchange Server 2010, it would help if you knew exactly what needs to be on Windows 2008 and what needs to be on Windows 2003 (or higher). There are many components in a network from the server on which Exchange Server 2010 is installed to the Active Directory to which the Exchange server is connected. Specifically, the various components of a network with which Exchange Server interacts include the following:

▶ Server operating system

▶ Domain functional level

▶ Flexible Single Master Operations roles

▶ Forest functional level

NOTE

References throughout this chapter to Windows Server 2008 and Active Directory 2008 also refer to Windows Server 2008 R2 and Active Directory 2008 R2. In general, this chapter just notes 2008, not 2008 R2, however what typically applies to Windows and Active Directory 2008 also directly applies to Windows 2008 R2 and Active Directory 2008 R2 unless directly specified.

Exchange Server 2010 on a Windows Server 2008 Operating System

Exchange Server 2010 runs only on a Windows 2008 (or higher) operating system (OS)—it won't run on Windows 2003 Server or any other version of Windows. More specifically, Exchange Server 2010 requires an x64-bit version of Windows 2008 or higher to run on because Exchange Server 2010 is a 64-bit application. Therefore, the migration path from Exchange Server 2003 or 2007 to Exchange Server 2010 requires a transition (movement of mailboxes) between old Exchange servers to new Exchange Server 2010 servers. There is no in-place upgrade option to get to Exchange Server 2010.

Exchange Server 2010 in a Windows 2003 Server Native Functional Level Domain

In addition to running on a Windows 2008 (or higher) x64-bit operating system, Exchange Server 2010 needs to be installed in a domain that is running at a functional level of Windows 2003 native mode. This means that the domain can no longer have Windows NT 4.0 or Windows 2000 domain controllers. The domain controllers in the domain must be running Windows 2003 or higher. This has confused many organizations as a Windows 2003 native functional level DOES NOT mean that all Windows NT 4.0 and Windows 2000 workstations or servers must be replaced, just the domain controllers need to be updated to at least Windows 2003. A Windows 2003 functional level domain can have Windows NT 4.0 and Windows 2000 servers and workstations as member servers and systems in the domain.

Importance of Windows Server 2003 Relative to Flexible Single Master Operation Roles

The Windows domain that Exchange Server 2010 is installed in needs to have specific Flexible Single Master Operations (FSMO) roles. The domain controller that is the Schema Master of the forest where Exchange Server 2010 will reside must be running on a system that has Windows 2003 SP1 or higher installed. This is because Exchange Server 2010 requires a version of the schema that is not supported by the attributes available on a

Windows 2000 Schema Master domain controller. As with the domain functional level, this does not mean ALL servers must be running Windows 2003 in the environment. Simply the domain controller holding the master schema for the network, which is typically the first domain controller that was used to create the Active Directory (AD) forest, needs to be running Windows 2003 SP1 or higher.

In addition, at least one global catalog server in every Active Directory site that Exchange Server 2010 is installed in needs to run Windows 2003 SP1 or higher. This is a requirement because Exchange Server 2010 gets its directory information for routing of messages as well as user and resource lookup through Active Directory objects that can only be queried on a Windows 2003 SP1 or higher global catalog system. This does not mean that every single global catalog server needs to be running Windows 2003 SP1 or higher, nor does it mean that every site needs to have a global catalog server. What this means is that every Active Directory site that has an Exchange Server 2010 installed in it must have a Windows 2003 SP1 or higher global catalog server.

> **NOTE**
>
> Although an actual Exchange Server 2010 server needs to run on Windows 2008 x64-bit edition, the domain controllers, global catalog servers, Schema Master server, or other Windows systems in a network can run a 32-bit version of Windows 2003 or Windows 2008. Only the actual Exchange Server 2010 servers need to be on a 64-bit platform. However in very large enterprise environments, performance metrics have found that a 64-bit global catalog server better serves the organization for directory look-up, so see Chapter 4, "Architecting an Enterprise-Level Exchange Server Environment" for more details.

Forest Functional Level Requirements for Server Exchange 2010

Lastly, the forest in which Exchange Server 2010 will reside needs to be at a forest functional level of Windows Server 2003. Promoting a forest to a Windows Server 2003 forest functional level is covered in the section "Upgrading Domain and Forest Functional Levels" later in this chapter.

In many ways, a migration from Active Directory 2000 or 2003 to Active Directory 2008 is more of a service pack upgrade than a major migration scenario. Different components can be upgraded to Windows 2003 whether it is the operating system or the functional level of the domain or forest. The differences between the operating systems are more evolutionary than revolutionary, and, consequently, there are fewer design considerations upgrading from Active Directory 2000 or 2003 to 2008 than with an upgrade from a Windows NT 4.0 domain.

This chapter focuses on the planning, strategy, and logistics of migration from Active Directory 2000 or 2003 to 2008. In addition, specialized procedures such as using Mixed-Mode Domain Redirect and migrating using the Active Directory Migration Tool (ADMT) are described, and step-by-step instructions complement these processes.

Understanding the Benefits to Upgrading Active Directory

The decision to upgrade Active Directory to a newer version is more than just making sure Active Directory is up to date; the organization should keep in mind some of the benefits it receives when migrating to a newer version of AD. If one or more of the improvements to Active Directory Domain Services justifies an upgrade, it validates the decision to migrate to AD 2008 or AD 2008 R2. Improvements were introduced in Windows Server 2003 and yet more improvements in Windows 2008 and Windows 2008 R2.

Benefits of Active Directory 2003

Active Directory 2000 was the first version of AD to ship from Microsoft and was the base configuration of the directory. Microsoft made a number of major updates to Active Directory 2003 extending the basic AD to include a number of needed features and functions. The following list details some of the many changes made to Active Directory in Windows Server 2003 that improved on the original Windows 2000 Active Directory:

▶ **Domain rename capability**—Windows Server 2003 Active Directory supported the renaming of either the NetBIOS name or the LDAP/DNS name of an Active Directory domain. The Active Directory domain rename tool can be used for this purpose, but only in domains that have completely upgraded to Windows Server 2003 or later domain controllers.

▶ **Cross-forest transitive trusts**—Windows Server 2003 supports the implementation of transitive trusts that can be established between separate Active Directory forests. Windows 2000 supported only explicit cross-forest trusts, and the trust structure did not allow for permissions to flow between separate domains in a forest. This limitation has been lifted in Windows Server 2003 or later.

▶ **Universal group caching**—One of the main structural limitations of Active Directory was the need to establish very "chatty" global catalog servers in every site established in a replication topology, or run the risk of extremely slow client logon times and directory queries. Windows Server 2003 or later enables remote domain controllers to cache universal group memberships for users so that each logon request does not require the use of a local global catalog server.

▶ **Intersite topology generator (ISTG) improvements**—The ISTG in Windows Server 2003 was improved to support configurations with extremely large numbers of sites. In addition, the time required to determine site topology has been noticeably improved through the use of a more efficient ISTG algorithm.

▶ **Multivalued attribute replication improvements**—In Windows 2000, if a universal group changed its membership from 5,000 users to 5,001 users, the entire group membership had to be re-replicated across the entire forest. Windows Server 2003 addressed this problem and allowed incremental membership changes to be replicated.

▶ **Lingering objects (zombies) detection**—Domain controllers that have been out of service for a longer period of time than the Time to Live (TTL) of a deleted object could theoretically "resurrect" those objects, forcing them to come back to life as zombies, or lingering objects. Windows Server 2003 properly identified these zombies and prevented them from being replicated to other domain controllers.

▶ **AD-integrated DNS zones in application partitions**—Replication of DNS zones was improved and made more flexible in Windows Server 2003 by storing AD-integrated zones in the application partition of a forest, thus limiting their need to be replicated to all domain controllers and reducing network traffic. Conversely, the DNS zones could be configured to replicate them to the entire forest if that was appropriate.

Benefits of Active Directory 2008

Five years after AD 2003 was released, Microsoft made a number of additional improvements to Active Directory with the release of AD 2008. Windows 2008 Active Directory retained all the updated features of Windows Server 2003 Active Directory and added several key new features. The updated AD 2008 features are as follows:

▶ **Fine-grained password policies**—Password policies can be customized to different users within the same Active Directory domain.

▶ **Read-Only Domain Controllers**—These domain controllers are designed for branch offices and for extranet scenarios, in that they allow directory information to be accessed but not changed. This adds an element of security to scenarios that require directory services but are not as secure as the corporate data center.

▶ **Granular auditing**—The Active Directory auditing is much more granular and allows tracking of some objects but not others. This reduces the volume of security logs; however, it provides less information for the auditor or analyst to review during an audit or information acquisition process.

▶ **Distributed File System Replication (DFSR)**—DFSR is now used for SYSVOL replication, replacing the File Replication Service (FRS) that is used to replicate SYSVOL in Windows 2000 Server and Windows Server 2003. This feature provides more robust and detailed replication of SYSVOL contents and is available when the domain functional level is raised to Windows Server 2008.

Benefits of Active Directory 2008 R2

Almost a decade after Active Directory was first released, Microsoft has once again updated the capabilities of Active Directory running on Windows 2008 R2. The Windows 2008 R2 Active Directory retained all the new features of Active Directory 2003 and Active Directory 2008, and added several key new features. The new AD 2008 R2 features are as follows:

▶ **Recovery of deleted objects**—Active Directory 2008 R2 has a recycle bin that allows an administrator to recover a deleted object and all of its corresponding and related objects.

15

▶ **Managed service accounts**—The maintenance of passwords relative to service accounts in Active Directory has always been a challenge for network administrators. As passwords expire, all applications utilizing service accounts had to be updated, usually resulting in service account passwords NOT being changed, which created a security issue for the organization. Active Directory 2008 R2 now supports managed service accounts where a password change to a service account invokes a feature that automatically updates the password for all services that use the service account.

▶ **Offline domain join**—With Active Directory 2008 R2, and administrator can take a workstation or server and join it to Active Directory without that system being connected to the network. An XML file is created that has all of the information for the target computer and generates a key that allows the target system to be added to the domain without even being connected to the network. During a system imaging or refresh process, the target system can be imaged and joined all offline so that the first time a user logs on to the network is the first time the system is physically connected to the network.

Beginning the Migration Process

Any migration procedure should define the reasons for migration, steps involved, fallback precautions, and other important factors that can influence the migration process. After finalizing these items, the migration can begin.

Identifying Migration Objectives

Two underlying philosophies influence technology upgrades, each philosophy working against the other. The first is the expression "If it ain't broke, don't fix it." Obviously, if an organization has a functional, easy-to-use, and well-designed Active Directory 2003 infrastructure, popping in a Windows Server 2008 or 2008 R2 DVD and upgrading the domain might not be so appealing. The second philosophy is something along the lines of "Those who fail to upgrade their technologies perish." Eventually, all technologies become outdated and unsupported, and a planned and staged update to the latest technologies keeps the organization's network current.

Choosing a pragmatic middle ground between these two philosophies effectively depends on the factors that drive an organization to upgrade. If the organization has critical business needs that can be satisfied by an upgrade, such an upgrade might be in the works. If, however, no critical need exists, it might be wise for an organization already on Active Directory 2003 to remain on Active Directory 2003 and not advance to Active Directory 2008 if they don't want to migrate since Exchange Server 2010 works fine in an Active Directory 2003 environment.

Establishing Migration Project Phases

After the decision is made to upgrade, a detailed plan of the resources, timeline, scope, and objectives of the project should be outlined. Part of any migration plan requires establishing either an ad-hoc project plan or a professionally drawn-up project plan. The migration plan assists the project managers of the migration project to accomplish the planned objectives in a timely manner with the correct application of resources.

The following is a condensed description of the standard phases for a migration project:

▶ **Discovery**—The first portion of a design project should be a discovery, or fact-finding, portion. This section focuses on the analysis of the current environment and documentation of the analysis results. Current network diagrams, server locations, wide area network (WAN) throughputs, server application dependencies, and all other networking components should be detailed as part of the Discovery phase.

▶ **Design**—The Design portion of a project is straightforward. All key components of the actual migration plan should be documented, and key data from the Discovery phase should be used to draw up design and migration documents. The project plan itself would normally be drafted during this phase. Because Active Directory 2008 is not dramatically different from Active Directory 2000 or 2003, significant reengineering of an existing Active Directory environment is not necessary. However, other issues such as server placement, new feature utilization, and changes in AD DS replication models should be outlined.

▶ **Prototype**—The Prototype phase of a project involves the essential lab work to test the design assumptions made during the Design phase. The ideal prototype would involve a mock production environment that is migrated from Active Directory 2000/2003 to Active Directory 2008. For Active Directory, this means creating a production domain controller (DC) and then isolating it in the lab and promoting it to the Operations Master (OM) server in the lab. The Active Directory migration can then be performed without affecting the production environment. Step-by-step procedures for the migration can also be outlined and produced as deliverables for this phase.

▶ **Pilot**—The Pilot phase, or Proof-of-Concept phase, involves a production "test" of the migration steps, on a limited scale. For example, a single server could be upgraded to Active Directory 2008 in advance of the migration of all other global catalog servers. In a slower, phased migration, the Pilot phase would essentially spill into Implementation, as upgrades of global catalog and domain controller servers are performed slowly, one by one.

▶ **Implementation**—The Implementation portion of the project is the full-blown migration of network functionality or upgrades to the operating system. As previously mentioned, this process can be performed quickly or slowly over time, depending on an organization's needs. It is, subsequently, important to make the timeline decisions in the Design phase and incorporate them into the project plan.

▶ **Training and Support**—Learning the ins and outs of the new functionality that Active Directory 2008 can bring to an environment is essential in realizing the increased productivity and reduced administration that the OS can bring to the environment. Consequently, it is important to include a Training portion into a migration project so that the design objectives can be fully realized.

For more detailed information on the project plan phases of a Windows 2008 migration, refer to Chapter 2, "Planning, Prototyping, Migrating, and Deploying Exchange Server 2010."

Comparing the In-Place Upgrade Versus New Hardware Migration Methods

Because the fundamental differences between Active Directory 2000/2003 and Active Directory 2008 are not significant, the possibility of simply upgrading an existing Active Directory 2000/2003 infrastructure is an option. Depending on the type of hardware currently in use in a Windows 2000/2003 network, this type of migration strategy becomes an option. Often, however, it is more appealing to simply introduce newer systems into an existing environment and retire the current servers from production. This technique normally has less impact on current environments and can also support fall-back more easily.

> **NOTE**
>
> Windows 2000 domain controllers cannot be upgraded directly to Windows 2008. Migrating a Windows 2000 domain controller to be a Windows 2008 domain controller requires the Windows 2000 domain controller to be replaced, rather than upgraded.

Determining which migration strategy to use depends on one major factor: the condition of the current hardware environment. If Windows 2000/2003 is taxing the limitations of the hardware in use, it might be preferable to introduce new servers into an environment and simply retire the old Windows 2000/2003 servers. This is particularly true if the existing servers are veterans of previous upgrades, maybe transitioning from Windows NT 4.0 to Windows 2000 to Windows Server 2003. If, however, the hardware in use is newer and more robust, and could conceivably last for another two to three years, it might be easier to simply perform in-place upgrades of the systems in an environment.

In most cases, organizations take a hybrid approach to migration. Older hardware or Windows 2000 domain controllers are replaced by new hardware running Windows 2003 or 2008. Newer Windows 2003 systems can more easily be upgraded in place to Windows 2008. Consequently, auditing all systems to be migrated and determining which ones will be upgraded and which ones will be retired are important steps in the migration process.

Identifying Migration Strategies: "Big Bang" Versus Phased Coexistence

As with most technology implementations, there are essentially two approaches in regard to deployment: a quick "Big Bang" approach or a slower phased coexistence approach. The Big Bang option involves the entire Windows 2000/2003 infrastructure being quickly replaced, often over the course of a weekend, with the new Windows 2008 environment; whereas the phased approach involves a slow, server-by-server replacement of Windows 2000/2003.

Each approach has its particular advantages and disadvantages, and key factors to Windows 2008 should be taken into account before a decision is made. Few Windows 2008 components require a redesign of current Windows 2000/2003 design elements. Because the arguments for the Big Bang approach largely revolve around not maintaining two conflicting systems for long periods of time, the similarities between Windows 2000/2003 and Windows 2008 make many of these arguments moot. Windows 2008 domain controllers can easily coexist with Windows 2003 and Windows 2000 domain controllers. With this point in mind, while coexistence of mixed domain controllers is possible, the quicker the organization migrates to a common platform, the less likelihood that domain controller version differences will create problems in domain controller replication and operations.

Big Bang Migration

The Big Bang approach to migrate from Windows 2003 to Windows 2008 is the most straightforward approach to migration. An upgrade simply takes any and all settings on the domain controllers and upgrades them to Windows 2008. If a Windows 2003 server handles Windows Internet Naming Service (WINS), domain name system (DNS), and Dynamic Host Configuration Protocol (DHCP), the upgrade process will upgrade all WINS, DNS, and DHCP components, as well as the base operating system. This makes this type of migration very tempting, and it can be extremely effective, as long as all prerequisites described in the following sections are satisfied.

The prerequisites are as follows:

▶ The operating system on the domain controllers is Windows Server 2003 SP1 or higher.

▶ The domain controller hardware exceeds the Windows 2008 requirements and all software is compatible with Windows 2008, including antivirus software and drivers.

▶ There is enough disk space free to perform the operating system and Active Directory upgrade. Specifically, verify that your free space is at least twice the size of your Active Directory database plus the minimum 8GB needed to install the operating system.

▶ The upgrade from 32-bit goes to 32-bit, and 64-bit goes to 64-bit as an in-place upgrade from 32-bit Windows to 64-bit Windows is not supported.

▶ The current domain functional level is Windows 2000 Native or Windows Server 2003. You cannot upgrade directly from Windows NT 4.0, Windows 2000 Mixed, or Windows Server 2003 interim domain functional levels.

Often, upgrading any given server can be a project in itself. The stand-alone member servers in an environment are often the workhorses of the network, loaded with a myriad of different applications and critical tools. Performing an upgrade on these servers would be simple if they were used only for file or print duties and if their hardware systems were all up to date. Because this is not always the case, it is important to detail the specifics of each server that is marked for migration.

Verifying Hardware Compatibility

It is critical to test the hardware compatibility of any server that will be directly upgraded to Windows 2008. The middle of the installation process is not the most ideal time to be notified of problems with compatibility between older system components and the drivers required for Windows Server 2008. Subsequently, the hardware in a server should be verified for Windows 2008 on the manufacturer's website or on Microsoft's Hardware Compatibility List (HCL), currently located at www.microsoft.com/whdc/hcl.

Microsoft suggests minimum hardware levels on which Windows 2008 will run, but it is highly recommended that you install the OS on systems of a much higher caliber because these recommendations do not take into account any application loads, domain controller duties, and so on. The following is a list of Microsoft's minimum (and recommended) hardware levels for Windows 2008:

- ▶ 1GHz x86 or 1.4GHz x64 processor (2GHz or faster)
- ▶ 512MB of RAM (2GB of RAM or more)
- ▶ 20–30GB free disk space

That said, it cannot be stressed enough that it is almost always recommended that you exceed these levels to provide for a robust computing environment. See Chapter 7, "Installing Exchange Server 2010," for additional details on hardware requirements.

NOTE

One of the most important features that mission-critical servers can have is redundancy. Putting the operating system on a mirrored array of disks, for example, is a simple yet effective way of increasing redundancy in an environment.

Verifying Application Readiness

Nothing ruins a migration process like discovering a mission-critical application is not certified to run in Active Directory 2008 mode. Subsequently, it is very important to identify and list all applications in an environment that will be required in the new environment. Typically only applications that leverage Active Directory schema need to be checked and tested. Standalone applications that do not query Active Directory at all typically have no impact whether the organization is running one version of AD or another.

> **NOTE**
>
> One of the most common vendors with application compatibility challenges with Active Directory 2008 was Cisco and their Unified Communications platform. Many of the earlier versions of Cisco Unified Messaging (that is, v4.2(1) or earlier) are not supported with AD 2008, and through most of 2009, many of the mobile communications solutions required an update to the latest release. So many organizations migrating to the latest version of Exchange Server may find remaining on Active Directory 2003 is driven by the vendor support for other applications with versioning and testing confirmed before migrating Active Directory. Again, AD 2008 is not a requirement for a migration to Exchange Server 2010, so validate that the addition of the migration to AD 2008 to the project does not impact the success of the Exchange Server 2010 migration project.

Backing Up and Creating a Recovery Process

It is critical that a migration does not cause more harm than good to an environment. Subsequently, we cannot stress enough that a good backup system is essential for quick recovery in the event of upgrade failure. Often, especially with the in-place upgrade scenario, a full system backup might be the only way to recover; consequently, it is very important to detail fallback steps in the event of problems. The backup should include the files and the System State.

Virtual Domain Controller Rollback Option

It is always good to have several fallback options, in case one of the options is unsuccessful. Another option to consider, in addition to a full backup, is to create a virtual domain controller. Using a virtual server platform such as Hyper-V or VMware Server, you can create a domain controller for little or no cost.

A virtual machine is created on the host, which can be an existing installation or even on a desktop with Virtual PC or VMware Workstation. This virtual machine is then joined to the domain and promoted to be a global catalog server.

Prior to the upgrade, the virtual global catalog server is shut down. Backup copies of the virtual server files can even be made for safekeeping.

In the event of a major failure in the upgrade process, the virtual global catalog server can be used to rebuild the domain. If the upgrade is successful, the virtual sever can either be turned back on and demoted, or simply be deleted and cleaned from the domain.

Performing an Upgrade on a Single Domain Controller Server

After all various considerations regarding applications and hardware compatibility have been thoroughly validated, a stand-alone server can be upgraded.

The health of the domain controllers should be verified prior to upgrading the domain controllers. In particular, the Domain Controller Diagnostics (DCDIAG) utility should be run and any errors fixed before the upgrade. The Windows Server DCDIAG utility is part of the Support Tools, which can be found on the installation media under

\support\tools\. The Support Tools are installed via an MSI package named
SUPTOOLS.MSI. After installing the tools, the DCDIAG utility can be run. Verify that all
tests passed.

The Active Directory Domain Services forest and the domain need to be prepared prior to
the upgrade. This installs the schema updates that are new to Windows 2008 Active
Directory. The following steps should be run on the Flexible Single Master Operations
(FSMO) role holder, specifically the infrastructure master role holder. In a small environment or a single domain, all these roles are typically on the same domain controller. To
prepare the forest and domain, execute the following steps on the domain controller
with the roles:

1. Insert the Windows Server 2008 DVD into the drive. If the Install Windows autorun
   page appears, close the window.

NOTE

Be sure to use the appropriate media for the operating system of the domain controller, specifically 32-bit or 64-bit.

2. Select Start, Run.

3. Enter `d:\sources\adprep\adprep.exe /forestprep` and click OK, where d: is the
   DVD drive.

4. A warning appears to verify that all Windows 2000 domain controllers are at Service
   Pack 4 or later. Enter `C` and press Enter to start the forest preparation.

5. Enter `d:\sources\adprep\adprep.exe /domainprep /gpprep` and click OK.

6. Enter `d:\sources\adprep\adprep.exe /rodcprep` and click OK. This update allows
   Read-Only Domain Controllers.

Now that the schema updates have been installed and the domain preparation is done,
the domain is ready to be upgraded. Follow these steps to upgrade:

1. Insert the Windows Server 2008 DVD into the DVD drive of the server to be upgraded.

NOTE

Be sure to use the appropriate media for the operating system of the domain controller, specifically 32-bit or 64-bit. If you have Windows 2003 32-bit, you cannot do an
in-place upgrade to x64-bit Windows 2008. And an x64-bit version cannot be changed
to a 32-bit version of the operating system. Only 32-bit to 32-bit, or 64-bit to 64-bit
upgrades are allowed.

2. The Install Windows page should appear automatically. If not, choose Start, Run and
   then type `d:\Setup`, where d: is the drive letter for the DVD drive.

3. Click Install Now.

4. Click the large Go Online to Get the Latest Updates button. This ensures that the
   installation has the latest information for the upgrade.

5. Depending on your license rights, enter your product key if prompted and click Next

6. Select I Accept This Agreement on the License page, and click Next to continue.

7. Click the large Upgrade button.

8. Review the compatibility report and verify that all issues have been addressed. Click Next to continue.

9. The system then copies files and reboots as a Windows 2008 server, continuing the upgrade process. After all files are copied, the system is then upgraded to a fully functional install of Windows 2008 (see Figure 15.1) and will then reboot again. All this can take some time to complete.

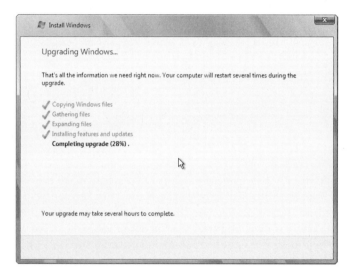

FIGURE 15.1   Big Bang upgrade.

10. After the final reboot, the domain controller will be at the familiar Ctrl+Alt+Del screen. After logon, the domain controller will open to the Server Manager console, as shown in Figure 15.2. The domain controller upgrade is complete.

The upgrade process shown in steps 1 through 10 is then repeated for each of the remaining Windows Server domain controllers.

Phased Migration

For many organizations, a slower or more planned or phased migration to the latest Active Directory makes more sense. This might be because the organization has many Active Directory domains that would need to be staged and migrated, or because the organization has a lot of domain controllers in remote offices that would need to be staged for the upgrade, or merely because the organization wants to be more methodical in the upgrade process.

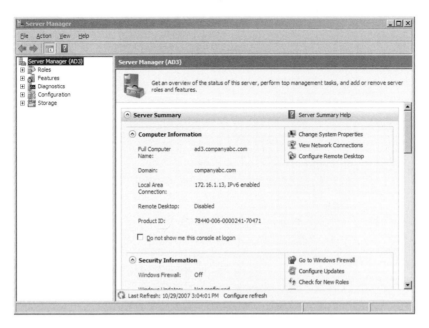

FIGURE 15.2   Server Manager console after upgrade.

Key to note is that a phased migration of Active Directory doesn't necessarily make the
migration "safer" in that the first domain controller to be updated advances key components of the domain and/or forest into the updated Active Directory level. The update
occurs immediately upon the first system update and thus the impact of the new Active
Directory takes place immediately and does not require all domain controllers to be
updated before the effect is seen throughout the enterprise. However, the phased migration controls the number of systems that have been physically updated or need to be
updated, and thus controls the number of systems directly being updated.

Because Active Directory is one of the most important portions of a Microsoft network, it
is subsequently one of the most important areas to focus on in a migration process. In the
phased migration scenario covered in this section, there are two domains
(companyabc.com and asia.companyabc.com), which are members of the same forest
(shown in Figure 15.3). The companyabc.com domain has all Windows 2000 SP4 domain
controllers and the asia.companyabc.com domain has all Windows Server 2003 SP2
domain controllers. The entire forest will be upgraded to Windows 2008, but they need to
be migrated over time. Thus, a phased migration will be used.

Migrating Domain Controllers

There are two approaches to migrating domain controllers, similar to the logic used in the
"Performing an Upgrade on a Single Domain Controller Server" section. The domain
controllers can either be directly upgraded to Windows 2008 or replaced by newly introduced Windows 2008 domain controllers. The decision to upgrade an existing server
largely depends on the hardware of the server in question. The rule of thumb is, if the

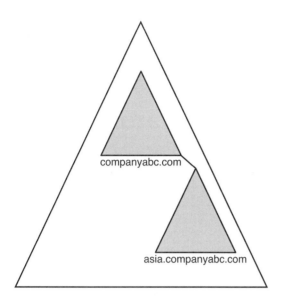

FIGURE 15.3   CompanyABC forest.

15

hardware will support Windows 2008 now and for the next two to three years, a server can be directly upgraded. If this is not the case, using new hardware for the migration is preferable.

The prerequisites for upgrading an Active Directory forest and domain discussed earlier still apply. The prerequisites to upgrade to Windows 2008 and Windows 2008 R2 Active Directory are as follows:

- ▶ The operating system on the domain controllers is Windows Server 2003 SP1 or higher.

- ▶ The current domain functional level is Windows 2000 Native or Windows Server 2003. You cannot upgrade directly from Windows NT 4.0, Windows 2000 Mixed, or Windows Server 2003 interim domain functional levels.

- ▶ All Windows 2000 Server domain controllers have Service Pack 4 (SP4) installed.

These prerequisites are required to upgrade to Windows 2008 and are separate from the decision to upgrade or replace any given domain controller.

NOTE

A combined approach can be and is quite commonly used, as indicated in Figure 15.4, to support a scenario in which some hardware is current but other hardware is out of date and will be replaced. Either way, the decisions applied to a proper project plan can help to ensure the success of the migration.

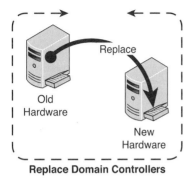

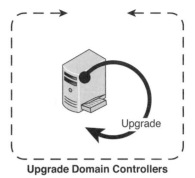

Replace Domain Controllers   Upgrade Domain Controllers

FIGURE 15.4   Combined approach to the upgrade process.

The scenario in this section will use the combined approach to the upgrade, replacing the
Windows 2000 SP4 companyabc.com domain controllers and upgrading the Windows
Server 2003 asia.companyabc.com domain controllers.

The health of the domain controllers should be verified prior to upgrading the domain
controllers. In particular, the Domain Controller Diagnostics (DCDIAG) utility should be
run and any errors fixed before the upgrade. The Windows Server DCDIAG utility is part
of the Support Tools, which can be found on the installation media under
\support\tools\. The Support Tools are installed via an MSI package named
SUPTOOLS.MSI. After installing the tools, the DCDIAG utility can be run. The dcdiag /e
option should be used to check all domain controllers in the enterprise. Verify that all
tests passed.

Preparing the Forest and Domains Using adprep

The introduction of Windows Server 2008 domain controllers into a Windows 2000/2003
Active Directory requires that the core AD database component, the schema, be updated to
support the increased functionality. In addition, several other security changes need to be
made to prepare a forest for inclusion of Windows 2008. The Windows Server 2008 DVD
includes a command-line utility called adprep that will extend the schema to include the
extensions required and modify security as needed. Adprep requires that both forestprep
and domainprep be run before the first Windows 2008 domain controller can be added.

The adprep utility must be run from the Windows Server 2008 DVD or copied from its
location in the \sources\adprep\ folder. This installs the schema updates that are new to
Windows 2008 Active Directory. The following steps should be run on the Flexible Single
Master Operations (FSMO) role holder, specifically the schema master role holder:

1. Insert the Windows Server 2008 DVD into the drive. If the Install Windows autorun
   page appears, close the window.

NOTE

Be sure to use the appropriate media for the operating system of the domain controller, specifically 32-bit or 64-bit.

2. Select Start, Run.

3. Enter `d:\sources\adprep\adprep.exe` `/forestprep` and click OK, where d: is the DVD drive.

4. A warning appears to verify that all Windows 2000 domain controllers are at Service Pack 4 or later. Enter `C` and press Enter to start the forest preparation.

> **NOTE**
>
> Any previous extensions made to a Windows 2000/2003 Active Directory schema, such as those made with Exchange Server 2003 or Exchange Server 2007, are not affected by the adprep procedure. This procedure simply adds additional attributes and does not change those that currently exist.

Now that the schema updates have been installed, the domain is ready to be prepared. The adprep/domainprep/gpprep operation must be run once in every domain in a forest. It must be physically invoked on the server that holds the infrastructure master Operations Master (OM) role. The steps for executing the domainprep procedure are as follows:

1. On the Operations Master domain controller, insert the Windows Server 2008 DVD into the drive. If the Install Windows autorun page appears, close the window.

> **NOTE**
>
> Be sure to use the appropriate media for the operating system of the domain controller, specifically 32-bit or 64-bit.

2. Select Start, Run.

3. Enter `d:\sources\adprep\adprep.exe` `/domainprep` `/gpprep` and click OK, where d: is the DVD drive.

4. Enter `d:\sources\adprep\adprep.exe` `/rodcprep` and click OK. This update allows Read-Only Domain Controllers by updating the permissions on all the DNS application directory partitions in the forest and allows them to be replicated by all RODCs that are also DNS servers.

Repeat steps 1 through 4 for each domain that will be upgraded.

After the forestprep and domainprep operations are run, the Active Directory forest will be ready for the introduction or upgrade of Windows 2008 domain controllers. The schema is extended and includes support for application partitions and other enhancements. After these updates have had sufficient time to replicate across all domains, the process of upgrading the domain controllers to Windows 2008 can commence.

Upgrading Existing Domain Controllers

If the decision has been made to upgrade all or some existing hardware to Windows 2008, the process for accomplishing this is straightforward. However, as with the standalone server, you need to ensure that the hardware and any additional software components are compatible with Windows 2008. The requirements for the server to upgrade are as follows:

▶ The operating system on the domain controllers is Windows Server 2003 SP1 or higher.

▶ The domain controller hardware exceeds the Windows 2008 requirements and all software is compatible with Windows 2008, including antivirus software and drivers.

▶ There is enough disk space free to perform the operating system and Active Directory upgrade. Specifically, verify that your free space is at least twice the size of your Active Directory database plus the minimum 8GB needed to install the operating system.

After establishing this, the actual migration can occur. The procedure for upgrading a domain controller to Windows Server 2008 is nearly identical to the procedure outlined in the previous section "Performing an Upgrade on a Single Domain Controller Server." Essentially, simply insert the DVD and upgrade, and an hour or so later the machine will be updated and functioning as a Windows 2008 domain controller.

The specific steps are as follows:

1. Insert the Windows Server 2008 DVD into the DVD drive of the server to be upgraded.
2. The Install Windows page should appear automatically. If not, choose Start, Run and then type d:\Setup, where d: is the drive letter for the DVD drive.
3. Click Install Now.
4. Click the large Go Online to Get the Latest Updates button. This ensures that the installation has the latest information for the upgrade.
5. Depending on your license rights, enter your product key if prompted and click Next.
6. Select I Accept This Agreement on the License page, and click Next to continue.
7. Click the large Upgrade button.
8. Review the compatibility report and verify that all issues have been addressed. Click Next to continue.
9. The system then copies files and reboots as a Windows 2008 server, continuing the upgrade process. After all files are copied, the system is then upgraded to a fully functional install of Windows 2008 and then reboots again. All this can take some time to complete.
10. After the final reboot, the domain controller will be at the familiar Ctrl+Alt+Del screen. After logon, the domain controller opens to the Server Manager console. The domain controller upgrade is complete.

Repeat for all domain controllers that will be upgraded.

Replacing Existing Domain Controllers

If you need to migrate specific domain controller functionality to the new Active Directory environment but plan to use new hardware, you need to bring new domain controllers into the environment before retiring the old servers.

Windows 2008 uses a roles-based model. To make a Windows 2008 server a domain controller, the Active Directory Domain Services role is added. This is the most thorough approach, and the following steps show how to accomplish this to establish a new Windows 2008 domain controller in a Windows 2000/2003 Active Directory domain:

> **NOTE**
>
> This procedure assumes that the Windows 2008 operating system has been installed on the server. The server does not need to be a domain member.

1. Log on to the new server as an administrator.
2. Launch Server Manager.
3. Select the Roles node.
4. Click Add Roles.
5. Click Next.
6. Select the Active Directory Domain Services check box, and click Next.
7. Click Next on the Information page.
8. Click Install to install the role. This installs the binaries necessary for the server to become a domain controller.
9. Click Close on the Installation Results page.
10. In the Server Manager console, expand the Roles node and select the Active Directory Domain Services node.
11. In the Summary section, click the Run the Active Directory Domain Services Installation Wizard (dcpromo.exe) link.
12. Click Next on the Welcome page.
13. Select the Existing Forest option button.
14. Select the Add a Domain controller in an Existing Domain option button, and click Next.
15. Enter the name of the domain.
16. Click Set to specify alternate credentials to use for the operation.
17. Enter the credentials of a domain administrator in the target domain, and click OK.
18. Click Next to continue.
19. Select the appropriate domain for the new domain controller, and click Next. In this example, the companyabc.com domain is used.

20. Select a site for the domain controller, and click Next.

21. Select the Additional Domain Controller Options, which are DNS Server and Global Catalog by default. The Read-Only Domain Controller option is not available, as this is the first Windows 2008 domain controller in the domain. Click Next.

22. Select locations for the database, log files, and the SYSVOL, and then click Next.

23. Enter the Directory Services Restore Mode administrator password, and then click Next.

24. Review the summary, and then click Next. The Installation Wizard creates the domain controller and replicates the Active Directory database, which might take some time depending on the network and the size of the Active Directory database.

25. After the wizard completes the installation, click Finish.

26. Click Restart Now to reboot the new domain controller.

This process should be repeated for each new replacement domain controller.

Moving Operation Master Roles

Active Directory Domain Services sports a multimaster replication model, in which any one server can take over directory functionality, and each full domain controller contains a read/write copy of directory objects. There are, however, a few key exceptions to this, in which certain forestwide and domainwide functionality must be held by a single domain controller in the forest and in each domain respectively. These exceptions are known as Operation Master (OM) roles, also known as Flexible Single Master Operations (FSMO) roles. There are five OM roles, as shown in Table 15.1.

TABLE 15.1   FSMO Roles and Their Scope

FSMO Roles	Scope
Schema master	Forest
Domain naming master	Forest
Infrastructure master	Domain
RID master	Domain
PDC emulator	Domain

If the server or servers that hold the OM roles are not directly upgraded to Windows 2008 but will instead be retired, these OM roles will need to be moved to another server. The best tool for this type of move is the NTDSUTIL command-line utility.

Follow these steps using NTDSUTIL to move the forestwide OM roles (schema master and domain naming master) to a single Windows 2008 domain controller:

1. Open a command prompt (choose Start, Run, type cmd, and press Enter).

2. Type ntdsutil and press Enter. The prompt will display ntdsutil:.

3. Type `roles` and press Enter. The prompt will display fsmo maintenance:.

4. Type `connections` and press Enter. The prompt will display "server connections:".

5. Type `connect to server <Servername>`, where <Servername> is the name of the target Windows 2008 domain controller that will hold the OM roles, and press Enter.

6. Type `quit` and press Enter. The prompt will display fsmo maintenance:.

7. Type `transfer schema master` and press Enter.

8. Click Yes at the prompt asking to confirm the OM change. The display will show the location for each of the five FSMO roles after the operation.

9. Type `transfer naming master` and press Enter.

10. Click OK at the prompt asking to confirm the OM change.

11. Type `quit` and press Enter, then type `quit` and press Enter again to exit the NTDSUTIL.

12. Type `exit` to close the Command Prompt window.

Now the forestwide FSMO roles will be on a single Windows 2008 domain controller.

The domainwide FSMO roles (infrastructure master, RID master, and PDC emulator) will need to be moved for each domain to a domain controller within the domain. The steps to do this are as follows:

1. Open a command prompt (choose Start, Run, type `cmd`, and press Enter).

2. Type `ntdsutil` and press Enter.

3. Type `roles` and press Enter.

4. Type `connections` and press Enter.

5. Type `connect to server <Servername>`, where <Servername> is the name of the target Windows 2008 domain controller that will hold the OM roles, and press Enter.

6. Type `quit` and press Enter.

7. Type `transfer pdc` and press Enter.

8. Click OK at the prompt asking to confirm the OM change.

9. Type `transfer rid master` and press Enter.

10. Click OK at the prompt asking to confirm the OM change.

11. Type `transfer infrastructure master` and press Enter.

12. Click Yes at the prompt asking to confirm the OM change.

13. Type `quit` and press Enter, then type `quit` and press Enter again to exit the NTDSUTIL.

14. Type `exit` to close the Command Prompt window.

The preceding steps need to be repeated for each domain.

Retiring Existing Windows 2000/2003 Domain Controllers

After the entire Windows 2000/2003 domain controller infrastructure is replaced by Windows 2008 equivalents and the OM roles are migrated, the process of demoting and removing all down-level domain controllers can begin. The most straightforward and thorough way of removing a domain controller is by demoting them using the dcpromo

utility, per the standard Windows 2000/2003 demotion process. After you run the
dcpromo command, the domain controller becomes a member server in the domain. After
disjoining it from the domain, it can safely be disconnected from the network.

Retiring "Phantom" Domain Controllers

As is often the case in Active Directory, domain controllers might have been removed
from the forest without first being demoted. They become phantom domain controllers
and basically haunt the Active Directory, causing strange errors to pop up every so often.
This is because of a couple remnants in the Active Directory, specifically the NTDS Settings
object and the SYSVOL replication object. These phantom DCs might come about because
of server failure or problems in the administrative process, but you should remove those
servers and remnant objects from the directory to complete the upgrade to Windows
2008. Not doing so will result in errors in the event logs and in the DCDIAG output.

Simply deleting the computer object from Active Directory Sites and Services does not
work. Instead, you need to use a low-level directory tool, ADSIEdit, to remove these
servers properly. The following steps outline how to use ADSIEdit to remove these
phantom domain controllers:

1. Launch Server Manager.
2. Expand the Roles node and select the Active Directory Domain Services node.
3. Scroll down to the Advanced Tools section of the page and click on the ADSI Edit link.
4. In the ADSIEdit window, select Action, Connect To.
5. In the Select a Well Known Naming Context drop-down menu, select Configuration, and click OK.
6. Select the Configuration node.
7. Navigate to Configuration\CN=Configuration\CN=Sites\CN=<Sitename>\ CN=Servers\CN=<Servername>, where <Sitename> and <Servername> correspond to the location of the phantom domain controller.
8. Right-click the CN=NTDS Settings, and click Delete, as shown in Figure 15.5.
9. At the prompt, click Yes to delete the object.
10. In the ADSIEdit window, select the top-level ADSIEdit node, and then select Action, Connect To.
11. In the Select a Well Known Naming Context drop-down menu, select Default Naming Context, and click OK.
12. Select the Default Naming Context node.
13. Navigate to Default naming context\CN=System\CN=File Replication Service\CN=Domain System Volume(SYSVOL share)\CN=<Servername>, where <Servername> corresponds to the name of the phantom domain controller.
14. Right-click the CN=<Servername>, and select Delete.
15. At the prompt, click Yes to delete the object.
16. Close ADSIEdit.

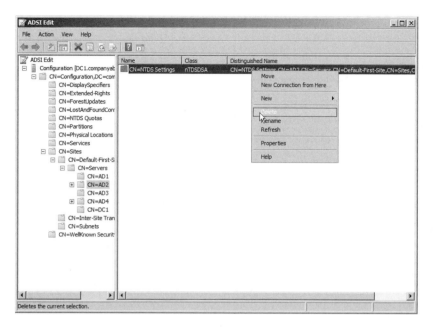

FIGURE 15.5   Deleting phantom domain controllers.

At this point, after the NTDS Settings are deleted, the server can be normally deleted from the Active Directory Sites and Services snap-in.

> **NOTE**
>
> ADSIEdit was included in the Support Tools in Windows Server 2000/2003, but is now included in the AD DS Tools that are installed automatically with the Active Directory Domain Services role in Windows 2008.

Upgrading Domain and Forest Functional Levels

Windows 2008 Active Directory Domain Services does not immediately begin functioning at a native level, even when all domain controllers have been migrated. The domains and forest will be at the original functional levels. You first need to upgrade the functional level of the domain to Windows Server 2008 before you can realize the full advantages of the upgrade.

> **NOTE**
>
> The act of raising the forest or domain functional levels is irreversible. Be sure that any Windows 2000/2003 domain controllers do not need to be added anywhere in the forest before performing this procedure.

After all domain controllers are upgraded or replaced with Windows 2008 domain
controllers, you can raise the domain level by following these steps:

1. Ensure that all domain controllers in the forest are upgraded to Windows 2008.

2. Launch Server Manager on a domain controller.

3. Expand the Roles node and then expand the Active Directory Domain Services node.

4. Select the Active Directory Users and Computers snap-in.

5. Right-click on the domain name, and select Raise Domain Functional Level.

6. In the Select an Available Domain Functional Level drop-down menu, select
   Windows Server 2008, and then select Raise, as shown in Figure 15.6.

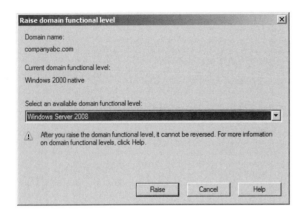

FIGURE 15.6   Raising the domain functional level.

7. Click OK at the warning and then click OK again to complete the task.

Repeat steps 1 through 7 for each domain in the forest. Now the forest functional level
can be raised. Although this does not add any new features, it does prevent non-Windows
Server 2008 domain controllers from being added in the future. To raise the forest functional level, execute the following steps:

1. Launch Server Manager.

2. Expand the Roles node and select the Active Directory Domain Services node.

3. Scroll down to the Advanced Tools section of the page, and click on the AD
   Domains and Trusts link.

4. With the topmost Active Directory Domains and Trusts node selected, select Action,
   Raise Forest Functional Level.

5. In the Select an Available Forest Functional Level drop-down menu, select Windows
   Server 2008, and then select Raise.

6. Click OK at the warning and then click OK again to complete the task.

After each domain functional level is raised, as well as the forest functional level, the
Active Directory environment is completely upgraded and fully compliant with all the AD
DS improvements made in Windows 2008.

Moving AD-Integrated DNS Zones to Application Partitions

The final step in a Windows 2008 Active Directory upgrade is to move any AD-integrated DNS zones into the newly created application partitions that Windows 2008 uses to store DNS information. To accomplish this, follow these steps:

1. Launch Server Manager on a domain controller.

2. Expand the Roles node and then expand the DNS Server node.

3. Select the DNS snap-in.

4. Navigate to DNS\<Servername>\Forward Lookup Zones and select the zone to be moved.

5. Right-click the zone to be moved, and click Properties.

6. Click the Change button to the right of the Replication description.

7. Select either To All DNS Servers in This Forest or To All DNS Servers in This Domain, depending on the level of replication you want, as shown in Figure 15.7. Click OK when you are finished and click OK again to save the changes.

Repeat the process for any other AD-integrated zones.

FIGURE 15.7   Moving AD-integrated zones.

Multiple Domain Consolidation Migration

There are cases when it is better to migrate to a new forest and domain, rather than bring along the baggage of a legacy Active Directory. This includes needing to consolidate names, concerns with the legacy Active Directory schema, or simply to consolidate Active Directory services. The consolidation migration allows an administrator to, in effect, start fresh with a clean installation of Active Directory. Figure 15.8 shows an example of the migration scenario used in this section, where the companyabc.com and asia.companyabc.com will be consolidated to a new forest with the domain companyxyz.com.

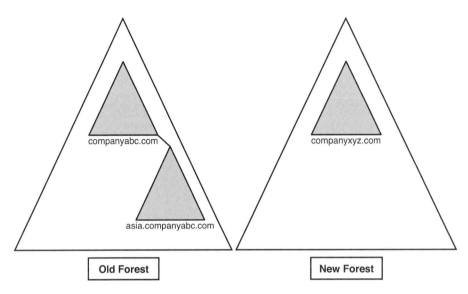

FIGURE 15.8   CompanyXYZ forest.

However, this can be disruptive to the users and applications if not handled carefully. Migrating to a new domain and forest results in changes to the security identifiers, which can impact access. It can also result in password changes, making it difficult for users. However, there are tools and techniques, which are explored in this section, to mitigate the impact to the users and applications.

The development of Windows 2008 coincides with improvements in the Active Directory Migration Tool, a fully functional domain migration utility. ADMT version 3.1 allows Active Directory users, computers, and groups to be consolidated, collapsed, or restructured to fit the design needs of an organization. In regard to Windows 2000/2003 migrations, ADMT v3.1 provides for the flexibility to restructure existing domain environments into new Windows 2008 Active Directory environments, keeping security settings, user passwords, and other settings.

Understanding ADMT v3.1 Functionality

ADMT is an effective way to migrate users, groups, and computers from one domain to another. It is robust enough to migrate security permissions and Exchange Server mailbox domain settings. ADMT is composed of the following components and functionality:

▶ **ADMT migration wizards**—ADMT includes a series of wizards, each specifically designed to migrate specific components. You can use different wizards to migrate users, groups, computers, service accounts, and trusts.

▶ **Low client impact**—ADMT automatically installs a service on source clients negating the need to manually install client software for the migration. In addition, after the migration is complete, these services are automatically uninstalled.

▶ **SID History and security migrated**—Users can continue to maintain network access to file shares, applications, and other secured network services through migration of the SID History attributes to the new domain. This preserves the extensive security structure of the source domain.

> **NOTE**
>
> One unfortunate change in ADMT v3.1 is the removal of the test migration and rollback functionality that was present in ADMT v2. Microsoft had numerous difficulties with it and chose to deprecate the features rather than resolve the issues.

ADMT v3.1 installs very easily but requires a thorough knowledge of the various wizards to be used properly. In addition, best-practice processes should be used when migrating from one domain to another.

The migration example in the following sections describes the most common use of the Active Directory Migration Tool: an interforest migration of domain users, groups, and computers into another domain. This procedure is by no means exclusive, and many other migration techniques can be used to achieve proper results. Subsequently, matching the capabilities of ADMT with the migration needs of an organization is important.

Using ADMT in a Lab Environment

You can develop the most effective lab by creating new domain controllers in the source and target domains and then physically segregating them into a lab network, where they cannot contact the production domain environment. The Operations Master (OM) roles for each domain can then be seized for each domain using the NTDSUTIL utility, which effectively creates exact replicas of all user, group, and computer accounts that can be tested with the ADMT.

ADMT v3.1 Installation Procedure

The ADMT component should be installed on a domain controller in the target domain, where the accounts will be migrated to. To install, follow these steps:

1. Download ADMT 3.1 from the Microsoft Download site.

2. Choose Start, Run. Then browse to the download location, select admtsetup.exe, and click Open. Click OK to launch the setup.

3. On the Welcome page, click Next to continue.

4. Accept the end-user license agreement (EULA), and click Next to continue.

5. Microsoft SQL Server Desktop Edition will be automatically installed (or choose an existing SQL Server if applicable). Accept the default database selection, and click Next to continue

6. Leave the default No, Do Not Import Data from an ADMT 2.0 Database. Click Next to continue.

7. After installation, click Finish to close the wizard.

ADMT Domain Migration Prerequisites

As previously mentioned, the most important prerequisite for migration with ADMT is lab verification. Testing as many aspects of a migration as possible can help to establish the procedures required and identify potential problems before they occur in the production environment.

That said, several technical prerequisites must be met before the ADMT can function properly. These are as follows:

▶ **Create two-way trusts between source and target domains**—The source and target domains must each be able to communicate with each other and share security credentials. Consequently, it is important to establish trusts between the two domains before running the ADMT.

▶ **Assign proper permissions on source domain and source domain workstations**—The account that will run the ADMT in the target domain must be added into the Builtin\Administrators group in the source domain. In addition, each workstation must include this user as a member of the local Administrators group for the computer migration services to be able to function properly. Domain group changes can be easily accomplished, but a large workstation group change must be scripted, or manually accomplished, prior to migration.

▶ **Create the target OU structure**—The destination for user accounts from the source domain must be designated at several points during the ADMT migration process. Establishing an organizational unit (OU) for the source domain accounts can help to simplify and logically organize the new objects. These objects can be moved to other OUs after the migration and this OU collapsed, if you want.

Exporting Password Key Information

The Password Export Server (PES) service is used to migrate passwords during interforest migrations. This service must be installed on the source domain and uses a password key generated previously.

A 128-bit encrypted password key must be installed from the target domain on a server in the source domain. This key allows for the migration of password and SID History information from one domain to the next.

To create this key, follow these steps from the command prompt of a domain controller in the target domain where ADMT is installed:

1. Insert a floppy disk into the drive to store the key. (The key can be directed to the network but, for security reasons, directing to a floppy is better.)

2. Open a command prompt.

3. Type `admt key /option:create /sourcedomain:<SourceDomainName> /keyfile:a:\key.pes /keypassword:*`, where <SourceDomainName> is the NetBIOS name of the source domain and a: is the destination drive for the key. Then press Enter.

4. The utility prompts for the password and confirmation of the password. Then the utility creates the password onto the floppy.

5. Upon successful creation of the key, remove the floppy and keep it in a safe place.

This needs to be repeated for each domain to be migrated.

Installing PES on the Source Domain

After exporting the password key from the target domain, the encrypted password key needs to be installed on a server in the source domain. The procedure uses the key generated previously. The following procedure outlines this installation:

1. Insert the floppy disk with the exported key from the target domain into the server's disk drive.

2. Download the Password Migration from Microsoft at www.microsoft.com/downloadS/details.aspx?familyid=F0D03C3C-4757-40FD-8306-68079BA9C773&displaylang=en.

3. Start the Password Migration Utility by choosing Start, Run and browsing to find PwdMig.msi. Click OK to run it.

4. On the Welcome page, click Next.

5. Enter the location of the key that was created on the target domain; normally, this is the A: floppy drive. Click Next to continue.

6. Enter the password twice that was set on the target domain, and click Next.

7. On the Verification page, click Next to continue.

8. Select the account for the service in the form domain\account and the password, and then click OK.

9. Click Finish after the installation is complete.

10. The system must be restarted, so click Yes when prompted to automatically restart. Upon restarting, the proper settings will be in place to make this server a Password Export Server.

The account used for the service will be granted the Logon As a Service right. This needs to be installed on at least one source domain controller in each domain to be migrated.

Setting Proper Registry Permissions

The installation of the proper components creates special Registry keys, but leaves them disabled by default for security reasons. One of these is the AllowPasswordExport value. You need to enable this Registry key on the source domain to allow passwords to be exported from the Password Export Server. The following procedure outlines the use of the Registry Editor to perform this function:

1. On a domain controller in the source domain, open the Registry Editor (Start, Run, Regedit).

2. Navigate to HKEY_LOCAL_MACHINE\SYSTEM\CurrentControlSet\Control\Lsa.

3. Double-click the AllowPasswordExport DWORD value.

4. Change the properties from 0 to 1 (Hexadecimal).

5. Click OK and close the Registry Editor.

6. Reboot the machine for the Registry changes to be enacted.

This allows passwords to be exported from the source domain to the target domain.

Configuring Domains for SID Migration

Migration of the source security identifiers (SIDs) into the target domain SID History allows the security assigned in access control lists (ACLs) to work transparently after the migration. This gives the administrator time to reset ACLs on a gradual basis or even after all objects are migrated.

There are several settings that need to be configured to allow for the SIDs to be transferred. These settings include creating a local group in the source domain for auditing, enabling TCP/IP client support on the source PDC emulator, and, finally, enabling auditing on both the source and target domains.

To create the local group on the source domain for auditing, execute the following steps:

1. Log on to a domain controller on the source domain.

2. Launch Active Directory Users and Computers.

3. Create a domain local group named SourceDomain$$$, where SourceDomain is the NetBIOS name of the source domain. For example, the local group for the companyabc.com domain would be companyabc$$$.

Do not add any members to the group, or the migration process will fail.

To enable TCP/IP client support, execute the following steps:

1. Log on to the PDC emulator domain controller in the source domain.

2. Launch the Registry Editor.

3. Navigate to \HKEY\LocalMachine\System\CurrentControlSet\Control\LSA.

4. Create the value TcpipClientSupport REG_DWORD and assign it a value of 1.

5. Exit the Registry Editor.

To enable auditing in Windows Server 2008 domains, execute the following steps:

1. Select Start, Administrative Tools, Default Domain Controller Security Settings.

2. Expand the Local Policies.

3. Select the Audit Policy node.

4. Double-click on the Audit Account Management policy.

5. Check the Define These Policy Settings and select both Success and Failure.

6. Click OK to save the changes.

7. Exit the Group Policy Object Editor.

Now the source and target domains will be prepared to transfer SIDs into the SID History.

Migrating Groups

In most cases, the first objects to be migrated into a new domain should be groups. If users are migrated first, their group membership will not transfer over. However, if the groups exist before the users are migrated, they will automatically find their place in the group structure. To migrate groups using ADMT v3.1, use the Group Account Migration Wizard, as follows:

1. Open the ADMT MMC snap-in (Start, All Programs, Administrative Tools, Active Directory Migration Tool).

2. Right-click Active Directory Migration Tool in the left pane, and choose Group Account Migration Wizard.

3. Click Next to continue.

4. Select the source and destination domains, and click Next to continue.

5. Choose the Select Groups from Domain option, and click Next.

6. On the subsequent page, you can select the group accounts from the source domain. Select all the groups required by using the Add button and selecting the objects. After you select the groups, click Next to continue.

7. Enter the destination OU for the accounts from the source domain by clicking Browse and selecting the OU created in the steps outlined previously. Click Next to continue.

8. On the following page, there are several options to choose from that determine the nature of the migrated groups. Clicking the Help button details the nature of each setting. In the sample migration, choose the settings, as shown in Figure 15.9. After choosing the appropriate settings, click Next to continue.

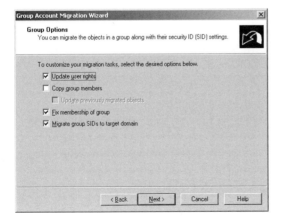

FIGURE 15.9   Setting group options.

9. Enter a user account with proper administrative rights on the source domain on the following page. Then click Next to continue.

10. The subsequent page allows for the exclusion of specific directory-level attributes from migration. If you need to exclude any attributes, they can be set here. In this example, no exclusions are set. Click Next to continue.

11. Naming conflicts often arise during domain migrations. In addition, different naming conventions might apply in the new environment. Objects will not be migrated if conflicts occur. Click Next.

12. The verification page is the last wizard page you see before any changes are made. Once again, make sure that the procedure has been tested before running it because ADMT will henceforth write changes to the target Windows 2008 Active Directory environment. Click Finish when you're ready to begin group migration.

13. The group migration process then commences. The window shows the migration progress. Click Close when it completes.

The group(s) is (are) now migrated to the new domain.

Migrating User Accounts

User accounts are the "bread and butter" of domain objects and are among the most important components. The biggest shortcoming of older versions of ADMT was their inability to migrate passwords of user objects, which effectively limited their use. However, ADMT v3.1 does an excellent job of migrating users, their passwords, and the security associated with them. To migrate users, follow these steps:

1. Open the ADMT MMC snap-in (Start, All Programs, Administrative Tools, Active Directory Migration Tool).

2. Right-click the Active Directory Migration Tool, and choose User Account Migration Wizard.

3. Click Next on the Welcome page.

4. Select the source and target domains on the subsequent page, and click Next to continue.

5. Choose the Select Users from Domain option, and click Next.

6. The following page allows you to choose user accounts for migration. Just click the Add button and select the user accounts to be migrated. After you select all the user accounts, click Next to continue.

7. The next page allows you to choose a target OU for all created users. Choose the OU by clicking the Browse button. After you select it, click Next to continue.

8. Select Migrate Passwords and then select the server in the source domain in which the Password Export Server (PES) service was installed, as covered in the "Installing PES on the Source Domain" section. Click Next to continue.

9. On the Account Transition Options page, leave the default transition options, and click Next.

10. Enter the account to use when adding SID History, which has to have administrative rights on the source domain. Then click Next.

11. The subsequent page deals with User Options settings. Click Help for an overview of each option. Select Translate Roaming Profiles. Then click Next to continue.

12. The next page is for setting exclusions. Specify any property of the user object that should not be migrated here. In this example, no exclusions are set. Click Next to continue.

13. Naming conflicts for user accounts are common. Designate a procedure for dealing with duplicate accounts in advance and enter such information on the next wizard page. Select the appropriate options for duplicate accounts and click Next to continue.

14. The following verification page presents a summary of the procedure that will take place. This is the last page before changes are written to the target domain. Verify the settings and click Finish to continue.

15. The Migration Progress status box displays the migration process as it occurs, indicating the number of successful and unsuccessful accounts created. When the process is complete, review the log by clicking View Log and verify the integrity of the procedure. Click Close when you finish.

> **NOTE**
>
> Depending on if other wizards have already been run, there might be additional steps at this point that happen one time only to set up proper Registry settings, reboot DCs, and create special groups.

Migrating Computer Accounts

Another important set of objects that must be migrated is also one of the trickier ones. Computer objects must not only be migrated in AD, but they must also be updated at the workstations themselves so that users will be able to log on effectively from their consoles. ADMT seamlessly installs agents on all migrated computer accounts and reboots them, forcing them into their new domain structures.

The account running the ADMT must have local administrator rights to the computers being migrated. The agents must also be accessible over the network, so any firewalls should be disabled for the migration or grant exceptions.

Follow these steps to migrate computer accounts:

1. Open the ADMT MMC snap-in (Start, All Programs, Administrative Tools, Active Directory Migration Tool).

2. Right-click the Active Directory Migration Tool, and choose Computer Migration Wizard.

3. Click Next on the Welcome page.

4. Type the names of the source and destination domains in the drop-down boxes on the next page, and click Next to continue.

5. Choose the Select Computers from Domain option, and click Next.

6. On the following page, select the computer accounts that will be migrated by clicking the Add button and selecting the appropriate accounts. Click Next to continue.

7. Select the OU the computer accounts will be migrated to, and click Next to continue.

8. The next Translate Objects page allows for the option to specify which settings on the local clients will be migrated. Click the Help button for a detailed description of each item. In this example, select all items, as shown in Figure 15.10. Click Next to continue.

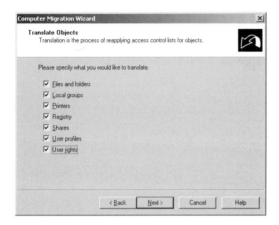

FIGURE 15.10   Specifying objects that will be translated.

9. The subsequent page prompts to choose whether existing security will be replaced, removed, or added to. In this example, replace the security.

   Click Next to continue.

10. A prompt then informs you that the user rights translation will be performed in Add mode only. Click OK to continue.

11. The next page is important, as it allows an administrator to specify how many minutes a computer will wait before restarting itself (the default is 5 minutes). Click Next to continue.

12. Just as in the previous wizards, exclusions can be set for specific attributes in the following wizard page. Select any exclusions needed and click Next to continue.

13. Naming conflicts are addressed on the subsequent page. If any specific naming conventions or conflict resolution settings are required, enter them here. Click Next to continue.

14. The Completion page lists a summary of the changes that will be made. Review the list and click Finish when you are ready. All clients that will be upgraded are subsequently rebooted.

15. When the migration process is complete, you can view the Migration log by clicking the View Log button. After verifying all settings, click Close.

16. The ADMT Agent Dialog window opens. This tool allows the administrator to control the agent operations. Click Start to run pre-check. This identifies any potential issues with the agent migration. The results of the pre-check will be displayed in the Pre-check column. Verify that all computers passed.

17. In the Agent Actions box, select the Run Pre-check and Agent Operations option button. Then click Start to perform the migration operations.

18. The client agents are subsequently distributed to all clients that have been migrated. Click Close on the ADMT MMC snap-in to end the wizard.

Each agent is installed automatically and counts down until the designated time limit set during the configuration of the Computer Migration Wizard. Then the migrated computers reboot into the new domain with the designated settings migrated.

Migrating Other Domain Functionality

In addition to the Group, User, and Computer Migration Wizards, several other wizards can be used to migrate specific domain-critical components. These wizards operate using the same principles as those described in the preceding sections, and are as straightforward in their operation. The following is a list of the additional wizards included in ADMT v3.1:

- ▶ Security Translation Wizard

- ▶ Reporting Wizard

- ▶ Service Account Migration Wizard

- ▶ Exchange 5.5 Mailbox Translation Wizard

- ▶ Retry Task Wizard

- ▶ Password Migration Wizard

Virtually all necessary functionality that needs replacing when migrating from one domain to another can be transferred by using ADMT v3.1. It has proven to be a valuable tool that gives administrators an additional option to consider when migrating and restructuring Active Directory environments.

Summary

Although Windows 2000/2003 and Windows Server 2008 are close cousins in the operating system family tree, there are some compelling reasons to upgrade to Windows 2008 Active Directory Domain Services. The evolutionary nature of Windows 2008 makes performing this procedure more straightforward because the upgrade does not require major changes to Active Directory architecture or the operating system design.

For most organizations, the migration from Active Directory 2000 or 2003 to Active Directory 2008 or 2008 R2 is merely extending the schema and upgrading or replacing old domain controllers with updated domain controllers.

For organizations collapsing domains or making more complex migrations to Active Directory 2008, advanced tools such as ADMT v3.1 provide for a broad range of options to bring organizations to Windows 2008 functionality and closer to realizing the benefits that can be obtained through a migration.

Best Practices

The following are best practices from this chapter:

- ▶ Ensure that one of the postupgrade tasks performed is an audit of all services so that servers that need IIS have the service reenabled after migration.

- ▶ Because prototype phases of a project are essential to test the design assumptions for a migration or implementation, create a production domain controller and then isolate it in the lab for testing.

- ▶ Test the hardware compatibility of any server that will be directly upgraded to Windows 2008 against the published Hardware Compatibility List from Microsoft.

- ▶ Because the decision to raise the forest or domain functional levels is final, ensure that there is no additional need to add Windows 2000/2003 domain controllers anywhere in the forest before performing this procedure.

- ▶ If the server or servers that hold the OM roles are not directly upgraded to Windows Server 2008 but will instead be retired, move these OM roles to another server.

- ▶ When using ADMT, migrate groups into a new domain first to keep users' group membership intact.

CHAPTER 16

Transitioning from Exchange Server 2003/2007 to Exchange Server 2010

In this day and age, most organizations already have some form of email in their environment. Some have been using Microsoft Exchange Server since its infancy, some have only recently started to use it, and others have used other messaging platforms. In many of these cases, these organizations might decide to transition to the latest Microsoft messaging offering, Exchange Server 2010. That said, a transition is a fundamental change in infrastructure, and it is important to understand fully how an organization can transition to the new version.

This chapter makes a differentiation between *migrations* and *transitions* to Exchange Server 2010. Microsoft defines a transition as moving between one version of Exchange Server to the next, whereas a migration is a move from a different vendor's messaging platform to Exchange Server 2010. This chapter focuses on Exchange Server 2010 transitions. Covered are transition scenarios from Exchange Server 2003 directly to Exchange Server 2010, and transition from Exchange Server 2007 directly to 2010. The bulk of the chapter deals with the Exchange Server 2003 to 2010 scenario because the transition process is nearly identical to an Exchange Server 2007 to 2010 transition. The later parts of the chapter outline any differences that might be encountered on a 2007 to 2010 migration.

The focus of this chapter is on the free tools available from Microsoft, and the process involved in using the tools based on tips, tricks, and lessons learned from previous transitions leveraging the built-in tools from Microsoft. This chapter does not cover migration from non-Microsoft messaging platforms, only transitions from older versions of Exchange Server to Exchange Server 2010.

High-Level Guide for Transition from Exchange Server 2003 to Exchange Server 2010

Although this chapter explains the transition process in detail, this first section gives a high-level overview of the process to help conceptualize it. Specific detail on each step is provided in subsequent sections of the chapter. This list can later be used as a checklist for the actual transition process.

Ultimately, a transition to Exchange Server 2010 from Exchange Server 2003 is not a terribly complex endeavor. Simply put, it requires the following fundamental steps:

1. Bring the Exchange organization to Exchange Native Mode.
2. Upgrade all Exchange Servers to Exchange Server 2003 Service Pack 2.
3. Bring the AD forest and domains to Windows Server 2003 Functional (or higher) levels.
4. Upgrade at least one Global Catalog domain controller in each AD site that will house Exchange Server to Windows Server 2003 SP2 or greater.
5. Prepare a Windows Server 2008 (RTM or R2) x64 edition server for the first Exchange 2010 server.
6. Install the AD LDIFDE tools on the new Exchange 2010 server (to upgrade the schema).
7. Install any necessary prerequisites (WWW for CAS server role).
8. Run setup on the Exchange 2010 server, upgrade the schema, and prepare the forest and domains. (Setup runs all in one step or separate at the command line.)
9. Install CAS server role servers and configure per 2010 design. Validate functionality.
10. Transfer OWA, ActiveSync, and Outlook Anywhere traffic to new CAS servers.
11. Install Hub Transport role and configure per 2010 design.
12. Transfer inbound and outbound mail traffic to the HT servers.
13. Install mailbox servers and configure Databases (DAG if needed).
14. Create public folder replicas on Exchange 2010 servers using `pfmigrate.wsf` script, `AddReplicaToPFRecursive.ps1`, or Exchange 2010 Public Folder tool.
15. Move mailboxes to Exchange Server 2010 using Move Mailbox Wizard or PowerShell.
16. Rehome the Offline Address Book (OAB) generation server to Exchange Server 2010.
17. Rehome the public folder hierarchy on the new Exchange Server 2010 admin group.
18. Transfer all Public Folder Replicas to Exchange Server 2010 Public folder store(s).
19. Delete Public and Private Information Stores from Exchange 2003 server(s).
20. Delete Routing Group Connectors to Exchange Server 2003.
21. Delete Recipient Update Service agreements using ADSIEdit.
22. Uninstall all Exchange 2003 servers.

For more information on specifics for each of these steps, refer to subsequent sections of this chapter.

High-Level Guide for Transition from Exchange Server 2007 to Exchange Server 2010

Exchange Server 2007 and Exchange Server 2010 are closer in architecture to each other than they are to Exchange Server 2003, so the transition process is more straightforward. The following checklist illustrates a typical transition from Exchange Server 2007 to 2010:

1. Upgrade all Exchange Servers to Exchange Server 2007 Service Pack 2.
2. Bring the AD forest and domains to Windows Server 2003 Functional (or higher) levels.
3. Upgrade at least one Global Catalog domain controller in each AD site that will house Exchange Server to Windows Server 2003 SP2 or greater.
4. Prepare a Windows Server 2008 (RTM or R2) x64 edition server for the first Exchange 2010 server.
5. Install the AD LDIFDE tools on the new Exchange 2010 server (to upgrade the schema).
6. Install any necessary prerequisites (WWW for CAS server role).
7. Run setup on the Exchange 2010 server, upgrade the schema, and prepare the forest and domains. (Setup runs all in one step or separate at the command line.)
8. Install CAS server role servers and configure per 2010 design. Validate functionality.
9. Transfer OWA, ActiveSync, and Outlook Anywhere traffic to new CAS servers.
10. Install Hub Transport role and configure per 2010 design.
11. Transfer inbound and outbound mail traffic to the 2010 HT servers.
12. Install mailbox servers and configure Databases (DAG if needed).
13. Create public folder replicas on Exchange 2010 servers using `AddReplicaToPFRecursive.ps1` or Exchange 2010 Public Folder tool.
14. Move mailboxes to Exchange 2010 using Move Mailbox Wizard or PowerShell.
15. Rehome the Offline Address Book (OAB) generation server to Exchange Server 2010.
16. Transfer all Public Folder Replicas to Exchange Server 2010 Public folder store(s).
17. Delete Public and Private Information Stores from Exchange 2007 server(s).
18. Uninstall all Exchange 2007 servers.

For more information on specifics for each of these steps, refer to subsequent sections of this chapter.

16

Understanding How to Transition to Exchange Server 2010

Before getting too far into the tools and process of transitioning to Exchange Server 2010, it is important to understand, from a high level, the strategy on how to transition to Exchange Server 2010. The transition strategy could be as simple as effectively moving everything from Exchange Server 2003 or 2007 straight into Exchange Server 2010 without making drastic modifications. Or it could mean a complex Exchange Server environment restructuring is performed as part of the transition process.

It is not required to completely restructure Exchange Server as part of the transition. In fact, if an Exchange Server 2003 or 2007 environment is working fine today, then just a simple transition is all that is required. The reason this book even addresses organizational restructuring as a potential option is that over the years with mergers, acquisitions, downsizing, or business changes, many organizations have Exchange Server structures that are not appropriate for the ongoing needs of an organization. Possibly, the organizational structure worked fine for years for the organization; however, a redesign is now needed because of a change in how the organization does business. These types of changes can make the transition process more complex as are transitions that take place from a messaging system other than Exchange Server 2003/2007. Some of the transition changes are things that could take place before or after the transition to Exchange Server 2010. This chapter itself covers the general process of transitioning to Exchange Server 2010.

Simple Transition from Exchange Server 2003 to Exchange Server 2010

For organizations that have a working Exchange Server 2003 environment that is happy with the architecture and operation of their Exchange Server environment and simply want to move to Exchange Server 2010, the transition process is a relatively simple and methodical process. In a condensed format, the process involves replacing Exchange Server 2003 front-end servers with Exchange Server 2010 Client Access Server (CAS) role systems, replacing bridgehead servers with Hub Transport (HT) servers, adding new Exchange Server 2010 mailbox servers, and moving the mailboxes from the old server, or servers, to the new server, or servers. It's not quite that simple, however, because there are several preparation steps that need to be conducted, a handful of test procedures that can assist the organization in the event of a transition failure that requires rolling back during the transition process. However, to transition to Exchange Server 2010 from an already operational Exchange Server 2003 environment just requires following the step-by-step procedure outlined in the "Transitioning from Exchange Server 2003 to Exchange Server 2010" portion of this chapter.

Restructuring Exchange Server as Part of the Transition to Exchange Server 2010

For organizations that have undergone business changes since the installation of Exchange Server, or that have an Exchange Server environment that is not architected properly for the current and near-future business environment of the organization, they might choose to restructure Exchange Server as part of their transition to Exchange Server 2010. The restructuring can occur with Exchange Server 2003 prior to the transition, the restructuring can occur during the Exchange Server 2010 transition, or the restructuring can occur after Exchange Server 2010 has been put in place.

The deciding factor on when the restructure occurs depends on the effort involved to perform the restructuring. Some organizations will consolidate servers as part of their restructuring process. This is a simple process that can usually be done during the transition where, for example, several Exchange Server 2003 back-end servers are consolidated into a smaller number of Exchange Server 2010 mailbox servers. As mailboxes are moved from the old Exchange Server to the new Exchange Server, they can be moved from multiple systems to a single system. This restructuring is easy to do as part of the transition process.

Some transition processes are more complex—for example, if the organization wants to completely collapse remote site servers and bring all of the servers into a centralized Exchange Server environment model. From an Exchange Server perspective, collapsing sites is one of the restructuring options that can be done as part of the transition; however, the challenge is typically trying to move large amounts of email over a wide area network (WAN) connection. If a remote site has several gigabytes or even tens or hundreds of gigabytes, it is unrealistic to transition that amount of mail over a WAN connection as part of a transition process. In many cases, the actual server, hard drives of the server, or backup of the databases are physically brought into the centralized data center, and the data is transitioned in the data center. Although a logistical shuffle to physically move servers or data during the transition process, this is not an insurmountable process than trying to move large sets of data across a slow WAN link connection.

The more complex restructuring model is required when an organization wants to add some sites, remove some sites, consolidate other sites, and completely redo sites that already exist. The choice of when to do the changes depends on the length and scope of the Exchange Server transition. If the scope and goal of the transition is to do the restructuring in the Exchange Server transition project, plan the process and proceed with a restructuring of Exchange Server as part of the transition to Exchange Server 2010. However, if the restructuring would be nice to have, but not significant to the scope of the project, you might choose to consolidate servers and transition to Exchange Server, and then perform the restructuring after Exchange Server 2010 has been installed.

Transitioning to a Brand-New Exchange Server 2010 Organization

Another method for transitioning to Exchange Server 2010 is one where a brand-new Exchange Server 2010 server is built from scratch, and then data is moved into the new Exchange Server environment. An organization might choose to use this method if there are significant problems with their existing Exchange Server 2003 environment, or if the configuration of their existing Exchange Server environment is not ideally suited for Exchange Server 2010. This is a significant transition task and requires serious consideration regarding whether this is the best option. Instead, perhaps the Exchange Server 2003 environment can be cleaned up to a state where a simpler transition could take place. In nearly all scenarios, this is not a recommended option.

When building a new Exchange Server 2010 environment, data can be exported and imported from an old Exchange Server environment to a new one; however, there will be many user interruptions and impacts. At a minimum, the Outlook profiles on user systems will need to be changed to point the user to a completely new Exchange server. Anyone with offline stores or cached-mode Exchange Server configurations will need to completely rebuild their offline Outlook databases. Furthermore, in cases where the new Exchange Server has a completely new organizational structure, links such as appoint-ments or meeting requests will be disconnected from the person who invited them to the appointment because the new calendar might have different usernames, site configura-tions, and so on.

In addition, with a clean installation of Exchange Server 2010, the organization will not be able to add back in an Exchange Server 2003 or Exchange Server 2007 system. Old Exchange server versions are only supported in an Exchange Server 2010 environment that was transitioned from the old version to the new version of Exchange Server. When Exchange Server 2010 is installed from scratch, none of the legacy backward-compatibility tools are installed or configured to work.

So, a brand-new Exchange Server 2010 installation is a drastic move for an organization that already has Exchange Server 2003. If the organization can do one of the transition methods and then clean up the model after transition, it would be easier to perform the transition.

Transitioning from Exchange Server 5.5 or Exchange 2000 Server

A transition from Exchange 5.5 or Exchange 2000 Server directly to Exchange Server 2010 is not supported and requires a transition first to Exchange Server 2003. After successfully transitioning to Exchange Server 2003, the organization can then execute the subsequent transition to Exchange Server 2010. For more information on performing a 5.5 to Exchange 2003 transition, refer to the SAMS Publishing book, *Exchange Server 2003 Unleashed*, Second Edition.

Migrating from Lotus Notes, Novell GroupWise, and Sendmail

The migration scenarios to Exchange Server involve an organization with an existing non-Exchange Server environment, such as Lotus Notes, Novell GroupWise, or Sendmail. A migration from a non-Microsoft Exchange Server messaging platform is not covered in this chapter. The process of migrating from a non-Exchange Server environment is one that requires tools to transition user email, calendars, contacts, shared folders, and other information stored in the old email system to Exchange Server 2010. This type of migra-tion usually starts with the installation of a completely clean Exchange Server 2010 envi-ronment in which user data is then migrated into the new environment. If Microsoft tools are used for these types of migration, they must be performed first to Exchange Server 2003 and then subsequently transitioned to Exchange Server 2010, as the Microsoft offer-ings for migrating from these platforms to Exchange Server 2010 are either weak or nonexistent. Many organizations look to third-party companies to fill this niche, or migrate first to Exchange Server 2003 before transitioning to Exchange Server 2010.

Transitions Involving a Limited Number of Servers

Beyond just transitioning from one version of messaging to Exchange Server 2010, the destination environment of Exchange Server 2010 can depend on the size and architectural structure of the resulting Exchange Server 2010 environment. For a small organization, the destination Exchange Server environment could be a single server where the various Exchange Server 2010 roles are all on a single system. If there is no need to add additional server systems to the environment, then having a limited number of servers and placing server roles on a single system is easy to do.

The Hub Transport, Client Access, and Mailbox server roles of Exchange Server 2010 can all be placed on a single server; however, if the organization wants to add an Edge Transport server role to the organization, the Edge Transport server needs to be on a separate server. This is done for security purposes to isolate the Edge Transport server from other servers in the Exchange Server 2010 organization that host production data.

Transitions Involving a Distributed Server Strategy

For larger organizations, the various server roles will likely be applied to systems dedicated to a particular server role for purposes of performance and scalability. In many cases, a larger organization will already have existing roles for front-end and back-end servers, as well as bridgehead servers. In these larger environments, assuming that separate servers will be retained, the Exchange Server 2010 server roles will replace the existing Exchange Server 2003 server systems with a similar distribution of server systems.

When transitioning to an Exchange Server 2010 environment with individual servers, the process of transitioning involves the following:

1. Transition of the Client Access Server roles first.
2. Replace the Hub Transport role with Exchange 2010 servers next.
3. Next, move mailboxes to new Exchange 2010 Mailbox role servers.
4. And finally, install server roles such as Edge Transport servers and Unified Messaging servers, if required.

Understanding What's New and What's Different with Exchange Server 2010

This section covers what is new and what is different with Exchange Server 2010, not from a product function and feature basis, which is covered in Chapter 1, "Exchange Server 2010 Technology Primer," but rather how certain changes in Exchange Server 2010 impact the transition process to Exchange Server 2010. This includes things such as the support for only 64-bit hardware, elimination of storage groups, routing groups, and administrative groups and the removal of support for specific Exchange Server 2003 components.

Exchange Server 2010 on x64-bit

One of the first things most organizations become aware of about Exchange Server 2010 is that it only supports x64-bit hardware running the Windows Server 2008 x64-bit or Windows Server 2008 x64 R2 edition operating system. Exchange Server 2007 was also 64-bit only, but supported Windows Server 2003 as well. This means that, during a transition from Exchange Server 2003 to Exchange Server 2010, in-place upgrades are not supported, and that, in many cases, new hardware is required for the transition to Exchange Server 2010.

Most organizations transitioning to Exchange Server 2010 have found that the transition process between servers is relatively simple, so there hasn't been any major concerns transitioning from Exchange Server 2003 to Exchange Server 2010 from one server to another. And because 64-bit Exchange Server 2010 is significantly more reliable and has better performance and scalability benefits, the requirement to forego in-place upgrades has been far outweighed by the enhancements 64-bit has brought to Exchange Server 2010.

Back to Just the EDB Database (STM Is Gone)

Another thing you will notice in a transition from Exchange Server 2003 to Exchange Server 2010 is that the STM database disappears. It originally was removed with Exchange Server 2007, and the contents of the STM databases were folded into the traditional EDB jet database. Because the EDB database is new and improved, you cannot mount an Exchange Server 2003 database on Exchange Server 2010; during the transition process, if you find that there is no STM database on your server, don't worry that you have lost any data.

No Routing Groups in Exchange Server 2010

Exchange Server 2010 has also brought about the elimination of the concept of a routing group in Exchange Server. Routing groups were used in Exchange Server 2003 to allow Exchange Server administrators to create groups of servers that communicated with each other and to identify common routes in which the servers in a group communicated with servers in another group. Exchange Server 2010 now uses Active Directory Sites and Services to identify subnets, where servers on the same subnet are, by default, part of the same routing communication group, but not as a formal group that requires specific administration or management. If an Exchange server is moved to a different subnet, the Exchange server acknowledges a new subnet from Active Directory Sites and Services, and associates itself with the servers on the same subnet if they exist.

The Hub Transport server role replaces the old Exchange Server 2003 bridgehead server, and the Hub Transport server knows which Exchange servers it is servicing by the identification of the subnets that the Hub Transport server is configured to service. It's much easier to just set a table of servers and how they communicate with one another than to create specific groups and then move the servers within a group or between groups to meet the needs of the organization.

The elimination of the routing group requires that a temporary routing group connector be configured between Exchange Server 2010 and the old Exchange Server 2003 environment. During the installation of Exchange Server 2010, as it is joined to an Exchange

Server 2003 organization, the installation process prompts for the name of the Exchange Server 2003 server from which the new Exchange Server 2010 server will route its messages to and from. The purpose of this special routing group connector is to ensure proper mail flow between Exchange Server 2010 and the older Exchange Server 2003 environment. This routing group connector shows up as "Exchange Routing Group (DWBGZMFD01QNBJR)."

> **NOTE**
>
> Some have asked how Microsoft came about naming the temporary routing group connector with DWBGZMFD01QNBJR attached to the connector name. If you advance each letter in that routing group by one letter (D becomes an E, W becomes an X, B becomes a C, and so on), DWBGZMFD01QNBJR becomes EXCHANGE12ROCKS. The same concept applies for the new admin group created, which is named FYDIBOHF23SPDLT. Microsoft chose this naming convention to avoid a naming conflict with any potential Exchange Org worldwide.

No Administrative Groups in Exchange Server 2010

In addition to having routing groups removed in Exchange Server 2010, Microsoft has also removed administrative groups from Exchange Server 2010. As part of the administrative model in Exchange Server 2003, the concept of having administrative groups was to have resources placed in the administrative groups for easier administration and management. This allowed certain Exchange Server administrators to manage the associated resources in their group. Rather than creating a special administrative role with resources associated with the administrative group, Exchange Server 2010 has done away with the administrative group and just has administration associated with user accounts or groups, and not as a special group to create, manage, and administer.

No Link State Updates Required in Exchange Server 2010

Because Exchange Server 2010 no longer requires routing group connectors other than to communicate between Exchange Server 2010 and earlier Exchange Server 2003 servers, the link state update process needs to be suppressed during the coexistence of Exchange Server 2010 with earlier versions of Exchange Server. Link state updates were needed in Exchange Server 2003 to establish a rerouting process if a routing group connector was down and messages needed to be rerouted in the Exchange Server organization.

Exchange Server 2010 uses Active Directory Sites and Services site links and site link bridge information to determine the best routing communications of messages, and it leverages Active Directory (AD) to determine the best way to reroute messages should a link be unavailable.

Elimination of the Recipient Update Service (RUS) in Exchange Server 2010

Exchange Server 2010 also eliminated the Recipient Update Service (RUS) in Exchange Server 2003. The RUS was the function that took a user account created in Active Directory Users and Computers and completed the provisioning process by autogenerating the user's email objects, such as the user's email address. Many Exchange Server 2003 and 2003 administrators never understood why after creating a user in Active Directory that many times the user's email address wasn't created and sometimes it would be created. It was because Active Directory Users and Computers was not the tool that generated the address information—the RUS created it. Depending on how busy the RUS was on a system, it could take a while for the email address information to show up for a newly created user.

In Exchange Server 2010, email recipients are now fully provisioned at the time a user is created in the Exchange Management Console or from the Exchange Management Shell. During the coexistence of an Exchange Server 2010 and Exchange Server 2003 environment, the RUS still needs to be created and present for each domain that has Exchange servers and users; however, you must use the Exchange System Manager from Exchange Server 2003/2007 to provision the RUS because the provisioning service cannot be configured from within the Exchange Management Console or Exchange Management Shell tools of Exchange Server 2010.

> **NOTE**
>
> Although the Recipient Update Service (RUS) needs to be created from the Exchange System Manager utility (found in Exchange Server 2003) for each domain in which an Exchange server or user resides, you cannot make an Exchange Server 2010 server the RUS. RUS will only work on an Exchange Server 2003 server system. If you create the RUS on an Exchange Server 2010 system, RUS will stop working altogether for the domain in which RUS on the Exchange Server 2010 server was created. As a rule of thumb, RUS is already configured and working in the existing Exchange Server 2003 environment. During the transition to Exchange Server 2010, keep the RUS server(s) in each domain operating and only remove those servers in each domain as the cleanup process to go to a native Exchange Server 2010 environment.

Coexistence in a Mixed Exchange Server Environment

During the coexistence between Exchange Server 2003 and Exchange Server 2010, an administrator needs to be mindful which administration tool to use for which function. This is a confusing task because many functions that no longer exist in Exchange Server 2010 require the administrator to go back to the Exchange System Manager tool in Exchange Server 2003 to perform tasks. This is why the shorter the coexistence between Exchange Server 2003 and Exchange Server 2010, the better.

The following list discusses some of the administrative tasks that need consideration for environments where Exchange Server 2003, 2007, and 2010 are coexisting:

▶ Exchange Server 2010 mailboxes must be managed with the Exchange Management Console or Exchange Management Shell found in Exchange Server 2010. Many objects in Exchange Server 2010 are not exposed in Exchange System Manager, and if mailboxes are created using Exchange System Manager for an Exchange Server 2010 user, certain objects will not be provisioned.

▶ Mailboxes on Exchange Server 2003 must be created using the Exchange System Manager found in Exchange Server 2003. Just as the Exchange System Manager doesn't fully support Exchange Server 2010 object creation, the creation of Exchange Server 2003 mailboxes needs the RUS process to fully provision an Exchange Server 2003 mailbox from the Exchange System Manager tool.

▶ The Exchange Management Console will successfully manage an Exchange Server 2003 mailbox. So, as long as the mailbox has been created with the Exchange System Manager tool, thereafter the mailbox can be managed or administered from either tool.

▶ Moving mailboxes between Exchange Server 2003 and Exchange Server 2010 (either way) must be done with the Exchange Management Console tool. Do not use the Exchange System Manager tool to move mailboxes to or from Exchange Server 2010 because certain components are not in the Exchange System Manager tool to successfully complete the mailbox move process.

No Support for Certain Exchange Server 2000 and 2003 Components

Several components in Exchange Server 2000 and 2003 are no longer supported in Exchange Server 2010. Most of these components weren't supported in a native Exchange 2003 environment either, and an organization needs to take this into consideration when transitioning to Exchange Server 2010. The following Exchange Server 2000 and 2003 components are no longer supported in Exchange Server 2010:

▶ Key Management Service (KMS)

▶ Microsoft Mobile Information Service

▶ Exchange Instant Messaging Service

▶ Exchange Chat Service

▶ Exchange Server 2003 Conferencing Service

▶ MS-Mail Connector

▶ cc:Mail Connector

These services do not exist in Exchange Server 2010, and an organization requiring functionality of these services needs to keep Exchange 2000 or 2003 Servers in the organization long enough to retain the service or replace the service with an Exchange Server
2010–supported equivalent service.

For services such as the MS-Mail Connector and cc:Mail Connector, those services can run
for a while on an Exchange Server 2003, even if all the users' mailboxes have been transitioned to Exchange Server 2010. However, services keyed to user mailboxes, such as the
Exchange Server 2003 Conferencing Service, Chat, Instant Messaging, Mobile Information
Service, or Key Management Service, will cease to work for each user as their mailboxes are
transitioned to Exchange Server 2010.

Deploying a Prototype Lab for the Exchange Server 2010 Transition Process

Regardless of the method that is chosen to transition Exchange Server, care should be
taken to test design assumptions as part of a comprehensive prototype lab. A prototype
environment can help simulate the conditions that will be experienced as part of the transition process. Establishing a functional prototype environment also can help reduce the
risk associated with transitions. In addition to traditional approaches for creating a prototype lab, which involves restoring from backups, several techniques exist to replicate the
current production environment to simulate transition.

Creating Temporary Prototype Domain Controllers to Simulate Transition

Construction of a prototype lab to simulate an existing Exchange Server infrastructure is
not particularly complicated, but requires thought in its implementation. Because an exact
copy of the Active Directory is required, the most straightforward way of accomplishing
this is by building a new domain controller in the production domain and then isolating
that domain controller in the lab to create a mirror copy of the existing domain data. DNS
and global catalog information should be transferred to the server when in production, to
enable continuation of these services in the testing environment.

> **NOTE**
>
> You should keep several considerations in mind if planning this type of duplication of
> the production environment. First, when the temporary domain controller is made into
> a global catalog server, the potential exists for the current network environment to
> identify it as a working global catalog server and refer clients to it for directory
> lookups. When the server is brought offline, the clients would experience connectivity
> issues. For these reasons, it is good practice to create a temporary domain controller
> during off-hours.

A major caveat to this approach is that the system must be completely separate, with no
way to communicate with the production environment. This is especially the case because

the domain controllers in the prototype lab respond to requests made to the production domain, authenticating user and computer accounts and replicating information. Prototype domain controllers should never be added back into a production environment.

Seizing Operations Master (OM) Roles in the Lab Environment

Because Active Directory is a multimaster directory, any one of the domain controllers can authenticate and replicate information. This factor is what makes it possible to segregate the domain controllers into a prototype environment easily. There are several different procedures that can be used to seize the OM (also referred to as Flexible Single Master Operations [FSMO]) roles. One approach uses the `ntdsutil` utility, as follows:

1. Open a command prompt by selecting Start, Run, typing `cmd` in the Open text box, and then clicking OK.

> **CAUTION**
>
> Remember, this procedure should only be performed in a lab environment or in disaster recovery situations. Never perform it against a running production domain controller unless the intent is to forcibly move OM roles.

2. Type `ntdsutil` and press Enter.
3. Type `roles` and press Enter.
4. Type `connections` and press Enter.
5. Type `connect to server` SERVERNAME (where SERVERNAME is the name of the target Windows Server 2003/2008 domain controller that will hold the OM roles), and press Enter.
6. Type `quit` and press Enter.
7. Type `seize schema master` and press Enter.
8. Click Yes at the prompt asking to confirm the OM change.
9. Type `seize domain naming master` and press Enter.
10. Click Yes at the prompt asking to confirm the OM change.
11. Type `seize pdc` and press Enter.
12. Click OK at the prompt asking to confirm the OM change.
13. Type `seize rid master` and press Enter.
14. Click OK at the prompt asking to confirm the OM change.
15. Type `seize infrastructure master` and press Enter.
16. Click OK at the prompt asking to confirm the OM change.
17. Exit the command prompt window.

After these procedures have been run, the domain controllers in the prototype lab environment will control the OM roles for the forest and domain, which is necessary for additional transition testing.

> **NOTE**
>
> Although the temporary domain controller procedure just described can be very useful toward producing a copy of the AD environment for a prototype lab, it is not the only method that can accomplish this. The AD domain controllers can also be restored via the backup software's restore procedure. A third option—which is often easier to accomplish but is somewhat riskier—is to break the mirror on a production domain controller, take that hard drive into the prototype lab, and install it in an identical server. This procedure requires the production server to lose redundancy for a period of time while the mirror is rebuilt, but is a "quick-and-dirty" way to make a copy of the production environment.

Restoring the Exchange Server Environment for Prototype Purposes

After all forest and domain roles have been seized in the lab, the Exchange server or servers must be duplicated in the lab environment. Typically, this involves running a restore of the Exchange server on an equivalent piece of hardware. All the major backup software implementations contain specific procedures for restoring an Exchange Server 2003 environment. Using these procedures is the most ideal way of duplicating the environment for the transition testing.

Validating and Documenting Design Decisions and Transition Procedures

The actual transition process in a prototype lab should follow, as closely as possible, any design decisions made regarding an Exchange Server 2003 implementation. It is ideal to document the steps involved in the process so that they can be used during the actual implementation to validate the process. The prototype lab is not only an extremely useful tool for validating the upgrade process, but it can also be useful for testing new software and procedures for production servers.

The chosen transition strategy—whether it be an in-place upgrade, a move mailbox method, or another approach—can be effectively tested in the prototype lab at this point. Follow all transition steps as if they were happening in production.

Transitioning to a Brand-New Exchange Server 2010 Environment

One of the transition options to get to Exchange Server 2010 is to build a brand-new Exchange Server 2010 environment, and then import any existing data into the new Exchange Server environment. This scenario is not much of a transition being that a brand-new environment is created. The only transition addressed by this scenario is potentially that of having user data such as email messages, calendar appointments, and contacts imported into the new environment.

This scenario is typically limited to organizations that might have one of the following environments:

▶ An organization that has never had email, such as a brand-new organization

▶ An organization that is migrating from a completely non-Microsoft environment where a brand-new Exchange Server 2010 is installed, and then data from the old non-Microsoft messaging system is transitioned to the new Exchange Server 2010 environment

▶ An organization that is undergoing a drastic business change that dictates the need to start from scratch with a new Exchange Server 2010 configuration, such as a merger of two companies with a third company emerging that has a completely different business name and organizational structure

This scenario is not expanded on further in this chapter, as the transition process really mirrors that of a brand-new installation of Exchange Server 2010 (covered in Chapter 7, "Installing Exchange Server 2010") with the process of importing old data, if desired, into the new environment.

The new Exchange Server 2010 environment should be designed and implemented to meet the needs of the new organization, through the use of third-party transition tools; even tools made available from Microsoft on the downloads page, http://technet. microsoft.com/en-us/exchange/bb456976.aspx, can be used to assist with the import of data to the new environment.

Transitioning from Exchange Server 2003 to Exchange Server 2010

For organizations that currently have Exchange Server 2003 looking to transition to Exchange Server 2010, the transition strategy pretty much involves replacing front-end servers with client access servers, bridgehead servers with Hub Transport servers, back-end servers with mailbox servers and moving the mailboxes, and then finally adding in Edge Transport and Unified Messaging servers as desired. There is a very specific order that works best in the transition process as well as tips and tricks that help you navigate around known transition challenges. These tips, tricks, and best practices for transitioning from Exchange Server 2003 to Exchange Server 2010 have been documented in this section of the chapter.

> **NOTE**
>
> There can be several variations of an existing Exchange Server 2003 environment where the organization has clustered back-end servers, or has an SMTP relay server ahead of the Exchange Server environment, or has servers residing in different physical sites that can still use this transition process. There are no transition limitations that prevent an organization from using this transition strategy and making variations to it, including transitioning onto a clustered mailbox server, adding Hub Transport or client access servers, or consolidating servers as part of the transition process.

Planning Your Transition

The planning process in transitioning from an environment that has Exchange Server 2003 to Exchange Server 2010 involves ensuring that the existing environment is ready for a transition, and that the hardware necessary to accept the transitioned server roles is compatible with Exchange Server 2010. The planning process to Exchange Server 2010 proceeds using the following path:

1. Review Chapter 3, "Understanding Core Exchange Server 2010 Design Plans," to become familiar with terminology used in Exchange Server 2010 design architecture.

2. Confirm that you want to do a one-to-one transition of servers from Exchange Server 2003 to Exchange Server 2010 (that is, Exchange Server 2003 front-end servers become Exchange Server 2010 client access servers, and Exchange Server 2003 back-end servers become Exchange Server 2010 mailbox servers).

NOTE

As part of this transition, you can do server consolidation by moving mailboxes from multiple servers to fewer servers, transition from shared storage cluster mailbox servers to servers running Exchange 2010 Database Availability Groups (DAGs), or add in Edge Transport or Unified Messaging server role systems as part of the transition process. These variations just need to be slipped in to the transition plan. For implementation of Hub Transport servers, see Chapter 17, "Implementing Client Access and Hub Transport Servers." For implementation of Edge Transport servers, see Chapter 8, "Implementing Edge Services for an Exchange Server 2010 Environment." And for implementation of DAGs, see Chapter 31, "Database Availability Group Replication in Exchange Server 2010."

---

3. Select the proper version of Exchange Server 2010 on which you will be implementing Exchange Server 2010, whether it is the Standard Edition or the Enterprise Edition of the server software.

Choosing Between Standard and Enterprise Editions

The Exchange Server 2010, Standard Edition is the basic messaging server version of the software. The Standard Edition supports five data stores and has full support for web access, mobile access, and server recovery functionality. The Standard Edition is a good version of Exchange Server to support a messaging system for a small organization, or as a dedicated Edge Transport, Hub Transport, or client access server for a larger environment. Many small and medium-sized organizations find the capabilities of the Standard Edition sufficient for most messaging server services, and even large organizations use the Standard Edition for message routing servers or as the primary server in a remote office. The Standard Edition meets the needs of effectively any environment wherein a server with a limited database storage capacity is sufficient.

The Exchange Server 2010, Enterprise Edition is focused at server systems that require more Exchange Server messaging databases. With support for up to 150 databases per server, the Enterprise Edition of Exchange Server 2010 is the appropriate version of messaging system for organizations that have a lot of mailboxes or a lot of mail storage, and for an organization that wants to set up clustering for higher reliability and redundancy of the Exchange Server environment.

4. The next step is to acquire the appropriate hardware necessary to implement the new Exchange Server 2010 environment. Remember that Exchange Server 2010 now requires x64-bit hardware and Windows Server 2008 RTM/R2 x64-bit edition operating system software.

> **NOTE**
>
> The variables to an Exchange Server 2010 environment are random access memory (RAM) and disk storage. Because 64-bit systems now support more than 4GB of RAM, it has been found that most Exchange Server 2010 servers have 16GB to 32GB of RAM in the system as the base configuration (more memory for servers hosting thousands of users). Instead of spooling or caching transactions primarily to disk, Exchange Server 2010 takes advantage of memory for caching transactions. For disk storage, Exchange Server 2010 does not require more disk storage than previous versions of Exchange Server. Therefore, as a rule of thumb, choose Exchange Server 2010 server hardware that has enough storage space to hold the current Exchange Server database plus plenty of additional storage space for the growth needs of the organization. Storage needs might grow when deploying DAGs as well. For more details on Exchange Server 2010 server sizing and optimization, see Chapter 34, "Optimizing an Exchange Server 2010 Environment."

16

5. Confirm that the current Exchange Server 2003 environment server components are compatible with Exchange Server 2010. This means checking to see if there are Exchange Server 2003 components referenced in the section "No Support for Certain Exchange Server 2000 and 2003 Components" earlier in this chapter running in the current Exchange Server environment. If there are components in use that are no longer supported, those services need to be eliminated or transitioned before migrating to Exchange Server 2010 or a third-party product might need to be purchased and used.. In the two sections referenced in this paragraph, workarounds are noted to address these issues.

6. Validate that add-ons and utilities used in the existing Exchange Server 2003 environment are compatible with Exchange Server 2010 or upgraded to support Exchange Server 2010. This includes products like BlackBerry services, Cisco Unity voice mail services, tape backup software, and so on.

> **NOTE**
>
> If a software program is not compatible with Exchange Server 2010, many times you can keep the software operating on an older Exchange Server 2003 server, and transition the rest of the environment to Exchange Server 2010. This can typically be done for gateway tools that route information into or out of an Exchange Server environment.

7. Make sure to bring the Exchange Server 2003 environment into Exchange Native mode, effectively eliminating any Exchange 5.5 compatibility components for the environment.

8. Test the transition process in a lab environment to confirm all the steps necessary in transitioning to Exchange Server 2010. The test transition is covered in the next section.

Testing the Transition Process

Part of any transition best practice is to perform the transition in a test lab prior to performing the transition in a real production environment. The test lab allows the person performing the transition to test and validate assumptions. Effectively, if it works in the lab, you have a higher level of confidence that it will work in the production environment. At a minimum, after walking through the transition process, you will understand the steps necessary to perform the transition, become familiar with the steps, work through problems if they arise, and correct problems so that if or when they happen in the production transition, you will already be prepared for the necessary action. In addition, testing the transition process provides you with a timeline to know how long it will likely take to transition the databases into the Exchange Server 2010 environment.

The test lab creation process is covered in detail earlier in this chapter in the section "Deploying a Prototype Lab for the Exchange Server 2010 Transition Process." This section addresses getting a copy of an Active Directory global catalog (GC) server and seizing the roles to make this GC replica the master global catalog for the lab environment. This section also addresses getting a copy of the current Exchange Server 2003 server data into the lab.

Key to the test lab process is to validate the operation of your third-party add-ons, utilities, backup software, and so on to confirm that all of the components in your current Exchange Server environment will successfully transition to Exchange Server 2010. Take this chance to confirm whether you need to download any patches or hotfixes from the third-party product vendors, and whether you can simply reinstall the third-party products on an Exchange Server 2010 server, or whether you need to keep a legacy Exchange Server 2003 server in your environment to maintain backward compatibility for a while.

When the lab is ready, you can run through the processes outlined in the following step-by-step sections to confirm that the processes outlined work as planned in your transition environment. Again, make note of all problems you run into and document the workarounds you come up with in the lab so that when you get into the production transition, you will have step-by-step notes on how to work through problems that come up. And also keep track of how long it takes processes to complete so you are prepared for how long the production transition process will take to complete.

Backing Up Your Production Environment

When you are ready to perform the transition in your production environment, you need to have a complete backup of the critical components that you will be working on just in case you need to roll back your environment. The expectation is that if your test lab replicated as much of your production environment as possible, then there should be no surprises in your production transition. However, as a best practice, make a backup of your Active Directory global catalog server, all of your Exchange servers, and all of the servers that interoperate with Exchange Server, such as gateway systems or replicated directory servers.

It is also a best practice to turn off any replication to other environments during the transition process, such as Forefront Identity Manager (previously named ILM, MIIS, IIFP, and MMS), Services for UNIX or Services for NetWare synchronization, or other directory synchronization tools.

Preparing the Exchange Server 2010 Server with Windows

Each Exchange Server 2010 server in the new environment needs to have Windows Server 2008 x64 Standard or Enterprise Edition installed on the system. Either the RTM or the R2 editions of Windows Server 2008 will work with Exchange Server 2010. The Exchange Server 2010 should also be joined to the expected Active Directory domain.

Preparing Exchange Server 2003

Whether you are performing this transition in a lab environment or in production, after performing a backup of your production environment, the first step in the transition process is to extend the Active Directory schema. This readies Active Directory and Exchange Server 2003 to integrate Exchange Server 2010 in the existing Exchange Server environment. This is necessary because during the transition process, or potentially in a long-term coexistence between Exchange Server 2003 with Exchange Server 2010, the old and new environments need to support each other.

The first time Exchange Server 2010 setup is run in an existing Exchange Server organization, it runs a set of prerequisite checks against the AD forest and the organization itself. If all prerequisites are satisfied, the setup utility enables an administrator to prepare the forest, domain, and existing Exchange organization for Exchange Server 2010. Administrators see a dialog box similar to Figure 16.1, which indicates that when setup proceeds, it modifies the Active Directory schema and extends it with the new Exchange Server 2010 schema.

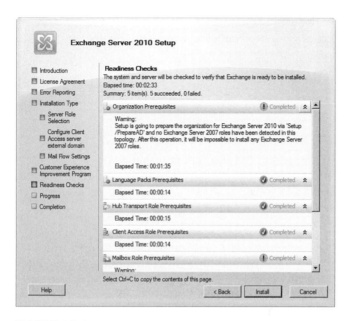

FIGURE 16.1   Running org prerequisite checks before the Exchange 2010 schema upgrade.

NOTE

An Active Directory schema update is no minor task and should be fully tested in the Prototype lab environment in advance. The account running setup must also be an Enterprise Admin and Schema Admin for the forest and an Exchange Full Administrator for the organization. If there are separate accounts for these roles, the schema upgrade portion of the installation can be run from the command prompt using the `setup.exe /prepareAD` switch.

Installing Exchange Server 2010 on a Server

The overall process for installing Exchange Server 2010 is outlined in Chapter 7, "Installing Exchange Server 2010." For purposes of a transition, after the schema has been upgraded, setup can commence on the Exchange 2010 server. This might be part of the same step, or it can be separated if using the `setup.exe /PrepareAD` option.

Server Sequencing

If you have various existing Exchange Server 2003 server roles, such as bridgehead servers, front-end servers, and back-end servers, the process is to transition each server role in a logical sequence. The proper sequence is as follows:

1. Transition all front-end servers to Exchange Server 2010 client access servers.

2. Transition all bridgehead servers to Exchange Server 2010 Hub Transport servers.

3. Transition back-end servers to Exchange Server 2010 mailbox servers.

The reason you need to transition Exchange Server 2003 front-end servers to Exchange Server 2010 client access servers first is because an Exchange Server 2010 client access server can fully host Exchange Server 2003 front-end services as well as Exchange Server 2010 client access server functions. In contrast, an Exchange 2003 front-end server can only host the front-end process of an Exchange 2003 back-end server. Before you can transition mailboxes from Exchange Server 2003 to Exchange Server 2010, the front-end server supporting the back-end server needs to be replaced with an Exchange Server 2010 client access server.

After the front-end servers have been replaced, proceed with the installation of bridge-head servers being replaced one for one with Hub Transport servers. Hub Transport servers will service all Exchange Server 2003, 2007, and 2010 routing functions. Unlike the requirement for front-end servers to be replaced by Exchange client access servers before mailboxes are moved to Exchange Server 2010, all bridgehead servers do not necessarily need to be replaced by Hub Transport servers before the transition of mailboxes. Bridgehead servers will continue to successfully route information for both the Exchange Server 2003 and Exchange Server 2010 environment as long as at least one routing group connector exists between each Exchange Server routing group in the organization.

After the front-end and bridgehead servers are replaced by CAS and Hub Transport servers, install Exchange Server 2010 mailbox server systems and move mailbox data to the new servers.

16

After replacing an old Exchange Server 2003 front-end server with an Exchange Server 2010 client access server, confirm you can render an Outlook Web Access page on the new client access server to mailboxes on the old Exchange Server 2003 mailbox server. After you confirm that all functions of the new client access server seem to operate, you can remove the old Exchange Server 2003 front-end server for Exchange Server. To remove the server, see the section "Uninstalling Exchange from Old Exchange Server 2003 Servers."

NOTE

Exchange Server 2003 OWA uses different IIS virtual directories than Exchange Server 2007 or Exchange Server 2010, namely /exchange, /public, and /exchweb compared to /owa. For a transition, it is important to point all users to /exchange because Exchange Server 2010 mailboxes will redirect to /owa, and Exchange Server 2003 mailboxes will proxy to Exchange 2003 back-end servers.

Continue to install new Exchange Server 2010 client access servers to replace all Exchange Server 2003 front-end servers, and then proceed with the same steps to install new Exchange Server 2010 mailbox servers, this time choosing a custom installation of a mailbox server. When a new Exchange Server 2010 mailbox server has been added to the organization and you are ready to move mailboxes from Exchange Server 2003 to Exchange Server 2010, proceed to the next section.

Moving Mailboxes

After a new Exchange Server 2010 server has been installed into an existing Exchange Server 2003 organization, the movement of mailboxes from an old Exchange Server back-end server to a new Exchange Server 2010 mailbox server is as simple as selecting the mailbox or mailboxes, and through a few mouse clicks, selecting the new destination server. The specific process is as follows:

1. Launch the Exchange Management Console (EMC) on an Exchange Server 2010 server.

2. Expand the recipient configuration, and click on the mailbox container. You will see a list of mailboxes. In the Recipient Type Details column, you will notice some of the mailboxes are flagged as Legacy Mailbox and some of the mailboxes are flagged as User Mailbox. Those flagged as Legacy Mailbox are still on Exchange Server 2003 and need to be transitioned to Exchange Server 2010. Those mailboxes already on Exchange Server 2010 are flagged as Mailbox User.

3. Click on a mailbox, or alternately hold down the Shift key and select a group of mailboxes, or hold down the Ctrl key and click on specific mailboxes that you want to transition.

4. Right-click and select New Local Move Request. (A remote move is a move to a server in a different Exchange Server organization.)

5. A New Local Move Request Wizard appears, and you are prompted with the option of choosing which mailbox database you want to move the mailbox to. Choose the database and review the settings, similar to what is shown in Figure 16.2. Choose the destination of the mailbox(es), and then click Next.

6. You are prompted with a Move Options screen to choose to Skip the Mailbox or to Skip the Corrupted Messages if corrupted messages are found during the move process. Usually, you would want to choose to skip the corrupt messages so you can complete the transition; however, if you want to problem-solve the corrupt messages, you can skip the transition of the mailbox, and then debug the mailbox problem and try the transition of the mailbox later. Click Next to continue.

7. A summary screen is shown that summarizes the choices made. Review the source and destination of the mailboxes that will be moved, and either click Back and make any desired changes, or click New to submit the request and begin the movement of mailboxes to the Exchange Server 2010 environment.

The move time will vary based on the amount of data to be moved, and the bandwidth between the source and destination server. This is something that should be tested in the lab to determine whether all the mailboxes desired to be moved at any one time can be

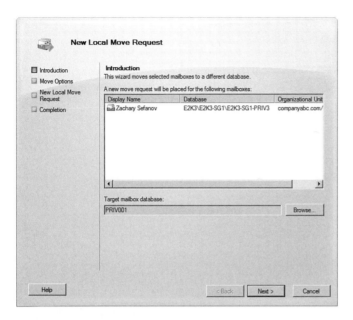

FIGURE 16.2   Choosing the Exchange Server 2010 database for mailbox moves.

accomplished in the time available. Organizations with a lot of data to move choose to install gigabit Ethernet adapters in servers and place systems on the same subnet to efficiently move large sets of data.

This is also something to ensure if mirrored in the test environment, as some organizations test the movement of mail on an isolated gigabit test lab switch with fast results, and then when performing the real transition, are working across a slower WAN backbone with very slow performance speeds. After the Move Request is submitted, it can be monitored and cancelled from the Move Request node in the Recipient Configuration console section.

Changing User Profile Configuration

Even after the Exchange Server mailboxes have been successfully moved from the old Exchange Server 2003 server(s) to the new Exchange Server 2010 server(s), keep the old Exchange Server 2003 servers running on the network for typically two weeks. The reason is that in Outlook, the mail profile on each user's system is keyed to a server— in this case, the old Exchange Server 2003 server. If you remove the old server immediately after the mailboxes are moved, the next time the users launch Outlook, their profiles will look for the old server, not find the server, and the users will not have access to email. You need to go to each user's Outlook profile and enter in the name of the new server so that the Outlook client can find the new mailbox server where the user's mailbox contents are stored.

16

However, if you leave the old server running, when the user launches Outlook, the Outlook profile connects the user to the old Exchange Server 2003 server. The old server tells the Outlook client that the user's mailbox has been moved to a new server, and the user's profile is automatically updated on each user's client system to now find the user's mailbox on the new server. When this is done once for each user, it never needs to be done again. The user's Outlook client profile is set to find the user's mailbox on the new server. The idea of leaving the old server running for two weeks is that usually within a couple of weeks, all users will have launched Outlook once and their profile will automatically change. After two weeks, you can remove the old Exchange Server 2003 server. See the section on "Cleaning Up the Exchange Server 2003 Environments" for the process to properly remove an Exchange server from the network.

If a user had not launched Outlook in the two-week timeframe that you had the old server running, such as an individual on maternity leave, on a sabbatical, or on an extended leave of absence, you will need to go back to the user's system and manually change the user's Outlook profile to connect the user to the new Exchange Server 2010 server. This will likely be done for a very limited number of users. Obviously, the old Exchange Server 2003 server can remain on for a very long time with no mailboxes on the system, but merely be there to redirect users to the new system. However, it is usually recommended to remove the old server just so that objects can be removed from Exchange Server and the organization doesn't have to patch, maintain, and manage a server in the environment beyond a reasonable operating timeframe.

Adding Unified Messaging and Edge Transport Servers and Enterprise Policies

After the core Exchange Server 2003 front-end and back-end servers have been transitioned to applicable Exchange Server 2010 client access and mailbox servers, additional server roles such as Unified Messaging servers, Edge Transport servers, or Hub Transport servers, including servers managing enterprise policies, can be added to the new Exchange Server 2010 organization. Because the addition of these additional server roles are not directly related to the transition of mail from Exchange Server 2003 to Exchange Server 2010, usually it is recommended to wait a few days and make sure that Exchange Server 2010 is operating smoothly in its new environment before adding more to the network.

The addition of enterprise policies on a Hub Transport server or security policies on a Edge Transport server in an Exchange Server 2010 environment might cause mail to be filtered, blocked, or altered as part of a spam filtering or policy management rule. This might appear to be a problem with basic Exchange Server 2010 functionality, whereas it is a function of a change in content filtering added to the new Exchange Server environment. Allowing Exchange Server 2010 to operate for a week or two as a basic Exchange Server 2010 environment provides the Exchange Server administrators as well as Exchange Server users time to become familiar with the operation of the new Exchange Server 2010 environment before changes are made in applying filters, new routes, or new operational structure changes.

Changing the Offline Address Book Generation Server

The server responsible for Offline Address Book (OAB) generation must be changed to an Exchange Server 2010 system before removing Exchange Server 2003 from an organization. To do this, select the Mailbox node under the Organization Configuration section and navigate to the Offline Address Book tab. Select the OAB to be moved and click on the Move action. The wizard move screen, as shown in Figure 16.3, enables you to select a server to become the new OAB generation server.

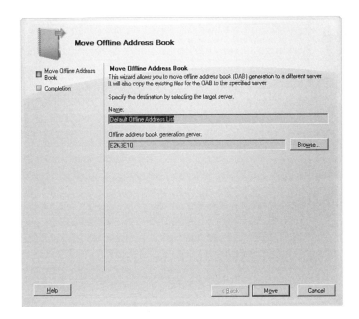

FIGURE 16.3   Changing the OAB generation server using the Configure External Client Access Wizard.

Replicating Public Folders from Exchange Server 2003 or Exchange Server 2003 to Exchange Server 2010

Just as mailboxes are transitioned from Exchange Server 2003 servers to Exchange Server 2010 systems, public folders need to be replicated before retiring the old Exchange Server 2003 servers. In the past, this procedure involved a manual replication of folder hierarchy, which could prove to be a tedious process. Microsoft addressed this drawback with a utility on the Exchange Server 2003 CD called PFMigrate. PFMigrate can create public and system folder replicas on new systems, and remove them from old servers. The following procedure outlines how to use PFMigrate to transition from an Exchange Server 2003 server to an Exchange Server 2010 system:

1. Open a command prompt (select Start, Run, type cmd, and click OK).

2. Type cd D:\support\Exdeploy and press Enter.

3. To create a report of current public folder replication, type the following:

   ```
   pfmigrate.wsf /S:OLDSERVERNAME /T:NEWSERVERNAME /R /F:c:\LOGNAME.log
   ```

   This generates a report named `LOGNAME.log` on the C: drive. `OLDSERVERNAME` should
   be the name of the old Exchange Server 2003 system, and `NEWSERVERNAME` should be
   the new Exchange Server 2010 system.

4. To replicate system folders from the Exchange Server 2003 server to the Exchange
   Server 2010 server, type the following:

   ```
   pfmigrate.wsf /S:OLDSERVERNAME /T:NEWSERVERNAME /SF /A /N:10000
      /F:c:\LOGNAME.log
   ```

5. To replicate public folders from Exchange Server 2003 to Exchange Server 2010, type
   the following:

   ```
   pfmigrate.wsf /S:OLDSERVERNAME /T:NEWSERVERNAME /A /N:10000
      /F:c:\LOGNAME.log
   ```

> **NOTE**
>
> The /N:#### field determines how many public folders should be addressed by the
> tool. If a larger number of public folders than 10,000 exists, the parameter should be
> increased to match.

6. After all public folders have replicated, the old replicas can be removed from the
   Exchange Server 2003 servers by typing the following:

   ```
   pfmigrate.wsf /S:OLDSERVERNAME /T:NEWSERVERNAME /D
   ```

7. The `LOGNAME.log` file can be reviewed to ensure that replication has occurred successfully and that a copy of each public folder exists on the new server.

> **TIP**
>
> Public Folder management is easier from the Exchange Server 2003 side, which is why
> the pfmigrate.wsf tool is an Exchange 2003 tool. For 2007 or 2010 public folder repli-
> ca creations, consider the use of the PowerShell AddReplicaToPFRecursive.ps1 script
> included on a deployed server.

Cleaning Up the Exchange Server 2003 and Exchange Server 2003 Environments

After a new Exchange Server 2010 server is added to the network to functionally replace
an old Exchange 2003 server, there comes a time when the old server should be removed.
As noted in the sidebar "Changing User Profile Configuration," the Exchange Server 2003
mailbox servers should remain on the network for two weeks after the transition of mailboxes to ensure that users connect to the new Exchange Server 2010 mailbox server at
least once to automatically change the users' Outlook profiles on their client system.

For front-end servers, however, they can be removed as soon as a new Exchange Server 2010 client access server is added to the network—the new Exchange Server 2010 client access servers will host both Exchange Server 2003 back-end servers, as well as Exchange Server 2010 mailbox servers.

The removal process is more than just powering off the system and disconnecting it from the network. It is very important that the old Exchange servers are properly removed from the Exchange Server organization; otherwise, Exchange Server does not know that a server has been removed, and the server remains in the Exchange Server organization configuration tables. As an example, if you have a bridgehead server that used to route mail messages between sites and you just unplugged the server without properly removing it, Exchange servers in the organization will not know that the server has been removed, and will continue to try to route messages to the server. This could cause messages to pile up in a queue, and unless the Exchange servers can recalculate a new message route for messages, the lack of removing a specific server can prevent messages from ever routing within the organization until the server is properly removed.

The proper process of removing an old Exchange Server 2003 server is a multistep process:

1. Delete or transition all mailboxes and public folders from the Exchange 2003 Server.
2. Move the public folder hierarchy to the Exchange Server 2010 admin group.
3. Remove all routing group connectors to the server.
4. Remove the Recipient Update Service (RUS) using ADSIEdit.
5. Uninstall Exchange Server from the server.
6. Remove routing groups.

Move the Public Folder Hierarchy to Exchange Server 2010

A critical step that must be taken before completing a move to Exchange Server 2010 is the task of moving the public folder hierarchy to the newly created admin group in which all Exchange Server 2010 systems exist. To do this, perform the following tasks:

1. In ESM, navigate to Administrative Groups; then right-click on Exchange Administrative Group (FYDIBOHF23SPDLT) and choose New—Public Folders Container.
2. Locate the Exchange Server 2003 legacy administrative group, expand the folders, and then drag the Public Folders container under the Exchange Server 2010 admin group.

Deleting Mailbox and Public Folder Stores

Before an Exchange Server 2003 system can be retired, any and all public folder stores and mailbox databases must be removed from the server. If a mailbox store is empty, this simply involves right-clicking and deleting the database. For public folder stores, however, you must first right-click and choose Move All Replicas, as shown in Figure 16.4. This ensures that all public folder replicas have been moved to the new Exchange 2010 servers.

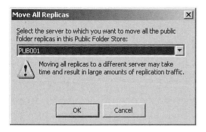

FIGURE 16.4   Moving all public folder replicas to Exchange Server 2010.

Note that this process might take several days to fully complete before the public store can be removed. After all replicas are gone, the public folder store can be deleted from the server.

Removing Routing Group Connectors to Servers

The removal process of an Exchange Server 2003 server continues with the removal of routing group connectors from the server being removed. It is important to confirm that the routing group connector that is being removed is not serving a key communication route for a site or for the organization. As an example, if the routing group connector is the only link for a server to another site in the organization, the removal of the routing group connector will have messages cease being sent or received to the remote site. Alternatively, if the routing group connector is the link between Exchange Server 2003 and Exchange Server 2010, and if there are no other routing group connectors between Exchange Server 2003 and Exchange Server 2010, the removal of the routing group connector will effectively prevent any communications between the old and new Exchange Server environment.

If you are certain that the routing group connector serves no purpose, remove the routing group connector so that you can remove the Exchange server from the organization.

TIP

If you aren't sure whether a routing group connector serves an important function in the network, and cannot figure out through looking at architectural or mail flow diagrams of the organization whether the RGC is of value, just stop the Routing Group Connector (RGC) service. On the Exchange Server 2003 server, click on Start, Programs, Administrative Tools, Service. Right-click on the Microsoft Exchange Routing Engine, and choose Stop. Wait a few hours or days to see if anybody complains that their messages aren't being transmitted properly. If after a few days no one has complained, you can probably assume the RGC is not serving any valuable function.

To remove a routing group connector, do the following:

1. On the Exchange Server 2003 server on which you plan to remove the routing group connector, launch the Exchange Server 2003 System Manager program.

2. Expand the Administrative Groups container.

3. Choose and expand the administrative group where the server that you are on resides.

4. Choose and expand the Routing Groups container.

5. Choose and expand the routing group that holds the routing group connector you want to remove.

6. Choose and expand the Connectors container.

7. Right-click on the routing group connector you want to remove, and choose Delete. Confirm Yes that you want to remove the routing group connector.

Note that Exchange Server connectors are usually created in pairs because each is one-directional. Make sure to remove both connectors to a server before removing the server.

This process removes the routing group connector, and you can now proceed with removing the server itself from Exchange Server.

Removing the Recipient Update Service Using ADSIEdit

The Recipient Update Service is used only for Exchange Server 2003 mailboxes and is not needed with Exchange Server 2007 or 2010. Because the uninstallation program for Exchange Server 2003 will not enable you to remove a server that is used for RUS; however, you must first remove the RUS connections using ADSIEdit, the low-level editor for AD objects.

To remove the RUS objects, open ADSIEdit on a domain controller and navigate to the following location in the Configuration naming context: CN=Configuration, DC=*DomainName* - CN=Services - CN=Microsoft Exchange - CN=*ExchangeOrgName* - CN=Address Lists Container- CN=Recipient Update Services. In the result pane, right-click Recipient Update Service (Enterprise Configuration), click Delete, and then click Yes to confirm the deletion. Repeat for any other RUS objects in the results pane.

Uninstalling Exchange Server from Old Exchange 2003 Servers

Rather than simply removing or disconnecting an old Exchange server from the network, it is important to uninstall Exchange Server from the old server system. The uninstall process doesn't just remove the Exchange Server software off the hard drive of the system; it performs a very important task of properly removing that Exchange server from the Exchange Server directory.

After all mailboxes, public folder replicas, and connectors have been moved off an old Exchange Server 2003 system, the server can be retired and removed from service. The easiest and most straightforward approach to this is to uninstall the Exchange Server 2003 component via the Add/Remove Programs applet in Windows. To perform this operation, do the following:

1. On the Exchange server, select Start, Control Panel.

2. Double-click Add/Remove Programs.

3. Select Microsoft Exchange and click Change/Remove.

4. Click Next at the welcome screen.

16

5. Under Action, select Remove from the drop-down box, and click Next to continue.

6. At the summary screen, click Next to continue. The Exchange server will then be uninstalled.

7. Repeat the process for any additional Exchange Server 2003 servers.

As Exchange Server 2003 servers are removed from Exchange Server 2003 routing groups, upon the removal of the last Exchange Server 2003 system from a routing group, the routing group itself can be removed.

Upon removal of the last Exchange Server 2003 server, the environment should be completely void of any Exchange Server 2003 functionality. There is no Native Exchange Server 2010 mode. The removal of the last Exchange Server 2003 routing group clears legacy mail routing that is no longer needed in Exchange Server 2010.

Transitioning from Exchange Server 2007 to Exchange Server 2010

In many ways, a transition from Exchange Server 2007 to Exchange Server 2010 is similar to a transition from Exchange Server 2003 to Exchange Server 2010—so similar that it would be redundant to rewrite many of the steps from the preceding sections of this chapter. Subsequently, it is more important to note what is different about a 2007 to 2010 transition process.

The following key factors differentiate a 2007 to 2010 transition from a 2003 to 2010 transition:

▶ Exchange admin groups and routing groups are already out of the picture.

▶ The Recipient Update Service is no longer part of the transition process.

▶ Exchange Server 2007 servers must be updated to Exchange Server Service Pack 2 in advance of the transition.

▶ The public folder hierarchy does not need to be rehomed. Indeed, because public folders are not required for Exchange Server 2007, they might not even be part of the transition.

Otherwise, the transitions look similar and have an identical process. Transition starts with the CAS role, moves to the Hub Transport role, and then proceeds to the Mailbox role and finally Unified Messaging and Edge Transport.

One added advantage of transition from Exchange Server 2007 to Exchange Server 2010: if Outlook clients are at 2007 levels or above, the move mailbox process does not result in downtime, making the end user transition experience completely transparent.

Summary

A transition to Exchange Server 2010 is relatively straightforward, provided the proper thought goes into execution of the tasks required. Effectively, the process merely involves adding Exchange Server 2010 servers to an existing Exchange Server 2003 or 2007 environment, and moving server roles and mailbox data to the new servers. This chapter covered several other prerequisite processes, along with tips and tricks needed to have a higher success factor in the transition process. With proper thought put into how to make the process seamless, a transition from Exchange Server 2003 or 2007 to Exchange Server 2010 can be made relatively painless.

Best Practices

The following are best practices from this chapter:

▶ Use the high-level transition checklists from the beginning of this chapter as a guide to the transition process.

▶ Key to a successful transition to Exchange Server 2010 is to properly plan and test the transition process to ensure that all data as well as server role functions have a successful transition to the new environment. See Chapters 3 and 4 of this book on design and architecture best practices prior to performing a transition to Exchange Server 2010.

▶ Because Exchange Server 2010 does not support certain Exchange Server 2003 functions, an Exchange Server 2003 server may need to exist in the organization after the transition or until that functionality is no longer required.

▶ Before transitioning to Exchange Server 2010, the Active Directory schema needs to be updated. Be sure to test this process in a prototype lab in advance of the transition.

▶ Before transitioning to Exchange Server 2010, be sure to bring the Exchange Server organization into Exchange Native mode and the AD forest and domains to Windows Server 2003 Functional level or higher.

▶ Being that Microsoft does not provide a direct transition from Exchange Server 5.5 or Exchange 2000 Server to Exchange Server 2010, the organization should plan their transition from Exchange 5.5/2000 to Exchange 2003 as a separate step before transitioning to Exchange Server 2010.

▶ Test the transition process in a lab environment before implementing the transition in production. A test transition confirms that all data successfully transitions to the new environment (that is, there is no mailbox corruption that can halt the transition process). In addition, by running through the process in a lab, you gain experience on the transition process and gain a good sense of how long it will take to complete the transition at the time of the live transition.

▶ When transitioning to an Exchange Server 2010 environment that will have distributed server roles (that is, not all server roles will reside on a single server), the proper order of implementation is client access server, Hub Transport server, and then mailbox server.

▶ Because Exchange Server 2010 client access servers can serve as Exchange Server 2003 front-end servers, transition all front-end servers to CAS role systems, and remove all front-end servers as one of the first server transition steps in the transition process.

▶ Keep in mind that if a brand-new Exchange Server 2010 environment is implemented as a clean installation of Exchange Server, it must be noted that a clean Exchange Server 2010 environment cannot have Exchange 2003 or Exchange 2007 servers added into the new Exchange 2010 organization. Related to this, if Exchange Server 2010 is installed directly into an Exchange 2003 organization that has never had Exchange 2007 in place, no Exchange 2007 servers can be added after the fact.

CHAPTER 17

Implementing Client Access and Hub Transport Servers

Two new roles within the Microsoft Exchange Server 2010 family are the client access server (CAS) and the Hub Transport server. In reality, these two roles are really specializations and evolutions of the original Exchange Server front-end and bridgehead server concepts, along with the Edge Transport server.

Exchange Server 2010 CAS and Hub Transport roles have a number of new features that improve the reliability and user experience. These new features include the following:

▶ Exchange Control Panel

▶ Enhanced Outlook Web App

▶ Client Throttling

▶ Shadow Redundancy

▶ Enhanced Disclaimers

▶ Moderated Transport

To see the place that the CAS and the Hub Transport server role hold in the constellation of Exchange Server 2010 roles, refer to Figure 17.1.

In this chapter, the discussion focuses on the CAS and Hub Transport server features. These two servers play pivotal roles in client access and routing within the Exchange Server 2010 infrastructure. The Edge Transport server is discussed at length in Chapter 8, "Implementing Edge Services for an Exchange Server 2010 Environment."

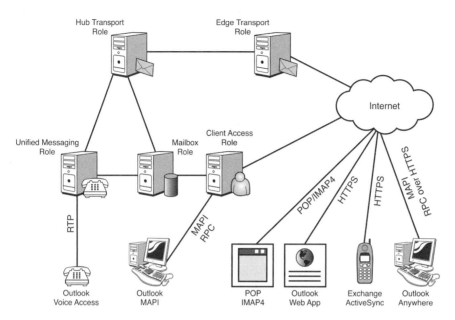

FIGURE 17.1   Exchange 2010 server roles and relationships.

Understanding the Client Access Server

The Exchange Server 2010 CAS role is an evolution of the same role in Exchange Server 2007. It still provides client access services for clients but now also includes clients that use MAPI clients (for example, Outlook 2007) and client-oriented services such as the Autodiscover service.

Clients can access their mailboxes using Messaging Application Programming Interface (MAPI), voice access, Hypertext Transfer Protocol (HTTP), RPC over HTTP, ActiveSync, Post Office Protocol (POP), or Internet Message Access Protocol version 4 (IMAP4). Exchange Server 2010 consolidates the client store access paths by folding in the last remaining client (MAPI) into the CAS server. Now all client access is mediated by the client access server, which thus lives up to its name.

There are seven client types, shown in Table 17.1. These seven client types connect to the CAS in various ways using various protocols, as shown in Figure 17.2.

TABLE 17.1   Client Types

Client	Protocol
Outlook	MAPI over RPC
Outlook Voice Access	RTP
Outlook Web App	HTTP/HTTPS
Exchange ActiveSync	HTTP/HTTPS

TABLE 17.1   Client Types

Client	Protocol
Outlook Anywhere	MAPI over RPC over HTTP/HTTPS
POP Client	POP3 (receive) / SMTP (send)
IMAP Client	IMAP4 (receive) / SMTP (send)

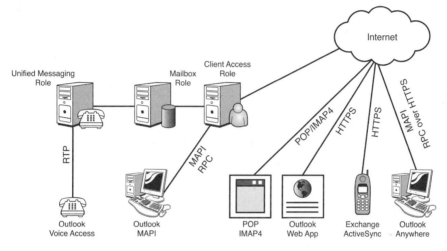

FIGURE 17.2   Client type connections to the CAS.

A CAS must exist in every Exchange Server 2010 organization and, in Exchange Server 2010, there must be a CAS in every AD site where there is a mailbox server. A best practice is to have a CAS in every Active Directory (AD) site, where AD sites represent contiguous areas of high bandwidth. Additional CASs can be deployed for performance and fault tolerance.

As indicated before, the CAS is used for the following clients and services:

▶ Outlook MAPI

▶ Outlook Anywhere

▶ Availability service

▶ Autodiscover service

▶ Outlook Web App (OWA)

▶ ActiveSync

▶ POP3 and IMAP

Basically, the CAS role handles the communications for all client access except for the voice access. Outlook Voice Access clients are essentially telephone access, which is handled by the UM role. Each of the client access methods supported by the CAS role is discussed individually in the following sections. For a detailed discussion of the design and implementation of client mobility features, see Chapter 23, "Designing and Implementing Mobility in Exchange Server 2010." For a detailed discussion of the Outlook Voice Access client, see Chapter 24, "Designing and Configuring Unified Messaging in Exchange Server 2010."

Outlook MAPI

In Exchange Server 2007, Outlook MAPI clients connected directly to the Mailbox role servers. In Exchange Server 2010, Outlook MAPI clients connect to the CAS role servers. This provides a consistent connection point and a single point to manage client access, performance, and compliance.

This is by far the most common access client because most Outlook clients in a company's internal network are Outlook MAPI clients. Outlook MAPI is also sometimes referred to as Outlook RPC because RPC is the connection protocol.

> **NOTE**
>
> The Messaging Application Programming Interface (MAPI) is technically not a protocol but is rather a general framework. This is implemented as the Exchange Server remote procedure calls (RPC) protocol in Exchange Server 2003, 2007, and 2010. So, technically, the protocol used by Outlook clients is called Exchange RPC.
>
> However, the term MAPI is used synonymously and more commonly in place of Exchange RPC.

Outlook MAPI is commonly supported by Microsoft Outlook 2007 and Microsoft Outlook 2003.

Outlook Anywhere

Outlook Anywhere is the Exchange Server 2010 name for the original RPC over HTTP feature in Exchange Server 2003. It essentially enables remote procedure calls (RPC) clients such as Outlook 2003 and Outlook 2007 to traverse firewalls by wrapping the RPC traffic in HTTP. This enables traveling or home users to use the full Outlook client without the need for a dedicated virtual private network (VPN) connection, which is frequently blocked by firewalls.

For security, the Outlook Anywhere protocol is always implemented with Secure Sockets Layer (SSL) to secure the transport, so it is actually RPC over HTTPS. This ensures that the confidentiality and integrity of the Outlook Anywhere traffic is protected.

> **NOTE**
>
> The idea of allowing RPC over the Internet is anathema to many organization's security groups. In the past decade, a number of well-publicized vulnerabilities occurred in the native RPC protocol, which gave it a bad reputation.

With the evolution of the RPC protocol and the securing of the transport with SSL, the Outlook Anywhere feature provides as much security as Outlook Web App (OWA) or ActiveSync. Outdated security concerns should not prevent an organization from deploying Outlook Anywhere.

Outlook Anywhere is enabled by default in Exchange Server 2010, albeit with a self-signed certificate. It is important to decide the certificate strategy and install the correct certificate type to ensure seamless access for clients. See Chapter 12, "Integrating Certificate-Based Public Key Infrastructure (PKI) in Exchange Server 2010," for a detailed discussion of certificates and PKIs.

Availability Service

The Availability service is the name of the service that provides free/busy information to Outlook 2007 and Outlook Web App clients. It is integrated with the Autodiscover service (discussed in the following section) and improves on the Exchange Server 2003 version.

In Exchange Server 2003, the free/busy information was published in local public folders. In Exchange Server 2010, the Availability service is web-based and is accessed via a uniform resource locator (URL). The service can be load-balanced with Network Load Balancing (NLB) and can provide free/busy information in trusted cross-forest topologies.

The Autodiscover service provides the closest availability service URL to the client in the XML file. It does the following tasks for the Outlook and OWA clients:

▶ Retrieve current free/busy information for Exchange Server 2010 mailboxes

▶ Retrieve current free/busy information from other Exchange Server 2010 organizations

▶ Retrieve published free/busy information from public folders for mailboxes on servers that have versions of Exchange Server that are earlier than Exchange Server 2007

▶ View attendee working hours

▶ Show meeting time suggestions

The Availability service is installed by default on each CAS. Interestingly, there are no Exchange Management Console options for the Availability service. All interaction with the service is through the Exchange Management Shell.

Autodiscover Service

In previous versions of Exchange Server, profiles were a frequent source of headaches for administrators. The Exchange Server 2010 Autodiscover feature automatically generates a profile from the user's email address and password. The service works with the clients and protocols listed in Table 17.2.

TABLE 17.2   Autodiscover Supported Clients and
Protocols

Client	Protocol
Outlook 2007	MAPI (Exchange RPC)
Outlook Anywhere	Exchange RPC over HTTPS
ActiveSync	ActiveSync

The Autodiscover service provides the following information to the clients:

▶ The user's display name

▶ Separate connection settings for internal and external connectivity

▶ The location of the user's mailbox server

▶ The URLs for various Outlook features

▶ Outlook Anywhere server settings

Autodiscover is an evolution of the Exchange Server 2003 MAPI referral feature, which would redirect the user to the appropriate Exchange Server back-end server and modify the user's profile. All that the users needed to provide was their alias and the name of any Exchange server. This was a useful feature if the location of a user's mailbox would change from one server to another, as it would automatically redirect the user and permanently change the profile. This was a marked improvement over the Exchange 2000 profile generation, which would simply fail if the server or alias were not specified correctly. Any Exchange server would do, and the user could type their full name, the account name, or even their email address. However, in Exchange Server 2003, the user still had to enter the information to get access.

With Outlook 2007 and Exchange Server 2010, it gets even better. The user simply provides authentication credentials, and the Autodiscover service determines the user's profile settings. Then, the Autodiscover function of Outlook 2007 configures the user's profile automatically, basically filling in the information automatically. No manual entry of the server name or username is needed.

When the CAS is installed, a virtual directory is created in the default website on the CAS server. The CAS role also creates Service Connection Point (SCP) objects in Active Directory.

When a client is domain joined and domain connected, the Outlook 2007 client looks up the SCP records in AD. The client picks the one in its site or a random one if there is none in its site. It then communicates with the CAS and gets an XML file with profile information. The Outlook client consumes this XML file to generate or update its profile.

The Autodiscover service can also be used by Outlook Anywhere and ActiveSync clients over the Internet, which requires SSL for security. The Outlook 2007 client uses the domain portion of the Simple Mail Transfer Protocol (SMTP) address of the user to locate the Autodiscover service. When the client communicates with the Autodiscover service over the Internet, the Outlook 2007 client expects that the URL for the service will be https://domain/autodiscover or https://autodiscover.domain/autodiscover/. For example, for the user chrisa@companyabc.com, the Autodiscover service URL will be https://companyabc.com/autodiscover/ or https://autodiscover.companyabc.com/autodiscover/.

The Autodiscover service requires the CAS. The Autodiscover service also requires that the forest in which it resides has the Exchange Server 2010 AD schema changes applied.

The functionality of the Autodiscover service and the Autodiscover feature can be tested using the Outlook 2007 client. The steps are as follows:

1. Launch Outlook 2007.
2. Press and hold the Ctrl key, and then select the Outlook icon in the system tray.
3. Select Test E-Mail AutoConfiguration in the menu.
4. The email address should already be populated, so enter the user's password.
5. Uncheck the Use Guessmart check box.
6. Click the Test button.
7. Review the Results, Log, and XML tabs.

The log should show a series of three lines in the log with the text:

```
Attempting URL https://ex1.companyabc.com/Autodiscover/Autodiscover.xml found
➥through SCP
Autodiscover to https://ex1.companyabc.com/Autodiscover/Autodiscover.xml starting
Autodiscover to https://ex1.companyabc.com/Autodiscover/Autodiscover.xml succeeded
➥(0x00000000)
```
This shows that the Autodiscover URL was identified from the SCP record in AD. The client then attempts the autodiscovery and is finally successful in the last line.

The XML tab shows (data shown next) the actual file that is returned by the Autodiscover service. This not only includes information such as the user's server and display name, but also information such as the URLs for the Availability service, Unified Messaging server, Exchange Control Panel (ECP), and OWA:

```
<?xml version="1.0" encoding="utf-8"?>
<Autodiscover xmlns="http://schemas.microsoft.com/exchange/
➥autodiscover/responseschema/2006">
 <Response xmlns="http://schemas.microsoft.com/exchange/
➥autodiscover/outlook/responseschema/2006a">
 <User>
 <DisplayName>Rand Morimoto</DisplayName>
 <LegacyDN>/o=CompanyABC/ou=Exchange Administrative Group
➥(FYDIBOHF23SPDLT)/cn=Recipients/cn=Rand Morimoto</LegacyDN>
 <DeploymentId>84834df8-edb1-4b31-8bd5-610b1f9b4633</DeploymentId>
 </User>
 <Account>
```

17

```
<AccountType>email</AccountType>
<Action>settings</Action>
<Protocol>
<Type>EXCH</Type>
<Server>EX1.companyabc.com</Server>
<ServerDN>/o=CompanyABC/ou=Exchange Administrative Group
➥(FYDIBOHF23SPDLT)/cn=Configuration/cn=Servers/cn=EX1</ServerDN>
<ServerVersion>7380826D</ServerVersion>
<MdbDN>/o=CompanyABC/ou=Exchange Administrative Group
➥(FYDIBOHF23SPDLT)/cn=Configuration/cn=Servers/cn=EX1/cn=Microsoft
➥Private MDB</MdbDN>
<AD>DC2.companyabc.com</AD>
<ASUrl>https://ex1.companyabc.com/EWS/Exchange.asmx</ASUrl>
<EwsUrl>https://ex1.companyabc.com/EWS/Exchange.asmx</EwsUrl>
<EcpUrl>https://ex1.companyabc.com/ecp</EcpUrl>
<EcpUrl-um>?p=customize/voicemail.aspx&amp;exsvurl=1</EcpUrl-um>
<EcpUrl-aggr>?p=personalsettings/EmailSubscriptions.slab&amp;
➥exsvurl=1</EcpUrl-aggr>
<EcpUrl-mt>PersonalSettings/DeliveryReport.aspx?exsvurl=1&amp;IsOWA=&lt;
➥IsOWA&gt;&amp;MsgID=&lt;MsgID&gt;&amp;Mbx=&lt;Mbx&gt;</EcpUrl-mt>
<EcpUrl-sms>?p=sms/textmessaging.slab&amp;exsvurl=1</EcpUrl-sms>
<OOFUrl>https://ex1.companyabc.com/EWS/Exchange.asmx</OOFUrl>
<UMUrl>https://ex1.companyabc.com/EWS/UM2007Legacy.asmx</UMUrl>
<OABUrl>http://ex1.companyabc.com/OAB/542fc47a-c163-4af9-8491-
➥d3ea54c52cd6/</OABUrl>
</Protocol>
<Protocol>
<Type>WEB</Type>
<Internal>
<OWAUrl AuthenticationMethod="Basic,
➥Fba">https://ex1.companyabc.com/owa/</OWAUrl>
<Protocol>
<Type>EXCH</Type>
<ASUrl>https://ex1.companyabc.com/EWS/Exchange.asmx</ASUrl>
</Protocol>
</Internal>
<External>
<OWAUrl AuthenticationMethod="Fba">
➥https://ex1.companyabc.com/owa/</OWAUrl>
</External>
</Protocol>
</Account>
</Response>
</Autodiscover>
```

This information is presented in a neater form on the Results tab, as shown in Figure 17.3. You can clearly see the Display Name, Protocol, Server, Login Name, and the various URLs.

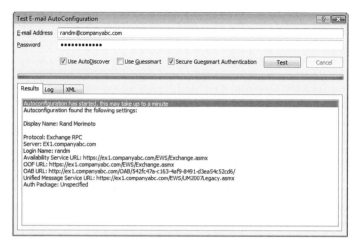

FIGURE 17.3   Autodiscover Results tab.

Outlook Web App

The Outlook Web App (OWA) is the full-featured Exchange Server 2010 web-based client. It is a component of the CAS server role. This client enables a user with a web browser to access the Exchange Server 2010 infrastructure from the intranet or the Internet. This is done securely using HTTPS and is supported by a wide range of browsers, including the following:

▶ Internet Explorer (IE)

▶ Firefox

▶ Safari

In addition to the email, calendaring, tasks, notes, and file access features, Exchange Server 2010 includes a number of new features for the OWA client. These new features include the following:

▶ Conversation View

▶ Presence and IM

▶ UM Voice Mail

▶ Calendar Sharing

▶ SMS Message Synchronization

▶ Improved Searching and Filtering

▶ Favorites Folders

▶ Message Delivery Reports

▶ Mail Tips Information

▶ Rights Management

▶ Group Management

These features and enhancements put the Outlook Web Mail client on par with the Outlook RPC client for the vast majority of users. OWA is an important client and has a dedicated chapter in this book. See Chapter 28, "Leveraging the Capabilities of the Outlook Web App (OWA) Client," for more information on the OWA client.

OWA uses forms-based authentication by default. This requires that users enter their credentials in the format "domain\username" and their password. A common issue in large organizations is that users might forget to enter their domain and fail their authentication, leading to unnecessary help desk calls. OWA forms-based authentication supports three different logon formats to enable the organization flexibility in the logon. The three logon formats follow:

▶ **Domain\user name**—This is the default logon format and requires the user to enter their domain and their username. For example, `companyabc\chrisa`.

▶ **User principal name (UPN)**—This enables the users to use their email address and the logon format. For example, chrisa@companyabc.com.

▶ **User name only**—This enables users to just enter their username to logon. For example, `chrisa`. This is the simplest option for the user, especially for organizations with only one Active Directory domain.

To set the logon format for User Name Only, do the following steps:

1. Launch the Exchange Management Console.
2. Expand the Server Configuration folder.
3. Select the Client Access folder.
4. In the top-right pane, select the CAS server to be changed.
5. In the bottom-right pane, select the Outlook Web App tab.
6. Right-click the website to be changed and select Properties.
7. Select the Authentication tab.
8. Select the User Name Only option.
9. Click Browse to find the domain.
10. Select the domain and click OK. The result should look like Figure 17.4.
11. Click OK to save the settings.
12. At the warning that IIS needs to restart, click OK.
13. Open a command prompt on the CAS server.
14. Run `iisreset /noforce` to reset IIS.

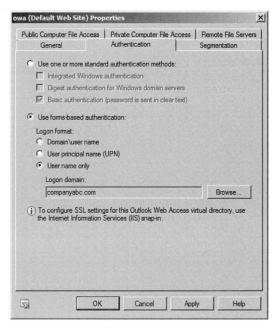

FIGURE 17.4   OWA Logon format setting.

The OWA client now prompts for only the username, as shown in Figure 17.5. This makes
the logon process simpler for users in organizations with a single domain name.

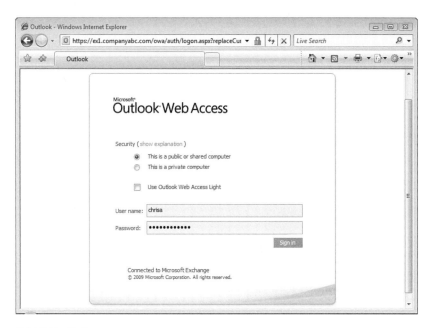

FIGURE 17.5   User Name Only Logon format in OWA.

Exchange Control Panel

The Exchange Control Panel (ECP) is hosted on the CAS server role and is an exciting new tool in Exchange Server 2010. The ECP is a browser-based Management client for end users, administrators, and specialists. This provides a new way to administer a subset of Exchange Server features and is completely RBAC integrated.

This new ECP web utility provides a great self-provisioning portal for administrators and a simplified user experience for common management tasks. It is accessible directly via URL, Outlook Web App (OWA), and Outlook Server 2010. Figure 17.6 shows the start page of the interface from an administrator role.

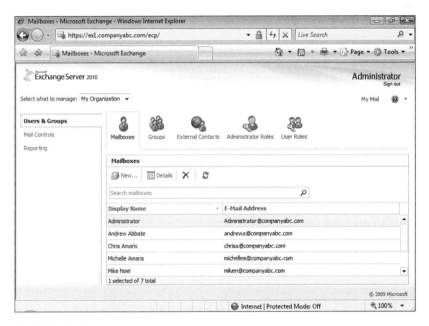

FIGURE 17.6   Exchange Control Panel.

The ECP is AJAX-based, is deployed as a part of the Client Access server role, and shares some code with OWA. However, the two are separate applications and sites.

The Exchange Control Panel can be used in a variety of scenarios. Administrators can delegate to permissions in role to support a variety of administrators, specialists, and users. These include the following types of scenarios:

▶ Administrators

▶ Helpdesk Specialists

▶ Auditors

▶ End Users

▶ Customers in a Hosted Environment

The scenarios are configured in the RBAC interface, which is itself based in the Exchange Control Panel.

Administrators would launch the ECP tool directly from the ECP link (https://<server-name>/ecp) where <servername> is an Exchange Server 2010 CAS. End users would access the ECP tool from within OWA, which launches from the Options link. Although it launches from the OWA web page (https://<servername>/owa), the link is to the ECP web page (https://<servername>/ecp). The security is completely integrated, enabling the end-user experience to be completely seamless.

The browser support for the ECP is the same as for OWA premium. Supported browsers are as follows:

- ▶ Internet Explorer (IE)

- ▶ Firefox

- ▶ Safari

The Exchange Control Panel is covered in detail in Chapter 18, "Administering an Exchange Server 2010 Environment."

ActiveSync

Exchange ActiveSync is a synchronization protocol that allows mobile devices to synchronize the user's Exchange Server mailbox, including email, calendar, contacts, and tasks. It is based on HTTP and Extensible Markup Language (XML). ActiveSync supports the following devices:

- ▶ Windows Mobile 6.x and 5.0

- ▶ Pocket PC 2003

- ▶ Pocket PC 2002

Unlike Exchange Server 2003, in Exchange Server 2010, the ActiveSync feature is enabled by default. The Exchange Server 2010 ActiveSync has a number of new features and improved features over the Exchange Server 2003 version, including the following:

- ▶ Support for HTML messages

- ▶ Support for follow-up flags

- ▶ Support for fast message retrieval

- ▶ Meeting attendee information

- ▶ Enhanced Exchange Search

- ▶ Windows SharePoint Services and Universal Naming Convention (UNC) document access

- ▶ PIN reset

- ▶ Autodiscover for over-the-air provisioning

▶ Support for Out of Office configuration

▶ Support for tasks synchronization

▶ Support for Direct Push

Some of the new features, such as Direct Push and Autodiscover, require Windows Mobile 5.0 with the Messaging and Security Feature Pack (MSFP) or Windows Mobile 6.x installed on the device to function.

Exchange Server 2010 ActiveSync also has a number of new security features, including the following:

▶ Exchange ActiveSync mailbox policies

▶ Device password policies

▶ Remote Device Wipe

These new security features allow Exchange Server 2010 administrators to effectively manage the security of their mobile devices. Settings like allowing the use of Bluetooth (a frequent security risk), the camera, and other new settings enable the Exchange Server 2010 administrator much more control over the devices. The settings available in the ActiveSync mailbox policy are listed here:

The General policy settings control overall policy settings, such as the policy refresh interval. General security policy settings include the following:

▶ **Allow Nonprovisionable Devices**—Specifies whether older devices that might not support application of all policy settings are allowed to connect to Exchange Server 2010 by using Exchange ActiveSync.

▶ **Refresh Interval (Hours)**—Defines how frequently the device updates the Exchange ActiveSync policy from the server.

▶ **Windows File Shares**—Enables access to files that are stored on Windows file share (UNC) shares.

▶ **Windows SharePoint Services**—Enables access to files that are stored in Microsoft Windows SharePoint Services document libraries.

Password policy settings control the password requirements for the mobile devices. Password policy settings include the following:

▶ **Require Password**—Enables the device password.

▶ **Required Alphanumeric Password**—Requires that a password contains numeric and nonnumeric characters.

▶ **Enable Password Recovery**—When this setting is enabled, the device generates a recovery password that's sent to the server. If the user forgets their device password, the recovery password can be used to unlock the device and enable the user to create a new device password.

▶ **Require Encryption on Device**—Specifies whether device encryption is required. If checked, the device must support and implement encryption to synchronize with the server.

▶ **Require Encryption on Storage Card**—Specifies whether the storage card must be encrypted. Not all mobile phone operating systems support storage card encryption. For more information, see your device and mobile operating system for more information.

▶ **Allow Simple Password**—Enables or disables the ability to use a simple password such as 1234. This option is checked by default.

▶ **Number of Failed Password Attempts Allowed**—Specifies how many times an incorrect password can be entered before the device performs a wipe of all data.

▶ **Minimum Password Length**—Specifies the minimum password length.

▶ **Time Without User Input Before Password Must Be Re-Entered (in Minutes)**—Specifies the length of time that a device can go without user input before it locks.

▶ **Password Expiration (Days)**—Enables the administrator to configure a length of time after which a device password must be changed.

▶ **Enforce Password History**—Prevents the user from reusing the past number of passwords specified when changing passwords on the device.

The Sync Setting policy settings control the synchronization behavior of the mobile devices. Sync Settings policies include the following:

▶ **Include Past Calendar Items**—Specifies the maximum range of calendar days that can be synchronized to the device. The default is All.

▶ **Include Past Email Items**—Specifies the maximum number of days' worth of email items to synchronize to the device. The default is All.

▶ **Limit Email Size to (KB)**—Specifies the size beyond which email messages are truncated when they are synchronized to the device. The value is specified in kilobytes (KB).

▶ **Allow Direct Push When Roaming**—Specifies whether the device must synchronize manually while roaming. Allowing automatic synchronization while roaming can frequently lead to larger-than-expected data costs for the mobile phone plan.

▶ **Allow HTML-Formatted Email**—Specifies whether email synchronized to the device can be in HTML format. If this setting is unchecked, all email is converted to plain text.

▶ **Allow Attachments to Be Downloaded to Device**—Enables attachments to be downloaded to the mobile phone.

▶ **Maximum Attachment Size (KB)**—Specifies the maximum size of attachments that are automatically downloaded to the device.

17

The Device policy settings control what device features are enabled by the organization. These features can be a source of consternation for security professionals, including cameras used to capture inappropriate information or Bluetooth-enabled devices hacked in coffee shops. The device policy settings enable Exchange Server 2010 administrators to disable device features as needed. Device policy settings include the following:

▶ **Allow Removable Storage**—Specifies whether the mobile phone can access information that is stored on a storage card.

▶ **Allow Camera**—Specifies whether the mobile phone camera can be used.

▶ **Allow Wi-Fi**—Specifies whether wireless Internet access is allowed on the device.

▶ **Allow Infrared**—Specifies whether infrared connections are allowed to and from the mobile phone.

▶ **Allow Internet Sharing from Device**—Specifies whether the mobile phone can be used as a modem for a desktop or portable computer.

▶ **Allow Remote Desktop from Device**—Specifies whether the mobile phone can initiate a remote desktop connection.

▶ **Allow Desktop Synchronization**—Specifies whether the mobile phone can synchronize with a computer through a cable, Bluetooth, or IrDA connection.

▶ **Allow Bluetooth**—Specifies whether a mobile phone enables Bluetooth connections. The available options are Disable, HandsFree Only, and Allow.

NOTE

The Device policy settings are premium Exchange ActiveSync features and require an Exchange Enterprise Client Access License for each device covered by the policy in which these are enabled.

The Device Application settings control how the devices use applications. These policies include the following:

▶ **Allow Browser**—Specifies whether Pocket Internet Explorer is enabled on the mobile phone. This setting doesn't affect third-party browsers installed on the device.

▶ **Allow Consumer Mail**—Specifies whether the mobile phone user can configure a personal email account (either POP3 or IMAP4) on the device.

▶ **Allow Unsigned Applications**—Specifies whether unsigned applications can be installed on the device.

> ▶ **Allow Unsigned Installation Packages**—Specifies whether an unsigned installation package can be run on the device.

NOTE

The Device Applications policy settings are premium Exchange ActiveSync features and require an Exchange Enterprise Client Access License for each device covered by the policy where these are enabled.

The policies under the Other tab control allowed and blocked applications. Specifically, those policies follow:

> ▶ **Approved Applications**—Stores a list of approved applications that can be run on the device.

> ▶ **Blocked Applications**—Specifies a list of applications that cannot be run on the device.

NOTE

The Other policy settings are premium Exchange ActiveSync features and require an Exchange Enterprise Client Access License for each device covered by the policy in which these are enabled.

These policies are much more comprehensive than in previous versions of Exchange Server and address concerns of many organizations about the twin demons of proliferation and lack of control of mobile devices. Exchange Server 2010 give administrators the policy tools they need to control what the devices can do and enforce the organizations written security policies.

To use the password policy features and the Remote Device Wipe, you need to create and associate the user with an Exchange ActiveSync mailbox policy. By default, all users are associated with the Default policy that is created at install.

Different policies can be created to meet the needs of different user communities. For example, an organization might have one general user ActiveSync mailbox policy with default password settings that require a minimum of four characters. A second ActiveSync mailbox policy for executives with higher security requirements and more secure password settings might require a minimum of 10-character passwords. These policies would be assigned to the appropriate mailboxes. During CAS installation, a Default ActiveSync mailbox policy is created. This policy enables most of the features of ActiveSync devices, so it is not restrictive at all. The policy can be adjusted or new policies created.

To create a new ActiveSync mailbox policy, execute the following steps:

1. Expand the Organization Configuration folder.
2. Select the Client Access folder.

17

3. In the actions pane, select New Exchange ActiveSync Mailbox Policy.

4. Enter the policy name, such as Default Exchange ActiveSync Mailbox Policy.

5. Click New to create the policy.

6. Click Finish to close the wizard.

To associate a user with an Exchange ActiveSync mailbox policy, execute the following steps:

1. Expand the Recipient Configuration folder.

2. Select the Mailbox folder.

3. Select the mailbox.

4. Select Properties in the actions pane.

5. Select the Mailbox Features tab.

6. Select Exchange ActiveSync and click Properties.

7. Click Browse and select a policy, such as the Default Exchange ActiveSync Mailbox Policy created earlier.

8. Click OK three times to save the settings.

Now, the user's mobile device will have the policies applied and can be managed remotely, as is evidenced by the Manage Mobile Device selection in the mailbox actions pane.

ActiveSync Remote Wipe

The ActiveSync Remote Wipe function deletes the data off the device. Applications and other program data remain on the system, only the data is removed. To administratively remote wipe a device:

The Exchange Management Console can be used to wipe a device. This would typically be done by an administrator after a device has been lost. To use the EMC to perform a remote device wipe, go through the following steps:

1. Open the Exchange Management Console.

2. Under Recipient Configuration, select Mailbox.

3. Select the user from the Mailbox window.

4. In the action pane, click Manage mobile device, or right-click the user's mailbox, and then click Manage mobile device.

5. Select the mobile device you want to clear all data from.

6. In the Actions section, click Clear.

7. Click Clear again.

The device will be wiped the next time it synchronizes. There might be an ActiveSync warning dialog box on the mobile device saying "Exchange Server must enforce security policies on your device to continue synchronizing. Do you want to continue?" The user must select OK or Cancel. If the user selects OK, the device restarts and comes up in a clean default Windows Mobile 6.x state. If the user selects Cancel, the device does not synchronize any new data. However, the user can still continue to look at the information already there.

> **NOTE**
>
> After the wipe is successful, the device needs to be removed from the list of user devices. If this is not done, the device continues to wipe every time it synchronizes.

The Outlook Web App client can also be used to wipe a device remotely. This would typically be done by the user rather than the administrator. To use Outlook Web App to perform a remote device wipe, run the following steps:

1. Open Outlook Web App.
2. Log on to the device owner's mailbox.
3. Click Options.
4. In the Navigation pane, select Mobile Devices.
5. Select the ID of the device that you want to wipe and remove from the list.
6. Click Wipe all data from device.
7. Click OK.
8. Click Remove Device from List (after the status changes to successful).

Note that the status changes to pending wipe. After the device synchronizes, the status changes to wipe successful. Once again, the device needs to be removed from the users list if it will be used again.

POP and IMAP

Post Office Protocol (POP) and Internet Message Access Protocol (IMAP) are legacy messaging protocols that are used mostly by home users and some third-party applications.

Exchange Server 2010 supports them for backward compatibility and the services are disabled by default. To use these protocols, the services must be started on the CAS.

Client Throttling

Client Throttling policies control the performance of the Exchange Server infrastructure by controlling the connection bandwidth. The feature does this on a component-by-component basis, allowing fine-grained control of the impact that clients have on the infrastructure.

Clients controlled by the policies are the following:

- ▶ Microsoft Exchange ActiveSync
- ▶ Exchange Web Services
- ▶ Outlook Web App
- ▶ IMAP4
- ▶ POP3
- ▶ PowerShell
- ▶ Unified Messaging (UM)

At installation time, a default throttling policy is created. The default policy can be adjusted and new polices can be created. Policies are set on a user-by-user basis. If no policy is explicitly set on the user, they are implicitly assigned the default throttling policy.

There are a set of new cmdlets to create, modify, and remove throttling policies. These new cmdlets are as follows:

- ▶ New-ThrottlingPolicy—Creates a new throttling policy.
- ▶ Remove-ThrottlingPolicy—Removes a throttling policy.
- ▶ Get-ThrottlingPolicy—Lets you view the settings of a throttling policy.
- ▶ Set-ThrottlingPolicy —Modifies all available settings for a throttling policy.

The parameters for the throttling policy cmdlets are less than straightforward. This is because each client can be controlled independently and the cmdlets use acronyms to specify which client is adjusted. The parameters for controlling client access follow:

- ▶ **<XXX>MaxConcurrency**–This is the maximum number of concurrent connections that the user can have for the specified service.
- ▶ **<XXX>PercentTimeInCAS**–This is the percentage of a minute that a user can spend executing CAS code. This is a combined set of PercentTimeInAD and PercentTimeInMailboxRPC.
- ▶ **<XXX>PercentTimeInAD**–This the percentage of a minute that a user can spend executing LDAP requests.
- ▶ **<XXX>PercentTimeInMailboxRPC**–This the percentage of a minute that a user can spend executing mailbox RPC requests.

Where <XXX> is the acronym of the service being throttled. The service acronyms are the following:

- ▶ **EAS**—Exchange ActiveSync Users
- ▶ **EWS**—Exchange Web Services Users

- **OWA**—Outlook Web App Users

- **POP**—POP3 Users

- **UM**—Unified Messaging Users

- **IMAP**—IMAP4 Users

The PercentTimeInCAS is the sum of PercentTimeInAD and PercentTimeInMailboxRPC plus time executing on the CAS. It is possible for the percent times to be higher than 100 due to concurrent connections. For example, if a user running an OWA session consumes 42 seconds out of a minute, their OWAPercentTimeInCAS would be 70%. If they open a second OWA session on another system that consumes 30 seconds out of a minute, their total OWAPercentTimeInCAS would be 70% + 50% or 120%.

Interestingly, PowerShell has its own set of throttling parameters, as follows:

- **PowerShellMaxConcurrency**—This is the number of remote PowerShell sessions that a user can have open at the same time.

- **PowerShellMaxCmdlets**—This specifies the number of cmdlets that the user can execute in the time period specified by the PowerShellMaxCmdletsTimePeriod parameter. The two should be set at the same time.

- **PowerShellMaxCmdletsTimePeriod**—The time period in seconds for which the PowerShellMaxCmdlets parameter is enforced.

- **PowerShellMaxCmdletQueueDepth**—This is the number of operations allowed to be executed by the user. This should be set to at least three times the value of PowerShellMaxConcurrency.

The default policy values for some of the key parameters are given in Table 17.3. These default values can be adjusted by either adjusting the default policy using the Set-ThrottlingPolicy cmdlet or by creating a new throttling policy with the New-ThrottlingPolicy cmdlet and then assigning it to a user with the Set-ThrottlingPolicy cmdlet.

TABLE 17.3   Key Default Throttling Policy Values

Parameter	Default Values
EASMaxConcurrency	5
EASPercentTimeInCAS	75
EWSMaxConcurrency	10
EWSPercentTimeInCAS	90
IMAPMaxConcurrency	20
IMAPPercentTimeInCAS	150

17

TABLE 17.3   Key Default Throttling Policy Values

Parameter	Default Values
OWAMaxConcurrency	5
OWAPercentTimeInCAS	150
POPMaxConcurrency	20
POPPercentTimeInCAS	150
PowerShellMaxConcurrency	18
PowerShellMaxCmdlets	

Throttling policy is assigned using the Set-Mailbox cmdlet. For example, to assign a throttling policy named ThrottlingPolicy1 to a user chrisa, run the following commands:

```
$tp = Get-ThrottlingPolicy ThrottlingPolicy1;
Set-Mailbox -Identity chrisa -ThrottlingPolicy $tp;
```

To reset a user's policy to the default policy, you have to explicitly set the user's throttling policy to the default policy. The commands to do this for the user chrisa are as follows:

```
$defaultpolicy = Get-ThrottlingPolicy ¦ where-object {$_.IsDefault -eq $true}
Set-Mailbox -Identity chrisa -ThrottlingPolicy $defaultpolicy;
```

The user chrisa now has the default throttling policy assigned to her account. The effect of an implicitly assigned default throttling policy and an explicitly assigned default throttling policy is the same.

Installing the Client Access Server

The installation of the Exchange Server 2010 CAS role is a straightforward task. This section covers the installation and configuration of a basic system to illustrate the concepts.

The installation of the CAS role assumes that Exchange Server 2010 is already installed on the target server. For detailed instructions on installing Exchange Server 2010, see Chapter 7, "Installing Exchange Server 2010."

Memory and CPU maximum recommendations for the CAS role are shown in Table 17.4. Beyond these capacities, there will be diminishing returns. These are based on the Exchange Server product group testing.

TABLE 17.4   CAS Role Server Resources

Configuration	Processor	Memory	Storage
Minimum	2 cores	2GB	2GB
Maximum	12 cores	16GB	N/A

TABLE 17.4   CAS Role Server Resources

Configuration	Processor	Memory	Storage
Recommended	8 cores	2GB per core	32GB

Installation of the CAS role modifies the base installation of Exchange Server 2010 and is done in what is termed Exchange Maintenance mode. The procedures in this section step through the build of a basic Exchange Server 2010 CAS system.

Installing the Client Access Server Role

This procedure assumes that the Exchange Server 2010 server has already been installed. The steps to add the CAS role are as follows:

1. In the Control Panel, double-click Programs and Features.

2. Select Microsoft Exchange Server 2010.

3. Click Change to enter Exchange Maintenance mode.

4. Click Next.

5. Select the Client Access Role check box (shown in Figure 17.7), and click Next.

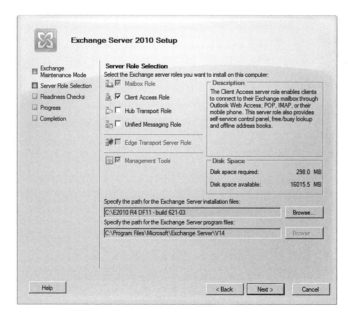

FIGURE 17.7   Client Access server role installation.

6. If the CAS server will be Internet-facing, check the box and enter in the external FQDN of the CAS server. Click Next.

7. The installer will conduct readiness checks. Remediate any findings, such as missing Web services features or configuring the Net. Tcp Port Sharing Service to start automatically.

8. Click Install to install the CAS role.

9. After the installation has successfully completed, click Finish.

Understanding the Hub Transport Server

The Hub Transport server is part of the internal Exchange Server infrastructure. The Hub Transport server role handles all internal mail flow, applies transport rules and journaling policies, and delivers mail to the Mailbox server role for placement in the user's mailbox. It also receives Internet mail from the Edge Transport server role, though the Hub Transport can also be configured to receive mail directly from the Internet. It is the evolved form of the bridgehead server in Exchange Server 2003, which was really the name of a configuration rather than a specific server component. The Hub Transport server has been developed to provide a number of key features that Exchange Server customers have long been clamoring for, such as disclaimers and transport rules.

The Hub Transport server provides four major services:

▶ Mail flow

▶ Categorization

▶ Routing

▶ Delivery

These services can collectively check mail for any problems such as spam or viruses, check mail for appropriateness, append any information that the organization needs, and finally route mail to the correct destination. New to Exchange Server 2010 is the Shadow Redundancy feature, which ensures delivery of messages by retaining a shadow copy and verifying delivery before releasing the shadow copy.

There should be a Hub Transport server in every AD site where there is a mailbox server for mail to flow and route correctly. Additional Hub Transport servers can be deployed for fault tolerance and load balancing, especially when paired with an Edge Transport server.

Mail Flow

The Hub Transport server is responsible for processing all mail that is sent within an Exchange Server 2010 organization. There is no exception to this. This allows the Hub Transport server to accomplish its other functions, such as categorization and routing.

It is important to understand that there are no exceptions to this rule. Thus, all mail flows through the Hub Transport servers. This ensures that the features that Hub Transport servers provide, such as transport rules, disclaimers, and journaling, are applied uniformly across the entire Exchange Server 2010 infrastructure.

Categorization

The categorizer does all the address lookups, route determination, and conversion of the content of messages. It is at this stage that the various agents, such as the transport rules agent and the journaling agent, process mail as well. It determines where the messages are destined to and what transport rules and journaling policies apply to the messages (see Chapter 14, "Understanding Exchange Policy Enforcement Security").

Although antispam and antivirus protection is provided by default at the Edge Transport server role, the Hub Transport server role can also be optionally configured to perform the scanning. This would take place at the categorization stage as well.

Routing

The Hub Transport server determines the path to route mail to. This applies to all messages that are not destined for mailbox servers in the local site. Messages that are destined for a mailbox server that is in another AD site are routed to a Hub Transport server in that site, whereas messages destined for external recipients are routed to Edge Transport servers.

Microsoft Exchange Server 2010 is AD site aware and uses the AD site topology for routing internally. It computes the most efficient—that is, lowest cost—route based on the sites and site links that it reads from Active Directory.

> **NOTE**
>
> It is critical to define the sites and the subnets that are associated with the sites for Exchange Server 2010 to route mail properly. These are fundamentally Active Directory design and deployment tasks, but not having it done properly can result in incorrect routing of email.
>
> This is true for all Active Directory–aware applications, such as Exchange Server 2010, System Center Configuration Manager (SCCM), distributed file system (DFS), and even Active Directory itself. Without a properly designed and deployed site and subnet infrastructure, they will fail or perform inefficiently.

17

The Hub Transport servers are intelligent and understand the architecture of the network based on the information in the sites and IP site links. If a message is destined for two different recipients, the Hub Transport servers will delay bifurcation of the message until the last possible hop.

This is illustrated in Figure 17.8. The user Chris in San Francisco sends a message to Sophia and Mike, who are in different locations (London and Frankfurt) and, thus, in different AD sites. A single message is routed through the transport from San Francisco to New York until it reaches Paris, which is the last possible hop for the message to split. The

Paris Hub Transport server then bifurcates the message and sends one to London and one to Frankfurt.

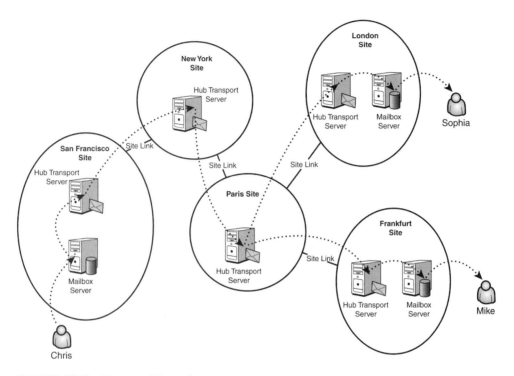

FIGURE 17.8   Message bifurcation.

Delivery

If the categorizer determines that the recipient of the messages is on a mailbox server in the local AD site, the message is delivered directly to the mailbox server.

Shadow Redundancy

The Shadow Redundancy feature in Exchange Server 2010 gives message routing a fault tolerance capability. The concept behind shadow redundancy is that a message is not deleted from the queue until the next hop has confirmed delivery to the subsequent hop. If confirmation is not received, the message is resubmitted. If the next hop server is down, the message is resubmitted to another server.

> **NOTE**
>
> Assured delivery requires that there be redundant Hub Transport and Edge Transport servers to resubmit to if a failure of any given transport server occurs.

The components of the shadow redundancy follow:

- **Primary Message**—The original message submitted to transport for delivery.

- **Shadow Message**—The copy of a message that a transport server retains until it confirms that all the next hops for that message have successfully delivered it.

- **Primary Server**—The transport server that is currently processing a message.

- **Shadow Server**—The transport server that holds shadow copies of a message after delivering the message to the primary server.

- **Shadow Queue**—The queue that a transport server uses to store shadow messages. A transport server will have separate shadow queues for each primary server to which it delivered the primary message.

- **Discard Status**—The information a transport server maintains for shadow messages that indicates when a message is ready to be discarded.

- **Discard Notification**—The response a shadow server receives from a primary server indicating a message is ready to be discarded.

- **Shadow Redundancy Manager**—The transport component that manages shadow redundancy.

- **Heartbeat**—The process of transport servers verifying the availability of each other.

A mail flow with shadow redundancy is given in the following example. In the example, Chris with mailbox on Exchange Server 2010 mailbox server MB1 is sending a message to Michelle with a mailbox on Exchange Server 2010 mailbox server MB2. There are two Exchange Server 2010 Hub Transport servers: HT1 and HT2. The process is as follows:

1. **Chris submits message**—The message is submitted to MB1. MB1 becomes the primary server for the message.

17

> **NOTE**
>
> Client submissions such as MAPI, Windows Mobile, or SMTP client are not redundant until the message is successfully stored on the mailbox or hub transport server. Then the Exchange Server high-availability features take effect.

2. **MB1 submits to HT1**—The message is submitted by MB1 to HT1. HT1 becomes the primary server and MB1 becomes a shadow server. However, HT1 subsequently fails and never acknowledges the delivery of the message to MB2. MB1 times out and becomes the primary server.

3. **MB1 submits to HT2**—The message is resubmitted by MB1 to the redundant HT2. HT2 becomes the primary server and MB1 becomes a shadow server.

4. **HT2 submits to MB2**—The message is submitted to by HT2 to MB2. MB1 confirms that HT2 has delivered the message, deletes the message from its shadow queue, and is no longer a shadow server.

5. **Michelle receives message**—The message is received by Michelle.

The process is diagrammed in Figure 17.9.

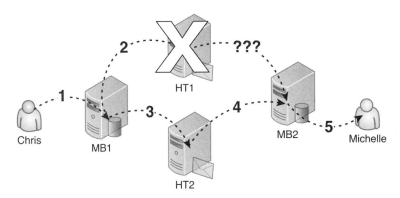

FIGURE 17.9   Shadow Redundancy example.

Shadow redundancy gives the Exchange Server 2010 self-healing capabilities for mail flow. It enables the infrastructure to intelligently fail over between redundant paths if messages have not been delivered in a timely manner.

Transport Pipeline

The transport pipeline reflects the internal routing of messages within the Hub Transport server. The elements of this are shown in Figure 17.10. These consist of the following:

- ▶ SMTP Receive
- ▶ Submission queue
- ▶ Categorizer
- ▶ Mailbox delivery queue
- ▶ Remote delivery queue

The figure also illustrates the relationships that the Hub Transport server role has with the other Exchange Server 2010 roles.

Messages get into the transport pipeline onto a Hub Transport server through one of four ways, as shown in Figure 17.10:

- ▶ Through the SMTP Receive Connector
- ▶ Through files being placed in the pickup or replay directories

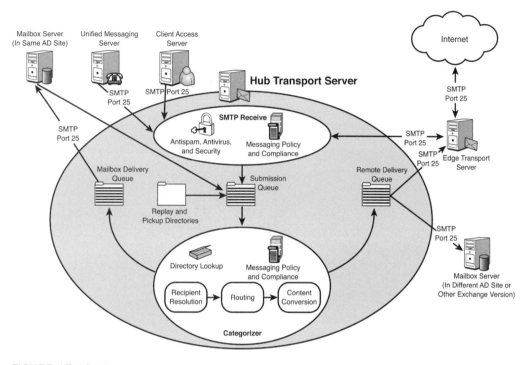

FIGURE 17.10   Transport pipeline.

▶ Through the submission queue by the mailbox store driver

▶ Through submission from an agent (not shown)

After the messages have gotten into the pipeline, they flow through the pipeline. The various segments of that pipeline are discussed in the following sections.

SMTP Receive Connector

In the Hub Transport server, the SMTP Receive Connector accepts SMTP (port 25) messages. Basic server-level policies are applied, such as the authorization of the remote IP address of the server and authentication of the server.

If installed on the Hub Transport server, the messages coming into the SMTP Receive Connector are also processed by antivirus and antispam services.

If they pass the SMTP Receive Connector, the messages flow down the transport pipeline to the submission queue.

Submission Queue

The submission queue takes messages from the SMTP Receive Connector, as well as from the mailbox store driver, the pickup and replay directories, and from agents such as the transport rules agent.

When messages enter the submission queue, the `OnSubmittedMessage` event activates. This triggers the journaling agent.

The messages are held in the submission queue until they are pulled out one at a time (first in, first out) by the categorizer.

Categorizer

The categorizer processes each message that it retrieves from the submission queue. The categorizer does four main steps:

- ▶ Resolving recipient addressing
- ▶ Determining routes to recipients
- ▶ Converting message content
- ▶ Rules processing

The last step, rule processing, is where the agents that trigger on the `OnRoutedMessage` event activate. On the Hub Transport server, that is all the default agents, including the rules transport agent, the journaling agent, and the AD RMS Prelicensing agent.

Mailbox Delivery Queue

The mailbox delivery queue handles messages that are destined for local delivery—that is, messages for recipients in mailbox servers in the same site as the Hub Transport server.

These messages are pulled off the queue one by one and delivered to the user's mailbox by the store driver.

Remote Delivery Queue

The remote delivery queue handles messages to be routed to other Hub Transport servers within the forest for messages destined for other mailbox servers within the organization but in a different AD site. The remote delivery queue also handles messages destined for external mail systems in other forests and for the Edge Transport servers.

Messages in the remote delivery queue are sent out via the SMTP Send Connector.

Installing the Hub Transport Server

The installation of the Exchange Server 2010 Hub Transport server role is a straightforward task. This section covers the installation and configuration of a basic system to illustrate the concepts.

The installation of the Hub Transport role assumes that Exchange Server 2010 is already installed on the target server. For detailed instructions on installing Exchange Server 2010, see Chapter 7.

Resource recommendations for the Hub Transport server role are shown in Table 17.6.

TABLE 17.6   Hub Transport Role Server Resources

Configuration	Processor	Memory	Storage
Minimum	1 core	2GB	2GB
Maximum	12 cores	16GB	—
Recommended	4 cores	1GB per core	32GB

Beyond these recommended capacities, there will be diminishing returns. These are based on the Exchange Server product group testing.

The first step is to install the Hub Transport server role. The following procedure assumes that the Exchange Server 2010 server has already been installed. The steps to add the Hub Transport server role are as follows:

1. In the Control Panel, double-click on Programs and Features.
2. Select Microsoft Exchange Server 2010.
3. Click Change to enter Exchange Maintenance mode.
4. Click Next.
5. Select the Hub Transport Role check box (shown in Figure 17.11), and click Next.
6. The installer will conduct readiness checks. Remediate any findings, such as the KB950888 hotfix requirement.
7. Click Install to install the Hub Transport server role.
8. After the installation has successfully completed, click Finish.

Configure SMTP Send Connectors

When a Hub Transport server is installed, there is no SMTP Send Connector installed. Without an SMTP Send Connector, the Hub Transport server can receive mail but not send mail.

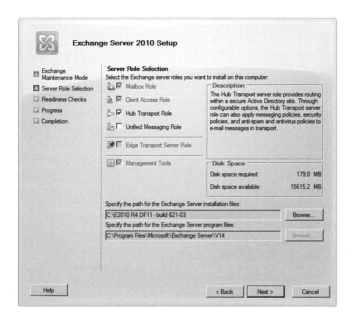

FIGURE 17.11   Hub Transport role installation.

The SMTP Send Connector can be configured as follows:

▶ **Internal**—For routing to other Hub Transport servers and Edge Transport servers

▶ **Internet**—For routing to nonconnected mail systems over the Internet

▶ **Partner**—For routing to a domain with mutual TLS authentication

▶ **Custom**—For routing to non-Exchange servers or across a forest trust

The steps to configure the SMTP Send Connector are as follows:

1. Launch the Exchange Management Console.
2. Expand the Organization Configuration branch, and select the Hub Transport folder.
3. In the actions pane, select New Send Connector.
4. Enter in a name for the connector.
5. Enter in the intended use of the connector, such as Custom, click Next.
6. Add the address space for which the SMTP connector will send mail to, typically "*".
7. Click Next.
8. Click Next to route using the domain name system (DNS).
9. Click Next to use the current server as the source server.
10. Click New to create the SMTP Send Connector.
11. Click Finish to close the wizard.

Test Cmdlets for CAS and Hub Transport Servers

Built into the Exchange Server 2010 are a number of PowerShell cmdlets to test the Client Access server and Hub Transport server roles. These enable an administrator to easily verify settings, certificates, and port access for the services. This can save an immense amount of troubleshooting time or having to set up a test infrastructure.

These cmdlets are used by the System Center Operations Manager 2007 R2 Exchange Server 2010 management pack to perform synthetic transactions. These provide the OpsMgr infrastructure with data for monitoring thresholds and producing performance reports. See Chapter 20, "Using Operations Manager to Monitor Exchange Server 2010," for more details on OpsMgr and the Exchange Server 2010 management pack.

There are cmdlets that specifically test the CAS functions and cmdlets that specifically test the Hub Transport functions.

The CAS test cmdlets are listed here:

- **Test-OutlookWebServices**—Tests Autodiscover Settings.

- **Test-WebServicesConnectivity**—Tests Exchange Web Services (EWS) functionality.

- **Test-ActiveSyncConnectivity**—Tests ActiveSync functionality.

- **Test-OwaConnectivity**—Tests Outlook Web App (OWA) functionality.

- **Test-ImapConnectivity**—Tests the IMAP4 functionality for a user or all mailboxes.

- **Test-PopConnectivity**—Tests the POP3 functionality for a user or all mailboxes.

- **Test-EcpConnectivity**—Tests that the Exchange Control Panel (ECP) is accessible.

- **Test-PowerShellConnectivity**—Tests PowerShell remote shell connectivity from a URI or a NetBIOS name.

The Hub Transport test cmdlets are listed here:

- **Test-Mailflow**—Tests if mail can be sent from the system mailbox to another mailbox server and to external addresses.

- **Test-Message**—Tests the transport rules for a test message and emails a report to the designated mailbox.

- **Test-EdgeSynchronization**–Tests the Edge synchronization status for a subscription and for a specific user.

The following sections give examples of the more useful HUB/CAS test cmdlets.

The `Test-OutlookWebServices` Cmdlet

The `Test-OutlookWebServices` cmdlet verifies the Autodiscover service settings for Outlook on an Exchange server that has the Client Access server role installed. The `Test-OutlookWebServices` cmdlet uses a specified email address to verify that the Outlook provider is configured correctly.

An example of the Test-OutlookWebServices cmdlet is shown in Listing 17.1.

LISTING 17.1   Test-OutlookWebServices Example

```
[PS] C:\>Test- OutlookWebServices –Identity:chrisa@companyabc.com
RunspaceId : 79f1e2b4-2db8-44c6-aa11-87464151c696
Id         : 1003
Type       : Information
Message    : Autodiscover is about to be tested with the e-
             mail address chrisa@companyabc.com.

RunspaceId :
79f1e2b4-2db8-44c6-aa11-87464151c696
Id         : 1006
Type       : Information
Message    : Contacted the Autodiscover service at https://
             EX1.companyabc.com/Autodiscover/Autodiscover.x
             ml.

RunspaceId : 79f1e2b4-2db8-44c6-aa11-87464151c696
Id         : 1016
Type       : Success
Message    : [EXCH]-Successfully contacted the AS service a
             t https://ex1.companyabc.com/EWS/Exchange.asmx
             . The elapsed time was 109 milliseconds.

RunspaceId :
79f1e2b4-2db8-44c6-aa11-87464151c696
Id         : 1015
Type       : Success
Message    : [EXCH]-Successfully contacted the OAB service
             at https://ex1.companyabc.com/EWS/Exchange.asm
             x. The elapsed time was 0 milliseconds.

RunspaceId :
79f1e2b4-2db8-44c6-aa11-87464151c696
Id         : 1014
Type       : Success
Message    : [EXCH]-Successfully contacted the UM service a
             t https://ex1.companyabc.com/EWS/UM2007Legacy.asm
             x. The elapsed time was 31 milliseconds.
```

```
RunspaceId :
79f1e2b4-2db8-44c6-aa11-87464151c696
Id        : 1006
Type      : Success
Message   : Autodiscover was tested successfully.
```

As can be seen from the output, all the tests completed successfully.

The Test-OwaConnectivity Cmdlet

The Test-OwaConnectivity cmdlet can be used to test Outlook Web App connectivity for all Microsoft Exchange Server 2010 virtual directories on a specified client access server for all mailboxes on servers running Exchange Server that are in the same Active Directory site. The Test-OwaConnectivity cmdlet can also be used to test the connectivity for an individual Exchange Outlook Web App URL.

An example of the Test-OwaConnectivity cmdlet used to test access to an OWA URL (https://ex1.companyabc.com) using the user companyabc\chrisa credentials is shown in Listing 17.2.

LISTING 17.2   Test-OwaConnectivity Example

```
[PS] C:\>Test-OwaConnectivity
-URL:https://ex1.companyabc.co
m/owa -MailboxCredential:(get-credential companyabc\chrisa)
 -TrustAnySSLCertificate ¦ fl


RunspaceId               :
79f1e2b4-2db8-44c6-aa11-87464
                           151c696
AuthenticationMethod     : FBA
MailboxServer            :
LocalSite                : Default-First-Site-Name
SecureAccess             : True
VirtualDirectoryName     :
Url                      : https://ex1.companyabc.com/ow
                           a/
UrlType                  : Unknown
Port                     : 0
ConnectionType           : Plaintext
ClientAccessServerShortName :
LocalSiteShortName       : Default-First-Site-Name
ClientAccessServer       :
Scenario                 : Logon
ScenarioDescription      : Log on to Live and verify the
                             response page.
```

```
PerformanceCounterName      : Logon Latency
Result                      : Success
Error                       :
UserName                    : chrisa
StartTime                   : 7/28/2009 8:10:27 PM
Latency                     : 00:00:00.3750144
EventType                   : Success
LatencyInMillisecondsString : 375.01
Identity                    :
IsValid                     : True
```

The command will prompt for the password of the user chrisa during the run of the command. Note that the –TrustAnySSLCertificate parameter was used to bypass certificate checks.

The Test-ActiveSyncConnectivity Cmdlet

The Test-ActiveSyncConnectivity cmdlet performs a full synchronization between a mobile device and a specified mailbox to test the functionality of Exchange ActiveSync. If the synchronization fails, a message is displayed in the Exchange Management Shell.

The example shown in Listing 17.3 shows the Test-ActiveSyncConnectivity cmdlet used to test ActiveSync for the user chrisa.

LISTING 17.3   Test-ActiveSyncConnectivity Example

```
[PS]    C:\>Test-ActiveSyncConnectivity -MailboxCredential (get-credential
companyabc\chrisa) -TrustAnySSLCertificate

WARNING: column "Error" does not fit into the display and w
as removed.
```

CasServer	LocalSite	Scenario	Result	Latency(MS)
ex1	Default-Fi...	Options	Success	15.63
ex1	Default-Fi...	FolderSync	Success	406.26
ex1	Default-Fi...	First Sync	Success	93.75
ex1	Default-Fi...	GetItemEstimate	Success	78.13
ex1	Default-Fi...	Sync Data	Success	156.26
ex1	Default-Fi...	Ping	Success	1515.75
ex1	Default-Fi...	Sync Test Item	Success	1375.02

During the run of the command, the get-credential cmdlet inline in the Test-ActiveSyncConnectivity command prompts for the credentials of the test user. The results of the seven tests were "success."

The Test-Mailflow Cmdlet

The Test-Mailflow cmdlet tests mail submission, transport, and delivery for Hub Transport role servers. The cmdlet verifies that each mailbox server can successfully send itself a message. You can also use this cmdlet to verify that the system mailbox on one mailbox server can successfully send a message to the system mailbox on another mailbox server.

The Test-Mailflow cmdlet example in Listing 17.4 shows testing mailflow between the mailbox server EX1 to the mailbox server EX2.

LISTING 17.4   Test-Mailflow Example

```
[PS] C:\>Test-Mailflow ex1 -TargetMailboxServer ex2
RunspaceId         : 79f1e2b4-2db8-44c6-aa11-87464151c696
TestMailflowResult : Success
MessageLatencyTime : 00:00:02.8297541
IsRemoteTest       : True
Identity           :
IsValid            : True
```

The TestMailflowResult: Success shows that the mail flow was successful.

The Test-EdgeSynchronization Cmdlet

The Test-EdgeSynchronization is a diagnostic cmdlet that provides a report of the synchronization status of subscribed Edge Transport servers. You can use the VerifyRecipient parameter with this cmdlet to verify that a single recipient has been synchronized to the Active Directory Lightweight Directory Services (AD LDS) directory service. This task provides useful information to the administrator when it is run manually.

The command must be run on a Hub Transport role server that is within the Active Directory site that the Edge Transport server is subscribed to. Listing 17.5 shows the results of testing the synchronization status of edge synchronization.

LISTING 17.5   Test-EdgeSynchronization Example

```
[PS] C:\>Test-EdgeSynchronization -MaxReportSize 500
-MonitoringContext $true

RunspaceId              : 79f1e2b4-2db8-44c6-aa11-87464
                          151c696
```

17

```
UtcNow                         : 7/29/2009 4:45:32 AM
Name                           : EX3
LeaseHolder                    : CN=EX1,CN=Servers,CN=Exchange
                                 Administrative Group (FYDIBO
                                 HF23SPDLT),CN=Administrative
                                 Groups,CN=CompanyABC,CN=Micro
                                 soft Exchange,CN=Services,CN=
                                 Configuration,DC=companyabc,D
                                 C=com
LeaseType                      : Option
ConnectionResult               : Succeeded
FailureDetail                  :
LeaseExpiryUtc                 : 7/29/2009 5:43:49 AM
LastSynchronizedUtc            : 7/29/2009 4:43:49 AM
CredentialStatus               : Synchronized
TransportServerStatus          : Synchronized
TransportConfigStatus          : Synchronized
AcceptedDomainStatus           : Synchronized
RemoteDomainStatus             : Synchronized
SendConnectorStatus            : Synchronized
MessageClassificationStatus    : Synchronized
RecipientStatus                : Synchronized
CredentialRecords              : Number of credentials 3
CookieRecords                  : Number of cookies 2
**** TRUNCATED ****
```

The truncated results of the Test-EdgeSynchronization -MaxReportSize 500 -
MonitoringContext $true command shows that all components are synchronized.

The cmdlet can also be used to test the synchronization status for an individual user. The
Listing 17.6 shows the results of an example test.

LISTING 17.6   Test-EdgeSynchronization User Example

```
[PS] C:\> Test-EdgeSynchronization -VerifyRecipient chrisa@companyabc.com


RunspaceId                     :
79f1e2b4-2db8-44c6-aa11-87464
                                 151c696
UtcNow                         : 7/29/2009 4:54:50 AM
Name                           : EX3
LeaseHolder                    : CN=EX1,CN=Servers,CN=Exchange
                                 Administrative Group (FYDIBO
                                 HF23SPDLT),CN=Administrative
                                 Groups,CN=CompanyABC,CN=Micro
```

```
                              soft Exchange,CN=Services,CN=
                              Configuration,DC=companyabc,D
                              C=com
LeaseType                   : Option
ConnectionResult            : Succeeded
FailureDetail               :
LeaseExpiryUtc              : 7/29/2009 5:52:51 AM
LastSynchronizedUtc         : 7/29/2009 4:52:51 AM
CredentialStatus            : Skipped
TransportServerStatus       : Skipped
TransportConfigStatus       : Skipped
AcceptedDomainStatus        : Skipped
RemoteDomainStatus          : Skipped
SendConnectorStatus         : Skipped
MessageClassificationStatus : Skipped
RecipientStatus             : Synchronized
CredentialRecords           : Number of credentials 3
CookieRecords               : Number of cookies 2
```

The results show that the RecipientStatus is synchronized for the user chrisa@companyabc.com.

Summary

The improved roles in Exchange Server 2010 are the CAS and Hub Transport server roles. In reality, these two roles are really specializations and evolutions of the original Exchange Server front-end and bridgehead server concepts, along with the Edge Transport server. The CAS and the Hub Transport server provide both sophisticated external client access and controlled routing and delivery throughout the organization.

The two roles within the Exchange Server 2010 family offer a wealth of features and functions that Exchange Server administrators have been clamoring for. Ranging from the transport rules, shadow redundancy, and journaling on the Hub Transport servers to Remote Wipe and Client Throttling on the CAS servers, these features make Exchange Server 2010 the premier messaging system.

Best Practices

The following are best practices from this chapter:

▶ Have a CAS in every AD site to ensure that users connect to the CAS closest to their mailbox.

▶ For client access to work correctly, you must install a CAS in each AD site that has a mailbox server.

▶ Deploy Exchange ActiveSync mailbox policies to ensure remote management of mobile devices.

▶ Deploy redundant Hub Transport and Exchange Transport role servers to take advantage of Shadow Redundancy and mail flow self-healing.

▶ For email messages to flow correctly, you must install the Hub Transport server role in each AD site.

▶ Given the dependence of the Hub Transport server on AD sites for routing email, it is critical to correctly design and deploy the AD site architecture.

▶ Create ActiveSync mailbox policies to ensure the manageability of the users' mobile devices.

CHAPTER 18

Administering an Exchange Server 2010 Environment

Administrators who have worked with Exchange Server over the years are used to change. With each major release, Microsoft evaluates what works well (and what works "not so well") and uses this information to refine future revisions of the product.

Exchange Server 2003 had the Exchange System Manager and utilized Exchange Administrative Roles to grant administrative permissions. Exchange Server 2007 introduced us to the Exchange Management Console and the Exchange Management Shell and relied primarily on Access Control Lists (ACLs) to manage permissions. The Exchange Management Shell, a utility welcomed by administrators everywhere, was built on Microsoft Windows PowerShell technology and allowed administrators to manage virtually every aspect of their Exchange Server environment from a command line.

With the introduction of Exchange Server 2010, Microsoft reminds us that "The more things change, the more they stay the same."

Introduction to Role Based Access Control

One of the administrative shortcomings of Exchange Server has been the ability to control precisely *who* can administer *what*. Granting a group of administrators the necessary permissions to create mailboxes anywhere in an Exchange Server environment might be practical for a small organization, but what about a large company with a worldwide presence? Do you actually want the support staff in one country to administer (and have access to) the mailboxes in another country? Do you actually want your tier 1 help desk personnel, staffed by junior administrators, to have the same access to Executive mailboxes as they do to Sales? And what about your user community? Just because an organization wants to allow their users to change their own phone number in the GAL, must they be allowed to change their display name as well?

Controlling administrative permissions to this level of granularity was often desired but difficult (or impossible) to implement with the permissions model in Exchange Server 2007—so Microsoft threw it out and started over.

In Exchange Server 2010, by implementing Role Based Access Control (RBAC), Microsoft has empowered organizations to not only dictate precisely *who* can access *what,* but also *where.*

With RBAC, the permission to perform tasks is assigned to specific *roles.* Administrators and users are assigned to appropriate roles, and through their membership in the role, they acquire the necessary permissions to perform the desired task. This does not only apply to administrators; RBAC also controls the extent to which end users can self-administer their own accounts.

The RBAC permissions model consists of four components:

- ▶ **Management role group**—A special universal security group (USG) in Active Directory (AD) that can be composed of mailboxes, users, other USGs, and other role groups. All members of a role group are assigned the same set of roles, and members are added to a management role group to assign the desired permissions.

- ▶ **Management role**—A container that holds management group entries. Management roles define the actual tasks that can be performed by members of the associated role group. A *management role entry* is a cmdlet (a specialized command in the PowerShell environment) and its parameters that are added to a management role. This process grants rights to manage or view the objects associated with that cmdlet.

- ▶ **Management role assignment**—Links a management role to a management role group. This grants the users assigned to the group the ability to perform the actions assigned to the role group.

- ▶ **Management role scope**—Defines the scope of influence that a role assignment has. A management role scope can include servers, organizational units, filters on server or recipient objects, and more.

And thus, we achieve the ability to control *who* (via management role group and management role assignment) can do *what* (via management role and management role entries) and *where* (via management role scope). Exchange Server administration can now be as granular or as broad as the needs of the organization mandate, and with RBAC, organizations can more closely align the permissions assigned to users and administrators to the roles they actually hold.

Understanding Management Role Groups

A *management role group* is a universal security group that is part of the RBAC permissions model. A management role group simplifies the assignment of management roles to a user or group of users. Management roles are assigned to the entire role group, so all members of a particular role group share the same set of roles.

Role groups are assigned both administrator and specialist roles. These define the major administrative tasks in Exchange Server and enable an organization to assign a broader set of permissions to a group of administrators, specialists, or even end users.

Understanding Management Roles

As previously stated, *management roles* act as logical groupings of all the pieces that define what a user is allowed to do in an Exchange Server 2010 environment, whether they are a senior Exchange Server architect, a junior help desk employee, or an end user.

Microsoft has provided dozens of built-in management roles that meet the basic needs of most environments. These roles cannot be modified, nor can the management role entries that are configured for them, but the *scope* can be modified. Some examples of built-in management roles include

- ► Reset Password
- ► Transport Rules
- ► Move Mailboxes

By adding users or groups of users to these management roles, the permissions needed to perform tasks can easily be assigned. So, if you want your tier 1 support staff to manage recipients and change their passwords, you would assign the Mail Recipients and Reset Password roles to the role group.

Although management roles can be directly assigned to users, it is recommended that role groups and role assignment policies are utilized to simplify the permissions model.

Understanding Management Role Assignments

A *management role assignment* is the connector between a *role* and a *role assignee*. A *role assignee* can be a role group, role assignment policy, user, or universal security group. Before a role can take effect, it must be assigned to a role assignee.

By adding, removing, or modifying a role assignment, administrators can control what permissions are given to other administrators and users. This effectively enables (or disables) management capabilities for the user.

Role assignments come in two flavors: Regular role assignments and Delegating role assignments.

Regular role assignments enable the assignee to access the management role entries made available by the associated management role. Management role entries are aggregated (combined), so if an assignee has several role assignments, all of the associated management roles are given.

Delegating role assignments do not give access to manage features; instead, they give a role assignee the ability to assign the specified role to other role assignees.

Understanding Management Role Scopes

A *management role scope* enables administrators to define the specific range of impact or influence that a management role has once a management role assignment has been created. By applying a role scope, the role assignee can modify only the objects contained within the scope.

Every management role, whether built in or custom, is governed by its associated management role scope. Scopes can be inherited from the management role, specified as a predefined relative scope for a particular management role assignment, or created using custom filters and added to a management role assignment. Those that are inherited from management roles are called *implicit* scopes, whereas the predefined and custom scopes are called *explicit* scopes.

There are two types of management role scope:

Regular role scopes are not exclusive. They determine where, in AD, objects can be viewed or modified by users assigned the associated management role. To put it simply, the management role dictates *what* objects a user can create or modify, and the management role scope dictates *where* the user can create or modify them. Regular scopes can be either implicit or explicit scopes.

Exclusive role scopes behave similarly to regular scopes, except that they provide the ability to deny users access to objects if the users aren't assigned a role associated with the exclusive scope. All exclusive scopes are explicit scopes.

Shared Versus Split Permissions Models

Both AD and Exchange Server environments require administrators with specialized knowledge to administer them. In some organizations, the responsibility for managing these two environments is shared by the same personnel. Other organizations have separate departments for managing AD and Exchange Server.

Exchange Server 2010 enables organizations to use either a shared permissions or a split permissions model. By default, the shared permissions model is deployed.

Shared Permissions Model

Organizations that want to use a shared permissions model don't need to change anything because this is the default model used in Exchange Server 2010. There is no separation of the management of Exchange Server and AD objects from within the Exchange Server management tools: the Exchange Management Console, the Exchange Management Shell, or the Exchange Control Panel (introduced later in this chapter). Administrators using these tools can create security principles in AD *and* manage the configuration of those objects in Exchange Server.

Split Permissions Model

In the split permissions model, a distinction is made between the creation of security principals in AD (such as users and security groups) and the configuration of those objects. Proper implementation of a split permissions model allows organizations to minimize the risk of unauthorized access to the network by limiting the ability to create objects to a small group of authorized personnel.

Using this model, one group of administrators (AD admins) can create security principals in AD, whereas another (Exchange Server admins) can manage specific attributes on existing AD objects.

Organizations desiring to implement a split permissions model should give serious thought as to whether this model will truly work in their environment. Under this model, AD admins need to create new users but *cannot* configure the Exchange Server attributes on the objects. Exchange Server admins can configure the attributes but *cannot* create new accounts. Under the split permissions model, Exchange Server admins can no longer use any of the following cmdlets:

- ▶ New-Mailbox or Remove-Mailbox

- ▶ New-MailUser or Remove-MailUser

- ▶ New-MailContact or Remove-MailContact

- ▶ New-LinkedUser or Remove-LinkedUser

- ▶ Add-MailboxPermission

- ▶ Add-MailboxFolderPermission

Exchange Server admins can still create and manage Exchange Server-specific objects, such as transport rules, distribution groups, and so on.

Configuring Exchange Server 2010 for Split Permissions

To implement a split permissions model, the Mail Recipient Creation and Security Group Creation and Membership roles must be assigned to a newly created role group. This role group contains users who are AD admins. Then, the assignments between those roles and any role group or universal security group (USG) that contains Exchange Server admins must be removed.

To perform this task using the Exchange Management Shell, perform the following steps: (The Exchange Management Shell commands are in *italics*.)

1. Create a new role group for the AD admins and create regular role assignments between the new role group and the Mail Recipient Creation and Security Group Creation and Membership roles.

   New-RoleGroup "Active Directory Administrators" -Roles "Mail Recipient
   ➥Creation", "Security Group Creation and Membership"

2. Create a delegating role assignment between the new role group and the Mail Recipient Creation role.

18

```
New-ManagementRoleAssignment "Mail Recipient Creation_AD Administrators_
➥Delegating" -Role "Mail Recipient Creation" -SecurityGroup "Active
➥Directory Administrators" -Delegating
```

3. Create a delegating role assignment between the new role group and the Security Group Creation and Membership role.

```
New-ManagementRoleAssignment "Security Group Creation and Membership_Org
➥Mgmt_Delegating" -Role "Mail Recipient Creation" -SecurityGroup
➥"Active Directory Administrators" -Delegating
```

4. Add the Active Directory admins to the new role group.

```
Add-RoleGroupMember "Active Directory Administrators" -Member <user to add>
```

5. Replace the delegate list on the new role group so that only members of the role group can add or remove members:

```
Set-RoleGroup "Active Directory Administrators" -ManagedBy "Active Directory
➥Administrators"
```

> **NOTE**
>
> Individuals who are members of the Organization Management role group, or those assigned the Role Management role either directly or indirectly, can bypass this security check. To prevent Exchange Server administrators from adding themselves to the new role group, the role assignment between the Role Management role and any Exchange Server administrator must be removed and assigned to another group.

6. Find all the regular and delegating role assignments to the Mail Recipient Creation role.

```
Get-ManagementRoleAssignment -Role "Mail Recipient Creation"
```

7. Remove all the regular and delegating role assignments to the Mail Recipient Creation that aren't associated with the new role group or any other role groups, USGs, or direct assignments that will remain.

```
Remove-ManagementRoleAssignment <Mail Recipient Creation role assignment to
➥remove>
```

8. Find all of the regular and delegating role assignments to the Security Group Creation and Management role.

```
Get-ManagementRoleAssignment -Role "Security Group Creation and Membership"
```

9. Remove all the regular and delegating role assignments to the Security Group Creation and Management that aren't associated with the new role group or any other role groups, USGs, or direct assignments you want to keep.

```
Remove-ManagementRoleAssignment <Security Group Creation and Membership role
➥assignment to remove>
```

Benefits of RBAC

One of the goals that Microsoft worked toward with the design and creation of Exchange Server 2010 is the capability to decrease support costs. Early in the process, it realized that one way to significantly reduce the administrative overhead in an environment was to empower users to perform specific tasks for themselves, rather than go through the time-consuming and resource-intensive process of requesting assistance to complete relatively minor changes.

Granting users the administrative rights to perform certain low-level tasks, while still preventing them from accessing (and potentially damaging) configuration settings that could impact the entire organization was extremely difficult, if not impossible, using the ACL-based model of previous Exchange Server versions.

Now with RBAC, employees can be given permission to track the status of messages that they have sent, create and manage their own distribution lists, and update certain aspects of their account information.

RBAC focuses on the effective and efficient distribution of administrative permissions. In previous versions of Exchange Server, granting help desk personnel (for example) the ability to create new mailboxes in one site gave them (by default) the ability to create new mailboxes anywhere in the environment. Locking down these permissions to one specific site was time-consuming and complicated—and there are *many* different scenarios that had to be identified, evaluated, and resolved before administrators could be sure they had matched the appropriate personnel with the appropriate access.

Another example of the benefits of RBAC is in the area of eDiscovery—granting permissions to a group of users (such as members of the HR department) to view the contents of a particular set of mailboxes (such as those located in the Marketing OU).

Using RBAC, administrators can grant the necessary access to allow the members of the HR department to review the mailboxes of the Marketing users but *not* those in sales (located in another OU).

These permissions can easily be delegated using RBAC for the duration of the discovery period and then removed until needed again.

18

NOTE

When creating a new OU in a Windows 2008 Active Directory environment, you might notice a new and welcome feature; when naming the OU, the option to Protect Container from Accidental Deletion is present and automatically selected. This places an explicit Deny permission on the object for the group "everyone," preventing accidental deletion of the object. To remove this (for intentional deletion), go to Active Directory Users and Computers, select View \ Advanced Features; then view the properties of the OU. Under the Object tab, you can see the Protect Object from Accidental Deletion check box and de-select it.

Administrative Tools

Exchange Server 2010 provides administrators with three primary administrative tools: The first two, the Exchange Management Shell and the Exchange Management Console, were both introduced with Exchange Server 2007. The third, the Exchange Control Panel, is new to Exchange Server 2010 and provides some exciting possibilities.

The Exchange Management Shell is a command-line interface, allowing administrators to run single commands or complex scripts to simplify redundant tasks. The Exchange Management Shell can be utilized to configure every aspect of an Exchange Server environment.

The Exchange Management Console has a graphical user interface (GUI). Nearly as powerful as the Shell, the Console can be used to configure *most* of the aspects of an Exchange Server environment.

New to Exchange Server 2010 is the Exchange Control Panel, which enables personnel to administer some aspects of the Exchange Server environment through a web interface. Unlike the Management Console or the Management Shell, which are designed and intended to be used only by Exchange Server administrators, the Exchange Control Panel is designed to also enable end users to self-manage certain aspects of their accounts.

Exchange Management Shell

The Exchange Management Shell (EMS) is the engine that powers all Exchange Administrative tools. A powerful management tool in its own right; the EMS is also utilized by both the Exchange Management Console and the Exchange Control Panel to process actions initiated in their interfaces.

Introduced in Exchange Server 2007, the Exchange Management Shell is a command-line management interface. Administrators had been screaming for years for a command-line tool that was powerful enough to enable scripted changes of Exchange Server objects, and the Exchange Management Shell was well received.

Tasks that had to be done manually within the confines of the GUI management application in pre-2007 versions could now be scripted, allowing administrators increased flexibility for repetitive tasks. The Exchange Management Shell looks similar to the DOS command prompt (`cmd.exe`), in that it opens a window with a black background and a text interface. However, you notice immediately that certain commands and errors are highlighted in yellow or red text rather than the traditional monochromatic command prompt.

With the Exchange Management Shell, administrators can manage every aspect of Exchange Server including the creation and management of new email accounts, the configuration of Simple Mail Transfer Protocol (SMTP) connectors and transport agents, or properties of database stores. In fact, every task that can be accomplished with the Exchange Management Console can be accomplished from the command line in the EMS, but the opposite is not true.

NOTE

When the EMS was first released, there were many commands that *had* to be performed in the shell because many configuration options were not available in the EMC. As much as administrators enjoyed the new capabilities of the command-line interface, they did not like being told "you have to use it all the time." Over time, more and more functionality was added back into the Exchange Management Console.

With the EMS, administrators have a powerful yet flexible scripting platform that is much easier to take advantage of than using Microsoft Visual Basic scripts—previously the only way to script changes in the Exchange Server environment. As described by Microsoft, "What once took hundreds of lines in Visual Basic scripts can now be accomplished easily with as little as one line of code."

The EMS uses an object model that is based on the Microsoft .NET platform. This enables the shell commands to apply the output from one command to subsequent commands when they are run.

Whereas Exchange Server 2007 used PowerShell v1, Exchange Server 2010 is built on PowerShell v2, which has several enhancements that distinguish it from the previous version.

Exchange Server 2010 also utilizes Windows Remote Management (WinRM) 2.0. Whether an administrator is connecting to a local server or one halfway around the world, EMS always connects to the desired Exchange Server 2010 server via a remote connection utilizing an Internet Information Server (IIS) virtual directory. This holds true even when administrators are running the PowerShell command against the server they are currently logged on to. Due to this capability, the ability to perform PowerShell-based Exchange Server management does not require Exchange Server binaries to be installed on the requesting client, so 32-bit clients that have PowerShell v2 with WinRM 2.0 installed can be used for remote PowerShell administration.

The supported client OS platforms include the x86 and x64 versions of Windows Vista, Windows Server 2008, Windows Server 2008 R2, Windows 7, Windows Server 2003, Windows Server 2003 R2, and Windows XP.

18

Exchange Management Shell Basic Concepts

The Exchange Management Shell has a number of command functions, support options, and customization features. The following is a list of some of the basic concepts administrators should be aware of:

▶ **Objects**—The collection of properties that represents each of the pieces that make up an Exchange Server environment. An object can refer to a user mailbox, a server, a connector, or one of many other configurable items.

▶ **Cmdlets**—A cmdlet, pronounced "command-let," is a specialized .NET class that performs a particular operation. Cmdlets are the smallest unit of functionality in the EMS. Similar in appearance to the built-in commands in other shells (such as the DIR or CD commands in a Microsoft command prompt), cmdlets can be run individually or combined in scripts. There are hundreds of cmdlets provided for Exchange Server-specific management tasks.

▶ **Parameters**—Parameters are elements that provide information to the cmdlet. Parameters can either identify an object or its attributes to act upon or can control how the cmdlet performs its task.

▶ **Restricted PSSession**—By implementing the RBAC control model, the EMS can restrict available cmdlets and parameters to only those that the user has access to run. For example, if the user does not have the access to create new mailboxes, the New-Mailbox cmdlet will not be presented to them.

▶ **Identity**—Identity is a special parameter that can be used with most cmdlets to give access to the unique identifiers that refer to a particular object. By using the identity parameter, administrators can specify the particular object they want to retrieve, modify, or delete. To reduce unnecessary keystrokes, the identity parameter was created as a positional parameter. When running a cmdlet, the first argument is assumed to be the identity parameter, so running the command get-mailbox –identity "linkin" will produce the same results as get-mailbox "linkin".

▶ **Pipelining**—Before the EMS, one of the biggest shortcomings of scripting in the Exchange Server environment was the lack of ability to take the output of one command and utilize it directly as the input for other commands. Within the EMS, pipelining allows exactly that. Administrators have the ability to string cmdlets together, using one cmdlet to gather data, passing the results to a second cmdlet that filters the data to a smaller subset, and then supplying the result to a third cmdlet to act on.

▶ **Object-oriented data handling**—Because the resulting output from any cmdlet in the Exchange Management Shell is an object, all output can be acted upon and processed by other commands with little to no changes. Commands that are intended to work together on particular feature sets accept the output from other commands in the same feature set.

▶ **Access cmd.exe commands**—All the commands available in the Windows command prompt (cmd.exe) are also available to the EMS. Administrators can not only run these commands, but also can take the output from those commands and perform actions based on that output.

▶ **Trusted scripts**—Administrators have long been concerned that the ability to run scripts in an organization (especially when logged in with administrative credentials) could have disastrous results. To prevent this from happening, the Exchange Management Shell requires that all scripts be digitally signed before they are allowed to run. This feature is intended to prevent malicious users from inserting a dangerous or harmful script in the EMS. Before a script can be run, the administrator must specifically "trust" it, helping to protect the entire organization.

▶ **Profile customization**—The EMS provides a powerful, easy-to-use interface with the default installation, but administrators might want to customize the appearance of the interface, create shortcuts for commonly used commands, or specify specific commands to automatically run when the EMS starts. All these items can be configured using a customized Exchange Management Shell profile.

▶ **Tip of the day**—Although perhaps not as impressive as the preceding features, a welcome feature of the EMS is the display of a Tip of the Day each time the Exchange Management Shell is opened. The Tip of the Day offers advice on how to perform specific tasks within the shell, listing commands and proper syntax for their use.

Exchange Management Console

With the release of Exchange Server 2007, Microsoft introduced the Exchange Management Console, its new Microsoft Management Console (MMC) snap-in that provided a graphical user interface (GUI). This product had a completely redesigned interface that was much easier to navigate than the previous administration tool, the Exchange System Manager.

The Exchange Management Console (EMC) remains in Exchange Server 2010. It has been refined and updated but has the same look and feel as it did in Exchange Server 2007, and administrators familiar with the older version can find their way around with little wasted effort. The EMC utilizes remote PowerShell commands to perform the actual work, and relies on RBAC to determine what level of administration accessing users can accomplish.

The EMC is installed on all Exchange 2010 servers. When utilized on Exchange servers housing the Exchange Hub Transport, Client Access, Unified Messaging, and/or Mailbox server roles, the console displays all servers in the organization that house these roles. However, if the Exchange server has the Edge Transport server role installed, the console displays only the Edge Transport server role.

Exchange Server 2007 required a 64-bit platform to install the server roles but enabled the administrative tools to be installed on 32-bit systems. Exchange Server 2010, however, does not. To deploy the Exchange Server 2010 EMC you must be running one of the supported x64 platforms:

▶ Vista x64 SP1 or later

▶ Windows Server 2008 x64 SP2 or later

▶ Windows Server 2008 x64 R2

▶ Windows7 x64 Client

The EMC Hierarchy

Opening the EMC, as shown in Figure 18.1, presents administrators with a graphical interface that consists of three primary sections.

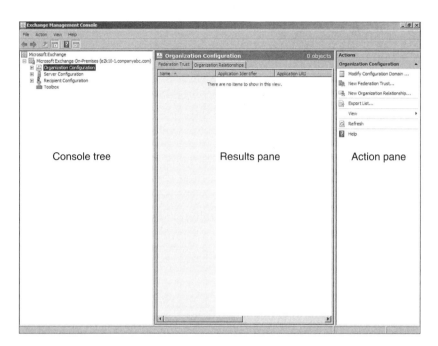

FIGURE 18.1   Exchange Management Console components.

The Console Tree (on the left) shows a hierarchy containing categories of objects that can
be managed. This is how administrators navigate through the various containers and
objects in their environment. The Console Tree can be shown or hidden by clicking the
Show/Hide Console Tree icon on the EMC toolbar.

The results pane, located in the center of the console, displays a collection of objects that
an administrator can select. This collection varies based on the object that is selected in
the Console Tree.

The action pane is located on the right side of the console. This pane lists all actions that
are available to administrators based on the items selected in the Console Tree or results
pane. Like the Console Tree, the action pane can be shown or hidden by clicking
Show/Hide Action Pane on the console toolbar. Even with the action pane hidden, administrators can still access relevant actions through context menus available by right-clicking
the object.

In the Console Tree, the hierarchy of the management containers displays. There are some
changes to the hierarchy that reflect new features and capabilities in the EMC.

Microsoft Exchange Node

As in Exchange Server 2007, the first node in the hierarchy is the Microsoft Exchange node. Selecting this node presents two tabs in the results pane: Post-Installation Tasks and Community Resources.

The Post-Installation Tasks tab details steps that are recommended by Microsoft whenever new Exchange servers are installed, or whenever new roles are added to existing servers. These Post-Installation Tasks include

▶ **Finalize Deployment Tasks**—Lists tasks that are *required* to complete the deployment of Exchange Server 2010, including features that are enabled by default but require manual configuration. Some tasks that might need to be reviewed follow:

> ▶ Configure domains for which you will accept email.
>
> ▶ Subscribe the Edge Transport server.
>
> ▶ Create a postmaster mailbox.

Administrators are strongly encouraged to review this section thoroughly.

▶ **End-to-End Scenario Tasks**—Provides a list of *recommended* tasks to perform after deploying Exchange Server 2010 to configure specific end-to-end scenarios. Some areas covered include the following:

> ▶ Managing Outlook Anywhere
>
> ▶ Configuring Monitoring for Exchange servers
>
> ▶ Securing your Exchange server from viruses, worms, and other malware
>
> ▶ Configuring your system for the Rights Management Services (RMS) Policy Application Agent

As with the Finalize Deployment page, these items should be reviewed for applicability in your environment.

▶ **Additional Post-Installation Tasks**—Provides a checklist of *optional* steps for configuring Exchange Server 2010 features and a checklist of optional tasks to perform after the Exchange Server 2010 installation is complete.

The Community Resources tab is new to Exchange Server 2010 and will be populated by Microsoft with links to various community resources that share information about the Exchange Server product. Some examples of possible entries here include links to recent posts on the Microsoft Exchange Server Team Blog and links to technical articles from Microsoft TechNet. The Community Resources tab can be a helpful reference for administrators wishing to keep up with new product announcements and features.

When the Microsoft Exchange node is selected, the action pane shows a new available action: Add Exchange Forest. This action heralds a major change in the Exchange world, the ability to manage multiple Exchange Server 2010 forests from a single Exchange

Management Console. This not only enables connecting to a secondary forest in the same organization, but also the ability to connect to and manage mailboxes that are hosted online with a hosted solution. Up to 10 forests can be added to the EMC.

NOTE

Before an Exchange Server forest can be added to the EMC, administrators must establish a federated trust or an Active Directory trust to the target forest.

Microsoft Exchange On-Premises Node

The next node in the hierarchy is new to Exchange Server 2010: the Microsoft Exchange On-Premises node. This is the default first forest that is installed with Exchange Server 2010, and the name cannot be changed. Selecting the node brings up two tabs in the results pane: The Organizational Health and Customer Feedback tabs.

The Organizational Health tab provides administrators with an Organizational summary that includes information about their environment. Although most of this information could be gathered in the Exchange 2007 EMC, it had to be done manually and was not offered in an "at-a-glance" presentation.

In a new installation, the data in the summary must be populated—to do so, click the link that says "Data is unavailable. Click here to access the latest data." Administrators are presented with the "Collect Organizational Health Data Wizard," which walks them through the data collection process. When completed, click Finish.

The tab provides a Database Summary, which tells how many databases and database copies exist in the environment, and how many of those database copies are unhealthy.

There is a License Summary for Exchange Server 2010 users that tells how many client access licenses (CALs) are needed for the environment. A Servers Summary lists the total number of Exchange servers (2010, 2007, and 2003) in the environment and how many there are of each version. The Servers Summary also breaks out how many Mailbox, Client Access, Hub Transport, and Unified Messaging servers are in the organization. Finally, there is a Recipients Summary that tells the total number of recipients, user mailboxes, distribution groups, dynamic distribution groups, mail contacts, and mail users in the organization. The Recipients Summary also tells how many users are messaging records management, journaling, OWA, ActiveSync, and Unified Messaging users, and how many have MAPI, POP3, and IMAP4 enabled.

The next tab on the On-Premises screen is the Customer Feedback tab, which enables administrators to configure their level of participation in the Microsoft Customer Experience Improvement Program. This program collects anonymous information about how Exchange Server is used in the organization and presents it to Microsoft; it evaluates the data and determines which areas they need to focus on for improvement. Administrators can also connect to the Exchange Tech center to view documentation and get the latest software updates. Finally, administrators can submit suggestions and report bugs to the Exchange Server team, directly from within the EMC interface.

Organization Configuration Node

This section configures global data for the Exchange Server organization. Global data applies to all servers in your organization that hold a particular role, such as the Mailbox, Client Access, Hub Transport, or Unified Messaging roles.

One notable change in the Organization Configuration Node—the Exchange 2010 Mailbox Databases, which used to be viewed in the *Server Configuration* node, have been relocated to the Organization Configuration node. By clicking on the Mailbox role, new tabs are visible that control Database Management and Database Availability Group management. This is because Exchange Server 2010 now considers databases to be *Global* objects. In addition, items such as email address policies and the Offline Address Book (OAB) can be managed from this node.

Server Configuration Node

The Server Configuration node is used to manage the configuration of all Exchange 2010 servers and the associated child objects. By clicking on the Server Configuration tab, administrators can see a full list of the Exchange 2010 Servers in their environment, and by right-clicking the tab, the list of servers can be exported to a .txt or .csv file. Exchange 2003 and 2007 servers cannot be administered using the Exchange 2010 Management Console, so these servers are not listed. This is by design.

The Server Configuration node enables administrators to view and configure server certificates as well, performing tasks that had to be done from the EMS in Exchange Server 2007.

> **NOTE**
>
> In mixed Exchange 2007/2010 environments, administrators may receive an error when clicking the Client Access node under Server Configuration. The error reads "AN IIS directory entry couldn't be created...". To resolve this issue, add the "Exchange Trusted Subsystem" as a member of the local admin group on all Exchange 2007 servers in the environment and reboot the systems.

18

Recipient Configuration Node

This section manages settings for Exchange email recipients throughout your organization. Exchange Server mailboxes, distribution groups, contacts, and disconnected mailboxes can be managed from this node.

Recipient administration is also performed here. Object properties can be modified, and the objects themselves can be moved, disabled, or deleted.

The Recipient Configuration node also contains a new container: Move Request. This is a container that keeps track of current, pending, and past mailbox moves, enabling administrators to view information about the moves and cancel pending requests if wanted. Information gathered in the Move Request container remains there until manually cleared by the administrator. To view the status of a move request, select the request in the Move Request folder and click Properties from the action pane.

Toolbox Node

The last of the nodes is the Toolbox node. The Toolbox includes additional tools that are extremely useful when managing an Exchange Server organization. Several configuration management, performance, and security tools, including utilities to manage public folders, troubleshoot mail flow, view message queues, and monitor server performance are found here.

The toolbox also houses the Exchange Best Practices Analyzer; one tool that should be run in every Exchange Server environment. The BPA checks the configuration and health of an Exchange Server topology by programmatically collecting settings and values from multiple sources—the Exchange servers and their registries, AD, performance monitors, and others—and compares what it finds to Microsoft's recommended best practices. Upon completion of each of the checks, administrators are presented with a detailed report stating warnings and problems that were found and recommended steps for resolving them. The BPA should be run after every new server deployment and should be run as part of a regularly scheduled maintenance routine.

The Exchange Management Shell Command Log

When administrators perform tasks in the EMC, the commands are actually carried out using the EMS using PowerShell cmdlets.

By having access to these PowerShell commands, administrators can copy the commands, modify them, and reuse them from the command line or within scripts, without having to manually figure out all the possible parameters.

In Exchange Server 2010, administrators can now capture all the PowerShell commands that are launched during their EMC session in a single location using the new Exchange Management Shell Command Log.

Before the Exchange Management Shell Command Log can be used, it must be enabled. To do so

1. In the EMC, select View, View Exchange Management Shell Command Log.

2. In the Exchange Management Shell Command Log, select Action, Start Command Logging.

3. To modify the number of Windows PowerShell commands to log, select Action, Modify the Maximum Number of Windows PowerShell Commands to Log. Enter a number between 1 and 32767. (The default is 2048.)

When enabled, the Exchange Management Shell command log tracks all PowerShell commands run from the Exchange Management Console.

> **NOTE**
>
> The Exchange Management Shell Command Log is cleared every time the Management Console is closed. If left "enabled," the Exchange Management Shell Command Log begins tracking commands automatically when the EMC is opened.

When viewing the Exchange Management Shell Command Log, detailed information can be viewed about each command by simply selecting the command and reviewing the results in the results pane below. Administrators can also copy a particular command (or multiple commands) to the clipboard by highlighting them and selecting Action, Copy Commands.

Additionally, administrators can clear the command log by selecting Action, Clear Log and can export the contents of the command log by selecting Action, Export List. Exported logs can be saved in any of the following formats:

- Text (Tab Delimited) (`*.txt`)

- Text (Comma Delimited) (`*.csv`)

- Unicode Text (Tab Delimited) (`*.txt`)

- Unicode Text (Comma Delimited) (`*.csv`)

To stop recording commands, select Action, Stop Command Logging. Newly issued commands will not be written to the log, but already captured commands will not be cleared until the administrator closes the EMC. You can resume logging commands by following Step 2 of the preceding procedure.

Bulk Recipient Editing

Another welcome addition to the EMC is the ability to edit certain object properties on multiple objects simultaneously, directly from the Management Console. For example, imagine that a request comes down notifying you that your company's East Coast Mergers department, consisting of 150 users, decided to rebrand itself as the East Coast Mergers and Acquisitions department. In Exchange Server 2007, you would have to a) figure out the PowerShell command to change this entry and the script needed to change it for the selected users or b) open each user one at a time and manually make the change.

With Exchange Server 2010, administrators can edit multiple objects at the same time. To perform the same task, simply perform a search for all users where Department = East Coast Mergers, select all users, right-click and select Properties, and enter the new department name. Click on the OK button, and you are presented with a Bulk Edit Summary, as shown in Figure 18.2.

18

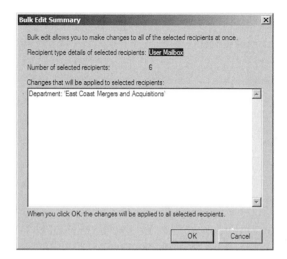

FIGURE 18.2   Bulk Edit Summary.

After you review the proposed changes, click Cancel to back out or OK to apply the changes to all selected recipients.

Property Dialog Command Exposure
As mentioned in the section on the Exchange Management Shell Command Log, administrators often want to know what commands the Shell is going to run in the background to accomplish tasks they perform in the Management Console. In Exchange Server 2007, the command was sometimes presented "after the fact"—when an administrator clicked OK, the associated Wizard showed what PowerShell command had been executed. Administrators could then copy the information and paste it elsewhere.

With Property Dialog Command Exposure, administrators can view the Shell commands that will be executed when the command is run. This information can be copied by right clicking and selecting Copy and then pasted elsewhere.

The Shell command to be run can be viewed by clicking the command-line icon that is located in the bottom-left corner of the dialog box, as shown in Figure 18.3. This icon is grayed out until a change is made that requires a shell command to be run.

Using the Exchange Management Console
To use the Exchange Management Console, the administrator selects either the Organization, Server, or Recipient Configuration node, depending on the desired action. The desired server role is then selected, and a list of the servers in the organization that hold that role is shown in the results pane. From there, the administrators can select the specific service they want to administer and view the available options in the action pane.

Items in the results pane can be filtered based on several expressions. This enables an administrator to focus on a subset of items that meet specific criteria. Filters can be made up of one or more expressions and allow minute control over which items are displayed in the results pane.

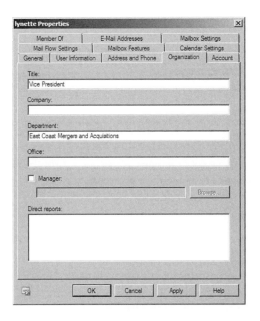

FIGURE 18.3   Property Dialog Command Exposure.

To create a filter, click Create Filter located in the upper-left corner of the results pane. A filter consists of one or more administrator-defined expressions. Each expression contains three parts: an attribute, an operator, and a value.

The attributes that are available are determined by the object for which you create a filter. For example, when selecting a mailbox server, the available attributes are Database Availability Group, Domain, Edition, Name, Product ID, Role, Site, and Version.

The operators that are available are based on the attribute you select. Some of the possible operators are Equals, Does Not Equal, Contains, Does Not Contain, Is Present, Starts With, Ends With, and others.

Finally, the list of values is also based on the selected attribute. Some values, such as Name or Site, can be typed in to match the name or site of an object in your organization. Others, such as when selecting the attribute of Edition or Role, are selected from a drop-down list.

To add additional expressions (and make the filter more restrictive), click the Add Expression box and input another attribute, operator, and value.

After you have set the expressions that you want, you can click Apply Filter. The expressions you configured are applied to the results pane, effectively filtering the results so that only the objects that match the expression are shown.

Applied expressions can be modified on-the-fly—simply click on the attribute, operator, or value, make the changes you want, and click Apply Filter. This feature can be extremely useful when you make a mistake and find that you have "filtered" yourself into an empty results pane.

To remove any of the created expressions, simply click Remove Expression located to the right of it. This button resembles a red X. However, after you have removed an expression, you must click Apply Filter again to implement the change.

Exchange Control Panel

New in Exchange Server 2010, the Exchange Control Panel can be considered by some to be the *least* and *most* powerful of all the administrative tools. It can be considered the *least* powerful because the scope of objects that can be managed is much more limited than in the EMS or EMC, and it can be considered the *most* powerful because it provides the potential for all users in your Exchange Server organization to have the ability to self-manage aspects of their own accounts.

The ECP is primarily targeted to be used by

- ▶ **End users**—Personnel granted the authority to self-manage aspects of their accounts such as the ability to track messages they have sent and received, create and manage distribution lists, or edit aspects of their personal account information.

- ▶ **Hosted tenants**—Tenant administrators for hosted customers.

- ▶ **Specialists**—Personnel such as Help Desk operators, Department Administrators, and eDiscovery Administrators who have had the appropriate level of access delegated by administrators.

The ECP can be accessed through Outlook Web App 2010 by logging into OWA and selecting the Options link. It can also be accessed directly via a URL which, by default, is located at https://CASServerName/ecp. Additionally, the ECP will be able to be accessed from Outlook 2010 when it is released.

The Exchange Control Panel (ECP) is a web-based management console that can be accessed from web browsers that have no Exchange Server–specific client-side software installed. It can be accessed from the same Internet browsers that support the Outlook Web App premium client—Internet Explorer 7+, Mozilla Firefox, and Apple Safari 3+. This AJAX-based application is built into the Client Access server role in an Exchange environment and, although it shares some code with OWA, it is a separate application.

It is important to note the Exchange Control Panel is RBAC-aware, meaning that administrative options are available only to those who have the appropriate permissions to utilize them. This can be seen by comparing Figure 18.4, which shows a user logged in with full administrative access (note the Select What to Manage option in the top-left corner and the Manage your Organization option in the bottom-right corner) and Figure 18.5, which shows the same interface as viewed by a standard user.

By default, standard users do have the ability to self-administer certain aspects of their accounts, as shown by the Edit link that, when clicked, allows users to modify certain aspects of their contact information. This default ability can be removed (or limited to certain fields only) using RBAC. For example

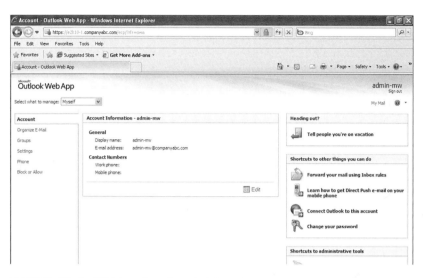

FIGURE 18.4   ECP interface for administrative account.

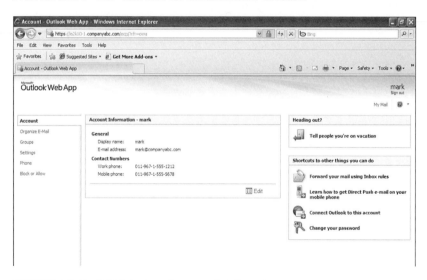

FIGURE 18.5   ECP interface for nonadministrative user account.

- ▶ If a user has been restricted from message tracking, that button does not appear in the ECP.

- ▶ If a user can edit mailboxes, but not create new ones, the New mailbox button will not display, but the Details button does.

- ▶ If users are allowed to edit their department but not their display name, the display name is visible but grayed out and read-only.

After an administrator elects to manage My Organization, the four main components of the Exchange Control Panel display, as shown in Figure 18.6. These components are

▶ **UI Scope Control**—At the top of the screen, identified by the text stating "elect What to Manage" (and the drop-down box beside it), the UI Scope Control enables those with the appropriate RBAC permissions to select whether they want to manage themselves, their organization, or another user.

▶ **Primary Navigation Panel**—To the left of the screen is the Primary Navigation panel, enabling administrators to select which area of administration they want to work with.

▶ **Secondary Navigation Panel**—Next to the Primary Navigation Panel and identified by icons in the figure labeled Mailboxes, Groups, External Contacts, and so on, is the Secondary Navigation Panel, which enables the user to further specify the area to administer.

▶ **The Slab**—At the bottom of the pane, identified in the figure by the list of Display Names and E-mail addresses, is the slab—the list of items that can be administered based on the preceding selections.

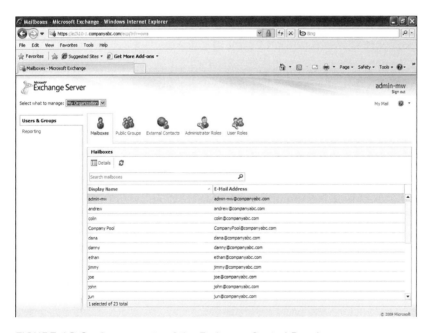

FIGURE 18.6   Components of the Exchange Control Panel.

Performing Common Tasks

With three different tools to choose from, determining which to use for a particular task is up to the person performing the task. The decision is based primarily on two questions:

1. What tools can perform the activity? Some activities, such as creating a new *user* mailbox, can be performed from EMC, the EMS, or the ECP, whereas others, such as creating a new *room* mailbox, can be accomplished only in the EMC and the EMS.

2. Which tool is most convenient for the task? If creating a new mailbox user, it might be easier to simply log on through a browser and create the account, whereas creating 100 new accounts would be easier using a script in the EMS.

Some tasks can be performed in the ECP, *more* tasks can be performed in the EMC, and *all* tasks can be performed in the EMS—but for something as simple as changing the department for a single user, determining the PowerShell cmdlet and parameters might be more challenging than simply using the GUI or Web interfaces.

Creating User Mailboxes

The creation of a new user mailbox, either for an existing user or in conjunction with the creation of a new user, is an example of a task that can be accomplished from any of the three administrative tools. For this example, we show how to perform the task using all three tools.

Exchange Server 2010 allows for the creation of four different types of mailboxes:

1. **User Mailbox**—Owned by a user and used to send and receive messages. This mailbox cannot be used for resource scheduling.

2. **Room Mailbox**—Intended for room scheduling and not owned by a user. A user account is created with the mailbox, but the account is disabled.

3. **Equipment Mailbox**—Intended for equipment scheduling. Like the room mailbox, this is not owned by an active user. The associated user account that is created will automatically be disabled.

4. **Linked Mailbox**—Accessed by a user in a separate, trusted forest.

However, only a *user* mailbox can be created with the ECP. For our following examples, we create a User Mailbox for a user named Oscar B. Hayve.

Creating a New Mailbox in the Exchange Management Console

Creating a new mailbox using the GUI interface of the EMC is easy and familiar to those who have worked with previous versions of Exchange Server. To do so

1. Start the Exchange Management Console.

2. In the Console Tree, navigate to the Recipient Configuration node.

3. In the action pane, click New Mailbox. The New Mailbox Wizard appears. Alternatively, administers can select New Mail User, which defaults to creating an actual user mailbox (as opposed to a room, equipment, or linked mailbox) and skips step 4.

4. On the Introduction page, as shown in Figure 18.7, select User Mailbox, and then click Next.

18

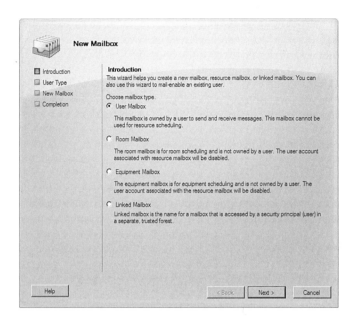

FIGURE 18.7   New Mailbox Introduction page.

5. On the User Type page, click New User, and then click Next.

6. On the User Information page, complete the following fields:

▶ **Specify the organizational unit rather than using a default one**—Select this box if you want to specify a particular organizational unit. If checked, click the Browse button and select the desired OU for the user account. For our example, we leave this box unchecked.

▶ **First name**—Type the first name of the user. This field is optional.

▶ **Initials**—Type the initials of the user. This field is optional.

▶ **Last name**—Type the last name of the user. This field is optional.

▶ **Name**—By default, this field is populated with the user's first name, initials, and last name, if entered. You can modify the name in this field or type one manually if no previous fields were populated.

▶ **User logon name (User Principal Name)**—This is the name that the user uses to log on to the mailbox. The user logon name consists of a username and a suffix. Typically, the suffix is the domain name in which the user account resides.

▶ **User logon name (pre-Windows 2000)**—This is also known as the Security Account Manager Account Name (SAMAccountName) and is used for Windows Internet Naming Service (WINS) name resolution. This name must be unique within the domain and is, by default, automatically populated based on the preceding User Principal Name.

- ▶ **Password**—Type the password that the user must use to log on to his mailbox.

- ▶ **Confirm Password**—Retype the password that you entered in the Password field.

- ▶ **User Must Change Password at Next Logon**—Select this check box if you want to require users to reset the password after their first logon (recommended).

7. When finished, click Next.

8. On the Mailbox Settings page, complete the following fields:

   - ▶ **Alias**—Enter the desired alias for the user, based on your organization's policies. For our example, we use the user's first initial, middle initial, and last name—OBHayve.

   - ▶ **Specify the mailbox database rather than using a database automatically selected**—If desired, select this option and use the Browse button to select a specific database. For our example, we leave this option blank.

   - ▶ **Managed folder mailbox policy**—If desired, select this box and click the Browse button to select the MRM mailbox policy to be associated with this mailbox. For our example, we leave this option blank.

   - ▶ **Exchange ActiveSync mailbox policy**—To specify an Exchange ActiveSync mailbox policy, select this check box, and then click Browse to select the Exchange ActiveSync mailbox policy to be associated with this mailbox. For our example, we leave this option blank.

9. When finished, click Next.

10. New to Exchange Server 2010 is the Archive Settings page. Selecting the box beside Create an Archive Mailbox for This Account will, as indicated, create a link to an online archive for the mailbox. Items will be moved automatically from the primary user mailbox to the archive based on the default retention policy settings or those defined by the administrator. For our example, we leave this option blank.

11. On the New Mailbox page, review the Configuration Summary. To make any configuration changes, click Back. To create the new mailbox, click New.

12. On the Completion page, the summary states whether the mailbox was successfully created. The summary also displays the Exchange Management Shell command that was used to create the mailbox. This command can be copied and pasted into a text editor as the first step toward creating future mailboxes from the command line interface of the EMS.

13. Click Finish.

Creating a New Mailbox in the Exchange Management Shell

Creating a new mailbox from the EMS can be complicated because there are so many parameters to consider. However, by copying the EMS Shell command created by the Management Console in the previous steps, we can now paste that command into a text editor and modify the contents, allowing us to create our next test user.

Note that we must also remove the Password System.Security.SecureString and ResetPasswordOnNextLogon $true portions of the command because these were created in the EMC command to populate the password for the account.

We can create our new user, Yasmine B. Guud, by using the following command:

```
New-Mailbox -Name 'Yasmine B. Guud' -Alias 'YBGuud' -UserPrincipalName
➥'YBGuud@companyabc.com' -SamAccountName 'YBGuud' -FirstName 'Yasmine'
➥-Initials 'B' -LastName 'Guud'
```

After running the preceding command in the Exchange Management Shell, we are prompted for the Password. Enter the desired password (carefully, there will not be an option to confirm it) and press Enter.

As you can see, every option configured during the creation of the account in the GUI interface, with the exception of the user password, can be replicated using the Exchange Management Shell command.

Creating Multiple Mailboxes in the Exchange Management Shell

Given the complexity of creating a new mailbox in the EMS, why would anyone want to do so? Generally, they wouldn't. But what if your Human Resources department handed you a list of 50 new employees and requested that you create new mailboxes for all of them? Doing so through the GUI interface of the EMC would not only take hours, but would also result in the increased likelihood that misspellings or mistakes might occur.

That's where the power of the EMS comes into play.

By putting the list of names in a .csv file, we can quickly create multiple accounts from only two lines of code. To do so, perform the following steps:

1. Create a text file called newusers.csv in a directory called (for our example) c:\scripts.

2. For our example, we create several column names and populate the data, as shown in Figure 18.8. The columns we will populate are Name, Alias, UPN, First, Middle, and Last. Additional column names can be added, if desired, to populate more data in the user accounts.

FIGURE 18.8   Creating the .csv file for multiple mailbox creation.

3. When the .csv file is complete, we are ready to begin. Each user account will be created with a default password, with the user required to reset the password when

they first log in. From the Exchange Management Shell, type the following command. (Type it word-for-word, do not attempt to enter the password yet.)

```
$Password = Read-Host "Enter Password" -AsSecureString
```

And press Enter. You will be presented with a prompt stating Enter Password. Type the password you want to apply to all your newly created users and press Enter. Your password will now be assigned to the variable $Password for use in our script.

4. Next, we run two cmdlets, piping the results of the first into the second, to create the new mailboxes from the .csv file. The syntax will be as follows:

```
Import-Csv "c:\scripts\newusers.csv" ¦ foreach { New-Mailbox –name $_.Name
➥-alias $_.Alias –UserPrincipalName $_.UPN -FirstName $_.First -Initials
➥$_.Middle -LastName $_.Last -Password $Password
➥-ResetPasswordOnNextLogon:$true}
```

The result, as shown in Figure 18.9, is the creation of the new mailboxes. The existence can be confirmed by viewing the mailboxes in the Exchange Management Console. (Remember to refresh the screen if you already had it open.)

FIGURE 18.9   End result of multiple mailbox creation script.

Again—while this is a significant amount of work for three users, the same concept can be used to create 50 users (or 500) and can prove to be a valuable time saver.

Creating a New Mailbox in the Exchange Control Panel

Before administrators can create a new mailbox in the Exchange Control Panel, they must be granted the rights to do so using RBAC.

Once they have the appropriate permissions, creating a new mailbox in the Exchange Control Panel is so easy that it's hardly worth the time to explain it. However, because the ECP is brand new, this section runs through the process to show how quick and easy it is.

To create a new mailbox user in the Exchange Control Panel, perform the following steps:

1. Log in to the OWA server with administrative credentials.
2. From the OWA page, select Options.

3. Select Manage Your Organization.

4. Ensure My Organization is selected in the UI Scope Control, Users & Groups is selected in the Primary Navigation Panel, and Mailboxes is selected in the Secondary Navigation Panel.

5. Click the New Mailboxes icon.

6. On the New Mailbox page, enter the information for the new account. Those marked with asterisks (*) are required fields. An example of the New Mailbox page is shown in Figure 18.10.

FIGURE 18.10   Creating New Mailbox with Exchange Control Panel.

7. When finished, click the Save button.

The ECP passes the information on to the CAS server, which, in turn, uses Remote PowerShell commands to perform the actual operation and create the account.

Understanding Distribution Groups

In Exchange Server 2010, distribution groups serve two primary purposes: They can be used as email distribution groups created to expedite the mass sending of email messages, calendar invitations, and other information within an Exchange Server organization, or a security group to assign permissions to a shared resource. Whether you create a distribution group or a security group, the same utility (New Distribution Group) is utilized.

Whether a distribution group or a security group is wanted, the group is created as a mail-enabled Active Directory group object. When a sender sends a message to a distribution group, the server takes the original message, accesses the distribution group membership, and sends the message to each recipient in the membership list; this is known as "distribution group expansion." In Exchange Server 2010, distribution groups are configured to use any Hub Transport server as the distribution group expansion server. Although this default behavior can be modified, this default setting is a recommended best practice.

By default, distribution groups created in Exchange Server 2010 require that all senders be authenticated. This prevents external senders from sending messages to distribution groups. To configure a new distribution group to accept messages from all senders, you must modify the message delivery restriction settings on the object.

To create or modify distribution groups, the user must be assigned to either the Organization Management or Recipient Management role.

Creating Distribution Groups in the EMC

To create a new distribution group in the Exchange Management Console, perform the following steps:

1. Start the Exchange Management Console.

2. In the Console Tree, navigate to the Recipient Configuration \ Distribution Group node.

3. In the action pane, click New Distribution Group. The New Distribution Group Wizard appears.

4. On the Introduction page, select New Group, and then click Next.

5. On the Group Information page, complete the following fields:

   ▶ **Group Type**—To create a distribution group, select Distribution. To create a security group, click Security. The remaining steps are identical, regardless of which type of group you create.

   ▶ **Organizational Unit**—By default, the New Distribution Group is created in the Users Organizational Unit (OU) in Active Directory. To change the default OU, select the box labeled Specify the Organizational Unit Rather Than Using a Default One; then click Browse and select the desired OU.

   ▶ **Name**—Enter the desired name for the group.

   ▶ **Name (pre-Windows 2000)**—By default, the group name for pre-Windows 2000 operating systems is automatically generated to be the same as the group name. You can modify the name in this field (not recommended).

   ▶ **Alias**—Enter the desired alias for the group. This is the name used to generate the default email address for the distribution group, so it must contain only characters that can be used in a valid SMTP address. (For example, no spaces can be used.) If you select an invalid character, the wizard notifies you. Enter the desired alias.

6. Click Next.

18

7. On the New Distribution Group page, review the Configuration Summary. To make any configuration changes, click Back. To create the new distribution group, click New.

8. On the Completion page, the summary states whether the distribution group was successfully created. The summary also displays the Exchange Management Shell command that was used to create the distribution group.

9. Click Finish.

Creating Distribution Groups in the EMS

To create a new distribution group in the Exchange Management Shell, you can use the following command syntax:

```
New-DistributionGroup -Name "GroupNameHere" -OrganizationalUnit
➥"companyabc.com/users" -Type "Distribution OR Security" -SamAccountName
➥"GroupNameHere" -Alias "AliasHere"
```

Creating Distribution Groups in the ECP

New in Exchange Server 2010 is the ability to create and manage distribution lists from within the Exchange Control Panel web interface.

Before we discuss the process, there are a few items to note:

▶ Although both Mail Universal Distribution Groups and Mail Universal Security Groups are visible from within the ECP, there is no noticeable differentiation between the two.

▶ All distribution groups created from within the ECP are created as Mail Universal Distribution Groups; there is no option to create a security group.

▶ Dynamic Distribution Groups are not visible from within the ECP, nor can new ones be created there.

The ability to create new groups using the ECP is governed by RBAC. Users must be granted the permission to do so before the following process can be accomplished.

To create a new distribution group in the ECP, perform the following steps:

1. Connect to the ECP by logging into OWA as an administrator and selecting the Options page, clicking Manage Your Organization, and selecting the Groups icon. Alternatively, you can go directly to https://{your CAS server name}/ecp and authenticate through OWA.

2. Under Groups, click the New button.

3. In the New Group window, as shown in Figure 18.11, complete the following fields:

▶ **Display Name—(Required)**—This name must be unique in the domain. This is the name that displays in the address book and on the To: line when mail is sent to the group. The display name should be user-friendly to help people recognize the purpose or membership of the group.

FIGURE 18.11   Create a new group with the Exchange Control Panel.

▶ **Alias—(Required)**—This is the name portion of the email address that appears to the left of the @ symbol. The alias must be unique in the domain and, because it is part of the email address, cannot contain any spaces.

▶ **Description—(Not Required)**—This description populates the Notes field for the object. This descriptive name can be viewed by employees who view the properties of the distribution list. If populated, the field should describe the purpose or membership of the group.

▶ **Ownership—(Required)**—Owners can add members to the group, approve or reject requests to join, and approve or reject messages sent to the group. By default, the person creating the group is added as a group owner. If an administrator creates the group at the request of an employee, the administrator can add the employee as an owner and then remove herself.

▶ **Membership—(Not Required)**—By default, all group owners are added as group members. If this behavior is not desired, deselect the check box for this option. Add or remove members to the group as desired.

▶ **Membership Approval—(Required)**—New to distribution groups in Exchange Server 2010 is the ability for users to self-manage their distribution lists, joining those that interest them and leaving those that don't. During the

18

creation of the distribution group using the ECP, the following options are available:

- **Owner Approval—Open**—Anyone can join the group without being approved by the group owners.

- **Owner Approval—Closed**—Members can be added only by the group owners. All requests to join will be rejected automatically.

- **Owner Approval—Owner Approval**—All requests are approved or rejected by the group owners.

- **Group Open to Leave—Open**—Anyone can leave the group without being approved by the group owners.

- **Group Open to Leave—Closed**—Members can be removed only by the group owners. All requests to leave will be rejected automatically.

4. After all fields have been populated and all options selected, click Save to create the distribution group.

Dynamic Distribution Groups

Unlike a regular distribution group, a *dynamic distribution group,* as the name implies, is dynamic in nature. Whereas a regular distribution group is composed of a defined set of members, the membership list for a dynamic distribution group is calculated every time a message is sent to it. This is accomplished by utilizing a Lightweight Directory Access Protocol (LDAP) query that has been defined and assigned to the group. For example, you can build a dynamic distribution group that is intended to include all recipients in a particular state. Each time the list is accessed, the membership would be built based on information gathered from the AD.

Dynamic distribution groups require less maintenance than standard groups because the query is defined once, and the membership is built automatically every time the group is called. However, a performance cost is associated with their use, especially if the query produces a large number of results. Every time an email is sent to a query-based distribution group, server and domain resources are utilized to determine its membership. Dynamic distribution groups are an extremely functional tool but should be used with discretion.

Creating Dynamic Distribution Groups in the EMC

To create a new dynamic distribution group in the Exchange Management Console, perform the following steps:

1. Start the Exchange Management Console.

2. In the Console Tree, navigate to the Recipient Configuration \ Distribution Group node.

3. In the action pane, click New Dynamic Distribution Group. The New Dynamic Distribution Group Wizard appears.

4. On the Introduction page, complete the following fields:

  ▸ **Organizational Unit**—By default, the New Distribution Group will be created in the Users Organizational Unit (OU) in AD. To change the default OU, select the box labeled Specify the Organizational Unit Rather Than Using a Default One; then click Browse and select the desired OU.

  ▸ **Name**—Enter the desired name for the group.

  ▸ **Alias**—Enter the desired alias for the group. This is the name that will be used to **generate** the default email address for the distribution group, so it must only contain characters that can be used in a valid SMTP address. (For example, no spaces can be used.) If you select an invalid character, the wizard notifies you. Enter the desired alias.

5. Click Next.

6. On the Filter Settings page, complete the following fields:

  ▸ **Recipient container**—By default, recipients from the entire organization are eligible as members of the distribution list. However, you can specify to include only members from a specific OU, if your OU structure matches the needs of the distribution list. For example, if you have an OU container for all employees in Europe, and you create a distribution group that contains only employees in Europe, specifying that OU prevents the list from searching the rest of AD every time a message is sent to the list. If you select an OU here, that OU and all OUs under it are included. To select an OU, click Browse and do so.

  ▸ **Include these recipient types**—Either leave the default All Recipient Types, or, if desired, you can limit the group membership to one of the following categories:

    ▸ Users with Exchange Mailboxes

    ▸ Users with external email addresses

    ▸ Resource mailboxes

    ▸ Contacts with external email addresses

    ▸ Mail-enabled groups

    ▸ Or any combination of the above

7. When you are ready, click Next to continue.

8. On the Conditions page, you can select the conditions that will build the LDAP query that will identify the recipients to be included in the list. Select one or more conditions by placing a check in the associated box and then editing the conditions by selecting an underlying value. For example, if you were to select Recipients in a State or Province, you would then click the highlighted word and enter the value (example: Florida).

18

9. When you are ready, click the Preview button to test the query you created and ensure the membership of the list is populated as you expect. Click OK and, if all is as expected, click Next.

10. Review the configuration summary. If all is well, click New.

11. On the Completion page, the summary states whether the distribution group was successfully created and shows the Exchange Management Shell command that was used to create the distribution group. When ready, click Finish.

Creating Dynamic Distribution Groups in the EMS

To create a new distribution group in the Exchange Management Shell, a sample command is shown here:

```
New-DynamicDistributionGroup -Name "Florida Employees" -RecipientContainer
➥"companyabc.com/Users" -IncludedRecipients "MailboxUsers"
➥-ConditionalStateOrProvince "Florida" -OrganizationalUnit
➥"companyabc.com/Users" -Alias "Florida_Employees"
```

Managing Distribution Groups

As organizations grow, they might find that the number of distribution groups maintained can get extremely large. As the membership of these groups can change often, the maintenance of them can take a significant amount of administrative resources.

With Exchange Server 2010, users can now be granted the ability to self-manage their distribution groups. This is intended to decrease the maintenance costs associated with the upkeep of these groups.

Users who have the appropriate RBAC permissions can create and manage their groups using the ECP through their OWA interface. By default users can join or leave groups using the ECP interface.

Message Delivery Restrictions

Often, distribution lists are created with a specific user base in mind. For example, although you might want any employee in the company to send to your Employee Suggestions mailbox, you might want to restrict who can send to All Employees, or All District Managers.

To restrict who can send to a particular distribution group, perform the following actions:

1. Start the Exchange Management Console.

2. In the Console Tree, navigate to the Recipient Configuration \ Distribution Group node.

3. From the results pane, select the distribution group you want to manage.

4. In the action pane, click Properties.

5. Select the Mail Flow Settings tab, and then double-click the Message Delivery Restrictions option.

6. By default, All Senders is selected, allowing all senders in the organization to send to the distribution list. To restrict this, select the Only Senders in the Following List radio button and click the Add button. Allowed senders can now be selected from the GAL. To select multiple senders, hold the CTRL key as you select each additional user.

7. Click OK three times to save the changes and exit.

When an unauthorized sender creates and sends an email to a restricted distribution group, a message similar to the one shown in Figure 18.12 will be received by the sender.

FIGURE 18.12   Undeliverable message from restricted group.

Other delivery restriction options include Require that all senders are authenticated (enabled by default on groups created in Exchange Server 2010), which prevents anonymous users from sending messages to the distribution group and Reject messages from, which enables you to configure specific users or groups that are restricted from sending messages to the group. In addition, message size restrictions can be placed on the distribution group, allowing only messages smaller than the mandated size to be delivered.

NOTE

When an OWA 2010 user attempts to send to a distribution list to which they do not have permissions, a MailTip is displayed in the OWA window notifying them that You Do Not Have Permission to Send To the distribution list, as shown in Figure 18.13. The MailTips feature is enabled with OWA 2010 but does *not* work with Outlook 2007 or OWA 2007.

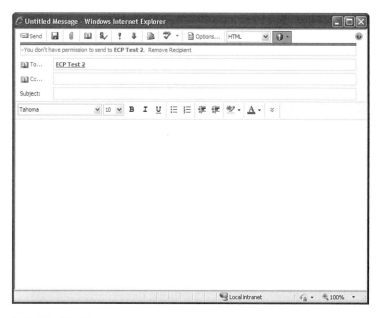

FIGURE 18.13   MailTip generated by restricted recipient.

Message Moderation

New in Exchange Server 2010 is the ability to configure Message Moderation settings on a distribution list. These settings are configured when creating the list using the ECP but are not populated when creating the distribution list from the EMC interface.

To configure these settings from the EMC interface, perform the following steps:

1. Start the Exchange Management Console.

2. In the Console Tree, navigate to the Recipient Configuration \ Distribution Group node.

3. From the results pane, select the distribution group you want to manage.

4. In the action pane, click Properties.

5. Select the Mail Flow Settings tab, and then double-click the Message Moderation option.

6. Administrators can configure the distribution group to require moderator approval for all messages, group moderators can be defined, senders that do not require

approval can be specified, and moderation notification messages can be configured. These settings are shown in Figure 18.14.

FIGURE 18.14   Message moderation configuration settings.

7. Click OK when finished.

Creating Mail Contacts

There are many times when an organization has the desire or need to communicate with users external to the Exchange Server organization but still have that user show up in the GAL. When this situation occurs, it is an ideal opportunity to utilize a mail contact.

Known as a custom recipient in some older versions of Exchange Server, this functionality has existed for some time, but the creation and management process has changed slightly from revision to revision.

To create a mail contact in the Exchange Management Console, perform the following steps:

1. Start the Exchange Management Console.
2. In the Console Tree, navigate to the Recipient Configuration \ Mail Contact node.
3. In the action pane, click New Mail Contact; this starts the New Mail Contact Wizard.
4. On the Introduction page, you can select whether you are creating a new contact or choosing to mail-enable a contact that exists in your organization but was previously not mail-enabled. For this instruction, select New Contact, and then click Next to continue.

18

5. On the Contact Information page, fill out the following fields:

   ▶ **Organizational Unit**—Select the Specify the Organizational Unit check box if you want the contact to reside in a specific OU. The default location is in the Users container.

   ▶ **First Name, Initials, Last Name**—Enter the appropriate information in these fields.

   ▶ **Name**—This field will automatically be populated based on the information entered in the First name, Initials, and Last name fields. You can change this setting to match your company standards if needed.

   ▶ **Alias**—Enter the desired alias for the contact.

   ▶ **External E-Mail Address**—Click the Edit button to enter the SMTP address for your mail-enabled contact (example, remote.user@yahoo.com). Click OK to continue.

6. Click Next to continue.

7. Review the Configuration Summary and click New to accept the current configuration and create the mail contact.

8. On the Completion page, review the summary and ensure the item was created without error. Click Finish to continue.

> **NOTE**
>
> Mail contacts can also be created and edited in the Exchange Management Shell and in the new Exchange Control Panel interfaces.

Managing Disconnected Mailboxes

Exchange Server 2003 introduced an exciting concept in mailbox administration: the Mailbox Recovery Center. Utilizing this feature, administrators could identify disconnected mailboxes (those no longer associated with a user account) and perform a variety of actions—including recovering the mailbox by connecting it to a new or existing user.

In Exchange Server 2007 and Exchange Server 2010, this process has been greatly simplified by the addition of a Disconnected Mailbox node located in the Recipient Configuration node of the Exchange Management Console.

With this utility, you can quickly and easily recover a mailbox that has been disassociated from a corresponding user mailbox. To reconnect a disconnected mailbox, perform the following procedure:

1. Start the Exchange Management Console.

2. In the Console Tree, navigate to the Recipient Configuration \ Disconnected Mailbox node.

3. In the action pane, click Connect to Server, and then click Browse. Select the Exchange server in which the mailbox resides, click OK, and then click Connect.

4. In the results pane, select the disconnected mailbox that you want to reconnect; then in the action pane, click Connect. This starts the Connect Mailbox Wizard.

5. On the Introduction page, select the type of mailbox you are reconnecting. By default, User Mailbox is selected, regardless of the mailbox type of the original mailbox. Click Next to continue.

6. On the Mailbox Settings page, fill out the following fields:

   ▶ **Matching User**—If the Exchange server located a matching user object in AD, this field will be prepopulated. There are times that a matching user exists, but Exchange Server does not locate it—in those instances, you can click Browse and, if found, you can insert the user by selecting it and clicking OK.

   ▶ **Existing User**—If you want to connect the mailbox to another existing user (but not a "matching" user), select this option button. Click Browse and select the user from those shown. After selecting the option, click OK to continue.

   ▶ **Alias**—The Alias is automatically filled in based on the alias of the account you have selected previously.

   ▶ **Managed Folder Mailbox Policy and Exchange ActiveSync Mailbox Policy**—Select the associated check boxes for these items if you want to associate the mailbox with an existing policy. The policy can be selected by clicking the Browse button.

7. Click Next to continue.

8. View the Configuration Summary and ensure all is correct. If you need to make any changes, use the Back button. After all the information is correct, click Connect.

9. From the Completion page, review the Completion Summary and ensure the reconnection was successful. Click Finish to close the wizard.

Moving Mailboxes

Administrators need to move mailboxes between databases for a variety of reasons such as a user being transferred to a different department or location or receiving a promotion (or demotion).

Additionally, mailboxes might need to be moved from one database to another to improve the load balancing of users across multiple Exchange servers (moving mailboxes from an overutilized server to an underutilized one).

Mailbox moves can also be extremely useful when implementing new Exchange Server hardware. The new server can be built in the existing environment, mailboxes can be moved to the new location, and the old server hardware can be decommissioned, all with minimal impact on the user community.

One other situation when the ability to move multiple mailboxes is helpful is during an upgrade to a newer version of Exchange Server; for example, when migrating your organization from Exchange Server 2007 to Exchange Server 2010. Administrators can install the new Exchange Server 2010 server, move all user mailboxes from your old environment to your new one, and then decommission your older Exchange servers when they are no longer needed.

Mailboxes are moved from a source mailbox database to a target mailbox database. The target mailbox database can be on the same server, on a different server, in a different domain, in a different active directory site, or in another forest.

New in Exchange Server 2010 is the concept of *asynchronous* mailbox moves. Asynchronous moves enable the user's mailbox to be kept online during the move. Mailbox moves between Exchange Server 2010 servers are asynchronous, but mailbox moves from previous versions (Exchange Server 2003 and Exchange Server 2007) to Exchange Server 2010 are NOT. In nonasynchronous moves, the user cannot access his mailbox during the move.

When moving from one Exchange Server 2010 database to another, a new cmdlet (New-MoveRequest) is used. The cmdlet can perform an asynchronous move because it is not actually *performing* the move. The action move is performed by the Mailbox Replication Service (MRS), which is a new service running on Exchange Server 2010 client access servers.

The old cmdlet used for mailbox moves, Move-Mailbox, operates differently, logging into both the source and target databases and moving the contents from the source to the destination. Administrators must keep the Shell open during the move or the process will fail.

Which cmdlet should an administrator use? This depends on the version of Exchange Server housing the source and destination mailboxes. This is explained in Table 18.1.

TABLE 18.1 Supported Mailbox Move Scenarios for Single-Forest Moves

Moving From	Moving To	New-MoveRequest Cmdlet	Move-Mailbox Cmdlet
E2010	E2010	Supported in the Exchange Management Shell and used by the Exchange Management Console	Not needed
E2007	E2010	Not supported	Supported
E2010	E2007	Not supported	Supported
E2003	E2010	Not supported	Supported
E2010	E2003	Not supported	Supported

Preparing for Mailbox Moves

Before moving mailboxes, some standard tasks should be completed in advance to minimize the potential for data loss and to streamline the process. These two primary tasks are as follows:

▶ **Backing Up Exchange Mailboxes**—Before performing any major work on a messaging system, it is a good practice to back up the message store. In the event of serious problems, you can always recover to your last known good backup.

▶ **Performing Mailbox Cleanup**—User mailboxes can grow rather large in size over time. Storing important messages, especially when there are attachments included, can take up a significant amount of disk space. Because moving larger mailboxes takes longer than smaller ones, it is always a good idea to have users clean up their mailboxes prior to moving them. One easy way to accomplish this is with the Mailbox Cleanup utility in Outlook. With this tool, users can view their current mailbox size, search for items older than, or larger than, a specified date and size, or run the autoarchive utility. Users can also empty their deleted items permanently because there is no need to waste time and bandwidth to move unwanted messages with the mailbox. Lastly, the utility enables users to delete all alternative versions of items in their mailbox. By cleaning up user mailboxes prior to moving them, you can significantly decrease the amount of time and resources needed to accomplish the task.

Performing the Mailbox Move

The following section discusses a mailbox move from one Exchange Server 2010 database to another using the Exchange Management Console. This process will, as previously described, utilize the `New-MoveRequest` cmdlet.

Mailbox moves are performed in the EMC using the Mailbox Move wizard. This process is so self-explanatory that we will bypass the step-by-step procedures and discuss, instead, the theory of what is happening.

When a new mailbox move request is generated by the Move Mailbox wizard, the source and target databases are selected. If both are on Exchange Server 2010 servers, the new cmdlet `New-MoveRequest` is utilized. If either the source or destination is on a legacy Exchange server, the `Move-Mailbox` cmdlet is used.

After a move request is started, the request and the current status can be viewed in the Recipient Configuration \ Move Request node in the EMC. Anytime between the time the move is requested and the time it is completed, the request can be canceled by selecting the request in this node and clicking Remove Move Request. This performs the EMS cmdlet `Remove-MoveRequest`.

When a Move Request has been completed, it can still be viewed in the Move Requests node until the administrator clears the move request. Mailboxes that have been moved have a different icon in the EMC, differentiating them from other mailboxes. This unique

18

icon, shown on users kevin, linkin, and logan in Figure 18.15, remains in place until the move request has been cleared at which point it reverts to a normal icon.

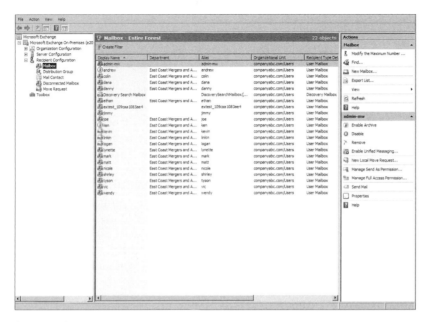

FIGURE 18.15   Custom icon for moved mailboxes.

This custom icon enables administrators to identify which mailboxes have recently been moved to prevent accidentally moving them a second time.

Recipient Configuration

Administrators can utilize any of the three administrative tools to perform a wide variety of user-specific configurations on an individual mailbox. As has been stated before, the ECP enables access to *some* of the settings, the EMC enables access to *more* of the settings, and the EMS enables access to *all* the settings. When it comes to administering nondisplay type data, the ECP gets left behind by the EMC and EMS.

Each mail-enabled object in an Exchange Server environment has specific settings that can be configured, enabling users in the same database to have different settings, even if a default setting is already applied to the database.

Several mailbox configurable properties are available on individual user mailboxes, including mailbox settings, mail flow settings, and mailbox features.

Mailbox Settings

Mailbox settings address storage quotas and records management functionality. Some of the detailed functions covered in mailbox settings are as follows:

- **Messaging Records Management**—Messaging Records Management (or MRM) policies assist organizations to comply with legal or regulatory requirements for their organization. Administrators can configure a Managed folder mailbox policy that varies from the database default. This setting can be turned on for all messages or particular start and end dates and times can be specified.

- **Federated Sharing**—New in Exchange Server 2010, the Federated sharing setting enables users to collaborate with organizations and users external to the Exchange Server organization by sharing personal information management (PIM) information such as free/busy data or contacts.

- **Storage Quotas**—By default, mailboxes are configured to adhere to the storage quota settings for the database on which they reside. By default, these quotas are set to

    - **Issue warning at**—1,991,680 KB (1,945 MB or approximately 1.9 GB). This is not a "hard" limit, but a warning threshold. When this limit has been exceeded, the user gets a message warning them.

    - **Prohibit send at**—2,097,152 KB (2,048 MB or 2 GB). This is a "hard" limit. When a mailbox exceeds this threshold, the user will be unable to send mail. This does not impact the user's ability to receive mail, ensuring users do not miss any messages while scurrying to clean up their mailbox.

    - **Prohibit send and receive at**—2,411,520 KB (2,355 MB or approximately 2.3 GB). This is also a "hard" limit. When the mailbox exceeds this limit, the user can no longer send or receive messages. Incoming mail destined for this mailbox will be returned to the sender.

> **TIP**
>
> Many organizations choose to disable the Prohibit Send and Receive option, preferring to allow a mailbox to exceed the desired maximum size rather than return messages to the sender. This can enable some users, such as IMAP users, to bypass storage quotas completely if the IMAP user is configured to send mail through an alternate SMTP server. With this configuration, users can allow their mailboxes to grow as large as they want, without ever being impacted by the storage quotas.
>
> Organizations should *always* configure a Prohibit Send and Receive quota, even if the quota is double (or triple) the desired maximum mailbox size.

To view existing quotas on a particular database in the EMC, navigate to the Organization Configuration \ Mailbox node and select the Database Management tab. Select the desired database and select Properties from the action pane. Select the Limits tab to review the settings.

To view existing quotas on a particular database in the EMS, use the following command:

```
Get-MailboxDatabase "database name here" ¦ fl *quota*
```

As previously stated, individual mailboxes can be configured to override the default database quotas. This is accomplished using the Storage Quotas option in the Mailbox Settings tab of the mailbox properties. To do so, remove the checkmark from the Use Mailbox Database Defaults box and configure the customized limits.

Deleted item retention settings are also configured using the Storage Quotas tab.

▶ **Archive Quota**—Also new to Exchange Server 2010, a mailbox archive is a secondary mailbox that is configured by the administrator that "archives" user data onto potentially cheaper storage than that used by the primary mailbox. Archive quotas can be set to a different level than the primary mailbox. This option is only available for configuration if the mailbox has an archive mailbox enabled.

Mail Flow Settings

Also configurable from the Properties of a mailbox object, mail flow settings can be modified to enable for changes in delivery options, message size restrictions, and message delivery restrictions. Some specifics on the mail flow settings are as follows:

▶ **Delivery Options**—Utilizing this tab, administrators can enable other users to Send on Behalf of this user. Messages that are "sent on behalf" show the recipient both who the message was sent on behalf of AND who actually sent the message. Additional settings on the Delivery Options tab can allow the mailbox to forward messages to another mailbox in the organization, and the administrator can specify whether to Deliver Message to Both Forwarding Address and Mailbox. Finally, an option exists to specify the Maximum recipients the mailbox can send to at one time.

▶ **Message Size Restrictions**—Administrators can mandate the maximum message size that a user can send or receive, overwriting the settings configured at the organizational level. The Maximum send and receive sizes should generally be the same, or users could have a situation in which they can receive a message but cannot forward it (or reply with the original message attached). Likewise, if the Receive limits are lower than the Send limits, the user might send a message to a fellow employee but not receive a reply that includes the original message.

The default quotas set at the organizational level are

   ▶ Maximum receive size (KB)—10,240KB (10MB).

   ▶ Maximum send size (KB)—10,240KB (10MB).

   ▶ Maximum number of recipients—5,000.

There are several places in an Exchange Server environment in which message size limits can be applied:

▶ **Individual Mailbox Level**—Viewed in EMC from the message size restrictions or can be viewed in EMS with the following command:

```
Get-Mailbox "username" | fl *size*
```

▶ **Organizational Level**—Viewed in EMC by navigating to the Organization Configuration \ Hub Transport node and select the Global Settings tab. Select Transport Settings object and select Properties from the action pane. Select the General tab to review the settings. Can be viewed in EMS with the following command:

```
Get-TransportConfig | fl *size*
```

▶ **Send and Receive Connectors**—Can be viewed in the EMC by navigating to the Organization Configuration \ Hub Transport node and selecting Send Connectors, or by the Server Configuration \ Hub Transport node and selecting Receive Connectors. Can be viewed in EMS with the following commands:

```
Get-ReceiveConnector –id "receive connector name" | fl *size*
Get-SendConnector –id "receive connector name" | fl *size*
```

NOTE

Setting a higher message size limit on an Exchange Recipient bypasses the maximum message size settings at the organizational level. However, this is for internal messages only—messages sent outside of the organization are still subject to the organizational limits.

▶ **Message Delivery Restrictions**—With this feature, you can dictate whether an individual mailbox can receive messages from all senders or only specified senders, and whether those senders are required to be authenticated. Additionally, you can configure the mailbox to reject messages from particular senders.

Mailbox Features

Several property options for mailbox features enable for changes in settings for Outlook Web App (OWA), Exchange ActiveSync, unified messaging, and the Messaging Application Programming Interface (MAPI) communications protocol. Specific details on these mailbox feature properties are as follows:

▶ **Outlook Web App**—This tab is used to enable or disable access to the Exchange servers via Outlook Web App for the user. Additionally, there is a new property for the object that allows the administrator to specify that the account must use a particular Outlook Web App mailbox policy, if one has been created. By default, OWA access is enabled for all user mailboxes.

18

▶ **Exchange ActiveSync**—This feature can be enabled or disabled for an individual mailbox. If enabled, you have the option in the properties to apply an Exchange ActiveSync mailbox policy for the mailbox. By default, Exchange ActiveSync is enabled for all user mailboxes.

▶ **Unified Messaging**—You have the option to enable or disable unified messaging for the mailbox using this feature setting.

▶ **MAPI**—With this setting, you can dictate whether the user can access his mailbox from a MAPI-enabled client. You have the option to enable or disable MAPI access. By default, MAPI access is enabled for all user mailboxes.

▶ **POP3**—With this setting, you can dictate whether the user can access his mailbox with POP3, an application-layer Internet standard protocol used to retrieve email from a remote server. This option is enabled by default for all user mailboxes.

▶ **IMAP4**—With this setting, you can dictate whether the user can access his mailbox with Internet Message Access Protocol Version 4 Rev1 (IMAP4). IMAP4 is an application-layer Internet protocol that enables a local client to access email on a remote server. By default, IMAP4 access is enabled for all user mailboxes.

▶ **Archive**—By enabling the Archive option, administrators can require that items be automatically moved from the primary mailbox to the archive using the configured policy.

Calendar Settings

New to Exchange Server 2010, the Calendar Settings tab enables administrators to modify the way that automatic processing of calendar items by the Calendar Attendant is handled. The following options are available:

▶ **Enable the Calendar Attendant—Enabled by default**—This option enables or disables the Calendar Attendant, which decides whether any of the remaining features on the tab are available. If the Calendar Attendant is disabled, none of the following features can be enabled.

▶ **Remove meeting forward notifications to the Deleted Items folder—Disabled by default**—When selected, this option takes meeting forward notifications and deletes them when they have been processed by the Calendar Attendant.

▶ **Remove old meeting requests and responses—Enabled by default**—When selected, this option allows the Calendar Attendant to remove old and redundant updates and responses.

▶ **Mark new meeting requests as Tentative—Enabled by default**—If selected, new meeting requests are marked as tentative in the user's calendar. If not selected, pending requests are marked as free.

▶ **Process meeting requests and responses originating outside the Exchange Organization—Disabled by default**—If selected, the Calendar Attendant will process meeting requests that originate from outside of the Exchange Server organization.

Managing Email Addresses

When a new mail-enabled user is created in an Exchange Server 2010 environment, the creation of the primary SMTP address is controlled by a recipient policy. By default, the recipient policy creates a primary SMTP address that is formatted as Alias @ your default organization. For example, user John Doe in companyabc.com, with an alias of JDoe, would have the default SMTP address of JDoe@companyabc.com.

However, the default behavior of this recipient policy can easily be modified to create primary SMTP addresses that conform to your organization's standard. For example, if your organization uses FirstName.LastName@companyname.com as its standard SMTP address, you can configure the recipient policy to generate this address for you when the user mailbox is created. To do so, perform the following procedure:

1. Start the Exchange Management Console.
2. In the Console Tree, select Organization Configuration; then select Hub Transport.
3. In the results pane, select the E-Mail Address Policies tab, and then highlight the default policy.
4. In the action pane, click Edit.
5. On the Introduction page, when modifying the Default Policy, all the options are read-only and cannot be changed. If you create an additional policy, these settings can be modified. Click Next to continue.
6. On the Conditions page, when editing the default policy, the options are read-only. When creating a new policy, the policy can be specified to apply to recipients based on a particular State or Province, a specific department, or several other criteria. Click Next to continue.
7. On the E-Mail Addresses page, under SMTP, select the policy and click Edit.
8. By default, the E-Mail Address Local Part is set to Use alias. To modify the policy, click the E-Mail Address Local Part check box, and select the desired SMTP naming standard for your organization. For available options, see Figure 18.16. In the example, we are changing the policy to create email addressed in the format of First name.last name, so John Doe would get the default email address of John.Doe@companyabc.com. Select the desired entry, and then, either select the Select the Accepted Domain for the E-mail Address radio button and choose your domain by clicking the Browse button, or (simpler) ensure the radio button for Specify the Custom Fully Qualified Domain Name is selected and type the desired domain there. When ready, click OK to continue.

18

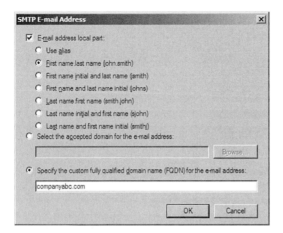

FIGURE 18.16   SMTP E-mail Address options.

9. You should now be back at the E-Mail Addresses page with the format for the desired custom address populated. In our example, this would be presented as %g.%s@companyabc.com (%g is the variable for Given Name and %s is the variable for Surname). Click Next to continue.

10. On the Schedule page, specify when the email address policy will be applied. Note that if you select a time and date in the future, the wizard remains open until the countdown has completed. Select the appropriate option, and click Next to continue.

11. On the Edit E-Mail Address Policy page, the Configuration Summary is shown. Review the policy to ensure all is correct, and then click Edit to continue.

12. On the Completion page, a summary is shown informing you how many items were modified, how many succeeded, and how many failed. Click Finish to continue.

After this policy has been applied, existing users will have a new SMTP e-mail address generated that conforms to the policy, and it will be set as their primary (reply-to) address. Previously assigned addresses remain in place as secondary addresses. Users created from this point on, however, have only the new address, and it is set as their primary SMTP address.

> **NOTE**
>
> If your existing email address policy was created in a legacy version of Exchange Server, it must be upgraded before you can edit it using the previous procedure. To upgrade your policy, you must use the Set-EmailAddressPolicy command from the Exchange Management Shell. The following example shows how this command can be used.
>
> From the Exchange Management Shell—for a policy named "Default Policy" that should apply to all users in the environment, the command would read:
>
> ```
> Set-EmailAddressPolicy "Default Policy" -IncludedRecipients allrecipients
> ```

After hitting Enter, the administrator will see the following:

```
To save changes on object "Default Policy", the object must be upgraded to the
current Exchange version. After the upgrade, this object cannot be managed by
an earlier version of Exchange Management Tools. Do you want to continue to
upgrade and save the object?
```

Select "Y" for "Yes" and hit Enter.

The policy can now be edited from within the Exchange 2010 Management Console.

Understanding Journaling

Journaling and archiving are two concepts that are often confused for one another. Both have to do with the retention of data, but the purpose behind the concepts is the defining factor.

Journaling is the process of recording all inbound and outbound email communications in an organization to meet email retention or archival strategy.

Archiving is the process of managing the size of an environment's data store by taking a backup copy of historical data, removing it from its native environment, and storing it elsewhere.

Each of these strategies can be used for meeting certain regulatory requirements, and journaling can often be used as a tool in an organization's archiving strategy.

The Benefits of Journaling

Over the past several years, there has been a significant increase in regulations requiring organizations to maintain records of communication—especially relating to the financial services, insurance, and health-care industries. Additionally, many companies have found that maintaining accurate and complete records of employee communications can assist them in the legal arena, whether they are defending against or initiating lawsuits.

For example, a disgruntled former employee might file a lawsuit against a company for wrongful termination, stating that he had never been notified that his behavior or performance was unsatisfactory. If the organization has an email journaling solution in place, they could go through the historical data and show specific examples where the behavior problems were discussed with the employee. More and more courts are accepting, and often insisting on, historical corporate messaging data to determine culpability.

Some of the more well-known U.S. regulations that, in recent years, have specified requirements that might rely on journaling technology follow:

▶ **Sarbanes-Oxley Act of 2002 (SOX)**—One of the most widely known regulatory acts, the Sarbanes-Oxley Act is a U.S. federal law that requires the preservation of records by certain Exchange Server members, brokers, and dealers. This act was passed into law in response to a number of major corporate and accounting scandals that resulted in a decline of public trust in corporate accounting and reporting practices.

▶ **Security Exchange Commission Rule 17a-4 (SEC Rule 17a-4)**—A U.S. Security and Exchange Rule that provides rules regarding the retention of electronic correspondence and records.

▶ **National Association of Securities Dealers 3010 & 3110 (NASD 3010 & 3110)**—The NASD details requirements for member firms that include the supervision of registered representatives, including inbound and outbound electronic correspondence with the public. In addition, the NASD details how long this information must be maintained and what conditions must be met.

▶ **Health Insurance Portability and Accountability Act of 1996**—More commonly known as HIPAA, this U.S. federal law provides rights and protections for participants and beneficiaries in group health plans.

▶ **Uniting and Strengthening America by Providing Appropriate Tools Required to Intercept and Obstruct Terrorism Act of 2001**—Better known as the Patriot Act, this U.S. federal law expands the authority of U.S. law enforcement for the stated purpose of fighting terrorist acts in the United States and abroad.

Additionally, there are regulations imposed outside of the U.S. that organizations with a worldwide presence might need to adhere to, such as the following:

▶ **The European Union Data Protection Directive (EUDPD)**–A directive that standardizes the protection of data privacy for citizens throughout the European Union (EU) by providing baseline requirements that all member states must adhere to.

▶ **Japan's Personal Information Protection Act**—A law created and enforced by the Japanese government to regulate the collection, use, and transfer of personal information. The Personal Information Protection Act applies to government or private entities that collect, handle, or use personal information of 5,000 or more individuals.

Using journaling technology is one way that companies can work toward meeting these (and other) regulatory requirements.

The Journaling Agent

In an Exchange Server 2010 environment, all email is processed by at least one Hub Transport server. This includes messages that are sent to or received from external organizations, mail sent from a mailbox on one server to a mailbox on another, or even mail sent between mailboxes located on the same server. All mail must pass through a Hub Transport server for delivery.

The *Journaling agent* is an agent that processes messages on Hub Transport (HT) servers that is focused on compliance.

In Exchange Server 2010, there are two journaling options:

▶ **Standard journaling**—Configured on a mailbox database. Standard journaling enables the Journaling agent (on the HT server) to journal all messages that are sent to or from any mailbox on that particular database. If an organization wants to journal all mail sent and received by all mailboxes in their environment, journaling must be configured on each mailbox database in the organization.

▶ **Premium journaling**—Enables the creation and implementation of journaling rules that enable the Journaling agent to be more specific about what is and isn't journaled. Rather than capturing all mail to all mailboxes in a database, journal rules can be configured to only journal specific mailboxes, or the mailboxes of all members in a distribution group. The implementation of premium journaling requires an Exchange Enterprise client access license (CAL).

Journal rules are comprised of three key components:

1. **The Journal Rule Scope**—Defines what messages are journaled by the Journaling agent.

2. **Journal Recipients**—The SMTP address of the recipient to be journaled

3. **Journaling Mailbox**—One or more mailboxes that are used for collecting journal reports.

Journal Rule Scope

When configuring a journal rule, the scope of the rule defines what type of messages will be journaled. You can choose from the following three scopes:

▶ **Internal**—When journaling entries are based on the Internal scope, messages that are sent and received by mailboxes within the Exchange Server organization are journaled.

▶ **External**—When journaling entries are based on the External scope, messages that are sent to recipients outside the Exchange Server organization, or that are received from senders outside of the Exchange Server organization, are journaled.

▶ **Global**—When journaling entries are based on the Global scope, all messages that pass through a server with the Hub Transport server role are journaled.

> **NOTE**
>
> When the Global scope is selected, the Hub Transport servers journal ALL messages that pass through. This includes messages that might or might not have been journaled already by rules in the Internal and External scopes.

Journal Recipients

In addition to the journaling scopes just discussed, specific SMTP addresses can be targeted for journaling. This can be helpful when your organization has specific individuals or positions that are subject to regulatory requirements that are more stringent than other personnel in your organization. In addition, this feature can be extremely useful when an individual is investigated for a legal proceeding and your organization wants to track his or her messages to be used as evidence.

Because every journaled message takes up storage space, customizing your journaling environment to match the actual needs of your organization, rather than simply turning it on for "everyone" can go a long way toward minimizing your costs.

All messages sent to or from the journaling recipients specified in a journaling rule are journaled. If a distribution group (rather than an individual user) is specified in the rule, all messages to and from members of the group are journaled. If a journal rule recipient is not specified, all messages sent to or from recipients that match the criteria of the journal rule scope are journaled.

For organizations that also utilize Unified Messaging to consolidate their voice mail and fax infrastructure into their email system, they must evaluate if they want to journal their voice mail and missed call notifications as well. Voice mail messages can be significant in size, and costly in terms of disk space, so if there is no specific requirement for your organization to save these messages, you might not want to do so. However, messages that contain faxes and that are generated by a Unified Messaging server are always journaled, even if you disable journaling of unified messaging voice mail and missed call notifications.

When you enable or disable the journaling of voice mail and missed call notification messages, your change is applied to all Hub Transport servers in your organization.

Journaling Mailboxes

All of these journaled messages must reside somewhere if they are ever to be utilized; a journaling mailbox is one that is used only for collecting journal reports. In Exchange Server, you have the flexibility to create a single journaling mailbox to store all journal reports, or you can create separate journaling mailboxes for each journal rule (or set of journal rules) that you configure. This flexibility even enables you to configure multiple journal rules to use one specific journaling mailbox and then configure other rules to each use their own specific one. How you configure your journaling mailboxes depends on your organization's policies and regulatory and legal requirements.

It is important to note that journaling mailboxes collect messages that are sent to and from recipients in your organization, and that these messages might contain sensitive information, might be used as part of legal proceedings, or might be used to meet regulatory requirements. Various laws are in place that mandate that these messages remain tamper-free if they are to be used by an investigatory authority. Administrators should work closely with the legal department in their organization (if one exists) to develop policies that specify who can access this data, and security measures to ensure these policies are enforced. Access to the journaling mailboxes should be limited to those with the "need to know" so to speak. When a journaling solution is put in place, it should be reviewed and certified by your legal representatives to make sure it complies with all the laws and regulations that govern your organization.

Journal Rule Replication

When a journal rule is created, modified, or deleted on a Hub Transport server, the change is replicated to all Active Directory servers in the organization. All Hub Transport servers in the organization get these new configuration changes from AD and apply the new or modified rules to messages that pass through them. Every time the Hub Transport server retrieves a new journal rule, an event is logged in the Security log of the Event Viewer.

By utilizing replication of journal rules throughout the organization, Exchange Server 2010 ensures a consistent set of rules are utilized throughout. All messages passing through the Exchange Server organization are subject to the same journaling rules.

> **NOTE**
>
> Journal rule replication relies on AD replication. Administrators should take link speeds and replication delays into consideration when implementing new or modified journal rules.

To reduce the number of requests that Hub Transport servers must make to AD, each one maintains a recipient cache that is used to look up recipient and distribution list information. This cache is updated every 4 hours, and the update interval cannot be modified. Changes to journal rule recipients might not be applied to journal rules until this cache is updated. To force an immediate update of the recipient cache, the Microsoft Exchange Transport service must be restarted on every Hub Transport server that you want to immediately update the cache.

Journal Reports

A journal report is the message that Exchange Server generates when a message is submitted to the journaling mailbox. Exchange Server 2010 supports envelope journaling only, which means that the original message matching the journal rule is included (unaltered) as an attachment to the journal report. The body of the journal report contains associated information such as the sender email address, message subject, message ID, and recipient address of the original message.

Creating a New Journal Rule

Unlike previous versions of Exchange Server, the Journaling agent is a built-in agent that is no longer visible in the Transport Agents tab in the EMC. It is also not included in the results when running the `Get-TranportAgent` cmdlet in the EMS. The Journaling agent is enabled by default in Exchange Server 2010, so administrators do not need to enable it before use.

To create a journal rule in the Exchange Management Console, follow these steps:

1. Open the Exchange Management Console on the Hub Transport server.
2. In the console tree, navigate to the Organization Configuration \ Hub Transport node.

18

3. In the results pane, select the Journal Rules tab, and then in the action pane, click New Journal Rule.

4. In the New Journal Rule dialog box, enter a name for your journaling rule.

5. In the Send Journal Reports to E-mail Address field, click Browse and select the recipient who will receive the journal reports.

6. Under Scope, select the scope to which the journal rule should be applied. See the previous section titled The Scope of a Journal Rule if you are unsure which scope to select.

7. If you want to target a specific recipient, select the option for Journal Messages for Recipient and click the Browse button. Select the desired recipient.

8. By default, the rule will be enabled upon completion. If you do not want the rule enabled, remove the check mark from the Enable Rule check box.

9. Click New to create the new journal rule, and then click Finish.

Understanding Archiving

As previously stated, *archiving* is the process of managing the size of an environment's data store by taking a backup copy of historical data, removing it from its native environment, and storing it elsewhere.

By integrating archiving directly into Exchange Server, Microsoft has enabled organizations to store this historical data without the complex administration and (often significant) additional licensing costs that can come with the integration of third-party applications.

The Benefits of Archiving

As users send and receive messages, maintaining older messages for historical purposes results in the mailbox (and the associated database) continuing to grow in size. Where users once could function with mailboxes that were measured in the tens (or at the most, hundreds) of megabytes, Exchange Server 2007 and Exchange Server 2010 provide users with a default mailbox size of 2 gigabytes, and it is not unusual for users to fill this space completely and require more.

With the growing need for larger and larger mailboxes comes a need to systematically archive historical data, freeing up space inside the user's mailbox to enhance performance, while retaining access to the historical data when it is needed.

Archiving can also help organizations better address compliance and legal electronic discovery requirements by allowing the historical data to be easily managed and searched.

Users with an archive enabled can perform searches on both the primary mailbox AND the archive mailbox at once—searching through all subfolders for the desired message.

Exchange Server 2010 now features new archiving capabilities that combine with additional enhanced mailbox management features that include the capability to perform advanced multi-mailbox searches and apply legal hold and granular retention polices for individual mailboxes.

Archiving in Exchange Server 2010 is composed of four main concepts:

▶ **Personal Archive**—A personal archive is an additional mailbox that is associated with a user's primary mailbox. It appears beneath the primary mailbox folders in Outlook Web App 2010 (similar to the way .pst archives were shown) and is labeled Online Archive – Username. This enables the user to have direct access to email within the archive just as they would their primary mailbox. Users can drag and drop PST files into the Personal Archive, for easier online access—and more efficient discovery by the organization. Mail items from the primary mailbox can also be offloaded to the Personal Archive automatically, using Retention Polices, reducing the size and improving the performance of the primary mailbox. With a personal archive, users can now have access to their archived mail without having to have local access to a .pst file and can access the archived mail from anywhere in the world using Outlook Web App.

▶ **Retention policies**—Retention policies are utilized to enable and enforce desired retention settings to specific items or folders in a mailbox. These policies are configured by the Exchange Administrator and are displayed inside each email, along with a header stating the applied policy and delete date. Utilizing retention policies makes it easy for a user to identify when an email is set for expiration—and the user has the ability to apply a new expiration policy if the email needs to be retained for a longer period. Administrators can set also a default policy that can move messages from the primary mailbox to the Archive automatically, removing the responsibility for maintaining the archive from the user.

▶ **Multi-Mailbox Search**—In Exchange Server 2010, the ability to search for mailbox items across multiple mailboxes, including email, attachments, calendar items, tasks, contacts, and IRM-protected files, is a welcome addition to those who specialize in eDiscovery. Multi-mailbox search searches both the primary and archive mailboxes for a user simultaneously and utilizes an easy-to-use control panel. Utilizing this feature, authorized personnel (such as HR representatives, legal, and compliance users) perform searches as needed, without the extremely time-consuming involvement of your already overworked IT staff. Mail that is located through a mailbox search can be copied and moved to a specified mailbox or external store for further investigation.

▶ **Legal Hold**—Placing a legal hold on a mailbox enables immediate preservation of a user's mailbox, including deleted and edited mailbox emails, appointments, tasks, and contacts. This hold is applied to both the primary mailbox and Personal Archive. A legal hold can be set on individual mailboxes or across the enterprise. Additionally, administrators have the option to automatically alert the users that a hold has been placed on their mailbox or not, as desired.

Enabling Archiving on a Mailbox

There are few things in the world that are simpler than enabling an archive for an Exchange Server 2010 mailbox. By navigating to the user mailbox (EMC \ Recipient Configuration \ Mailbox \ select mailbox), administrators can right-click on the mailbox and select Enable Archive.

The administrator is presented with a notification that informs them that an Exchange Enterprise client access license (CAL) is required to enable the online archive and asks if they want to proceed. Clicking Yes creates and enables the archive. The archive mailbox can be created only on the same mailbox database as the primary mailbox.

Administrators can, if they want, go into the mailbox properties and select the Mailbox Settings tab and double-click Archive Quota to place a quota on the archive. The quota is enabled by selecting the Issue Warning at (MB) check box and entering the quota size. This quota, placed on the Archive Mailbox, is completely separate from any quotas placed on the primary mailbox.

When a mailbox in Exchange Server 2010 has the archive enabled, the icon associated with the mailbox changes to a white circle with a blue "i" in the middle. An example of the new icon can be seen by looking at the mailboxes for users andrew and ken in Figure 18.15 earlier in this chapter.

Accessing the Mailbox Archive

Archived messages are of little use to the end user if they cannot access them. With an Exchange Server 2010 archive, the user can view the contents (and search through the contacts) while connected to the network with Outlook 2010 or Outlook Web App 2010. Earlier versions of Outlook and OWA (2003 and 2007) cannot access the archive mailbox.

As the archive mailbox node is stored on the Exchange server, it is not accessible by offline users, even those in cached mode.

Because messages that are auto-archived retain the same folder structure in the archive that they had in the primary mailbox, users with complex folder structures are unable to maintain them, and searches can be conducted that span both the primary and archive mailbox at the same time.

Using the Exchange Server 2010 Toolbox

The Exchange Management Console includes a Toolbox with several tools that can assist administrators with the identification and resolution of common Exchange Server problems. The Toolbox can be accessed from the Exchange Management Console in the Console Tree. Included in the Toolbox are a series of tools to assist with enhancing the Configuration, Performance, and Security of the environment.

The Toolbox is extensible, meaning that additional tools can be added to it from within the Toolbox by clicking the Open Tools Website. However, this toolbox is for Microsoft provided tools only; third-party tools cannot be added. Some of the utilities are locally installed applications, some are MMC 3.0 snap-ins, and some connect to the Internet to run remotely.

Another feature of several of the tools in the Toolbox is that each time the utility is launched, a connection is made to Microsoft to determine if the utility is up to date. If it is not, the latest version is downloaded and installed, ensuring that administrators always have access to the most current version of the utility. This feature is not available for all tools in the toolbox as of yet.

Following is a list of tools available and some information about the use of each.

Exchange Best Practices Analyzer

At Microsoft, when customers need urgent assistance with problems that affect their business and end users, they refer to the issue as a "critical situation" or CritSit. In 2003, the Microsoft Exchange Server Team noticed that more than 60% of these situations were caused by a configuration error in the environment.

From this discovery, the decision was made to design and implement a utility that would gather information about an organization's Exchange Server and AD implementation and compare what was found against Microsoft recommended best practices. And thus, with the release of Exchange Server 2007, the Exchange Best Practices Analyzer (ExBPA) was born.

By default, the ExBPA uses the credentials of the currently logged-on account, so the account that you are logged on with must have read access to AD and administrator access to each of the Exchange servers viewed. If it is necessary to run the ExBPA using different credentials, that can be configured in the Advanced Login options.

There are several tests that can be run against the Exchange Server and Active Directory environments. These tests are simple to configure and run, and the reports are easy to understand. Errors and warnings are presented, arranged by severity, with descriptions of each problem and its resolution. Additionally, there are often hyperlinks included that direct you to the latest information on the error from the Microsoft website. Reports can be saved for future viewing and trending.

Details Templates Editor

The details template editor enables for the management of Exchange Server Details Templates. Details Templates are client-side graphical user interface (GUI) presentations of object properties that are accessed through Microsoft Outlook.

When a user opens an address list in Outlook, the properties of each object are presented as defined by the details template for the Exchange Server organization.

The Details Template Editor can customize the following objects:

- Users

- Groups

- Public Folders

- Mailbox Agents

▶ Contacts

▶ Search Dialogs

Using the editor, administrators can customize field sizes, can add or remove fields and tabs, and rearrange the fields, and the layout of the templates can vary by language.

To restore a template to its original (default) configuration, select it from the list and click the Restore button in the action pane.

Public Folder Management Console

The Public Folder Management Console is an MMC 3.0 based interface that offers administrators a GUI to manage their public folder infrastructure. Administrators can use the console to create, configure, or maintain public folders.

The Public Folder Management Console displays the public folder hierarchy with two primary subtrees:

▶ **Default Public Folders**—Public folders that users can connect to directly using client applications such as Microsoft Outlook

▶ **System Public Folders**—Not accessible directly by users, the System Public Folders enable client applications to store information such as free/busy data, offline address books (OABs) and organizational forms. The system public folders container also stores configuration information that is used by Exchange Server itself.

The OAB and Schedule+ Free Busy information is important for environments with legacy (Outlook 2003 and before) client applications.

Remote Connectivity Analyzer

New to the toolbox in Exchange Server 2010 is the Remote Connectivity Analyzer (RCA). This web-based tool enables administrators to verify that Internet facing services such as Exchange ActiveSync, AutoDiscover, Outlook Anywhere, and inbound email are set up and configured properly.

Unlike the `test-ActivesyncConnectivity` and `test-OWAConnectivity` cmdlets in the Exchange Management Shell, which can only run from inside the network and only test internal connectivity, the Remote Connectivity Analyzer, as the name suggests, enables administrators to verify the connectivity to these features from outside the network.

The RCA provides the following tests:

▶ Microsoft Exchange ActiveSync Connectivity Tests

  ▶ Exchange ActiveSync with AutoDiscover

  ▶ Exchange ActiveSync

- ▶ Microsoft Exchange Web Services Connectivity Tests

    - ▶ ActiveSync Provider AutoDiscover

    - ▶ Outlook Provider AutoDiscover

- ▶ Microsoft Office Outlook Connectivity Tests

    - ▶ Outlook Anywhere with AutoDiscover

    - ▶ Outlook 2003 RCP/HTTP

- ▶ Internet Email Tests

    - ▶ Inbound SMTP Email Test

Role Based Access Control (RBAC) User Editor

Also new to the toolbox is the Role Based Access Control User Editor. With the change in Exchange Server 2010 from using access control lists (ACLs) to RBAC, administrators need to assign users to RBAC groups and roles. Although this can be done from the EMS, the cmdlets and parameters will all be new to administrators, so Microsoft has provided an Editing tool to assist administrators with this task.

The RBAC User Editor is a web-based interface that utilizes the new Exchange Control Panel. Clicking the icon opens a web browser, enabling the administrator to authenticate through OWA. When logged in, the administrator is taken to the Administrator Roles editor in which he can view the properties of existing role groups and add or remove members as needed.

Although much of the RBAC configuration still needs to be accomplished using the Exchange Management Shell, the ECP enables basic configuration changes to be made.

Mail Flow Troubleshooter

The Mail Flow Troubleshooter is a wizard-based application, similar in design to the Exchange Best Practices Analyzer, which provides easy access to various data sources that are necessary to troubleshoot common problems with mail flow such as messages backed up in mail queues, slow delivery of messages, or unexplained nondelivery reports.

The Mail Flow Troubleshooter enables the administrator to diagnose problems based on the symptoms observed. After selecting the observed symptom from a drop-down box, the utility gathers data and automatically diagnoses it—presenting a report that contains possible root causes. The utility also suggests corrective actions and guides administrators through the correct troubleshooting path.

18

Message Tracking

The message tracking utility has been around in one form or another since Exchange Server 5.5, but it has always been rather complicated to use. In Exchange Server 2010, the message tracking utility is now a web-based utility, utilizing the new Exchange Control Panel, and the interface couldn't be simpler.

> **NOTE**
>
> Before the Message Tracking tool can be run, administrators must configure their browser security—setting both "Run ActiveX Controls and Plug-Ins" and "Active Scripting" to Enable. Some administrators will not be comfortable negating these security measures on their Exchange server. Because this tool uses the Exchange Control Panel, administrators access the same interface directly from their workstation browser by logging into OWA, selecting Options, Organize E-Mail, Delivery Reports and selecting My Organization from the UI Scope Control option (labeled Select What to Manage).

Clicking the link opens a browser window, enabling the administrator to log in to the Exchange Control Panel and utilize the Delivery Reports feature. By selecting either My Organization or Another User from the drop-down box in the UI Scope Control (identified by the text stating Select What to Manage), administrators can search for delivery information about messages sent to or from a specific person in the past 2 weeks. Additionally, the administrator can narrow the search to messages with certain keywords in the subject field.

The Search Results lists all emails found that meet the search criteria and shows four columns: From, To, Subject, and Sent Time. Administrators can select a particular message and view the details of the message, including the number of recipients and the number that were delivered.

An example of the Delivery Report is shown in Figure 18.17.

Queue Viewer

The Exchange Queue Viewer is a Microsoft Management Console snap-in that is added to the Toolbox when an Exchange Server 2007 Hub Transport or Edge Transport server role is installed.

The Queue Viewer is a graphical interface that enables administrators to view information about mail queues and mail items on a transport server. In addition, administrators can perform management actions on these items.

Often used for troubleshooting mail flow and identifying spam messages, the viewer can also be used by administrators to easily perform intrusive actions against the queuing databases, such as suspending or resuming a queue or removing messages.

Using the Queue Viewer requires certain administrative permissions. To use Queue Viewer on a computer that has the Edge Transport server role, you must use an account that is a member of the local Administrators group on that computer. To use Queue Viewer on a

FIGURE 18.17   Sample Delivery Report.

computer that has the Hub Transport server role, the account you use must also be a domain account that is a member of the Server Management role.

By default, the Queue Viewer connects to the queuing database on the server on which the application is run. Administrators can use the tool to connect to any Hub Transport server in the organization and, by opening multiple instances of the utility and tiling the windows, administrators can easily monitor queues on several servers simultaneously.

To connect to a remote Hub Transport server, perform the following steps:

1. Open the Exchange Management Console.

2. In the Console Tree, click Toolbox.

3. In the results pane, click Queue Viewer.

4. In the action pane, click Connect to server.

5. In the Connect to server window, click Browse to view a list of the available Hub Transport servers.

6. In the Select Exchange Server window, select a Hub Transport server. To search for a Hub Transport server to connect to, use one of the following procedures:

   ▶ Enter the exact server name or the first few letters of the server name in the Search: field, and then click Find Now. Select a server from the results pane.

▶ Select the View menu, and then click Enable Column Filtering. In the Name column or Version column, click the filter icon, and then select the filter operator. Type the filter criteria in the Enter text here field. Press ENTER. Select a server from the results pane. If you want, you can select the check box stating Set as Default Server to ensure that the Queue Viewer focuses on this server whenever the application is launched.

7. Click OK to close the Select Exchange Server window.

8. In the Connect to server window, click Connect.

By viewing the Message Count in each of the queues, administrators can determine if mail is flowing through the queues. Using the F5 key or the Refresh button in the action pane refreshes the view.

Routing Log Viewer

As with the preceding Queue Viewer, the Routing Log Viewer is available in the toolbox of servers that have the Hub Transport or Edge Transport server role installed.

In previous versions of Exchange Server, administrators could connect to the Exchange Routing Engine service on port 691 using the WinRoute tool. However, as there is no Routing Engine in Exchange Server 2010, the Routing Log Viewer enables administrators to open a routing log file that contains information about how the routing topology appears to the server. Administrators can also open a second lot to determine what changes have occurred within the routing topology between the two time periods.

Tracking Log Explorer

The Message Tracking utility discussed earlier is, as stated, a simplified tool for confirming delivery of messages utilizing the ECP interface. However, with its simplicity comes a lack of detail that administrators occasionally need when tracking messages. The Tracking Log Explorer is the utility formerly known as the Message Tracking utility in Exchange Server 2007.

This utility enables administrators to search for messages and determine the actual path they took through the Exchange Server environment. This is accomplished by searching through the records of SMTP transport activity of all messages entering or leaving an Exchange Hub Transport, Edge Transport, or mailbox server.

By default, message tracking is enabled on all Exchange 2007 and Exchange 2010 Hub Transport, Edge Transport, and Mailbox servers. To confirm or modify the status of the message tracking log, administrators can use the following commands from the Exchange Management Shell:

To view the status of all transport servers in the organization:

```
Get-TransportServer
```

and look under the MessageTrackingLogEnabled column.

To view the status of a particular transport server:

```
Get-TransportServer "ServerName"
```

where "ServerName" is the name of the server.

To view the status of a particular mailbox server:

```
Get-MailboxServer "ServerName" ¦fl
```

and confirm "MessageTrackingLogEnabled" = "True"

To disable the message tracking log on a particular server:

```
Set-TransportServer "ServerName" -MessageTrackingLogEnabled $false
```

or

```
Set-MailboxServer "ServerName" -MessageTrackingLogEnabled $false
```

To enable the message tracking log on a particular server:

```
Set-TransportServer "ServerName" -MessageTrackingLogEnabled $true
```

or

```
Set-MailboxServer "ServerName" -MessageTrackingLogEnabled $true
```

The message tracking utility is intended primarily for mail flow analyses, reporting, and (of course) determining the status of a message that has been reported as undelivered.

Administrators can search for messages based on any combination of the following fields:

- ▶ Recipients
- ▶ Sender
- ▶ Server
- ▶ EventID
- ▶ MessageID
- ▶ InternalMessageID
- ▶ Subject
- ▶ Reference

In addition, the administrator can specify a Start and End date and time to search for the message. In organizations with large message stores, it can be extremely beneficial to narrow the scope of the search as much as possible because sorting through all messages in the environment to look for a particular one can take a significant amount of time.

18

At the bottom of the pane, the Exchange Management Shell command that will be utilized for the search displays.

Double-click the Tracking Log Explorer icon to launch the tool. A wizard walks you through the steps for tracking messages.

Exchange Server Performance Monitor

One of the most powerful, yet often overlooked, utilities available is the Exchange Server Performance Monitor, labeled simply as *Performance Monitor* in the toolbox. This tool is essentially the same as the Windows Performance Monitor, but it has a series of predefined counters that are related specifically to Exchange Server, including message traffic sent or received per second, Average Disk Queue Length, and several counters to monitor remote procedure calls (RPC) traffic. Of course, the old favorites are still there, including memory, processor, hard drive, and network utilization.

This utility is somewhat less intuitive than others in the toolbox because there is no built-in wizard to assist with its configuration, but a great deal of information can be gathered about your Exchange Server environment.

Virtually every measurable aspect of an Exchange server can be monitored using this tool. The data collected can be presented in a variety of forms, including reports, real-time charts, or logs. Using the Exchange Server Performance Monitor, administrators can take baseline readings on server and network performance and compare them over time to spot trends and plan accordingly, but it is most commonly used to view parameters while troubleshooting performance problems.

Double-click the Performance Monitor icon to launch the tool. It automatically starts displaying a live graph of the key performance indicators for the machine on which the tool is launched. More information on the usage of the tool can be found by clicking the Help icon within the utility and from the Microsoft website.

Performance Troubleshooter

With an interface that looks similar to the Exchange Mail Flow Troubleshooter and the ExBPA, the Performance Troubleshooter is designed to help administrators identify andlocate performance issues that have a negative impact on their Exchange Server environment.

Like the Mail Flow Troubleshooter, administrators begin by selecting the symptoms they are experiencing. Based on these systems, the utility identifies potential bottlenecks in the messaging system and outlines a troubleshooting path for the administrators to follow.

Double-click the Performance Troubleshooter icon to launch the utility, bringing up a wizard that walks you through the steps necessary to perform an analysis and view the results.

Exchange Server Coexistence

There is no way to upgrade an Exchange Server 2003 or 2007 server to Exchange Server 2010. The changes in the database structure alone are enough to preclude such a possibility.

However, that does not mean that there is no upgrade *path* for environments with legacy mailbox installations. The key to transitioning to Exchange Server 2010 lies in the concept of coexistence.

Exchange Server 2010 can be installed into an existing Exchange Server 2003/2007 messaging system. When Exchange Server 2010 has been introduced into the legacy environment, the organization is considered to be in a state of coexistence.

Table 18.2 lists the supported coexistence scenarios with earlier versions of Exchange Server.

TABLE 18.2   Supported Coexistence Scenarios

Exchange Server Version	Exchange Organization Coexistence
Exchange 2000 Server	Not Supported
Exchange Server 2003	Supported
Exchange Server 2007	Supported
Mixed Exchange Server 2003/2007	Supported

Before you can deploy Exchange Server 2010 in a legacy environment, the organization must be operating in native mode. If the organization is already running Exchange Server 2007, it is already in native mode. For Exchange Server 2003, you can go to native mode using the Exchange System Manager by performing the following steps:

1. Start Exchange System Manager. Click Start, point to Programs, point to Microsoft Exchange, and then click System Manager.
2. Right-click the organization and then click Properties.
3. Click the General tab, and then, under Change Operations Mode, click Change Mode. Click Yes if you are sure that you want to permanently switch the organization's mode to native mode.

Additionally, all Exchange 2007 servers in the existing environment must have Exchange Server 2007 Service Pack 2 installed before Exchange 2010 can be deployed. Attempts to deploy Exchange 2010 into an environment with even one Exchange 2007 server that is pre-SP2 will fail.

Once Exchange 2010 mailbox servers have been installed into the legacy Exchange Server organization, mailboxes can be moved from the old environment to the new. Once Exchange 2010 Client Access and Hub Transport servers have been deployed, email

18

address policies and Transport rules can be updated or recreated. Once all functionality provided by the legacy servers has been replicated in the new environment, the legacy boxes can be retired.

Server Administration

Exchange Server 2007, administrators were constantly reminded that to take advantage of the improvements in high-availability technology, there should only be one storage group per database. If having several databases in a storage group complicated high-availability scenarios and made single-database restores more complex, why bother having them at all?

Apparently Microsoft agreed: In Exchange Server 2010 the concept of the storage group is no more.

Databases are now considered to be "global objects" that are no longer tied specifically to particular mailbox servers. Where administrators used to go to the Server Configuration \ Mailbox node in the EMC to view and modify databases, they now must go to the Organization Configuration \ Mailbox node.

And where Exchange Server 2007 allowed up to 50 databases per server, Exchange Server 2010 now allows 150.

That's right—150 databases per server. This does not mean, however, that administrators should run out and create 150 new databases on each of their servers; rather, the intention is to enable organizations to take advantage of database availability groups, or DAGs. With a DAG, organizations can create up to 16 copies of a database and have them replicated across multiple servers. For more information on DAGs, refer to Chapter 31, "Database Availability Group Replication in Exchange Server 2010."

Creating a New Database

Creating a new mailbox database in Exchange Server 2010 is a straightforward process. Below are the steps to create a new database in the EMC.

1. Start the Exchange Management Console.

2. In the Console Tree, navigate to Organization Configuration, and select the Mailbox node.

3. In the action pane, click either New Mailbox Database or New Public Folder Database, depending on the type you want to create. This launches the New Database Wizard.

4. Enter the Mailbox database name. As there are no more storage groups to differentiate one database from another, each database name must be unique within the organization. Click the Browse button to select which server will house the new database and click Next to continue.

5. Enter the file location's Database and Log folder paths. Note that the option to Mount This database is selected by default. If you do not want the database to mount automatically upon creation, deselect this option. Click Next to continue.

6. Review the Configuration Summary and, if all is correct, click New to create the database.

7. Review the Completion page and ensure all steps were completed successfully. Click Finish when done.

To create a new database from the EMS, a sample command is shown here:

```
new-mailboxdatabase -Server 'E2010-1' -Name 'Mailbox Database 2' -EdbFilePath
➥C:\Program Files\Microsoft\Exchange Server\V14\Mailbox\Mailbox Database 2\
➥Mailbox Database 2.edb' -LogFolderPath 'C:\Program Files\Microsoft\
➥Exchange Server\V14\Mailbox\Mailbox Database 2'
```

To mount the newly created database, use

```
mount-database -Identity 'Mailbox Database 2'
```

To dismount the database, use

```
dismount-database -Identity 'Mailbox Database 2'
```

Setting Limits on Databases

After you create a database, you can customize the maximum storage limits and deletion settings for mailboxes stored on that database. Although some organizations consider placing limits of any kind on mailboxes to be draconian, most understand that preventing users from storing unlimited amounts of archaic data and enforcing the regular automatic purging of deleted items helps to ensure a healthy and happy messaging system that benefits the entire organization.

By default, these settings apply to all user mailboxes stored on that database. However, specific limits on individual mailboxes can be configured to override these database-wide settings. This can be useful when you want to set a limit for all users on a particular database, but you have one user who needs more (or less) restrictive settings. To configure these options, perform the following tasks:

1. Start the Exchange Management Console.

2. In the Console Tree, navigate to the Organization Configuration and select the Mailbox node.

3. In the results pane, select the database you want to configure.

4. In the action pane, click Properties to open the database properties sheet. Note: There are two properties options in the action pane. One for the database, co-located with Dismount Database and Move Database Path, enables you to configure the properties of the object. The other is associated with the database copy and offers general information about the database copy such as the server status, latest available log time, and other information. For our purposes, we select the former. Alternatively, you can simply locate the database you want to modify and double-click it in the results pane.

5. Select the Limits tab.

18

6. Several limits are available to configure for the database. You can configure any of the following settings on the database:

- **Storage Limits**—The storage limits section enables you to configure restrictions on all mailboxes located within that database. The available storage limits options are as follows:

  - **Issue warning at**—1,991,680KB (1,945MB or approximately 1.9GB). This is not a "hard" limit, but a warning threshold. When this limit has been exceeded, the user will get a message warning them.

  - **Prohibit send at**—2,097,152 KB (2,048 MB or 2 GB). This is a "hard" limit. When a mailbox exceeds this threshold, the user is unable to send mail. This does not impact the user's ability to receive mail, ensuring the user does not miss any messages while scurrying to clean up their mailbox.

  - **Prohibit send and receive at**—2,411,520 KB (2,355MB or approximately 2.3GB). This is also a "hard" limit. When the mailbox exceeds this limit, the user can no longer send or receive messages. Incoming mail destined for this mailbox will be returned to the sender.

- **Warning Message Interval**—By default, storage limit warning messages are sent daily at 1:00 a.m. This selection can be customized to perform the warning at a different time of the day, or even to send multiple messages at various times of the day. Click Customize to change the default setting.

- **Deletion Settings**—The deletion settings dictate how deleted items and mailboxes in the database will be dealt with. The available deletion settings options are as follows:

  - **Keep Deleted Items for (Days)**—By default, mailbox databases are configured to keep deleted items for 14 days.

NOTE

There is often some user confusion as to what messages can be recovered using the Tools, Recover Deleted Items option in Outlook. There are two types of deletion: Hard (or physical) deletion and Soft (or logical) deletion. When users delete an item, it goes to their Deleted Items folder and can be recovered simply by dragging and dropping it back into their Inbox. If users go to the Deleted Items folder, and again delete the message, or if they select Tools, Empty Deleted Items Folder, the item has been soft deleted and can be recovered using the Tools, Recover Deleted Items option. This recovery can be accomplished if it is initiated within the window set in the Keep Deleted Items for (Days) section field. However, if a user enters the Recover Deleted Items utility and selects to purge a message, or if the Keep Deleted Items for (Days) period has expired, the item is hard deleted and cannot be recovered without resorting to backup/restore methods.

- **Keep Deleted Mailboxes for (Days)**—In Exchange Server 2010, as it was in Exchange Server 2007, deleting a mailbox does not mean that it is permanently purged from the database immediately. The mailbox is flagged for deletion and can no longer be accessed by users. After the mailbox retention period controlled by this setting has been reached, the mailbox is then purged from the system. This option is extremely useful if a user deletion occurs that is the result of a mistake and enables the administrator to re-create the user object and reconnect the deleted mailbox. By default, this setting is set to 30 days. It can be configured anywhere from 0 (immediate purge upon deletion) to 24,855 days. It is unlikely you will ever need the upper limit (equivalent to a little more than 68 years), but this setting can be adjusted to meet your organization's needs. Unless disk space becomes an issue, it is recommended that you do not disable the deleted mailbox retention feature.

- **Don't permanently delete items until the database has been backed up**—This final setting is not enabled by default. By checking this option, you instruct Exchange Server to not delete items or mailboxes, even after the retention period has expired, until the database has been successfully backed up. By selecting this option, you ensure that you can recover critical items or mailboxes from backup tape, even after the purge has been completed.

Summary

The Microsoft Exchange Server platform has grown over the years, becoming more and more powerful to meet the growing needs of organizations and their desire for a reliable and feature laden messaging system.

The administrative tools available for managing the environment have improved with every revision, and things that would have been impossible a few revisions ago can now be done quickly and easily.

With the introduction of the Role Based Access Control (RBAC) security model and the Exchange Control Panel (ECP), end-users can now participate in the administration of the environment, albeit to a limited degree.

Changes in the way that databases are managed, the release of PowerShell v2 and the concept of Remote PowerShell administration, the retirement of storage groups, the creation of the new Exchange Management Shell Command Log, new toolbox utilities— Exchange Server just keeps getting better and better.

Whether dealing with users and mailboxes, distribution groups, or monitoring and analyzing the environment for performance bottlenecks, Exchange Server 2010 has tools and utilities that give administrators more control over their Exchange Server environments than ever before.

18

Best Practices

The following are best practices from this chapter:

▶ Review the Finalize Deployment and End-to-End Scenario Guides tabs in the Exchange Management Console carefully. The tasks and documentation there might prove to be invaluable when verifying your Exchange Server 2010 implementation.

▶ For scripting routine or repetitive tasks, consider performing the task once in the Exchange Management Console and, when possible, copy the associated Exchange Management Shell command that is automatically generated by the wizard. This can give you a starting point for creating your scripts.

▶ Restrict access to large distribution groups to those who truly need it. Leave the default setting requiring that all senders are authenticated in place whenever possible.

▶ Use dynamic distribution lists with caution if they will be frequently used. The list is re-created every time it is accessed, requiring both server and domain resources to determine the membership.

▶ Implement storage limits on user mailboxes. Use the Issue Warning option to warn the users and the Prohibit Send option to enforce the limits

▶ Implement the Prohibit Send and Receive option, even if you must configure it with a size that is three or more times your expected maximum mailbox size. Leaving mailboxes "open ended" can be dangerous.

▶ Do not use circular logging. Circular logging was sometimes necessary in older versions of Exchange Server because log files could quickly grow to a size that would fill up the Exchange server hard drives. With today's technology, and with hard drive space relatively inexpensive, there are rarely situations where circular logging is needed.

▶ Stagger database maintenance so that all storage groups are not attempting to run maintenance at the same time.

▶ Keep deleted items for at least 14 days, and deleted mailboxes for at least 30 days. Use the option to not remove the items permanently until the store has been backed up.

▶ Use the Exchange Best Practices Analyzer tool whenever you install a new Exchange server, upgrade an existing server, or make configuration changes to your environment.

▶ Periodically, run the Exchange Best Practices Analyzer tool against your Exchange Server environment, simply to look for anything out of place.

▶ Regularly launch the tools in the Exchange Management Console Toolbox, allowing them to check for updates from the Microsoft website. Whenever the Exchange Best Practices Analyzer is updated, run it against your Exchange Server environment to check if there are any new/updated recommendations that you can implement that will improve performance and reliability for your organization.

CHAPTER 19

Exchange Server 2010 Management and Maintenance Practices

Organizations have become increasingly reliant on email as a primary method of communication and, as such, the messaging system in most environments has come to be considered a mission-critical application. Any messaging downtime results in frustrated calls to the help desk. For most organizations, gone are the days where the email system can be taken offline during business hours for configuration changes.

To ensure the dependability and reliability of any application, proper maintenance and upkeep is vital, and Exchange Server 2010 is no exception. By implementing and performing proper management and maintenance procedures, administrators can minimize downtime and keep the system well tuned.

Exchange Server 2010 has advanced the health of the messaging system through the introduction of continuous online defragmentation, compaction, and contiguity maintenance. This has eliminated the need for routine offline database maintenance, which dramatically reduces the need for planned downtime.

This chapter focuses on recommended best practices for an administrator to properly maintain an Exchange Server 2010 messaging environment.

Proper Care and Feeding of Exchange Server 2010

This section is not about how to perform common, albeit necessary, management tasks such as using the interface to add a database. Instead, it focuses on concepts such as identifying and working with the server's functional roles in the network environment, auditing network activity and usage, and monitoring the health and performance of your messaging system.

With each new iteration of Exchange Server, Microsoft has greatly improved the tools and utilities used to manage the environment. Exchange Server 2010 is no exception. Exchange Server 2010 management can be done locally or remotely. The administration can even be done through firewalls. There are primary management interfaces, the Exchange Management Console, the Exchange Control Panel, and the Remote Exchange Management Shell, and new tools and utilities to assist administrators in the upkeep of their environment. The remote capabilities of these tools have been greatly enhanced, as discussed in Chapter 21, "Remote Administration of Exchange Server 2010 Servers."

Managing by Server Roles and Responsibilities

Key in Exchange Server 2010 is the concept of role-based deployment, allowing administrators to deploy specific server roles to meet the requirements of their environment. Exchange Server 2010 provides five distinct server roles: Edge Transport, Hub Transport, Client Access, Mailbox, and Unified Messaging.

The Edge Transport Server Role

The Edge Transport server role is responsible for all email entering or leaving the Exchange Server organization. To provide redundancy and load balancing, multiple Edge Transport servers can be configured for an organization.

The Edge Transport role is designed to be installed on a standalone server that resides in the perimeter network. As such, it is the only Exchange server designed to NOT be a member of the Active Directory (AD) domain. Synchronization with Active Directory is provided through the use of Active Directory Application Mode (ADAM) and a component called EdgeSync.

Edge Transport servers can provide antispam and antivirus protection, as well as the enforcement of Edge Transport rules based on Simple Mail Transfer Protocol (SMTP) and Multipurpose Internet Mail Extensions (MIME) addresses, particular words in the subject or message body, and a Spam Confidence Level (SCL) rating. In addition, Edge Transport servers can provide address rewriting—an administrator can modify the SMTP address on incoming and outgoing messages.

It is possible for an organization to avoid the use of an Edge Transport server completely and simply configure a Hub Transport server to communicate directly with the Internet. However, this scenario is not recommended because it exposes your Hub Transport server to potential attack. The Edge Transport server has a reduced attack surface to protect against these external threats.

The Hub Transport Server Role

The Hub Transport role is responsible for managing internal mail flow in an Exchange Server organization and is installed on a member server in the AD domain.

The Hub Transport role handles all mail flow within the organization, as well as applying transport rules, journaling policies, and delivery of messages to recipient mailboxes. In addition, Hub Transport agents can be deployed to enforce corporate messaging policies such as message retention and the implementation of email disclaimers.

Hub Transport servers accept inbound mail from the Edge Transport server(s) and route them to user mailboxes. Outbound mail is relayed from the Hub Transport server to the Edge Transport server and out to the Internet.

The Hub Transport role can be installed on the same hardware with any other nonclustered internal server role or as a dedicated Hub Transport server. It cannot be installed on the same hardware as an Edge Transport server role.

Each AD site that contains a Mailbox server role must contain at least one Hub Transport server role.

The Client Access Server Role

The Client Access Server (CAS) role is similar to the front-end server in Exchange Server 2000/2003. New to Exchange Server 2010 is that all clients communicate through the CAS. This is different than in Exchange Server 2007, where Outlook clients using MAPI would access the mailbox servers directly. Now the CAS mediates all client traffic, providing a single point of communication that can be monitored to ensure consistent compliance and security across all types of clients.

The Mailbox Server Role

The Mailbox role will be the most familiar to administrators with previous Exchange Server experience. As the name implies, the mailbox role is responsible for housing mailbox databases which, in turn, contain user mailboxes. The Mailbox server role also houses public folder databases if they are implemented in the environment.

The Mailbox server role integrates with the directory in the Active Directory service much more effectively than previous versions of Exchange Server allowed, making deployment and day-to-day operational tasks much easier to complete. The Mailbox server role also provides users with improved calendaring functionality, resource management, and Offline Address Book downloads.

The Unified Messaging Server Role

The Unified Messaging server role is responsible for the integration of Office Communication Server Voice over IP (VoIP) technology into the Exchange Server messaging system. When implementing Unified Messaging with Exchange Server 2010, users can have access to voice, fax, and email messages all in the same mailbox, and these messages can be accessed through multiple client interfaces.

Managing by User Roles

Exchange Server 2010 introduces role-based access control (RBAC) to the Exchange Server platform. This new permissions model applies to the Mailbox, Hub Transport, Unified Messaging, and Client Access Server roles. RBAC has replaced the permission model used in Exchange Server 2007. RBAC is not used on the Edge Transport role because the Edge Transport security is not integrated with the other roles and is based on the Local Administrators group.

The new role-based model enables administrators to easily assign staff to one of the predefined roles or to create a custom role that meets the organizations unique requirements. The RBAC permissions model is used by Exchange Management Console (EMC), the Exchange Management Shell (EMS), and the Exchange Control Panel (ECP).

There are eleven predefined administrative roles:

- Delegated Setup
- Discovery Management
- Help Desk
- Hygiene Management
- Organization Management
- Public Folder Management

- Recipient Management
- Records Management
- Server Management
- UM Management
- View-Only Organization Management

There are seven predefined user roles to allow user self administration. This allows users to self-update things such as their phone number, address, and mailbox settings through the web interface. The predefined users roles are as follows:

- My Distribution Groups
- My Distribution Group Membership
- My Profile Information
- My Contact Information

- My Base Options (Use PowerShell to set)
- My Text Messaging (Use PowerShell to set)
- My Voice Mail (Use PowerShell to set)

The administrative and user predefined roles cannot be changed. However, new roles can be created to define precise or broad roles and assignments based on the tasks that need to be performed in a given organization. This is done through the RBAC User Editor.

Maintenance Tools for Exchange Server 2010

Several new and improved tools are available to administer and manage an Exchange Server 2010 environment. There are Microsoft Management Console snap-ins, an automation and scripting shell, and several tools native to the Windows Server 2008 operating system and the Exchange Server 2010 application. There is also the new Exchange Control Panel web tool, which provides a cool role-based access control (RBAC) administration.

The Exchange Management Console

The Exchange Management Console (EMC) shown in Figure 19.1 is one of the primary tools provided with Exchange Server 2010. This utility replaces the Exchange System Manager (ESM) from Exchange Server 2000/2003 and can be used to manage Exchange Server 2010, Exchange 2007, and Exchange Server 2003 servers in the organization.

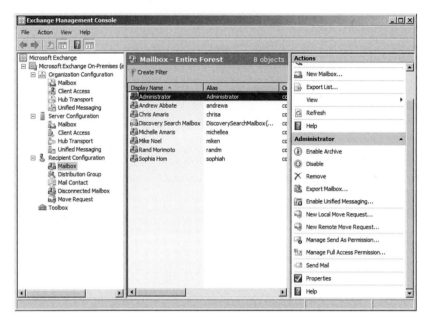

FIGURE 19.1   Exchange Server 2010 Exchange Management Console.

Improvements to the console in Exchange Server 2010 include the following:

▶ Built on Remote PowerShell with remote server administration

▶ Role-based access control (RBAC)

▶ Multiple forest support

▶ Cross-premises Exchange Server 2010 management including mailbox moves between organizations

▶ Recipient bulk edit

▶ PowerShell command logging

▶ New feature support such as High Availability

19

The Exchange Management Console is a Microsoft Management Console 3.0 snap-in. Prerequisites for the Exchange Management Console include the following:

▶ A 64-bit operating system

▶ Microsoft .NET Framework 3.5 Service Pack 1

▶ Windows Remote Management

▶ PowerShell v2

All of Exchange Server 2010 is 64-bit only, so all administration using the management tools is 64 bit. The management console also requires a 64-bit OS. Supported OS platforms for the Exchange Management Console include the following:

▶ Vista x64 SP1/2

▶ W2k8 x64 SP2

▶ W2k8 R2 x64

▶ Windows7 x64

Unlike the Exchange System Manager, which allowed administrators to access all configuration settings of their Exchange Server 2003 environment, the Exchange Management Console is designed to allow administrators access to common configuration settings from the familiar graphical user interface (GUI). However, many aspects of the environment cannot be viewed or modified with this utility. For such configuration settings, the command line Exchange Management Shell, which is discussed next, must be used.

For more in-depth information on using the Exchange Management Console, refer to Chapter 18, "Administering an Exchange Server 2010 Environment."

The Remote Exchange Management Shell

The second utility for managing an Exchange Server 2010 environment is an automation and scripting tool called the Exchange Management Shell (EMS), shown in Figure 19.2. This shell is a command-line management interface that can be used to administer servers in an Exchange Server 2010 organization. It enables administration of the Exchange Server 2010 environment without the Exchange management tools such as the EMC, albeit via a command-line interface. Built on Microsoft Windows PowerShell v2 technology, the Exchange Management Shell can perform any task that can be accomplished in the Exchange Management Console, and a lot more. In fact, many configuration settings in an Exchange Server 2010 environment can only be accomplished using the Exchange Management Shell.

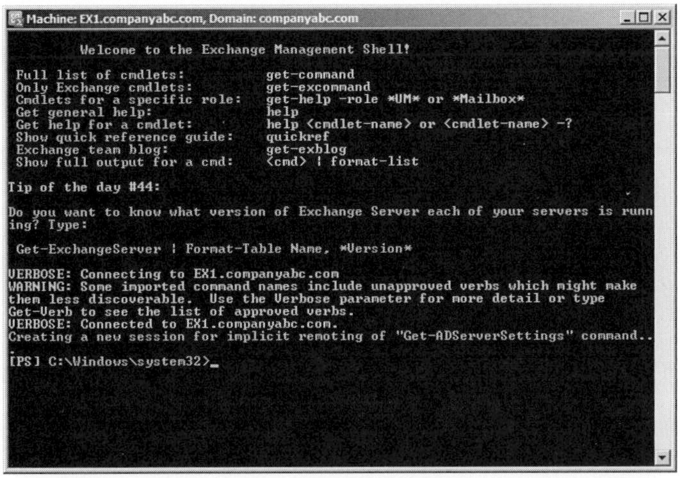

FIGURE 19.2   Exchange Server 2010 Remote Exchange Management Shell.

New to Exchange Server 2010 is the ability to access all the familiar Exchange Server cmdlets remotely, leveraging the PowerShell v2 remote capabilities. This enables cmdlets and scripts to run across multiple servers in a single EMS instance. It also enables administrators to run the shell from their workstation and connect remotely to the Exchange Server 2010 servers. Given the limitation of the Exchange Management Console to run only on 64-bit systems, the EMS also enables 32-bit clients to connect to the servers.

The EMS does not require Exchange Server binaries to be installed on the client, making deployment much easier.

Supported client OS platforms for the Exchange Management Shell are as follows:

▶ Vista (32-bit or 64-bit)

▶ W2k8 (32-bit or 64-bit)

▶ W2k8 R2 (86-bit or 64-bit)

▶ Win7 (32-bit or 64-bit)

▶ W2k3 (32-bit or 64-bit)

▶ XP (32-bit or 64-bit)

For more in-depth information on using the Exchange Management Shell, refer to Chapter 9, "Using Windows PowerShell in an Exchange Server 2010 Environment."

19

The Exchange Control Panel

The Exchange Control Panel (ECP) is an exciting new tool in Exchange Server 2010. The ECP is a browser-based Management client for end users, administrators, and specialists. This provides a new way to administer a subset of Exchange Server features and is completely RBAC-integrated.

This new ECP web utility provides a great self-provisioning portal for administrators and a simplified user experience for common management tasks. It is accessible directly via URL and Outlook Web App (OWA). Figure 19.3 shows the start page of the interface from an administrator role.

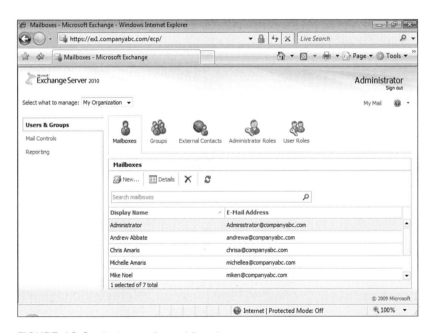

FIGURE 19.3   Exchange Control Panel.

The ECP is AJAX-based, deployed as a part of the Client Access Server role, and shares some code with OWA. However, the two are separate applications and sites.

The Exchange Control Panel can be used in a variety of scenarios. Administrators can delegate to permissions in role to support a variety of administrators, specialists, and users. These include the following types of scenarios:

▶ Administrators

▶ Helpdesk specialists

- Auditors

- End users

- Customers in a hosted environment

The scenarios are configured in the RBAC interface, which is based in the Exchange Control Panel.

Administrators would launch the ECP tool directly from the ECP link (https://<server-name>/ecp) where <servername> is an Exchange 2010 CAS. End users would access the ECP tool from within OWA, which launches from the Options link. Although it launches from the OWA web page (https://<servername>/owa), the link is to the ECP web page (https://<servername>/ecp). The security is completely integrated, enabling the end-user experience to be completely seamless.

The browser support for the ECP is the same as for OWA premium. Supported browsers are as follows:

- Internet Explorer (IE)

- Firefox

- Safari

The Exchange Control Panel is covered in detail in Chapter 18.

Exchange Best Practices Analyzer

The Exchange Best Practices Analyzer (ExBPA) is included in Exchange Server 2010 and can be found in the Exchange Management Console toolbox.

The ExBPA can be used to run health checks on an Exchange Server environment, and can also run performance checks, permissions checks, and connectivity tests to assist when troubleshooting problems.

The ExBPA should be run whenever a new server is added to an Exchange Server 2010 environment, or whenever configuration changes are made. More information on this utility can be found in Chapter 18.

Remote Connectivity Analyzer

The Remote Connectivity Analyzer is new to Exchange Server 2010 and allows administrators to test services from outside their organization. The tool essentially launches a browser to the website https://www.testexchangeconnetivity.com/, shown in Figure 19.4. The website is maintained by Microsoft and is not technically a component of Exchange Server 2010, although the console has a link to it.

19

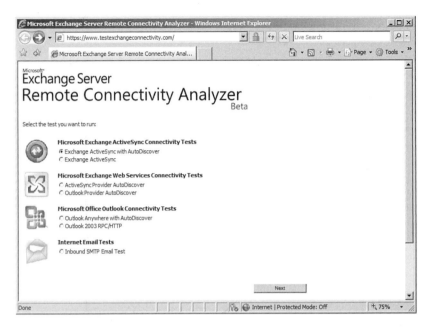

FIGURE 19.4   Remote Connectivity Analyzer website.

The tests that can be launched from the site include the following:

- ▶ Microsoft Exchange ActiveSync Connectivity Tests

- ▶ Microsoft Exchange Web Services Connectivity Tests

- ▶ Microsoft Office Outlook Connectivity Tests

- ▶ Internet Email Tests

This site performs a valuable service by testing actual client access from a third party (that is, Microsoft). This simulates a client and exposes configuration or connectivity problems. For example, the Internet Email Tests use SMTP to send email to a user, verifying the MX record, name resolution, SMTP, and if the gateway is an open relay. Another example is ActiveSync Provider AutoDiscover, which tests the notoriously difficult to test ActiveSync autodiscover services. As shown in Figure 19.5, the site prompts for email address, domain credentials, and verification. On clicking Perform Test, the site tests ActiveSync autodiscover and presents the results.

The tool does require domain credentials to test the various services, so security measures are built into the product. The site uses the HTTPS protocol, so the confidentiality of the transmissions are protected by SSL encryption. The site prompts human verification, reading, and entering distorted text to ensure that the system is not hijacked by bots. And the site has a privacy statement indicating that the information collected is not retained after the tool is used. All that said, it is recommended that dummy test accounts and credentials be used to execute the tests. And that those accounts be disabled or deleted following the tests.

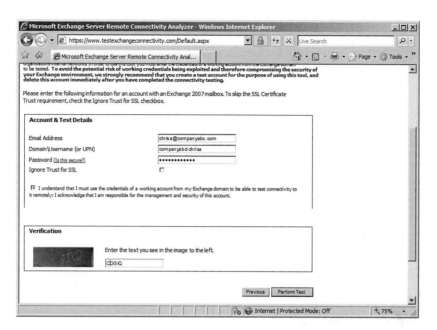

FIGURE 19.5   Remote Connectivity Analyzer ActiveSync Autodiscover Test setup.

Disaster Recovery Tools

Also included in the Exchange Management Console toolbox are two utilities designed to analyze and maintain Exchange Server databases. The Database Troubleshooter can inspect existing databases and available transaction logs and report on any problems found. The tool also offers recommended steps that should be taken to ensure the database is healthy.

The Database Recovery Management utility is intended to assist administrators when a database is unable to mount. This tool also generates recommended step-by-step instructions to follow to bring the database back online.

Mail Flow Tools

The Mail Flow Troubleshooter is a utility that assists with troubleshooting common mail flow issues in an Exchange Server environment. Administrators can input the issues they are encountering, and the utility gathers information, diagnoses the environment, and presents a recommended plan of action.

The Tracking Log Explorer utility allows administrators to search for messages and track them through the Exchange Server environment. Message tracking can be extremely useful for determining where a message was delayed or "stuck" in the messaging environment.

The Message Tracking launches a browser into the Exchange Control Panel message tracking section, enabling an administrator to search the mail store for messages that meet a certain criteria.

The Mail Flow Troubleshooter, the Tracking Log Explorer, and the Message Tracking utility are all included in the Exchange Server 2010 Exchange Management Console toolbox. For more information on these three utilities, refer to Chapter 18. For information on configuring message tracking logs, refer to the "Message Tracking" section later in this chapter.

Exchange Queue Viewer

The Exchange Queue Viewer is another utility included in the Exchange Management Console toolbox that is added to an Exchange server when the Hub Transport or Edge Transport role is installed. The Exchange Queue Viewer is used to view the contents of the queues for each particular protocol on a server. Although this tool is more of a troubleshooting tool, it is important to periodically check protocol queues (for example, SMTP or X.400 queues) to ensure that no delivery problems exist.

Performance Tools

The Exchange Management Console toolbox includes two tools that are designed to monitor and troubleshoot performance issues in an Exchange Server environment.

The Exchange Server Performance Monitor is based on the Windows Performance Monitor, but includes a series of predefined counters that are specifically related to an Exchange Server environment.

The Performance Troubleshooter is designed to help administrators identify and locate performance issues that are impacting the Exchange Server environment.

More information on these tools can be found in Chapter 18.

Windows Server 2008 Backup

Windows Server 2008 includes a Windows Server Backup feature that allows the native VSS backup of a local Exchange Server 2010 server and files. The Windows Server Backup is added via the Add Features Wizard or command-line. Support for a local Exchange Server backup was absent from Windows Server 2008 until Exchange Server 2007 Service Pack 2 and now Exchange Server 2010.

The Windows Server Backup in Windows Server 2008 provides an important low-cost backup tool for small organizations or branch office scenarios in which a local backup is an important part of the organization's recovery strategy.

Third-party software vendors, such as EMC Legato and Symantec, produce Exchange Server backup and restore agents for the purpose of Exchange database backup and recovery.

For more detailed information on Exchange Server 2010 backup and recovery, refer to Chapter 31, "Database Availability Group Replication in Exchange Server 2010," Chapter 32, "Backing Up the Exchange Server 2010 Environment," and Chapter 33, "Recovering from a Disaster in an Exchange Server 2010 Environment," respectively.

Active Directory Database Maintenance Using ntdsutil

Exchange Server 2010 uses Windows Server 2003 or 2008 AD to store all its directory information. As a result, it is important to keep AD as healthy as possible to ensure that Exchange Server 2010 remains reliable and stable.

Windows Server 2003 and Windows Server 2008 automatically perform maintenance on Active Directory by cleaning up the AD database on a daily basis. The process occurs on domain controllers approximately every 12 hours. One example of the results of this process is the removal of tombstones, which are the "markers" for previously deleted objects. In addition, the process deletes unnecessary log files and reclaims free space.

The automatic daily process does not, however, perform all maintenance necessary for a clean and healthy database. For example, the maintenance process does not compress and defragment the Active Directory database. To perform this function, the `ntdsutil` command-line utility is needed.

> **CAUTION**
>
> To avoid possible adverse affects with the AD database, run `ntdsutil` in Directory Service Restore mode. Reboot the server, press the F8 key, and then select this mode of operation.

To use `ntdsutil` to defragment the Windows Server 2008 AD database, perform the following steps:

1. Restart the domain controller.
2. When the initial screen appears, press the F8 key.
3. From the Windows Advanced Options menu, select Directory Services Restore Mode.
4. Select the Windows Server 2008 operating system being used.
5. Log on to the Windows Server 2008 system.
6. Click OK when the informational message appears.
7. At a command prompt, create a directory where the utility can store the defragmented file. For example, `C:\NTDS`.
8. At a command prompt, type `ntdsutil` files, and then press Enter.
9. At the file maintenance prompt, type `compact to <TargetDirectory>`, where `<TargetDirectory>` identifies the empty directory created in step 7. For example:

    ```
    compact to c:\ntds
    ```

    This invokes the `esentutl.exe` utility to compact the existing database and write the results to the specified directory.
10. If compaction was successful, copy the new `ntds.dit` file to `%systemroot%\NTDS`, and delete the old log files located in that directory.
11. Type `quit` twice to exit the utility.
12. Restart the domain controller.

This typically needs to be done only following a large migration or reorganization of the Active Directory forest, rather than on a routine basis.

19

Integrity Checking with the `isinteg` Utility

The Information Store Integrity Checker (`isinteg.exe`) is a command-based utility that finds and eliminates errors from mailbox and public folder databases at the application level. Although this tool is not intended for use as a part of routine Information Store maintenance, it is mentioned here because it can assist in disaster recovery situations.

`isinteg` is most often used in conjunction with the `eseutil` repair operation, and can recover data that the `eseutil` tool cannot. The `isinteg` tool repairs the contents of the mailbox and public folder databases (messages, links, and attachments), whereas the `eseutil` tool repairs the mailbox and public folder databases (database files, tables, and indexes).

> **CAUTION**
>
> Using this utility in any mode other than Test mode results in irreversible changes to the database.
>
> It is best to restore a copy of a suspected corrupt database in a lab environment, and then run `isinteg` against that copy prior to any attempts to use it in a production environment.

Dismount the Exchange Server databases on which you plan to perform maintenance and stop the Microsoft Exchange Information Store service prior to running this utility. Keep in mind that this makes the databases unavailable to users until after the maintenance has been completed.

Database table integrity problems are caused by corruption, which can occur if the server is shut down improperly, if the drive or controller fails, and so forth.

To view the command-line help about usage of the `isinteg` utility, type the following command from a command prompt: `isinteg /?`

For more information on using `isinteg`, refer to Chapter 33.

Database Maintenance with the `eseutil` Utility

The `eseutil` utility is a database-level utility that is not application-specific. It can, for example, be used to maintain, test, and repair both AD and Exchange Server databases. More specifically, `eseutil` is used to maintain database-level integrity, perform defragmentation and compaction, and repair even the most severely corrupt databases. It is also the utility to use when maintaining Exchange Server 2010 transaction log files to determine which transaction logs need to be replayed or which log file the `Edb.chk` file points to.

> **CAUTION**
>
> Using the `eseutil` utility on an AD or Exchange Server database can produce irreversible changes.

As with the `isinteg` utility, it is best to restore a copy of a suspected corrupt database in a lab environment, and then run `eseutil` against that copy prior to any attempts to use it in a production environment.

NOTE

`eseutil` investigates the data that resides in the database table for any corruption or errors, which is why it is called a database-level utility. The `eseutil` options are shown in Table 19.1.

TABLE 19.1   `eseutil` Syntax

Mode of Operation	Syntax
Defragmentation	ESEUTIL /d <database name> [options]
Recovery	ESEUTIL /r <logfile base name> [options]
Integrity	ESEUTIL /g <database name> [options]
Checksum	ESEUTIL /k <filename> [options]
Repair	ESEUTIL /p <database name> [options]
File dump	ESEUTIL /m[mode-modifier] <filename>
Copy file	ESEUTIL /y <source file> [options]
Restore	ESEUTIL /c[mode-modifier] <pathname> [options]

The `eseutil` tool repairs the mailbox and public folder databases (database files, tables, and indexes), whereas the `isinteg` tool repairs the contents of the mailbox and public folder databases (messages, links, and attachments).

For more information on using `eseutil`, refer to Chapter 33.

Auditing the Environment

Various methods of auditing the Exchange Server environment exist to gather and store records of network and Exchange Server access and to assist with the monitoring and tracking of SMTP connections and message routing.

Typically used for identifying security breaches or suspicious activity, auditing has the added benefit of allowing administrators to gain insight into how the Exchange Server 2010 systems are accessed and, in some cases, how they are performing.

This chapter focuses on three types of auditing:

▶ **Audit logging**—For security and tracking user access

▶ **SMTP logging**—For capturing SMTP conversations between messaging servers

▶ **Message tracking**—For tracking emails through the messaging environment

Audit Logging

In a Windows environment, auditing is primarily considered to be an identity and access control security technology that can be implemented as part of an organization's network security strategy. By collecting and monitoring security-related events, administrators can track user authentication and authorization, as well as access to various directory services (including Exchange Server 2010 services).

Exchange Server 2010 relies on the audit policies of the underlying operating system for capturing information on user access and authorization. Administrators can utilize the built-in Windows Server event auditing to capture data that is written to the security log for review.

Enabling Event Auditing

Audit policies are the basis for auditing events on Windows Server 2003 and Windows Server 2008 systems. Administrators must be aware that, depending on the policies configured, auditing might require a substantial amount of server resources in addition to those supporting the primary function of the server. On servers without adequate memory, processing power or hard drive space, auditing can potentially result in decreased server performance. After enabling auditing, administrators should monitor server performance to ensure the server can handle the additional load.

To enable audit policies on a Windows Server 2008 server, perform the following steps:

1. On the server to be audited, log on as a member of the local Administrators group.

2. Select Start, Administrative Tools, and launch the Local Security Policy snap-in.

3. Expand Local Policies and select Audit Policy.

4. In the right pane, double-click the policy to be modified.

5. Select to audit Success, Failure, or both.

6. Click OK to exit the configuration screen, and then close the Local Security Policy tool.

Figure 19.6 shows an example of typical auditing policies that might be configured for an Exchange server.

These audit policies can be turned on manually by following the preceding procedure, configuring a group policy, or by the implementation of security templates.

> **NOTE**
>
> After enabling audit policies, Windows event logs (specifically the security log) will capture a significant amount of data. Be sure to increase the "maximum log size" in the security log properties page. A best practice is to make the log size large enough to contain at least a week's worth of data, and configure it to overwrite as necessary so that newer data is not sacrificed at the expense of older data.

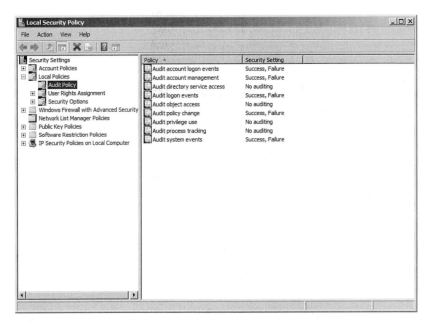

FIGURE 19.6   Windows Server 2008 audit policy setting example.

Viewing the Security Logs

The events generated by the Windows Server 2003 and Windows Server 2008 auditing policies can be viewed in the security log in the Event Viewer.

Understanding the information presented in the security log events can be a challenge. The event often contains error codes, with no explanation on their meaning. Microsoft has taken strides to make this easier by providing a link to the Microsoft Help and Support Center within the event.

When an administrator clicks on the link, the Event Viewer asks for permission to send information about the event to Microsoft. Administrators can select the option to always send information if they want, and can then click Yes to authorize the sending of the data. A connection is made to the Help and Support Center, and information about the Event ID is displayed. This information can be invaluable when trying to decipher the sometimes cryptic events in the security log.

Administrators can use the Filter feature (from the View menu) to filter the events based on various fields. In addition, when searching for a specific event within a specific time frame, administrators can select a specific window of time to filter on.

For an extensive list of security event IDs and their meaning in Windows Server 2008, go to http://support.microsoft.com/kb/947226.

The information supplied here on viewing security log Event IDs is intended to help administrators get a basic understanding of the topic. There is much more that can be learned on the subject of security auditing and event monitoring, and the Microsoft website is an excellent resource for doing so.

19

SMTP Logging

Logging SMTP protocol activity provides administrators with a powerful tool when troubleshooting issues with message delivery. By enabling SMTP logging, administrators can capture the SMTP conversations with email servers during message transport. Each Receive and Send Connector in an Exchange Server 2010 environment has the capability of logging SMTP activity, providing information regarding messaging commands that a user sends to the Exchange Server 2010 server. This includes, but is not limited to, such information as IP address, bytes sent, data, time, protocol, and domain name.

To enable SMTP protocol logging, administrators must enable the feature on each Send and Receive Connector on each 2010 Exchange server where logging is desired. By default, SMTP logging is disabled on all Send and Receive Connectors.

Configure SMTP Logging from the Exchange Management Console

The configuration of SMTP protocol logging utilizing the Exchange Management Console is limited to enabling or disabling the feature. To enable or disable SMTP protocol logging from the Exchange Management Console, perform the following tasks:

1. Start the Exchange Management Console.

2. Locate the Send or Receive Connector on which you want to enable logging.

   ▶ **For Hub Transport Send Connectors**—In the console tree, select Organization Configuration, then Hub Transport. In the results pane, click the Send Connectors tab, and then select the appropriate Send Connector.

   ▶ **For Hub Transport Receive Connectors**—In the console tree, select Server Configuration, then Hub Transport. Select the appropriate server in the results pane, and then select the appropriate connector in the bottom half of the results pane.

   ▶ **For Edge Transport Connectors**—On the Edge Transport server, select Edge Transport in the console tree. Select the appropriate server in the results pane, and then select the Receive Connectors or Send Connectors tab in the bottom half of the results pane. Select the desired connector from those displayed.

3. After you have selected the appropriate connector, select Properties from the action pane.

4. On the General tab, configure the desired protocol logging level. By default, all connectors are set to None. The only other option is Verbose.

Changing the Protocol Log Path

Exchange Server 2010 allows administrators to specify the location of the Send and Receive log files. The log files for all Send Connectors on a particular server are in one location, and the log files for all Receive Connectors are in another.

By default, these files are located in the following locations:

   ▶ **Receive log**—`C:\Program Files\Microsoft\Exchange Server\V14\TransportRoles\Logs\ProtocolLog\SmtpReceive`

▶ **Send log**—`C:\Program Files\Microsoft\Exchange Server\V14\TransportRoles\Logs\ProtocolLog\SmtpSend`

To change the default location for these log files, use the following commands in the Exchange Management Shell.

Change log file location for the Receive Connectors:

```
Set-TransportServer <Identity> -ReceiveProtocolLogPath <LogPath>
```

Change log file location for the Send Connectors:

```
Set-TransportServer <Identity> -SendProtocolLogPath <LogPath>
```

Sample command: To set the Receive SMTP protocol log path for all Receive Connectors on Server1 to `C:\SMTP Receive Logs`, use the following command:

```
Set-TransportServer Server1 -ReceiveProtocolLogPath "C:\SMTP Receive Logs"
```

Configuring Log File and Log Directory Maximum Size

To prevent log files from growing so large that they deplete all available disk space, Exchange Server 2010 allows administrators to configure maximum log file and directory sizes. This configuration setting is a per-server setting and, by default, the maximum directory size is 250MB, whereas the maximum log file size is 10MB. When the maximum file size is reached, Exchange Server opens a new log file. When the maximum directory size is reached, Exchange Server overwrites the log files, starting with the oldest logs first.

To configure SMTP protocol log directory and file sizes, use the following commands in the Exchange Management Shell. Be aware, these commands must be performed for each server that you want to modify. The `<DirectorySize>` and `<FileSize>` arguments should be entered as a number followed by one of the following:

▶ B (bytes)

▶ KB (kilobytes)

▶ MB (megabytes)

▶ GB (gigabytes)

▶ TB (terabytes)

Change maximum size for Receive SMTP protocol log directory:

```
Set-TransportServer <Identity> -ReceiveProtocolMaxDirectorySize <DirectorySize>
```

Change maximum size for Send SMTP protocol log directory:

```
Set-TransportServer <Identity> -SendProtocolMaxDirectorySize <DirectorySize>
```

Change maximum size for Receive SMTP protocol log files:

```
Set-TransportServer <Identity> -ReceiveProtocolMaxFileSize <FileSize>
```

Change maximum size for Send SMTP protocol log files:

```
Set-TransportServer <Identity> -SendProtocolMaxFileSize <FileSize>
```

Sample command: To set the maximum size for the Receive SMTP protocol log directory on Server1 to 1 Gigabyte, use the following command:

```
Set-TransportServer Server1 –ReceiveProtocolMaxDirectorySize 1GB
```

Configuring the Maximum Age for the SMTP Protocol Log

In addition to having the ability to configure the maximum file and directory sizes for SMTP protocol logs, administrators can also configure a maximum age for each SMTP protocol log file. The default age for all log files is set to 30 days, and any log files that exceed this age are deleted by Exchange Server.

To change the maximum age of SMTP protocol log files, use the following commands in the Exchange Management Shell. The <Age> argument is entered in the following format: DD.HH:MM:SS, for Days, Hours, Minutes, Seconds.

Change maximum age for the Receive SMTP protocol log file:

```
Set-TransportServer <Identity> -ReceiveProtocolLogMaxAge <Age>
```

Change maximum age for the Send SMTP protocol log file:

```
Set-TransportServer <Identity> -SendProtocolLogMaxAge <Age>
```

Sample command: To set the maximum age of the Send SMTP protocol log file on Server1 to 60 days, use the following command:

```
Set-TransportServer Server1 –SendProtocolLogMaxAge 60.00:00:00
```

Message Tracking

Of the auditing techniques available in Exchange Server, message tracking is by far the least resource-intensive and will likely be the most commonly used by administrators. Because this feature has proven to be so valuable in previous versions of Exchange Server, Microsoft has enabled it by default in Exchange Server 2010. Previously, message tracking was disabled by default, and had to be enabled on a server-by-server basis.

Administrators can use message tracking logs for message forensics, reporting, and troubleshooting, as well as analyzing mail flow in an organization.

Message tracking records the SMTP transport activity of all messages sent to or from any Exchange Server 2010 Hub Transport, Edge Transport, or mailbox server.

To perform these procedures on a computer with the Hub Transport or mailbox server role installed, administrators must be logged on using an account that is a member of the Exchange Administrators group. The account must also be a member of the local

Administrators group on that computer. For a computer with the Edge Transport server role installed, administrators must be logged on using an account that is a member of the local Administrators group on that computer.

Enabling or Disabling Message Tracking

As previously stated, by default, message tracking is enabled on all Exchange Server 2010 computers that deal with message transport. This includes Hub Transport, Edge Transport, and mailbox servers. Message tracking can prove to be extremely useful, and administrators should avoid disabling the feature unless there are overwhelming reasons.

To set or review the message tracking on a Hub Transport server, use the following procedure:

1. Open the Exchange Management Console.
2. Expand the Server Configuration folder and select the Hub Transport folder.
3. In the right pane, right-click on the Exchange server to configure and select Properties.
4. Select the Log Settings tab to access the Message tracking log settings.

The message tracking can also be set via command-line. All commands must be run from the Exchange Management Shell. As in other shell commands, the <Identity> argument is replaced by the server name. To enable the feature, use the $true argument, and to disable it use $false.

To enable or disable message tracking on a Hub Transport or Edge Transport server:

```
Set-TransportServer <Identity> -MessageTrackingLogEnabled:<$true or $false>
```

To enable or disable message tracking on a mailbox server:

```
Set-MailboxServer <Identity> -MessageTrackingLogEnabled:<$true or $false>
```

Sample command: To disable message tracking on a mailbox server named Server1, use the following command:

```
Set-MailboxServer Server1 –MessageTrackingLogEnabled:$false
```

> **NOTE**
>
> If a server has both the Mailbox server role and the Hub Transport server role installed, you can use either the Set-MailboxServer or Set-TransportServer cmdlet.

Changing the Location of Message Tracking Logs

Exchange Server 2010 allows administrators to specify the location of the message tracking logs. The new location becomes effective immediately upon the completion of the command; however, any existing log files are not copied to the new directory—they will remain in the old directory.

By default, these files are located in the `C:\Program Files\Microsoft\Exchange Server\V14\TransportRoles\Logs\MessageTracking` directory.

When creating a new directory, the following permissions are required:

- **Administrator**—Full Control
- **System**—Full Control
- **Network Service**—Read, Write, and Delete Subfolders and Files

The location can be set on the properties of the Hub Transport or Edge Transport server in the Exchange Management Console using the procedure previously described. To change the default location for these log files via command-line, use the following commands in the Exchange Management Shell.

Change message tracking log file location for a Hub Transport server or an Edge Transport server:

```
Set-TransportServer <Identity> -MessageTrackingLogPath <LocalFilePath>
```

Change message tracking log file location for a mailbox server:

```
Set-MailboxServer <Identity> -MessageTrackingLogPath <LocalFilePath>
```

Sample command: To change the location of the message tracking log to `D:\Message Tracking` on an Exchange Server 2010 Hub Transport server named Server1, use the following command:

```
Set-TransportServer Server1 –MessageTrackingLogPath "D:\Message Tracking"
```

Configuring Message Tracking Log File and Log Directory Maximum Size

To prevent log files from growing so large that they deplete all available disk space, Exchange Server 2010 allows administrators to configure maximum log file and directory sizes. This configuration setting is a per-server setting and, by default, the maximum directory size is 250MB, whereas the maximum log file size is 10MB. When the maximum file size is reached, Exchange Server opens a new log file. When the maximum directory size is reached, Exchange Server overwrites the log files, starting with the oldest logs first.

To configure message tracking log directory and file sizes, use the following commands in the Exchange Management Shell. This cannot be done with the Exchange Management Console. Be aware that these commands must be performed for each server you want to modify. The `<DirectorySize>` and `<FileSize>` arguments should be entered as a number followed by one of the following:

- B (bytes)
- KB (kilobytes)
- MB (megabytes)
- GB (gigabytes)
- TB (terabytes)

Change maximum size for message tracking log directory on a Hub Transport or Edge Transport server:

```
Set-TransportServer <Identity> -MessageTrackingLogMaxDirectorySize <DirectorySize>
```

Change maximum size for message tracking log directory on a mailbox server:

```
Set-MailboxServer <Identity> -MessageTrackingLogMaxDirectorySize <DirectorySize>
```

Change maximum size for individual message tracking log files on a Hub Transport or Edge Transport server:

```
Set-TransportServer <Identity> -MessageTrackingLogMaxFileSize <FileSize>
```

Change maximum size for individual message tracking log files on a mailbox server:

```
Set-MailboxServer <Identity> -MessageTrackingLogMaxFileSize <FileSize>
```

Sample command: To set the maximum size for the message tracking log directory on a Hub Transport server named Server1 to 500MB, use the following command:

```
Set-TransportServer Server1 –MessageTrackingLogMaxDirectorySize 500MB
```

Configuring the Maximum Age for the Message Tracking Logs

In addition to having the ability to configure the maximum file and directory sizes for message tracking logs, administrators can also configure a maximum age for each message tracking log file. The default age is set to 30 days, and any log files that exceed this age are deleted by Exchange Server.

To change the maximum age of message tracking log files, use the following commands in the Exchange Management Shell. This cannot be done with the Exchange Management Console. The <Age> argument is entered in the following format: DD.HH:MM:SS, for Days, Hours, Minutes, Seconds.

Change maximum age for the message tracking log files on a Hub Transport or Edge Transport server:

```
Set-TransportServer <Identity> -MessageTrackingLogMaxAge <Age>
```

Change maximum age for the message tracking log files on a mailbox server:

```
Set-MailboxServer <Identity> -MessageTrackingLogMaxAge <Age>
```

Sample command: To set the maximum age of the message tracking log files on an Exchange Server 2010 mailbox server named Server1 to 45 days, use the following command:

```
Set-MailboxServer Server1 –MessageTrackingLogMaxAge 45.00:00:00
```

19

Best Practices for Performing Database Maintenance

The Exchange Server storage system is a database and requires routine maintenance to perform efficiently and prevent failures. In the old days, this required routine maintenance and planned downtime. Exchange Server 2010 does away with all that by fully automating the routine maintenance tasks of defragmentation and compaction. Exchange Server 2010 has advanced the health of the messaging system through the introduction of the following:

▶ Continuous online database defragmentation

▶ Continuous online database compaction

▶ Continuous online database contiguity maintenance

This has eliminated the need for routine offline database maintenance, which dramatically reduces the need for planned downtime.

As messaging environments have evolved from "nice to have" to "business critical," database maintenance has evolved from "should be done" to "must be done." Any database that is not regularly maintained will suffer from some level of corruption and, if left unchecked, might fail. Hence, the automatic daily maintenance that Exchange Server 2010 performs is invaluable to maintaining a healthy messaging environment.

However, there are other potential causes of database corruption. These include the following:

▶ Improper shutting down of the system, including unexpected power outages

▶ A poorly maintained disk subsystem

▶ Hardware failures

▶ Failure to use or review systems or operational management tools

▶ Manual modification of Exchange Server databases

▶ Deletion of Exchange Server transaction logs

Sometime, administrators still need to perform manual maintenance using the `isinteg` and `eseutil` tools.

Automatic Database Maintenance

Exchange Server 2010 automatically performs database maintenance procedures on a nightly basis during the scheduled maintenance window. Exchange Server 2010 performs two distinct activities: Online Maintenance (OLM) and Online Defragmentation (OLD). OLM starts by default at 1:00 a.m. every day, whereas OLD is continuous.

NOTE

This is different than in Exchange Server 2007, in which OLD ran during the OLM process. This led to a fragmented database during operations with the attendant drop in performance.

The following tasks are automatically performed by these processes (OLM and OLD):

1. **Cleanup (deleted items/mailboxes)**—Cleanup also happens during OLM. Cleanup is performed at run time when hard deletes occur.

2. **Space Compaction**—Database is compacted and space reclaimed at run time. Auto-throttled to avoid performance impact on end users.

3. **Maintain Contiguity**—Database is analyzed for contiguity and space at run time and is defragmented in the background. Auto-throttled to avoid performance impact on end users. The contiguity maintenance is new to Exchange Server 2010 and improves performance significantly.

4. **Database Checksum**—There are two options for the database checksum tasks: either run the background 24x7 (the default) or run during the OLM window. In both cases, the task runs against both Active and Passive copies of the database.

By default, the OLM maintenance schedule is set to run daily from 1:00 a.m. to 5:00 a.m. Because the maintenance cycle can be extremely resource intensive, this default schedule is intended to perform the maintenance during periods when most of an organization's mail users are not connected. However, organizations should also take their Exchange Server backup schedules into consideration.

The OLD task runs continuously but is auto-throttled to prevent impact to the end user.

Taken together, the new automatic maintenance regime is much more effective at keeping the database healthy and performing. In particular, the contiguity maintenance of Exchange Server 2010 reduces the I/O of the database immensely.

Configuring Database Maintenance Schedules

Administrators can stagger the maintenance schedules for different databases. For example, database 1 might have the maintenance cycle performed from 1:00 a.m. to 2:00 a.m., and the next store from 2:00 a.m. to 3:00 a.m., and so on. To view or change the default maintenance schedule on a database, perform the following steps:

1. Open the Exchange Management Console.

2. In the console tree, expand Organization Configuration and select Mailbox.

3. Select the Database Management tab and then select the appropriate database.

4. In the action pane, click Properties.

5. On the Maintenance tab, locate the Maintenance Schedule.

6. To change the default schedule, select one of the options from the drop-down box, or click Customize to create your own schedule.

Prioritizing and Scheduling Maintenance Best Practices

Exchange Server 2010 is a very efficient messaging system. However, as mailboxes and public folders are used, there is always the possibility of the logical corruption of data contained within the databases. It is important to implement a maintenance plan and schedule to minimize the impact that database corruption will have on the overall messaging system.

This section focuses on tasks that should be performed regularly—on a daily, weekly, monthly, and quarterly schedule. Besides ensuring optimum health for an organization, following these best practices will have the additional benefit of ensuring that administrators are well informed about the status of their messaging environment.

> **TIP**
>
> Administrators should thoroughly document the Exchange Server 2010 messaging environment configuration and keep it up to date. In addition, a change log should be implemented that is used to document changes and maintenance procedures for the environment. This change log should be meticulously maintained.

Daily Maintenance

Daily maintenance routines require the most frequent attention of an Exchange Server administrator. However, these tasks should not take a significant amount of time to perform.

Verify the Online Backup

One of the key differences between disaster and disaster recovery is the ability for an organization to resort to backups of their environment if the need arises. Considering the potential impact to an environment if the data backed up is not recoverable, it is amazing to see how often backup processes are ignored. Many organizations implement a "set it and forget it" attitude, often relying on nontechnical administrative personnel to simply "swap tapes" on a daily basis.

Whatever method is used to back up an Exchange Server environment, daily confirmation of the success of the task should be mandatory. Although the actual verification process will vary based on the backup solution being utilized, the general concept remains the same. Review the backup program's log file to determine whether the backup has successfully completed. If there are errors reported or the backup job set does not complete successfully, identify the cause of the error and take the appropriate action to resolve the problem.

Some best practices to keep in mind when backing up an Exchange Server environment are as follows:

▶ Include System State data to protect against system failure.

▶ Keep note of how long the backup process is taking to complete. This time should match any service level agreements that might be in place.

▶ Determine the start and finish times of the backup process. Attempt to configure the environment so that the backup process completes before the nightly maintenance schedule begins.

▶ Verify that transaction logs are successfully truncated upon completion of the backup.

Check Free Disk Space

All volumes that Exchange Server 2010 resides on (Exchange Server system files, databases, transaction logs, and so forth) should be checked on a daily basis to ensure that ample free space is available. If the volume or partition runs out of disk space, no more information can be written to the disk, which causes Exchange Server to stop the Exchange Server services. This can also result in lost data and the corruption of messaging databases.

Although it is possible to perform this process manually, it is easily overlooked when "hot" issues arise. As a best practice, administrators can utilize System Center Operations Manager 2007 (OpsMgr) or a third-party product to alert administrators if free space dips below a certain threshold.

For organizations without the resources to implement such products, the process can be accomplished utilizing scripting technologies, with an email or network alert being generated when the free space falls below the designated threshold.

Review Message Queues

Message queues should be checked daily to ensure that the mail flow in the organization is not experiencing difficulties. The Queue Viewer in the Exchange Management Console toolbox can be accomplished for this task.

If messages are found stuck in the queue, administrators can utilize the Message Tracking and Mail Flow Troubleshooter to determine the cause.

Check Event Viewer Logs

On Exchange Server 2010 servers, the application log within the Event Viewer should be reviewed daily for any Warning or Error level messages. Although some error messages might lead directly to a problem on the server, some might be symptomatic of other issues in the environment. Either way, it is best to evaluate and resolve these errors as soon as possible.

Filtering for these event types can assist with determining if any have occurred within the last 24 hours.

Alternatively, if a systems or operational management solution (such as System Center Operations Manager 2007) is utilized, this process can be automated, with email or network notifications sent as soon as the error is generated.

Weekly Maintenance

Tasks that do not require daily administrative input, but that still require frequent attention, are categorized as weekly maintenance routines. Recommended weekly maintenance routines are described in the following sections.

19

Document Database File Sizes

In an environment without mailbox storage limitations, the size of the mailbox databases can quickly become overwhelmingly large. If the volume housing the databases is not large enough to accommodate the database growth beyond a certain capacity, services can stop, databases can get corrupted, performance can get sluggish, or the system can halt.

Even with mailbox size limitations implemented, administrators should be aware of and document the size of databases so that they can determine the estimated growth rate.

By documenting the size of all mailbox databases on a weekly basis, administrators can have a more thorough understanding of the system usage and capacity requirements in their environment.

Verify Public Folders Replication

Many environments rely on public folders to share information, and the public folder configurations can vary widely from environment to environment.

With environments that replicate public folder information among different Exchange Server servers, administrators should inspect the replication to ensure all folders are kept up to date.

There are several ways to perform quick tests to determine if a public folder is replicating properly. Among these are manual testing and reviewing the `Ex00yymmdd.log` and `Ex01yymmdd.log` files. If problems exist, administrators can use these logs to troubleshoot.

Verify Online Maintenance Tasks

Exchange Server 2010 records information in the application log about scheduled online maintenance processes. Check this event log to verify that all the online maintenance tasks are being performed and that no problems are occurring.

Using the filtering capabilities of the Event Viewer (View, Filter), administrators can apply a filter to search for specific events, and can specify a date (and time) range to search for these events. For example, it is easy to filter the events to view all events with an ID of 1206 that have occurred in the past week.

Alternatively, in the right pane of the Event Viewer, click on the Event column to sort events by their ID number; however, this view is more challenging to read because you must then verify the dates of the events as well.

The following Event IDs should be regularly reviewed:

- ▶ **Event ID 1206 and 1207**—These IDs give information about the start and stop times for the cleanup of items past the retention date in Item Recovery.

- ▶ **Event ID 700 and 701**—These IDs indicate the start and stop times of the online database defragmentation process. Administrators should ensure that the process does not conflict with Exchange Server database backups and make sure that the process completed without interruptions.

- ▶ **Event IDs 9531–9535**—These IDs indicate the start and end times of the cleanup of deleted mailboxes that are past the retention date.

Analyze Resource Utilization

To keep any environment healthy, overall system and network performance should be regularly evaluated. An Exchange Server 2010 environment is no exception.

At a minimum, administrators should monitor system resources at least once a week. Primary areas to focus on include the four common contributors to bottlenecks: memory, processor, disk subsystem, and network subsystem.

Ideally, utilizing a monitoring utility such as Microsoft OpsMgr 2007 to gather performance data at regular intervals is recommended because this data can be utilized to discover positive and negative trends in the environment.

Check Offline Address Book Generation

An Offline Address Book (OAB) is used by Outlook to provide offline access to directory information from the Global Address List (GAL) when users are working offline or in Cached Exchange mode. When a user starts Outlook in Cached Exchange mode for the first time, the user's Exchange Server mailbox is synchronized to a local file (an .ost file) and the offline address list from the Exchange server is synchronized to a collection of files (.oab files) on the user's computer.

By default, the OAB is updated daily at 5:00 a.m. if there are changes. Administrators can use the Exchange Management Console to determine the last time it was updated to ensure remote users have a valid copy to update from. To do so, follow these steps:

1. Open the Exchange Management Console.

2. In the console tree, expand Organization Configuration and select Mailbox.

3. In the results pane, select the Offline Address Book tab. Select the address book you want to view, and then, in the action pane, click Properties.

4. Check the Modified field to determine when the Offline Address Book was last updated.

5. If you want to modify the default update schedule, that can be accomplished on this page as well. Select one of the predefined schedules from the drop-down box, or click Customize to create your own schedule.

6. Click OK to exit the configuration.

NOTE

If you are experiencing problems with OAB generation, enable diagnostic logging and review the application log for any OAB generator category events.

Monthly Maintenance

Recommended monthly maintenance practices for Exchange Server 2010 do not require the frequency of daily or weekly tasks, but they are, nonetheless, important to maintaining the overall health of the environment. Some general monthly maintenance tasks can be quickly summarized; others are explained in more detail in the following sections.

19

General tasks include the following:

▶ Perform a reboot on the Exchange Server 2010 servers to free up memory resources and kick-start online maintenance routines. This procedure can usually coincide with the implementation of any necessary hotfixes and/or service packs.

▶ Install approved and tested service packs and updates.

▶ Schedule and perform, as necessary, any major server configuration changes, including hardware upgrades.

Run the Exchange Best Practices Analyzer

Administrators should run the Exchange Best Practices Analyzer (ExBPA) in their environments on a regular basis to determine if there are any configurations or settings that are not in line with Microsoft recommended best practices. This utility and its configuration files are updated often with new and improved settings, and available updates are installed every time the utility is run.

Administrators should perform a health check, permissions check, and connectivity test at regular intervals, and the quarterly maintenance period is an ideal time to do so.

During the health check, a two-hour performance baseline can be gathered as well.

The results of these scans can be saved and compared from month to month to determine when particular issues might have occurred.

Test Uninterruptible Power Supply

Uninterruptible Power Supply (UPS) equipment is commonly used to protect the server from sudden loss of power. Most UPS solutions include supporting management software to ensure that the server is gracefully shut down in the event of power failure, thus preserving the integrity of the system. Each manufacturer has a specific recommendation for testing, and the recommended procedures should be followed carefully. However, it should occur no less than once per month, and it is advantageous to schedule the test for the same time as any required server reboots.

Quarterly Maintenance

Although quarterly maintenance tasks are infrequent, some might require downtime and are more likely to cause serious problems with Exchange Server 2010 if not properly planned or implemented. Administrators should proceed cautiously with these tasks.

General quarterly maintenance tasks include the following:

▶ Check the Property pages of mailbox and public folder stores to verify configuration parameters, review usage statistics, determine mailbox sizes, and more.

▶ Evaluate the current rate of growth on server hard drives to ensure there is adequate space available on all volumes. This evaluation is based on the information gathered during the weekly maintenance tasks.

Validate Information Store Backups

As previously mentioned, the backing up of an environment's data is one of the most important steps an organization can take to ensure recoverability in the event of a disaster.

However, simply backing up the data, and assuming the ability to recover it is inadequate.

Backups should be regularly restored in a test environment to ensure the recoverability of systems. By performing regular restores in a test environment, administrators are providing several services:

▶ Confirmation that the data is truly being backed up successfully

▶ Verification of the actual restore procedures

▶ Training for new Exchange Server administrators, or practice for existing ones, in the steps needed to recover an Exchange Server environment

Organizations that do not implement regular testing of restore procedures often find that, in the time of actual need, restorations take significantly longer than necessary because of missing hardware, missing software, inadequate or inaccurate procedures, administrators unfamiliar with the process, or, worst of all, backup sources that had been reported good, but are unable to be restored.

TIP

Backup and recovery procedures are one of the most critical documents in an Exchange Server organization. These procedures should be thoroughly tested and updated whenever changes to the process occur. And remember, it is not enough to store copies of this documentation electronically on network shares or (worse) within the messaging system. If these procedures can't be quickly accessed when they are most needed, they are practically useless.

Post-Maintenance Procedures

Post-maintenance procedures are designed to quickly and efficiently restore Exchange Server operations to the environment following any offline maintenance. Devising a checklist for these procedures ensures that the systems are brought back online quickly and efficiently, without time wasted because of minor errors. The following is a sample checklist for maintenance procedures:

1. Start all the remaining Exchange Server services.
2. Test email connectivity from Outlook, Outlook Web App, Outlook Anywhere, and ActiveSync.
3. Perform a full backup of the Exchange Server 2010 server(s).
4. Closely review backup and server event logs over the next few days to ensure that no errors are reported on the server.

19

Reducing Management and Maintenance Efforts

As you have seen throughout the chapter, numerous utilities are available with Exchange Server 2010 for managing, maintaining, and monitoring the messaging system. These utilities can often help administrators avoid problems, and can save time and energy addressing those that arise.

In any messaging environment, administrators should always attempt to develop processes and procedures that can reduce maintenance efforts while maximizing effectiveness and efficiency. Many management and maintenance procedures can be streamlined, or even automated, ensuring a maximum return for minimum time spent, resulting in a significant monetary savings for the organization. Equally important, proper upkeep of the Exchange Server environment ensures administrators are one step ahead of preventable issues, allowing more time for proactively managing the environment, and less time reacting to problems.

Using Microsoft System Center Operations Manager 2007 R2

Microsoft System Center Operations Manager 2007 R2 (OpsMgr) is one tool that can be used to streamline and automate many of an administrator's messaging responsibilities. More specifically, the OpsMgr Exchange Server management pack provides the key features required to manage, maintain, and monitor the Exchange Server 2010 environment. More on OpsMgr in Chapter 20, "Using Operations Manager to Monitor Exchange Server 2010."

Key features to consider evaluating include, but are not limited to, the following:

▶ Provides monitors, rules, and scripts to track Exchange Server performance, availability, and reliability of all Exchange Server-related components, including Internet-related services, Extensible Storage Engine, System Attendant, Microsoft Exchange Information Store service, and SMTP.

▶ Sends test synthetic emails to verify operations and measures actual delivery times.

▶ Gathers Exchange Server data and provides technical reports on Exchange Server service delivery, traffic, storage capacity, and usage.

▶ Alerts administrators when various thresholds are met, such as resource utilization statistics or capacity.

▶ Performance baselining and continuous monitoring of system resources and protocols.

▶ Trend analysis of usage and performance.

▶ A full knowledge base of Exchange Server-specific solutions tied directly to over 1,700 events.

▶ Reporting on usage, problems, security-related events, and much more.

Summary

Most organizations consider their email systems to be one of the most mission-critical applications in their environment. Message delays, nondeliveries, and unscheduled downtime are usually considered unacceptable, and administrators who cannot maintain their environments well enough to meet service level agreements and management expectations are often quickly out of a job.

For a messaging environment to perform well, remain reliable, and continue to provide full functionality, it must be properly managed and maintained. Exchange Server 2010 provides tools and utilities to assist in this endeavor, but they must be used properly and regularly to be effective.

Exchange Server 2010 brings some impressive advancements to the task of maintaining the Exchange Server environment, including the new continuous online database maintenance features and the new remote management tools. These advancements help the organization maintain a healthy environment.

With proper care and feeding, Exchange Server 2010 can meet and exceed the messaging needs for just about any organization.

Best Practices

The following are best practices from this chapter:

- ▶ Manage Exchange Server 2010 based on server roles and responsibilities with the new role-based access control (RBAC) features.

- ▶ Utilize the Exchange Best Practices Analyzer on a monthly basis to evaluate the current environment and compare it to Microsoft recommended best practices.

- ▶ Audit the messaging environment using Windows auditing.

- ▶ Use Exchange Server 2010 protocol logging and diagnostic utilities for troubleshooting purposes.

- ▶ Install the Exchange Management Console and the Exchange Management Shell on a client computer to remotely administer Exchange Server 2010.

- ▶ Keep AD well tuned using `ntdsutil` because Exchange Server 2010 relies heavily on it.

- ▶ Avoid possible adverse affects with the AD database by running `ntdsutil` in Directory Service Restore mode.

- ▶ Use `isinteg` in Test mode unless there is a specific problem reported.

19

▶ Never manually modify Exchange Server 2010 databases or transaction log files.

▶ Thoroughly document the Exchange Server 2010 messaging environment and configuration. Create and maintain change logs to document changes and maintenance procedures.

▶ Document the process of restoring Exchange Server 2010 databases thoroughly and completely. If documentation already exists, verify that the existing process has not changed. If it has changed, update the documentation.

▶ Store printed copies of the Exchange Server 2010 restoration process in an easy-to-access location.

▶ Create post-maintenance procedures to minimize time needed for restoration.

▶ Include the System State data in daily backup routines. Be sure to back the System State up with a separate backup job if using the ntbackup utility.

▶ Implement System Center Operations Manager 2007 R2 with the available Exchange Server management packs to minimize administrative overhead for daily routines.

CHAPTER 20

Using Operations Manager to Monitor Exchange Server 2010

System Center Operations Manager (OpsMgr) 2007 R2 provides the best-of-breed approach to monitoring and managing Exchange Server 2010 within the environment. OpsMgr helps to identify specific environmental conditions before they evolve into problems through the use of monitoring and alerting components.

OpsMgr provides a timely view of important Exchange Server 2010 conditions and intelligently links problems to knowledge provided within the monitoring rules. Critical events and known issues are identified and matched to technical reference articles in the Microsoft Knowledge Base for troubleshooting and quick problem resolution.

The monitoring is accomplished using standard operating system components such as Windows Management Instrumentation (WMI), Windows event logs, and Windows performance counters, along with Exchange Server 2010 specific API calls and PowerShell cmdlets. OpsMgr-specific components are also designed to perform synthetic transaction and track the health and availability of network services. In addition, OpsMgr provides a reporting feature that allows administrators to track problems and trends occurring on the network. Reports can be generated automatically, providing network administrators, managers, and decision makers with a current and long-term historical view of environmental trends. These reports can be delivered via email or stored on file shares for archive to power web pages.

The following sections focus on defining OpsMgr as a monitoring system for Exchange Server 2010. This chapter provides specific analysis of the way OpsMgr operates and presents OpsMgr design best practices, specific to deployment for Exchange Server 2010 monitoring.

OpsMgr Exchange Server 2010 Monitoring

The Operations Manager 2007 R2 includes one of the best management packs for monitoring and maintaining Exchange Server 2010. This management pack was developed by the product group and includes deep knowledge about the product.

The Exchange Server 2010 management pack monitors all the Exchange Server 2010 server roles and has separate views for each of the roles to enable for targeted monitoring in the console. The Exchange Server 2010 management includes the following features:

▶ **Exchange Server 2010 Client Access server role**—The management pack includes Exchange ActiveSync and Outlook Web App (OWA) connectivity monitoring, synthetic transactions that are enabled through new management pack templates. It does comprehensive performance measuring and alerting.

▶ **Exchange Server 2010 Edge Transport server role**—The management pack does extensive performance measuring and alerting on queues and critical events.

▶ **Exchange Server 2010 Hub Transport server role**—The management pack does extensive performance measuring and alerting on queues and critical events.

▶ **Exchange Server 2010 Mailbox server role**—The management pack includes information store monitoring for performance and load. It also does mail flow monitoring, including synthetic transactions that are enabled through the new R2 management pack templates. It also does MAPI connectivity monitoring to measure client latency.

▶ **Exchange Server 2010 Unified Messaging server role**—The management pack does Unified Messaging connectivity monitoring, including synthetic transactions. It also does performance measuring and alerting on critical events.

▶ **Configuration and Security**—The management pack regularly runs the Exchange Best Practices Analyzer (ExBPA) tool and converts the output to alerts and warnings. This gives best practices guidance on security, performance, configuration, and a host of other parameters.

▶ **Exchange Server 2010 Event Log monitoring**—The management pack has comprehensive rules for Exchange Server 2010 that alert on problem conditions. These alerts contain detailed product knowledge about the events to assist in troubleshooting and resolving the issues.

The management pack includes a comprehensive set of reports that are specific to Exchange Server 2010. These include reports on client performance, top users, mail flow statistics, and protocol availability for the various roles. These reports can be generated ad hoc, scheduled for email delivery on a regular basis, or even generated into web pages for portal viewing. Figure 20.1 shows an SLA report for the major mail services (OWA, Outlook, and Mailbox Databases). The report shows that the overall service level of 96.65 percent falls below the targeted 99.90 percent SLA. It also clearly shows that the mailbox database is the problem area.

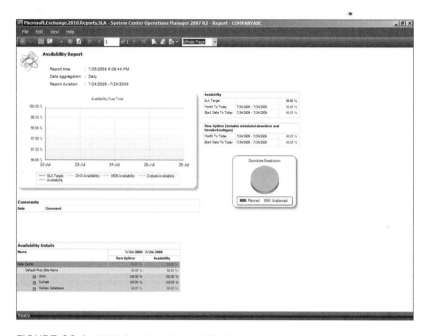

FIGURE 20.1   Mail Services Availability Report.

This kind of summary availability report is invaluable to reporting on the Exchange Server 2010 infrastructure and ties together the low-level technical monitoring into a high-level view that executives and management can use.

In addition, the OpsMgr platform monitors the Exchange Server 2010 dependencies to ensure that the Exchange Server 2010 infrastructure doesn't fail due to a failure of the dependant systems such as the operating system, AD, DNS, and IIS. The features of the management packs for the following major systems follow:

▶ **Windows Operating System Management Pack**—Monitors and alerts all the major elements of the Windows server that Exchange Server 2010 runs on, including processor, memory, network, disk, and event logs. It gathers performance metrics and alerts on thresholds and critical events.

20

▶ **Active Directory Management Pack**—Monitors and alerts on AD key metrics such as replication latency, domain controller response times, and critical events. The management pack generates synthetic transactions to test the response time of the PDC, LDAP, and other domain services.

▶ **DNS Management Pack**—Monitors and alerts on DNS servers for resolution failures and latency and critical events.

▶ **IIS Management Pack**—Monitors and alerts on IIS services, application pools, performance, and critical events.

On all these elements, administrators can generate availability reports to ensure that the servers and systems are meeting the Service Level Agreements (SLAs) set by the organization.

What's New in OpsMgr R2

System Center Operations Manager 2007 R2 was released in Spring 2009, and includes many new improvements on the previous version, Operations Manager 2007 Service Pack 1. Some of these improvements include:

▶ **Cross Platform Support**—This is support for non-Microsoft platforms such as UNIX and Linux. This enables administrators to have a single-pane view of their entire IT environment in OpsMgr.

▶ **Integration with System Center Virtual Machine Manager 2008**—This integrates with the VMM 2008 and enables synergies such as Performance Resource and Optimization (PRO) Tips, which provide virtual machine recommendations based on observed performance and the ability to implement the recommendation at the click of a button.

▶ **Notifications**—The notification system has been revamped and now sports an Outlook rule style interface. And notifications can be generated for specific alerts, and notifications can be sent out as high-priority emails.

▶ **Overrides View**—Rather than hunt for overrides within all the management packs, OpsMgr R2 has an authoring view that shows all the overrides defined in the system.

▶ **Improved Management Pack Maintenance**—OpsMgr 2007 R2 enables Microsoft management packs to be browsed, downloaded, and imported directly from the console. It even includes versioning and dependency checks, and the ability to search from management pack updates.

▶ **Service Level Monitoring**—Applications can be defined from various monitored objects and the service level of the application and be monitored and reported on against defined target SLAs.

▶ **Better Scaling of URL Monitoring**—The URL monitor now scales to thousands of websites without undue performance impact.

▶ **Improved Database Performance**—The overall performance of the database and console has been dramatically improved.

These improvements bring the platform to a new level of performance and interoperability, while retaining the look and feel of the original Operations Manager 2007 tool.

Explaining How OpsMgr Works

OpsMgr is a sophisticated monitoring system that effectively allows for large-scale management of mission-critical servers. Organizations with a medium to large investment in Microsoft technologies will find that OpsMgr allows for an unprecedented ability to keep on top of the tens of thousands of event log messages that occur on a daily basis. In its simplest form, OpsMgr performs two functions: processing monitored data and issuing alerts and automatic responses based on that data.

The model-based architecture of OpsMgr presents a fundamental shift in the way a network is monitored. The entire environment can be monitored as groups of hierarchical services with interdependent components. Microsoft, in addition to third-party vendors and a large development community, can leverage the functionality of OpsMgr components through customizable monitoring rules.

OpsMgr provides for several major pieces of functionality as follows:

▶ **Management packs**—Application-specific monitoring rules are provided within individual files called management packs. For example, Microsoft provides management packs for Windows server systems, Exchange Server, SQL Server, SharePoint, DNS, DHCP, along with many other Microsoft technologies. Management packs are loaded with the intelligence and information necessary to properly troubleshoot and identify problems. The rules are dynamically applied to agents based on a custom discovery process provided within the management pack. Only applicable rules are applied to each managed server.

▶ **Event monitoring rules**—Management pack rules can monitor for specific event log data. This is one of the key methods of responding to conditions within the environment.

▶ **Performance monitoring rules**—Management pack rules can monitor for specific performance counters. This data is used for alerting based on thresholds or archived for trending and capacity planning. A performance graph, as shown in Figure 20.2, shows MAPI Logon Latency data for a couple of databases on the EX1 server. There was a brief spike in latency at approximately 9:45 a.m., but the latency is normally under less than 25.

20

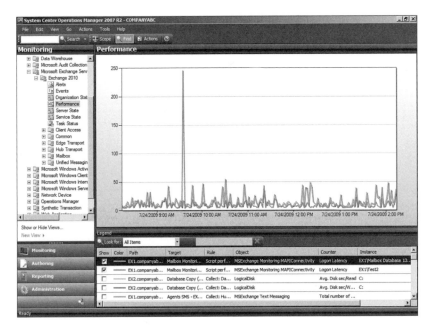

FIGURE 20.2   Operations Manager 2007 R2 Performance Charts.

▶ **State-based monitors**—Management packs contain monitors, which allow for advanced state-based monitoring and aggregated health rollup of services. Monitors also provide self-tuning performance threshold monitoring based on a two- or three-state configuration.

▶ **Alerting**—OpsMgr provides advanced alerting functionality by enabling email alerts, paging, short message service (SMS), instant messaging (IM), and functional alerting roles to be defined. Alerts are highly customizable, with the ability to define alert rules for all monitored components.

▶ **Reporting**—Monitoring rules can be configured to send monitored data to both the operations database for alerting and the reporting database for archiving.

▶ **End-to-end service monitoring**—OpsMgr provides service-oriented monitoring based on System Definition Model (SDM) technologies. This includes advanced object discovery and hierarchical monitoring of systems.

Processing Operational Data

OpsMgr manages Exchange Server 2010 infrastructures through monitoring rules used for object discovery, Windows event log monitoring, performance data gathering, and application-specific synthetic transactions. Monitoring rules define how OpsMgr collects, handles, and responds to the information gathered. OpsMgr monitoring rules handle incoming event data and allow OpsMgr to react automatically, either to respond to a predetermined problem scenario, such as a failed hard drive, with predefined corrective and diagnostics actions (for example, trigger an alert, execute a command or script) to provide the operator with additional details based on what was happening at the time the condition occurred.

Generating Alerts and Responses

OpsMgr monitoring rules can generate alerts based on critical events, synthetic transactions, or performance thresholds and variances found through self-tuning performance trending. An alert can be generated by a single event or by a combination of events or performance thresholds. Alerts can also be configured to trigger responses such as email, pages, Simple Network Management Protocol (SNMP) traps, and scripts to notify you of potential problems. In brief, OpsMgr is completely customizable in this respect and can be modified to fit most alert requirements. An example alert is shown in Figure 20.3. The alert is indicating that the database Test on EX2 is dismounted. Note also that this is a correlated alert, which is an Exchange Server management pack specific function that reduces spurious alerts. A root cause alert is generated, but correlated alerts are suppressed by the management pack to avoid alert noise.

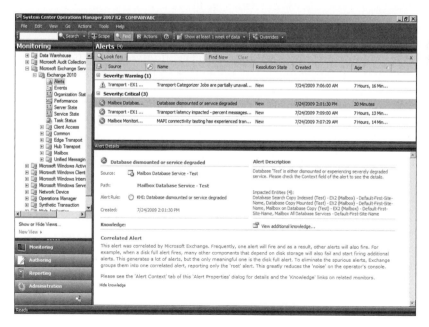

FIGURE 20.3   Operations Manager 2007 R2 Exchange Server 2010 Correlated Alert.

20

Outlining OpsMgr Architecture

OpsMgr is primarily composed of five basic components: the operations database, reporting database, Root Management Server, management agents, and Operations Console. These components make up a basic deployment scenario. Several optional components are also described in the following bulleted list; these components provide functionality for advanced deployment scenarios.

OpsMgr was specifically designed to be scalable and can subsequently be configured to meet the needs of any size company. This flexibility stems from the fact that all OpsMgr components can either reside on one server or can be distributed across multiple servers.

Each of these various components provides specific OpsMgr functionality. OpsMgr design scenarios often involve the separation of parts of these components onto multiple servers. For example, the database components can be delegated to a dedicated server, and the management server can reside on a second server.

The following list describes the different OpsMgr components:

▶ **Operations database**—The operations database stores the monitoring rules and the active data collected from monitored systems. This database has a 7-day default retention period.

▶ **Reporting database**—The reporting database stores archived data for reporting purposes. This database has a 400-day default retention period.

▶ **Root Management Server**—This is the first management server in the management group. This server runs the software development kit (SDK) and Configuration service and is responsible for handling console communication, calculating the health of the environment, and determining what rules should be applied to each agent.

▶ **Management server**—Optionally, an additional management server can be added for redundancy and scalability. Agents communicate with the management server to deliver operational data and pull down new monitoring rules.

▶ **Management agents**—Agents are installed on each managed system to provide efficient monitoring of local components. Almost all communication is initiated from the agent with the exception of the actual agent installation and specific tasks run from the Operations Console. Agentless monitoring is also available with a reduction of functionality and environmental scalability.

▶ **Operations Console**—The Operations Console is used to monitor systems, run tasks, configure environmental settings, set author rules, subscribe to alerts, and generate and subscribe to reports.

▶ **Web console**—The Web console is an optional component used to monitor systems, run tasks, and manage maintenance mode from a web browser.

▶ **Audit Collection Services**—This is an optional component used to collect security events from managed systems; this component is composed of a forwarder on the agent that sends all security events, a collector on the management server that receives events from managed systems, and a special database used to store the collected security data for auditing, reporting, and forensic analysis.

▶ **Gateway server**—This optional component provides mutual authentication through certificates for non-trusted systems in remote domains or workgroups.

▶ **Command shell**—This optional component is built on PowerShell and provides full command-line management of the OpsMgr environment.

▶ **Agentless Exception Monitoring**—This component can be used to monitor Windows and application crash data throughout the environment and provides insight into the health of the productivity applications across workstations and servers.

▶ **Connector Framework**—This optional component provides a bidirectional web service for communicating, extending, and integrating the environment with third-party or custom systems.

The Operations Manager 2007 architecture is shown in Figure 20.4, with all the major components and their data paths.

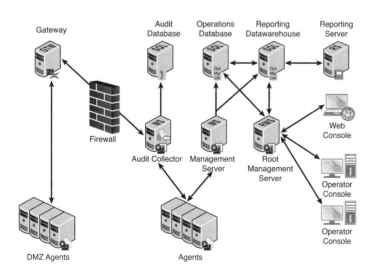

FIGURE 20.4   Operations Manager 2007 R2 architecture.

Understanding How OpsMgr Stores Captured Data

OpsMgr itself utilizes two Microsoft SQL Server databases for all collected data. Both databases are automatically maintained through OpsMgr-specific scheduled maintenance tasks.

The operations database stores all the monitoring rules and is imported by management packs and operational data collected from each monitored system. Data in this database is retained for 7 days by default. Data retention for the operations database is lower than the reporting database to improve efficiency of the environment. This database must be installed as a separate component from OpsMgr but can physically reside on the same server, if needed.

The reporting database stores data for long-term trend analysis and is designed to grow much larger than the operations database. Data in the reporting database is stored in three states: raw data, hourly summary, and daily summary. The raw data is only stored for 14 days, whereas both daily and hourly data are stored for 400 days. This automatic summarization of data allows for reports that span days or months to be generated very quickly.

Determining the Role of Agents in System Monitoring

The agents are the monitoring components installed on each managed computer. They monitor the system based on the rules and business logic defined in each of the management packs. Management packs are dynamically applied to agents based on the different discovery rules included with each management pack.

Defining Management Groups

OpsMgr utilizes the concept of management groups to logically separate geographical and organizational boundaries. Management groups allow you to scale the size of OpsMgr architecture or politically organize the administration of OpsMgr.

At a minimum, each management group consists of the following components:

- ▶ An operations database
- ▶ An optional reporting database
- ▶ A Root Management Server
- ▶ Management agents
- ▶ Management consoles

OpsMgr can be scaled to meet the needs of different sized organizations. For small organizations, all the OpsMgr components can be installed on one server with a single management group. In large organizations, on the other hand, the distribution of OpsMgr components to separate servers allows the organizations to customize and scale their OpsMgr architecture. Multiple management groups provide load balancing and fault tolerance within the OpsMgr infrastructure. Organizations can set up multiple management servers at strategic locations, to distribute the workload among them.

Understanding How to Use OpsMgr

Using OpsMgr is relatively straightforward. The OpsMgr monitoring environment can be accessed through three sets of consoles: an Operations Console, a Web console, and a command shell. The Operations Console provides full monitoring of agent systems and administration of the OpsMgr environment, whereas the Web console provides access only to the monitoring functionality. The command shell provides command-line access to administer the OpsMgr environment.

Managing and Monitoring with OpsMgr

As mentioned in the preceding section, two methods are provided to configure and view OpsMgr settings. The first approach is through the Operations Console and the second is through the command shell.

Within the Administration section of the Operations Console, you can easily configure the security roles, notifications, and configuration settings. Within the Monitoring section of the Operations Console, you can easily monitor a quick "up/down" status, active and closed alerts, and confirm overall environment health.

In addition, a web-based monitoring console can be run on any system that supports Microsoft Internet Explorer 6.0 or higher. This console can be used to view the health of systems, view and respond to alerts, view events, view performance graphs, run tasks, and manage maintenance mode of monitored objects. New to OpsMgr 2007 R2 is the ability to display the health explorer in the Web console.

Reporting from OpsMgr

OpsMgr management packs commonly include a variety of preconfigured reports to show information about the operating system or the specific application they were designed to work with. These reports are run in SQL Reporting Services. The reports provide an effective view of systems and services on the network over a custom period, such as weekly, monthly, or quarterly. They can also help you monitor your networks based on performance data, which can include critical pattern analysis, trend analysis, capacity planning,

20

and security auditing. Reports also provide availability statistics for distributed applications, servers, and specific components within a server.

Availability reports are particularly useful for executives, managers, and application owners. These reports can show the availability of any object within OpsMgr, including a server (shown in Figure 20.5), a database, or even a service such as Exchange Server 2010 that includes a multitude of servers and components. The availability report shown in Figure 20.5 shows that the EX2 server was showing as up until a bit after 7:00 a.m. and then was down through 5:30 p.m.

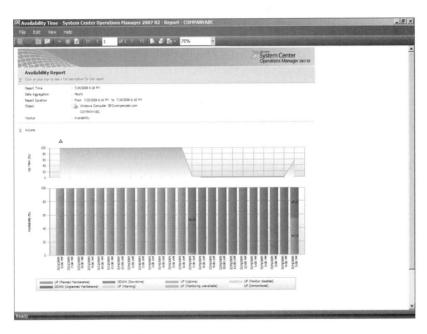

FIGURE 20.5   Availability report.

The reports can be run on demand or at scheduled times and delivered via email. OpsMgr can also generate HTML-based reports that can be published to a web server and viewed from any web browser. Vendors can also create additional reports as part of their management packs.

Using Performance Monitoring

Another key feature of OpsMgr is the capability to monitor and track server performance. OpsMgr can be configured to monitor key performance thresholds through rules that are set to collect predefined performance data, such as memory and CPU usage over time. Rules can be configured to trigger alerts and actions when specified performance thresholds have been met or exceeded, allowing network administrators to act on potential performance issues. Performance data can be viewed from the OpsMgr Operations Console.

In addition, performance monitors can establish baselines for the environment and then alert the administrator when the counter subsequently falls outside the defined baseline envelope.

Using Active Directory Integration

Active Directory integration provides a way to install management agents on systems without environmental-specific settings. When the agent starts, the correct environmental settings, such as the primary and failover management servers, are stored in Active Directory. The configuration of Active Directory integration provides advanced search and filter capabilities to fine-tune the dynamic assignment of systems.

Integrating OpsMgr Non-Windows Devices

Network management is not a new concept. Simple management of various network nodes has been handled for quite some time through the use of the SNMP. Quite often, simple or even complex systems that utilize SNMP to provide for system monitoring are in place in an organization to provide for varying degrees of system management on a network.

OpsMgr can be configured to integrate with non-Windows systems through monitoring of syslog information, log file data, and SNMP traps. OpsMgr can also monitor TCP port communication and website transaction sequencing for information specific data management.

New to OpsMgr 2007 R2 is the ability to monitor non-Microsoft operating systems such as Linux and UNIX, and the applications that run on them such as Apache and MySQL. OpsMgr monitors the file systems, network interfaces, daemons, configurations, and performance metrics. Operations Manager 2007 R2 supports monitoring of the following operating systems:

▶ HP-UX 11i v2 and v3 (PA-RISC and IA64)

▶ Sun Solaris 8 and 9 (SPARC) and Solaris 10 (SPARC and x86)

▶ Red Hat Enterprise Linux 4 (x86/x64) and 5 (x86/x64) Server

▶ Novell SUSE Linux Enterprise Server 9 (x86) and 10 SP1 (x86/x64)

▶ IBM AIX v5.3 and v6.1

These operating systems are "first-class citizens" in Microsoft's parlance, meaning they are treated as equals with the Windows operating systems. Agents can be pushed from the console, operations data is collected automatically, tasks can run against the agents, and all major functions are supported.

Special connectors can be created to provide bidirectional information flows to other management products. OpsMgr can monitor SNMP traps from SNMP-supported devices as well as generate SNMP traps to be delivered to third-party network management infrastructures.

20

Exploring Third-Party Management Packs

Software and hardware developers can subsequently create their own management packs to extend OpsMgr's management capabilities. These management packs extend OpsMgr's management capabilities beyond Microsoft-specific applications. Each management pack is designed to contain a set of rules and product knowledge required to support its respective products. Currently, management packs have been developed for APC, Cisco, Citrix, Dell, F5, HP, IBM, Linux, Oracle, Solaris, UNIX, and VMware to name a few. A complete list of management packs can be found at the following Microsoft site: http://technet. microsoft.com/en-us/opsmgr/cc539535.aspx.

Understanding OpsMgr Component Requirements

Each OpsMgr component has specific design requirements, and a good knowledge of these factors is required before beginning the design of OpsMgr. Hardware and software requirements must be taken into account, as well as factors involving specific OpsMgr components, such as the Root Management Server, gateway servers, service accounts, mutual authentication, and backup requirements.

Exploring Hardware Requirements

Having the proper hardware for OpsMgr to operate on is a critical component of OpsMgr functionality, reliability, and overall performance. Nothing is worse than overloading a brand-new server only a few short months after its implementation. The industry standard generally holds that any production servers deployed should remain relevant for three to four years following deployment. Stretching beyond this time frame might be possible, but the ugly truth is that hardware investments are typically short term and need to be replaced often to ensure relevance. Buying a less-expensive server might save money in the short term but could potentially increase costs associated with downtime, troubleshooting, and administration. That said, the following are the Microsoft-recommended minimums for any server running an OpsMgr 2007 server component:

▶ 2.8 GHz processor or faster

▶ 20GB of free disk space

▶ 2GB of random access memory (RAM)

These recommendations apply only to the smallest OpsMgr deployments and should be seen as minimum levels for OpsMgr hardware. More realistic deployments would have the following minimums:

▶ 2–4 2.8GHz Cores

▶ 64-bit Windows Operating System

▶ 64-bit SQL Server

▶ 60GB free disk space on RAID 1+0 for performance

▶ 4–8GB RAM

Operations Manager 2007 R2 is one of Microsoft's most resource-intensive applications, so generous processor, disk, and memory are important for optimal performance. Future expansion and relevance of hardware should be taken into account when sizing servers for OpsMgr deployment to ensure that the system has room to grow as agents are added and the databases grow.

Determining Software Requirements

OpsMgr components can be installed on either 32-bit or 64-bit versions of Windows Server 2008. The database for OpsMgr must be run on a Microsoft SQL Server 2005 or Microsoft SQL Server 2008 server. The database can be installed on the same server as OpsMgr or on a separate server, a concept that is discussed in more detail in following sections.

OpsMgr itself must be installed on a member server in a Windows Active Directory domain. It is commonly recommended to keep the installation of OpsMgr on a separate server or set of dedicated member servers that do not run any other applications that could interfere in the monitoring and alerting process.

A few other factors critical to the success of an OpsMgr implementation are as follows:

▶ Microsoft .NET Framework 2.0 and 3.0 must be installed on the management server and the reporting server.

▶ Windows PowerShell

▶ Microsoft Core XML Services (MSXML) 6.0

▶ WS-MAN v1.1 (for UNIX/Linux clients)

▶ Client certificates must be installed in environments to facilitate mutual authentication between non-domain members and management servers.

▶ SQL Reporting Services must be installed for an organization to be able to view and produce custom reports using OpsMgr's reporting feature.

OpsMgr Backup Considerations

The most critical piece of OpsMgr, the SQL databases, should be regularly backed up using standard backup software that can effectively perform online backups of SQL databases. If integrating these specialized backup utilities into an OpsMgr deployment is not possible, it becomes necessary to leverage built-in backup functionality found in SQL Server.

20

Understanding Advanced OpsMgr Concepts

OpsMgr's simple installation and relative ease of use often belie the potential complexity of its underlying components. This complexity can be managed with the right amount of knowledge of some of the advanced concepts of OpsMgr design and implementation.

Understanding OpsMgr Deployment Scenarios

As previously mentioned, OpsMgr components can be divided across multiple servers to distribute load and ensure balanced functionality. This separation allows OpsMgr servers to come in four potential "flavors," depending on the OpsMgr components held by those servers. The four OpsMgr server types are as follows:

▶ **Operations database server**—An operations database server is simply a member server with SQL Server 2005 installed for the OpsMgr operations database. No other OpsMgr components are installed on this server. The SQL Server 2005 component can be installed with default options and with the system account used for authentication. Data in this database is kept for 4 days by default.

▶ **Reporting database server**—A reporting database server is simply a member server with SQL Server 2005 and SQL Server Reporting Services installed. This database stores data collected through the monitoring rules for a much longer period than the operations database and is used for reporting and trend analysis. This database requires significantly more drive space than the operations database server. Data in this database is kept for 13 months by default.

▶ **Management server**—A management server is the communication point for both management consoles and agents. Effectively, a management server does not have a database and is often used in large OpsMgr implementations that have a dedicated database server. Often, in these configurations, multiple management servers are used in a single management group to provide for scalability and to address multiple managed nodes.

▶ **All-in-one server**—An all-in-one server is effectively an OpsMgr server that holds all OpsMgr roles, including that of the databases. Subsequently, single-server OpsMgr configurations use one server for all OpsMgr operations.

Multiple Configuration Groups

As previously defined, an OpsMgr management group is a logical grouping of monitored servers that are managed by a single OpsMgr SQL database, one or more management servers, and a unique management group name. Each management group established operates completely separately from other management groups, although they can be configured in a hierarchical structure with a top-level management group able to see "connected" lower-level management groups.

The concept of connected management groups allows OpsMgr to scale beyond artificial boundaries and also gives a great deal of flexibility when combining OpsMgr environments. However, certain caveats must be taken into account. Because each management group is an island in itself, each must subsequently be manually configured with individual settings. In environments with a large number of customized rules, for example, such manual configuration would create a great deal of redundant work in the creation, administration, and troubleshooting of multiple management groups.

Deploying Geographic-Based Configuration Groups

Based on the factors outlined in the preceding section, it is preferable to deploy OpsMgr in a single management group. However, in some situations an organization needs to divide its OpsMgr environment into multiple management groups. The most common reason for division of OpsMgr management groups is division along geographic lines. In situations in which wide area network (WAN) links are saturated or unreliable, it might be wise to separate large "islands" of WAN connectivity into separate management groups.

Simply being separated across slow WAN links is not enough reason to warrant a separate management group, however. For example, small sites with few servers would not warrant the creation of a separate OpsMgr management group, with the associated hardware, software, and administrative costs. However, if many servers exist in a distributed, generally well-connected geographical area, that might be a case for the creation of a management group. For example, an organization could be divided into several sites across the United States but decide to divide the OpsMgr environment into separate management groups for East Coast and West Coast, to roughly approximate their WAN infrastructure.

Smaller sites that are not well connected but are not large enough to warrant their own management group should have their event monitoring throttled to avoid being sent across the WAN during peak usage times. The downside to this approach, however, is that the reaction time to critical event response is increased.

Deploying Political or Security-Based Configuration Groups

The less common method of dividing OpsMgr management groups is by political or security lines. For example, it might become necessary to separate financial servers into a separate management group to maintain the security of the finance environment and allow for a separate set of administrators.

Politically, if administration is not centralized within an organization, management groups can be established to separate OpsMgr management into separate spheres of control. This would keep each OpsMgr management zone under separate security models.

As previously mentioned, a single management group is the most efficient OpsMgr environment and provides for the least amount of redundant setup, administration, and troubleshooting work. Consequently, artificial OpsMgr division along political or security lines should be avoided, if possible.

Sizing the OpsMgr Database

Depending on several factors, such as the type of data collected, the length of time that collected data will be kept, or the amount of database grooming that is scheduled, the size of the OpsMgr database will grow or shrink accordingly. It is important to monitor the

20

size of the database to ensure that it does not increase well beyond the bounds of acceptable size. OpsMgr can be configured to monitor itself, supplying advance notice of database problems and capacity thresholds. This type of strategy is highly recommended because OpsMgr could easily collect event information faster than it could get rid of it.

The size of the operations database can be estimated through the following formula:

```
Number of agents x 5MB x retention days + 1024 overhead = estimated database size
```

For example, an OpsMgr environment monitoring 1,000 servers with the default 7-day retention period will have an estimated 35GB operations database:

```
(1000 * 5 * 7) + 1024 = 36024 MB
```

The size of the reporting database can be estimated through the following formula:

```
Number of agents x 3MB x retention days + 1024 overhead = estimated database size
```

The same environment monitoring 1,000 servers with the default 400-day retention period will have an estimated 1.1TB reporting database:

```
(1000 * 3 * 400) + 1024 = 1201024 MB
```

It is important to understand that these estimates are rough guidelines only and can vary widely depending on the types of servers monitored, the monitoring configuration, the degree of customization, and other factors.

Defining Capacity Limits

As with any system, OpsMgr includes some hard limits that should be taken into account before deployment begins. Surpassing these limits could be cause for the creation of new management groups and should subsequently be included in a design plan. These limits are as follows:

▶ **Operations database**—OpsMgr operates through a principle of centralized, rather than distributed, collection of data. All event logs, performance counters, and alerts are sent to a single centralized database, and there can subsequently be only a single operations database per management group. Considering the use of a backup and high-availability strategy for the OpsMgr database is, therefore, highly recommended, to protect it from outage. It is recommended to keep this database with a 50GB limit to improve efficiency and reduce alert latency.

▶ **Management servers**—OpsMgr does not have a hard-coded limit of management servers per management group. However, it is recommended to keep the environment between three to five management servers. Each management server can support approximately 2,000 managed agents.

▶ **Gateway servers**—OpsMgr does not have a hard-coded limit of gateway servers per management group. However, it is recommended to deploy a gateway server for every 200 non-trusted domain members.

- ▶ **Agents**—Each management server can theoretically support up to 2,000 monitored agents. In most configurations, however, it is wise to limit the number of agents per management server, although the levels can be scaled upward with more robust hardware, if necessary.

- ▶ **Administrative consoles**—OpsMgr does not limit the number of instances of the Web and Operations Console; however, going beyond the suggested limit might introduce performance and scalability problems.

Defining System Redundancy

In addition to the scalability built in to OpsMgr, redundancy is built in to the components of the environment. Proper knowledge of how to deploy OpsMgr redundancy and place OpsMgr components correctly is important to the understanding of OpsMgr redundancy. The main components of OpsMgr can be made redundant through the following methods:

- ▶ **Management servers**—Management servers are automatically redundant and agents will failover and failback automatically between them. Simply install additional management servers for redundancy. In addition, the RMS server acts as a management server and participates in the fault tolerance.

- ▶ **SQL databases**—The SQL database servers hosting the databases can be made redundant using SQL clustering, which is based on Windows clustering. This supports failover and failback.

- ▶ **Root Management Server**—The RMS can be made redundant using Windows clustering. This supports failover and failback.

Having multiple management servers deployed across a management group allows an environment to achieve a certain level of redundancy. If a single management server experiences downtime, another management server within the management group will take over the responsibilities for the monitored servers in the environment. For this reason, it might be wise to include multiple management servers in an environment to achieve a certain level of redundancy if high uptime is a priority.

The first management server in the management group is called the Root Management Server. Only one Root Management Server can exist in a management group and it hosts the software development kit (SDK) and Configuration service. All OpsMgr consoles communicate with the management server so its availability is critical. In large-scale environments, the Root Management Server should leverage Microsoft Cluster technology to provide high availability for this component.

Because there can be only a single OpsMgr database per management group, the database is subsequently a single point of failure and should be protected from downtime. Utilizing Windows Server 2008 clustering or third-party fault-tolerance solutions for SQL databases helps to mitigate the risk involved with the OpsMgr database.

20

Monitoring Nondomain Member Considerations

DMZ, Workgroup, and Non-Trusted domain agents require special configuration; in particular, they require certificates to establish mutual authentication. Operations Manager 2007 requires mutual authentication, that is, the server authenticates to the client and the client authenticates to the server to ensure that the monitoring communications are not hacked. Without mutual authentication, a hacker can execute a man-in-the-middle attack and impersonate either the client or the server. Thus, mutual authentication is a security measure designed to protect clients, servers, and sensitive AD domain information, which is exposed to potential hacking attempts by the all-powerful management infrastructure. However, OpsMgr relies on Active Directory Kerberos for mutual authentication, which is not available to nondomain members.

> **NOTE**
>
> Edge Transport role servers are commonly placed in the DMZ and are by definition not domain members, so almost every Exchange Server 2010 environment needs to deploy certificate-based authentication.

In the absence of AD, trusts, and Kerberos, OpsMgr 2007 R2 can use X.509 certificates to establish the mutual authentication. These can be issued by any PKI, such as Microsoft Windows Server 2008 Enterprise CA. See Chapter 12, "Integrating Certificate-Based Public Key Infrastructure (PKI) in Exchange Server 2010," for details on PKI and Exchange Server 2010.

Installing agents on Edge Transport servers is discussed later in the chapter in the section "Installing Edge Transport Monitoring Certificates."

Securing OpsMgr

Security has evolved into a primary concern that can no longer be taken for granted. The inherent security in Windows 2008 is only as good as the services that have access to it; therefore, it is wise to perform a security audit of all systems that access information from servers. This concept holds true for management systems as well because they collect sensitive information from every server in an enterprise. This includes potentially sensitive event logs that could be used to compromise a system. Consequently, securing the OpsMgr infrastructure should not be taken lightly.

Securing OpsMgr Agents

Each server that contains an OpsMgr agent and forwards events to management servers has specific security requirements. Server-level security should be established and should include provisions for OpsMgr data collection. All traffic between OpsMgr components, such as the agents, management servers, and database, is encrypted automatically for security, so the traffic is inherently secured.

In addition, environments with high security requirements should investigate the use of encryption technologies such as IPSec to scramble the event IDs that are sent between agents and OpsMgr servers, to protect against eavesdropping of OpsMgr packets.

OpsMgr uses mutual authentication between agents and management servers. This means that the agent must reside in the same forest as the management server. If the agent is located in a different forest or workgroup, client certificates can be used to establish mutual authentication. If an entire non-trusted domain must be monitored, the gateway server can be installed in the non-trusted domain, agents can establish mutual authentication to the gateway server, and certificates on the gateway and management server are used to establish mutual authentication. In this scenario, you can avoid needing to place a certificate on each non-trusted domain member.

Understanding Firewall Requirements

OpsMgr servers that are deployed across a firewall have special considerations that must be taken into account. Port 5723, the default port for OpsMgr communications, must specifically be opened on a firewall to allow OpsMgr to communicate across it.

Table 20.1 describes communication for this and other OpsMgr components.

TABLE 20.1   OpsMgr Communication Ports

From	To	Port
Agent	Root Management Server	5723
Agent	Management server	5723
Agent	Gateway server	5723
Agent (ACS forwarder)	Management server ACS collector	51909
Gateway server	Root Management Server	5723
Gateway server	Management server	5723
Management or Gateway server	UNIX or Linux computer	1270
Management or Gateway server	UNIX or Linux computer	22
Management server	Operations Manager database	1433
Management server	Root Management Server	5723, 5724
Management server	Reporting data warehouse	1433
Management server ACS collector	ACS database	1433
Operations console	Root Management Server	5724
Operations console (reports)	SQL Server Reporting Services	80
Reporting server	Root Management Server	5723, 5724
Reporting server	Reporting data warehouse	1433

TABLE 20.1   OpsMgr Communication Ports

From	To	Port
Root management server	Operations Manager database	1433
Root management server	Reporting data warehouse	1433
Web console browser	Web console server	51908
Web console server	Root Management Server	5724

The agent is the component that ports need to be opened most often, which is only port 5723 from the agent to the management servers for monitoring. Other ports, such as 51909 for ACS, are more rarely needed. Figure 20.6 shows the major communications paths and ports between OpsMgr components.

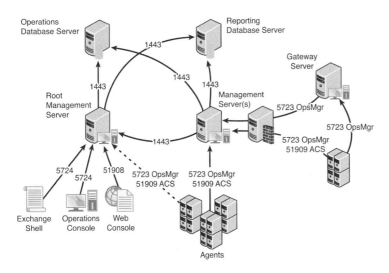

FIGURE 20.6   Communications ports.

Outlining Service Account Security

In addition to the aforementioned security measures, security of an OpsMgr environment can be strengthened by the addition of multiple service accounts to handle the different OpsMgr components. For example, the Management Server Action account and the SDK/Configuration service account should be configured to use separate credentials, to provide for an extra layer of protection in the event that one account is compromised.

▶ **Management Server Action account**—The account responsible for collecting data and running responses from management servers.

▶ **SDK and Configuration service account**—The account that writes data to the operations database; this service is also used for all console communication.

- **Local Administrator account**—The account used during the agent push installation process. To install the agent, local administrative rights are required.

- **Agent Action account**—The credentials the agent will run as. This account can run under a built-in system account, such as Local System, or a limited domain user account for high-security environments.

- **Data Warehouse Write Action account**—The account used by the management server to write data to the reporting data warehouse.

- **Data Warehouse Reader account**—The account used to read data from the data warehouse when reports are executed.

- **Run As accounts**—The specific accounts used by management packs to facilitate monitoring. These accounts must be manually created and delegated specific rights as defined in the management pack documentation. These accounts are then assigned as run-as accounts used by the management pack to achieve a high-degree of security and flexibility when monitoring the environment.

Installing Operations Manager 2007 R2

As discussed in the previous section, Operations Manager 2007 R2 is a multitier and multicomponent application that can be deployed in a variety of architectures. This enables OpsMgr to support scaling from a small organization to a large enterprise.

For the purposes of this chapter, an all-in-one single-server install is used. This allows for monitoring of small- to medium-sized Exchange Server 2010 organizations spanning a handful of servers to up to 50 servers.

Single Server OpsMgr 2007 R2 Install

This section steps through the install of OpsMgr and Reporting on a single-server configuration. The specification for a single-server configuration to support 50 Exchange Server 2010 servers would be

- 2 x 2.8GHz Cores

- 8GB RAM

- 4 Drive RAID 0+1 Disk (200+ GB Space)

These hardware requirements ensure that the system can perform to specification. Note that the Exchange Server 2010 servers generate a heavier load than other server types such as domain controllers or web servers. This configuration can support 50 Exchange Server 2010 servers or 250 servers of other types.

NOTE

If the configuration were to be virtualized on a Windows Server 2008 Hyper-V host or a VMware ESX host, a single server configuration is not recommended. Instead, a two-server configuration would be recommended, and the SQL Server 2008 should be installed on the second server to balance the load.

The steps in this section assume that the single server has been prepared with the following:

▶ Windows Server 2008 operating system installed.

▶ Web role with the appropriate features installed.

NOTE

To install SQL Reporting Services and the Web components of OpsMgr 2007 R2, the following Windows Server 2008 web role features need to be installed: Static Content, Default Document, HTTP Redirection, Directory Browsing, ASP, ASP.Net, ISAPI Extension, ISAPI Filters, Windows Authentication, IIS Metabase, and IIS 6 WMI.

▶ Windows PowerShell feature installed.

▶ SQL Server 2008 with Reporting Services installed.

▶ Create an OpsMgr service account with local administrator rights to the server and system administrator rights to the SQL Server 2008.

This prepares the system for the install of OpsMgr R2. See the following prerequisite checker information for additional requirements and how to check them.

Before installing, it is important to run the built-in prerequisite checker. This utility is available on the OpsMgr installation media and confirms a host of software perquisites before attempting the actual installation. This gives the administrator time to download and install the necessary software, rather than have the installation bomb out in the middle after entering a lot of configuration information.

This section assumes a Windows Server 2008 and SQL Server 2008 server will be used for the single-server installation, but the prerequisite checker looks at more general requirements based on the OpsMgr supported platforms. The prerequisite checker looks for the following software on a single-server configuration:

▶ Windows Server 2003 Service Pack 1 or Windows Server 2008

▶ Microsoft SQL Server 2005 Service Pack 1 or SQL Server 2008

▶ Microsoft SQL Server 2005 Reporting Services Service Pack 1 or SQL Server 2008 Reporting Services

▶ World Wide Web Service running and set for automatic startup

- WS-MAN v1.1

- .NET Framework 2.0 and .NET Framework 3.0 components

- Windows PowerShell

- Key Hotfixes

To use the Prerequisite Viewer for a single-server configuration, run the following steps:

1. Log on with an account that has Administrator rights.
2. Insert the Operations Manager 2007 R2 installation media.
3. The setup starts automatically or launches the SetupOM.exe.
4. Click Check Prerequisites to start the Prerequisite Viewer.
5. Select Operational Database, Server, Console, Power Shell, Web Console, Reporting, and Data Warehouse, and then click Check.

> **NOTE**
>
> The prerequisite checker findings display and have active links that can be clicked to get specific guidance, and links to download software and hotfixes.

6. When you finish with the Prerequisite Viewer, click Close.

Remediate all the guidance in the prerequisite checker before proceeding to the installation. Some of the guidance will be warnings, particularly with some of the hotfixes. Leaving out hotfixes might enable the installation to proceed but might make the OpsMgr application less stable. It is highly recommended that all the recommendations be applied to ensure the most stable platform possible. If any of the installations require a reboot, it is recommended to run the prerequisite checker again.

When the server meets all the prerequisites and is ready for installation, the steps to run the install are as follows:

1. Log on with the OpsMgr service account.
2. Launch SetupOM.exe from the OpsMgr installation media.
3. Click Install Operations Manager 2007 R2.
4. Click Next.
5. Accept the license agreement and click Next.
6. Enter the CD key if required and then click Next.
7. When the Custom Setup page displays, leave the components set to their defaults, and then click Next.
8. Type the management group name in the Management Group box and click Next.
9. Select the instance of SQL Server on which to install the Operations Manager 2007 R2 database (the local system because this is a single server install) and then click Next.

20

10. Leave the default database size of 1,000MB, and then click Next.

11. Select Domain or Local Computer Account, type the User Account and Password, select the Domain or local computer from the list, and then click Next.

12. On the SDK and Config Service Account page, select Domain or Local Account, type the User Account and Password, select the Domain or local computer from the list, and then click Next.

13. On the Web Console Authentication Configuration page, select Use Windows Authentication and click Next.

14. On the Operations Manager Error Reports page, leave Do You Want To Send Error Reports to Microsoft cleared and click Next to not send Operations Manager 2007 R2 error reports to Microsoft.

15. On the Customer Experience Improvement Program page, leave the default option of I Don't Want to Join the Program selected and then click Next.

16. On the Ready to Install page, click Install.

17. When the Completing the System Center Operations Manager 2007 R2 Setup Wizard page appears, leave the Backup Encryption Key box selected to back up the encryption key.

> **NOTE**
>
> A copy of the encryption key is needed to promote a management server to the role of the Root Management Server if a failure of the RMS occurs.

18. Leave Start the Console selected to open the Operations console.

19. Click Finish.

Operations Manager 2007 R2 is now installed in a single-server configuration. This configuration can manage up to 50 Exchange servers or 250 non-Exchange servers.

Importing Management Packs

After the initial installation, OpsMgr includes only a few management packs. The management packs contain all the discoveries, monitors, rules, knowledge, reports, and views that OpsMgr needs to effectively monitor servers and applications. One of the first tasks after installing OpsMgr 2007 is to import management packs into the system.

There is a large number of management packs in the Internet catalog on the Microsoft website. These include updated management packs, management packs for new products, and third-party management packs. It is important to load only those management packs that are going to be used because each additional management pack increases the database size, adds discoveries that impact the performance of agents, and in general clutters up the interface.

The key management packs for an Exchange Server 2010 environment follow:

► Windows Server Core OS

► Windows Server Active Directory

► Windows Server Domain Naming Service

► Windows Server IIS

► SQL Server

► ForeFront for Exchange

► Exchange Server

For each of these management packs, it is important to load the relevant versions only. For example, if the environment includes Windows Server 2008 only, load only the Windows Server Core OS 2008 management pack. If the environment includes both Windows Server 2003 and Windows Server 2008, load both the Windows Server Core OS 2003 and the Windows Server Core OS 2008.

In versions of OpsMgr prior to R2, the management packs had to be downloaded from the Microsoft website one by one, the MSI installed one by one, and the management packs imported one by one. Dependencies would not be checked unless additional steps were taken to consolidate the management pack files prior to importing. This was a labor-intensive process. Also, there was no easy way to check for updates to already installed management packs.

In OpsMgr 2007 R2, a new Management Pack Import Wizard was introduced. This wizard connects directly to the Microsoft management pack catalog and downloads, checks, and imports management packs. It even does version checks to ensure that the management packs are the latest versions. This is a huge improvement over the old method to import management packs.

To import the key management packs, use the following steps:

1. Launch the Operations Console.
2. Select the Administration section.
3. Select the Management Packs folder.
4. Right-click the Management Packs folder and select Import Management Packs.
5. Click the Add button and select Add from Catalog.
6. Click the Search button to search the entire catalog.

20

NOTE

The View pull-down in the Management Pack Import Wizard includes four options, which are All Management Packs in the Catalog, Updates Available for Installed Management Packs, All Management Packs Released in the Last 3 Months, and All Management Packs Released in the Last 6 Months. The Updates option will check against the already installed management packs and enable the download of updated versions of those.

---

7. Select the key management packs from the preceding bulleted list and click Add for each of them. Each of the major management packs might include a number of submanagement packs for discovery, monitoring, and other breakdowns of functionality.

8. When done adding management packs, click OK.

9. The wizard now validates the added management packs, checking for versions, dependencies, and security risks. It allows problem management packs to be removed and dependencies to be added to the list.

10. Click Install to begin the download and import process. Progress will be shown for each of the management packs imported.

11. After all the management packs complete, click Close to exit the wizard.

After the import completes, the management packs take effect immediately. Agents begin discovering based on the schedule specified in the management packs and monitors and rules begin deploying.

Deploying OpsMgr Agents

OpsMgr agents are deployed to all managed servers through the OpsMgr Discovery Wizard, or by using software distribution mechanisms such as Active Directory GPOs or System Center Configuration Manager 2007. Installation through the Operations Console uses the fully qualified domain name (FQDN) of the computer. When searching for systems through the Operations Console, you can use wildcards to locate a broad range of computers for agent installation. Certain situations, such as monitoring across firewalls, can require the manual installation of these components.

The Discovery Wizard can discover and configure monitoring for Windows computers, UNIX/Linux computers, and for Network devices. It pushes agents to Windows and UNIX/Linux computers, if the proper rights are provided such as an account with local administrator rights or a root account.

To install domain member agents using the Discovery Wizard, follow these steps:

1. Launch the Operations Console and select the Administration section.

2. Right-click on the top-level Administration folder and select Discovery Wizard.

3. Select the Windows computers and click Next.

4. Select Automatic computer discovery and click Next. This scans the entire Active Directory domain for computers.

5. Leave the Use selected Management Server Action Account and click Discover. This starts the discovery process.

6. After the discovery runs (this might take a few minutes), the list of discovered computers displays. Select the devices that should have agents deployed to them, as shown in Figure 20.7.

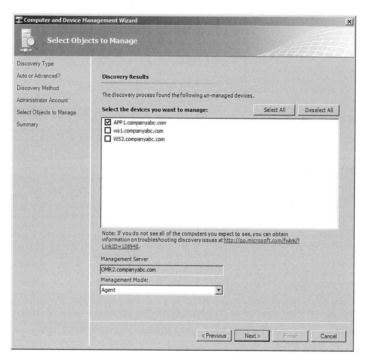

FIGURE 20.7   Discovered computers.

7. Click Next.

8. Leave the Agent installation directory and the Agent Action Account at the defaults; then click Finish.

9. The Agent Management Task Status window appears, listing all the computers selected and the progress of each installation. As shown in Figure 20.8, the APP1.companyabc.com agent installation task started.

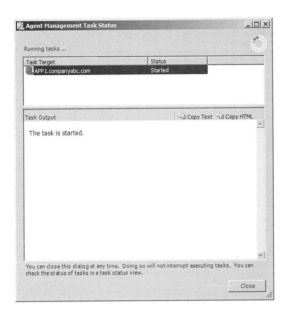

FIGURE 20.8   Agent Installation Progress.

10. Click Close when the installation completes.

Even if the window is closed before the installs complete, the results of the installs can be viewed in Task Status view in the Monitoring section of the Operations Console.

The agent deployment is efficient, and a large number of computers can be selected for deployment without any issues. The agents start automatically and begin to be monitored as they are discovered.

After installation, it might be necessary to wait a few minutes before the information from the agents is sent to the management server.

During the next few minutes after installation, the agent contacts the management server and establishes a mutually authenticated, encrypted communication channel with the assigned management server. If the agent was pushed through a software delivery system such as System Center Configuration Manager 2007, the agent determines the management server through AD integrated discovery.

The agent downloads rules to discover the various applications and components it's hosting, enabling the correct application-specific management packs to be applied. This discovery process runs periodically to ensure the correct rules are always applied to the server.

Installing Edge Transport Monitoring Certificates

Monitoring the Edge Server role requires an install of certificate-based mutual authentication. This process has a lot of steps but is straightforward. To install and configure certificates to enable the Edge Transport servers to use mutual authentication, there are five major tasks to be completed. These tasks follow:

1. Create a Certificate Template to issue the right format of X.509 certificates for Operations Manager to use for mutual authentication.

2. Request the Root CA certificate to trust the CA and the certificates it issues. This is done for each Edge Transport server and possibly for the management servers if not using an enterprise CA.

3. Request a certificate from the Root CA to use for mutual authentication. This is done for each Edge Transport server and for each management server.

4. Install the Operations Manager agent manually. This is done for each Edge Transport server.

5. Configure the agent to use the certificate. This is done for each Edge Transport server and for each management server.

These various X.509 certificates are issued from a certificate authority. This is a good use of the CA created as part of Chapter 12.

Create Certificate Template

This step creates a certificate template named Operations Manager that can be issued from the Windows Server 2008 certification authority web enrollment page. The certificate template supports Server Authentication (OID 1.3.6.1.5.5.7.3.1) and Client Authentication (OID 1.3.6.1.5.5.7.3.2), and enables the name to be manually entered rather than auto-generated from Active Directory because the Edge Transport will not be an AD domain member.

The steps to create the security template follow:

1. Log on to CA, which is DC1.companyabc.com in this example.

2. Launch Server Manager.

3. Expand Roles, Active Directory Certificate Services, and select Certificate Templates (*fqdn*).

4. Right-click the Computer template and select Duplicate Template.

5. Leave the version at Windows 2003 Server, Enterprise Edition and click OK.

6. In the General tab in the Template display name, enter Operations Manager.

7. Select the Request Handling tab and mark the Allow Private Key to Be Exported option.

20

8. Select the Subject Name tab and select Supply in the request. Click OK at the warning.

9. Select the Security tab, select Authenticated Users, and select the Enroll checkbox.

10. Click OK to save the template.

11. Select the Enterprise PKI to expose the CA.

12. Right-click the CA and select Manage CA.

13. In the certsrv console, expand the CA; right-click the Certificates Templates and then select New, Certificate Template to Issue.

14. Select the Operations Manager certificate template and click OK.

The new Operations Manager template is now available in the Windows Server 2008 web enrollment page.

Request the Root CA Server Certificate

This enables the Edge Transport server to trust the Windows Server 2008 CA. This does not need to be done on the OpsMgr management servers because the Windows Server 2008 CA is an Enterprise CA, and all domain members automatically trust it. If the CA is not an enterprise CA, the steps need to be completed for the management servers as well.

To request and install the Root CA certificate on the Edge Transport server, execute the following steps:

1. Log on to the Edge Transport server (EX3.companyabc.com in this example) with local administrator rights.

2. Open a web browser and point it to the certificate server, in this case https://dc1.companyabc.com/certsrv. Enter credentials if prompted.

3. Click the Download a CA Certificate, Certificate Chain, or CRL Link (shown in Figure 20.9).

4. Click the Download CA certificate link. Note: If the certificate does not download, add the site to the Local Intranet list of sites in IE.

5. Click Open to open the CA certificate.

6. Click Install Certificate to install the CA certificate.

7. At the Certificate Import Wizard screen, click Next.

8. Select Place all certificates in the following store radio button.

9. Click Browse.

10. Click the Show physical stores check box.

11. Expand the Trusted Root Certification Authorities folder and select the Local Computer store.

12. Click OK.

13. Click Next, Finish, and OK to install the CA certificate.

14. Close any open windows.

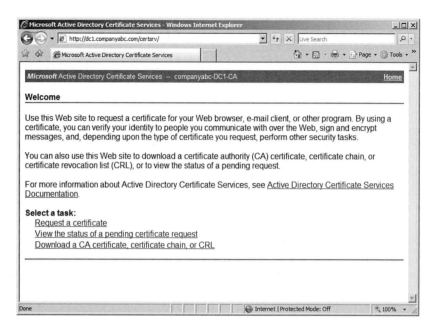

FIGURE 20.9   Download Root CA certificate.

Repeat for all Edge Transport servers. Now the Edge Transport servers trust certificates issued by the certification authority. The next step is to request the certificates to use for the mutual authentication for all servers.

Request a Certificate from the Root CA Server

Each of the management servers and the servers in the DMZ (that is, the Edge Transport servers) need to be issued certificates to use for communication.

The steps to request a certificate follow:

1. Log in as an administrator and then open a web browser and point it to the certificate server (in this case https://dc1.companyabc.com/certsrv).

2. Click the Request a Certificate link.

3. Click the advanced certificate request link.

4. Click the Create and Submit a request to this CA link.

5. In the Type of Certificate Template field, select Operations Manager.

6. In the Name field, enter the FQDN (Fully Qualified Domain Name) of the target server.

NOTE

Go to the actual server to get the name! On the server, go to Computer Properties, Computer Name. Copy the Full Computer Name and paste it into the Name Field of the form.

20

7. Click Submit.

8. Click Yes when you get the warning pop-up.

9. Click Install this certificate.

10. Click Yes when you see the warning pop-up. The certificate is now installed in the user certificate store.

NOTE

The certificate was installed in the user's certificate store but needs to be in the local computer store for Operations Manager. The ability to use the web enrollment to directly place the certificate into the local computer store was removed from the Windows Server 2008 web enrollment, so the certificate needs to be moved manually.

---

11. Select Start, Run, and then enter mmc to launch an MMC console.

12. Select File and Add/Remove Snap-In.

13. Select Certificates and click Add.

14. Select My User Account and click Finish.

15. Select Certificates again and click Add.

16. Select Computer account and click Next.

17. Select the Local computer; click Finish and then OK.

18. Expand the Certificates – Current User, Personal, and select the Certificates folder.

19. In the right pane, right-click the certificate issued earlier (in this example EX3.companyabc.com) and select All Tasks, Export. The certificate can be recognized by the certificate template name Operations Manager.

20. At the Certificate Export Wizard, select Next.

21. Select Yes, export the private key. Click Next.

22. Click Next.

23. Enter a password and click Next.

24. Enter a directory and filename (such as c:\EX1cert.pfx) and click Next.

25. Click Finish to export the certificate. Click OK at the pop-up.

26. Expand the Certificates (Local Computer), Personal, and select the Certificates folder.

NOTE

If this is the first certificate in the local computer store, the Certificates folder will not exist. Simply select the Personal folder instead, and the Certificates folder will be created automatically.

---

27. Right-click in the right pane and select All Tasks, Import.

28. At the Certificate Import Wizard, select Next.

29. Click Browse to locate the certificate file saved earlier. Change the file type to Personal Information Exchange (pfx) to see the file. Click Next.

30. Enter the password used earlier, select the Mark This Key as Exportable, and click Next.

31. Click Next.

32. Click Finish and then OK at the pop-up to complete the import.

The results for EX1.companyabc.com are shown in Figure 20.10. Note that EX1 also has a self-signed certificate that was created when the Exchange Server 2010 Edge Transport role was installed.

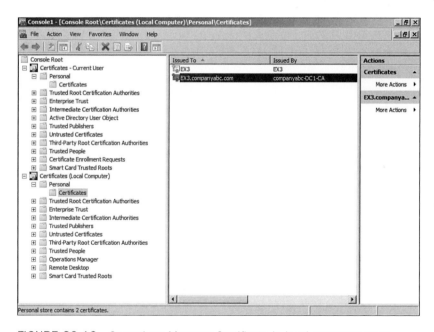

FIGURE 20.10   Operations Manager Certificate in local computer store.

The previous steps need to be completed for each Edge Transport server and for each management server.

Install the Agent on the Edge Transport

The agent needs to be installed manually on each Edge Transport server. Normally agents would be pushed by the Operations Manager console, but Edge Transport servers typically reside in the DMZ and are not members of the domain.

The steps to manually install the agent follow:

1. Log on as an administrator and insert the OpsMgr 2007 R2 installation media.

2. At the AutoPlay menu, select Run SetupOM.exe.

20

3. Select Install Operations Manager 2007 R2 Agent from the menu.

4. Click Next.

5. Click Next to accept the default directory.

6. Click Next to specify Management Group information.

7. Type in the Management Group Name and FQDN of the Management Server. Keep the default Management Server port as 5723. The example shown in Figure 20.11 has COMPANYABC as the management group name and omr2.companyabc.com as the management server.

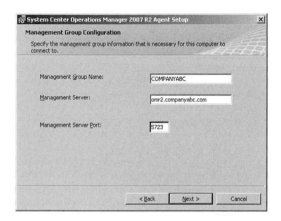

FIGURE 20.11   Manually entered Management Group information.

8. Click Next.

9. Click Next at the Agent Action Account page to leave the Local System as the action account.

10. Click Install to complete the installation.

11. When the installer finishes, click Finish.

The previous steps need to be completed for each Edge Transport server.

The agent is installed but will not communicate correctly with the management server. This is because the agent has not been configured to use the certificate for mutual authentication. This will be done in the next section.

Configure the Agent to Use the Certificate

After the agent is installed, the agent still needs to be configured to use the correct certificate. The OpsMgr installation includes a utility called MOMCertImport.exe that configures the agent to a) use certificates for authentication and b) select which certificate in the local computer store to use. The tool does not do any validation checking of the certificate itself, so care needs to be taken that the correct certificate is selected.

The steps to configure the agent to use a certificate follow:

1. Log on as an administrator on the Edge Transport server and insert the OpsMgr 2007 R2 installation media.
2. At the AutoPlay menu, select Run SetupOM.exe.
3. Select Browse This CD from the menu.
4. Select the SupportTools directory and then the AMD64 directory.

> **NOTE**
>
> Exchange Server 2010 is a 64-bit application, so the AMD64 is the correct folder for the 64-bit binaries. If the procedure is run for other servers, select the appropriate directory for the binaries such as i386.

5. In the directory, double-click MOMCertImport.exe.
6. In the pop-up window, select the certificate issued previously and click OK. The View Certificate button can be used to view the certificate details if the correct certificate is not obvious.

The Operation Manager service restarts automatically to have the certificate selected take effect. The preceding steps need to be repeated for each Edge Transport server and for each management server.

The Operations Manager event log can be viewed with the Windows Event Viewer. It is named Operations Manager and is located in the Applications and Services Logs folder in the tool. Any problems with the certificate are shown in the log immediately following the start of the System Center Management service.

Summary

System Center Operations Manager 2007 is key to managing Exchange Server 2010. It can also be used in Windows 2000/2003 or mixed environments to provide for automated monitoring of all vital operating system, application, and network functionality. This type of functionality is instrumental in reducing downtime and getting the most out of an Exchange Server 2010 investment. Briefly, OpsMgr is an effective way to gain proactive, rather than reactive, control over the entire environment.

20

Best Practices

The following are best practices from this chapter:

▶ Deploy System Center Operations Manager 2007 R2 for monitoring Exchange Server 2010.

▶ Install the Windows Operating System, Active Directory, DNS, IIS, and Exchange 2010 management packs into OpsMgr to monitor network systems and applications that Exchange Server 2010 depends on.

▶ Deploy Operations Manager Components on Windows 64-bit and SQL 64-bit for optimal performance.

▶ Create override management packs for each application management pack, such as the Exchange Server 2010 management pack. Don't use the Default Management Pack.

▶ Take future expansion and relevance of hardware into account when sizing servers for OpsMgr deployment.

▶ Keep the installation of OpsMgr on a separate server or set of separate dedicated member servers that do not run any other separate applications.

▶ Use SQL Server Reporting Services to produce custom reports using OpsMgr's reporting feature.

▶ Start with a single management group and add on additional management groups only if they are absolutely necessary.

▶ Use a dedicated service account for OpsMgr.

▶ Allocate adequate space for the databases depending on the length of time needed to store events and the number of managed systems.

▶ Monitor the size of the OpsMgr database to ensure that it does not increase beyond the bounds of acceptable size.

▶ Leverage the reporting database to store and report on data over a long period.

▶ Modify the grooming interval to aggressively address environmental requirements.

▶ Configure OpsMgr to monitor itself.

CHAPTER 21

Remote Administration of Exchange Server 2010 Servers

To keep maintenance and administration costs down and promote efficiency in any Microsoft Exchange Server 2010 messaging environment, you must have a secure and reliable means of managing the servers remotely. Because most servers are hosted in data center environments or are virtual machines, physical access to a server is the exception rather than the rule. Remote access to servers is the de facto standard method of access.

Windows Server 2008 and Exchange Server 2010 have these remote access capabilities built in so that you do not have to rely on third-party solutions. Methods of remote access to manage Exchange Server are mainly the following:

▶ Exchange Management Console (EMC)

▶ Remote Exchange Management Shell (EMS)

▶ Exchange Control Panel (ECP)

▶ Remote Desktop Protocol (RDP)

EMC is now completely remote-capable. The Exchange Server console is based on PowerShell, so the console can natively take advantage of the remote capabilities of PowerShell v2. Remote shell capability is new to Exchange Server 2010, and its remote capabilities are a function of PowerShell v2, which enables remote execution of PowerShell commands.

ECP is a new feature to Exchange Server 2010. It is a web-based front end that facilitates easy role-based access control, enabling users to manage their personal settings and administrators to manage the organization. This can be done from a web browser from any system on the network.

You can manage Exchange Server systems remotely using Terminal Services in different ways, and it is important to understand not only what these options are, but also which one is best for your particular environment. This chapter complements Chapter 19, "Exchange Server 2010 Management and Maintenance Practices," and expands on the different remote management capabilities and when to use them.

There are two Terminal Services functions within Windows Server 2008: Remote Desktop for Administration and Terminal Services (formerly known as Terminal Services Application Mode). Remote Desktop for Administration mode is installed (but not enabled) by default; Terminal Services is a Windows Server 2008 role and must be manually installed and configured.

Certificates, Trust, and Remote Administration

The various remote administration methods (EMS, EMC, ECP, and even RDP) in this chapter rely on certificates for encryption and authentication. This is the trend in the industry, to rely on X.509 certificates and PKI to transparently secure computer systems across platforms such as Windows and Linux operating systems and across applications such as Internet Explorer and Safari browsers.

The procedures in this chapter assume that the target Exchange Server 2010 server has a certificate that is issued by a trusted certification authority—that is, a certificate authority trusted by the client. This will not be the case if the Exchange Server 2010 server uses a self-signed certificate. If that's the case, the self-signed certificate needs to be imported into the trusted certification authority list of the client certificate store.

On the Exchange Server 2010 server, execute the following steps to export the self-signed certificate:

1. Click Start, and in the Start Search box, type mmc and press Enter.

2. From the File menu, select Add/Remove Snap-In.

3. Add the Certificates snap-in and select to manage certificates for the Computer account. When prompted to select a computer, select the local computer and click Finish and OK.

4. In the Certificate Manager console, open the Personal node and then select Certificates.

5. In the right pane, right-click the certificate with the server name of the Exchange 2010 server in Issued To column, select All Tasks, and then select Export.

6. In the Certificate Export Wizard, click Next.

7. On the Export Private Key page, select No, Do Not Export the Private Key and click Next.

8. On the Export File Format page, select Cryptographic Message Syntax Standard - PKCS #7 Certificates (.P7B) and select Next.

9. On the File to Export page, specify a path and filename to export the certificate to— for example, c:\EX1SelfSignedCert.p7b. After you specify a path and filename, click Next and then click Finish.

On the client computer, execute the following steps to import the certificate:

1. Copy the certificate file from the previous steps to the client computer.

2. Click Start for the Windows Vista pearl, and in the Start Search box, type `mmc` and press Enter.

3. From the File menu, select Add/Remove Snap-In.

4. Add the Certificates snap-in and select to manage certificates for the Computer account. When prompted to select a computer, select the local computer and click Finish and OK.

5. In Certificate Manager, open Trusted Root Certification Authorities and then select Certificates.

6. Right-click Certificates; then select All Tasks and then select Import.

7. In the Certificate Import Wizard, click Next.

8. On the File to Import page, specify the path and filename of the certificate file you copied to the client computer—for example, `c:\EX1SelfSignedCert.p7b`. After you specify the path and filename of the certificate file, click Next.

9. On the Certificate Store page, select Place All Certificates in the Following Store; then click Browse and select Trusted Root Certification Authorities. Click OK and then click Next.

10. Click Finish to import the certificate into the client computer.

11. A security warning appears that asks Do You Want to Install This Certificate?. Respond Yes to the security warning.

Now the Exchange Server 2010 self-signed certificate will be trusted by the client system.

Using the Exchange Management Console Remotely

EMC is supported on all computers that have any supported combination of server roles installed. On computers that have any combination of Client Access, Hub Transport, Mailbox, and Unified Messaging server roles installed, the EMC displays all servers in the organization and includes all console tree nodes. However, for computers that have the Edge Transport server role installed, EMC displays only the Edge Transport server role.

However, it can be used to remotely access another server in the organization or to remotely access another Exchange Server organization.

Using the Remote Exchange Management Shell

New to Exchange Server 2010 is the ability to access all the familiar Exchange Server cmdlets remotely, leveraging the PowerShell v2 remote capabilities. This enables cmdlets and scripts to run across multiple servers in a single EMS instance. It also enables administrators to run the shell from their workstation and connect remotely to the Exchange Server 2010 servers. Given the limitation of the EMC to run only on 64-bit systems, the EMS also enables 32-bit clients to connect to the servers.

Supported client OS platforms for the EMS are the following:

▶ Vista (32-bit or 64-bit)

▶ W2k8 (32-bit or 64-bit)

▶ W2k8 R2 (86-bit or 64-bit)

▶ Win7 (32-bit or 64-bit)

▶ W2k3 (32-bit or 64-bit)

▶ XP (32-bit or 64-bit)

The software requirements for the EMS are as follows:

▶ Windows PowerShell v2

▶ WinRM 2.0

The remote EMS does not require any Exchange Server binaries to be installed on the client, making deployment much easier.

The New-PSSession and the Import-PSSession cmdlets establish a remote session. The New-PSSession cmdlet establishes a secure persistent connection to the remote computer. A number of security options to the command support a variety of authentication and transmission options. The Import-PSSession cmdlet imports commands such as cmdlets, functions, and aliases from the remote computer into the local client. This includes all the Exchange Server 2010 cmdlets. The imported commands actually run in the remote session—that is, on the remote Exchange Server 2010 server rather than the local client.

To access an Exchange Server 2010 server from another system using the remote shell, execute the following commands:

1. Launch PowerShell.

2. Execute the cmdlet $UserCredential = Get-Credential. This prompts for credentials to use with the shell and store them in the variable.

3. Execute the cmdlet $Session = New-PSSession -ConfigurationName Microsoft.Exchange -ConnectionUri http://EX1.companyabc.com/PowerShell/ -Credential $UserCredential. Make sure to replace the FQDN of the target server in this example. This cmdlets establishes a connection with the Exchange Server 2010 server.

4. Execute the cmdlet Import-PSSession $Session. This imports the server-side session from the Exchange Server 2010 server.

Exchange Server 2010 commands can now be executed remotely. Figure 21.1 shows an example of a remote session connection and the execution of a sample Get-Mailbox cmdlet executed from the remote system.

The preceding example was executed on a 32-bit Windows Vista system running WinRM 2.0 and PowerShell v2.

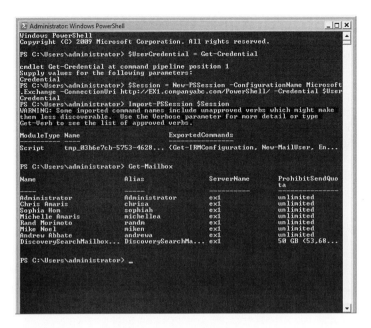

FIGURE 21.1   Setting up a remote shell session.

The certificate requirement can be bypassed using the SkipCACheck, SkipCNCheck, and SkipRevocationCheck options. These are a little tricky to generate because the options need to be stored in an object prior to executing the cmdlet. Here are the steps:

1. Launch PowerShell.

2. Execute the cmdlet $SkipCert = New-WSManSessionOption -SkipCACheck -SkipCNCheck –SkipRevocationCheck. This captures the option to skip the certificate check in the $SkipCert variable.

3. Execute the cmdlet $UserCredential = Get-Credential. This prompts for credentials to use with the shell and store them in the variable $UserCredential.

4. Execute the cmdlet $Session = New-PSSession -ConfigurationName Microsoft.Exchange -ConnectionUri http://EX1.companyabc.com/PowerShell/ -Credential $UserCredential -SessionOption $SkipCert. Make sure to replace the FQDN of the target server in this example. This cmdlets establishes a connection with the Exchange 2010 server.

5. Execute the cmdlet Import-PSSession $Session. This imports the server-side session from the Exchange 2010 server.

To get help with remote operations in PowerShell, use the get-help about_Remote_Troubleshooting command. This has extensive troubleshooting information and helpful tips. Use get-help New-PSSession to get help on the New-PSSession cmdlet, which includes quite a few options.

Using the ECP Remotely

ECP is a fully HTML-based application. It is secured with SSL and certificates and securely transmitted via the HTTPS protocol. As such, it is an excellent candidate for remote access.

The ECP can be accessed by an administrator or specialist from any client using a supported browser via the https://<servername>/ecp URL. End users can access the ECP from within the Outlook Web App (OWA) client by clicking on the Options link, which redirects the end user to the https://<servername>/ecp, as shown in Figure 21.2.

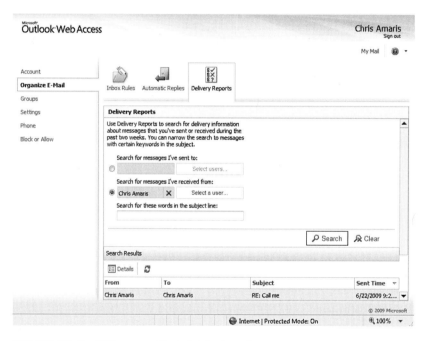

FIGURE 21.2   ECP user self-administration view.

The ECP also functions across a firewall, similar to Outlook Web App. It is recommended to proxy the HTTPS traffic through an application level proxy firewall such as Microsoft ISA 2006. Figure 21.3 shows an example of ECP access using an ISA proxy firewall.

The diagram in Figure 21.3 shows clearly that the ECP traffic goes to the Exchange Server 2010 CAS role.

RDP with Exchange Server 2010

RDP access to an Exchange server is one of the most common methods to remotely access a server. With most servers hosted in data centers that might be halfway around the world, RDP give administrators a fast, easy, and secure method to get complete console access.

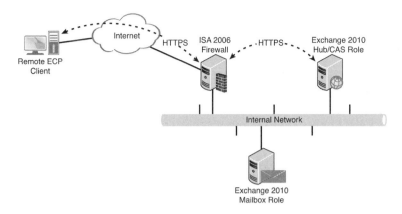

FIGURE 21.3   Exchange Control Panel network path.

In this section, two methods of using RDP are discussed. The first is Remote Desktop for Administration, which enables a maximum of two connections and has no licensing implications. This is great for basic access to the Exchange Server 2010 server remotely. The second is Terminal Services, which enables many users to connect and has licensing costs associated with it. This is great for setting up a jump box to enable many administrators to use an SMC.

Planning and Using Remote Desktop for Administration

As mentioned earlier, Remote Desktop for Administration is included and installed with the Windows Server 2008 operating system and needs only to be enabled. This eases automated and unattended server deployment by enabling an administrator to deploy servers that can be managed remotely after the operating systems have completed installation. This enables Exchange Server administrators in central offices to manage servers in branch offices or Exchange Server administrators in one region (such as the America region) to manage servers in another region (such as the Asian region). This can reduce the required headcount to manage Exchange Server infrastructure and facilitate a follow-the-sun model of global support.

This model can also be used to manage a headless server, which can reduce the amount of space needed in any server rack. More space can be dedicated to servers instead of switch boxes, monitors, keyboards, and mouse devices.

This also provides for an improved security model because Exchange Server administrators can administer the Exchange servers without having to get physical access to the servers. This is an effective security strategy for large data centers with various application servers that might be collocated in the same racks as the Exchange servers. It enables the Exchange Server administrators to perform their job functions without needed access to the data center.

Remote Desktop for Administration limits the number of terminal sessions to two, with only one RDP or Secure Sockets Layer (SSL) for remote administration connection per network interface. Only administrators can connect to these sessions. No additional licenses are needed to run a server in this Terminal Services mode, which enables an administrator to perform almost all the server management duties remotely.

Even though Remote Desktop for Administration is installed by default, this mode does need to be enabled. Some organizations might see Remote Desktop for Administration as an unneeded security risk and choose to keep it disabled. This function can easily be disabled throughout the entire Active Directory (AD) forest by using a Group Policy setting to disable administrators from connecting through Remote Desktop for Administration.

Planning for Remote Desktop for Administration Mode

Unless Remote Desktop for Administration is viewed as a security risk, you should enable it on all internal servers to allow remote administration. For servers that are on the Internet or for demilitarized zone (DMZ) networks, Remote Desktop for Administration can be used, but access should be even more restricted. For example, consider limiting access to a predefined IP address or set of IP addresses, using firewall access control lists (ACLs) to eliminate unauthorized attempts to log on to the server. Another option is to limit connections to the server based on protocol.

> **NOTE**
>
> The level of encryption for remote sessions by default is 128-bit (bidirectional). It is also important to note that some older Terminal Services clients might not support that level of encryption. See the section "Securing Remote Desktop for Administration" for more details and how to increase the security.

Enabling Remote Desktop for Administration

Remote Desktop for Administration mode is installed on all Windows Server 2008 servers by default and needs only to be enabled. To manually enable this feature, follow these steps:

1. Launch Server Manager.
2. In the Server Summary, Computer Information section, click the Configure Remote Desktop link.
3. In the Remote Desktop section, check Allow Connections from Computers Running Any Version of Remote Desktop (Less Secure), as shown in Figure 21.4 (or alternately choose Allow Connections Only from Computers Running Remote Desktop with Network Level Authentication (More Secure) if you have a more current version of the RDP client that supports network level authentication).
4. At the Remote Desktop Firewall exception will be an enabled pop-up; click OK to allow the firewall exception to be made.
5. Click OK on the Systems Properties page to complete this process.

The connection can be tested by launching the Remote Desktop Client from Start, All Programs, Accessories and selecting the Remote Desktop Connection icon. Enter in the name of the Exchange server to connect to.

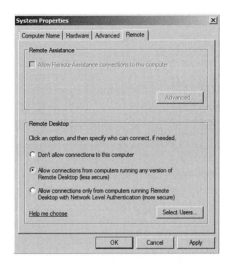

FIGURE 21.4   Enabling users to connect to the system remotely.

Enabling Remote Desktop for Administration After the Fact

Sometimes, an Exchange server is built and deployed, but the Remote Desktop option is not enabled. This is a problem when subsequently attempting to remotely administer the server. The Terminal Services Client will behave as if the server could not be found.

Even though Remote Desktop is not enabled, the Exchange server can still be accessed administratively. In particular, the Registry can still be modified remotely and the Remote Desktop setting can be enabled using the RegEdit tool.

To enable Remote Desktop remotely on a Windows Server 2008-based Exchange Server 2010 server, complete the following steps:

1. From a domain member computer, log on as a user with Administrator privileges on the server.
2. Launch `regedit.exe`.
3. Click File and then select Connect Network Registry.
4. Enter the name of the server on which you want to enable Remote Desktop, and click OK.
5. Under the Exchange server tree, go to the key `HKLM\System\CurrentControlSet\ Control\Terminal Services\`.
6. Change the value `fDenyTSConnections` from 1 to 0.
7. Close `regedit.exe`.
8. The change takes effect immediately.

The server now accepts Terminal Services connections.

Remote Desktop Client Command-line Options

The Remote Desktop Connection client (`mstsc.exe`) can be launched from the command line for additional control.

The command line for the Remote Desktop Client is as follows:

```
mstsc.exe {ConnectiᴜnFile ¦ /v:ServerName[:Port]} [/console] [/f]
➥[/w:Width/h:Height]
```

A handful of switch commands for the Remote Desktop Client can be used to choose specific servers and options. The commands are as follows:

▶ `/v:ServerName[ :Port]`—Specifies the remote computer and, optionally, the port number to which you want to connect.

▶ `/admin`—Connects to the console session of the specified Windows Server 2008 family operating system.

▶ `/f` —Starts the Remote Desktop connection in full-screen mode.

▶ `/w:Width/h:Height`—Specifies the dimensions of the Remote Desktop screen.

In particular, the `/admin` switch setting is useful. It enables the Exchange Server administrator to connect directly to the console session on the Exchange server, which is the session used when logging on at the keyboard of the Exchange server. This, in effect, enables the Exchange Server administrator to assume control of the keyboard of the Exchange server.

Remote Desktop Administration Tips and Tricks

You should consider several key points before using Remote Desktop for Administration, including, but not limited to, the following:

▶ **Make sure resources are available**—What information technology (IT) personnel resources, if any, are available at the remote location or at the Exchange server's location? If a problem arises with the connection to the remote Exchange server or the server itself (for example, a disconnection), contingency plans should be available to recover and continue to remotely manage the system. Generally speaking, it is a good idea to have someone in the vicinity who can assist the administrator.

▶ **Use care when modifying network configurations**—With any remote administration tool, you are dependent upon the connectivity between the client computer and the Exchange server that is remotely managed. If network configuration settings must be modified remotely, consider having alternative methods of access. For instance, dial-up or a separate network connection might minimize downtime or other issues stemming from loss of connectivity.

▶ **Use disconnect and reset timeout values**—Anytime a connection is accidentally broken or an administrator disconnects, the remote session is placed into a disconnected state that can later be reconnected and used to manage a server remotely. Disconnect and reset timeouts are not configured by default for Remote Desktop administration tools. These values can be used to ensure that administrators are not unintentionally locked out (for example, when there are two remote sessions that are active but in a disconnected state). Generally speaking, using a five-minute timeout value allows enough time for administrators to reconnect if they were accidentally disconnected. Moreover, it helps minimize the number of sessions that are disconnected and not used.

▶ **Coordinate remote administration efforts**—The number of remote administration connections is limited to a precious two. Therefore, plan and coordinate efforts to reduce the number of attempts to access Exchange servers remotely. This also helps ensure that remote administration activities do not conflict with other administrators and sessions or, in the worst of cases, corrupt information or data on the server.

Remote Desktop Administration Keyboard Shortcuts

The keyboard shortcuts that work on the server have equivalents when running in Terminal Services. Table 21.1 lists the most common ones.

TABLE 21.1   Keyboard Shortcuts in a Remote Desktop Session

Windows Keyboard Shortcut	Terminal Services Keyboard Shortcut	Description
Alt+Tab	Alt+Page Up	Switches between programs from left to right
Alt+Shift+Tab	Alt+Page Down	Switches between programs from right to left
Alt+Esc	Alt+Insert	Cycles through the programs in the order they were started
	Ctrl+Esc	Switches the client between a window and full screen
Ctrl+Esc	Alt+Home	Displays the Start menu
	Alt+Delete	Displays the Windows menu
Prnt Scrn	Ctrl+Alt+Minus (–) symbol on the numeric keypad	Places a snapshot of the active window in the Remote Desktop session on the Clipboard
Ctrl+Alt+Del	Ctrl+Alt+End	Displays the Task Manager or Windows Security dialog box
Alt+Prnt Scrn	Ctrl+Alt+Plus (+) symbol on the numeric keypad	Places a snapshot of the entire Remote Desktop session window on the Clipboard

These keyboard shortcuts can be handy when working within Terminal Services sessions to capture a screen for documentation, check the performance in Task Manager, or quickly switch between windows in the session.

Planning and Preparing Terminal Services for Exchange Administration

Terminal Services mode is available in all editions of Windows Server 2008 (that is, Standard, Enterprise, and DataCenter) except the Web Edition. It enables any authorized user to connect to the server and run a single application or a complete desktop session from the client workstation.

Because the applications are loaded and running on the Terminal Services server, client desktop resources are barely used; all the application processing is performed by the Terminal Services server. This enables companies to extend the life of old, less-powerful workstations by running applications only from a Terminal Services server session.

Terminal Services is generally not considered a viable technology to manage Exchange Server remotely. Although it is possible to use Terminal Services to manage Exchange Server 2010, several planning considerations must be addressed to determine whether Terminal Services is suitable in your environment.

The narrow use for Terminal Services is in the case of a centralized tool platform where multiple administrators (more than two at a time) log on and use the administration tools. Terminal Services in this case allows the organization to set up a central server or set of servers with all the tools that the administrators use. This server is sometimes referred to as a Jump Server, as administrators establish a Remote Desktop to the system, and then they jump to other servers using console administration applications.

Planning Considerations for Using Terminal Services

Terminal Services can require a lot of planning, especially when you're considering whether to use it to manage Exchange Server remotely. Because Terminal Services is intended to make applications available to end users rather than serve as a remote management service, security, server performance, and licensing are key components to consider before using it in a production environment.

Terminal Services Security

Terminal Services servers should be secured following standard security guidelines defined in company security policies and as recommended by hardware and software vendors. Some basic security configurations include removing all unnecessary services from the Terminal Services nodes and applying security patches for known vulnerabilities on services or applications that are running on the terminal server.

Terminal Services in Windows Server 2008 supports three different security levels. The main difference is in the support for Network Level Authentication, which uses certificates to authenticate the server identity to the client. This prevents man-in-the-middle attacks. The three security levels follow:

▶ **RDP Security**—This is the native RDP encryption and does not support Network Level Authentication.

▶ **SSL (TLS 1.0)**—Network Level Authentication is performed to verify the identity of the server to the client. Certificates are used to secure the transmission and to perform Network Level Authentication.

▶ **Negotiate**—The most secure level that the client supports will be used. If the client supports SSL (TLS 1.0), that will be used. If not, then RDP security will be used. This is the default setting.

In addition to the security levels, Windows Server 2008 terminal services can be run in four different encryption levels to provide the transmission protection appropriate for the organization. The four levels of encryption follow:

► **Low**—Encryption is performed at the highest level supported by the client, but only on the data sent from the client to the server. Data sent from the server to the client is not encrypted. This is insecure and not recommended.

► **Client Compatible**—Encryption is performed at the highest level supported by the client, but all data between the client and server is encrypted.

► **High**—128-bit encryption is performed on all data between the client and the server. If the client cannot support 128-bit encryption, the connection is refused by the server.

► **FIPS Compliant**—Federal Information Process Standard (FIPS) 140-1 validated encryption is performed on all data between the client and the server. If the clients cannot support FIPS encryption, the connection is refused by the server.

An administrator can use Group Policy to limit client functionality as needed to enhance server security, and if increased network security is a requirement, can consider requiring clients to run sessions in 128-bit high-encryption mode.

In addition to the more common security precautions that are recommended for Terminal Services, you must also consider how running Terminal Services on an Exchange Server 2010 server affects security. Using a server with both Terminal Services and Exchange Server 2010 roles and responsibilities can be a dangerous combination and should be considered only in the smallest of environments with very relaxed security requirements. In any circumstance, the combination is not recommended.

Combining the two services and configuring Terminal Services to remotely manage Exchange Server can result in many security-related hazards, including the following:

► A single misconfiguration or setting can enable users to change specific Exchange Server settings or parameters.

► Users authorized to shut down or restart the system might inadvertently do so, causing messaging downtime.

► Application-specific security might conflict or, in some cases, unintentionally allow or restrict access to messaging components on the server.

Terminal Server Licensing

Terminal Services requires the purchase of client access licenses (CALs) for each client device or session. A Terminal Services License Server also must be available on the network to allocate and manage these CALs. When a Terminal Services server is establishing a session with a client, it checks with the Terminal Services License Server to verify whether this client has a license. A license is allocated if the client does not already have one.

> **NOTE**
>
> Using Terminal Services to connect to and remotely manage an Exchange Server 2010 server does not exempt you from needing a Terminal Services CAL. This adds to the overall cost of supporting Exchange Server 2010.

To install licenses on the Terminal Services License Server, the Terminal Services License Server must first be installed and then activated online. The Terminal Services License Server requires Internet access or dial-up modem access to activate the CALs added to the server.

When a Terminal Services server cannot locate a Terminal Services License Server on the network, it still allows unlicensed clients to connect. This can go on for 120 days without contacting a license server, and then the server stops serving Terminal Services sessions. It is imperative to get a license server installed on the network as soon as possible—before Terminal Services servers are deployed to production.

Installing Terminal Services for Remote Administration

To install Terminal Services, a network administrator can use the Server Manager as follows:

1. Launch Server Manager. Right-click on Roles and select Add Roles.
2. Click Next.
3. Select the Terminal Services role and click Next.
4. Click Next at the Introduction page.
5. Select Terminal Server for the role services and click Next.
6. Click Next.
7. Select the Authentication Method for the Terminal Server and click Next.
8. Select the Licensing Mode and click Next.
9. Select the User Groups that can connect to the Terminal Server and click Next.
10. Click Install to complete the installation of Terminal Services.
11. Click Close to finish. A reboot might be required.

Terminal Services is now accessible.

Accessing a Server Using the Remote Desktop Client

A Windows Server 2003 or Windows Server 2008 system with Terminal Services installed can be accessed from a variety of clients.

Accessing Terminal Services Using the Windows Remote Desktop Protocol (RDP) Client

All Windows Server 2003 server, Windows Server 2008 server, Vista, and Windows XP Professional versions include a terminal server client called Remote Desktop Connection.

This full-featured client enables end users to tune their connections to run in Full-screen mode, utilizing advanced features, such as server audio redirection, true-color video, and local disk, COM port, and printer redirection. Remote Desktop Connection can also be optimized to run over a slow connection.

Down-level client workstations can get the RDP client as a free download from the Microsoft website.

Accessing Terminal Services Using the Web Client

Terminal Services provides a web-based client that can easily be distributed through a web browser. Connecting to a terminal server using this client requires a web port connection to the terminal server logon web page and also access to TCP port 3389 on the terminal server. The web-based client still uses the RDP native to Windows Server 2008 Terminal Services.

Contrary to many terminal server administrators' beliefs, the web server system hosting the web client pages does not need to be running on the terminal server. If there is no particular reason to run a web server on the terminal server, for security and performance reasons, place the terminal server web client on a separate web server.

To install the web server client on a web server system, do the following:

1. Launch Server Manager. Right-click on Roles and select Add Roles.
2. Click Next.
3. Select the Terminal Services role and click Next.
4. Click Next.
5. Select TS Web Access role service and click Next. The wizard might prompt to add the Web Services role if it is not already installed.
6. Click Install to complete the installation of TS Web Access.
7. Click Close to finish. A reboot might be required.

To access this page, open a web browser and type `https://<servername>/ts`. This can be accessed through a firewall as well.

Using the Remote Desktops MMC (`Tsmmc.msc`)

Remote Desktop is a utility that provides a way to manage several Terminal Services sessions from within one window. This utility still uses RDP to connect to servers and workstations, but it allows an administrator to switch between terminal sessions by clicking a button instead of having to switch windows. Also, because the console settings can be saved, a new terminal session can also be established with the click of a button.

Remotely Connecting to a Terminal Server Console

Administrators can connect to terminal server consoles remotely by using the Remote Desktop Connection client or the Remote Desktops MMC snap-in. With remote console access, administrators can use Terminal Services to log on to the server remotely as though they were logged on at the console.

Using the Remote Desktops MMC snap-in, administrators can configure remote desktop sessions that always connect to the terminal server console session. This enables administrators to successfully install and update the operating system and applications remotely.

CAUTION

You need to know whether to leave the console session logged on and/or locked. If a user logs off the session, the console will also be logged off. So, you need to be informed and be safe.

To connect to a terminal server console using Remote Desktop Connection, run `mstsc.exe` from the command prompt with the `/admin` switch to gain console access.

Securing Remote Desktop for Administration

The security of the Remote Desktop for Administration can be adjusted in a variety of ways to enhance the security of the sessions. All of these settings are configured in the Terminal Services Configuration MMC snap-in, which is, by default, installed in the Administrative Tools, Terminal Services folder. The security settings are properties of the RDP-Tcp connection under the Connections folder in the tool.

These settings ensure that the Remote Desktop for Administration is secure.

Encryption Layer

The Encryption Level setting can be used to change the encryption from the RDP Security Layer to SSL. This supports the use of certificates. This is a little-used feature of Remote Desktop for Administration but can be used to enhance or standardize security.

Terminal Services in Windows Server 2008 supports three different security levels. The main difference is in the support for Network Level Authentication, which uses certificates to authenticate the server identity to the client. This prevents man-in-the-middle attacks. The three security levels follow:

- ▶ **RDP Security**—This is the native RDP encryption and does not support Network Level Authentication.

- ▶ **SSL (TLS 1.0)**—Network Level Authentication is performed to verify the identity of the server to the client. Certificates are used to secure the transmission and to perform Network Level Authentication.

- ▶ **Negotiate**—The most secure level that the client supports will be used. If the client supports SSL (TLS 1.0), that will be used. If not, RDP security will be used. This is the default setting.

Encryption Level

In addition to the security levels, Windows Server 2008 terminal services can be run in four different encryption levels to provide the transmission protection appropriate for the organization. The four levels of encryption follow:

▶ **Low**—Encryption is performed at the highest level supported by the client, but only on the data sent from the client to the server. Data sent from the server to the client is not encrypted. This is insecure and not recommended.

▶ **Client Compatible**—Encryption is performed at the highest level supported by the client, but all data between the client and server is encrypted.

▶ **High**—128-bit encryption is performed on all data between the client and the server. If the client cannot support 128-bit encryption, the connection is refused by the server.

▶ **FIPS Compliant**—Federal Information Process Standard (FIPS) 140-1 validated encryption is performed on all data between the client and the server. If the clients cannot support FIPS encryption, the connection is refused by the server.

The various options are shown in Figure 21.5.

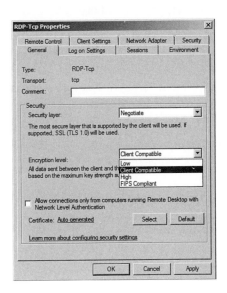

FIGURE 21.5   Encryption level security setting.

An administrator can use Group Policy to limit client functionality as needed to enhance server security and, if increased network security is a requirement, can consider requiring clients to run sessions in 128-bit high-encryption mode.

The sessions can be made more secure by changing the setting to High, which ensures that the clients will always connect at 128-bit. Older clients that don't support 128-bit or clients that are hard-coded for 56-bit will fail.

Remote Control

The Terminal Services connection allows the sessions to be remotely controlled, meaning that a third party can view and possibly interact with the Terminal Services session. Although this can be useful for training and support by facilitating support, it can also present a security risk.

The ability to use remote control can be disabled by selecting the Do Not Allow Remote Control check box on the Remote Control tab.

Disable Mappings

Another feature of the Terminal Services connection is to map local drives, printers, LPT ports, COM ports, the Clipboard, and the audio. These allow for a much richer experience by allowing the administrator to copy files from local drives, print to the local printer, and cut/paste from the Terminal Services session to the local system.

However, these features could also be security risks as they allow direct interaction between the client and the Terminal Services session. These mapping features can be disabled as needed on the Client Settings tab in the Connection Properties dialog box. By default, all are allowed except the Audio mapping.

Always Prompt for Password

The Terminal Services Client can be configured to save the logon password and allow for automatic logon to the Exchange server. This is very convenient for the Exchange Server administrator, who can just launch the Terminal Services client and get access to the Exchange server without being prompted to enter credentials.

However, this is a very bad security practice because any user can click on the icon and then have full access to the Exchange server. Unfortunately, the password is saved at the client level and not on the server side.

Fortunately, the Terminal Services connection can be configured to always prompt for a password regardless of whether one is supplied automatically. The Always Prompt for Password feature can be enabled on the Logon Settings tab of the Connection Properties dialog box.

Session Disconnect

If an Exchange Server administrator's Terminal Services session breaks, the session is normally left in a disconnected state. This allows the Exchange Server administrator to reconnect to the session and pick up where he left off. The Exchange Server administrator can also choose to disconnect rather than log off a session. This is frequently done when a long-running process is started on the Exchange server, such as a migration of a large mailbox.

Although the disconnected session is convenient, it might also be considered a security risk to have active sessions left unattended so to speak. If this is a security concern, the connection can be configured on the Sessions tab to end a disconnected session after a period of time, as shown in Figure 21.6. The session is ended after being in a disconnected state for five minutes, which gives the Exchange Server administrator ample time to reconnect following connection problems.

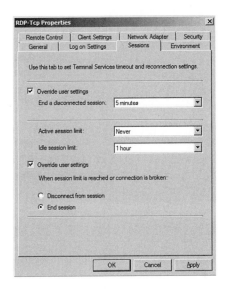

FIGURE 21.6   Idle session limit configuration.

Other session limits can be configured on this tab as well, such as ending or disconnecting a session that has been active too long (not recommended) or that has been idle too long.

Permissions

By default, only members of the local Administrators group or the local Remote Desktop Users group are able to access the server via the Remote Desktop for Administration. These permissions can be customized to explicitly grant access or explicitly deny access. The permissions for the connection can be accessed in the RDP-Tcp connection properties on the Security tab.

Using the Remote Desktop Tool for Remote Exchange Management

The Remote Desktop tool comes standard with all Windows 2003 and Windows Server 2008 implementations and facilitates managing multiple Exchange servers. As shown in Figure 21.7, multiple console screens can be defined for each server in the tool, as well as multiple connections can be established simultaneously to various servers in the environment. The left pane shows a list of servers that can be connected to and switched between. The credentials for each session can optionally be saved to have the sessions automatically connect.

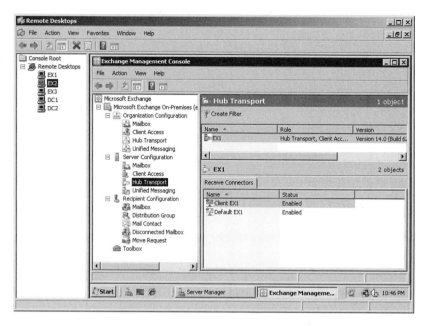

FIGURE 21.7   Managing Exchange Server 2010 servers using the Remote Desktop tool.

The multiple connections can be toggled between quickly simply by clicking on their icon or even arranged in multiple panes on a single screen. A large display is very effective for this.

Another interesting Remote Desktop tool feature is that the tool has an option to connect to the console session rather than establish a new session. This allows the Exchange Server administrator to connect directly to the console session and interact with any applications that were started at the server keyboard.

The Remote Desktop configuration can be saved in Microsoft Management Console files (*.msc) to be quickly launched. This allows the Exchange Server administrator to create different custom consoles with the appropriate Terminal Services sessions for the task at hand, such as when doing mailbox maintenance or troubleshooting front-end problems.

Summary

Many messaging environments today require an easy and effective way to remotely manage and maintain systems. Microsoft Exchange Server 2010 has a number of remote options for administering the Exchange Server messaging system, including the Exchange Management Console, the Remote Exchange Management Shell, and the Exchange Control Panel. Terminal Services provides an excellent mechanism to accomplish this.

Windows Server 2003 and Windows Server 2008 have a variety of tools built-in that administrators can use to securely manage and maintain Exchange Server from any location using Terminal Services.

Best Practices

The following are best practices from this chapter:

- ▶ Use the Exchange Control Panel to provide secure RBAC to administrative functions.

- ▶ For 32-bit systems, leverage the Remote Exchange Management Shell or the Remote Desktop Protocol to Provide Remote Administrative Access.

- ▶ Use certificates from trusted CAs or import the self-signed certificates into the trusted root certification authorities of the workstation.

- ▶ Carefully plan which Exchange servers should use Remote Desktop for Administration for remote management.

- ▶ Restrict Remote Desktop for Administration access on Exchange Server 2010 servers that are facing the Internet (for example, limiting access to a predefined IP address or set of IP addresses).

- ▶ Use High or FIPS level encryption on the RDP sessions for Internet-facing Exchange servers, such as Edge Transport roles.

- ▶ Have a person in the vicinity of the server that is being managed remotely assist the administrator in case network connectivity is lost.

- ▶ Use care when modifying network configurations over a Remote Desktop for Administration connection.

- ▶ Use disconnect and reset timeout values for Remote Desktop for Administration connections.

- ▶ Plan and coordinate remote administration efforts to reduce the number of attempts to access Exchange servers remotely.

- ▶ Do not implement Terminal Services on an Exchange server solely to manage Exchange Server remotely.

CHAPTER 22

Documenting an Exchange Server 2010 Environment

Documentation is the cornerstone for building and maintaining a streamlined Microsoft Exchange Server 2010 environment. Documentation is not only an integral part of the installation or design of an Exchange Server 2010 environment, but it is also important for the maintenance, support, and recovery of new or existing environments.

Documentation serves several purposes throughout the life cycle of Exchange Server 2010 and is especially critical on a per-project basis. In the initial stages of a project, it serves to provide a historical record of the options and decisions made during the design process. During the testing and implementation phases, documents such as step-by-step procedures and checklists guide project team members and help ensure that all steps are completed. When the implementation portion of the project is complete, support documentation can play a key role in maintaining the health of the new environment. Support documents include administration and maintenance procedures, checklists, detailed configuration settings, and monitoring procedures.

In the discovery stages of the project, documentation serves to record the key elements of a successful implementation:

▶ Organizational goals and objectives

▶ Business requirements

▶ Technical specifications

It quickly becomes apparent how the documents become building blocks for the remaining documentation needs. By defining the organizational goals and objectives, the business requirements can be identified. After the business requirements are listed, the technical specifications are developed to support them.

This chapter is dedicated to providing the breadth and scope of documentation for an Exchange Server 2010 environment. Equally important, it provides considerations and best practices for keeping your messaging environment well documented, maintained, and manageable.

Benefits of Documentation

Although many of the benefits of Exchange Server 2010 documentation are obvious and tangible, others can be harder to identify. A key benefit to documentation is that the process of putting the information down on paper encourages a higher level of analysis and review of the topic at hand. The process also encourages teamwork and collaboration within an organization and interdepartmental exchange of ideas.

Documentation that is developed with specific goals, and goes through a review or approval process, is typically well organized and complete, and contributes to the overall professionalism of the organization and its knowledge base. The following sections examine some of the other benefits of professional documentation in the Exchange Server 2010 environment.

In today's world of doing more with less, the intangible benefits of good documentation can become a challenge to justify to upper management. Some key benefits of documentation include the following:

- ▶ **Collaboration**—Producing the documentation to support a good Exchange Server 2010 implementation requires input from departments across the organization. This teamwork encourages deeper analysis and more careful review of the project goals. With better base information, the project team can make more informed decisions and avoid having to go back to the drawing board to address missed objectives.

- ▶ **Historical records**—Implementation projects are composed of several different stages where goals are identified and key decisions are made to support them. It is important to make sure these decisions and their supporting arguments are recorded for future reference. As the project moves forward, it is not uncommon for details to get changed because of incomplete information being passed from the design stage onto the implementation stage.

- ▶ **Training**—Life is ever changing. That might sound a bit philosophical for a book on technology, but when it comes to people, we know that some of them move on to other challenges. And that is when good documentation will become an invaluable tool to provide information to their replacement. This is equally true for the executive sponsor, the project manager, or the engineer building the Exchange server.

Knowledge Sharing and Knowledge Management

The right documentation enables an organization to organize and manage its data and intellectual property. Company policies and procedures are typically located throughout multiple locations that include individual files for various departments. Consolidating this information into logical groupings can be beneficial.

> **TIP**
>
> Place documentation in at least two different locations where it is easily accessible for authorized users, such as on the intranet, in a public folder, or in hard-copy format. Also consider using a document management system such as Microsoft Office SharePoint Services 2010.

A complete design document consolidates and summarizes key discussions and decisions, budgetary concerns, and timing issues. This consolidation provides a single source of information for questions that might emerge at a later date. In addition, a document that describes the specific configuration details of the Exchange server might prove very valuable to a manager in another company office when making a purchasing decision.

All the documents should be readily available at all times. This is especially critical regarding disaster recovery documents. Centralizing the documentation and communicating the location helps reduce the use of out-of-date documentation and reduce confusion during a disaster recovery. It is also recommended that they be available in a number of formats, such as hard copy, the appropriate place on the network, and even via an intranet.

Financial Benefits of Documentation

Proper Exchange Server 2010 documentation can be time consuming and adds to the cost of the environment and project. In lean economic times for a company or organization, it is often difficult to justify the expense of project documentation. However, when looking at documents, such as in maintenance or disaster recovery scenarios, it is easy to determine that creating this documentation makes financial sense. For example, in an organization where downtime can cost thousands of dollars per minute, the return on investment (ROI) in disaster recovery and maintenance documentation is easy to calculate. In a company that is growing rapidly and adding staff and new servers on a regular basis, tested documentation on server builds and administration training can also have immediate and visible benefits.

Financial benefits are not limited to maintenance and disaster recovery documentation. Well-developed and professional design and planning documentation helps the organization avoid costly mistakes in the implementation or migration process, such as buying too many server licenses or purchasing too many servers.

Baselining Records for Documentation Comparisons

Baselining is a process of recording the state of an Exchange Server 2010 system so that any changes in its performance can be identified at a later date. Complete baselining also pertains to the overall network performance, including wide area network (WAN) links, but in those cases it might require special software and tools (such as sniffers) to record the information.

An Exchange Server 2010 system baseline document records the state of the server after it is implemented in a production environment and can include statistics such as memory use, paging, disk subsystem throughput, and more. This information then allows the administrator or appropriate IT resource to determine at a later date how the system is performing in comparison to initial operation.

Using Documentation for Troubleshooting Purposes

Troubleshooting documentation is a record of identified system issues and the associated resolution. This documentation is helpful both in terms of the processes that the company recommends for resolving technical issues and a documented record of the results of actual troubleshooting challenges. Researching and troubleshooting an issue is time consuming. Documenting the process followed and the results provides a valuable resource for other company administrators who might experience the same issue.

Exchange Server 2010 Project Documentation

An Exchange Server 2010 implementation is a complex endeavor that should be approached in phases. First and foremost, a decision should be made on how the project will be tracked. This can be done using a simple Microsoft Excel spreadsheet, but a tool like Microsoft Project makes mapping out the tasks much easier. Also, the first round of mapping out a project will most likely have at most 15-20 lines of tasks. Using a tool like Microsoft Project makes it easier to fill in more line items as you progress in the design and planning stages.

With the tracking method in place, you can move on to address the documents that are typically created for an Exchange Server 2010 implementation:

- ▶ Design and planning document
- ▶ Communication plan document
- ▶ Migration plan document
- ▶ Training plan document
- ▶ Prototype lab document
- ▶ Pilot test document
- ▶ Support and project completion document

This chapter examines each of these documents individually and focuses on their key elements.

Design and Planning Document

One of the concepts discussed earlier in the chapter was that of documents being used as building blocks. Continuing with that idea, the Exchange Server 2010 design and planning document is considered the foundation for all the documentation created from this point forward. The design and planning document takes the original business requirements, matches them to the technical specifications, and then maps out how to produce the end product. It cannot be stressed enough the importance of a well-developed design and planning document.

The Exchange Server 2010 design and planning document is the outcome of the design sessions held with the subject matter expert (SME) and the technical staff within the organization. A standard Exchange Server 2010 design and planning document contains the following information:

Executive Summary
> Project Overview

Project Organization
> Resources

> Costs

> Risk Assessment

Existing Environment
> Network Infrastructure

> Active Directory Infrastructure

> Exchange Topology

> Backup and Restore

> Administrative Model

> Client Systems

Exchange Server 2010 Environment
> Goals and Objectives

Exchange Server 2010 Architecture
> Server Placement

> Exchange Version

> Databases

> Database Availability Groups

> Recipient Policies

> Connectors

22

Global Catalog Placement

Groups

Hardware Configuration and Capacity Planning

Client Access and Hub Servers

Outlook Web App

Edge Services

Unified Messaging Services

Exchange Server 2010 Security

Exchange Roles and Advanced Security Delegation

Edge Security

Disabling Unnecessary Services/Protocols

IPSec

Antivirus/Antispam/Antiphishing

Project Plan

Blackout Dates

Vacation Schedules

Additional Projects Overlap

Documentation Plan

Design

Plan

Build Guides

Migration Guides

Administration Guides

Maintenance Guides

As Builts

Disaster Recovery Guides

User Guides

Training Plan

Users

Administrators

Migration Team

Communication Plan

Communication Plan Document

The detail of the communication plan depends on the size of the organization and management requirements. From the project management perspective, the more communication, the better! This is especially important when a project affects something as visible as the email system.

Mapping out the how, when, and who to communicate with allows the project team to prepare well-thought-out reports and plan productive meetings and presentations. This also provides the recipients of the reports the chance to review the plan and set their expectations. Once again, no surprises for the project team or the project sponsor.

A good communication plan should include the following topics:

▶ Audience

▶ Content

▶ Delivery method

▶ Timing and frequency

Table 22.1 gives an example of a communication plan. To make the plan more detailed, columns can be added to list who is responsible for the communication and specific dates for when the communication is delivered.

TABLE 22.1   Communication Plan

Audience	Content (Message)	Delivery Method	Timing Stage/Frequency
Executive sponsor	Project status	Written report	Weekly in email
Project team	Project status	Verbal updates	Weekly in meeting
IT department	Project overview	Presentation	Quarterly meeting

Migration Plan Document

After the design and planning document has been mapped out, the project team can begin planning the logistics of implementing Exchange Server 2010. This document is a guide that contains the technical steps needed to implement Exchange Server 2010 from the ground up. However, depending on how the migration team is set up, it can also include logistical instructions such as the following:

▶ Communication templates

▶ Location maps

▶ Team roles and responsibilities during the implementation

In a large organization, a session or sessions will be held to develop the migration plan. An agenda for the development of the plan might look similar to the following:

Goals and Objectives

Migration Planning—E2010

New Exchange Organization Versus Upgrade

Exchange 2010 Directory Cleanup/One-to-One Mapping

Migration Tools

Migration Using the AD Connector (ADC)

ForestPrep/DomainPrep

Rolling Migration

Gateway Migration

Special Considerations: Third-Party Add-Ins (Fax, Voicemail, Apps)

Rollback Planning

Backup and Restore

Phased Migration Rollback

Training

Users

Administrators

Communications

Status Meetings

Open Issues Log

Administration and Maintenance

Administration

Maintenance

Disaster Recovery

Guides

Periodic Schedules

Daily/Weekly/Monthly

Planned Downtime

Checklists

Test

Project Management

Phased Approach

Phase I—Design/Planning

Phase II—Prototype

Phase III—Pilot

Phase IV—Implement

Phase V—Support

Timelines

Resource Requirements

Risk Management

Interactive Refinement of Plan

Migration Planning—AD

In Place Versus Restructuring

Account Domains

Resource Domains

Active Directory Migration Tool (ADMT)

DNS Integration

Switching to Native Mode

Deployment Tools

Scripting

Built-In

Third-Party

Building

Normalize Environment

Data Center First

Branch Offices Second

Deployment Strategies

Staged Versus Scripted Versus Manual

Documentation

Design

Plan

Build Guides

Migration Guides

Administration Guides

Maintenance Guides

As Builts

Disaster Recovery Guides

User Guides

Training

Users

Administrators

Migration Team

Technical Experts

Communications

Migration Team

Executives and Management

Administrators

Users

Methods

Frequency

Detail Level

Administration and Maintenance

Administration

Maintenance

Disaster Recovery

Guides

Periodic Schedules

Daily/Weekly/Monthly

Planned Downtime

Checklists

Testing

Note that many of the agenda topics are stated in a way that facilitates discussion. This is a great way to organize discussion points and at the same time keep them on track.

Training Plan Document

When creating a training plan for an Exchange Server 2010 implementation, the first thing that needs to be identified is the target audience. That determines what type of training needs to be developed. Some of the user groups that need to be targeted for training are as follows:

▶ **End users**—If the implementation is going to change the desktop client, the end user must receive some level of training.

▶ **Systems administrators**—The personnel involved in the administration of the messaging systems must be trained.

▶ **Help desk**—In organizations where the support is divided among different teams, each team must be trained on the tasks they will be carrying out.

▶ **Implementation team**—If the implementation is spread across multiple locations, some project teams choose to create implementation teams. These teams must be trained on the implementation process.

After the different groups have been identified, the training plan for each one can be created. The advantage of creating a training plan in-house is the ability to tailor the training to the organization's unique Exchange environment. The trainees will not have to go over configurations or settings that do not apply to their network.

As a special note, if the systems administrators and implementation team members can be identified ahead of time, it is wise to have them participate in the prototype stage.

The implementation team can assist by validating procedures and through the repetitive process can become more familiar with the procedures. After the prototype environment is set up, administrators and help desk resources can come in to do the same for the administrative procedures.

This provides the necessary validation process and also allows the systems groups to become more comfortable with the new tools and technology.

Prototype Lab Document

Going in to the prototype stage, experienced engineers and project managers are aware that the initial plan will probably have to be modified. This is because of a range of factors that can include application incompatibility, administrative requirements, or undocumented aspects of the current environment.

So, if it was important to start out this stage with a well-documented plan, the most important documentation goal for the prototype is to track these changes to ensure that the project still meets all goals and objectives of the implementation.

The document tool the project team will use to do this is the test plan. A well-developed test plan contains a master test plan and provides the ability to document the test results for reference at a later date. This is necessary because the implementation procedures might change from the first round of testing to the next and the project team will need to refer to the outcome to compare results.

A prototype lab test plan outline contains the following:

Summary of What Is Being Tested and the Overall Technical Goals of the Implementation

Scope of What Will Be Tested

Resources Needed

Hardware

Software

Personnel

Documentation

What Will Be Recorded

Test Plan Outline

Operating System

Hardware Compatibility

Install First Domain Controller

Test Replication

Install Additional Domain Controllers

Client Access

Role-Based Configuration

DNS

WINS

DHCP

IIS

Domain Controller

Exchange

Group Policy

New Settings

GPMC

RSoP

Antivirus

Password Policy

Security Templates

File Migration

Print Migration

DFS

Remote Assistance

UPS Software

Applications Testing

Exchange Server 2010

Exchange Install and Configuration

Exchange Migration

OWA

Functionality

Forms-Based Authentication

Individual Mailbox/Message Restores

Database Restore

Antivirus

Exchange Management Console

Functionality

Backup and Restore

SCOM Agents

Administrative Rights

Each individual test should be documented in a test form listing the expected outcome and the actual outcome. This becomes part of the original test plan and is used to validate the implementation procedure or document a change.

A sample prototype lab test form is shown in Table 22.2.

TABLE 22.2   Sample Test Form

Test Name:

Hardware Requirements:

Software Requirements:

TABLE 22.2   Sample Test Form

Other Requirements:

Expected Outcome:

Actual Outcome:

Test Name:

Tester:

Date:

_____

At the end of the stage, it should be clearly documented what, if anything, has changed. The documentation deliverables of this stage are as follows:

▶ Test plan

▶ Implementation plan

▶ Pilot implementation plan

▶ Rollback plan

Pilot Test Document

Documenting a pilot implementation has special requirements because it is the first time the implementation will touch the production environment. If the environment is a complex one where multiple applications are affected by the implementation, all details should be documented along with the outcome of the pilot.

This is done by having a document similar in content to the prototype lab test plan form and tracking any issues that come up.

In extreme cases, the project team must put the rollback plan into effect. Before starting the pilot implementation, the team should have an escalation process, along with contact names and phone numbers of the personnel with the authority to make the go-no-go decision in a given situation.

Support and Project Completion Document

An Exchange implementation should include a plan for handing off administration to the personnel who will be supporting the messaging environment after the implementation is complete—especially if the SMEs are brought in to implement the Exchange messaging infrastructure and will not be remaining onsite to support it.

The handoff plan should be included in the original project plan and have a timeline for delivery of the administrative documentation, as well as training sessions if needed.

Exchange Server 2010 Environment Documentation

As the business and network infrastructure changes, it is common for the messaging infrastructure to change as well. Keep track of these changes as they progress through baselines (how the Exchange Server 2010 environment was built) and other forms of documentation, such as the configuration settings and connectivity diagrams of the environment.

Documents that map out the Exchange Server 2010 environment will prove to be an invaluable tool for maintaining, expanding, or troubleshooting the messaging infrastructure.

These documents should provide information on the physical setup of the network, such as server configuration and location, and also go over the logical elements such as mail flow.

Some of the key documents that are used for this include the following:

- **Network diagrams**—To give a visual of the messaging infrastructure. This should show mail flow, location of front-end servers, site connectors, and WAN topology. A large or very complex organization might prefer to have this information mapped out in several different diagrams.

- **Server builds**—The server builds are guides that instruct on how to build the server from the ground up. These guides are key in ensuring standardized builds during an implementation, as well as recovering from a major server crash or for use during a disaster recovery scenario.

Another document that is especially useful in larger organizations is the roles and responsibilities guide that outlines the administrative model used in the Exchange infrastructure.

> **NOTE**
>
> A great tool for examining the Exchange Server 2010 environment is the Exchange Best Practices Analyzer (ExBPA). This Microsoft tool can be run from the Exchange Management Console (EMC) and produces reports on a variety of topics.

Server Build Procedures

The server build procedure is a detailed set of instructions for building the Exchange Server 2010 system. This document can be used for troubleshooting and adding new servers, and is a critical resource in the event of a disaster.

The following is an example of a table of contents from a server build procedure document:

Windows Server 2008 Build Procedures

    System Configuration Parameters

    Configure the Server Hardware

        Install Vendor Drivers

        Configure Storage

    Install and Configure Windows Server 2008

        Using Images

        Scripted Installations

    Applying Windows Server 2008 Security

        Using a Security Template

        Using GPOs

        Configuring Antivirus

        Installing Service Packs and Critical Updates

    Backup Client Configuration

Exchange Server 2010 Build Procedures

    System Configuration Parameters

    Configuring Exchange as a Mailbox Server

        Creating Storage Groups

        Creating Databases

    Configuring Exchange as an Edge, Client Access, or UM Server

Configuration (As-Built) Documentation

The configuration document, often referred to as an as-built, details a snapshot configuration of the Exchange Server 2010 system as it is built. This document contains essential information required to rebuild a server.

The following is an Exchange Server 2010 server as-built document template:

Introduction

The purpose of this Exchange Server 2010 as-built document is to assist an experienced network administrator or engineer in restoring the server in the event of a hardware failure. This document contains screenshots and configuration settings for the server at the time it was built. If settings are not implicitly defined in this document, they are assumed to be set to defaults. It is not intended to be a comprehensive disaster recovery with step-by-step procedures for rebuilding the server. For this document to remain useful as a recovery aid, it must be updated as configuration settings change.

System Configuration

    Hardware Summary

    Disk Configuration

        Logical Disk Configuration

    System Summary

    Device Manager

    Windows Server 2008 TCP/IP Configuration

    Network Adapter Local Area Connections

Security Configuration

    Services

    Lockdown Procedures (Checklist)

    Antivirus Configuration

Share List

Applications and Configurations

Topology Diagrams

Network configuration diagrams and related documentation generally include local area network (LAN) connectivity, wide area network (WAN) infrastructure connectivity, IP subnet information, critical servers, network devices, and more. Having accurate diagrams of the new environment can be invaluable when troubleshooting connectivity issues. For topology diagrams that can be used for troubleshooting connectivity issues, consider documenting the following:

- Internet service provider contact names, including technical support contact information

- Connection type (such as frame relay, ISDN, OC-12)

22

- ▶ Link speed

- ▶ Committed Information Rate (CIR)

- ▶ Endpoint configurations, including routers used

- ▶ Message flow and routing

Exchange Server 2010 Administration and Maintenance Documents

The administrative documents are designed to provide information for the ongoing support and administration of the Exchange Server 2010 environment. Most of the diagrams and guides created to document the environment (discussed in the previous section) will also be used for reference in the day-to-day administration. These documents should address the basic administrative tasks, such as adding a user and troubleshooting documents.

It is a best practice to have one location where all the documents are consolidated to make it easy to find any one of them. This also facilitates replication of the directory to a website or a share on another server for disaster recovery purposes.

Administration Manual

The administration manual is the main tool for the administrative group. All the Exchange tasks are documented with the organization-specific details. A well-prepared administration manual can also be used for training new administrators.

Some of the documents that are typically consolidated into the enterprise Exchange Server 2010 administration manual are as follows:

Exchange User Administrative Tasks

Creating a Mailbox

Creating a Shared Mailbox

Modifying Mailbox Permissions

Moving an Exchange Mailbox

Reconnecting a Deleted Exchange Mailbox

Hiding and Unhiding a User

Setting User-Specific Storage Limits

Contacts

Creating a Contact

Deleting a Contact

Modifying a Contact

Although the outline provided is a pretty complete example, some additional documents are outlined in more detail in the following sections.

Troubleshooting Guide

Troubleshooting documents are especially useful for larger organizations where multiple administrators are working together. Providing the information to all administrators can potentially shorten or avoid server downtime and user impact.

Procedural Documents

An important aspect of creating the administrative documentation is that it is mainly procedural. These are step-by-step guides that walk the administrator through any given task, and it is imperative that the documents are validated. This is a collaborative effort in which one person writes the document and another validates the procedures, noting any differences so that they can be corrected. These are living documents that change along with the environment, and updates to the documents should be routinely included as a part of changes or updates to the infrastructure or administrative model.

Exchange Server Maintenance

In most organizations, email is one of the most visible, if not number one, business applications. How to keep email up and running is the topic of many technical and business discussions. To keep the Exchange Server 2010 infrastructure up and running, the main goal of an Exchange administrator should be to be proactive. This is achieved by setting up a well-thought-out maintenance plan that checks all of the components of the Exchange infrastructure and addresses issues before they affect the email system causing downtime.

The maintenance plan should include daily, weekly, monthly, and quarterly tasks. The execution and status or outcome of the tasks should be documented and archived for historical reference. The best way to do this is by using checklists that can be easily followed and signed off on when the tasks are completed.

A standard maintenance schedule includes, but is not limited to the following:

Exchange Server Maintenance

Exchange Status Monitor

> Monitoring Tool

> Monitoring Services with the Computer Management Console

Daily Tasks

> Examine Performance Counters

> Monitor Services and Links

> Check Server Mail Queues

> SMTP Log Files

> Check Daily Backup Logs

> Check Available Disk Space

> Verify the Alerter Service Is Running

> Physical Server Check

Weekly Tasks

> Check Event Logs for Errors and Warnings

> Check for Message Tracking Log File Buildups

Monthly Tasks

> Validate Exchange Backup

Quarterly Tasks

> IS Maintenance

> Check Mailbox Usage

Event Logs

> Checking Event Log Events

> Tools for Troubleshooting Event Log Messages

>> Microsoft Online TechNet Website

Disaster Recovery Documentation

Creating and maintaining a disaster recovery plan for the Exchange Server 2010 infrastructure requires the commitment of IT managers as well as the systems administrators in charge of the messaging systems. This is because creating a disaster recovery plan is a complex process, and after it is developed, the only way of maintaining it is by practicing the procedures on a regular schedule. This, of course, involves the administrative personnel and should be worked into their scheduled tasks.

The initial steps of creating the disaster recovery plan involve determining the desired recovery times. Then, the team moves on to discuss possible disaster scenarios and maps out a plan for each one. The following table of contents outlines the different topics that are addressed when creating the disaster recovery plan:

> Executive Summary or Introduction
>
> Disaster Recovery Scenarios
>
> Disaster Recovery Best Practices
>
>> Planning and Designing for Disaster
>
> Business Continuity and Response
>
>> Business Hours Response to Emergencies
>>
>> Recovery Team Members
>>
>> Recovery Team Responsibilities
>>
>> Damage Assessment
>>
>> Off-Hours Response to an Emergency
>>
>> Recovery Team Responsibilities
>>
>> Recovery Strategy
>>
>> Coordinate Equipment Needs
>
> Disaster Recovery Decision Tree
>
> Software Recovery
>
> Hardware Recovery
>
> Server Disaster Recovery
>
> Preparation
>
>> Documentation
>>
>> Software Management
>>
>> Knowledge Management

Server Backup

    Client Software Configuration

Restoring the Server

    Build the Server Hardware

    Post Restore

Recovering Data

    Continuous Replication

Exchange Disaster Recovery

    Disaster Recovery Service-Level Agreements

    Exchange Disaster Recovery Plan

    Exchange Message/Mailbox Restore Scenario

    Complete Disk Failure

    Network Operating System Partition Failure

    Complete System Failure

    NIC, Storage Controller Failures

Train Personnel and Practice Disaster Recovery

Disaster Recovery Planning

The first step of the disaster recovery process is to develop a formal disaster recovery plan. This plan, although time consuming to develop, serves as a guide for the entire organization in the event of an emergency. Disaster scenarios, such as power outages, hard drive failures, and even earthquakes, should be addressed. Although it is impossible to develop a scenario for every potential disaster, it is still helpful to develop a plan to recover from different levels of disaster. It is recommended that organizations encourage open discussions of possible scenarios and the steps required to recover from each one. Include representatives from each department because each department will have its own priorities in the event of a disaster. The disaster recovery plan should encompass the organization as a whole and focus on determining what it will take to resume normal business function after a disaster.

Backup and Recovery Development

Another important component of a disaster recovery development process is the evaluation of the organization's current backup policies and procedures. Without sound backup policies and procedures, a disaster recovery plan is useless. It is not possible to recover a system if the backup is not valid.

A backup plan does not just encompass backing up data to tape or another medium. It is an overarching plan that outlines other tasks, including advanced system recovery, offsite storage, testing procedures, and retention policies. These tasks should be carefully documented to accurately represent each backup methodology and how it's carried out. Full documentation of the backup process includes step-by-step procedures, guidelines, policies, and checklists.

Periodically, the backup systems should be reviewed and tested, especially after any configuration changes. Any changes to the system should be reflected in the documentation. Otherwise, backup documents can become stale and can add to the problems during recovery attempts.

Recovery documentation complements backup documentation. The primary purpose of the documented backup process is to provide the ability to recover that backup in the event of an emergency. Recovery documentation should outline where the backup data resides and how to recover from various types of failures, such as hard drive failure, system failure, and natural disasters. Just like backup documentation, recovery documentation takes the form of step-by-step procedures, guidelines, policies, and checklists.

Exchange System Failover Documentation

Many organizations use Database Availability Groups in their Exchange environment to provide failover and redundancy capabilities for their messaging systems. When a system or database fails over, having fully tested and documented procedures helps get the system back up and running quickly. Because these procedures are not used often, they must be thoroughly tested and reviewed in a lab setting so that they accurately reflect the steps required to recover each system.

Performance Documentation

Performance documentation helps monitor the health and status of the Exchange environment. It is a continuous process that begins by aligning the goals, existing policies, and service-level agreements of the organization. When these areas are clearly defined and detailed, baseline performance values can be established, using tools such as the System Monitor, Microsoft System Center Operations Manager (SCOM), or other tools (such as PerfMon). These tools capture baseline performance-related metrics that can include indicators such as how much memory is being used, average processor use, and more. They also can illustrate how the Exchange Server 2010 environment is performing under various workloads.

After the baseline performance values are documented, performance-related information gathered by the monitoring solution should be analyzed periodically. Pattern and trend analysis reports need to be examined at least on a weekly basis. This analysis can uncover current and potential bottlenecks and proactively ensure that the system operates as efficiently and effectively as possible. These reports can range from routine reports generated by the monitoring solution to complex technical reports that provide detail to engineering staff.

Routine Reporting

Although built-in system monitoring tools log performance data that can be used in reports in conjunction with products such as Excel, it is recommended that administrators use products such as SCOM for monitoring and reporting functionality. SCOM can manage and monitor the Exchange systems and provide preconfigured graphical reports with customizable levels of detail. SCOM also provides the framework to generate customized reports that meet the needs of the organization.

Management-Level Reporting

Routine reporting typically provides a significant amount of technical information. Although helpful for the administrator, it can be too much information for management. Management-level performance reporting should be concise and direct. Stakeholders do not require the specifics of performance data, but it's important to take those specifics and show trends, patterns, and any potential problem areas. This extremely useful and factual information provides insight to management so that decisions can be made to determine proactive solutions for keeping systems operating in top-notch condition.

For instance, during routine reporting, administrators identify and report to management that Exchange Server processor use is on the rise. What does this mean? This information by itself does not give management any specifics on what the problem is. However, if the administrator presents graphical reports that indicate that if the current trends on Exchange Server processor use continue at the rate of a 5% increase per month, an additional processor will be required in 10 months or less. Management can then take this report, follow the issue more closely over the next few months, and determine whether to allocate funds to purchase additional processors. If the decision is made to buy more processors, management has more time to negotiate quantity, processing power, and cost instead of having to pay higher costs for the processors on short notice.

Technical Reporting

Technical performance information reporting is much more detailed than management-level reporting. It goes beyond the routine reporting to provide specific details on many different components and facets of the system. For example, specific counter values might be given to determine disk subsystem use. This type of information is useful in monitoring the health of the entire Exchange environment. Trend and pattern analysis should also be included in the technical reporting process to not only reflect the current status, but to allow comparison to historical information and determine how to plan for future requirements.

Security Documentation

Just as with any other aspect of the Exchange environment, security documentation also includes policies, configurations and settings, and procedures. Administrators can easily feel that although documenting security settings and other configurations are important, it might lessen security mechanisms established in the Exchange Server 2010 environment. However, documenting security mechanisms and corresponding configurations are vital to administration, maintenance, and any potential security compromise. Security documentation, along with other forms of documentation—including network diagrams and configurations—should be well guarded to minimize any potential security risk.

A network environment might have many security mechanisms in place, but if the information—such as logs and events obtained from them—isn't reviewed, security is more relaxed. Monitoring and management solutions can help consolidate this information into reports that can be generated on a periodic basis. These reports are essential to the process of continuously evaluating the network's security.

In addition, management should be informed of any unauthorized access or attempts to compromise security. Business policy can then be made to strengthen the environment's security.

Change Control

Although the documentation of policies and procedures to protect the system from external security risks is of utmost importance, internal procedures and documents should also be established. Developing, documenting, and enforcing a change control process helps protect the system from well-intentioned internal changes.

In environments where there are multiple administrators, it is very common to have the interests of one administrator affect those of another. For instance, an administrator might make a configuration change to limit mailbox size for a specific department. If this change is not documented, a second administrator might spend a significant amount of time trying to troubleshoot a user complaint from that department. Establishing a change control process that documents these types of changes eliminates confusion and wasted resources. The change control process should include an extensive testing process to reduce the risk of production problems.

Procedures

Although security policies and guidelines comprise the majority of security documentation, procedures are equally as important. Procedures include not only the initial configuration steps, but also maintenance procedures and more important procedures that are to be followed in the event of a security breach.

Additional areas regarding security that can be documented include, but are not limited to, the following:

- ▶ Auditing policies including review
- ▶ Service packs (SPs) and hot fixes
- ▶ Certificates and certificates of authority

- Antivirus configurations

- Bitlocker

- Password policies (such as length, strength, and age)

- Group Policy Object (GPO) security-related policies

- Registry security

- Lockdown procedures

Training Documentation

Training documentation for a project can be extensive and ranges from user training to technical training. The most important aspect of training documentation is to make sure that it meets the needs of the individual being trained. The two key documents created and used in organizations are focused for the benefit of end users, and technical documents are focused toward administrators.

End User

Proper end-user training is critical to the acceptance of any new application. Developing clear and concise documentation that addresses the user's needs is key in providing proper training. As discussed earlier, developing specific documentation goals and conducting an audience analysis are especially important to the development of useful training materials.

Technical

Administrators and engineers are responsible for the upkeep and management of the Exchange environment. As a result, they must be technically prepared to address a variety of issues, such as maintenance and troubleshooting. Training documentation should address why the technologies are being taught and how the technologies pertain to the Exchange environment. In addition, the training documentation should be easy to use and function as a reference resource in the future.

Summary

The development of documentation for the Exchange Server 2010 environment is important not only to establishing the environment, but also to the health, maintenance, and ongoing support of the system. After this documentation is developed, it must be thoroughly tested—preferably by a disinterested party—and maintained. Every change that is made to the environment should be changed in the documentation.

Best Practices

The following are best practices from this chapter:

- ▶ Determine the business needs for documentation.
- ▶ Determine the goals of each document.
- ▶ Determine the audience and the need for each document.
- ▶ Validate and test the documentation.
- ▶ Develop audience level-specific training materials.
- ▶ Establish a documentation update process.

22

CHAPTER 23

Designing and Implementing Mobility in Exchange Server 2010

Microsoft Exchange Server 2010 was specifically designed to expand beyond the traditional boundaries that previously defined the messaging experience. No longer are users limited to receiving and responding to messages while in the office. Today's fast-paced information society requires more immediate capabilities of gaining access to mail data, enabling information workers to get anytime, anywhere access to their messages.

Exchange Server 2010 greatly enhances the capabilities of information workers to stay in touch, through enhancements to the ways that they receive and respond to emails. Exchange Server now allows for an unprecedented seamless integration between handheld mobile devices such as Pocket PCs, Smartphones, Apple iPhones, and an Exchange Server mailbox, through an improved Exchange ActiveSync application.

This chapter covers the details of deploying Microsoft Exchange ActiveSync with Exchange Server 2010 and Windows Mobile devices. Step-by-step examples of ActiveSync deployments are outlined, and varying approaches are compared.

Understanding Mobility Enhancements in Exchange Server 2010

Microsoft Exchange ActiveSync is a technology that allows information workers to gain access to their messaging data, calendaring, and other information from a handheld device. ActiveSync works by tunneling the data over Hypertext Transfer Protocol (HTTP), the same one used for web traffic on the Internet.

Using ActiveSync in an Exchange Server 2010 environment gives organizations unprecedented control over the management of the remote devices and over their security, allowing for lost or stolen devices to be wiped, and enforcing policies that require encryption of data and passwords to be used.

Outlining the History of Exchange Server Mobility Enhancements

ActiveSync was originally released as an add-on product to Exchange 2000 Server known as Mobile Information Server (MIS). MIS was the first foray Microsoft had into syncing handheld devices and saw limited deployment.

Exchange Server 2003 was the first release of the Exchange Server messaging platform that included built-in ActiveSync functionality, though it had to be enabled in a separate step. The first versions of the software in 2003 did not support automatically pushing emails out to the handhelds, with the exception of a concept called Always Up to Date that would notify the device via a short message service (SMS) text message. The device would then dial in and sync. This was time and battery consuming and costly.

Service Pack 2 for Exchange Server 2003 introduced the concept of Direct Push technology, similar to BlackBerry-style technology, where messages were automatically pushed out to a handheld as they were received. This improvement was warmly received.

At the same time, Windows Mobile, the handheld operating system formerly known as Windows CE and PocketPC, was evolving. The Messaging Security and Feature Pack (MSFP) for Windows Mobile 5.0 allowed for built-in, file-level encryption for the devices, and integrated them with 2003 SP2's abilities to provision and deprovision devices over the air.

Exchange Server 2010 expands even further beyond 2003 SP2's Direct Push technology, allowing for other improvements, such as the ability to automatically configure a handheld, encrypt connections, reset passwords, and view file data on a SharePoint server.

Exploring Exchange ActiveSync

Exchange ActiveSync is a service that runs on a client access server (CAS) in an Exchange Server 2010 topology. It uses the same virtual server that other HTTP access methods to Exchange Server use, such as Outlook Web App and Outlook Anywhere. In ActiveSync's case, however, it uses its own virtual directory, named Microsoft-Server-ActiveSync.

Because it uses the same type of access mechanism as Outlook Web App (OWA) does, ActiveSync can be designed using the same CAS considerations that OWA and Outlook Anywhere does. In most cases, it is deployed as an ancillary service to these offerings. In any case, when it is deployed, it becomes a vital service to the organization.

Enabling ActiveSync in Exchange Server 2010

In Exchange Server 2010 ActiveSync, the application itself has become more integrated with the rest of Exchange Server functionality. After the CAS role has been assigned to a server, the server is closely positioned to enable ActiveSync support. That said, several configuration steps can be taken to improve and streamline ActiveSync access, per Microsoft best practices.

Working with ActiveSync Settings in the Exchange Management Console

Many of the ActiveSync settings on a CAS can be modified within the Exchange Management Console, from the Client Access node, as shown in Figure 23.1. The console allows for ActiveSync to be disabled, or for individual ActiveSync settings to be modified on individual recipient mailboxes.

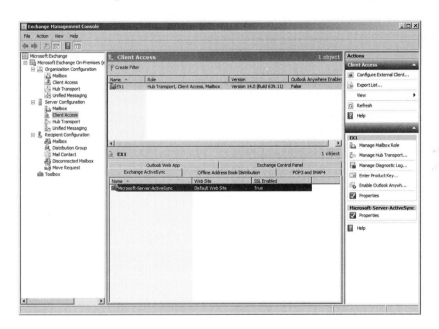

FIGURE 23.1   Administering ActiveSync settings.

Right-clicking on the Microsoft-Server-ActiveSync listing in the details pane and choosing Properties allows for several other ActiveSync settings to be modified, such as the following:

▶ **External url**—This setting allows an administrator to enter in the fully qualified domain name (FQDN) that will be used to access ActiveSync from the Internet. An example of this is https://mail.companyabc.com/Microsoft-Server-ActiveSync.

▶ **Authentication**—Authentication methods for the ActiveSync virtual directory can be entered here. This tab allows an administrator to configure the server to use Basic authentication, which is commonly used with Secure Sockets Layer (SSL) encryption.

There is also an option to define whether dual-factor authentication using client certificates is required or accepted.

▶ **Remote File Servers**—This tab, shown in Figure 23.2, introduces some of the new functionality in Exchange Server 2010 in regard to Windows Mobile access to file data in shares via Universal Naming Convention (UNC) paths, or on Windows SharePoint Services Sites.

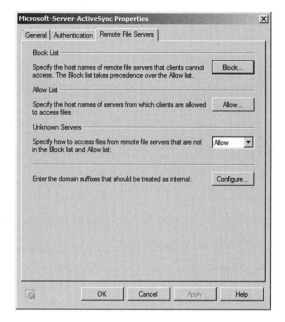

FIGURE 23.2   Configuring Remote File Servers options in ActiveSync.

> **NOTE**
>
> The functionality on the Remote File Servers tab can only be taken advantage of if the Windows Mobile device supports it. Currently, the minimum required version is Windows Mobile 6.0.

Configuring Per-User ActiveSync Settings

Individual mailbox settings can be configured for ActiveSync in the Mailbox node under Recipient Configuration in the console pane, shown in Figure 23.3. Enabling and disabling ActiveSync on an individual mailbox can be controlled from here, as well as the ability to add a mailbox to a specific ActiveSync mailbox policy, a concept further defined in the section titled "Working with ActiveSync Policies."

Right-clicking on an individual mailbox and choosing Properties invokes the Properties dialog box. Choosing the Mailbox Features tab, shown in Figure 23.4, allows for Exchange ActiveSync to be enabled or disabled for that particular mailbox. In addition, clicking the

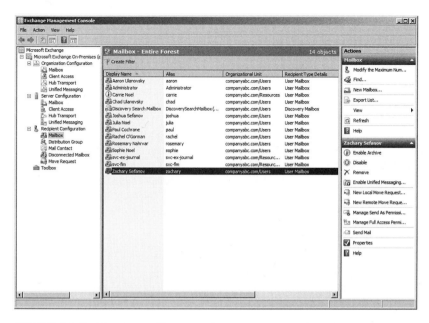

FIGURE 23.3   Viewing mailboxes in Exchange Management Console.

Properties button gives the option to join the mailbox to a specific ActiveSync policy, as mentioned earlier.

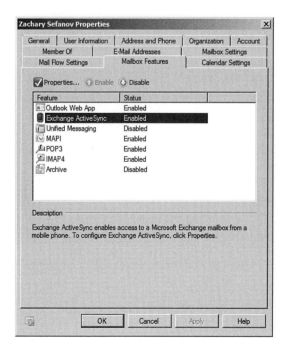

FIGURE 23.4   Enabling or disabling ActiveSync on a mailbox.

Securing Access to ActiveSync with Secure Sockets Layer Encryption

By default, ActiveSync is configured to use Integrated Windows authentication. This form of authentication works fine if access to the server is over a trusted internal network, but is not feasible for access over the Internet, which is where most mobile devices originate from.

Because of this limitation, a form of authentication that can be sent across the Internet must be used. This effectively limits the ActiveSync server to using Basic authentication, which is supported by most web browsers and devices. The problem with Basic authentication, however, is that the username and password that the user sends is effectively sent in clear text, and can be intercepted and stolen in transit. In addition, mail messages and other confidential information are transmitted in clear text, which is a huge security issue.

The solution to this problem is to use what is known as Secure Sockets Layer (SSL) encryption on the traffic. SSL encryption is performed using Public Key Infrastructure (PKI) certificates, which work through the principle of shared-key encryption. PKI SSL certificates are widely used on the Internet today, any website starting with an https:// uses them, and the entire online merchant community is dependent upon the security of the system.

For ActiveSync, the key is to install a certificate on the server so that the traffic between the device and the server is protected from prying eyes. There are effectively two options to this approach, as follows:

▶ **Use a third-party certificate authority**—A common option for many organizations is to purchase a certificate for ActiveSync (and other Exchange HTTP access methods such as OWA) from a third-party trusted certificate authority (CA), such as VeriSign, Thawte, or others. These CAs are already trusted by a vast number of devices, so no additional configuration is required. The downside to this option is that the certificates must be purchased and the organization doesn't have as much flexibility to change certificate options.

▶ **Install and use your own certificate authority**—Another common approach is to install and configure Windows Server 2003/2008 Certificate Services to create your own CA within an organization. This gives you the flexibility to create new certificates, revoke existing ones, and not have to pay immediate costs. The downside to this approach is that no browsers or mobile devices will recognize the CA, and error messages to that effect will be encountered on the devices unless the certificates are trusted.

Each of these options is outlined in the subsequent sections of this chapter.

Installing a Third-Party CA on a CAS

If a third-party certificate authority will be used to enable SSL on a server with the CAS role, a certificate request must first be generated directly from the CAS. After this request has been generated, it can be sent to the third-party CA, who will then verify the identity of the organization and send it back, where it can be installed on the server.

When deciding which CA to use, keep in mind that Windows Mobile devices automatically trust the certificate authorities of the following organizations:

▶ VeriSign

▶ Thawte

▶ GTE CyberTrust

▶ GlobalSign

▶ RSA

▶ Equifax

▶ Entrust.net

▶ Valicert (Windows Mobile 5.0 and up only)

If an internal CA will be utilized, this section and its procedures can be skipped, and you can proceed directly to the subsequent section titled "Using an Internal Certificate Authority for OWA Certificates."

To generate an SSL certificate request for use with a third-party CA, you can create a certificate from the Exchange Management Shell using the New-ExchangeCertificate applet, or you can create the request directly from IIS. For optimal flexibility, use the PowerShell applet because it enables you to create multiple Subject Alternative Name (SAN) entries in the certificate, enabling the Exchange server to impersonate multiple FQDNs, such as mail.companyabc.com, autodiscover.companyabc.com, activesync.companyabc.com, and so on.

After the certificate request has been generated, the text file, which will look similar to the one shown in Figure 23.5, can then be emailed or otherwise transmitted to the certificate authority via their individual process. Each CA has a different procedure, and the exact steps need to follow the individual CA's process. After an organization's identity has been proven by the CA, they will send back the server certificate, typically in the form of a file, or as part of the body of an email message.

FIGURE 23.5   Viewing a certificate request file.

The certificate then needs to be installed on the server itself. If it was sent in the form of a `.cer` file, it can simply be imported via the process described next. If it was included in the body of an email, the certificate itself needs to be cut and pasted into a text editor such as Notepad and saved as a `.cer` file. After the `.cer` file has been obtained, it can be installed on the CAS using the Import-ExchangeCertificate applet.

Using an Internal Certificate Authority for OWA Certificates

If a third-party certificate authority is not utilized, an internal CA can be set up instead. There are several different CA options, including several third-party products, and it might be beneficial to take advantage of an existing internal CA. Windows Server 2008 also has a very functional CA solution built into the product, and one can be installed into an organization.

> **CAUTION**
>
> Proper design of a secure PKI is a complex subject, and organizations might want to spend a good amount of time examining the many factors that can influence CA design. This sample scenario assumes a very basic design, with an enterprise CA installed directly into a domain. Most enterprise CAs want to consider a stand-alone root CA and a second or even third tier of intermediate and issuing enterprise CAs, depending on the organization.

The following types of CAs are available for installation:

▶ **Enterprise Root CA**—An enterprise root CA is the highest level CA for an organization. By default, all members of the forest where it is installed trust it, which can make it a convenient mechanism for securing OWA or other services within a domain environment. Unless an existing enterprise root CA is in place, this is the typical choice for a homegrown CA solution in an organization.

▶ **Enterprise Subordinate CA**—An enterprise subordinate CA is subordinate to an existing enterprise root CA, and must receive a certificate from that root CA to work properly. In certain large organizations, it might be useful to have a hierarchy of CAs, or the desire might exist to isolate the CA structure for OWA to a subordinate enterprise CA structure.

▶ **Stand-Alone Root CA**—A stand-alone root CA is similar to an enterprise root CA, in that it provides for its own unique identity, and can be uniquely configured. It differs from an enterprise root CA in that it is not automatically trusted by any forest clients in an organization.

▶ **Stand-Alone Subordinate CA**—A stand-alone subordinate CA is similar to an enterprise subordinate CA, except that it is not directly tied or trusted by the forest structure, and must take its own certificate from a stand-alone root CA.

After the internal CA is in place, the CAS can automatically use it for generation of certificates.

After being placed on a server, SSL encryption will be made available on the CAS. If the enterprise CA was installed in an Active Directory domain, all the domain members will include the internal CA as a trusted root authority and connect to OWA via SSL with no errors. External or nondomain members, however, will need to install the enterprise CA into their local trusted root authorities. This includes Windows Mobile devices as well. The procedure for installing a third-party certificate for a Windows Mobile device is covered in the next section of this chapter titled "Installing a Root Certificate on a Windows Mobile Device."

Installing a Root Certificate on a Windows Mobile Device

If a third-party or self-generated certificate authority is used for ActiveSync, Windows Mobile devices must be configured to trust that CA. If they are not configured like this, they will error out with something similar to the error shown in Figure 23.6 when attempting to connect via ActiveSync.

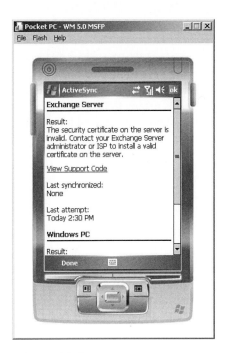

FIGURE 23.6   Error received when Windows Mobile device does not trust the root of the CA.

For Windows desktops and laptops, this task is relatively straightforward, and involves simply installing the enterprise root CA for this third-party certificate into the Trusted Root Certificate Authority group for the machine.

NOTE

Be sure to select the root certificate, and not the actual certificate used for the virtual server

For Windows Mobile devices, however, the enterprise root certificate must first be exported to a .cer file. After the certificate has been exported, it must be copied to the Windows Mobile device, either through the Explore button in Microsoft ActiveSync (while the device is cradled), or via a memory chip.

After the .cer file is installed, clicking on it using the File Explorer in Windows Mobile (Start, Programs, File Explorer) invokes a dialog box, warning that you are about to install the certificate. Click Yes and the certificate will be automatically installed and ActiveSync over SSL can be performed.

Securing Access to ActiveSync Using Internet Security and Acceleration (ISA) Server 2006

Allowing your information workers to have access to a technology like ActiveSync can do wonders for productivity, but can also potentially expose your organization to threats from the outside. Just like Outlook Web App or Outlook Anywhere, ActiveSync requires a web connection to be available to a CAS. Because ActiveSync is meant to be used when out of the office, the web traffic must go over the Internet and must be accessible without requiring a specific virtual private network (VPN) client to be utilized.

This creates somewhat of a dilemma, as the HTTP used by ActiveSync can be subject to attack, potentially exposing your organization to unnecessary risk. Fortunately, however, Microsoft Exchange Server 2010 can be readily secured against these types of attack with the use of an application-layer inspection product such as the Internet Security and Acceleration (ISA) Server 2006 product available from Microsoft.

Note that ISA Server 2006 does not include native understanding of Exchange Server 2010, but rules can be created for Exchange Server 2007 ActiveSync that apply to Exchange Server 2010 as well. When the new version of ISA server is released, currently named Forefront Edge Threat Management Gateway (TMG), it is recommended to use this Exchange Server 2010-aware version to replace ISA Server 2006.

Understanding How ISA Server 2006 Can Protect ActiveSync

ISA Server 2006 is an application-layer aware firewall that can filter HTTP traffic for exploits and scumware. It can reside inline to the ActiveSync traffic (as a traditional firewall), or as a dedicated reverse proxy system that sits in the demilitarized zone (DMZ) of a packet-filter firewall.

In this scenario, the client believes it is directly accessing the CAS, but it is instead being secretly authenticated and scanned at the ISA server itself. Using this scenario or the inline firewall scenario with ISA Server 2006 is a highly useful way to secure the ActiveSync traffic.

Creating an ActiveSync Securing Rule in ISA Server 2006

This section of the chapter briefly explains how to create a web publishing rule with ISA Server 2006 for ActiveSync. For more detailed information on using ISA Server with Exchange Server 2010, reference Chapter 13, "Securing Exchange Server 2010 with ISA Server."

To create the rule in the ISA Server console, perform the following steps:

1. Open the ISA Management Console and navigate to the Firewall Policy node in the console pane.

2. On the Tasks tab of the tasks pane, click the Publish Exchange Web Client Access link.

3. Enter a descriptive name in the welcome dialog box, such as `ActiveSync Rule`, and click Next.

4. In the Select Services dialog box, shown in Figure 23.7, change the Exchange Server version to Exchange Server 2007 (this works for Exchange Server 2010 as well), and then check the Exchange ActiveSync check box. Click Next to continue.

FIGURE 23.7   Creating an ActiveSync rule with ISA Server 2006.

5. In the Publishing Type dialog box, click the Publish a Single Web Site or Load Balancer, and click Next to continue.

6. In the Server Connection Security dialog box, shown in Figure 23.8, click the Use SSL to Connect to the Published Web Server or Server Farm option. This creates an end-to-end SSL connection. Click Next to continue.

FIGURE 23.8   Securing the ISA rule with SSL.

7. For the internal site name, enter the FQDN that clients use to connect to the CAS, as shown in Figure 23.9. In this case, the name should match what the external clients use, as problems can be encountered when using SSL if the names do not match. If internal DNS does not forward that FQDN to the CAS, you might need to fool the ISA server by using a hosts file to make it resolve the FQDN to the CAS. Click Next to continue.

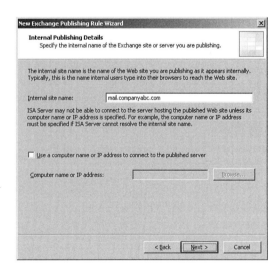

FIGURE 23.9   Creating an ActiveSync securing rule with ISA.

8. Under Public Name Details, enter "This domain name" and then type in the FQDN of the public name, such as mail.companyabc.com. Click Next to continue.

9. For Web Listener, either choose an existing listener that can be used for OWA or Outlook Anywhere, or click the New button. This scenario assumes you are creating a new listener. Click the New button.

10. At the start of the Web Listener Wizard, enter a descriptive name for the listener, such as Exchange HTTP/HTTPS Listener, and click Next to continue.

11. A prompt appears to choose between SSL and non-SSL. This prompt refers to the traffic between the client and ISA, which should always be SSL whenever possible. Click Next to continue.

12. Under Web Listener IP addresses, select the External Network, and leave it at All IP Addresses. Click Next to continue.

13. Under Listener SSL Certificates, click Select Certificate.

14. Select the `mail.companyabc.com` certificate. If the certificate is not on the ISA server, it must be installed into the Certificates store of the ISA server via a process outlined in Chapter 3, "Understanding Core Exchange Server 2010 Design Plans."

15. Click Next to continue.

16. For the type of authentication, choose HTTP Authentication and then check the Basic check box, as shown in Figure 23.10. Leave Windows (Active Directory) selected, and click Next.

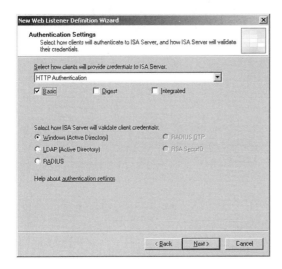

FIGURE 23.10   Selecting Basic authentication for the ISA ActiveSync rule.

17. Click Next at the Single Sign on Settings dialog box. SSO is not available with Basic authentication.

18. Click Finish to end the wizard.

19. Click Next after the new listener is displayed in the Web Listener dialog box.

20. Under Authentication Delegation, choose Basic from the drop-down list. Basic is used as the secured transport mechanism chosen. Click Next to continue.

21. Under User Sets, leave All Authenticated Users selected. In stricter scenarios, only specific AD groups can be granted rights to OWA using this setting. In this case, the default is fine. Click Next to continue.

22. Click Finish to end the wizard.

23. Click Apply in the details pane, and then click OK when you are finished to commit the changes.

The ActiveSync Policy will then show up in the details pane, as shown in Figure 23.11. Further customization of the rule can take place if necessary.

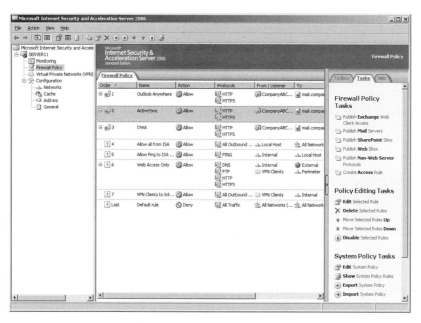

FIGURE 23.11   Viewing the ActiveSync rule in ISA Server 2006.

Working with ActiveSync Policies

ActiveSync in Exchange Server 2010 allows for an unprecedented level of control over the security and management of devices. It allows an administrator to create ActiveSync mailbox policies that force devices to comply with specific restrictions, such as requiring a complex password, or requiring file encryption.

In addition, Exchange Server 2010 ActiveSync now allows an administrator to create multiple policies in an organization. This enables specific types of users to have more restrictive policies placed on their handheld devices, whereas other users are not as restricted. For example, a hospital could stipulate that all the devices that have confidential patient data on them be forced to be encrypted and password protected, while other users are not forced to the same standards.

Creating ActiveSync Mailbox Policies

Creating a new ActiveSync mailbox policy in Exchange Server 2010 is not a complex task. To do so, follow this procedure:

1. From Exchange Management Console, expand Organization Configuration in the console pane, and click Client Access.

2. In the tasks pane, click the New Exchange ActiveSync Mailbox Policy link.

3. Enter a descriptive name for the policy, such as Manager's ActiveSync Mailbox Policy. Set password settings, such as that shown in Figure 23.12, and click New.

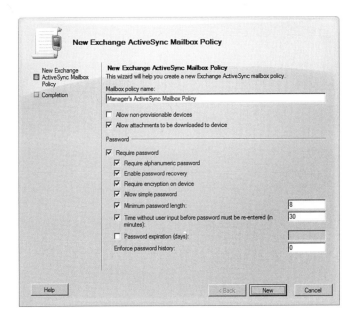

FIGURE 23.12   Creating an ActiveSync mailbox policy.

4. Click Finish.

Applying Mailbox Policies to Users

After a specific policy has been created, it can be added to mailboxes, either during the provisioning process or after the mailbox has already been created. For existing mailboxes, perform the following steps:

1. From the Exchange Management Console, expand Recipient Configuration, and then click Mailbox.

2. Right-click on the mailbox to be added, and click Properties.

3. Select the Mailbox Features tab, click Exchange ActiveSync, and then click the Properties button.

4. Check the Apply an Exchange ActiveSync Mailbox Policy check box, and then click the Browse button.

5. Select the policy from the list, such as that shown in Figure 23.13, and then click OK.

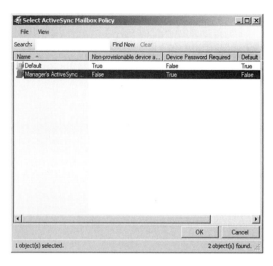

FIGURE 23.13   Applying an ActiveSync mailbox policy to a mailbox.

6. Click OK two more times to save the changes.

Adding multiple mailboxes to a specific mailbox policy is best done from the PowerShell console.

Wiping and Resetting ActiveSync Devices

One of the advantages to Exchange Server 2010's ActiveSync is the optimized management capabilities available. With ActiveSync and the proper Windows Mobile devices, passwords can be reset remotely, and devices can be wiped clean of data in the event that they are lost or stolen. This concept—combined with the encryption capabilities of the Messaging Security Feature Pack—allows an organization to deploy ActiveSync without fear of data compromise.

Invoking this function is as simple as right-clicking on a mailbox user under the Mailbox area of the Recipient Configuration node and choosing Manage Mobile Device. In addition, users can remotely wipe their own devices via Outlook Web App.

Working with Windows Mobile Pocket PC and Smartphone Editions

Exchange Server 2010 ActiveSync supports synchronization with multiple client types, including some non-Microsoft device operating systems. In general, however, the best feature set support comes from the Windows Mobile 5.0/6.0 devices. Windows Mobile 5.0

devices can be integrated with the Messaging Security Feature Pack to encrypt data and to allow for remote password reset and remote wipe capabilities. Windows Mobile 6.0 has added capabilities, such as the ability to access file data via UNC paths and document management capabilities via Microsoft Office SharePoint Server 2007 Document libraries.

There are two flavors of Windows Mobile available that can be synchronized with Exchange Server. Windows Mobile Pocket PC Edition is for full Pocket PC devices, many equipped with a stylus and/or a keyboard. The other version supported is the Windows Mobile Smartphone Edition, which is limited to traditional smaller phones, such as clamshell flip phones and non-keyboard units. The configuration steps for both versions of the OS are outlined in this section.

Setting Up Windows Mobile Pocket PC Edition for ActiveSync

Windows Mobile Pocket PC Edition is widely used on many cutting-edge devices and provides for a larger screen than most cellphones. Many of the systems also have a full-sized keyboard. To configure a Windows Mobile Pocket PC Edition phone for ActiveSync to an Exchange server, perform the following steps:

1. From the Windows Mobile screen, click Start, Programs.

2. Select ActiveSync.

3. When prompted about syncing options, choose the Set Up Your Device to Sync with It link.

4. Enter the FQDN of the ActiveSync server into the dialog box shown in Figure 23.14 and make sure the This Server Requires an Encrypted (SSL) Connection check box is checked. The FQDN should match the name on the certificate. Click Next to continue.

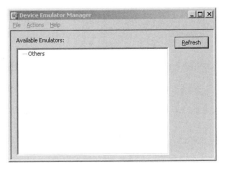

FIGURE 23.14   Configuring server settings with ActiveSync.

5. Enter a valid username, password, and domain, and then choose to save the password. Click Next to continue.

6. Choose which types of data will be synchronized from the dialog box shown in Figure 23.15. Clicking on Calendar or E-mail and choosing Settings allows for customization of the amount of data to be synchronized. Click Finish when you are done.

FIGURE 23.15   Syncing calendar, mail, and contact information with ActiveSync.

7. Click the Sync button to connect to the Exchange server.

The Mobile device will start synchronizing automatically. Synchronizing can be enacted manually, or if the Windows Mobile device supports Direct Push, the emails will be automatically pushed out to the phone.

Setting Up Windows Mobile Smartphone Edition for ActiveSync

Many traditional-style mobile phones (no keyboard, stylus, or large Pocket PC display) are configured with the Windows Mobile 5.0 or 6.0 Smartphone Edition operating system, which allows the operator to synchronize the phone with Exchange Server 2010 and ActiveSync. The procedure for setting up this type of synchronization is very similar to the procedure for Windows Mobile 5.0 Pocket PC Edition, with a few minor exceptions as follows:

> **NOTE**
>
> The hardware on many smartphones is different, and some of the button options in this step-by-step procedure might vary. The overall concept should apply to any Windows Mobile system, however.

1. From the smartphone, press the button corresponding to the Start command.
2. Navigate to ActiveSync and press Select/Enter.
3. When prompted with the dialog box shown in Figure 23.16, select the Set Up Your Device to Sync with It link.

FIGURE 23.16   Setting up Windows Smartphone Edition for ActiveSync.

4. Enter the FQDN of the ActiveSync server, such as mail.companyabc.com. Check the box to require SSL, and press Next.
5. Enter a valid username, password, and domain, and check the Save Password check box, as shown in Figure 23.17. Press Next.

FIGURE 23.17   Entering credentials for ActiveSync.

6. Select which data will be synchronized from the subsequent dialog box, such as contacts, calendar, email, or tasks. Press Finish.

The phone will then begin syncing with the ActiveSync server. A similar process works for
Apple iPhones and other ActiveSync-enabled devices—simply enter the FQDN of the
ActiveSync presence on the Internet and enter a username and password.

Summary

The concept of the "office without walls" is fast becoming a reality, as information
workers now have a myriad of options available to connect with their co-workers using
Exchange Server 2010 technologies such as ActiveSync. ActiveSync in Exchange Server
2010 also allows for unprecedented management and security capabilities, allowing organizations to take advantage of the improved productivity these devices give, but without
sacrificing security in the process.

Best Practices

The following are best practices from this chapter:

- ▶ Always use SSL encryption with ActiveSync technologies.

- ▶ Consider the use of ActiveSync mailbox policies to gain granular control over password and encryption settings of the mobile devices.

- ▶ If using a smartphone or phone PDA device to sync a mailbox to ActiveSync, consider purchasing an unlimited data plan from the mobile phone provider, as the amount of data to be transferred can be great.

- ▶ Consider the use of a third-party trusted root CA for SSL with ActiveSync to avoid having to install a certificate on every mobile device.

- ▶ Secure the ActiveSync HTTP traffic to CAS systems by implementing ISA Server 2006 to monitor the traffic with application-layer inspection capabilities.

23

CHAPTER 24

Designing and Configuring Unified Messaging in Exchange Server 2010

Microsoft Exchange Server 2010 unified messaging (UM) delivers voice messaging, fax, and email into a unified Inbox. These messages can be accessed from a telephone or a computer. Exchange Server 2010 unified messaging integrates with the telephony systems, operating fundamentally as a voice mail server using the Exchange Information Store as a repository for the messages.

Unified messaging was launched in Exchange Server 2007. Exchange Server 2010 represents the natural evolution of the UM platform. This chapter focuses on the design and configuration of the unified messaging capabilities built in to Exchange Server 2010. This includes telephony concepts, server specifications, installation and configuration considerations, and monitoring of the unified messaging services.

Unified Messaging Features

Exchange Server 2010 extends the UM features first introduced in Exchange Server 2007. Unified messaging seamlessly integrates voice messaging, faxing, and electronic mail into a single Inbox. This frees up the user from having to manage separate accounts and Inboxes for these three types of messages. With the new role, there are a number of new features.

Telephony Integration

With unified messaging, Exchange Server is integrated into the telephony world. This integration takes place between the Exchange Unified Messaging server and gateways or Private Branch Exchanges (PBXs).

In a classic set of telephony and electronic mail systems, shown in Figure 24.1, there are two separate networks that deliver voice messages and electronic messages (email). In the telephony system, there are separate components for the PBX, voice mail, external lines, and phones. As shown in the figure, calls from the Public Switched Telephone Network (PSTN) come into a PBX device. Typically, an incoming call is routed by the PBX to the telephone. If the phone does not answer or is busy, the call is routed to the voice mail system. Similarly, email from the Internet arrives at the Exchange messaging server. Note that in the classic system, there is no integration or connectivity between the telephony and electronic mail systems.

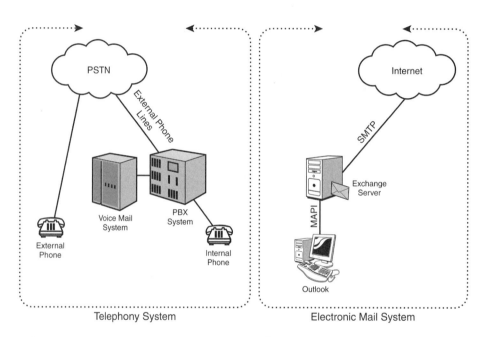

FIGURE 24.1   Classic telephone and electronic mail systems.

With Exchange Server 2010 and unified messaging, these two disparate systems are integrated, as shown in Figure 24.2. Although the UM server does not connect directly with a traditional PBX, it does integrate with PBXs via gateways. The combination of the PBX and the Internet Protocol (IP) gateway can also be replaced by an IP-PBX, which provides both sets of functionality.

One such IP-PBX option is Microsoft Office Communications Server, OCS. Integrating these two Microsoft platforms provides a powerful enterprise voice solution that can replace most modern PBXs at a fraction of the cost.

Notice that, in effect, the Unified Messaging server has replaced the voice mail server in the classic system. The new Microsoft Exchange Server 2010 Unified Messaging server is a voice mail server.

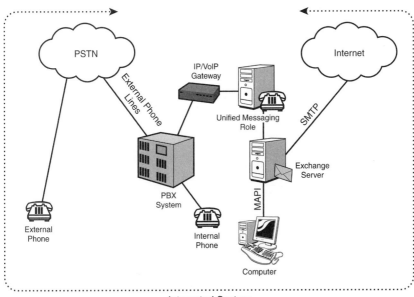

FIGURE 24.2   New integrated system.

The more detailed view with all the Exchange Server 2010 server roles is shown in Figure 24.3. This figure also includes the various ways that a user can interact with the integrated system.

This diagram is discussed in more detail in later sections of this chapter.

Single Inbox

The Unified Messaging server enables the true unification of email messages, voice mail messages, and fax messages into a single Inbox. Messages from all these disparate sources are stored in the user's Inbox and are accessible through a wide variety of interfaces, such as Outlook, a telephone, a web browser, or even a mobile PDA.

The Inbox can be managed just like a traditional email Inbox, with folders, Inbox rules, message retention, and so on. Exchange Server administrators can back up and restore Inboxes with all these forms of data just as they do with email data. This reduces the complexity and ease of use for both users and administrators.

Call Answering

Call answering picks up incoming calls for a user who does not answer their phone. It plays their personal greeting, records voice messages, and converts the voice messages to an email message to be submitted to the user's Exchange Server mailbox.

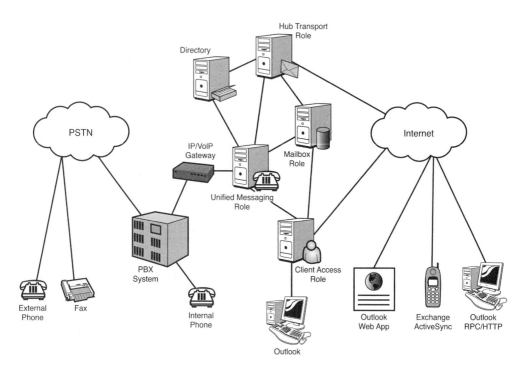

FIGURE 24.3   Detailed architecture diagram.

Fax Receiving

If the incoming call is from a fax machine, the server can recognize this and accept the
fax. The fax is then converted to an email message and submitted to the user's Exchange
Server mailbox. The user can then read the fax as an attachment to the message.

Subscriber Access

The subscriber access feature allows a user to access their Exchange Server mailbox using a
phone. This access mechanism is called Outlook Voice Access.

With Outlook Voice Access, a user can access their Exchange Inbox with the telephone to
do the following:

- ► Listen to and forward voice mail messages.
- ► Listen to, forward, and reply to email messages.
- ► Listen to calendar information.
- ► Access or dial contacts.
- ► Accept or cancel meeting requests.
- ► Notify attendees that the user will be late.
- ► Set a voice mail Out-of-Office message.
- ► Set user security preferences and personal options.

This, in effect, gives the user working access to their Exchange Inbox while out in the field with only a telephone.

The system not only recognizes dual tone multiple frequency (DTMF) key presses from the phone, but also understands voice commands. The system guides the user through the prompts responding to voice commands, giving the user complete hands-free operation.

For example, a user might be on the freeway running late for a lunch meeting. Not remembering the exact time, the user calls into the subscriber access and says "Today's Calendar." The unified messaging system speaks the summary of the next meeting, which is at 12 p.m. Recognizing that the traffic will force him to be 20 minutes late, the user says "I'll be 20 minutes late for this appointment." The unified messaging system confirms and then sends a message to all the attendees.

The speech recognition is remarkably effective and able to recognize commands even over cell phones and with background noise.

Outlook Play on Phone

The Exchange Server 2010 Outlook Web App client and the Outlook 2007 client both support a feature called Play on Phone. This feature allows users to play voice mail on a phone rather than through the computer. The user opens the voice mail message, selects the Play on Phone option, enters the number to play the message on, and clicks the Dial button.

This allows the user to send the audio stream of the voice mail message to a phone for more privacy or to allow a third party to hear the message. The system also provides prompts over the phone following the playback with message handling options.

Outlook Voice Mail Preview

Outlook voice mail preview is a new feature to Exchange Server 2010 unified messaging. In Exchange Server 2007 UM, you would see caller information and message priority. Exchange Server 2010 kicks it up a notch with speech-to-text functionality. Before the voice mail message arrives in your inbox, Exchange Server UM transcribes the voice mail and puts the text in the body of the email. Though not perfect, it's quite accurate. This is especially helpful for "spam" voice mail with "anonymous" caller information. Using this function a user can save time, and frustration, by deleting unwanted messages without listening to them with no fear of deleting a legitimate message.

Call Answering Rules

New to Exchange Server 2010 is the concept of call answering rules. A user can configure basic call workflows using Outlook Web App. By default, no call answering rules are configured. However, users can browse to the phone tab and then select voice mail in the OWA options menu. See an example in Figure 24.4.

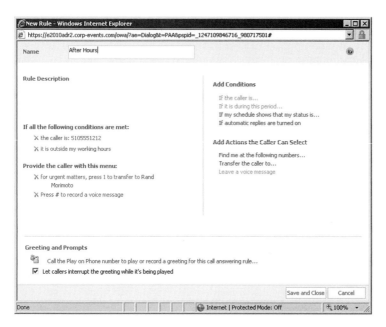

FIGURE 24.4   Call answering rules.

For example, let's say you want your kids to reach you at anytime, but you don't want coworkers to reach you after 5 p.m. You could set a rule to allow calls from the numbers your children would call from to come through to Communicator and then also ring your mobile phone or another phone. You could also set a rule to force any calls from a business associate or coworker to be forwarded directly to voice mail after 5 p.m. The interface is reminiscent of Outlook Web App email rules and should be familiar to most users. Even after rules are created, they can be disabled or enabled through the Outlook Web App Voice Mail menu. Rules, by default, are created as enabled.

Intelligent call routing, a more generic term for Microsoft's call answering rules, was a frequently noted omission in Exchange Server 2007. Its inclusion in Exchange Server 2010 and Exchange Server 2010 UM's tight integration with Office Communications Server 2007 R2 offers a rich voice platform capable of being a full PBX replacement.

Auto Attendant

The auto attendant, as shown in Figure 24.5, is like a secretary, providing voice prompts to guide an external or internal caller through the voice mail system. The system can respond to either telephone keypad presses or voice commands.

The auto attendant features include the following:

▶ A customizable set of menus for external users

▶ Greetings for business hours and nonbusiness hours

▶ Hours of operation and holiday schedules

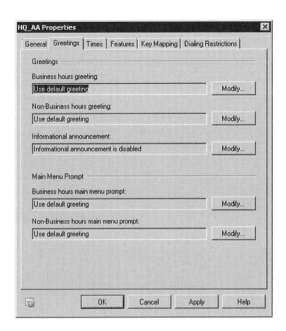

FIGURE 24.5   Auto Attendant menu.

▶ Access to the organization's directory

▶ Access for external users to the operator

The voice prompts that provide the preceding information can be customized to suit the organization.

Unified Messaging Architecture

The Exchange Server 2010 unified messaging features and telephony integration bring a whole new set of concepts, terminology, and architectural elements to the Exchange Server platform. This section explores these different components, objects, protocols, and services.

Unified Messaging Components

The central repository for all the unified messaging components is Active Directory. The schema extensions that are installed as part of the Exchange Server 2010 prerequisites add a variety of objects and attributes that support the UM functionality. These objects are as follows:

▶ Dial plan objects

▶ IP gateway objects

▶ Hunt group objects

▶ Mailbox policy objects

▶ Auto Attendant objects

▶ Unified Messaging server objects

The objects and their relationships are illustrated in the example shown in Figure 24.6. The
example consists of two locations, San Francisco (SFO) and Paris (PAR), with an integrated
Exchange Server 2010 unified messaging infrastructure. The unified messaging objects are
shown with a dotted line around them to separate them from the telephony objects.

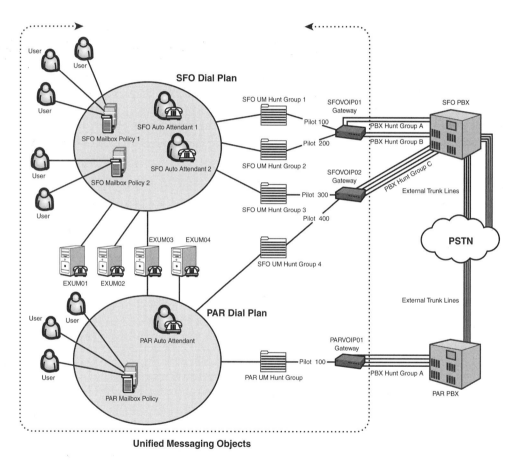

FIGURE 24.6   Unified messaging objects and relationships.

When a UM hunt group is created manually, not only does the associated UM IP gateway
and the associated UM dial plan get specified, but also a pilot identifier is specified.

This diagram is referenced in the subsequent sections describing the various unified
messaging objects and components.

Dial Plan Objects

Dial plans are the central component of the Exchange Server 2010 unified messaging architecture. A UM dial plan essentially logically corresponds to PBX or subsets of extensions within a PBX. The UM dial plan objects can be found in the Exchange Management Console on the UM Dial Plan tab of the Organization, Unified Messaging container.

Different PBXs with an organization, such as between SFO and PAR in Figure 24.6, can have overlapping extensions. For example, a user in San Francisco might have extension 150 and a user in Paris might also have extension 150. Because the two users are on different PBXs, there is no inherent conflict. However, when Exchange Server 2010 unified messaging is deployed and the telephony infrastructure is unified in Active Directory, then there would be a conflict.

Dial plans ensure that all extensions are unique within the architecture by mapping a dial plan to a PBX. Extensions within a dial plan must be unique. However, extensions between different dial plans do not have to be unique. A user can only belong to a single dial plan and will have an extension number that uniquely identifies him within the dial plan.

In the figure, there is one dial plan for each location. In the example, San Francisco is the large office with more users and Paris is smaller. There could be multiple dial plans per location.

Dial plans also provide a way to set up common settings among a set of users, such as the following:

- Number of digits in an extension
- Ability to receive faxes
- Subscriber greetings
- Whom caller can contact within the dial plan
- User's call restrictions (international calls)
- Languages supported

These settings should not be confused with UM mailbox policies, which are covered in the "Mailbox Policy Objects" section later in this book.

> **NOTE**
>
> When a new UM dial plan object is created, a default UM mailbox policy object is also created and associated with the dial plan.

The dial plan also associates the extension for the subscriber access to Outlook Voice Access.

There can be multiple dial plans within an architecture and even associated with the same PBX.

UM IP Gateway Objects

The UM IP gateway object is the logical representation of the next hop in the VoIP chain. It can be either a media gateway connected to the PSTN or a PBX such as Microsoft Office Communications Server 2007 R2. The UM IP gateway object is a critical component, in that it specifies the connection between the UM dial plan and the physical IP/VoIP gateway. The major configuration of the UM IP gateway object is the IP address of the IP/VoIP gateway device it represents and the associated dial plan. The UM IP gateway objects can be found in the Exchange Management Console on the UM IP Gateway tab of the Organization, Unified Messaging container.

The UM IP gateway is created as enabled. The gateway can be disabled, either immediately (which disconnects any current calls) or by specifying to disable after completing calls. The latter mode disables the gateway for any new calls but does not disconnect any current calls.

If a UM IP gateway object is not created or is deleted, the Unified Messaging servers in the dial plan will not be able to accept, process or place calls.

Within the same Active Directory, there can only be one UM IP gateway object for each physical IP/VoIP gateway, and it is enforced through the IP addresses; however, multiple UM IP gateway objects might be defined within the Exchange Management Console for redundancy or advanced call routing.

UM IP gateway objects can be associated with multiple dial plans. This is accomplished by creating multiple hunt groups, as discussed in the following section.

Hunt Group Objects

In the telephony world, hunt groups are collections of lines that a PBX uses to organize extensions. The hunt group collections allow the system to treat the extensions as a logical group. Hunt groups are used for incoming lines, for outgoing lines, and to route calls to groups of users such as the Sales department. The UM hunt group objects can be found in the Exchange Management Console on the UM IP Gateway tab of the Organization, Unified Messaging container. They are listed under each of the UM IP gateways.

Calls with a hunt group can be routed using different methods or algorithms, such as the following:

▶ **Rollover**—The PBX starts with the lowest numbered line each time and increments until it finds a free line.

▶ **Round-robin**—The PBX rotates equally among all the lines when starting and then rolls over from that starting point. This ensures that the calls are distributed evenly within the hunt group.

▶ **Utilization**—The PBX tracks extension utilization and routes the call to the least utilized line first, and then rolls over to the next least busy line.

These algorithms basically encode what the organization deems the appropriate behavior for the routing.

Each hunt group has an associate pilot number, which is the extension that is dialed to access the hunt group. This is frequently the lowest numbered extension in the set of extensions because the most common implementation of a hunt group is rollover.

Within Exchange Server 2010, the UM hunt group object performs a different function. Essentially, the UM hunt group object maps the IP/VoIP gateway and an extension to a UM dial plan.

NOTE

If a default hunt group is created when the UM IP gateway object is created, that UM hunt group will not have a pilot extension associated with it. This creates call routing problems if you create additional hunt groups, so it is best to remove the default hunt group. When a new UM hunt group is created after that, the pilot identifier must be specified.

24

Additional UM hunt groups can be created to route different incoming extensions to different UM dial plans.

There is no limit to the number of UM hunt group objects that can be created. There must be at least one hunt group per UM IP gateway object for calls to be routed to a dial plan.

Mailbox Policy Objects

Mailbox policy objects control unified messaging settings and security for users. The UM mailbox policy objects can be found in the Exchange Management Console on the UM Mailbox Policies tab of the Organization, Unified Messaging container.

These settings include the following:

▶ Maximum greeting duration

▶ Message text for UM generated messages to users

▶ PIN policies

▶ Dialing restrictions

Mailbox policies are created to control security and provide customized messages to users. For example, in Figure 24.6 the SFO Mailbox Policy 1 is a general user policy with default PIN settings that require a minimum of 6 characters. The second policy, SFO Mailbox Policy 2, is for executives with higher security requirements and more secure PIN settings that require a minimum of 10 characters.

The UM mailbox policy is associated with one and only one UM dial plan, but dial plans can be associated with multiple mailbox policies. This allows the dial plan to be associated to the users associated with the mailbox policy. Each user will be associated with one and only one UM mailbox policy object, but many users can be associated with a single mailbox policy object.

There is no limit to the number of UM mailbox policy objects that can be created.

Auto Attendant Objects

The auto attendant provides an automated phone answering function, essentially replicating a human secretary. The auto attendant answers the incoming calls, provides helpful prompts, and directs the caller to the appropriate services. The UM auto attendant objects can be found in the Exchange Management Console on the UM Auto Attendant tab of the Organization, Unified Messaging container.

The auto attendant supports both phone key press (DTMF) and voice commands. This sophisticated voice recognition technology allows the caller to navigate the menus and prompts with nothing more than their voice if they want to.

The auto attendant objects support the following configurable features:

▶ Customized greetings and menus for business hours and nonbusiness hours

▶ Predefined and custom schedule to specify business hours and time zone

▶ Holiday schedule for exceptions to the business hour schedule

▶ Operator extension and allowing transfer to operator during business and nonbusiness hours

▶ Key mapping to enable the transfer of callers to specific extensions or other auto attendants based on hard-coded key presses or voice commands.

> **NOTE**
>
> Everyone has felt the frustration of moving through an automated call system and not being able to reach an operator or a live person. With unified messaging, the Exchange Server administrator now has control over that behavior.
>
> The auto attendant can allow or disallow transfer to the operator by specifically allowing or disallowing transfer to the operator during business and nonbusiness hours.
>
> The author's recommendation is to allow transfers to the operator at least during business hours to reduce caller frustration.

Each auto attendant can be mapped to specific extensions to provide a customized set of prompts. For example, an organization could set up one auto attendant to support the sales organization calls with specific prompts for handling calls to sales. The organization could then set up a second auto attendant to support the service organization with specific prompts for technical support and help. These would service different pilot numbers, depending on the number that the caller used.

A front-end menu can be created with key mapping and an auto attendant with customized prompts. This allows the organization in the previous example to create a top-level auto attendant that would prompt callers to "Press or say 1 for Sales or 2 for Service" and then perform the appropriate transfer. Figure 24.7 shows the key mapping configuration, which would be accompanied by customized prompts.

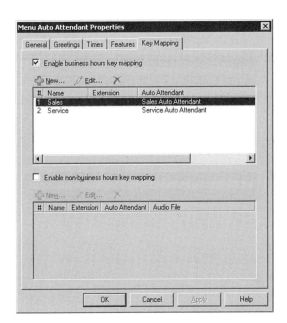

FIGURE 24.7   Key mapping example.

The initial greeting can be customized as well. There are two default greetings, one for business hours and a second for off-hours. By default the system says Welcome to Microsoft Exchange Server. In most implementations you want to customize this to your company name and include other relevant information. Customized greetings must be in a specific format. They must be saved as PCM/16bit/8kHz/Mono .WAV files. Each auto attendant can have a unique set of customized greetings and prompts.

There is no limit to the number of auto attendants that can be created in Active Directory. An auto attendant can only be associated with a single dial plan, though a dial plan can be associated with multiple auto attendants.

Unified Messaging Server Objects

In Active Directory, the Unified Messaging server object is a logical representation of the physical Exchange Server 2010 Unified Messaging server. The UM server objects can be found in the Exchange Management Console in the Server Configuration, Unified Messaging container.

The Microsoft Exchange Unified Messaging service (`umservice.exe`) is the service that instantiates the unified messaging functionality that runs under the Local System account. It is dependent on the Microsoft Exchange Active Directory Topology service and the Microsoft Exchange Speech Engine service.

The major configuration task for the Unified Messaging server object is to specify the associated dial plans, of which there can be more than one. The Unified Messaging server must be associated with a dial plan to function. The other configurable parameters for the service are the maximum concurrent calls (default is 100) and maximum concurrent faxes (default is 100).

The Unified Messaging server checks for changes when the service is started and every 10 minutes thereafter. Changes take effect as soon as they are detected by the server.

After determining the dial plans for which it is associated, the server then locates and establishes communications with the appropriate IP/VoIP gateways.

Much like the UM IP gateway, the Unified Messaging server is created as enabled. The server can be disabled via the Exchange Management Console or via the Exchange Management Shell for graceful shutdown or maintenance. This can be executed either immediately (which disconnects any current calls) or by specifying to disable after completing calls. The latter mode disables the server for any new calls but does not disconnect any current calls. Any current calls will be allowed to complete.

Unified Messaging Users

There is actually not an Active Directory object for unified messaging users. Rather, the unified messaging properties are stored in the Active Directory user account and the Exchange Server 2010 mailbox. Voice mail messages and fax mail messages are stored in the user's mailbox.

These properties can be found in the Exchange Management Console in the properties of the user's account in the Recipient Configuration, Mailbox folder. Within the user account properties, the unified messaging settings are under the Mailbox Features tab in the properties of the Unified Messaging feature. After navigating to the Unified Messaging feature, the properties button is clicked to access the feature properties.

When enabling a user for unified messaging, the associated UM mailbox policy and extension must be specified. The link to the mailbox policy provides a one-to-one link to the UM dial plan.

The user's mailbox quotas apply to both voice mail messages and fax messages. If the user's quota settings prevent the user from receiving email (that is, the user's mailbox is full), then unified messaging functionality will be impacted. Callers attempting to leave a message will not be allowed to leave a message and will be informed that the user's mailbox is full.

NOTE

Interestingly, if a user's mailbox is almost full, a caller will be allowed to leave a message for the user even if that message will cause the mailbox to exceed its quota. For example, consider a user who only has 25KB before they exceed their quota and are prevented from receiving messages. A caller could leave a minute long 100-KB voice message. However, the next caller would not be able to leave a message for the user.

Exchange Server 2010 unified messaging includes a number of features to control the size of voice mail messages to help control the storage impacts.

UM Web Services

A component that is not represented in Active Directory is the UM Web Services. This is a web service that is installed on Exchange Server 2010 servers that have the Client Access role.

The service is used for the following:

- ▶ Play on Phone Feature for both Outlook Server 2010 and Exchange Server 2010 Outlook Web App
- ▶ PIN Reset feature in Exchange Server 2010 Outlook Web App

This service requires that at least one Exchange Server 2010 server run the Client Access, Hub Transport, and mailbox server roles in addition to the Unified Messaging role.

Audio Codecs and Voice Message Sizes

Codec is a contraction of coding and decoding digital data. This is the format in which the audio stream is stored. It includes both the number of bit rate (bits/sec) and compression that is used.

The codec that is used by the Unified Messaging server to encode the messages is one of the following four:

- ▶ **Windows Media Audio (WMA)**—16-bit compressed
- ▶ **GSM 06.10 (GSM)**—8-bit compressed
- ▶ **G.711 PCM Linear (G711)**—16-bit uncompressed
- ▶ **Mpeg Audio Layer 3 (MP3)**—16-bit compressed

The Exchange Server 2010 unified messaging default is MP3. This is a change from Exchange Server 2007 in which the default was WMA. Although using WMA results in slightly smaller file sizes, most people prefer the universal nature of MP3. This enables a much larger number of mobile devices to play voice mail messages. The Audio Codec setting is configured on the UM dial plan on the Settings tab.

> **NOTE**
>
> A dirty little secret is that the digital compression can result in loss of data. When the data is compressed and decompressed, information can be lost. That is, bits of the conversation or message can be lost. This is a trade-off that the codec makes to save space. This is why the G.711 codec is available, which doesn't compress data and doesn't lose data but at a heavy cost in storage.

These are stored in the message as attachments using the following formats:

- ▶ **Windows Media Audio Format (.wma)**—For the WMA codec
- ▶ **RIFF/WAV Format (.wav)**—For GSM or G.711 codecs
- ▶ **Mpeg Audio Layer 3 (.mp3)**—For the MP3 codec

The choice of the audio codec impacts the audio quality and the size of the attached file. Table 24.1 shows the approximate size of data in the file attachment for each codec.

TABLE 24.1   Audio Size for Codec Options

Codec Setting	Approximate Size of 10 Sec of Audio
WMA	11,000 bytes
G.711	160,000 bytes
GSM	16,000 bytes
MP3	19,500 bytes

The G.711 audio codec setting results in a greater than 10:1 storage penalty when compared to the WMA audio codec setting. Although the GSM audio codec setting results in approximately the same storage as the WMA codec setting, this comes at a cost of a 50% reduction in audio quality. MP3 provides similar audio quality to WMA at an acceptable file size. The ubiquitous nature of the MP3 codec makes it the preferred choice for Exchange Server 2010.

> **NOTE**
>
> The .wma file format has a larger header (about 7KB) than the .wav format (about 0.1KB). So for small messages, the GSM files will be smaller. However, after messages exceed 15 seconds, the WMA files will be smaller than the GSM files.

Operating System Requirements

This section discusses the recommended minimum hardware requirements for Exchange Server 2010 servers.

Exchange Server 2010 unified messaging supports the following processors:

- ▶ x64 architecture-based Intel Xeon or Intel Pentium family processor that supports Intel Extended Memory 64 Technology
- ▶ x64 architecture-based computer with AMD Opteron or AMD Athlon 64-bit processor that supports AMD64 platform

The Exchange Server 2010 unified messaging memory requirements are as follows:

- ▶ 2GB of RAM minimum
- ▶ 4GB of RAM recommended

The Exchange Server 2010 unified messaging disk space requirements are as follows:

- ▶ A minimum of 1.2GB of available disk space
- ▶ Plus 500MB of available disk space for each unified messaging language pack

▶ 200MB of available disk space on the system drive

▶ DVD drive

As features and complexity of the applications such as Exchange Server 2010 have grown, the installation code bases have grown proportionally. Luckily, so have the hardware specifications of the average new system, which now typically includes a DVD drive.

Exchange Server 2010 unified messaging supports the following operating system and Windows components:

▶ Windows Server 2008, x64 Standard Edition with service pack 2

▶ Windows Server 2008, x64 Enterprise Edition with service pack 2

▶ Windows Server 2008, x64 R2 Standard Edition

▶ Windows Server 2008, x64 R2 Enterprise Edition

Exchange Server 2010 unified messaging requires the following components to be installed:

▶ Microsoft .NET Framework Version 3.5

▶ Windows PowerShell 2.0

▶ Windows Remote Management (WinRM) 2.0

▶ Extensions for ASP.NET AJAX 1.0

▶ Desktop Experience operating system feature

▶ Microsoft Management Console (MMC) 3.0.

Out of the box, an Exchange Server 2010 Unified Messaging server is configured for a maximum of 100 concurrent calls. This is enough to support potentially thousands of users, given that the number of calls and voice messages per day is a fraction of the number of users and is spread out throughout the day.

Supported IP/VoIP Hardware

Exchange Server 2010 unified messaging relies on the ability of the IP/VoIP gateway to translate time-division multiplexing (TDM) or telephony circuit-switched based protocols, such as Integrated Services Digital Network (ISDN) or QSIG, from a PBX to protocols based on voice over IP (VoIP) or IP, such as Session Initiation Protocol (SIP), Real-Time Transport Protocol (RTP), or T.38 for real-time facsimile transport.

Although there are many types and manufacturers of PBXs, IP/VoIP gateways, and IP/PBXs, there are essentially two types of IP/VoIP gateway component configurations:

▶ **IP/VoIP Gateway**—A legacy PBX and an IP/VoIP gateway provisioned as two separate devices. The Unified Messaging server communicates with the IP/VoIP gateway.

▶ **IP/PBX**—A modern IP-based or hybrid PBX such as a Cisco CallManager. The Unified Messaging server communicates directly with the PBX.

24

Table 24.2 lists the currently supported IP/VoIP gateways.

TABLE 24.2   Supported IP/VoIP Gateways for Exchange Server 2010 UM

Manufacturer	Model	Supported Protocols
AudioCodes	MediaPack 114, MediaPack 118	Analog with In-Band or SMDI
AudioCodes	Mediant 1000/2000	T1/ or E1 with CAS—In-Band or SMDI, T1/E1 with Primary Rate Interface (PRI) and Q.SIG or Analog PSTN
Dialogic	1000/2000	T1/ or E1 with CAS—In-Band or SMDI, T1/E1 with Primary Rate Interface (PRI) and Q.SIG or Analog PSTN
Ferrari AG	OfficeMaster 3.2	PSTN Analog
Net	VX1200	T1/ or E1 with CAS—In-Band or SMDI, T1/E1 with Primary Rate Interface (PRI) and Q.SIG or Analog PSTN
Nortel	CS1000	Direct SIP
Quintum	Tenor-series	Analog PSTN

To support Exchange Server 2010 unified messaging, one or both types of IP/VoIP device configurations are used when connecting a telephony network infrastructure to a data network infrastructure.

All these solutions must communicate with the unified messenger via SIP over TCP (TLS encrypted) and SRTP.

Telephony Components and Terminology

With the integration of Exchange Server 2010 into the telephony world, it is important for the Exchange Server administrator to understand the various components and terminology of a modern telephone system.

The following are some of the common components and terms that are critical to understand:

▶ **Circuit**—A circuit is a connection between two end-to-end devices. This allows the device to communicate. A common example of this is a telephone call where two people are talking, in which a circuit is established between the two telephones.

▶ **Circuit-switched networks**—Circuit-switched networks consist of dedicated end-to-end connections through the network that support sessions between end devices. The circuits are set up end-to-end through a series of switches as needed and torn down when done. While the circuit is set up, the entire circuit is dedicated to the devices. A common example of a circuit-switched network is the PSTN.

▶ **DTMF**—The Dual Tone Multiple frequency (DTMF) signaling protocol is used for telephony signaling and call setup. The most common use is for telephone tone dialing and is known as Touch-Tone. This is used to convey phone button key presses to devices on the network.

▶ **IP/PBX**—With the advent of high-speed ubiquitous packet-switched networks, many corporations have moved from legacy PBXs to modern IP-based PBXs known as Internet Protocol/Private Branch Exchange (IP/PBX). These devices come in a myriad of forms, including true IP/PBXs that only support IP protocols to hybrid devices that support both circuit-switched and packet-switched devices. A major advantage of the IP/PBXs is that they are typically much easier to provision and administer. Rather than having to add a separate physical line to plug a phone into, IP phones are simply plugged into the Ethernet jack. Rather than being provisioned by the physical line they are plugged into, the IP phones are provisioned by their own internal characteristics such as the MAC address. This allows for more flexibility.

▶ **IP/VoIP gateways**—Connecting legacy circuit-switched networks to packet-switched networks, IP/VoIP gateways provide connections between the new packet-switched VoIP protocols and the circuit-switched protocols. These gateways can connect the PSTN to an IP/PBX or a legacy PBX to VoIP devices. In the case of Exchange Server 2010 unified messaging, the IP/VoIP gateway connects the Unified Messaging server to the legacy PBX. This is not typically needed if the PBX that the Unified Messaging server is connecting to is an IP/PBX.

▶ **Packet-switched networks**—In packet-switched networks, there is no dedicated end-to-end circuit. Instead, the sessions between devices are disassembled into packets and transmitted individually over the network, then reassembled when they reach their destination. All sessions travel over the shared network. A common example of a packet-switched network is the Internet.

▶ **PBX**—In all but the smallest companies, there is a device that takes incoming calls from the circuit-switched telephone network and routes them within the company. This device is called a Private Branch Exchange or PBX. In the old days, this was done by an operator who plugged in the lines manually. The PBX also routes internal outgoing calls, calls between internal phones, and calls to other devices such as the voice mail system.

▶ **POTS**—The Plain Old Telephone System (POTS) is the original analog version of the PSTN. The term originally referred to Post Office Telephone Service, but morphed into the current definition when control of the telephone systems was removed from national post offices.

▶ **PSTN**—The Public Switched Telephone Network (PSTN) is the circuit-switched network to which most telephones connect. It can be either analog, digital, or a combination of the two.

24

▶ **TDM**—Time-division multiplexing (TDM) is a digital, multiplexing technique for placing multiple simultaneous calls over a circuit-switched network such as the PSTN.

▶ **VoIP**—Voice over Internet Protocol (VoIP) is the use of voice technologies over packet-switched networks using TCP/IP transport protocols rather than circuit-switched networks like the PSTN. This takes advantage of and reflects the trend toward a single, ubiquitous packet-switched network. The local area network (LAN) and wide area network (WAN) are used not only for data traffic, but also for voice traffic. VoIP is not a single technology, but rather a collection of different technologies, protocols, hardware, and software.

Unified Messaging Protocols

The Exchange Server 2010 Unified Messaging servers use several telephony-related protocols to integrate and communicate with telephony devices. These protocols are listed and discussed in the following list:

▶ **SIP**—Session Initiation Protocol (SIP) is the signaling protocol that is used to set up and tear down VoIP calls. These calls include voice, video, instant messaging, and a variety of other services. The SIP protocol is specified in RFC 3261 produced by the Internet Engineering Task Force (IETF) SIP Working Group. SIP is only a signaling protocol and does not transmit data per se. After the call is set up, the actual communications take place using the RTP for voice and video or T.38 for faxes.

> **NOTE**
>
> Exchange Server 2010 only supports SIP over TCP. SIP can be configured to run over User Datagram Protocol (UDP) or Transmission Control Protocol (TCP). UDP is connectionless and does not provide reliability guarantees over the network. TCP is connection-oriented and provides reliability guarantees for its packets.

▶ **RTP**—Real-Time Transport Protocol (RTP) is a protocol for sending the voice and video data over the TCP/IP network. The protocol relies on other protocols, such as SIP or H.323, to perform call setup and teardown. It was developed by the IETF Audio-Video Transport Working Group and is specified in RFC 3550. There is not a defined port for the RTP protocol, but it is normally configured to use ports in the range 16384–32767. The protocol uses a dynamic port range, so it is not ideally suited to traversing firewalls.

▶ **T.38**—The Real-Time Facsimile Transport (T.38) protocol is an International Telecommunication Union (ITU) standard for transmitting faxes over TCP/IP. The protocol is described in RFC 3362. Although it can support call setup and teardown, it is normally used in conjunction with a signaling protocol such as SIP.

It is important to note that the Exchange Server 2010 Unified Messaging server is also a Windows server, a web server, and a member of the Active Directory domain. There are a myriad of protocols, including domain name system (DNS), Hypertext Transfer Protocol (HTTP), Lightweight Directory Access Protocol (LDAP), remote procedure calls (RPC), and Simple Mail Transfer Protocol (SMTP) among others, that the servers use to communicate with other servers in addition to the telephony communications.

TABLE 24.3   Ports Used for Unified Messaging Protocols

Protocol	TCP Port	UDP Port	Can Ports Be Changed?
SIP-UM Service	5060		Ports are hard-coded.
SIP-Worker Process	5061 and 5062		Ports are set by using the Extensible Markup Language (XML) configuration file.
RTP		Port range above 1024	The range of ports can be changed in the Registry.
T.38		Dynamic port above 1024	Ports are defined by the system.
UM Web Service	Dynamic port above 1024		Ports are defined by the system.

Unified Messaging Port Assignments

Table 24.3 shows the IP ports that unified messaging uses for each protocol. The table also shows if the ports can be changed and where.

Unified Messaging Installation

The installation of Exchange Server 2010 is surprisingly easy, although the configuration can be tricky. This section covers the installation and configuration of a basic system to illustrate the concepts.

The installation of the Unified Messaging server role assumes that Exchange Server 2010 is already installed on the target server. For detailed instructions on installing Exchange Server 2010, see Chapter 7, "Installing Exchange Server 2010."

Installation of the Unified Messaging server role modifies the base installation of Exchange Server 2010 and is done in what is termed Maintenance mode. The procedures in this section step through the build of a basic Exchange Server 2010 unified messaging system, as shown in Figure 24.8.

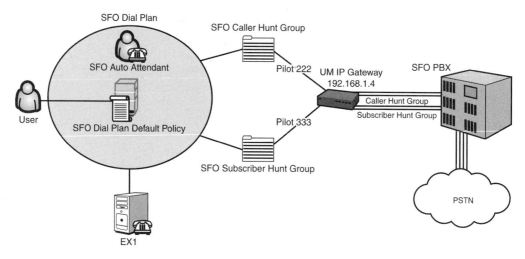

FIGURE 24.8   Sample Exchange Server 2010 UM system.

Installation Prerequisites

Before starting the installation, it is important that the user's mailboxes that will be serviced by the Unified Messaging server are on Exchange Server 2010 servers. In other words, Exchange Server 2010 UM cannot service users with mailboxes on an Exchange 2007 mailbox server. Of course, the requirements (such as PowerShell) for any Exchange Server 2010 server role apply to the Unified Messaging server.

Telephony Prerequisites

As the Exchange Server 2010 Unified Messaging server is essentially a voice mail system, all the other components must be in place and operational before introducing it. This includes the following:

▶ **PBX**—The existing PBX must be configured with the appropriate hunt groups to route calls correctly.

▶ **Hunt groups**—The hunt groups and pilot numbers should be provisioned in the PBX. The Auto Attendant pilot numbers and the subscriber access pilot numbers should be part of a rollover group, so that if one number is busy, the call will roll over to the next line.

NOTE

Set up separate hunt groups and pilot access numbers on the PBX for the Auto Attendant and the subscriber access lines.

▶ **IP/VoIP gateway**—The IP gateway must be configured to route calls from the pilot extensions to the Exchange Server 2010 UM server IP address. The gateway must also be configured to use SIP over TCP, rather than SIP over UDP. Some gateways will attempt UDP first and then try TCP, resulting in strange connection behavior such as delays in initiating calls.

▶ **Phones**—The phones must be provisioned and assigned to users. At the very least, at least two test phones should be available.

▶ **External lines**—External lines must be provisioned within the PBX.

▶ **The Early Media setting** is not supported in Exchange Server 2010 unified messaging.

See the manufacturer's documentation for specific details of the configuration for each of the telephony components.

Installing the Unified Messaging Role

The first step is to install the Unified Messaging role. This procedure assumes that the Exchange Server 2010 server has already been installed. To add the Unified Messaging server role, complete the following steps:

1. In Control Panel, select Programs and Features.

2. Select Microsoft Exchange Server 2010.

3. Click the Change button to enter Exchange Maintenance mode.

4. Click Next.

5. Select the Unified Messaging Role check box, as shown in Figure 24.9, and click Next.

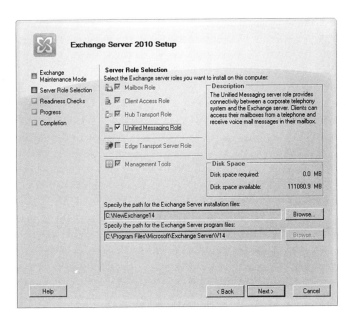

FIGURE 24.9   Choosing the Unified Messaging Role from the setup screen.

6. The installer conducts readiness checks.

7. Click the Install button to install the Unified Messaging server role.

8. After the installation has successfully completed, click Finish.

The basic software has been installed, but the UM server needs to be configured post-installation to function properly.

Postinstall Configuration

After the server has the Unified Messaging server role installed, you need to complete several postinstall configuration tasks for a basic installation:

▶ Create a UM dial plan.

▶ Associate subscriber access numbers.

▶ Create a UM IP gateway.

▶ Associate the UM server with the dial plan.

▶ Create a UM Auto Attendant.

▶ Create the hunt groups.

▶ Enable mailboxes for UM.

▶ Test functionality.

Following these tasks results in a functioning Exchange Server 2010 Unified Messaging system. The remainder of this section details the installation steps for each task.

Creating a UM Dial Plan

The first task is to create the central organizing element of the Exchange Server 2010 UM infrastructure—the dial plan shown in Figure 24.10.

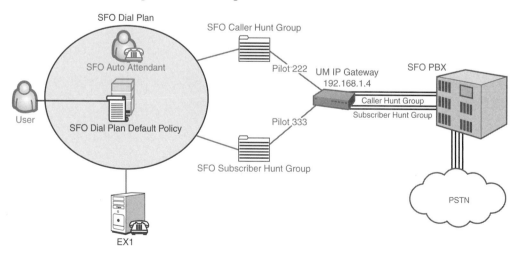

FIGURE 24.10   Creating the dial plan.

To create a dial plan, execute the following steps:

1. Launch the Exchange Management Console.
2. Under the Organization Configuration folder, select the Unified Messaging container.
3. Select the UM Dial Plan tab.
4. In the Action menu, select New UM Dial Plan.
5. Enter the dial plan name, such as SFO Dial Plan.
6. Enter the number of digits in the PBX extensions, such as 3.
7. Enter the Country/Region code, such as 1 for the United States.
8. Click New to create the UM dial plan.
9. Click Finish to close the wizard.

The newly created dial plan should be shown in the results pane. Notice that the default mailbox policy (SFO Dial Plan Default Policy) was automatically created at the same time.

Associating Subscriber Access Numbers

For subscribers to access their mailbox, one or more subscriber access numbers must be specified in the dial plan. This should be the pilot number for the PBX hunt group that the subscribers will use.

To associate a subscriber access extension to the dial plan, execute the following steps:

1. Launch the Exchange Management Console.
2. Under the Organization Configuration folder, select the Unified Messaging container.
3. Select the UM Dial Plan tab.
4. Select the dial plan in the results pane, such as SFO Dial Plan.
5. In the Action menu, select Properties.
6. Select the Subscriber Access tab.
7. Enter the extension that subscribers will use to access their mailboxes, such as 333.
8. Click Add.
9. Click OK to close the window.

The UM server will now recognize that subscribers will use the extension to access their mailboxes.

Creating a UM IP Gateway

The next task is to create an UM IP gateway to link the dial plan with the IP/VoIP gateway and the PBX. This is shown in Figure 24.11.

To create the UM IP gateway, execute the following steps:

1. Launch the Exchange Management Console.
2. Under the Organization Configuration folder, select the Unified Messaging container.
3. Select the UM IP Gateway tab.
4. In the Action pane, click New UM IP Gateway.

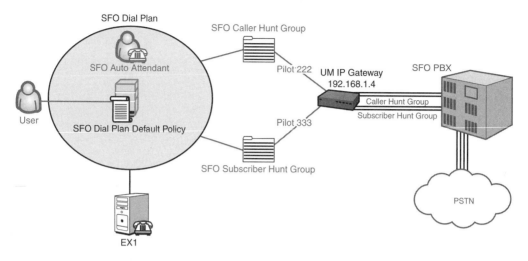

FIGURE 24.11   Creating an IP gateway.

5. Enter the IP gateway name, such as SFO IP Gateway.

6. Enter the IP address for the IP gateway, such as 192.168.1.4 shown in Figure 24.12.

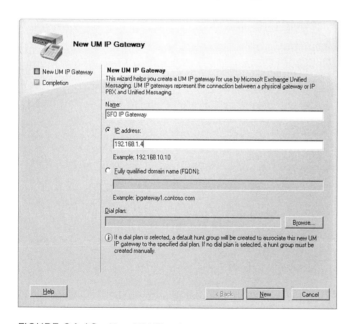

FIGURE 24.12   New UM IP gateway.

7. Click Browse.

8. Select a dial plan to associate the IP gateway with, such as the SFO Dial Plan.

9. This also creates a default hunt group (which will be deleted later).

10. Click OK.

11. Click New to create the UM IP gateway.

12. Click Finish to close the wizard.

The newly created UM IP gateway should be shown in the results pane. The default hunt group will be removed and a new one created in a later task.

Associating the UM Server with the Dial Plan

The dial plan needs to be associated with the UM server that was installed in the first task. This eventually causes the UM server to register with the IP/VoIP gateway to receive calls.

To associate the UM server with the new dial plan, execute the following steps:

1. Launch the Exchange Management Console.

2. Under the Server Configuration folder, select the Unified Messaging container.

3. Select the Unified Messaging server.

4. In the actions pane, click Properties.

5. Select the UM Settings tab.

6. Click Add.

7. Select the dial plan to associate, such as the SFO Dial Plan.

8. Click OK.

9. Click OK to close the Properties dialog box.

The pilot number will now be associated to the dial plan for subscriber access.

Create a Unified Messaging Auto Attendant

For the UM server to answer callers, a UM Auto Attendant must be created and associated with a dial plan. This allows incoming calls to be answered and directed to the appropriate voice mailbox.

To create an Auto Attendant and associate it with a dial plan, execute the following tasks:

1. Launch the Exchange Management Console.

2. Under the Organization Configuration folder, select the Unified Messaging container.

3. Select the UM Auto Attendants tab.

4. In the actions pane, click New UM Auto Attendant.

5. Enter the name of the Auto Attendant, such as SFO Auto Attendant.

6. Click Browse.

7. Select a dial plan, such as the SFO Dial Plan.

8. Click OK.

9. Enter the pilot extension number, such as 222, and click Add.

10. Check the Create Auto Attendant as Enabled check box.

11. Check the Create Auto Attendant as Speech-Enabled check box, shown in Figure 24.13, if you want the Auto Attendant to accept voice commands.

FIGURE 24.13   Creating an Auto Attendant.

12. Click New.

13. Click Finish to close the wizard.

The newly created auto attendant should be shown in the results pane.

> **NOTE**
>
> If the Auto Attendant is created as speech-enabled, a secondary fallback Auto Attendant that is not speech-enabled should be created and that option configured on the primary Auto Attendant. If a user cannot use voice commands, he can use DTMF commands on the secondary Auto Attendant. Although the speech-enabled Auto Attendant accepts DTMF commands, the user is not notified this is possible unless a DTMF fallback Auto Attendant is configured.

Creating the Hunt Groups

The default hunt group that is created with the UM IP gateway does not contain a pilot number. To have the system handle incoming calls correctly, the default hunt group should be deleted and new ones created for the caller and subscriber hunt groups.

To accomplish the creation of the hunt groups, execute the following steps:

1. Launch the Exchange Management Console.

2. Under the Organization Configuration folder, select the Unified Messaging container.

3. Select the UM IP Gateway tab.

4. Select the Default Hunt Group in the results pane.

5. In the actions pane, under the section for the selected hunt group, click Remove.

6. At the prompt, click Yes.

7. Select the UM IP gateway, such as SFO IP Gateway.

8. In the actions pane, click New UM Hunt Group.

9. Enter the caller hunt group name, such as SFO Caller Hunt Group.

10. Click Browse.

11. Select the dial plan to associate, such as SFO Dial Plan.

12. Click OK.

13. Enter the hunt group pilot number, such as 222.

14. Click New.

15. Click Finish.

16. Repeat steps 7 through 14, using SFO Subscriber Hunt Group as the name and 333 as the hunt group pilot.

The result of the configuration is shown in Figure 24.14, including the new hunt groups.

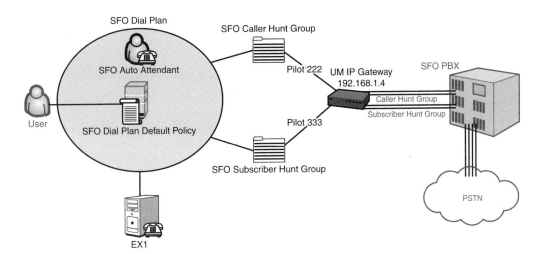

FIGURE 24.14   Creation of hunt groups.

The system is now configured and ready for the final configuration step in the basic configuration—the enabling of a user for unified messaging.

Enabling Mailboxes for UM

The last task is to enable a user's mailbox. This associates the user with a mailbox policy and, therefore, to the rest of the unified messaging infrastructure.

To enable a user, execute the following steps:

1. Launch the Exchange Management Console.
2. Under the Recipient Configuration folder, select the Mailbox folder.
3. In the results pane, select the user to be enabled.
4. In the actions pane, select Enable Unified Messaging.
5. Click Browse.
6. Select the UM policy, such as the SFO Dial Plan Default Policy.
7. Click OK.
8. Click Next.
9. Enter the extension, such as 100, shown in Figure 24.15.

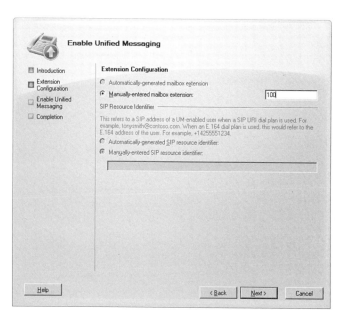

FIGURE 24.15   Enabling a user for unified messaging.

10. Click Next.

11. Click Enable.

12. Click Finish to close the wizard.

A simple welcome email message with the extension and their confidential PIN will be automatically sent to their Exchange Server mailbox.

Testing Functionality

The final step is to make sure that it is all working. This could be the most difficult testing tasks for an average Exchange Server administrator, as they will be the least familiar with the telephony elements of the infrastructure.

It is important to make sure that these critical functions be tested:

▶ The UM server is operating.

▶ The UM server can connect to the gateway and PBX.

▶ The UM server can be reached from an internal phone.

▶ The UM server can be reached from an external phone.

Figure 24.16 shows the paths of the critical tests.

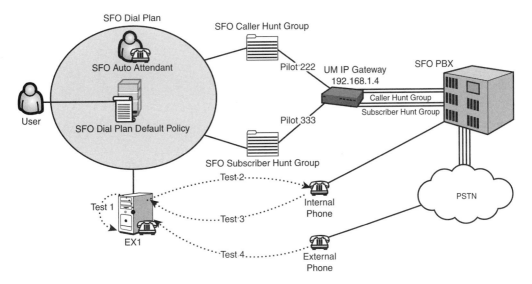

FIGURE 24.16   Paths of the critical tests for UM testing.

The specific commands and steps for testing are discussed in the following sections.

Testing Unified Messaging Server Operation

The Unified Messaging server operations test needs to run on the local UM server in the Exchange Management Shell. The shell command is:

```
Test-UMConnectivity
```

This command attempts a diagnostic SIP call and reports back on the success. Figure 24.17 shows the result of a successful test. Specifically, the value of `EntireOperationSuccess` is True.

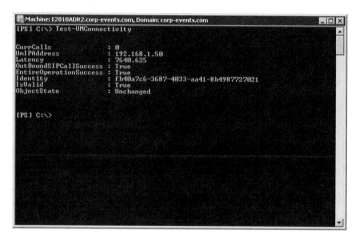

FIGURE 24.17   Testing the UM server.

Testing Unified Messaging Server Connectivity

This test shows if the UM server can communicate with the PBX and access a phone. Specifically, it causes the internal phone to ring.

The command needs to be run from the Exchange Management Shell. The command syntax is:

```
Test-UMConnectivity -IPGateway "IP Gateway Name" -Phone extension
```

For example, the command might be:

```
Test-UMConnectivity -IPGateway "SFO IP Gateway" -Phone 102
```

The results for a successful test are shown in Figure 24.18. The phone at the extension should ring. If the test is successful, it will show that "The call was disconnected by the other party" at the end of the test.

To show the results of an unsuccessful test, enter the command:

```
Test-UMConnectivity -IPGateway "SFO IP Gateway" -Phone 104
```

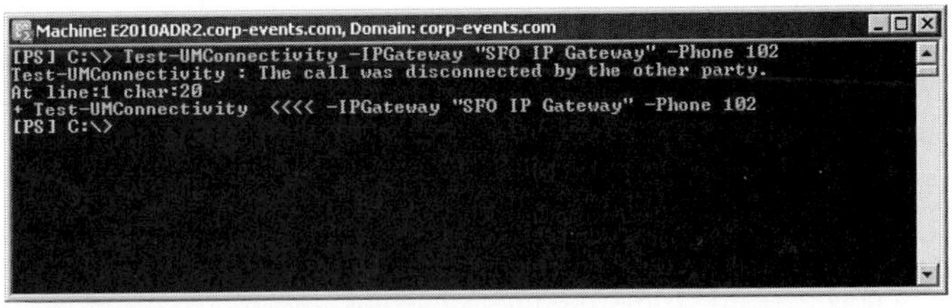

FIGURE 24.18   Connectivity success.

This command specifies a nonexistent extension. The results are shown in Figure 24.19. It shows that the requested operation failed.

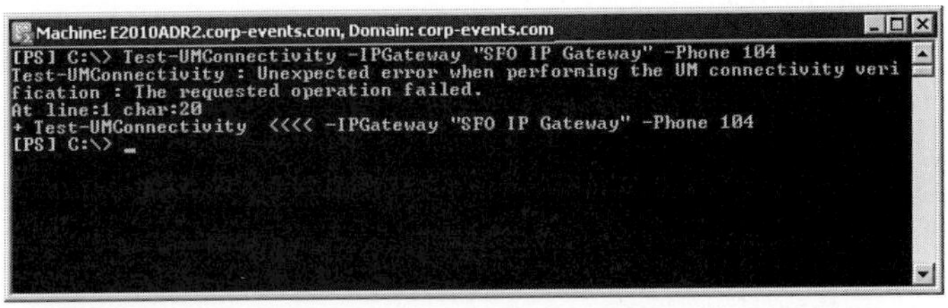

FIGURE 24.19   Connectivity failure.

Testing Unified Messaging Server with an Internal Phone

To test the Unified Messaging server from a phone, pick up a phone from within the dial plan and dial the pilot number.

For example, from the phone at extension 102, dial the pilot number 222. The Auto Attendant should pick up and prompt the caller.

Leave a message for a test user and then hang up.

Dial the pilot number for subscriber access (for example, extension 333) and check the message. Alternatively, check the message using Outlook or Outlook Web App.

Testing Unified Messaging Server with an External Phone

Use an outside line to call the company number that the PBX routes to the caller hunt group. Say the user's name. Press # to leave a message and leave a message for the user.

To verify the message was received, dial the external number for subscriber access and check the message. Alternatively, check the message using Outlook or Outlook Web App.

Data Storage in Unified Messaging

Unified messaging stores data in a variety of locations and formats. The different types of data include custom audio prompts, incoming calls, configuration, and setup.

It is important to understand where the data is stored, the relative importance of backing it up, and the method of restoring the data. Tables 24.4, 24.5, 24.6, and 24.7 list the relevant data storage information for each type of data.

TABLE 24.4   Custom Audio Prompt Data

Data Type	Custom audio files (.wav) for UM dial plans and UM Auto Attendants
	Custom audio files (.wav) for telephone user interface (TUI) and Outlook Voice Access
Storage	File system in \UnifiedMessaging\Prompts
Backup	File-level backup is only needed on the prompt publishing server
Restore	File-level restore is only needed on the prompt publishing server
Data Type	Custom audio files (.wav) for UM dial plans and UM Auto Attendants
	Custom audio files (.wav) for telephone user interface (TUI) and Outlook Voice Access
Storage	File system in \UnifiedMessaging\Prompts

TABLE 24.5   Incoming Call Data

Critical Data	Incoming calls: .eml and .wma files for each voice mail
Storage	File system \UnifiedMessaging\temp
Backup	None
Restore	None

TABLE 24.6   Server Configuration Data

Critical Data	Server configuration data, including all objects and settings
Storage	Active Directory configuration container
Backup	Backup method is domain controller replication or Active Directory backup
Restore	This data is reapplied to the server during a setup /m:recoverserver restore

TABLE 24.7   Setup Data

Critical Data	Limited information is stored in the Registry by Setup that is not essential to server restore
Storage	HKLM\SOFTWARE\Microsoft\Exchange
	HKLM\SYSTEM\currentcontrolset\Services
Backup	Backup method is System State backup or Registry export
Restore	Restore method is System State restore or Registry import

Monitoring and Troubleshooting Unified Messaging

A number of tools are built in to the Exchange Server 2010 unified messaging platform to support the troubleshooting and monitoring of the services.

First and foremost, it is highly recommended that administrators deploy Microsoft System Center Operations Manager (SCOM) 2007 to monitor the Exchange Server 2010 infrastructure. There is a management pack specific to the Exchange Server 2010 platform with a wealth of knowledge built in. See Chapter 20, "Using Operations Manager to Monitor Exchange Server 2010," for more details on SCOM and Exchange Server 2010.

That said, it is still important for the Exchange Server administrator to have a good knowledge and familiarity with the tools that are available to monitor Exchange Server 2010 unified messaging. These tools include the following:

- ▶ Exchange Management Shell test cmdlets
- ▶ Performance Monitor objects and counters
- ▶ Event log messages
- ▶ Removing the first UM server

These tools and techniques are covered in the next sections.

Active Calls

The system can provide information on active calls, which is very useful for monitoring and troubleshooting the unified messaging system. The Get-UMActiveCalls cmdlet returns information about the calls that are active and being processed by the Unified Messaging (UM) server. The syntax for the cmdlet is given in Table 24.8.

TABLE 24.8   Get-UMActiveCalls cmdlets

Syntax
Get-UMActiveCalls [-Server <ServerIdParameter>]
Get-UMActiveCalls -InstanceServer <UMServer>
Get-UMActiveCalls -DialPlan <UMDialPlanIdParameter>
Get-UMActiveCalls -IPGateway <UMIPGatewayIdParameter>

Figure 24.20 shows two instances of the command. In the first execution of the command, it shows an active call with the DialedNumber of 333, indicating that it has come in via the subscriber access line configured in the example installation. In the second execution of the command, it shows that the caller has dialed extension 102.

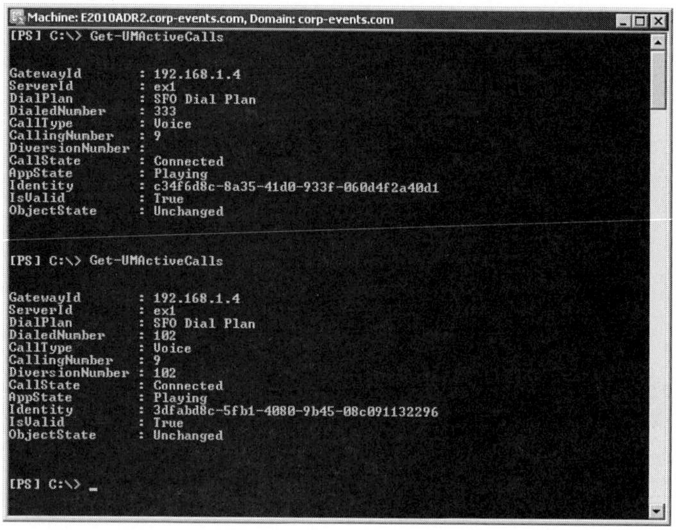

FIGURE 24.20   Active calls.

Connectivity

Connectivity to the IP/VoIP gateway can be one of the most troublesome aspects of the deployment and support of a unified messaging system. The Test-UMConnectivity cmdlet can be used to test the operation of a computer that has the Unified Messaging server role installed. The syntax for the cmdlet is given in Table 24.9.

TABLE 24.9   Test-UMConnectivity cmdlet

Syntax
test-UMConnectivity [-Fax <$true ¦ $false>] [-ListenPort <Int32>] ➥[-MonitoringContext <$true ¦ $false>] [-Secured <$true ¦ $false>] [-Timeout <Int32>] Test-UMConnectivity -IPGateway <UMIPGatewayIdParameter> -Phone <String> ➥[-Fax <$true ¦ $false>] [-ListenPort <Int32>] [-MonitoringContext <$true ¦ $false>] ➥[-Secured <$true ¦ $false>] [-Timeout <Int32>]

This test was used in the installation section of this chapter to test the functionality of the UM server. See the section "Testing Functionality" earlier in this chapter for details of the command usage.

Performance Monitors

Unlike many applications, the Exchange Server 2010 unified messaging application is very well instrumented.

Tables of the counters for each of the monitored objects are noted in the balance of this section.

General Performance Counters for Unified Messaging

The counters listed in Table 24.10 are under the MSExchangeUMGeneral performance object and are useful for monitoring and troubleshooting general problems with the Exchange 2010 UM server.

TABLE 24.10   Counters for the MSExchangeUMGeneral Object

Performance Counter	Description
Total Calls	The number of calls since the service was started.
Total Calls per Second	The number of new calls that arrived in the last second.
Calls Disconnected by User Failure	The total number of calls disconnected after too many user entry failures.
Calls Rejected	The total number of new call invitations that have been rejected.
Calls Rejected per Second	The number of new call invitations that have been rejected in the last second.
Current Calls	The number of calls currently connected to the UM server.
Current Voice Calls	The number of voice calls currently connected to the UM server.
Current Fax Calls	The number of fax calls currently connected to the UM server. Voice calls become fax calls after a fax tone is detected.
Current Auto Attendant Calls	The number of Auto Attendant calls that are currently connected to the UM server.
Current Play on Phone Calls	The number of outbound calls initiated to play back messages.
Current Unauthenticated Pilot Number Calls	The number of voice calls to the pilot number that have not yet been authenticated.
Total Play to Phone Calls	The total number of Play to Phone calls that were initiated since the service was started.
Average Call Duration	The average duration, in seconds, of calls since the service was started.
Average Recent Call Duration	The average duration, in seconds, of the last 50 calls.
User Response Latency	The average response time, in milliseconds, for the system to respond to a user request. This average is calculated over the last 25 calls. This counter is limited to calls that require significant processing.
Delayed Calls	The number of calls that experienced one or more delays longer than 2 seconds.

TABLE 24.10   Counters for the MSExchangeUMGeneral Object

Performance Counter	Description
Call Duration Exceeded	The number of calls that were disconnected because they exceeded the UM maximum call length. This number includes all types of calls, including fax calls.
Current Prompt Editing Calls	The number of logged on users who are editing custom prompts.
Current Subscriber Access Calls	The number of logged on subscribers who are currently connected to the UM server.
OCS User Event Notifications	The number of OCS User Event notifications that have occurred since the service was started.
Current CAS Connections	The number of connections that are currently open between the UM server and client access servers.

Call Answering Performance Counters for Unified Messaging

The counters listed in Table 24.11 are under the MSExchangeUMCallAnswering performance object and are useful for monitoring and troubleshooting call answering problems with the Exchange Server 2010 UM server.

TABLE 24.11   Counters for the MSExchangeUMCallAnswering Object

Performance Counter	Description
Call Answering Calls	The number of diverted calls that were answered on behalf of subscribers.
Call Answering Voice Messages	The total number of messages that were submitted because the calls were answered on behalf of subscribers.
Call Answering Voice Messages per Second	The number of messages that were submitted because the calls were answered on behalf of subscribers.
Call Answering Missed Calls	The number of times a diverted call was dropped without a message being left.
Call Answering Escapes	The number of times a caller pressed the * key to connect to another user rather than leaving a message.
Average Voice Message Size	The average size, in seconds, of voice messages left for subscribers.
Average Recent Message Size	The average size, in seconds, of the last 50 voice messages left for subscribers.
Average Greeting Size	The average size, in seconds, of recorded greetings that have been retrieved by the UM server.
Calls Without Personal Greetings	The number of diverted calls received for subscribers who did not have recorded greeting messages.

TABLE 24.11   Counters for the MSExchangeUMCallAnswering Object

Performance Counter	Description
Fetch Greeting Timed Out	The number of diverted calls for which the subscriber's personal greeting could not be retrieved within the time allowed.
Calls Disconnected by Callers During UM Audio Hourglass	The number of calls during which the caller disconnected while Unified Messaging was playing the audio hourglass tones.
Calls Disconnected by UM on Irrecoverable External Error	The number of calls that have been disconnected after an irrecoverable external error occurred.
Call Failed Because Transport Unavailable	The number of calls that failed because the transport service is not available to submit the message.
Diverted Extension Not Provisioned	The number of calls received for which the diverted extension supplied with the call is not a UM subscriber extension.

Subscriber Access Performance Counters for Unified Messaging

The counters listed in Table 24.12 are under the MSExchangeUMSubscriberAccess performance object and are useful for monitoring and troubleshooting subscriber access problems with the Exchange Server 2010 UM server.

TABLE 24.12   Counters for the MSExchangeUMSubscriberAccess Object

Performance Counter	Description
Subscriber Authentication Failures	The number of authentication failures that have occurred since the service was started. This number is incremented once for every failed authentication. It's possible that a single phone call could generate several authentication failures.
Subscriber Logons	The number of UM subscribers who have successfully authenticated since the service was started.
Subscriber Logon Failures	The number of authentication failures since the service was started. This number is incremented once when all three per-call logon attempts fail.
Average Subscriber Call Duration	The average duration, in seconds, that subscribers spent logged on to the system. This timer starts when logon completes.
Average Recent Subscriber Call Duration	The average length of time, in seconds, that subscribers spent logged on to the system for the last 50 subscriber calls.

24

TABLE 24.12   Counters for the MSExchangeUMSubscriberAccess Object

Performance Counter	Description
Voice Message Queue Accessed	The number of times subscribers accessed their voice message queues using the telephone user interface.
Voice Messages Heard	The number of voice messages played to subscribers. This count is incremented as soon as playback starts. The subscriber does not need to listen to the entire message.
Voice Messages Sent	The number of voice messages sent by authenticated UM subscribers.
Average Sent Voice Message Size	The average size, in seconds, of voice messages that are sent. This size does not include any attachment data.
Average Recent Sent Voice Message Size	The average size, in seconds, of the last 50 voice messages that were sent.
Voice Messages Deleted	The number of voice messages that were deleted by authenticated subscribers.
Reply Messages Sent	The number of replies sent by authenticated subscribers.
Forward Messages Sent	The number of messages forwarded by authenticated subscribers.
Email Message Queue Accessed	The number of times subscribers accessed their email message queue using the telephone user interface.
Email Messages Heard	The number of email messages heard by authenticated subscribers.
Email Messages Deleted	The number of email messages deleted by authenticated subscribers.
Calendar Accessed	The number of times subscribers accessed their calendars using the telephone user interface.
Calendar Items Heard	The number of calendar items heard by authenticated subscribers.
Calendar Late Attendance	The number of messages sent to inform the organizer of a meeting that the subscriber will be late.
Calendar Items Details Requested	The number of times a subscriber requested additional details for a calendar item.
Meetings Declined	The number of Meeting Declined messages sent by subscribers.
Meetings Accepted	The number of Meeting Accepted messages sent by subscribers.

TABLE 24.12   Counters for the MSExchangeUMSubscriberAccess Object

Performance Counter	Description
Called Meeting Organizer	The number of times subscribers called the meeting organizer.
Replied to Organizer	The number of times subscribers sent reply messages to meeting organizers.
Contacts Accessed	The number of times subscribers accessed the Main Menu Contacts option using the telephone user interface.
Contact Items Heard	The number of times authenticated subscribers listened to directory details.
Launched Calls	The number of subscriber calls that resulted in an outbound call being placed.
Calls Disconnected by Callers During UM Audio Hourglass	The number of times callers disconnected while Unified Messaging was playing the audio hourglass tones.
Calls Disconnected by UM on Irrecoverable External Error	The number of subscriber calls that have been disconnected after an irrecoverable external error occurred.
Directory Accessed	The number of times subscribers accessed the Main Menu Directory option using the telephone user interface.
Directory Accessed by Extension	The number of directory access operations in which the user supplied the extension number.
Directory Accessed by Dial by Name	The number of directory access operations where the subscriber used the Dial by Name feature.
Directory Accessed Successfully by Dial by Name	The number of dial by name directory access operations that completed successfully on behalf of subscribers.
Directory Accessed by Spoken Name	The number of directory access operations in which the subscriber spoke a recipient name.
Directory Accessed Successfully by Spoken Name	The number of speech-recognition directory access operations that completed successfully on behalf of subscribers.

The variety of counters in the subscriber access area is impressive and can really aid in the understanding of the behavior of the subscribers.

Unified Messaging Auto Attendant Performance Counters

The counters listed in Table 24.13 are under the MSExchangeUMAutoAttendant performance object and are useful for monitoring and troubleshooting Auto Attendant problems with the Exchange Server 2010 UM server.

TABLE 24.13   Counters for the MSExchangeUMAutoAttendant Object

Performance Counter	Description
Total Calls	The number of calls that have been processed by this Auto Attendant.
Business Hours Calls	The number of calls processed by this Auto Attendant during business hours.
Out of Hours Calls	The number of calls processed by this Auto Attendant outside of business hours.
Disconnected Without Input	The number of calls that were dropped without any input being offered to the Auto Attendant prompts.
Transferred Count	The number of calls that were transferred by this Auto Attendant. This number does not include calls that were transferred by the operator.
Directory Accessed	The number of directory access operations performed by this Auto Attendant.
Directory Accessed by Extension	The number of directory access operations in which the user supplied the extension number.
Directory Accessed by Dial by Name	The number of directory access operations in which the subscriber used the Dial by Name feature.
Directory Accessed Successfully by Dial by Name	The number of successful directory access operations in which the caller used the Dial by Name feature.
Directory Accessed by Spoken Name	The number of directory access operations in which the subscriber spoke a recipient name.
Directory Accessed Successfully by Spoken Name	The number of successful directory access operations in which the caller used the Spoken Name feature.
Operator Transfers	The number of calls that were transferred to the operator.
Menu Option 1 Used	The number of times that a caller has chosen option 1 from the custom menu. This value is always zero if no menu or option is defined.
Menu Option 2 Used	The number of times that a caller has chosen option 2 from the custom menu. This value is always zero if no menu or option is defined.
Menu Option 3 Used	The number of times that a caller has chosen option 3 from the custom menu. This value is always zero if no menu or option is defined.
Menu Option 4 Used	The number of times that a caller has chosen option 4 from the custom menu. This value is always zero if no menu or option is defined.

TABLE 24.13   Counters for the MSExchangeUMAutoAttendant Object

Performance Counter	Description
Menu Option 5 Used	The number of times that a caller has chosen option 5 from the custom menu. This value is always zero if no menu or option is defined.
Menu Option 6 Used	The number of times that a caller has chosen option 6 from the custom menu. This value is always zero if no menu or option is defined.
Menu Option 7 Used	The number of times that a caller has chosen option 7 from the custom menu. This value is always zero if no menu or option is defined.
Menu Option 8 Used	The number of times that a caller has chosen option 8 from the custom menu. This value is always zero if no menu or option is defined.
Menu Option 9 Used	The number of times that a caller has chosen option 9 from the custom menu. This value is always zero if no menu or option is defined.
Menu Option Timed Out	The number of times that the system has timed out waiting for a caller to select an option from the custom menu. This value is always zero if no menu is defined.
Average Call Time	The average length of time that callers interacted with the Auto Attendant.
Calls with DTMF Fallback	The total number of times a caller has been passed the DTMF fallback auto attendant. This happens only for speech-enabled auto attendants.
% Successful Calls	% Successful Calls calculates the success rate of the auto attendant.
Calls Disconnected by UM on Irrecoverable External Error	The total number of calls disconnected after an irrecoverable external error occurred.
Average Recent Call Time	The average length of time, in seconds, of the last 50 Auto Attendant calls.
Calls with Speech Input	The total number of calls during which the caller is determined to have spoken at least once.
Calls with Sent Message	The total number of calls in which the caller has sent a voice message.
Calls with Spoken Name	The total number of calls to this Auto Attendant in which a caller has spoken a name at least once.
Custom Menu Options	The total number of times callers have selected custom menu options.

24

TABLE 24.13 Counters for the MSExchangeUMAutoAttendant Object

Performance Counter	Description
Disallowed Transfers	The number of times a caller was transferred to the operator because the user identified was configured to only accept calls from logged on users.
Operator Transfers Requested by user	The number of times a caller to this Auto Attendant has asked to be transferred to an operator.
Operator Transfers Requested by User from Opening Menu	The number of times a caller to this Auto Attendant has asked to be transferred to an operator while at the opening menu.
Sent to Auto Attendant	The number of times a caller has used the custom menu to go to an Auto Attendant.
Ambiguous Name Transfers	The number of times that a caller was transferred to the operator because the name that they spelled or spoke was too common in the search results.

The variety of counters in the Auto Attendant area is impressive and can really aid in the understanding of the behavior of the callers, the menu choices they make, how long they stay in the system, and their preferred method of access to the menus.

System Resources and Availability Counters for Unified Messaging

The counters listed in Table 24.14 are under the MSExchangeAvailability performance object and are useful for monitoring and troubleshooting system resource and availability problems with the Exchange Server 2010 UM server.

TABLE 24.14 Counters for the MSExchangeAvailability Object

Performance Counter	Description
Directory Access Failures	The number of times that attempts to access Active Directory failed.
Hub Transport Access Completed	The number of times that the Hub Transport server was accessed successfully.
Hub Transport Access Failures	The number of times that attempts to access a Hub Transport server failed. This number is only incremented if all Hub Transport servers were unavailable.
Mailbox Server Access Failures	The number of times the system failed to access a mailbox server.
Maximum Calls Allowed	The length of time, in seconds, that the server was concurrently processing the maximum number of calls allowed.
Worker Process Recycled	The number of times a new UM worker process has been started.

TABLE 24.14   Counters for the MSExchangeAvailability Object

Performance Counter	Description
Failed to Redirect Call	The number of times the unified messaging service failed to redirect calls to a UM worker process.
Total Worker Process Call Count	The total number of calls handled by this UM worker process.
Unhandled Exceptions per Second	The number of calls that encountered an unhandled exception in the last second.
Incomplete Signaling Information	The number of calls for which the signaling information was missing or incomplete.
Calls Disconnected by UM on Irrecoverable External Error	The number of calls disconnected after an irrecoverable external error occurred.
Calls Disconnected by UM on Irrecoverable External Error/sec	The number of calls disconnected after an irrecoverable external error occurred in the last second.
Calls Disconnected on Irrecoverable Internal Error	The number of calls disconnected after an internal system error occurred.
Call Answer Queued Messages	The number of messages created and not yet submitted for delivery.
Spoken Name Accessed	The number of times the system retrieved the recorded name of a user.
Name TTSed	The number of times the system used text-to-speech to create an audio version of the display name of a subscriber.
Queued OCS User Event Notifications	The number of notifications that have been created and not yet submitted for delivery.

Unified Messaging Performance Monitoring Counters

The counters listed in Table 24.15 are under the MSExchangeUMPerformance performance object and are useful for monitoring and troubleshooting server latency problems with the Exchange Server 2010 UM server. These counters measure the time in number of seconds that server operations took. This is an important measure of the time that callers are waiting for the UM server to complete a task.

TABLE 24.15   Counters for the MSExchangeUMPerformance Object

Performance Counter	Description
Operations over Two Seconds	The number of all UM operations that took between 2 and 3 seconds to complete. This is the time during which a caller was waiting for UM to respond.
Operations over Three Seconds	The number of all UM operations that took between 3 and 4 seconds to complete. This is the time during which a caller was waiting for UM to respond.

24

TABLE 24.15   Counters for the MSExchangeUMPerformance Object

Performance Counter	Description
Operations over Four Seconds	The number of all UM operations that took between 4 and 5 seconds to complete. This is the time during which a caller was waiting for UM to respond.
Operations over Five Seconds	The number of all UM operations that took between 5 and 6 seconds to complete. This is the time during which a caller was waiting for UM to respond.
Operations over Six Seconds	The number of all UM operations that took more than 6 seconds to complete. This is the time during which a caller was waiting for UM to respond.
Operations under Two Seconds	The number of all UM operations that took less than 2 seconds to complete. This is the time during which a caller was waiting for Unified Messaging to respond.

Event Logs

Event logs are important for troubleshooting Microsoft Exchange Server unified messaging. Each of the different aspects of a Unified Messaging server generate their own set of error messages. The tables of events show the errors and events that could be generated for each of the following categories:

▶ Call answering

▶ Call transfer

▶ Subscriber access

▶ Auto Attendant

▶ Active Directory

▶ Prompt Publishing

▶ Outdialing

▶ Administrative

▶ Speech grammar

▶ System

▶ Performance

The event log messages are very detailed and specific to many conditions, making it very easy to understand, audit, troubleshoot, and instrument the Unified Messaging server.

Although there are hundreds of event IDs related to unified messaging, a few common events are reviewed here for help in troubleshooting.

Call Answering

Unified messaging generates call answering events to help troubleshoot call answering features and issues. A good example is when a call is directed to a user that is not enabled for unified messaging. Exchange Server UM logs an 1169 event in Event Viewer with the extension number of the affected user. To resolve this issue, enable the user for Exchange Server unified messaging.

Call Transfer

Unified messaging generates call transfer events for actions related to call transfers in unified messaging. Event IDs 1025 and 1136 are often found together and relate to a failure in Exchange Server UM to transfer a call. Relevant information such as call ID and destination number are included in the body of the event logged in Event Viewer.

Subscriber Access

Exchange Server 2010 unified messaging generates events based on subscriber access behavior. This relates mostly to user induced events such as event ID 1012 that indicates a user has entered his PIN incorrectly more times than is allowed by the policy and has been locked out. Reset the user's PIN to allow him to log in again.

Another common event is ID 1080 that indicates the UM service could not process a message for a user because her mailbox is over quota. In this situation the administrator can either raise the quota, or the user must delete messages from her mailbox to get under her allowed quota limit.

Auto Attendant

The Exchange Server 2010 Unified Messaging Auto Attendant is one of the most important functions within UM. It is almost always a caller's entryway to the system. As such, any warnings or errors encountered should be taken seriously. Event ID 1128 indicates that an operator extension has not been defined. The UM service cannot forward a call to an operator. This means calls will simply be disconnected if they are not routed through the Auto Attendant. To resolve this issue, assign an operator extension using the UM portion of the Exchange Management Console.

Active Directory

Every part of Exchange Server 2010 is tightly coupled with Active Directory, and Exchange Server 2010 Unified Messaging is no exception. If the UM service cannot contact Active Directory for lookup or authentication data, a warning or error is logged. If Active Directory is unavailable on start up of the UM service, the service fails to start.

Prompt Publishing

Exchange Server 2010 Unified Messaging enables a number of custom prompts to be configured. Although this enables a lot of flexibility, it can also be a source of errors. The UM service logs alerts and errors for events related to custom prompts. Any update of custom prompts is logged. For example, Event ID 1100 indicates a successful publishing whereas Event ID 1099 indicates that a failure occurred and provides information on where the failure happened.

Outdialing

Exchange Server 2010 UM enables users to dial out from the system dependent on policy. This includes the Play on Phone functionality. Most of the events in this section focus on the dialing rules set in Exchange Server UM. The dialing rules might be different depending if the next hop is a PBX or a media gateway. An example of a warning is Event ID 1076 that indicates the UM service cannot complete a Play on Phone request due to improperly configured dialing rules. To resolve the issue, review and make the appropriate changes to your dialing rules.

Administrative

The administrative events logged for Exchange Server 2010 unified messaging are all administrative. They indicate actions such as enabling or disabling a user for Exchange Server UM or the changing of a PIN. They are often good to check when you make an administrative change if you suspect that change was not successful.

Speech Grammar

Exchange Server 2010 unified messaging has a built-in speech grammar file for understanding Automatic Speech Recognition (ASR) commands. If this file is not present or is malformed, a warning or error is logged. Event ID 1086, for example, indicates that the speech grammar files cannot be found, and ASR will be disabled. To resolve this issue, place a valid speech grammar file in the default location and restart the service.

System

The large majority of events logged for Exchange Server 2010 unified messaging fall under the System category. The events range from informational such as when the UM worker process successfully starts to significant failures such as TLS certificate failures. Other events that are important are those related to the UM IP gateway such as Event IDs 1124 and 1165 that indicate no IP gateways were found. To resolve this issue, ensure the UM server is configured to the correct IP gateway and the gateway is operational.

Performance

There are only two performance-related events for Exchange Server unified messaging. Event ID 1054 is informational and indicates the UM worker process was terminated because the startup time exceeded the maximum. Event ID 1089 is a warning and indicates the IP gateway did not respond promptly to a SIP request issued by the UM server.

Removing the First UM Server in a Dial Plan

The unified messaging prompt publishing point for a dial plan is automatically set at the time that the first Unified Messaging server joins the dial plan. Before you can remove the first Unified Messaging server, you need to migrate all of the custom prompts and then set the new server as the prompt publishing point.

For each dial plan that has a prompt publishing point on the server to be removed, run the following Exchange Management Shell command:

```
Set-UMDialPlan -Identity <Dial_Plan_Name> -PromptPublishingPoint
➥<UNC_Path_to_PromptPublishingPoint_Share_On_New_Server>
```

Then copy all of the contents of the old Universal Naming Convention (UNC) path to the new UNC path. The first Unified Messaging server can now be removed safely.

Unified Messaging Shell Commands

Sometimes, just finding commands in the PowerShell can be a daunting task. In this section, each of the unified messaging commands is listed by verb.

For each of the commands, the detailed syntax can be obtained by executing the command help *cmdlet*. For example, to get help on the cmdlet Add-ADPermission, execute the command help adpermission in the Exchange Management Shell interface shown in Figure 24.21.

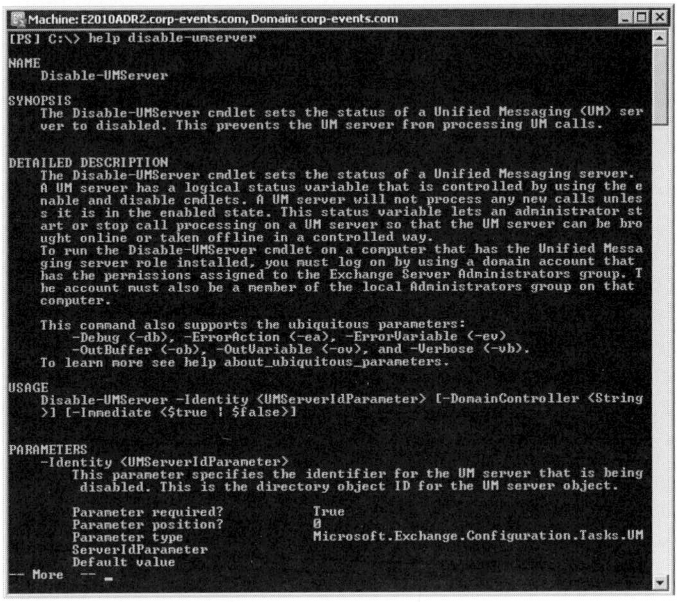

FIGURE 24.21   PowerShell Help.

Add/Remove Verb Cmdlets

Table 24.16 lists all the Exchange Server 2010 unified messaging specific add/remove verb cmdlets.

TABLE 24.16   Add/Remove Cmdlets

Verb	Noun	Cmdlet Name
Add	ADPermission	Add-ADPermission
Add	ExchangeAdministrator	Add-ExchangeAdministrator
Remove	ADPermission	Remove-ADPermission
Remove	UMAutoAttendant	Remove-UMAutoAttendant
Remove	UMDialPlan	Remove-UMDialPlan
Remove	UMHuntGroup	Remove-UMHuntGroup
Remove	UMIPGateway	Remove-UMIPGateway
Remove	UMMailboxPolicy	Remove-UMMailboxPolicy

Get/Set Verb Cmdlets

Table 24.17 lists all the Exchange Server 2010 unified messaging specific get/set verb cmdlets.

TABLE 24.17   Get/Set Cmdlets

Verb	Noun	Cmdlet Name
Get	ADPermission	Get-ADPermission
Get	UMActiveCalls	Get-UMActiveCalls
Get	UMAutoAttendant	Get-UMAutoAttendant
Get	UMDialPlan	Get-UMDialPlan
Get	UMHuntGroup	Get-UMHuntGroup
Get	UMIPGateway	Get-UMIPGateway
Get	UMMailbox	Get-UMMailbox
Get	UMMailboxPIN	Get-UMMailboxPIN
Get	UMMailboxPolicy	Get-UMMailboxPolicy
Get	UmServer	Get-UmServer
Set	EventLogLevel	Set-EventLogLevel
Set	UMAutoAttendant	Set-UMAutoAttendant
Set	UMDialPlan	Set-UMDialPlan
Set	UMIPGateway	Set-UMIPGateway
Set	UMMailbox	Set-UMMailbox

TABLE 24.17   Get/Set Cmdlets

Verb	Noun	Cmdlet Name
Set	UMMailboxPIN	Set-UMMailboxPIN
Set	UMMailboxPolicy	Set-UMMailboxPolicy
Set	UmServer	Set-UmServer

Test Verb Cmdlets

Table 24.18 lists all the Exchange Server 2010 unified messaging specific test verb cmdlets.

TABLE 24.18   Test Cmdlets

Verb	Noun	Cmdlet Name
Test	SystemHealth	Test-SystemHealth
Test	UMConnectivity	Test-UMConnectivity

Enable/Disable Verb Cmdlets

Table 24.19 lists all the Exchange Server 2010 unified messaging specific enable/disable verb cmdlets.

TABLE 24.19   Enable/Disable Cmdlets

Verb	Noun	Cmdlet Name
Enable	UMAutoAttendant	Enable-UMAutoAttendant
Enable	UMIPGateway	Enable-UMIPGateway
Enable	UMMailbox	Enable-UMMailbox
Enable	UMServer	Enable-UMServer
Disable	UMAutoAttendant	Disable-UMAutoAttendant
Disable	UMIPGateway	Disable-UMIPGateway
Disable	UMMailbox	Disable-UMMailbox
Disable	UMServer	Disable-UMServer

Copy Verb Cmdlet

Table 24.20 lists the only Exchange Server 2010 unified messaging specific copy verb cmdlet.

TABLE 24.20   Copy Cmdlet

Verb	Noun	Cmdlet Name
Copy	UMCustomPrompt	Copy-UMCustomPrompt

24

New Verb Cmdlets

Table 24.21 lists all the Exchange Server 2010 unified messaging specific new verb cmdlets.

TABLE 24.21   New Cmdlets

Verb	Noun	Cmdlet Name
New	UMAutoAttendant	New-UMAutoAttendant
New	UMDialPlan	New-UMDialPlan
New	UMHuntGroup	New-UMHuntGroup
New	UMIPGateway	New-UMIPGateway
New	UMMailboxPolicy	New-UMMailboxPolicy

SIP Protocol

Session Initiation Protocol (SIP) is an Application-layer signaling protocol for creating, modifying, and terminating sessions with one or more participants.

Given the importance of SIP in the Exchange Server 2010 unified messaging system, it is important to understand the protocol in some detail. This assists in troubleshooting integration problems between the Unified Messaging server and the IP/VoIP gateway, which is a frequent source of problems.

SIP Terminology

SIP uses specific terminology to define the elements and devices in a SIP call. Table 24.22 lists the various SIP terms and definitions.

TABLE 24.22   SIP Terminology

Term	Description
Methods	SIP commands and messages.
Result codes	Responses to SIP methods indicating success, failure, or other information.
User Agent	Endpoint devices that can issue or respond to SIP protocol methods (such as the UM server or IP gateway).
User Agent Client	Devices such as phones or PDAs.
Server	An application that can accept or respond to SIP methods (for example a UM server).

TABLE 24.22   SIP Terminology

Term	Description
Gateway	A gateway that can convert SIP methods and result codes to another protocol (for example an IP gateway).
Proxy server	A server that can make requests on behalf of other clients.

SIP Methods

SIP uses a number of commands or methods within the protocol. Table 24.23 lists the methods that SIP uses.

TABLE 24.23   SIP Methods

Method	Description
REGISTER	Registers a user with a registrar.
INVITE	Session setup request or media negotiation. Used also to hold and retrieve calls.
CANCEL	Used to cancel an in-progress transaction.
ACK	Acknowledgement for an INVITE transaction.
BYE	Terminates a session.
OPTIONS	Used for the remote device status and capabilities.
INFO	Used for mid-call signaling information exchange.
SUBSCRIBE	Request notification of call events.
NOTIFY	Event notification after a subscription.
REFER	Call transfer request.

This table can be useful when doing a protocol trace of a SIP session to determine what the session is doing.

SIP Response Codes

SIP uses a number of response codes, both informational and error related. Table 24.24 lists the response codes that SIP uses.

Basic Call Example

The SIP protocol is used to set up calls between and then hands the communication over to the RTP protocol. A basic call sequence for a SIP call setup and teardown in unified messaging looks like the example in Table 24.25.

TABLE 24.24   SIP Response Codes

Response Code	Description
100	Trying
180	Ringing
181	Call is being forwarded
182	Call is being queued
183	Session progress
200	OK
302	Moved temporarily, forward call to a given contact
305	Use proxy: repeat same call setup using a given proxy
400	Bad Request
401	Unauthorized Request
404	Not Found
408	Request Timeout
486	Busy
5xx	Server Failure
6xx	Global Failure

TABLE 24.25   Basic SIP Call Example

IP Gateway	Direction	UM Server
INVITE	——>	
	<——	180 Ringing
	<——	200 OK
ACK	——>	
RTP	<——>	RTP
	<——	BYE
200 OK	——>	

Notice that after the IP Gateway sends a SIP ACK method back to the Unified Messaging server, the call is handed off to the RTP protocol. After the call is complete, the Unified Messaging server sends a SIP BYE method to terminate the communication.

Summary

Exchange Server 2010 raises the bar for Microsoft unified messaging. It builds on the rich feature set of Exchange Server 2007 UM and adds a host of new features. The interface and management should be familiar to seasoned Exchange Server 2007 professionals making it easy to roll out new features in the course of an upgrade. Or for those who haven't worked with Exchange Server 2007, the way the Exchange Server 2010 administrative interface is set up, the configuration is well organized to speed up the learning curve. If you are new to Exchange Server's telephony features, they might seem intimidating at first; however, by following the steps in this chapter, you can get the Exchange Server 2010 UM role up and running so that you can begin your testing of unified messaging in the new Exchange Server environment.

Best Practices

The following are best practices from this chapter:

▶ Allow transfers to the operator at least during business hours to reduce caller frustration.

▶ Be careful when implementing mailbox quotas because it can impact the ability of users to receive voice mail.

▶ Create a secondary Auto Attendant that is not speech-enabled and configure the primary Auto Attendant to fallback to it.

▶ Create separate PBX hunt groups for the caller lines and the subscriber lines with separate pilot numbers.

▶ Have two test internal phones available for testing the new unified messaging system.

▶ Leave the audio codec setting on MP3 for small file sizes and playback on the largest number of mobile devices.

▶ Move users' mailboxes to an Exchange Server 2010 mailbox server in advance of the unified messaging deployment.

▶ Remove the default hunt groups and create specific ones for maximum control over call routing.

▶ Use key mapping to create helpful front-end menus for callers.

▶ Use the disable after completing call feature when disabling UM IP gateways or UM servers.

CHAPTER 25

Collaborating Within an Exchange Server Environment Using Microsoft Office SharePoint Server 2007

Exchange Server is the messaging component of the Microsoft product stack; it focuses on providing tools for knowledge workers to communicate with each other using email and other unified messaging capabilities. Collaboration is not only limited to messaging, however, and many organizations are looking into document management and workflow solutions to provide for a higher degree of collaboration in their messaging environments.

The Microsoft product line that provides for a near seamless integration of document management into a Microsoft Exchange Server 2010 environment is composed of several technologies collectively referred to as SharePoint. This chapter focuses on understanding the latest SharePoint products, formally named Microsoft Office SharePoint Server (MOSS) 2007 and Windows SharePoint Services (WSS), and how they can integrate into an Exchange Server 2010 environment.

Understanding the History of SharePoint Technologies

SharePoint technologies have a somewhat complicated history. Multiple attempts at rebranding the applications and packaging them with other Microsoft programs has further confused administrators and users alike. Consequently, a greater understanding of what the SharePoint products are and how they were constructed is required.

WSS's Predecessor: SharePoint Team Services

In late 1999, Microsoft announced the digital dashboard concept as the first step in its knowledge management strategy, releasing the Digital Dashboard Starter Kit, the Outlook 2000 Team Folder Wizard, and the Team Productivity Update for BackOffice 4.5. These tools leveraged existing Microsoft technologies, so customers and developers could build solutions without purchasing additional products. These tools, and the solutions developed using them, formed the basis for what became known as SharePoint Team Services (STS), the predecessor of Windows SharePoint Services (WSS).

With the launch of Office XP, SharePoint Team Services was propelled into the limelight as the wave of the future, providing a tool for non-IT personnel to easily create websites for team collaboration and information sharing. Team Services, included with Office XP, came into being through Office Server Extensions and FrontPage Server Extensions. The original server extensions were built around a web server and provide a blank default web page. The second generation of server extensions provided a web authoring tool, such as FrontPage, for designing web pages. Team Services was a third-generation server extension product, with which a website could be created directly out of the box.

Understanding the Original MOSS Application

Microsoft Office SharePoint Server (MOSS) 2007 is the enterprise-level entry of the SharePoint product, building on top of the base Windows SharePoint Services 3.0 functionality. MOSS 2007 further extends the capabilities of WSS, allowing for multiple WSS sites to be indexed and managed centrally.

In 2001, Microsoft released the predecessor to MOSS 2007, SharePoint Portal Server 2001. The intent was to provide a customizable portal environment focused on collaboration, document management, and knowledge sharing. The product carried the "Digital Dashboard" Web Part technology a step further to provide an out-of-the-box solution. SharePoint Portal Server was the product that could link together the team-based websites that were springing up.

Microsoft's initial SharePoint Portal product included a document management system that provided document check-in/check-out capabilities, as well as version control and approval routing. These features were not available in SharePoint Team Services. SharePoint Portal also included the capability to search not only document libraries, but also external sources such as other websites and Exchange Server public folders.

Because the majority of the information accessed through the portal was unstructured, the Web Storage System was the means selected for storing the data, as opposed to a more structured database product such as Structured Query Language (SQL), which was being used for SharePoint Team Services. The Web Storage System, incidentally, is the same technology that is used by Microsoft Exchange Server. Further SharePoint implementations use the same SQL database as WSS does, however.

Differences Between the Two SharePoint Products

As SharePoint Team Services was available at no extra charge to Office XP/FrontPage users, many organizations took advantage of this "free" technology to experiment with portal usage. STS's simplicity made it easy to install and put into operation. Although functionality was not as robust as a full SharePoint Portal Server solution, knowledge workers were seeing the benefits of being able to collaborate with team members.

Adaptation of SharePoint Portal Server progressed at a slower rate. In a tight economy, organizations were not yet ready to make a monetary commitment to a whole new way of collaborating, even if it provided efficiency in operations. In addition, the SharePoint Portal interface was not intuitive or consistent, which made it difficult to use.

Having two separate products with similar names confused many people. "SharePoint" was often discussed in a generic manner, and people weren't sure whether the topic was SharePoint Portal or SharePoint Team Services, or the two technologies together. Even if the full application name was mentioned, there was confusion regarding the differences between the two products, and about when each was appropriate to use. People wondered why SharePoint Team Services used the SQL data engine for its information store, whereas SharePoint Portal Server used the Web Storage System. It appeared as though there was not a clear strategy for the product's direction.

Examining Microsoft's Next-Generation SharePoint Products: SPS 2003 and WSS 2.0

Microsoft took a close look at what was happening with regard to collaboration in the marketplace and used this information to drive its SharePoint technologies. Microsoft believed that in the world of online technology and collaboration, people need to think differently about how they work. The focus was to develop a suite of products to better handle this collaboration.

In addition to looking closer at how people collaborate, Microsoft also analyzed what had transpired with its SharePoint products. The end result was that Microsoft modified its knowledge management and collaboration strategy. Microsoft began talking about its "SharePoint technology," with a key emphasis on building this technology into the .NET Framework, and, thus, natively supporting XML Web Services.

In 2003, Microsoft released the 2.0 generation of SharePoint Products. SharePoint Team Services was rebranded as Windows SharePoint Services 2.0, the engine for the team-collaboration environment. Windows SharePoint Services included many new and enhanced features, some of which were previously part of SharePoint Portal Server. Windows SharePoint Services was also included as an optional component to the Windows Server 2003 operating system at the same time.

SharePoint Portal Server 2001 was released as Microsoft Office SharePoint Portal Server 2003. It built on the Windows SharePoint Services technology and continued to be the enterprise solution for connecting internal and external sources of information. SharePoint Portal Server allowed for searching across sites, and enabled the integration of business applications into the portal.

Unveiling the Third Wave of SharePoint: MOSS 2007 and WSS 3.0

As adoption of SharePoint technologies increased, Microsoft put more and more emphasis on the product line as collaboration functionality became increasingly important for organizations. Organizations were increasingly excited about the 2003 product line, but there were some functional disadvantages to the platform, which held many organizations back from a full deployment of the product or forced them to purchase third-party add-ons to the suite. Workflow, navigation components, and administration were all weaker than many organizations needed, and Microsoft began work on the 3.0 generation of SharePoint products.

Along with the new generation came another rebranding of the product. SharePoint Portal Server became Microsoft Office SharePoint Server (MOSS) 2007. Windows SharePoint Services retained the same name and simply incremented the version number to 3.0.

MOSS 2007 and WSS 3.0 introduced several functional enhancements to SharePoint, including the following:

▶ **Integrated business process and Business Intelligence**—A significant portion of the development time for SharePoint was spent focused on improving the business workflow functionality of SharePoint. MOSS 2007 introduces a multitude of business process and Business Intelligence improvements that allow organizations to increase the efficiencies in their tasks.

▶ **Consolidated administrative tools**—Previous versions of SharePoint proved to be a headache to administer, as administrative tools and interfaces were scattered throughout the product. MOSS 2007 consolidates these admin interfaces into a single location, and provides for additional administrative tools as well.

▶ **Improved Office integration**—MOSS 2007 has further improved the tight integration between Office and SharePoint by allowing for advanced functionality, such as direct editing from Microsoft Excel, and offline capabilities in Microsoft Outlook and Groove.

▶ **Extranet and single sign on enhancements**—SharePoint 2007 allows for more secure and functional extranet deployment scenarios, so that internal MOSS sites can be utilized from the Internet without compromising safety or violating governmental regulations.

Microsoft SharePoint Server 2010

The tightest integration with Exchange Server 2010 and the 2010 line of Office products can be found within the SharePoint Server 2010 wave of SharePoint products and technologies. Many of the details of this new wave of SharePoint were not publicly available at the time of the printing of this book, and this chapter subsequently deals with MOSS 2007 and WSS 3.0. Some features of this new line of SharePoint products has been announced, however, and includes the following improvements:

- 64-bit only infrastructure, both on SharePoint and on the database back-end

- Inclusion of the Office ribbon for performing common Office tasks from within the browser

- Improved and consolidated administration from SharePoint Central Admin

- Improvements in business data tools

- Many other improvements to the platform, most of which will be announced in the near future

Look for subsequent versions of this book to include more information on SharePoint Server 2010, or refer to the upcoming book by SAMS, *SharePoint 2010 Unleashed*.

Identifying the Need for MOSS 2007

SharePoint is one of those services that is greatly misunderstood. Much of the confusion over the previous branding of the product has contributed to this, but a fundamental shift in thinking is required to effectively utilize the platform. An understanding of what SharePoint is and how it can be fully utilized is an important step toward realizing the efficiency the system can bring.

Changing Methodology from File Servers to a MOSS Document Management Platform

MOSS expands beyond its origins as a web team site application into a full-fledged documentation platform with the new functionalities introduced. These capabilities, previously only available with the full-functioned SharePoint Portal Server product, allow MOSS to store and manage documents efficiently in a transaction-oriented Microsoft SQL Server 2000 environment. What this means to organizations is that the traditional file server is less important, and effectively replaced, for document storage. Items such as Microsoft Word documents, Excel spreadsheets, and the like are stored in the MOSS database.

Along with these document management capabilities comes the realization by users that their standard operating practice of storing multiple versions of files on a file server is no longer feasible or efficient. Using MOSS effectively subsequently requires a shift in thinking from traditional approaches.

Enabling Team Collaboration with MOSS

MOSS 2007 and Windows SharePoint Services have demonstrated how web-based team sites can be effectively used to encourage collaboration among members of a team or an organization. Content relevant to a group of people or a project can be efficiently directed to the individuals who need to see it most, negating the need to have them hunt and peck across a network to find what they need.

After being deployed, the efficiency and collaboration realized is actually quite amazing. A good analogy to SharePoint can be found with email. Before using email, it's hard to understand how valuable it can be. After you've used it, however, it's hard to imagine not having it. The same holds true for SharePoint functionality. Organizations that have deployed WSS or the full-functioned MOSS 2007 product have a hard time imagining working without it.

Customizing SharePoint to Suit Organizational Needs

If the default functionality in SharePoint is not enough, or does not satisfy the specific web requirements of an organization, SharePoint can easily be customized. Easily customizable or downloadable Web Parts can be instantly "snapped-in" to a site, without the need to understand Hypertext Markup Language (HTML) code. More advanced developers can use ASP.NET or other programming tools to produce custom code to work with MOSS. Further enhancement of MOSS sites can be accomplished using SharePoint Designer 2007, which allows for a great deal of customization with relative ease. In general, if it can be programmed to work with Web Services, it can interface with SharePoint.

Exploring Basic MOSS Features

A SharePoint deployment can be used to create websites, manage documents, and provide other capabilities. Understanding and testing the features available in MOSS is an important prerequisite step toward effectively using MOSS, and a walk-through of those features should subsequently be performed.

The next sections walk through the features that are readily available to an employee using Microsoft Word 2007 when MOSS 2007 is installed on the network. Note that shared workspaces can be created from other Microsoft Office applications, including Excel, PowerPoint, and Visio.

Creating a Shared Workspace from MOSS

When a document is opened or created in Word 2007, click on the Office button followed by the Publish link and then Create Document Workspace. When selected, the Document Workspace interface appears on the right side of the screen. The user is prompted to name the workspace—the default is the document name—and enter the URL of the SharePoint site where the workspace will reside. The user can then add members to the site by entering either a domain and username, an email address, or both to define who will be included in the workspace. The level of participation for those members can also be set on the site with varying levels of authority, such as Reader, Contributor, Web Designer, or Administrator.

Six tabs in the Shared Workspace area provide information and tools to the user who created the site, as well as other users who open the file:

- ▶ **Status**—Provides errors or restrictions regarding the file

- ▶ **Members**—Provides a list of the different members of the workspace, and whether they are online

- ▶ **Tasks**—Allows the user to view tasks assigned to members of the site or create new ones

- **Documents**—Displays any other documents or folders available in the workspace, and allows the addition of other documents or folders to the workspace

- **Links**—Displays any URL links on the site and allows the addition of new URL links to the workspace

- **Document Information**—Displays basic information about the file such as who created or edited it, and allows viewing of the revision history

These features give the user a "dashboard," providing valuable information about the document, and help other users collaborate on the document.

> **TIP**
>
> Online presence can be enabled on a virtual server basis when Office 2003/2007 and Microsoft Office Communications Server 2007 R2 are installed. Smart Tags using the Person Name object type become active when the mouse pointer is hovering over a site member's name. Additional tools are made available when the down arrow is clicked, such as a notification as to whether the person is online or available for instant messaging. Other options include Schedule a Meeting, Send Mail, or Edit User Information.

Working Within the MOSS Site

A MOSS 2007 environment is composed of multiple WSS sites, which are essentially individual workspaces that contain the knowledge worker content, such as document libraries, lists, document workspaces, and so on. Figure 25.1 illustrates a document workspace in MOSS 2007.

Understanding Document Libraries

Document libraries may well be the feature most often used, as it is the location where documents and folders can be stored and managed, and document libraries offer a number of features not available in a standard server file share.

The team members who are working on one of the documents in the document library can upload related items to this library for reference purposes. This eliminates the step of printing out copies of supporting documentation for an in-person meeting, or emailing the actual files or hyperlinks via email.

A number of actions can be performed on the document from the Shared Documents page, as shown in Figure 25.2:

- **View Properties**—Show the document filename and title assigned to the document (if any), who created the document and when, as well as who modified the document and when.

- **Edit Properties**—Change the name of the file that SharePoint is storing and the title of the document.

- **Manage Permissions**—Change who has rights to the document.

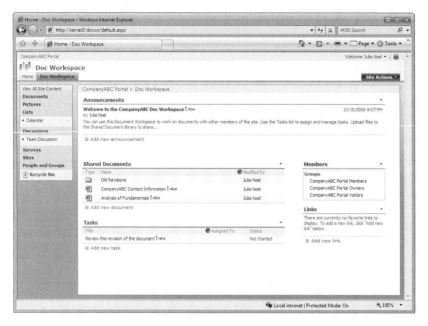

FIGURE 25.1   The MOSS 2007 document workspace.

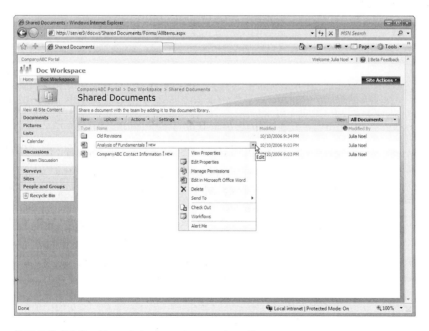

FIGURE 25.2   Shared documents page in a library.

▶ **Edit in Microsoft Word**—Modify a document that the user has editing rights in the Shared Document library. The document can be opened and edited in Microsoft Word. Note that if the document is a Microsoft Office document, the appropriate application will be listed, such as Excel or PowerPoint.

▶ **Delete**—Delete the file if you (the user) have deletion rights in the Shared Document library.

▶ **Send To**—Move the document to another location, email it to someone, create a document workspace, or download a local copy of the document.

▶ **Check Out**—Retrieve a document that is reserved for the individual who has checked it out, and only that person can modify the document. So even if that person doesn't have the document open, no one else can edit it. An administrator of the site can force a document check-in.

▶ **Workflows**—Invoke the Workflow Wizard, which allows for special document workflow processes, such as approval routing or feedback collection.

▶ **Alert Me**—Notify the user with an email alert if changes are made to the file.

25

> **NOTE**
>
> Alerts are an extremely powerful feature in MOSS. A user can set an alert on an individual item stored in a SharePoint list, such as a document, so that if the document is changed, users receive an email letting them know of the change. Alternatively, an alert can be set for the whole document library, so if any items are changed, added, or deleted, users receive an email. The emails can be sent immediately, or in a daily or weekly summary. This is the primary way MOSS pushes information to the users of its sites, enhancing the flow of information.

Other capabilities in the Shared Documents page include creating a new document, uploading other documents to the site, creating a new folder, filtering the documents, or editing the list in a datasheet.

Using Picture Libraries

A picture library can include a wide variety of file types, including JPEG, BMP, GIF, PNG, TIF, WMF, and EMF. Examples are photos of members of the team, or screenshots of documents from software applications that might not be available to all users. For instance, a screen capture from an accounting application could be saved to the library in BMP format so that any of the users of the site could see the information.

Similarly, a Visio diagram or Project Gantt chart could be saved to one of these formats, or as an HTML file and then saved to a picture library and thereby made accessible to users of the site who might not have these software products installed on their workstations. By providing a graphical image rather than the native file format, the amount of storage space required can be reduced in many cases, and there is no easy way for users to change the content of the documents.

Maps of how to find a client's office or digital photos of whiteboards can also be included. Some editing features are available using the Microsoft Picture Library tool (if Office 2007 is installed), which include brightness and contrast adjustment, color adjustment, cropping, rotation and flipping, red-eye removal, and resizing.

Pictures can be emailed directly from the library, or a discussion can be started about a photo as with other documents in libraries. Pictures can be sorted using the filter tool by file type, viewed in a slideshow format, and checked out for editing; the version history can be reviewed; or alerts can be set.

Although this type of library might not be useful in every collaborative workspace, it provides a set of tools that are well suited to newsletter creation, complex document publication, or less formal uses, such as company events.

Working with SharePoint Lists

Lists are used in many ways by MOSS, and a number of the Web Parts provided in the default workspace site are, in fact, lists. Some of the list options available are listed as follows:

▶ **Links**—These lists can contain either internal or external URL links, or links to networked drives.

▶ **Announcements**—These lists typically contain news that would be of interest to the employees accessing the site, and can be set to expire at predefined times.

▶ **Contacts**—Contacts can be created from scratch using the provided template, or can be imported from Outlook. This type of list can help clarify who is involved with a particular project or site, what their role is, how to contact them, and can contain custom fields.

▶ **Events**—Events can be created in the site complete with start and stop times, descriptions, location information, and its rate of recurrence. The option to create a workspace for the event is provided when it is created. Events can be displayed in list format or in a calendar-style view. Events can be exported to Outlook, and a new folder will be added to the calendar containing the events. Note that this calendar will be read-only in Outlook.

▶ **Tasks**—Each task can be assigned to a member of the site and can have start/due dates and priority levels set, and the percentage complete can be tracked. These tasks do not link to Outlook, however, so they're specific to the SharePoint site.

▶ **Issue tracking**—Slightly different from tasks, issues include category references, and each receives its own ID number. Individuals assigned to an issue can automatically be sent email notification when an issue is assigned to them, and will receive emails if their assigned issue changes.

▶ **Custom list options**—If one of the template lists doesn't offer the right combination of elements, one can be created from scratch. This allows the individual creating the list to choose how many columns make up the list, determine what kind of data each column will contain, such as text, choices (a menu to choose from), numbers, currency, date/time, lookup (information already on the site), yes/no, hyperlink or picture, or calculations based on other columns. With this combination of contents available and the capability to link to other data contained in the site from other lists, a database of information that pertains to the site can be created that can get quite complex. For example, a custom list could include events from the Events list, tracking the cost of each event and which task corresponds to the event.

▶ **Data imported from a spreadsheet**—Rather than creating a list from scratch, data can be imported from a spreadsheet (ideally Excel). The data can then be used actively within the site without the file needing to be opened in Excel. It can then be exported for use in other applications.

With any list, additional options are available to users of the site. Figure 25.3 shows a simple task list open in Datasheet view (Office 2003/2007 is required for this feature), as well as the additional options available when the Task Pane option is selected.

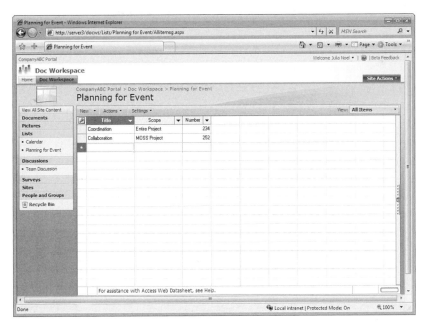

FIGURE 25.3   Simple task list in Datasheet view.

After the list is displayed in Datasheet view, new rows can be added by either selecting this option in the toolbar, or by clicking in the row that starts with the asterisk. Totals of all columns can be displayed by clicking the Totals option.

Using SharePoint Discussions

The next option in the Quick Launch toolbar is for discussions, which are a key component for online collaboration. Although email is well suited to conversations involving a handful of people, it becomes unwieldy when there are too many participants, as multiple threads of conversations can easily get started and the original point of the discussion can get lost. With a bulletin board or threaded discussion, the high-level topics can be viewed at the same time, and readers can choose the topics of interest and see any responses to the initial item. With email, individuals have no control over which emails they receive, whereas a discussion Web Part in SharePoint allows the user to decide which items to read and which ones to respond to.

Members with the appropriate rights can also manage the discussions to remove topics or responses that are not appropriate to the discussion, or remove threads when they have been completed. This level of control facilitates effective communication and encourages participation by the various team members.

Figure 25.4 shows a sample of a discussion concerning a proposal that is about to be sent out. Other responses have been posted.

FIGURE 25.4   Sample discussion board.

Discussions can also take place on any Office document posted to a SharePoint site. The data is stored in the SharePoint database, not in the document itself. This encourages team members to share their input and thoughts about a document in a controlled environment that is directly associated with the document.

Depending upon which site group participants are members of, they might only be able to view threaded discussions, or they might be able to participate, edit, and even delete portions of the conversation.

The alerts feature is very useful with discussions, as users can choose when and if they want to be alerted about changes to a specific discussion thread. This eliminates the need for participants to check a number of different discussions on a regular basis, as they can receive an email informing them if changes have been made.

Understanding Surveys

An entry for surveys also appears in the Quick Launch area in the document workspace. With MOSS, it's easy to quickly create a survey to request input from site users on any number of topics. They can be configured to request input on any topic imaginable, such as the functionality of the site, the information contained in it, or any business-related topics. As well as collecting the information from the surveys, the results can be viewed individually, displayed graphically, or exported to a spreadsheet for further analysis.

Surveys can be configured to be anonymous, so no information is saved or provided about the individual who responds to the survey, or the information can be displayed. In addition, both multiple responses and single responses are possible. Other options include allowing survey users to see other responses or only their own, or allowing them to edit their own and others' responses (or none at all). Common sense would dictate that users should not be able to edit a survey after it's submitted, but in some situations, it might make sense to allow a person to go back and change input at a later date.

Exploring End-User Features in MOSS

The previous versions of SharePoint brought confusion to end users. The user interface was inconsistent, and it was difficult to maneuver between pages. For example, some pages had a Back button, some had menu items on the page that you could click and go back to, and some had nothing to get you "back," and you had to use the browser's Back feature or type in the URL to get back to where you wanted to go. In addition, there were some functions that had to be performed outside of SharePoint, some could only be done from within, and some could be done either way.

MOSS 2007 has a better user interface, and also has tighter integration with Microsoft Office. A user working on a document in Word 2007 can decide that collaboration is necessary and create a shared workspace, invite users to participate, and set up some milestone tasks without ever leaving Office 2007.

MOSS provides the end user with a much better set of features for customizing and personalizing sites. Users can create their own personal sites containing their own documents, their own links, and other content that is meaningful to them, as opposed to having to live with a "generic" website with "generic" content that might not be applicable to their position in the organization.

Some of the new and improved features available for enhancing the end-user experience are discussed in the following sections.

Expanding Document Management Capabilities

Previous versions of SharePoint, particularly the 1.0 versions of the product line, had some limitations with their document management capabilities. MOSS 2007, however, has become much more of an enterprise document management (DM) solution, including features such as the following:

▶ Document check-in/check-out to ensure that revisions are not overwritten by another user

▶ Ability to maintain versions of documents for tracking changes

▶ Ability to require approval when checking a document back in for quality control

▶ Improved document workflow capabilities

In addition to these features, MOSS provides the user with the flexibility to create a structured document storage environment, as opposed to the relatively flat view of the document space in older versions. MOSS is also more tightly integrated with Microsoft Office 2007, providing enhanced features available directly from the Office interface. Features in these areas include the capability to perform the following tasks:

▶ Create folders within a document library, and view all documents in a library, including those in subfolders.

▶ Create a MOSS document workspace directly from Word 2007, providing a means for easily setting up collaboration sites.

▶ Easily save and retrieve SharePoint documents from Office 2007 applications. Improvements in Microsoft Office 2007 and MOSS make saving documents to a workspace as easy as saving them to a file share.

▶ Access document libraries in the same manner as file shares through HTTP DAV Web Folder support, preventing users from having to learn a whole new set of commands.

▶ View Office documents through the browser without having Office installed on the client computer. This enables the remote and mobile user to view documents stored in SharePoint when on the road from a client's computer, when sitting at an airport kiosk, or when having a cup of coffee at an Internet café.

Introducing Meeting Workspaces

When organizations have meetings, there is generally an agenda for the meeting, some type of document or documents associated with the meeting, and often follow-up tasks. Although email can be used to send out agendas and documents prior to the meeting, and to send out follow-up tasks and meeting notes, a better solution is to have all of the information associated with the meeting available in one place. Meeting workspaces in MOSS provide this capability—a place for managing all of the documentation and tasks associated with a meeting. Meeting workspaces can be created from the site or from the "schedule meeting" function in Outlook 2003/2007. When a meeting is scheduled using Outlook 2003/2007, an option is available for creating a MOSS meeting workspace to store the meeting agenda, a list of attendees, documents relevant to the meeting, and any action items that result from the meeting.

Several meeting templates are available when creating the meeting workspace. In addition to a "standard" single meeting workspace, the other types of meeting workspaces include the following:

- ▶ Decision meeting workspaces

- ▶ Social meeting workspaces

- ▶ Multiple meeting workspaces

Figure 25.5 shows some of the different templates that can be chosen when creating a new site.

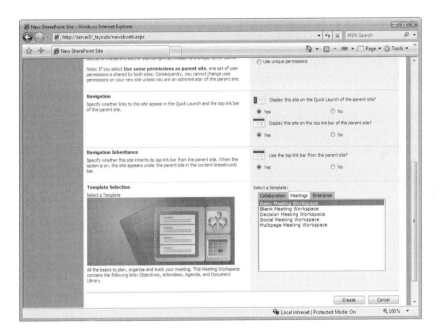

FIGURE 25.5   Templates for new SharePoint sites.

Integrating with Microsoft Office 2007

A key design goal for MOSS 2007 was to have it even more tightly integrated with Microsoft Office. Although SharePoint technologies support earlier versions of Office, such as Office 2000 or Office 2003, improvements and enhancements in both WSS 3.0 and in Microsoft Office 2007 provide a more efficient way for users to access shared document workspaces and team sites. This ease of use for accessing information encourages users to share, collaborate, and communicate together on projects, initiatives, or ideas. For example, instead of simply opening up a document in an older version of Office and working on the document, a user opening the same document off a SharePoint server with

Microsoft Office 2007 is presented with not only the document, but also a new task pane that lists the members of the team site where the document is stored (showing presence information about the users), the status of the document, as well as any tasks and links associated with the document. Specifically, Microsoft Office 2007 integration means that

▶ The entire setup of the document workspace can be done from the Word 2007 interface. Using the Shared Workspace task pane, the document workspace can be created, users granted access, links pertaining to the document added, and tasks created.

▶ The document workspace is accessible through the task pane whenever the document is opened in Word 2007. The status of the members is displayed (such as whether they are online); messages can be sent to the members, links browsed to, and tasks viewed and updated.

▶ When a meeting is created using Outlook 2007, a SharePoint meeting workspace can also be created for storing content related to the meeting.

▶ SharePoint contacts can be viewed directly from Outlook 2007.

▶ Metadata and file properties are copied from Office documents to SharePoint libraries—therefore, file information doesn't have to be reentered into SharePoint if it has already been entered in Office.

▶ SharePoint documents can be attached to mail messages as shared attachments. When the user receives the message, there is a link to the workspace where the shared attachment can be accessed.

▶ MOSS sites can be searched from the Office 2007 Research and Reference tool pane.

▶ Documents stored in SharePoint picture libraries can be edited with an Office 2007 picture-editing tool.

Personalizing MOSS 2007

MOSS 2007 includes many ways in which users can personalize a SharePoint environment. Some forms of personalization can originate from Office 2007, and some features are accessed directly through MOSS. The following list includes various ways in which users can personalize the SharePoint experience:

▶ Users can create private sites and private views with their own personalized look and feel, in a way that makes sense for the way they work. Changes to team sites are stored with the user's profile and will be applied each time the user visits the site.

▶ News can be targeted to users based on their audience affiliation. Considering the amount of information available, this is an efficiency feature that streamlines the content based on user interest.

▶ Users can be given the capability to create sites without involving IT personnel. A typical scenario in today's world, where the organization does not have a portal application such as MOSS, might go something like this:

A user decides that a website would be helpful for collaborating on a project. The user presents the justification of the website to and obtains the approval of the department manager. The department manager submits a request to the IT department to have the site created. The IT manager reviews the request and places it low on the priority list because it will take time to develop the site, and the users can collaborate in the current environment using email and shared network drives. By the time IT gets to the project, the users have already completed the work and no longer need the collaboration site.

If users can create shared sites and workspaces on their own, and don't have to wade through the red tape of getting IT personnel to create them, they will be more likely to use them and realize the benefits they can provide.

Using Lists with MOSS

Each list in MOSS is a Web Part; therefore, they can be easily customized from the browser. Lists have been enhanced in many ways, including support for additional field types such as rich text, multivalue fields, and calculated fields. Field values can also be calculated. Field types can be changed after the list has been created, thus providing a means for accommodating data that is not particularly stable.

MOSS also has many new options for viewing lists. Filtered list views can also be created based on a calculation. For example, all events within the next week can be viewed by setting up a filter based on the date being greater than the current date plus seven. Another new view is the Event Calendar view, which enables displaying any list that has a date and time field in it using the daily, weekly, or monthly calendar view. Aggregated views enable totaling data into a number field and displaying the value. Totals can be based on the entire view or a subset of it. Group-by views enable grouping by one column, and then sorting within each group.

A picture library is a new kind of list. Graphics and photos can be stored in a picture library and optionally viewed as a filmstrip or as thumbnails in views automatically generated by SharePoint.

For Microsoft Office 2003/2007 users, lists can be edited in Datasheet view. This option presents the data in spreadsheet style and provides spreadsheet types of editing features, such as copy and paste, adding rows, and fill options. Using the Datasheet view can be faster then the traditional SharePoint list editing style for some types of data entry and editing.

MOSS includes security features for lists. Permissions can be applied to the list so that only specific people can change it. Also included is the capability for the list owner to approve or reject items that are submitted to the list.

Other new list features include the following:

- ▶ Users can create their own personal lists that are not visible to other users.

- ▶ Alert notifications for lists include the name of the user who made the change to the list and which item in the list was changed.

- ▶ Attachments can be added or removed from a list item dependent on whether the attachment is required or not.

▶ Recurring events can be set up on an event list when an event occurs on a regularly scheduled basis.

Improving on SharePoint Alerts

Alerts in MOSS 2007 are what used to be called notifications in previous versions. Alerts have been improved to identify whether the alert was sent because content was changed or added, and now include the tracking of additional items. Prior versions of SharePoint tracked search queries and documents. In addition to these items, MOSS alerts track the following:

▶ News listings

▶ Sites added to the site directory

▶ SharePoint lists and libraries

▶ List items

▶ Site users

▶ Backward-compatible document library folders

Microsoft Outlook 2007 can be used to view MOSS alerts, and it includes rules to sort and filter them into special folders.

Exploring Additional New/Enhanced End-User Features

Many other new and enhanced features improve the end-user experience. These include the following:

▶ A site directory that lists all MOSS sites.

▶ The capability for users to create a SharePoint site from the Sites Directory page, to indicate whether they want the site added to the directory, and whether they want the site content to be indexed. This provides a level of security for protecting sensitive information, such as human resources data.

▶ Support for multiple file uploads. Older versions required files to be uploaded individually. MOSS supports multiple file uploads (such as an entire directory or folder). This is a great time-saver for organizations that are migrating large numbers of documents to SharePoint.

▶ The capability to select from one of several site templates when creating a new site. Organizations can also create their own site templates (such as with the organization logo and color theme) for providing a level of consistency among different types of sites within the site.

▶ The capability to create surveys and have the results automatically calculated and made available.

▶ Additional improvements in the survey process. The survey feature now supports responding to a question using a scale, and the capability for users to select all answers that might apply to a survey question.

▶ Everywhere a member name appears in a MOSS site, a user presence menu is available. The presence menu can be integrated with Active Directory, Exchange Server 2010, and Office Communications Server 2007 for providing information such as office location and free/busy status. It can be used for scheduling meetings and sending email.

▶ Team discussions that can be expanded and collapsed.

Customizing and Developing MOSS Sites

MOSS has many out-of-the-box new features that make it easier to customize using the browser interface. This provides nonprogrammers with a mechanism to create and customize sites to meet their needs.

For developers, the following provides an overview of the SharePoint technical structure. MOSS is built on the .NET platform. Use of the .NET platform enables SharePoint to assimilate information from multiple systems into an integrated solution. ASP.NET contains many new features, and it is more responsible, secure, and scalable than ASP. Using ASP.NET reduces the amount of code that needs to be written over similar ASP solutions.

SharePoint's SQL back end provides access to internal database components using industry-standard tools. From an application standpoint, integration with BizTalk provides access to over 300 application connectors using Web Services calls.

In MOSS, sites and lists can be saved as templates, stored in a Site or List Template library, and then made available to all sites in the collection. There is also a library for Web Parts that can be shared across all sites in the collection.

Features such as these provide an environment for developing fully customized MOSS solutions. Additional customization and development features are highlighted in the following sections.

Using the Browser to Customize SharePoint

Through the browser, you can add a logo to the team site, apply a theme, modify a list, or create a new Web Part page.

In SharePoint Team Services, there was a template that contained three "zones" for placing Web Parts, producing a three-column view. In MOSS, there are additional zone layouts to choose from, making customization much more user friendly.

The new Web Part tool pane is a feature that enables users to easily customize sites. It provides the ability to do the following:

▶ Drag/drop Web Parts onto a page

▶ Customize Web Parts

▶ Change the home page site logo

The site administrator can control what goes into the Web Part libraries and who has access to the libraries for adding Web Parts to a site. Figure 25.6 illustrates the Web Part

25

tool pane with its various Web Part libraries and the capability to display the contents of
the library.

FIGURE 25.6   Displaying the Web Part tool pane for access to Web Part libraries.

Development Enhancements for Site Templates

MOSS includes multiple templates that can be used when you create a new site. Each
template includes a set of features from MOSS to satisfy a specific collaboration need.
Templates are included for the following:

- ▶ Document collaboration
- ▶ Team collaboration
- ▶ Wiki sites
- ▶ Blogs
- ▶ Records repositories
- ▶ Publishing sites
- ▶ Basic meetings
- ▶ Decision meeting workspaces

▶ Social meeting workspaces

▶ Multipage meeting workspaces

▶ Document centers

▶ Personalization sites

▶ Report center sites

If these don't satisfy the organization's requirements, customized templates can easily be put together using the browser-based customization features, using SharePoint Designer 2007 or some other web design tool, or using programming. For example, if an organization always put its company logo on the home page and used specific Web Parts that were unique to their organization, it could save the site as a template and then just duplicate the template when necessary to maintain consistency and security.

Editing MOSS 2007 with SharePoint Designer 2007

With SharePoint Team Services, it was difficult to modify SharePoint sites. SharePoint 2003 made it easier with the use of FrontPage 2003, but performance was affected by editing sites directly. With MOSS 2007, a new product, SharePoint Designer, shown in Figure 25.7, is more tightly integrated with Windows SharePoint Services and Microsoft Office SharePoint Server 2007 and fully supports Web Parts, Web Part pages, and Web Part zones. This means that Web Parts can be added and customized using SharePoint Designer to provide the look, feel, and content to meet organizational requirements.

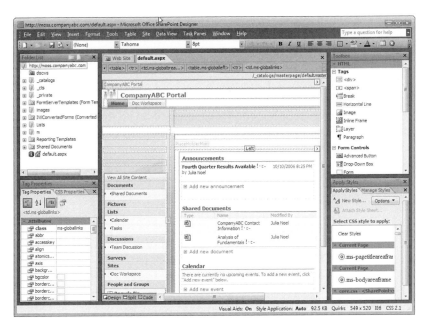

FIGURE 25.7   Working with SharePoint Designer 2007.

25

Web Parts can be previewed in SharePoint Designer before being published to the SharePoint site, thus providing an "audit" to ensure that the changes have the desired effect. The SharePoint Designer client can be used to back up and restore MOSS sites, providing a much-needed feature that was lacking in older versions of the product.

Other features provided in SharePoint Designer 2007 include the ability to do the following:

▶ Deploy a site throughout the organization using solution packages. This provides a means for implementing changes and modifications to organizations that have multiple sites and servers.

▶ Search Web Part libraries directly. This enables the product to be a complete editing source for web pages, as opposed to a two-step process in which the Web Parts would be added using the MOSS interface, and then further modifications made in SharePoint Designer.

▶ Create list templates and create, edit, and delete SharePoint list views. For experienced SharePoint Designer users, the SharePoint interface might be cumbersome for performing functions such as these. Therefore, SharePoint Designer can be more efficient for these users when creating templates and managing list views.

▶ Connect Web Parts across pages or on the same page to create a new user interface. Because SharePoint Designer is a web development tool, it has more capabilities and is more flexible than SharePoint; thus, features such as these are available for more complete customization.

▶ Use an Extensible Stylesheet Language (XSL) data view Web Part that can bring data from external sources into SharePoint sites. This is a great new integration feature that shows Microsoft's commitment toward a truly integrated Office solution.

Summary

Microsoft Office SharePoint Server 2007 is an excellent way to extend the capabilities of an Exchange Server 2010 messaging environment. Installation of MOSS 2007 allows a server to become an enterprise-level document management and collaboration system. Enhanced capabilities within MOSS and strong integration with Microsoft Office 2007 allow organizations to realize improvements in productivity and quality quickly. In addition, the scalability of MOSS and its reliability on the robust Microsoft SQL database provide strong incentive to deploy and utilize MOSS technology.

Best Practices

The following are best practices from this chapter:

▶ Consider using a full version of SQL Server 2005/2008 for any MOSS 2007 implementation with greater than 10 sites.

- ▶ Highly consider 64-bit architecture for SharePoint servers to ease the transition to SharePoint 2010 technology, which will be 64-bit only.

- ▶ Use document versioning sparingly in MOSS document libraries to ensure that the SQL database does not grow too large.

- ▶ Keep a MOSS server up to date with all Windows Server 2003/2008 and SQL Server patches and updates to reduce the risk of attacks or malfunctions.

- ▶ Deploy MOSS server(s) to replace file servers for document storage to take advantage of the newly integrated document management features MOSS offers.

- ▶ Use SharePoint Designer 2007 to provide advanced administration, site maintenance, and backup and restore capabilities.

CHAPTER 26

Integrating Office Communications Server 2007 in an Exchange Server 2010 Environment

Microsoft Exchange Server 2010 is the messaging muscle to the Microsoft unified communications platform. In addition to messaging functionality, however, many organizations are looking to improve the ability of their knowledge workers to collaborate with each other, particularly when they might be remote. They have found that email, although a time-saving and ideal mechanism for certain types of communications, is not the best medium to transmit real-time conversations between knowledge workers.

From a business perspective, many processes can be made more efficient through real-time communications. These efficiencies fall under the umbrella of communications-enabled business processes and often result in substantial cost-savings and increased productivity. Adding real-time communications functionality to Exchange Server 2010 adds tangible business value to the network.

In the Microsoft suite of applications, real-time communications are addressed by Office Communications Server 2007 R2 (OCS), which provides presence, instant messaging, web conferencing, voice over IP (VoIP), and videoconferencing. It tightly integrates with Exchange Server 2010 for unified messaging and extended voice capabilities. At the same time, it also provides for mechanisms to secure and audit these activities.

This chapter covers the products that comprise the Microsoft Unified Communications strategy: Office Communications Server 2007 R2, Office Live Meeting, and the Communicator 2007 client. Step-by-step guides on how to install, use, and administer these applications are presented, and best practices in their deployment and architecture are outlined.

Understanding Microsoft's Unified Communications Strategy

Microsoft has placed considerable emphasis on its unified communications (UC) strategy in Exchange Server 2010. Microsoft is positioning several products as solutions to the various types of communications that knowledge workers use, such as phone, email, instant messaging, videoconferencing, and voice mail. By default, Exchange Server 2010 includes built-in support for email, voice mail, and limited voice capabilities through the Unified Messaging server role and Mailbox role. Instant messaging, enterprise voice, data, and audio and videoconferencing, however, require the addition of Office Communications Server 2007 R2.

Office Communications Server 2007 R2 works closely with Exchange Server 2010 to further extend the capabilities of the environment and to further improve the efficiencies gained when communications barriers are broken down in an organization.

Outlining the History of the Unified Communications Products

Microsoft has made several forays into the videoconferencing and instant messaging space, which have eventually led to the current state of the product today. What we now know as the Office Communications Server (OCS) 2007 R2 product was originally part of the Exchange 2000 Beta Program (Platinum) but was removed from the application before it went to market. It was then licensed as a separate product named Mobile Information Server (MIS) 2000. MIS has some serious shortcomings, however, and adoption was not high.

Microsoft rebranded the application upon the release of Exchange Server 2003 by naming it Live Communications Server (LCS) 2003. This version was deployed much more extensively than the previous versions, but still suffered from limited integration with Exchange Server.

The LCS product was updated two years later as Live Communications Server 2005, with an SP1 version coming later that added some additional functionality. This version of the product was widely deployed, and was the most solid implementation to date.

Timed to release with Exchange Server 2007, the new version of LCS was named the Office Communications Server (OCS) 2007. This version marked the ascension of the technology as a core component to many organizations' collaboration designs.

Two years later, Microsoft released Office Communications Server (OCS) 2007 R2. This enhanced the voice and data functionality of OCS 2007 and became the first product to seriously be considered as a PBX replacement. It also became the first true, single platform, unified communications solution on the market. The adoption rate is high and should continue to increase with the adoption of Exchange Server 2010.

Exploring the Office Communications Server (OCS) 2007 R2 Product Suite

OCS 2007 builds upon some impressive capabilities of its predecessors, while at the same time adding additional functionality. The following key features of the application exist:

▶ **Web conferencing**—OCS has the capability to centrally conference multiple users into a single virtual web conference, allowing for capabilities such as whiteboard, chat, and application sharing. In addition, these conferences can be set up and scheduled from within the users' Outlook clients. OCS utilizes the Microsoft Live Meeting client to connect to web conferences; however, the transition between clients is seamless.

▶ **Audio conferencing**—OCS added audio conferencing in the R2 release of the product. Tightly integrated with Outlook 2007/2010, it enables users to schedule conference calls from Outlook or have ad-hoc meetings based on a meeting code and PIN.

▶ **Videoconferencing**—In addition to standard web conferencing, OCS allows for videoconferencing between members of a conference. It also enables interoperability with other platforms such as Tandberg videoconference rooms and HP Halo Telepresence rooms. OCS 2007 R2 introduced support for HD-quality video on the desktop.

▶ **Instant messaging**—The OCS server also acts as an instant messaging server, providing for centralized IM capabilities as well as the ability to archive IM traffic and to filter it for specific information. OCS allows an organization to gain more control over the instant messaging traffic that is being used.

▶ **Presence information**—Tied into the instant messaging functionality of OCS is the ability of the software to provide presence information for users. For example, within Outlook, a user can determine whether the sender of the message is online by hovering over their name.

▶ **Public IM Connectivity**—Microsoft, Yahoo!, and AOL recently agreed to make it easier to interoperate between their various IM tools. In response to this agreement, Microsoft made it possible to integrate a corporate IM platform on OCS with external private IM clients on the MSN, Yahoo!, or AOL platforms. The way that OCS does this is through the concept of a Public IM Connectivity (PIC) license.

▶ **IM federation**—OCS also has the ability to tie a corporate IM environment into the OCS or LCS environment at another organization, through a process known as IM federation. A federation proxy running on the edge server role is used to mediate secure communications between federation partners.

▶ **Contact management**—OCS integrates Exchange Server contacts with IM contacts, providing the ability to integrate them into a common list.

▶ **Outlook integration**—OCS now offers the ability for the IM functionality to be tied into the Free/Busy and Out of the Office functionality of Outlook and Exchange

26

Server 2010. This allows users to determine the status of a user directly from the IM client and the client to auto-update presence status based on free/busy information.

The product is available in the following two versions:

▶ **Standard Edition**—The Standard Edition of OCS 2007 R2 allows for a single server to be deployed using a Microsoft SQL Express database. It supports up to 5,000 concurrent users.

▶ **Enterprise Edition**—The Enterprise Edition allows for pools of servers connected to a common SQL Server database to be utilized, allowing for up to 300,000 users. Enterprise Edition can be deployed in a consolidated manner similar to Standard Edition; however, it also enables the flexibility to split the functional roles out onto separate servers for additional scalability. Multiple Enterprise Edition front-end servers can be members of the same pool.

Server roles are defined for OCS servers, just as Exchange Server 2010 defines server roles. A single server can hold multiple roles, and multiple servers can be deployed with a single role, as necessary. The following server roles exist in OCS:

▶ **Front-End server**—The default server role for OCS handles presence, IM, audio/web/videoconferencing, and voice routing for either Standard edition or a consolidated enterprise edition deployment.

▶ **Communicator Web Access server**—Enables users to log in to OCS using a web client instead of the full Microsoft Office Communicator (MOC) client. Although presence, IM, and desktop sharing are available, voice and video are not supported using the web client.

▶ **Archiving server**—An OCS Archiving server archives instant messages and specific usage information and stores it in a SQL database.

▶ **Monitoring server**—The Monitoring server collects performance and CDR information related to voice calls. It records information for both PC2PC and PSTN calls. The server role requires a SQL database and SQL reporting services.

▶ **Mediation server**—The Mediation server proxies communication between the OCS pool and either a PBX or a media gateway out to the PSTN. It converts voice communications from RTAudio to a traditional codec like G.711 and passes it along to the next hop following configurable routing rules.

▶ **Edge server**—An OCS Edge server creates an encrypted, trusted connection point for traffic to and from the Internet. It serves as a method of protecting internal servers from direct exposure and is often placed into a demilitarized zone (DMZ) of a firewall. It also enables users to connect to OCS from outside the trusted network, extending phone, video, and collaboration functionality to wherever a user might be. The Edge server can create encrypted connections to partner through federation enabling inter-organization communication.

The OCS product is central to Microsoft's unified communications strategy, as it serves as a mechanism to unite the various products such as Exchange Server and SharePoint by providing information about when a user is online, and providing ideal mechanisms to communicate with them.

Viewing the Communicator 2007 Client

On the client side of the unified communications equation, Microsoft has released a new version of the corporate instant messaging client. This version is known as Microsoft Office Communicator (MOC) 2007. The Communicator client provides the end user with a mechanism to conduct instant messaging conversations with users, to share their desktop or an application with another user or with a group of users, and to transfer files and conduct videoconferences.

The Communicator client serves as a replacement for free Internet instant messaging clients, which can serve as a conduit for viruses and spyware. In addition, the Communicator client does not include any type of advertising in its console, as do the public IM clients for MSN, Yahoo!, and AOL. More information on installing and using the Communicator client are provided in later sections of this chapter.

Exploring the Office Live Meeting Client

The same Microsoft Live Meeting client that is used for the Microsoft-hosted service can also be used to connect to the web conferencing portion of Office Communications Server 2007 R2. The connection information is usually included in the meeting invitation so that the client requires no configuration to switch between on-premise and off-premise services.

More information on how to use the Office Live Meeting product is presented in later sections of this chapter.

Installing OCS 2007 R2

OCS 2007 has a surprisingly complex installation process at first glance. What Microsoft has done, however, has been to divide up the installation process into multiple sections, providing for checks along the way so that there is less room for error. Because the installation requires an Active Directory schema upgrade, it is important that the process run smoothly, so it is good that this process is designed the way it is. It is important to note that OCS 2007 R2 is a 64-bit-only application and requires a 64-bit version of Windows Server to be installed.

This section of the chapter focuses on the installation of the Standard Edition of OCS 2007. The Enterprise Edition installation routine is similar, but with more emphasis on multiple redundant server deployment and on the use of a full remote SQL database.

Extending the Active Directory (AD) Schema

OCS 2007 integrates deep into an existing AD environment. It integrates so deeply, in fact, that an extension of the underlying AD schema is required before the product can be installed. AD schema upgrades are no small thing, of course, so it is wise to become familiar with the consequences of extending the schema and to make sure that a backup of the domain takes place first. To start the installation process, perform the following steps:

1. When you insert the OCS media, the AutoRun brings you to a menu with a choice to install Standard Edition or Enterprise Edition.

2. From this menu, click the Deploy Standard Edition Server link.

3. You will be asked to install Microsoft Visual C++ and then the .Net Framework 3.5 from the media. Click Yes on both to continue. A reboot might be required when the installation finishes.

4. Review the steps on the subsequent dialog box for the Deployment Wizard, shown in Figure 26.1. Click Prepare Active Directory.

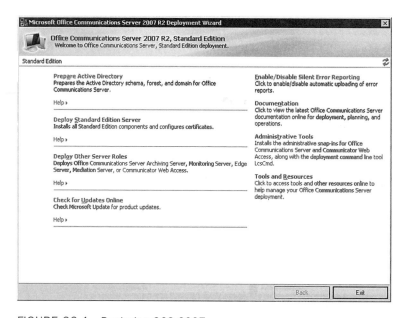

FIGURE 26.1   Deploying OCS 2007.

CAUTION

Installation of Office Communications Server 2007 R2 requires an AD schema upgrade to the AD forest. It is important to fully understand the consequences of a schema upgrade in advance, as an upgrade will replicate to all domain controllers in a forest. If there is already Office Communications Server 2007 in the forest, the schema update is still required for OCS 2007 R2.

5. In the subsequent dialog box, shown in Figure 26.2, click Run to start the schema upgrade process.

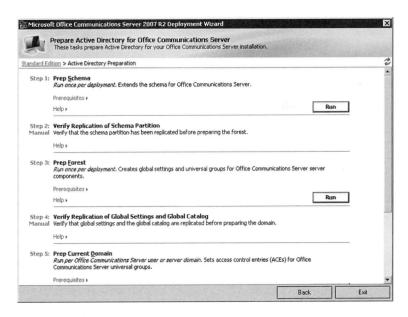

FIGURE 26.2   Starting the schema upgrade process.

6. At the Schema Preparation Wizard welcome screen, click Next to begin the process.

7. In the Schema File Location dialog box, leave the default location selected, and click Next.

8. At the review screen, review the settings and, keeping in mind the caution previously given about schema upgrades, click Next to continue.

9. The schema upgrade process will begin. When it is complete, click Finish.

After the schema update has run, be sure you wait until the new schema extensions have replicated to all domain controllers in the forest. After this has been verified, return to the Deployment Wizard to continue.

Preparing the AD Forest

After the schema extension is complete, perform the following steps:

1. Return to the Deployment Wizard and click Run under Step 3: Prep Forest, as shown in Figure 26.3.

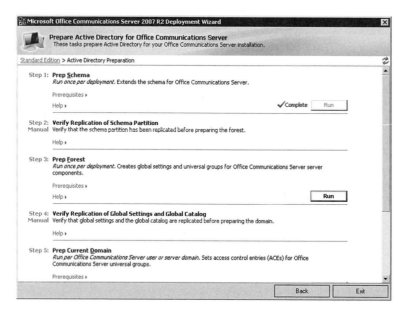

FIGURE 26.3   Prepping the forest.

2. Click Next at the welcome screen of the Forest Preparation Wizard.

3. The subsequent dialog box, shown in Figure 26.4, gives you the option to choose between storing the global settings in the root domain, or in the configuration partition. In a single domain forest, choose the system container. In a multiple domain forest, choosing the configuration partition has some advantages.

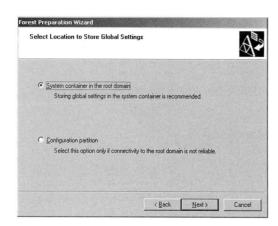

FIGURE 26.4   Choosing where to store global settings.

4. Under Domain, choose the domain where OCS will create the groups used by the server. This is typically the main resource domain where the servers are installed into. Click Next to continue.

5. Accept the default selection for the SIP Domain used for Default routing.

6. At the review screen, click Next to continue.

7. Click Finish.

After this step is complete, ensure that replication of the newly created objects has occurred on all domain controllers in the forest and proceed to the next step.

Prepping the Domain

The following procedure must be run on each domain in the forest where OCS will be installed:

1. Click Run under the Prep Current Domain listing in the Deployment Wizard, as shown in Figure 26.5.

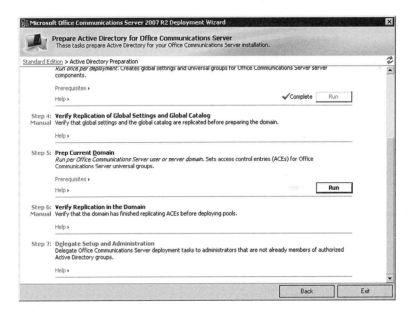

FIGURE 26.5   Prepping the domain.

2. From the Domain Preparation Wizard, click Next to continue.

3. From the Domain Preparation Information dialog box, review the warning illustrated in Figure 26.6, and click Next to continue.

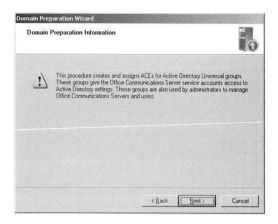

FIGURE 26.6   ACEs notification.

4. Click Next at the review dialog box.

5. Click Finish.

Again, make sure replication takes place before advancing to the next step in the installation process.

Delegating Setup and Administrative Privileges

To continue the installation process, perform the following steps:

1. From the Deployment Wizard, click on Delegate Setup and Administration under
   Step 7.

2. Click the Run button underneath Delegate Setup Tasks.

3. At the Setup Delegation Wizard welcome dialog box, click Next to continue.

4. At the Authorize Group dialog box, shown in Figure 26.7, choose the Trustee
   domain and enter a name of an existing Universal Security group. Members of that
   group will receive permissions to activate the server. Click Next to continue.

NOTE

The group chosen must be a Universal Security group, or installation will fail.

5. At the OU Location dialog box, enter the full distinguished name (DN) of the organizational unit (OU) where the OCS Server computer accounts will be located. For
   example, the following DN was entered in this example:

   `OU=OCS,OU=Servers,CN=Computers,DC=corp-events,DC=com`

6. After entering the DN of the server's OU, click Next to continue.

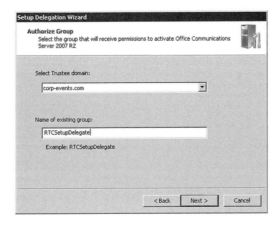

FIGURE 26.7   Delegating setup and administrative privileges.

7. Enter the name of service accounts that will be used for the session initiation proto-col (SIP) and components services, such as that shown in Figure 26.8. These accounts should be created in advance in AD.

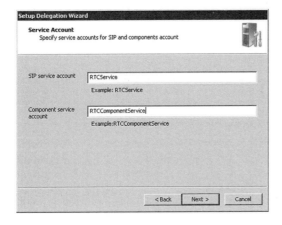

FIGURE 26.8   Entering in service account information.

8. Review the information in the subsequent dialog box, and then click Next to begin setup.

9. Click Finish.

At this point, setup of the Active Directory portion of the OCS Enterprise is complete, and individual servers can now be deployed.

26

Configuring Prerequisites

The installation of the server portion of the process requires that certain prerequisites be installed. Although the Add Roles Wizard can be used, as shown in Figure 26.9, it is easier to install everything needed from a script:

```
Servermanagercmd -i web-server
Servermanagercmd -i web-webserver
Servermanagercmd -i web-common-http
Servermanagercmd -i web-static-content
Servermanagercmd -i web-dir-browsing
Servermanagercmd -i web-http-errors
Servermanagercmd -i web-http-redirect
Servermanagercmd -i web-health
Servermanagercmd -i web-http-logging
Servermanagercmd -i web-request-monitor
Servermanagercmd -i web-security
Servermanagercmd -i web-basic-auth
Servermanagercmd -i web-windows-auth
Servermanagercmd -i web-digest-auth
Servermanagercmd -i web-filtering
Servermanagercmd -i web-performance
Servermanagercmd -i web-stat-compression
Servermanagercmd -i web-mgmt-tools
Servermanagercmd -i web-mgmt-console
```

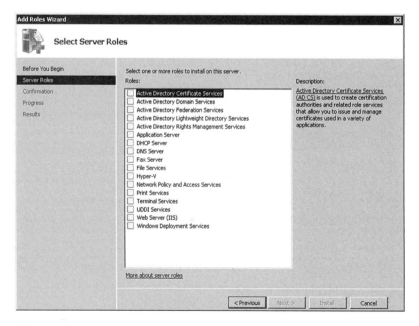

FIGURE 26.9   Add Roles Wizard.

```
Servermanagercmd -i web-mgmt-compat
Servermanagercmd -i web-metabase
Servermanagercmd -i web-wmi
Servermanagercmd -i web-lgcy-scripting
Servermanagercmd -i web-lgcy-mgmt-console

Servermanagercmd -i rsat
Servermanagercmd -i rsat-addc
Servermanagercmd -i rsat-role-tools
Servermanagercmd -i rsat-web-server

Servermanagercmd -i was
Servermanagercmd -i was-process-model
Servermanagercmd -i was-config-apis
```

Take the preceding code and copy it in Notepad.exe. Save the file on the root of the C: drive and call it OCSPreReq.bat. The script running on the server can be seen in Figure 26.10. A reboot will be required when the script completes.

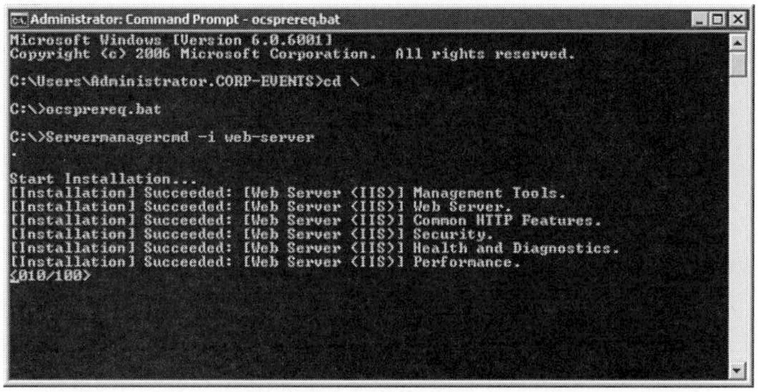

FIGURE 26.10   OCS Prerequisites Script.

Deploying an OCS 2007 Server

After all the prerequisites have been satisfied and the AD schema has been extended, the process for installing an OCS 2007 standard server can begin. To begin this process, perform the following steps:

1. From the Deployment Wizard, click Deploy Standard Edition Server.

2. Under Step 2, click Run.

3. Click the Run button in the Deploy Server section at the screen that appears, as shown in Figure 26.11.

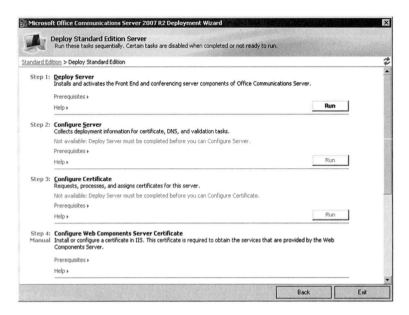

FIGURE 26.11   Deploy server.

4. Click OK if prompted to install Media Format Runtime. If a reboot is required, reboot the server and repeat steps 1 through 3.

5. Click Next on the first screen, accept the license agreement, and click Next. Leave the installation folder at the default, and click Next to continue.

6. Select the appropriate Application Configuration. The default is All Services Selected.

7. At the account information field, select Use an Existing Account, and enter the service account information entered in the previous steps for delegation.

8. At the Component Service Account dialog box, choose Use an Existing Account, and then enter the second service account created during the delegation steps and its password. Click Next to continue.

9. In the Web Farm FQDNs dialog box, shown in Figure 26.12, enter the external FQDN of the farm as it will be made available to Internet users (if applicable). Click Next to continue.

10. Enter the database and log information into the fields in the Database File dialog box. Click Next to continue.

NOTE

For best performance, separate the RTCDYN and RTC logs onto physically separate drive sets.

---

11. Click Next at the Ready to Deploy Server dialog box.

12. Click Finish.

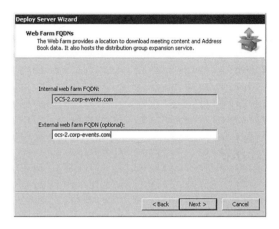

FIGURE 26.12   Entering web farm FQDN settings.

Configuring the Server

After the server software has been installed, OCS services are not started by default. Instead, the Deployment Wizard encourages administrators to configure certain settings first before doing so. To configure these settings, follow this procedure:

1. From the Deployment Wizard, click Run under Step 2 (Configure Server).

2. Click Next at the welcome screen.

3. Select the appropriate pool from the drop-down list shown in Figure 26.13, and click Next to continue.

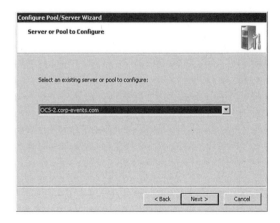

FIGURE 26.13   Configuring the OCS server.

4. If any additional SIP domains are needed in the environment, enter them in the subsequent dialog box. If not, accept the default of the domain name (for example, corp-events.com), and click Next.

5. Under Client Logon Settings, select that all clients will use DNS SRV records for auto logon, and click Next to continue.

6. Check the domain or domains that will be used for SIP automatic logon, such as that shown in Figure 26.14, and click Next to continue.

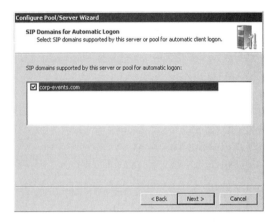

FIGURE 26.14   Selecting SIP domains for automatic logon.

7. In the External User Access Configuration dialog box, select to not configure external user access now. External user access can be configured at a later date from the Admin tool. Click Next to continue.

8. Click Next at the Verification dialog box.

9. Click Finish.

Configuring Certificates for OCS

Communications to and from the OCS server should ideally be encrypted and the user should also be able to trust that they are actually accessing the server that they expect. For this reason, Microsoft made it part of the installation process to install certificates onto the OCS server. To start the process of installing a certificate on the server, perform the following steps:

1. From the Deployment Wizard, click Run under Step 3 (Configure Certificate).

2. Click Next at the welcome screen.

3. From the list of available tasks, shown in Figure 26.15, select Create a New Certificate, and click Next.

4. Select Send the Request Immediately to an Online Certification Authority, and click Next to continue.

> **NOTE**
>
> This step assumes that a trusted Windows Enterprise certificate authority exists in the organization. If not, the request must be sent to a globally trusted third-party certificate authority.

FIGURE 26.15   Creating a new certificate for the OCS server.

5. Type a descriptive name for the certificate; leave the bit length at 1024 and the certificate as exportable but select Include client EKU in the certificate request, and click Next to continue.

6. Enter the organization and OU of your organization. It should exactly match what is on file with the CA. Click Next to continue.

7. At the Your Server's Subject Name dialog box, enter the subject name of the server (FQDN in which it will be accessed), such as that shown in Figure 26.16. Enter any subject alternate names as well, such as sip.domain.com and sipinternal.domain. com. It is recommended to check Automatically Add Local Machine Name to Subject Alt Name check box. Click Next to continue.

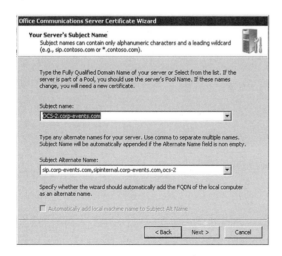

FIGURE 26.16   Entering the server's subject name.

8. Enter the appropriate country, state, and city information into the Geographical Information dialog box, bearing in mind that abbreviations cannot be used. Click Next to continue.

9. Select the local CA from the drop-down list, and click Next to continue.

10. Click Next at the Verification dialog box.

11. In the Success dialog box, click Assign certificate immediately; click Next.

12. Click Next to acknowledge that the settings were applied.

13. Click Finish to exit the wizard.

14. Next, assign the certificate in IIS using the IIS Manager Console.

After the certificate is installed, check to make sure that the changes have replicated.

Starting the OCS Services on the Server

After the certificate has been installed, the services for OCS can be started via the Deployment Wizard via the following process:

1. From the Deployment Wizard, click Run under Start Services.

2. On the wizard welcome screen, click Next.

3. Review the list of services to be started, as shown in Figure 26.17. Click Next to continue.

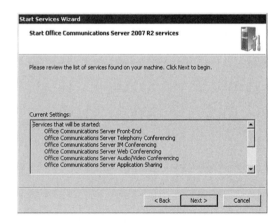

FIGURE 26.17   Starting the services.

4. Click Finish when the wizard is complete.

Validating Server Functionality

The Deployment Wizard contains a useful mechanism for running a series of tests against the server to ensure that everything was set up properly. To run this wizard, do the following:

1. From the Deployment Wizard, click Run under Step 7 (Validate Server Functionality).

2. This brings up a number of different validation tests, as shown in Figure 26.18.

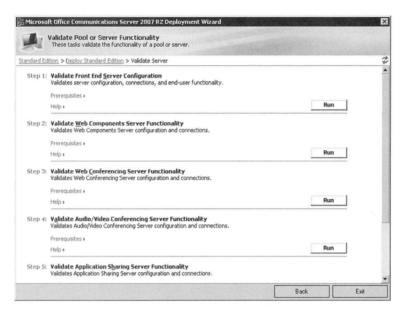

FIGURE 26.18   Validate server functionality.

3. Run through each of the tests examining the logs for any errors or warnings.

Installing the Admin Tools

The administrative tools are not installed by default. To install the admin tools, navigate to the main installation menu and choose Install Administration Tools from the right-column menu. The admin tools can be installed on Windows XP SP2 or higher or Windows Server 2003 SP2 or higher. To install Admin tools, do the following:

1. From the initial Deployment Wizard screen, click the Administrative Tools link.

2. Select I Accept for the license terms, and click Next.

3. Click Next to start the installation.

Exploring Office Communications Server Tools and Concepts

After OCS 2007 R2 has been installed in an organization, the job of administering the environment comes into play. Basic OCS functionality is not difficult to grasp, but it is important to have a good grasp on several key concepts in how to administer and maintain the OCS environment. Key to these concepts is a familiarity with the OCS Admin tools, as illustrated in the following sections.

Administering Office Communications Server

Administration of an OCS 2007 environment is composed of two components: user administration and server administration. Basic user administration is primarily concerned with enabling users for OCS access, giving them a SIP account, moving them from one server to another, and enabling or disabling public IM connectivity and federation.

Adding Users to OCS

The Office Communication Server 2007 Admin tool allows for both user and server administration. Enabling a user account for OCS access, however, requires the use of the Active Directory Users and Computers (ADUC) tool, which can be downloaded from Microsoft as part of the Windows Server 2003 Service Pack 1 Admin Pack (adminpak.msi). Installing it on the server that runs OCS allows for additional tabs for OCS to be displayed, and allows for new drop-down menu options that enable and disable OCS access.

To enable a user account for OCS access, perform the following steps from the ADUC tool on the OCS server:

1. From Active Directory Users and Computers, right-click on the user to be enabled, and choose Enable Users for Communications Server.
2. Click Next at the welcome screen.
3. Select the server pool from the list, and click Next to continue.
4. In the dialog box shown in Figure 26.19, specify how to generate the SIP address for the user. Click Next to continue.
5. Click Next to confirm the operation and then click Finish.

Configuring User Settings from the OCS Admin Tool

After a user account has been provisioned for OCS access using the ADUC tool, it will show up in the Users container underneath the server name icon in the console pane of the Admin tool. Right-clicking on the user and selecting Configure Users invokes a wizard with the dialog box shown in Figure 26.20.

Clicking on the Properties option also opens up advanced options, such as Federation and Public IM options. The OCS console allows for OCS users to be deleted or moved to other servers.

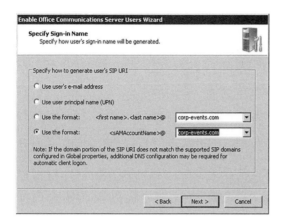

FIGURE 26.19   Enabling a user for OCS.

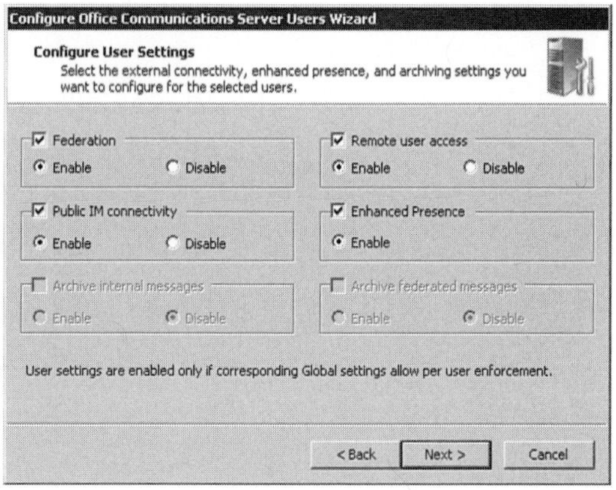

FIGURE 26.20   Modifying user settings in OCS 2007.

Configuring Server Settings from the OCS Admin Tool

Server-specific settings can be configured from the OCS Admin tool by right-clicking the pool name and choosing Properties, <Server Role> (where Server Role is the role that will be configured, such as Front End, Web Conferencing, A/V, or Web Component). The dialog box shown in Figure 26.21 displays some of the settings that can be manipulated here.

Using the Instant Messenger Filter in OCS 2007

OCS 2007 also includes a built-in instant messenger filter, shown in Figure 26.22, that gives organizations control over what type of traffic is being sent through IM. This allows administrators to limit the risk that IM clients can pose, particularly with spyware and other vulnerabilities. It also includes a file transfer filter that can be modified to block specific file extensions.

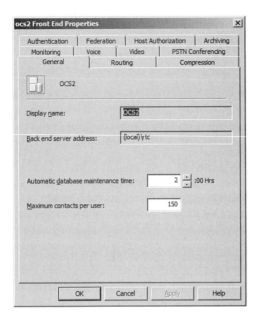

FIGURE 26.21   Changing server settings in the OCS Admin tool.

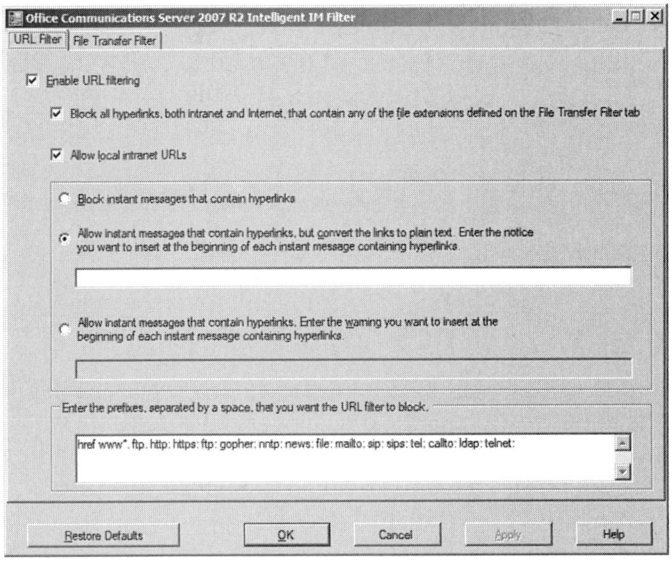

FIGURE 26.22   Viewing the IM filter in OCS.

Together with a Public IM Connectivity (PIC) license running on an OCS Edge Proxy
server, this allows an organization to let employees use the IM client for external IM functionality, but without exposing them to unnecessary risks.

The client version can disallow legacy clients and force an update through the front-end server's client autoupdate function.

OCS 2007 R2 Integration with Exchange Server 2010 Outlook Web Access

Exchange Server 2010 offers additional integration with OCS 2007 R2. Although users could see another user's presence from the Outlook client, Exchange Server 2010 brings similar functionality to OWA. Just like in the full Outlook client, presence icons display for users next to their name in OWA for Exchange Server 2010.

To enable this functionality, simply run the Integration Wizard from the Exchange Server 2010 CAS server. When the wizard is complete, you need to restart IIS on the CAS server, or reboot, for the changes to take effect.

> **NOTE**
>
> Specific step-by-step procedures on configuring Exchange Server 2010 to support the integration of OCS 2007 R2 instant messaging into the Outlook Web App interface is covered in Chapter 28, "Leveraging the Capabilities of the Outlook Web App (OWA) Client," in the section "Configuring OWA and IM Integration."

Installing and Using the Communicator 2007 Client

The client component of an OCS 2007 implementation is the Communicator 2007 client. This client is essentially the business version of Microsoft's IM client, which provides for instant messaging capabilities, as well as conferencing, video, and audio capabilities.

The Communicator client, shown in Figure 26.23, communicates to the OCS 2007 server via an encrypted Transport Layer Security (TLS) channel, securing the traffic from prying eyes. Users can set their presence information directly from the client, allowing other users in the OCS system to view whether they are online and available for conversations.

Installing the Communicator 2007 Client

The Communicator 2007 client can be installed as part of a deployment package in an application such as Systems Management Server (SMS) 2003 or System Center Configuration Manager 2007, or it can be manually deployed to desktops. The following procedure illustrates how to manually install the client on a desktop:

1. Run the Communicator 2007 client setup from the client media.
2. Click Next at the welcome screen.
3. Select I Accept for the license terms, and click Next.
4. Enter a patch for the application (typically accept the default path given), and click Next to continue.
5. Click Finish.

FIGURE 26.23   Viewing the Communicator 2007 client.

Web Conferencing

Office Communications Server 2007 R2 can replace expensive hosted offerings such as
Microsoft Live Meeting. This on-premise conferencing solution can be extended to
include external and anonymous guests through the OCS edge server as well. The web
conferencing component of OCS utilizes the same Live Meeting client on the desktop for
connectivity.

Installing the Live Meeting 2007 Client

OCS web conferencing sessions can be attended with the Live Meeting Client. The client
installation is straightforward and does not require any immediate configuration. Meeting
information is included in the invitation so that no additional client reconfiguration is
required to utilize OCS web conferencing or migrate from off-premise Live Meeting.

Working with Live Meeting

A web conferencing session, shown in Figure 26.24, allows for a presenter to share applications with end users, chat with them over text or audio, share video with the users, and
interact with them in a question-and-answer format.

Invitations to the web conference can be easily sent via email through an Outlook add-in,
and attendees need only click on the link in the email to join. Users who have attended
Microsoft Webcasts in the past might recognize many of the features, as similar technology has been used for this purpose. OCS web conferencing enables organizations to
quickly and easily hold online web conferences on the fly.

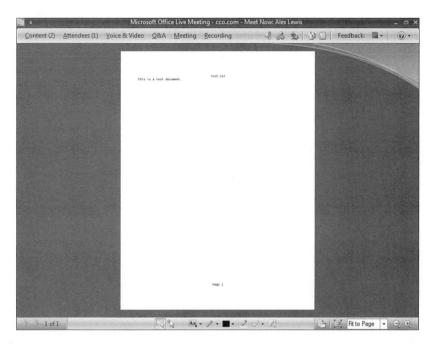

FIGURE 26.24   Viewing a web conference.

Summary

The Real-Time Communications functionality that Microsoft has designed into Office Communications Server 2007 and the Office Live Meeting, and Communicator 2007 clients are ideal for organizations looking to get more productivity out of their Exchange Server 2010 environment. Tight integration with Exchange Server 2010, Outlook, and other Microsoft technologies makes them an ideal match for organizations because they allow for improved efficiencies in communications between knowledge workers.

Best Practices

The following are best practices from this chapter:

- ► Take care when installing OCS 2007 R2 because it extends the AD schema. Be sure to fully understand the implications of a schema change before doing so.

- ► Deploy the Enterprise Edition of OCS 2007 R2 if greater than 5,000 users will be using the environment or if redundancy of server components is required.

- ► Use the instant messaging filter in OCS 2007 R2 to filter out potential spyware and unwanted files from users.

- ► Consider the use of a Public IM Connectivity (PIC) license to allow internal corporate IM users access to public instant messaging clients, such as MSN, Yahoo!, and AOL.

CHAPTER 27

Getting the Most Out of the Microsoft Outlook Client

Microsoft Outlook is a personal information manager that provides access to email messages, calendar appointments, contacts, tasks, and various other types of communications.

Unlike Outlook Web App (which is discussed in Chapter 28, "Leveraging the Capabilities of the Outlook Web App [OWA] Client"), the Outlook client is a full-fledged messaging client that runs locally on the user's workstation. It is packaged as part of the Microsoft Office Suite but can also be purchased and used separately.

This chapter focuses on the current iteration of the product, Microsoft Outlook 2007. Outlook 2007 has been around for a few years; it was originally released about the same time as Exchange Server 2007. Users and administrators will be glad to hear that it plays well with Exchange Server 2010 as well.

In short, there is no better client for accessing email located on an Exchange server because Outlook 2007 was built from the ground up to work hand-in-hand with both Microsoft Exchange Server and Microsoft's Active Directory.

Outlook over the Years

As previously stated, Outlook was built to work hand-in-hand with both Microsoft Exchange and Active Directory. This was not always the case.

In the early days of Microsoft, the developers of the client-side applications, such as Office and Outlook, did not work closely with the developers of the server-side applications, such as Exchange Server. The Office suite focused on individual productivity, whereas the server team focused on building software that facilitated collaboration.

Starting with Outlook 98, these two groups started to work more closely together and Outlook began to take on the characteristics of a collaboration tool, enabling users to more easily share information with one another. The results are self-evident with Outlook 2007 because Exchange Server and Outlook now have greater integration, enhanced functionality for the end user, and improved collaborative tools.

The Evolution of a Messaging Client

Over the years, the developers at Microsoft have been listening attentively to their user community, and the Outlook client has evolved based on the recommendations of these users. Popular features have remained, and new ones have been added to support the ever-changing messaging needs of the business community.

Although the early versions of Outlook were focused almost entirely on messaging and calendaring, the later generations have added tools such as forms and rules to enhance the user's ability to manage their information. Microsoft has also developed the Outlook client to integrate closely with SharePoint, Microsoft's enterprise information portal, enabling organizations to create resources for collaboration in SharePoint and have the user community access these resources through the familiar interface of Outlook.

Microsoft has put a significant amount of effort into improving the security of its product as well. By implementing Information Rights Management, for example, users can create email messages that are restricted–helping to prevent them from being forwarded, printed, and having the information copied and pasted into new documents. Additionally, documents created in Microsoft Office 2007 are automatically restricted when attached to a message with restricted permissions.

The look and feel of the Outlook product has evolved over the years as well. The interface has become less and less "cluttered" as the developers discovered ways of presenting more information with greater organization. Improvements have been made in the prioritizing of to-do items, the ability to create Internet calendars has been added, and enhanced search capabilities enable users to more easily locate messages in their mailboxes.

With each new version of Outlook, the underlying focus has been to streamline information, add new functionality, and make Outlook a more collaborative business tool.

The Basic Features of Outlook

Since the inception of Outlook, the most basic features of messaging, calendaring, and task tracking have been available. Each revision has improved the capabilities of these basic functions while adding additional features. Outlook has long supported protocols such as Messaging Application Programming Interface (MAPI), Internet Message Access Protocol version 4 (IMAP4), and Post Office Protocol version 3 (POP3) to enable users to access messaging functions. Storage in local files and local archival has existed in each version of Outlook. As Outlook has evolved, it has become easier to access these functions, and they have become more powerful.

Outlook has always offered contact management from both a local and centralized stand-point, and later versions of Outlook have offered users the ability to search their messages. As Outlook has evolved, these functions have become faster and easier to access.

Security in Outlook

Security has always been a concern for Information Technology (IT) departments, and Outlook 2007 offers cutting-edge security functions to help protect data from prying eyes. These functions range from support for Secure/Multipurpose Internet Mail Extensions (S/MIME) encrypted messaging to integrated antispam and antiphishing technologies. Outlook has always made an effort to reduce the exposure of the user by blocking Hypertext Markup Language (HTML) content and preventing embedded scripts from launching when messages are previewed. The past few versions of Outlook have prevented third-party applications from accessing it to help protect a user's email and the Exchange server itself.

Collaborating with Outlook

The word "collaboration" comes from the Latin word "collaborare" that means "labor together." Organizations have found that their users, when working together with tools that enable them to share information easily, can be more productive than individuals working alone. The ability for users to collaborate with one another by using Microsoft Outlook is a major reason companies leverage the client as their standard calendaring and messaging application. With each new version, the collaborative power of Outlook has grown, and although many tools are available for an Outlook user when partnered with an Exchange server, greater integration with Microsoft Office and Microsoft's SharePoint Portal product has greatly increased the possibilities.

Other Enhancements in Outlook

Each new version of the Outlook client has introduced new or improved features to enhance functionality and enhance the end-user experience. By making the product faster, sleeker, and more intuitive, each version of Outlook has surpassed the previous one in usability and integration, not only with the Exchange Server product, but also with other applications. This chapter covers many of the most popular features available with Outlook 2007 and shows the user how to leverage some of the more powerful features of the product.

Highlighted Features in Outlook 2007

As previously mentioned, new versions of Outlook continue to provide new features and functionality, in addition to enhancing existing features. In this section, administrators can find information covering some of the new features that organizations might find beneficial, along with new tools for the end user.

Understanding the Outlook 2007 Interface

There is a lot of information kept in Exchange Server mailboxes these days, and the Outlook interface has changed to improve the organization and presentation of this data. Additionally, the price of large screen monitors has come down significantly, and they are in ever-widening use, giving many users more "real estate" to work with.

In Outlook 2007, Microsoft divided the Outlook view into four main sections: the navigation pane, the message index pane, the reading pane (also sometimes called the preview pane), and the To-Do bar, as shown in Figure 27.1.

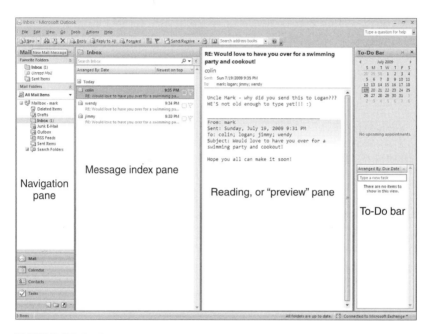

FIGURE 27.1 The Outlook 2007 interface.

The Navigation Pane

The navigation pane is primarily used to view, open, and manage individual folders that make up the user's mailbox. It enables the user to add or remove favorites, which are shortcuts to commonly accessed folders. There is also a shortcuts section, which allows single-click access to the various areas of the Outlook client. The navigation pane can be minimized or turned off completely. Under the View menu, click Navigation Pane, and select either Normal, Minimized, or Off. Alternatively, the user can toggle through these choices by pressing the Alt+F1 keys.

The Message Index Pane

To the right of the navigation pane is the message index pane. This display box shows a summary for each message contained in the folder that is currently viewed (the folder currently selected in the navigation pane). This summary typically includes the Sender's address, the date and time the message was received, and a portion of the information contained in the Subject.

When a user clicks a message in the index pane one time, they select the message, and a preview of the message displays in the reading pane. When the user double-clicks a message instead, Outlook 2007 opens that message in a separate window.

The message index pane can be resized by hovering the mouse on the border of the pane until the pointer turns into a double-headed arrow. Click the left mouse button and hold it while dragging the border to the desired location.

The Reading Pane

The reading pane enables the user to preview the contents of a message without opening the message completely. In addition to the convenience of this method, there is a security related benefit as well—potentially malicious scripts or attachments are not activated or opened automatically in the reading pane.

Users can also view attachments in the reading pane. After the user clicks the attachment in the reading pane, they are warned, You Should Only Preview Files from a Trustworthy Source. The user can then click Preview File and view the contents of the attachment.

NOTE

For users to preview an attachment, they must have an application installed on their workstation that is capable of *opening* the attachment. For example, to preview an Excel spreadsheet, users must have Excel installed.

In addition to viewing attachments, the reading pane also enables users to follow embedded hyperlinks, use voting buttons, view follow-up information, and respond to meeting requests.

The reading pane can be enabled or disabled by clicking Reading Pane in the View menu. When enabled, the reading pane can be located to the right of the message index pane or underneath it. As with the preceding index pane, the reading pane can be resized by dragging and dropping the borders to the desired location.

27

The To-Do Bar

On the right edge of the main Outlook page is the To-Do bar. By default, the To-Do bar displays a Date Navigator, which is a calendar of the current month. Dates shown in **bold** are dates where the user has at least one meeting scheduled. By clicking any date on the date navigator, the users are taken immediately to the selected date in their own Calendar inside of Outlook. Next, the pane shows the user's next three appointments and a list of outstanding tasks.

Any of these three features can be disabled, and the To-Do bar minimized or turned off completely, by going to the View menu and clicking To-Do Bar. Alternatively, the user can minimize the To-Do bar, turn it off completely, or restore it, by pressing the Alt+F2 keys.

Similarities with Outlook Web App

The Outlook 2007 graphical user interface (GUI) is similar to the GUI for Outlook Web Access users on an Exchange Server 2007 environment. It is similar to OWA 2010 as well, in the general layout, but Outlook 2007 cannot take advantage of some of the new features that Exchange Server 2010 provides, such as viewing the Presence status of fellow employees and the MailTips feature. These features are discussed in overview of Outlook Web App in Chapter 28.

Methods for Highlighting Outlook Items

Each new version of Outlook has improved the methods for organizing and finding messages. As email becomes a more and more common way of sharing information, the volume of mail received by end users will continue to increase. With Outlook 2007, users are given enhanced methods for organizing, categorizing, and flagging messages when working with Outlook and Exchange Server.

Using Quick Flags to Tag Messages

Using quick flags has changed in Outlook 2007. End users used to assign a colored flag to a message to help them organize messages. In previous versions of Outlook, these flags had no predetermined meanings. This meant the user was free to use them in whatever manner they wanted. In Outlook 2007, the flags now have some predefined meanings for follow-up tasks. Flags can be set for when a message must be dealt with and setting these flags results in a new entry in the Tasks area of the To-Do Bar.

To set quick flags in the Outlook 2007 client, complete the following:

1. Right-click on the gray flag icon on the far-right side of the email message in the Inbox to access the flag options.

2. Choose the flag you need to use.

Flags can also be used to configure a reminder. The option for using reminders with flags allows users to configure information and a due date associated with each flag. To configure a reminder, complete these steps:

1. Flag the message.

2. Right-click on the flag and choose Add Reminder.

3. Choose the reason to flag the message and then choose a due date.

4. Choose the date and time for the reminder, and click OK when you are finished.

If you have the To-Do bar enabled, you will now see your flagged message in the task area, similar to that shown in Figure 27.2, showing the flag, the category, and a bell to represent that there is a reminder set.

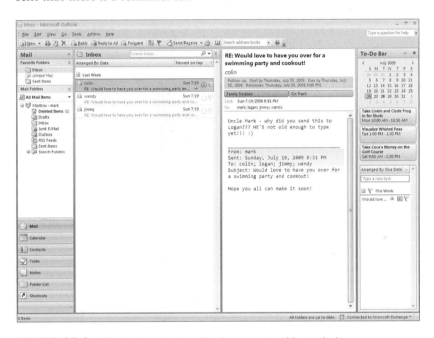

FIGURE 27.2   Flagged and categorized message with reminder.

In addition to flags, Outlook 2007 supports color-coded Categories that can be assigned to items. Categories have no predefined meaning, so users can implement them however they want. For example, a user might decide that the Yellow category references projects that are in danger, and Red refers to projects that are over budget. By simply right-clicking the rounded square to the left of the flag, the user can tag the message with the desired color. Additionally, multiple categories can be assigned to messages, as shown in our example.

To help users remember what their color categories mean, they can be renamed. To do so, right-click on a category and select All Categories. Select the category to be changed and click Rename; then click the OK button. As can be seen in Figure 27.2, these category names display in the preview pane when looking at a message.

NOTE

A flag with an associated reminder provides the end user a standard Outlook reminder pop-up balloon when the preconfigured reminder comes due.

Like any column in Outlook, the flag and category columns can be used as a sorting point for arranging messages. To do so, simply click the desired column header in the index pane.

Making Key Appointments Stand Out with Color

Using the Outlook 2007 calendar, this feature allows for the customization and organization of appointments using colors, allowing end-user appointments to stand out when viewing the calendar.

To choose a color and label an appointment, follow these steps:

1. Open the appointment in the calendar and select the multicolored button labeled Categorize. Alternatively, right-click the message in the calendar view and select Categorize.

2. Choose the category you want to apply.

3. Close the calendar item.

The calendar item will now appear with the color you selected, similar to what is shown in Figure 27.3.

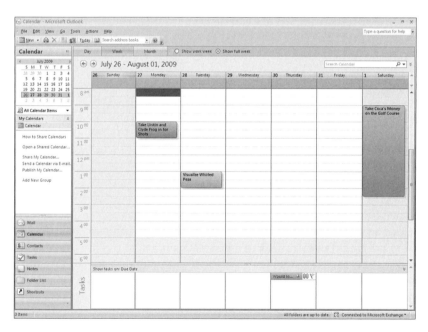

FIGURE 27.3   Calendar items with categories.

Creating Meetings Based on Time Zone

In older versions of Outlook, users who travel often found it difficult to schedule meetings when their destination was in another time zone. Outlook (and most computers, email servers, and email clients) uses Coordinated Universal Time (UTC) for appointments and adjusts the time of the meeting based on the current time zone for the computer.

Users found that they would create a meeting while sitting in one time zone, for a date in the future when they would be in another time zone. At what time should they set the meeting? And if they changed their time zone on their computer when they arrive, will it adjust the meeting time?

Outlook 2007 helps with this problem with the addition of a Time Zone option from within meeting requests. To utilize this feature, open a new meeting request and complete the following:

1. Toward the right side of the main set of buttons, find the Globe icon labeled Time Zones.

2. Click the Time Zones icon and a new drop-down is created next to the start and end times.

3. Via the drop-down, select the time zone where the meeting is going to occur.

4. Select the start and stop times as usual.

5. Invite your attendees and click Send when you are finished.

By selecting the time zone that the meeting will be held in when creating the meeting request, users find it much easier to set the appointments for the proper time.

Using the New Search Functionality

Outlook 2007 makes it easier than ever to search through large mailboxes and calendars. Users can save searches that are commonly used and can leverage the flag and category functions mentioned earlier to provide very powerful ways of managing messages, appointments, or tasks.

Using the Query Builder
The query builder is easily accessible from the top of the toolbar above the message pane. To perform a search, do the following:

1. Enter the word(s) to search for in the Search Inbox box and matches will immediately highlight.

2. Click the double-down arrow next to Search Inbox to expand the query builder.

3. Click Add Criteria to add additional fields to search against.

Typing in the search area updates the results in near real time.

Saving Commonly Used Searches
To save a search, the search must be started from within the Folder list under Search Folders. To do so, complete the following steps:

1. Right-click on Search Folders and choose New Search Folder.

2. Within the New Search Folder pop-up window, choose the search folder and criteria for your search. Depending on what selection is made, the user might be presented with more options to complete before commencing the search. Choose also what part of Outlook to search.

3. Click OK when you are finished.

4. The search completes and the results are displayed in the center pane. In addition, the search is saved under the Search Folders area in the Folder list.

5. To delete the saved search, click on it and choose Delete.

> **TIP**
>
> Saved searches are also available when using Outlook Web App (OWA). For saved searches to be accessed via Outlook Web App, a user must create the saved search in Outlook 2007 first.

Managing Multiple Email Accounts from One Place

Outlook 2007 allows the end user to access multiple email accounts from the same Outlook client, including IMAP, POP3, and Hypertext Transfer Protocol (HTTP) mail accounts.

To configure Outlook to access multiple mailboxes, do the following:

1. From Outlook 2007, select Tools; then select Account Settings.

2. From the E-mail tab, click New.

3. Select the Microsoft Exchange, POP3, IMAP, or HTTP radio button and click Next.

4. Enter the appropriate information for the email account so that it can be properly connected.

   If your server does not support autodiscovery (that is, Exchange 2000 Server or Exchange Server 2003), you need to check the box for Manually Configure Server Settings.

5. Click Next.

6. Click Finish, completing the account setup.

Taking Advantage of the Trust Center

Outlook 2007 adds a new function called the Trust Center. The Trust Center is a centralized location for the management of security-related functions in Outlook 2007. This includes the following:

► Trusted Publishers

► Add-ins

► Privacy Options

► Email Security

► Attachment Handling

► Automatic Download

► Macro Security

► Programmatic Access

By placing these functions under a single interface, it is much easier to manage the security functions in Outlook 2007.

Introducing RSS Feeds

New to Outlook 2007 is the ability to subscribe to RSS feeds. RSS stands for Really Simple Syndication. Many blogs and news sites are offering RSS feeds as a way to disseminate information. RSS feeds are a concept similar to the old Network News Transfer Protocol (NNTP).

To subscribe to an RSS feed, simply do the following:

1. In Outlook 2007, select Tools; then Account Settings.
2. From the Account Settings window, click the RSS Feeds tab.
3. Click New.
4. Enter the uniform resource locator (URL) to the RSS feed you want to add, and click Add.
5. If the URL is valid, you will see the RSS Feed Options page. Choose the settings you want for this feed, similar to those shown in Figure 27.4, and click OK.

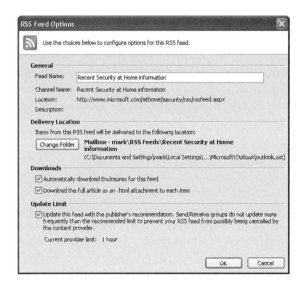

FIGURE 27.4   Sample RSS Feed Options page.

6. Click Close and then click OK.

Security Enhancements in Outlook 2007

Microsoft announced its Secure Computing initiative in 2002 and has continued to improve the security of their products ever since. For Outlook 2007, this means a great increase in the number of security and antispam features available when using the

Outlook 2007 client partnered with Exchange Server. Similarly, improvements have been made in the area of preventing unwanted viruses or malicious scripts from executing when a message is received or previewed. Microsoft continues to integrate advanced email security features such as digital signing of messages, mail encryption, and Information Rights Management.

Support for Secured Messaging

Microsoft's Outlook 2007 development team has taken the feedback from IT groups as well as from end users and has recognized the ever-increasing need for secured messaging. To stay ahead of competitors, Outlook 2007 expanded its support for secured messaging, including S/MIME, digital signing, message encryption, and smart card support.

S/MIME Support, Digital Signatures, and Email Encryption

Though S/MIME support has been available in previous versions of Outlook, Outlook 2007 provides updated support for the latest S/MIME functionality. Using S/MIME, email messages are encrypted by the recipient's public key and can be decrypted, and, therefore, made accessible, only with the recipient's private key. This private/public key exchange is critical for secure email correspondence.

Use of S/MIME support requires that the Outlook 2007 client have a certificate for cryptography on the client computer (and is stored locally either in the Microsoft Windows certificate store or on a smart card), and can be pushed through Registry settings or via Group Policy to easily implement S/MIME throughout an organization. This type of internal certificate use is usually performed via an internal Public Key Infrastructure (PKI). The creation of an internal PKI goes beyond the scope of this book and is not included here.

S/MIME support also includes digital signing. Digital signing allows for security labels and signed secure message receipts. This is a way for a message recipient to be sure that the message came from the person who claimed to send it. Using Outlook 2007, enterprisewide security labels are enforced such as "For Internal Use Only" or labeling messages to restrict the forwarding or printing of messages through Information Rights Management. In addition, users can now request S/MIME affirmation of receipt of a message. By requesting a receipt, the sender confirms that the recipient recognized and verified the digital signature because no receipt is received unless the recipient, who should have received the message, actually does receive the message. Only then does the sender receive the digitally signed read receipt. This allows email users to more safely trust the information they receive via email. This can be especially valuable when email is used for workflow or approval processes.

Setting Email Security on a Specific Message

Security such as payload encryption or digital signing can be set for an individual email using the options available when creating an email message. Clicking on the Options button opens the Message Options dialog box. There, the user can access the Security Properties page to set the security for the message. The user can choose to encrypt the message and/or add a digital signature, request S/MIME receipt, and configure the security settings.

To do this, follow these steps:

1. Open a new message.
2. Click the Options tab and click the arrow in the bottom-right corner of the More Options box.
3. Click the Security Settings button.
4. Add security settings as desired, similar to the ones shown in Figure 27.5.

FIGURE 27.5   Security Properties page in Outlook.

5. Click OK when you are finished.
6. Continue composing the message as normal.

Setting Email Security on the Entire Mailbox
Security settings can also be globally configured for the entire mailbox so that they apply at all times.

To do this, follow these steps:

1. Go to Tools, and select Trust Center.
2. Select Email Security from the left pane.

3. Enable the choices desired for security for the entire mailbox:

   ▶ Encrypt Contents and Attachments for Outgoing Messages

   ▶ Add Digital Signature to Outgoing Messages

   ▶ Send Clear Text Signed Messages When Sending Signed Messages (picked by default). (This allows users who don't have S/MIME security to read the message.)

   ▶ Request S/MIME Receipt for All S/MIME Signed Messages

4. For all choices (except the third choice) to work properly, the user must get a digital certificate provided by the administrator. This can be imported by clicking on the Import/Export button at the bottom of the window beneath Digital IDs (Certificates) or by clicking on Get a Digital ID.

5. After you import the digital certificate, the security functionality is complete.

6. Click OK when you are finished.

Attaching Security Labels to Messages

Also a feature in Outlook 2007, security labels can be configured by the administrator and used by the end user to add security messages to the heading of any email messages. Security labels require digital certificates and denote the sensitivity and security of an email. This functionality leveraged Information Rights Management functions made possible by Exchange Server and Active Directory. Security labels include information in the email header such as "Do not forward outside of the company" or "Confidential." They can be configured on a message-by-message basis or for the entire mailbox.

To configure a security label for a single message, follow these steps:

1. Open a new message.

2. Click the Options tab and click More Options.

3. Click Security Settings from the Message Options window.

4. Click the Add Digital Signature to This Message check box.

5. Choose the security label, classification, and privacy mark that apply to the message.

6. Click OK when you are finished.

To configure a security label for all messages in the mailbox, follow these steps:

1. Go to Tools, Trust Center.

2. Click Email Security in the left pane.

3. Click Settings.

4. Click Security Labels.

5. Choose the policy module, classification, and privacy mark that will apply to all messages.

6. Click OK three times when you are finished.

Using Junk Email Filters to Reduce Spam

Improved antispam and antiphishing filters have now been integrated into Outlook 2007. With these features, the end user can configure the level of antispam filtering desired and control the level of restriction in which messages will be checked. These local functions work in tandem with antispam settings on the Exchange server.

In today's business environment, organizations often find that more than 90% of the mail coming into their environment is spam. Rather than burden the end user with the task of reviewing and deleting spam messages, Outlook 2007 is able to determine if a message is spam and prevent the user from having to deal with it. This can be especially helpful as spam messages are often infected with viruses or contain materials that would be inappropriate in the workplace. Occasionally, Outlook 2007 misses some messages that are actually spam, but the user has the ability to help improve the system when using Exchange Server. By tagging a message as spam, Exchange Server will be more likely to catch a similar spam message in the future. This can benefit an entire network when users tag spam messages in this way.

With the Outlook 2007 Junk E-mail filter, messages are reviewed when the client receives them to determine if the message should be treated as junk or valid email. To do this, the filter analyzes each message based on a class or criteria and imported spammer list. When Outlook is initially installed, the default setting is Low, which catches only the most obvious junk email. This setting is configurable by the end user and can be changed to increase the level of sensitivity on the junk email feature. This catches more unwanted email but increases the chance of false positives. False positives are valid messages that are mistakenly junked. It is important to occasionally check the Junk Mail folder to ensure that no valid messages were accidentally junked. Messages caught by the filter and determined to be junk mail are moved to a Junk E-mail folder in the Outlook 2007 client. The end user can and should review emails checking for false positive emails that were accidentally specified as junk. Optionally, the end user can configure the option to permanently delete junk email messages as they arrive and not save them to the folder at all. This setting should be used with caution.

To configure junk email filtering, follow these steps:

1. In Outlook 2007, select Actions, Junk E-mail, and then Junk E-mail Options.

2. On the Options tab shown in Figure 27.6, choose the level of blockage desired. Use caution when increasing the level of blockage because missing valid messages that are incorrectly categorized as spam can at times be more of a problem than removing a few spam messages per day from your inbox.

27

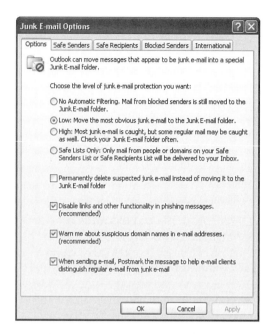

FIGURE 27.6   Junk E-Mail filtering options in Outlook.

3. Click OK when you are finished.

Utilizing the Safe Senders List

If the Outlook 2007 Junk E-mail filter incorrectly determines that a message is junk, the end user can add the sender's email address to a Safe Senders list. This list prevents the filter from identifying any new emails from that sender to be classified as junk mail. This function is also referred to as a "whitelist." The Safe Senders list supports both email addresses and wildcard domains for safe senders. So, a user could add andrew@companyabc.com to allow that individual to send them messages, or the user could add @companyabc.com to allow any user from companyabc.com to send them a message.

The Safe Senders tab has two additional useful options. The first is Also Trust E-mail from My Contacts that ensures that messages sent from email addresses in the user's Contacts folder can bypass the Outlook antispam efforts. However, this useful feature can cause an often overlooked problem. Spammers rarely send out spam with a valid From address. They often *spoof* the address to match that of the person they are sending to—so a message sent TO mark@companyabc.com will also appear to be FROM mark@companyabc.com. Now—if this user has a contact for himself in his Contacts folder and selects Also Trust E-mail from My Contacts—any mail with this address in the From field will be whitelisted—including some of the most prevalent spam. When selecting this option, users should make sure they do not have a contact for themselves.

The other tab, Automatically Add People I E-mail to the Safe Senders List, is also useful. When users have more stringent settings in their Junk E-mail options, selecting this option builds a whitelist of anyone that the user sends an email to–working on the premise of "If you send to them, you probably want to receive from them."

Utilizing the Safe Recipients List

The Safe Recipients list performs a very similar function to the Safe Senders list. The Safe Recipients list allows the user to configure email lists or mail-enabled groups of which they are a member. Any messages sent from these email groups are automatically considered "safe" and bypass Outlooks antispam efforts.

Utilizing the Blocked Senders List

The opposite of the Safe Senders list is the Blocked Senders list. This concept is often referred to as a "blacklist." By entering email addresses or wildcard domains, a user can tell Outlook 2007 to automatically junk any and all messages received from the blocked senders. This tab is not useful when it comes to fighting spam, however, because the worst offenders change their email addresses (and usually domain names) with every round of messages.

TIP

It is important to understand that Blocked Sender rules are based only on the Reply-to addresses given in the email. Reply-to addresses are usually forged in an attempt to slip around antispam systems.

Populating the Lists

To add users to the Safe Senders, Safe Recipients, or Blocked Senders lists, users can do the following:

1. In Outlook 2007, select Actions, Junk E-mail, and then Junk E-mail Options.
2. Choose one of the tabs (Safe Senders, Safe Recipients, Blocked Senders, or International), and then click Add to insert the user to the appropriate list.
3. Type in the SMTP email address of the sender (or their domain) in the following format: jdoe@companyabc.com or @companyabc.com.
4. Click OK when you finish.

Alternatively, any of these lists can be populated with an initial set of addresses by using a combination of Group Policy and the Office Outlook 2007 template. However, when added, administrators cannot REMOVE an entry using GPO. If an invalid entry is distributed, it can be deleted by the user or the entire list can be overwritten by pushing another list via GPO.

Some organizations have been known to add their own domain to the Safe Senders list and push it out to all users. This can be a huge mistake, as much of what the spam users are faced with are messages that are spoofed with a "from" address that matches the "to" address, and this setting leaves the door wide open.

> **TIP**
>
> Many services provide lists of junk senders for import into a Blocked Senders list. These lists are created based on known spammers. If your organization wants to provide the end users with a list of trusted or junk senders, the end user can easily import the list by clicking on the Import from File button. However, as previously stated, this option is of little value because the spammers change their address constantly.

Utilizing the International List

Outlook 2007 also has the ability to flag messages as junk based on where they came from. The International tab allows a user to block entire top-level domains or to block messages in particular languages. This is a more encompassing option than blocking by domain name but is often not an option for organizations with a large international presence.

Avoiding Web Beaconing

Web beaconing refers to the use of references to external content via email to identify a message as having been read. This allows a spammer to validate their list of addresses by identifying the messages that reached a valid user and were opened. When the end user opens the message or views it in the preview pane, the computer retrieves this external content. Outlook 2007 has the ability to block web beaconing, which can help reduce the chances of a user getting onto more spam lists.

To enable web beacon filtering from Outlook 2007, do the following:

1. Click Tools and then click Trust Center.
2. Select Automatic Download in the left pane.
3. Check the Don't Download Pictures Automatically in HTML E-Mail Messages or RSS Items check box.
4. Click OK when you are finished.

Implementing Outlook Anywhere

In Exchange Server 2010, the Outlook Anywhere feature (formerly known as RCP over HTTP) enables Outlook 2007 (and Outlook 2003) clients to connect to their Exchange server over the Internet by using the RPC over HTTP Windows networking component. By wrapping Remote Procedure Calls (RCPs) with a HyperText Transfer Protocol (HTTP) layer, the communication between the Outlook client and the Exchange server can go through network firewalls without requiring RPC ports to be opened. Users can have the benefits of a native MAPI connection to the Exchange server without having to utilize a virtual private network. Additionally, as HTTP protocols were designed to function on networks with unreliable connectivity (such as the Internet), Outlook Anywhere enables users with higher latency to connect to Exchange Server, in which MAPI (for example) functions unreliably when the latency goes above 250ms.

Administrators should configure at least one CAS server per site that is dedicated to providing client access to the Exchange Server 2010 mailbox server. For improved performance and redundancy, multiple CAS servers can be configured.

Additionally, Microsoft recommends that Outlook Anywhere be enabled on at least one CAS server per site. This enables Outlook 2007 clients to connect to the CAS server that is in the same site as their mailbox and minimizes the risks that come from using RPCs across the Internet, which can negatively impact performance.

Enabling Outlook Anywhere—Server Side

Enabling Outlook Anywhere in Exchange Server 2010 is much simpler to configure and manage RPC over HTTP than in Exchange Server 2003. Outlook Anywhere can be enabled using the Enable Outlook Anywhere Wizard from the Exchange Management Console. To do so, navigate to the following container in the Exchange Management Console:

1. Go to Microsoft Exchange\Microsoft Exchange On-Premises\Server Configuration\Client Access.

2. Select the CAS server that you are enabling Outlook Anywhere on and, in the actions pane on the right side, select Enable Outlook Anywhere.

3. Define the External host name. This is the name that users will use to connect to the Exchange Server. In our example we use webmail.companyabc.com.

4. Select the Client authentication method. Administrators can select different authentication as follows:

   ▶ **Basic Authentication**—Username and password are sent in clear text. The users are required to enter their domain, username, and password every time they connect to the Exchange server.

   ▶ **NTLM Authentication**—The user's credentials are never sent over the network. The client computer and server exchange hashed values of the user's credentials, or NTLM can utilize the current system logon information from the client's Windows operating system. Using NTLM is more secure than Basic Authentication, but it might not work with firewalls that examine and modify traffic. NTLM can be used with an advanced firewall server, such as Microsoft's Internet Security and Acceleration (ISA) server.

   ▶ **Allow secure channel (SSL) offloading**—This option can be used in environments in which a separate server handles the Secure Sockets Layer (SSL) encryption and decryption.

Connecting to Outlook Anywhere with Outlook 2007

After Outlook Anywhere is configured on the CAS servers, the Outlook client can be configured to connect to Exchange Server via RPC over HTTPS.

For Outlook 2007 to use RPC over HTTPS, the workstation should be running Windows XP or higher, with the latest available service packs.

27

To install the required patch and configure the Outlook 2007 client for RPC over HTTP access, complete the following:

1. In Outlook 2007, select Tools; then select Account Settings.
2. Highlight the Exchange Server connection, and click Change.
3. On the Change E-mail Account screen, click More Settings.
4. Click the Connection tab.
5. Place a check mark in the box labeled Connect to Microsoft Exchange Using HTTP.
6. Click Exchange Proxy Settings.

On the Exchange Proxy Settings screen, configure the following:

1. For Connection Settings, enter the URL of the Exchange server that has been configured as the RPC proxy server.
2. Click Connect using SSL only.
3. Click the two boxes to use HTTP as the first choice for both fast and slow connections, as shown in Figure 27.7. Click OK, and then click OK again.

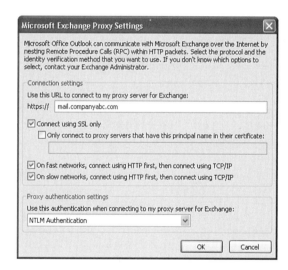

FIGURE 27.7   Outlook Anywhere client configuration.

4. Click OK to accept the information box about restarting Outlook.
5. Click Next, click Finish, and then click Close.
6. Exit the Outlook application, and open it again to apply the new settings.

TIP

To ensure that Outlook 2007 is now using RPC over HTTPS, hold the Ctrl key and right-click the Outlook icon in the taskbar. Select Connection Status. This screen shows you the connection type to the Exchange server, which should state HTTPS.

The most secure method of connecting uses the following settings, which are also the default settings when RPC over HTTP is first configured:

▶ Connect with SSL Only

▶ Mutually Authenticate the Session When Connecting with SSL

▶ Password Authentication is NTLM

Deploying Outlook 2007

To take advantage of all the features of Outlook 2007, you need to deploy Outlook 2007 to your users. The deployment can be performed with many tools such as Systems Management Server 2003 or though Group Policy Objects. This section focuses on how to preconfigure Outlook 2007 so that it will be deployed with the functions and settings that you need.

Utilizing the Office Customization Tool

The Office Customization Tool (OCT) is a new application included in Office 2007. The OCT allows an administrator to preconfigure components and settings within the Office 2007 suite to simplify deployments of Office 2007 applications.

The OCT is accessed in the following manner:

1. Launch a command prompt.
2. Browse to the drive containing the Office install files.
3. Browse to the directory containing the `setup.exe` file.
4. Type `Setup.exe /admin`.

Running the OCT in this way allows you to either create a new setup customization file or to modify an existing one. If you are creating a new file, the OCT displays a list of the products available on the network installation point. You must select a single product that you want to customize.

After running the wizard, you can save your customizations in the Updates folder. Setup will look into this folder to find customizations when you run the setup.

Alternatively, you can save your customizations in another location and reference them during the install. For example:

```
Setup.exe /adminfile \\server\share\OCT\remoteusers.msp
```

This is an exceptionally powerful ability as you can create different custom settings for different types of users.

27

Taking Advantage of OCT for Outlook 2007

Although the OCT offers customizations for all Office 2007 components, this section examines some of the settings available specifically for Outlook 2007. Some of the more useful settings include the following:

▶ **Use existing profile**—This setting retains the existing profile or prompts the user to create a profile the first time Outlook is started.

▶ **Modify profile**—This setting modifies the default profile or makes changes to profiles that you specify. If there isn't a default profile or no profile by the name that you specify, Outlook creates a profile based on settings you choose in the other areas of the OCT.

▶ **New profile**—This setting creates a new profile and sets it as the default profile. If a profile already exists, it is not removed and is still available to the user. You need to enter a name in the Profile name box, which appears in the E-Mail Accounts dialog box in Outlook. The new profile is created based on the options you choose in the other areas of the OCT.

▶ **Apply PRF**—This setting imports an Outlook profile (PRF) file to define a new default profile. You can use any profile created for Outlook 2007. Enter a name and path for the profile in the Apply the Following Profile (PRF File) field. If you created a PRF file for a previous version of Outlook, you can import it to Office Outlook 2007, provided it uses only MAPI services.

▶ **Do not configure Cached Exchange mode**—This setting configures Outlook 2007 to only attach to the Exchange Server mailboxes directly from the Exchange server, as opposed to being cached on users' computers in an Offline Folder file (OST file).

▶ **Configure Cached Exchange mode**—This setting creates an OST file or uses an existing OST file. This results in users working with a local copy of their Exchange Server mailbox. When selecting Use Cached Exchange mode, you can configure the following options.

   ▶ **Download only headers**—Download copies of headers only from users' Exchange Server mailboxes.

   ▶ **Download headers followed by the full item**—Download copies of headers from users' Exchange Server mailboxes, and then download copies of messages.

   ▶ **Download full items**—Download copies of full messages (headers and message bodies) from users' Exchange Server mailboxes.

   ▶ **On slow connections, download only headers**—When a slow network connection is detected, download copies of headers only from users' Exchange Server mailboxes.

   ▶ **Download public folder favorites**—Download the list of public folder favorites.

Using Outlook 2007

Like every evolution of Outlook, Outlook 2007 expands on the collaborative tools available to the end user when connecting to an Exchange server. This section covers many of these collaborative tools and new collaborative features available in the Outlook 2007 client.

Viewing Shared Calendars in Multiple Panes

Tracking appointments and setting meetings have quickly become high priorities for employees in today's business world. To simplify these types of functions, Outlook 2007 allows a user to view multiple Exchange Server calendars in a shared pane. In previous versions of Outlook, an additional calendar would be opened in a new window. In Outlook 2007, if a user has configured their calendar with View rights, other users can view those calendars as well as their own at the same time lined up side by side to view or compare them.

To open additional calendars, perform the following steps:

1. Choose File, Open, Other User's Folder.

2. Choose the name of the user and select Folder Type: Calendar. The calendar opens in the main window and automatically removes the mailbox owner's calendar.

   New to Outlook 2007 is a prompt to allow a user to request access to a calendar to which they don't currently have access.

3. To view both your own calendar and the additional calendar, look at the left pane. There is an area under the monthly calendar that provides check boxes for what calendars the end user wants to view. This is split into My Calendars and Peoples Calendars. Check the My Calendar check box and another check box to view both your own calendar and an additional calendar.

TIP

When viewing multiple calendars, keep in mind that each additional calendar is shown in a different color; also note that the corresponding check box on the left is seen in the same color.

---

4. Continue to add the desired calendars, and click on the check boxes to remove or add calendars to the view.

5. When you are finished, click the My Calendar check box and deselect all the additional calendars.

> **TIP**
>
> When in the Calendar view, you can click the Open a Shared Calendar hyperlink and you will be prompted to enter the name of the user whose calendar you want to view. Enter the name of the calendar to open and click OK. This automatically shows both the mailbox owner's calendar and the new calendar(s).

Enabling Calendar Sharing in Outlook 2007

By default, the full details of a user's calendar are not shared. Other users in the organization have the ability to view free/busy information, but that is all. If the calendar owner wants to allow others to view the full details of their calendar, or to write to their calendar, the default permissions must be modified.

To enable the mailbox owner's calendar to be shared, follow these steps:

1. From the Folder List view, right-click Calendar in the navigation pane (if you don't see Calendar in the list, click the Folder List icon at the bottom of the navigation pane).

2. Click Change Sharing Permissions.

3. From the Calendar Properties page, on the Permissions tab, click Add.

4. Browse or enter the name of the user who will get access to the calendar, and click Add.

5. Click OK when the users have been added.

6. The user must now specify what permissions are to be granted. Outlook provides predefined roles for permissions that appear in the Permission Level box. Clicking the drop-down menu and choosing a predefined permission level shows what permissions are being granted, making it easy to choose the desired permissions. To create a unique set of permissions, choose an initial permission level and then check the boxes and radio buttons to assign the unique permissions, as shown in Figure 27.8.

7. Click OK when finished. The user(s) specified will have those rights to the end user's calendar until the end user specifically removes them by going through the same process mentioned, and then clicking on the user or group with permissions to the calendar and choosing Remove.

> **NOTE**
>
> When you grant another user Read access to your calendar, they will be able to read your calendar entries. They will not, however, be able to read calendar items that are marked as Private.

Sharing Other Personal Information

Outlook 2007 allows users to share their personal information (such as the Inbox, contacts, and tasks) with other users. This is done via the same method listed previously with the difference being that the permissions are set for the Inbox, Contacts, or Tasks folders.

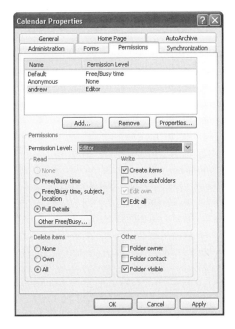

FIGURE 27.8   Changing calendar permissions.

To enable Inbox sharing, for example, follow these steps:

1. Right-click on the Inbox in the Folder view.

2. Choose Change Sharing Permissions.

3. Add the users or groups and set their permissions as described previously in the "Enabling Calendar Sharing in Outlook 2007" section.

Delegating Rights to Send Email "On Behalf Of" Another User

In some situations, such as when a user has an administrative assistant, they might want to give someone the ability to send messages or meeting requests on their behalf. This results in a message that will come from "user B on behalf of user A." To enable a user to send email on someone else's behalf, follow these steps:

1. Go to Tools, Options, and select the Delegates tab.

2. Click Add.

3. Add the name of the user or group that needs the rights.

4. When finished, click OK.

5. Choose the permission level for each component of Outlook.

6. If desired, select Automatically Send a Message to the Delegate Summarizing These Permissions.

7. If desired, select Delegate Can See My Private Items.

8. Click OK when finished.

27

9. From the Options page, select how meeting requests should be delivered. The available options are shown in Figure 27.9. The default setting for the delivery of meeting requests is "My delegates only, but send a copy of meeting requests and responses to me." This is the recommended setting.

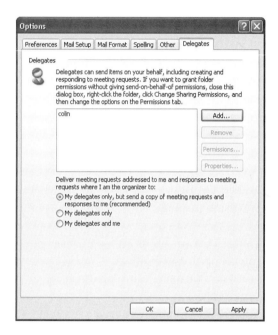

FIGURE 27.9   Adding permissions to delegates.

> **NOTE**
>
> Although Outlook does not have a predefined maximum number of delegates that can be assigned, Microsoft performed its tests with a maximum of four delegates. Best practices recommend that users assign only one other user with Editor Permissions. Adding additional editors is a common cause of unpredictable behavior with meetings and appointments in Outlook.

Sharing Information with Users Outside the Company

In response to more advanced needs of users, Outlook 2007 has provided functions to help extend familiar collaboration tools into unfamiliar areas. Much of the functionality available among users of the same Exchange Server environment is now available across the Internet. This is a great enabler for users because it is now easier to collaborate with colleagues from other companies.

Configuring Free/Busy Time to Be Viewed via the Internet

In the past, it required specialized software and connectors to exchange free/busy information with another Exchange Server organization. Free/busy information is what tracks the availability of users in terms of having appointments, being in meetings, or having free time available. Exchange Server administrators and mailbox owners can publish this free/busy information outside of their Exchange Server environment to more easily set up meetings with other organizations. If this functionality is needed, this information can be published to a web server available to both organizations. In the past, you could use a service provided by Microsoft called the Microsoft Office Internet Free/Busy Service, but this service is no longer available. This service has been replaced by Office Online. By publishing free/busy information to a shared website, users outside of the Exchange Server organization can view published free/busy information over the Internet. They can also use the same website to schedule meetings with recipients from the participating organizations. This option is available for users accessing Exchange Server with the Outlook 2002 or later clients.

To configure free/busy time to be displayed on the Internet with a custom server, follow these steps:

1. Right-click the calendar to be shared.
2. Choose Publish to Internet and Publish to WebDAV Server.
3. Enter the URL to which you will publish your information.
4. Choose the time frame you want to publish as well as the options and upload method, similar to the information shown in Figure 27.10.

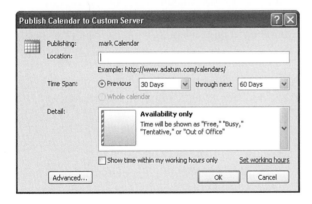

FIGURE 27.10   Publishing Calendars.

5. Click OK.

To stop sharing this information on the custom server, complete the following steps:

1. Right-click the shared calendar.
2. Choose Publish to Internet.
3. Choose Remove from Server.
4. Click Yes.

To publish a calendar to Office Online, follow these steps:

1. Right-click the calendar to be shared.

2. Choose Publish to Internet and then click Publish to Office Online.

3. Register for Office Online if you do not already have a Windows Live ID.

4. Choose the time frame you want to publish and the options and upload method, similar to that shown in Figure 27.10.

5. Click OK and information will be published.

6. Optional: Send invites to contacts to share your information.

To stop sharing this information on Office Online:

1. Right-click the shared calendar.

2. Choose Publish to Internet.

3. Choose Remove from Server.

4. Click Yes.

Viewing Free/Busy Time via the Internet

If granted necessary permissions, Outlook users from one organization can view free/busy information from another organization's users via the shared website. The user can send meeting requests, add the user to a group schedule, and see free/busy time just as they could with users from their own organization. To do this, the end user must access the free/busy information website, click on View Free/Busy Times on the Web, and enter the email address of the user whose free/busy time is to be viewed.

The user also has the option to see a free/busy search path for their contacts. To do so, follow these steps:

1. In the navigation pane, click Contacts, and then double-click an entry to open a contact.

2. Click the Details tab.

3. Under the text that reads Internet Free-Busy, type the fully qualified path of the location that you want to search for this contact's free/busy information in the Address box. You can use any valid URL format, such as: http://..., file://\\..., or ftp://..., as shown in Figure 27.11.

To let other users know about your shared calendar information, you can do the following:

1. Right-click the shared calendar.

2. Click Publish to Internet.

3. Click Share Published Calendar.

4. Enter the email addresses of the people with whom you want to share your free/busy information.

5. Click Send.

The person who will be accessing the shared calendar will also need a Windows Live logon.

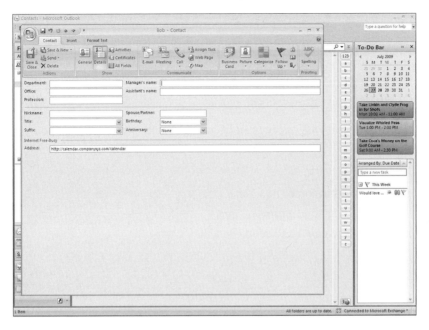

FIGURE 27.11   External Free/Busy Path.

They will receive a message similar to the following:

```
Mark has invited you to add the "Mark_Calendar" Internet Calendar subscription to
Microsoft Office Outlook.
You can open this calendar on any computer with an Internet calendar compatible
program installed, such as Microsoft Office Outlook 2007.
```

Sending Contact Information to Others

As the business world becomes more and more electronic, old customs such as the exchange of paper business cards are being replaced by more modern methods. Virtual Business Cards, or vCards, have greatly increased in popularity. These vCards enable an Outlook user to send anyone a small file containing their contact information. Because of the vCard format, this contact information can then be imported into the recipient's contact list. The vCard can contain common information such as the following:

▶ Name

▶ Address

▶ Phone numbers

▶ Email address

▶ Job title

Going beyond the concepts of a typical business card, a vCard can also include the following:

▶ A picture of the contact

▶ A public key for encryption or digital signing

▶ A link to Internet published free/busy information

vCards can be emailed as attachments or they can be automatically attached to outgoing messages as part of a signature file.

To email a vCard, follow these steps:

1. Open the contact that will become the vCard.
2. Click Actions; then select Send as Business Card.
3. Input information into the email and send the email.

When the user receives the card, he can open it and Save and Close into his own contacts area.

To include a vCard in an AutoSignature, follow these steps:

1. Click Tools, Options.
2. Click the Mail Format tab and click Signatures.
3. Edit an existing AutoSignature or create a new one.
4. In the toolbar above the text window, click the Business Card icon.
5. Select the business card from your contacts, and click OK.
6. Click OK.

Using Public Folders to Share Information

Public folders have long been a staple of collaborative work via Outlook. Outlook 2007 continues to support easy access of public folders. Public folders are often used where mailing lists would be overkill. Rather than flooding mailboxes of dozens of users with back-and-forth discussions, public folders are used as a single storage point for these types of messages and various users are granted access to read or write to these folders. Public folders are also a great place to store common contacts or common calendar items. This makes it easier to share information within a subset of users in Exchange. Outlook 2007 makes it easy to access this information centrally without it cluttering the global resources.

Using Group Schedules

Group schedules are a fairly new feature and are only available to Outlook 2003 and 2007 clients. Group schedules enable the user to create groups of users enabling a quick view of their calendars. The Group Schedules features also allow a user to send all the members of the Group Schedule an email or a meeting request using a single address. This makes it very easy for a user to group together commonly used resources for a quick view of availability. This might include a list of conference rooms in a given building or could be members of a team for a project they are working on. By arranging these resources together into a group schedule, the user can avoid the tedious process of inviting all of the resources individually to a meeting to see when they are available.

Configuring Group Schedules

Users can create multiple group schedules to help them organize resources into logical groups.

To create a new group schedule, follow these steps:

1. From the Calendar view, click Actions; then click View Group Schedules. The Group Schedules dialog box opens.
2. Click New.
3. Name the group schedule and click OK.
4. The Customized Group Schedules dialog box opens.
5. Click Add Others and select Add from Address Book or Add Public Folder
6. Type the name of the user(s) in the Type Name or Select from List box, and click To after each user has been selected. Alternatively, select the user from the list and double-click the name to add him to the To field. When finished, click OK.
7. Click Save and Close.

After the group schedule has been created, to view it and work with it, follow these steps:

1. From the Calendar view, click Actions; then click View Group Schedules. The Group Schedules dialog box opens.
2. Select the group schedule to view and click Open.
3. A screen similar to the one shown in Figure 27.12 appears.

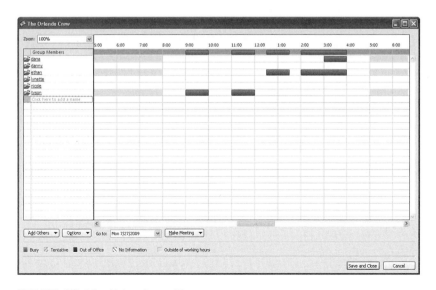

FIGURE 27.12   Using Group Views.

Sending Email or Meeting Requests to Group Schedules

Organizing subsets of user or resources into group schedules can also be very useful for sending emails or meeting requests. In this sense, the group schedule acts similarly to a distribution group.

To schedule a meeting, follow these steps:

1. Click Make Meeting from within the Group Schedule view for the specific group.

2. Choose New Meeting to just send the meeting request to one member or select New Meeting with All to send the meeting request to all members of the group schedule.

3. Fill out the meeting request as you normally would.

To send an email, follow these steps:

1. Click Make Meeting.

2. Choose New Mail Message to send to an individual member of the group, or select New Mail Message to All to send to the whole group.

3. Fill out the email message as you normally would, and send the message.

> **NOTE**
>
> It is important to realize that group schedules created in this way are only available to the user who created them. Other members of the group schedule who wanted similar functionality would have to create their own group schedule.

Using Cached Exchange Mode for Offline Functionality

Outlook 2007 continues to support Cached Exchange mode. Cached Exchange mode, or Cached mode for short, refers to a configuration where Outlook is storing the messages and calendar items locally. Unlike the old Personal folder file (PST) storage method, Cached mode utilizes an OST file. This file is synchronized with the Exchange server on a regular basis. This means that there are two copies of the mailbox at all times. One copy lives on the Exchange server and one copy lives on the Outlook client.

This configuration has many advantages in terms of performance and reliability. For example, imagine that a user is connecting to their Exchange server over a dial-up connection and isn't running Cached mode. The user receives a message with a large attachment. The user sees the new message and opens the attachment. Now, the message has to be downloaded to the user's computer. This takes several minutes because of the size of the file and the relatively slow link speed. This usually results in unhappy users because they had to wait several minutes between wanting to open the attachment and the attachment actually opening.

Now, let's view this same scenario with Cached mode. In Cached mode, the attachment is downloaded in the background when the message arrives, assuming the Outlook client is attached to the server. The message with the attachment doesn't appear in the mailbox until the contents have been downloaded and cached locally. Now, when the user sees the message appear in the Inbox, the files associated with the attachment are already on the local system. The user opens the attachment and it opens immediately. This results in a happier user.

The truth of the matter is that the download time of the message was exactly the same in both scenarios. However, the perceived difference is that the Cached mode situation was faster because the user doesn't know when the message was sent. This situation also takes great advantage of the idle time of the user. Most messages arrive and are fully downloaded to the client while the user is away from their system or doing other things. This means that when the user is actively working with email, there aren't any delays in moving data.

Because the data downloaded is only a mirror of the Exchange Server mailbox, the content available via OWA is exactly the same. Similarly, if the user were to get another computer or a new computer, Outlook simply creates another copy of the data locally to keep in sync.

With the OST file locally stored, the user is able to work with the contents of their mailbox even when not connected to the Exchange server. Changes made locally will sync back to the Exchange server. Like most replication performed by Microsoft, the newest copy always wins and overwrites older changes. This allows a traveling user to reply to messages, organize folders, and create calendar entries while away from the office. Upon connecting to the Exchange server, their local changes get applied to the Exchange server copy. This is really an optimal configuration for traveling users and users who have limited connectivity.

The User Experience in Cached Exchange Mode

When the user is connected to the Exchange server, the phrase "Connected to Microsoft Exchange" appears in the lower-right corner of the Outlook 2007 window. The message "All Folders Are Up to Date" should also be displayed when synchronization is up to date.

When connectivity is lost, the message says "Disconnected" and gives the date and time the offline folders were last updated.

When connectivity is first restored, the message says "Trying to Connect." As connectivity is reestablished, the phrase "Connected to Microsoft Exchange" reappears, and to the left are updates informing the user what is automatically occurring to get the mailbox up to date.

These messages could be any of the following:

▶ Waiting to Update the Full Items in Inbox

▶ Sending Complete

▶ All Folders Are Up-to-Date

The user might occasionally find that people appear to be missing from the Global Address List (GAL). While running in Cached mode, Outlook 2007 no longer gets its GAL from the global catalog. The client downloads the Offline Address Book. This is what allows the user to look up addresses while not connected to the network. The user can trigger a download of the OAB at any time. Important to realize is that, by default, Exchange Server only updates the OAB every 24 hours. As such, it's possible for a user to be added to Exchange Server after the OAB generation has occurred. Users not running in Cached mode would see the new user in the GAL but the Cached mode users wouldn't see them until the OAB was updated and they downloaded the latest copy.

Deploying Cached Exchange Mode

Cached mode can be deployed by using the Office Customization Tool or through enabling this option using domain Group Policy. Be aware that setting it via Group Policy on a large number of users drastically increases network traffic to the Exchange server. Outlook in Cached mode has to download the entire mailbox. Environments where mailbox size limits aren't set are especially impacted by this. Imagine 200 users logon on Monday morning and a GPO sets their Outlook to Cached mode. If each user had 100MB of mail in their mailbox, there would be 20GB of data being copied from the Exchange server. This could be especially impacting if some of those users were coming across WAN connections to get to Exchange Server.

If possible, only set a user to Cached mode when they are on the same LAN of the Exchange server or when they are first created in Exchange Server. This reduces the traffic at the Exchange server.

Deploying Cached Exchange Mode Manually

When configuring a user's Outlook profile manually, it's possible to configure Cached mode at that time.

To configure Cached mode manually, do the following:

1. Begin configuring a user profile in the standard manner.

2. When the E-Mail Accounts page is reached, make sure the Use Cached Exchange Mode check box is checked.

3. Finish configuring the Outlook profile.

Deployment Considerations for Cached Exchange Mode

Because enabling Cached mode forces the end users to synchronize a full copy of their mailbox to a local OST file as well as a full copy of the OAB, the demand on an Exchange server can be quite high. If a large number of users must be configured to use Cached mode at one time, the best choices for configuring Cached mode are as follows:

▶ Only enable Cached mode if the user will benefit from it. This would include traveling users or users who are on slow connections.

▶ Deploy Cached mode to groups of users at a time rather than to the whole enterprise.

▶ Encourage users to clean up their mailboxes prior to enabling Cached mode. Sent and Deleted items often account for 50% of the size of a mailbox.

▶ Deploy Cached mode sooner rather than later. The smaller the mailbox at the time of the OST creation, the less data needs to be moved.

Using Cached Exchange Mode

Because Cached mode acts somewhat differently from a traditional mailbox, an administrator might consider some additional user training for those with Cached mode. This helps users recognize those differences and should result in fewer calls to the help desk. Some of these differences are mentioned in the following sections.

The Send/Receive Button

For users in Cached mode, it is unnecessary to click the Send/Receive messages button regularly when synchronizing with the new Cached mode functionality. This now happens automatically and clicking Send/Receive doesn't accomplish anything.

RPC Over HTTPS and the Cached Exchange Mode

It is recommended that users running RPC over HTTPS also run with Cached Exchange mode enabled. This is because Cached Exchange mode deals better with "slow links and disconnections" to Exchange Server. Because RPC over HTTPS accesses Exchange Server information via the Internet, these users are more likely to experience network latency and slowness.

Slow-Link Connection Awareness

Cached mode was originally designed to address the challenges associated with links 128Kbps or slower. When slow-link connection awareness is enabled, it automatically implements the following email-synchronization behaviors:

▶ OAB is not downloaded (neither partial nor full download).

▶ Mail headers only are downloaded.

▶ The rest of the mail message and attachments are downloaded when the user clicks on the message or attachment to open it.

To change the slow-link configuration, perform the following steps:

1. Click File.
2. Choose Cached Exchange Mode.
3. Uncheck On Slow Connections Download Only Headers.

Cached Exchange Mode and OSTs and OABs

Using Cached mode downloads a full copy of the user's mail to the OST file stored locally on the user's hard drive. However, administrators need to be aware of some considerations regarding OSTs and Cached mode to plan and make their configuration choices for these Exchange Server clients allowing optimal performance and efficient connectivity.

Cached Exchange Mode OST Considerations

OST files in Outlook 2007 use the new Unicode format. This allows them to go beyond the 2-GB limitation of the old American National Standards Institute (ANSI) format. However, be sure to account for the potential size of the OST file when planning your desktop or laptop images. Older notebooks might not have enough space locally to support a large OST file if you aren't limiting the size of mailboxes on the Exchange server.

Cached Exchange Mode and Outlook Address Book (OAB) Implications

When using Cached mode, it is possible to download a No Details Outlook address book. However, users in Cached mode should download the Full Details OAB. This is because they can experience significant delays when they access the OAB when the full details are not locally accessible. When this situation occurs, the user's workstation must contact the Exchange server to provide full data for the OAB. This results in delays for the user during the download.

When Cached mode is enabled, the OAB is synchronized every 24 hours, by default. If there are no updates to the server OAB, there will be no updates to the offline OAB. When there are changes to the OAB, only the differences are downloaded. This results in a faster update to the OAB for the Cached mode user.

Outlook Features That Decrease Cached Exchange Mode's Effectiveness

Cached Exchange mode is easy to configure and provides many benefits to the occasionally offline user. It is important to try to keep the Cached mode experience as positive as possible for the user. Thus, it is useful to know that several Outlook 2007 features can actually decrease the effectiveness of Cached mode. The features discussed in the following sections all result in Outlook 2007 sending calls to the Exchange server for information when in Cached mode. For users using Cached mode, these calls can greatly decrease the effectiveness and performance of the client and, therefore, should be avoided if possible.

Delegate Access and Accessing Shared Folders or Calendars

These two items both require access to the Exchange server to view other users' Outlook items. Cached mode does not download another user's data to the local OST, so this nullifies the use of Cached mode when the functionality is required. These functions will work while the Cached mode user is connected to the Exchange server, but it can result in attempted external connections that will fail when the user is offline. This results in the interface waiting for a timeout before continuing with its processes.

Outlook Add-ins

Outlook add-ins such as ActiveSync can result in Outlook not utilizing important items, such as the Download Headers Only functionality that allows Cached mode to work so well. They also can cause excessive calls to the Exchange server or network. Avoid Outlook add-ins, if possible. Third-party add-ins should be tested with Cached mode for both online and offline behaviors to see if they are making calls to nonlocal data that could impact Cached mode users while they are offline.

Digital Signatures

Verification of digital signatures requires Outlook to verify a valid signature for messages sent using digital encryption, requiring a server call as well. Be sure to test such configurations to ensure that signed or protected content can still be accessed while a user is offline.

Noncached Public Folders

This, too, requires bandwidth and a call to the server. Consider synchronizing frequently used public folders to the OST through the use of Public Folder Favorites. Be careful not to cache too much public folder information because it inflates the size of the OST file.

Including Additional Searchable Address Books

If the enterprise includes custom address books and contact lists that are enabled to be searchable and usable for email addressing, this results in the client/server communications. These types of address lists are not cached by Outlook.

Customizing the User Object Properties

If the enterprise has created customized items on the General tab of the properties box of a user, this always requires a call to the server: When user properties are displayed, the General tab is always displayed first. Therefore, if these are necessary, consider placing any customized fields on a different tab on the user properties pages requiring a call to the server only when that tab is accessed, not every time the user properties are accessed.

Summary

Outlook 2007 has been around for a few years now, but it remains the most fully featured and capable email client around.

When Microsoft releases Outlook 2010, the product will take advantage of the new features enabled by Exchange Server 2010–Conversation grouping, ignoring conversations, MailTips, Presence, and others. All of these are wonderful and exciting features, but until the new product releases, it's good to know that Outlook 2007 can function with Exchange Server 2010 and will continue to provide an outstanding messaging experience.

Users can continue to benefit from the powerful collaboration functions of Outlook 2007 and to enjoy the fantastic improvements in the area of calendar interactions. Scheduling meetings with users from other Exchange Server organizations always proved difficult in the past, requiring the configuration of complex connectors. But by taking advantage of the enhancements provided by Internet-based calendaring, users can empower themselves to make their free/busy information available to selected partners when needed, and just as easily revoke access to that information when the project is completed.

Somehow, Microsoft made the Search functionality more powerful than ever, while simplifying the use of the feature at the same time. Near real-time searches of the entire mailbox are made possible through configurable indexing, enabling users to find a particular message quickly and easily–even with today's larger and larger mailboxes. The search capabilities are further enhanced by enabling users to include calendar items and tasks in the search results.

As more and more unethical people attempt to assault us with spam and phishing attacks, Outlook 2007 fights back by adding improved capabilities, helping the user avoid these annoying and potentially dangerous email messages. By integrating with the message filtering functions of Exchange Server, Outlook 2007 allows the end users to do their part to help protect the company as a whole by acting as a secondary layer in the spam blocking by flagging messages that snuck through the primary filter.

Entirely new functions such as the ability to subscribe to RSS (Really Simple Syndication) feeds gives the Outlook 2007 user access to whole new worlds of information.

Security enhancements in Outlook 2007 include improvements for encrypted client-to-server communications by using RPC over HTTPS to connect to Exchange Outlook Anywhere. And the ability to add security to specific messages through Information Rights Management and the capability to set security for an entire mailbox give users a much more secured environment for enabling business processes.

Finally, a Cached mode method of access enables a user to access mail, calendar appointments, and other content within Outlook, regardless of whether they are connected to Exchange Server. Cached mode access provides remote and roving users an improved user experience by placing data local to their system making accessing large attachments significantly faster than if they were accessing them from the Exchange server.

All the powerful and useful features built into Outlook 2007 make it the latest and truly greatest version of Outlook—until the next one.

Best Practices

The following are best practices from this chapter:

- ▶ Quick flags should be used to flag messages that require follow-up or other attention.

- ▶ Key appointments can be categorized with colors to draw attention to appointments in user calendars.

- ▶ Using the enhanced search capabilities of Outlook 2007 can dramatically decrease the time it takes for a user to find messages or information within Outlook.

- ▶ Instead of establishing a VPN before accessing an Exchange server from a remote Outlook 2007 client, the RPC over HTTPS should be enabled to provide SSL-based 128-bit encrypted end-to-end communication from client to server.

- ▶ Outlook Anywhere provides the best performance on unreliable or high-latency links. However, it takes roughly twice the bandwidth to move the same amount of data. Take this into consideration when deploying Outlook Anywhere.

- ▶ Calendars can be set up in group schedules to provide a side-by-side view of appointment calendars for individuals or groups of users.

- ▶ Free/busy times can be configured to be viewable from the Internet, to provide external users access and views to appointment schedules.

- ▶ Cached mode can be used to support users accessing Exchange Server across WAN links, saving bandwidth for other network needs such as business application access.

- ▶ Make sure there is at least one CAS server per site. Additional CAS servers per site can provide redundancy and improved performance.

- ▶ When deploying Outlook Anywhere, enable it on at least one CAS server in each site.

CHAPTER 28

Leveraging the Capabilities of the Outlook Web App (OWA) Client

As email communication has become more entrenched in the daily business (and personal) lives of people throughout the world, the ability to *access* their email from alternative locations has stopped being a "want" for many users and has become a "need."

Outlook Web App (OWA) has provided this functionality in one form or another since Exchange Server 5.0 and, with each new release, the product has improved in functionality, ease of administration, and ease of use.

However, with Exchange Server 2010, Microsoft has changed the name of this key product—Outlook Web Access is now known as Outlook Web App. Fortunately, with this name change the old and familiar abbreviation still applies, allowing administrators and users to accurately continue to refer to the product as OWA.

The earliest versions of OWA were often criticized as providing a "watered down" version of the Microsoft Outlook client. These criticisms were justified because these early releases lacked the functionality and polish that could be found in Outlook. The most recent versions of OWA, however, have provided a user experience that rivals that of a locally installed client.

With Exchange Server 2010, Microsoft continues to improve Outlook Web App by incorporating many new features that appeal to both the administrator and user communities.

This chapter focuses on providing information for both Administrators and users on the configuration and use of OWA 2010, including both basic and advanced features.

Understanding Microsoft's Direction on OWA

As with previous versions of OWA, Microsoft has attempted to implement new feature sets and functionality into the product, while keeping the interface of the application as similar to previous versions as possible. By maintaining a familiar "look and feel," Microsoft enables organizations to minimize the need to incur the costs of retraining the user community each time a new version is released.

By allowing organizations to provide a full-featured email client to roaming users, Microsoft can further cement Exchange Server as the messaging system of choice for corporate America.

The OWA 2010 interface is extremely intuitive. Those with prior experience using OWA or Outlook will feel right at home, and those with little to no experience can quickly and easily take advantage of many of the capabilities of the product with little to no formal training.

Leveraging a Common Interface

For those familiar with OWA in Exchange Server 2007, Exchange Server 2010 does not appear to have changed much at first glance. However, although the basic components of the two products are similar, the layout, as shown in Figure 28.1, feels less "cluttered" than before.

On the left side, the navigation pane lists the folders in the mailbox. At the bottom of the navigation pane are shortcuts for some of the more commonly used items. For those who have a long list of folders and need more space, the shortcuts display can be minimized by clicking the dotted line above the Mail shortcut. At the top of the navigation pane, OWA 2010 adds a Favorites section. The Favorites section is configurable, and users can add their most commonly accessed folders by simply right-clicking them and selecting Add to Favorites.

In the middle of the screen, the view pane shows the list of messages in the selected folder, collated in the new conversation view. At the top of the view pane is the OWA toolbar with icons and drop-down menus to assist with creating and deleting messages, checking for new mail, moving messages, changing how the messages are arranged, applying filters, and so on.

On the right, we have the reading pane. Of the three panes, the reading pane has changed the most. Where it used to show a single message, the conversation view enables multiple messages in a thread to be viewed simultaneously.

As with previous versions, the borders between each pane can be adjusted by hovering the mouse over the border until the double arrow appears, clicking the left mouse key, and dragging the border to the desired location.

Although OWA is designed to replicate the experience users have when utilizing the actual Outlook client, the users are likely to notice a few differences here and there. The two products are intentionally kept as similar as possible to ensure that users familiar with one interface will be comfortable in the other.

FIGURE 28.1   OWA Main page.

TIP

OWA 2010 has a useful feature that also existed in OWA 2007 but that some users never noticed. In the navigation pane, users can hover the mouse pointer over their Display Name. After a second or two, a box appears showing how much mailbox space the users are currently using, and at what point the messaging quotas will go into effect.

For example, the message might say 273.82MB of Mailbox Space Used. At 2GB You Will Not Be Able to Send Mail.

A Feature-Rich Web Client Is Still a Web Client

Although OWA 2010 provides much of the functionality of a full-fledged Outlook client, one basic capability differentiates the two: OWA has no provisions for enabling users to access their mail or calendar data while offline.

Enabling users to access their mailbox from various locations, including public kiosks and workstations, necessarily precludes keeping a local copy of the messages on the accessing workstation, so the data can be accessed while online only.

What's New in OWA 2010?

With Exchange Server 2010, Microsoft has provided a much-improved Outlook Web App client. There are many enhanced features that members of the user community have been requesting over the years, and Microsoft has clearly shown that it has been listening.

With OWA 2010, users have the ability to access and manage their messages from a remote web client as effectively as they can from their desktop at the office.

(Real) Multi-Browser Support

Since Exchange 2000 Server, Microsoft has provided two different flavors of the OWA interface with each release of Exchange Server. The Premium user interface enabled clients with recent versions of Internet Explorer to connect with a user experience that rivaled the Outlook email client in both usability and available features. The Light user interface was available for older versions of IE and non-Microsoft browsers. Although the Light version improved with each new revision, it was always several steps behind the Premium version in functionality and was considered by many to be inadequate for regular use.

Now, with Exchange Server 2010, users of Safari and Firefox no longer need to feel like second-class citizens. Outlook Web App provides the same Premium experience for users of Safari 3 (and later) and Firefox 3 (and later) that it does for Internet Explorer, including the ability to print daily, weekly, or monthly calendars, right-click on actionable items, and receive calendar reminders and pop-ups.

Conversation View

The default message view in OWA 2010 is the conversation view. Although a conversation view was available in OWA 2007, the layout was not the same as it is now.

The conversation view groups all the messages in a conversation together and shows them one after the other in the reading pane, allowing users to quickly and easily follow the thread of a conversation in chronological order and view all the responses in one place. Even if various messages in the thread are moved to different folders, their position in the conversation view is kept intact.

Single Page of Messages

In previous versions of OWA, the user's inbox displayed in chunks—up to 50 messages at a time. If a user wanted to scroll farther down the message queue, they had to click to go to the next page, and the next page, and so on.

With OWA 2010, messages are delivered in a single page and the user has the ability to access all messages in a folder using the scroll bar.

Message Filters

OWA users have long had the ability to sort messages in their inbox, but until now, they could not apply filters to their inbox and view the results.

By selecting the Filter button from the toolbar, uses can show a subset of messages that were sent to or CC'd to them, which are flagged or marked with high importance or that meet any of several other criteria.

Using filters can help users quickly locate messages and organize their mailbox in ways they never could before.

Administrative Capabilities

OWA 2010 allows those with the appropriate permissions to administer certain portions of the Exchange Server environment from within OWA.

For those with the appropriate permissions assigned, clicking Options in the top-right corner of the main OWA page and selecting the Account tab presents administrators with several items—one of which is titled Shortcuts to Administrative Tools. In that section, clicking the link called Manage Your Organization offers the ability modify user mailboxes. Modifications include setting or changing the attributes of existing mailboxes, performing tasks such as adding or removing secondary email addresses, changing the user's display name and contact information, or adding MailTips (discussed next). Additionally, administrators can add or remove members from administrative and user roles.

The ability to perform administrative tasks from within the mail client is a welcome addition to the OWA client.

MailTips

Another new feature in Exchange Server 2010 that OWA 2010 can leverage is MailTips. A MailTip is automated or configurable information about a mailbox that can help senders decide if they want to send the message.

Some examples of an automated MailTip include

▶ You are blind carbon copied (BCC'd) on an email and you inadvertently press the Reply to All button. MailTips notifies you that Your address was hidden when this message was sent. If you Reply All, everyone will know you received it.

▶ You're about to send a message to a fellow employee on a time-sensitive matter. When you enter the user's name in OWA, you receive a MailTip that this user is out of the office for the next two weeks and will not be checking email. Prior to MailTips, you needed to send the message and receive an Out of Office reply before you knew this information.

Some examples of a configurable MailTip include

▶ You are about to send an email to a distribution list in your organization called SalesPeople@CompanyABC.com. However, you were not aware that this distribution list goes to 2,500 employees worldwide. If a MailTip has been configured for that distribution list, you could be notified of this before you inadvertently send your query to all those people.

28

▶ You are sending to John Doe and are selecting his name from the GAL. However, there are two John Does in the company. When you resolve the name, you get a message that states "I'm in New Orleans—if you want the John Doe in Albuquerque, you've got the wrong man."

These are only a few examples of the possible uses of MailTips in Exchange Server 2010.

> **NOTE**
>
> MailTips are an Exchange Server feature that can be used with Outlook 2010, and OWA 2010. Legacy Outlook and OWA versions are not supported.

Integrated Instant Messaging

OWA can be combined with a Microsoft Office Communications Server (or the Windows Live Messenger service) to integrate Instant Messaging within the OWA client. OWA 2010 users can tell which employees are logged into the instant messenger service and send and receive IMs within the OWA client.

Integrated SMS Capabilities

When some people think of "texting," they think of teenagers zipping messages back and forth by the hundreds—but there is much more to it than that. Short Message Service (SMS) text messaging is the most widely used data application on the planet, with more than 2 billion active users representing almost 75 percent of all mobile phone users.

Exchange Server 2010 provides the ability to utilize the SMS messaging capabilities of mobile devices from within OWA. Using the OWA 2010 interface, users can configure their email client to send SMS text messages for calendar reminders and voice mail notifications (among other things). This is extremely useful to users who have not embraced smart phones that run the Microsoft Windows Mobile operating system.

Forward as Attachment

Previous versions of OWA allowed users to add attachments to messages, such as photos, documents, spreadsheets, and text files; just about any nonexecutable (program) file could be sent. However, users could NOT take an existing message from their inbox and send it as an attachment in a new message (unless they had installed the S/MIME control discussed later in the chapter).

Now they can. By right-clicking a message in OWA, one of the options is Forward as Attachment. This embeds the original message as an attachment in the new message, preserving the original message's header information intact. This is especially helpful for administrators who work on an issue in which they need to view the header information for the problematic email message.

Users can also drag-and-drop the message they want to forward into a new message. By simply arranging the view so that they can see both the inbox and the new message side by side, the user can select the message they want to forward as an attachment and drop it into the new message. The user can finalize the addressing and content of the message and click Send.

Understanding Available Versions and Security Options

Traditionally, OWA is published to the Internet so that users can access their mailboxes from any Internet-connected browser.

In most cases, the user accesses OWA via forms-based authentication (FBA), which publishes a web page with several options to choose from. (This is the default setting in Exchange Server.) These options determine some basic behaviors of the client and the features the user has access to.

There are two very different OWA versions and two Security Levels to choose from.

Understanding OWA Versions

OWA provides two different versions that have very different capabilities, the Premium version and the Light version.

Premium Version

The default version of OWA is the Premium version, as shown in Figure 28.2. The Premium version is the most functional version of the OWA client. From Exchange 2000 Server through Exchange Server 2007, the Premium version was always restricted to users of later versions of Internet Explorer—those using non-Microsoft browsers could not enjoy the enhanced features that were bundled into the Premium version.

With Exchange Server 2010, the Premium version can now be accessed from a wider range of browsers, including Mozilla's Firefox and Apple's Safari, and most users will want to use this version whenever possible.

Light Version

The Light version enables access to an Exchange Server mailbox with basic functionality, allowing users to navigate through their mail folders, read, reply, and forward messages, search for messages in a mailbox, and view and create new meeting requests and appointments. However, the Light version does not enable users to take advantage of many of the enhanced features that the Premium version enables.

Despite the limited feature set, there are still times when selecting the Light version is recommended. The Light version offers faster logon times for users with slow connections and provides a better accessibility experience for blind and low-vision users. The Light version also is more likely to function on Internet kiosks and in other environments that have strict workstation or network security policies in place.

An example of the Light version is shown in Figure 28.3.

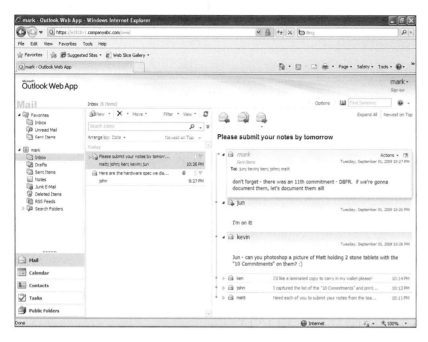

FIGURE 28.2   OWA 2010 Premium version.

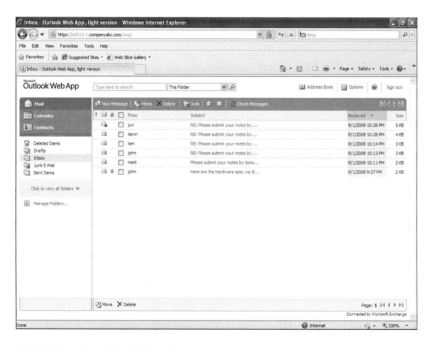

FIGURE 28.3   OWA 2010 Light version.

Differences Between Premium and Light Versions

Some of the differences between the Premium and Light versions of OWA are highlighted here:

- **Reading pane**—The Premium version gives the option of a reading pane that shows selected messages without having to open the message. There is no reading pane in the Light version.

- **Conversation view**—In the Premium version, the default view is the conversation view that groups messages in an email thread together for ease of reading and performing maintenance tasks that apply to the entire thread. The conversation view is not available in the Light version.

- **Tasks module**—Access to the Tasks module is only available in the Premium version.

- **Rules**—The Premium version has full access creating, enabling, disabling, and editing mailbox rules. The Light version has no rules interface.

- **Message formats**—The Premium version enables users to compose messages in either HTML or plain text. The Light version enables message composition in plain text only.

- **Arrange by view**—In the Premium version, messages can be sorted by Date, From, Size, Subject, and several other categories. In the Light version, messages can be sorted only on the From, Subject, Received, and Size categories.

- **Access to public folders**—The Premium version enables access to an organization's public folder infrastructure. The Light version does not.

- **Calendar views**—The Premium version provides different views of the calendar including Day, Work Week, Week, and Monthly views. The Light version offers only a daily view of the calendar.

- **Start and end times**—The Premium version allows users to set any start and finish time that they want (such as 3:15 PM, or 9:05 AM). The Light version enables users to select only start and finish times from a drop-down box, with the available options being on the hour or half hour only (10:00 AM or 10:30 AM, but not 10:15 AM).

- **Reminders**—The Premium version enables users to set meeting reminders and enables pop-up reminders. The Light version doesn't enable these features.

- **Scheduling assistant**—The Premium version offers a fully functional scheduling assistant, with clear and easy-to-use visibility of other users' free/busy times. The Light version offers similar functionality but with a less-intuitive interface.

- **Right-click context menus**—In the Premium version, users can right-click messages or folders and perform various actions such as creating new folders, marking items as read, replying to or forwarding messages, creating new rules, adding the sender to the Blocked or Safe senders list, ignoring a conversation, and many others. In the Light version, there are no right-click capabilities.

▶ **Drag-and-Drop**—The Premium version enables full drag-and-drop capabilities, including the ability to move messages from one folder to another, drag meeting requests and drop them in a new time, and so on. There are no drag-and-drop capabilities in the Light version.

▶ **Spell check**—The Premium version enables users to spell check messages before sending. (Though it does not natively tag misspelled words until the user clicks the spell check button.) The spell check option is not available in the Light version.

There are many other differences between the Premium and Light versions. As can easily be seen, the Premium version offers a significantly enhanced experience over the Light version.

> **NOTE**
>
> As the Premium version is the more fully featured of the two versions, most of the sections in this chapter will be reviewed using that interface. The experience for a user accessing OWA via the Light version will vary significantly.

Understanding Security Options

In addition to selecting between the Premium and Light versions, users logging on to OWA are also presented with two security options that control their connection. The available options are This Is a Public or Shared Computer and This Is a Private Computer.

Public or Shared Computer

This is the initial default setting in OWA and should be used whenever users are on a computer that is not under their direct control. When users log on with the This Is a Public or Shared Computer option, they are telling the Exchange server that they are on a computer that other people have access to and that might or might not meet an organization's recommended security measures.

With this setting, Exchange Server takes a more restrictive stance in some areas of security. Most notably, the user's session will time out after several minutes of inactivity. By default, this timeout period is set to 15 minutes, although organizations can configure the timeout to meet their needs. The timeout for disconnect is only enforceable on sessions using FBA.

Although the timeout lessens the risk of unauthorized personnel accessing an employee's mailbox, it does not eliminate it entirely. Employees should be trained and encouraged to always log out of a public or shared computer and close all browser windows when leaving their session unattended.

Private Computer

If users select This Is a Private Computer when logging on to OWA via FBA, they will, by default, have fewer restrictions placed on them than they would in Public mode. The user's session is allowed to remain active for 12 hours with the private security option, though organizations can change this default setting.

Most organizations enable this because users should select only this option when they are on workstations that nonemployees do not have ready access to.

Using OWA 2010

Outlook Web App provides a powerful and functional web interface that enables users to access email, voice mail, instant messaging, and SMS text messages that are stored in their Microsoft Exchange Server mailbox.

Signing In to OWA

The default location to access OWA is https://servername/owa, in which *servername* is the name of the CAS server hosting OWA. The default authentication method, and the one most commonly used, is Forms-Based Authentication (FBA). If the organization is using FBA for the authentication method, the Sign in screen looks like the one shown in Figure 28.4.

FIGURE 28.4   OWA sign-in screen.

As can be seen from the screenshot, users no longer Log On to OWA; they now Sign In. The users have the choice to select the type of computer they are on (public or private), whether they want to use the Premium version (default) or the Light version, and a place to enter their domain\username and password.

These options are discussed in greater detail in the previous section "Understanding Available Versions and Security Settings." For the rest of this chapter, we work from the Premium version.

Using the New Conversation View

After users log in to OWA, one of the first things they notice (if the mailbox is already populated with messages) is the new default layout, the conversation view.

As shown in Figure 28.5, message threads are viewed in the reading pane on the right side of the screen. This view shows the thread collapsed—where only the initiating email is shown in the inbox pane, but the thread is expanded in the reading pane.

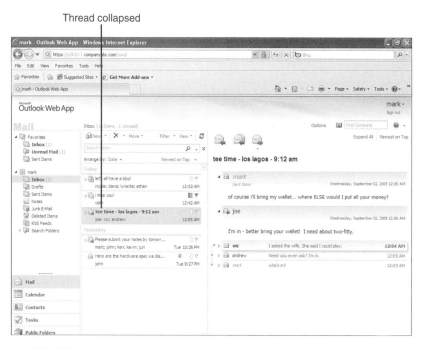

FIGURE 28.5   The conversation view with thread collapsed.

Messages from other users that have been read have a normal font. (See the messages from Joe.)

Unread messages are shown with a bold font. (See the messages from Vic.) Although they are unread, they can still be viewed in the conversation pane.

The thread can also be expanded in the inbox pane by clicking the arrow to the left of the subject line. The expanded view, as shown in Figure 28.6, still shows the unread messages in a bold font in both the view and reading panes.

Because the entire conversation is grouped together and treated as a unit, the entire conversation can easily be moved to another folder, deleted, or ignored completely.

Thread expanded

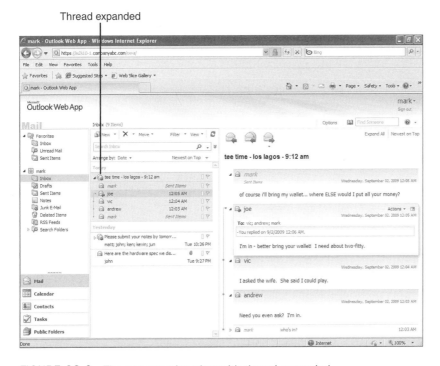

FIGURE 28.6   The conversation view with thread expanded.

Ignoring a Conversation

Users can often find themselves involved in a message thread that no longer applies to or interests them. With the conversation view, it is simple to opt out of the conversation and no longer view messages in that thread.

By right-clicking a message or thread and selecting Ignore Conversation, users can effectively elect to mute all messages within that thread. When a user chooses to ignore a conversation, they see a pop-up (as shown in Figure 28.7) notifying them that OWA will delete all the messages in that thread, except for the ones located in the user's Sent Items. Future messages from the thread will be automatically deleted upon receipt. Users might want to leave this check box unchecked, allowing OWA to remind them when they are deleting an entire conversation and not just a single message.

The messages remain in the users' deleted items folder, so if they decide that they want to review the messages, they can still see them there.

Canceling Ignore Conversation

Of course, there's always the possibility that the user's boss (or the user's boss's boss) will get involved in the thread and ask for input. Should this happen, the user might need to get caught up on the previous messages in the thread quickly!

To unmute the message thread, the user can select one of the messages in the thread in the user's deleted items folder, right-click on it, and select Cancel Ignore Conversation. This moves all the existing items in the conversation out of the Deleted Items folder and

28

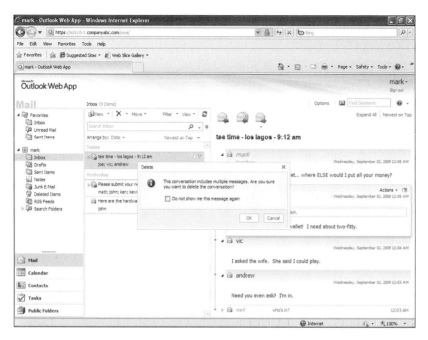

FIGURE 28.7   Results of ignoring a conversation.

back into the previous location and stops the deletion of new items in the conversation thread.

Creating New Folders

Creating new folders to aid in the organization of mail is a basic task, so we won't spend too much time on it here. Suffice to say, if users want to create new folders, they can right-click on the folder that will house the subfolder, click Create New Folder, and name the folder appropriately.

As basic as this sounds, the ability to right-click and perform ANY task does not exist in the Light version of the OWA client, so those new to the Premium version might not be aware of the functionality.

Customizing the Favorites Folder

The Favorites folder at the top of the navigation pane comes with shortcuts to three default folders: Inbox, Unread Mail, and Sent items. Users can configure the Favorites shortcuts to suit their particular needs.

Don't want a folder in the Favorites section? Right-click the folder and select Remove from Favorites.

Want to add a new folder to the favorites? Right-click the desired folder and select Add to Favorites, or grab the folder and drag-and-drop it to the Favorites section.

Want the folders in the Favorites section to show in a different order? Grab the folder you want to move, drag it to the desired location and drop it.

OWA remembers the user's Favorites, even when they log in from another computer. It should be noted that not all items can be added to the Favorites section. Notes, for example, does not have an Add to Favorites option.

Accessing Public Folders

After Microsoft removed the ability to access public folders through OWA in Exchange Server 2007, an extremely vocal user base complained about the decision and it was quickly reversed. The ability to access public folders from OWA was added back in with Exchange Server 2007 SP1, and that ability remains in OWA 2010.

Accessing public folders from OWA 2010 is simple because there is a shortcut for Public Folders at the bottom of the navigation pane.

Using Filters

OWA 2010 now has the ability to filter messages in the mailbox, showing only the messages that match the desired filter. Available options are Sent to Me, Cc'd to Me, and Unread. Additionally, users can filter on a particular color category, on messages from a particular sender, on flagged messages, those marked as high importance, or those with attachments.

Users can also apply multiple filters. For example, a user could elect to look only at messages that are Sent to Me AND that have attachments. For further specificity, filters can be combined with the following search feature.

Searching for Messages

The search feature in OWA 2010 works the same way as it did in OWA 2007. Type the search criteria in the Search Inbox box and click the magnifying glass. If the user wants to change the parameters of the search, he can click the arrow at the right side of the box and change his search parameters to This Folder, This Folder and Subfolders, or Entire Mailbox. He can also set his default setting to any of the preceding three options.

Clicking the double arrow at the far right of the search box shows additional search options. Users can elect to search for the desired terms in the Subject and message body (default), Message body only, or Subject only. Users can also specify to search only for emails with certain words in the From or Sent to fields, or search for messages for which a particular color category has been assigned.

Boolean arguments can be used for advanced searches as well—for example, if users wanted to pull up emails with the words "server" and "specs" but NOT "CompanyXYZ," they could enter a search for `server +specs -companyabc`.

Using the combination of Filters and the Search feature, users can quickly and easily locate messages that they might otherwise have to hunt for manually.

Utilizing the Presence Capabilities

As previously mentioned, OWA 2010 has the ability to be integrated with Office Communications Server (OCS). This enables users to view the "presence" (availability) of other users.

As shown in Figure 28.8, a user can view the presence status of other users in his or her contact list in the navigation pane (left side), and see the presence of email recipients in a message viewed in the reading pane. Different color icons represent different status messages (available, busy, and such), and users can hover their mouse over the icon for a description of the status.

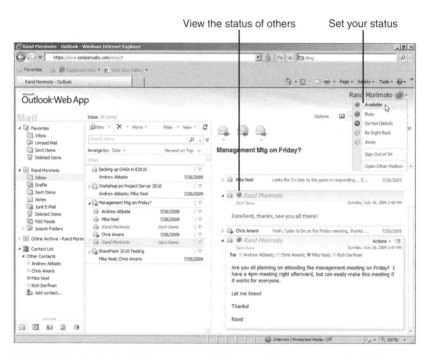

FIGURE 28.8   Instant Messaging and "Presence" integrated with OWA.

By clicking the circle in the top-right corner of the OWA screen, users can easily change their status, allowing other users to easily view their availability.

Integrating Instant Messaging capabilities with OWA requires a functioning Office Communications Server in the environment. There must also be some tweaking done to allow Exchange Server to work with OCS. The steps necessary are covered later in this chapter in the "Configuring OWA and IM Integration" section.

Creating an Email

To create a new email message, navigate to the Inbox view and click the New icon in the toolbar above the view pane. This icon has a picture of a mail message on it. If in the Calendar, Contacts, or Tasks view, users can click the down arrow *next* to the New button and select Message.

Addressing an Email

When opening a new message, by default, the To and CC (carbon copy) fields are available for use. If users want to BCC (blind carbon copy) a recipient, they must click the Options tab and select Show Bcc.

Commonly accepted email etiquette for addressing messages is shown here:

▶ If the message is being sent to only one person, use the To field.

▶ If the message is being sent to several people:

   ▶ Populate the To field with the primary recipients—those to whom the message is directed, who have an action item in the email, or from whom you expect a reply.

   ▶ Populate the CC field with secondary recipients—those who are included for notification purposes only and from whom you do not expect a reply.

   ▶ Last—utilize the BCC field when you want someone to receive a copy of the message but you don't want the other recipients to KNOW the person received a copy. If any of the recipients on the To or CC lines reply to the message, the reply will NOT go to the originally BCC'd user.

> **NOTE**
>
> Over the years, there have been some uncomfortable situations arising from the use of the BCC feature. If BCC recipients have an auto reply set that is configured to reply to all messages, their mailbox might automatically reply to all the original recipients. Also, users receiving a message in which they were BCC'd might not *realize* it and might reply to all users by mistake. Either of these situations could show all the users that the original sender had used the BCC feature.
>
> With the new MailTips feature, if users are BCC'd on an email message and they click Reply to All, a MailTip warns of the action that they are about to take.

There are several ways to address an email message. The most basic is to enter the SMTP email address for the recipient. This is necessary when the user is not inside of your organization's Global Address List (GAL) or within your own contacts list. The sender can also type in the display name or alias of a user in his organization or contacts list. Multiple names can be entered into any of the To, CC, or BCC fields, as long as they are separated by a semicolon (;).

After names or partial names have been entered, the user can click the Check Names button to have OWA check against the Global Address List (GAL) to find the closest match. If several matches are available, they will be displayed and the user can click the correct address.

When typing in the name of a previously used recipient, OWA provides a shortcut to the full name.

Adding a Recipient Using the OWA Address Book

With OWA 2003 and earlier, users trying to locate someone in the corporate Global Address List (GAL) had to enter a name to search on. If the user did not know how to spell the recipient's name, finding him or her could be extremely challenging as there was no Browse feature.

With OWA 2007, Microsoft introduced the ability to browse the address book. Additionally, it added additional features, such as showing the user's free/busy information in the search results. Prior to this feature, users had to open a new meeting request and add the recipient to the meeting request to view the free/busy information.

The address book can be accessed by opening a new mail message or meeting request and clicking on the To CC or BCC fields. The OWA 2010 address book looks almost identical to OWA 2007 and functions in the same way.

An example of the results of a search in the address book (including the user's contact information and free/busy information) is shown in Figure 28.9.

Removing a User from the To, CC, or BCC Fields in a Message

If a user finds that he has accidentally added an incorrect recipient (or if he changes his mind about a recipient), there is no need to cancel the message. A recipient can be removed from any of the three fields by right-clicking the recipient name or email address and selecting Remove from the available choices, or by highlighting the recipient's name and pressing the Delete key.

Adding Attachments

Email has proven to be an extremely effective tool for sharing documents, spreadsheets, photographs, and other files. By attaching them to email messages, users can distribute files to people anywhere in the world.

Attaching files to an email message is easy to do in OWA; however, users should realize that uploading the file from the local machine to the OWA client can take some time if the file is large, if the users connect via a slow link, or both.

Users should also be aware of any message or attachment size restrictions set by their organization. Also, the message must be smaller than the maximum receive size of the recipient's organization.

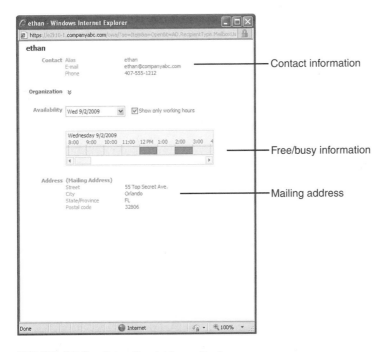

FIGURE 28.9   Using the Address Book.

To determine the MaxSendSize for the organization, administrators can use the get-transportconfig command from the Exchange Management Shell. By default, Exchange Server 2010 has a MaxSendSize and MaxReceiveSize of 10MB.

To attach a file, perform the following steps:

1. Click the paper clip icon on the toolbar at the top of the new message. The Attachment dialog box opens.

2. Browse to the file to be attached, highlight it, and then click Open. Multiple files can be selected and attached by highlighting them together and clicking Open.

3. To add additional attachments, click on the paper clip again and select the desired files.

To make this simple process even *more* convenient, users can drag-and-drop attachments into a message. Simply select the message from the desktop or other location, drag it to the opened new message, and release.

Utilizing the Check Spelling Feature

The Check Spelling feature is heavily relied upon by some users. The Check Spelling feature is accessed when composing a new message and can be activated by clicking the icon in the toolbar with ABC and a check mark.

28

If users need to change the default language used by the spell checker, they can click the down arrow attached to the Spell Check icon and select from one of more than 20 languages.

When activated, the Check Spelling feature reviews the body of the message and underlines any words it cannot identify. The user can right-click on the underlined word and choose from a list of suggested alternatives. Additionally, the user can elect to Ignore the unidentified word or Ignore All instances of the word within the message.

A few things to remember:

▶ The Subject Line is NOT spell-checked.

▶ In the OWA Options section, on the Settings \ Spelling page, the user has the ability to change the behavior of the Check Spelling feature, including instructing the spell checker to 1) Ignore words in UPPERCASE, 2) Ignore words with numbers, and 3) Always check spelling before sending.

▶ The spell checker does not do a grammar check; it will not identify words that are spelled correctly but used incorrectly. For example, if the user were to type "I went too the store," the spell checker will not identify "too" and suggest the proper word "to."

Configuring Message Options: Importance, Sensitivity, and Tracking Options

When creating a new message, additional options can be applied to the message. These options can be accessed when editing a new message by clicking the Options button in the toolbar.

It should be noted that all the settings discussed next are reliant on the ability of the recipient's messaging system to utilize the settings.

Clicking the Options button presents the user with several available settings.

Importance

The message can be sent with one of three levels of importance: Low, Normal, or High. By default, messages are marked as Normal. Configuring a message as Low Importance causes a down-pointing blue arrow icon to appear to the left of the message when the recipient receives the message. Configuring an email message as High Importance attaches a red exclamation mark (!) icon to the message that appears in the message list when the user receives the message.

Setting a level of importance has no impact on the delivery time of the message; it simply creates a visual indicator for the recipient that shows the importance of the message in the opinion of the sender.

Sensitivity

Adding a sensitivity setting to a message is a way for the sender to alert the recipient that the information provided in the email is not for general distribution. When a sensitivity level is set for the message, a visual clue appears at the top of the message (above the Sent and To boxes). The sensitivity setting also appears in the reading pane when the message is highlighted.

As with the Importance option, setting a Sensitivity level is for information only and does not affect the message behavior in any way.

Tracking Options

Setting a Tracking Option enables the sender to request a Delivery Receipt or a Read Receipt for the message sent.

Both the Delivery Receipt and Read Receipt options are *requests*; both rely on the ability of the recipient's email system to actually generate the requested receipt. Some mail systems (and some users) elect NOT to send receipts of any kind, nullifying the request.

Senders should note that receiving a Read Receipt does not necessarily ensure the message has been read, as some rules mark messages as Read even though the user has never laid eyes on them.

Email Security

If the sending users have installed the S/MIME controls in their OWA, the option to Encrypt Message Contents and Attachments and Add a Digital Signature to This Message appears on the Message Options page.

Other Available Options

When composing an email in HTML format, the user can change the font type, size, and color, and apply properties to the font, such as making the text **bold**, *italicized*, or underlined—or ***all of the above***. Users can add bullet points, numbered lists, insert a signature into the message, and perform several other available actions. There are several other options available in the formatting toolbar, and users familiar with Microsoft products will find most of them familiar.

Sending the Email

When the message has been addressed, the desired subject line and body have been composed, and any files have been attached, the email can be sent by clicking the Send button at the top of the window. At this time, if there are any issues with the names in the To, CC, or BCC boxes, OWA presents a dialog box highlighting the names to be resolved. Unresolved recipients can be modified or removed.

After all addresses are resolved, click Send again and the message is sent.

Reading an Email

When a new message arrives in the user's mailbox, there are three visible cues, as shown in Figure 28.10. First, a New Message notification pops up and remains for 4 to 5 seconds. Second, the Unread Message Count is incremented, and third, the message appears in the inbox view as unread (unless the user has rules in place to move the message elsewhere or mark it as read).

Message count
showing number of
unread messages

New message notification

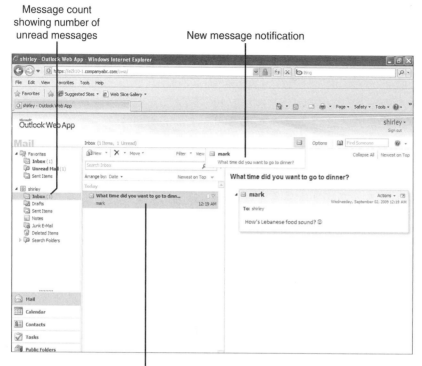

Unread messages appear in bold font.

FIGURE 28.10   New message notifications.

OWA checks for new messages frequently, and the user does not have to refresh the screen to see them. However, users can elect to manually initiate a new message check by clicking the Check Messages button in the toolbar, which is the icon with two curved arrows in a circle next to the View tab.

If a new message arrives that Exchange Server or Outlook has classified as a Junk E-Mail and placed into the Junk E-Mail folder, the new message pop-up window does not appear.

To read an email, users can select the message with the mouse and view it in the reading pane. Alternatively, users can double-click the message to open it in its own window.

Flagging Messages and Applying Categories

OWA enables users to manage their messages by Flagging them or Applying Categories to the message. Both of these features are available from the toolbar when viewing an open message.

Flagging Messages

Messages can be flagged for follow up by clicking the Flag icon in the toolbar. Available time frames include Today, Tomorrow, This Week, or Next Week, or the user can select a custom date from a calendar.

Messages that have been Flagged for Follow Up have a visual indicator (a flag) attached to the message in the inbox. The message also appears in the Tasks folder.

When the flag is no longer needed, the user can simply click on it in the navigation pane, the reading pane, or in the open message to mark it as Complete.

Categories

Categories can be applied to a message as well—another visual indicator in the navigation and reading panes to help the user remember the importance of a message. Various colors can be applied to the category, selecting them from the toolbar while viewing a message. A single message can have multiple categories assigned to it.

> **NOTE**
>
> The colors used for categories have no assigned significance within OWA or Outlook. Each user or organization can choose to designate certain colors for different levels of importance or classification. The colored rectangles merely designate similarities or differences between messages.

When a categorized message no longer needs to be singled out, the user can right-click the colored rectangle and choose Clear Categories, returning it to a grayed-out rectangle.

Figure 28.11 shows examples of a message with a follow-up flag and assigned categories.

Replying to or Forwarding an Email

Users can reply to a message or forward it to other recipients. As shown in Figure 28.12, several choices are available to perform these actions: Reply, Reply to All, Forward, and Forward as Attachment.

- ▶ Reply:
  - ▶ Represented by a single envelope with a left-facing blue arrow.
  - ▶ A new email is generated that has the To: field preaddressed with the address of the sender of the original message.
  - ▶ The original message is included in the body of the new email (at the bottom), and the subject line is prepended with RE:.
  - ▶ Attachments sent in the original email are NOT included in a reply.
- ▶ Reply to All:
  - ▶ Represented by a double envelope with a left-facing blue arrow.
  - ▶ A new email is generated with the To: field preaddressed with the sender of the original message AND all recipients that were in the To: field of the original message. The CC: field is preaddressed with recipients in the CC: field of the original message.
  - ▶ The original message is included in the body of the new email (at the bottom) and the subject line is prepended with RE:.

28

Follow-up flags

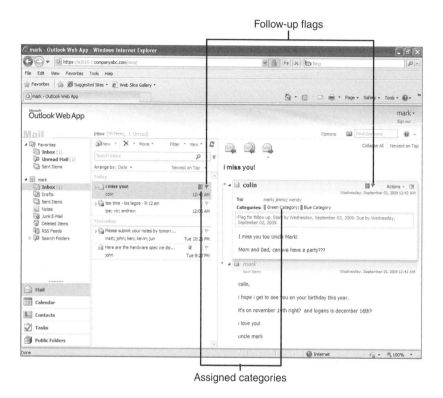

Assigned categories

FIGURE 28.11   Message with follow-up flags and assigned categories.

- ▶ Attachments sent in the original email are NOT included in a Reply to All.
- ▶ Forward:
  - ▶ Represented by a single envelope with a right-facing blue arrow.
  - ▶ A new email is generated, but no addressing fields are preaddressed.
  - ▶ The original message is included in the body of the new email (at the bottom), and the subject line is prepended with FW:.
  - ▶ Attachments sent in the original email ARE included in the Forward.
- ▶ Forward as Attachment:
  - ▶ Accessed by clicking the downward pointing arrow on the Forward icon in the reading pane.
  - ▶ A new email is generated, but no addressing fields are preaddressed.
  - ▶ The original message is included as an attachment of the new message.
  - ▶ Attachments sent in the original email remain in the original email, which is in turn forwarded as an attachment of the new message.

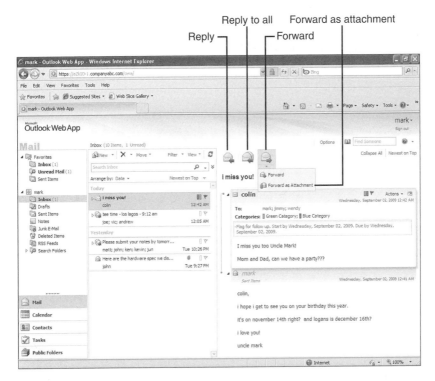

FIGURE 28.12   Reply, Reply to All, Forward, and Forward As Attachment options.

All these options are also available by right-clicking a message in the view pane and selecting from the available action items, or by right-clicking the envelope icon in the message in the reading pane.

Marking Messages as Read or Unread

Some users choose to manage the Read status of messages to aid in their message organizing or to remind themselves to follow up on the message. For example, if a user reads a message from his or her boss stating, "Please contact me regarding this tomorrow," the user might want to leave the message marked Unread so he or she can remember to look at it the next day.

To change the status of a message, simply right-click the message. If the message is already Read, the option to Mark as Unread appears in the action pane. If the message is Unread, the option to Mark as Read appears.

Viewing User Properties

When viewing a message from another member of their organization, the recipients can click on the sender's name to bring up available information about the sender.

When the user Properties page appears, some of the information available includes

- ▶ Sender Name (first and last)

- ▶ Alias

- ▶ Email address

- ▶ Phone numbers

- ▶ Job title

- ▶ Department

- ▶ Company

- ▶ Manager

- ▶ Availability (if calendar path is known and published)

- ▶ Mailing address

If the sender is a member of the user's organization, this information is pulled from the Active Directory. If not, any available information is pulled from the user's contacts list.

Deleting Email

Due to the implementation of the conversation view in OWA, deleting a message can be a little trickier than before. Emails can be deleted from the navigation pane by right-clicking and selecting Delete or by selecting the message and clicking the Delete icon, represented by a big X.

Selecting a top-level message in a conversation and selecting Delete brings up a warning message that states, "This conversation includes multiple messages. Are you sure you want to delete the conversation?" If deleting the conversation was the intent, the user can click OK and continue. Messages that have been deleted still show up in the conversation view, as long as the conversation itself has not been deleted. However, they show their current location as Deleted.

Messages can be deleted from the reading pane as well. Right-click the envelope icon in the top-left corner of the message and select Delete from the Action menu.

To delete a message while it's open, click the icon with the black X in the open email message.

Recover Deleted Items

Unlike previous versions of OWA, OWA 2010 enables users to Recover Deleted Items by right-clicking on the Deleted Items folder. In OWA 2007, users had to go in through the options pane to access this feature. Users can recover items that were recently permanently deleted or emptied from the Deleted Items folder. When recovering these messages, users can recover them to a folder of their choice.

To do so, right click the Deleted Items folder and click Recover Deleted Items. From the recoverable items folder, users can select a message (or messages) and recover them or purge from their mailboxes completely. To recover the message, select it and click the Recover Selected Items icon, identified by a yellow envelope with a curved blue arrow.

Reading Attachments

When a message arrives with an attachment, the message displays with a paper clip icon next to the subject line. In the reading pane or in an opened email, attachments appear shown next to the word Attachments.

Some attachments, such as executable programs, might be blocked by the security policies of your organization. Additionally, some attachments might be removed or blocked by the organization's antivirus software. Bear in mind, these attachments might be blocked or stripped by the policies of the *sender's* organization as well.

Additional restrictions on attachments can be placed by the organization on OWA sessions from "public" computers. Because opening documents within OWA can potentially leave copies of the file in the accessing computer's pagefile or browser cache, some organizations limit the type of attachments that can be accessed from public computers.

There are several methods available to access attachments:

▸ **Open the attachment**—Double-clicking the attachment gives the user the option to Open or Save the attachment. If the user selects Open, OWA attempts to download the file and open it for viewing. For many proprietary file types (Microsoft Office Documents, Adobe .PDF files, and such), the computer must have an application associated with the file type that is capable of opening the attachment. For example, if you choose to open a Microsoft Word document, the computer must have Microsoft Word installed to open the attachment when it is downloaded.

▸ **Save the attachment**—Double-clicking the attachment also gives the option to save the attachment. This option enables the user to save the attachment to a drive on the computer accessing OWA. Users should be extremely cautious because downloading documents onto public workstations could put private intellectual property at risk. As previously mentioned, to view the attachment after it has been saved locally, the computer must have an application capable of opening the file.

▸ **Open as web page**—OWA enables many file types to be opened with a built-in feature called WebReady Document Viewing. This feature enables OWA to convert supported document types into an HTML file and display them within a browser window. If the document type accessed is supported, beside the attachment name the user can see a link that says Open as Web Page. Clicking this link opens the supported attachment within a browser window for viewing.

Using the Calendar in OWA

Outlook 2010 provides a fully functional calendar for managing personal meeting appointments, group appointments, and recurring events. The Calendar feature in OWA includes the same functionality as the Outlook client, including appointment views, meeting creation, and editing.

28

Sharing Your Calendar

New in OWA 2010 is a long-awaited feature: the ability to share your calendar with others from within OWA. This capability has been available in the full-blown Outlook client, but now users can configure access to their calendar from a new and easy-to-use interface.

From within the Calendar view, there is a button in the toolbar labeled Share. Clicking this button brings up three options: Open a Shared Calendar, Share a Calendar, and Change Sharing Permissions.

Open a Shared Calendar

Selecting this option enables the user to open other users' calendars in a side-by-side view, as shown in Figure 28.13. The requesting user must have access to the requested calendar for this feature to work. By default, users within an organization have the ability to view other users' free/busy information, but details about the other users' meetings are not shared.

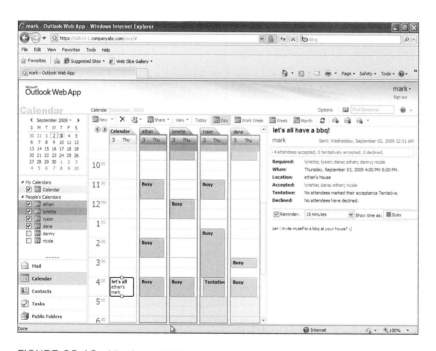

FIGURE 28.13   Viewing multiple calendars.

Up to five calendars can be viewed simultaneously, in any of the available views (Day, Work Week, Week, Month). After five calendars have been selected, the user must deselect one if they want to add another.

When the user exits OWA and logs back in again, the calendar reverts to viewing his or her calendar only; however, the other users who have been added remain in the People's Calendars section in the left pane, ready to be selected again.

Share a Calendar

Selecting Share a Calendar opens a new window, as shown in Figure 28.14. Users can type the name of the person that they want to share their calendar with (or select it from the GAL by clicking the TO button). The default subject, which states "I'd like to share my calendar with you" can be changed if desired, and the level of access can be selected. The available options follow:

- Share Free/Busy Information

- Share Free/Busy Information Including Subject and Location

- Share All Information

Additionally, the user can select the option that states "I want to request permission to view the recipient's Calendar folder."

Body text can be added to the message as well, if desired, and the user then clicks Send.

The recipient receives an email message that enables him or her to click an icon that states Add This Calendar. Upon clicking the icon, the sender's calendar will be added to the People's Calendar section for the recipient. When selected, the appropriate level of access is available.

If the request for reciprocation was included, the recipient also has an icon that states Share My Calendar in the email message. Upon clicking this icon, the Share a Calendar page shown in Figure 28.14 is shown again, allowing this user to select the appropriate

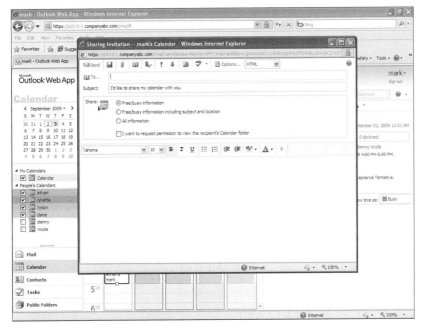

FIGURE 28.14   Sending an invitation to share calendar information.

level of access. As before, an email is sent with an icon enabling the original sender to Add This Calendar.

This process sounds much more complicated than it is in practice, and the feature is a welcome addition and great enhancement to the OWA calendaring utility.

Change Sharing Permissions

The third option, Change Sharing Permissions, opens a new pane that enables users to see what other users have been granted access to their calendars. Two columns appear: Shared With and Permission Granted.

Users can select someone with access to their calendar and click the Delete button, identified by a large X, to stop sharing their calendar with that individual.

When this occurs, the deleted user reverts back to the permissions allowed to all users in the organization (by default, the ability to view free/busy, but no meeting details).

Using Views

Users can view their calendars in several different ways. By selecting the appropriate icon in the toolbar, users can select either

- ▶ **Today**—The Today view jumps directly to the current date in the Day view.

- ▶ **Day**—The Day view displays one day at a time. Users can change the day they view by either selecting the desired day from the calendar in the left pane or by clicking the left and right (Previous and Next) arrows under the New icon.

- ▶ **Work Week**—The Work Week view displays a full week as defined in the user's Options\Settings\Calendar tab (for example, Mon–Fri).

- ▶ **Week**—The Week view displays one week at a time (Sun–Sat).

- ▶ **Month**—The Month view shows the entire month with brief information about each of the meetings in each day.

It might go without saying, but as the user changes from one view to the next, if more days are shown, less information about individual meetings might be shown. For the greatest detail, use the Day view and select the desired day from the calendar.

Scheduling Meetings in OWA

When scheduling meetings or appointments in OWA 2010, users can see that little has changed since Outlook 2007—another area where Microsoft already "had it right" and needed little improvement.

When scheduling a meeting, the familiar Scheduling Assistant is there to help. Users can add recipients and/or meeting rooms to their invitation, view the free/busy time for all people and resources, and select a recommended time for the meeting. Attendees can be marked as Required or Optional, which factors in to the attempt to find a free time that works for the largest number of people.

Suggested times are automatically displayed and tell the user how many of the invited people are free at that time (such as "3 of 3 free" or "2 of 3 free") and whether the rooms selected are available.

To schedule a meeting using the Scheduling Assistant, as shown in Figure 28.15, perform the following steps:

1. From OWA, click the Calendar button in the Outlook toolbar and click New Meeting Request. (Alternatively, users can select the drop-down arrow next to New on the main page and select Meeting Request.)

2. Click the Scheduling Assistant tab; then type in the names of the attendees for the meeting, clicking the arrows next to their names to determine if they are Required Attendees, Optional Attendees, or Resources.

3. Choose a Suggested Time that best meets the requirements; then click the Appointments tab.

4. Enter the remaining meeting information, including Subject, Location, a Reminder time frame, and so on and click Send.

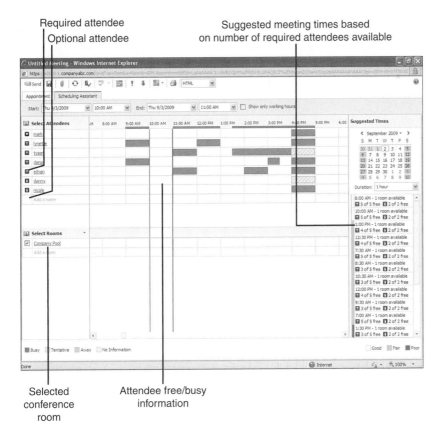

FIGURE 28.15   Scheduling a new meeting request with Scheduling Assistant.

Changing Meeting Times in OWA

To reschedule a meeting in OWA, users can open the appointment, change the time in the appointment, and send an update. Alternatively, users can simply select the appointment and drag-and-drop it in the newly selected time slot. The appointment relocates and gives the user the option to Send Meeting Updates or Cancel. If the user selects Cancel, the meeting is returned to its former time.

Receiving Task and Calendar Reminders

The premium version of OWA enables users to receive pop-up reminders when meetings or tasks are coming due. A dialog box appears listing current reminders. Users can either double-click the item to open it in a new window or click one of the following buttons:

▶ **Dismiss All**—All reminders shown in the current window will be dismissed. No further reminders for these items will be displayed.

▶ **Dismiss**—Selecting this button will dismiss the highlighted (selected) item. No further reminders will be displayed for this item.

▶ **Open Item**—Same as double-clicking the item. This option opens the appointment/task in a new window for review.

▶ **Snooze**—One other option is available. Under the statement Click Snooze to be Reminded Again In, there is a drop-down box with various time frames. The user can select one of the time frames (the default is the ever-useful "5 Minutes Before Start") and click the Snooze button. Like the Snooze button on an alarm clock, this temporarily dismisses the reminder and allows it to pop up again 5 minutes before the appointment—just in time for the user to attend/dial in promptly.

To view current/undismissed reminders at any time, users can click the alarm icon at the top of the page (next to the Options button) while in the Calendar view.

Using Tasks in OWA

The Tasks option in OWA is like an electronic to-do list, enabling the user to track start dates, due dates, reminders, and associated notes. Tasks can be created, viewed, and organized. Additionally, email messages with a Follow Up flag configured appear in the Tasks view as a visual reminder to address the issue.

The Tasks feature is one of the most underutilized of the Outlook and OWA features. Many users simply do not understand how helpful the feature can be and how easy it is to use.

Creating Tasks

Users can create tasks in OWA 2010 just as they do in Outlook. Tasks can remind users of jobs that must be completed by a certain date or time, to document the percentage of a task that has been completed, or to track billable hours and mileage driven for particular clients.

Users can also set reminders on tasks that generate a pop-up message in OWA.

To create a task:

1. Open the Tasks Interface from the main OWA page.
2. Click the New button.
3. Enter the Subject of the task and populate desired fields such as Start date, Due date, Status, Priority, and others.
4. If desired, set a reminder on the task to enable a Pop Up reminder in OWA.
5. When finished, click Save and Close.

Task Views

Users can configure the Tasks page, electing to show All tasks or only those that are Active, Overdue, or Complete. Tasks can be sorted by Due Date, Subject, or several other categories and can have categories assigned to them for easier identification.

In addition, Emails that have been flagged for follow up can be replied to or forwarded from within the tasks view.

Using Contacts in OWA

The Contacts feature enables users to create a personal address book to keep track of people and their phone numbers, email addresses, physical address, and many other attributes. By entering users into the Contacts list, users can easily send emails and meeting requests to those contacts, populating their address in an email message by simply entering their name in the To: field. Users can also create personal Groups, a collection of recipients from inside and outside the organization.

As with the Tasks feature, creating a new contact is a basic task that consists of clicking New Contact, populating the data, and saving the contact.

User can elect to show All contacts, only the contacts classified as People, or only contacts classified as Groups.

Using Keyboard Shortcuts

Many of the familiar keyboard shortcuts used in Microsoft Outlook can be used while working in OWA. Table 28.1 shows some of the keyboard shortcuts that OWA 2010 recognizes.

TABLE 28.1   Keyboard Shortcuts Available in the OWA Client

Shortcut	Option
In the Inbox View	
Ctrl+N	Open a new message window.
Ctrl+Q	Mark message as read.

28

TABLE 28.1   Keyboard Shortcuts Available in the OWA Client

Shortcut	Option
Ctrl+U	Mark message as unread.
Ctrl+R	Reply to message.
Ctrl+Shift+F	Forward the selected message.
In Opened Message, While Creating a Message	
Ctrl+S	Save the message.
Ctrl+Enter or Alt+S	Send the message.
[F7]	Activate Spell Check.
Ctrl+K	Check names in the address boxes.
In Calendar View	
Ctrl+N	Create a new appointment.
In Contracts View	
Ctrl+N	Create a new contact distribution list.
In Task View	
Ctrl+N	Create a new task.

The Options Page

Like the main Inbox view, the options page has a similar look and feel to that of OWA 2007. Again, the view is less cluttered and easy to navigate. However, there are quite a few new options available to the user.

Clicking on Options in the top-right part of the OWA screen takes the user to the Options page. The home view of the Options page is the Account tab.

The Account Tab

In the Account tab, users have access to view/edit their general account information. Additionally, there are several shortcuts to other commonly used tasks.

Account Information

In the Account Information section, as shown in Figure 28.16, users can view their existing Display name, E-mail address, and Contact Numbers. Users can also quickly and easily update particular aspects of their personal contact information, changing their Contact Location and Contact numbers and storing the updated information in the GAL. This

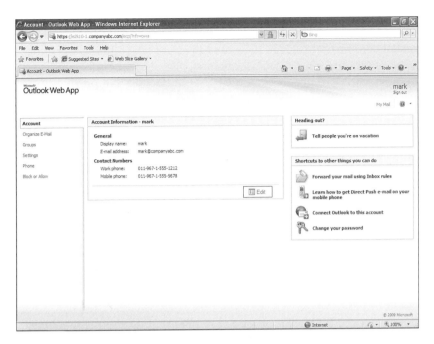

FIGURE 28.16   The Account tab.

feature enables users to modify their information without requesting assistance from a help desk—a process that is time-consuming and prevents the help desk from focusing on more critical tasks. Some of these fields are enabled by default, and modifying which fields are accessible can be accomplished by using the Role Based Access Control (RBAC).

> **NOTE**
>
> The ability of users to edit each of these fields is controlled by using the Role Based Access Control (RBAC). Organizations that do not want users to edit their work phone number (for example) can disable this feature for some or all users.

Shortcuts to Other Things You Can Do

The account page also has shortcuts to some specific help topics and several tasks that users often use.

The help topics include Learn How to Get Direct Push E-mail on Your Mobile Phone and Connect Outlook to This Account.

The other shortcuts (Organize Your Inbox with Rules and Change Your Password) are links to other sections of the Options tab. Each of these is covered in the following paragraphs.

The Organize E-Mail Tab

On the Organize E-Mail tab, the user is given the ability to create Inbox Rules and configure Automatic Replies. Additionally, users can now request Delivery Reports for messages that they have sent or received, placing a task in the hands of the user that previously would have required administrative intervention.

Inbox Rules

The first of the available Organize E-Mail utilities is the Organize Your Inbox with Rules link, OWA 2010's interface for creating, editing, enabling, disabling, or deleting mailbox rules.

The Rule Wizard is easy to use, and rules can be created that adhere to many situations. Many of the messaging fields are actionable, allowing rules to be written based on the sender or recipient address, specific words in the subject or body, if the message is marked urgent, if the message has an attachment, and several other options.

Various action items are available, including moving, copying or deleting the message, marking the message as read, or forwarding or redirecting the message to other users.

Exceptions can be built into the rule as well, allowing further specificity in the rule creation. The list of possible exceptions is as extensive as the list of previously mentioned possible actionable items.

Users should remember that rules are applied in order. An action item in the first rule might be negated by an action item in a later rule, unless the user has Stop Processing More Rules selected at the end of the rule creation. This was an option in previous versions of OWA but was hidden away under the Perform Other Actions screen and was NOT enabled by default.

In OWA 2010, the option to Stop Processing More Rules is now selected by default and is visible on the New Inbox Rule front page.

> **NOTE**
>
> With Exchange Server 2010's capability to send and receive text messages, a user can even create a rule that says, "If the Incoming Message Meets These Certain Criteria, Send a Text Message to a Particular Phone Number," an extremely useful tool for users who are often away from their computer.

Automatic Replies

The next item in the Organize E-Mail tab is the Automatic Replies option, which is OWA 2010's version of the Out of Office Assistant. Users can configure automatic replies by either turning on the feature immediately or by configuring a period of time when the automatic replies should start and end.

Users have the option to reply only to senders from inside of their organization or to both internal and external senders. If electing to reply to external senders, there is the further option to reply to *all* external senders, or only those in the user's contacts list.

If the users decide to reply to both internal and external senders, the users can then create custom replies for each group. This can be helpful when there is information the users want to share with their co-workers during an absence (such as emergency contact information), but that they do NOT want to share with the rest of the world.

In the early days of automatic replies, administrators had to be on the alert for *mail storms* that could be created by dueling automatic replies. For example, UserA sends a message to 5 people (or 50 people). UserB, one of those recipients, has an automatic reply that replies to all recipients of the message, including UserC. UserC also has automatic replies enabled and sends the message back to UserB. UserB and UserC automatically replying to each other could potentially create thousands and thousands of messages, bringing the messaging system to its knees, before the problem was discovered and shut down.

To prevent this situation (and others like it) OWA and Outlook have, for the past several revisions, allowed only one automatic reply per sender during each out-of-office period.

Delivery Reports

The Delivery Reports option is new in OWA 2010 and is a welcome addition. As shown in Figure 28.17, the Delivery Reports option enables users to search for delivery information on messages that they have sent or received during the previous 2-week period.

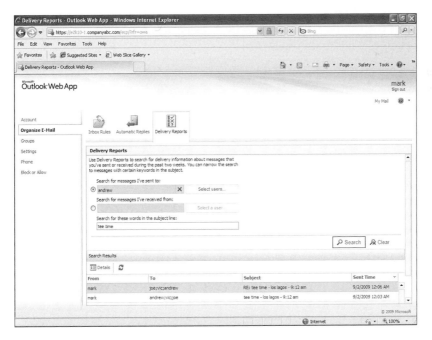

FIGURE 28.17   Searching for a Sent Message using OWA Delivery Reports.

Users can either type the SMTP email address (user@companyabc) in the I've Sent To or I've Received From fields or select the user from the Global Address List (GAL) by clicking the Add Users button. Multiple addresses can be separated by a comma.

Additionally, users can be more specific in their search by looking for messages with specific words in the subject line.

The Groups Tab

Another area where users can utilize the new self-service tools built into Exchange Server 2010 is in the Groups tab.

In keeping with Microsoft's new concept of enabling users to self-manage basic tasks, the Groups tab enables users to see what Public Groups they are a member of, to join or leave Public Groups that already exist, and to create new Public Groups. By default, users only have the ability to join or leave groups that already exist. The creation of new groups from the OWA interface is restricted using Role Based Access Control (RBAC). To give users the ability to create new public groups, the administrator can edit the Default Role Assignment Policy under User Roles. Placing a check mark in the box next to My Distribution Groups allows users to create and manage their own groups.

A user with the ability to create new public groups is shown in Figure 28.18. The pane is split into two parts: Public Groups I Belong To and Public Groups I Own.

In the Public Groups I Belong To section, users can join or leave a group, search for a group, or view the details of a group.

In the Public Groups I Own section, users can create or delete a group that they own or view/change the details of a group that they own.

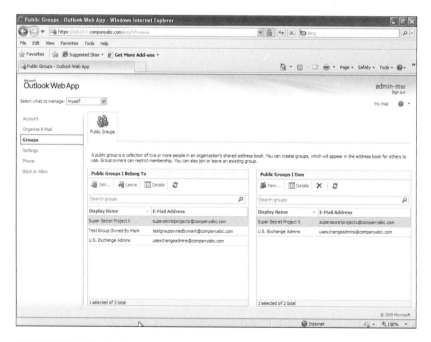

FIGURE 28.18   Public Groups management.

To create a new Public Group

1. Click on the New button.

2. Enter a Display name for the group. This is the name that will appear in the Global Address List (GAL) and will appear on the To line when an email is sent to the group. This name can be user-friendly so that people can identify the purpose of the group.

3. Enter the Alias. The alias will be part of the groups email address, so it must adhere to the RFC specifications for SMTP addresses. The alias can contain

   ▶ Uppercase and lowercase English letters (a–z, A–Z)

   ▶ Digits 0 through 9

   ▶ Characters ! # $ % & ' * + - / = ? ^ _ ` { | } ~

   ▶ Character . (the period) if it is not the first or last character and does not appear two or more times consecutively

   ▶ When given free reign, users often begin their email addresses with a special character so that it appears at the top of the GAL. Of course, after a thousand users have done so, the benefit is lost. Administrators should develop a naming convention for email addresses and enforce it strictly.

4. Enter a description. The description field can be seen by users when they double-click the alias in an email they are composing. Users should always enter a description that is accurate and thorough.

5. If necessary, modify the Ownership. By default, the creator of the group will be the Owner. Users can add other users as owners of the group (and remove them after) if they want.

6. Confirm/modify the group Membership. By default, group owners will be added as members of the new group. If this is not desired, remove the check mark for that selection. To populate the group with users, click the Add button. Members of the organization can be added to the group by searching and selecting them from the GAL. Alternatively, the group creator can leave the group empty and allow people to add themselves if they want.

7. Set the appropriate setting for Membership Approval. The available options follow:

   ▶ **Open:** Anyone can join this group without being approved by the group owners.

   ▶ **Closed:** Members can be added only by the group owners. All requests to join will be rejected automatically.

   ▶ **Owner Approval:** All requests are approved or rejected by the group owners.

8. Click Save to create the group.

After the group has been created, additional options can be configured. By looking in the Public Groups I Own section, selecting the group, and clicking Details (or double-clicking

28

the group), owners can modify the preceding items or configure any of the following additional settings:

▶ **Delivery Management:** The default (empty) enables anyone to send to the group, whether they are members of that group. Users can elect to add individuals or other groups in this field, but only those users can send messages to the group. One common scenario is to select the name of the group; this enables only members of the group to send messages to the group.

▶ **Message Approval:** By placing a check mark in Messages Sent to This Group Have to Be Approved by a Moderator and adding a user (or users), the group becomes a Moderated group in which messages are sent to the moderators for approval *before* being sent to the group members. Additionally, when the group becomes Moderated, there are three options for what should be done with messages that aren't approved:

  ▶ Notify all senders when their messages aren't approved.

  ▶ Notify senders in your organization only when their messages aren't approved.

  ▶ Don't notify anyone when a message isn't approved.

▶ **MailTip:** The group owner can create a MailTip that will be displayed when people send email to the group. The MailTip will appear in the infobar of senders with Outlook 2010/OWA 2010 or later. Although users can enter up to 492 characters in the MailTip field (including HTML tags), only 175 characters (including spaces) will appear in the infobar.

When a user addresses an email to the Public Group, they can double-click the group name to find out details about the group, including the current members.

> **NOTE**
>
> As with the ability for users to edit their own Account Information, the ability of users to create and edit Public Groups is managed utilizing the Role Based Access Control (RBAC).

The Settings Tab

Under the Settings tab, users can customize their mailbox configuration to suit their own preferences. There are many options available, some of which follow.

Mail

In the Mail section, users can assign an E-Mail signature, configure the Message Format, configure notifications or sounds for new messages, configure the behavior of the reading pane, and modify the behavior of the conversation view.

Setting a Default Signature

Users can configure an E-Mail Signature that can be manually entered when creating an email or added automatically to all emails the users send. Signatures usually provide personal information about the sender—such as name, company, title, and phone number—allowing the user to configure the information once and have it included in emails without typing it over and over. To configure an E-Mail signature

1. Enter the Options page by clicking the Options link in the top-right corner of the inbox page.

2. Click Settings in the far-left pane and select the Mail tab.

3. In the E-Mail Signature area, enter the content of the signature utilizing the editing options available in the toolbar.

4. If desired, select the option to Automatically Include My Signature on Messages I Send.

5. Click the Save button in the bottom-right corner.

If the Automatically Include My Signature on Messages I Send option is selected, the signature appears on any messages created from scratch, forwarded, or replied to. If that option is not checked, the user can add the signature on a message-by-message basis when composing an email. To add the signature manually, begin editing a message and then click the icon in the toolbar that is shown as a sheet of paper with a hand holding a pen.

Message Format

Users can instruct OWA to always show the BCC and/or From fields when creating a new email message. By showing the From field, users can elect to send the message as an account other than their own. The user MUST have Send As permissions to that other account for this option to work.

Users can also elect to compose new messages in HTML format (the default), or in plain text, and can select the default font they would like to compose messages in.

Read Receipts

By default, OWA is configured to ask the user before sending a response to a read receipt request. Users can change this default behavior by selecting Always Send a Response to automatically respond to these requests, or Never Send a Response to stop prompting the user to determine if they want to allow the read receipt to go out.

Reading Pane

The default behavior of the reading pane can be configured in this section, enabling users to select under what circumstances they want messages marked as Read.

If the user selects Mark the Item Displayed in the Reading Pane as Read, the user can then configure the default wait period that states how long the item must be viewed in the reading pane before being marked as Read.

Users can also elect to Mark the Item as Read When the Selection Changes, the default behavior in OWA. When users have a message in the reading pane and then change to another message, the one they were reading gets marked as Read.

Lastly, the user can elect to Don't Automatically Mark Items as Read. This option requires the user to manually mark the item as Read or the message will be marked as Read when the message is actually opened and viewed.

Conversations

The last of the configurable items in the Mail tab is the Conversations feature. Users can elect whether they want messages in the reading pane sorted with the Newest Message on Top (the default setting) or the Newest Message on Bottom.

Users can also select how to sort the messages in the list view in an expanded conversation: either "Match the Sort Order of the Reading Pane" (default) or "Show the Conversation Tree."

Lastly, users can elect to Hide Deleted Items in the conversation view.

Spelling

As you might imagine, in the Spelling section users can modify the behavior of the built-in spell check feature, including selecting which language dictionary they want to use and what types of words should be ignored. Users can also configure Outlook to Always Check Spelling Before Sending, which is a useful option for those whose spelling skills are less than optimal.

Calendar

The appearance of the calendar can be modified here, including setting the days of the week and hours of the day that are the normal working hours for the user. Accurately setting these options helps ensure others will not schedule meetings during the user's regular time off.

Users can configure the behavior of their Reminders and the Automatic Processing of Meeting Requests here as well.

Two new features have been added in the OWA 2010 Calendar Options section: Text Messaging Notifications and a Calendar Troubleshooting utility.

Text Messaging Notifications

The user can elect to set up Text Messaging notifications, which involves selecting the Locale (country or region that the mobile phone is registered in) and Mobile operator (company that provides the user's cell phone service). Next, the user enters the telephone number for the cell phone, including Area Code.

A six-digit passcode will be generated and sent to the user's cell phone. Upon receipt, that passcode is entered into OWA to finalize the setup. After text messaging notifications have been configured, users can opt to receive SMS text messages when the calendar is updated, when meeting reminders are triggered, or messages that contain their daily calendar agenda.

Calendar Troubleshooting Utility

There are as many different ways to use the calendaring capabilities of Exchange Server as there are users. With so many available options, sooner or later many users find their calendar is not acting as they feel it should. With the Calendar Troubleshooter, OWA can access the users' calendar logs. Users can enter the subject of the meeting they have a question about and click Send My Calendar Logs, and Exchange Server will locate the logs associated with that meeting request and contact the users when complete.

General

The General section enables users to configure whether name resolution should first check the Global Address List (GAL) or their personal Contacts. Users can also elect to utilize the Blind and Low Vision Experience. However, selecting this option requires the users to log off and back on, and the users are redirected to the Light version of OWA which, as stated before, enables significantly fewer features and capabilities.

Regional

In the Regional Settings section, users can configure their preferred language, date format, time format, and current time zone. As remote users travel to different regions, they can easily update their configuration with their current time zone, displaying message delivery times and calendar items in the appropriate time for their location.

Password

In the Password section, as you would expect, users are presented with the option to change their password.

As basic as this capability is, users who have been using OWA through all its past iterations know that this feature was not always included. It could be enabled in OWA 2003 through some rather complicated steps and was included by default for the first time in OWA 2007.

Changing the password requires three common steps. The users enter their old (current) password, new password, and new password a second time to Confirm New Password. By typing the password twice, the chance that the users mistyped the password is greatly reduced.

Click on Save to update the password.

S/MIME

OWA 2010 supports the ability for users to elect to encrypt and digitally sign messages that they send. As with previous versions of OWA, the users must download the S/MIME control to enable this functionality. S/MIME, which stands for Secure/Multipurpose Internet Mail Extensions, is a standard for public key encryption and signing of messages encapsulated in MIME. When utilizing this security feature, outgoing messages (and attachments) are encrypted so that only the intended recipient can read them.

To enable this feature, perform the following steps:

1. Click on Download the S/MIME control.
2. On the File Download–Security Warning screen, click Save.
3. On the Save As screen, select the location on the computer in which the file should be saved and click Save.
4. On the Download Complete screen, click Run. Then click Run again on the Internet Explorer–Security Warning screen.

When the S/MIME control has been installed, two new options appear in the S/MIME section: Encrypt Contents and Attachments of All Messages I Send, and Add a Digital Signature to All Messages I Send. Users can select either or both of these options to have the security settings applied to all outgoing messages.

28

If users do not elect to apply the enhanced security to ALL outgoing messages, they can still utilize S/MIME on individual outgoing messages. When composing a new message, under the Options tab, a new section called E-Mail Security shows two new options: Encrypt Message Contents and Attachments and Add a Digital Signature to This Message.

The Phone Tab

Under the Phone tab, the user can manage mobile devices that are configured to synchronize with Exchange Server via ActiveSync and configure Text Messaging.

Mobile Phones

In the Mobile phones section, users can view the devices that are configured to synchronize with their Exchange Server account, delete configured devices, display their Recovery Password, or initiate a remote device wipe or a block on a misplaced phone.

The page also displays the Last Synch Time and Status of the mobile device. The status includes information such as the date and time when the first sync occurred, the date and time of the last successful sync, the Device ID, and the User Agent.

Text Messaging

In the Text Messaging section, users can turn on notifications for enabled devices and configure Calendar and E-mail notifications.

Calendar Notifications

The configurable options in this section are the same as they are on the Settings tab in the Calendar section previously described.

Unified Messaging

When Unified Messaging is installed, a new tab is available that enables the user to configure voice mail settings and options specific to the Unified Messaging features.

E-mail Notifications

The E-Mail Notifications page enables the user to configure rules to send text notifications when certain messages arrive.

The Block or Allow Tab

Under the Block or Allow tab, users can configure their Junk E-Mail settings. Users can elect to disable their junk email filtering altogether by selecting Don't Move Mail to My Junk E-Mail Folder; with unsolicited bulk email (UBE) constantly on the rise, few users are likely to elect to do so.

When the Automatically Filter Junk E-Mail option is selected, users can add email addresses or domains to the Safe Senders and Recipients section, formerly known as the Safe Senders list. Configuring this option enables messages from the listed senders to bypass the junk email filters. This practice is also known as *whitelisting*.

There is also the option to Trust E-Mail from My Contacts. When this option is selected, email from addresses in the users contacts list are automatically whitelisted and bypass the junk email filters.

Users can also add email addresses or domains to the Blocked Senders list. Configuring this option automatically sends mail from the listed senders straight to the Junk E-Mail folder, regardless of the content. This practice is also known as *blacklisting*.

Lastly, there is a check box that states "Don't Trust E-Mail Unless It Comes from Someone in My Senders I want to E-Mail with List or Local Senders." This option is the most restrictive of the Junk E-Mail options. With this option selected, only mail from local senders and trusted senders will be processed. All other messages go directly to the Junk E-Mail folder.

Getting Help

As with all Microsoft applications, information on how to use the product is available by clicking the Help button. The Help button is a blue circle with a question mark (?) and is located in the top-right portion of the page.

The Help feature is web-based and delivers information through a pop-up window. Users might need to make adjustments to their Internet Explorer settings to use the feature. Adding http://help.outlook.com to the allowed sites in the pop-up blocker (if enabled) and adding http://help.outlook.com as a trusted site within Internet Explorer should do the trick.

The Help pages provide information on features, and step-by-step instructions for performing tasks such as Create a Message, Search for an Item, and Learn About Inbox Rules.

Opening Another User's Inbox or Mailbox

There are several reasons why one user might need access to the data stored in another mailbox: Administrators who are troubleshooting delivery issues, administrative assistants who are gathering information for their bosses, or even a user accessing a "shared" team mailbox.

Whereas previous versions of OWA enabled access to other mailboxes, OWA 2010 improves the experience by enabling two different methods for accessing the data, with two different results.

Opening Another User's Mailbox

As in OWA 2007, OWA 2010 enables users who have the appropriate permissions to open another user's mailbox, granting access to the inbox, calendar, deleted items, and so on.

To open another user's mailbox with OWA, perform the following steps:

1. In the primary OWA window, in the top-right corner, click on the display name to bring up the Open Other Mailbox window.

2. Type the display name, alias, or SMTP email address of the mailbox that is to be opened and press Enter to resolve the name. Ensure the name has resolved successfully (the font will change colors and become underlined); then click Open.

3. If the user has not been granted the appropriate permissions, he or she receives an error. See the upcoming "Granting Full Access to a Mailbox" section.

4. The browser window will open the requested mailbox, granting access to all of the target folders.

28

Opening Another User's Inbox

While opening another user's mailbox is a useful feature, there are times in which users just need to open/monitor the Inbox of another mailbox. Often, it is helpful if they can do so from within their own mailbox, allowing them to switch back and forth between the two. Users have enjoyed this capability for years in Outlook, but it has never been available in OWA before. Now, it is.

To open another user's inbox with OWA, perform the following steps:

1. In the navigation pane on the primary OWA window, users should right-click their display name in the folder list (above Inbox).

2. Select Open Other User's Inbox.

3. Type in the display name, alias, or SMTP email address of the mailbox that is to be opened and press Enter to resolve the name. Alternatively, users can click Name and select the desired user account from the address book. Ensure the name has resolved successfully (the font will change colors and become underlined); then click OK.

4. If the users do not have the appropriate permissions, they receive an error. See the following "Granting Full Access to a Mailbox" section.

5. Unlike opening another user's mailbox, the users now have full access to their own mailbox, and the other user's inbox is added to the folder list on the left side. As previously stated, this grants access only to the requested Inbox, not to the other mailbox folders.

Granting Full Access to a Mailbox

Before a user can access another user's mailbox from within OWA, he must be granted Full Access to the target mailbox. By granting Full Access, the user can open and read the contents of the target mailbox but cannot send as the mailbox without additional permissions.

To grant Full Access from the Exchange Management Console

1. Start the Exchange Management Console and, in the console tree, click Recipient Configuration.

2. In the result pane, select the target mailbox (the mailbox that the user will be opening).

3. In the action pane (under the mailbox name) click Manage Full Access Permission. The Manage Full Access Permission Wizard opens.

4. On the Manage Full Access Permission page, click Add.

5. In Select User or Group, search for and select the user who will be accessing the target mailbox and then click OK.

6. Click Manage.

7. On the Completion page, confirm whether permission was successfully granted. The summary also displays the Exchange Management Shell command that was used to grant the Full Access permission.

8. Click Finish.

To grant Full Access from the Exchange Management Shell

1. Run the following command to add the Full Access permission directly to the mailbox:

    ```
    Add-MailboxPermission "Mailbox" -User "Trusted User" -AccessRights FullAccess
    ```

    Where *Mailbox* is the alias for the mailbox modified and *Trusted User* is the alias for the user being granted full access.

    Example:

    ```
    Add-MailboxPermission "shirley" -User "admin" -AccessRights FullAccess
    ```

    would grant user "admin" full access and the ability to open mailbox "shirley."

2. View the results in the Management Shell console and ensure Full Access permissions were granted.

Signing Out of OWA 2010

Just as users Sign In to OWA instead of Log On, they now Sign Out instead of Log Off. The Sign Out link is located at the top-right corner of the screen, under the name of the Signed In user.

After clicking Sign Out, a screen appears to remind the user to close all browser windows, as shown in Figure 28.19. Users should be trained to always close all browser windows when they finish with an OWA session.

FIGURE 28.19   Reminder to close the browser window when finished.

Configuring OWA and IM Integration

Exchange Server 2010 enables the integration of OWA and Instant Messaging, utilizing Office Communications Server (OCS) R2. However, for the feature to work, the OWA server must be configured to communicate with the OCS server.

There are four high-level steps needed:

▶ Configure the Exchange Client Access Server.

▶ Configure the OCS Server.

▶ Modify Windows Firewall on the Client Access Server.

▶ Confirm User Configuration.

Configure the Exchange Client Access Server

There are five steps that must be taken to configure the Exchange Server 2010 Client Access Server:

1. Copy OCS 2007 R2 Web Service Provider Files.
2. Gather Information about the certificate used by the Client Access Server.
3. Edit the OWA Web Config file.
4. Enable OCS Integration.
5. Restart Internet Information Services.

Step 1: Copy OCS 2007 R2 Web Service Provider Files

Three OCS 2007 R2 files must be copied to the Client Access server to enable IM integration. They are

▶ SIPEPS.dll

▶ Microsoft.Rtc.Collaboration.dll

▶ Microsoft.Rtc.UCWeb.dll

These files can be obtained from Microsoft and must exist in the following directory on the Client Access server:

    C:\Program Files\Microsoft\Exchange Server\V14\ClientAccess\Owa\Bin

Step 2: Gather Certificate Information

The Client Access Server needs to use a certificate that is trusted by the OCS server.

> **NOTE**
>
> To simplify the configuration, the certificate used by the Client Access Server should be issued by the same Issuer as the certificate used by OCS 2007 R2. The configuration of the certificate on the Client Access Server is not covered in this chapter. The following steps assume that the certificate configuration is already in place.

Using Exchange PowerShell, gather the certificate information by running the following command:

```
Get-ExchangeCertificate ¦ fl
```

(The last character of the command is an L, not a one.)

Sample Output, with only relevant information shown:

```
IsSelfSigned    : False
Issuer          : CN=ca1, DC=companyabc, DC=com
SerialNumber    : 71652G3R00000000001A
Services        : IMAP, POP, IIS, SMTP
Status          : Valid
Subject         : CN=e2010w2k8
```

Locate the certificate that will be used and make note of the following information:

▶ **Issuer** of the certificate

▶ **Serial Number** assigned to the certificate

▶ **Subject** of the certificate

Document this information for use in later steps.

Step 3: Edit the OWA Web Config File

On the Client Access Server, navigate to the following directory:

C:\Program Files\Microsoft\Exchange Server\V14\ClientAccess\OWA

Open the `web.config` file using Notepad and perform the following steps:

1. Search for OCSServerName. You see the following three entries:

   ```
   <add key="OCSServerName" value="" />
   <add key="OCSCertificateIssuer" value="" />
   <add key="OCSCertificateSerialNumber" value=""/>
   ```

2. Populate the server name:

   In the <add key="OCSServerName" section, insert the FQDN of the OCS server between the final two quotes. For our example, the line will look like this:

   ```
   <add key="OCSServerName" value="ocs-1.companyabc.com" />
   ```

3. Populate the Certificate Issuer:

   In the <add key="OCSCertificateIssuer" section, insert the issuer of the certificate (gathered earlier) between the final two quotes. For our example, the line will look like this:

   ```
   <add key="OCS CertificateIssuer" value=" CN=ca1, DC=companyabc, DC=com " />
   ```

4. Populate the Certificate SerialNumber:

   In the <add key="OCSCertificateSerialNumber" section, insert the certificate serial number between the final two quotes. For our example, the line would look like this:

   ```
   <add key="OCSCertificateSerialNumber" value="71 65 2G 3R 00 00 00 00 00 1A" />
   ```

   Important: You must manually add spaces in the Serial Number string to separate each octet or the system cannot locate the certificate.

5. Save and close the Web.config file.

28

Step 4: Edit the OCS Integration

To enable the OWA Virtual Directory to use OCS IM integration, from Exchange PowerShell, type the following command:

```
(Get-OwaVirtualDirectory).Identity ¦ Set-OwaVirtualDirectory
➥-InstantMessagingType OCS
```

Step 5: Restart Internet Information Services

Although the preceding changes should be detected automatically, administrators might need to restart IIS on the Client Access Server. However, doing so can cause any current OWA sessions to be logged off, so care should be taken.

From the command prompt on the Client Access server, issue the IISRESET command to restart the services.

Configure the OCS Server

The Exchange Server 2010 OWA IM integration component is implemented as an OCS 2007 end-point. For the integration component to sign in to OCS 2007 R2, the OCS server must be configured to trust the Client Access Server.

This is accomplished by adding the Exchange Client Access Server as a trusted server on the OCS 2007 R2 front end. To do so, perform the following steps:

1. While logged in as an OCS administrator, start the OCS Management Console by selecting the following:

   Start\All Programs\Administrative Tools\Office Communicator Server 2007 R2

2. Navigate to the OCS 2007 R2 Pool. Right-click the OCS Pool name and select Properties; then select Front End Properties

3. Click on the Host Authorization tab; then click the Add button.

4. In the Add Authorized host window

   ▶ Select the FQDN radio button.

   ▶ Type the name of the Client Access Server. This name must reflect the Subject name of the certificate for the CAS server. Depending on the configuration of your environment, this name might not be fully qualified. Using the IP address button instead of the FQDN button is possible but is less secure as it does not rely on certificate authentication.

   ▶ Select the following options: Treat as Authenticated and Throttle as Server.

   There must be an entry created for every Client Access Server that has the IM Integration components installed.

5. Click OK to save the configuration changes.

6. To allow changes to take effect immediately, stop and restart the OCS front-end services; however, this disconnects any active users.

Troubleshooting the Installation

Next are a few troubleshooting steps that can assist with some of the more common problems encountered with Exchange/OCS integration.

Configuring the Firewall on the CAS Server

If the Client Access Server has the Windows Firewall enabled, it might need an exception to enable OCS 2007 R2 to communicate with it. To create the exception, perform the following steps:

1. From the Control Panel, open Windows Firewall.
2. On the left side of the Windows Firewall window, click Allow a Program Through Windows Firewall.
3. Click Add Program; then click Browse.
4. Browse to C:\Windows\System32\inetsrv and select w3wp.exe.
5. Click Open and then click OK twice to apply changes and close the window. Be sure to perform this step on all CAS servers with IM integration enabled.

User Configuration

Before the user community can utilize the IM features, they must be "provisioned" for Office Communications Server R2 and must be enabled for Enhance Presence. When the user is initially enabled on OCS 2007 R2, he will automatically be enabled for Enhanced Presence.

Users must also have a valid SIP proxy address for the OWA IM integration component to enable the IM Integration UI.

Instant Messaging Not Available

When attempting to view the Instant Messaging contact list, a user might receive a notification that states:

Instant Messaging Isn't Available Right Now. The Contact List Will Appear When the Service Becomes Available.

If this occurs, perform the following steps:

1. Using the same user account, confirm that you can access the IM services using the Office Communicator 2007 R2 client.
2. If functional, confirm that the OCS Server name is properly entered in the Web.Config file of the CAS server.
3. Also confirm the configuration of the Authorized Hosts option on the OCS pool contains all IM Integrated Client Access Servers.

OWA Certificate Error

If OWA cannot locate the certificate, an error stating The Local Certificate Specified Was Not Found in the Store for the Local Computer appears.

In this case, confirm that the value of the OCSCertificateIssuer and OCSCertificateSerialNumber fields in the Web.Config file are correct. Also ensure that there are blank spaces between every two characters in the serial number to separate octets in the string.

Summary

Exchange Server 2010 Outlook Web App is the most powerful and capable OWA client to date. With each new version, Microsoft adds capabilities that improve collaboration and make the product easier to use, and OWA 2010 is no exception.

As the Premium version becomes available to a wider user base through the support of non-IE browsers, OWA is positioned to meet the needs of more and more users. Additionally, there are enhancements in OWA 2010 that make the product, in ways, more powerful than the existing Outlook client, Outlook 2007.

When planning and deploying Client Access Servers, administrators should do so with an eye toward their OWA deployment and make sure the new capabilities are fully implemented.

Despite the simplified appearance, OWA 2010 is more powerful than ever before, and the user community is going to appreciate that fact.

Best Practices

The following are best practices from this chapter:

▶ Use the Premium version of the OWA client whenever practical. It has significant improvements over the Light version.

▶ Get familiar with the Scheduling Assistant. Proper use makes scheduling meetings significantly easier.

▶ Use Ctrl or Shift when selecting emails for deletion; this speeds up the process of deleting several messages at the same time.

▶ Use categories or flags to create reminders or to bring attention to a message for Outlook users.

▶ Use keyboard shortcuts to simplify menu button tasks or functions.

▶ Take advantage of the new MailTips features and apply MailTips to large distribution lists, lists that contain external members, and users with similar names to show where they are located.

▶ To simplify the integration of OWA with OCS to enable Instant Messaging and Presence, make sure to request the CAS certificate from the same issuer as the OCS certificate.

CHAPTER 29

Using Non-Windows Systems to Access Exchange Server 2010

In today's business networks, Exchange Server 2010 administrators are challenged with a variety of compatibility issues. One of the biggest challenges is the need to support today's complex, mixed-Exchange client platforms often found when implementing or upgrading to Microsoft Exchange Server 2010. With a diversity of different client needs attached to Exchange Server data, administrators and information technology (IT) managers are constantly challenged with the complexities of providing client access to corporate mail systems for a variety of different clients, including those running non-Windows–based client operating systems.

When administrators need to meet these specific requirements and the many challenges involved with connecting non-Windows–based clients to Exchange Server 2010 mail information, they can become overwhelmed with using the built-in functionality of Windows Server 2003, Windows Server 2008, and Exchange Server 2010 technologies. Combining Microsoft technologies, administrators can provide support and establish compatibility to alternative messaging clients using remote technologies, Internet solutions, and Microsoft-developed alternative clients. This makes Exchange Server 2010 an effective all-in-one corporate mail solution to support non-Windows-based client operating systems, such as Apple's Mac platform and UNIX-based platforms.

Using the information in this chapter, administrators will learn the options available for connecting these non-Windows–based client systems and the applications available to provide access to Microsoft Exchange Server 2010 mailbox information.

This chapter discusses applications—such as Outlook Web App (OWA), Mac OS X Mail, Outlook Express, Post Office Protocol 3 (POP3)/Internet Message Access Protocol (IMAP) clients, and Entourage for the Mac—that provide connectivity for non-Windows–based clients to Exchange Server 2010 mail data. Each option is reviewed and discussed in detail to determine the different functions available with each solution and the compatibility when being used to connect Exchange Server 2010 with the different alternative operating systems.

In addition to functionality and the conventional client/server connectivity methods, this chapter also provides systems administrators with the step-by-step instructions to configure access to Exchange Server 2010, using concepts such as Remote Desktop and Windows 2008 Terminal Services.

Understanding Non-Windows–Based Mail Client Options

In most enterprise network environments today, the need to support non-Microsoft Windows client operating systems is almost guaranteed; administrators must plan and support alternative means of access to Exchange Server mail information.

To accomplish this goal, administrators can use several options available to provide Exchange Server data and calendaring information to a variety of alternative non-Windows–based clients systems. Leveraging the built-in compatibility and functionality of Exchange Server 2010, access can be accomplished using any one or combination of multiple familiar client options, depending on the operating system being used and the functionality needed by the individual client.

One of the huge improvements an administrator will find when working with Exchange Server 2010 is the enhanced support for non-Windows-based mail systems. With a movement away from a proprietary WebDAV standard to a broader industry supported Web Services standard for Outlook Web App, users running Apple Mac Safari or FireFox for Windows will experience "Premium Client" support that was previously provided only to users of the Microsoft Internet Explorer browser. This, along with a number of other improvements, provides a better experience for non-Windows mail client users.

Using Exchange Server client options such as Mac OS X Mail, Entourage 2008, Outlook Web App, Windows-based Remote Desktop, and others listed later in this chapter, administrators can identify the best solution available to provide Exchange Server 2010 server connectivity based on the operating system being used and functionality of each solution.

In addition, because these types of clients are usually the minority in most Microsoft Exchange Server environments, administrators can evaluate the functionality available with each of these client solutions and implement any specific one based on the requirements of the client accessing Exchange Server information.

Supporting Mac Clients with Microsoft Solutions

When determining which Exchange Server client is best for supporting Mac users and desktops, the most important consideration is the required functionality of the client user and the limitations involved with each available option.

To support Mac desktops with Exchange Server 2010, Microsoft provided a few options, including Entourage 2008 and Outlook Express clients designed specifically for the Macintosh desktop operating system. A very popular option for Macintosh support to Exchange Server is to use the built-in Mac Mail, iCal, and Address Book client that comes with OS X and fully supports access to Exchange Server.

Using any of these options, administrators can support internal network access and remote connectivity to Exchange Server 2010 using applications installed directly on the client desktop using protocols already enabled to support their Windows-based Outlook client cousins.

Supporting Outlook Options

For additional information on Entourage 2008 and support for Mac clients in an Exchange Server 2010 environment, Microsoft provides comprehensive information and instructions through the Mactopia support website at www.microsoft.com/mac/default.mspx.

Though most Windows users are familiar with the name Outlook and Outlook Express, Microsoft also provides another very powerful client option for connecting Macintosh clients to Exchange Server 2010. Using the Entourage 2008 client, Mac users can get a robust set of client options, such as mail and calendaring synchronization, junk email filtering, and contact management with the look and feel more familiar to Macintosh users. Not the Outlook client, this alternative to Outlook is available individually or as part of the Office 2008 Mac client suite or can be downloaded independently.

Providing Full Functionality with PC Virtualization and Remote Desktop for Mac

What is probably the simplest and most popular option when supporting Mac clients in a predominantly Windows-based environment is using the PC virtualization tool (such as Microsoft Virtual PC for the Mac, Parallels, or VMware Fusion) and Remote Desktop Client for Mac. Using these Mac client options provides any Mac user with the full functionality of the Windows-based Outlook 2007 and Outlook 2003 clients on the Mac desktop. These are two options that can be easily implemented and allow Mac users full access to Windows client tools and functionality. Using this option, administrators can not only provide access to Microsoft Outlook, but they can also provide full functionality to Windows desktop applications and tools directly to the Mac client.

Using PC virtualization for the Mac, users can launch and work in a fully functional virtual Windows-based PC loaded on the Mac desktop. Effective for Mac users with Windows experience, PC virtualization provides cross-platform functionality for users by allowing features such as access to Mac desktop peripherals, cut-and-paste features between the Virtual PC and the Mac OS, no-configuration printing, and access to Windows network-based shares.

> **NOTE**
>
> Unlike the RDP client, PC virtualization runs the applications on the local Mac client. This means that any data, including saved files and offline folders, is also stored on the local Mac desktop.

Using the Remote Desktop Client, Mac users can access a Windows desktop functionality through sessions based on Terminal Services functionality, allowing full functionality in Windows through a remote connection. This function also gives Mac clients the ability to cut and paste information from the Remote Desktop Connection to the Mac operating system, full printing functionality to local connected Mac printers, and the ability to provide network access to shared Windows resources. The difference in these two options is the default storage of Exchange Server data and saved work; with the RDP client, when the RDP session is disconnected, all saved information remains on the network and not on the attached client.

Using the Internet for Exchange Server Connectivity

When access to Exchange Server information is all that is required, the most effective option available is leveraging the Outlook Web App (OWA) functionality built in to the Exchange Server 2010 operating system. Because using this option is normally enabled for standard Windows-based remote access from the Internet, Mac users and UNIX/Linux users can also access OWA as they access a web page from both the internal network and the Internet.

By using web-based access to provide Exchange Server 2010 client functionality, administrators can consider this solution for a variety of different non-Windows–based client systems with Internet browsing enabled. With the release of Exchange Server 2010 and its support for Web Services, Outlook Web App 2010 provides full "Premium client" support for Apple Mac Safari users. This provides Mac users with full Web access just like Windows Internet Explorer users. This includes more than 90% of the capabilities of a full Outlook 2007 or Outlook 2003 client with Outlook Web App features, such as spell checking, calendar appointments, the Rules Wizard, and more. Even more important, this option requires no additional client software to be installed on any non-Windows–based client.

> **NOTE**
>
> Microsoft initially released support for Apple Mac Safari and FireFox for Windows; however, additional browser support will continue to expand the platform support for the Premium Client experience for Outlook Web App users. See Chapter 28, "Leveraging the Capabilities of the Outlook Web App (OWA) Client," for more information on Outlook Web App.

Comparing Client Functionality and Compatibility

With each option and method of access to Exchange Server 2010, different options and functionality are available. As mentioned in the review of each method of access, some methods enable full functionality and others are limited.

Review the operating system requirements in Table 29.1 to determine whether the Mac operating systems meet the required revision for the method of access being considered.

TABLE 29.1   Client Functionality

Requirement	Outlook Express	Remote Desktop	Entourage 2008	OWA
Email	X	X	X	X
Calendaring	No	X	X	X
Contacts	X	X	X	X
Directory search	X	X	X	X
Offline access	X	X	X	No
PST archive	No	X	X	No
PST import/export	No	X	X	No
Junk mail filtering	No	X	X	X
SSL security	No	X	X	X

Determine the required functionality by using this table to compare the features of each client access method. Review the functionality of each method and compare the result with the Mac OS you are working with.

Outlook Express

A common client used by many users to access Exchange Server from a non-Windows perspective has been the use of the Outlook Express client shown in Figure 29.1. However, a few years ago, Microsoft chose to abandon the further development of Outlook Express and focused their support in development of the Outlook client for Windows, as well as a better OWA client for non-Windows users. Outlook Express remains a viable remote client solution for Exchange Server supporting IMAP and POP3 access, and Outlook Express is available for Macintosh, UNIX/Linux, and Windows support.

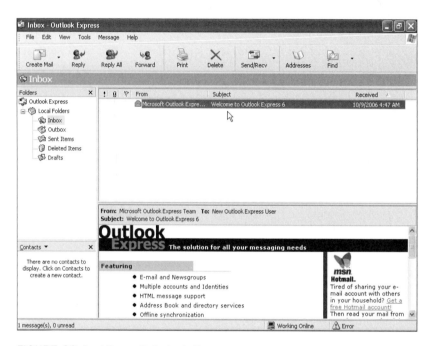

FIGURE 29.1   Microsoft Outlook Express.

With Microsoft not advancing the development of Outlook Express, organizations can choose other IMAP or POP3 clients available on the marketplace, such as the free Mac Mail utility found directly in the operating system on Macintosh systems, or any of a number of IMAP/POP3 clients for Linux (see http://www.emailman.com/unix/clients.html for a series of mail clients downloadable off the Internet).

However, because Outlook Express is still a commonly used client, some features/functions of Outlook Express are covered here in this section. Outlook Express offers support with the basic needs for mail and address books, such as the following:

▶ **Email support**—Access to Exchange Server email using the Simple Mail Transfer Protocol (SMTP) and Post Office Protocol (POP).

▶ **Address books**—Email addresses are stored in address books locally and within the Outlook Express client.

Messages accessed through Outlook Express via POP3 are downloaded to the local client and, by default, are removed from the local server. Because client messages, by default, are downloaded and stored on the local client only if a user wants to keep their mail on the Exchange server, choose the option in Outlook Express (varies by Outlook Express versions) that typically resides in the account settings or profile configuration option of Outlook Express to Keep a Copy of Mail on the Server.

▶ **Contact address list**—Outlook Express supports contacts and address lists, which can be used to select addresses when creating and sending messages and to store personal contact information.

▶ **LDAP support**—Lightweight Directory Access Protocol (LDAP) support enables an Outlook Express client's access to view information such as the Global Address List (GAL) of an Exchange Server 2010 organization.

▶ **POP support**—POP is the primary method of supporting Outlook Express clients when accessing Exchange Server from the Internet. This option requires POP to be enabled on Exchange Server 2010 and might require additional configuration of the firewall to enable pass-through of POP.

▶ **Password support**—Usernames and passwords can be configured in advance, enabling users to open Outlook Express and access mail with a preconfigured account name and password.

Installing and Enabling Support for Outlook Express

This section reviews the tasks required to configure Outlook Express to support communication with Exchange Server 2010 from the internal network location and the Internet. Although each version of Outlook Express, depending on the operating system, is slightly different, the instructions might also be a little different; however, for the most part, these instructions provide general installation and configuration guidance.

One common task when enabling support for Outlook Express is to enable support for the client to use TCP/IP to communicate with and access Exchange Server mail.

Using TCP/IP enables client access from the internal network and from the Internet. This configuration is not the same as the protocol that will be used to access Exchange Server 2010 mail.

When installing Outlook Express, the installation file can be downloaded free from the Microsoft website at www.microsoft.com/downloads/Search.aspx?displaylang=en.

Configuring POP Access with Outlook Express

In this scenario, you can configure the Outlook Express client to connect to Exchange Server 2010 through an Internet connection using the Post Office Protocol. This enables Outlook Express to access the Exchange Server 2010 server and authenticate downloading messages.

NOTE

Before configuring client connectivity to Exchange Server 2010 using POP, additional configuration of the Exchange server is required to enable the protocol for the individual mail and server. In addition, if accessing with POP from the Internet, the network firewall should be configured to enable POP access, and the domain name for the Exchange Server 2010 POP server should be populated to the Internet.

For more information on domain name system (DNS), see Chapter 6, "Understanding Network Services and Active Directory Domain Controller Placement for Exchange Server 2010."

For information on configuring your firewall and security best practices when enabling support with POP, consult the firewall manufacturer's product information.

To configure Outlook Express to connect an Exchange Server 2010 server using POP, begin by opening Outlook Express and follow these steps:

1. From the Tools menu, select Accounts.

2. On the Internet Accounts tab, click the Mail tab and select New.

3. To create a new email account, enter the name for the account in the Display Name dialog box, enter the name for the account being created, and click Next.

4. On the email screen, select the I Already Have an Email Address That I'd Like to Use option, and enter the email address for the user being configured. Click Next to continue.

5. At the Email Server Information page, type POP under the My Incoming Mail Server selection.

6. Enter the fully qualified mail server name as listed in the following example; then click Next to continue.

   Example:

   Incoming Mail Server = Mail.CompanyABC.com

   Outgoing Mail Server = SMTP.CompanyABC.com

NOTE

The incoming and outgoing mail server names should be added and populated to the Internet for proper DNS name resolution.

When configuring this option for Internet access, the outgoing mail server might need to be configured to point to the outgoing mail server of the Internet service provider (ISP) being used.

7. At the authentication screen, enter the logon name and password for the account accessing the Exchange Server 2010 POP server, as shown in the following example.

   Example:

   Account Name = User@CompanyABC.com

   Password = ***********

8. To enhance security and limit the ability of others to access the Exchange Server POP account, uncheck the Save Password check box and click Next to continue.

Password and Best Practices

To enhance security, leave the password entry blank; this requires users to enter the password each time they access Exchange Server.

In addition, when accessing Exchange Server through POP, it is best practice to use strong passwords to enhance security. Use the Active Directory Users and Computers management console to create a strong password for accounts using this method of access.

9. Complete the installation by entering the account name for the account being used, and then click Next to complete the installation.

10. Test accessing the Exchange Server 2010 POP services by selecting Send/Receive on the Outlook Express toolbar.

Migrating and Backing Up Personal Address Books

One of the most common tasks when managing Outlook Express clients is backing up the contacts from the Outlook Express 5 client. When performing this task, administrators can export contact information and create comma-separated files for import into other mail programs and Outlook clients.

To complete the export of contact information for backup and migration reasons, follow the example in the next section. In this scenario, you back up the Outlook Express 5 contacts to a comma-delimited CSV file.

Backing Up Outlook Express Contacts

To begin, open the Outlook Express 5 client and complete the following steps to create a full backup of all the contact information:

1. From the File menu, select the Export Contact option.

2. In the Save dialog box, select the location where the export file will be saved by modifying the default Desktop location.

3. In the Name dialog box, enter the name for the Export file to create.

> **NOTE**
>
> By default, export files are created as comma-delimited files only and are placed on the desktop.

4. Click the Save button to create the export file and back up the Outlook Express contacts.

Mac Mail, iCal, and Address Book

With the release of OS X 10.6 Snow Leopard, users of Macintosh computers can use the built-in Mail, iCal, and Address Book client that provides a tightly integrated support for email access and synchronization of email messages, address book information, and calendar information.

Mac OS X Mail uses IMAP as the standard communication method between Mac Mail and Exchange Server. A Macintosh user can access Exchange Server content, transfer the information to the Macintosh, or download the information and leave a copy of the information on the Exchange server.

> **NOTE**
>
> Usually, users download their information to their Mac Mail and leave a copy on the Exchange server, so that if the user needs to access his email from the Microsoft Exchange OWA client, or uses a different mail client on a different system, all of the user's information remains on the Exchange server for subsequent download and access.

Understanding Mac Mail Support for Exchange Server

Mac OS X Mail is simply an IMAP mail client for Exchange Server and requires the Macintosh computer to have TCP/IP connectivity to the Exchange server and Active Directory authentication to the Active Directory network in which Exchange Server resides. This allows for the support of Mac-to-Exchange integration while a Macintosh is on the local area network (LAN) backbone or while the Macintosh user is mobile.

To access the Exchange server on the LAN, a user needs to have TCP/IP access to the Exchange server, whether that is directly on the network subnet as the Exchange server, or with appropriate routes from where the user is connected to the Exchange server.

While mobile, the TCP/IP access of the Macintosh user is handled through the same network connection address as OWA. OWA should be configured with Secure Sockets Layer (SSL)–encrypted access for improved security. As long as users can access their mailbox externally using OWA, they can configure their Macintosh to access the OWA port to download and synchronize mail to the Mac OS X Mail client.

Configuring Mac Mail Support on Exchange Server 2010

To configure support for Mac Mail on the Exchange Server 2010 side, all the organization needs to do is set up Exchange Server 2010 to support OWA and enable IMAP on Exchange Server. OWA is configured by default in Exchange Server 2010, and most organizations already have OWA operating in the environment. With OWA already functional in an Exchange Server 2010 environment, all that needs to be done is to configure and enable IMAP support on Exchange Server.

Unlike the RTM release of Exchange Server 2007 that did not provide IMAP configuration support from the graphical user interface (GUI), Exchange Server 2007 SP1, SP2, and Exchange Server 2010 provide direct GUI configuration settings within the Exchange Management Console to enable IMAP support. Configuration of a user client to support IMAP in Exchange Server 2010 using the Exchange Management Shell is as follows:

```
set-CASMailbox testmbx -ImapEnabled:$True
```

where `testmbx` is the name of the mailbox being enabled for IMAP support.

Configuring Mac Mail on a Mac OS X System

With IMAP support enabled on Exchange Server 2010, the user just needs to configure the Mac Mail client on OS X. To configure the Mac Mail client on Mac OS X, do the following:

1. Launch Mac Mail on an OS X system.
2. Click Mail, Preferences, and then click Accounts.
3. Click Add Account.

29

4. When prompted to choose an account type, click up and down on the scroll option and select Exchange, similar to what is shown in Figure 29.2.

Welcome to Mail

You have no email accounts configured to use Mail. Please enter the following information to send and receive email.

Full Name:	Amy Citizen
Email Address:	abc1234@rit.edu
Incoming Mail Server:	mymail.rit.edu
Account Type:	Exchange
User Name:	abc1234
Password:	
Outgoing Mail Server (SMTP):	smtp–server.rit.edu
Outlook Web Access Server:	mymail.rit.edu

Quit   OK

FIGURE 29.2   Configuring Mac Mail for Exchange Server support.

5. On the Accounts Information page, type the name of the Outlook Web App server used by users to access Outlook Web App in the Incoming Mail Server field (such as owa.companyabc.com).

6. Enter the user's logon name and password to access Exchange Server.

7. In the Outlook Web App Server field, type the name of the Outlook Web App server, which will likely be the exact same name as referenced in step 5.

8. Click OK and then click OK again to save the settings.

After the Mac Mail configuration settings have been set, the user can now synchronize with the Exchange server to download Exchange Server content information with the network.

Because of the simplicity of the Mac Mail client, and also because it is included free with the Mac OS X operating system and provides direct support right to Exchange Server, most organizations use the Mac Mail client as a simple and effective mail client for Exchange Server.

Configuring and Implementing Entourage for the Mac

Understanding the need for a more comprehensive functional solution for Mac, Microsoft provides a powerful Exchange Server client for the Macintosh as part of their Office 2008 package called Entourage 2008. This option is very effective for Mac users' internal and external connectivity needs because it provides the same look and feel that Mac users are familiar with and many of the enhanced functions of the latest Windows-based Outlook client.

The most compatible platform with the Mac operating system, Entourage 2008 provides support for email, calendaring, contact management, junk email filtering, synchronization, and even support for handheld devices when combined with Exchange Server 2010. Exchange Server administrators can now leverage the Entourage client to provide Mac users with a familiar look and feel while delivering full integration with added features and access to Exchange Server 2010 data.

Features and Functionality

The Entourage 2008 client software combined with the Exchange Server 2010 platform and latest service packs can provide enhanced functionality for the Mac user in many areas not before available. The Entourage 2008 for Mac Web Services edition update provides Entourage users access to synchronize tasks, store attachments in calendar appointments, and other features that were not supported in the original release of the Entourage 2008 application. To download the latest Entourage updates, go to www.microsoft.com/mac/downloads.mspx.

When combined with the Exchange Server update, Entourage provides extensive support and enhanced functionality in the following areas:

▶ **Enhanced Autodiscover capability**—Autodiscover is a feature added to Exchange Server 2007 (and continued in Exchange Server 2010) that provides automatically failover intelligence for client systems to connect to a surviving Exchange server node if a server failure occurs. With Autodiscover enabled, when an Exchange Server 2010 server fails over to another server, the client will reconnect to Exchange Server automatically.

▶ **Full synchronization support**—With the Web Services edition, an Entourage client will synchronize tasks, notes, and categories, features that weren't synchronized with the original release of Entourage 2008.

▶ **Attachment support**—The Web Services edition also supports the synchronization of calendar appointments that have attachments.

Deploying Entourage 2008

Requirements for installing Entourage 2008 vary slightly from the requirements of Outlook and other Exchange Server solutions. Before installing and configuring Entourage 2008 clients, administrators must ensure that minimum hardware requirements at the Mac desktop are met and the Exchange Server 2010 prerequisites have been configured. In addition, the client must be updated and installed with the required updates and software to ensure proper functionality and connectivity when accessing Exchange Server mail data.

Before installing Entourage, ensure that the following requirements and configurations have been enabled on the Exchange server:

- ▶ Microsoft Exchange Server 2010 with the latest updates

- ▶ IMAP/SMTP/LDAP

- ▶ Outlook Web App

Though most of these settings are already enabled to support Windows-based client connectivity to Exchange Server, review and address any of the hardware and software requirements for installing Entourage by reviewing Table 29.2 and the software prerequisites for Exchange Server 2010.

TABLE 29.2   Entourage 2008's Mac Hardware Requirements

Processor	Memory	Hard Disk Space
Intel or PowerPC G4 or G5 (500MHz or faster)	512MB	1.5GB available disk space

Other Requirements

Mac OS X installed
Mac OS X 10.4.9 or later
Version of Entourage installed
Office for Mac 2008 Standard or Special
Media Edition

Verify that the Mac client desktop hardware you are installing meets the minimum hardware requirements to install Entourage 2008, as listed in Table 29.2. If you do not know what hardware is installed on the Mac client, use the Mac System Profiler available on the Tools menu of the Mac desktop to display and evaluate the hardware installed on the Mac desktop.

After the Exchange server has been prepared and the hardware requirement for Entourage has been addressed, the next components to support Entourage are the updates and software requirements for the Mac client. Before the installation of Entourage 2008 can be completed, the following components must be installed or updated in the Mac client:

- ▶ **Office 2008 for Mac**—To install Entourage 2008, the Microsoft Office 2008 for Mac suite must be installed.

- ▶ **Install Updates**—Because upgrades can be completed after the installation of Office 2008 for Mac, administrators can install any available updates before running the Upgrade Wizard or configuring any identities.

- ▶ **Microsoft Exchange Update**—When connecting Entourage 2008 to Exchange Server 2010, be sure to install the latest Office 2008 Service Pack on the client computer that includes the Web Services edition for Entourage 2008.

TIP

To address Office 2008 updates, Microsoft provides an autoupdate feature for the Office for Mac suite. Download and install the latest update version from Microsoft at www.microsoft.com/mac/downloads.aspx.

To provide functionality for junk email filtering with the latest definition files, install the junk email filter update from Microsoft at http://www.microsoft.com/mac/downloads.aspx.

After all updates have been completed and requirements met, the installation of Entourage 2008 can be completed, and the Entourage client can be connected to Exchange Server. To configure the Entourage client for Exchange Server support, follow these steps:

Enhancing Authentication with NTLM V2

To further leverage the available features of Windows and Exchange Server, administrators can enable NTLM version 2 for authentication of Mac users when connecting with Entourage clients.

To encrypt a password using NTLM V2, select the properties of the Exchange Server mail account and select the Advanced Features tab. Enable password encryption by selecting the Always Use Secure Passwords option.

Entourage 2008 does not support NTLM version 1; ensure that the default domain policy is configured to support NTLM version 2 before connecting Entourage 2008 clients.

1. Launch the Entourage 2008 client, and select Tools, Accounts.

2. Select the Mail tab, select New from the New drop-down box, and enter the account type for connecting to Exchange Server.

3. Enter the user information for the account connecting to Exchange Server with the client:

   ▶ **Account Name**—Enter the name of the account created in Active Directory for the Mac user to connect to Exchange Server.

   ▶ **Password**—Provide the password for the Active Directory account or leave this entry blank to prompt the user to log on when connecting to Exchange Server.

   ▶ **Domain Name**—Enter the name of the Active Directory domain where the account is a member.

Remote Desktop Connection Client for Mac

The Remote Desktop Connection Client for Mac, shown in Figure 29.3, can be considered and planned in the same manner as its Windows counterpart. When the prerequisites are met, administrators can use the Remote Desktop Connection Client to provide full Windows and application functionality to Mac users requiring Exchange Server services and more.

29

FIGURE 29.3   Remote Desktop Client for the Macintosh.

Through Terminal Services technology, Mac users are able to fully access the Windows client and Outlook application with all the features and functionality of Windows-based users, including network shares and printers.

Compatibility, Features, and Functionality

Because this Remote Desktop Connection for Mac uses Windows Terminal Services, the only compatibility concern to be considered is the actual connection manager. All applications, when being run, are executed remotely and do not require additional compatibility between Windows-based applications, such as Outlook and the Mac client.

The Remote Desktop Connection manager is compatible with the Mac OS X 10.4.9 (Tiger) or later. If required on an earlier version of the Mac client, upgrade the Mac operating system to meet the operating system requirements (or consider searching the Internet and downloading and installing an older v1.x version of the Remote Desktop Connection Client for the Mac). Also ensure that the Mac client hardware meets the minimum hardware requirements for installing the Remote Desktop Connection for Mac, as shown in Table 29.3.

TABLE 29.3   Remote Desktop Hardware Requirements

Processor	Memory	Hard Disk Space
Intel or PowerPC G4 or G5 (500MHz or faster)	128MB	3MB for installation 1.1MB after installation

One of the biggest benefits to the Remote Desktop Connection client for the Mac is its integration with Windows and Mac clients. Because of this compatibility, Mac users are able to leverage the functionality and features of Microsoft Outlook when accessing Exchange Server information and also leverage some of the following enhanced features when integrating Mac clients into a Windows Terminal Services environment:

▶ **Access to Windows**—The Remote Desktop Connection for Mac provides full access for Mac users into the Windows environment. This connection can be configured to the Windows desktop or restricted to an application such as Outlook.

▶ **Printing**—Through the Terminal Services connection, Mac users can access network printing and print information from applications to a networked Windows printer. To further enhance this feature, Mac users can print Windows information to the local Mac printer.

▶ **Access to data**—Through the copy feature, Mac users are fully enabled to copy and paste data between the Mac client and the Windows Terminal Services session.

Before beginning any installation of the Remote Desktop Connection for Mac, Microsoft Windows Terminal Services and remote access must be enabled for supporting a remote connection with one or more of the following Microsoft Windows operating systems:

▶ **Windows XP, Vista, or Windows 7**—Supported only through the Remote Desktop Connection feature of Windows XP, Vista, or Windows 7, this method is limited to one concurrent connection.

▶ **Windows 2003, 2008, or 2008 R2**—Supported in all versions of Windows Server 2003, 2008, and 2008 R2, Terminal Services (or now called Remote Desktop Services in Windows 2008 R2) can be enabled to support remote access for multiple, simultaneous connections.

▶ **Windows 2000**—Included in Windows 2000 Enterprise, Standard, and Datacenter Editions, the Terminal Service Application mode component must be enabled and will support multiple, simultaneous connections.

TIP

When using Terminal Services for multiple client connections from Mac and Windows users, performance is dependent on the total amount of simultaneous connections and the total amount of available hardware resources installed in the server.

29

Installing the Remote Desktop Connection Client

To install and configure the Remote Desktop Connection for Mac, let's begin with a simple scenario of creating a one-to-one connection. In this scenario, you configure a Windows desktop and a Mac client to provide remote desktop connectivity to Microsoft Outlook.

Preferably, you should have a Windows Terminal Services or Remote Desktop Services server available to run remote guest RDC client connections. This provides a one-server-to-many client connection for remote access.

Alternatively, for a single guest session from a Mac to a Windows client system, enable the Remote Desktop feature of the Windows desktop client by following these steps:

1. From the Windows desktop, select Start, My Computer and open the Properties page by right-clicking the Remote Desktop icon and selecting Properties.
2. Select the Remote tab and check the Allow Users to Connect Remotely to This Computer check box.
3. Next, assign the account that may access the desktop remotely by clicking the Select the Remote Users button. Assign or create an account for the Mac users to authenticate with when accessing the Windows client system remotely.

After the remote desktop configuration is complete and the client permissions to access Windows remotely have been configured, begin the installation of the Remote Desktop Connection for Mac by ensuring that the Mac client can communicate via TCP/IP on the network. Follow these steps to configure TCP/IP on the Mac client:

1. From the Apple menu, select Control, TCP/IP properties.
2. In the TCP/IP dialog box, configure the TCP/IP properties. In this scenario, configure the TCP/IP properties using a Static setting. Select the Connect Via option and select Ethernet.
3. From the Configure tab, select Manual.
4. Enter the TCP/IP properties for the client and the DNS address being used on your network.
5. Close the TCP/IP properties and reboot the Mac system.

To install the Remote Desktop Connection for Mac, download the installation file from Microsoft and place the file on the local Mac client where it will be installed.

To install the client, complete the following steps:

1. Expand the downloaded installation file by double-clicking it.
2. Go to the Mac desktop and open the Remote Desktop Connection volume. Copy the Remote Desktop Connection folder into the local disk of the Mac client.
3. Remove the Remote Desktop Connection volume and the original installation file by placing them in the Desktop Trashcan.
4. Launch the Remote Desktop Connection from the Remote Desktop Folder, and enter the name of the system to which you are connecting. Click Connect to establish the remote connection.
5. When prompted, enter the name and password of the account you configured to allow remote access to this desktop system.

Understanding Other Non-Windows Client Access Methods

In addition to the Mac operating systems, Exchange Server 2010 can support a variety of clients by using virtual machines on the Mac client and leveraging support for IMAP, SMTP, and POP. Using these protocols, Exchange Server administrators can provide limited email functionality and support a variety of clients throughout the Exchange Server environment for email and communication purposes.

PC Virtualization Access to Exchange Server

Most effective for users who are familiar with operating and working within Windows PC-based operating systems, the PC virtualization (that is, Virtual PC for the Mac, Parallels, or VMware Fusion) provide the same full functioning of a Windows PC client on the Mac OS desktop. Using this option allows Mac users who are comfortable working in Windows Microsoft Office and Outlook applications the ability to use a Microsoft client from the Mac. Running within a virtual machine, a Windows domain client PC can allow the same features to a Mac desktop as any Windows domain client.

With a virtual PC machine, the latest version of Outlook for Windows can be used on the Mac client desktop, accessing Exchange Server 2010 data with full Windows-based support in areas such as offline files, multiple profiles, and Windows domain network resources.

POP3 Access to Exchange Server

POP3 is a popular method of providing mail services over the Internet. POP3 is highly reliable but has limited functionality. Users who access email using POP3 are limited to downloading all messages to the local client and can only send and receive messages when a connection is established with the POP3 server.

Unlike the RTM release of Exchange Server 2007 that did not provide POP3 configuration from the graphical user interface (GUI), Exchange Server 2007 SP1, SP2, and Exchange Server 2010 provide direct GUI configuration settings within the Exchange Management Console to enable POP3 support. Configuration of a user client to support POP3 in Exchange Server 2010 using the Exchange Management Shell is as follows:

```
set-CASMailbox testmbx -PopEnabled:$True
```

where `testmbx` is the name of the mailbox being enabled for POP3 support.

When enabled with Exchange Server 2010, POP3 can be leveraged to provide email support to additional non-Windows–based clients' platforms. Through the common method of sending mail, multiple client platforms can communicate over email regardless of the actual desktop operating system and client mail software being used.

The POP3 functionality of Exchange Server 2010 can support multiclient environments, including the Eudora Mail client, the Thunderbird Mail client, and other POP-compatible

29

nonspecific client platforms. This protocol is best used when supporting single-client systems that download mail and store mail information locally.

IMAP Access to Exchange Server

As covered in the section "Mac Mail, iCal, and Address Book," IMAP is a fully supported method that allows access from non-Windows–based client systems to access Exchange Server 2010 information. Designed to allow access to Information Stores located on a remote system, IMAP can also be used to support the Linux-based Thunderbird Mail clients.

Using the Thunderbird Mail client, FireFox users can access, collaborate, and store information on the Exchange Server 2010 server with the IMAP support built in to Thunderbird. With this functionality, networks can now incorporate additional operating systems, such as Linux with Thunderbird Mail, and still support email functionality between all network users.

Use the Preferences option on the Thunderbird Mail client to configure and enable support for IMAP communication with Exchange Server 2010.

Windows Mobile/Pocket PC Access

Client mobile access is now fully integrated and supported when the Exchange Server 2010 server is installed. Remote and mobile users can use the Outlook Mobile version to send, receive, and synchronize mail, calendaring, and task information, using the Windows Mobile and Pocket PC platform over mobile information services built in to Exchange Server 2010. In addition, Apple iPhone users now have ActiveSync support for access to Exchange Server.

For more information regarding the options and configuration to support Windows Mobile, Pocket PC, and iPhone access to Exchange Server 2010, see Chapter 23, "Designing and Implementing Mobility in Exchange Server 2010."

HTML Access

Another feature with Exchange Server 2010 is HTML access. With this feature, administrators can use Internet-ready cellular telephones to provide HTML access to Exchange Server information for mobile users regardless of where they might be.

By providing additional mobile services and client permissions through Active Directory, alternate access can be granted to email and Exchange Server using Internet-ready mobile phone devices over HTML access.

For more information regarding HTML access options and configurations, see Chapter 23.

Outlook Web App

Another very effective method of allowing access to Exchange Server information is OWA. Enhanced greatly in Exchange Server 2010, OWA can be used to provide browser access to Exchange Server mailboxes from inside the network and from the Internet. As previously noted in this chapter, Microsoft has greatly enhanced Outlook Web App in Exchange

Server 2010 to support non-Internet Explorer browsers in Premium client mode. This allows support for Apple Mac Safari, FireFox for Windows, and other browsers to have full OWA support, with additional browsers being added to the list of Premium client support.

Even for browsers that do not have Premium support, OWA is nondiscretionary as to which type of Internet browser can be used to access it. Effective in functionality just like the full Outlook client, Linux-based users and others using non-Windows–based systems can access OWA for email and calendar management using the Light mode for client access, still with extensive support in terms of features and functions.

For more information regarding OWA and enabling support, see Chapter 28.

Summary

In a Microsoft-centric environment, administrators of networks often focus solely on Windows-based connections to Exchange Server, spending little time on options for non-Windows–based users. When accessing Exchange Server 2010, many options are available for non-Windows users, including a whole suite of clients for the Macintosh—such as Entourage 2008, Outlook Express, and the Remote Desktop Connection. In addition, Outlook Express is still available on other non-Windows platforms. For UNIX and Linux clients, several mail clients are available that support IMAP and POP3, that can access Exchange Server 2010 or OWA from any browser, and that provide full support for email, calendars, and contacts.

By choosing any one of a variety of client applications to access Exchange Server, an organization can leverage the capabilities of Exchange Server 2010 beyond just Windows-based users and provide seamless messaging communications throughout an entire enterprise. Depending on the client application selected, some options provide just email communications and others provide the full suite of Outlook and Exchange Server business productivity functions, such as calendaring, contacts, notes, to-do lists, journals, public folder access, offline files, junk email filtering, and more.

Using the information in this chapter, an organization should not be limited in its ability to extend Exchange Server 2010 to all users within the enterprise, and with the implementation of new client access capabilities, an organization can greatly improve its reach to all users in an organization well beyond Windows.

Best Practices

The following are best practices from this chapter:

▶ When choosing a client configuration for Exchange Server, an organization should evaluate the different solutions available for non-Windows client connectivity.

▶ To achieve the full Outlook functionality of Windows users, a non-Windows client might consider using a Terminal Services or the PC virtualization on a Mac, which provides complete support to a full Windows client that is identical to the one Windows users access.

▶ Users who want calendar integration access or are using a system running Mac OS X will not want to use Outlook Express, which lacks calendar support, and should consider using the built-in Mac Mail, iCal, and Address Book built into the Apple OS X operating system.

▶ The built-in Mac Mail client has direct Exchange Server support, synchronizes mail, calendar, and address book information, and closely integrates with the Apple OS X operating system.

▶ For IMAP or POP3 to work in Exchange Server 2010, the functions need to be enabled. However, if IMAP and/or POP3 will not be used, the services should be disabled on Exchange Server to minimize any security risk to unauthorized access to Exchange Server 2010.

▶ To improve security, leave the password entry on any client options configuration page blank so that the user will be prompted for a password every time logon is executed.

▶ Because different versions of client software for the Macintosh have different support requirement for various versions of the Mac OS, make sure to verify compatibility before installing any client software.

▶ To provide authentication to Entourage clients, NTLM v2 must be enabled on the default domain policy for access to the Exchange Server 2010 server.

CHAPTER 30

Deploying the Client for Microsoft Exchange Server 2010

Whether you implement a new Microsoft Exchange Server 2010 environment or upgrade your organization from a previous version of Microsoft Exchange Server, deploying the email client to your user community is a task that you must accomplish to provide full email functionality.

Many options are available for deploying the Microsoft Exchange Outlook client, and administrators can utilize one or all of them to distribute the client software to their user community.

This chapter is intended to assist administrators with the planning and deploying of the Outlook client. It provides information about possible deployment alternatives and shares best practices to ease the process.

Outlook 2007 Auto Account Setup

Regardless of the method used to get Outlook to the desktop, when an administrator combines Exchange Server 2010 and Outlook 2007, the configuration of the Outlook client is easier than ever before. Outlook 2007 and Exchange Server 2010 include a feature called autoconfiguration that enables the Outlook 2007 client to automatically detect and configure the Outlook profile.

Outlook 2007 Autoconfiguration

The first time a user opens Outlook 2007 on a workstation, the client utilizes a new technology called the Autodiscover service to help with the client configuration. The Outlook client checks the credentials of the logged-on user and automatically fills in the username and email address, as shown in Figure 30.1.

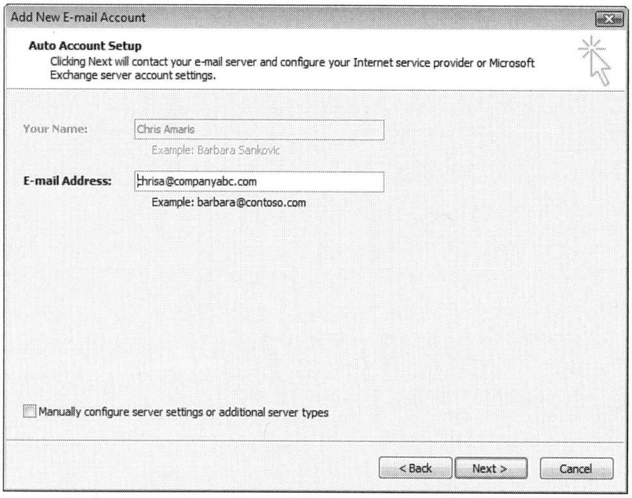

FIGURE 30.1   Autodiscover of username and email address.

After the username and mailbox have been selected, the user clicks Next, and the Autodiscover feature continues with the client setup—establishing a network connection to the Exchange server, searching for the username, and logging on to the messaging server. All remaining client configuration is completed automatically, as shown in Figure 30.2.

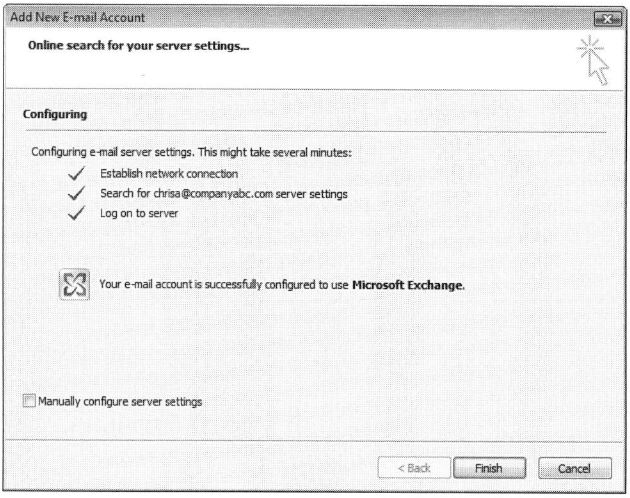

FIGURE 30.2   Email client configuration.

Users no longer have to remember complicated server names because the location of the user mailbox is automatically managed by Outlook and Exchange Server. Even if a user mailbox is moved to a new location, all user configuration information is updated automatically thanks to the autodiscover technology.

Troubleshooting Auto Account Setup

Outlook 2007 includes a built-in set of tools to test the autoconfiguration setup and to show the connection status. These tools enable testing to be done from the client perspective to ensure that the service works end to end.

To test the autoconfiguration setup from the Outlook 2007 client, execute the following steps:

1. Launch Outlook 2007.
2. Hold the Ctrl key and right-click the Outlook icon in the system tray.
3. Select Test E-mail AutoConfiguration from the menu.
4. Enter the email address of the account to use for the test.
5. Enter the password for the account.
6. Click the Test button to start the test.

The results are shown in Figure 30.3. The test shows the protocol as Exchange RPC, the user's server name, login name, and the various URLs for the services. More important, it shows that the autodiscover service works.

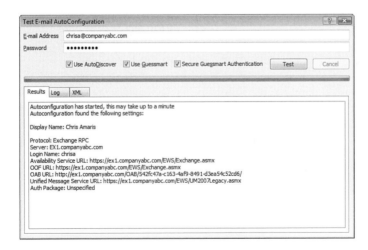

FIGURE 30.3   Test E-mail AutoConfiguration.

A variety of errors can be presented by the tool. The errors and their possible causes are listed in Table 30.1.

TABLE 30.1   Autoconfiguration Error Codes in Outlook 2007

Error Code	Error Name	Description
0x80072EE7	ERROR_INTERNET_NAME_NOT_RESOLVED	Caused by a missing or misconfigured DNS entry for the Autodiscover service
0X80072F17	ERROR_INTERNET_SEC_CERT_ERRORS	Due to an incorrect certificate configuration on the Exchange Server 2010 CAS
0X80072EFD	ERROR_INTERNET_CANNOT_CONNECT	Due to DNS issues
0X800C820A	E_AC_NO_SUPPORTED_SCHEMES	Due to misconfigured security settings in Outlook 2007

You can view the connection status of the Outlook 2007 client:

1. Launch Outlook 2007.

2. Hold the Ctrl key and right-click the Outlook icon in the system tray.

3. Select Connection Status from the menu.

The connection status for the Outlook 2007 client displays. This shows the server names for the directory, mail and public folders (if appropriate), interface on which it is communicating, connection (TCP/IP or HTTPS), and some communications statistics. A sample view is shown in Figure 30.4.

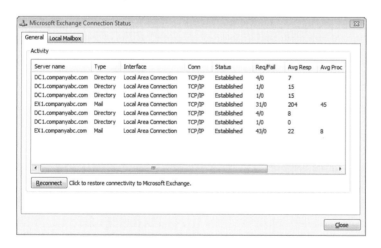

FIGURE 30.4   Connection status.

Figure 30.4 shows that the Outlook 2007 client is connected to the DC1.COMPANYABC.COM server for directory services and to the EX1.COMPANYABC.COM server for mail services.

The autoconfiguration test and connection status are useful for troubleshooting problems with client connectivity.

Understanding Deployment Options

When deploying the Outlook client, administrators can take advantage of several existing Microsoft technologies that have been designed for software distribution. In addition, by utilizing tools found in the installation media and the Microsoft Office Resource Kit (ORK), custom installations and settings can be preconfigured and deployed using one of several software distribution methods.

As organizations begin the planning process, administrators can pick and choose from the available deployment methods and can implement custom client installations that are based on the specific need for each type of client desktop. This chapter explores the different options available for deploying the Outlook client software to desktops in the enterprise.

Available Methods of Deployment

With Outlook 2003 and Outlook 2007, the installation of the client software to the desktop can be performed in ways not available for previous versions. By implementing the tools available in the installation media of Office 2007 or the Microsoft ORK, administrators can elect to use one or more of the following methods for deploying the Outlook client:

▶ **Manual installation**—Manual installation enables administrators to incorporate wizards, profile generation tools, and configuration files into the client installation process. Using these methods, administrators can define baseline settings and standard configuration settings, and they can manually test the installation when complete.

▶ **Windows Server 2008 or Windows 2003 Group Policy**—Leveraging Windows Group Policy Software deployment technologies and Microsoft Office Security Templates, Outlook clients and client updates can be pushed to desktop systems on the network. Using Group Policy, administrators can also centrally configure Outlook security and user options to enforce a baseline configuration to all client systems on the enterprise.

▶ **Imaging technologies**—Whether upgrading to a newer version of Outlook or deploying Outlook in a new environment, organizations can image the Outlook clients to the desktop or refresh the entire desktop image to implement updates or the latest company standards.

▶ **System Center Configuration Manager**—Using Microsoft System Center Configuration Manager (SCCM), you can centrally deploy and push the Outlook client and updates to large numbers of desktop systems in multiple locations throughout the enterprise. This option also enables tracking and reporting information to manage a full Exchange Outlook client deployment.

Outlook Profile Generation

Often, one of the biggest challenges Exchange Server administrators face when deploying Outlook is configuring the profiles to communicate with the Exchange server. To automate this task, profiles can be scripted using tools available with the installation media of Office 2007 or the ORK from Microsoft.

Outlook 2003 client profiles and their associated Exchange server settings can be configured using the Office 2003 Custom Installation Wizard (CIW) and configuration files can be created with Outlook option settings.

Outlook 2007 can be similarly prepared utilizing the new Office Customization Tool (OCT). The OCT is a new application that is included with Microsoft Office 2007. With the OCT, administrators can preconfigure components and settings within the Office 2007 suite to simplify deployments.

Creating Custom Profiles by Using PRF Files

By creating an Outlook profile (PRF) file, administrators can quickly create Messaging Application Programming Interface (MAPI) profiles for Microsoft Office Outlook users. A PRF file is a text file that contains syntax that Microsoft Outlook uses to generate a profile. By utilizing a PRF file, an administrator can configure new profiles, or modify existing ones, without affecting other parts of your Outlook (or Office) installation. PRF files can be manually edited to include custom Outlook settings or MAPI services that are not included in the Custom Installation Wizard interface.

Because Outlook PRF files are executable, administrators can update profiles by double-clicking the filename to run the file directly. When executing a PRF file, Outlook ensures that services that should be unique are not added more than once.

The easiest way to create a PRF file is by using the Custom Installation Wizard (CIW) for Office 2003, or the OCT for Office 2007. Administrators can specify the settings desired, and then export the settings to a PRF file. The PRF file can then be manually edited if the need should arise, for example, if your organization wants to add a new service that is not included in the CIW or OCT. The PRF file can be manually edited in any text-editing application (such as notepad.exe).

To create a PRF file with Office 2007, use the setup.exe file on the installation media. The steps to create a PRF file follow:

1. From the root of the Office 2007 media, enter setup.exe /admin to launch the Office Customization Tool.

2. Click OK to create a new setup customization file.

3. Select the Outlook profile under Outlook from the left tree.

4. Select either the Modify Profile radio button to use the default profile named Default Outlook Profile or the New Profile radio button to create a different named profile.

5. Select Specify Exchange Server settings under Outlook from the left tree.

6. Select the Configure an Exchange Server connection radio button.

7. Enter the Exchange Server name.

8. Select Remove Accounts & Export Settings under Outlook from the left tree.

9. Click the Export Profile Settings button.

10. Browse to a save location and enter a filename to save the PRF to.

You can use the resulting PRF file to set the profile automatically.

You can set additional settings to customize even further. PRF files can be applied to Outlook in several ways:

▶ Import the PRF file in the CIW or the OCT to specify profile settings in a transform, and then include the transform when you deploy Outlook.

▶ Specify the PRF file as a command-line option for outlook.exe, without prompting the user, as follows:

```
outlook.exe /importprf \\server1\share\outlook.prf
```

▶ Specify the PRF file as a command-line option for outlook.exe, but prompt the user before importing the PRF file, as follows:

```
outlook.exe /promptimportprf \\localfolder\outlook.prf
```

NOTE

Although the PRF file can be located on a network share (as shown in the first example), it will not be applied if the file is not found or if the user account used to execute the installation process does not have the appropriate permissions to access the file.

▶ Administrators can also configure the Registry to trigger Outlook to import the PRF file upon startup. Both the CIW and the Custom Maintenance Wizard contain a feature that allows you to Add/Remove Registry Entries.

Using the CIW or the OCT to preconfigure Outlook options and apply the initial profile configuration through PRF files is a very effective means of deploying Outlook profiles.

> **NOTE**
>
> The CIW and Microsoft Exchange Profile Update tool, along with additional utilities, can be found in the ORK, which can be downloaded from Microsoft. These are needed for configuring Outlook 2003. The tools for Outlook 2007, such as the OCT, are included in the Outlook 2007 setup program and you can access them by running `setup.exe /admin`.

Configuring Outlook Client Options

Even after the Outlook client software has been installed, administrators can define configuration settings and apply them dynamically to the existing clients. This task can be accomplished in one of several ways.

Custom Installation Wizard

To deploy the Outlook 2003 client to desktops on the network with configuration options predefined, powerful tools such as the CIW, along with Office configuration files such as PRF files, can be leveraged to define Outlook client options for large deployments that have the need to specify client user options. Using these tools can potentially eliminate the need for administrators to visit each desktop to configure profile settings and Outlook options.

The resulting files are Microsoft Windows Installer Transform (MST) files.

Office Customization Tool

What the CIW is to Office 2003, the OCT is to Office 2007. Administrators can preconfigure components and settings to simplify the deployment of the product. The resulting files are Microsoft Windows Installer Patch (MSP) files.

Windows Server Group Policy

Another effective configuration option is the centralized management available through security templates for Outlook. With the Group Policy feature of Windows Server 2008 or Windows Server 2003, standard and advanced options can be configured and established after the client software has been deployed.

This option can also be useful when deploying new settings to existing clients after a policy change.

Deploying Non-Windows Systems

In organizations with non-Windows–based systems, such as a Macintosh desktop, special considerations must be made for accessing an Exchange Server environment. To understand the installation and configuration process for non-Windows systems, refer to Chapter 29, "Using Non-Windows Systems to Access Exchange Server 2010."

Planning Considerations and Best Practices

Before deploying the Microsoft Outlook client, organizations should carefully evaluate their messaging needs and take a good look at their existing environment. There are many facets to the deployment of any software solution, and organizations with complex environments and messaging needs will only be successful in their implementation if they plan accordingly.

Identifying and documenting various client needs, reviewing the overall network topology, and reviewing recommended best practices can allow administrators to greatly enhance the performance of each deployment and ensure a transparent client installation.

Network Topology Bandwidth Consideration

When planning the deployment of Outlook clients to end users, administrators should take their existing network environment into account to avoid network disruptions or bandwidth saturation that could impact their user community.

When evaluating the network environment in a single-site deployment, the primary focus should be on ensuring adequate bandwidth for the client deployment. By planning the deployment in small groups, or after normal business hours, administrators can avoid negatively impacting their user community.

With multisite organizations, administrators must review the available network bandwidth on wide area network (WAN) links. Because these types of connections are generally significantly slower than local area network (LAN) connections, it can be challenging to deploy multiple Outlook clients simultaneously without negatively impacting the overall WAN performance. If this is done during normal working hours, or during periods of high network utilization (during the evenings when network backups are being performed, for example), communication problems can result.

One way to avoid passing large amounts of data across the WAN is through the use of administrative distribution points that contain copies of the files necessary for installation. By placing an administrative distribution point at each remote location, deployments can be managed centrally while minimizing the traffic across the WAN link. This can help avoid bandwidth saturation and can improve overall implementation times.

Planning Best Practices

To assist in the planning process when deploying the Outlook client, the following best practices are offered for review:

- ▶ Deploy the Outlook client with the Microsoft Office suite to provide enhanced functionality, such as the ability to utilize Microsoft Word as the Outlook client email editor.

- ▶ Be sure to document all profile settings and configuration options for each transform, PRF, and custom installation file.

▶ Always test deployment options and profile generations in a lab environment prior to deploying to actual clients.

▶ Deploy Outlook and preconfigured settings to a pilot group prior to full deployment. Administrators should work with these pilot users on testing all aspects of the application prior to widespread distribution.

▶ Break users into small, easily managed groups for deployment. Deploy the client software in phases to these groups to ensure "morning-after" supportability.

▶ When creating and naming configuration files, use unique naming conventions based on the group or configuration options being focused on. For example, when configuring options for workstations in the Public Relations department, you can name the file public_relations.prf to avoid confusing it with other configuration files.

Addressing Remote and Mobile Client Systems

When planning the Outlook client deployment, special attention must be paid to the needs of remote and mobile clients. With remote and mobile users accessing the business network environment using many different methods, administrators should consider what might happen to clients who access the network over low-bandwidth links, such as virtual private network (VPN) or Remote Access Server (RAS) dial-up links.

One method to avoid this problem is to schedule remote and mobile users to come to a location where administrators can perform the installation manually. This can be accomplished during monthly or quarterly meetings or during sales calls near a corporate office. Alternatively, user workstations can be shipped to a central location where administrators can install the application and return the machine to the user. This method is often used during full software upgrades, or in situations where the installation process requires special know-how beyond the average end user.

As an additional alternative, rarely used except with senior executives, administrators can travel to the client location to perform the needed work.

Managing the Outlook Deployment

Managing the deployment of Outlook clients can be much easier when utilizing a software deployment tool, such as Microsoft System Center Configuration Manager 2007 (SCCM). With Microsoft SCCM, deployments can be tracked and managed down to the desktop level. Administrators can identify which desktops need the Outlook client, deploy the Outlook client, and even identify and track any failed installations utilizing the reporting functionality built in to SCCM 2007.

When options such as SCCM are not available, it can be extremely difficult to track the deployment of the client and determine overall progress. The tools available in the ORK do not present any evidence on the installation progress, nor does the use of Windows

2003 or Windows Server 2008 Group Policy. However, you can use the following methods to gather a limited amount of information:

▶ When using Windows Server Group Policy, administrators can filter the server Application Event Logs to search for any events generated by the MSI Installer.

▶ On the local machine, administrators can use the Add or Remove Programs application in Control Panel to determine if the Outlook update package is listed. By utilizing the Remote Desktop feature built in to Windows Vista, this option can be accomplished remotely.

Preparing the Deployment

As the planning phase of the deployment comes to a close, administrators can focus on preparing the different areas of the Outlook client deployment.

Each of the different methods that will be utilized to deploy the software should be reviewed and tested to ensure a seamless installation.

Outlook Systems Requirements

Prior to deploying the Outlook client to user desktop systems on the network, the desktop hardware must be evaluated to determine whether it meets the recommended Microsoft hardware and software requirements to support the client.

> **TIP**
>
> Utilizing Microsoft System Center Configuration Manager 2007, administrators can conduct remote hardware inventories on managed systems. SCCM can then create a report detailing the current status of all hardware, software, and available drive space on these systems.

Ensure that the desktop systems meet the minimum installation requirements by reviewing Table 30.2.

TABLE 30.2   Outlook System Requirements

Requirement	Outlook 2003	Outlook 2007
Client operating system	Microsoft Windows 2000 SP3 or later	Microsoft Windows Vista, Windows XP2 or later
Processor speed	233-MHz processor or higher	500-MHz processor or higher

TABLE 30.2   Outlook System Requirements

Requirement	Outlook 2003	Outlook 2007
Memory	128MB of RAM or higher	256MB of RAM or higher
Hard disk space	400MB	2GB required for installation
Messaging system	Microsoft Exchange Server 5.5 or greater	Microsoft Exchange 2000 Server or greater
Monitor resolution	800x600 or higher recommended	Minimum 800x600; 1024x768 recommended
Additional components	Microsoft Internet Explorer 5.01 or higher	Microsoft Internet Explorer 6.0 or higher

Although the installation of Outlook 2007 requires 2GB of hard disk space, a portion of that space will be released after installation if the original download package is removed from the hard drive.

> **NOTE**
>
> If installing Microsoft Office Outlook 2007 with Business Contact Manager, a 1-GHz processor and 512MB of RAM or higher is required. Also, prior to installing Outlook 2007 with Business Contact Manager, administrators will first have to install Outlook 2007.

Planning Predefined Configuration Options

Another area to understand when planning for the deployment of the Outlook client is what options can be configured using the CIW and transform configuration files.

Understanding how to utilize PRF files, transforms, and various ORK utilities enables Exchange Server administrators to create a baseline plan detailing what options will be used prior to actually creating the individual configuration files.

Using the Office 2003 Resource Kit tool CIW, you can configure the following features:

- ▶ **Outlook User Profile Settings**—Administrators can specify how users' profiles will be created. Using this option, administrators can set new profiles, modify existing profiles, or add additional user profiles.

▶ **Exchange Server Settings**—Settings defining Exchange server names and specific options, such as Exchange Server connection options, can also be defined.

▶ **Installation States for Outlook and Features**—Using the installation options, administrators can define installation states to make individual features available, available at first use, or not available.

▶ **Mail Options**—Options such as PST and OST settings and synchronization options can be defined using the CIW.

▶ **Settings and Options**—Many of the options available when configuring Outlook from within the application can be defined when creating custom installation files.

▶ **Installation Path**—Ensure that the installation directory path on the desktop where the Outlook client will be installed contains enough free disk space to complete the installation.

Using the Office 2007 OCT, the following features are configurable:

▶ **Outlook Profile**—Customizes the user default Outlook or customized profile.

▶ **Specify Exchange Settings**—Configures the user Microsoft Exchange Server settings in a new or modified Outlook profile.

▶ **Exchange Server connection**—Configures an Exchange Server connection for new or existing profiles.

▶ **Cached Exchange Mode**—Configures users' Outlook profiles to use a local copy of the Exchange Server mailbox.

▶ **More Exchange Server Settings**—Configures Exchange Server offline use options and the Outlook Anywhere features.

▶ **Add Accounts**—Includes additional Outlook email accounts in the user profile, such as a shared helpdesk mailbox.

▶ **Remove Accounts and Export Settings**—Removes existing email accounts and exports settings to a PRF file. Under Remove the Following Accounts if They Exist, select Lotus cc:Mail or Microsoft Mail to remove these accounts from users' computers when Outlook first starts. More important, used to save the Outlook profile settings to a PRF file.

Creating Administrative Installation Points

If the deployment requires administrative installation points, administrators can create them using the setup.exe program of the Outlook or Office installation software and utilizing the /a switch. Outlook 2003 files are compressed on the media and need to be uncompressed to support network installations. Outlook 2007 installations are done from the compressed source files, so no special preparation is needed for the files for a network installation.

To create the administrative installation point for Outlook 2003, complete these steps:

NOTE

In the following example, the administrative installation point is created using the Microsoft Office 2003 installation media.

1. Insert the installation CD-ROM into the systems where the installation point will be created. Click Start, Run, type `setup.exe /a` in the Open text box, and then click OK to continue.

2. When prompted, enter the product key that came with the Office 2003 installation software, and click Next to continue.

NOTE

Use the Install Location option on this screen to change the installation path that Outlook will use when being deployed.

3. Accept the End User License Agreement (EULA) and select Install; this begins the installation process.

4. Select the installation state for Outlook and Outlook options; click Next to continue.

The Outlook 2003 installation files will be uncompressed and copied to the share. For Outlook 2007, simply copy the files to the share directly.

Automating Outlook Profile Settings

You have multiple options for configuring Outlook profiles when deploying. The most commonly used are the PRF files that generate Outlook profiles and apply Outlook settings.

To configure profile settings using PRF files, administrators can use the CIW or the OCT. Profile settings are defined on the Outlook: Customize Default Profile page. This section guides administrators through the standard configuration of the PRF file to generate a user's profile dynamically after the Outlook client installation has completed. In this scenario, you configure a single PRF file and create the Outlook profile for any user when the Outlook client is launched for the first time.

To create a new profile, open the CIW by selecting Start, Run, Microsoft Office, Microsoft Office Tools, Microsoft Office ORK, Custom Installation Wizard. Then follow these steps:

1. Select the default options until the Outlook: Customize Default Profile page appears. Select the New Profile option, enter Outlook for the profile name, and click Next.

TIP

To configure the PRF file to run when Outlook is launched for the first time, use the Add/Remove Registry Entries page of the Custom Installation Wizard.

To enable the run-once option, make the following Registry changes:

1. Delete the following key:

HKEY_CURRENT_USER\Software\Microsoft\Office\10.0\Outlook\Setup\First-Run

2. Expand the Registry tree to the following:

HKEY_CURRENT_USER\Software\Microsoft\Office\10.0\Outlook\Setup

3. Add the string value and enter the path of the PRF file share created earlier.

2. To configure the PRF file to dynamically configure each user profile, enter the %username% variable in the User Name field. Also, enter the name of your Exchange server.

3. Because this PRF file is a default profile configuration file, click Next at the Add Accounts screen.

4. On the Remove Accounts and Export Settings screen, select the Export Profile Settings option. Enter the name "Outlook" for the name of the new PRF file and save the file to the desired location. Select Finish to complete the PRF file creation.

NOTE

Microsoft PRF files can also be configured with additional Outlook profile settings, such as Personal folders and Outlook option settings. To understand more about configuring PRF files, go to www.microsoft.com/office/ork and search for .PRF.

Creating Transforms and Profile Files for Office 2003

Several different types of configuration files can be used to deploy Outlook 2003 client configurations to the desktop. In this section, you complete the steps needed to configure Outlook using the CIW to create transforms and PRF files.

Creating Transforms

Transform files, designated with a .MST extension, are created using the Office CIW. Transforms can be used to create detailed custom settings when installing and configuring the Outlook client.

NOTE

Use the Transform option when extensive settings are required for the Outlook deployment and when deploying Outlook with the Office application suite. Transforms can be configured with custom settings and Outlook profile information, making this option the most comprehensive of all configuration options when deploying.

Be sure to document all settings expected to be used when creating configuration transform files.

To create a transform file, download and install the appropriate ORK, launch the utility, and then follow these steps:

1. From the Welcome to Microsoft Office Custom Installation Wizard screen, click Next.
2. On the Open the MSI File page, enter the path and filename for the Outlook MSI Installation package. Use the Browse button to locate the MSI installation package being used for this Microsoft Transform file. Click Next to continue.
3. Because this scenario is creating a new Transform file, on the Open the MST File page, click the Create a New MST File option, and click Next.
4. Select the location where the new MST file will be created, and click Next.
5. Enter the location where the Outlook installation will be placed on the desktop when the client is deployed, and then enter the name of the organization that will be used for registration information.
6. If previous installations of Outlook and Microsoft Office exist on the desktop, select which installation version to remove.

> **NOTE**
>
> Selecting the option to remove a previous version of Outlook removes the selected version and all components of the Microsoft Office suite existing on the client desktop prior to installation of the new Outlook client or Office Suite.

7. On the Set Feature Installation States page, select the Outlook components that will be installed. Select the Microsoft Outlook for Windows and the Run from My Computer options.
8. Use the Custom Default Application Settings page to define and add an Office Application Settings (OSP) file. If upgrading, select the Migrate User's Settings check box to maintain the existing user-defined options after the upgrade.
9. Use the Change the Office User Settings page to define the settings and options to be applied to Outlook after the installation is finished.
10. Use the Options pages to modify the Outlook installation; continue through the configuration pages to create the transform files.

Continue through the installation and configure the following:

1. Add/remove additional custom installation files.
2. Add/remove custom Registry entries.
3. Modify shortcuts and Outlook icons.
4. If deploying across WAN links, select an additional installation point for the deployment.
5. Establish Outlook security settings.
6. Add additional programs to be installed with Outlook.

NOTE

For more information regarding options on each page and additional settings, use the Help option on each page to review the Microsoft Custom Installation Wizard help file.

Configuring Profiles with Transforms

Customizing the configuration of a profile during the installation can be accomplished using the Customize Default Profiles page. Using the options available, administrators can select the method in which to create the client profile with the Outlook Deployment tool.

For this transform, select Apply PRF File and select the PRF file created in the previous section. If you want to use an existing profile, modify an existing profile, or create a new profile, you can select one of those options instead.

▶ **Use Existing Profile**—Use when upgrading the Outlook client; this option maintains the existing settings.

NOTE

When Use Existing Profile is selected and no profile is found on the client desktop, this option prompts the user to create the profile.

▶ **Modify Profile**—Select this option to customize profile information and Exchange Outlook options.

▶ **New Profile**—Use this option to create a single new profile and configure connection settings.

Additional options are available, such as Send and Receive Options and Mail settings; continue through the configuration screens by choosing the desired options for your organization's deployment. The creation of the PRF file can be completed at any time by clicking the Finish button on any setup screen.

After the PRF has been created, the command syntax required to implement the transform file will be shown for you. Copy the command as it is shown for future reference.

Creating Patch and Profile Files for Office 2007

You can use several different types of configuration files to deploy Outlook 2007 client configurations to the desktop. In this section, you complete the steps needed to configure Outlook using the Office Customization Tool (OCT) to create patch and PRF files for Outlook 2007 clients.

Creating Patch Files

You create Microsoft Patch files, designated with a .MSP extension, using the Office OCT. Use Patch files to create detailed custom settings when installing and configuring the Outlook 2007 client.

> **NOTE**
>
> Use the MSP option when extensive settings are required for the Outlook 2007 deployment and when deploying Outlook 2007 with the Office 2007 application suite. Patch files can be configured with custom settings and Outlook profile information, making this option the most comprehensive of all configuration options when deploying.
>
> Be sure to document all settings expected to be used when creating configuration transform files.

To create a Patch file, follow these steps:

1. From the root of the Office 2007 media, enter `setup.exe /admin` to launch the Office Customization Tool.

2. Click OK to create a new setup customization file.

3. Select the Install location and organization name under Setup from the left tree. Configure the Default installation path and the Organization name settings.

4. Select the Licensing and user interfaces under Setup from the left tree. Configure the Product key setting, and check the I Accept the Terms in the License Agreement box.

5. On the Set Feature Installation States page, select the Outlook components that will be installed. Select the Microsoft Office Outlook and the Run All from My Computer options.

6. Select the Modify User Settings page. Expand the Microsoft Office Outlook 2007 folder in the right window. Review all the customizable settings that can be incorporated in the MSP.

7. To save the MSP, select File, Save and save the MSP.

Configuring Profiles with Patch Files

You can customize the configuration of a profile during the installation using the Outlook pages in the Office Customization Tool. Using the options available, administrators can select the method in which to create the client profile with the Outlook Deployment tool, as covered earlier in the chapter in the "Creating Custom Profiles by Using PRF Files" section.

The profile settings will be saved with the MSP file and applied at installation.

Installing the Outlook Client for Exchange Server

The option that requires the most administrative attention—manually installing the Outlook client—is often a necessary choice for deploying the Outlook client. After considering all available options, administrators must determine which option best fits the deployment needs by determining the overall effort required for each.

Any or all of the options can be utilized for an organization-wide deployment—utilizing each where it best fits. In this section, you review the basic steps for installing the Outlook client to desktop systems using transforms, PRF files, and the switches available when using these options.

Using Transforms and PRF Files When Installing Outlook

When the options are not available to push the installation to client systems, administrators can still install the Outlook client and save valuable keystrokes and time by predefining profile information. Using these options with a manual installation scenario can greatly reduce the overall amount of time required to install the Outlook client manually. Administrators can now incorporate the manual installation process with preconfiguration files, such as PRF files and transforms, and save time on each installation by avoiding the necessity of manually configuring each installation after completion.

When the required functionality is the client profile configuration setting and limited configuration options, the manual installation can easily be completed by using a simple PRF file. PRF files are simple to incorporate into the installation and require only the addition of a command-line switch with the setup.exe installation program to deploy.

With more complex installation needs, administrators can create MST files to define Outlook settings, security profiles, and user options. This option is most effective and enables administrators to continue with installations rather than manually configure each client setting individually.

Installing the Outlook Clients with PRF Files

After creating a PRF file by following the steps detailed in the previous section, administrators can copy the file to an installation share for use when manually installing Outlook. This allows administrators to avoid the necessity of manually configuring each Outlook profile after installation.

To understand more about using PRF files when using the Windows installation program, complete these steps:

1. Create a folder share and place the Outlook.PRF file in the folder where it can be accessed from any location on the network.

> **TIP**
>
> When creating shares to support installs and PRF configuration file access, grant the account being used to install the client with Full Control permissions to the PRF file and installation share.

2. To open a command prompt and begin an installation in Outlook using PRF files, begin by selecting Start, Run, enter command in the Open text box, and then click OK to continue.

3. At the command prompt, type

```
d:\setup.exe /ImportPRF \\Outlook Files\Outlook.PRF
```

where d: represents the location of the Outlook installation files and Outlook Files is the name of the folder share created to host the PRF configuration files.

When errors occur or it appears that the Outlook profile has not been set correctly, the PRF file can be run by using the Open command and manually installing the configuration information.

Manually Installing Outlook 2003 with Transforms

Transforms offer administrators the most functionality and flexibility when predefining Outlook 2003 settings and profile information. By utilizing transforms, administrators can leverage multiple options and even combine multiple transforms to configure Outlook 2003 clients. To understand the command lines and syntax used when installing the Microsoft Outlook client with MST files, review the examples listed in the following sections.

Applying Transforms with the Outlook Setup.exe

In these examples, administrators should use the `OutlookSet1.MST` transform filename to customize the Outlook installation. To incorporate transforms into the Outlook installation, use the following command:

```
Example: D:\setup.exe TRANSFORMS=OutlookSet1.mst
```

Administrators can also use multiple transforms when necessary. At times, organizations create individual transforms to configure specific settings. By combining these individual transforms, administrators can "pick and choose" which settings they do or do not want to apply.

For example, an organization creates a baseline transform that defines settings to be applied to all users. They then create individual transforms for specific settings for particular departments. These transforms can be applied to a single installation, creating customized Outlook settings that are configurable and easily redeployed if necessary. Using a `Setup.ini` file with the proper syntax, administrators can link and apply transforms in a very effective manner.

Manually Installing Outlook 2007 with MSPs

MSPs offer administrators the most functionality and flexibility when predefining Outlook 2007 settings and profile information. By utilizing MSP files, administrators can leverage multiple options and even combine multiple transforms to configure Outlook 2007 clients. To understand the command lines and syntax used when installing the Microsoft Outlook client with MSP files, review the examples listed in the following sections.

Applying Transforms with the Outlook Setup.exe

In this example, administrators should use the `CompanyABC.MSP` to customize the Outlook installation. To incorporate transforms into the Outlook installation, use the following command:

```
Example: D:\setup.exe /adminfile CompanyABC.MSP
```

Administrators can also use multiple MSPs when necessary. At times, organizations create individual MSPs to configure specific settings. By combining these individual MSPs, administrators can "pick and choose" the settings they want to apply. In this situation, the MSPs can be placed in the Updates folder in the installation media or network install point, and they will be applied as part of the default installation. Multiple MSP files can be placed into the Updates folder to chain together a set of configurations.

> **TIP**
>
> Every time a customization file is saved in the OCT, the tool updates the customization file's patch sequencing number with the current computer date and time stamp and generates a new patch globally unique identifier (GUID). The OCT MSP files are applied chronologically according to their time stamp.

Pushing Outlook Client Software with Group Policies

Using Windows Server 2008 or Windows Server 2003 Group Policy management tools, administrators can easily and inexpensively deploy the Outlook client to desktops throughout their organization by minimizing the tasks that require manual intervention.

Group policies can provide extremely powerful administration and management options when deploying the Outlook client. Use the information provided in this section to set up and deploy the `Outlook.MSI` package.

Deploying Outlook with Group Policy Overview

Using Group Policy to deploy the Outlook client is one of the most effective and flexible options administrators can leverage.

However, before creating deployment packages, administrators should understand the basic functionality of Group Policy in Windows Server 2003. Review the information and overview provided in the next sections before planning and setting up Windows Server 2003 Group Policy to support the Outlook client deployment.

Exchange Client Policy Options

When utilizing Group Policy functionality to deploy Outlook clients, Microsoft provides predefined administration templates (ADM) for managing Outlook on the domain.

This template enables administrators to centrally manage and configure many of the security functions and preferences normally required to be configured at each individual Outlook client. Using the security template, administrators can fully manage and configure the following areas defined by domain clients:

▶ **Outlook preferences**—The preferences options available with the security template can be enabled in the same manner as using the Options tab available on the Tools menu of the Outlook desktop client. When defining preferences, administrators can control the standard look and feel of each component available with Outlook.

Options include areas for enforcing items, such as spell check and email format, calendaring views, contacts options, and more.

▶ **Exchange settings**—Configuration items, such as Outlook user profile configurations and auto archiving, can now be centrally configured.

▶ **Intranet and SharePoint Portal Server settings**—In addition to the Outlook client settings, using the templates enables administrators to configure access to internal business information and SharePoint Portal Server resources through Outlook client folders.

Though the template enables you to configure many important options and preferences with the Outlook Exchange Server client, not all areas are available using the template.

Adding the Outlook Administrative Template

Because the additional administrative templates are not configured by default when Windows Server 2008 or Windows Server 2003 is installed, administrators must download or install the administrative Outlook template manually. For Outlook 2003, this file is called `Outlk11.adm` and is available in the ORK. For Office 2007, the Outlook template is named `outlk12.adm` and is available at the Microsoft download site. During installation, the `.adm` files are placed on the local drive of the systems on which they are installed.

To begin setting up the Outlook security template `Outlk12.adm`, start by installing the Group Policy Management Console (GPMC) on the domain controller on which the policy will be administered. GPMC is installed natively in Windows Server 2008 but needs to be downloaded in Windows Server 2003.

Next download and install the Microsoft Administrative Template files on a system on which the template can be accessed from a domain controller for import into the Domain Group Policy.

NOTE

The Office 2007 Administrative Templates, the GPMC for Windows 2003, and the ORK can be downloaded from Microsoft at www.microsoft.com/downloads.

In the Search field, simply type `Office 2007 Administrative Templates`, `Office Resource Kit` or `GPMC` to find the latest revisions. The Administrative Templates are typically updated for each Office Service Pack release.

A file named `AdminTemplates.exe` will be downloaded and will expand into directories for the Administrative Template files (ADM, ADMX, and ADML) and for the updated Office Customization Tool (OCT). The Administrative Template files will be in the \ADM directory.

To import the Outlook security template Outlk12.adm into a new Group Policy Object using the GPMC, use the following steps:

NOTE

When importing the Outlk12.adm administration template, it is a best practice to import the template to a new Group Policy Object. This enables administrators to easily control the new group policy. Review the event logs on additional domain controllers or use the Replmon tool available with Windows 2003 support tools to ensure the replication of the domain policy to all domain controllers occurs correctly.

---

1. From a Windows Server 2008 domain controller in the domain where the policy will be applied, open the Server Manager console.

2. Expand the Features node to access the Group Policy Management Console. Expand the Forest node and then the Domains node.

3. Select the location in which the new Group Policy Object will be created in the OU tree, in this case the WS organizational unit in the domain companyabc.com.

4. Right-click the selected OU and select Create a GPO in This Domain, and Link It Here. Name the new GPO Outlook Group Policy Object and click OK to create it.

5. Select the new Outlook Group Policy Object in which Outlk12.adm will be imported to, as shown in Figure 30.5.

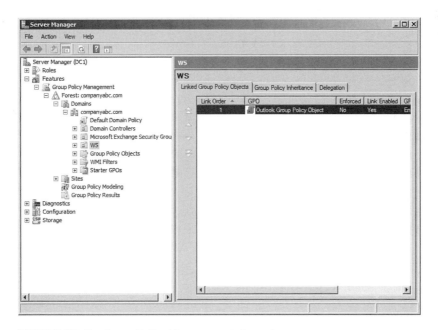

FIGURE 30.5   Group Policy Management Console.

6. Right-click the Outlook Group Policy Object, select Edit; this opens the Group Policy Object Editor window.

7. In the Group Policy Object Editor, right-click Administrative Templates under the User Configuration, Polices option and choose Add/Remove Templates, as shown in Figure 30.6.

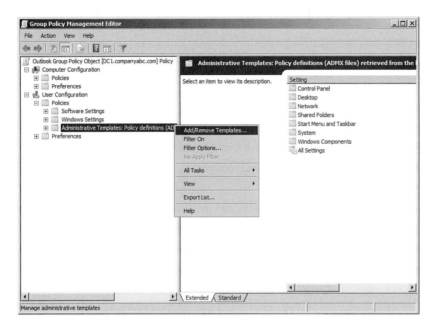

FIGURE 30.6   Group Policy Object Editor.

8. From the Add/Remove Templates dialog box, click the Add button.

9. Navigate to the location in which Outlk12.adm was placed, as noted in step 2. Select the template to import Outlk12.ADM and click the Open button.

10. Ensure that the outlk12 template has been added to the Add/Remove Templates dialog box, and click Close to continue.

You should now see the Microsoft Office Outlook 2007 template under the Administrative Templates, Classic Administrative Templates (ADM) folder in the Group Policy Object Editor.

Administrative Options

Delegating the proper rights for administrators to manage and manipulate Group Policy when deploying Outlook clients is important. With the Delegation Wizard available in the Windows Group Policy snap-in, administrative rights can be assigned to Exchange Server administrators to manage and control the deployment of Outlook to the desktop without interfering with the day-to-day operations of the Windows systems. By using the

Delegation Wizard to assign rights, administrators can grant permissions to individual accounts, groups, and Exchange server administrators.

Deployment Options

With Group Policy, the Outlook client can be deployed to the desktop using any of the following deployment methods:

▶ **Assigned to Computers**—This method of installation creates an Outlook installation package that is applied to workstations when a user logs on to the desktop. Using this option, all users have access to the Exchange Server client software after it's installed.

▶ **Assigned to Users**—When the installation package is assigned to users, application shortcuts are placed on the desktop of the user's profiles and in the Start menu of the individual user's profile. When these shortcuts are selected, the application installation is launched and completed.

▶ **Publishing the Installation**—When Outlook client software packages are published, the installation package is displayed in the Add/Remove Programs Group in the local desktop system Control Panel. Users can then initiate the installation by selecting the Install option.

With each method, Outlook administrators use the MSI installation file format to push the Outlook client's software packages from a central location or from administrative installation points to the workstations or users on the network.

Pushing Outlook Client

The steps in this scenario enable administrators to push the Outlook client package to workstations on the domain.

To create Outlook client software Group Policy Objects (GPOs), complete the following steps:

1. From a Windows Server 2008 domain controller in the domain in which the policy will be applied, open the Server Manager console.

2. Expand the Features node to access the Group Policy Management Console. Expand the Forest node and then the Domains node.

3. Select the location in which the new Group Policy Object will be created in the OU tree, in this case the WS organizational unit in companyabc.com.

4. Right-click the selected OU, select Create a GPO in This Domain, and Link It Here. Name the new GPO Outlook Client Install Group Policy Object and click OK to create it.

5. Right-click the Outlook Client Install Group Policy Object, select Edit; this opens the Group Policy Object Editor window.

6. Select Computer Configuration, Policies, Software Settings, and then Software Installation.

7. Right-click Software Installation and select New, Package.

8. Navigate the Open dialog box to the network share where the Outlook.MSI was placed, and select the MSI package being applied. Select Open to continue.

NOTE

If prompted that the Group Policy Object Editor cannot verify the network location, ensure that the share containing the installation files has the permissions configured to allow user access. Select Yes to continue when confirmed.

---

9. At the Deploy Software dialog box, select Advanced and click OK to continue. Windows Server 2008 will verify the installation package; wait for the verification to complete before continuing to the next step. The Package Properties window opens.

10. On the Package Properties page, select the Deployment tab. Review the configuration, click Assign, and ensure that the Install this Package at Logon option is selected. Click OK when you are finished.

When the new package is ready to deploy, test the package install by moving a workstation into the WS organizational unit, logging on to the workstation, and verifying that the package has installed correctly using the steps listed in the next section. If problems exist, redeploy the package by selecting the software update; click Action, All Tasks, Redeploy Application to force the deployment.

The Group Policy Objects previously created can be expanded to the rest of the environment by linking the GPOs to other OUs. Alternatively, the GPO ACLs can be set to limit the application of the group policy, and the GPO can be linked at the domain level.

Verifying the Outlook Client Deployment

When using Group Policy, administrators cannot determine whether a software package was pushed successfully the way management software such as Microsoft System Center Configuration Manager (SCCM) can. Evidence of the success of a client installation using Group Policy can only be determined by reviewing the client desktop. Using the following two areas on the client desktop, administrators can determine whether a software installation was successful:

▶ View the client application logs for MSI Installer events.

▶ On the local machine, view Add/Remove Programs to see whether the Outlook update package is listed.

Updates and Patch Management with Group Policies

One other advantage to using Group Policy is the centralized deployment options available to distribute the Outlook client updates and patches to domain workstations. Using any one of the following options, including a combination of each, Exchange Server administrators can use Group Policy to deploy updates using Microsoft MSI installation packages or Windows Updates security templates to push updates to the Microsoft

Outlook client. Using GPOs, installation of software updates can be deployed from the centralized administrative installation point to a predefined set of workstations or, in the case of a WAN, from any remote installation point or Windows Update site configured in the GPO settings.

Deployment Options When Updating Outlook Clients

Using Group Policy, the Outlook client can be upgraded and patched using one of the following deployment methods:

▶ **Assigned to Computers**—This method of installation uses the Outlook Installation package on the workstation and is available when the workstation is restarted. Using this option, all users have access to the Exchange Server client software after it is installed.

▶ **Assigned to Users**—When the installation package is assigned to users, application shortcuts are placed on the desktop of the user's profile and on the Start menu. When these shortcuts are selected, the application installation will be completed.

▶ **Publishing the Installation**—This option requires additional configuration at the desktop level to allow users the ability to install published packages on client systems. When a software package is published, the installation package is displayed in the Add/Remove Programs group in the local desktop system Control Panel. Users can then initiate the installation by selecting the update.

▶ **Using Windows Update Services**—This might be the most common method of deploying software updates to client desktop systems on any enterprise. Using Windows Server Update Services technology and Group Policy, security updates, patches, and critical updates can be deployed for Microsoft Office platforms to the client workstation.

Each method enables Exchange Server administrators to deliver update packages to the Outlook client using a push or pull method. These updates can be configured for deployment from a central location or from an administrative installation point located on the network to allow for ease of download to the workstation anywhere in the enterprise.

CAUTION

When deploying updates with GPOs, do not assign the option to install updates to users and computers at the same time. Assigning both options can create conflicts as to how updates are installed and possibly corrupt the installation of the Outlook client.

Group Policy Best Practices

As with all aspects of Group Policy, the choices and configuration options available when deploying clients or updates are numerous. Regardless of which type of package is being pushed, some basic best practices apply and can help make the process easier and less troublesome:

▶ When configuring clients to use update methods such as Windows Server Update Services, configure clients to use installation points that will allow clients to update systems from the local LAN rather than over WAN links.

▶ Software packages pushed with GPOs must be in the format of an MSI package. Any other format type than an MSI cannot be pushed using Group Policy. Using additional tools such as Marovision's Admin Studio can help administrators convert other update formats such as .exe files to customized MSI installation packages as well as custom configuration of predefined installation choices.

▶ Don't modify the default Group Policy Objects, the Default Domain Policy, and the Default Domain Controllers Policy. Instead, always create new Group Policy Objects. This helps organize the setting and makes it clear which GPOs contain which settings.

▶ When configuring software pushes using GPOs, configure the GPO at the highest levels possible in the domain tree. If the push is going out to more than one group or OU, the software update should be configured to be pushed at the domain level. If the software update is being pushed to only a few groups or one OU, or if multiple update packages are being pushed, configure the push at the group or OU level.

▶ Configure software pushes to the Computer Configuration settings rather than the User Configuration settings. This way, if users log on to multiple computer systems, updates are not applied more than once to the same system.

▶ When pushing updates to multiple locations, use technologies such as administrative distribution points and distributed file system (DFS). This allows software updates to be installed from packages and sources close to the client being updated.

Pushing Client Updates

With the options available and a good understanding of the best practices for deploying software using GPOs, the next step is to configure a GPO to push an update directly to the Outlook client. The steps in this scenario enable administrators to push a small update package to the Outlook 2007 client workstations on the domain.

Begin by downloading an update to use for this exercise ensuring an MSI format. Some updates, such as Office 2007 Service Pack 2, download as EXE files and need to be extracted with the /extract:path option to expose the MSI packages. Also, create a share on the network folder where the update will be placed and deployed. To create an Outlook client software update GPO, follow these steps:

1. From a Windows Server 2008 domain controller in the domain in which the policy will be applied, open the Server Manager console.

2. Expand the Features node to access the Group Policy Management Console. Expand the Forest node and then the Domains node.

3. Select the location in which the new Group Policy Object will be created in the OU tree, in this case the WS organizational unit in companyabc.com.

4. Right-click the selected OU and select Create a GPO in This Domain, and Link It Here. Name the new GPO Outlook Client Update Group Policy Object and click OK to create it.

5. Right-click the Outlook Client Update Group Policy Object and select Edit; this opens the Group Policy Object Editor window.

6. Select Computer Configuration, Policies, Software Settings, and then Software Installation.

7. Right-click Software Settings and select New, Package.

8. Navigate the Open dialog box to the network share where the Office 2007 update was placed, and select the MSI package being applied. Select Open to continue.

> **NOTE**
>
> If prompted that the Group Policy Object Editor cannot verify the network location, ensure that the share containing the installation files has the permissions configured to enable user access. Select Yes to continue when confirmed.

9. At the Deploy Software dialog box, select Advanced and click OK to continue. Windows Server 2008 verifies the installation package; wait for the verification to complete before continuing to the next step. The Package Properties window will open.

10. On the Package Properties page, select the Deployment tab. Review the configuration, click Assign, and ensure that the Install this Package at Logon option is selected. Click OK when you finish.

When the new package is ready to deploy, test the package install by moving a workstation into the WS organizational unit, logging on to the workstation and verifying that the package has installed correctly. If problems exist, redeploy the package by selecting the software update; click Action, All Tasks, Redeploy Application to force the deployment.

You can expand the Group Policy Objects previously created to the rest of the environment by linking the GPOs to other OUs. Alternatively, the GPO ACLs can be set to limit the application of the group policy, and the GPO can be linked at the domain level.

Deploying with Microsoft System Center Configuration Manager 2007

The most comprehensive option to deploy the Outlook client is Microsoft System Center Configuration Manager 2007 (SCCM). With the powerful software deployment functionality and management tools incorporated with SCCM, this method becomes the best solution for deploying the Outlook client software to medium and large organizations.

Planning and Preparing Outlook Deployments with SCCM 2007

To prepare the Outlook client installation for use with SCCM 2007, administrators must plan and prepare the deployment in many of the same ways as when using other options.

This section reviews and outlines the following options and deployment preparation tasks involved with using SCCM 2007:

▶ **Software distribution**—Plan and create administrative installation points to support software pushes in remote locations and on separate subnets. SCCM site servers and distribution points can be used to support software distribution, while preventing pushes over WAN links.

▶ **Evaluate client needs**—Determine the specific client installation needs and document the deployment plan.

▶ **Inventory using SCCM collections**—Leveraging the powerful functionality of SCCM collections, administrators can perform detailed inventories of desktop hardware and software and precise targeting of software deployments.

Deploying with System Center Configuration Manager

When deploying the Outlook client with Microsoft System Center Configuration Manager, SCCM leverages the Windows Installer to enhance the functionality of the deployment. Furthermore, SCCM incorporates the capability to report on and recover from failed installations.

When leveraging Windows Installer and SCCM to push client software, the following options are available:

▶ **Predefined Configuration Support**—Administrators can incorporate transforms and PRF files with the distribution of the MSI package.

▶ **Per System Pushes**—Users can establish a connection to the website without providing credentials

▶ **Unattended Installation**—Using the /qb option with the installation syntax for the MSI package, administrators can force an unattended installation to the Outlook client.

▶ **Administrative Installation Points**—As with other options, remote locations and alternate locations can be defined to support client pushes over slower connections.

▶ **Advertised and Silent Installation**—Administrators can choose between the options of advertising the installation package in the SCCM Advanced Client or forcing the installation without user intervention.

Configuring the SCCM Package for an Unattended Installation

Using the property pages of the Outlook MSI package used with SCCM to deploy Outlook clients, administrators can define the options to be used and how the package will be installed.

In this scenario, an administrator can configure the basic installation package for an unattended installation with SMS:

1. Open the SCCM 2007 Console.

2. Expand the Computer Management, Software Distribution, and select the Packages folder.

3. Right-click the Packages folder and select New, Package from Definition.

4. Click Next.

5. Click Browse and navigate to the Office 2007 Outlook MSI file.

6. Select the Outlook MSI and click Open.

7. Select Create a compressed version of the source files and click Next.

8. Click Next to accept the source directory.

9. Click Finish to create the package.

Because the package was created from the MSI, it already contains the deployment options for the following deployment methods or programs:

▶ Per-system attended

▶ Per-system unattended

▶ Per-system uninstall

▶ Per-user attended

▶ Per-user unattended

▶ Per-user uninstall

You can use these deployment methods to deploy the Outlook client to workstations in a flexible manner. Now that the installation package has been prepared, SCCM can be configured to push Microsoft Outlook clients to the desktop. The package can be distributed to locations where it will be installed from, targeted at collections of desktops or users, and the progress of the deployments can be tracked and reported on in detail.

Managing Post-Deployment Tasks

Overall, without deployment and management software such as SCCM 2007, administrators are very limited in options for managing and validating Outlook client deployments. This section reviews methods and functionality of Exchange Server that can be leveraged to help determine the overall success of a deployment and troubleshoot common deployment issues.

Validating Successful Installations

When SCCM 2007 is not available for managing and determining the success of the Outlook client deployments, administrators must use the standard tools and functionality available with Windows Server and Exchange Server. Administrators can use several methods to review and validate client installations and ensure that the client can authenticate after the Outlook client is deployed into the production environment.

Review the following options to determine methods and tricks that can assist in validating Outlook client functionality after the deployment is complete:

▶ Installations can be validated by reviewing the Application Event Logs of the client systems and identifying MSI Installer events that are written into the event logs.

▶ On the local machine, view Add/Remove Programs to see whether the Outlook update package is listed.

▶ Enable diagnostic logging on the Exchange server to monitor `MSExchangeIS` events when deploying clients.

Summary

When planning a deployment of Outlook clients, organizations can leverage different options depending on the type of client and the specific needs identified during the discovery. If using manual installation, Windows Server 2003 or 2008 Group Policy, or System Center Configuration Manager 2007, extensive planning and testing of Outlook client transforms and Outlook profiles should be performed prior to deploying any clients to the production environment.

Regardless of the deployment method, configuration settings and procedures should be documented and the deployment of Outlook clients should be staged in groups for manageability.

Best Practices

The following are best practices from this chapter:

▶ Use the Group Policy Management Console (GPMC) to plan and test policies prior to installation, as well as to debug policy problems after implementation.

▶ The Resultant Set of Policies (RSoP) should be used to analyze policy enforcement.

▶ Administrators should delegate rights to distribute the management and enforcement of group policies.

▶ Don't modify the default Group Policy Objects, the Default Domain Policy, and the Default Domain Controllers Policy. Instead, always create new Group Policy Objects. This can help organize the settings and make it clear which GPOs contain which settings.

▶ Document configuration settings being applied to Outlook transform and PRF files.

▶ If possible, use System Center Configuration Manager 2007 (SCCM) to deploy the Outlook 2007 client. It provides the best deployment options and reporting on the progress and success of the deployment.

▶ With Microsoft SCCM inventories can be conducted on network desktop systems to identify hardware and software installed on each.

▶ To enhance functionality when using Windows Server 2003 Group Policy, download and install the GPMC from Microsoft. This is not necessary for Windows Server 2008, which include the GPMC by default.

▶ Enable diagnostic logging on the Exchange server to monitor `MSExchangeIS` events when deploying clients.

▶ Leverage built-in functionality such as Remote Desktop and the Computer Management snap-in to review the success and failures of client installations.

CHAPTER 31

Database Availability Group Replication in Exchange Server 2010

One of the most interesting changes in Microsoft Exchange Server 2010 is the replacement of Cluster Continuous Replication (CCR) and Standby Continuous Replication (SCR) with Database Availability Group Replication. Unlike Exchange Server 2003 in that it no longer requires shared storage between the two nodes and ran a single copy cluster, or Exchange Server 2007 which was capable of running an active/passive pair where each node maintained an independent copy of the Exchange Server databases, Exchange Server 2010 changes the paradigm yet again and allows an administrator to replicate a database to as many as 16 geographically dispersed mailbox servers. The identity of the mail server no longer needs to be maintained by the cluster resources and move back and forth between the cluster nodes. In Exchange Server 2010, the model moves more toward a traditional multi-tier web application where a presentation layer is accessed by clients and that presentation layer tracks which database it needs to talk to in order to find an object. Database Availability Groups allow that presentation tier to make decisions about which copy of the backend data should be accessed. If a failure were to occur on the "preferred" copy of the mailbox database, another copy would be selected based on a priority value set on replicas that were established by the email administrator. In this way, mailbox redundancy scales beyond the 2 copies offered by CCR and improves to as many as 16 copies. While SCR previously allowed an administrator to store mailbox replicas in more than 2 places, the recovery via SCR was always a manual process while DAG is an automatic occurrence. This ability to replicate and automatically attach to a valid copy of the data has tremendous implications for today's email administrators ranging from simple geographic redundancy all the way to fundamentally changing the way storage for Exchange Server is designed. Having so many potential copies of mailbox data, coupled with mailbox retention policies, could completely eliminate the need for nightly backups for Exchange Server data. Do note, however, that these new abilities come with a price. Replication, while efficient, still requires bandwidth. Replicating daily Exchange Server 2010 traffic to as many as 16 WAN attached locations will eat up a significant amount of bandwidth and must be planned for appropriately.

Network Load Balancing (NLB) is as important as ever in the Exchange Server 2010 world because it allows various services such as Post Office Protocol version 3 (POP3), Internet Message Access Protocol version 4 (IMAP4), or Outlook Anywhere to enjoy redundancy as well. As Exchange Server 2010 has greatly improved OWA experiences for "non-Internet Explorer" browsers, email administrators can expect an increase in the number of users that access OWA for remote access to their email. As such, the ability to load balance web based services becomes even more critical. Even the latest version of Entourage for the Macintosh utilizes Web Services now rather than WebDAV and those users can enjoy the redundancy that comes with using NLB to load balance Client Access Servers.

This chapter further details these new functions and offers advice on how best to utilize them. Step-by-step installation and configuration instructions are included where appropriate.

Understanding Database Availability Groups

A Database Availability Group is a group of up to 16 Exchange Server 2010 mailbox role servers that replicate mailbox data to each other and that can perform automated recovery at the mailbox database level in the event of a hardware, storage, or network failure. They utilize a subset of Windows 2008 failover clustering in order to monitor each other's health. This allows them to determine which node should be primary for a given database.

To understand Database Availability Groups and how they work, it's important to understand the various technologies that are involved with making this work. DAGs take advantage of

- ▶ Windows 2008 Clustering

- ▶ Database Portability

- ▶ Log Shipping Replication

- ▶ Shadow Redundancy

- ▶ Incremental Reseeding

- ▶ Removal of Storage Groups

While Exchange Server 2010 DAGs aren't built on a traditional Windows cluster, DAGs do take advantage of Windows 2008 failover clustering in order to establish a heartbeat amongst them and to monitor the availability of each other. Unlike earlier versions of Exchange Server, Exchange Server 2010 does not require the administrators to manage resources at the cluster level. The installation of failover clustering features and the management of failover clustering is handled entirely "under the hood" by Exchange Server 2010.

Database Portability is a concept that was introduced in Exchange Server 2007. In short, it effectively uncoupled the Exchange server's identity from the security settings on the mailbox database. This allowed an Exchange Server 2007 server to host a mailbox database that was originally owned by a different server. In versions of Exchange Server prior to 2007, this concept didn't exist and as a result, recovering mailbox databases on new servers was a rather painful exercise. In Exchange Server 2010, this concept is what allows multiple Exchange Server 2010 mailbox servers to be effectively authoritative for the same mailbox database information.

> **NOTE**
>
> Because a single mailbox database can be replicated across multiple servers, it is required by Exchange Server 2010 that all mailbox databases be created with unique names. In older versions of Exchange Server, it was acceptable to reuse a database name because they were always referenced by "Server name\Storage Group name\ Database name" which made them unique within the Exchange Server organization. In Exchange Server 2010, this is not the case as a replica could potentially have a name conflict with a local database.

Log Shipping Replication was introduced into Exchange Server 2007 with the creation of Clustered Continuous Replication and was later reused in Standby Continuous Replication. The same base technology is used to replicate mailbox database transactions between members of a Database Availability Group. This replication has been improved in terms of resiliency and recovery through the introduction of Shadow Redundancy and Incremental Reseeding.

Shadow Redundancy is the name given to a new process in Exchange Server 2010. Similar to the Transport Dumpster function in Exchange Server 2007, wherein a message that was sent via a Hub Transport role was saved for a period of time in case it needed to be resent after a CCR or SCR failover, Shadow Redundancy ensures that a message is not deleted from a transport database until after it has received a confirmation of receipt from the next hop. If the next hop doesn't confirm receipt, the message is resubmitted for delivery. This is especially useful in high traffic environments where large numbers of messages are potentially "in flight" on a hub transport server. If that server was to fail and the messages were not sent to their next hop, the mailbox server would detect this and resubmit the unconfirmed messages to another available Hub Transport server. Should those messages later become available through a "fix" of the failed Hub Transport, the destination would recognize them as duplicates and suppress them from the target mailbox.

Incremental Reseeding is another new function of Exchange Server 2010 that reduces the impact of replicating mailbox data to a database that was offline for a period of time. In Exchange Server 2007, if a CCR or SCR replica was too far out of sync, the only solution was to delete the database and start replication from scratch. This resulted in potentially hundreds of gigabytes of data being replicated in order to get the database back to a point where it could accept and process log files. During this time, the databases were no longer redundant and the mailbox data was at risk. With Incremental Reseeding, the out of sync database is compared to the source database and only the necessary updates are sent to the database in order to bring it back to a level where replication can resume normally. This greatly reduces the time taken to reseed a database and thus reduces the windows of exposure for the mailbox data.

The last piece of Database Availability Groups was the removal of the concept of a Storage Group from Exchange Server 2010. In Exchange Server 2007, any of the replication technologies required that the system be configured with only one database per storage group. Log files for all databases within a storage group were grouped together and recovery of a database read the log files from this storage group. In Exchange Server 2010 DAG, because the databases are no longer associated with a specific server, the need to manage by Storage Group was removed. Databases are now associated with the DAG instead.

> **NOTE**
>
> Database replication within a DAG is only supported between mailbox servers with less than 250ms of round trip latency. As such, it's important to be aware of the typical latency between sites that might potentially house replicas of your mailbox data. Although physics tells us that electricity can travel the circumference of the earth in around 135ms, network induced latency as well as indirect paths can make this number significantly higher.

Deploying a Database Availability Group

Deployment of a Database Availability Group (DAG) is a fairly straightforward process but it does have several steps that must occur in the correct order. By becoming familiar with the requirements and the process, the implementation should be fairly uneventful.

Because a DAG doesn't require a Windows 2008 Cluster to be prebuilt, the instructions will assume that the administrator has already built a basic Exchange Server 2010 mailbox server. For detailed instructions on building an Exchange Server 2010 mailbox server, see Chapter 4, "Architecting an Enterprise-Level Exchange Server Environment."

Requirements for DAG

You will need two or more servers that are capable of supporting the Exchange Server 2010 Mailbox role. You don't need shared storage with a DAG because the transactions are shipped to the replicas and applied locally. This allows up to 16 independent databases and sets of log files on up to 16 different servers with independent media. You will want to follow the same standards as you would with a normal mailbox server in terms of database sizes and hardware specifications to support your anticipated user load.

To set up a DAG, you need the following:

- ▶ Two or more servers running Windows Server 2008, Enterprise Edition
- ▶ Two network interfaces per server
- ▶ Exchange Server 2010 Enterprise Edition
- ▶ 1 File share witness per DAG
- ▶ No longer limited to a single AD site

You need to pre-create the file share that will be used as the file share witness by the cluster. The permissions on the share will be configured for you by Exchange Server 2010. The file share witness cannot be hosted on a member of the DAG.

Creating the File Share Witness

While a Database Availability Group isn't a cluster in the traditional sense, it does utilize some of the functions of Windows 2008 clustering in order to track system availability. One of the components required for this function is a file share witness. Administrators familiar with Exchange Server 2007 may recall that a file share witness acts like a voting node in a cluster, specifically a Majority Node Set cluster. This allows a cluster to have as few as 2 traditional nodes with the FSW acting like a 3rd node. This allows the cluster to achieve a majority if a node were to fail. Were there only 2 voting nodes total, the majority of two is two, so only one being up and running wouldn't constitute a majority and it wouldn't be able to make cluster related decisions. Each Database Availability Group will need its own file share witness. To create this share, follow these steps:

1. Create a directory on a Hub Transport server or a File server.
2. Right-click the directory, and choose Share.
3. Click Share.
4. Click Done.

The configuration of the Database Availability Group will configure the necessary permissions on the share for you.

Creating the DAG via GUI

Once the Exchange Server mailbox servers are prepared, they can be joined into a new Database Availability Group by performing the following steps:

1. Launch the Exchange Management Console.
2. Expand Organization Configuration.
3. Click Mailbox.
4. In the middle pane, click the Database Availability Group tab (see Figure 31.1).

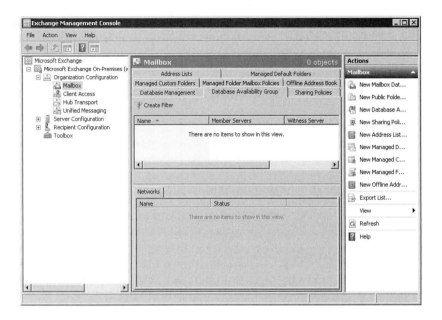

FIGURE 31.1   Creating the DAG.

5. In the right pane, click New Database Availability Group.

6. When prompted, enter a unique name for the Database Availability Group along with the file share witness path and directory that were created earlier (see Figure 31.2). Click New.

7. When the wizard has completed, click Finish.

At this point, the DAG has been created, however it has no members. Add member mailbox servers to the DAG with the following steps:

1. Launch the Exchange Management Console.

2. Expand Organization Configuration.

3. Click Mailbox.

4. In the middle pane, click the Database Availability Group tab.

5. Right click the DAG created in the previous steps and choose Manage Database Availability Group Membership.

6. When the wizard appears, click Add and choose the mailbox servers from the list that you want to join to the DAG (see Figure 31.3). Click Manage.

7. The wizard might take several minutes to complete. When it has added all the necessary nodes, click Finish (see Figure 31.4).

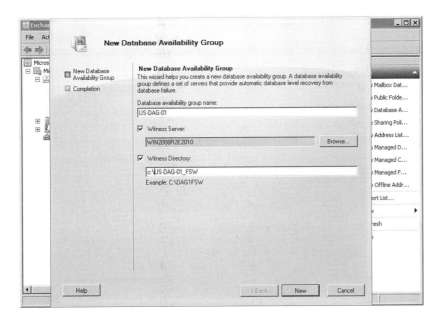

FIGURE 31.2   Entering the information for a new DAG.

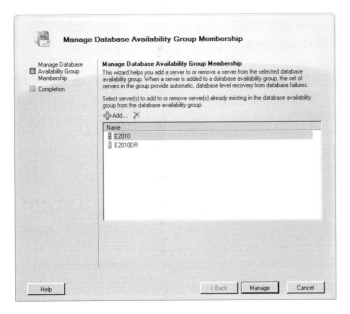

FIGURE 31.3   Adding members to the DAG.

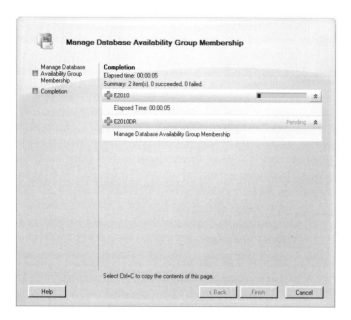

FIGURE 31.4 Completing the new DAG member wizard.

When this process has been completed on both nodes, the systems are ready for the rest of the configuration process to continue.

1. Return to Exchange Management Console and expand Organization Configuration.

2. Click Mailbox. In the middle pane, click the Database Management tab (see Figure 31.5).

3. In the lower pane, right-click the database you wish to replicate within the DAG.

4. Choose Add Mailbox Database Copy.

5. When the wizard launches, browse for the server in the DAG to which you want to replicate the mailbox database. Pick a Replay Lag Time and a Truncation Lag Time (see Figure 31.6).

6. Enter a unique preferred list sequence number and click Add.

7. When the wizard completes, click Finish.

When the Database Availability Group is created, a computer object is created in Active Directory to represent the Failover cluster virtual network name account. If a DAG is going to be recreated with the same name, it is necessary to disable or delete this computer account or the process will error out and fail.

Suspending and Reseeding a Database

In the event that a replica of a mailbox database should become out of sync with the primary copy, it becomes necessary to reseed the database in order to resume the replication of log files. There are a few situations that can cause the need to sync the databases:

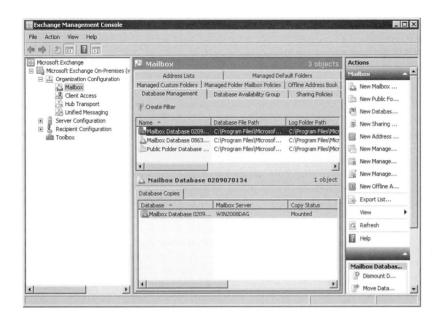

FIGURE 31.5   The newly created DAG.

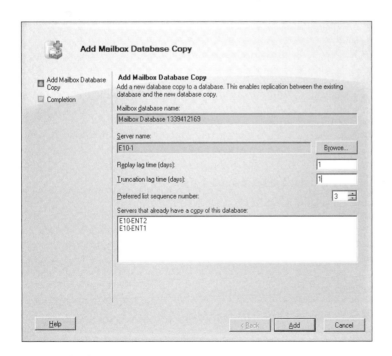

FIGURE 31.6   Adding a DAG replica.

▶ Bringing a replica back online after extended downtime

▶ Corruption of log files

▶ Corruption of a database

▶ An extended WAN outage

The easiest way to determine if a database needs to be resynchronized is to look at its current replication status:

1. Launch Exchange Management Console.

2. Expand Organization Configuration.

3. Click Mailbox.

4. In the middle pane, click the Database Management tab.

5. Click the database whose replication status you want to check.

6. In the lower pane, look at the Copy Status on the replicas in question. If they are in a Failed state, they will likely need to be reseeded.

> **NOTE**
>
> If you have a large number of mailbox databases, it may behoove you to take advantage of the filter function. This allows you to match based on Master, Mounted, Mounted on Server or Name. You can use the browse button to look for specific Exchange Server names to match against.

If the database is found to be in a failed state, it can be reseeded in the following manner:

1. Launch Exchange Management Console.

2. Expand Organization Configuration.

3. Click Mailbox.

4. In the middle pane, click the Database Management tab.

5. Click the database whose replication status you wish to fix.

6. In the lower pane, click the database replica that is in a failed state.

7. Right-click the database and select Suspend Database Copy. Enter an optional comment if you want, then click Yes.

8. The Copy Status should update to read Suspended (see Figure 31.7).

9. Right-click the suspended database and select Update Database Copy.

10. Enter a hostname to specify which cluster networks should be used for seeding (see Figure 31.8). Click Add.

11. Click Update.

12. The update might take a while depending on how big the database is and how many log files have been created since the database was last in sync (see Figure 31.9).

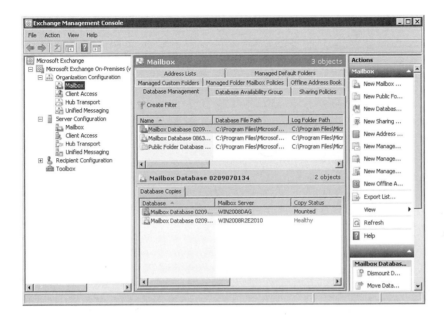

FIGURE 31.7   Viewing the Summary Copy Status.

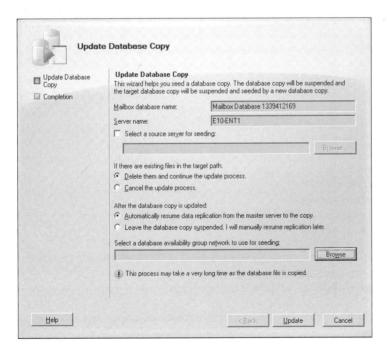

FIGURE 31.8   Updating the database copy.

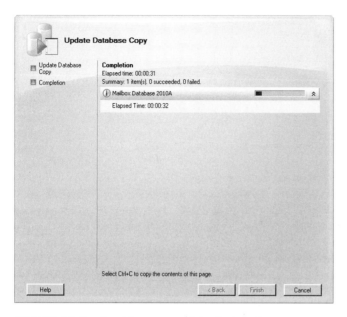

FIGURE 31.9   Checking status of the Update Database Copy Wizard.

13. When the wizard finishes, click Finish.

14. Refresh the view in EMC, and the database should now have a status of Healthy (see Figure 31.10).

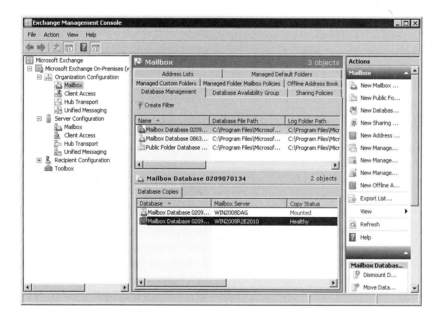

FIGURE 31.10   Viewing the Summary Copy Status.

The same process of suspending and updating the Database Copy can be performed via Powershell:

1. Launch Exchange Management Shell.

2. Type `Suspend-MailboxDatabaseCopy-Identity` DatabaseName\ReplicaServer where DatabaseName and ReplicaServer are the names of the DB you want to update and the server holding the replica that is to be reseeded. Answer Yes when prompted.

3. Type `Update-MailboxDatabaseCopy-Identity` DatabaseName\ReplicaServer-DeleteExistingFiles. Answer Yes when prompted (see Figure 31.11).

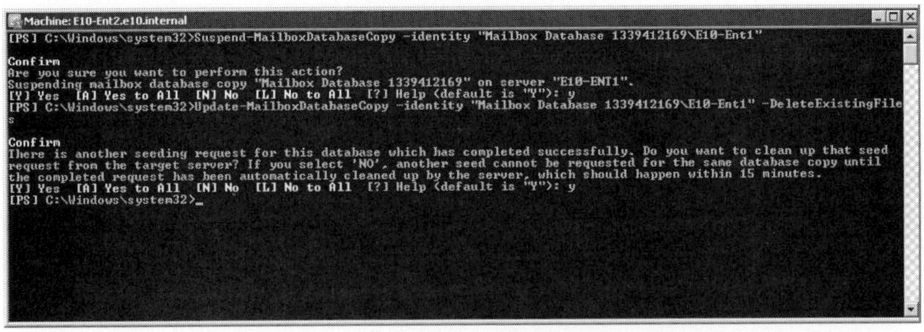

FIGURE 31.11   Updating from Exchange Management Shell.

Creating the DAG via Exchange Management Shell

Many Exchange Server administrators have embraced the Exchange Management Shell as the preferred tool for configuration. Doing things via the shell has many advantages. The primary advantage being that it is very easy to script configuration and deployment which ensures that all systems are configured correctly and that no human error occurs while following a set of directions. To create a DAG via the Exchange Management Shell, perform the following steps:

1. Launch Exchange Management Shell.

2. Type `New-DatabaseAvailabilityGroup-Name` *name*`-FileShareWitnessDirectory` *DirectoryPath*`-FileShareWitnessShare` *UNCPath*`-DomainController` *DC*.

   For example, `New-DatabaseAvailabilityGroup-Name US-DAG-01-FileShareWitnessDirectory` c:\FSW`-FileShareWitnessShare` \\hotspace\FSW`-DomainController` Coldspare (see Figure 31.12).

Adding Nodes to the DAG via Exchange Management Shell

When the Database Availability Group has been created via Exchange Management Shell, the same shell can be used to add members to the DAG via the following steps:

1. Launch Exchange Management Shell.

2. Type `Add-DatabaseAvailabilityGroupServer-Identity` *DAGName*`-MailboxServer` *firstnode*.

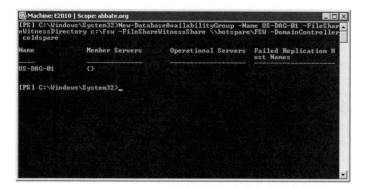

FIGURE 31.12   Adding a DAG replica from Exchange Management Shell.

For example, `Add-DatabaseAvailabilityGroupServer-Identity US-DAG-01-MailboxServer E2010` (see Figure 31.13).

FIGURE 31.13   Adding a node to an existing DAG via Exchange Management Shell.

3. Add any additional nodes with the same command; simply replace the name of the node to be added.

Adding a Database Copy to a DAG via Exchange Management Shell

With the Database Availability Group configured and functional, you can add database copies to DAG members by following these steps:

1. Launch Exchange Management Shell.

2. Type `Add-MailboxDatabaseCopy-Identity` *DatabaseName*`-MailboxServer` *ReplicaServer*`-ActivationPreference` number.

For example, Add-MailboxDatabaseCopy-Identity Mailbox Database
2010A-MailboxServer E2010DR-ActivationPreference 2 (see Figure 31.14).

FIGURE 31.14   Seeding a DAG replica via Exchange Management Shell.

3. The database will begin seeding.

4. When the seeding is completed, the database replica will be in a suspended state.
   Resume the replication by typing Resume-MailboxDatabaseCopy-Identity
   DatabaseName-MailboxServer *ServerToResume*.

   For example, Resume-MailboxDatabaseCopy-Identity Mailbox Database
   2010A-MailboxServer E2010DR.

Monitoring the Health of DAG Replication

When a Database Availability Group has been established and replicas added to it, it is
useful for administrators to be able to check on the health of the replication. Should this
replication fail for any reason, the sooner an Administrator can be aware of it, the better
their chance is to fix the replication before a reseed becomes necessary.

The health of the replication can be checked in two ways, through the GUI by using
Exchange Management Console or from the command line by using Exchange
Management Shell.

To check the health of a replica via the GUI, follow these steps:

1. Launch Exchange Management Console.

2. Expand Organization Configuration.

3. Click mailbox.

4. Click the Database Management tab.

5. Highlight the Database whose status you wish to check. If there are a large number of databases in your environment, consider using the Filter option to narrow your view.

Additional status information is available by right-clicking the database copy and choosing Properties. This will show the Copy and Replay queue lengths as well as show the Replay and Truncation lag settings. The Status tab will show log related information including the latest log file available, the time a log was last inspected, the time a log was last copied and the time a log was last replayed. This information can be useful in determining the cause of replication problems.

To perform a similar task in Exchange Management Shell, perform the following steps:

1. Launch Exchange Management Shell.

2. Type Get-DatabaseCopyStatus-MailboxServer *ReplicaServer*.

    For example, Get-DatabaseCopyStatus-MailboxServer E2010DR (see Figure 31.15).

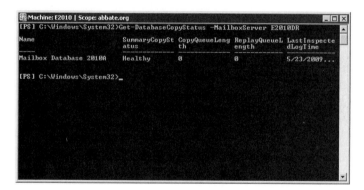

FIGURE 31.15   Checking replication status via Exchange Management Shell.

This shows the current status of the replication and will show the Copy Queue Length and the Replay Queue Length. This makes it easy to see if a copy is in sync or if not, how far behind it is.

There are several advantages to querying the replication status via the Management Shell. For example, while at first the output from the command would seem to suggest that there is less information available than what is shown by the GUI, this is actually not the case. If one were to pipe the output of Get-DatabaseCopyStatus to a formatted list, one would find that there are 44 parameters that are tracked by this command.

Get-DatabaseCopyStatus-MailboxServer E2010DR ¦ FL

This can be exceptionally useful when one needs to query a large number of systems for any errors. By querying all of your mailbox servers and filtering out just ones where a particular parameter is returning a specific status, you can quickly find all servers matching those criteria.

For example, an administrator might want to generate a real time report showing all mailbox servers who have a database status of Failed = true. This can be written fairly easily in Exchange Management Shell:

```
del c:\users\Administrator \Documents\FailedState.csv
$mailboxservers = Get-MailboxServer
Foreach ($server in $mailboxservers)
{
$var=Get-DatabaseCopyStatus -mailboxserver $server ¦ where {$_.Failed -match "True"}
$status=$Var.Failed
$ID=$Var.Databasename
$log=$var.LastCopiedLogTime
Add-content c:\users\Administrator \Documents\FailedState.csv "$server,$ID,
➥$Status, $Log"}
```

This will produce a list showing replica servers who have one or more databases in a Failed state. It will show specifically which databases are in that Failed state and will show the timestamp of the last log which was shipped. This type of a script could be scheduled to run hourly to allow for an up-to-date view of replication across the whole environment.

Moving the Active Copy of the Database

When, in the course of administrator events, it becomes necessary for one to perform maintenance on a member of a Database Availability Group, it might be necessary to move the active copy of a given database from one server to another. Although taking down a node that is currently the active copy causes the second priority node to activate, the process is cleaner and smoother if it is initiated intentionally.

Given that the active copy of the database is effectively the source of replication, it is important to consider that the site holding a given copy of the database will experience an increase in bandwidth usage if there are multiple copies of a database distributed across the environment. As such, it is recommended to move the active copy to a well connected site whenever possible.

To make a replica the active copy of a mailbox database, perform the following steps:

1. Launch Exchange Management Console.
2. Expand Organization Configuration.
3. Click mailbox.
4. Click the Database Management tab.
5. Right-click the database copy you want to make the active copy.
6. Select Activate Database Copy (see Figure 31.16).

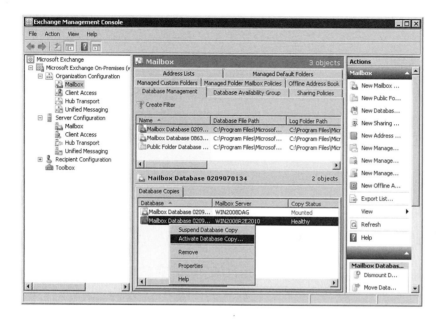

FIGURE 31.16   Active Database Copy.

7. When the wizard launches, confirm the mount dial override and click OK.

The same process can be done entirely from the Exchange Management Shell as well by following these steps:

1. Launch Exchange Management Shell.

2. Type Move-ActiveMailboxDatabase-Identity *DBName*-ActivateOnServer *NewServer*.

For example, Move-ActiveMailboxDatabase-Identity Mailbox Database 2010A-ActivateOnServer E2010.

NOTE

It is of value to point out that when the active copy status is moved from one host to another, several things happen automatically. Replication from active copy to replicas automatically resumes from the new source, and Client Access Servers automatically connect to the copy of the database that is now active. OWA clients might see a small hiccup in service, stating that their mailbox is not mounted, but simply refreshing the browser will reconnect the session.

Changing Priorities on Replicas of Mailbox Databases

As an Exchange Server 2010 environment grows and evolves, you might want to alter the initial distribution of mailbox database replicas in terms of the preferred replacement if a failure occurs. For example, an environment may start off with an active copy of a database in San Francisco with a replica copy in an office in New York. Some time down the road a new office, say in Denver, might be brought online. Based on latency, it might be more desirable for Denver to be the secondary site for San Francisco rather than New York. Denver could be added as a replica using the steps shown earlier in this chapter and it would default to being the third in the list of preferred replicas. To change this replica to preference 2, simply follow these steps:

1. Launch Exchange Management Console.

2. Expand Organization Configuration.

3. Click mailbox.

4. Click the Database Management tab.

5. Right-click the database copy whose preference you wish to change and select Properties.

6. Change the Preferred List Sequence Number, in this case from 3 to 2 (see Figure 31.17).

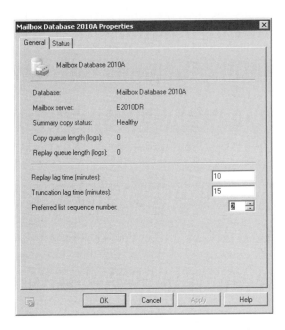

FIGURE 31.17   Viewing Mailbox Database Copy properties.

7. Click OK.

The same change can be performed via the Exchange Management Shell by following these steps:

1. Launch Exchange Management Console.

2. Type Set-mailboxDatabaseCopy -Identity *DBName* -MailboxServer *ServerWithCopyToChange* -ActivationPreference *PreferenceNumber*.

For example, Set-MailboxDatabaseCopy-Identity SF-DB-01-MailboxServer EX-Denver-MB01-ActivationPreference 2.

This would take the copy of the database called SF-DB-01 that was living on Exchange DAG member EX-Denver-MB01 and alter its priority to 2–making it the copy that would become active if the current active copy were to become unavailable.

Hardware Considerations for Database Availability Group Members

With the evolutionary changes that come with Exchange Server 2010, there is a noticeable shift in recommendations around hardware that should be used to support Exchange Server, especially in the area of Database Availability Groups.

Administrators who were familiar with Clustered Continuous Replication in Exchange Server 2007 will immediately see the parallels between DAG and CCR. CCR introduced, and DAG continues to show, the benefits of directly attached storage for Exchange Server. Older versions of Exchange Server required very high levels of I/O to be provided in order for users to get good performance. Similarly, older versions of Exchange Server were dependent on shared storage to allow for redundancy at the mailbox level. DAG creates a situation in which there is no requirement to share any storage whatsoever across the nodes that form a DAG. This means that DAG members are free to utilize directly attached storage. This also means that because many DAG members are comprised mostly of mailbox databases that aren't being directly accessed, their I/O requirements tend to be relatively low. This, coupled with the changes in architecture within Exchange Server 2010 that further lower I/O requirements through the use of larger blocks of data being transferred, further reduces the need for high performance disk subsystems.

Another factor that heavily influenced the hardware used for Exchange Server in the past was the requirements around localized redundancy and fault tolerance. Traditionally Exchange servers were built with multiple sets of disks for the operating system, the database files and the transaction logs. The logic was that by mirroring the operating system, one could protect against a server failure due to a failed hard drive. Similarly, logs were always kept separate from the databases so that if a database failed, the data could be restored from a backup and the current log files could be replayed to bring the database back to a current state. In a Database Availability Group, the Exchange Server mailbox servers become a disposable resource. Not unlike domain controllers in Active Directory, there is very little need to ever restore a failed DAG member, so long as at least one other DAG member exists with a replica of the mailbox databases. One simply installs a fresh Exchange Server 2010 mailbox server and adds it to the appropriate DAG and then adds that server to the list of replicas for the databases that were previously hosted in that site. The data is replicated and the level of redundancy and fault tolerance is restored to its previous state.

Based on this ability to quickly and easily replace a lost DAG member, the requirements around local redundancy are effectively removed. Money that previously would have been used to purchase multiple disks and very high performance disks can now be used to instead purchase commodity hardware to act as an additional DAG member with replicas of databases. Microsoft has gone as far as to recommend building mailbox servers with no

RAID whatsoever. The redundancy is effectively moved from the storage layer to the application layer.

When planning for the hardware to deploy an Exchange Server 2010 environment, keep in mind that the old CCR model of active/passive is no longer a limiting factor in your planning. For example, in Exchange Server 2007, if one were to build in redundancy for a site, they would have to build a stretched CCR pair where one system was active for all its users and the other system sat by just dealing with replication. Often administrators would take the hardware for CCR and utilize Hyper-V or VMWare to effectively turn each system into two systems. Each host would have two guest systems where one was the active CCR node for its own site and the other guest was the passive node for its partner site. This meant that each system had to be built with enough available performance to host all users from both sites. In a Database Availability Group, this 1 for 1 relationship isn't necessarily a requirement. Imagine a 3 site DAG where each host is running at 66% capacity. Each site has 10 databases that are active copies and each site is replicated to every other site. In the event of a failure, rather than having all 10 databases fail over to a single site, a clever administrator might have set 5 of the databases to priority 2 in "site B" and priority 3 in "Site C" with the other 5 set to priority 3 in "site B" and priority 2 in "Site C." In this scenario, the 66% load is spread evenly to the other two sites, resulting in each site being capable of handling the load. This level of granularity in determining where loads will go in the case of a failure is exactly what Exchange Server 2007 administrators were wishing for.

This concept can be carried further in the case of smaller sites that are replicated to a centralized disaster recovery site. While an environment might have a dozen sites with say 500 users each, one doesn't necessarily build their disaster recovery site to handle 6,000 users. If, by some terrible series of events, all 12 sites suffered simultaneous failures, the odds of all 6,000 users being able to access their email would be very low. One might instead plan the capacity from a performance standpoint to handle say 2,000 users but build the storage to replicate the mailboxes for all 6,000 users.

In older versions of Exchange Server, supporting 6,000 users required a fair amount of spindles on the disk subsystem. Exchange Server 2003, for example, recommended about 0.75 disk i/o per second per user. With a 6,000 user load, this meant about 4500 i/o per sec. Given that a typical 10,000rpm disk can provide 110 i/o at an acceptable disk latency (under 20ms) it required 41 disks to provide this level of performance. If one needed the storage to be redundant, and most did, this requirement jumped to 82 disks to provide the i/o in a RAID0+1 configuration. It was in these days that SAN reigned supreme as it was otherwise unrealistic to present 82 disks to an Exchange server. In Exchange Server 2010, the i/o requirement is more like 0.1 i/o per sec per user, due to the larger transfer block size and the amount of data that is cached. The cache of mailbox information is significantly larger due to the ability to access large amounts of memory, made possible by the 64-bit architecture. In this scenario, the same 6,000 users would require 600 i/o per sec, which could be provided by 6 spindles. Assuming one was planning to replicate the data via a Database Availability Group, the local requirement would literally be for 6 disks, in RAID0. The cost of a SAN plus the 82 disks minus the costs of the 6 local disks would more than cover the price of a second server with 6 disks to provide the replica. It becomes easy to see that Exchange Server 2010 has the potential to be a much lower cost to deploy, and become a much faster return on investment.

The logical extension of the reduction in resources required to support Exchange Server 2010 in a Database Availability Group model is the concept of virtualization for the hosts. Depending on one's level of trust and expertise with virtualization, it might make sense to initially virtualize one set of the replicas in order to gain knowledge and trust in managing a virtualized environment. For those who have already headed down a path of virtualization, all the roles in Exchange Server 2010 are very good candidates for virtualization.

Perhaps the simplest point to take away from this discussion is that the old days of needing identical hardware across all cluster nodes is no longer the case. Database Availability Groups, while loosely dependent on Windows clustering services, have no requirements for the hardware to be identical, or even similar for that matter. Mixing and matching levels of performance, processor architecture, and storage types are completely supported. Just make sure a given system has enough performance to perform its primary job and to take over any additional loads that you're planning it to be redundant for.

> **NOTE**
>
> Administrators who are considering virtualization of very large Exchange Server 2010 servers should be aware of performance issues surrounding non uniform memory access (NUMA) boundaries. The short version is that host system memory divided by the number of processor cores is the size of a NUMA boundary on that system. Guest virtual machines that are allocated memory larger than a single NUMA boundary will suffer a performance loss compared to a virtual system whose memory allocation is equal to or smaller than a NUMA boundary.

Dedicating a Network to Log Shipping for DAG Replication

Many companies that run Exchange Server have invested in very high performance WAN connections. MPLS networks have become something of a corporate standard due to their performance and stability. The drawback to these high speed MPLS networks is often the cost. While bandwidth has become steadily more affordable, the connections and high bandwidth is nonetheless a large portion of most IT groups' budgets. Many companies have moved toward a strategy of utilizing the high performance MPLS network for servicing end users and have moved their replication to lower cost networks, such as IPSec or VPN tunnels running across the Internet. Environments who run these multi-tiered networks will likely wish to take advantage of Exchange Server 2010's capability to specify a network to be used for DAG replication. In Exchange Server 2007, one had to create additional network interfaces as cluster resources and associate them with each cluster group and then utilize host files so that the CCR or SCR targets always resolved their sources by the dedicated replication interfaces. Exchange Server 2010 makes this significantly easier by allowing an administrator to define a database availability network.

To create a Database Availability Group network via the GUI, follow these steps:

1. Launch Exchange Management Console.
2. Expand Organization Configuration.

3. Click mailbox.

4. Click the Database Availability Group tab.

5. Right-click the DAG for which you need to define a replication network.

6. Choose New Database Availability Group Network.

7. Enter a Network Name of up to 128 characters.

8. Enter a Network Description of up to 256 characters.

9. Click Add to add subnets to the DAG network.

10. Check the box for Enable replication.

11. Click New.

To create a Database Availability Group network via the Exchange Management Shell, follow these steps:

1. Launch Exchange Management Shell.

2. Type `New-DatabaseAvailabilityGroupNetwork –DatabaseAvailabilityGroup` *DAG* `–Name` *DAGNet* `–Description "`*description*`" –Subnets "#.#.#.#/#" –ReplicationEnabled:$true`.

   For example, `New-DatabaseAvailabilityGroupNetwork-DatabaseAvailabilityGroup US-DAG-1 –Name DAGNetworkSFtoNY-Description "dedicated replication network via IPSec tunnel from SF to NY"–Subnets "192.168.1.0/24" –ReplicationEnabled:$true`.

Using DAG to Provide a "Tiered Services" Model

One of the limitations of Clustered Continuous Replication in Exchange Server 2007 was that you didn't have any level of granularity in which content got replicated. It was really an all or nothing configuration. Database Availability Groups give you the ability to determine which database should be replicated and how often. This allows an administrator to create an interesting tiered services model that allows them to establish parameters around classes of mailboxes.

For example, one might wish to replicate all mailboxes locally to allow for simplified maintenance windows. One can simply alter a replica to be the current active copy and perform maintenance on the previously active copy. When that maintenance is completed, the administrator can optionally reactivate the previous replica, after it has had a chance to get back into sync. This is likely to be a common scenario as it accomplishes redundancy and allows for quick maintenance without incurring a lot of overhead expense. LAN bandwidth isn't much of a concern in most environments and the total cost to provide this level of convenience and protection is simply an additional server and its associated licenses.

In more advanced environments there may be a requirement to replicate mailbox data offsite to protect against a failure of an entire site or perhaps even an entire geographic region. In some cases, this need for geographic redundancy may really only be appropriate for specific types of users. While managers and executives may have a requirement for nearly 100% mailbox availability, it might not be required for resource mailboxes or for part time workers or perhaps for factory floor users whose jobs aren't dependent on email access. For these types of situations, administrators can take advantage of the granularity of Database Availability Groups to set different replication rules for different databases. By organizing users into databases by job types, one can easily increase the number of replicas for specific groups to provide the level of protection they need without incurring the overhead of having to replicate an entire server.

Comparing and Contrasting DAG Versus CCR/SCR/SCC

For administrators coming from an Exchange Server 2003 or Exchange Server 2007 environment looking to upgrade to Exchange Server 2010, it may prove useful to compare and contrast Database Availability Groups to existing replication technologies that one might already be familiar with.

In Exchange Server 2003, the only clustering option available was Single Copy Cluster. Exchange Server 2003 could withstand a hardware failure of a mailbox server because another node in the cluster could take over the identity and host the Exchange Virtual Server. DAG provides a similar ability to recover from a failed server though it does so without the need for a shared identity or for shared storage.

Exchange Server 2007 brought about the concept of Clustered Continuous Replication which, like SCC, provided protection against the failure of a server. It did so by sharing the identity between two hosts. It surpassed SCC by providing two copies of the Exchange Server mailbox database, which protected Exchange Server from a storage failure or a database corruption. DAG utilizes the same log shipping and replay process that was introduced by CCR to perform its replication of mailbox databases. Many of the same concepts such as Suspend-StorageGroupCopy and Update-StorageGroupCopy are still present and accomplish essentially the same tasks. The names have been updated to reflect the fact that the storage group is no longer the root of the replication but instead it occurs at the database layer. As readers may recall, storage groups no longer exist in Exchange Server 2010 as the databases belong to the Database Availability Group or to the Exchange Organization. Administrators with experience in maintaining a CCR environment will likely have an easy transition to DAGs.

Exchange Server 2007 also offered Standby Continuous Replication, which while similar to CCR, didn't utilize a shared identity. It used the same log shipping and replay technologies to keep a remote Exchange Server 2007 in sync with the primary copy of data but it was up to the client to make a determination about where the mailbox was currently located. The other drawback to SCR as opposed to CCR was that SCR required an administrator to make manual changes to the systems in order to bring up a remote copy of the mailbox database. DAG made an important improvement by moving the logic for finding the active copy of the database from the client to the client access servers. In this manner, clients that could not previously redirect themselves based on information in Active

31

Directory can now successfully connect to their mailbox when the primary copy is moved to another location. Like SCR, DAG doesn't need to share the identity of the server as the middle tier of this application architecture is able to determine that automatically.

Backing Up a Database Availability Group

While Chapter 32, "Backing up the Exchange Server 2010 Environment," will cover this concept in more detail, there are some interesting implications of Database Availability Groups in the area of backing up Exchange Server 2010. Exchange Server 2010 provides no native methods to backup mailbox data in the traditional sense. Even for third party backups, the old style of streaming backups is no longer supported. The only option is to utilize a VSS based backup. However, consider the possibility that with Database Availability Groups and an appropriate retention policy, it might not be necessary to backup Exchange Server 2010 at all.

Consider, for example, an environment with a written policy that "no email shall be retained for more than 30 days in a backup." For companies that don't have specific regulatory requirements for mail retention, this is actually a fairly common situation. Now imagine that Exchange Server 2010 mailbox databases are configured with a retention of 30 days. This is to say that a user can use Outlook to "undelete" a message that has cleared the Deleted Items folder for up to 30 days. This means that the only thing a backup needs to protect against is a failure of the database or the storage, as accidental deletions are covered for up to 30 days. By definition, DAG is providing a remote backup that is an independent copy of the mailbox database. This means that if the active database copy were corrupted or if there was a hardware or storage failure of the active copy, the next priority copy of the mailbox database would automatically take over and there would be no loss of messages. Similarly, because there are multiple replicas of the mailbox databases, there would really never be a situation in which it was necessary to restore a mailbox database. Not unlike a domain controller, an administrator would simply build a new one and let it replicate with the other copies.

This ability to replicate rather than restore replicas offers an interesting possibility. In older versions of Exchange Server, one could restore a mailbox server to current by restoring an older database from tape and replaying the log files, assuming the log files were still available on the system. This is why it was always critical to store the log files separately from the databases. In an Exchange Server 2010 DAG, there is no need to restore from tape and replay logs, which raises the question, why bother to maintain log files?

One could configure their environment to have three or more DAG nodes and enable circular logging for the Exchange Server databases. This would eliminate the need to perform log truncations, which is one of the primary reasons that backups are run in Exchange Server 2007 and older environments.

For longer term backups, one could dismount the databases on an inactive DAG replica and simply copy those files to another location. Now there would be a point in time backup that could be stored long term. One could even use something like Single Mailbox

Recovery tool from NetApp to mount the edb file directly and recover individual messages without even having to put it back onto Exchange Server.

A similar option would be to snapshot the storage if one were using a SAN to host the Exchange Server 2010 data and that SAN supported snapshots.

Load Balancing in Exchange Server 2010

Another high-availability technology provided with the Windows Server 2008 platform is Network Load Balancing (NLB). NLB clusters provide high network performance and availability by balancing client requests across several server systems. When the client load increases, Windows NLB clusters can easily be scaled out by adding more nodes to the NLB configuration, to maintain an acceptable client response time to client requests.

Using NLB offers administrators the ability to leverage two dynamic features: First, to implement Windows NLB clusters, no proprietary hardware is required and NLB clusters can be implemented and configured through Windows management interfaces fairly easily and quickly.

NLB clusters are most effectively used to provide front-end support for web applications, virus scanning, and Simple Mail Transfer Protocol (SMTP) gateways. Because they are a very effective solution when used for web application functionality, NLB technology is a very effective solution for front-end access to Exchange Outlook Web App and terminal servers maintaining Exchange Server client software.

NLB clusters can grow to 32 nodes, and if larger cluster farms are necessary, the Microsoft Application Center server can be considered as an option for server platform support, along with technologies such as domain name system (DNS) round-robin to meet larger client access demands.

NLB Modes and Port Configuration Overview

In Unicast mode, clients and servers maintain a one-to-one relationship when communicating. In Multicast mode, servers respond by broadcasting a single, multicast address, which clients attach to when accessing information such as websites. NLB groups configured in Unicast mode will have a tendency to flood the switch to which they are connected, as the switch will need to pass traffic to all ports to be sure that all potential NLB nodes see the requests. If one plans to utilize Unicast mode NLB, it is recommended to place the NLB hosts onto their own VLAN to limit the scope of this broadcast traffic. Systems configured with Multicast mode will likely require minor changes to be made to the network switches to bind the virtual MAC address in the ARP tables and to define which ports should be forwarded traffic destined for that MAC address. Systems configured in Multicast mode should have two or more NICs installed to be properly supported.

For example, on a Cisco switch running IOS, to configure an NLB group with a virtual MAC address of 00-1D-60-18-83-83 and an IP address of 10.1.1.100:

```
Arp 10.1.1.100 001D.6018.8383
Mac-address-table static 001D.6018.8383 vlan 1 interface fa4/5 fa5/5
```

Where the VLAN value matches the VLAN assigned to the ports to which the NLB hosts are attached. Similarly, the "interface" will reference the ports to which the NLB hosts are attached.

Another option when configuring NLB with Outlook Web App is the ability to define the ports in which NLB cluster members will respond to client requests. This option is effective for the scenario because administrators can restrict and allow access to ports such as Hypertext Transfer Protocol (HTTP) port 80 and Secure Sockets Layer (SSL) port 443.

NLB Installations

One of the first steps when configuring NLB cluster nodes in Windows 2008 is the installation of Network Load Balancing as a feature. In Windows 2008, this isn't turned on by default and must be installed via the following steps:

1. From the Start menu, right click Computer and choose Manage.
2. In the left pane, click Features.
3. In the right pane, click Add Features (see Figure 31.18).

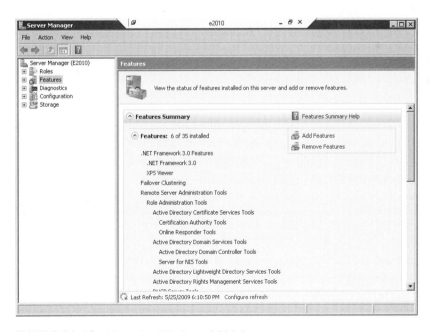

FIGURE 31.18   Managing Windows 2008 features.

4. Check the box for Network Load Balancing and click Next.
5. Confirm the installation selections and click Install (see Figure 31.19).

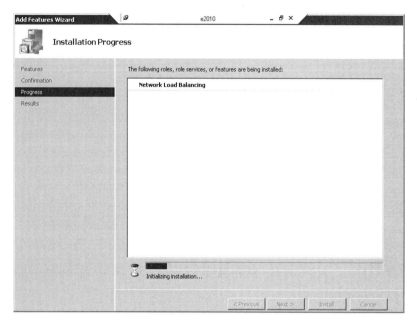

FIGURE 31.19   Installing NLB as a feature.

6. When the installation is completed, click Close.

7. Repeat these steps for all nodes of the NLB group.

Next is the configuration of the NICs in each server. A configuration of network cards can be completed using the NLB Manager and the TCP/IP properties of each node's network interface. One other option for configuring NICs is the command-line tool `nlb.exe`. This utility enables administrators to configure TCP/IP properties on NLB cluster nodes remotely and through the command line.

Configuring Network Load Balancing with Client Access Servers

Using the NLB Manager is the simplest method in configuring Client Access Servers into a load-balanced cluster configuration. When using the Network Load Balancing Manager, all information regarding the NLB cluster and load-balancing TCP/IP addresses is added dynamically to each cluster node when configured. Using the NLB Manager also simplifies the tasks of adding and removing nodes by enabling administrators to use the NetBIOS name or TCP/IP address to identify nodes.

TIP

To effectively manage NLB clusters on remote servers, install and configure two NICs on the local NLB Manager system.

In the following example, NLB services will be implemented to provide support with two separate Outlook Web App servers. This scenario assumes that each Outlook Web App server (client access server) has already been installed and configured and is functioning.

To begin, configure the network cards for each Outlook Web App system that you plan to configure in the NLB cluster:

1. Log on to the local console of an NLB node using an account with local Administrator privileges.

2. Select Start, right-click Network and choose Properties.

3. In the tasks list, click Manage network connections.

4. Right-click the interface that will participate in the NLB group and choose Properties.

5. Check the box labeled Network Load Balancing (NLB).

6. Click OK.

7. Repeat this process on all nodes that will participate in this NLB group.

TIP

It is a good practice to rename each network card so you can easily identify it when configuring interfaces and troubleshooting problems.

After Network Load Balancing has been enabled on each node, it is time to configure the NLB rules. This is most easily configured via the Network Load Balancing Manager. To configure the NLB hosts, perform these steps:

1. Log on to the local console of an NLB node using an account with local Administrator privileges.

2. From the Start menu, click Run and type `nlbmgr.exe`.

3. From the Cluster menu, click New (see Figure 31.20).

4. Enter the name of one of the hosts that will form the NLB group and click Connect.

5. Highlight the interface that will be used for NLB and click Next.

6. Set the Priority (this acts as a unique identifier) to a unique value for the NLB group and click Next.

7. Click Add and enter an IP address and subnet mask for the NLB group to use. Click OK. Click Next.

8. Enter a name for the NLB group to be known by. Set the cluster operation mode to the mode desired. Click Next.

9. Highlight the defined port rule and click Edit. Set the port range to the range needed (i.e. 443 to 443). Click OK.

10. If additional ports are needed to be load balanced, click Add and repeat step 9.

11. Click Finish.

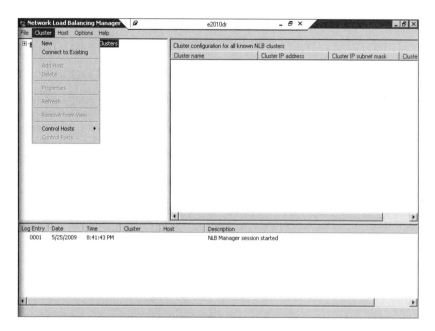

FIGURE 31.20   Creating an NLB cluster.

NOTE

A Windows 2008 host that has the Windows Cluster services installed cannot be a member of an NLB group. This means that a DAG member, while capable of running the CAS and/or HT roles, cannot load balance those roles.

Additional CAS servers can be added to the NLB group by following these steps at any time.

1. Log on to the local console of an NLB node using an account with local Administrator privileges.

2. From the Start menu, click Run and type `nlbmgr.exe`.

3. Right click the existing NLB group and choose Add Host.

4. Type in the name of the host to add to the NLB group and click Add.

5. Click Finish.

Validate that the state of the clustered NLB system is listed in the NLB Manager as Started, and close the Manager to complete the configuration of additional servers.

Summary

As you have seen in this chapter, Microsoft has replaced several different methods of providing high availability and disaster recovery with a single unified solution. By disassociating mailbox database from storage groups and instead associating them with Database Availability Groups, they have further improved the flexibility around high availability and disaster recovery. The limitation of CCR in terms of being required to replicate an entire server has been bypassed by DAG and the ability to replicate database by database and, in fact, to configure replications differently for different mailbox databases. Microsoft has given administrators enough granularity to finally configure their Exchange Server implementation specifically for their own unique needs. DAG does an excellent job of replacing both CCR and SCR by providing for the best of both worlds; the ability to automatically fail mailbox services from one host to another without the complexity and limitations of a traditional Windows cluster.

Microsoft has also opened up a whole new world of options for Exchange Server backups by introducing an environment that could conceivably operate without any backups whatsoever. By replicating the mailbox database information to multiple geographic locations and by avoiding log generation through the use of circular logging, Exchange Server 2010 Database Availability Groups, combined with prudent deleted item retention, could eliminate the need for traditional backups. Taking a replica offline to simply copy the databases in an acquiesced state would still allow an Administrator to maintain a long term copy of Exchange Server 2010 in the way that was traditionally performed by tape backups.

While some might wonder why Microsoft deprecated Clustered Continuous Replication and Standby Continuous Replication, one can easily see how those two technologies evolved into Database Availability Groups and can hopefully see the inherent advantages to this technology. Exchange Server administrators are highly encouraged to consider the implementation of Database Availability Groups in their Exchange Server 2010 deployments to provide the levels of high availability and disaster recovery that are demanded by modern business. As companies become more and more dependant on email and calendaring, Microsoft continues to raise the bar to make Exchange Server more resilient and easier to manage than ever.

Best Practices

The following are best practices from this chapter:

- Run an additional NIC in DAG member nodes to properly support Windows clustering.

- Ensure that hardware is chosen to not only support its dedicated load, but to take over additional loads when it's acting as a replica for other master copies of a mailbox database.

- Base your disk subsystem primarily on storage, as the performance requirements have dropped drastically.

▶ Always plan for a sufficient amount of TCP/IP addresses in advance to support current and future cluster needs.

▶ Do not run both clustering and NLB on the same computer; it is unsupported by Microsoft because of potential hardware-sharing conflicts between MSCS and NLB.

▶ Always plan for the additional WAN traffic created by adding another DAG replica that isn't on the local LAN.

▶ To avoid unwanted failover, power management should be disabled on each of the cluster nodes, both in the motherboard BIOS and in the power applet in Control Panel.

▶ Thoroughly test failover and failback mechanisms after the configuration is complete and before migrating users to a Database Availability Group.

▶ Make sure that mailbox databases have unique names.

▶ When utilizing load balancing, make sure to only load balance the ports necessary. This will avoid the possibility of network related issues when talking to Active Directory.

▶ Be sure to regularly monitor replication between DAG nodes to ensure that replication is healthy.

▶ Periodically test the move of master status between various copies of mailbox database groups to ensure that the data is valid and the cluster is working correctly.

CHAPTER 32

Backing Up the Exchange Server 2010 Environment

Although the key to implementing technologies is to install the software in a production environment, making sure the new technology environment is properly backed up is just as important for the organization. This chapter covers the proper planning, implementing, testing, and support of a properly backed-up environment. Organizations should spend as much time planning and implementing their backup processes as they do implementing the core environment. This can ensure that if there are any problems with the systems, servers, and sites that a successful recovery process can be initiated.

Understanding the Importance of Backups

Through various improvements and changes in the JET database engine and storage, Microsoft Exchange Server 2010 offers the most stable and resilient database of any Exchange Server implementation to date. The database can recover from dirty shutdowns, hardware failures, and power outages. The database enables both users and administrators to recover recently deleted items. Exchange Server 2010 even introduces new replication options that result in up to 16 independent copies of mailbox data spread across the world. However, even with all this functionality, it is still necessary to perform backups of the Exchange server to address long-term archival, legal discovery, and protection against malicious attacks on the Exchange Server environment.

Traditionally, backups are performed and maintained for three primary purposes:

- ▶ Recovering deleted items past the retention period
- ▶ Offline extraction of messages
- ▶ Disaster recovery

In modern environments, a fourth common purpose can be added with the purpose of electronic discovery. Legal departments regularly need to access historic email for groups of users to utilize in legal proceedings. Because maintaining a deleted item retention of multiple years isn't realistic, it falls to the traditional backup to provide this data over the years. To support these functions, it is critical to not only perform the regular backups, but to also understand what it is you are backing up, how often you are backing it up, and exactly what recovery scenarios you can support. It is equally critical to ensure that a retention policy is clearly defined and that it is supported by both information technology and the legal departments within a company. The job of IT is to use technology to support and enforce the retention policies set forth by legal. This means not only ensuring that enough data is available, it is also making sure that no data beyond that which is allowed is still resident in the environment.

The goal of this chapter is to show an administrator how to do the following:

- ▶ Evaluate their needs for backup
- ▶ Capture all the necessary information for disaster recovery
- ▶ Properly document their environment
- ▶ Determine a reasonable service level agreement (SLA)
- ▶ Design their backup strategy to support that SLA
- ▶ Build policies and procedures around backup processes
- ▶ Determine what data to back up
- ▶ How to take advantage of new backup technologies available in Exchange Server 2010

The process of restoring data within Exchange Server 2010 is covered in Chapter 33, "Recovering from a Disaster in an Exchange Server 2010 Environment."

> **NOTE**
>
> Exchange Server 2010 running on Windows Server 2008 does not provide any native backup functionality. Exchange Server 2010 supports only Volume Shadowcopy Services (VSS)-based backup technologies. This means that Exchange Server 2010 requires a separate product to perform backups. This can be at the storage level, such as NetApp's SnapManager for Exchange Server, or it can be at the application level, such as Microsoft's SCDPM 2010 or Symantec's NetBackup.

Establishing Service Level Agreements

The most common question from Exchange Server administrators is "How should I be doing my backups?" The answer to this question is quite simple. You should be doing them so that they support your service level agreements around recoverability and retention for Exchange Server services.

Based on this concept, it quickly becomes apparent that the first step in planning out your backups is to determine exactly what you've committed yourself to. This is commonly referred to as a service level agreement or simply an SLA.

Establishing a Service Level Agreement for Each Critical Service

Exchange Server 2010 is often deployed so that roles are distributed across multiple servers. This distribution of roles might vary from site to site. However, the SLAs will likely remain constant across the enterprise as the goal is actually to keep messaging alive and available to the end users.

It is important to understand the implication of SLAs for each aspect of Exchange Server 2010 because the SLA drives your design and must be considered upfront and not as an afterthought to a deployed Exchange Server 2010 environment. Too often, IT groups implement Exchange Server and later go back to determine how quickly they can restore services or rebuild a failed system. The correct methodology is to determine recovery time objectives and uptime goals and then design the architecture to enable those goals.

Determining SLAs for Mailbox Servers

One of the most important aspects of Exchange Server 2010 is the mailbox server. If the mailbox server isn't up, users can't access their mail. This is usually the first thing that triggers the help desk phone to ring. Most companies start their SLAs around the mailbox servers. In most environments, a two-hour recovery for a mailbox database is acceptable. This means that if your database fails, you need to recover that data within two hours. If you know that your system is capable of restoring 100GB of data per hour, you know that, based on your backup process, you can support only 200GB per database.

If your SLA for an entire mailbox server recovery is four hours and you know that it takes two hours to rebuild a new server with Exchange Server 2010, you have only two hours to restore data; based on the preceding example, this means you can have only 200GB of data on the server. If you planned to allow users 2000MB of storage each, this limits the server to 100 users. If you want to support more users per server, you either need to alter the SLA or you need to change your backup strategy to allow you to restore more data in the same period of time. This is what enables you to safely support large numbers of users with good SLAs. This is where you have to balance the costs of the backup/restore system with the cost of adding additional servers.

Luckily Exchange Server 2010 offers technologies that enable you to run a significantly tighter SLA. For example, Database Availability Groups enable a replica server to take over for a failed server within a matter of minutes. This would be a prime technology to implement if you have an SLA that allows mailbox access to be down for only a number of minutes.

Determining SLAs for Client Access Servers

Another major component of Exchange Server 2010 is the Client Access server (CAS). These are the systems that enable mobile devices and web browsers to access users' email. In Exchange Server 2010, the functions of the Client Access servers are greatly extended. Exchange Server 2010 utilizes MAPI on the middle tier that puts a much greater importance on CAS roles always being available. When determining SLAs for this function, it is helpful to view the service and the servers as two entities. Although you likely want high availability on the service, you can likely worry less about the servers individually if they are designed with redundancy in mind. So, if you have at least one more Client Access server than you need for performance purposes, you have plenty of time to rebuild one server if it fails because there is already another that is taking up the load. Keep this in mind when designing your Exchange Server environment. Also keep in mind that the data on a CAS is mostly static. Building a new CAS is often faster than restoring an existing one.

Determining SLAs for Edge Transport Servers

For systems such as the Edge Transport servers in Exchange Server 2010, it is more useful to view the SLA for this role as being for the service as opposed to the servers themselves. In the case of Edge Transport servers, the service they provide is to send and receive external email to and from the Internet. In this sense, most companies try to enforce a fairly aggressive SLA on the service itself. For example, if Internet mail connectivity were to fail, they'd want the service restored within one to two hours. In most environments, this is fairly easy to accomplish because there is typically two or more Edge Transport servers to provide redundancy and minimize wide area network (WAN) traffic. In the case of the SLAs on the servers themselves, typically a one-day recovery is acceptable. Because the Edge Transport servers don't hold any unique data, they can easily be replaced a failure occurs.

Remember that the Edge Transport service is dependent on the network itself. If the Edge Transport servers are running but the Internet connection is down, they can't do their job. One easy way to improve availability and thus support a tight SLA for Edge Transport is to have multiple entry points from the Internet. This can protect against Internet or Internet service provider issues by enabling Internet mail to enter from another location and simply ride the corporate WAN to reach the appropriate Exchange Server 2010 server. The simplest way to do this is to advertise multiple Mail Exchanger records (MX) in Domain Name Services (DNS) on the Internet.

Determining SLAs for Hub Transport Servers

The role of the Hub Transport server is to transfer mail from one site to another connected site. As such, when a Hub Transport server fails, the site it served is effectively cut off from other sites. Moreover, because the architecture of Exchange Server 2010 requires that all messages first pass through a Hub Transport, if this role were unavailable in a site, users cannot send to each other even though they are hosted on the same mailbox server. As such, a company would most likely want a fairly aggressive SLA on the Hub Transport servers. In most environments, the Hub Transport server role is combined with other roles because, in most cases, it won't justify being on an isolated server. As such, the SLA for recovery is often overwritten by the SLA for another role that it supports. As such, it is recommended that, when possible, two or more systems per site should host the Hub Transport server role.

Supporting Backups with Documentation

Performing trustworthy backups is a critical process in any Exchange Server environment. One of the simplest ways to ensure that your backups are done properly is to document your requirements and your processes.

A mechanism needs to be in place to track the success of backups and a process to follow if a backup fails. Sticking to this process and not conflicting with the set policies ensures that backups are valid and recoverable if a failure occurs.

Companies that are publicly traded follow a set of rules around documentation of processes and proof of following those processes. This is primarily dictated by Sarbanes-Oxley, or SOX. For privately held companies, although they are not legally required to follow SOX standards, they nonetheless serve as an excellent example of best practices around maintaining an IT environment and should be strongly considered.

Documenting Backup Policy and Procedures

When building your documentation around your backups, it is best to start with a policy that supports not only the SLAs for your Exchange Server environment but one that also complies with any existing rules from your Information Security group or Regulatory Compliance group.

Management should review and approve your backup policies to ensure that they are in line with any established SLAs. Policies should include items such as the following:

- ▶ Frequency and type of backups
- ▶ Acceptable standards for offsite storage and retrieval
- ▶ Escalation path for failed backups
- ▶ Decision criteria for overrun jobs
- ▶ Clear statement of what is and isn't backed up
- ▶ Whether the backups are password protected
- ▶ Data retention periods

In this way, everyone knows what is and isn't covered by Exchange Server backups, and there are no surprises in the future. Having this policy documented is also helpful if you are required to pass any audits or verify regulatory compliance.

Maintaining Documentation on the Exchange Server Environment

Systems such as Exchange Server often outlast the employees who built them. This means that it's easy to lose track of exactly how systems are deployed, where various roles are located, and the specific needs of each participating system. For this reason, it is extremely important to maintain accurate documentation for the server configurations, the network, and the path of mail flow. In addition, you need to track the configuration of firewalls and switches that can potentially impact the overall Exchange Server environment if they were to fail and need to be replaced.

Server Configuration Documentation

Server documentation is essential for any environment regardless of size, number of servers, or disaster recovery budget. A server configuration document contains a server's name, network configuration information, hardware and driver information, disk and volume configuration, or information about the applications installed. This complete server configuration document contains all the necessary configuration information a qualified administrator needs if the server needs to be restored and the operating system cannot be restored efficiently. A server configuration document can also be used as a reference when server information needs to be collected.

The Server Build Document

A server build document contains step-by-step instructions on how to build a particular type of server for an organization. The details of this document should be tailored to the skill of the person intended to rebuild the server. For example, if this document were created for disaster recovery purposes, it might be detailed enough that anyone with basic computer skills could rebuild the server. This type of information can also be used to help information technology (IT) staff follow a particular server build process to ensure that when new servers are added to the network, they all meet company server standards.

Hardware Inventory

Documenting the hardware inventory of an entire network might not be necessary. If the entire network does need to be inventoried, and if the organization is large, the Microsoft System Center Configuration Manager can help automate the hardware inventory task. If the entire network does not need to be inventoried, hardware inventory can be collected for all the production and lab servers and networking hardware, including specifications such as serial numbers, amount of memory, disk space, processor speed, and operating system platform and version. By knowing all the hardware involved, the restore process becomes much simpler, especially in situations in which hardware needs to be replaced as part of the restoration.

Network Configurations

Network configuration documentation is essential when network outages occur. Current, accurate network configuration documentation and network diagrams can help simplify and isolate network troubleshooting when a failure occurs.

WAN Connection

WAN connectivity should be documented for enterprise networks that contain many sites to help IT staff understand the enterprise network topology. This document is helpful when a server is restored and data should be synchronized enterprisewide after the restore. Knowing the link performance between sites helps administrators understand how long an update made in Site A will take to reach Site B. This document should contain information about each WAN link, including circuit numbers, Internet service provider (ISP) contact names, ISP technical support phone numbers, and the network configuration on each end of the connection, and can be used to troubleshoot and isolate WAN connectivity issues.

A strong understanding of the network is also critical to the process of initially creating the backups. By understanding the implication of backups over the network or how bandwidth would be affected after replacing a failed Database Availability Group replica, you can account for periods of time in which the environment might not have the normal level of redundancy that it was designed for and backups might potentially need to be altered to account for it.

For example, if an environment were using database availability groups to place replicas of mailbox data into two locations, they might feel that they were protected against system failures; combined with a 30-day deleted item retention, they might only do traditional backups once a month. If a DAG replica failed and would take two days to reseed due to a total replacement of the failed replica, they would be at risk for those two days because only one copy of the mailbox databases would be available. During this period of time, they might alter their backup schedule to perform backups nightly until the additional replica was returned to service.

Router, Switch, and Firewall Configurations

Firewalls, routers, and, sometimes, switches can run proprietary operating systems with a configuration that is exclusive to the device. During a system recovery, certain gateway connections, configuration routing information, routing table data, and other information might need to be reset on the restored server. Information should be collected from these devices, including logon passwords and current configurations. When a configuration change is planned for any of these devices, the newly proposed configuration should be created using a text or graphical editor, but the change should be approved before it is made on the production device. A rollback plan should be created first to ensure that the device can be restored to the original state if the change does not deliver the desired results.

Updating Documentation

One of the most important, yet sometimes overlooked, areas around documentation is maintaining accuracy as changes are applied to server systems. Documentation is tedious, but outdated documentation can be worthless if changes have occurred to a server's software configuration since the document was created. For example, if a server configuration document were used to re-create a server from scratch but many changes were applied to the server after the document was created, the correct security patches might not be applied, applications might be configured incorrectly, or data restore attempts could be unsuccessful. Whenever a change will be made to a network device, printer, or server, documentation outlining the previous configuration, proposed changes, and rollback plans should be created before the change is approved and carried out on the production device. After the change is carried out and the device is functioning as needed, the documentation associated with that device or server should be updated.

Logging Daily Backup Results and Evaluation

When running regular backups of mission-critical systems, you need to monitor the process to ensure that backup jobs are running properly. You also need to ensure that the data backed up can actually be restored.

Tracking Success and Failure

Most third-party backup software packages have the capability to send a summary of the result of the backup job to the administrator. This is a critical function because failures or inconsistent results need to be immediately brought to the attention of the administrator who is responsible for backups.

The results of these nightly backups should be reviewed each day to ensure not only the success of the backup process, but also to sanity-check the results. For example, if your backup normally ran for 6 hours and filled up 800GB of space, you should be suspicious of a 16-hour job of the same size or a 1-hour job that backed up only 120GB of data. Because either of those results can show up as a successful run of the backup job, it is critical for an administrator to review the results.

If using a backup software package that doesn't send this level of information, you need to check the event logs each day on the Exchange Server 2010 mailbox servers. The event log tracks any issues with the backup as the software in question must utilize the VSS Application Programming Interface (API) to back up Exchange Server 2010. The old style legacy "streaming" backups are no longer supported in Exchange Server 2010.

Validating Your Backups

The benefit of backing up data to a remote location or media is the ability to recover the data at a later time. As such, you need to regularly validate that your backups are valid and can be successfully restored. It is recommended that you adopt a practice of randomly pulling backups and picking random databases to perform a restore to a nonproduction location. After the restore, verify that you can access the data successfully. This process helps ensure that your data can be restored if an emergency occurs. For more information on restoring Exchange data specifically, see Chapter 33.

There are many third-party utilities, such as NetApp's Single Mailbox Recovery Tool or Quest's Recovery Manager for Exchange Server, that enable an administrator to bypass the recovery storage group process and attach directly to an .edb file off disk or even directly off tape to recover individual mailbox items from a backup. This is a great way to test the restore process and to restore individual items without having to restore an entire database. Best of all, it doesn't require an Exchange server.

Roles and Responsibilities

With any process that is likely to include more than one person, it is useful to clearly define the roles and responsibilities of those people. This ensures that the people involved know what is expected of them and they know who to go to in various situations.

Separation of Duties

A typical Exchange Server environment involves members from potentially many groups. For example, one group might be responsible for Exchange Server services and configuration, whereas another group might be tasked with management of Windows and security patches. Often, yet another group is responsible for performing backups of the systems. Each of these groups must be aware of what other groups are doing. For example, if the Windows group needs to install Windows patches on the Exchange servers, the backup group also needs to be aware of this because they might need to change the scheduling of the backup job. This type of interdependency must be taken into account when configuring the backup schedule.

Escalation and Notification

If a backup job fails, it is critical for the support staff to know what they are supposed to do and who they should contact. It is recommended to build a matrix of common issues and create an escalation path for various events. It is also quite useful to have those events automatically notify the responsible party. For example, the server monitoring group might be told that in the event of a backup failure, they should do the following:

▶ Contact the backup group to alert them of the failed job.

▶ Contact the Exchange Server group to alert them of the failed job.

▶ If neither group contacts you within 30 minutes, contact the IT manager.

▶ If the IT manager doesn't contact you within 60 minutes, contact the IT director.

By knowing who to call, it is easier to get a qualified party to look at the issue and potentially fix the issue in time to allow another backup job to be attempted before the backup window is expired.

Developing a Backup Strategy

Developing an effective backup strategy involves detailed planning around the logistics of backing up the necessary information or data via backup software, media type, and accurate documentation. To truly be effective, organizations should not limit a backup strategy by not considering the use of all available resources for recovery.

Along with planning and documentation, other aspects of a backup strategy include assigning specific tasks and responsibilities to individual IT staff members, considering the best person to be responsible for backing up a particular service or server and ensuring that documentation is accurate and current depending on their strengths and area of expertise.

What Is Important to Exchange Server Backups?

In general, the critical thing to capture in an Exchange Server backup is any unique data whose loss would impact users. This typically means that you need to back up the mailbox databases, public folder databases, and the log files that go with them. Files such as the operating system or the System State data are less important. As you'll find out in

Chapter 33, this information can be easily recovered because it is stored in the Active Directory (AD). In the case of Database Availability Groups, the backup of log files is less important because multiple copies of the databases and logs are in other locations that can take over if the primary replica fails. In these configurations, the primary purposes for the backups is to enable for long-term storage of data to protect against deletion and to truncate log files so that servers don't run out of space and shut down Exchange Server.

Creating Standard Backup Procedures

Creating a regular backup procedure helps ensure that the entire enterprise is backed up consistently and properly on a regular basis. When a regular procedure is created, the assigned staff members soon become accustomed to the procedure because they are given a guide that walks through each required step. If there is no documented procedure, certain items might be overlooked and not be backed up, which can be a major problem if a failure occurs. For example, a regular backup procedure for an Exchange Server 2010 server might back up the Exchange Server databases on the local drives every night, and perform a System State backup with Windows Server Backup Features once a month and whenever a hardware change is made to a server. These differences might be overlooked if no one is following regular change control and documented procedures.

> **TIP**
>
> It is a best practice to add documentation updates into standard server change control processes. This ensures that any modifications to server configurations also get added into server build documents.

Protecting Data if a System Failure Occurs

Server failures are the primary concern most organizations plan for, because a complete system failure creates the most impact and, ultimately, a scenario in which data needs to be restored from backup tape. Server hardware failures include failed motherboards, processors, memory, network interface cards, disk controllers, power supplies, and, of course, hard disks. Each of these failures can be minimized through the implementation of RAID-configured hard disk drives, error-correcting memory, redundant power supplies, or redundant controller adapters. In a catastrophic system failure, however, it is likely that the entire data backup would need to be restored to a new system or repaired server.

Because data is read and written to hard drives on a constant basis, hard drives are frequently singled out as the most possible cause of a server hardware failure. To address this, Windows Server 2008 supports hot-swappable hard drives and RAID storage systems, enabling for the replacement of the drive without server downtime. However, this is only if the server chassis and disk controllers support such a change. Windows Server 2008 supports two types of disks: Basic disks, which provide backward compatibility, and Dynamic disks, which enable software-level disk arrays to be configured without a separate disk controller. Both Basic and Dynamic disks, when used as data disks, can be moved to other servers easily. This provides data or disk capacity elsewhere if a system hardware failure occurs and the data on these disks needs to be made available as soon as possible.

NOTE

If hardware-level RAID is configured, the controller card configuration should be backed up using a utility available through the vendor.

With most array controllers today, dynamic reading of the disk configuration can be done if the disks are placed into a new system using the same disk order. If this is not supported, the controller can be moved to the new systems, or the configuration might need to be re-created from scratch to complete a successful disk move to a new machine.

This process should always be tested, verified, and documented in a lab environment before being considered as a valid recovery option.

32

To protect against a system failure, organizations need to have a full image backup that can then be restored in its entirety to a new or repaired server system. This also requires completing and documenting these steps in advance to ensure that it can be completed and administrators understand the steps involved.

Protecting Data if a Database Corruption Occurs

Data recovery also is needed if a database corruption occurs in Exchange Server. Unlike a catastrophic system failure, which can be restored from the last tape backup, data corruption creates a more challenging situation for information recovery. If data is corrupt on the server system, a restore from the last backup might also contain corrupt information in its database, so a data restore needs to predate the point of corruption. This typically requires the capability to restore the database from an older full backup tape and then recover incremental data since the clean database restoral.

Providing the Ability to Restore a Message, Folder, or Mailbox

In other situations, an organization might need to recover a single message, folder, or mailbox rather than a full database. With most full backups of an Exchange server, the restore process requires a full restore of all messages, folders, and mailboxes. If an administrator needs to work with only a full image backup, typically a full restore must be performed on a spare server and information extracted from the full restore as necessary.

If message, folder, or mailbox recovery is required on a regular basis, the organization might elect to back up information in a format or process that provides an easier method of information recovery. This might involve the purchase and use of a third-party tape backup system, or a combination of various utilities available in Exchange Server 2010 to restore individual sets of information.

Assigning Tasks and Designating Team Members

Each particular server or network device in the enterprise has specific requirements for backing up and creating documentation around hardware and the service it provides. To make sure that a critical system is backed up properly, IT staff should designate a single individual to monitor that device and ensure the backup is completed and documentation is accurate and current at all times. Assigning a secondary staff member who has the same set of skills to act as a backup if the primary staff member is unavailable is a wise decision, to ensure that there is no point of failure among IT staff performing these tasks.

Assigning only primary and secondary resources to specific devices or services helps improve the overall security and reliability of the device and services provided to network users. By limiting who can back up and restore data—and even who can manage servers and devices—to just the primary and secondary qualified staff members, the organization can be assured that only competent, trained individuals work on systems they are assigned to manage. Even though the backup and restore responsibilities lie with the primary and secondary resources, the backup and recovery plans should still be documented and available to the remaining IT staff for additional training and a final means of support if needed.

Selecting the Best Devices for Your Backup

Each device used on any network could have specific backup requirements. As mentioned earlier, each assigned IT staff member should also be responsible for researching and learning the backup and recovery requirements of each device to ensure that all backups have everything that is necessary to also recover from a device failure.

As a rule of thumb for network devices, the device configuration should be backed up whenever possible—using the device manufacturer's configuration software whenever possible or just by documenting the configuration for use as a reference should a device require reconfiguration.

TIP

It is also a best practice to evaluate the hardware used in your environment to determine which areas might be the most likely points of failure. Having spare devices can reduce the overall downtime in case of a failure. When dealing with Exchange Server 2010 considerations, these spare hardware devices can be pieces such as hard drives to support a failed drive in a RAID configuration.

Understanding How Devices Affect Backups

Depending on how a given environment is architected, there might be several different options on how it will be backed up. Administrators lucky enough to have network attached storage (NAS) or storage area networks (SANs) for their Exchange Server 2010 servers might have significantly faster options for performing backups than administrators who use direct attached storage (DAS). Many times, the NAS or SAN devices can perform local snapshots, or the SAN might be backed up by a tape device that is plugged directly into the Fibre Channel fabric. This has great advantages when compared to backing up an Exchange Server 2010 server over the network. For example, Gigabit Ethernet enables for 1Gb/sec of throughput. Fibre Channel not only offers speeds of 4Gb/sec to 8Gb/sec but is also a more efficient protocol.

One way to drastically speed up backups performed is to use a faster media for the final destination. Although current AIT and LTO tape technologies are very fast, they still can't compare to an array of hard drives for the destination. Technologies such as System

Center Data Protection Manager can take regular snapshots of Exchange Server 2010 and store them on disks. Longer-term backups are made from the disk images to tape. Because this transfer from disk to tape happens on the backup server, it can be done during the day without impacting end users or interfering with the regular backups. Technologies exist for most backup software in the form of virtual tape libraries that are actually files within a set of disks that can enable you to retain the normal methodologies of traditional tape backup while taking advantage of the speed and size of modern hard drives to drastically shrink the backup window on network attached backups.

Determining Backup Speeds and Times

The time needed to perform a backup of Exchange Server 2007 is influenced mostly by the speed of the backup device. Although vendors quote values for MB per minute that their device can back up, this isn't always an accurate value when backing up an Exchange Server 2010 server. It is always recommended to perform test backups of Exchange servers to determine the speed at which they can be backed up. By knowing how long jobs take, an administrator can better select the backup window in which the backups occur. As Exchange servers grow in terms of the storage used by mail data, the backups take longer to occur. Pay careful attention to the network utilization and to the backup device utilization so that you can watch for bottlenecks that cause backup jobs to take too long.

> **TIP**
>
> Consider backing up Exchange Server 2010 to a backup server that uses disks as the media for the backup. This is typically the fastest media that you can utilize for "over the network" backups. Then take the locally stored backup and back that up to tape. Because you are backing up "cold" data, there is no concern about performing the backup during the day. This allows you to keep your backup window relatively short. The side benefit is that if you ever experience a failure that requires you to restore from the backups, you'll be doing a disk-to-disk restore, which is much faster than a tape-to-disk restore.

Validating the Backup Strategy in a Test Lab

Regardless of what methodology you choose for backups of your Exchange Server 2010 environment, it is critical to test the processes in a lab environment. The goal of this validation is not only to prove that data can be backed up and restored, but also to refine and document the exact steps used. It is much easier to figure out how to perform a restore in the lab than it is in production when hundreds or thousands of mailbox users are down. The goal of a production restore is to follow accurate, validated instructions and not have to figure out what you need to do on-the-fly.

What to Back Up on Exchange Servers

With the various roles available on Exchange servers, the process of backing them up is no longer a one-size-fits-all proposition. Different Exchange Server 2010 roles have different needs and different options on what to back up and how to back it up. This section highlights the needs of the various Exchange Server roles.

What to Back Up on Mailbox Servers

When planning backups for an Exchange server, you must first determine the critical data that is stored on that particular system. For a mailbox server, the critical data present is as follows:

- ▶ Exchange database files—mailboxes
- ▶ Exchange database files—public folders
- ▶ Exchange transaction log files
- ▶ Full-text indexing information
- ▶ Free/busy information
- ▶ Offline Address Book

Of these items, the index information, the free/busy information, and the Offline Address Book can all be regenerated so that they do not need to be backed up. This leaves the databases and the transaction logs. If you use a certified Exchange Server 2010–compatible backup software product, you can always back up the databases and the log files as logical devices.

If you should ever need to back up the databases or log files at a flat-file level, be sure to stop all the Exchange Server services. These files can be found by running the Exchange Management Shell and typing the following:

```
Get-mailboxdatabase –server <server_name> ¦ fl name,edbfilepath,logfolderpath
```

What to Back Up on Hub Transport Servers

When planning for backups on a Hub Transport server, the critical data located on this role includes the following:

- ▶ Message tracking logs
- ▶ Protocol logs

The logs contained on the Hub Transport server are not critical for a restore of an Exchange Server 2010 environment; however, these logs might be useful for troubleshooting or for forensics and can be backed up at a file level. The logs are located below the directory in which Exchange Server was installed in \Transportroles\logs.

What to Back Up on Client Access Servers

Generally speaking, there is no need to back up the CAS. This is because the CAS merely acts as a pass-through to get to Exchange Server data. This was also the case in previous versions of Exchange Server. Typically, multiple CAS servers are deployed for redundancy, so rapid restoration is rarely needed. Typically, if a CAS server fails, it would be rebuilt from scratch and would not need any data restored to it.

If there is only a single CAS server in the environment, it might be worthwhile to back up the POP/IMAP configuration stored in \ClientAccess\PopImap. Optionally, you can just document the Post Office Protocol (POP) and Internet Message Access Protocol (IMAP) settings and reset them if a CAS were rebuilt.

If your environment requires auditing of client or mobile device access to Exchange Server 2010, it might be of value to back up the IIS logs because they track this information.

On a related note, CASs can generate a large volume of IIS logs. Typically, these log files are forgotten about until they fill the drive they are on and cause an outage. Typically CASs are built with a single drive and the IIS log files default is stored on the C: drive. If the C: drive fills up, the Exchange Server services stop and stop serving clients. These log files can be pruned with a simple batch file that should be scheduled to run nightly:

```
FORFILES -p c:\inetpub\logs\logfiles\w3svc1 -s -m*.log -d -30 -c "CMD /C del @FILE"
-p = path
-s = include subdirs
-m = match filetype
-d = age in days (can also be set as an absolute date ie DDMMYYYY)
-c = command to execute
```

What to Back Up on Edge Transport Servers

When backing up the Edge Transport server, the unique Protocol Log data should be captured.

To back up the protocol logs, follow the steps given for Hub Transport servers in the previous section.

What to Back Up on Unified Messaging Servers

When planning for backups on a Unified Messaging server, the critical data located in the Custom Audio Prompts should be included in the backup.

This information is stored under the Exchange Server file structure in \UnifiedMessaging\ Prompts and is needed only on the prompt publishing server. Not unlike a CAS server, its configuration is stored in AD, and it acts as a pass-through to the .wav files stored in the users' mailboxes.

Directory Server Data

As was the case with the previous version of Exchange Server, Exchange Server 2010 stores the vast majority of its configuration information in Active Directory. This allows Exchange Server 2010 servers to easily read the configurations of other systems in the environment and provides an easy mechanism to restore the configuration of a rebuilt server. For this reason, it is critical to ensure that at least one domain controller in the root of the forest is backed up regularly.

To back up a Windows 2008 domain controller, from the domain controller, follow these steps:

1. Make sure the Windows Backup features have been installed (ServerManager, Features, Windows Server Backup Features).

2. Start, Program Files, Administrative Tools, Windows Server Backup.

3. Choose Actions, Backup Once.

4. Choose Different Option, and then click Next.

5. Choose Custom; then click Next.

6. Make sure your C> volume is selected and Enable System Recovery is selected; then click Next.

7. Typically choose a remote shared folder or possibly a local drive other than the C> that you are backing up from, and then click Next.

8. Choose the drive or path you want to save to. Typically also choose Do Not Inherit so that you can choose the authorized user(s) who can access the backup. Click Next.

9. Typically choose VSS Full Backup, assuming you are not using any other backup product on the system. Click Next.

10. Click Backup to begin.

Common Settings and Configuration Data

Be aware of any additional dependencies that would need to be backed up to fully restore the Exchange Server environment. This can include things such as the following:

▶ SSL certificates

▶ S/MIME certificates

▶ IIS metabase

▶ Custom Outlook Web App pages

▶ Third-party applications

The Need for Backups with Database Availability Groups

Exchange Server 2010 introduced a new concept in backups for the databases due to the inclusion of Database Availability Groups, or DAGs. This new technology has the potential to drastically change your strategies for backup. DAGs are more thoroughly covered in Chapter 31, "Database Availability Group Replication in Exchange Server 2010." In short, a DAG is a real-time replica of a mailbox database that is replicated to up to 15 other mailbox servers. As a result, if the master copy of a DAG goes offline, the next highest-priority copy of the mailbox database will become the master copy, and the users hosted on that mailbox database continue to function normally. Rather than restoring a failed DAG, you can simply rebuild the DAG replica and let the database replicate to it. This is similar to the situation you have with domain controllers in which the data replication effectively becomes a distributed backup. Not unlike in the case of domain controllers, the purpose of the backup shifts from being a tool for recovery to a tool for historic storage.

By maintaining a relatively long deleted item retention, you can protect against the need to restore data from tape. Because up to 16 copies of a mailbox database are in a DAG, it is statistically unlikely that all 16 copies would fail simultaneously. This leaves relatively few reasons to need to perform backups:

- ▶ Reseeding
- ▶ Long-term storage/eDiscovery
- ▶ Truncating log files

Exchange Server 2010 introduced the ability to perform an incremental reseeding of a database that has gotten too far out of sync with the master copy. In Exchange Server 2007, a database had to be copied in its entirety if it became too far out of sync. In Exchange Server 2010, only the deltas of the database need to be copied before normal log shipping can resume. Although this is a noticeable improvement, it does not help in a situation in which the delta is the entire database. Imagine a situation in which a new DAG replica is built and it asks to replicate copies of 10 different 100GB databases. The delta in this situation is 1TB. This could take a long time to replicate over a WAN connection and would eat up a lot of bandwidth. In this situation, pre-seeding the database replicas via a backup/restore process would take a huge strain off the network and would potentially occur in a much shorter time frame. Something as simple as backing up the databases to an external hard drive and shipping the hard drive to the remote location would likely be accomplished in a single day, whereas for the same amount of data to replicate over the WAN in 24 hours, you would need just under 100Mbps/sec of dedicated bandwidth.

Another situation involving DAG in which you would still need regular backups would be in the case of needing to store mail data for a period of time longer than what would be maintained in the deleted item retention. This might be to protect against an accidental deletion of items or more commonly it might be to maintain a source of data for legal discovery. It is not unusual for a legal department to request all mailbox data for a set of users over a period of several months. If you weren't maintaining long-term backups, there would be no ability to recover messages that had been deleted by the users when the deleted item retention period had been exceeded.

The last situation that is not obviated by the use of DAGs as a distributed backup is the need to truncate log files. Because you would not likely restore a DAG member, if you were comfortable that they had enough replicas of a mailbox database, the need to truncate log files could be addressed by enabling circular logging.

Backing Up Windows Server 2008 and Exchange Server 2010

As previously mentioned, the use of DAGs in Exchange Server 2010 mostly eliminates the need to perform backups of the Exchange servers because the data is already replicated to multiple locations. The individual identity of the mailbox, Client Access, Hub Transport, and Unified Messenger servers becomes much less important because there is no "unique" data store on them. This said, it is necessary to realize that not all environments will be large enough to justify the use of DAGs to provide protection against system failures. Smaller deployments will still need to be backed up to allow for recovery of failed systems.

The Windows Server 2008 operating system and the Exchange Server 2010 messaging system contain several features to enhance operating system stability, provide data and service redundancy, and deliver feature-rich client services. Windows Server 2008 continues to provide additional services such as Volume Shadow Copy Service, or VSS, which works to enhance backup capabilities when organizations use third-party backup products. Additional information about working with VSS is covered in the "Volume Shadow Copy Service and Exchange Server 2010" section later in this chapter.

Though other options have been mentioned, this section discusses ways to back up a Windows Server 2008 system, including key components of Exchange Server 2010. Because there are no built-in backup utilities available with the Windows Server 2008 operating system that are compatible with Exchange Server 2010, it is necessary to utilize a third-party backup utility.

By preparing for a complete server failure and using the information in this section, an organization is more likely to successfully recover from a failed server, restoring it to its previous state.

Backing Up Boot and System Volumes

A backup strategy for every nonredundant Exchange Server 2010 system should always include the boot and system disk volumes of the server. For most Exchange server installations, the boot and system volume are the same, but in some designs they are located on completely separate volumes—as usually is the case for dual-boot computers. For the rest of this section and discussion, assume that they are both on the same partition. This volume contains all the files necessary to start the core operating system. It should be backed up before and after a change, such as the application of service packs, is made to the operating system and once every 24 hours, if possible.

When Exchange Server is installed on a Windows 2008 server, the installation, by default, installs on the system partition unless a different location is specified during installation. On average, the amount of information stored on the system volume, with applications, services, and all service packs installed, is typically approximately 15GB.

NOTE

When system volumes are backed up, the System State should also be included in the backup at the same time to simplify recovery and restoration of the system to its original state, if a server needs to be recovered from scratch.

Backing Up Windows Server 2008 Services

Many Windows Server 2008 services store configuration and status data in separate files or databases located in various locations on the system volume. If the service is native to Windows Server 2008, performing a complete server backup on all drives and the System State almost certainly backs up the critical data. A few services provide alternative backup and restore options. The procedures for backing up these services are outlined in the "Backing Up Specific Windows Services" section later in this chapter. The classic NTBackup utility has been replaced in Windows Server 2008 with the new Windows Server Backup that is installed as a feature. Although this utility is incapable of backing up Exchange Server 2010, it is also capable of backing up Windows 2008.

Backing Up the System State

The System State of a Windows Server 2008 system contains, at a minimum, the system Registry, boot files, and the COM+ class registration database. Backing up the System State creates a point-in-time backup that can be used to restore a server to a previous working state. Having a copy of the System State is essential if a server restore is necessary.

How the server is configured determines what will be contained in the System State, other than the three items listed previously. On a domain controller, the System State also contains the Active Directory database and the SYSVOL share. On a cluster, it contains the cluster quorum data. When services such as Certificate Services and Internet Information Services, which contain their own service-specific data, are installed, these databases are not listed separately but are backed up with the System State.

Even though the System State contains many subcomponents, using the programs included with Windows Server 2008, the entire system can be backed up only as a whole. When recovery is necessary, however, there are several different options. Recovering data using a System State backup is covered in Chapter 33.

The system should be backed up every week to prepare for several server-related failures. A restore of a system backup is powerful and can return a system to a previous working state if a change needs to be rolled back or if the operating system needs to be restored from scratch after a complete server failure.

Volume Shadow Copy Service and Exchange Server 2010

Before discussing the backup process using Windows Server Backup, it is important for Exchange Server administrators to understand what Windows 2008 Volume Show Copy Service is used for. With limited native support for backing up Exchange Server 2010, most organizations use third-party backup products. Backup products for Exchange Server 2010 must utilize VSS because legacy style "streaming" backups are no longer supported.

The Volume Shadow Copy Service is a server service in Windows 2008 and is available as part of the operating system. Alone, VSS is a service, but when combined with backup applications, VSS become a vital part of every organization's backup strategy and recovery plan.

32

What Role VSS Plays in Backup

Microsoft created VSS to provide application platforms and infrastructures to enhance functionality when working with Microsoft services such as Exchange Server 2010. The key to VSS is its capability to act as a go-between or coordinator for service providers (backup applications) and service writers (Exchange Server 2010 databases).

It is important to know that VSS does not function alone; VSS is designed to provide application developers a platform in which to build applications to create Exchange Server snapshots.

Shadow Copies and Snapshots

This capability enabled third-party backup applications to create shadow copies or mirrors of the Exchange Server database and enabled administrators to design more dynamic backup strategies and reduce the overall cost of restoring servers. Using Shadow Copies (Mirror Copies) and Snapshots (Point in Time Mirror Copies), daily backups can be much smaller and for vital messaging systems, and snapshots can be taken several times a day.

VSS Requirements and Prerequisites

When looking at third-party products as an option for backups with VSS technology, you must evaluate the products to ensure that they are compatible with VSS. Compatibility is based on three specific areas:

▶ Backups of the Exchange Server 2010 database, logs, and checkpoint files must be completed by the application writer (Exchange Server 2010).

▶ The application must complete a full validation of the backup.

▶ When restoring data in Exchange Server, this must also be completed by the application writer (Exchange Server 2010).

VSS and third-party applications also require hardware compatibility. This is especially true when backing up to disk subsystems, such as NAS and SAN solutions. To verify this information, review the application vendor support pages and verify that the application and hardware meet all requirements.

TIP

For more information regarding Volume Shadow Copy Service, Microsoft published several articles over the years on the Microsoft web page. The content is at http://support.microsoft.com/?kbid=822896 and http://technet.microsoft.com/en-us/library/dd233256.aspx.

Backing Up Specific Windows Services

Most Windows Server services that contain a database or local files are backed up with the System State but also provide alternate backup and restore options. Because the system restore from Windows Server Backup is usually an all-or-nothing proposition, except when it comes to cluster nodes and domain controllers, restoring an entire system might deliver undesired results if only a specific service database restore is required. This section outlines services that either have separate backup/restore utilities or require special attention to ensure a successful backup.

Disk Configuration (Software RAID Sets)

Disk is not a service but should be backed up to ensure that proper partition assignments can be restored. When Dynamic disks are used to create complex volumes—such as mirrored, striped, spanned, or RAID-5 volumes—the disk configuration should be saved. This way, if the operating system is corrupt and needs to be rebuilt from scratch, the complex volumes need to have only their configuration restored, which could greatly reduce the recovery time. Only a full system backup can back up disk and volume configuration.

Certificate Services

Installing Certificate Services creates a certificate authority (CA) on the Windows Server 2008 system. The CA is used to manage and allocate certificates to users, servers, and workstations when files, folders, email, or network communication needs to be secured and encrypted. In many cases, the CA is a completely separate secured CA server; however, many organizations use their Exchange server as a CA server. This might be because of a limited number of servers with several different roles and services installed on a single server, or because the organization wants to use Secure Sockets Layer (SSL) and forms-based authentication (FBA) for secured Outlook Web App and to support encrypted connections from Outlook 2007 or higher to the Client Access servers, so they install Certificate Services on an Exchange server. Whatever the case, the CA needs to be backed up whether on the Exchange server or on any other server; if the CA server crashes and needs to be restored, it can be restored so that users can continue to access the system after recovery.

> **CAUTION**
>
> For security purposes, it is highly recommended that Certificate Services be enabled on a server other than the Exchange server. Definitely do not have the CA services on an Outlook Web App server that is exposed to the Internet. The integrity of certificate-authenticated access depends on ensuring that certificates are issued only by a trusted authority. Any compromise to the CA server invalidates an organization's capability to secure its communications.

When the CA allocates a certificate to a machine or user, that information is recorded in the certificate database on the local drive of the CA. If this database is corrupted or deleted, all certificates allocated from this server become invalid or unusable. To avoid this problem, the certificates and Certificate Services database should be backed up frequently. Even if certificates are rarely allocated to new users or machines, backups should still be performed regularly.

Certificate Services can be backed up in three ways: backing up the CA server's System State, using the CA Microsoft Management Console (MMC) snap-in, or using the command-line utility Certutil.exe. Backing up Certificate Services by backing up the System State is the preferred method because it can be easily automated and scheduled. But using the graphic console or command-line utility adds the benefit of restoring Certificate Services to a previous state without restoring the entire server System State or taking down the entire server for the restore.

To create a backup of the CA using the graphic console, follow these steps:

1. Log on to the CA server using an account with local Administrator rights.

2. Open Windows Explorer and create a folder named CaBackup on the C: drive.

3. Select Administrative Tools, Certificate Authority.

4. Expand the Certificate Authority server, and select the correct CA.

5. Select Action, All Tasks, Back Up CA.

6. When the backup wizard launches, click Next.

7. On the Items to Back Up page, check the Private Key and CA Certificate check box and the Certificate Database and Certificate Database Log check box.

8. Specify the location to store the CA backup files. Use the folder created in the beginning of this process. Click Next to continue.

9. When the CA certificate and private key are backed up, this data file must be protected with a password. Enter a password for this file, confirm it, and click Next to continue.

> **NOTE**
>
> To restore the CA private key and CA certificate, you must use the password entered in step 9. Store this password in a safe place, possibly with the master account list.

10. Click Finish to create the CA backup.

Internet Information Services (IIS)

Internet Information Services 7.0 (IIS) is the Windows Server 2008 web and FTP services that support websites like OWA. It is included on every version of the Windows Server 2008 platform. IIS stores configuration information for web and FTP site configurations and security, placing the information into the IIS metabase. The IIS backup methodology has changed quite a bit from IIS 6.0.

In IIS 7.0, all the configuration data is stored in %windir%/system32/inetpub/config. If you have a backup of that directory, the configuration can be restored by simply returning the files to this location. A more automated process can be performed by utilizing the appcmd.exe function.

To backup an IIS configuration, simply run appcmd.exe add backup "IIS Backup".

To restore an IIS configuration, simply run `appcmd.exe restore backup "IIS Backup"`.

By creating and scheduling a batch file to perform the backup, you can take regular snapshots of the IIS configuration. This can be useful to perform right before making a change to IIS settings on a Client Access Server so that if the changes cause any problems, the configuration can be quickly restored.

Backing up Exchange Server 2010 with Windows Server Backup

Although the native Windows Server Backup is fairly basic in its functionality for Exchange Server 2010, it can, nonetheless, be used to perform a backup of Exchange Server 2010 data via the following steps:

1. Click Start, All Programs, Administrative Tools, Windows Server Backup.
2. In the right pane, click Backup Schedule.
3. When the wizard launches, click Next.
4. When prompted to select your backup configuration, choose Custom and click Next.
5. Select the volumes you want to back up and click Next.
6. Choose the time at which you'd like the backups to run and click Next.
7. Select the disk on which you want to store the backup. Click Next.
8. Note: The disk you select for the destination will be reformatted and all data will be lost. Make sure there is no important data on this volume.
9. View the label of the destination disk and click Next.
10. Confirm the backup settings and click Finish.

Recovery of Exchange Server data from this type of backup is covered in Chapter 33.

Summary

Microsoft has pushed the role of backup and restore away from Exchange Server and Windows and more toward the third party. Newer backup systems such as Microsoft's System Center Data Protection Manager 2010 and the newest versions of third-party packages such as NetBackup or CommVault utilize VSS to correctly interface with Exchange Server 2010 to perform backups that can be successfully restored. Microsoft introduced Database Availability Groups to drastically reduce the need for backups by making the data redundant across up to 16 servers. Backup has been deprecated from the role of primary disaster recovery to more of a historic storage of messages for purposes of eDiscovery. Depending on the needs of your environment and your regulatory compliance requirements, you might perform fewer backups than in the past. Depending on whether you build stand-alone Exchange Server 2010 servers or implement Database Availability Groups has a huge impact on your backup strategy.

Exchange Server 2010 has taken a philosophy to improve the overall backup process by offering more scenarios in which you can restore or recover data without having to resort to restoring from tape. This means that Exchange Server 2010 administrators can put more faith into the stability and recoverability of Exchange Server 2010 by utilizing native retention functions, archiving, and data replication.

Although the backup mechanisms are mostly unchanged, this means that it is still easy to back up Exchange Server 2010 data to disk or tape for long-term storage if you implement a supported backup solution. VSS is still utilized for backups, and is the interface of choice for third-party backup applications as legacy style streaming backups are no longer supported. Advanced features such as backing up a "non-master" replica gives administrators increased flexibility with the ability to back up Exchange Server 2010 mailbox database during business hours with greatly reduced impact to end users. This can be especially helpful in situations in which a backup job fails and the administrator has to make a choice between impacting end users' performance or skipping a backup.

Backups continue to be the safety net that enables administrators to operate knowing that in any situation, they can restore a message, a mailbox, or an entire server. Careful planning and regular verification of backups enable an administrator to sleep at night knowing their Exchange Server environment is safe.

Best Practices

The following are best practices from this chapter:

▶ When budget and bandwidth allows for it, implement Database Availability Groups to replicate data to multiple locations to allow for near-instant recovery of failed services.

▶ Try to run the Hub Transport role on more than one server per site.

▶ Mailbox servers should be backed up often enough to meet any Recovery Point Objectives enforced by the environment.

▶ Always check the status of backup jobs to ensure they run properly.

▶ Maintain a list of who to contact if errors occur during the backup process.

▶ Always follow the documented process for performing backups. If the process changes because of a change in the environment or backup product, be sure to update the documentation.

▶ Always perform a full backup before making major changes to an Exchange server.

▶ Perform a weekly system backup of key systems to enable rapid restore in the case of a major failure if you are not running redundant CAS/HT along with DAG.

► When possible, perform backups to disk for speed and spool them to tape during the day.

► Define your SLAs before determining your backup strategy because the SLA will heavily influence your choices.

► Clearly define the roles and responsibilities of the people who are involved in backups of Windows and Exchange Server.

► Always take your third-party Exchange Server

► Always take your third-party Exchange 2010 applications into account when planning your backup strategy.

► Be sure to configure new databases for DAG if that is your backup strategy.

► Be sure to update your backup jobs when new databases are added.

32

CHAPTER 33

Recovering from a Disaster in an Exchange Server 2010 Environment

Most companies have found that over the years, email has become the primary form of communication in their environment. As they've become more and more dependent on email as a business-critical communication and collaboration tool, their tolerance for downtime has decreased at a similar rate. As such, it is more important than ever to understand how to return an Exchange Server environment to a working state as quickly as possible and with as little data loss as possible. Depending on the type of failure that took down all or part of the Exchange Server environment, you can use one of several approaches to recover the environment and restore the flow of mail and access to existing messages.

Unfortunately, most organizations do not proactively create an environment with disaster-recovery processes in place. As a result, this chapter takes into account the information in Chapter 31, "Database Availability Group Replication in Exchange Server 2010," and Chapter 32, "Backing Up the Exchange Server 2010 Environment," and also provides recommendations based on possible disaster scenarios. Recommendations in this chapter will be based on two different approaches to Exchange Server 2010: DAG and non-DAG. A DAG-based infrastructure seeks to mostly obviate the need for performing recoveries of individual systems through redundancy and retention policies. That said, the need for long-term backup for legal purposes isn't directly covered by the use of DAG. For those needs and for environments that can't justify a DAG deployment, more traditional methods of disaster recovery will be covered.

Identifying the Extent of the Problem

Before attempting to perform a recovery, it is important to first determine the type and extent of the problem. If the problem is not properly identified, you run the risk of performing an incorrect action that could actually make the problem worse. Equally important is to choose the most appropriate solution available. For example, restoring an entire server when only a single database failed would impact users who otherwise could have continued to use Exchange Server, and it would take significantly longer than restoring just the necessary database. Even though both plans of action would fix the issue, one is much simpler with less impact than the other.

Mailbox Content Was Deleted, Use the Undelete Function of Exchange Server and Outlook

When information is deleted from a user's mailbox, whether it is an email message, a calendar appointment, a contact, or a task, the information is not permanently deleted from the Exchange server. Deleted items go into the Deleted Items folder in the user's Outlook mailbox. The information is actually retained on the Exchange server for 30 days after deletion, even when it is supposedly permanently deleted from the Deleted Items folder.

> **TIP**
>
> Environments that are utilizing Database Availability Groups as their primary form of DR might consider increasing the Deleted Item Retention period to further reduce the likelihood of needing to restore data. Make sure the disk storage planning takes this into account because it will result in mailboxes that can take up more space in the database than their limits would suggest.

With a little training and documentation, end users can recover their own deleted mail items with ease. To recover mailbox items that have been deleted within Outlook, follow these steps:

1. Highlight the Deleted Items folder.
2. Click Tools, Recover Deleted Items.
3. In the Recover Deleted Items From – Deleted Items window, select the items that you want to restore.
4. Click the Recover Selected Items button.

If the item was "Shift-deleted," which bypasses the Deleted Items folder, the message is not lost. Follow these instructions to enable recovery of hard-deleted items:

1. Click Start, Run, type Regedt32.exe in the Open text box, and then click OK.

2. Browse to the following key in the Registry:

   HKEY_LOCAL_MACHINE\SOFTWARE\Microsoft\Exchange\Client\Options

3. On the Edit menu, click Add Value, and then add the following Registry value:

   Value name: DumpsterAlwaysOn

   Data type: DWORD

   Value data: 1

4. Quit Registry Editor.

With this key set, you can highlight any folder in Outlook and use the Recover Deleted Items tool. This ability to restore items that users thought they had permanently deleted can drastically reduce the level of involvement of the helpdesk when users need to recovery messages that they accidentally deleted.

Data Is Lost, Must Restore from Backup

If data is lost and the undelete function does not recover the information, the information might need to be restored from a backup. Depending on how much information was lost, this might involve a full recovery of the Exchange server from tape or snapshot, or it might involve restoring just a single mailbox, folder, or message. The key to restoring information is determining what needs to be restored. If just a single message needs to be restored, there is no reason to recover the entire server in production. In many cases, when full tape backups have been conducted of an Exchange server, a restore of the storage group containing the missing data can be performed. In the past, this was done with the recovery storage group and the missing content merged back into the production databases. This functionality is no longer available in Exchange Server 2010. Although you can restore a database and its logs to an alternate location, you would need to use a third-party utility like Single Mailbox Recovery Tool or Quest's Recovery Manager for Exchange Server. These tools have the capability to recover individual items directly from an unmounted EDB file without having to involve Exchange Server 2010.

Data Is Okay, Server Just Doesn't Come Up

The failure of a server does not necessarily mean that the data needs to be restored completely from tape. Often, a server goes down because of a failure with the power supplies, a motherboard failure, or even a processor failure. In a situation where the hard drives on a dead server are still operational, the hard drives should be moved to an operational server or, at the very least, the data should be transferred to a different server. By preserving the data on the drives, an organization can minimize the need to perform more complicated data reconstruction from a tape restore, which could result in the loss of data from the time of the last backup. Restoring from tape should always be considered a final option.

The process of recovering data from a drive and recovering a failed server is covered in the section "Performing a Restore of Only Exchange Server Database Files," later in this chapter.

This type of a failure is an excellent example of where you can take advantage of a Database Availability Group architecture. When utilizing a DAG, the failure of a mailbox server doesn't actually prevent the users from accessing their email. When the master copy of the mailbox replica fails, the second priority copy becomes the master copy, and replication to any additional replicas continues. In this scenario, there would be no need to restore the failed server. Rather, you would simply build a new server from scratch at their convenience and add it back to the replica list. When replicated, you can choose to make this copy the master copy again. Similarly, if the failed system were a client access server or a Hub Transport server, if there were more than one server in that role in the site, the overall Exchange Server 2010 services would still be available when a single system failed. Rather than being restored, this system could be rebuilt and would take up its share of the load.

Data Is Corrupt—Some Mailboxes Are Accessible, Some Are Not

Data corruption typically occurs on Exchange servers when the time period since the last database maintenance is too long or maintenance has been neglected altogether. Without periodic maintenance, covered in Chapter 19, "Exchange Server 2010 Management and Maintenance Practices," the databases in Exchange Server are more susceptible to becoming corrupt. Exchange Server database corruption that is not repaired can make individual messages or entire portions of mailboxes stored on an Exchange server to become inaccessible.

When a mailbox or multiple mailboxes are corrupt, the good data in the mailboxes can be extracted with minimal data loss. By isolating the corruption and extracting good data, an organization that might not need to recover the lost data can typically continue to operate with minimal downtime.

The process of extracting mail from an Exchange Server database is covered in the section "Recovering from Database Corruption," later in this chapter.

Data Is Corrupt, No Mailboxes Are Accessible

Depending on the condition of an Exchange Server database, the information might be so corrupt that none of the mailboxes are accessible. Recovering data from a corrupt database that cannot be accessed is a two-step process. The first step is to conduct maintenance to attempt to repair the database; the second step is to extract as much information from the database as possible.

The process of performing maintenance and extracting data from a corrupt database is covered in the section "Recovering from Database Corruption," later in this chapter.

In the case of a DAG configuration, if the database became unavailable due to localized corruption, you could simply make a different replica of the master copy and services would be restored. The steps to perform this are covered in Chapter 31.

Exchange Server Is Okay, Something Else Is Preventing Exchange from Working

If you know that the Exchange server and databases are operational and something else is preventing Exchange Server from working, the process of recovery focuses on looking at things such as Active Directory, Internet Information Services (IIS), the domain name system (DNS), and the network infrastructure, as with site-to-site connectivity for replication.

The process of analyzing the operation of other services is covered in the sections "Recovering Windows Server 2008 Domain Controllers" and "Recovering Active Directory," later in this chapter.

Mail Is Not Flowing Between Sites

If users can access their mailboxes normally and mail can be sent between users of the same site, odds are the issue is with the Hub Transport server. In larger implementations of Exchange Server 2010, the Hub Transport server role is likely to be run on a system that doesn't host mailboxes. Generally speaking, backups are not performed on a Hub Transport server as it contains no unique information. To restore these services, simply rebuild the Hub Transport server. Installing with a /recoverserver switch enables the server to recover its configuration from Active Directory, saving some configuration steps. This assumes the server is built with the same name.

If you need the transport services up rapidly, consider adding the Hub Transport server role to an existing system. To add this role, follow these steps:

1. From an existing Exchange Server 2010 server, open a command prompt.
2. Navigate to Program Files, Microsoft, Exchange Server, bin.
3. Type `exsetup.exe /mode:install /role:hub`.

Internet Mail Is Not Flowing

If you cannot send mail to the Internet or receive mail from the Internet, there is a good chance that the issue is a failure with the Edge Transport server. Most environments should run more than one Edge Transport server, preferably in different locations. But if an Edge Transport server fails, it should be rebuilt as they are typically not backed up. Installing with a /recoverserver switch enables the server to recover its configuration from Active Directory, saving some configuration steps. This assumes the server is built with the same name.

If you need the transport services up rapidly, consider adding the Edge Transport server role to an existing system. To add this role, follow these steps:

1. From an existing Exchange Server 2010 server, open a command prompt.
2. Navigate to Program Files, Microsoft, Exchange Server, bin.
3. Type `exsetup.exe /mode:install /role:et`.

33

> **NOTE**
>
> If you place the Edge Transport role on a new system, you need to make sure that incoming Simple Mail Transfer Protocol (SMTP) mail from the Internet reaches this system. This might involve a change in configuration of MX records, firewall rules, Network Address Translation (NAT), or your antispam/antivirus gateway. Be sure you understand the implications of putting the Edge Transport role on another system before attempting this fix.

What to Do Before Performing Any Server-Recovery Process

If a full server recovery will be performed, or if a number of different procedures will be taken to install service packs, patches, updates, or other server-recovery attempts such as an attempt to recover the server, a full backup should be performed on the server.

At first, it might seem unnecessary to back up a server that isn't working properly, but during the problem-solving and debugging process, it is quite possible for a server to end up in even worse shape after a few updates and fixes have been applied. The initial problem might have been that a single mailbox couldn't be accessed, and after some problem-solving efforts, the entire server might be inaccessible. A backup provides a rollback to the point of the initial problem state. When making changes in an attempt to fix a server, you always want a way to roll back a change if it turns out to make the situation worse. When the backup is complete, verify that the backup is valid, ensuring that no open files are skipped during the backup process or that, if the files are skipped, they are backed up in other open file backup processes. This way, you will always have the ability to return to your starting point in case you need to try a different method to fix the server.

> **CAUTION**
>
> When performing any recovery of an Exchange server or resource, be careful what you delete, modify, or change. As a rule of thumb, never delete objects that are known throughout the directory; otherwise, you cannot restore the object because of the uniqueness of each object. As an example, if you plan to restore an entire server from tape, you do not want to first delete the server and then add the server back during the restoration process. The restoration process requires the existence of the old server in the directory. Deleting the server object and then adding the object again later gives the object a completely different globally unique identifier (GUID). Even though you restore the entire Exchange server from tape, the ID of the server and all the objects in the server will be different, making it more difficult to recover the server. Other replicable objects that should not be deleted include public folders, public folder trees, groups, and distribution lists.

Validating Backup Data and Procedures

Another important task that should be done before doing any maintenance, service, or repairs on an Exchange server is to validate that a full backup exists on the server, test the condition of the backup, and then secure the backup so that it is safe. Far too many organizations proceed with risky recovery procedures, believing that they have a fallback position by restoring from tape, only to realize that the tape backup is corrupt or that a complete backup does not exist. Equally important is to be sure that the tape you might need is actually onsite. Many companies send tapes offsite for storage. If you depend on a particular backup tape for your rollback, be sure it is readily accessible.

If the administrators of the network realize that there is no clean backup, the procedures taken to recover the system might be different than if a backup had existed. If a full backup exists and is verified to be in good condition, the organization has an opportunity to restore from tape if a full restore is necessary. This requirement is somewhat lessened in an environment where Database Availability Groups are utilized because those configurations can suffer a failure of a system should something go wrong during an upgrade or maintenance.

Preparing for a More Easily Recoverable Environment

Steps can be taken to help an organization more easily prepare for a recoverable environment. This involves documenting server states and conditions, performing specific backup procedures, and setting up new features in Exchange Server 2010 that provide for a more simplified restoration process. By maintaining these processes and performing regular test restores, a company can feel confident that they can quickly and easily recover from a disaster. Most notably is the use of Database Availability Groups to provide for redundant mailbox services. Because the failover to another replica within a DAG is essentially transparent to the end users, it is considered a best practice with Exchange Server 2010 to utilize DAGs.

Documenting the Exchange Server Environment

Key to the success of recovering an Exchange server or an entire Exchange Server environment is having documentation on the server configurations. Having specific server configuration information documented helps to identify which server is not operational, the routing of information between servers, and, ultimately, the impact that a server failure or server recovery will have on the rest of the Exchange Server environment. By having a complete understanding of the Exchange Server environment as a whole, an administrator can often bring up temporary services to alleviate a failure and give themselves more time to fix the issue and determine the root cause.

> **NOTE**
>
> A utility called ExchDump can assist an administrator with baselining and improving the environment. Use ExchDump to export and document a server's configuration. The ExchDump utility can be downloaded from the Microsoft Exchange Server download page at www.microsoft.com/exchange/downloads/2003/default.mspx.
>
> Although this utility was originally written for Exchange Server 2003, it works fine for extracting the same information from an Exchange Server 2010 server.

Some of the items that should be documented include the following:

- Server name
- Server roles held
- Version of Windows on servers (including service pack)
- Version of Exchange Server on servers (including service pack)
- Organization name in Exchange Server
- Site names
- Database names
- Location of databases
- Size of databases
- When database maintenance was last run
- Public folder tree name
- Replication process of public folders
- Security delegation and administrative rights
- Names and locations of global catalog servers

Documenting the Backup Process

To simplify a restore of an Exchange Server environment, it is important to start with a clean backup. A clean backup is performed when the proper backup process is followed. Create a backup process that works, document the step-by-step procedures to back up the server, follow the procedures regularly, and then validate that the backups have been completed successfully.

Also, when configurations change, the backup process and system configurations should be documented and validated again, to make sure that the backups are completed properly.

Documenting the Recovery Process

An important aspect of recovery feasibility is knowing how to recover from a disaster. Just knowing what to back up and what scenarios to plan for is not enough. Restore processes should be created and tested to ensure that a restore can meet service level agreements (SLAs) and that the staff members understand all the necessary steps.

When a process is determined, it should be documented, and the documentation should be written to make sense to the desired audience. For example, if a failure occurs in a satellite office that has only marketing employees and one of them is forced to recover a server, the documentation needs to be written so that it can be understood by just about anyone. If the information technology (IT) staff will be performing the restore, the documentation can be less detailed, but it assumes a certain level of knowledge and expertise with the server product. The first paragraph of any document related to backup and recovery should be a summary of what the document is used for and the level of skill necessary to perform the task and understand the document.

The recovery process involved in resolving an Exchange Server problem should also be focused not only on the goal of getting the entire Exchange server back up and operational, but also on considering smaller steps that might help minimize downtime. As an example, if an Exchange server has failed, instead of trying to restore 10TB of mail back to the server, which can take hours, if not days, to complete, an organization can choose to restore just the user Inboxes, calendars, and contacts. After a faster system recovery of core information on a server, the balance of the information can be restored over the next several hours.

The other advantage of having a properly documented restore procedure is that it greatly reduces the chances of human error occurring during a restore. Recovering a failed server while hundreds or possibly thousands of email users are affected is a stressful situation. This isn't the time to learn how to perform a restore. The goal in this situation is for the administrator to follow a clearly documented and well-tested process to ensure that no steps are missed and that no information is entered incorrectly. Having well-documented steps can greatly reduce the stress of this situation and increase the chances of a successful restore.

Even if an environment is utilizing DAG as their primary form of disaster recovery, there should still be a documented procedure of what to do in this situation. Although the rebuild of redundant systems can be delayed, the longer the delay, the more data will have to be incrementally reseeded and the longer a company is at a higher risk should other replicas fail.

Including Test Restores in the Scheduled Maintenance

Part of a successful disaster recovery plan involves periodically testing the restore procedures to verify accuracy and to test the backup media to ensure that data can actually be recovered. Most organizations or administrators assume that if the backup software reports "Successful," the backup is good and data can be recovered. If special backup consideration is not addressed, the successful backup might not contain everything necessary to restore a server if data loss or software corruption occurs.

Restores of file data, application data, and configurations should be performed as part of a regular maintenance schedule to ensure that the backup method is correct and that disaster recovery procedures and documentation are current. Such tests also should verify that the backup media can be read from and used to restore data. Adding periodic test restores to regular maintenance intervals ensures that backups are successful and familiarizes the administrators with the procedures necessary to recover so that when a real disaster occurs, the recovery can be performed correctly and efficiently the first time.

These test restores should occur in a lab environment in which end users won't be affected. The restores should vary in type, testing single mailbox restores, complete server restores, and full site restores in which even domain controllers might need to be restored from scratch. This helps ensure that staff members are comfortable with the process and will have no problem performing a restore in production should the occasion ever arise.

Recovering from a Site Failure

When a site becomes unavailable because of a physical access limitation or a disaster such as a fire or earthquake, steps must be taken to provide the recovery of the Exchange server in the site. Exchange Server does not have a single-step method of merging information from the failed site server into another server, so the process involves recovering the lost server in its entirety.

To prepare for the recovery of a failed site, an organization can create redundancy in a failover site. With redundancy built into a remote site, the recovery and restore process can be minimized if a recovery needs to be performed.

For environments in which SLAs offer little time to bring up a recovery location, administrators should strongly consider implementing Database Availability Groups, a new feature of Exchange Server 2010 that replaces CCR and SCR. For details on building this type of Exchange Server cluster, see Chapter 31.

Creating Redundant and Failover Sites

Redundant sites are created for a couple of different reasons. First, a redundant site can have a secondary Internet connection and bridgehead routing server so that if the primary site is down, the secondary site can be the focus for inbound and outbound email communications. This redundancy can be built, configured, and set to automatically provide failover in case of a site failure. See Chapter 7, "Installing Exchange Server 2010," for details on creating Send/Receive Connectors and configuring Hub Transport servers.

The other reason for a redundant site is to provide geographic failover to allow for transparent disaster recovery. In Exchange Server 2010, although you could build a "warm standby" site in which you would install Exchange Server 2010 when needed for recovery, that would provide no benefits versus building a redundant site that is already replicated with the mailbox data. This is exactly what Database Availability Groups provide when placed in a site that also has the Client Access Server and Hub Transport Server roles available.

If you plan to utilize redundant DR sites, be sure to update those sites with patches and applications as you apply them to the production systems. This ensures that the remote replicas are usable should you have a failure in the primary location.

Creating the Failover Site

When an organization decides to plan for site failures as part of a disaster recovery solution, many areas need to be addressed and many options exist. For organizations looking for redundancy, network connectivity is a priority, along with spare servers that can accommodate the user load. The spare servers need to have enough disk space to accommodate a complete restore. As a best practice, to ensure a smooth transition, the following list of recommendations provides a starting point:

▶ Allocate the appropriate hardware devices, including servers with enough processing power and disk space to accommodate the restored machines' resources.

▶ Host the organization's external DNS zones and records using primary DNS servers located at an Internet service provider (ISP) collocation facility, or have redundant DNS servers registered for the domain and located at both physical locations.

▶ Publish the recovery site's IP address as a lower-priority MX record. This way, when the recovery server comes online, you won't have to wait for DNS propagation to advertise the new MX record.

▶ Ensure that network connectivity is already established and stable between sites and between each site and the Internet.

▶ Create at least one copy of backup tape medium for each site. One copy should remain at one location, and a second copy should be stored with an offsite data storage company. This is necessary only if recovery of mailbox data beyond the internal retention policies is needed.

▶ Have a copy of all disaster recovery documentation stored at multiple locations and at the offsite data storage company. This provides redundancy if a recovery becomes necessary.

When the systems are in place in the failover site and configured to support a Database Availability Group, the data will automatically be replicated from the master copy and will be available when needed. Be sure to account for the amount of replication traffic that will be passed over the WAN to the disaster recovery site. Although the log files are compresses, they are still potentially a large source of data. To get an idea of the amount of data that will be replicated, look at the volume of log files generated on the primary server each day. That is the amount of data that will be replicated to each replica. For sites running multiple replicas across WAN connections, this can be a significant volume of data.

Failing Over Between Sites

When utilizing Database Availability Groups with replicas in a failover site that also has CAS and HT roles available, the process of failing services from the primary site to the DR site is easy:

1. Launch Exchange Management Console.
2. Expand Organization Configuration.
3. Click mailbox.
4. Click the Database Management tab.
5. Right click the database copy you'd like to activate.
6. Select Activate Database Copy.
7. When the wizard launches, if desired, enter an override mount dial for the operation; click OK.
8. When the wizard is completed, click Finish.

The same process can be done entirely from the Exchange Management Shell as well by following these steps:

1. Launch Exchange Management Shell
2. Type `Move-ActiveMailboxDatabase -Identity DBName -ActivateOnServer` *NewServer*.

    For example, `Move-ActiveMailboxDatabase -Identity 'Mailbox Database 2010A' -ActivateOnServer E2010`.

If, on the other hand, the failover isn't a planned event, the mailbox databases within a DAG will be automatically failed over to the site holding the second highest-priority copy of the mailbox database. The preceding steps would primarily be used for DR testing or to move services to enable systems to be patched or upgraded in some manner.

Failing Back After Site Recovery

When the initial site is back online and available to handle client requests and provide access to data and networking services and applications, it is time to consider failing back the services. This process is greatly improved in Exchange Server 2010 through the use of Database Availability Groups. Unlike SCR, which was used for DR in Exchange Server

2007, there is no need to reestablish the replication relationship. A DAG simply continues to replicate mailbox data to all other replicas. This means that if mailbox master status is moved from ServerA to ServerB, ServerB will replicate to ServerA. If, on the other hand, ServerA were unavailable for an extended period of time and ServerB were to become too far out of sync and ServerA needed to be reseeded, Exchange Server 2010 supports the concept of incremental reseeding; the amount of data that would need to be sent back to ServerA would be significantly less than it would have been in Exchange Server 2007 with SCR.

Questions to consider for failing back are as follows:

▶ Will downtime be necessary to restore databases between the sites?

▶ When is the appropriate time to fail back?

▶ Is the failover site less functional than the preferred site? In other words, are only mission-critical services provided in the failover site, or is it a complete copy of the preferred site?

The answers lie in the complexity of the failed-over environment. If the cutover is simple, there is no reason to wait to fail back.

Providing Alternative Methods of Client Connectivity

When failover sites are too expensive and are not an option, it does not mean that an organization cannot plan for site failures. Other lower-cost options are available but depend on how and where the employees do their work. For example, many times users who need to access email can do so without physically being at the site location. Email can be accessed remotely from other terminals or workstations.

The following are some ways to deal with these issues without renting or buying a separate failover site:

▶ Consider renting racks or cages at a local ISP to co-locate servers that can be accessed during a site failure.

▶ Have users dial in from home to a terminal server hosted at an ISP to access Exchange Server.

▶ Set up remote user access using Terminal Services or Outlook Web App at a redundant site so that users can access their email, calendar, and contacts from any location.

▶ Configure Outlook to utilize Outlook Anywhere on "slow" connections. This enables them to connect normally while in the office but can utilize "public" connections to connect should the office be unavailable.

▶ Rent temporary office space, printers, networking equipment, and user workstations with common standard software packages such as Microsoft Office and Microsoft Internet Explorer. You can plan for and execute this option in about one day. If this is an option, be sure to find a computer rental agency first and get pricing before a failure occurs, and you have no choice but to pay the rental rates.

Recovering from a Disk Failure

Organizations create disaster recovery plans and procedures to protect against a variety of system failures, but disk failures tend to be the most common in networking environments. The technology used to create processor chips and memory chips has improved drastically over the past couple decades, minimizing the failure of system boards. And although the quality of hard drives has also drastically improved over the years, because hard drives are constantly spinning, they have the most moving parts in a computer system and tend to be the items of most failure.

Key to a disk fault-tolerant solution is creating hardware fault tolerance on key server drives that can be recovered in case of failure. Information is stored on system, boot, and data volumes that have varying levels of recovery needs. Many options exist such as storage area networks (SANs) or various RAID levels to minimize the impact of drive failures.

Important to note is that Exchange Server 2010 environments built with a DAG architecture are much less impacted by single server failures. Microsoft suggests doing away with local RAID configurations and utilizing the application layer redundancy to protect against system failures. In some cases, the reduction in disks and expensive RAID controllers will offset the costs associated with building servers for a redundant site. This should be taken into consideration when designing for server resilience.

Hardware-Based RAID Array Failure

Common uses of hardware-based disk arrays for Windows servers include RAID 1 (mirroring) for the operating system and RAID 5 (striped sets with parity) for separate data volumes. Some deployments use a single RAID-5 array for the OS, and data volumes for RAID 0+1 (mirrored striped sets) have been used in more recent deployments.

RAID controllers provide a firmware-based array-management interface, which can be accessed during system startup. This interface enables administrators to configure RAID controller options and manage disk arrays. This interface should be used to repair or reconfigure disk arrays if a problem or disk failure occurs.

Many controllers offer Windows-based applications that can be used to manage and create arrays. Of course, this requires the operating system to be started to access the Windows-based RAID controller application. Follow the manufacturer's procedures on replacing a failed disk within hardware-based RAID arrays.

> **NOTE**
>
> Many RAID controllers enable an array to be configured with a hot spare disk. This disk automatically joins the array when a single disk failure occurs. If several arrays are created on a single RAID controller card, hot spare disks can be defined as global and can be used to replace a failed disk on any array. As a best practice, hot spare disks should be defined for arrays.

System Volume

If a system disk failure is encountered, the system can be left in a completely failed state. To prevent this problem from occurring, the administrator should always try to create the system disk on a fault-tolerant disk array such as RAID 1 or RAID 5. If the system disk was mirrored (RAID 1) in a hardware-based array, the operating system will operate and boot normally because the disk and partition referenced in the boot.ini file will remain the same and will be accessible. If the RAID-1 array was created within the operating system using Disk Manager or `diskpart.exe`, the mirrored disk can be accessed upon bootup by choosing the second option in the `boot.ini` file during startup. If a disk failure occurs on a software-based RAID-1 array during regular operation, no system disruption should be encountered.

Boot Volume

If Windows Server 2008 has been installed on the second or third partitions of a disk drive, a separate boot and system partition will be created. Most manufacturers require that for a system to boot up from a volume other than the primary partition, the partition must be marked active before functioning. To satisfy this requirement without having to change the active partition, Windows Server 2008 always tries to load the boot files on the first or active partition during installation, regardless of which partition or disk the system files will be loaded on. When this drive or volume fails, if the system volume is still intact, a boot disk can be used to boot into the OS and make the necessary modification after changing the drive.

Data Volume

A data volume is by far the simplest of all types of disks to recover. If an entire disk fails, simply replacing the disk, assigning the previously configured drive letter, and restoring the entire drive from backup restores the data and permissions.

A few issues to watch out for include the following:

▶ Setting the correct permissions on the root of the drive

▶ Ensuring that file shares still work as desired

▶ Validating that data in the drive does not require a special restore procedure

Recovering from a Boot Failure

Occasionally, a Windows Server 2008 system can suffer a service or application startup problem that could leave a server incapable of completing a normal bootup sequence. Because the operating system cannot be accessed in this case, the system remains unavailable until this problem can be resolved.

Windows Server 2008 includes a few alternative bootup options to help administrators restore a server to a working state. Several advanced bootup options can be accessed by pressing the F8 key when the boot loader screen is displayed. If the Recovery Console was previously installed, it is listed as an option in the boot loader screen. The advanced boot options include the following:

▶ **Safe Mode**—Starts the operating system with only the most basic services and hardware drivers, and disables networking. This enables administrators to access the operating system in a less functional state to make configuration changes to service startup options, some application configurations, and the system Registry.

▶ **Safe Mode with Networking**—The same as Safe Mode, but networking drivers are enabled during operation. This mode also starts many more operating system services upon startup.

▶ **Safe Mode with Command Prompt**—Similar to the Safe Mode option; however, the Windows Explorer shell is not started by default.

▶ **Enable Boot Logging**—Boots the system normally, but all the services and drivers loaded at startup are recorded in a file named `ntbtlog.txt`, located in the `%systemroot%` directory. The default location for this file is `C:\Windows\ntbtlog.txt`. To simplify reading this file, the administrator must delete the existing file before a bootup sequence is logged so that only the information from the last bootup is logged.

▶ **Enable low-resolution video**—Loads the current display driver, but it displays the desktop at the lowest resolution. This mode is handy if a server is plugged into a different monitor that cannot support the current resolution.

▶ **Last Known Good Configuration**—Starts the operating system using Registry and driver information saved during the last successful logon.

▶ **Directory Services Restore Mode**—Only for domain controllers and enables for maintenance and restoration of the Active Directory database or the SYSVOL folder.

▶ **Debugging Mode**—Sends operating system debugging information to other servers through a serial connection. This requires a server on the receiving end with a logging server that is prepared to accept this data. Most likely, standard administrators will never use this mode.

▶ **Start Windows Normally**—As the name states, this mode loads the operating system as it would normally run.

▶ **Reboot**—Reboots the server.

> ▶ **Return to OS Choices Menu**—Returns the screen to the boot loader page so that the correct operating system can be chosen and started.

The Recovery Console

The Recovery Console provides an option for administrators to boot up a system using alternate configuration files to perform troubleshooting tasks. Using the Recovery Console, the bootup sequence can be changed, alternate boot options can be specified, volumes can be created or extended, and service startup options can be changed. The Recovery Console has only a limited number of commands that can be used, making it a simple console to learn. If Normal or Safe Mode bootup options are not working, the administrator can use the Recovery Console to make system changes or read the information stored in the boot logging file using the `type` command. The boot logging file is located at `C:\Windows\ntbtlog.txt` by default and exists only if someone tried to start the operating system using any of the Safe Mode options or the boot logging option.

Recovering from a Complete Server Failure

Because hardware occasionally fails and, in the real world, operating systems do have problems, a server-recovery plan is essential, even though it might never be used. The last thing any administrator wants is for a server failure to occur and to end up on the phone with Microsoft technical support asking for the server to be restored from backup when no plan is in place. To keep from being caught unprepared, the administrator should have a recovery plan for every possible failure associated with Windows Server 2008 systems.

Restoring Versus Rebuilding

When a complete system failure occurs, whether it is because of a site outage, a hardware component failure, or a software corruption problem, the method of recovery depends on the administrator's major goal. The goal is to get the server up and running, of course, but behind the scenes, many more questions should be answered before the restore is started:

> ▶ How long will it take to restore the server from a full backup?

> ▶ If the server failed because of software corruption, will restoring the server from backup also restore the corruption that actually caused the failure?

> ▶ Will reloading the operating system and Exchange Server manually followed by restoring the System State be faster than doing a full restore?

Loading the Windows Server 2008 operating system and Exchange Server 2010 software can be a relatively quick process. This ensures that all the correct files and drivers are loaded correctly and all that needs to follow is a System State restore to recover the server configuration and restore the data. One of the problems that can occur is that, upon installation, some applications generate Registry keys based on the system's computer name, which can change if a System State restore is performed.

Exchange Server 2010 has a setup /recoverserver installation option and does not need the server's System State restore—just the original computer name and domain membership, as long as computer and user certificates are not being used. Using this switch also prevents the Exchange Server computer from creating the default storage groups and databases. This simplifies the process of restoring the server later.

The key to choosing whether to rebuild or restore from backup is understanding the dependencies of the applications and services to the operating system, and having confidence in the server's stability at the time of the previous backups. The worst situation is attempting a restore from backup that takes several hours, only to find that the problem has been restored as well.

Keep in mind that if one is utilizing redundant systems with a DAG configuration, the decision of restore versus rebuild is almost entirely a question of which is faster. Environments not based on DAG are more dependent on the identity of the individual servers and tend to favor restores.

Manually Recovering a Server

When a complete server system failure is encountered and the state of the operating system or an application is in question, the operating system can be recovered manually. Locating the system's original configuration settings is the first step. This information is normally stored in a server build document or wherever server configuration information is kept.

Because each system is different, as a general guideline for restoring a system manually, perform the following steps:

1. Install a new operating system on the original system hardware and disk volume, or one as close to the original configuration as possible. Be sure to install the same operating system version—for example, Windows Server 2008, Enterprise or Standard Edition.

2. During installation, name the system using the name of the original server, but do not join a domain.

3. Do not install additional services during installation, and proceed by performing a basic installation.

4. When the operating system completes installation, install any additional hardware drivers as necessary and update the operating system to the service pack and security patches that the failed server was expected to have installed. To reduce compatibility problems, install the service packs and updates as outlined in the server build document to ensure that any installed applications will function as desired. During a restore is not the time to roll out additional system changes. The goal is to get the system back online, not to upgrade it.

5. Using the Disk Management console, create and format disk volumes and assign the correct drive letters as recorded in the server build document.

6. If the server was originally part of a domain, join the domain using the original server name. Because many Windows Server 2008 services use the server name or

require the service to be authorized in a domain, perform this step before installing any additional services or applications.

7. Install any additional Windows Server 2008 services as defined in the server build document.

8. Install Exchange Server 2010 using the same version of Exchange Server (Standard or Enterprise) that was originally installed. Apply any Exchange service packs and updates that were expected to be on the original server as well. When installing Exchange Server, use the setup /recoverserver installation process that will install Exchange Server but will not add new databases.

9. Restore Exchange Server data to the new server.

10. Test functionality, add this system to the backup schedule, and start a full backup.

> **NOTE**
>
> If certificates were issued to the previous server, the new server must import the same certificates or enroll with the certificate authority (CA) for a new certificate before encrypted communication can occur.

Recovering Exchange Server Application and Exchange Server Data

To recover an Exchange server, there are several different ways of rebuilding the core Exchange server and restoring the Exchange Server data. The restoration of Exchange Server databases must be done to a server with the exact same server name as the original server from which the databases were backed up.

After the Active Directory and base Windows servers have been installed, the first process is installing or restoring the Exchange Server application software; the second process is installing the data files for Exchange Server.

Recovering Using Windows Server Backup in Windows 2008

When program and data files are corrupt or missing, or a previously backed-up copy is needed, the information can be restored using Windows Server Backup if a previous backup were performed using this utility. The following process should be followed:

1. Log on to the server using an account that has at least the privileges to restore files and folders. Backup Operators and Local Administrator groups have this right, by default.

2. Click Start, All Programs, Administrative Tools, Windows Server Backup.

3. In the right pane, click Recovery Wizard.

4. Choose the server for which to recover files and click Next.

5. Select the backup from which you want to recover and click Next.

6. When prompted to select a recovery type, choose Applications and click Next.

7. Select Exchange as your application and click Next.

8. When prompted to specify recovery options, choose to recover to another location. Click Browse to pick a location for the restored files. Click Next.

9. Review the restore information and click Recover.

10. When the restore is completed, click Close.

To recover items from the restored database, you need to create a recovery database. This process is a bit different from Exchange Server 2007 and is best performed via the Exchange Management Shell:

1. Launch Exchange Management Shell.

2. Create a recovery database by typing `new-mailboxdatabase -Recovery <databaseIdParameter> -Server <StoreMailboxIdParameter>`.

3. To extract the data, use `Restore-mailbox -Identity <MailboxIdParameter> -RecoveryDatabase <DatabaseIdParameter> -Recoverymailbox <StoraMailboxIdParameter>`.

   The `restore-mailbox` commandlet can be used with switches to be more specific about the data being extracted. For example:

   ```
   Restore-Mailbox -Identity Andrew -RSGDatabase RecoveredDB -SubjectKeywords
   ➥"Take over world" -IncludeFolders \Inbox, \Calendar, \SecretPlans
   ```

   Or for a bulk extraction, you could use the following:

   ```
   Get-Mailbox -Database AccountingDB ¦ Restore-mailbox -RSGDatabase
   ➥RecoveredAccountingDB
   ```

   This would allow you to extract information for all users in the AccountingDB from the restored copy of the Accounting DB.

Performing a Restore of Only Exchange Server Database Files

For environments that are not utilizing Database Availability Groups, situations might occur in which Exchange Server 2010 is still running properly but one or more databases might have become corrupted and cannot be fixed via the utilities. In these situations, you might need to restore from a backup and overwrite the existing database. To perform this task, follow these steps:

1. Launch Exchange Management Console.

2. Expand the Organization Configuration and click Mailbox.

3. From the Database Management tab, right-click the database you want to restore and click Properties.

4. On the Maintenance tab, check the box for This Database Can Be Overwritten by a Restore.

5. Click OK.

6. Click Start, All Programs, Administrative Tools, Windows Server Backup.

7. In the right pane, click Recovery Wizard.

8. Choose the server for which to recover files and click Next.

9. Select the backup from which you want to recover and click Next.

10. When prompted to select a recovery type, choose Applications and click Next.

11. Select Exchange as your application and click Next.

12. When prompted to specify recovery options, choose to recover to the original location. Click Next.

13. Review the restore information and click Recover.

14. When the restore is completed, click Close.

Recovering from Database Corruption

If an Exchange Server database is corrupt, it is not extremely effective to restore the corrupt database to a production server. The server might continue to operate, but database corruption never goes away on its own, and you eventually need to repair the database. In fact, when minor database corruption is not repaired, the corruption can get to the point that entire sections of the Exchange Server database become inaccessible.

A couple of methods can be used to repair a corrupt Exchange Server database, or at least restore the database and extract good information from the database. Key to the successful recovery of as much information as possible is using the right tool. In many cases, administrators jump right into using the ESEUTIL /p repair command; instead of repairing the Exchange Server database to 100% condition, the utility finds a corrupt section of the database and deletes all information from that portion of the database on. So, although the Exchange Server system becomes 100% clean, the utility deleted 20%–30% of the data that was in the database to get the database to a clean state. The ESEUTIL /P command is the task of last resort: Other tools work around corrupt database areas and enable the administrator to recover as much of the data as possible.

Going all the way back to the start of the chapter in the "What to Do Before Performing Any Server-Recovery Process" section, this is where having a complete backup of the databases in Exchange Server is really important. If a process to repair or recover information causes more harm to the database than good, there is still a backup copy to restore and start again.

Exchange Server 2010 makes this process easier for the new administrator by introducing the Database Recovery Management tool that analyzes the failed databases for the administrator and choose what tools to run against them.

Flat-File Copying the Exchange Server Databases

One of the best techniques Exchange Server experts use when working to recover corruption in a database is to make a flat-file copy of the Exchange Server databases. A flat-file copy is merely an exact copy of the Exchange Server databases copied to another portion of the server hard drive or to another server. To do a manual copy of the databases, do the following:

1. Dismount the Exchange Server database stores by going into the Exchange System Manager. Traverse the tree past Administrative Groups, Servers, Storage Group. Right-click on the mailbox store, and select Dismount Store.

2. Dismount the store for all mailbox stores you will be working on.

3. Copy (using Windows Explorer, or XCOPY) the `*.edb` files to a safe location.

NOTE

If the databases need to be manually restored, a simple XCOPY (or Windows Explorer copy) of the databases back to the original subdirectories will bring the data back to the condition the databases were in at the time the databases were copied off the system. If the Exchange Server databases were properly dismounted before they were copied, the logs would have already been committed to the database, and the database can be remounted exactly where it left off.

Moving Mailboxes to Another Server in the Site

One way of extracting mail from a corrupt database is to move the mailbox or mailboxes to a different server in the site. Instead of trying to run utilities to fix the corruption in the database, which can take several hours (or even days, depending on the size of the database and the amount of corruption that needs to be fixed), an administrator can set up another server in the Exchange Server site and move the mailboxes to a new server.

Moving mailboxes grabs all the mail, calendar, contacts, and other mailbox information from one server and moves the information to a new server. As the information is written to the new server, the information is automatically defragmented, and corruption is not migrated. In addition, mailboxes can be moved from one server to another without ever having to bring down the production server. A mailbox user must be logged off Outlook and must not be accessing Exchange Server before the mailbox can be moved. However, if mailboxes are moved when individuals are out of the office, at lunch, or on weekends, the mailboxes can be moved without users ever knowing that their information was moved from one system to another.

The two caveats to moving mailboxes are these: Corrupt mailboxes will not move, and user Outlook profiles will be changed. For Outlook profiles, because a user's Outlook profiles point to a specific server, when a mailbox is moved from one server to another, the user's profile also needs to point to the new server. Fortunately, with Exchange Server and Outlook, when a user's mailbox is moved, Outlook tries to access the mailbox on the original server, and the server notifies Outlook that the mailbox has been moved to a new Exchange server. The user's Outlook profile automatically changes to associate the profile to the new server where the user's mailbox resides. So, as long as the old server remains operational and the user attempts to access email from the old server, the profiles will be automatically changed the next time the user tries to access email. Typically, within one to two weeks after moving mailboxes from one server to another, the user profiles are all automatically changed.

As for corrupt mailboxes, unfortunately, Exchange Server typically does not move a corrupt mailbox. So, if a user's mailbox has been corrupted, the mailbox remains on the old server. Moving the data from the corrupt mailbox needs to be handled in a manner specified in the following section, "Recovering Data with a Recovery Storage Group." However, if 80%–90% of the user mailboxes can be moved to a new server, the administrators are trying to recover only a handful of mailboxes instead of all mailboxes on a server. This could mean far less downtime for all users who had mail on the server and could limit the exposure of data loss to a limited number of users. It will also result in much faster results when running the database recovery tools as the database will be much smaller.

To move mailboxes between servers in a site, do the following :

1. Open the Exchange Management Console.
2. Expand Recipient Configuration and click Mailbox.
3. Highlight the mailboxes to be moved.
4. From the Action menu, choose New Local Move Request.
5. Select the destination for the mailbox to be moved, and click Next.
6. Choose how you want the tool to deal with corrupted messages, and click Next.
7. Review the proposed changes and if you are satisfied that they are correct, click New.
8. You can review the status and results of the move request in the newly added Move Request section by expanding Recipient Configuration in Exchange Management Console.

Running the ISINTEG and ESEUTIL Utilities

When a database is determined to be corrupt, usually an administrator is directed to run the built-in utilities on Exchange Server to run maintenance on the databases. The utilities are the ISINTEG ("eye-ess-in-tehg") and ESEUTIL ("ee-ess-ee-u-tihl"). However, depending on the condition of the database, a corrupt database can take several hours to run, only to result in the loss of data. Some administrators are incorrectly told to never run the utilities because they will always result in loss of data. It's typically just a lack of knowledge of how the utilities work that leads to misunderstanding the potential results of the databases.

As noted in the previous two sections, there might be better options for recovering information from a corrupt database. Instead of trying to fix a known corrupt database, simply migrating the information off a server or extracting information from corrupt databases is frequently a better fix. However, if the determination is to run the utilities, a few things should be noted:

▶ The ISINTEG utility is a high-level utility that checks the consistency of the database, validating the branches of the database that handle data, data directory tables, attachment objects, and the like. Fixing the database table makes way for a more intensive data integrity check of the database.

▶ The ESEUTIL utility is a low-level utility that checks the data within the database. ESEUTIL does not differentiate between a corrupt section of the database and how that section impacts mailboxes or messages. So, when a complete repair is performed using ESEUTIL, entire mailboxes can be deleted, or all attachments for the entire database can be eliminated to fix the corruption. This is why running ESEUTIL to repair a database is a function of last resort.

▶ To run ISINTEG on a database takes around one hour for every 10GB scanned for a moderately corrupt database. The repairs are done relatively quickly, and the database is ready for more extensive scanning.

▶ Running ESEUTIL on a database takes anywhere from one hour for every 10GB to up to one hour per 1GB, depending on the level of repair performed. It is not unreasonable to see a relatively corrupt 30GB database take more than 24 hours to complete the repair.

▶ ISINTEG and ESEUTIL can be performed only offline, meaning that the Exchange server is offline during the process. Users cannot access their mailboxes during the ISINTEG and ESEUTIL processes. Thus, if it takes 20 to 40 hours of downtime to complete the repair of a database, the Move Mailbox method that can be run without bringing servers offline is frequently a more palatable solution.

▶ However, if run on a regular basis, the ISINTEG and ESEUTIL utilities can clean up an Exchange Server database before serious corruption occurs. Administrators who get scared off performing maintenance because of the potential threat of losing data could actually minimize their chance of data corruption if the utilities are run regularly. See Chapter 19 for recommended maintenance practices.

The common parameters used for the ISINTEG and ESEUTIL utilities are as follows. For regular maintenance, such as checking the database structure's integrity and performing defragmentation of the database, the following commands should be run:

```
isinteg -s SERVERNAME -test allfoldertests
eseutil /d priv1.edb
```

NOTE

The ISINTEG and ESEUTIL utilities typically reside in the \Program Files\Microsoft\Exchange Server\V14\Bin directory of the Exchange server.

When a database needs to be repaired, eseutil /p priv1.edb can be run. Beware: The /p repair command is a brute-force repair and deletes sections of the database to make the integrity of the database clean. A message provides an additional warning about ESEUTIL. When running the /p command in ESEUTIL, entire sections of the database might be deleted to repair and recover the state of the database.

> **NOTE**
>
> Prior to a disaster, if the `ISINTEG` or `ESEUTIL` utilities have not been run against an Exchange Server database for a long period of time, restore the database from tape to an Exchange server in a lab environment to run tests. These tests can tell you how much corruption might be present and give an indication of how long it might take to repair the database.

Recovering Internet Information Services

When Internet Information Services (IIS) data is erased or the service is not functioning as desired, restoring the configuration might be necessary. Backup and restore of IIS configurations is simpler than ever in Windows 2008. To restore the IIS 7 configuration, perform the following step:

1. From a command prompt, type `%windir%\system32\inetsrv\appcmd.exe restore backup "My Backup"`.

   This assumes that you've taken backups of IIS by using `%windir%\system32\inetsrv\appcmd.exe add backup "My Backup"` as detailed in Chapter 32.

Recovering IIS Data and Logs

IIS web and FTP folders are stored in the `C:\InetPub\` directory. The default location for the IIS logs is `C:\Windows\system32\LogFiles`. To recover the IIS website, FTP site, or IIS logs, restore the files using either shadow copy data or a backup/restore tool such as `Ntbackup.exe`.

Recovering Windows Server 2008 Domain Controllers

When a Windows Server 2008 domain controller fails, the administrator needs to either recover this server or understand how to completely and properly remove this domain controller from the domain. The following are some questions to consider:

- ▶ Did this domain controller host any of the domain or forest Flexible Single Master Operations (FSMO) roles?

- ▶ Was this domain controller a global catalog (GC) server, and, if so, was it the only GC in a single Active Directory site?

- ▶ If the server failed because of Active Directory corruption, has the corruption been replicated to other domain controllers?

- ▶ Is this server a replication hub or bridgehead server for Active Directory site replication?

Using the preceding list of questions, the administrator can decide how best to deal with the failure. For example, if the failed domain controller hosted the PDC emulator FSMO role, the server could be restored or the FSMO role could be manually seized by a separate domain controller. If the domain controller was the bridgehead server for Active Directory site replication, recovering this server might make the most sense so that the desired primary replication topology remains intact. The administrator should recover a failed domain controller as any other server would be recovered, restore the OS from an ASR restore, or build a clean server, restore the System State, and perform subsequent restores of local drive data as necessary.

Recovering Active Directory

When undesired changes are made in Active Directory or the Active Directory database is corrupted on a domain controller, recovering the Active Directory database might be necessary. Restoring Active Directory can seem like a difficult task, unless frequent backups are performed and the administrator understands all the restore options.

The Active Directory Database

The Active Directory database contains all the information stored in Active Directory. The global catalog information is also stored in this database. The actual filename is `ntds.dit` and, by default, is located in `C:\Windows\NTDS\`. When a domain controller is restored from server failure, the Active Directory database is restored with the System State. If no special steps are taken when the server comes back online, it will ask any other domain controllers for a copy of the latest version of the Active Directory database. This situation is called a nonauthoritative restore of Active Directory.

When a change in Active Directory needs to be rolled back or the entire database needs to be rolled back across the enterprise or domain, an authoritative restore of the Active Directory database is necessary. Recovery of this type is a combination of two events: first, a system state restore of the domain controller, followed by NTDSUTIL commands to tell the newly restored information to overwrite existing information in the directory.

To perform an authoritative restore of the Active Directory database, follow these steps:

1. Log on to the Windows Server 2008 system with an account with administrator privileges.
2. Click Start, click All Programs, click Administrative Tools, and select System Configuration.
3. Select the Boot tab. In the Boot Options section, check the Safe Boot check box, select the Active Directory Repair option button, and then click OK.
4. The System Configuration utility asks for a reboot, and if there are no additional tasks to perform, click the Restart button to boot the system into DSRM.

5. When the system completes a reboot, log on as administrator with the DSRM password. Make sure to specify the local server as the logon domain—for example, server1\administrator instead of companyabc\administrator.

6. Click Start, click All Programs, click Accessories, and select Command Prompt.

7. At the command prompt, type wbadmin get versions and press Enter. This returns a list of the known backups. The most recent backup is the last one listed.

8. In the Command Prompt window, select the desired backup version that can recover the System State by highlighting the version identifier and pressing Enter to store the version name on the Clipboard. For this example, use the version identifier of 02/02/2009-17:00.

9. If the System State is restored to recover Active Directory, in the Command Prompt window, type wbadmin Start SystemStateRecovery -version:02/02/2007-17:00 and press Enter.

10. If the System State is being recovered to recover the SYSVOL, in the Command Prompt window, type wbadmin Start SystemStateRecovery -version: 20/02/2007-17:00 -authsysvol and press Enter.

11. If the command was entered properly, a confirmation will be required to start the System State recovery. Type in Y to accept the System State recovery, and press Enter to start the System State recovery process.

12. The System State recovery will take several minutes to complete. Do not reboot.

13. If an authoritative restore of Active Directory objects is required, perform that task now as outlined in a proceeding section. If an authoritative restore of Active Directory objects is not required, click Start, click Administrative Tools, and select System Configuration.

14. Select the Boot tab. In the Boot Options section, uncheck the Safe Boot check box, and click OK to save the settings.

15. Reboot the domain controllers into normal Boot mode.

16. After the system reboots, verify functionality. If everything is working fine, perform a full backup.

When Active Directory has been modified and needs to be restored to a previous state, and this rollback needs to be replicated to all domain controllers in the domain and possibly the forest, an authoritative restore of Active Directory is required. An authoritative restore of Active Directory can include the entire Active Directory database, a single object, or a container, such as an organizational unit including all objects previously stored within the container. To perform an authoritative restore of Active Directory, perform the System State restore of a domain controller, but when you are finished, do not reboot and perform these additional steps:

1. Open a command prompt on the domain controller that is running in DSRM and has just completed a System State recovery, but has not yet been rebooted.

2. In the Command Prompt window, type NTDSUTIL and press Enter.

3. Type Activate Instance NTDS and press Enter.

4. Type `Authoritative Restore` and press Enter.

5. To restore a single object, type `Restore Object` followed by the distinguished name of the previously deleted object. For example, to restore an object named Omar in the Users container of the companyabc.com domain, the command would be `Restore Object "cn=Omar,cn=Users,dc=companyabc,dc=com"`.

6. To restore a container or organizational unit and all objects beneath it, replace the "restore object" with "restore subtree" followed by the appropriate distinguished name.

7. After the appropriate command is typed in, press Enter. A window opens, asking for confirmation of the authoritative restore; click the Yes button to complete the authoritative restore of the object or subtree.

8. The NTDSUTIL tool displays the name of the text file that might contain any back-links for objects just restored. Note the name of the file and whether any back-links were contained in the restored objects.

9. Type `quit` and press Enter; type `quit` again to close out of the NTDSUTIL tool.

10. Close the command prompt and open the System Configuration utility to change the boot option back from a safe boot to a normal boot, and reboot the domain controller.

11. After the domain controller reboots, log on to verify that the authoritatively restored objects are replicating to the other domain controllers. If things are working properly, run a full backup of the domain controller and log off.

Global Catalog

No special restore considerations exist for restoring a global catalog server other than those outlined for restoring Active Directory in the previous sections. The global catalog data is re-created based on the contents of the Active Directory database.

Summary

As you've seen in this chapter, Exchange Server 2010 offers a number of different ways to recover from different types of disasters. Dealing with these disasters is much like being a doctor. You start off with preventative measures to try to greatly reduce the risk of having a failure. If you do encounter a failure, you always start with the least intrusive actions so as not to make the problem worse. Only when other options have been exhausted do you revert to a tape backup. In this way, you can reduce the impact of the failure and improve your chances of not losing any data.

Recovering from a disaster can often go beyond the scope of just the Exchange server because it might have been a full site failure. By having written procedures that have been well tested and practiced, you can quickly recover from major failures.

You've also seen how to deal with minor issues such as corrupted messages in otherwise healthy servers and have seen how similar processes can enable for easy extraction of archived messages or how to recover something that was accidentally deleted.

By utilizing the advanced data protection features of Exchange Server 2010 such as Database Availability Groups and maintaining a reasonable retention period for deleted items, Exchange Server administrators can greatly reduce the chances of having to restore from tape. Similarly, this type of architecture bridges the gap between High Availability and Disaster Recovery and turns a recovery site into a useful maintenance tool by allowing administrators to use that site to pick up services when the local systems need to be patched or upgraded. By maintaining best practices around database maintenance and proactive monitoring, you can also greatly reduce your chances of encountering corrupted data in Exchange Server. Coupling this with the enhancements in the Jet database, managing an Exchange Server 2010 environment should be more uneventful than ever.

Best Practices

The following are best practices from this chapter:

- ▶ If not utilizing DAG, always separate your logs and databases onto different physical drives. This way, if you need to restore a database from the night before, the logs can be replayed to bring the database back to current.

- ▶ Consider multiple alternatives beyond restoring an entire server or running the built-in Exchange Server utilities when analyzing recovery methods.

- ▶ Have good documentation on the Exchange Server environment to make for an easier time in recovering from system failures.

- ▶ Use the setup /recoverserver command to greatly simplify the recovery process in Exchange Server.

- ▶ Perform an offline copy of the database using XCOPY before performing any maintenance.

- ▶ Move mailboxes from an old server with corrupt databases to a new server in the same site to minimize downtime.

- ▶ Run the ISINTEG and ESEUTIL utilities on a regular basis to maintain the integrity of Exchange Server databases.

- ▶ Use a recovery storage group whenever possible to simplify the recovery of information from backup.

- ▶ Take advantage of the new Database Availability Groups to greatly reduce your dependency on traditional backups.

- ▶ Test recovery procedures in a lab before they are needed in production.

- ▶ Test your recovery procedures quarterly in production to ensure that your methods are effective.

33

CHAPTER 34

Optimizing an Exchange Server 2010 Environment

As the latest version of Microsoft Exchange Server, Exchange Server 2010 offers several enhancements over previous versions of Exchange Server. These enhancements improve the messaging environment's reliability, availability, and scalability as well as giving additional flexibility in how these improvements are utilized. To be able to make use of these features, however, you must carefully plan the deployment and implementation of Exchange Server 2010 with a strong understanding of your environment's needs. Any good implementation of Exchange Server 2010 includes an optimization phase. This involves baselining the performance of the "out-of-the-box" build and applying best practices and tweaks to improve the performance of the environment. Through careful analysis of capacity and testing with the available tools, a clever administrator can wring additional performance out of an Exchange Server 2010 environment.

Capacity analysis, stress testing, and performance optimization processes and procedures are, most often, low-priority tasks for most IT organizations. This is frequently because productivity is regularly measured by what can be achieved now and not always what can be properly planned or designed. The benefits of capacity analysis and performance monitoring can be obtained in the short term, but they are more important when established over longer periods of time. As a result, the main focus of most Information Technology (IT) departments shifts to the more immediate and more tangible day-to-day processes and IT needs. Companies that focus on the performance optimization of their Exchange Server 2010 environment will find that it requires upgrades less often and it offers a better experience to the user community.

The results of capacity analysis and performance optimization save organizations of all sizes time, effort, and expenditures. This chapter is designed to provide best practices for properly and proactively performing capacity analysis and performance optimization so that IT personnel and end users can work more effectively and efficiently.

Examining Exchange Server 2010 Performance Improvements

Before delving into ways to tweak Exchange Server 2010 performance, it is useful to have an understanding of the performance improvements that have been made since its predecessor, Exchange Server 2007. Although some of these performance improvements are more noticeable than others, Exchange Server 2010 has been designed to scale into the enterprise and beyond. Even prior to its release, Exchange Server 2010 was used to host literally millions of mailboxes via Microsoft's Live@edu offering, which provided email services to students and gave Microsoft an impressive opportunity to load test Exchange Server 2010 in a real world implementation.

Architectural Improvements

Like Exchange Server 2007, Exchange Server 2010 is built on a 64-bit architecture. This provides Exchange Server 2010 with scalability and performance that was not available with 32-bit code. By eliminating the legacy limitation of a 3GB memory space, the Exchange Server engine is able to cache very large amounts of data. This means that Exchange Server is no longer as limited by disk input/output (I/O) performance. When configured with sufficient memory, Exchange Server 2010 can reduce its disk I/O requirements by as much as 66% over the already impressive numbers offered by Exchange Server 2007. This allows administrators to be much more efficient in their use of disks. Given the impressive rate of growth of capacity of hard drives as opposed to the fairly stagnant growth of I/O capacity, Exchange Server 2010 continues to drive a paradigm shift toward low cost direct attached disk.

The improved internal architecture of Exchange Server 2010 also allowed Microsoft to raise the limits on the number of databases that could be hosted by a single Exchange server. Whereas Exchange Server 2003 was only capable of a total of 20 databases (spread out across four storage groups) and Exchange Server 2007 was able to host as many as 50 databases (spread out across 50 storage groups), Exchange Server 2010 again raises the bar by allowing for 150 databases, which are no longer tied to storage groups. This again offers administrators greater flexibility in how they design their Exchange Server 2010 servers, which can result in increased performance if it is designed correctly. This topic is covered in greater detail later in this chapter.

Database Engine Improvements

Microsoft has continued to make great strides with the JET database. JET is the database used by Exchange Server 2010, as well as in previous versions of Exchange Server, to store mailbox data and public folder data. In the latest 64-bit version of JET offered by

Exchange Server 2010, the JET engine is able to take advantage of the lift in restrictions on memory space and it allows JET to allocate significantly more cache for the Exchange Server store. This means that users have access to more cache and this greatly increases the likelihood that data requested by a user is already in memory and doesn't have to be read from disk. This results in quicker response times for the end users. Similarly, the database page size in Exchange Server 2010 has been increased from 8KB to 32KB. Although this might not seem significant, the result is that more messages are able to fit into a single database page and, as a result, the Exchange server uses fewer I/O operations to gather the requested information. This helps to significantly reduce the overall I/O requirements of the Exchange Server 2010 server.

TIP

To take best advantage of the larger block size used by Exchange Server 2010 when accessing databases, consider formatting hard drives that will host Exchange Server 2010 mailboxes with a larger block size. This will reduce fragmentation within the disk and will reduce overall I/O usage by reducing the number of disk blocks that have to be read for each transaction.

Exchange Server 2010 has an entirely new Store schema that is significantly flatter than the Store schema used by Exchange Server 2007. The changes in the Store schema allow for 100,000 items in a single folder within the mailbox as opposed to 20,000 in Exchange Server 2007. While this will alleviate a source of pain for many "power users," it is still recommended to encourage users to organize their mailbox and to delete unneeded items in order to keep their performance as high as possible.

Exchange Server 2010 has also made some changes to offer what's called the Personal Archive. This functionality creates a folder within the mailbox that is actually located in a secondary mailbox. The functionality works very similarly to the concept of opening 2 mailboxes simultaneously, which is a fairly common situation for Executive Admins or for IT members who monitor a common mailbox. By creating this secondary mailbox, Exchange Server 2010 is able to reduce the load on the more commonly accessed mailbox by allowing a user to offload the bulk of their messages into an archive. The user is still able to access all the messages, but the loads are effectively separated from each other. Enabling this Personal Archive also prevents the user from creating PST files, which can be a very useful control for IT departments who need to control where potentially sensitive email information is stored.

Transport Pipeline Improvements

The transport pipeline refers to the collection of server roles as well as various queues, components, and connections within Exchange Server that work together to transport messages to the message categorizer in the Hub Transport server. The job of this categorizer is to deliver mail to the appropriate location within the Exchange Server environment. This process has been greatly improved in Exchange Server 2010 and is able to handle significantly more messages than earlier versions of Exchange Server.

Exchange Server 2010 introduces the concept of cross premises mail routing, wherein an Exchange Server 2010 environment can be built with a combination of onsite servers combined with off premises hosted servers, all acting as part of the same Exchange Server organization.

A very useful improvement in the Hub Transport functionality is changes to appended disclaimers, performed by Hub Transport rules. The improved disclaimers can now support hyperlinks and images as well as accessing fields in AD to populate the disclaimers. This is exceptionally useful for Exchange Server 2010 organizations that span multiple countries. For example, the European Union requires that email messages sent outside an organization must contain the physical address of the sending company's offices. In Exchange Server 2007, this required the creation of multiple disclaimers and required administrators to manage them such that they were attached to the members of the correct offices. In Exchange Server 2010, a single disclaimer could be utilized that queried Active Directory to find the appropriate office address to use in the disclaimer.

Exchange Server 2010 also introduces moderated transport, which allows Hub Transport rules to enforce a workflow for various messages. This would allow Exchange Server 2010 to provide process routing so that one or more parties would have to approve messages before they got to their final destination. This can be a very effective way to control the usage of managed distribution groups.

Shadow redundancy is a new feature introduced by Exchange Server 2010 that serves to ensure that messages are correctly routed within an organization. When a message is sent, it isn't considered truly sent until there is a confirmation from the next hop that the message was passed along. For example, if a message leaves a mailbox server and reaches a Hub Transport server, the mailbox server doesn't consider the message sent until the Hub Transport server tells it that it was successfully sent to the next hop. If, for example, the Hub Transport server were to crash before it was able to pass the message along, the mailbox server would see that it never got a confirmation that the message left the Hub Transport server and it would resend the message via another Hub Transport server, assuming one were available, and would wait for the next hop confirmation. This prevents messages "in flight" from being lost due to a hardware or storage failure.

Exchange Server 2010 also introduces a feature called MailTips. MailTips present the user with useful information that will potentially change the way they send messages. MailTips give administrators a way to warn users about the action they are about to perform. For example, if a user is sending to a distribution list, the MailTips will tell the user the number of recipients that are about to get the message. In many cases, users don't necessarily understand the scope of a DL that they are about to use. By knowing the actual audience, they may think twice about sending that email about having kittens to give away. The MailTips can also give users "what if" types of information. For example, if a user were typing an email to a user who is out of office, the MailTips would preview that target user's OOF message even before the first user sent a message. This would often result in the first user not wasting the time to type a message to a user that isn't going to get it any time soon. It would also reduce the number of messages waiting for the second user upon their return.

Perhaps the most useful feature of the MailTips is the ability for the Exchange Server 2010 system to quickly identify a recipient that isn't in the organization and can alert users to this fact. By knowing that someone in the "Reply All" is from outside their organization, users are less likely to include information that isn't supposed to be told to people outside the organization.

Security Improvements

Exchange Server 2010 has offered administrators greater integration with Rights Management Services by allowing one to create Hub Transport rules that will enable RMS protection on messages. This is a huge boon to administrators as traditionally the biggest challenge with RMS is getting employees to actually use it. By triggering the use of RMS based on text patterns or on specific recipients, RMS can be activated automatically.

Exchange Server 2010 also offers much more granular control in the area of delegating permissions within Exchange Server. This should simplify the adoption of role based administration with Exchange Server 2010.

Accessibility Improvements

Lack of support for non-Internet Explorer browsers for use with OWA has long been a complaint of Exchange Server administrators. While OWA works in other browsers, it was always a neutered set of functionality with a less than impressive appearance. Exchange Server 2010 has finally overcome that limitation and now offers the full experience to all browsers. This will allow Exchange Server administrators to overcome a large adoption hurdle by finally being able to fully support Macintosh and Linux clients as well as PC users that prefer to use web browsers other than Internet Explorer.

Exchange Server 2010 has also introduced support for Text messaging (SMS) integration. This allows Outlook Web App users to send SMS messages to phones.

The new Conversation View allows email messages to be grouped together as a logical conversation thread even if the messages are currently stored in different folders. This simplifies tracking information in a conversation where some participants might delete portions of the thread.

Analyzing Capacity and Performance

Capacity and performance analysis for an Exchange Server 2010 environment requires a well-established understanding of the business and messaging needs of the organization and a well-documented outline of the organization's expectations of its messaging environment. The capacity of an Exchange Server environment is directly dependent on the expected level of performance. It is important to understand exactly what it is you are expecting from the system in terms of storage per user, level of responsiveness of the server, and room for anticipated expansion. When armed with these concepts, you can more accurately determine what your current capacity is.

The first step in capacity analysis is to grasp an understanding of these concepts and define performance expectations. This can be done by establishing policies and service level agreements (SLAs). It is in these policies and SLAs that an administrator can outline acceptable performance thresholds and more accurately gauge the capacity needs of Exchange Server 2010. These thresholds can also be used to accurately establish performance baselines from which to analyze the requirements against available resources.

To help develop the policies and SLAs, use questionnaires, interviews, business objectives, and the like along with performance measurements via the Performance Monitor, Exchange Best Practices Analyzer, or third-party analysis tools. This allows you to combine realistic expectations with concrete data to see where you are relative to where you want to be.

Establishing Baselines

The importance of establishing meaningful baselines of the messaging environment cannot be underscored enough. Baselines are particularly important in the sense that they are the measurable tools that can be used to balance what is required of Exchange Server 2010 with what resources are needed to fulfill those requirements. Achieving this balance can be made simpler if an administrator consults performance metrics, such as industry-standard benchmarks. By starting with an accurate baseline of system performance, you can quickly and easily test changes in the environment to see if they have made things better or worse. Accurate baselines are also very helpful when troubleshooting problems and you can quickly determine which subsystems are not performing the way they normally do. A clear baseline allows you to determine whether a server that "seems slow" really is slower than the way it usually runs.

> **NOTE**
>
> Use ExchDump to assist with baselining the environment. ExchDump exports a server's configuration, which can be useful to determine whether the build follows company standards. This is particularly important with Exchange Server clusters because each node in the cluster should be a replica of the other.

To establish an accurate baseline of Exchange Server 2010, a number of tools can help an administrator in this process. These tools are discussed in detail in the following sections. Some of these capacity analysis tools are built in to Windows Server 2008, and others are built in to Exchange Server 2010. Many third-party tools and utilities are also available for the careful measurement of Exchange Server 2010 capacity requirements and performance analysis.

Using the Exchange Best Practices Analyzer Tool

The Exchange Best Practices Analyzer (ExBPA) is a utility provided by Microsoft that analyzes an Exchange server's configuration and informs administrators of possible configuration changes that can be made to improve performance or mitigate problems. More specifically, ExBPA can be used to perform a health check, a health and performance check, a connectivity test, and a baseline test. This tool, which was a download in previous versions of Exchange Server, is now a built-in tool. To access the Best Practices Analyzer, perform the following steps:

1. Launch Exchange Management Console.
2. If the left pane, scroll down and select Toolbox.
3. In the center pane, double click Best Practices Analyzer.
4. When the Best Practices Analyzer tool launches, check the Check for Updates on Startup check box, and click Check for Updates Now. Joining the Microsoft Customer Experience Improvement Program is optional.
5. If there are updates available, click Download the Latest Updates. This will ensure you have the latest version of the tool and any of the latest updates to their configuration rules.
6. After being updated, the tool closes, and you have to click it again.
7. Choose Go to Welcome Screen.
8. Click Select Options for a New Scan.
9. Type the name of your closest global catalog, and click Connect to the Active Directory Server.
10. Enter a label for this scan, choose the systems you want to scan, choose Health Check, and click Start Scanning.
11. When the tool has finished, click View a Report of This Best Practices Scan.

When viewing the report, an administrator is able to see any critical issues, nondefault settings, or recent changes to the system. This quickly identifies configuration settings that might be detrimental to the overall performance of the system. Be sure to always update the Best Practices Analyzer before running it because Microsoft is constantly adding new information to this tool.

The Informational Items tab offers a convenient and consolidated view of information that is typically captured in Exchange Server documentation. Take advantage of this view when tracking the configuration of your Exchange Server 2010 servers.

The Best Practices Analyzer also allows administrators to run a multi-hour performance baseline that serves as an excellent way to track overall changes in the performance of servers. By looking at several hour blocks of time and running the tool at the same time on the same day of the week, administrators can get a very accurate view of how the loads on their servers are affecting performance.

Planning for Growth

One of the easiest ways to maintain the performance of an Exchange Server 2010 server is to plan ahead for the growth of the environment. Too many administrators have a tendency to build an Exchange Server infrastructure that meets the storage and performance requirements of today but that fails to account for the growth of the company.

Typically, when designing an Exchange Server 2010 infrastructure, you should try to look ahead roughly 3 years to predict the size to which the company will grow. This is a good time to talk to groups such as Human Resources and Finance to see the rate at which the company has grown historically. This will give you a good idea of how many employees would be utilizing the Exchange Server environment in 3 years. This process should also uncover specific expansion plans for the company. For example, if the company were going to grow from 10,000 employees to 13,000 employees in 3 years, you would naturally consider that a 30% growth and would allow for an extra 30% capacity on servers. However, if the case were that 2,000 of those employees would be in a new facility in Japan that was going to be online in 2 years, it would really be a 10% growth across the enterprise and potentially a very large increase in capacity needs in Asia or perhaps an entirely new Exchange Server site in Japan.

Understanding these types of growth allow you to more easily plan for capacity growth and understand how the increase in user load will affect the performance of your Exchange Server 2010 servers in various sites.

The other thing to consider when planning for growth is the increases in usage of the Exchange Server environment. It is common to see companies increase the storage limits for users without changing the number of users on a server. There are also third-party technologies that might be in your 3-year plan that will leverage Exchange Server 2010 as a storage or transport. Voice mail systems, Structured Query Language (SQL), or Oracle implementations could quickly increase the loads placed on your Exchange Server 2010 servers.

The reason it is important to predict, as best you can, these anticipated growths is because it is often easier to account for these needs at the time of the Exchange Server 2010 design. Most companies are using storage area networks (SANs) or network attached storage (NAS) for the mailbox stores in Exchange Server. Although these systems do have the ability to resize their LUNs to offer additional storage, this is a very time-consuming process and it directly impacts the users on the server. Similarly, because these are usually shared storage devices, there is likely not enough spare capacity on the shelf or device to allocate more space to the Exchange servers. This results in the SAN or NAS administrator having to allocate additional space in a nonoptimal way, which can affect the performance of all the applications that attach to the NAS or SAN. That said, Exchange Server 2010 utilizing direct attached storage can generally be expanded easily by simply adding more disks, assuming the subsystem has room to allow for more disks. Based on this ability, administrators should consider avoiding deploying all 100 databases on a server from day 1.

Optimizing Exchange Server 2010 Servers

With the separation of various roles in Exchange Server 2010, individual optimizations vary from role to role. The following sections address the various roles in Exchange Server 2010 and how to optimize the performance of those roles.

Optimizing Mailbox Servers

Of all the servers in an Exchange Server 2010 environment, the Mailbox server role is the one that will likely benefit the most from careful performance tuning.

Mailbox servers have traditionally been very dependent on the disk subsystem for their performance. Although this has changed in Exchange Server 2010, it is important to understand that this change in disk behavior is very dependent on memory. As such, the general rule for performance on an Exchange Server 2010 Mailbox server is to configure it with as much memory as you can. For example, in Exchange Server 2003, if you had a load of 2,000 users that generated an average of 1 disk I/O per second and you were running a RAID 0+1 configuration, you would need 4GB of memory and 40 disks (assuming 10k RPM disk and 100 random disk I/O per disk) to get the performance you'd expect out of an Exchange server. In Exchange Server 2010, the I/O load per user would be closer to 0.15 disk I/O per second and you could reduce the number of disks required by roughly 85% if you increased the system memory to 12GB of memory.

As you can see, with a mailbox server, the trick is to balance costs against performance. In large implementations, it is less expensive to replace high-performance disks with memory. This makes direct attached disks a viable choice for Exchange Server 2010 mailbox servers. In modern servers, configurations of 16GB or more are becoming commonplace and are quite affordable.

Another area where a mailbox server benefits in terms of performance is the disk subsystem. Although you've just seen that the disk requirements are lower than previous versions of Exchange Server, this doesn't mean that the disk subsystem is unimportant. This is another area where you must create a careful balance between cost, performance, and recoverability. The databases benefit the most from a high-performance disk configuration. Consider using 15k RPM drives because they offer more I/O performance per disk; generally 50% more random I/O capacity versus a 10k RPM disk. Given the reduction in disk needed to support the databases, you should consider using RAID 0+1 rather than RAID 5 so as not to incur the write penalties associated with RAID 5. The log files also need fast disks to be able to commit information quickly, but they have the advantage of being sequential I/O rather than random. That is, the write heads don't have to jump all around the disk to find the object to which they want to write. The logs start at one point on the disk and they write sequentially without having to modify old logs.

Exchange Server 2010 has also implemented several changes that specifically improve performance when utilizing SATA disks. By altering the I/O pattern within Exchange Server 2010, the disk writes are better spread out and are less "bursty" than before. This makes SATA a very viable choice for Exchange Server 2010.

Another interesting performance benefit available in Exchange Server 2010 is the potential to eliminate RAID entirely on the Exchange Server 2010 server. If one is using Database Availability Groups with 3 or more replicas of mailbox databases, there is enough redundancy in the system as a whole to allow one to eliminate redundancy at the individual

34

server level. If the 30 second "blip" in services is acceptable within one's Service Level Agreements, one could potentially remove all redundant disks and power supplies and NICs from their Exchange Server 2010 mailbox servers. This would greatly reduce the number of disks that the server needs to be able to support, often resulting in the ability to deploy less expensive servers and thus to deploy more of them. So while one isn't likely to save money in hardware, as there is a need to deploy additional disks, one can likely create a significantly more resilient environment for approximately the same cost. The easiest way to look at this idea of redundancy at the application level rather than redundancy at the server level is to think about Active Directory. In AD, if a domain controller fails, it's generally not a big deal so long as there are other DCs to take over the load. Rather than fixing a DC, one simply builds a new one and lets it replicate the directory. The same philosophy can apply to Exchange Server 2010 where if a DAG member fails, rather than restore it, one simply builds a new one and lets it replicate the data. Another DAG member would have already taken over for the failed node and services would not be significantly interrupted. For more details on creating and using DAGs, see Chapter 31, "Database Availability Group Replication in Exchange Server 2010."

In a perfect world, the databases and logs are all on their own dedicated disks. Although this isn't always possible, it does offer the best performance. In the real world, you might have to occasionally double up databases or log files onto the same disk. Be aware of how this affects recoverability. For performance, always separate the logs from the databases as their read/write patterns are very different. It also makes recovery of a lost database much easier.

Mailbox servers also deal with a large amount of network traffic. Email messages are often fairly small and as a result, the transmission of these messages isn't always as efficient as it could be. Whenever possible, equip your mailbox servers with Gigabit Ethernet interfaces. If possible, and if you aren't clustering the mailbox servers, try to run your network interfaces in a teamed mode. This improves both performance and reliability.

As mailbox servers also hold the public folder stores, consider running a dedicated public folder server if your environment heavily leverages public folders. Public folder servers often store very large files that users are accessing, so separating the load of those large files from the mailbox servers results in better overall performance for the user community.

For companies that only lightly use public folders, it requires some investigation of the environment to see if it is better to run a centralized public folder server or if it is better to maintain replicas of public folders in multiple locations. This is usually a question of wide area network (WAN) bandwidth versus usage patterns.

Optimizing Database Availability Groups

Mailbox servers in Exchange Server 2010 offer a new function known as Database Availability Groups. In a DAG configuration, mailbox data is replicated across multiple hosts. As such, it becomes less important to build in system level redundancy. The best analogy is to think of DAG nodes like domain controllers. As long as there's at least one up and running, your users are still accessing their mail normally. If one were to fail, rather than rebuild it, one simply builds another node, adds it as a replica, and lets the data replicate to it. This allows an administrator to drastically change the way they deploy servers. Rather than have to struggle with the price versus performance tradeoffs of RAID5 vs. RAID0+1, administrators can consider just running basic disks with no redundancy whatsoever. This makes smaller servers viable as one isn't likely to need nearly as many disks in the chassis. This makes it even easier for administrators to move away from complex and expensive SANs back toward direct attached storage. In this case, optimizing doesn't always mean making things faster and more scalable, sometimes optimizing is about doing more with less.

When configuring a DAG, consider utilizing a separate network for replication. DAGs offer the ability to configure the nodes to use a specific network for their replication traffic. This offers two potential benefits. Number one, in a LAN scenario, it means that clients aren't competing with replication traffic for access to their mailboxes over the LAN. In a WAN configuration, it means that if an environment has access to multiple networks, they can potentially move replication traffic to a lower cost network. Consider a typical scenario where a large enterprise has their offices connected via an MPLS network. MPLS provides excellent bandwidth and performance but is generally somewhat expensive. Many of these large enterprises also have IPSec tunnels set up across Internet connections to provide a secondary network to use in case of a failure of the MPLS links. These cheaper IPSec tunnels can be used to offload the DAG replication. This reduces the load on the "production" network and at the same time, saves money by utilizing a lower tier of bandwidth.

The other way to optimize DAG members is to balance the load across multiple DAG replicas. This is a concept that is new compared to CCR in Exchange Server 2007. In Exchange Server 2010, the replication is done at the database level rather than at the server level. This means that rather than running in Active/Passive pairs, one can effective be active for one or more databases and passive for others on the same server. So a site might have 3 DAG members in a single location for redundancy and could run $1/3^{rd}$ of the databases as "master" on node 1, $1/3^{rd}$ on node 2 and the remaining $1/3^{rd}$ on node 3, with replicas going to the other 2 nodes. Node 1 might be "master" for databases 1-5, the 2nd priority for databases 6-10 and 3rd priority for databases 11-15. This means that if a node failed, the load would double on the remaining 2 servers rather than tripling on a single node. This allows administrators to get the best performance out of their hardware by carefully planning out loads for both a "normal" and a "DR" situation.

Optimizing Client Access Servers

Client access servers (CASs) tend to be more dependent on CPU and memory than they are on disk. Because their job is to simply proxy requests back to the mailbox servers, they don't need much in the way of local storage. The best way to optimize the client access server is to give it enough memory that it doesn't need to page very often. By monitoring the page rate in the Performance Monitor, you can ensure that the CAS is running optimally. If it starts to page excessively, you can simply add more memory to it. Similarly, if the CPU utilization is sustained above 65% or so, it might be time to think about more processing power.

Unlike mailbox servers, client access servers are usually "commodity" class servers. This means they aren't likely to have the capacity for memory or CPU that a mailbox server might have. It is typical to increase the performance of the client access servers by simply adding more servers into a load-balanced group.

This is a good example of optimizing a role as opposed to a server that holds a role. As you start to add more services to your client access servers, such as Outlook Anywhere or ActiveSync, you will see an increase in CPU usage. Be sure to monitor this load because it allows you to predict when to add capacity to account for the increased load. This prevents your users from experiencing periods of poor performance.

Exchange Server 2010 utilizes the client access servers much more than Exchange Server 2007 did. This is because the new Exchange Server 2010 architecture utilizes what is called MAPI on the Middle Tier. This means that Outlook clients no longer talk directly to the mailbox server role. They instead talk to the Client Access server role. The reason this change was made was to support Database Availability Groups. Rather than requiring Outlook to determine which copy of a database is currently the master copy, the client access servers perform that role. As such, Outlook merely needs to find an available client access server to make its connections. As a result of this architectural change, the ratio of client access servers to mailbox servers has gone up noticeably. It is now recommend to run a ratio of 3 CAS processor cores for every 4 mailbox processor cores. Maintaining this ratio will ensure sufficient performance for Outlook users.

It is also recommended to always run at least 2 client access servers per site to ensure uninterrupted services for users.

Generally speaking a client access server should run at least 2GB of memory and 2GB per processor core are recommended. Client access servers don't scale well beyond 8 cores.

Another way in which the Client Access server role can be optimized is in the area of how users attach to it. One of the most common requests in Exchange Server from and OWA perspective is to configure things such that users don't have to remember the full URL for connecting to OWA. For example, your users might need to type https://webmail.companyabc.com/owa to get to their OWA page, but many users will type https://webmail.companyabc.com instead. In the past, it was recommended to utilize a customized ASP page to make the redirection. In Windows 2008, the redirection functionality is built it. When configuring IIS for Exchange Server 2010 CAS, be sure to include the HTTP Redirection feature. With this available, one can reconfigure the IIS site as follows:

1. Launch the Internet Information Services (IIS) Manager.
2. Expand the left pane to Default Web Site.
3. Click the Features View and Group by No Grouping.
4. Double click HTTP Redirect, as shown in Figure 34.1.
5. Check the box for Redirect Requests to This Destination, as shown in Figure 34.2, and set the destination to the /owa sub site.
6. Check both boxes in the Redirect Behavior section.
7. Click Apply.
8. Uncheck the redirection settings from all sub sites in IIS.

FIGURE 34.1   Choosing HTTP Redirect.

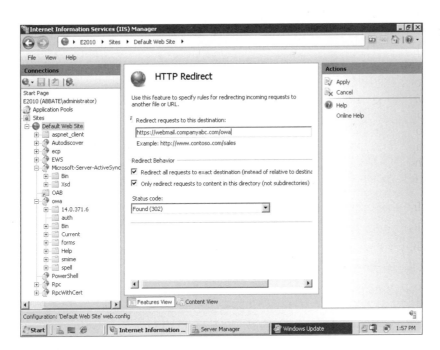

FIGURE 34.2   HTTP Redirect.

Optimizing Hub Transport Servers

The goal of the Hub Transport server is to transfer data between different Exchange Server sites. Each site must have a Hub Transport server to communicate with the other sites. Because the Hub Transport server doesn't store any data locally, its performance is based on how quickly it can determine where to send a message and send it off. The best way to optimize the Hub Transport role is via memory, CPU, and network throughput. The Hub Transport server needs ready access to a global catalog server to determine where to route messages based on the recipients of the messages. Placing a global catalog (GC) in the same site as a busy Hub Transport server is a good idea. Ensure that the Hub Transport server has sufficient memory to quickly move messages into and out of queues. Monitoring available memory and page rate gives you an idea if you have enough memory. High-speed network connectivity is also very useful for this role. If you are running a dedicated Hub Transport server in a site and you find that it's overworked even though it has a fast processor and plenty of memory, consider simply adding a second Hub Transport server to the site because they automatically share the load.

Disk performance is potentially a concern in environments that send very high volumes of messages. The Hub Transport maintains the SMTP queues on disk and the faster they can be processed, the faster mail can flow. In older versions of Exchange Server it was recommended to run redundant disks for the SMTP queues. This was because if a Hub Transport lost the disks on which the SMTP queues lived, the messages would be lost. In Exchange Server 2010, the shadow redundancy feature protects against this type of message loss. Basically, when the mailbox server hands a message to the Hub Transport, the mailbox server doesn't consider the message as "sent" until the Hub Transport reports back that it successfully handed the message off to someone else. This means that if the message were sitting in the queue on the Hub Transport and that Hub Transport failed, the mailbox server would know the message never got past the Hub Transport and it would attempt to resend the message via another Hub Transport in the site. When the Hub Transport reports that it's handed the message to another hop, either to another mailbox server or to another Hub Transport, it would report back and the message would be "sent" from the perspective of the mailbox server. This means that administrators can design their Hub Transport servers without the requirement for redundant disks for the SMTP queues. By taking the approach of building Hub Transports on non-redundant commodity hardware, one can likely build two Hub Transports for about the same cost as one highly redundant Hub Transport. This makes it easy to build sites with multiple Hub Transport servers to provide redundancy. This means that administrative and maintenance tasks can be done at any time without interrupting services for an Exchange Server 2010 site.

As was the case with Exchange Server 2007, in Exchange Server 2010, all messages, regardless of destination, must first pass through a Hub Transport server. This means that the Hub Transport server is the logical choice for where to place anti-virus scanning. When planning out a Hub Transport server, make sure you account for your anti-virus product. This may mean adding additional memory or processing power to the Hub Transport server. Also, keep in mind, if you are anticipating utilizing a large number of Hub Transport rules, that may result in a need for faster processors or more memory.

Generally speaking, a Hub Transport should run at least 2GB of memory and 1GB per processor core is recommended.

Optimizing Edge Transport Servers

The Edge Transport server is very similar to the Hub Transport server, with the key difference being that it is the connection point to external systems. As such, it has a higher need for processing power because it needs to convert the format of messages from Simple Mail Transfer Protocol (SMTP) to Messaging Application Programming Interface (MAPI) for internal routing. Edge Transport servers are often serving "double duty" as antivirus and antispam gateways, thus increasing the need for CPU and memory. The Edge Transport role is one where it is very common to optimize the service by deploying multiple Edge Transport servers. This not only increases a site's capacity for sending mail into and out of the local environment, but it also adds a layer of redundancy.

To fully optimize this role, consider running Edge Transport servers in two geographically disparate locations. Utilize multiple MX records to balance out the load of mail coming into the company. Use your route costs to control the outward flow of mail such that you can reduce the number of hops needed for mail to leave the environment.

Keep a close eye on CPU utilization as well as memory paging to know when you need to add capacity to this role. Utilizing content-based rules or running message filtering increases the CPU and memory requirements of this role.

Generally speaking, an Edge Transport should run at least 2GB of memory and 1GB per processor core is recommended.

Optimizing Unified Messaging Servers

The Unified Messaging server is still supported in the Exchange Server 2010 world to act as a connector to voice mail systems to allow voice mail to be stored in and accessed through the users' mailboxes. In the past, this type of functionality was always performed by a third-party application. In Exchange Server 2010, this ability to integrate with phone systems and voice mail systems in built in. As you might expect, to optimize this role, you must optimize the ability to quickly transfer information from one source to another. This means that the Unified Messaging role needs to focus on sufficient memory, CPU, and network bandwidth. To fully optimize Unified Messaging services, strongly consider running multiple network interfaces in the Unified Messaging server. This allows one network to talk to the phone systems and the other to talk to the other Exchange servers. Careful monitoring of memory paging, CPU utilization, and NIC utilization allows you to quickly spot any bottlenecks in your particular environment.

Generally speaking, a Unified Messaging server should run at least 4GB of memory and 1GB per processor core is recommended.

Deployment Ratios

To summarize the deployment ratios of various roles within Exchange Server 2010:

▸ 7 mailbox server processor cores per 1 Hub Transport server processor core

▸ 4 mailbox processor cores per 3 client access server processor cores

▸ 4 mailbox processor cores per 1 global catalog processor core (32-bit GC)

▸ 8 mailbox processor cores per 1 global catalog processor core (64-bit GC)

General Optimizations

Certain bits of advice can be applied to optimizing any server in an Exchange Server 2010 environment. For example, the elimination of unneeded services is one of the easiest ways to free up CPU, memory, and disk resources. Event logging should be limited to the events you care about and you should be very careful about running third-party agents on your Exchange Server 2010 servers.

Event logs should be reviewed regularly to look for signs of any problems. Disks that are generating errors should be replaced and problems that appear in the operating system should be addressed immediately.

You should regularly review the performance counters identified in this chapter to see how your systems are running compared to what you'd expect. Always investigate any anomalies to determine if things have been changed or if you are suffering a potential problem. By staying on top of your systems and knowing how they should run, you can more easily keep them running in an optimal manner.

The Security Customization Wizard should be run to ensure that correct network ports for Exchange Server 2010 roles are available. While many administrators are tempted to simply disable the Windows 2008 firewall, it is important to realize that the Windows Filtering Platform is still running and can potentially interrupt traffic.

Optimizing Active Directory from an Exchange Server Perspective

As you likely already know, Exchange Server 2010 is very dependent on Active Directory for routing messages between servers and for allowing end users to find each other and to send each other mail. The architecture of Active Directory can have a large impact on how Exchange Server performs its various functions.

When designing your Exchange Server 2010 environment, consider placing dedicated global catalog servers into an Active Directory site that contains only the GCs and the local Exchange servers. Configure your site connectors in AD with a high enough cost that the GCs in this site won't adopt another nearby site that doesn't have GCs. This ensures that the GCs are only used by the Exchange servers. This can greatly improve the lookup performance of the Exchange server and greatly benefits your OWA users as well.

In the case of a very large Active Directory environment, for example 20,000 or more objects, consider upgrading the domain controllers to run Windows Server 2003 64-bit or

Windows Server 2008 64-bit. This is because a directory this large can grow to be larger than 3GB. When the Extensible Storage Engine database that holds Active Directory grows to this size, it is no longer able to cache the entire directory. This increases lookup and response times for finding objects in Active Directory. By running a 64-bit operating system on the domain controller, you can utilize the larger memory space to cache the entire directory. The nice thing in this situation is that you retain compatibility with 32-bit domain controllers, so it is not necessary to upgrade the entire environment, only sites that will benefit from it.

Monitoring Exchange Server 2010

A variety of built-in Microsoft tools are available to help an administrator establish the baseline of the Exchange Server 2010 environment. Among these, the Performance Monitor Microsoft Management Console (MMC) snap-in is one of the most common tools used to measure the capacity requirements of Exchange Server 2010. This MMC tool is built in to Windows Server 2008.

Using the Performance Monitor Console

The Performance snap-in enables an in-depth analysis of every measurable aspect of the Exchange server. The information that is gathered using the Performance snap-in can be presented in a variety of forms, including reports, real-time charts, or logs, which add to the versatility of this tool. The resulting output formats enable an administrator to present a baseline analysis in real time or through historical data. The Performance snap-in, shown in Figure 34.3, can be launched from the Start, Administrative Tools menu.

Using Task Manager

Task Manager displays real-time performance metrics, so an administrator can quickly get an overall idea of how the Exchange Server 2010 server is performing at any given time. Its biggest downfall, however, is that it does not store any historical data, so it is not a suitable tool for capacity-analysis purposes. Task Manager is typically used as a quick check to see if anything is out of the ordinary. If a server appears to be running slow, using Task Manager and using the Processes tab allows you to sort the processes by CPU or Memory use and quickly see if something is noticeably different from its baseline value. This is a quick way to spot common issues like an antivirus scanner taking up all the CPU time or an lsass.exe process using an excessive amount of memory.

Analyzing and Monitoring Core Elements

The capacity analysis and performance optimization process can be intimidating because there can be an enormous amount of data to work with. In fact, it can easily become unwieldy if not done properly. The process is not just about monitoring and reading counters; it is also an art.

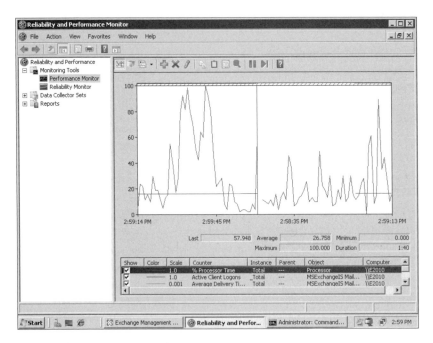

FIGURE 34.3   The Performance snap-in.

As you monitor and catalog performance information, keep in mind that more information does not necessarily yield better optimization. Tailor the number and types of counters that are being monitored based on the server's role and functionality within the
network environment. It's also important to monitor the four common contributors to
bottlenecks: memory, processor, disk, and network subsystems. When monitoring
Exchange Server 2010, it is equally important to understand the various Exchange roles to
keep the number of counters being monitored to a minimum.

Memory Subsystem Optimizations

At the risk of sounding cliché, forget everything you knew about memory optimization in
32-bit Windows. Because Exchange Server 2010 is a 64-bit application, it requires a 64-bit
operating system. 64-bit Windows 2008 deals with memory in an entirely different way
than Windows 2003 32-bit did. The concepts of Physical Addressing Extensions (PAE) have
gone away, as there are now enough bits to natively address memory, and the old tricks
such as "/3GB" and "/USERVA=3030" in the boot.ini files have gone away. Table 34.1
summarizes some of the key improvements in memory management that will greatly
enhance the performance of Exchange Server 2007.

Virtual memory refers to the memory space made from a combination of physical
memory and swap file space. Each process in Windows is constrained by this virtual
memory size. In 32-bit Windows, this meant that the store.exe, traditionally the largest

TABLE 34.1   Key Improvements in Memory Management with 64-bit Windows

Architectural Component	64-bit Windows	32-bit Windows
Virtual memory	16TB	4GB
Paging file size	512TB	16TB
Hyperspace	8GB	4MB
Paged pool	128GB	470MB
Non-paged pool	128GB	256MB
System cache	1TB	1GB
System PTEs	128GB	660MB

consumer of memory in Exchange Server, was limited to 4GB of address space. In 64-bit Windows, store.exe can access 16TB of address space. This gives store.exe 4,096 times as much memory space as before. This means Exchange Server 2010 can utilize significantly more physical memory and use the page file, consisting of much slower disks, less often. By being able to cache more of the Exchange Server database in this larger memory space, the requirements for disk I/O are greatly reduced.

The page file refers to the disk space allocated for scratch space where the operating system will place "memory pages" when it no longer has room for them and they aren't being actively used. This increased value allows for the support of the greater virtual memory size.

Hyperspace is the special region that is used to map the process working set list. It is also used to temporarily map other physical pages for such operations as zeroing a page on the free list, invalidating page table entries in other page tables, and for setting up the address space of a new process.

Paged pool is the region of virtual memory that can be paged in and out of the working set of the system process. It is used by Kernel mode components to allocate system memory.

Non-paged pool is the memory pool that consists of ranges of system virtual addresses. These virtual addresses are guaranteed to be resident in physical memory at all times. Thus, they can be accessed from any address space without incurring paging I/O to the disks. This pool is also used by Kernel mode components to allocate system memory.

System cache refers to the pages that are used to map open files in the system cache.

System PTEs are the Page Table Entries that are used to map system pages. 64-bit programs use a model of 8TB for User and 8TB for Kernel, whereas 32-bit programs use 2GB for User and 2GB for Kernel.

With the Performance Monitor console, a number of important memory-related counters can help in establishing an accurate representation of the system's memory requirements. The primary memory counters that provide information about hard pages (pages that are causing the information to be swapped between the memory and the hard disk) are as follows:

▶ **Memory**—Pages/sec—The values of this counter should range from 5 to 20. Values consistently higher than 10 are indicative of potential performance problems, whereas values consistently higher than 20 might cause noticeable and significant performance hits. The trend of these values is impacted by the amount of physical memory installed in the server.

▶ **Memory**—Page Faults/sec—This counter, together with the Memory—Cache Faults/sec and Memory—Transition Faults/sec counters, can provide valuable information about page faults that are not committed to disk. They were not committed to disk because the memory manager allocated those pages to a standby list. Most systems today can handle a large number of page faults, but it is important to correlate these numbers with the Pages/sec counter as well to determine whether Exchange Server is configured with enough memory.

Improving Virtual Memory Usage

Calculating the correct amount of virtual memory is one of the more challenging parts of planning a server's memory requirements. While trying to anticipate growing usage demands, it is critical that the server has an adequate amount of virtual memory for all applications and the operating system. This is no different for Exchange Server 2010.

Virtual memory refers to the amount of disk space that is used by Windows Server 2008 and applications as physical memory gets low or when applications need to swap data out of physical memory. Windows Server 2008 uses 1.5 times the amount of random access memory (RAM) as the minimum paging file size by default, which for many systems is adequate. However, it is important to monitor memory counters to determine whether this amount is truly sufficient for that particular server's resource requirements. Another important consideration is the maximum size setting for the paging file. As a best practice, this setting should be at least 50% more than the minimum value to enable paging file growth, should the system require it. If the minimum and maximum settings are configured with the same value, there is a greater risk that the system could experience severe performance problems or even crash.

The most indicative sign of low virtual memory is the presence of 9582 warning events logged by the Microsoft Exchange Information Store service that can severely impact and degrade the Exchange server's message-processing abilities. These warning events are indicative of virtual memory going below 32MB. If unnoticed or left unattended, these warning messages might cause services to stop or the entire system to crash.

TIP

Use the Performance snap-in to set an alert for Event ID 9582. This helps proactively address any virtual memory problems and possibly prevent unnecessary downtime.

To get an accurate portrayal of how Exchange Server 2010 is using virtual memory, monitor the following counters within the `MSExchangeIS` object:

▶ **VM Largest Block Size**—This counter should consistently be above 32MB.

▶ **VM Total 16MB Free Blocks**—This counter should remain over three 16MB blocks.

▶ **VM Total Free Blocks**—This value is specific to your messaging environment.

▶ **VM Total Large Free Block Bytes**—This counter should stay above 50MB.

Other important counters to watch closely are as follows:

▶ **Memory**—Available Bytes—This counter can be used to establish whether the system has adequate amounts of RAM. The recommended absolute minimum value is 4MB.

▶ **Paging File**—% Usage—% Usage is used to validate the amount of the paging file used in a predetermined interval. High usage values might be indicative of requiring more physical memory or needing a larger paging file.

Monitoring Processor Usage

Analyzing the processor usage can reveal valuable information about system performance and provide reliable results that can be used for baselining purposes. Two major Exchange-related processor counters are used for capacity analysis of an Exchange Server 2007:

▶ **% Privileged Time**—This counter indicates the percentage of nonidle processor time spent in privileged mode. The recommended ideal for this value is under 55%.

▶ **% Processor Time**—This counter specifies the processor use of each processor or the total processor use. If these values are consistently higher than 50%–60%, consider upgrade options or segmenting workloads.

Tracking these values long term, for trend analysis, makes it much easier to spot accountable anomalies, such as a processor time spike during the online defragmentation or interactions with other systems. Tracking a "weighted average" of these processor values allows you to predict the point in time at which a system needs to be upgraded or when an additional system needs to be deployed to share the load.

Monitoring the Disk Subsystem

Exchange Server 2010 relies heavily on the disk subsystem and it is, therefore, a critical component to properly design and monitor. Although the disk object monitoring counters are, by default, enabled in Windows Server 2008, it is recommended that these counters be disabled until such time that an administrator is ready to monitor them. The resource requirements can influence overall system performance. The syntax to disable and enable these counters is as follows:

```
diskperf -n (to disable)
diskperf -y [\\computer_Name] (to reenable)
```

34

Nevertheless, it is important to gather disk subsystem performance statistics over time.

The primary Exchange-related performance counters for the disk subsystem are located within the Physical and Logical Disk objects. Critical counters to monitor include, but are not limited to, the following:

▶ **Physical Disk**—% Disk Time—This counter analyzes the percentage of elapsed time that the selected disk spends on servicing read or write requests. Ideally, this value should remain below 50%.

▶ **Logical Disk**—% Disk Time—This counter displays the percentage of elapsed time that the selected disk spends fulfilling read or write requests. It is recommended that this value be 60%–70% or lower.

▶ **Current Disk Queue Length (Both Physical and Logical Disk Objects)**—This counter has different performance indicators depending on the monitored disk drive (Database or Transaction Log volume). On disk drives storing the Exchange Server database, this value should be below the number of spindled drives divided by 2. On disk drives storing transaction log data, this value should be below 1.

If there appears to be an excessive load on the disks, consider adding more memory to the Exchange Server 2010 server. Improvements in cache in the Exchange Server database engine allow more information to be read and cached into memory. This decreases the workload on the disks and might alleviate the need to add more disks. For large Exchange Server 2010 servers, it is usually less expensive to add more memory than to add more disks to address this type of issue.

Monitoring the Network Subsystem

The network subsystem is one of the more challenging elements to monitor because a number of factors make up a network. In an Exchange Server messaging environment, site topologies, replication architecture, network topologies, synchronization methods, the number of systems, and more are among the many contributing factors.

To satisfactorily analyze the network, all facets must be considered. This most likely requires using third-party network monitoring tools in conjunction with built-in tools such as the Performance snap-in and Network Monitor. The current version of Network Monitor is 3.3 and can be downloaded from Microsoft at the following URL:

http://www.microsoft.com/downloads/details.aspx?FamilyID=983b941d-06cb-4658-b7f6-3088333d062f&displaylang=en

From a performance standpoint, consider implementing Gigabit Ethernet adapters in your Exchange Server 2010 servers. Given the amount of memory and disk likely to be in the server, it would easily saturate a 100-MB connection. If your server hardware offers it, consider using fault-tolerant configurations for your Ethernet connections that will not be participating in clusters or load-balance groups. Most of the fault-tolerant configurations on the market today separate out input and output to different interfaces, resulting in better overall throughput for the network interfaces.

If you are connecting your storage via iSCSI, strongly consider running dedicated Gigabit Ethernet interfaces for the connection to the iSCSI network with an appropriate Device Specific Module (DSM) to support MultiPath I/O (MPIO). This separates the load of the iSCSI from the load for the users and results in better overall performance for the users.

Properly Sizing Exchange Server 2010

Before delving into recommended configurations for Exchange Server 2010, it is essential to not only understand the fundamentals of this messaging system, but to also understand the dependencies and interactions those components have with the underlying operating system (that is, Windows Server 2008). Being a client/server messaging application, maximizing Exchange Server 2010 involves fine-tuning its entire core and extended components. Optimization of each of these components affects the overall performance of Exchange Server.

The core components of Exchange Server (for example, the Information Stores, connectors, transaction logs, and more) have a direct bearing on gauging resource requirements. The number of users in a messaging environment and the various Exchange Server functions are equally influential.

Expected User Loads

In Exchange Server 2010, one can predict with fair accuracy the load that will be generated by various types of users. Consider the following information when planning out CPU and disk configurations for an Exchange 2010 Mailbox server:

- ▶ Light user – 5 receive/20 send – 0.5 MCycles/user – 0.04 IO/user/sec

- ▶ Average user 10/40 – 0.9 MCycles/user – 0.08 IO/user/sec

- ▶ Heavy user – 20/80 – 1.8 MCycles/user – 0.15 IO/user/sec

- ▶ Very Heavy – 30/120 – 2.7 MCycles/user – 0.23 IO/user/sec

In this context, MCycles/user is the number of Mhz of processing time consumed by a user.

Mhz / MCycles per user * desired utilization = users

So a light user consuming 0.5 MCycles / user means that a 1Ghz (1,000 Mhz) CPU would support 2,000 light users at 100% CPU load. Similarly, it would only support 370 Very Heavy users at 100% CPU load. To put things into a more realistic perspective, a dual core 3.0Ghz processor would support:

2*3*1000 = 6,000 Mhz / (1.8 MCycles per user) * 0.6 (desired 60% CPU utilization) = 2000 users.

This formula is generally more accurate than a flat claim of "500 users per core" as it will take into account the fact that a 3.2Ghz processor will support more users than a 2.0Ghz processor.

Optimizing the Disk Subsystem Configuration

Many factors, such as the type of file system to use, physical disk configuration, database size, and log file placement, need to be considered when you are trying to optimize the disk subsystem configuration. The desire for performance must also be balanced with the requirements for redundancy and revocability.

Choosing the File System

Among the file systems supported by Windows Server 2008 (that is, FAT and NTFS), it is recommended to use only NTFS on all Exchange Server 2010 servers. NTFS provides the best security, scalability, and performance features. For instance, NTFS supports file- and directory-level security, large file sizes (files of up to 16TB), large disk sizes (disk volumes of up to 16TB), fault tolerance, disk compression, error detection, and encryption.

Choosing the Physical Disk Configuration

Windows Server 2008, like its predecessors, supports RAID (Redundant Array of Inexpensive Disks). The levels of RAID supported by the operating system are as follows:

- RAID 0 (Striping)

- RAID 1 (Mirroring)

- RAID 5 (Striping with parity)

Various other levels of RAID can be supported through the use of hardware-based RAID controllers.

The deployment of the correct RAID level is of utmost importance because each RAID level has a direct effect on the performance of the server. From the viewpoint of pure performance, RAID level 0 by far gives the best performance. However, fault tolerance and the reliability of system access are other factors that contribute to overall performance. The skillful administrator strikes a balance between performance and fault tolerance without sacrificing one for the other. The following sections provide recommended disk configurations for Exchange Server 2010.

> **NOTE**
>
> As mentioned earlier, various levels of RAID are available, but for the context of Exchange Server 2007, there are two recommended basic levels to use: RAID 1 and RAID 5. Other forms of RAID, such as RAID 0+1 or 1+0, are also optimal solutions for Exchange Server 2007. These more advanced levels of RAID are supported only when using a hardware RAID controller. As a result, only RAID 1 and 5 are discussed in this chapter.

Disk Mirroring (RAID 1)

In this type of configuration, data is mirrored from one disk to the other participating disk in the mirror set. Data is simultaneously written to the two required disks, which means read operations are significantly faster than systems with no RAID configuration or with a greater degree of fault tolerance. Write performance is slower, though, because data is being written twice; once to each disk in the mirror set.

Besides adequate performance, RAID 1 also provides a good degree of fault tolerance. For instance, if one drive fails, the RAID controller can automatically detect the failure and run solely on the remaining disk with minimal interruption.

The biggest drawback to RAID 1 is the amount of storage capacity that is lost. RAID 1 uses 50% of the total drive capacity for the two drives.

> **TIP**
>
> RAID 1 is particularly well suited for the boot drive and for volumes containing Exchange Server 2010 log files.

Disk Striping with Parity (RAID 5)

In a RAID-5 configuration, data and parity information is striped across all participating disks in the array. RAID 5 requires a minimum of three disks. Even if one of the drives fails within the array, the Exchange Server 2010 server can still remain operational.

After the drive fails, Windows Server 2008 continues to operate because of the data contained on the other drives. The parity information gives details of the data that is missing because of the failure. Either Windows Server 2008 or the hardware RAID controller also begins the rebuilding process from the parity information to a spare or new drive.

RAID 5 is most commonly used for the data drive because it is a great compromise among performance, storage capacity, and redundancy. The overall space used to store the striped parity information is equal to the capacity of one drive. For example, a RAID-5 volume with three 200-GB disks can store up to 400GB of data.

> **TIP**
>
> Although RAID 5 has a significant performance penalty for disk activity that has a large percentage of writes, this can be mostly compensated for via caching on the RAID controller. This allows the writes to be done in cache and later be committed to disk. If you are going to utilize write caching on your RAID controller, ensure that the cache is protected by a battery. Otherwise a system failure could result in cached information never getting written to disk. This is a sure way to corrupt a database.

Hardware Versus Software RAID

Hardware RAID (configured at the disk controller level) is recommended over software RAID (configurable from within the Windows Server 2008) because of faster performance, greater support of different RAID levels, support for caching, and capability of recovering from hardware failures more easily.

Database Sizing and Optimization

As mentioned throughout this book, Exchange Server 2010 is available in two versions: Standard and Enterprise. The Standard Edition supports 5 databases. The maximum

Information Store (database) size is not limited with Exchange Server 2010, Standard Edition. The Enterprise Edition provides support for up to 150 databases per server with unlimited database size.

The flexibility with the Enterprise Edition is beneficial not just in terms of growth but also in terms of performance and manageability. More specifically, the advantages for segmenting can include the following:

▶ Administrators are enabled to segment the user population on a single Exchange server.

▶ Multiple mailboxes can more evenly distribute the size of the messaging data and help prevent one database from becoming too large and possibly unwieldy for a given system.

▶ Multiple databases present greater opportunities for faster enumeration of database indexing.

▶ Multiple databases can be segmented onto different RAID volumes and RAID controller channels.

▶ Transaction logs can be segmented from other log files using separate RAID volumes.

▶ Failures such as database corruption affect a smaller percentage of the user population.

▶ If utilizing Database Availability Groups, there is plenty of room to support replicas for other servers.

▶ Offline maintenance routines require less scheduled downtime, and fewer users are affected.

TIP

If using the Enterprise Edition, the recommended best practice is to keep database sizes in the 100GB–120GB range. This will allow Eseutils to be run in a reasonable amount of time should they be needed. An administrator can use this guideline to gauge or plan for the number of users each database should optimally contain. This best practice is also useful in determining the appropriate number of Exchange Server 2010 mailbox servers that are required to support the number of users in the organization.

Determining the number of databases for Exchange Server 2010 mailbox servers should also be based on workload characterization. Users can be grouped based on how they interact with the messaging system (for example, in terms of frequency, storage requirements, and more). Users placing higher demands on Exchange Server 2010 can be placed into separate databases so that the greater number of read/write operations do not occur in the same database and are more evenly distributed. This is beneficial to performance only if the storage groups and databases are located on physically different disks.

If a deployment calls for a large number of databases, it is necessary to mount disks as mount points rather than as drive letters or you would quickly run out of drive letters before utilizing all 150 of your potential databases, depending on how the databases were laid out across your disks. This becomes very noticeable in situations where a SAN is utilized as most often the databases would live on unique LUNs within volumes to align with storage snapshot behaviors.

Optimizing Exchange Server Logs

Similar to the previous versions of Exchange Server, transaction log files should be stored on separate RAID volumes. This enables significant improvements in disk input/output (I/O) operations. Transaction logs are created on a per–storage group level rather than per database. Therefore, when you have multiple storage groups, multiple log files are created that enable simultaneous read and write operations. If the transaction logs are then placed on separate RAID volumes, there can be significant improvements to performance. This recommendation applies to Exchange Server 2010 mailbox servers that are not utilizing DAG.

> **TIP**
>
> Because transaction logs are as important to Exchange Server 2010 as the data contained in the databases, the most suitable RAID configuration to use for transaction log files is RAID 1. This provides suitable performance without sacrificing fault tolerance. Because the logs are written sequentially, they require significantly fewer disks than a database would to achieve sufficient I/O capacity.

Sizing Memory Requirements

The recommended starting point for the amount of memory for an Exchange Server 2010 server is 2GB of RAM per server + 2-4MB of RAM per user. The specific memory requirements naturally vary based on server roles, server responsibilities, and the number of users to support. In addition, some organizations define certain guidelines that must be followed for base memory configurations. A more accurate representation of how much memory is required can be achieved by baselining memory performance information gathered from the Performance snap-in or third-party tools during a prototype or lab testing phase.

Another important factor to take into consideration is when the organization adds functionality to Exchange Server 2010 or consolidates users onto fewer servers. This obviously increases resource requirements, especially in terms of adding more physical memory. In these scenarios, it is recommended to use the base amount of memory (for example, 8GB) and then add the appropriate amount of memory based on vendor specifications. It is also important to consult with the vendor to determine what the memory requirements might be on a per user basis. This way, the organization can plan ahead and configure the proper amount of memory prior to needing to scale to support a larger number of users in the future.

Sizing Based on Server Roles

Server roles can have a considerable bearing on both the performance and capacity of Exchange Server 2010. Based on the various roles of the Exchange servers, the strategic placement of Exchange Server services and functionality can greatly improve performance of the overall messaging system while reducing the need for using additional resources. By the same token, a misplaced Exchange Server service or functional component can noticeably add to network traffic and degrade the overall performance of the messaging system.

Servers are divided into five roles: client access servers, mailbox servers, Hub Transport servers, Edge Transport servers, and Unified Messaging servers.

Mailbox Server Sizing

Various factors affect the performance of a mailbox server, including the following:

▶ The number and type of protocols supported

▶ The number of users supported

▶ The authentication methods supported

▶ Encryption requirements

Table 34.2 shows the recommended resource requirements of mailbox servers. It is important to note that these guidelines are minimum recommendations, and actual requirements might vary depending upon the organization.

TABLE 34.2   Recommended Minimum Mailbox Server Configurations

Resource	Description
RAM	2GB + 2-4MB/user
Processor	Pentium IV 3.0GHz or higher processor with E64MT support or equivalent AMD processor
Hard disk	RAID 1 for Windows Server 2008 and Exchange Server 2010
	RAID 0+1 for mailbox data
Network	Gigabit Ethernet NIC(s)
Other considerations	If connections to this server are over SSL, consider using a NIC that off-loads SSL processing

Client Access Server Sizing

Various factors affect the performance of a client access server, including the following:

▶ The number and type of protocols supported

▶ The number of type of applications supported

- The number of users supported

- The authentication methods supported

- Encryption requirements

Table 34.3 shows the recommended resource requirements of client access servers. It is important to note that these guidelines are minimum recommendations, and actual requirements might vary depending upon the organization.

TABLE 34.3   Recommended Minimum Client Access Server Configurations

Resource	Description
RAM	2GB
Processor	Pentium IV 3.0GHz or higher processor with E64MT support or equivalent AMD processor
Hard disk	RAID 1 for Windows Server 2008 and Exchange Server 2010
Network	Gigabit Ethernet NIC(s)
Other considerations	If connections to this server are over SSL, consider using a NIC that off-loads SSL processing

Hub Transport Server Sizing

Various factors affect the performance of a Hub Transport server, including the following:

- The number and type of protocols supported

- The number of users supported

- The authentication methods supported

- Encryption requirements

Table 34.4 shows the recommended resource requirements of a Hub Transport server. It is important to note that these guidelines are minimum recommendations, and actual requirements might vary depending upon the organization.

TABLE 34.4   Recommended Minimum Hub Transport Server Configurations

Resource	Description
RAM	2GB
Processor	Pentium IV 3.0GHz or higher processor with E64MT support or equivalent AMD processor
Hard disk	RAID 1 for Windows Server 2008 and Exchange Server 2010
Network	Gigabit Ethernet NIC(s)

34

TABLE 34.4   Recommended Minimum Hub Transport Server Configurations

Resource	Description
Other considerations	If connections to this server are over SSL, consider using a NIC that off-loads SSL processing

Edge Transport Server Sizing

Various factors affect the performance of an Edge Transport server, including the following:

▶ The number of messages sent and received

▶ The types of rules implemented

▶ The types of filtering performed

▶ Encryption requirements

Table 34.5 shows the recommended resource requirements of an Edge Transport server. It is important to note that these guidelines are minimum recommendations, and actual requirements might vary depending upon the organization.

TABLE 34.5   Recommended Minimum Edge Transport Server Configuration

Resource	Description
RAM	2GB
Processor	Pentium IV 3.0GHz or higher processor with E64MT support or equivalent AMD processor
Hard disk	RAID 1 for Windows Server 2008 and Exchange Server 2010
Network	Gigabit Ethernet NIC(s)
Other considerations	If extensive content rules will be applied, consider a dual-core processor

Unified Messaging Server Sizing

Various factors affect the performance of a Unified Messaging server, including the following:

▶ The number and type of codecs supported

▶ The number of users supported

▶ The type of phone system integrated with

Table 34.6 shows the recommended resource requirements of a Unified Messaging server. It is important to note that these guidelines are minimum recommendations, and actual requirements might vary depending upon the organization.

TABLE 34.6   Recommended Minimum Unified Messaging Server Configurations

Resource	Description
RAM	2GB
Processor	Pentium IV 3.4GHz or higher processor with E64MT support or equivalent AMD processor
Hard disk	RAID 1 for Windows Server 2008 and Exchange Server 2007
Network	Gigabit Ethernet NIC(s)
Other considerations	Use of very high-compression audio codecs might increase the minimum CPU requirements

Combined Role Server Sizing

Various factors affect the performance of an Exchange Server 2010 server with combined roles, including the following:

- ▶ The number and type of protocols supported
- ▶ The number of users supported
- ▶ The authentication methods supported
- ▶ Encryption requirements

Table 34.7 shows the recommended resource requirements of a combined role Exchange Server 2010 server. It is important to note that these guidelines are minimum recommendations, and actual requirements might vary depending upon the organization.

TABLE 34.7   Recommended Minimum Combined Server Configuration

Resource	Description
RAM	4GB +2-4MB per user
Processor	Pentium IV 3.4GHz or higher processor with E64MT support or equivalent AMD processor
Hard disk	RAID 1 for Windows Server 2008 and Exchange Server 2010
	RAID 0+1 for mailbox data
Network	Gigabit Ethernet NIC(s)
Other considerations	If a large number of functions run on this system, consider implementing multi-core processors for added processing power

Optimizing Exchange Server Through Ongoing Maintenance

Through typical usage, Exchange Server databases become fragmented. This fragmentation gradually slows server performance and can also lead to corruption over extended periods of time. To ensure that an Exchange server continues to service requests in an optimized manner and the chances of corruption are minimized, it is important to perform regular maintenance on Exchange Server.

Although Exchange Server 2010 performs online maintenance tasks on a nightly basis, this accounts for roughly only 60%–70% of the maintenance tasks that are recommended. Offline maintenance, on the other hand, achieves the true optimization of the Information Stores, as well as prevents and fixes corruption. Offline optimization routines help keep the messaging server operating like a well-oiled engine and ensure that Exchange Server provides the highest serviceability and reliability.

> **CAUTION**
>
> It is of utmost importance to perform a full backup of Exchange Server 2010 prior to and immediately after running offline maintenance. After the backup has completed, it is equally important to verify the backups.

Because offline maintenance procedures require at least one database or that the entire server is offline, it is also important to schedule maintenance during the off-peak hours and notify the end users in advance.

The utilities to use for offline maintenance are ESEUTIL (ESEUTIL.EXE) and the Integrity Checker (ISINTEG.EXE). These utilities perform a number of functions, including, but not limited to, checking database and table integrity, identifying and correcting corruption, and defragmenting databases. For further information on the recommended best practices on maintaining Exchange Server 2010 and step-by-step instructions for offline maintenance, refer to Chapter 19, "Exchange Server 2010 Management and Maintenance Practices."

Monitoring Exchange Server with System Center Operations Manager

System Center Operations Manager (SCOM) is an application that can be used to actively monitor Exchange Server 2010. Employing SCOM in an Exchange Server messaging environment offers administrators the following benefits:

- ▶ SCOM has the capability of detecting even the smallest of problems that, if unnoticed, can lead to more complicated issues. Early detection of problems enables an administrator to troubleshoot the problem areas well in advance.

- ▶ SCOM can monitor all Exchange Server-related system health indicators.

▶ The Exchange Server 2010 Management Pack leverages all the new features of Exchange Server 2010.

▶ The Exchange Server 2010 Management Pack also includes the Microsoft Knowledge Base, which can be used for fast and reliable resolution of issues.

▶ SCOM can centrally manage a large number of Exchange Server 2010 servers over widely dispersed deployments.

▶ SCOM can actively monitor server availability by verifying that services are running, databases are mounted, messages are flowing, and users are able to log on.

▶ SCOM can actively monitor server health by monitoring free disk space thresholds, mail queues, security, performance thresholds, and more.

▶ SCOM provides detailed reports on database sizes, traffic analysis, and more.

▶ Alerts can be sent based on customized thresholds and events.

In short, SCOM is an excellent tool that administrators can use to proactively monitor the Exchange Server environment from a centralized location.

Summary

Despite all the performance, reliability, scalability, and availability enhancements of Exchange Server 2010, capacity analysis and performance optimization are still a necessity. The techniques and processes described in this chapter not only help you determine how to size a server or tweak it to operate optimally; they also reflect a methodology for continually monitoring a changing environment. By keeping one step ahead of the system, an organization can use resources more efficiently and effectively and in return save time, effort, and costs associated with supporting Exchange Server 2010.

Capacity must always be monitored and growth must be planned for. An efficient administrator will have a playbook built up for expanding the Exchange Server 2010 environment in a logical and effective manner. This includes plans for increasing capacity on existing servers, increasing capacity from a storage standpoint, and bringing up new Exchange Server 2010 sites when expansion requires it. By tying capacity expansion to company growth and expansion, Information Technology is able to stay in step with the needs of the business and fulfill its role as a business enabler rather than just being a support cost.

Best Practices

The following are best practices from this chapter:

▶ Begin capacity analysis and performance optimization sooner rather than later.

▶ Create performance baselines in which to gauge the changing requirements and performance levels of Exchange Server 2010.

▶ Use existing baselines to recognize changes in the performance or behavior of a server.

▶ Establish SLAs and other policies that reflect the business expectations of the messaging environment.

▶ Monitor only those counters that are pertinent to the server's configuration.

▶ Always monitor the four common contributors to bottlenecks: memory, disk subsystem, processor, and network.

▶ Run performance and stress tests in a lab environment prior to implementing in a production environment.

▶ Establish regular maintenance routines, including those for offline maintenance tasks.

▶ Set an alert for Event ID 9582 to proactively address any memory or virtual memory problems.

▶ Use enough physical memory in mailbox servers to reduce the requirement on the disk subsystem.

▶ Keep Exchange Server 2010 database sizes in the 100GB to 120GB range whenever possible.

▶ Choose hardware RAID over software RAID whenever possible.

▶ Use separate, hardware-based RAID-1 volumes for system files and transaction logs.

CHAPTER 35

Designing and Optimizing Storage in an Exchange Server 2010 Environment

A few years ago, storage area network (SAN) and network attached storage (NAS) devices were found only in high-end data centers and were generally used only in high-performance scenarios. Now, use of SAN and NAS devices has become much more common. SANs are extremely high-performance collections of disks that can be sliced and diced dynamically and attached to remote systems as though they were directly attached. SANs differ from traditional direct attached storage (DAS) in that the disks are no longer attached to the local system through SCSI or IDE connections. The SAN is viewed as a cloud and is literally a separate, high-speed network with the sole purpose of connectivity between hosts and high-speed disks. From the server's point of view, the remote disk acts exactly the same as the locally attached disk. By consolidating the disks into a central location, organizations can better manage their storage demands and storage management operations. NAS is similar with the key difference that the disks are presented via Ethernet rather than Fibre Channel. Many disk consolidation devices available today are a hybrid of the two, offering Fibre Channel Protocol and Internet SCSI (iSCSI) for connectivity. This gives you more options and enables you to control costs by using only the more expensive Fibre Channel when the situation calls for it.

Many applications take advantage of the performance and large number of spindles typically offered only via a SAN or NAS. Microsoft Exchange Server has traditionally been one such application because the Exchange Server database format has required a high-performance input/output (I/O) storage access model. However, with Exchange Server 2010, Microsoft dramatically improved the read/write performance of the Exchange Server database, and provides a replicated storage model that provides administrators high performance and high availability out of the box. The Database Availability Group (DAG) storage model was covered in detail in Chapter 31, "Database Availability Group Replication in Exchange Server 2010." Despite Microsoft providing DAG for better storage operations, many organizations continue to leverage SAN and NAS technologies, either in terms of consistency with other applications in the organization using SAN and NAS, or in terms of utilizing the external replication technologies of SAN and NAS storage systems.

This chapter highlights the use of SAN and NAS technologies for Exchange Server 2010 for organizations that continue to leverage the external storage solutions. Additionally, this chapter covers the advantages of one technology over another and explains the requirements of each technology to help you avoid common mistakes when choosing a storage technology. It also touches on industry best practices for using NAS and SAN technologies with Exchange Server 2010.

Defining the Technologies

To understand how and when to use technologies such as NAS or SAN, you need to understand what they are and what they offer. The technologies differ in how they are used and what advantages they provide. Many administrators assume that they need a SAN when often a NAS can suffice. Because information technology (IT) budgets are far from limitless, it is to your advantage to know that you aren't overbuying for your solution. By the same token, it is often less expensive to buy your solution all at one time rather than trying to expand it later.

What Is a SAN?

A SAN is a high-speed, special-purpose network or subnetwork that connects various data storage devices with associated data servers on behalf of a larger network of users. Typically, a SAN is part of an overall network of computing resources for an enterprise. A SAN is usually located in relative proximity to other computing resources, such as databases and file servers, but might also extend to remote locations for backup and archival storage. These remote locations traditionally connect via wide area network (WAN) carrier technologies, such as asynchronous transfer mode (ATM) or Synchronous Optical Networks (SONETs).

It is important to understand that the SAN is more than just the chassis that contains the disks. It includes the redundant array of inexpensive or independent disks or drives (RAID) controllers for the disks, the Fibre Channel switching fabric, and the host bus adapters (HBAs) that reside in the data servers. SANs are traditionally connected to hosts via Fibre Channel and talk via Fibre Channel Protocol. Although it can be fairly easy to support dual-arbitrated fiber loops in a corporate environment, keep in mind that one of the primary benefits of SAN is the capability to do block-level mirroring to another SAN. If this SAN is located remotely, up to 1,000km away with current fiber technology, a company needs to have fiber between the two locations. A fiber connection across those kinds of distances can be quite expensive.

SAN technologies excel in the area of disk performance. Fibre Channel networks regularly push 4–8Gb/sec of throughput. Although SCSI technologies can move data at up to 320Mb/sec and can be bonded together for higher throughput, they are limited to less than 25 feet of distance. SAN, not unlike SCSI, is seen by the host system as raw disk space. This is also referred to as a block-level technology. In the past, database applications required block-level access to the disk and the "near 0 latency" offered by SAN.

> **TIP**
>
> Although most SAN manufacturers refer to the performance of their products as having zero latency, it is important not to misinterpret this. Zero latency refers to the fact that Fibre Channel has extremely low overhead and doesn't add additional latency. The laws of physics, on the other hand, are still in effect. A 1,000-km fiber run between remote locations still takes 7 milliseconds round trip.

What Is NAS?

NAS is a hard disk storage technology that uses an Ethernet connection rather than being attached directly to the host computer that serves applications or data to a network's users. By removing storage access and its management from the host server, both application programming and files can be served faster because they do not compete for the same processor time. The NAS device is attached to a local area network (LAN) via Ethernet and given an IP address. File requests are mapped by the host server to the NAS device.

NAS consists of hard disk storage, including multidisk RAID systems and software for configuring and mapping file locations to the network-attached device. NAS software can usually handle a number of network protocols, including Microsoft's Internetwork Packet Exchange, Common Internet File System, and NetBEUI; Novell NetWare Internetwork Packet Exchange; and Sun Microsystems Network File System. Configuration, including the setting of user access priorities, is usually possible using a web browser though many NAS offerings require command-line configuration. Most NAS manufacturers include specialized software to allow specific applications such as Structured Query Language (SQL) or Exchange Server to take advantage of special functions provided by the NAS. These functions include things such as mirroring, failover, automated recovery, and snapshotting.

NAS has the advantage of using existing Ethernet technologies that are much less expensive than fiber technologies. With the availability of 10Gb Ethernet, NAS can compete with Fibre Channel–based technologies even with the added overhead of Ethernet over Fibre Channel. In most scenarios, Gigabit Ethernet is sufficient for Exchange 2010 servers, especially if multiple connections are employed.

Depending on the vendor you work with, you might hear the terms SAN and NAS used somewhat interchangeably when referring to the capability to support iSCSI. Network card vendors have even gone to the point of referring to TCP offloaded NICs as iSCSI HBAs.

When Is the Right Time to Implement NAS and SAN Devices?

There are many reasons to implement a NAS or SAN solution in favor of direct attached storage. For Exchange Server 2010, if the requirements for storage consolidation, reduction in mailbox server count, centralized management of disk resources, service level agreement (SLA) recoverability times, or near real-time mirroring of data justify the cost of a SAN or NAS solution, it is time to explore those options. To make an informed decision about when to make the switch within your Exchange Server 2010 environment, it is important for you to pass through several phases:

1. **Analyze**—Gather usage metrics and performance metrics. Determine how storage is used and how it affects the business processes. Determine if disk throughput is the bottleneck in your Exchange Server deployment.

2. **Plan**—Determine the current limitations of your storage solutions. Prioritize the problems and determine if there is a better way. Don't fall into the trap of doing things just because they were always done a particular way.

3. **Develop**—Build the proposed solution for testing. Perform benchmarking to show improvements over the old methods. Experiment with various functions of Exchange Server 2010 on different types of disks. Get a feel for the improvement versus the costs.

4. **Pilot**—Test the solution and improve it based on user feedback. Educate the user population on how to take full advantage of the new functions and determine the improvements in efficiencies.

5. **Deploy**—Deliver the solution to the masses.

Following this methodology not only streamlines the process of implementing new and more-efficient storage technologies, but also provides valuable data to help upper management buy into the upgrades and support the storage program for the Exchange Server environment.

Analyzing Your Storage Needs

The first phase of any good project is an in-depth analysis of the environment and its needs. For storage systems, it is critical to identify any systems with special requirements. This includes systems that require multiple layers of redundancy, systems that are under extremely tight SLAs, and systems that cannot tolerate a loss of data. For Exchange Server 2010 that is deployed by role, it is most likely only the Mailbox server role that can benefit significantly from using SAN or NAS technologies. Similarly, you might determine that it is less expensive to take advantage of the additional memory that can be used by Exchange Server 2010 because of its 64-bit architecture, to increase the caching of database transactions and, therefore, reduce the necessary number of disks. NAS and SAN solutions can be expensive compared to purchasing memory for a server. If the driving force toward a SAN or NAS is performance-based, consult Chapter 34, "Optimizing an Exchange Server 2010 Environment," for more information on the reduction in disk I/O that can be gained by increasing system memory. If your driving force is centralized disk management, enhanced capacity, or rapid restoration of data, SAN or NAS might be for you.

Another key area to understand is the capacity requirements of the enterprise. If an investment is going to be made in storage, it is a good idea to plan for several years of growth. Look at the number of servers in the environment. If additional servers have been added simply because that is the way things were always done, it is time to look at shifting the philosophy to doing things because it is the right way to do it.

> **TIP**
>
> Disk drives get larger, faster, and less expensive each year. When planning for the future, keep expandability in mind. By buying a partially filled chassis now and adding additional disks later, you can take advantage of falling disk prices and save money over the long run and still get the full capacity needed and the benefits of fewer chassis.

Planning the Storage Solution

Storage technologies can be confusing. In most situations, valid arguments can be made for using any of the available technologies. This is a situation in which it makes a lot of sense to get your vendors involved. Contact your potential vendors and let them know what your storage requirements are. Often, they have worked with other companies with similar needs and can provide valuable insight into what worked and what didn't. Given the costs of a large storage system, you can't afford to do it wrong.

After you have an idea of what you want to implement, find out if you can contact references to determine if they were happy with the solution they implemented. Some companies try to get you to commit to the latest and greatest versions of their software and firmware. Large storage environments are a big investment, and business processes depend heavily on it. Ensure that you implement a stable and well-tested solution.

> **TIP**
>
> A tremendous number of options are available for storage solutions. When in doubt about a decision, always refer to the original goals of the project and ask yourself, "Does this decision support the goals of the project?"

Developing the Storage Solution

After you determine the needs, explore the options, and devise a plan, the real fun begins. Any solution that becomes part of the critical path of business must be developed and tested in a controlled lab environment. This is the part of the project in which policies and procedures start to take form. Practice runs of mirroring, failing over of resources, and recovery of systems ensure that the solution can support the needs of the company.

During this development phase, practice connecting your servers to the SAN or NAS. Develop and document standards around HBAs or network interface cards (NICs), the versions of firmware that will be used, and the version of the drivers that will be used.

Most SAN and NAS manufacturers provide a detailed list of supported combinations of hardware, firmware, and software. Deviate from these approved lists at your own risk. The last thing you want to implement is an unstable storage environment because you chose not to follow the recommended configurations.

The development phase can identify several requirements that are not usually thought of during the planning phase. Most specifically, these requirements are in the area of facilities. Most SAN devices are fairly large. An EMC Symetrix and Connectix, for example, can take up a full rack each. With heat generation more than 3,000BTUs, HVAC resources need to be considered. Also keep in mind that most SAN and NAS solutions require 220V to run them. Ensure that planned data center locations have appropriate space, cooling, and power. Power should include not only the standard AC feed, but also battery backup. Be aware of any special requirements of the SAN or NAS. Some SAN devices on the market void their warranty if they are placed within 5 feet of any solid objects.

> **TIP**
>
> Be sure to carefully document the entire installation and configuration process. It not only makes troubleshooting easier, but it also provides the full road map for pilot implementation.

Designing the Right Data Storage Structure for Exchange Server 2010

Exchange Server 2010 provides administrators with a lot more options on how to configure their environment than previous versions of Exchange Server. When considering SAN or NAS for Exchange Server 2010, you need to understand the strengths and weaknesses of a given disk solution and ensure that you address all the potential concerns and gain all the potential benefits. This includes decisions regarding disk type, methods of connectivity, and the distribution of aggregates and logical unit numbers, or LUNs.

Choosing the Right Connectivity for NAS

All the high-speed disks in the world won't amount to much if you can't get the data to and from the Exchange servers quickly. In a NAS environment, the network itself is the biggest concern for performance. Most NAS devices on the market use fast heads that are literally dedicated computers with high-performance processors and loads of memory. With SCSI RAID controllers on board, they can easily saturate multiple 100-Mb Ethernet connections. Attaching such a device to a low-end switch would result in the NAS running in an extremely restricted manner. Strongly consider using a switch that can enable you to use a gigabit connection.

Consider creating a separate network for the NAS environment. Suppose, for example, that the NAS is going to support a number of Exchange servers. By multihoming the Exchange servers, one Ethernet connection can face the users and provide connectivity to the mail clients, whereas the other interface can be dedicated to NAS traffic. This enables each interface to run unfettered by the traffic associated with the other network. This also enables you to upgrade only a subset of the network to improve performance and save money. The traffic of the database transaction back to the NAS device by Exchange Server would be much greater than the traffic associated with users viewing their mail because the traffic that would normally go to the local disk would now be traveling across the Ethernet via the virtual disk driver that connects the NAS to the Exchange server. Similarly by using systems that support MultiPath I/O (MPIO), you can improve overall throughput while adding a layer of network resiliency to protect against connectivity failures.

When selecting network gear for a NAS out-of-band network, focus on packets per second. Whenever possible, build this NAS network with multiple switches that cross-connect. Connect each server to both switches with the NICs in a Teamed mode. This not only adds bandwidth, but also creates redundancy for the Network layer. Odds are if the application warranted the use of a NAS device, it deserves redundancy at the network level as well.

When selecting NICs for the servers, strongly consider the use of NICs that support Transmission Control Protocol (TCP) offload processing. This means that the work involved with network transfers is performed by the NIC itself rather then increasing the load on the server's CPUs. Because the NIC is designed with data transfer in mind, the result is the capability to move huge amounts of data without impacting the overall performance of the Exchange server. Because network overhead is associated with mounting NAS disks, this type of configuration can be helpful for the Exchange server.

Choosing the Right Connectivity for SANs

When attaching to a SAN, you use HBAs via Fibre Channel rather than NICs via Ethernet. HBAs can be relatively expensive, but they offer much greater throughput than NICs and NAS would offer. Between the higher speeds (4Gb for Fibre Channel versus 1Gb for Ethernet) and the lower overhead involved in the protocol, an HBA-attached SAN can move significantly more data in the same period of time. This can be especially useful in situations where a large number of disks are accessed.

SANs are generally attached to the HBAs via a Fibre Channel fabric, though iSCSI HBAs are growing in popularity. A Fibre Channel fabric is created by a set of interconnected HBAs, bridges, storage devices, and switches. Strongly consider implementing multiple fabrics for redundancy. Generally, a fabric can be thought of as a set of switches sharing interswitch links along with the devices to which they connect. A SAN with multiple switches not connected by interswitch links provides multiple fabrics.

The SAN connects to the switch fabric through controllers. These controllers are what combine the disks together into larger aggregates and servers as the entry and exit point for data. SAN controllers generally contain large caches of memory (typically 2–4GB) to improve performance. Multiple controllers are always recommended for redundancy and performance.

When thinking about the connectivity between the Exchange servers and the SAN, always try to use multiple LUNs and connect them so that half the LUNs prefer Controller A and half prefer Controller B. This helps even out the load across the controllers and increases

35

overall throughput of the SAN. In the event of controller failure or controller maintenance, the connectivity is picked up by the remaining controller.

When planning your SAN storage, be aware of how your particular SAN and switch fabric
deal with zoning. The concept of zoning is similar to the concept of virtual LANs (VLANs)
in networking. The objective is to ensure that only the necessary servers can see the disks
that will be provisioned to them. Depending on your particular solution, this is performed
via LUN masking, hard/soft zoning, port zoning, or through the use of worldwide names.
These concepts work as follows:

▶ **LUN masking**—LUN masking is a process that makes particular LUNs available to
some hosts but not to others. This process is akin to setting permissions on a
resource to determine which hosts are allowed to access them. This is particularly
important in Windows environments in which a server will attempt to write a signature to a newly discovered disk. This can render an existing LUN unavailable to its
originally intended host.

▶ **Hard/soft zoning**—In this context, hard and soft refer to the location of the implementation of this type of zoning. Hard zoning is done at a hardware level, and soft
zoning is done in software. Hard zoning physically blocks access to a zone from any
device outside of the zone. Soft zoning uses filters in the switch fabric that prevent
ports from being seen from outside of their assigned zones.

▶ **Port zoning**—Port zoning uses physical ports to define security zones. A user's
access to data is determined by what physical port he is connected to. The drawback
with port zoning is that zone information must be updated every time a user
changes switch ports. In addition, port zoning does not allow zones to overlap. Port
zoning is normally implemented using hard zoning but can also be implemented
using soft zoning.

▶ **World Wide Name (WWN) zoning**—WWN zoning uses name servers in the
switches to either allow or disallow access to particular WWNs in the fabric. A major
advantage of WWN zoning is the capability to modify the fabric without having to
redo the zone information. SAN-related devices such as HBAs are built with unique
WWNs installed into them, not unlike Media Access Control (MAC) addresses in
network interfaces.

Choosing the Right Type of Disks

When researching SAN and NAS devices, you discover that you have several types of disks
available to you. These disks vary by architecture (SCSI versus SATA versus SAS versus Fibre
Channel) and by size. Current disks are available in sizes ranging from 72GB to 1.5TB.

In terms of size, your decisions will be based on three factors:

▶ Price

▶ Capacity

▶ Performance

Generally speaking, the larger the disk, the more you pay for it. Capacity refers to the total amount of space you plan to deploy. If, for example, you need to deploy 2TB of space, you can use eight 250GB disks or 32 72GB disks. Why would you pick one configuration over the other?

If you opt to use 8 250GB disks, you use less capacity on your SAN or NAS device. If you expect to expand capacity in the future, you can expand further before needing to purchase additional disk shelves or chassis. The potential downside to this approach is that 8 250GB disks might be more expensive than 32 72GB disks. The other more noticeable impact is in the area of I/O performance. Assuming the spindle speeds were the same for both disks, you would get four times more I/O out of the 32 72GB disks than you would from the 8 250GB disks. Depending on whether your application needed the additional I/O, this might be a deciding factor.

> **TIP**
>
> If random access disk I/O performance is a concern, pay close attention to the spindle speed of the disks. Traditionally, the largest disks available to SAN or NAS applications operate at a lower revolutions per minute (rpm) than smaller disks. Typical random access I/O per second ratings of hard drives is roughly rpm/100. For example, a 15,000-rpm hard drive offers 150 random access disk I/O per second.

Useful to note is that with sufficient memory in an Exchange Server 2010 server, disk I/O requirements are roughly one-fourth what they were in an Exchange 2003 server with the same number of users. This behavior was specifically engineered into Exchange Server 2010 to take advantage of the ever-increasing capacity of hard disks. Hard disk capacity is increasing drastically every year with nearly no improvements in I/O performance. According to Seagate, although disk capacity increased 15,000 times from 1987 to 2004, the random I/O performance increased only 11 times during the same period.

In addition to choosing the size of the disks you deploy, you also have a choice in terms of the disk architecture. Your most common choices are as follows:

- ▶ Serial ATA (SATA)
- ▶ SCSI
- ▶ Serial attached SCSI (SAS)
- ▶ Fibre Channel

SATA is generally the least-expensive option. SATA disks provide excellent throughput, nearly equal to SCSI, at a much better price. High-capacity disks are usually available as SATA first because it is a more common market for disks. Newer implementations of SATA include high-performance functions such as command queuing, which give them performance that approaches that of SCSI.

SCSI disks have been around for decades. It's a well-proven technology and is known for having high performance and high reliability. SCSI disks are less expensive than Fibre

Channel disks but offer lower throughput through the bus. This results in needing more controllers to manage the disks themselves and lower performance than Fibre Channel disks.

SAS disks are growing in popularity due to their reduced form factor (typically 2.5") and their high performance. By virtue of their form factor, they actually achieve a higher level of I/O than a 3.5" disk of a similar rotational speed. This is because the read/write heads don't need to travel as far to get from one side of the disk to the other. They do suffer a bit in the area of overall throughput because the liner speed at the outer portions of the platter are lower than that would be on a 3.5" disk at the same rotational speed.

Fibre Channel disks are the highest-performance drives available today. They are also the most expensive and generally trail a full generation behind other formats in terms of capacity. If performance is your number-one concern, the Fibre Channel disk can't be beat.

> **TIP**
>
> Don't be afraid to mix and match disk types for different applications. A typical SAN or NAS supports multiple disk shelves of different types. Consider something such as Fibre Channel disks for the databases, SCSI drives for the logs, and Serial ATA disks for archive storage. A similar concept can be applied to disk sizes to maximize capacity where I/O loads are relatively low.

Slicing and Dicing the Available Disk

Simple physics tells you that you'll get improvements in performance as you add more disks to an array. Because each drive's read/write head can operate simultaneously, you get a fairly linear improvement as drives are added. NAS and SAN offer the advantage of dynamically increasing the size of a volume without taking the volume offline. This allows for the addition of even more spindles.

Although it's possible to later resize a volume from a NAS or SAN, you must be careful not to oversubscribe the device. Devices that support snapshots of the data reserve twice the volume size that they claim for capacity. So, to make 100GB available to a server, the NAS reserves 200GB on itself. This ensures that it can complete all transactions. This function can be disabled on most devices, but it is not recommended. This removes the protection from oversubscription of the disks.

When provisioning disk space for an Exchange server, you should consider a few rules of thumb when optimizing performance.

In a perfect world, an entire SAN or NAS would be dedicated to just the Exchange Server 2010 environment. This would reduce the possibility of contention with other applications. If your budget doesn't allow for this, be aware of what applications are shared with your SAN or NAS.

If you can't dedicate a SAN or NAS to your Exchange Server environment, build your aggregate from disks that are spread out across multiple shelves. This helps distribute the load across multiple backplanes and results in fewer spikes in performances.

Try not to make LUNs larger than they need to be. For example, if you plan to have four storage groups with 50GB of mail each, create four LUNs of 50GB each rather than a single LUN of 200GB. This enables you to separate the LUNs across both controllers and improves the performance of the system. The potential pitfall here is that you could run out of drive letters because Exchange Server 2010 allows for up to 150 databases in the Enterprise Edition. To work around this, mount the LUNs as mount points instead of drive letters. This can greatly simplify expansions of Exchange Server 2010 servers as you can place a storage group on a drive letter and then mount new LUNs as mount points for each new database that you need to bring online. This is exceptionally useful when using snapshot functions in NAS or SAN in which the database has to be dismounted for an integrity check because this typically occurs at the LUN level.

To mount a LUN as a mount point rather than a drive letter, perform the following steps:

1. Right-click My Computer and choose Manage on the shortcut menu.
2. Expand Storage and click Disk Management.
3. Right-click the unpartitioned space and select New Partition on the shortcut menu.
4. When the New Partition Wizard launches, click Next.
5. From the Select Partition Type screen, select Primary Partition, and click Next.
6. Choose the size of the partition desired, and click Next.
7. Select Mount in the Following Empty NTFS folder, and click Browse.
8. Select the folder that will host the new mount point, and click OK. Ensure that this folder is empty. Choose to create a new folder, if necessary. Click Next.
9. Choose to format the drive as NTFS. Label it to reflect the name of the data it will house. Click Next.
10. After the drive is formatted, click Finish.

> **NOTE**
>
> When configuring LUNs for a cluster, be sure to create them as basic disk in Windows; otherwise, the cluster cannot recognize the disks as potential cluster resources.

Predicting Disk Performance with Exchange Server 2010

When planning the number of disks to use for LUNs for various functions in Exchange Server 2010, the question that invariably comes up is "How many spindles do I need for good performance?" Although it is fairly straightforward to determine the I/O needs for various functions in Exchange Server 2010, it can be trickier to predict the effect that the disk configuration will have on the system. One of the most common configurations is to utilize RAID 5 to provide redundancy at the disk level. To understand the impact of RAID 5, consider the following:

RAID-5 performance can be approximated as %Reads * IOPS per disk * (disks-1)) + (%Writes * IOPS per disk * ((disks-1) / 4)) = Total IOPS

Or for the more mathematically oriented:

Total IOPS = (R * I(d-1)) + (W * I((d-1) / 4))

where:

- ▶ R = % Reads

- ▶ W = % Writes

- ▶ I = Input / Output operations per second (IOPS) per disk

- ▶ d = number of disks in RAID5

- ▶ T = Total IOPS

With typical IOPS performance per disk being:

- ▶ 140–150 Random IOPS from 15,000-RPM disks (@<20ms disk latency)

- ▶ 100–120 Random IOPS from 10,000-RPM disks (@<20ms disk latency)

- ▶ 75–100 Random IOPS from 7,200-RPM disks (@<20ms disk latency)

Adding in Fault Tolerance for External Storage Systems

When implementing centralized storage solutions, you are often placing a large number of important eggs into a single basket. This is usually the case in large virtualization farms in which virtual machine images are stored on a SAN to enable the virtualization hosts to dynamically move the loads across various members of the farm. SAN and NAS manufacturers understand this and have spent a lot of research and development dollars on building in fault tolerance into their offerings. Many options are available to the end user; some of the fault-tolerance options are as follows:

- ▶ **RAID configurations**—RAID levels 0+1 and 5 are most common. RAID level 6 offers the capability to lose two drives at a time and not lose data.

- ▶ **Triple mirroring**—This enables you to snap off a mirror so that data becomes static for purposes of backup. Meanwhile, the system still has mirrored drives for fault tolerance. This is most commonly used with databases.

- ▶ **Log shipping**—Most SAN and NAS devices can copy log files in near real time to another SAN or NAS so that databases can be copied regularly and log files can be kept in sync remotely.

- ▶ **Geographic mirroring**—SAN and NAS devices offer in-band and out-of-band options for mirroring data across wide distances. Whereas SCSI has a 25-foot limitation, Fibre Channel can locate a device up to 1,000km away.

- ▶ **Snapshotting**—By flagging disk blocks as being part of a particular version of a file and writing changes to that file on new blocks, a NAS or SAN device can take a snapshot of what the data looked like at a point in time. This enables a user to roll back a file to a previous version. It also enables you to roll an entire system back to a point in time almost instantly.

▶ **Clustering**—NAS devices that use heads to serve data offer dual heads so that if one fails, the other continues to serve data from the disks.

▶ **Redundant power systems**—Any good SAN or NAS offers multiple power supplies to protect against failure. Take advantage of the separate power supplies by attaching them to separate electrical circuits.

▶ **Redundant backplanes**—Many NAS and SAN devices offer redundant backplanes to protect against hardware failure.

▶ **Hot standby drives**—By having unused drives available in the chassis, the device can replace a failed disk instantly with one that is already present and ready for use. Be sure to monitor the SAN or NAS device to see if a disk has failed and been replaced. It can be easy to miss because there is no interruption to service.

Although Exchange Server 2010 offers functions such as Database Availability Groups to provide for server-level fault tolerance, it is still a good idea to provide disk-level redundancy for the individual servers to reduce the possibility of a failover occurring unexpectedly. With the reduced dependence on disk I/O in Exchange Server 2010 servers equipped with large amounts of system memory, RAID 5 will become a more common configuration on mailbox servers. If utilizing a caching controller for the RAID controller, be sure that the cache is protected by a battery backup. Failure to do so can result in lost data that was cached in the controller during a failure. If the cache isn't committed to the disk, the data will be in an inconsistent state and most likely will not be usable.

> **TIP**
>
> RAID 5 is not recommended for any application that performs write transactions more than approximately 30% of the time. This is because each write transaction requires reading multiple disks and recalculating and writing of parity bits.

Recommendations for SAN and NAS Solutions

SAN and NAS manufacturers have provided a number of technologies that make it easier to integrate their products with specific software products. Because these products have been available for a number of years, best practices around these implementations have been developed and can help you avoid common pitfalls with SAN and NAS usage.

Recommendations for Exchange Server with NAS/SAN Environments

When implementing a NAS or SAN solution in a Microsoft Exchange Server environment, many different interpretations abound on the best way to implement the solution. Some of the recommended best practices are as follows:

▶ Run multiple HBAs in each Exchange server with each HBA connected to a different Fibre Channel switch. This allows for failover if one of the Fibre Channel switches should fail, assuming your system can support MPIO with the appropriate Device Specific Module (DSM).

▶ Ensure that zoning of the SAN is configured correctly so that only the necessary systems can see the LUNs. In the case of a cluster, all nodes that might potentially own the disks should be in the same zone. If an unrelated Windows system sees the disks, it tries to write a new signature to the disk, which makes it unreadable by the intended hosts.

▶ Backups should be performed at the storage group level rather than at the mailbox level. Mailbox-level backups are processor-intensive for the Exchange server.

▶ If available, direct disk backup solutions are significantly faster than storage group level backups.

▶ If you implement third-party applications with your NAS or SAN for use with Exchange Server, make sure they are certified by Microsoft for use with Exchange Server 2010 and that they use the standard application programming interfaces (APIs), such as Volume Shadow Copy Services.

▶ Separate log files from databases onto different drive sets. This improves overall throughput and improves recoverability if a NAS/SAN failure occurs.

▶ Replicate databases hourly to another device for disaster recovery if you aren't performing an application level replication. Logs should be replicated every few minutes. This limits potential mail loss to one log replication interval.

▶ Always use integrated tools if they are available, such as Network Appliance's SnapManager for Exchange Server. They greatly simplify management and recoverability of the product for which they were designed.

▶ Always plan for space reservation on a volume. If the database will grow to 80GB and will have snapshots taken for recoverability, reserve 160GB of space on the device.

▶ When possible, expand capacity on the Exchange Server 2010 server via additional mailbox databases placed on new LUNs. Although LUNs can be dynamically grown, it is usually a time-consuming process and impacts system performance on the Exchange server. Bring up new LUNs to remove the dependency of reserving space on a shelf to resize LUNs hosted on that shelf.

▶ Be careful when placing multiple virtual logical disks or LUNs on the same RAID group because this can result in databases and log files being on the same RAID group. This would complicate system recoveries if the RAID group were to fail.

Consolidating the Number of Exchange Servers via NAS or SAN

Exchange servers were traditionally sized based not only on performance potential, but also on the time needed to recover a system. Administrators knew that if they had a 4-hour SLA for system recovery, they could count on using half that time to recover data from tape and half that time to perform the recovery tasks. This meant that they could have only as much local storage as they could recover in 2 hours. So, if a backup/restore system could restore 16GB of data in 2 hours and each user was allowed 100MB of storage, the maximum number of users on the system would be 160. For a company of 1,600 users, this would mean 10 Exchange servers would be required to support the 4-hour SLA.

By placing the mailbox stores onto a NAS or SAN device that can be mirrored and snap-shotted, the recoverability time for a 16-GB database would drop to mere minutes. Now the bottleneck would become the performance of the server itself and possibly the I/O rate of the NAS or SAN. Odds are that the systems that had been purchased for the capability to support 160 users would be dual-processor systems with 1 to 2GB of memory. By reducing the server count to two and fully populating those two systems with memory taken from the retired systems, the two systems with NAS- or SAN-based mailboxes could easily support the 800 users each and still meet the 4-hour recovery time required by the SLA. This would result in the reduction of eight Exchange servers, which would free up OS licenses and hardware and reduce the effort required to manage the data center.

Similarly, with the trend toward virtualization of Exchange Server 2010 servers rather than running physical servers, the SAN/NAS enables you to easily host a virtualization farm in which the virtual systems are stored on the SAN/NAS to enable loads to be quickly moved from one member of the farm to another based on performance or a desire to perform host-level maintenance without interrupting the Exchange Server 2010 services.

35

Making the Best Use of SAN/NAS Disks with Exchange Server 2010

SAN or NAS disks are generally more expensive than the disks used in DAS. As such, you can generally utilize the SAN/NAS storage only where it makes a significant difference in performance. Many aspects of Exchange Server 2010 utilize the disks but use them in different ways.

The largest consumer of disk performance is the Mailbox role. In Exchange Server 2010, it is common to run servers that are dedicated to doing nothing but hosting mailboxes. On these systems, several different consumers of disk resources would benefit from being placed on SAN or NAS, as discussed in the following sections.

Storage of Transaction Log Files (.log Files) and Database Files (.edb Files)

Changes made to the database are first committed to the transaction log. This results in a sequential write to the disk. Because sequential I/O is significantly higher per disk than random I/O, the logs do not benefit as much from being placed on SAN or NAS disks. For performance reasons and recoverability reasons, the logs should not be located on the same disks as the database. Similarly, the logs should not be on the same disk as the page file for the operating system.

To create a storage group with log files on a NAS or SAN disk, complete the following steps:

1. From the Start menu, select All Programs, Microsoft Exchange, Exchange Management Console.

2. Expand Organization Configuration, and then highlight Mailbox.

3. From the Database Management tab, click New Mailbox Database.

4. Enter the database name and browse to the server that will host it (see Figure 35.1). Click Next.

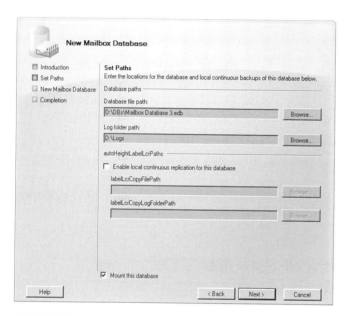

FIGURE 35.1   New Mailbox Database Wizard.

5. Click browse to choose the database path.

6. Navigate to the drive letter representing the SAN/NAS disk, and click OK.

7. Click browse to choose the log folder path.

8. Navigate to the drive letter representing the SAN/NAS disk, and click OK.

9. Click Next.

10. Click New to trigger the creation of the mailbox database.

Performing Content Indexing

The Search features have been significantly improved in Exchange Server 2010. Content indexing is a random access workload that should be placed on the same LUN as the database that it is indexing. Content indexing is usually approximately 10% of the database size. Exchange Search (formerly known as Content Indexing) runs in the background, indexing messages as they arrive and, as such, the disk I/O impact is minimal.

Exchange Search is enabled by default on all databases; to manage content indexing, perform the following:

1. From the Start menu, click Programs, Microsoft Exchange, Exchange Management Shell.

2. From the Exchange Management Shell, type the following:

```
Set-MailboxDatabase -Identity <Database Name> -IndexEnabled:$false¦$true
```

3. Press Enter.

When a process requests a page from memory and the system cannot find the page at the requested location, a page fault occurs. If the page is elsewhere in memory, the fault is a soft page fault. If the page must be retrieved from disk, the fault is a hard page fault. Most processors can handle large numbers of soft page faults without consequence. However, hard page faults can cause significant delays. Continuous high rates of disk paging indicate a memory shortage. If memory cannot be increased sufficiently to reduce the number of hard page faults, you must improve the speed of the disks that host the page file. In this scenario, the page file location could benefit from the improved performance of a SAN or NAS disk.

If you want to move your page file to a SAN or NAS attached disk, perform the following steps:

1. Right-click My Computer and select Properties on the shortcut menu.
2. Click the Advanced System Settings task.
3. In the Performance section, click Settings.
4. From the Performance Options pane, click the Advanced tab.
5. Near the bottom of the pane in the Virtual Memory section, click Change.
6. Uncheck Automatically Manage Paging File Size for All Drives.
7. Highlight the drive letter that represents the disk that should host the page file.
8. Click the Custom Size option button.
9. Enter an initial size of `1.5*system memory`.
10. Enter a maximum size of `1.5*system memory`, and then click Set.
11. Highlight the drive letter that previously held the page file.
12. Click the No Paging File option button, and then click Set.
13. Click Yes to accept the warning about the page file on the volume you are modifying, and then click OK.
14. Click OK again to accept the notification that you need to reboot for the settings to take effect.
15. Click OK twice to close the dialog box.
16. Click Yes to reboot if it is acceptable to reboot the system.

You might wonder why the page file was configured with the same value for initial and maximum sizes. By setting the range to a single value, the page file is initially created at a size that will never change. This allows the page file to be contiguous on the drive. A page file that is allowed to grow might grow to a new location on the hard drive. This results in fragmentation of the page file and causes a reduction in page file performance.

35

In Exchange Server 2010, significant improvements have been achieved in memory management because of the use of 64-bit code. This enables you to install enough memory to greatly reduce the need for the system to page to disk.

Content Conversion

Most content conversion performed in an Exchange Server 2010 environment is performed by the client access servers (CASs) and the Hub Transport servers. Legacy WebDAV content conversion, for legacy Outlook Web Access (OWA) clients, occurs on the Exchange 2010 mailbox server. When a client needs data that must be converted on a CAS, the data is pulled from the Exchange 2010 mailbox server, converted in the Exchange Server 2010 mailbox server's TMP folder, and sent to the CAS. To improve performance, the TMP folder should not be on the same LUN as the page file and operating system. If there is a large amount of legacy OWA clients supported, placement of the TMP folder on a NAS or SAN disk might result in improved performance.

Performing Database Maintenance

The Exchange Server 2010 Information Store performs periodic online maintenance against each database. The two tasks that impact disk I/O are the hard deletion of messages and mailboxes that are past their retention policy and online database defragmentation. Because a backup job will halt online defragmentation, you must be sure to give both database maintenance and backup jobs exclusive windows of time to finish their tasks or disk contention will result in greatly reduced performance for both tasks. If you cannot sufficiently separate these two events, the increased I/O load would benefit from the databases being located on SAN or NAS disks.

Backing Up and Restoring Data

Backing up data requires that data be read from both the database and transaction log volumes. This additional I/O can impact user response times and should be avoided during business hours. Placing the databases and log files on faster SAN or NAS disks can often result in faster backup and restore processes, assuming the destination location for the data is not the bottleneck. Backups that attach to the SAN or NAS directly are usually much faster than backing up Exchange Server 2010 via the network with an Exchange Server agent. Backups that are performed at the storage itself, usually called snapshots, can occur in literally seconds.

The process of performing a soft recovery in the case of a database restore requires that the JET engine plays back all the transaction log files. This results in a sequential read stream from the disks containing the associated log files. As a result, the recovery process can be faster if the transaction log files are on a disk with fast sequential disk access, such as SAN or NAS.

In addition to having similar needs for content conversion and paging, CASs also consume disk I/O in the process of protocol logging.

Enabling Protocol Logging

Protocol logging, if enabled, results in a sequential write that is a performance hit and consumes disk space to store the logs. Protocol logging is typically used to verify the performance of a given protocol or when you suspect attacks from the Internet.

Impact from Message Tracking Logs

Edge and Hub Transport servers maintain message tracking logs that result in sequential write traffic for the log files. Because sequential write performance is much higher than random access, these types of logs typically don't require high-performance disks.

Conversion of Incoming Mail

The Hub Transport server converts incoming mail into a Messaging Application Programming Interface (MAPI) format. This occurs in the TMP directory of the Hub Transport server. As such, it is important to ensure that the TMP directory is not located on the same LUN as the page file or the operating system. In environments that receive large amounts of Internet mail, it is beneficial to place this TMP directory on a SAN or NAS attached disk.

Events Trigged by Agents

Customization of the Transport server is done via bits of code more commonly referred to as agents. These agents run in the common language runtime environment and are triggered by specific events. Some agents write data to a log, which can result in a disk performance hit in addition to consuming disk space. If you find your environment taking performance hits because of agents, consider configuring them to place their logs on higher-performance NAS or SAN disks.

Summary

This chapter introduced the concepts of network attached storage and storage area networks as options to improve performance and manageability over traditional direct attached storage. You've seen how SAN and NAS can be used to manage data effectively through the reduction of servers. With Exchange Server 2010, administrators now have varying options for storage, either leveraging Database Availability Groups (DAGs) for high availability and storage replication using out-of-the-box server-to-server replication, or centralizing storage and usage SAN and NAS replication for storage availability.

For those organizations choosing to use SAN or NAS for replication in addition to or in place of DAG replication, you've seen how advanced technologies like SAN or NAS snapshotting enable you to back up Exchange Server data regularly on the device itself so that users can recover their own data without having to involve administrators. When coupled with technologies such as DAG replication, snapshotting can give administrators great peace of mind that they can recover quickly from a server or database failure.

This chapter discussed some of the specific functions within Exchange Server 2010 that work well with both NAS and SAN storage. You learned that SAN provides block-level access to the disk, whereas NAS provides file-level access. Some applications require SAN, but most can work with NAS.

SAN and NAS offer exceptional performance and enable you to perform geographic mirroring that was previously impossible for the application itself. As administrators leverage the new Exchange Database Availability Group technology, they might replace NAS or SAN replication. However, for organizations already using SAN and NAS for other storage operations, the organizations might choose to continue to leverage existing storage resources.

Best Practices

The following are best practices from this chapter:

- ▶ Leverage out-of-the-box Database Availability Group storage and replication for simplified storage redundancy and recovery.

- ▶ Implement a SAN or NAS solution when there is a need in the organization to utilize existing SAN or NAS technologies used in the organization.

- ▶ Analyze your storage needs so that you can size the storage system with the appropriate disk space necessary to meet current and project near-term future requirements.

- ▶ During the development and testing phase, connect and disconnect servers to the SAN and NAS system to confirm your knowledge and the practice of accessing external storage on the network.

- ▶ Choose the right type of connectivity based on the transaction throughput of data transmission that allows the SAN or NAS to keep up with the reading and writing of data to and from the servers.

- ▶ Acquire disks that are fast enough to keep up with the performance demand of the servers and of the network connectivity of the SAN or NAS.

- ▶ Use the formula in the section "Predicting Disk Performance with Exchange Server 2010" to calculate the I/O per second to determine disk performance and disk speed requirements of the disk subsystem.

- ▶ Add the appropriate fault tolerance to the storage system based on the disaster recovery and business continuity needs of the organization.

- ▶ Develop a backup strategy that matches the performance capabilities and the recovery time frame desired in the organization.

- ▶ Utilize SAN or NAS in virtualization farms to enable virtual guests to be moved between hosts without impacting the application or the users.

- ▶ Place the Exchange Server database files and the log files on the proper disk location of the SAN and NAS system for optimum performance and desired recoverability if a storage system failure occurs.

Index

A

B

IIS (Internet Information Services) 7.0, 1080-1081

information store backups, validating, 663

OpsMgr, 681

Outlook Express contacts, 982

production environment, 509

snapshots, 1166

validating backup data, 1091

verifying online backup, 658-659

Windows Server 2008

boot and system volumes, 1076

overview, 1075-1076

services, 1077

System State, 1077

Volume Shadow Copy Service, 1077-1078

with Windows Server 2008 Backup, 644

backplaces, redundant, 1161

backup and recovery development, 748-749

balancing, network load. See **NLB (Network Load Balancing)**

bandwidth issues, 1003

baselines

baselining records for documentation comparisons, 730

establishing, 1120

basic authentication, 323

Big Bang migration

backing up and creating recovery process, 465

prerequisites, 463-464

upgrades on single domain controller server, 465-467

verifying application readiness, 464-465

verifying hardware compatibility, 464

virtual domain controller rollback option, 465

blacklists, 346-347

Block List Providers, 226-227

Block Lists

configuring with EMC (Exchange Management Console), 225-226

configuring with EMS (Exchange Management Shell), 227-228

Blocked Senders list, 320, 324, 899

blocking

attachments, 316-317

read receipts, 321

blogs, Vivek Sharma, 298

boot process

advanced boot options, 1100-1101

boot failures, 1100-1101

boot logging, 1100-1101

boot volumes

backing up, 1076

disaster recovery, 1099

Bridging tag (rule settings), 412

browsers

customizing MOSS sites with, 851-852

multibrowser support in OWA, 924

budgets

estimating in Migration documents, 62

initial budget, summarizing in Statement of Work, 50-51

bulk recipient editing, 579-580

business unit messaging goals, 45-46

BYE method (SIP), 829

C

cache

overview, 1133

universal group caching for AD sites, 158-159, 458

How can we make this index more useful? Email us at indexes@samspublishing.com

public groups

creating, 959-960

options, 959-960

routing groups, 498-499

scope, 164-165

securing, 340-342

security groups, 163

growth, planning for, 1121-1122

GUI interface, installing Exchange Server 2010 from, 206-208

H

hard zoning, 1156

hardening Windows Server 2003, 331

hardware

compatibility, verifying, 464

disks. *See* disk subsystem

for enterprise-level environments

overview, 92

server memory and processor recommendations, 93

server number and placement, 92

server redundancy and optimization, 92

Entourage 2008 hardware requirements, 986

Exchange Server 2010 hardware requirements, 175-176

hardware considerations for DAG members, 1046-1040

hardware inventory, 1064

hardware versus software RAID, 1139

OpsMgr hardware requirements, 680-681

Outlook 2007 client hardware requirements, 1005-1006

Remote Desktop Connection Client for Mac hardware requirements, 988

requirements for Exchange Server 2010, 73

Health Insurance Portability and Accountability Act of 1996. *See* HIPAA (Health Insurance Portability and Accountability Act of 1996)

help

in EMS (Exchange Management Shell), 283-284

in OWA (Outlook Web App), 965

help command, 283-284

high availability, 174-175

High encryption level (Terminal Services), 717

high-level business goals, 43-44

high-level messaging goals, 44-45

HIPAA (Health Insurance Portability and Accountability Act of 1996), 612

early provisions, 431

implications for Exchange Server 2010 environments, 435-436

late provisions, 431

overview, 431

Privacy Rule, 432-434

Security Rule, 434-435

TCS (Transactions and Code Sets), 432

historical records, 728

history

of Exchange Server, 6

Exchange 2000 Server, 8

Exchange Server 2003, 8-9

Exchange Server 2003 Service Pack 2, 9

Exchange Server 2007, 10

Exchange Server 2007 Service Pack 1, 10-11

Exchange Server 4.0, 6-7

Exchange Server 5.0, 7

Exchange Server 5.5, 7-8

of LDAP (Lightweight Directory Access Protocol), 109-110

of mobility enhancements, 756

How can we make this index more useful? Email us at indexes@samspublishing.com

How can we make this index more useful? Email us at indexes@samspublishing.com

spam, protecting against

blacklists, 346-347

Exchange Server 2010 antispam features, 317-318, 344-346

junk email filters, 319-320

overview, 317, 330

OWA (Outlook Web App) junk email settings, 964-965

reporting spammers, 347

SMTP relay access, 347

third-party antispam products, 347

web beacon filtering, 318-319

for Terminal Services

disabling mappings, 722

encryption levels, 721-722

overview, 716-717, 720

passwords, 722

permissions, 723

Remote Control, 722

security levels, 720

session disconnect, 722-723

TLS (Transport Layer Security), 19

transport-level security

email encryption, 350-351

overview, 350

PKI (Public Key Infrastructure), 351

S/MIME support, 351

SSL (Secure Sockets Layer) encryption, 352

TLS (Transport Layer Security), 352

viruses, 329-330

antivirus outsourcing, 349-350

antivirus protection, 98

Exchange Server 2010 antivirus features, 347-348

Forefront Security, 348-349

third-party antivirus products, 349

Windows environments

client-based virus protection, 310-311

overview, 302-303

patches and updates, 307-310

Security Configuration and Analysis tool, 305-306

security templates, 305, 306-307

Windows 7, 304

Windows Firewall, 304

Windows lockdown guidelines and standards, 311

Windows Server 2008, 303

Security Configuration and Analysis tool, 305-306

Security Configuration Wizard (SCW), 86, 335-336

Security Development Lifecycle (SDL), 328

Security Exchange Commission Rule 17a-4, 612

security groups, 683

definition of, 163

mail-enabled security groups, 164

Security Rule (HIPAA), 434-435

security templates, 305, 306-307

self-signed certificates, 379

exporting, 706

importing, 707

Send Connectors (SMTP), 354

configuring on Edge Transport server, 361-362

creating automatically, 357-358

creating manually, 358

sender filtering, 228-229, 447-448

Sender Reputation Agent. *See* Sender/IP reputation

SenderID

configuration, 232-234, 237

overview, 231-232, 448

SenderID Agent, 236-237

V

W

Y

Z

UNLEASHED

Unleashed takes you beyond the basics, providing an exhaustive, technically sophisticated reference for professionals who need to exploit a technology to its fullest potential. It's the best resource for practical advice from the experts, and the most in-depth coverage of the latest technologies.

Microsoft Dynamics CRM 4 Integration Unleashed
ISBN-13: 9780672330544

OTHER UNLEASHED TITLES

Microsoft SQL Server 2008 Integration Services Unleashed
ISBN-13: 9780672330322

Microsoft SQL Server 2008 Analysis Services Unleashed
ISBN-13: 9780672330018

Windows PowerShell Unleashed
ISBN-13: 9780672329883

Windows Small Business Server 2008 Unleashed
ISBN-13: 9780672329579

ASP.NET 3.5 AJAX Unleashed
ISBN-13: 9780672329739

WPF Control Development Unleashed
ISBN-13: 9780672330339

ASP.NET MVC Framework Unleashed
ISBN-13: 9780672329982

Microsoft XNA Game Studio 3.0 Unleashed
ISBN-13: 9780672330223

Windows Server 2008 Hyper-V Unleashed
ISBN-13: 9780672330285

System Center Operations Manager 2007 Unleashed
ISBN-13: 9780672329555

Microsoft Dynamics CRM 4.0 Unleashed
ISBN-13: 9780672329708

LINQ Unleashed
ISBN-13: 9780672329838

Silverlight 2 Unleashed
ISBN-13: 9780672330148

Windows Communication Foundation 3.5 Unleashed
ISBN-13: 9780672330247

C# 3.0 Unleashed
ISBN-13: 9780672329814

Microsoft Expression Blend Unleashed
ISBN-13: 9780672329319

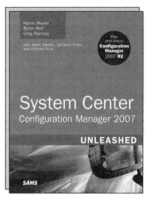

System Center Configuration Manager (SCCM) 2007 Unleashed
ISBN-13: 9780672330230

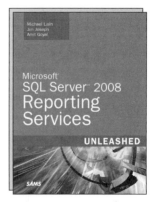

Microsoft SQL Server 2008 Reporting Services Unleashed
ISBN-13: 9780672330261

SAMS

informit.com/sams

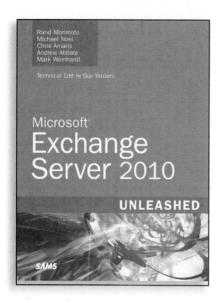

FREE Online Edition

Your purchase of **Microsoft® Exchange Server 2010 Unleashed** includes access to a free online edition for 45 days through the Safari Books Online subscription service. Nearly every Sams book is available online through Safari Books Online, along with more than 5,000 other technical books and videos from publishers such as Addison-Wesley Professional, Cisco Press, Exam Cram, IBM Press, O'Reilly, Prentice Hall, and Que.

SAFARI BOOKS ONLINE allows you to search for a specific answer, cut and paste code, download chapters, and stay current with emerging technologies.

Activate your FREE Online Edition at
www.informit.com/safarifree

STEP 1: Enter the coupon code: UJGAHAA.

STEP 2: New Safari users, complete the brief registration form.
Safari subscribers, just log in.

If you have difficulty registering on Safari or accessing the online edition, please e-mail customer-service@safaribooksonline.com